THE PALA
ENTERTA

The Paladin Video Home Entertainment Guide contains comprehensive information on more than 5500 video tapes and discs in the home entertainment field, including all the latest releases. Covering all forms of entertainment from feature films to opera, documentary to dance, cookery to physical fitness, *The Paladin Video Home Entertainment Guide* is the most practical and complete work of its kind.

The Paladin Video Home Entertainment Guide

PALADIN
Granada Publishing

Paladin Books
Granada Publishing Ltd
8 Grafton Street, London W1X 3LA

Published by Paladin Books 1985

Copyright © The National Video Clearinghouse, Inc. 1985

The National Video Clearing house, Inc.
100 Lafayette Drive
Syosset, NY 11791
(516) 364-3686
Telex: 6852011

ISBN 0-586-08541-6

Printed and bound in Great Britain by
Collins, Glasgow

Set in Helvetica

All rights reserved. No part of this publication may
be reproduced, stored in a retrieval system, or
transmitted, in any form, or by any means, electronic,
mechanical, photocopying, recording or otherwise,
without the prior permission of the publishers.

This book is sold subject to the conditions that it
shall not, by way of trade or otherwise, be lent,
re-sold, hired out or otherwise circulated
without the publisher's prior consent in any
form of binding or cover other than that in
which it is published and without a similar
condition including this condition being imposed
on the subsequent purchaser.

Table of Contents

Preface ix

Use Guide xi

New Releases xvii

Key xix

Programme Listings 1

Subject Category Index 743

Video Disc Index 808

Cast Index 812

Video Programmes Sources Index 832

Acknowledgements

This guide is an original work compiled by the staff of the National Video Clearinghouse, Inc.: George C. Hatch, Chairman of the Board; Harvey Seslowsky, President; David J. Weiner, Editor; Liz Doris, Publications Manager; Jill Lambert, Information Supervisor, UK Video Information Centre; Costas Mendonis, Graphic Designer; Mary S. Bean and Gregory P. Fagan, Editorial Coordinators; Meg Plastino and Debbie Freiberg, Editorial Secretaries.

PREFACE

The Paladin Video Home Entertainment Guide is designed to provide the home video viewer with information on nearly 6000 video programmes currently available. Most people know that they can obtain recent hit films, classics and even children's cartoons, but home video is much more. There are programmes on sports, health and physical fitness covering automobile racing to yoga; instructional programmes on everything from photography and flower arranging to hair dressing and how to train your dog; music videos from classical to contemporary; and even historical documentaries and current events programmes. Most of these will be available from your local video retailer (if he doesn't have them in stock, he can probably order them), while some are available through direct-mail order only. Either way, all programmes listed in this *Guide* are accessible to the home consumer.

Two special features of this publication which we are pleased to include are the Video Disc Index and the Cast Index. The Video Disc Index provides a listing of programmes available on video disc, and the companies that distribute them. The Cast Index, comprised of more than 270 actors, directors and personalities, should prove useful to you in locating videos of your favourite performers.

You will note that no prices have been included in the programme listings. Prices fluctuate rapidly in the video industry today, and many would be out of date before they were even printed.

The Paladin Video Home Entertainment Guide has been compiled from printed catalogues, supplementary lists and information supplied by the video programme sources. Distributors have not paid to have their video programmes listed, nor do the publishers pay them for information about their titles. The publishers are not responsible for any distributor changes, withdrawals or additions.

The Paladin Video Home Entertainment Guide has sought to provide the most comprehensive and up-to-date information available on home video. We hope you will find it a useful and welcome addition to your home library.

Use Guide

Introduction

The Paladin Video Home Entertainment Guide is divided into five major sections: (1) Programme Listings; (2) Subject Category Index; (3) Video Disc Index; (4) Cast Index; and (5) Video Programme Sources Index. A description of each section is given below.

I. Programme Listings

The main body of this book consists of nearly 6000 programme listings. Each entry may contain up to 22 different pieces of information, most of which is supplied by the distributor, or 'video programme source.' Standard film and video reference materials are utilized to obtain pertinent information when not supplied by the distributor. Full explanations of the information included are listed below; consult the key for illustrated examples.

ALPHABETIZATION
Each programme is listed alphabetically. 'A,' 'an' and 'the' and their foreign counterparts are ignored.

CATEGORY HEADINGS
Main Category: Each programme has been assigned a main category. The eight main category headings are:
1. Bus-Ind .... Business/Industry
2. Chl-Juv .... Children/Juvenile
3. Fil-Ent .... Films/Entertainment
4. Fin-Art .... Fine Arts
5. Gen-Edu .... General Interest/Education
6. How-Ins .... How-to/Instruction
7. Med-Sci .... Medicine/Science
8. Spo-Lei .... Sports/Leisure

Subject Category: Each title has been assigned a more specific subject heading, i.e. 'Comedy,' 'Gardening,' etc. This descriptive category will identify the contents of the programme. In some entries, a second subject category has also been assigned.

RELEASE DATES
'Release date' is defined as the year in which the film or programme was initally made available for public viewing. The known release date is listed as '72, indicating 1972. When the decade is known or determined, but not the precise year, the information is listed as '6?, indicating the decade of the 1960's. When neither the decade or the year can be determined, the listing indicates this by the annotation, '??.

ACCESSION NUMBER
Each title entry is assigned an accession number. The number is simply an identifying code number for the publishers and has no other meaning.

RUNNING TIMES
The running time of a programme is listed as '88 mins.' When edited or different versions of a programme are available, they are listed separately with the appropriate running times. In a series entry, the running time given is the average running time of each programme in the series. (See sub-heading 'Series: Number of Programmes.')

COLOUR AND BLACK AND WHITE
Each title listing indicates whether the programme is available in colour (C) or black and white (B/W).

FORMAT AVAILABILITY
Each entry includes the video formats available for that particular programme. The most common home video formats are VHS and Beta, although others are listed, when available. The popular V-2000 format is listed also, and it should be noted that many companies are now making all or some of their progammes available in this home format. Although the number of video discs currently on the market is relatively small, a notation for this format will be included in the appropriate programme entries as well. The format codes are as follows:

V2	V-2000
B	Beta
V	VHS
PH15	Phillips 1500
PH17	Phillips 1700
¾U	¾" U-matic cassette
CED	Capacitance electronic disc
LV	Laser optical video disc
FO	Formats other than those listed for the programme are available from the distributor by special arrangement.

CAST/STARS/HOSTS/GUESTS
The major stars or other members of the cast of dramatic television programmes or films are listed. In some instances the director is listed as well. For instructional, chat show, and documentary programmes, the host, narrator, or instructor may be given.

SERIES: NUMBER OF PROGRAMMES
The number of programmes in a generic series is listed as '5 pgms.' The individual titles of each programme within the series are listed in the sequence in which they are given by the distributor. When the distributor will make programmes available either as a series or individually, the individual programmes may also be listed in the main text.

PROGRAMME DESCRIPTION
The narrative programme descriptions are designed to briefly identify the major plot, subject, or theme of the programme.

AWARDS
The major awards and the year of the award are listed in each entry when applicable. Unless there is an obvious abbreviation for well-known awards, the awards are spelled out. Nominations are normally not listed. General generic awards are listed, followed by a colon and the specific award.

ANCILLARY MATERIALS
Brochures, study guides, and other printed and audio materials are occasionally available from the distributor to aid in the use of the programme. This is noted by the phrase 'AM Available.'

AUDIENCE RATING/DEMOGRAPHICS/PURPOSE
BBFC: For motion pictures, the standard British Board of Film Censors ratings are listed. BBFC ratings, preceded by 'BBFC,' are coded as follows:

Old System		New System	
U	All ages admitted.	U	Universal: suitable for all
A	Some material may not be suitable for children.	PG	Parental Guidance: some scenes may be unsuitable for young children
AA	Children under 14 not admitted.	15	Passed only for persons of 15 years and over
X	No one under 18 admitted.	18	Passed only for persons of 18 years and over
		R	Restricted 18: for restricted distribution only through segregated premises to which no one under the age of 18 is admitted

No self-imposed ratings are listed. The ratings listed are the last available from the distributor, and denote the rating given for theatrical release.

•

Demographics: To assist the user in identifying the intended audience level for the programme, an 'audience demographic' code has been assigned to each entry. The audience level listed ranges from pre-school to adult, and often contains more than one level, indicating the suitability of the programme for a broader audience. A maximum of two audience demographic codes are listed, indicating a span of ages such as 'S,A,' which indicates that the programme is appropriate from secondary school through adult levels. The following codes are used:

PS	Pre-school	C	College
I	Infant school	A	Adult
M	Middle school	F	Family
S	Secondary school		

Purpose: While the majority of programmes are entertainment in nature, other types of programmes have also been included. The demographic information is followed by one code which specifies the intended use of the programme. The following codes are used:

ED	Education	R	Religious
EN	Entertainment	SE	Special education
I	Instruction	TE	Teacher education
P	Professional	V	Vocational

Summary: The Audience Rating Demographics, and Purpose codes when applied in combination are designed to assist the reader im determining the nature and intended use of the programme, as in the following example:

BBFC: U   F   EN
           General Audience   Family   Entertainment

FOREIGN LANGUAGE

Virtually all titles found in this publication are available in English. Some foreign films have retained their original foreign language sound track; other English-language films have been dubbed into foreign languages. The availability of a foreign language version is indicated according to the following codes:

EL	English	FR	French	PR	Portuguese
AF	Afrikaans	GE	German	RU	Russian
AB	Arabic	GR	Greek	SE	Serbo Croatian
BE	Belgian	HE	Hebrew		
CH	Chinese	IT	Italian	SP	Spanish
CZ	Czech	JA	Japanese	SA	Swahili
DA	Danish	LA	Latin	SW	Swedish
DU	Dutch	LI	Lithuanian	TH	Thai
EG	Egyptian	NE	Nepalese	TU	Turkish
FI	Finnish	NO	Norwegian	WE	Welsh
FL	Flemish	PO	Polish		

When EL is not given along with a foreign language code, the programme is not available in English.

SILENT/DUBBED/SUB-TITLES
Silent films or those with dubbing or different language sound tracks are noted in the programme descriptions. Similarly, a programme with sub-titles is so indicated at the end of the programme description.

ORIGINAL PRODUCER
The original producer (studio, company, and/or individual person) is listed in each entry. When the actual producer cannot be determined, but the country of origin (other than Great Britain) is known, that information will be listed instead.

VIDEO PROGRAMME SOURCES
The video programme source, also known as the distributor, appears to the right of the original producer in the listing. The address and telephone number of each source can be found in the Video Programme Sources Index in the back of this book. Sources listed are generally the programme manufacturers of licenced representatives. Wholesalers, local retailers or video clubs are not listed unless they are the sole source of the programmme.

ACQUISITION AVAILABILITY
Video programmes may be acquired in several ways. The following codes are used to indicate the means by which the consumer may obtain the programme from the listed source or its assignee:

H	Hire (user may hire or lease the programme)
L	Loan (user may borrow the programme for a fee)
P	Purchase (user may purchase the programme)
S	Subscription (user may obtain the programme as part of a membership at an annual fee or through a club)
E	Exchange (user may exchange a purchased programme for a credit on another programme)
FL	Free Loan (user may borrow the programme for a postage or handling charge)
FD	Free Duplication (user may duplicate the programme at no additional charge)
DL	Duplication Licence (user may purchase a licence to duplicate the programme)

The information supplied in this coding is obtained from the video programme source.

DISTRIBUTORS' ORDER NUMBER
The distributors' order numbers, if available, will appear in italics on the last line of the entry. Two or more numbers separated by a slash (/) indicate that each format has a different order number, and the numbers will correspond to the formats listed in the entry. For example, a programme with B, V listed in the format line will have its corresponding order numbers listed as B101/V101. In a series entry where each individual programme has its own order number, all order numbers will be listed and will be separated by a semi-colon(;).

II. Subject Category Index

Each title in *The Paladin Video Home Entertainment Guide* has been assigned a subject category. A complete listing of all subjects and titles within them appears after the Programme Listings. When a programme is assigned two different subjects. that title is indexed under both. This index is designed to help the reader quickly locate programmes in his area of interest, be it drama, tennis, or any of more than 100 other subjects.

III. Video Disc Index

The Video Disc Index is a compilation of programmes available on video disc at the time of publication. Titles are grouped by distributor. For complete information on each title, see entries in the Programme Listings.

IV. Cast Index

We have compiled videographies of selected performers and directors. This cast listing is by no means complete, since it would be impossible to list every performer in every film available on video; however, more than 270 entertainers have been included.

V. Video Programme Sources Index

The full corporate name, address, telephone number(s), and policy information for each video programme source whose entries appear in *The Paladin Video Home Entertainment Guide* are listed alphabetically in the Video Programme Sources Index in the last section of this book. Most of the programmes listed herein are available through local video shops. Contact the individual programme sources for further information about their titles.

New Releases

As we go to press, the following new video releases have been announced:

BBC VIDEO
Doctor Who: Pyramids of Mars
Ensemble: L'Amour de la Vie
The Fall and Rise of Reginald Perrin
The Family-Ness
Hancock—The Blood Donor
Hancock—The Bowmans
Hancock—The Lift
Hancock—The Radio Ham
Ivor the Engine and the Elephants
The Moon Stallion
More Ripping Yarns
The Old Man of Lochnagar
Pigeon Street
Pride and Prejudice, Parts 1 & 2
Supercharged—The Grand Prix Car 1924-1939

GUILD HOME VIDEO

The All New Incredible Hulk, Cassette 1
The Amazing Spiderman, Cassette 6
Atom Ant, Cassette 4
Barry Manilow—Live at the Pittsburgh Civic Centre
Batfink, Cassette 3
Bolero
Carlene Carter: Live from London
An Evening with Johnny Morris
The Fabulous Fantastic Four, Cassette 4
Fearless Fly, Cassette 2
A Flock of Seagulls
Gary Numan: Berserker Tour
Hercules
The Invincible Iron Man, Cassette 4
King Kurt: Live from London
Making the Grade
The Metal Edge
Millie Jackson
The Naked Face
Over the Brooklyn Bridge
Record Shack
Spider Woman, Cassette 4
Spider Woman, Cassette 5
A Streetcar Named Desire (1951)
Thomas the Tank Engine and Friends, Cassette 1
Top Cat, Cassette 5

INTERVISION VIDEO
Best of Both Worlds
Caligula and Messalina
Crazed
Hot and Blue
Plunge into Darkness
Queen of Diamonds

MGM/UA HOME VIDEO

The Blood of Others
Deaf Smith and Johnny Ears
Dennis Brown Live at Montreux
Dirty Dingus Magee
Double Trouble
Heaven with a Gun
The Ice Pirates
It Happened at the World's Fair
Just the Way You Are
The Last Run
The Lone Ranger
The Pied Piper
Reckless
Royal Wedding
The Slams
Speedway

Take Me Out to the Ball Game
Terrytoons—Cartoon Capers Volume 2
Tom and Jerry: Four of the Best
Tom and Jerry: Tee for Two
Utu
Viva Las Vegas
Why Would I Lie?
The Wizard of Oz

ODYSSEY VIDEO
The Cartier Affair
Charlie's Balloon
Death Ride to Osaka
Louisiana
Richie

PALACE VIDEO
The Best of Elvis Costello, The Man
Jimi Hendrix Plays Berkeley
The Mission
Special AKA on Film
Terror in the Aisles

POLYGRAM
Bernard Manning—Ungagged
Best Revenge
Bronski Beat: The First Chapter
Daniel
David Essex—Live at the Royal Albert Hall
'Do They Know It's Christmas?'
Don't Watch That, Watch This, Volume 2
Law and Disorder
Lloyd Cole and the Commotions
Orange Juice: dAdA with Juice
Pursuit
Silent Kill
SK-1 'A One Way Ticket to Palookasville'
Stanley
The Stranger Within Us

PRECISION VIDEO
The Darts Live from London
Family Secrets
Invitation to Hell
The Music of Gerard Kenny
Musical Cartoon Shows, 1 & 2
The Old Testament
Secrets of a Married Man
79 AD
Summer Fantasy
Swinging UK

VESTRON VIDEO
Benji's Very Own Christmas Story
Breaking with the Mighty Poppalots
Candid Candid Camera
The Company of Wolves
Dead Easy
Hawmps!
The Little Prince, Tape 1
Mean Dog Blues
The Nighttime Concert
Sakharov
Street Music
Ultraflash
Walking Tall
Weekend Pass
Yor

VIDEOSPACE
An American Christmas Carol
Annie's Coming Out
Aurora
GCE O-Level Revision Video Tapes
Her Life As a Man
Love's Savage Fury
Monkey Grip
Shattered Vows
Winds of Jarrah

VIRGIN VIDEO
Another Country
The Comic Strip Presents I & II
Electric Dreams
Electric Dreams—The Video Soundtrack
Emerald Aisles
Meatloaf—Bad Attitudes Live
MI5's Official Secrets
1984
Stray Tracks
The World We Live In and Live in Hamburg

Key

This sample entry will assist the reader in interpreting the individual Programme Listings. For complete explanation of each code, please see the USE GUIDE.

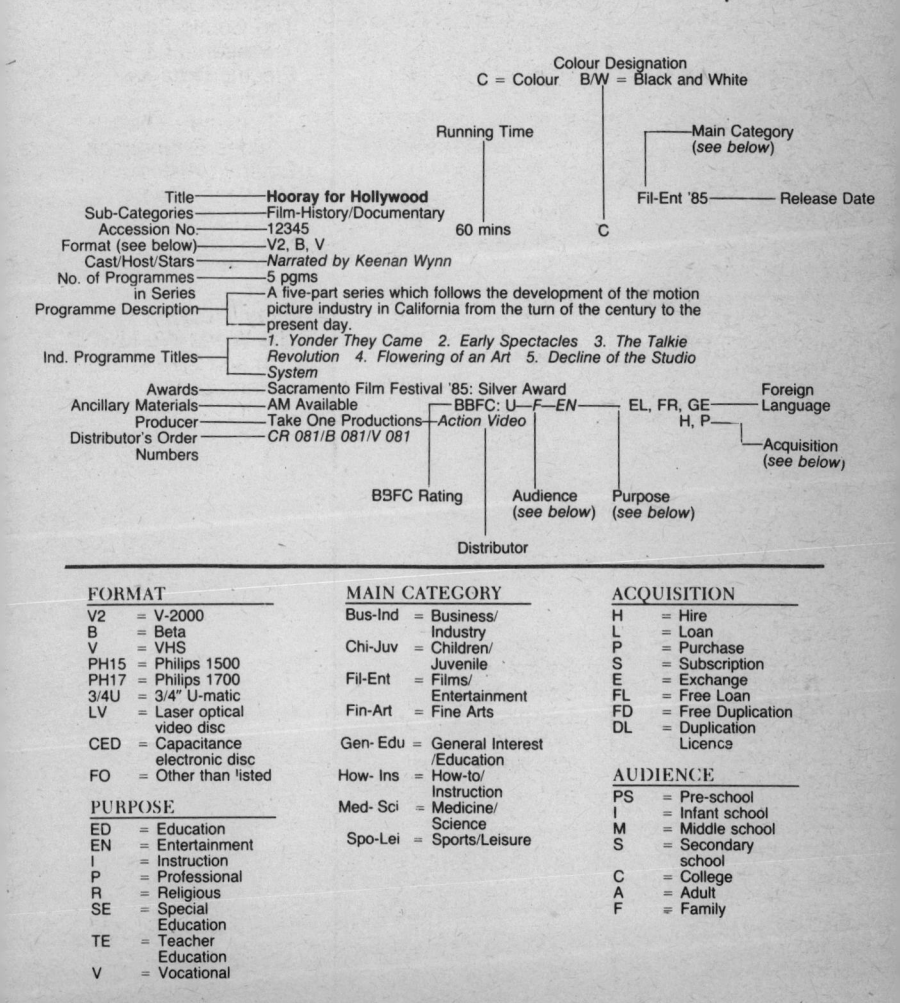

Colour Designation
C = Colour   B/W = Black and White

Running Time — Main Category (see below)

Title — **Hooray for Hollywood**
Sub-Categories — Film-History/Documentary
Accession No. — 12345   60 mins   C   Fil-Ent '85 — Release Date
Format (see below) — V2, B, V
Cast/Host/Stars — Narrated by Keenan Wynn
No. of Programmes — 5 pgms
in Series
Programme Description — A five-part series which follows the development of the motion picture industry in California from the turn of the century to the present day.
Ind. Programme Titles — 1. Yonder They Came 2. Early Spectacles 3. The Talkie Revolution 4. Flowering of an Art 5. Decline of the Studio System
Awards — Sacramento Film Festival '85: Silver Award   Foreign
Ancillary Materials — AM Available   BBFC: U—F—EN   EL, FR, GE — Language
Producer — Take One Productions — Action Video   H, P —
Distributor's Order — CR 081/B 081/V 081
Numbers   Acquisition
                                                                         (see below)
            BBFC Rating   Audience   Purpose
                          (see below) (see below)

Distributor

FORMAT

V2	= V-2000
B	= Beta
V	= VHS
PH15	= Philips 1500
PH17	= Philips 1700
3/4U	= 3/4" U-matic
LV	= Laser optical video disc
CED	= Capacitance electronic disc
FO	= Other than listed

PURPOSE

ED	= Education
EN	= Entertainment
I	= Instruction
P	= Professional
R	= Religious
SE	= Special Education
TE	= Teacher Education
V	= Vocational

MAIN CATEGORY

Bus-Ind	= Business/Industry
Chi-Juv	= Children/Juvenile
Fil-Ent	= Films/Entertainment
Fin-Art	= Fine Arts
Gen-Edu	= General Interest/Education
How-Ins	= How-to/Instruction
Med-Sci	= Medicine/Science
Spo-Lei	= Sports/Leisure

ACQUISITION

H	= Hire
L	= Loan
P	= Purchase
S	= Subscription
E	= Exchange
FL	= Free Loan
FD	= Free Duplication
DL	= Duplication Licence

AUDIENCE

PS	= Pre-school
I	= Infant school
M	= Middle school
S	= Secondary school
C	= College
A	= Adult
F	= Family

THE PALADIN VIDEO HOME ENTERTAINMENT GUIDE

A

Abba Music Show 1 Fil-Ent '8?
Music-Performance
06786   60 mins   C
V2, B, V
Abba
This chart-busting group performs a selection of their top hits.
S,A — EN
Polar — *Intervision Video*   H, P
ZC 9000

Abba Music Show 2 Fil-Ent '8?
Music-Performance
06787   60 mins   C
V2, B, V
Abba
A special performance by this popular group of seven of their hits including 'Dancing Queen.'
S,A — EN
Polar — *Intervision Video*   H, P
ZC 9001

Abba—The Movie Fil-Ent '79
Music-Performance
12235   90 mins   C
B, V
This film follows the group on its tour of Australia. Many of their songs are featured, including 'Take a Chance on Me,' 'The Name of the Game' and 'Thank You for the Music.'
F — EN
Warner Bros — *MGM/UA Home Video*   P
10215

Abbe Lane Show, The Fil-Ent '7?
Variety
04377   60 mins   C
B, V, PH17, 3/4U
Abbe Lane, Sandler and Young, Jose Greco
A variety show starring Abbe Lane and special guest stars.
F — EN
Unknown — *Vidpics International*   P

Abbott and Costello Fil-Ent '??
Cartoons/Comedy
06250   57 mins   C
B, V
Animated
This is a compilation of eleven cartoon episodes featuring the comic antics of Bud Abbott and Lou Costello.
F — EN
Hanna-Barbera — *VCL Video Services*   P
F192B

ABC's Mantrap Fil-Ent '??
Music-Performance
09888   60 mins   C
B, V, LV
This tape features music from ABC's celebrated No. 1 album, 'Lexicon of Love'. It follows the band from obscurity to international stardom against a series of lush European settings. Recorded in stereo.
F — EN
Unknown — *Polygram Video*   H, P
790 6714 / 790 6712 / 790 6711

Abducted Fil-Ent '8?
Drama
09057   87 mins   C
V
This film tells the horrifying tale of two brothers, who abduct and abuse the subjects who fall fate to their twisted and tormented needs, and where their sexual fantasies become a nightmare.
C,A — EN
Unknown — *Astra Video*   H, P

Abduction Fil-Ent '75
Crime-Drama
06213   94 mins   C
B, V
Judith-Marie Bergan, David Pendleton, Dorothy Malone, Lief Erickson, Gregory Rozakis, directed by Joseph Zito
The story of a kidnapping of a wealthy girl in California by a group of leftists. Eventually she converts to their revolutionary cause.
BBFC:X — A — EN
Venture Dist Inc; Kent E Carroll Prods — *VCL Video Services*   P
P193D

Abductors, The Fil-Ent '??
Suspense/Crime-Drama
05622   73 mins   C
V2, B, V
Larry Daniels, Andrews Calman, Susa Castura, Ann Vagena, Dennis Mitchel

PALADIN VIDEO HOME ENTERTAINMENT GUIDE

The story of a young undercover law enforcement agent and his battle with men of violence in international crime, where villains plot against each other to become leaders.
BBFC:X — A — EN
Unknown — Go Video Ltd   **P**
G0112

Abigail's Party   Fil-Ent '84
Drama/Comedy
13396   103 mins   C
B, V
Alison Steadman, directed by Mike Leigh
Middle class social manners are spotlighted in this savagely funny study of a social get-together in suburbia.
A — EN
Unknown — BBC Video   **H, P**
2011

Abilene Town   Fil-Ent '46
Western/Drama
06320   86 mins   B/W
B, V
Randolph Scott, Rhonda Fleming, Lloyd Bridges, Ann Dvorak
A Kansas town becomes the scene of conflict between cattlemen and homesteaders. The homesteaders construct barbed wire fences around their land and across the cattle trail when a cattle boss vows vengeance when he is thrown out of town, resulting in a stampede and shoot-out in the mainstreet.
F — EN
United Artists — VCL Video Services   **P**
0231G

Able to Fish   Gen-Edu '78
Learning disabilities
13533   102 mins   C
B, V
3 pgms
These films show how, with the help of special aids and devices, disabled adults and children are able to fish in the river and sea with success.
1.Coarse Angling 2.Game Fishing 3.Sea Angling
C,A — SE
Unknown — TFI Leisure Ltd   **H, P**

Above All   Gen-Edu '??
Aeronautics
09121   50 mins   C
B, V

This film demonstrates how flight has changed man's world. It describes how ever expanding technology has taken us from virtual box kites to the high speed jets.
S,A — EN
Unknown — Quadrant Video   **H, P**
AV1

Above Us the Waves   Fil-Ent '56
War-Drama
08034   96 mins   B/W
B, V
John Mills, John Gregson, Donald Sinden, James Robertson Justice, Michael Medwin, Lee Patterson, Lyndon Brook, directed by Ralph Thomas
This film tells of the dramatic World War II Operation to destroy the German battleship Tirpitz in a Norwegian fjord using midget submarines.
S,A — EN
Rank — Rank Video Library   **H, P**
0109 B

Absolution   Fil-Ent '81
Drama
05675   95 mins   C
B, V
Richard Burton, Billy Connolly, Dominic Guard, Dai Bradley, Andrew Keir, directed by Denis Holt
This story is set in a Roman Catholic School in England where tension runs high when reality is removed in this rule-bound atmosphere. Father Brown is a rigid opinionated master who affects the pupils with his discipline and power, favouring a few and rejecting others. Problems arise when one of his favourites is influenced by a free-wheeling, free-spirited long haired freak whose crucial life infects the boy with excitement.
BBFC:X — A — EN
Enterprise Pictures; Bulldog Productions Ltd — Home Video Holdings   **H, P**
032

Absurd   Fil-Ent '7?
Mystery/Suspense
09165   96 mins   C
V
George Eastman, Annie Belle, Charles Borrunel, Ian Danby
This is a thriller in a true sense of the word, containing brutal, shocking and violent sequences.
BBFC:X — A — EN
Unknown — Medusa Communications Ltd
H, P

PALADIN VIDEO HOME ENTERTAINMENT GUIDE

Acapulco Gold   Fil-Ent '??
Crime-Drama/Adventure
07811   105 mins   C
B, V
Marjoe Gortner, Robert Lansing, Ed Nelson
This film follows the outrageous smuggling activities of a gang who use helicopters, hydrofoils and a million ingenious means to get 'Acapulco Gold,' the most precious and dangerous commodity on the international drugs circuit.
S,A — EN
Unknown — *Video Tape Centre*   P
VTC 1015

Accident   Fil-Ent '67
Drama
07481   100 mins   C
B, V
Dirk Bogarde, Stanley Baker, Jacqueline Sassard, Michael York, Vivien Merchant, Delphine Seyrig, Alexander Knox, directed by Joseph Losey
This is a sensitive study of love and jealousy among the dons of Oxford. Two men are in love with the same girl; one pursues her with the pride of a natural predator, the other with guilty self-loathing. Their rival is a wealthy, blond, blue-blooded student whose 'accidental' death springs the trap of guilt, remorse and thwarted sexual ambition on all involved. Screenplay by Harold Pinter.
BBFC:A — S,A — EN
Royal Avenue Chelsea Productions Ltd — *THORN EMI*   P
TXB 90 0004 4/TVB 90 0004 2

Ace High   Fil-Ent '68
Western
13607   122 mins   C
B, V
Terence Hill, Bud Spencer, Steffan Zacharias, Eli Wallach, directed by Guiseppe Colizzi
When a philanthropist bandit joins forces with two con-men the results are funny, exciting and, of course, violent.
BBFC:15 — S,A — EN
Paramount — *CIC Video*   H, P
2116

Ace Up My Sleeve   Fil-Ent '8?
Drama
08990   90 mins   C
B, V
Omar Sharif, Karen Black, Joseph Bottoms

Based on a novel by James Hadley Chase, this film tells of a world of international high finance where corruption, power, money and lust are intermingled with nightmares.
S,A — EN
Unknown — *Polygram Video*   P
791 524

Aces High   Fil-Ent '76
War-Drama
04664   110 mins   C
B, V
Malcolm McDowell, Christopher Plummer, Simon Ward
The film tells the story of the young, newly commissioned pilot Stephen Croft who arrives as a replacement at the squadron in France commanded by Major John Gresham, who is clearly cracking under the strain.
C,A — EN
EMI; S Benjamin Fisz; Jacques Roitfeld — *THORN EMI*   H, P
TXC 90 0220 4/TVC 90 0220 2

Acorn Electron, The   Gen-Edu '8?
Electronic data processing
09996   60 mins   C
B, V
This tape demonstrates how to use the Electron in basic to help one write one's own programme. The tape is in four sessions. In the 1st session it introduces programme writing. In the 2nd programme it looks at designing a new programme. In the 3rd session it looks at graphics on the Electron and finally in the 4th session it looks at arrays and data.
S,A — I
Holiday Brothers Ltd — *Holiday Brothers Ltd*
P

Acquasanta Joe   Fil-Ent '??
Western
06082   90 mins   C
V2, B, V
Richard Harrison, Ty Hardin, Lee Banner
A bounty killer has his hard earned money stolen by a gang of outlaws. He swears revenge and sets out to track them down.
F — EN
Unknown — *Video Programme Distributors*
P
Cinehollywood—V100

Across the Great Divide   Fil-Ent '76
Adventure
08871   98 mins   C
V2, B, V
Robert Logan, George Flower, Heather Rattray, Mark Hall, directed by Stewart Raffill

(For Explanation of codes, see USE GUIDE and KEY)   3

PALADIN VIDEO HOME ENTERTAINMENT GUIDE

After the death of their grandfather and having been abandoned in the wilderness, two youngsters set out to cross the Rocky Mountains in order to claim their rightful inheritance, a 400 acre plot of land in Oregon.
BBFC:U — F — EN
Pacific International Enterprises — *Video Programme Distributors* **P**
Media 206

Act, The Fil-Ent '84
Suspense/Drama
13230   92 mins   C
B, V
Eddie Albert, Robert Ginty, Jill St. John, Pat Hingle, Sarah Langenfeld
Set in the world of politics, this film depicts the secret deals and cynical machinations behind the power struggle of a President up for re-election.
BBFC:15 — S,A — EN
Film Ventures International Production — *Entertainment in Video* **H, P**
EVB 1026/EVV 1026

Act Of Passion Fil-Ent '83
Drama
13680   95 mins   C
B, V
Kris Kristofferson, Marlo Thomas, directed by Simon Langton
A young girl's happiness is shattered when she is seized by the police and brutally interrogated as a suspect of a terrorist gang.
BBFC:18 — A — EN
John Nicolella — *CBS/Fox Video* **P**
3044

Act of Vengeance Fil-Ent '74
Drama
13456   88 mins   C
B, V
JoAnn Harris, Peter Brown, Jennifer Lee, Lisa Moore, Connie Strickland, Tony Young
A rape victim is so angered by the lack of police action that she forms her own vigilante force who wreak their own revenge.
BBFC:18 — A — EN
Orion Pictures — *Rank Video Library* **H, P**
0176 E

Adam Fil-Ent '83
Drama
13778   120 mins   C
B, V
JoBeth Williams, Daniel J. Travanti
This is the true story of a parent's fight against government agencies after their child had been abducted and murdered leading to the signing of the Missing Children Act by President Reagan in 1982.
BBFC:15 — S,A — EN
Alan Landsburg Productions — *Odyssey Video* **H, P**
6541

Adios Gringo Fil-Ent '65
Western
04297   100 mins   C
V2, B, V
Montgomery Wood, Evelyn Stewart
After killing in self-defense Brent Landers has to flee Johnson City to search for witness Gill Clowson to help clear his name. He meets up with Lucy Tillson, who recognizes Gill as one of a gang who had attacked her. Now, Brent with a price on his head and the girl with a special reason to catch up with the gang, set out together.
C,A — EN
Trans Lux Distributing — *Video Programme Distributors* **P**
Inter-Ocean—027

Adolph Hitler—Benito Mussolini Gen-Edu '??
History-Modern/World War II
06133   30 mins   B/W
V2, B, V
An authentic filmed document on the life of the two dictators: Adolf Hitler's career from childhood, his rise to power, the 'final solution' and his mysterious end; Benito Mussolini and his first Fascist movement, his career and his tragic death.
S,A — ED
Unknown — *Video Programme Distributors* **P**
Cinehollywood—V790

Adult Fairytales Fil-Ent '79
Fairy tales/Comedy
08906   82 mins   C
V2, B, V
Don Sparks, Brenda Fogarty
A prince, on his twenty-first birthday, is told that he has to produce an heir, or he will lose the kingdom. A beautiful young girl is brought in for him, but he explains that he loves Princess Beauty who disappeared many years ago. This programme is for adults only.
BBFC:X — A — EN
Fairytales Distributing Company — *Video Programme Distributors* **P**
Inter-Ocean 064

---

4   (For Explanation of codes, see USE GUIDE and KEY)

PALADIN VIDEO HOME ENTERTAINMENT GUIDE

Adventure in Ventana   Fil-Ent '74
Adventure/Documentary
06244   60 mins   C
B, V
Narrated by Doug McClure
A documentary set high in the peaks of California's Pacific Coastal mountains. One man alone and armed only with a tranquiliser gun tries desperately to save the ferocious Russian Black Boar from extinction.
F — EN
American Natl Entprs — *VCL Video Services*
P
F038

Adventurers, The   Fil-Ent '52
Adventure/Drama
01945   82 mins   B/W
B, V
Jack Hawkins, Dennis Price, Peter Hammond, Siobhan McKenna
Two Boers and a cashiered English officer search to recover stolen diamonds in South Africa, circa 1902.
F — EN
J Arthur Rank — *CBS/Fox Video*   **P**
3B-058

Adventures of a Plumber's Mate   Fil-Ent '7?
Comedy
06813   ? mins   C
V2, B, V
The amorous adventures of a plumber's helper.
BBFC:X — *A* — *EN*
Salon Productions — *Intervision Video*
H, P
A-A 0382

Adventures of a Private Eye   Fil-Ent '7?
Comedy
06815   ? mins   C
V2, B, V
Christopher Neil, Suzy Kendall, Harry H. Corbett
A clever detective 'uncovers' everyone.
BBFC:X — *A* — *EN*
Salon Productions — *Intervision Video*
H, P
A-A 0383

Adventures of a Taxi Driver   Fil-Ent '7?
Comedy
06814   ? mins   C
V2, B, V
Barry Evans, Judy Geeson, Adrienne Posta, Diana Dors
The story of a taxi driver who gets more than his fair share.
BBFC:X — *A* — *EN*
Salon Productions — *Intervision Video*
H, P
A-A 0381

Adventures of Buster the Bear, The   Chl-Juv '78
Cartoons/Adventure
09240   52 mins   C
B, V
Animated
This animated film follows the adventures of Buster the Bear who goes to live in the Green Forest. Joe the otter gets angry with him for eating the fish in the stream. Grandfather bullfrog steps in to help the two animals live happily together.
PS,M — EN
ZIV International — *Home Video Holdings*
H, P
040

Adventures of Captain Future I, The   Fil-Ent '80
Cartoons/Adventure
05752   54 mins   C
B, V
Animated
Captain Future and his crew travel through space helping to bring peace and harmony to all. In this adventure they use a time machine to go back a million years into the past to save a planet and encounter strange prehistoric creatures.
BBFC:U — *F* — *EN*
ZIV International; Family Home Entertainment — *Home Video Holdings*
H, P
030

Adventures of Captain Future II, The   Fil-Ent '80
Cartoons/Adventure
05753   54 mins   C
B, V
Animated
Once more Captain Future and his crew travel through time and space encountering the many hazards before them.
BBFC:U — *F* — *EN*
ZIV International; Family Home Entertainment — *Home Video Holdings*
H, P
029

(For Explanation of codes, see USE GUIDE and KEY)

PALADIN VIDEO HOME ENTERTAINMENT GUIDE

Adventures of Chip 'n' Dale
Chl-Juv '6?
Cartoons
13764   71 mins   C
B, V
Animated
Ten cartoons are featured on this cassette as Chip 'n' Dale, the two naughty chipmunks, bring havoc into the lives of all their friends.
BBFC:U — F — EN
Walt Disney Productions — *Rank Video Library*
P
233B

Adventures of Choppy and the Princess, The
Fil-Ent '7?
Cartoons/Fantasy
09047   80 mins   C
V
Animated
In the kingdom of Silverland it is law that only a male can succeed as heir to the throne. When a daughter is born, the king tells the people that he has a son, and must protect his secret from the court subjects. At the age of 12, pretending to be a boy together with Choppy, a protective leprechaun, they set off on an adventure, confronted by masked bandits, and a ravenous wolf.
F — EN
Unknown — *Astra Video*   H, P

Adventures of Choppy and the Princess—1, The
Fil-Ent '7?
Cartoons/Adventure
09048   52 mins   C
V
Animated
This tape contains two adventures of Choppy and the Princess. In 'Three Wishes' Choppy and the Princess discover an adorable Pixie who pleads with them to take him home to his island. They encounter a series of adventures on their journey. In the 'Flying Horse' Pegasus comes to Earth to teach the Princess how to be gentle. However the wicked Baron decides to capture the horse to trap the Princess into revealing her true identity.
F — EN
Unknown — *Astra Video*   H, P

Adventures of Choppy and the Princess—2, The
Fil-Ent '7?
Cartoons/Adventure
09049   52 mins   C
V
Animated
This tape contains two further adventures of Choppy and the Princess. In 'The Princess and the Beggar', the Princess changes places with a beggar boy envious of her Royal position. In 'The Sandman' the son of Jeralamon, demands strawberries in winter. The only place he can get them is in a wood, protected by the Sandman. The Princess is blamed for the theft.
F — EN
Unknown — *Astra Video*   H, P

Adventures of Choppy and the Princess—3, The
Fil-Ent '7?
Cartoons/Adventure
09050   52 mins   C
V
Animated
This tape contains two further adventures of Choppy and the Princess. 'The Magic Herb' finds them searching for an antidote to save the Queen, only to be confronted by an ice, then fire then water monster. In 'Rose Castle' the Grand Duke Jeralamon decides to destroy the castle belonging to two princes. They send a plea for help to the Princess.
F — EN
Unknown — *Astra Video*   H, P

Adventures of Curley and His Gang, The
Fil-Ent '47
Adventure/Comedy
07326   51 mins   C
B, V
Larry Olsen, Eileen Janssen, Frances Rafferty, Kathleen Howard
This film is one of the few Hal Roach comedies to be produced in colour. Curley and his gang plan a few tricks to play on a new teacher, but they all backfire. More trouble comes their way when two kids take Curley's rocket car on a crazy joy ride through hay stacks, the air and finally crashing into the school supervisor's new car.
BBFC:U — F — EN
United Artists — *Derann Film Services*   P
BDV 115B/BDV 115

Adventures of Frontier Fremont, The
Fil-Ent '76
Adventure/Biographical
08035   92 mins   C
B, V
Denver Pyle, Dan Haggarty, Tone Mirrati, directed by Richard Friedenberg
This film, set in the year 1835, tells the true story of a farmer who leaves his homestead to live in the moutains. He encounters fierce animals, a forest fire, rapids and Indians before finding a home.
BBFC:U — F — EN
Sunn Classic Productions — *Rank Video Library*   H, P
0057 C

(For Explanation of codes, see USE GUIDE and KEY)

PALADIN VIDEO HOME ENTERTAINMENT GUIDE

Adventures of Gumdrop, The Chl-Juv '??
Cartoons/Adventure
08320   51 mins   C
B, V
Animated, voices by Peter Hawkins, illustrated and written by Val Biro
Gumdrop is a trusty old car, and this tape features seven of its adventures: Gumdrop and the Secret Switches' (11 mins, 1981),'Gumdrop Finds a Ghost' (10 mins, 1980), 'Gumdrop and the Steamroller' (3 mins, 1976), 'Gumdrop Posts a Letter' (8 mins, 1976), 'Gumdrop in Double Trouble' (10 mins, 1975), 'Gumdrop Races a Train' (4 mins, 1982) and 'Gumdrop and Horace' (5 mins, 1982).
BBFC:U — M,S — EN
Val Biro; Nutland Video — *Nutland Video Ltd*
P

Adventures of Hambone and Hillie, The Fil-Ent '82
Drama
12830   90 mins   C
B, V
Lillian Gish, Candy Clark, O.J. Simpson, Robert Walker, Timothy Bottoms, directed by Roy Watts
A lovable shaggy dog is accidentally left behind in the confusion of a New York airport and encounters many adventures on his long trek home.
BBFC:PG — F — EN
Gary Gillingham; Sandy Howard — *Video Tape Centre*   P
1168

Adventures of Huckleberry Finn, The Fil-Ent '79
Adventure/Drama
07492   97 mins   C
B, V
Kurt Ida, Dan Monahan, Brock Peters, Forrest Tucker, Larry Storch
Based on the classic novel by Mark Twain that recounts boyhood misadventures, this film follows Huck's adventures as he travels down the Mississippi River on a home made raft. He has to cope with a greedy malicious father, two grasping con-men, the excitement of buried treasure, a gun-hungry posse, feuding neighbours and a hermit, all of which he takes in his stride.
F — EN
Sunn Classic — *Quadrant Video*   H, P
FF10

Adventures of King Rollo, The Chl-Juv '80
Cartoons
10004   60 mins   C
B, V
Animated
This tape contains twelve adventures of King Rollo and his friends, the Magician, Cook, Queen Gwen and Hamlet the Cat. King Rollo discovers he can do magic tricks, and makes Queen Gwen's birthday memorable.
M — EN
King Rollo Films; David McKee — *Longman Video*   P
LGBE 5015/LGVH 5015

Adventures of Kum Kum, The Chl-Juv '77
Cartoons
13301   87 mins   C
B, V
Animated
Set in Japan in stone age time, Kum Kum lives with his family in a small village with many interesting characters including an old sage, a witch, a giant and a gigantic tyrannosaurus.
PS,M — EN
Paramount — *CIC Video*   H, P
BER 2112/VHR 2112

Adventures of Little Lulu — Volume 1, The Fil-Ent '78
Cartoons
08590   48 mins   C
V2, B, V
Animated
This tape features two adventures of Little Lulu and her gang. In 'Good Luck Guard' Lulu tries to join Tubby's club for boys. In 'Operation Baby-Sitting' Lulu has to baby-sit for her best friend, Tubby.
F — EN
ZIV International — *Videomedia*   P
PVM 3117/BVM 3117/HVM 3117

Adventures of Little Lulu—Volume 2, The Fil-Ent '78
Cartoons
08591   47 mins   C
V2, B, V
Animated
This tape contains two further adventures of the rascals, Little Lulu and her gang. In 'Save the Prisoners', Tubby and the rest of the gang are captured by the dreaded Westside gang. Lulu comes to the rescue. In 'Little Angel' Lulu tries to become an angel by trying to solve other peoples' problems.
F — EN
ZIV International — *Videomedia*   P
PVM 3118/BVM 3118/HVM 3118

(For Explanation of codes, see USE GUIDE and KEY)

PALADIN VIDEO HOME ENTERTAINMENT GUIDE

Adventures of Little Lulu—Volume 3, The
Fil-Ent '78
Cartoons
08592   46 mins   C
V2, B, V
Animated
This tape contains two further adventures of Lulu and her gang. 'The Little Fireman' finds Lulu fooling all the boys and becoming the first one on the block to ride in a real fire engine. In 'The Endurance Test' Lulu gets back at Tubby when they go on an all-day hike, without any food for Tubby.
F — EN
Z/V International — *Videomedia*   P
PVM 3119/BVM 3119/HVM 3119

Adventures of Mole, The
Chl-Juv '84
Cartoons
13085   60 mins   C
B, V
Animated
This programme features seven slapstick cartoons with the ingenious and lovable Mole plowing his garden and sorting out the humans in his life.
PS,I — EN
Unknown — *Longman Video*   P
5026

Adventures of Peter Cottontail, The
Chl-Juv '7?
Fairy tales
02218   85 mins   C
V
Famous characters created by Thorton W. Burgess come to life in this delightful story.
M — EN
Unknown — *JVC*   P
PRT 28

Adventures of Popeye, The
Fil-Ent '3?
Cartoons
02464   52 mins   C
B, V
Animated
The humourous exploits of the famous sailorman, Olive Oyl, Bluto, and Wimpy. Contains several short cartoons produced by Max Fleischer.
F — EN
Max Fleischer; Paramount — *Mountain Video*
P

Adventures of Reddy the Fox, The
Chl-Juv '78
Cartoons/Adventure
09241   52 mins   C
B, V
Animated
Reddy the Fox has been told to be good while his Granny is away. The temptation to go and play with his friends proves too much. This film follows his adventures with Farmer Brown's sheep, Bowser the Dog and the Coyote.
PS,M — EN
ZIV International — *Home Video Holdings*
H, P
043

Adventures of Robin Hood, The
Fil-Ent '38
Adventure
13165   102 mins   C
B, V
Errol Flynn, Basil Rathbone, Claude Rains, Olivia DeHavilland, Alan Hale
The first technicoloured version of the Robin Hood legend.
BBFC:U — F — EN
Warner Bros — *Warner Home Video*   P
99234

Adventures of Sherlock Holmes' Smarter Brother, The
Fil-Ent '78
Comedy
01762   91 mins   C
B, V
Gene Wilder, Madeline Kahn, Marty Feldman, Dom DeLuise
The unknown brother of the famous Sherlock Holmes takes on some of his brother's more disposable excess cases and makes some hilarious moves.
F — EN
20th Century Fox — *CBS/Fox Video*   P
3A-035

Adventures of Sinbad the Sailor, The
Fil-Ent '75
Cartoons/Adventure
05755   87 mins   C
B, V
Animated
As a reward of saving his life, the Old Man of the Sea gives Sinbad a map to a treasure island. In his search, Sinbad falls in love with the King's daughter and is put in jail. An evil Prime Minister follows them to the island; the battle that follows causes the island to sink into the sea. Sinbad rescues the Princess and they live happily ever after.
BBFC:U — F — EN
ZIV International; Family Home Entertainment — *Home Video Holdings*
H, P
027

(For Explanation of codes, see USE GUIDE and KEY)

PALADIN VIDEO HOME ENTERTAINMENT GUIDE

Adventures of Superman, The
Fil-Ent '4?
Cartoons
02068   30 mins   C
B, V
Animated
The Man of Steel returns to the screen in three of the best colour cartoons by Dave Fleischer.
F — EN
Paramount — *VCL Video Services*   **P**

Adventures of the Wilderness Family
Fil-Ent '76
Adventure
08869   100 mins   C
V2, B, V
Robert F. Logan, Susan Damante Shaw, Holly Holmes, Ham Larsen, directed by Stewart Raffill
This is the true story of a modern-day pioneer family who become bored with the troubles of city life and head for life in the wilderness. It is the beginning of an incredible life with nature and the elements.
BBFC:U — F — EN
Pacific International Enterprises — *Video Programme Distributors*   **P**
Media 203

Adventures of the Wilderness Family—Part 2
Fil-Ent '77
Adventure
08870   104 mins   C
V2, B, V
Robert F. Logan, Susan Damante Shaw, Heather Rattray, Ham Larsen, George Flower, directed by Frank Zuniga
This is the continuing saga of the Robinson family who have to face their first winter in the wilderness, the worst for twenty years.
BBFC:U — F — EN
Pacific International Enterprises — *Video Programme Distributors*   **P**
Media 204

Adventures of Tom Sawyer, The
Fil-Ent '38
Adventure
04184   76 mins   C
B, V
Tommy Kelly, Jackie Moran, Ann Gillis, Walter Brennan, May Robson, Victor Jory
Colourful film version of Mark Twain's classic tale.
BBFC:U — F — EN
Selznick — *Guild Home Video*   **H, P**

Adventures of Ultraman, The
Fil-Ent '81
Cartoons/Adventure
09239   90 mins   C
B, V
Animated
This animated film follows the outer-space adventures of Ultraman as he battles to save mankind. His deadly enemy Starlord Barock has command of the evil powers of the Universe. Ultraman uses his Ultramind to fight Barock's invasion.
F — EN
Family Home Entertainment — *Home Video Holdings*   **H, P**
039

Affair, The
Fil-Ent '73
Romance/Drama
07341   74 mins   C
B, V
Natalie Wood, Robert Wagner, Bruce Davison, Jamie Smith-Jackson, Kent Smith, Kate Reid, directed by Gilbert Cates
A young woman, crippled since childhood by polio, becomes a successful composer of love songs without ever having been in love. Then a divorced lawyer with two children enters her life and she experiences the joys and sorrows of love for the first time.
BBFC:A — S,A — EN
Spelling-Goldberg Prods — *Precision Video Ltd*   **P**
BITC 2091/VITC 2091

Africa Express
Fil-Ent '73
Adventure/Suspense
08008   90 mins   C
V2, B, V
Ursula Andress, Giuliano Gemma, Jack Palance, directed by Michele Lupo
This is the tale of a young American out to make his fortune by running a small trucking line, helped by his intelligent chimp Biba, selling almost anything to the African natives. He encounters a disguised nun who is on the trail of an ex-Nazi, wanted for war crimes.
BBFC:U — F — EN
Unknown — *Iver Film Services*   **P**
187

Africa Screams
Fil-Ent '49
Comedy
06885   79 mins   C
V2, B, V
Bud Abbott, Lou Costello

(For Explanation of codes, see USE GUIDE and KEY)

PALADIN VIDEO HOME ENTERTAINMENT GUIDE

A series of hilarious adventures take place when Abbott and Costello go on safari with a secret map showing a spot where diamonds can be found.
M,A — EN
United Artists — European Video Company
P

Africa—Texas Style Fil-Ent '67
Adventure
04200   109 mins   C
B, V
Hugh O'Brian, John Mills
Kenya rancher hires two American cowboys to prove that the herding and domesticating of wild animals can help save African wildlife. A cattle rancher tries to sabotage his plan.
BBFC:U — F — EN
Paramount; Ivan Tors — Guild Home Video
H, P

African Queen, The Fil-Ent '51
Adventure/Romance
01027   105 mins   C
B, V
Humphrey Bogart, Katharine Hepburn, Robert Morley, Theodore Bikel, directed by John Huston
In the Congo during World War I, a spinster persuades a dissolute captain to try to destroy a German gunboat.
Academy Awards '51: Best Actor (Bogart).
F — EN
United Artists; Horizon Romulus
Prod — CBS/Fox Video   P
3B-001

African Waterhole Gen-Edu '7?
Wildlife/Africa
02274   25 mins   C
V
The story of a day at a waterhole in the African Savannah. This programme shows the extreme caution of the animals at the waterhole because of the presence of predators, but also how all of them are completely dependent on the waterhole.
F — ED
Unknown — JVC   P
PRT 13

Against a Crooked Sky Fil-Ent '75
Western/Adventure
12247   ? mins   C
B, V
Richard Boone, Stewart Peterson, Geoffrey Lard, directed by Earl Bellamy

Set against the rugged scenery of Death Horse Point, Utah, this film tells the story of an eleven year old boy's search for his sister who was captured by Indians.
F — EN
Lyman D Dayton; Cinema Shares — VCL Video Services   P

Agatha Christie Collection, Volume 1, The Fil-Ent '82
Mystery/Drama
12905   104 mins   C
B, V
Maurice Denham, Gwen Watford, Peter Jones, Nicholas Clay, Emma Piper, directed by Michael Simpson and Desmond Davis.
This tape contains two tales from the Agatha Christie Hour: 'The Case of the Middle-Aged Wife' and 'In a Glass Darkly.'
S,A — EN
EMI — THORN EMI   P
TXJ 90 17144/TVJ 90 17142

Age of Innocence Fil-Ent '78
Drama
06920   96 mins   C
B, V
David Warner, Honor Blackman, Trudy Young, Cec Linder, Tim Henry, Lois Maxwell, Robert Hawkins, directed by Alan Bridges
An Englishman takes a teaching job in Canada to escape persecution as a pacifist in the 1914-18 war. He soon faces a new moral dilemma when he falls in love with the headmaster's daughter. Despite the ridicule of his colleagues, the advances of a wealthy woman and the jealousy of the daughter's sweetheart, the relationship deepens. When he mistakenly voices his pacifist views he finds he is being persecuted all over again.
BBFC:AA — S,A — EN
Unknown — Rank Video Library   H, P
0067C

Agency Fil-Ent '81
Mystery/Drama
06149   110 mins   C
V2, B, V
Robert Mitchum, Lee Majors, Valerie Perrine, Alexandra Stewart
The Agency attempts, through the world of advertising, to influence and control the minds of millions of people exposed to the media. Hidden messages are sent to manipulate public behaviour and opinion to suit the Agency's mysterious purpose, which is not just selling a product.
BBFC:AA — S,A — EN
Lantas and Roth Prod — Guild Home Video
H, P, E

PALADIN VIDEO HOME ENTERTAINMENT GUIDE

Agony and the Ecstasy, The   Fil-Ent '65
Drama
05640   134 mins   C
V2, B, V
Charlton Heston, Rex Harrison, Diane Cilento
This film dwells on the relationship between the great Florentine painter, sculptor and architect Michelangelo and Pope Julius II over the painting of the Sistine Chapel ceiling. Based on the novel by Irving Stone.
S,A — EN
Twentieth Century Fox — CBS/Fox Video   P
4A-131

Agostini   Fil-Ent '7?
Motorcycles/Sports
07644   30 mins   C
B, V
Introduced by Mike Hailwood
This film is a tribute to Giacomo Agostini, his races and his courage. He won 15 World Championship titles between 1964 and 1975. He won 122 races in the world championship series between April 1965 and August 1976 including a record 19 in 1970.
F — EN
Unknown — VCL Video Services   P
S054A

Aguirre, Wrath of God   Fil-Ent '74
Drama/Adventure
07739   90 mins   C
B, V
Klaus Kinski, directed by Werner Herzog
A band of Spanish Conquistadors, lead by Aguirre and consisting of eleven hundred men, two women, horses, Llamas, pigs and rifles descend from the Andes in search of the fabled city of gold. Aguirre has brought with him his 14 year old daughter who he intends to marry and found a 'pure' race to rule the new empire. His megalomania turns the expedition into a death trip as the forest swallows them up. Not one of them returns alive.
S,A — EN
Werner Herzog — Palace Video Ltd   P

Aib Ya Loulou (Shame on You Loulou)   Fil-Ent '??
Comedy
06737   115 mins   C
V2, B, V
A girl decides to share a flat with three young men.
C,A — EN   AB
Unknown — Intervision Video   H, P
A-C 0147

Aida   Fin-Art '55
Opera
06810   96 mins   C
V2, B, V
Sophia Loren, Lois Maxwell
Verdi's opera transformed to the screen.
F — EN
IFE — Intervision Video   H, P
A-AE 0375

Aida   Fil-Ent '8?
Opera
08655   156 mins   C
B, V
Maria Chiara, Nicola Martinucci, Fiorenza Cossotto, Giuseppe Scandola, Alfredo Zanazzo
This is an opera by Giuseppe Verdi, written in 1870 for the new Cairo Opera House, built to commemorate the opening of the Suez Canal. This production of Aida was recorded in the Roman Arena of Verona in Italy. It is performed in four acts and conducted by Anton Guadagno.
S,A — EN
Unknown — Longman Video   P
LGBE 7001/LGVH 7001

Air Hawk   Fil-Ent '7?
Adventure
12171   92 mins   C
V2, B, V
Eric Oldfield, Louise Howill, Ellie Maclure, David Robson, directed by David Baker
A pilot's brother is killed and he finds he is their next victim. In this tale of diamond smuggling, death and destruction, he fights for his life.
BBFC:15 — S,A — EN
Unknown — Intervision Video   H, P
A-A 0496

Airplane II—The Sequel   Fil-Ent '82
Comedy-Drama
12046   82 mins   C
B, V
Robert Hays, Julie Hagerty, Peter Graves, Lloyd Bridges, Raymond Burr, directed by Ken Finkleman
The world's first commercial lunar shuttle leaves earth manned by a very peculiar group of people. With such an assorted bunch, trouble soon sets in with a computer malfunction which puts them on a collision course with the sun.
BBFC:PG — S,A — EN
Paramount — CIC Video   H, P
BER 2071/VHR 2071

Airport '80—The Concorde   Fil-Ent '79
Drama
07367   110 mins   C
B, V

(For Explanation of codes, see USE GUIDE and KEY)   11

PALADIN VIDEO HOME ENTERTAINMENT GUIDE

Alain Delon, Susan Blakely, Robert Wagner, Sylvia Kristel, George Kennedy, directed by David Lowell Rich
When a brilliant scientist is threatened with exposure, after selling arms illegally for foreign companies, he launches his Buzzard Attack Missile to intercept a Concorde flying from Washington to Paris. The passengers include the Russian Olympic team who are on a goodwill tour of the West.
S,A — EN
Universal — *CIC Video*   **H, P**
BEA 1023/VHA 1023

Airport '77   Fil-Ent '77
Drama/Suspense
05331   116 mins   C
V2, B, V
Jack Lemmon, Lee Grant, Brenda Vaccaro, Joseph Cotten, Olivia de Havilland, Darren McGavin, Christopher Lee, George Kennedy, James Stewart, directed by Jerry Jameson
A 747 jumbo jet crashes into the sea in the infamous Bermuda Triangle. The main body remains intact but they are unable to communicate with the outside world, their air supply is low and the fuselage is about to give way under pressure. With rescuers searching for the plane in the wrong area the survivors have to find their own way to safety.
S,A — EN
Universal — *CIC Video*   **H, P**
CRA1019/BEA1019/VHA1019

Airport SOS Hijack   Fil-Ent '73
Suspense/Drama
07818   90 mins   C
V2, B, V
Adam Roarke, Neville Brand, Jay Robinson, Lynn Borden, directed by Barry Pollack
An airliner is hijacked for the purpose of extorting a million dollar ransom to pay huge gambling debts owed to the Syndicate.
S,A — EN
Unknown — *Video Unlimited*   **H, P**
048

Airwolf   Fil-Ent '83
Adventure/Drama
13300   85 mins   C
B, V
Ernest Borgnine, David Hemmings, Jan-Michael Vincent, Alex Cord, directed by Donald P Bellisario
Two men are enlisted by the CIA to recapture a secret military helicopter which is in the hands of a power crazed pilot.
S,A — EN
Universal TV; Belisarius Productions — *CIC Video*   **H, P**
BET 1119/VHT 1119

Aladdin   Chi-Juv '7?
Fantasy/Fairy tales
01869   70 mins   C
V2, B, V
Animated, written by France and Jean Image
A classic fairy tale combining magic, a beautiful heroine, and Aladdin's attempt to retain his magic lamp.
I — EN
Films Jean Image Production — *Videomedia*
P
PVM 2110/BVM 2110/HVM 2110

Aladdin's Lamp   Chi-Juv '??
Fairy tales
01685   74 mins   C
V2, B, V
Aladdin's adventures with the powerful Genie of the Lamp are re-created in this version of the classic fairy story.
BBFC:U — F — EN
Unknown — *Intervision Video*   **H, P**
A-AE 0008

Alam Alhaiwan   Gen-Edu '??
Wildlife/Documentary
07999   ? mins   C
B, V
This programme produced entirely in Arabic is in four parts and looks at wildlife.
F — ED   AB
Unknown — *Motion Epics Video Company Ltd*
P

Alamo, The   Fil-Ent '61
Adventure/Western
13023   161 mins   C
B, V
John Wayne, Richard Widmark, Laurence Harvey, Frankie Avalon, directed by John Ford
The story of how, in 1936, a handful of assorted Americans defended a ramshackle mission against a 7,000 strong Mexican Army.
BBFC:A — A — EN
United Artists — *Warner Home Video*   **P**
99224

Alan Price   Fil-Ent '81
Music-Performance
06245   40 mins   C
B, V
This tape contains many of Alan Price's most popular songs shot entirely in Concert. Songs featured include: Lucky Man, Simon Smith and his Amazing Dancing Bear, Poor People, A Song of Love (Hi Lilly, Hi Lo).
F — EN
Unknown — *VCL Video Services*   **P**
V114B

PALADIN VIDEO HOME ENTERTAINMENT GUIDE

Alaska Wilderness Adventure, The — Fil-Ent '78
Documentary
06774   92 mins   C
V2, B, V
Fred and Elaine Meader
This production follows the Meader family through a year of their life in the Artic wilderness.
F — EN
Ron Wilton; Jon and Bunny Dana — *Intervision Video*   **H, P**
A-A 0334

Alcatraz — Fil-Ent '80
Drama
05633   108 mins   C
V2, B, V
Telly Savalas, Michael Beck, Will Sampson
This is the story of the two most famous breakouts from the prison that was designed as the most secure ever built, housing the hardest convicts in the U.S.A. Based on true life, the film traces the 1946 'Battle of Alcatraz.'
S,A — EN
Pierre Cossette;Mark E Massari — *Video Unlimited*   **H, P**

Alcatraz II—The Final Escape — Fil-Ent '80
Drama
07823   98 mins   C
V2, B, V
Michael Beck, Art Carney, Telly Savalas, Ronny Cox, Alex Karras
This film tells the true story of the most famous escape from Alcatraz.
S,A — EN
Pierre Cossette Productions; Mark E Massari — *Video Unlimited*   **H, P**
032

Alchemist, The — Fil-Ent '??
Horror
10181   84 mins   C
B, V
Robert Ginty, Lucinda Doaling, John Sanderford, Viola Kate Stimpson, Bob Glaudin, directed by Charles Band
On a dark night in 1871 a man attempts to save his wife from the powers of the Alchemist. Whilst trying to destroy the evil power he kills his wife and is condemned to eternal damnation. It is now 1955 and the Alchemist must be avenged before hell is let loose on the world.
BBFC:18 — *A — EN*
Ideal Films Inc; Manson Int'l — *Video Form Pictures*   **H, P**
MGS 28

'Alchemy'—Dire Straits Live — Fil-Ent '83
Music-Performance
12030   80 mins   C
B, V
This tape contains excerpts from the summer 1983 Dire Straits concert at London's Hammersmith Odeon and consists of ten tracks including 'Romeo and Juliet,' 'Private Investigations' and 'Sultans of Swing.'
F — EN
Mark Knopfler — *Polygram Video*   **H, P**
0402694/0402692

Alex and His Dog — Fil-Ent '??
Cartoons/History
06209   60 mins   C
B, V
Animated
A collection of stories made to introduce children to historical events. Stories include: How fire was discovered, How the Pyramids were built, How the Olympic Games started, The age of Chivalry, How America was discovered and The French Revolution.
F — EN
Unknown — *VCL Video Services*   **P**
F124B

Alexis Korner-Eat a Little Rhythm and Blues — Fil-Ent '84
Music-Performance
12730   71 mins   C
B, V
A celebration of Alexis Korner's 50th birthday, when he got together with other musician friends at Pinewood. This video serves as a tribute to the great man's work but also features many other famous musicians including Eric Clapton, Chris Farlowe, Paul Jones and Zoot Money.
F — EN
Peter Ruchel — *BBC Video*   **H, P**
3011

Alfie Darling — Fil-Ent '75
Comedy-Drama
05435   98 mins   C
B, V
Alan Price, Joan Collins, Jill Townsend, directed by Ken Hughes
Set in London during the 'swinging sixties' this is the story of a womanizing lorry driver with women up and down the motorways of Europe.

(For Explanation of codes, see USE GUIDE and KEY)

PALADIN VIDEO HOME ENTERTAINMENT GUIDE

The main object of this chauvinistic crusade is the sophisticated editor of a travel magazine who proves to be his downfall to the extent of him proposing marriage.
BBFC:X — A — EN
Signal Film Productions Ltd — THORN EMI
P
TXC 90 0327 4/TVC 90 0327 2

Alice Cooper   Fil-Ent '77
Music-Performance
07711   71 mins   C
B, V
This programme features the pioneer of 'shock rock,' Alice Cooper, in concert in San Diego during 1977.
S,A — EN
Independent — CBS/Fox Video   P
1064

Alice Doesn't Live Here Anymore   Fil-Ent '74
Comedy-Drama
06027   108 mins   C
B, V
Ellen Burstyn, Kris Kristofferson, Billy Green Bush, Diane Ladd, Jodie Foster, directed by Martin Scorsese
A young woman who is suddenly widowed is left with an 11 year old son to bring-up. The two of them set out for Monterey in California where she was once very happy and employed as a singer. She intends resuming her singing career but on the way she meets a young man and falls in love.
BBFC:AA — S,A — EN
Warner Bros; David Susskind and Audrey Maas Prods — Warner Home Video   P
WEX1034/WEV1034

Alice in the Cities   Fil-Ent '74
Comedy-Drama
08961   110 mins   C
B, V
Rudiger Vogeler, Yella Rottlander, Elizabeth Kreuzer, directed by Wim Wenders
This film tells the story of a young reporter who fails to submit a story after a confusing assignment in the USA, and his subsequent odyssey across Germany in the company of a little girl who has lost her mother. The film has German dialogue with English subtitles.
BBFC:U — F — EN   GE
Cinegate — Palace Video Ltd   P
PVC 2023A

Alice in Wonderland   Fil-Ent '77
Comedy
06730   75 mins   C
V2, B, V
Kristine DeBell
An adult musical comedy version of the classic tale starring Playboy cover girl Kristine DeBell.
BBFC:X — A — EN
General National Enterprises — Intervision Video   H, P
A-AE 0323

Alice in Wonderland   Chi-Juv '51
Cartoons
13443   74 mins   C
B, V
Animated
In this adaptation of Lewis Carroll's story, all his legendary fantasy characters are brought to life; Alice the White Rabbit, the Cheshire Cat, The Queen of Hearts and the Mad Hatter in a dream-like world.
BBFC:U — F — EN
Walt Disney Productions — Rank Video Library
P
VW 036

Alice's Restaurant   Fil-Ent '69
Comedy-Drama
12500   107 mins   C
B, V
Arlo Guthrie, Patt Quinn, James Broderick, directed by Arthur Penn
The extraordinary adventures of the famous folk singer Arlo Guthrie and his friends, based on his memorable song 'The Alice's Restaurant Massacre'.
BBFC:18 — A — EN
Hillard Elkins; Joe Manduke — Warner Home Video   P
99423

Alien   Fil-Ent '80
Science fiction
05649   111 mins   C
V2, B, V, LV
Yaphet Kotto, Ian Holm, John Hurt, Veronica Cartwright, Sigourney Weaver
In their battered commercial starship, seven astronauts are returning home from deep space. They receive a mysterious distress call, to which they respond, little knowing that they are to become the victims of a galactic creature of unspeakable horror.
BBFC:X — A — EN
Twentieth Century Fox — CBS/Fox Video
H
4A-128

Alien Attack   Fil-Ent '7?
Science fiction
00836   122 mins   C
B, V
Martin Landau, Barbara Bain, Barry Morse

PALADIN VIDEO HOME ENTERTAINMENT GUIDE

Suspected radiation leaks from nuclear waste containers on the moon is a prologue to catastrophe: man's most fantastic adventure is about to begin.
A — EN
ITC — Precision Video Ltd   P
BITC 3024/VITC 3024

Alien Encounters   Fil-Ent '??
Science fiction
08835   90 mins   C
B, V
A man loses his family in an explosion, which seems to be connected with a distant star. A scientist sets out to try to solve the mystery.
C,A — EN
Unknown — VCL Video Services   P
C025C

Alien Factor, The   Fil-Ent '78
Science fiction
07982   82 mins   C
B, V
Don Leifert, Tom Griffith, Mary Mertens
This film tells the story of an alien spacecraft which accidentally crashes on Earth, outside the city limits of a small town. It releases its dangerous live cargo, causing havoc and destruction as the authorities fight to control them.
C,A — EN
Unknown — AVI Video Ltd   P

Alien Terror   Fil-Ent '??
Science fiction/Horror
07810   102 mins   C
B, V
A space capsule returns to earth without the astronauts who have been victims of a bloodthirsty alien. The alien then traps six young cave explorers underground where they are eaten alive one by one; it then goes on to destroy a Californian community.
A — EN
Unknown — Video Tape Centre   P
VTC 1017

Aliens from Spaceship Earth   Fil-Ent '79
Science fiction
01153   93 mins   C
V2, B, V
Donovan, Lynda Day George

Are strange, celestial forces invading our universe? If they are, is man prepared to defend his planet against threatening aliens of unknown strength?
M,A — EN
Unknown — Intervision Video   P
A-AE 0192

Alison's Birthday   Fil-Ent '??
Horror
09005   95 mins   C
V2, B, V
Lou Brown, Joanne Samuel, Bunney Brooke, John Bluthal, Vincent Ball, directed by Ian Coughlan
This is a tale of the supernatural. Alison is warned at a seance that she must break away from her family before her nineteenth birthday. Her birthday celebrations herald the prophetic warnings as her nightmares become reality in a life and death struggle with evil.
A — EN
Unknown — Intervision Video   H, P
A-A 0474

All About Eve   Fil-Ent '50
Drama
01140   138 mins   B/W
B, V
Bette Davis, Anne Baxter, Gary Merrill, Celeste Holme, George Sanders, Marilyn Monroe, directed by Joseph L. Mankiewicz
An aspiring young actress ingratiates herself with a prominent group of theatre people, but passion to perform and jealousy consume her as she viciously betrays her colleagues in her struggle for success.
Academy Awards '50: Best Picture; Best Supporting Actor (Sanders); Best Direction (Mankiewicz); Best Screenplay (Mankiewicz).
F — EN
20th Century Fox — CBS/Fox Video   P
4A-087

All Coppers Are.....   Fil-Ent '74
Crime-Drama/Comedy
08036   84 mins   C
B, V
Julia Foster, Martin Potter
This tells the story of a young policeman who, because of a chance meeting with a girl, involves himself with robbery and violence.
BBFC:AA — S,A — EN
Rank — Rank Video Library   H, P
0123 C

All Creatures Great and Small   Fil-Ent '8?
Drama
10142   99 mins   C

(For Explanation of codes, see USE GUIDE and KEY)   15

PALADIN VIDEO HOME ENTERTAINMENT GUIDE

V2, B, V
Christopher Timothy, Robert Hardy, Peter Davison, Carol Drinkwater
This tape contains two episodes from the series-'It Takes All Kinds' and 'Advice and Consent'. Based on the books by James Herriot and set in the thirties it follows the adventures of a young vet in a friendly but eccentric practice.
F — EN
BBC — *BBC Video* **H, P**
BBCV 2006

All in a Night's Work   Fil-Ent '61
Mystery
01761   94 mins   C
B, V
Dean Martin, Shirley MacLaine, Cliff Robertson
The founder of a one-man publishing empire is discovered dead with a smile on his face.
BBFC:A — S,A — EN
Paramount; Hal Wallis Prod — *CBS/Fox Video* **P**
3B-002

All Night Long   Fil-Ent '81
Comedy
10110   96 mins   C
B, V
Barbara Streisand, Gene Hackman, directed by Jean-Claude Tramont
The trials of middle age are portrayed by a demoted businessman, who decides late in life to 'do his own thing', encouraged by his lover who he persuaded away from his son.
BBFC:15 — C,A — EN
Paramount — *CIC Video*   **H, P**
BEA 1076/VHA 1076

All Night Long   Fil-Ent '61
Drama
13765   95 mins   B/W
B, V
Patrick McGoohan, Richard Attenborough, Dave Brubeck, Johnny Dankworth, Keith Michell, directed by Basil Dearden
This is a tale of love and jealousy between two couples in the jazz scene and is played against the atmospheric music of such music greats as Dave Brubeck, John Dankworth, Charles Mingus and Tubby Hayes.
BBFC:A — C,A — EN
Basil Deardon; Michael Relph — *Rank Video Library* **H, P**
0208E

All of Me   Fil-Ent '84
Comedy
13691   88 mins   C

B, V
Steve Martin, Lily Tomlin, Victoria Tennant, directed by Carl Reiner
When a rich, eccentric woman dies, a crazy guru tries to transport her soul into another girl's body, but he makes a mistake.
BBFC:15 — S,A — EN
Stephen Friedman — *THORN EMI*   **P**
90 3086

All Quiet on the Western Front   Fil-Ent '7?
War-Drama
02036   123 mins   C
B, V
Donald Pleasence, Richard Thomas, Ernest Borgnine, Ian Holm, Patricia Neal
Six German schoolboys are whisked off to World War I where they are put through rigorous military drills. When they first view wounded men being rushed to hospital, they begin to realise the grim reality of war.
S,A — EN
Norman Rosemont — *Precision Video Ltd* **P**
BITC 3020/VITC 3020

All Quiet on the Western Front   Fil-Ent '30
War-Drama
12051   103 mins   B/W
B, V
Lew Ayres, Louis Walheim, directed by Lewis Milestone
This film is adopted from the novel and tells the story of seven German schoolboys who eagerly enlist in the 1914 war. They are quickly disillusioned by the hard facts of the war and one by one they go to their death in battle.
Academy Awards '31: Best Picture; Best Director (Milestone).   BBFC:U — F — EN
Universal — *CIC Video*   **H, P**
BEJ 1084/VHJ 1084

All That Jazz   Fil-Ent '80
Drama
05527   123 mins   C
V2, B, V, LV
Roy Scheider, Jessica Lange, Ann Reinking, Leland Palmer, directed by Bob Fosse
A Broadway choreographer and film director is overworking on a new musical show and a film. He keeps hallucinating that he is talking to the Angel of Death. His womanising, his daughter, smoking and pill taking with overwork cause him to have a heart-attack. After open-heart surgery

---

16   (For Explanation of codes, see USE GUIDE and KEY)

PALADIN VIDEO HOME ENTERTAINMENT GUIDE

he fantasises about production numbers and has a relapse. A song and dance finale takes him to his coffin and the hands of the Angel of Death.
A — EN
Twentieth Century Fox — *CBS/Fox Video* **H**

All the Kind Strangers Fil-Ent '74
Suspense/Drama
05632   90 mins   C
V2, B, V
Samantha Eggar, Stacy Keach, John Savage, Robby Benson, directed by Burt Kennedy
A story of an ordeal for a New York photographer when he innocently gives a lift to a small boy. The photographer is lured to the boy's home where seven strange orphans and their dogs are trying to find substitute parents. If the strangers fail to please they murder them and incinerate the bodies.
S,A — EN
Cinemation — *Video Unlimited* **H, P**

All the Loving Couples Fil-Ent '69
Comedy
07820   80 mins   C
V2, B, V
Scott Graham, Lynn Cartwright, Gloria Manon, Paul Comi, directed by Mack Bing
In this hilarious romp the personal and confidential desires of ordinary people are exposed as 'wife-swapping' and the sexual revolution engulfs suburbia.
BBFC:X — A — EN
U-M Productions — *Video Unlimited* **H, P**
030

All the President's Men Fil-Ent '76
Drama
07853   130 mins   C
B, V
Robert Redford, Dustin Hoffman, Jack Warden, Martin Balsam, Hal Holbrook, Jason Robards, Jane Alexander, Stephen Collins, Meredith Baxter, Ned Beatty, Penny Fuller, directed by Alan J. Pakula
Based on the book by Carl Bernstein and Bob Woodward, this film looks at the extensive investigative work by two young reporters from the Washington Post resulting in the exposure of the Watergate scandal.
BBFC:AA — S,A — EN
Warner Bros — *Warner Home Video* **P**
WEX 61018/WEV 61018

All the Right Moves Fil-Ent '83
Drama
13254   113 mins   C
B, V

Tom Cruise, Craig T. Nelson, Lea Thompson, Charles Cioffi, Chris Penn, directed by Michael Chapman
Set in a steel town in Pennsylvania, this film tells the story of a boy's determination to escape from his surroundings and win a football scholarship to university.
BBFC:15 — S,A — EN
Stephen Deutsch — *CBS/Fox Video* **P**
1299

All the Way Boys Fil-Ent '73
Adventure/Comedy
10077   88 mins   C
V2, B, V
Terence Hill, Bud Spencer
This duo of modern day outlaws are engaged in flying airplanes through the Amazonian Forest. Chaos in the form of emergency landings, burning planes, bank robberies, baddies versus goodies is caused as they search for adventure and fortune.
F — EN
Italo Zingarelli Film; Joseph E Levine; Avco Embassy — *Embassy Home Entertainment* **P**
2022

All You Need to Know How-Ins '81
About Dogs
Pets
05417   60 mins   C
B, V, FO
Presented by Lesley Judd
This is a comprehensive guide to choosing, feeding, training, breeding, showing and caring for your dog. Some of the world's leading experts, presented by Lesley Judd, help owners gain the greatest possible pleasure from having a dog in the family.
F — I
Commercial Video Limited; Pedigree Pet Foods Ltd — *Michael Barratt Ltd* **P**

Allan Sherman Show, The Fil-Ent '7?
Variety
04382   60 mins   C
B, V, PH17, 3/4U
Allan Sherman, Young Americans
A variety show starring Allan Sherman, featuring the Young Americans.
F — EN
Unknown — *Vidpics International* **P**

Allegheny Uprising/Back Fil-Ent '??
from Eternity
Western/Drama
05769   164 mins   B/W
B, V

(For Explanation of codes, see USE GUIDE and KEY)   17

PALADIN VIDEO HOME ENTERTAINMENT GUIDE

John Wayne, George Sanders, Claire Trevor, Brian Donlevy, Chill Wills, Wifrid Lawson, directed by William Seiter, Anita Ekberg, Rod Steiger, Robert Ryan, directed by John Farrow
Two films are contained on one cassette. 'Allegheny Uprising' (black/white, 71 mins, 1940) is set in 1759 a man clashes with a military commander in order to stop the sale of firearms to Indians. 'Back from Eternity' (black/white, 93 mins, 1957) is a suspense story in which an airliner crashes in Central American headhunter territory with eleven passengers on board, as the hunters close in to attack they discover that the plane is capable of taking off if three people remain behind.
S,A — EN
RKO; Universal — Kingston Video   H, P
KV13

Alley Cat   Fil-Ent '84
Drama
13228   84 mins   C
B, V
Karin Mani, Robert Torti, Brit Helfer, Michael Wayne, Jon Greene, directed by Edward Victor
Set in down-town Los Angeles, a young girl sets out to avenge the death of her grandparents by a brutal street gang but finds herself in trouble with the law.
BBFC:18 — A — EN
Film Ventures International — Entertainment in Video   H, P
EVB 1029/EVV 1029

Alligator   Fil-Ent '80
Suspense
07878   90 mins   C
V2, B, V
Robert Forster, Robin Riker, Dean Jagger, Sue Lyon
A little girl returns home one day having bought a baby alligator as a pet. Her father refuses to keep it and flushes it down the toilet. Twelve years later the town is thrown into utter chaos and devastation as a 20-ft monster alligator wreaks havoc, killing and mutilating the inhabitants.
S,A — EN
Brandon Chase — Intervision Video   H, P
A-A0395

Aloha, Bobby and Rose   Fil-Ent '75
Romance/Drama
06263   90 mins   C
B, V
Paul Le Mat, Dianne Hull, Tim McIntire, Leigh France, directed by Floyd Mutrux
A young couple meet by chance and fall in love on a rainy Californian night. They become inseparable, but a romantic prank results in tragedy and they go on their own to Mexico only to wait until death separates them. Sound track includes songs by Elton John, Stevie Wonder, Emerson Lake and Palmer and many others.
S,A — EN
Columbia Pictures — VCL Video Services
P
P195D

Alone in the Dark   Fil-Ent '8?
Horror
12759   90 mins   C
B, V, LV
Jack Palance, Martin Landau, Donald Pleasence, Dwight Schultz
There are terrifying consequences when the four most dangerous patients in a mental hospital escape and surround the hospital assistant's family home, believing that he has killed their benevolent director.
BBFC:18 — A — EN
Robert Shaye — Rank Video Library   H, P
2036

Alpha Beta   Fil-Ent '73
Drama
01679   65 mins   C
V2, B, V
Albert Finney, Rachel Roberts
This film depicts the frustration, disintegration, and final break-up of a marriage, despite the wife's efforts to the contrary. The effects of the break-up on family members are poignantly but dramatically shown.
BBFC:A — S,A — EN
Cine III — Intervision Video   H, P
A-A 0040

Alpha Incident, The   Fil-Ent '81
Science fiction
07907   81 mins   C
V2, B, V
Ralph Meeker
On returning from Mars a space probe is found to be contaminated with a deadly organism that could destroy all life on Earth. Scientists working to isolate the strain become infected and the Government is forced to take drastic measures to eliminate the germ and the carriers before civilisation is destroyed.
S,A — EN
Bill Rebane — Video Programme Distributors
P
Replay—1005

Alphaville   Fil-Ent '65
Science fiction
08962   180 mins   B/W
B, V

PALADIN VIDEO HOME ENTERTAINMENT GUIDE

Eddie Constantine, Anna Karina, Akim Tamiroff, directed by Jean-Luc Godard
This cassette contains both the English and the subtitled versions of the film, each 90 minutes long. A special agent travels across space to find out what had happened to his predecessor, and finds himself in a loveless society. His aim is to destroy the ruthless computer-controlled civilisation and rescue a girl.
BBFC:X — A — EN
Chaumiane; Filmstudio — *Palace Video Ltd*
P
PVC 2035A

Altered States   Fil-Ent '80
Fantasy
13051   103 mins   C
B, V
William Hurt, directed by Ken Russell
A research scientist experiments with the altered states of consciousness, discovering a mounting awareness of the wonder and ominous depths yet to be found within ourselves.
BBFC:X — A — EN
Warner Bros Inc — *Warner Home Video*
P
61076

Alvarez Kelly   Fil-Ent '66
Western
09275   116 mins   C
B, V
William Holden, Victoria Shaw, Janice Rule, Patrick O'Neil, Richard Widmark, Roger C. Carmel, directed by Edward Dmytryk
A gun-slinging maverick manages to find time for a little romance in between cattle raids and ferocious attacks from Union troops.
F — EN
Columbia — *RCA/Columbia Pictures Video UK*
H, P

Amanda Lear—Live in Concert   Fil-Ent '80
Music-Performance
04544   28 mins   C
B, V
Amanda Lear
This video cassette programme captures the sensational performance of Amanda Lear in concert in Hamburg and in Paris, singing all of her hits.
F — EN
VCL — *VCL Video Services*   P

Amag Elbehar   Gen-Edu '??
Documentary/Oceanography
07998   120 mins   C
B, V
This is an Arabic film about life under sea water.
F — ED   AB
Unknown — *Motion Epics Video Company Ltd*
P

Amateur, The   Fil-Ent '82
Drama/Adventure
12010   109 mins   C
B, V
John Savage, Christopher Plummer, directed by Charles Jarrott
An American who worked for the CIA travels to Czechoslovakia to avenge the murder of his girlfriend who was killed by a band of international terrorists.
S,A — EN
20th Century Fox — *CBS/Fox Video*   P
1147

Amazing Adventures of Baron Munchausen, The   Fil-Ent '43
Fantasy
05037   101 mins   C
B, V
Hans Albers, directed by Joseph von Baky
The story of the arch-storyteller and exaggerator of all time. The film was made in Germany.
F — EN
UFA — *THORN EMI*   P
TXB 90 0281 4/TVB 90 0281 2

Amazing Adventures of Joe 90, The   Fil-Ent '??
Science fiction/Puppets
07349   ? mins   C
B, V
This marionette production follows the adventures of the super-hero Joe 90.
F — EN
Gerry and Sylvia Anderson — *Precision Video Ltd*   P
BITC 2096/VITC 2096

Amazing Adventures of Morph: Volume 1, The   Chl-Juv '82
Cartoons/Fantasy
07423   27 mins   C
B, V
Animated, narrated by Tony Hart
This tape, the first of a series, features the bendy clay figure of Morph and his friends in his under-the-table world. The six stories on this

(For Explanation of codes, see USE GUIDE and KEY)

PALADIN VIDEO HOME ENTERTAINMENT GUIDE

tape are: 'Morph's Birthday Party,' 'Morph Plays Golf,' 'The Two Mountaineers,' 'The Day Morph Was Ill,' 'A Swimming Pool in the Garden' and 'The Double Decker Boot.'
PS,M — EN
Morph Ltd — *THORN EMI* **P**
TXF 90 0593 4/TVF 90 0593 2

Amazing Adventures of   Chl-Juv   '82
Morph: Volume 2, The
Cartoons/Fantasy
07424   28 mins   C
B, V
Animated, narrated by Tony Hart
This tape, the second in the series, features the bendy clay figure of Morph and his friends in his under-the-table world. The six stories on this tape are: 'The Baby-Sitters,' 'How It All Began,' 'The Strange Visitor,' 'Morph's Forgotten Dream,' 'Gobbledygook The Burglar,' 'Invisible Morph.'
PS,M — EN
Morph Ltd — *THORN EMI* **P**
TXF 90 0716 4/TCF 90 0716 2

Amazing Adventures of   Chl-Juv   '82
Morph: Volume 3, The
Cartoons/Fantasy
07425   30 mins   C
B, V
Animated, narrated by Tony Hart
This third tape in the series once more features the bendy clay figure of Morph and his friends in his under-the-table world. The six stories on this tape are: 'The Day Morph Went Skiing,' 'Morph and the Swoggle Flange,' 'The Abominable Snowman,' 'The Dog Show,' 'Morph the Weakling' and 'Green-A Very Small Creature.'
PS,M — EN
Morph Ltd — *THORN EMI* **P**
TXF 90 0739 4/TVF 90 0739 2

Amazing Adventures of   Chl-Juv   '82
Morph: Volume 4, The
Cartoons/Fantasy
08540   28 mins   C
B, V
Animated, narrated by Tony Hart
This fourth tape in the series features more of the antics of Morph and his friends, set in his under-the-table world. The six stories on this tape are 'Anyone for Cricket?', 'The Cowboys', 'A Game of Chess', 'The Day Nothing Happened', 'Grandmorph's Home Movies' and 'The Magic Wand'.
PS,M — EN
Morph Ltd — *THORN EMI* **P**
TXF 90 0758 4/TVF 90 0758 2

Amazing Adventures of   Chl-Juv   '84
Sherlock Holmes, The,
Cassette 1
Cartoons
13303   48 mins   C
B, V
Animated
Based on the stories of Sir Arthur Conan Doyle, The Hound, Sherlock Holmes and his doggy partner, Dr. Watson, use their detective powers to outwit Moriarty in 'The Blue Carbuncle' and 'The Little Client.'
BBFC:U — *F — EN*
Unknown — *CIC Video*   **H, P**
BER 3004/VHR 3004

Amazing Adventures of   Chl-Juv   '84
Sherlock Holmes, Volume
2, The
Cartoons
13606   48 mins   C
B, V
Animated
In the second cassette in this series the doggy duo encounter more adventure in two episodes titled 'Adventure of the Sea Bottom' and 'Adventure of the Sovereign Coins'.
BBFC:U — *F — EN*
CIC Video; Yoshimitusu Takahashi — *CIC Video*   **H, P**
3005

Amazing Adventures of   Chl-Juv   '84
Sherlock Holmes, Volume
3, The
Cartoons
13635   48 mins   C
B, V
Animated
Two more episodes are featured on this cassette for the doggy sleuths to solve titled 'The Adventure of Mrs. Hudson' and 'The Crown of Mazarine.'
BBFC:U — *F — EN*
Yoshimitsu Takahashi — *CIC Video*   **H, P**
3006

Amazing Dobermans, The   Fil-Ent   '76
Adventure
09961   90 mins   C
V2, B, V
Fred Astaire, James Franciscus, Barbara Eden
The owner of five trained dogs assists an undercover agent in foiling a small-time criminal's gambling and extortion racket.
BBFC:AA — *C,A — EN*
Golden Films — *Video Unlimited*   **H, P, E**
059

PALADIN VIDEO HOME ENTERTAINMENT GUIDE

Amazing Howard Hughes, The
Fil-Ent '77
Biographical
07453   119 mins   C
B, V
Tommy Lee Jones, Ed Flanders, James Hampton, Tovah Feldshuh, Lee Purcell, directed by William A. Graham
This film traces the life and career of Howard Hughes, the millionaire flyer, playboy and film maker. It follows Hughes from his early days, when at the age of 19 he inherited a fortune and went to Hollywood where, combining his obsession with aviation, he became a film producer. He set up world records as a pilot, formed his own company and gained control of TWA. But in 1946 he crashed while test-flying one of his own planes, which led to him becoming a total recluse.
S,A — EN
Roger Gimbel Productions; EMI Television Programmes — *THORN EMI*   P
TXB 90 0279 4/TVB 90 0279 2

Amazing Mr. Blunden, The
Fil-Ent '71
Fantasy/Fairy tales
07653   98 mins   C
B, V
Laurence Naismith, Lynne Frederick, James Villiers, Madeline Smith, Diana Dors, directed by Lionel Jeffries
This is the story of two children who are befriended by a kindly ghost. After the death of their father during World War I money was very scarce for the children. During a grim Christmas in a cold, dingy London house Mr. Blunden came to call: a strange old man whose eyes are transparent, whose shoes don't get wet and snowflakes don't settle on his coat.
F — EN
Hemdale — *VCL Video Services*   P
F186C

Amazing Spider-Man—Cassette 2, The
Fil-Ent '??
Cartoons/Adventure
08350   55 mins   C
V2, B, V
Animated
This tape contains six more episodes of Peter Parker, Spider-man. It includes spider-man meeting the Vulture Man and a metal-eating monster.
F — EN
Unknown — *Guild Home Video*   H, P, E

Amazing Spider-Man IV in Night of the Villains
Fil-Ent '7?
Cartoons/Adventure
12065   72 mins   C
V2, B, V
Animated
Eight exciting episodes in which Spider-Man continues his fight against evil characters like Vultureman and Dr Von Schlik.
BBFC:U — F — EN
Marvel Comics — *Guild Home Video*   H, P, E

Amazing Spider-Man-Cassette 3, The
Fil-Ent '??
Cartoons/Adventure
09427   63 mins   C
V2, B, V
Animated
This tape contains six more episodes, each 9 minutes long, of Peter Parker alias Spider-Man and his battle agains evil characters like, Electro, a human lightening bolt and the nasty Dr. Magneto. The episodes are 'The Kilowatt Kaper', 'The Peril of Parafino', 'Horn of the Rhino', 'The One-Eyed Idol', 'The Revenge of Dr. Magneto' and 'The Sinister Prime Minister'.
BBFC:U — F — EN
Marvel Comics — *Guild Home Video*   H, P, E

Amazing Spiderman in The Terrible Triumph of Dr. Octopus, The
Chl-Juv '84
Cartoons
13348   77 mins   C
B, V
Animated
This cassette contains eight episodes from Spider-Man, alias student Peter Parker who was given miraculous powers when bitten by a radio-active spider.
BBFC:U — F — EN
Marvel Comics — *Guild Home Video*   H, P, E
8432-7

Amazing World of Psychic Phenomena, The
Gen-Edu '77
Occult sciences
08064   93 mins   C
B, V
Hosted and narrated by Raymond Burr
This film looks at the mysteries of parapsychology
BBFC:U — F — EN
Sunn Classic — *Rank Video Library*   H, P
2012 B

Amazing Years of Early Cinema 1, The
Fil-Ent '??
Film-History
04689   50 mins   B/W

(For Explanation of codes, see USE GUIDE and KEY)   21

PALADIN VIDEO HOME ENTERTAINMENT GUIDE

B, V
Introduced and narrated by Douglas Fairbanks Jr.
With a number of mystifying examples, the first film on this cassette describes the importance of magic on the screen and reveals how some of the tricks were done. The second film investigates why the great epics were so quickly part of the cinema-goer's entertainment.
F — EN
Spectrum — *Polygram Video* **P**

Amazing Years of Early Cinema 2, The   Fil-Ent '??
Film-History
04688   50 mins   B/W
B, V
Introduced and narrated by Douglas Fairbanks Jr.
A look at the circus clowns who congregated to film in the early days and also the first cowboy films.
F — EN
Spectrum — *Polygram Video* **P**

Ambush Murders, The   Fil-Ent '82
Crime-Drama
09199   110 mins   C
B, V
James Brolin, Dorian Harewood, Alfred Woodward, Antonio Fargas
This film, based on a true story tells of a court case which is investigating the double murder of two white California policemen. Overzealous law officers arrest their primary suspect. After two years in jail, awaiting his third trial, his wife hires a compassionate lawyer, determined to prove his client's innocence to the jury.
S,A — EN
David Goldsmith Prods — *Video Form Pictures* **H, P**
DD2

America—Live in Central Park   Fil-Ent '81
Music-Performance
07476   60 mins   C
B, V
Directed by Peter Clifton
This film features the rock band 'America' recorded live at a concert held in New York's Central Park before an audience of 12,000 fans. With special effects, the band perform some of their well known hits including 'Horse With No Name,' 'Ventura Highway,' 'Sandman,' 'Tin Man' and 'All Night.'
S,A — EN
B C Productions Inc — *THORN EMI* **P**
TXE 90 0710 4/TVE 90 0710 2

America Screams   Fil-Ent '??
Adventure
06208   48 mins   C
B, V
Hosted by Vincent Price
A tour of America's scariest fun fair rides, including the giant roller coaster and the weirdest, wildest rides created with Vincent Price as guide.
S,A
Cyclone Productions — *VCL Video Services* **P**
F138B

American Candid Camera   Fil-Ent '8?
Comedy
09174   90 mins   C
B, V
Sheila Burnett, Dolly Parton
This is a compilation of funny sketches produced in America, such as having your shoes sold whilst trying on a new pair, seeing a Policeman doing the 'twist' whilst directing traffic, or the secretary that your were about to interview, suddenly lose her skirt and many more typical Candid Camera jokes.
F — EN
Unknown — *Video Form Pictures* **H, P**
MGS 14

American Candid Camera-Part 2   Fil-Ent '8?
Comedy
10182   90 mins   C
B, V
Muhammed Ali, Dolly Parton, Buster Keaton, Sheila Burnett
This is a further compilation of funny sketches produced in America where the unwitting public are subjected to various unlikely and crazy situations-their reactions being secretly filmed by a hidden camera.
F — EN
Unknown — *Video Form Pictures* **H, P**
MGS 23

American Candid Camera-Part 3   Fil-Ent '8?
Comedy
10183   90 mins   C
B, V
Sheila Burnett, Dolly Parton
A further compilation of the best extracts from American Candid Camera.
F — EN
Unknown — *Video Form Pictures* **H, P**
MGS 33

(For Explanation of codes, see USE GUIDE and KEY)

PALADIN VIDEO HOME ENTERTAINMENT GUIDE

American Challenge   Spo-Lei   '8?
Sports-Minor/Motorcycles
09105   65 mins   C
V2, B, V
This film features the attempts of two Americans, Steve Baker in 1978 and Freddie Spencer in 1982, to gain supremacy on the European Grand Prix scene. It shows the 1978 film 'Formula 750 Champion'depicting Baker in 500 and 750 cc action, at Imola, Spa Silverstore and Assen. Freddie Spencer gave Honda their first win for 15 years at the 1982 Belgium Grand Prix. The 250 and side car races are also covered.
S,A — EN
C H Wood Ltd — Duke Marketing Limited
P

American Friend   Fil-Ent   '77
Drama
08963   123 mins   C
B, V
Dennis Hopper, Bruno Ganz, directed by Wim Wenders
This film is an adaptation of Patricia Highsmith's novel, 'Ripley's Game'. It tells the story of a man, apparently dying of an incurable disease, and in order to leave his family with an inheritance he is persuaded to undertake a murder for the mysterious and affluent American, Ripley. It is a German film with English subtitles.
S,A — EN   GE
New Yorker Films — Palace Video Ltd   P
PVC 2011B

American Heartbeat   Fil-Ent   '84
Music-Performance/Music video
13260   40 mins   C
B, V
This video contains a collection of the very best in contemporary rock'n'roll and includes tracks from Toto, Split Enz and Asia.
F — EN
Unknown — CBS/Fox Video   P
6699

American in Paris, An   Fil-Ent   '51
Musical
13426   97 mins   C
B, V
Gene Kelly, Leslie Caron, Oscar Levant, directed by Vincente Minnelli
An ex-GI stays on in Paris after the war to study painting and falls in love with a young Parisienne who is engaged to his best friend. The music is scored by George Gershwin and includes an 18-minute ballet sequence choreographed by Gene Kelly.

Academy Awards '51: Best Picture; Best Story and Screenplay; Best Musical Scoring.
BBFC:U — F — EN
MGM — MGM/UA Home Video   P
10006

American Nightmare   Fil-Ent   '82
Horror
08996   85 mins   C
B, V
Lawrence Day, Lora Staley, directed by Don McBrearty
This is the brutally realistic story of urban degradation. Set against drug peddling, striptease, pornography and prostitution. It tells of a psychotically avenging moralist, an American 'Ripper'.
A — EN
Unknown — Video Programme Distributors
P
Media 216

American Raspberry   Fil-Ent   '??
Comedy
06938   72 mins   C
B, V
This film takes a wickedly satirical look at American television and the society it serves.
BBFC:X — A — EN
Unknown — Rank Video Library   H, P
1032C

American Werewolf in London, An   Fil-Ent   '81
Horror
07838   98 mins   C
B, V
David Naughton, Jenny Agutter, Griffin Dunne, John Woodvine, directed by John Landis
Two young American lads on a trip through Europe are attacked on a lonely moor. One survives and wakes up in a London hospital to be told that his friend's body has been flown home and that they were attacked by a lunatic. He insists that it was an animal. One night his hideously mutilated friend visits him to explain that they were attacked by a werewolf and that those who are killed become members of the undead, but those who survive become werewolves. He realises that the full moon is only two days away.
BBFC:X — A — EN
Lycanthrope Films Ltd — Polygram Video
H, P
790 404

American Wilderness   Fil-Ent   '??
Adventure
08875   110 mins   C
V2, B, V

(For Explanation of codes, see USE GUIDE and KEY)

PALADIN VIDEO HOME ENTERTAINMENT GUIDE

This is a true-life adventure of one man's travels through the Rockies, Baja California, British Columbia, and the northern country. In Alaska he pursues a huge polar bear.
BBFC:U — F — EN
Unknown — Video Programme Distributors P
Media 202

Americana   Fil-Ent '83
Drama/Romance
13240   91 mins   C
B, V
David Carradine, Barbara Hershey
A Vietnam veteran finds adjustment to the American way of life very difficult and devotes his time to restoring a broken down carousel with the help of a young girl whose shy approaches are frowned upon by the local community.
BBFC:15 — S,A — EN
David Carradine — CBS/Fox Video   P
6699

Americano, The   Fil-Ent '55
Drama/Adventure
08724   85 mins   C
B, V
Glenn Ford, Cesar Romero, Frank Lovejoy, Ursula Thiess, Abbe Lane
A cowpoke from Texas attempts to deliver prize Brahma bulls to South America. However, the bandit-infested Brazilian jungle causes problems, and he arrives to learn of the ranch owner's untimely death.
S,A — EN
RKO; Robert Stillman Prods — BBC Video
H, P
BBCV 8003

Americathon   Fil-Ent '79
Comedy-Drama
09458   80 mins   C
V2, B, V
Peter Riegart, Harvey Korman, Fred Willard, Zane Buzby, Nancy Morgan, John Ritter, Elvis Costello, Chief Dan George, Peter Marshall, Jay Leno
Set in the year 1998, the United States is bankrupt, fuelless and about to fall into the hands of the oil rich Arabs and Jews. It can only be saved by raising 400 billion dollars. President Chet Roosevelt finally hits on a solution, a 30 day non-stop telethon.
BBFC:PG — F — EN
Lorimar — Guild Home Video   H, P, E

Amigo   Fil-Ent '??
Cartoons/Geography
09972   60 mins   C
B, V
Animated
This film features Amigo as a guide to famous places of the world. In this cartoon it is discovered how the great Colorado River cuts its way through the Arizona desert forming the Grand Canyon, how the Statue of Liberty was given as a gift from France. Amigo also looks at the Tower of London, the Eiffel Tower and the Notre Dame.
F — EN
Unknown — Select Video Limited   P
3215/43

Amityville Horror, The   Fil-Ent '79
Horror/Suspense
08377   118 mins   C
V2, B, V
James Brolin, Margot Kidder, Rod Steiger, Murray Hamilton, Don Stroud
This film is based on a true story and tells the tale of the Lutz family and their supernatural experiences in their Long Island home, once the scence of a mass murder. It is based on the book by Jay Anson.
BBFC:X — A — EN
American International Pictures — Guild Home Video   H, P, E

Amityville III   Fil-Ent '84
Horror
12508   90 mins   C
B, V
Tony Roberts, Tess Harper, Robert Joy, Candy Clark, directed by Richard Fleisher
A story of an investigation which turns to horror with the discovery of the Gateway to Hell in the now infamous Amityville house.
BBFC:15 — S,A — EN
Stephen F Kesten — THORN EMI   P
TXA 90 2441 4/TVA 90 2441 2

Amityville II-The Possession   Fil-Ent '82
Horror
08523   100 mins   C
B, V
James Olson, Burt Young, Rutanya Alda, Andrew Prine, Jack Magnes Diane Franklin, Moses Gunn
This is a sequel to the film 'Amityville Horror' and shows what happened to the previous family who lived in the Long Island house in New York. The film includes Holy water turning into blood, crayons writing obscene graffiti and crashing mirrors.
BBFC:X — A
Orion — THORN EMI   P
TXA 90 1411 4/TVA 90 1411 2

24   (For Explanation of codes, see USE GUIDE and KEY)

PALADIN VIDEO HOME ENTERTAINMENT GUIDE

Amorous Milkman, The   Fil-Ent '7?
Drama/Comedy
08956   93 mins   C
V2, B, V
This film tells the story of a young milkman who sets out to have some fun. However, fun with one woman lands him in court defending a rape charge, fun with another woman puts him into the multiple fracture ward at the local hospital, but he still continues, heavily pursued by beautiful girls and their parents.
BBFC:X — A — EN
Unknown — Walton Film and Video Ltd
P

Amsterdam Kill   Fil-Ent '77
Crime-Drama
06914   86 mins   C
B, V
Robert Mitchum, Bradford Dillman, Richard Egan, Leslie Nielsen, Keye Luke
When a retiring godfather seeks safe passage to America he hires a discredited former drug enforcement agent to get him there. The job brings him face to face with more problems than he bargained for and he finds himself in a position to expose and destroy the world drug traffic at its nerve centre in Amsterdam.
BBFC:AA — S,A — EN
Columbia Pictures — Rank Video Library
H, P
0080C

Anatomy of a Seduction   Fil-Ent '79
Drama
12947   96 mins   C
B, V
Susan Flannery, Rita Moreno, Ed Nelson
This is the story of the lives and loves of two women divorcees and their sons.
C,A — EN
Filmways Productions — Video Form Pictures
H, P
MGS 18

Anchors Aweigh   Fil-Ent '45
Musical/Dance
12220   139 mins   C
B, V
Frank Sinatra, Gene Kelly, Kathryn Grayson, Dean Stockwell, Pamela Britton, directed by George Sidney
Two sailors on holiday in Los Angeles team up with a pretty Hollywood extra and promise to get her an audition with a famous musician.
F — EN
MGM — MGM/UA Home Video   P
10309

And Baby Comes Home   Fil-Ent '80
Drama
09466   91 mins   C
V2, B, V
Warren Oates, Colleen Dewhurst
In this, the sequel to 'And Baby Makes Six', Anna Kramer comes home with a new baby to find her once ordered and happy life drastically changed.
BBFC:PG — F — EN
Alan Landsburg Prods. — Guild Home Video
H, P, E

And Baby Makes Six   Fil-Ent '79
Drama
09418   93 mins   C
V2, B, V
Colleen Dewhurst, Warren Oates, Maggie Cooper, Al Corley, Tim Hutton, Allyn Ann McLerie, Mildred Dunnock, Mason Adams
A 46-yr-old woman is shocked to learn that she is pregnant. It leaves her family in conflict and even threatens her marriage. She faces the greatest decision whether one unborn child can make up for the loss of her family, love and happiness.
BBFC:PG — F — EN
Alan Landsburg Prods. — Guild Home Video
H, P, E

And Now For Something Completely Different   Fil-Ent '71
Comedy
12478   84 mins   C
B, V
John Cleese, Eric Idle, Michael Palin, Terry Jones, Terry Gilliam, Graham Chapman
This is a hilarious anthology of sketches from the BBC TV series of Monty Python's Flying Circus.
BBFC:15 — F — EN
Patricia Casey — RCA/Columbia Pictures Video UK   H, P
10064

And Now the Screaming Starts   Fil-Ent '73
Horror
06173   87 mins   C
V2, B, V
Peter Cushing, Herbert Lom, Patrick Magee, Ian Ogilvy, Stephanie Beacham, Geoffrey Whitehead, Guy Rolfe, directed by Roy Ward Baker

(For Explanation of codes, see USE GUIDE and KEY)

PALADIN VIDEO HOME ENTERTAINMENT GUIDE

A story of bizarre revenge set in a manor house in eighteenth century England. The doctor delves into the secrets of a curse, a dead hand that crawls, kills and lives. Not only is a bride-to-be faced with this disembodied hand but bloody faces at the window and five corpses.
BBFC:X — A — EN
Cinerama; Milton Subotsky; Max J Rosenberg Prods — *Guild Home Video*　　**H, P, E**

And Soon the Darkness　　Fil-Ent　'80
Drama
09817　　94 mins　　C
B, V
Pamela Franklin, Michele Dotrice, Sandor Eles
Two young nurses are enjoying a cycling holiday in France. One of them disappears at the spot of an old unsolved murder. Her friend is left alone, with a sex killer at large.
BBFC:15 — C,A — EN
Associated British Productions Ltd. — *THORN EMI*　　**P**
TXE 90 1552 4/TVC 90 1552 2

And Then There Were None　　Fil-Ent　'74
Mystery
08557　　94 mins　　C
B, V
Oliver Reed, Elke Sommer, Richard Attenborough, Stephane Audran, Herbert Lom, Gert Froebe, Maria Rohm, Adolfo Celi, directed by Peter Collinson
This film is an adaptation of Agatha Christie's novel 'Ten Little Indians.' The plot involves ten characters who gather at the mysterious request of a Mr. Owen. At the end of their welcoming meal they are violently interrupted by a recorded message charging each of them with an unpunished murder. One by one they start to disappear.
BBFC:U — F — EN
Filibuster Films Ltd — *THORN EMI*　　**P**
TXB 90 0764 4/TVB 90 0764 2

Andrea, the Nympho　　Fil-Ent　'7?
Drama
02397　　84 mins　　C
B, V
Dagmar Lassander, Joachim Hansen, directed by Hans Schott-Schobinger
The beautiful, young and willful Andrea leaves the desolate country home of her sick father to seek 'relationships' in the city.
A — EN
Unknown — *Derann Film Services*　　**H, P**
DV 126B/DV 126

Android　　Fil-Ent　'82
Science fiction
08009　　80 mins　　C
V2, B, V
Klaus Kinski, Brie Howard, Norbeth Weisser, Crofton Hardester, Kendra Kirchner, directed by Don Preston
This film is set in an experimental space station. It is invaded by three fugitives which, to the controller, or Daniels, is an advantage during his robot experiments with the near human Android Max.
C,A — EN
New World Pictures — *Iver Film Services*　　**P**
217

Andy Warhol and His Work　　Fin-Art　'73
Documentary/Arts
05856　　51 mins　　C
B, V
Directed by Lana Jokel
This film offers an insight into the world and the work of artist Andy Warhol seen through his own eyes and those of his friends.
S,A — ED
RM Productions — *Polygram Video*　　**P**
7901834/7901832

Andy Warhol Presents Lonesome Cowboys　　Fil-Ent　'79
Drama
12959　　105 mins　　C
B, V
Viva, Taylor Mead, Eric Emerson, Tom Hompertz, Joe Dallesandro, Louis Waldron
A camp and bizarre tale of a visit by a group of cowboys to a deserted western city.
BBFC:18 — A — EN
Paul Morrissey — *Virgin Video*　　**H, P**
VVA 035

Angel　　Fil-Ent　'82
Drama/Adventure
08964　　90 mins　　C
B, V
Stephen Rea, Honor Heffernan, Marie Kean, Ray McAnally, Donal McCann, directed by Neil Jordan
This film tells the story of a young, talented saxaphone player. He meets a deaf teen-ager at a dance at which he had been playing. However, he becomes witness to the bombing

PALADIN VIDEO HOME ENTERTAINMENT GUIDE

of the dance-hall, and the killing of the girl and his band's manager. He embarks on a journey of vengeance that comes slowly to dominate him.
BBFC:AA — C,A — EN
Motion Picture Company of Ireland; Irish Film Board — *Palace Video Ltd* **P**
PVC 2034 A

Angel Fil-Ent '83
Drama
12886   92 mins   C
B, V
Cliff Gorman, Susan Tyrrell, Dick Shawn, Donna Wilkes, directed by Robert Vincent O'Neil
A high school honours student becomes a hooker at night but a pathological killer is at loose on the streets.
BBFC:18 — A — EN
New World Pictures — *THORN EMI* **P**
TXA 90 24034/TVA 90 24032

Angel and the Badman Fil-Ent '47
Western
06326   100 mins   B/W
V2, B, V
John Wayne, Gail Russell, Bruce Cabot, Irene Rich
A notorious badman is humanised by he love of a young Quaker girl.
F — EN
Republic — *World of Video 2000* **H, P**
GF507

Angel City Fil-Ent '80
Drama
08695   100 mins   C
V2, B, V
Ralph Waite, Paul Winfield, Mitchell Ryan, Jennifer Warren
This film tells of the courageous story of a West Virginia family. Having been forced to sell their land and look for a better life, they discover that they are only a small part in a wave of immigrants from all over Appalachia. The family is tricked into joining 'Angel City', despite being warned by a kind neighbour. They become prisoners, forced to work long hours and be witness to murder.
C,A — EN
Factor-Newland Productions — *Video Unlimited* **H, P**
041

Angel of Vengeance Fil-Ent '81
Drama
12502   80 mins   C
B, V
Zoe Tamerlis, Steve Singer, Jack Thibeau, Peter Yellen, directed by Abel Ferrara
A mute young woman is raped brutally twice in a single evening and turns vigilante, gunning down lecherous men.
BBFC:18 — A — EN
Rochelle Weisberg — *Warner Home Video* **P**
61326

Angel on My Shoulder Fil-Ent '80
Fantasy/Drama
09215   96 mins   C
B, V
Peter Strauss, Richard Kiley, Barbara Hershey, Janis Paige, Seymor Cassel, Scott Colomby, Murray Matheson, directed by John Berry
A long-dead hoodlum through demonic intervention gets a second chance at life. He was executed for a murder he did not commit. He returns to Earth to take over the body of his 'look-alike', an incorruptible D.A., who is stamping out evil.
S,A — EN
Mace Neufeld Prod; Barney Rosenzweig and Beowolf Prods — *Video Form Pictures* **H, P**
MGD 3

Angelo Branduardi—Concerto Fil-Ent '??
Music-Performance/Documentary
06258   85 mins   C
B, V
Angelo Branduardi
This film features performances by Angelo Branduardi, a classical-rock musician from Italy, it highlights recent successes in France, Germany and Spain. As well as live concert performances the film includes behind-the-scenes glimpses capturing the public and private pressures placed on a major musician.
F — EN
Unknown — *VCL Video Services* **P**
V196C

Angels Die Hard Fil-Ent '??
Drama
08631   90 mins   C
V2, B, V
Tom Baker, Alan de Witt, William Smith, Gary Littlejohn
A pack of thirty 'Angels' arrive at the lakeside town, Kernville. They stop at a local bar, which ends in a wild street brawl. One of the Angels is taken as a hostage whilst the rest of the gang are led out of town. Two days later he is released, but as he passes the border he is brutally run off the road and killed.
A — EN
Unknown — *Hokushin Audio Visual Ltd* **P**
VM 56

(For Explanation of codes, see USE GUIDE and KEY)

PALADIN VIDEO HOME ENTERTAINMENT GUIDE

Angels in Hell Fil-Ent '77
Drama
05735   95 mins   C
V2, B, V
Victor Holchak, Lindsay Bloom, David Mclean, Royal Dano, Adam Roarke, directed by Larry Buchanan
A story based on the reflections and thoughts of Producer/Director Howard Hughes during the making and subsequent gala premiere of the film 'Hells Angels' in 1930 which starred Jean Harlow, with whom he had a love affair.
S,A — EN
Pro International — *Video Unlimited*   H, P

Angler's Choice Spo-Lei '82
Fishing
13551   33 mins   C
B, V
Four celebrated British Anglers, Billy Lane, Peter Hoyle, Dick Orton and Terry Thomas demonstrate their fishing techniques on this tape.
S,A — I
Unknown — *TFI Leisure Ltd*   H, P

Angler's Corner—Bream, Spo-Lei '7?
Tench, Roach, Chubb
Fishing
01262   45 mins   C
B, V
Three fifteen-minute programmes which include fishing tips for bream, tench, and chubb, and remarkable underwater scenes.
M,A — ED
Max Munden — *Quadrant Video*   H, P
A2

Angler's Spo-Lei '7?
Corner—Salmon,
Grayling, Trout
Fishing
04498   60 mins   C
B, V
The talents of three expert fishermen are displayed in this four-part programme about fishing for salmon, grayling, and trout in the rivers and streams of England.
F — EN
Max Munden — *Quadrant Video*   H, P
A1

Angry Breed, The Fil-Ent '69
Suspense
10214   89 mins   C
B, V
Jan Sterling, James MacArthur, Murray McLeod, William Windom, Jan Murray
This film set in Hollywood and Malibu Beach follows the rise to stardom of an aspiring young actor who has returned from service in Vietnam. An encounter with a motorcycle gang and his rescue of a beautiful girl involve him in the lives of her family. A series of bizarre events lead to intrigue and revenge involving the less savory characters of the movie industry.
BBFC:18 — A — EN
David Commons Assoc — *Video Form Pictures*   H, P
DIP 12

Angry Breed, The Fil-Ent '83
Drama
12922   91 mins   C
B, V
James MacArthur, Jan Sterling
A war hero rescues a beautiful girl from being raped and gets signed up for the screen by her film magnate father but the thugs who tried to attack her are out of revenge.
BBFC:15 — S,A — EN
Unknown — *Video Form Pictures*   H, P
CLO 016

Angry Dragon, The Fil-Ent '??
Martial arts/Adventure
05623   80 mins   C
V2, B, V
Cheong Lik, Christine Hui Shan, Lee Wan Chung
A police Chief Inspector, a Kung Fu hero, seeks to break up a gang involved in smuggling and kidnapping. The gang are opposed by the head of a Martial Arts Institute, his son and his pretty daughter. The film contains an almost continuous series of combat and set fights.
BBFC:X — A — EN
Unknown — *Go Video Ltd*   P
GO115

Angry Joe Bass Fil-Ent '??
Horror
07611   82 mins   C
V2, B, V
Henry Bal, Holly Mershon
In this film, small town racial prejudice leads to a climax of horror. A man who holds most of the financial interests in the town attempts to limit commercial fishing to promote sports fishing. The commercial fishermen, mostly American Indians, object, only to be terrorised by his men. To aggravate the situation the Indian's leader falls in love with the man's daughter.
BBFC:X — A — EN
Unknown — *Iver Film Services*   P
141

(For Explanation of codes, see USE GUIDE and KEY)

PALADIN VIDEO HOME ENTERTAINMENT GUIDE

Animal Alphabet Parade Chi-Juv '7?
Language arts
01973   120 mins   C
B, V
An entertaining and constructive programme intended for young children learning the alphabet.
PS,M — ED
Unknown — *Quadrant Video*   H, P

Animal Crackers   Fil-Ent '30
Comedy
13333   93 mins   B/W
B, V
Groucho, Harpo, Chico and Zeppo Marx, Margaret Dumont, directed by Victor Heerman
Groucho Marx's famous character, Captain Jeffrey Spaulding, was introduced in this, the second of their feature films, and it includes such cameos as Groucho's 'African Lecture' and Harpo and Chico in 'The Card Game.'
BBFC:U — F — EN
Paramount — *CIC Video*   H, P
BEJ 1107/VHJ 1107

Animal Farm   Fil-Ent '55
Satire
01121   75 mins   C
B, V
Animated
Tired of their cruel master's oppression, the farm animals stage a revolt, setting up a new society on the farm, which soon turns into a dictatorship. From George Orwell's political satire.
BBFC:U — F — EN
Louis de Rochemont; Halas and Batchelor — *Rank Video Library*   H, P
9001

Animal House   Fil-Ent '78
Comedy
01036   109 mins   C
B, V
John Belushi, Tim Matheson, John Verna, Donald Sutherland, Thomas Hulce, directed by John Landis
Every college tradition from fraternity rush week to the homecoming pageant is irreverently and relentlessly mocked in this wild comedy.
A — EN
Universal; Matty Simmons; Ivan Reitman — *CIC Video*   H, P

Animal Kingdom   Chi-Juv '??
Cartoons/Animals
06229   60 mins   C

B, V
Animated
Through these entertaining, yet educational films children can learn about African wildlife, the life-style, the habitat, enemies and behaviour. Animals featured include: the ostrich, the baboon, the crocodile, the hippo, the rhino, the secretary bird and the elephant.
PS,M — EN
Estudios Castilla SL — *VCL Video Services*
P
F120

Animal Magic Presents   Chi-Juv '84
Keeper (Johnny) Morris
Animals
12727   59 mins   B/W
B, V
The best and funniest moments from the TV series 'Animal Magic' as the famous zoo-keeper Johnny Morris travels to zoos around Britain and the world chatting to okapis in Paris, dragon fish and horseshoe crabs in Antwerp, Snowflake the white gorilla in Barcelona and Percy the Pelican in Plymouth, among others.
PS,M — EN
Douglas Thomas; George Inger — *BBC Video*
H, P
9013

Animalympics   Fil-Ent '80
Cartoons
05408   79 mins   C
B, V
Animated, voices by Billy Crystal, Gilda Radner, Harry Shearer, Michael Tremer, directed by Steven Lisberger, music by Graham Gouldman of 10cc
All the most influential animals in the world gathered together and decided that 1980 should be the year of the first Animal Olympics, the best animal architects are employed to build the Pawprint Stadium. There the animals stand side by side, united in a quest for world peace, everyone is a winner inspired by the new found brotherhood and the thrill of victory.
BBFC:U — F — EN
Lisberger Studios Film — *Precision Video Ltd*
P
BBPV 2555/VBPV 2555

Animates, The   Chi-Juv '78
Cartoons/Puppets
07852   57 mins   C
V2, B, V
Animated

(For Explanation of codes, see USE GUIDE and KEY)   29

PALADIN VIDEO HOME ENTERTAINMENT GUIDE

This entertaining and educational series of thirteen stories features the adventures of the Animates, a carefree bunch of characters, in the land of the Personates who are mean and grouchy. Written and created by Sylvia Anderson.
PS,M — EN
Animates Film Productions; RPTA — *RPTA Video Ltd*   **H, P**

Ann-Margret from Hollywood with Love   Fil-Ent '75
Music-Performance
04386   52 mins   C
B, V
Ann-Margret, Dean Martin, Lucille Ball
A musical spectacular from Hollywood—the talented Ann-Margret sings and dances—performing both up-tempo numbers and memorable ballads.
F — EN
Dwight Hemion — *VCL Video Services*   **P**

Anna Karenina   Fil-Ent '48
Drama
09861   110 mins   B/W
B, V
Vivien Leigh, Ralph Richardson, Kieron Moore, Martita Hunt
This is an adaptation of Tolstoy's classic story about a married woman's blinding passion for an army officer, an impossible love affair doomed to failure.
F — EN
MGM — *Polygram Video*   **H, P**
790 2484/790 2482

Anne of the Thousand Days   Fil-Ent '69
Drama
13639   140 mins   C
B, V
Richard Burton, Genevieve Bujold, directed by Charles Jarrott
This is the historical story of Henry VIII and the second of his wives, Anne Boleyn, for whom he divorced his first wife and broke with the Catholic Church, before beheading her.
BBFC:PG — S,A — EN
Hal B Wallis — *CIC Video*   **H, P**
1148

Annie Hall   Fil-Ent '77
Comedy
01051   94 mins   C
V2, B, V
Woody Allen, Diane Keaton, Paul Simon, Carol Kane, directed by Woody Allen
Autobiographical love story with incisive Allenisms on romance, relationships, fame, and other topics.
Academy Awards '77: Best Picture; Best Actress (Keaton); Best Direction (Allen); Best Screenplay (Allen, Brickman).
BBFC:AA — S,A — EN
United Artists; Jack Rollins; Charles H Joffe — *Intervision Video*   **H**
UA A B 5001

Annie Hall   Fil-Ent '77
Comedy/Romance
13037   93 mins   C
B, V
Woody Allen, Diana Keaton, directed by Woody Allen
This romantic comedy has a semi-autobiographical script and tells of the ups and downs in the relationship between a Jewish comedian and a mid-western girl.
BBFC:AA — C,A — EN
United Artists Corp — *Warner Home Video*   **P**
99252

Anonymous Avenger   Fil-Ent '75
Crime-Drama
08646   105 mins   C
V2, B, V
Franco Nero, Barbara Bach
This film follows the story of one man's fight against a deadly gang of hoodlums.
S,A — EN
Unknown — *Fletcher Video*   **H, P**
V189

Another Time, Another Place   Fil-Ent '8?
Drama/Romance
09398   ? mins   C
B, V
Set in the Highlands of Scotland during World War II, this film tells of impossible love and passionate desires.
BBFC:15 — C,A — EN
Gate Cinema — *VCL Video Services*   **P**
P376

Antagonists, The   Fil-Ent '81
Drama
13275   128 mins   C
B, V
Peter O'Toole, Peter Strauss, Timothy West, Anthony Quayle, Barbara Carrera, directed by Boris Sagal

(For Explanation of codes, see USE GUIDE and KEY)

PALADIN VIDEO HOME ENTERTAINMENT GUIDE

Set in Jesusalem 70 AD, a group of Jewish zealots are under seige from the Romans in the seemingly impregnable fortress of Masada.
BBFC:15 — S,A — EN
Universal — CIC Video   **H, P**
BEN 1101/VHN 1101

Anthropohagous the Beast   Fil-Ent '7?
Horror
09125   90 mins   C
V
George Eastman, Tisa Farrow
This is the horrific tale of The Beast as it gallops through, giving shock after shock, decapitating tourists and leaving a trail of devastation.
A — EN
Unknown — Video Film Promotions   **H, P**

Antony and Cleopatra   Fil-Ent '7?
Drama
02034   162 mins   C
B, V
Richard Johnson, Janet Suzman, The Royal Shakespeare Company
A dazzling production of William Shakespeare's romance-tragedy-drama which covers ground from Rome to Egypt, holding imaginations for numerous generations.
F — EN
Unknown — Precision Video Ltd   **P**
BITC 3025/VITC 3025

Antony and Cleopatra   Fil-Ent '71
Drama
05725   160 mins   C
V2, B, V
Charlton Heston, Hildegard Neil, Eric Porter, Freddie Jones
One of Shakespeare's greatest love epics, starring and directed by Charlton Heston.
F — EN
Unknown — Video Unlimited   **H, P**
001

Ants—Panic at Lakewood Manor   Fil-Ent '77
Horror
05499   110 mins   C
B, V
Robert Foxworth, Linda Day George, Suzanne Somers, Myrna Loy, Gerald Gordon, Bernie Casey, Barry Van Dyke, Karen Lamin, Anita Gilette, directed by Robert Sheerer
An old family residence has now been turned into an hotel by a young girl and her mother. A young couple with dishonest intentions are offering to buy the hotel. Amid the intrigue a man meets with an unexplainable fatal accident followed by several more. It appears they are being terrorised by poisonous ants which casts a curtain of fear over the hotel.
BBFC:A — S,A — EN
Alan Lansburg Prod — THORN EMI   **P**
TXB 90 1477 4/TVB 90 1477 2

Any Which Way You Can   Fil-Ent '80
Comedy/Adventure
07854   110 mins   C
B, V
Clint Eastwood, Sondra Locke, directed by Buddy Van Horn
This film follows further outrageous adventures with the love struck trucker and his orangutan companion. Sequel to 'Every Which Way But Loose.'
BBFC:AA — S,A — EN
Warner Bros — Warner Home Video   **P**
WEX 61077/WEV 61077

Any Which Way You Can   Fil-Ent '80
Comedy
13197   112 mins   C
B, V
Clint Eastwood, Sondra Locke, Ruth Gordon, directed by Buddy Van Horn
A good-natured knockabout follow-up to the huge blockbuster 'Every Which Way But Loose,' featuring many of the same characters, including the orangutan.
BBFC:AA — C,A — EN
Warner Bros — Warner Home Video   **P**
61077

Anzio   Fil-Ent '68
War-Drama
12476   112 mins   C
B, V
Robert Mitchum, Peter Falk, Arthur Kennedy, Robert Ryan
A realistic war film about an American war correspondent accompanying troops preparing for the Anzio assault in 1944.
BBFC:PG — F — EN
Columbia — RCA/Columbia Pictures Video UK **H, P**
10211

Apache Massacre   Fil-Ent '72
Western
13656   93 mins   C
B, V
Cliff Potts, Xochitl, Harry Dean Stanton, Don Wilbanks, directed by William A Graham

---

(For Explanation of codes, see USE GUIDE and KEY)   31

PALADIN VIDEO HOME ENTERTAINMENT GUIDE

Romance blossoms between an Indian woman who escapes from a massacre by a US Cavalry Unit and a Western gunman who befriends her and helps her to evade the platoon.
BBFC:18 — C,A — EN
Harvey Matofsky — CBS/Fox Video   P
5018

Ape and Super Ape   Fil-Ent   '??
Documentary/Animals
05852   97 mins   C
B, V
Bert Haanstra
This documentary looks at the evolution of the ape family. It compares animal behaviour, social, sexual and parental, with human beings to emphasise the parallels in order to gain a better understanding of our own behaviour.
F — EN
Bert Haanstra — Polygram Video   P
7901394/7901392

Apocalypse—The Untold Story   Fil-Ent   '80
War-Drama/Suspense
09131   100 mins   C
V2, B, V
This is a powerful and emotional story of war. It tells of the determination of the North Vietnamese as they take on the far superior United States Army. It describes the dramatic effects that the events have on ordinary people.
S,A — EN
Unknown — Go Video Ltd   P
GO 139

Apollo 4 Mission, The   Med-Sci   '68
Space exploration
04426   16 mins   C
B, V, PH15, PH17, 3/4U
The story of the launching of the first unmanned Apollo/Saturn V space vehicle.
C,A — ED
NASA — Istead Audio Visual   P
HQa 181

Apollo 9: The Space Duet of Gumdrop and Spider   Med-Sci   '69
Space exploration
01223   29 mins   C
B, V, PH15, PH17, 3/4U
A view of the Apollo 9 astronauts before, during, and after their Earth-orbital mission, concentrating on the rendezvous and docking of the command module and the lunar module.
M,A — ED
NASA — Istead Audio Visual   P
HQ 189

Apollo 10: Green Light for a Lunar Landing   Med-Sci   '69
Space exploration
01224   29 mins   C
B, V, PH15, PH17, 3/4U
Highlights of the second lunar orbital mission are seen—the docking and descent of the lunar module, and views of the moon and Earth. Columbus Film Festival '69: Chris Statuette.
M,A — ED
NASA — Istead Audio Visual   P
HQ 190

Apollo 12: Pinpoint for Science   Med-Sci   '69
Space exploration
01226   28 mins   C
B, V, PH15, PH17, 3/4U
Highlights of the second manned lunar landing in November, 1969 are seen, including placement of scientific equipment on the moon, collection of soil and rock samples, and investigation of a Surveyor spacecraft that had landed on the moon in 1967.
CINE Golden Eagle '70.   M,A — ED
NASA — Istead Audio Visual   P
HQ 197

Apollo 13: 'Houston, We've Got a Problem'   Med-Sci   '70
Space exploration
01227   28 mins   C
B, V, PH15, PH17, 3/4U
The dramatic struggle to return the crewmen of Apollo 13 safely to Earth after an explosion on board the service module is shown.
M,A — ED
NASA — Istead Audio Visual   P
HQ 200

Apollo 14: Mission to Fra Mauro   Med-Sci   '71
Space exploration
01238   28 mins   C
B, V, PH15, PH17, 3/4U
This programme explains the problems encountered on the way to the moon by this mission, as well as the astronauts' activities on the moon and the return flight.
CINE Golden Eagle '71; Columbus Film Festival '71: Chris Certificate.   M,A — ED
NASA — Istead Audio Visual   P
HQ 211

Apollo 15: In the Mountains of the Moon   Med-Sci   '71
Space exploration
01228   28 mins   C
B, V, PH15, PH17, 3/4U

(For Explanation of codes, see USE GUIDE and KEY)

PALADIN VIDEO HOME ENTERTAINMENT GUIDE

Coverage of the fourth lunar landing mission, detailing, the moon surface scientific expeditions and lunar orbital experiments.
CINE Golden Eagle Certificate '71; Columbus Film Festival '72: Chris Award.   M,A — ED
NASA — *Istead Audio Visual*   **P**
HQ 217

Apollo 16: Nothing So Hidden   Med-Sci '71
Space exploration
01229   28 mins   C
B, V, PH15, PH17, 3/4U

An account of the Apollo 16 lunar landing mission and exploration in the highland region near the crater Descartes. This programme includes some of most spectacular lunar photography of any Apollo mission.
CINE Golden Eagle '72.   M,A — ED
NASA — *Istead Audio Visual*   **P**
HQ 222

Apollo 17: On the Shoulders of Giants   Med-Sci '73
Space exploration
01230   28 mins   C
B, V, PH15, PH17, 3/4U

A view of the Apollo 17 mission—the final lunar landing scheduled in the Apollo programme.
Columbus Film Festival '73: Chris Bronze Plaque.   M,A — ED
NASA — *Istead Audio Visual*   **P**
HQ 227

Apple, The   Fil-Ent '80
Musical-Drama
08084   84 mins   C
B, V

Catherine Mary Stewart, Alan Love, Grace Kennedy
This is a futuristic musical drama featuring a singing duo who fall into the hands of an unscrupulous and evil rock promoter.
BBFC:AA — C,A — EN
Independent — *Rank Video Library*   **H, P**
7014 C

Apple Dumpling Gang, The   Fil-Ent '75
Comedy
12577   100 mins   C
B, V

Bill Bixby, Susan Clark

Three lively children strike it rich and set off the wildest bank robbery in the history of the West, where robbers get robbed and con-men get conned and desperados blow up a town.
F — EN
Walt Disney Productions — *Rank Video Library*   **H**
018

Apple Dumpling Gang Rides Again, The   Fil-Ent '79
Western/Comedy
13441   88 mins   C
B, V

Tim Conway, Don Knotts, Tim Matheson, Kenneth Mars, Jack Elam, Robert Pine, Harry Morgan
Another adventure about a bunch of former outlaws trying too hard to become honest citizens.
BBFC:U — F — EN
Walt Disney Productions — *Rank Video Library*   **P**
026

Apprenticeship of Duddy Kravitz, The   Fil-Ent '74
Comedy-Drama
08379   121 mins   C
V2, B, V

Richard Dreyfuss, Michelina Lanctot, Randy Quaid, Joseph Wiseman, Denholm Elliot, Joe Silver, Jack Warden, directed by Ted Kolcheff
A young Jewish man in Montreal in 1948 is driven by an insatiable need to be a 'somebody.' His father, a taxi driver, belittles him while favouring his medical student brother. Following his grandfather's advice he obtains some land and gradually gains credibility with his father.
BBFC:A — S,A — EN
Paramount — *Guild Home Video*   **H, P, E**

April Wine—Live in London   Fil-Ent '81
Music-Performance
07478   60 mins   C
B, V

Directed by Derek Burbidge
This film recorded at London's Hammersmith Odeon in January 1981, features thirteen hard-driving rock and roll numbers by the group April Wine. Songs include 'Big City Girls,' 'Crash and Burn,' 'Tellin' Me Lies,' 'Future Tense,' 'Ladies Man,' 'Caught in the Crossfire,' 'Bad Boys,' '21st Century Schizoid Man' and 'I Like to Rock.'
S,A — EN
Zoetrope Ltd — *THORN EMI*   **P**
TXE 90 0645 4/TVE 90 0645 2

(For Explanation of codes, see USE GUIDE and KEY)

PALADIN VIDEO HOME ENTERTAINMENT GUIDE

Arabian Adventure   Fil-Ent '79
Fantasy
05889   94 mins   C
B, V
Christopher Lee, Milo O'Shea, Oliver Tobias, directed by Kevin Connor
A colourful fantasy about a wicked sorcerer, a handsome Prince and a beautiful Princess.
F — EN
John Dark — THORN EMI   P
TXB 90 0308 4/TVB 90 0308 2

Arch of Triumph   Fil-Ent '48
Romance
04323   87 mins   B/W
V2, B, V
Ingrid Bergman, Charles Boyer, directed by Lewis Milestone
A couple meet on a bridge on a rainy night in Paris and a tale unfolds of high tension and drama.
A — EN
United Artists — Intervision Video   H, P
A-A 0130

Archie and Sabrina   Fil-Ent '83
Cartoons
12176   68 mins   C
B, V
Animated
Further adventures of Archie and his gang, this time joined by Sabrina, who livens up proceedings at the High School, ending up with a special party in a haunted house.
F — EN
The Archie Co; The Sabrina Co — Select Video Limited   P
3613/43

Archies, The   Fil-Ent '7?
Cartoons
09974   60 mins   C
B, V
Animated
Adapted from the comic strip series, this film features Archie and his gang, Betty, Veronica, Reggie and Jughead. The adventures of the gang include exploring a haunted mine, helping out at a dude ranch and dressing up as a spaceman for a fancy dress competition.
A — EN
Filmation — Select Video Limited
3605/43

Are You Being Served?   Fil-Ent '77
Comedy
05887   91 mins   C
B, V
Mollie Sugden, John Inman, Frank Thornton, Trevor Bannister, directed by Bob Kellett

A full-length film based on the television series. Grace Brothers sends its staff on a holiday abroad while the store is being decorated. The problems begin as soon as they arrive at the hotel.
F — EN
Andrew Mitchell — THORN EMI   P
TXC 90 0313 4/TVC 90 0313 2

Arena, The   Fil-Ent '73
Drama
05434   79 mins   C
B, V
Pam Grier, Margaret Markov, Lucretia Love, Daniel Vargos, directed by Steve Carver
The owner of a small and seedy arena in ancient Brundisium can't find anything to please his jaded customers. He decides with his henchmen to employ a group of slave-girls to fight each other. They prove smarter than their employers and eventually the owner discovers he has a female Spartacus on his hands.
BBFC:X — A — EN
New World Pictures — THORN EMI   P
TXC 90 0328 4/TVC 90 0328 2

Ark of the Sun God, The   Fil-Ent '83
Adventure
12831   30 mins   C
B, V
David Warbeck, John Steiner, directed by Anthony M. Dawson
The story of man's quest for fabulous treasure guarded by a golden door buried deep in the desert sands.
BBFC:15 — S,A — EN
Unknown — Video Tape Centre   P
1169

Arm of Fire   Fil-Ent '??
War-Drama
06295   87 mins   C
V2, B, V
Gordon Scott, directed by Richard McNamara
Set in 500 BC, this film follows the exploits of Caius Macius who became the last minute saviour of Rome. Beseiged and starving, Rome was about to surrender to Tarquin the Proud, who was banished from the throne by popular fury and had amassed a large army to reconquer his lost kingdom.
S,A — EN
Unknown — Video Programme Distributors
P
Inter-Ocean 089

Arrival, The   Fil-Ent '68
Crime-Drama
07357   90 mins   C
B, V

34   (For Explanation of codes, see USE GUIDE and KEY)

PALADIN VIDEO HOME ENTERTAINMENT GUIDE

Patrick McGoohan
This tape contains one episode from the highly successful television series 'The Prisoner.'
S,A — EN
Patrick McGoohan — *Precision Video Ltd*
P
BITC 2108/VITC 2108

Arthur   Fil-Ent '81
Comedy
13200   97 mins   C
B, V
Dudley Moore, Liza Minnelli, John Gielgud, directed by Steve Gordon
A rich and amiable drunk has his inheritance threatened unless he marries his fiancée Susan, but he then meets another girl.
BBFC:AA — C,A — EN
Orion Pictures Co — *Warner Home Video*
P
72020

Ascendancy   Fil-Ent '83
Drama
10015   85 mins   C
B, V
Julie Covington, Ian Charleson, John Phillips, directed by Edward Bennett
Set in Belfast during 1920, this film tells of the daughter of a shipbuilding tycoon, still mourning the death of her brother in the Great War. A young British Lieutenant is 'keeping the peace' but plunges her into great torment.
S,A — EN
British Film Institute — *Longman Video*
P
LGBE 7007/LGVE 7007

Ash Wednesday   Fil-Ent '73
Drama
05611   99 mins   C
B, V
Elizabeth Taylor, Henry Fonda, Helmut Berger, Keith Baxter, directed by Larry Peerce
A rich middle aged woman in an attempt to salvage her marriage undergoes massive and traumatic plastic surgery. While recovering at a ski resort she has an affair with a young man, but she finds that physical beauty is not enough.
S,A — EN
Paramount; Dominick Dunne — *Home Video Merchandisers*   H, P
009

Ash Wednesday   Fil-Ent '73
Drama
08708   99 mins   C
V2, B, V
Henry Fonda, Elizabeth Taylor, Helmut Berger, Keith Baxter, directed by Larry Peerce

An aging woman undergoes cosmetic surgery, in an attempt to salvage her marriage after she finds out that her husband is having an affair. She recuperates in a ski resort, and while waiting for her husband to join her, she has an affair with a handsome young man.
BBFC:AA — C,A — EN
Paramount; Dominick Dunne Prod — *Video Unlimited*   H, P
060

Ashes and Diamonds   Fil-Ent '58
Drama
09318   100 mins   B/W
B, V
Zbigniew Cybulski, directed by Andrzej Wajda
The final part of Andrzej Wajda's trilogy of films about the youth of the Polish resistance during and after World War II. Dialogue in Polish with English subtitles.
BBFC:X — A — EN   PO
Film Polski — *THORN EMI*   P
TXE 90 0731 4/TVE 90 0731 2

Ashford and Simpson   Fil-Ent '82
Video, The
Music-Performance
08567   60 mins   C
B, V
Nick Ashford, Valerie Simpson
The Music from Ashford and Simpson's 'Street Opera' album is featured on this tape, along with their classics such as 'Ain't No Mountain High Enough,' 'Found a Cure,' and 'Is It Still Good to Ya,' among many others.
F — EN
Capitol Records — *THORN EMI*   P
TXE 90 0985 4/TVE 90 0985 2

Asia in Asia   Fil-Ent '84
Music-Performance
12882   30 mins   C
B, V
Directed by Dave Mallet
This programme features a live performance by Asia from Tokyo, Japan, and includes a feature documentary of the band and backstage coverage before and after the show.
M,A — EN
Scott Millaney — *Vestron Video International*
P

Asiad Wa Abeed (Masters   Fil-Ent '??
and Slaves)
Drama
06736   140 mins   C
V2, B, V

(For Explanation of codes, see USE GUIDE and KEY)   35

PALADIN VIDEO HOME ENTERTAINMENT GUIDE

A political story set in a police state where people are thrown into prison merely for their political beliefs.
S,A — EN AB
Unknown — Intervision Video H, P
A-C 0150

Asphyx, The Fil-Ent '74
Science fiction
01035 91 mins C
V2, B, V
Robert Stevens, Robert Powell, Jane Lapotaire
The asphyx holds the key to eternal life, and once discovered, a scientist must protect it to achieve eternal life for himself and his loved ones.
BBFC:AA — F — EN
Paragon Pictures — Intervision Video P
A-A 0034

Assassin Fil-Ent '??
Martial arts
08693 88 mins C
V2, B, V
This film is set around a revolution, rising to the province where a former leader is imprisoned. His son, an expert in Kung-Fu, is persuaded to join the fight against the revolters. The action is amusingly interspersed with what's going-on behind governmental doors.
BBFC:X — A — EN
Unknown — Derann Film Services P
FGS902

Assassin of Youth Fil-Ent '35
Exploitation
07633 71 mins B/W
B, V
Luanna Walters, Arthur Gardner, directed by Elmer Clifton
This 1935 exploitation film tells of a girl who is induced to smoke marihuana. She becomes involved in the thrills of wild parties and unleashed passions. A reporter 'rescues' her and gets a gang of reefer pushers exposed.
S,A — EN
Unknown — VCL Video Services P
0240G

Assassination of Trotsky, The Fil-Ent '72
Drama
13139 99 mins C
B, V
Richard Burton, Alain Delon, directed by Joseph Losey

This film tells the story of the last days of Trotsky, one of the original conspirators behind the Bolshevik revolution.
BBFC:15 — S,A — EN
Cinerama; Valoria Films — Polygram Video P
790 4224/790 4222

Assassination Run, The Fil-Ent '8?
Crime-Drama
10146 108 mins C
V2, B, V
Malcolm Stoddard, Mary Tamm
A retired 'hit man' for British Intelligence has a deadly decision to make when his wife is kidnapped by a gang of young German terrorists. His wife will die if he fails to eliminate a West German newspaper magnate.
S,A — EN
BBC — BBC Video H, P
BBCV 2010

Assault Fil-Ent '70
Mystery/Suspense
06923 87 mins C
B, V
Lesley-Anne Down, Frank Finlay, James Laurenson, Suzy Kendall, Freddie Jones, Tony Beckley, directed by Sidney Hayer
A school girl is struck dumb by a vicious attack. Unable to help detectives, she struggles to live as the rapist turns killer and terrorises the girl's school. Those suspected include the doctor, a local reporter and the headmistress' husband. But the rapist's identity remains a mystery until the art teacher persuades the police to let her play a decoy game with the killer.
BBFC:X — A — EN
Rank — Rank Video Library H, P
0060B

Assault on Precinct 13 Fil-Ent '79
Crime-Drama
06081 91 mins C
B, V
Austin Stoker, Darwin Joston, Laurie Zimmer, directed by John Carpenter
This film builds up to a crescendo of irrational violence reflecting the fear of unmotivated attack. A gang swore a blood oath to destroy precinct 13 and every cop in it.
S,A — EN
Irwin Yablans — Video Programme Distributors P
Media—M132

Assignment, The Fil-Ent '77
Crime-Drama
07623 90 mins C
V2, B, V

PALADIN VIDEO HOME ENTERTAINMENT GUIDE

Christopher Plummer
A high ranking army officer is assassinated in Latin America, an act which triggers a wave of violence throughout the country. The Local Government assigns a Swedish Diplomat to mediate between two extremist political factions.
BBFC:A — *S,A* — *EN*
Nordisk Tonefilm; Swedish Film Institute — *Iver Film Services* **P**

Assignment, The   Fil-Ent '7?
Martial arts
09826   91 mins   C
B, V
After a long journey Ma Tsai-tung visits a restaurant. Having finished his meal he tells the owner that he cannot pay. A fierce fight breaks out, but he manages to escape. The restaurant owner swears he will track him down and make him pay with his life.
S,A — *EN*
Unknown — *Polygram Video*   **H, P**
790 4534/790 4532

Asterix and Cleopatra   Fil-Ent '??
Cartoons/Adventure
09982   70 mins   C
B, V
Animated
Asterix, the gallic hero, together with friends Obelix and Getafix, and their canine companion Dogmatic, journey to Egypt to help their friend, the architect Edifis. Queen Cleopatra has commanded that a new palace be built in three months; an impossible task without the help of our heroes aided by a little magic potion.
F — *EN*
Les Productions Dargaud — *Select Video Limited*   **P**
3002/43

Asterix the Gaul   Fil-Ent '??
Cartoons/Adventure
08315   67 mins   C
B, V
Animated
Asterix, a cunning little warrior, is the hero of these adventures. He achieves his superhuman strength from the magic potions brewed by Getafix the Druid. Obelix is Asterix's inseparable friend, always ready for a new adventure so long as there is plenty to eat, and plenty of fighting. Vitalstatistix is the chief of the tribe, a brave but hot-tempered old warrior.
F — *EN*
Les Production Dargaud — *Select Video Limited*   **P**
3001

Asterix the Gaul   Fil-Ent '8?
Cartoons
12236   67 mins   C
B, V
Animated
Asterix is the hero of these adventures; he gets his strength from a magic potion brewed by Getafix. Obelix is Asterix's inseparable friend. Panoramix the village druid brews potions and Tonabrix the tribal chief is a brave, hot-tempered warrior.
F — *EN*
Les Productions Dargaud — *Select Video Limited*   **P**
3001/43

Astro Zombies   Fil-Ent '69
Horror
02462   78 mins   C
B, V
John Carradine, Wendell Corey
Human transplants go berserk and threaten the safety of a city.
A — *EN*
Gemeni Films — *Mountain Video*   **P**

Asylum   Fil-Ent '72
Horror
06174   95 mins   C
B, V
Peter Cushing, Britt Ekland, Herbert Lom, Patrick Magee, Barry Morse, Barbara Parkins, Robert Powell, Charlotte Rampling, Sylvia Syms, Richard Todd, James Villiers
A young psychiatrist is faced with the task of identifying the former director of an Asylum who may possibly be one of the incurable lunatics. As the young doctor investigates, he unveils the secrets of four of the inmates, their cases revealed in flash-back of their crimes and retributions that lead to the loss of sanity.
BBFC:AA — *S,A* — *EN*
Cinerama; Amicus Prod — *Guild Home Video*
H, P, E

Asymmetric Cut (Two Styles), The   How-Ins '80
Beauty
02051   50 mins   C
B, V
Kevin Murphy
The first in the planned 'Advanced Hair Tek Ladies' Hairdressing' series.
C,A — *I*
Hair Tek Video — *VideoSpace Ltd*   **H, P**

At the Earth's Core   Fil-Ent '76
Science fiction/Fantasy
05041   86 mins   C
B, V

(For Explanation of codes, see USE GUIDE and KEY)

PALADIN VIDEO HOME ENTERTAINMENT GUIDE

Doug McClure, Peter Cushing, Caroline Munro, Cy Grant, Godfrey James, directed by Kevin Connor
Set in 1898, a scientist invents a burrowing machine to explore the center of the earth, and discovers a frightening new world.
F — EN
John Dark — *THORN EMI* P
TXB 90 0326 4/TVB 90 0326 2

At War with the Army Fil-Ent '50
Comedy
06883   90 mins   B/W
V2, B, V
Jerry Lewis, Dean Martin, Polly Bergen
In this classical comedy a sergeant in the U.S. Army tries to get a none-too-smart private to help him with a problem he has with a girl.
M,A — EN
Paramount — *European Video Company*
P

Atlantic Adventure Spo-Lei '8?
Boating/Adventure
13554   38 mins   C
B, V
Sir Francis Chichester
This is the story of the preparations and the crossing of the Atlantic in 1964 by Sir Francis Chichester from the start at Plymouth to the finish in Newport, USA.
F — EN
Unknown — *TFI Leisure Ltd*   H, P

Atlantic City Fil-Ent '81
Crime-Drama/Romance
05742   105 mins   C
B, V
Burt Lancaster, Susan Sarandon, Michel Piccoli, Hollis McLaren, Kate Reid, directed by Louis Malle
An ageing hard-up numbers runner is kept by his hypochondriac girlfriend. His luck changes when he meets a dope pedlar and his pregnant girlfriend; he is enlisted as delivery man. A pair of gangsters liquidates the pedlar and the numbers runner is left with the pregnant girlfriend who he protects by killing two hoods searching for stolen dope. The hypochondriac demands that he return to her; heartbroken, the pregnant girl leaves.
BBFC:AA — S,A — EN
CINE Neighbor Inc; Montreal Delta Selva Films — *Home Video Holdings*   H, P
001

Atlantis Interceptors, The Fil-Ent '83
Science fiction
12194   89 mins   C
V2, B, V
Christopher Connolly, Mike Miller, George Hilton
A massive radioactive leak from a nuclear submarine triggers the emergence of Atlantis from the ocean depths, and with it come the Interceptors. Two trained killers try to discover the source of the Interceptors' power.
BBFC:18 — A — EN
Regency Productions — *Medusa Communications Ltd*   H, P

Atom Ant—Cassette 1 Chl-Juv '66
Cartoons/Adventure
08358   84 mins   C
V2, B, V
Animated
This features the ant with atomic strength, who battles with ferocious flea and karate ant. It also contains 'Precious Pupp' and the 'Hillbilly Bears.'
PS,M — EN
Hanna-Barbera — *Guild Home Video*   H, P, E

Atom Ant—Cassette 2 Chl-Juv '66
Cartoons/Adventure
08359   64 mins   C
V2, B, V
Animated
This film follows more of the adventures of Atom Ant, battling with his opponents, Ferocious Flea and Karate Ant together with his friends Precious Pupp and the Hillbilly Bears.
PS,M — EN
Hanna-Barbera — *Guild Home Video*   H, P, E

Atom Ant in How Now Bow Wow Chl-Juv '6?
Cartoons
13364   82 mins   C
V2, B, V
Animated
Twelve more supersonic adventures featuring the Precious Pupp and the Hillbilly Bears.
BBFC:U — PS,M — EN
Hanna-Barbera — *Guild Home Video*   H, P, E

Ator, the Fighting Eagle Fil-Ent '83
Adventure/Fantasy
12534   98 mins   C
B, V
Miles O'Keeffe, Sabrina Siani, Warren Hillman, Brook Hart, Edmund Purdom, Ron Carter, directed by David Hills

38   (For Explanation of codes, see USE GUIDE and KEY)

PALADIN VIDEO HOME ENTERTAINMENT GUIDE

Born with the mark of Thoren upon his infant flesh, Ator was destined to assert his might over the terrible powers of darkness and avenge the death of his parents.
S,A — EN
Patrick Murphy; Comworld Pictures — *THORN EMI* **P**
TXA 90 1998 4; TVA 90 1998 2

Attack FORCE Z   Fil-Ent '??
War-Drama/Adventure
08386   92 mins   C
V2, B, V
John Phillip Law, Mel Gibson, Sam Neill, Chris Haywood, John Waters, Koo Chaun-Hsiung, Sylvia Chang
This is a true story of Z special force, a secret operation unit of the Australian armed forces in World War II. This group carried out 284 wartime missions in the Pacific.
BBFC:AA — C,A — EN
John McCallum Productions — *Guild Home Video*   **H, P, E**

Attack of the Killer Tomatoes   Fil-Ent '79
Comedy/Horror
06080   87 mins   C
B, V
David Miller, George Wilson, Sharon Taylor, Jack Riley, directed by John Debello
In this non-stop pace film, an average American housewife is confronted by a blood-thirsty tomato crawling out of her waste disposal unit.
S,A — EN
Steve Peace; J Bello — *Video Programme Distributors*   **P**
Media—M108

Attack of the Normans   Fil-Ent '61
Drama
04288   90 mins   C
V2, B, V
Cameron Mitchell, Genevieve Grad
The Norman Conquest of Britain created jealousy on the part of the Baron of Saxony. He plans to capture the King of England by dressing his troops in Norman guise, thus bringing about another war. His plot is thwarted but not before intrigue and torture have claimed the lives of many.
C,A — EN
American International — *Video Programme Distributors*   **P**
Inter-Ocean—031

Attic, The   Fil-Ent '??
Horror
06789   ? mins   C
V2, B, V
Carrie Snodgress, Ray Milland
Fantasy and nightmares meet in the attic, a dark and frightening place only thirteen steps away.
S,A — EN
Raymond M Dryden — *Intervision Video*   **H, P**
A-A 0380

Attica   Fil-Ent '79
Drama
12934   97 mins   C
B, V
George Grizzard, Charles Durning, Henry Darrow, Morgan Freeman, Anthony Zerbe
This is the true story of the events at Attica Prison in 1971 when the US government sent in New York State troopers to quell the rioting.
BBFC:PG — C,A — EN
Unknown — *Video Form Pictures*   **H, P**
MGS 045

Attila the Hun   Fil-Ent '55
Drama/Adventure
05556   88 mins   C
V2, B, V
Anthony Quinn, Sophia Loren, Irene Papas, directed by Pietro Francisci
Set during the onslaught by the barbarous Hun tribes on Europe. The Emperor of the Roman Empire's corrupt capital is ignoring all warnings and indulging in a huge feast. His sister takes the chance of seizing the throne by offering to become the Hun leader's bride. However contempt, humiliation and enslavement lie in wait for those who cross the sword of Attila the Hun.
BBFC:U — F — EN
Dino de Laurentiis and Carlo Ponti — *Videomedia*   **P**
PVM 5103/BVM 5103/HVM 5103

Audrey Rose   Fil-Ent '77
Drama/Mystery
12602   109 mins   C
B, V
Marsha Mason, Anthony Hopkins, directed by Robert Wise
A young couple are plunged into a nightmare of terror when a mysterious stranger tells them that their twelve year old daughter is the reincarnation of his long-dead child — and he seems to be telling the truth.
BBFC:15 — C,A — EN
Joe Wizan; Frank de Felitta — *Warner Home Video*   **P**
99362

Austrian Enduro   Spo-Lei '8?
Sports-Minor/Motorcycles
09106   62 mins   C   (PAL, NTSC)

(For Explanation of codes, see USE GUIDE and KEY)

PALADIN VIDEO HOME ENTERTAINMENT GUIDE

V2, B, V
This film features the 1981 Enduro Championships. It includes footage taken deep in the forest, often from within inches of passing bikes, and film record of some of the dubious tactics employed by some national teams.
S,A — EN
CH Wood Ltd — Duke Marketing Limited
P

Author! Author!   Fil-Ent '82
Comedy
12199   100 mins   C
V2, B, V
Al Pacino, Dyan Cannon, Tuesday Weld, Bob Dishey, directed by Arthur Hiller
An anxious playwright has a new play scheduled to open on Broadway. His unfaithful wife walks out on him and he suddenly finds he has to cope with looking after his five children.
C,A — EN
20th Century Fox — CBS/Fox Video   P
1181

Autobiography of a Princess   Fil-Ent '75
Drama
05679   59 mins   C
B, V
James Mason, Madhur Jaffrey, directed by James Ivory
An Indian princess entertains a former family retainer to tea in her now permanent London home. They watch nostalgic home movies of their past life in India which provoke not always pleasant memories. This film is a comment on the complexities and contradictions of the British Raj.
BBFC:A — S,A — EN
Merchant Ivory Production — Home Video Holdings   H, P
019

Autumn Sonata   Fil-Ent '78
Drama
05387   89 mins   C
B, V
Ingrid Bergman, Liv Ullman, Lena Nyman, Halvar Bjork, directed by Ingmar Bergman
An international concert pianist has just lost the man with whom she had been living for many years. His death leaves her lonely and bewildered. She is invited to stay with her daughter, who is married to a clergyman, in Norway. The film explores the relationship between the two women and the many aspects of love. This version is dubbed in English.
BBFC:AA — S,A — EN
Ingmar Bergman Production — Precision Video Ltd   P
BITC 2004/VITC 2004

Avalanche Express   Fil-Ent '79
Suspense
07699   88 mins   C
V2, B, V
Lee Marvin, Robert Shaw
A KGB agent who defects to the West has to be escorted by train across Europe, a journey which proves anything but simple.
S,A — EN
Twentieth Century Fox — CBS/Fox Video
P
1138

Avanti!   Fil-Ent '72
Comedy
12506   139 mins   C
B, V
Jack Lemmon, Juliet Mills, Clive Revill, Edward Andrews, directed by Billy Wilder
A stuffy American tycoon goes to Italy to collect the body of his father who was killed in a car crash and discovers that his mistress also perished in the accident. Then the woman's daughter arrives and the two fall in love.
BBFC:PG — F — EN
Billy Wilder — Warner Home Video   P
99369

Average White Band   Fil-Ent '7?
Music-Performance
01957   28 mins   C
B, V
The legendary Average White Band performs some of their most popular hits as captured on a European tour.
S,A — EN
Unknown — VCL Video Services   P

Avon Tour 1974/3 Days in August 1975   Spo-Lei '75
Automobiles-Racing
04510   27 mins   C
B, V
The official film of the 1974 Avon Tour of Britain is highlighted by interviews with winner Roger Clark, runnerup Gerry Marshall, and other star drivers including Toby Fall, James Hunt, and Jody Scheckter. In the second feature, Tony Pond, Brian Culcheth, and Colin Vandervell fight for victory in the 1975 Avon Tour.
F — EN
Avon Tyre — Quadrant Video   H, P
M22

Awakening, The   Fil-Ent '80
Suspense/Horror
05296   100 mins   C
B, V
Charlton Heston, Susannah York, Jill Townsend, Stephanie Zimbalist

PALADIN VIDEO HOME ENTERTAINMENT GUIDE

An evil Egyptian Queen with occult powers is reincarnated, after 3,800 years, into the body of an apparently still-born baby girl. As she grows up, she is compelled to re-enact the events of the queen's life.
BBFC:X — A — EN
Robert Solo — *THORN EMI*   **P**
TXB 90 0303 4/TVB 90 0303 2

AWOL   Fil-Ent '??
Comedy-Drama
09946   89 mins   C
V2, B, V
Russ Thacker, Lenny Baker, Glynn Turman, Isabella Kaliff, Stephen Eckman
AWOL (Absent Without Leave) is the bizarre adventure of an American deserter.
BBFC:X — A — EN
Unknown — *Video Unlimited*   **H, P, E**
097

Axe   Fil-Ent '??
Horror
07670   90 mins   C
B, V
Jack Canon, Leslie Lee, Ray Green, Frederick R. Friedel, Douglas Powers, Frank Jones, Carol Miller, Hart Smith, George Monaghan, directed by Frederick R. Friedel
A man on the run from police and his gang hide out in a peaceful-looking farmhouse where a little girl lives with her crippled grandfather. The young child is forced to use an axe to defend herself from the three killers.
A — EN
Boxoffice Intl Pictures — *Video Network*   **P**
0004

B

Baby, The   Fil-Ent '72
Suspense/Drama
08794   93 mins   C
B, V
Anjannette Comer, Ruth Roman, Marianna Hill, directed by Ted Post
A well-meaning, attractive social worker tries to free a mentally-retarded young man from his over protective mother and sisters. She later becomes a brutal murderess to keep 'baby' for herself.
BBFC:18 — S,A — EN
Scotia International Films — *VCL Video Services*   **P**
P341D

Baby Care   Gen-Edu '8?
Infants
09238   ? mins   C
B, V
Dr. Hugh Jolly
This video aimed at first-time parents explains the 'do's and dont's' of caring for a new baby. Dr. Jolly is an acknowledged authority on babies and is currently physician in charge of the Pediatric Dept. at Charing Cross Hospital. The tape explains why babies cry—and what to do, bathing technique, nappy changing, breast and bottle feeding, handling and play, health care, development, food, prevention of accidents, first aid and much more.
A — ED
Home Video Premier Productions — *Home Video Holdings*   **H, P**

Baby Love   Fil-Ent '69
Drama/Romance
08334   96 mins   C
V2, B, V
Linda Hayden, Lynn Baron, Keith Baron, Diana Dors, Dick Emery, Patience Collier, Derek Lamden, directed by Alastair Reid
This is the story of a pretty, illegitimate, love-hungry teenager who comes to live in the house of her dead mother's one time lover.
C,A — EN
AVCO Embassy — *Embassy Home Entertainment*   **P**
2052

Baby Love   Fil-Ent '83
Comedy
13366   80 mins   C
V2, B, V
Yftach Katzur, Zachi Noy, Jonathan Segall, directed by Dan Wolman.
With a backing of twenty-five musical hits from the fifties, this 'Popsicle' adventure shows Benji, Bobby and Huey concentrating on their two main obsessions, motorcycles and the fairer sex.
BBFC:18 — C,A — EN
Noah Films Ltd — *Guild Home Video*   **H, P, E**
8326-3

Baby Maker, The   Fil-Ent '70
Drama
12083   109 mins   C
V2, B, V
Barbara Hershey, Collin Wilcox-Horne, Sam Groom, Scott Glenn, directed by James Bridges

---

(For Explanation of codes, see USE GUIDE and KEY)

PALADIN VIDEO HOME ENTERTAINMENT GUIDE

A happily married couple discover that the wife is unable to have a baby. Not wanting to adopt, they find a girl willing to bear a child fathered by the husband and this is where the trouble begins.
BBFC:AA — A — EN
National General Pictures; Robert Wise Production — *Videomedia* **P**
PVM 0807/BVM 0807/HVM 0807

Baby Sister Fll-Ent '83
Drama/Romance
09368   90 mins   C
B, V
Ted Wass, Phoebe Cates, Pamela Bellwood, Efrem Zimbalist Jr.
An affair between a beautiful young woman and her sister's boyfriend threatens to destroy a family forever.
BBFC:PG — F — EN
Moonlight Prods II — *Precision Video Ltd* **P**
BITC 2138/VITC 2138

Babylon Fll-Ent '81
Drama
05424   90 mins   C
B, V
Brinsley Forde, Karl Howman
This film presents a harsh and uncompromising view of the lives of black youths living in South London. It centres around the battle between two rival sound-systems in the days leading up to the final play-off.
BBFC:X — A — EN
Chrysalis Group Ltd — *Chrysalis Video* **P**
CVID BE3/CVID VH3

Babysitter, The Fll-Ent '80
Drama
12918   96 mins   C
B, V
William Shatner, Patti Duke Astin, Stephanie Zimbalist, directed by Pete Medak.
An eighteen year old girl with angelic looks but devilish intentions starts to manipulate the lives of the family she becomes babysitter/housekeeper to.
BBFC:15 — S,A — EN
Moonlight Productions; Filmways — *Video Form Pictures* **H, P**
DIP 010

Back Roads Fll-Ent '81
Drama
12001   95 mins   C
B, V
Sally Field, Tommy Lee Jones, directed by Martin Ritt
This is the story of two losers who encounter violence, poverty and bigotry. An Alabama hooker and an ex-boxer are drawn together on their way to California.
C,A — EN
Ronald Sheldo — *CBS/Fox Video* **P**
7071

Back to Bataan/Roadblock Fll-Ent '??
War-Drama/Crime-Drama
05706   161 mins   B/W
B, V
John Wayne, Anthony Quinn, Beulah Bondi, Lawrence Tierney, directed by Edward Dmytryk, Charles McGraw, Joan Dixon, Milburn Stone, directed by Harold Daniels
Two films are featured on one cassette. 'Back to Bataan' (Black/white, 91 mins, 1946) is set in the battle-zones of the Philippines. A Colonel sees his men captured by the Japanese he forms a guerilla group and terrorises the Japanese occupiers until the American launch another offensive. 'Roadblock' (Black/white, 70 mins, 1952) features an insurance investigator who gives information to a gang in return for a share of the haul so he can marry a girl who has expensive tastes.
S,A — EN
RKO — *Kingston Video* **H, P**
KV36

Bad Boys Fll-Ent '83
Crime-Drama
09778   99 mins   C
B, V
Sean Penn, Reni Santoni, Jim Moody, Esai Morales, directed by Rick Rosenthal
A story of gang warfare set in a Juvenile Detention Centre. A young street outlaw finds there is no escape when faced with his deadly enemy behind bars, and a fight to the death ensues.
C,A — EN
EMI Films — *THORN EMI* **P**
TXA 90 19104/TVA 90 1910 2

Bad Timing Fll-Ent '80
Drama
08079   118 mins   C
B, V
Art Garfunkel, Theresa Russell, Harvey Keitel, Denholm Elliot
This is a terrifying love story concerning a moody psychiatrist's obsession with a fun-loving young girl. It leads to tragedy and suspicions of foul play.
BBFC:X — A — EN
World Northal — *Rank Video Library* **H, P**
0129 D

---

42 (For Explanation of codes, see USE GUIDE and KEY)

PALADIN VIDEO HOME ENTERTAINMENT GUIDE

Badge   Fil-Ent '73
Crime-Drama
13644   111 mins   C
B, V
Robert Duvall, Louis Cosentino, Verna Bloom, Marina Durell, directed by Howard W Koch
Three people are murdered, friends of a suspended New York cop, when he becomes involved with a gang of Puerto Rican revolutionaries.
BBFC:18 — C,A — EN
Paramount — CIC Video   **H, P**
2136

Badlands   Fil-Ent '74
Drama/Romance
06051   74 mins   C
B, V
Martin Sheen, Sissy Spacek, Warren Oates, directed by Terrence Malick
A story set in South Dakota where a rubbish collector falls in love with a wide-eyed 15 year old girl. What follows is a string of murders as they kill to stay together; the girl's father is the first victim when he tries to interfere with their romance.
BBFC:X — A — EN
Warner Bros; Terrence Malick Prods — Warner Home Video   **P**
WEX1135/WEV1135

Baffled   Fil-Ent '72
Drama/Suspense
07337   96 mins   C
B, V
Leonard Nimoy, Susan Hampshire, Vera Miles
An American racing driver keeps experiencing a series of visions during races. He meets up with a young woman who is an expert in the occult, and together they set out to find the origins of his visions.
S,A — EN
ATV — Precision Video Ltd   **P**
BITC 2063/VITC 2063

Bait, The   Fil-Ent '72
Drama
04273   72 mins   C
B, V
Donna Mills, William Devane, Michael Constantine, June Lockhart
A tense and realistic story of a courageous police-woman who risks her life as an undercover agent to lure a homicidal rapist into the arms of the law.
A — EN
Worldvision — Rank Video Library   **H, P**
0045

Bal du Moulin Rouge   Fil-Ent '??
Musical/Dance
08537   86 mins   C
B, V
This, filmed at the Sahara Reno Hotel, U.S.A., shows the famous performance of the legendary dancers of the Moulin Rouge. Thirty-two girls clothed in clouds of feathers perform many dance routines ending with the can-can. Choreography by Doris Haug and Ruggero Angeletti.
C,A — EN
Unknown — THORN EMI   **P**
TXB 90 09334 / TVB 90 0933 2

Balance, La   Fil-Ent '83
Suspense/Drama
13252   90 mins   C
B, V
Nathalie Baye, Phillipe Leotard, Richard Berry, Christophe Malavoy, directed by Bob Swaim
A police supergrass is murdered in the back streets of Paris and they recruit a pimp to take his place who becomes trapped in a world of vice facing death from both sides of the law.
BBFC:18 — A — EN
Spectra Films — CBS/Fox Video   **P**
6702

Balboa   Fil-Ent '80
Drama
13104   100 mins   C
B, V
Tony Curtis, Carol Lynley, Chuck Connors, Steve Kanaly
A steamy story of sex and power amongst the rich and beautiful is dipicted on this video when a man's partner is found dead and two men are rivals for his widow's affections.
C,A — EN
Unknown — Quadrant Video   **H, P**

Baldmoney, Sneezewort,   Fil-Ent '??
Dodder and Cloudberry
Cartoons/Fantasy
09452   140 mins   C
V2, B, V
Animated
Based on 'The Little Grey Men', this is the magic tale of the last four gnomes left in England. They live under an old oak tree on the banks of the Folly Brook.
BBFC:U — F — EN
Unknown — Guild Home Video   **H, P, E**

Ballad of Death Valley   Fil-Ent '7?
Western
04601   90 mins   C
V2, B, V

(For Explanation of codes, see USE GUIDE and KEY)

PALADIN VIDEO HOME ENTERTAINMENT GUIDE

Lee Calloway arranges a prison escape for the notorious Douglas gang in exchange for half the gold they have stolen. The brothers turn on Calloway and in the fight he kills one of the gang and escapes. Lee now becomes the hunted, and after being rescued from the desert by a mysterious woman, they search for the Douglas brothers.
C,A — EN
Unknown — Video Programme Distributors
P
Inter-Ocean—033

Ballad of Gregorio Cortez, The Fil-Ent '82
Western
13218   100 mins   C
V2, B, V
Based on the true story of one of the biggest manhunts in Texas in 1901, it tells of a young Mexican wrongly accused of murdering a sheriff and the eleven day hunt for him as he eludes his captors and becomes a national hero.
C,A — EN
Moctesuma Esparza Productions — Embassy Home Entertainment   P
2062

Ballad of Joe Hill, The Fil-Ent '71
Drama
05883   100 mins   C
B, V
Thommy Berggren, directed by Bo Widerberg
The story of a young Swedish immigrant to America in 1902, who became the organiser of a union with an anarchist reputation.
A — EN
Unknown — THORN EMI   P
TXB 90 0255 4/TVB 90 0255 2

Baltimore Bullet, The Fil-Ent '80
Comedy/Suspense
05244   100 mins   C
B, V, LV
James Coburn, Omar Sharif, Bruce Boxleitner, Ronee Blakley
It's one big hustle as 'poolroom jewel' Carolina Red teams up with The Baltimore Bullet and Billy Joe to finagle their way into every money making game they can find until they finally meet The Deacon in a tense yet explosively funny climax.
BBFC:AA — C,A — EN
Avco Embassy; John Brascia — Rank Video Library   H, P
0051

Bamboo Brotherhood, The Fil-Ent '??
Martial arts
06856   92 mins   C
V2, B, V
Yao Tien Lung, Tang Mei Fong, Lei Ming
A young man witnesses the killing of his parents by a Kung Fu gang. To take revenge he begins working for one of the gang in order to kill him and locate the other members. The leader discovers his intentions and sends the gang after him. They finally locate him in a brothel.
S,A — EN
Unknown — European Video Company
P

Banana Splits Adventure Show, The Fil-Ent '68
Cartoons
08387   90 mins   C
V2, B, V
Animated
This compilation of cartoon adventures features the mad antics of the Banana Splits—Snorky, Fleegle Bingo and Drooper. Includes three cartoons entitled 'The Arabian Knights', 'The Three Musketeers' and 'Micro Ventures'.
PS,S — EN
Hanna-Barbera — Guild Home Video   H, P, E

Banana Splits Adventure Show, Cassette 4 Chi-Juv '84
Cartoons
13374   90 mins   C
V2, B, V
Animated
Three episodes are featured on this cassette titled 'The Arabian Knights,' 'The Three Musketeers' and 'Micro Ventures.'
BBFC:U — F — EN
Hanna Barbera — Guild Home Video   H, P, E

Banana Splits Adventure Show-Cassette 2, The Fil-Ent '68
Cartoons/Adventure
09438   90 mins   C
V2, B, V
Animated
The four crazy animals are back again, a Dog, a Gorilla, a Lion and a baby Elephant better known as the Banana Splits. Their cartoon friends The Arabian Knights and The Three Musketeers are also featured.
BBFC:U — F — EN
Hanna Barbera — Guild Home Video   H, P, E

Banana Splits Adventure Show, Cassette 3, The Chi-Juv '68
Cartoons/Adventure
12063   95 mins   C

(For Explanation of codes, see USE GUIDE and KEY)

PALADIN VIDEO HOME ENTERTAINMENT GUIDE

V2, B, V
Animated
Four crazy animals who dance, sing and play rock music introduce us to exciting tales of swash-buckling adventure.
BBFC:U — *PS,S* — *EN*
Hanna Barbera — *Guild Home Video* **H, P, E**

Bananaman Chl-Juv '83
Cartoons
12902   60 mins   C
B, V
Animated
This cassette features a collection of adventures from the intrepid Bananaman.
PS,M — *EN*
Thames Video — *THORN EMI* **P**
TXE 90 26864/TVE 90 26862

Bananarama Fil-Ent '84
Music-Performance
13134   30 mins   C
B, V
This programme features ten tracks from Bananarama including 'Hot Line to Heaven,' 'Rough Justice,' 'Cruel Summer' and 'Really Saying Something.' It is recorded in stereo hi-fi.
F — *EN*
PMV — *Polygram Video* **P**
041 0564/041 0562

Bananas Fil-Ent '71
Comedy
13038   82 mins   C
B, V
Woody Allen, directed by Woody Allen
In this zany comedy Woody Allen plays a New Yorker who leaves his mundane job to pursue grandiose dreams of glory in Latin America.
BBFC:AA — *C,A* — *EN*
Rollins and Joffe Productions — *Warner Home Video* **P**
99215

Bad Man's River Fil-Ent '72
Western/Adventure
10205   90 mins   C
B, V
Gina Lollobrigida, Lee Van Cleef, James Mason
This story of greed centres around a lot of money: a Wild West outlaw with a price on his head; his wife who has him committed to an asylum whilst stealing his latest haul; and her new husband, a philosopher, adventurer, gentleman and scoundrel.
BBFC:PG — *S,A* — *EN*
Philip Yordan Prods — *Video Form Pictures* **H, P**
6263-SO

Band Reunion Concert, The Fil-Ent '84
Music-Performance
12927   85 mins   C
B, V
This programme contains 15 tracks from The Band and includes such numbers as 'Rag Mama Rag,' 'Up on Cripple Creek,' 'The Weight,' 'Java Blues' and 'Chest Fever.'
S,A — *EN*
Concert Productions International — *Video Form Pictures* **H, P**
VFX 13/VFV 13

Bandidos Fil-Ent '7?
Western
07791   95 mins   C
V2, B, V
Terry Jenkins, E.M. Salerno, Venantino Venantini
A man takes revenge on the leader of a bandit gang.
S,A — *EN*
Unknown — *Fletcher Video* **H, P**
V161

Bandits, The Fil-Ent '67
Western
04482   94 mins   C
V2, B, V
Robert Conrad, Jan-Michael Vincent, Manual Lopez Ochoa, Roy Jenson
Three American bandits are rescued by Mexican outlaws and help them recover a hidden fortune in gold.
A — *EN*
Alfredo Zacarias; EpicFilm — *Intervision Video* **P**
A-AE 0184

Bandits from Shantung Fil-Ent '71
Crime-Drama/Martial arts
06930   79 mins   C
B, V
When a man brings a valuable consignment of silver to a small town in Shantung, he attracts the attention of the deadly Green Dragon

(For Explanation of codes, see USE GUIDE and KEY)

PALADIN VIDEO HOME ENTERTAINMENT GUIDE

Association, who hold the townspeople in terror. A valiant knight comes to visit his fiancee, but when they take her hostage it unleashes a chain of events ending in a duel to the death.
BBFC:X — A — EN
Unknown — *Rank Video Library* H, P
0085C

Bandolero   Fil-Ent '68
Western
12201   106 mins   C
B, V
James Stewart, Dean Martin, Raquel Welch, George Kennedy, directed by Andrew V. McLaglen
Two robbers make off with a large amount of money, kidnap a Mexican widow and together with their outlaw gang, head for the border and safety pursued by the vengeful sheriff.
C,A — EN
20th Century Fox — *CBS/Fox Video*   P
1203

Bandwagon, The   Fil-Ent '53
Musical
10170   108 mins   C
B, V, LV
Fred Astaire, Jack Buchanan, Nanette Fabray, Cyd Charisse
A song and dance star sells everything he's got to finance a musical written by his two friends. The musical score of Schwartz-Dietz songs include 'Dancing in the Dark', 'Louisiana Hayride' and 'That's Entertainment'.
BBFC:U — F — EN
MGM — *MGM/UA Home Video*   P
UMB 10113/UMV 10113/UMLV 10113

Bang Bang Gang, The   Fil-Ent '??
Adventure/Suspense
09352   76 mins   C
B, V
Jae Miller, Marland Proctor, Mark Griffin, Revel Quinn
Two boys set out to rob a cafe, a quick way of earning themselves some money, only to find it is already being robbed by two women. The four of them decide to team up and become the 'Bang Bang Gang' which begins a wave of crime along the California coastline. While taking a rest, they become involved in a brawl with a local gang. After a night of terror the Bang Bangs are chased by both the local gang and the police.
BBFC:18 — A — EN
Unknown — *Precision Video Ltd*   P
BMPV 2598/VMPV 2598

Bang Bang Kid, The   Fil-Ent '67
Western/Comedy
09375   90 mins   C
B, V
Tom Bosely, Guy Madison
In the little town of Limerick, Arizona a wealthy mineowner, who sees himself as a medieval lord, is in control with the aid of a gang of ruffians. The citizens, led by the mayor, try to find a sheriff capable of standing up to him, but each is gunned down in turn. Things change on the arrival of Merriweather Newberry, who has invented a gun-toting robot.
F — EN
Foreign — *Precision Video Ltd*   P
BWPV 504/VWPV 5O4

Bang the Drum Slowly   Fil-Ent '73
Drama
07394   98 mins   C
V2, B, V
Robert DeNiro, Michael Moriarty, Vincent Gardenia, Phil Foster, Ann Wedgeworth, Patric McVey, Heather Macrae, Selma Diamond, directed by John Hancock
This is a fictionalised account of what might happen to a big league New York baseball team if a key member was suffering from a fatal disease. A bond of friendship exists between two players, one is successful, fashionable with a beautiful wife and the other is uneducated, unsophisticated, chews tobacco, falls in love with the wrong girls and is dying. Together they fight to keep his illness from their teammates.
BBFC:AA — S,A — EN
Paramount — *Guild Home Video*   H, P, E

Bar-b-q   Gen-Edu '??
Cookery
09908   60 mins   C
B, V
This programme gives a guide to make barbecuing as good as it should be. It looks at the different methods and the equipment to use, together with some special recipes.
C,A — I
Marlboro Video; Michael Barratt Ltd — *Michael Barratt Ltd*   P

Barbapapa   Chl-Juv '73
Fantasy/Cartoons
04465   53 mins   C
B, V
Animated

(For Explanation of codes, see USE GUIDE and KEY)

PALADIN VIDEO HOME ENTERTAINMENT GUIDE

This tape contains thirteen short cartoons which tell the continuing story of Barbapapa (a creature from space), his family, their problems adjusting to life in the city, and the children who befriend them.
PS,I — EN

Polyscope B V; Annette Tison and Talus Taylor — *Polygram Video*   **P**

Barbapapa Volume II   Chi-Juv '73
Fantasy/Cartoons
04687   60 mins   C
B, V
Animated
13 original cartoon stories. In this second volume of Barbapapa stories we see the different Barbababies at work and play.
PS,I — EN

Polyscope B V; Annette Tison and Talus Taylor — *Polygram Video*   **P**

Barbara McNair Show, The   Fil-Ent '7?
Variety
04378   60 mins   C
B, V, PH17, 3/4U
Barbara McNair, Duke Ellington and his Orchestra
A variety show with Barbara McNair and Duke Ellington.
F — EN

Unknown — *Vidpics International*   **P**

Barbara Woodhouse Goes to Beverly Hills   Fil-Ent '8?
Animals
12070   52 mins   C
V2, B, V

Britt Ekland, David Soul and William Shatner are just a few of the stars who meet Barbara Woodhouse and bring along their pampered pets.
F — EN

Unknown — *Guild Home Video*   **H, P, E**

Barbara Woodhouse's World of Horses and Ponies   Spo-Lei '8?
Animals
12056   60 mins   C
V2, B, V

Barbara Woodhouse gives the viewer an insight into the world of horses and ponies, going through many stages, from the selection and purchase of a pony, to grooming, schooling and training.
BBFC:U — F — EN
ON TV Productions Video — *Intervision Video*
H, P
A-A 0493

Barbarella   Fil-Ent '68
Fantasy
01216   98 mins   C
B, V
Jane Fonda, John Phillip Law, David Hemmings, directed by Roger Vadim
Based on the popular French sci-fi comic strip drawn by Jean-Claude Forest, this popular film stars Jane Fonda as a sexually emancipated space woman who vanquishes evil robots and monsters and rewards the many men she meets in her travels.
S,A — EN
Paramount — *CIC Video*   **H, P**

Barbarian, The   Fil-Ent '60
Drama
08866   83 mins   C
V2, B, V
Jack Palance, Melody O'Brien, Milly Vitae, Richard Wyler, Guy Rolfe, Deirdre Sullivan, Austin Willis, Joseph Cuby, directed by Rudolph Mate
During an invasion, the leader of a marauding race and his beautiful sister are captured and imprisoned. Their captor, in order to humiliate them further, directs his desires on the captured sister. To avoid this, she takes her own life. When her brother escapes he rows his revenge on his captor.
C,A — EN
Unknown — *Video Programme Distributors*
P
Replay 1017

Barbarosa   Fil-Ent '82
Western/Adventure
09365   85 mins   C
V2, B, V, LV
Willie Nelson, Gary Busey
Set in southern Texas, 1878, this film tells a tale of love and revenge. Barbarosa, born a survivor, becomes aware that his time is running out. For the past thirty years he has been pursued by the Zavalas, a close-knit Mexican clan.
BBFC:PG — F — EN
AFD-Universal — *Precision Video Ltd*   **P**
CRITC 2131/BITC 2131/VITC 2131/LVITC 0025

(For Explanation of codes, see USE GUIDE and KEY)

PALADIN VIDEO HOME ENTERTAINMENT GUIDE

Barcelona Kill, The   Fil-Ent '??
Mystery/Crime-Drama
06253   86 mins   C
B, V

Linda Hayden, John Austin, Simon Andrew, Maximo Valverde

Set in the alleys of Barcelona's gypsy quarter. A gruesome murder is yet another link in a chain of crime involving prostitution, smuggling, racketeering and drugs.

S,A — EN

Michael Klinger Production — *VCL Video Services*   P
C175C

Barclay James Harvest   Fil-Ent '??
Music-Performance
09887   51 mins   C
B, V, LV

This tape features Barclay James Harvest, from their concert for the people in Berlin. It contains many of their best loved hits. Recorded in stereo.

F — EN

Unknown — *Polygram Video*   H, P
790 4994/790 4992/790 4991

Bare Knuckles   Fil-Ent '78
Adventure/Drama
08855   86 mins   C
V2, B, V

Sherry Jackson, Robert Viharo, Gloria Henry

This film features a modern day bounty hunter. He makes his living by capturing small time criminals for a few hundred dollars. He has few friends, is hated by criminals, and distrusted by the authorities.

C,A — EN

Intercontinental Releasing Corp — *Video Programme Distributors*   P
Inter-Ocean 074

Barefoot in the Park   Fil-Ent '67
Comedy
10125   102 mins   C
B, V

Jane Fonda, Robert Recford, Charles Boyer, directed by Gene Saks

A newly married couple start their married life in a bleak apartment block. The wife is zany and fun loving, the husband solid and straight-laced and together they learn to come to terms with each other through a series of riotous escapades.

BBFC:PG — S,A — EN

Paramount — *CIC Video*   H, P
BEL 2065/VHL 2065

Barkleys of Broadway, The   Fil-Ent '49
Musical/Dance
12221   109 mins   C
B, V

Ginger Rogers, Fred Astaire, Oscar Levant, Billie Burke, directed by Charles Walters

The screen's most celebrated dancing partners sing and dance their way through this film; one of the highlights being Astaire's solo dance 'Shoes With Wings On,' a spectacular tap routine set in a shoe shop.

F — EN

MGM — *MGM/UA Home Video*   P
10321

Baron Blood   Fil-Ent '72
Horror
07385   90 mins   C
B, V

Joseph Cotton, Elke Sommer, directed by Mario Bava

A vampire baron's descendants decide to restore the old ancestral castle as a tourist attraction. However, the old Baron is disturbed in his place of rest. Recalled from the grave, his mutilated body wreaks revenge.

BBFC:AA — S,A — EN

American International Pictures — *Guild Home Video*   H, P, E

Barrel Full of Dollars, A   Fil-Ent '??
Western/Drama
05554   98 mins   C
V2, B, V

Klaues Kinski, Hunt Powers directed by Miles Deem

This story of a vendetta is set during the American Civil War. An outlaw's brothers have been killed by the Nevada Kid's family during a hold-up. He has taken refuge in a deserted village on the Mexican border to order the massacre of the Kid's entire family.

BBFC:X — A — EN

Unknown — *Videomedia*   P
PVM 6101/BVM 6101/HVM 6101

Barry Lyndon   Fil-Ent '75
Drama
13062   184 mins   C
B, V

Ryan O'Neal, Marisa Berenson, Patrick Magee, directed by Stanley Kubrick

48   (For Explanation of codes, see USE GUIDE and KEY)

PALADIN VIDEO HOME ENTERTAINMENT GUIDE

In this beautiful adaptation of the novel by Thackeray set in the eighteenth century, an Irishman has high social ambitions which provoke drama, adventure and ultimate sadness.
BBFC:A — C,A — EN
Warner Bros Inc — Warner Home Video **P**
61178

Barry Manilow in Concert at the Greek Theater   Fil-Ent '8?
Music-Performance
09419   ? mins   C
B, V

This concert was filmed during his live performance in Los Angeles and features many of his hits including 'Copacabana', 'Mandy', 'I Write the Songs', 'Even Now', 'It's a Miracle', 'Ready to take a Chance Again', 'Looks Like We Made It', 'I was a Fool (to Let You Go)' and 'Can't Smile Without You'.
F — EN
Unknown — Guild Home Video   **H, P, E**

Barry White   Fil-Ent '??
Music-Performance
06186   60 mins   C
B, V

Barry White performs live in Mexico backed by Love Unlimited. The programme includes for the first time 'Love's Theme with Words.' Other songs featured: I'm under the Influence of Love, I Can't Get Enough of Your Love, Babe, I'm Never Ever Gonna Give you Up, Baby What Am I Gonna Do With You, Let the Music Play On and more.
F — EN
Unknown — VCL Video Services   **P**
V156B

Basic Dressage   Spo-Lei '82
Sports
06837   70 mins   C
B, V
David Hunt
This video uses the expertise of professional dressage trainer David Hunt and gives a realistic impression of the problems any dressage rider can encounter, how they are to be coped with and what the rider should be aiming for.
S,A — I
IMPS Limited — TFI Leisure Ltd   **P**

Basic Introduction to Yoga, A   How-Ins '80
Yoga

06322   60 mins   C
V2, B, V

This film produced by Malcolm Strott, a tutor for yoga teachers, demonstrates a number of simple exercises that anyone of any age can easily follow.
F — I
Center for Conscious Living; Malcolm Strott — World of Video 2000   **H, P**
GFS18

Basketcase   Fil-Ent '82
Horror/Satire
08965   93 mins   C
B, V
Kevin Vanhentenryck, Terri Susan Smith, Beverly Bonner, directed by Henenlotter
This is an amusing black comedy horror film that tells of a man who carries a padlocked wicker basket with him everywhere he goes. Occasionally he turns it loose to wreak revenge on unscrupulous doctors.
C,A — EN
Edgar levins — Palace Video Ltd   **P**
PVC 2024A

Bassey and Basie   Fil-Ent '7?
Variety
04365   60 mins   C
B, V, PH17, 3/4U
Shirley Bassey, Count Basie and his Orchestra
A variety show with Shirley Bassey and Count Basie.
F — EN
Unknown — Vidpics International   **P**

Bat, The   Fil-Ent '59
Horror
05186   78 mins   B/W
B, V
Vincent Price, Agnes Moorehead, Gavin Gordon, John Sutton, Lenita Lane, Elaine Edwards
Vincent Price stars as Dr. Wells in this horror classic. A prowler invades a guarded house and a woman sets a trap for him, with a surprise climax.
BBFC:AA — C,A — EN
Allied Artists — Rank Video Library   **H, P**
2004

Bat People, The   Fil-Ent '74
Horror
06780   91 mins   C
V2, B, V
Stewart Moss, Marianne McAndrew

(For Explanation of codes, see USE GUIDE and KEY)   49

PALADIN VIDEO HOME ENTERTAINMENT GUIDE

A doctor is bitten by a bat and is then incriminated in a series of bizarre murders.
S,A — EN
American International — *Intervision Video*
H, P
A-A 0327

Batfink-Cassette 1   Chi-Juv '??
Cartoons/Adventure
09415   65 mins   C
V2, B, V
Animated, directed by Hal Seeger
The great little Batfink, with his wings of steel races to the scene of each adventure in his suped-up Batillac, with his powerful pal Karate right behind him.
BBFC:U — I,S — EN
Unknown — *Guild Home Video*   **H, P, E**

Batfink II in Bat Patrol   Chi-Juv '??
Cartoons/Adventure
12069   65 mins   C
V2, B, V
Animated
Fifteen episodes are contained in this cassette where the steel-winged champion of law and order strikes terror into the hearts of villains everywhere.
BBFC:U — I,S — EN
Unknown — *Guild Home Video*   **H, P, E**

Battle Beyond the Stars   Fil-Ent '80
Science fiction
07855   98 mins   C
B, V
Richard Thomas, Robert Vaughn, John Saxon
A tale of the ultimate space war and the fight for survival or extinction.
BBFC:A — S,A — EN
Warner Bros — *Warner Home Video*   **P**
WEX 74050/WEV 74050

Battle Creek Brawl   Fil-Ent '80
Martial arts
08346   95 mins   C
V2, B, V
Jackie Chan, Jose Ferrer, Kristine De Bell, Ron Max, David Sheiner, Rosalind Chao, Lenny Montana, Peter Marc
This film is set in America in the 1930's. It tells of a fight in which the toughest, roughest and meanest fighters are gathered, each aiming to win the huge cash prize.
BBFC:AA — C,A — EN
Unknown — *Guild Home Video*   **H, P, E**

Battle for the Falklands   Gen-Edu '82
Documentary/Armed Forces-GB
08538   110 mins   C
B, V
Narrated by Ian Holm
This film records the heroic battle of the Falkland Islands. It tells how the task force was created in days to sail 8,000 miles to win back the islands. It is compiled from the news coverage, filmed by the camera teams with the task force.
S,A — ED
ITN; Granada Television
International — *THORN EMI*   **P**
TXC 90 1005 4/TVC 90 1005 2

Battle for the Planet of   Fil-Ent '73
the Apes
Science fiction/Drama
07692   83 mins   C
V2, B, V
Roddy McDowall, Claude Akins, Natalie Trundy, Severn Darden, Lew Ayres, Paul Williams, Austin Stoker, directed by J. Lee Thompson
In this futuristic story of the earth, the ape civilization is trying to live peacefully with human beings who are atom bomb mutations. The humans plan an attack on the apes while they are trying to suppress a plan by one of their community to form a military dictatorship.
S,A — EN
Twentieth Century Fox — *CBS/Fox Video*
P
1134

Battle of Britain, The   Fil-Ent '69
War-Drama
13022   110 mins   C
B, V
Laurence Olivier, Michael Caine, Robert Shaw, Susannah York, directed by Guy Hamilton
A starry cast recreates the events leading up to and including that historic September day which in the words of Winston Churchill was the RAF's finest hour.
BBFC:U — C,A — EN
United Artists — *Warner Home Video*   **P**
99292

Battle of Okinawa   Fil-Ent '??
War-Drama
09912   150 mins   C
V2, B, V
This film depicts how this battle was fought, the savagery, the frenzy, the agony, the gore and how soldiers, civilians even women and children fought to the grim end against all impossible odds.
BBFC:18 — A — EN
Unknown — *Derann Film Services*   **P**
FCV 605

PALADIN VIDEO HOME ENTERTAINMENT GUIDE

Battle of San Pasquale, The   Fil-Ent '8?
War-Drama
09154   80 mins   C
V
John Agar, Richard Arlen, Pancho Magnolona, Alicia Vergel
Set during the year of 1902, this film tells of an unusual assignment of the US Cavalry, to restore law and order in the Philippines. One platoon is directed to occupy the town of San Pasquale, only to be confronted by a hostile population, a one-man rebellion by a renegade Army officer and trouble from the local natives.
S,A — EN
Unknown — *Cinema Indoors*   **H, P**

Battle of the Bulge   Fil-Ent '65
War-Drama
07856   135 mins   C
B, V
Henry Fonda, Robert Shaw, Robert Ryan, Telly Savalas, Dana Andrews, George Montgomery, Ty Hardin, Charles Bronson, James MacArthur, directed by Ken Annakin
During December 1944, the Allies take longer than expected to win a land battle in the Ardennes, due to a crack Nazi Panzer commander. Realising that the German weakness is lack of petrol, the commander of the Allies plays a strategic game of hide and seek in an attempt to deplete their fuel supply.
BBFC:A — *S,A — EN*
Warner Bros — *Warner Home Video*   **P**
WEX 61086/WEV 61086

Battle of the Commandos   Fil-Ent '71
War-Drama
09200   94 mins   C
B, V
Jack Palance, Curt Jurgens, Thomas Hunter, Robert Hundar
A small group of commandoes have to destroy a huge German cannon before it can operate effectively against the Allied Forces. To accomplish this task a beautiful French girl becomes the innocent pawn in the long-running private war between a British Colonel and the German Colonel. The mission is a success but the two enemies have to meet face to face.
S,A — EN
Commonwealth United — *Video Form Pictures*
H, P
MGS 11

Battle of the Japan Sea   Fil-Ent '??
War-Drama
09915   120 mins   C
V2, B, V
Toshiro Mifune
This film depicts the agony and the bloodshed of Japan's War with Russia, which started in 1904 and reached its final conflict in May of 1905, when the Imperial Japanese combined fleet met Russia's Baltic Fleet in the Straits of Tushima, for one of the most spectacular naval battles.
BBFC:AA — *C,A — EN*
Toho International — *Derann Film Services*
P
FCV 606

Battle of the Planets—Curse of the Cuttlefish   Chi-Juv '84
Cartoons/Science fiction
13090   90 mins   C
B, V
Animated
Four episodes featuring G-force are contained in this cassette titled 'The Curse of the Cuttlefish I & II', 'Peaks of Planet Odin' and 'Victims of the Hawk'.
I,M — EN
Unknown — *Longman Video*   **P**
4012

Battle of the Planets—G-Force Vs The Giant Insects   Chi-Juv '84
Cartoons/Science fiction
13093   90 mins   C
B, V
Animated
Four episodes featuring G-force are contained in this cassette titled 'A Swarm of Robot Ants', 'The Ghostly Grasshopper', 'Attack of the Alien Wasp' and 'Space Spider'.
I,M — EN
Unknown — *Longman Video*   **P**
4009

Battle of the Planets—The Jupiter Moon Menace   Chi-Juv '84
Cartoons/Science fiction
13091   90 mins   C
B, V
Animated
Four episodes featuring G-force are contained in this cassette titled 'The Jupiter Moon Menace', 'Secret Island', 'Siege of the Squids' and 'The Seals of Sytron'.
I,M — EN
Unknown — *Longman Video*   **P**
4011

(For Explanation of codes, see USE GUIDE and KEY)

PALADIN VIDEO HOME ENTERTAINMENT GUIDE

Battle of the   Chi-Juv '84
Planets—Zoltar, Evil
Master of Disguises
Cartoons/Science fiction
13092   90 mins   C
B, V
Animated
Four episodes featuring G-force are contained in this cassette titled 'Zoltar Strikes Out,' 'Museum of Mystery,' 'Island of Fear' and 'The Galaxy Girls.'
I,M — EN
Unknown — *Longman Video*   **P**
4010

Battle of the River Plate,   Fil-Ent '56
The
War-Drama
08037   114 mins   C
B, V
John Gregson, Anthony Quayle, Peter Finch, Ian Hunter, Bernard Lee
This film, set in the South Atlantic, gives an account of the 1939 trapping of the German pocket battleship, Graf Spee, in Montevideo harbour and her subsequent hounding by the British.
BBFC:U — F — EN
Rank — *Rank Video Library*   **H, P**
0134 B

Battle of the Stars   Fil-Ent '79
Science fiction
09359   93 mins   C
B, V
John Richardson, Jason Palance
Two alien spaceships attempt to break through the Earth's defense system. One is destroyed, but the other is successful and cannot be intercepted. Captain of the Earth Security Services is called in and given full authority to destroy the foreign spaceship. When all seems lost, two mysterious strangers, a man and a young boy, come to aid the earth men.
F — EN
Cinematografica International — *Precision Video Ltd*   **P**
BPMPV 2624/VPMPV 2624

Battle of the Stars   Fil-Ent '79
Adventure/Science fiction
12092   93 mins   C
B, V
West Buchanan, Yanti Somer

An alien spacecraft breaks through Earth's defence system and lands in Mexico. They start to build a vast underground city for use as a base for conquering the planet and it is up to a small band of people to thwart their plans.
BBFC:PG — F — EN
Cinematografica International — *Precision Video Ltd*   **P**
BPMPV 2624/VPMPV 2624

Battle on the River   Fil-Ent '69
Neretva, The
War-Drama
07941   127 mins   C
V2, B, V
Yul Brynner, Hardy Kruger, Franco Nero, Sylvia Koscina, Orson Welles, Curt Jurgens
This film follows the true story of a war-weary but valiant Yugoslav army marching to a bloody and decisive clash on the bridge of the river Neretva.
S,A — EN
American International — *Videomedia*   **P**
PVM 7103/BVM 7103/HVM 7103

Battle Robot   Fil-Ent '8?
Cartoons
12714   90 mins   C
B, V
Animated
The world's most advanced robot equipped with Laser Vision, Rocket Fists, Heat Ray, strength and speed beyond compare, battles with the Robots of Hell to save the future of Earth.
I,M — EN
Unknown — *Mountain/Graphic*   **P**
BGV 1002

Battle Squadron   Fil-Ent '??
War-Drama
08832   ? mins   C
B, V
During World War II most of Europe was occupied by the Nazis. In this film, a Partisan Airforce is formed to free the skies.
S,A — EN
Unknown — *VCL Video Services*   **P**
M333D

Battlestar Galactica   Fil-Ent '78
Science fiction
01057   125 mins   C
V2, B, V
Lorne Greene, Richard Hatch, Dirk Benedict, Ray Milland, directed by Richard A. Colla

PALADIN VIDEO HOME ENTERTAINMENT GUIDE

A spaceship tries a desperate attempt to reach the ancient planet called Earth. Spectacular special effects. A movie made for television.
F — EN
Glen Larson — CIC Video **H, P**
CRA 1006/BEA 1006/VHA 1006

Battletruck Fil-Ent '7?
Adventure
12170   89 mins   C
V2, B, V
Michael Beck, Annie McEnroe, James Wainwright
This film is set in 1994 after the oil wars and destruction of cities. A ruthless warlord rules what is left of a radioactive world in his bullet-proof truck.
Avoriaz International Film Festival 1983: Special Jury Prize.   BBFC:15 — S,A — EN
Unknown — Guild Home Video   **H, P, E**

BBC Children's Favourites Chl-Juv '81
Cartoons
04853   55 mins   C
V2, B, V, LV
Animated
This is a selection from BBC children's programmes, including 'Bagpuss,' 'Ivor the Engine' and 'Clangers.'
PS,M — EN
Oliver Postgate — BBC Video   **H, P**
BBCV 9000

BBC Micro Computer in Primary Education Gen-Edu '8?
Electronic data processing/Education
09989   60 mins   C
B, V
This tape demonstrates some of the uses to which the BBC Micro can be put to use in the classroom and how the teacher can expand the scope of the programme and evaluate their worth.
C,A — TE
Holiday Brothers Ltd — Holiday Brothers Ltd **P**

Beach Girls, The Fil-Ent '82
Comedy/Adventure
12515   89 mins   C
B, V
Debra Blee, Val Kline, Jeana Tomasina, James Daughton, Adam Roarke, directed by Pat Townsend

This is the story of a school girl, willingly led astray by her sexy friends, while enjoying a holiday at her uncle's Malibu beach-house.
BBFC:18 — A — EN
Crown International Pictures — THORN EMI **P**
TXB 90 21964/TVB 90 21962

Beach House Fil-Ent '84
Drama
13263   76 mins   C
B, V
Kathy McNecl, Richard Duggan, Ileana Seidel, John Cosola, directed by John Gallagher
The kids from Brooklyn and suburban Philadelphia get together in a beach house for the summer and indulge in slapstick fights, music, baseball games and romance galore.
BBFC:15 — S,A — EN
Marino Amoruso — CBS/Fox Video   **P**
3014

Beach of the War Gods Fil-Ent '74
War-Drama/Martial arts
06924   78 mins   C
B, V
Wang Yu, Lung Fei, Tien Yeh
This is the heroic story of a brave group of coastal villagers who fought to save the Chinese city of Hangchow from marauding Japanese pirates in the late Ming Dynasty.
BBFC:AA — S,A — EN
Unknown — Rank Video Library   **H, P**
0084B

Beany and Cecil, Volume 1 Chl-Juv '84
Cartoons
13081   41 mins   C
B, V
Animated
Beany and his sea serpent pal Cecil travel to the far ends of the earth and outer space, outwitting their arch-adversary Dishonest John.
BBFC:U — F — EN
Bob Clampett — RCA/Columbia Pictures Video UK   **H, P**
10317

Bear Island Fil-Ent '79
Adventure/Suspense
09276   102 mins   C
B, V
Donald Sutherland, Vanessa Redgrave, Richard Widmark, Christopher Lee, Barbara Parkins, Lloyd Bridges, directed by Don Sharp

(For Explanation of codes, see USE GUIDE and KEY)   53

PALADIN VIDEO HOME ENTERTAINMENT GUIDE

Based on the novel by Alistair MacLean, this film follows the adventures of a scientific expedition to an isolated Arctic island. As one death follows another it becomes clear that every member of the expedition is not what he or she seems.
S,A — EN
Selkirk Films; Columbia — *RCA/Columbia Pictures Video UK* **H, P**

Bears and I, The   Fil-Ent '74
Adventure
13440   88 mins   C
B, V
Patrick Wayne
Set in the Canadian outback, a man finds himself in charge of three bear cubs and upsets the local Taklute Indians at the same time.
BBFC:U — *F* — *EN*
Walt Disney Productions — *Rank Video Library*
P
109

Beast in the Cellar   Fil-Ent '70
Horror
02438   90 mins   C
B, V
Dame Flora Robson, Beryl Reid
A story of murder and lust, with two old ladies the cause of it all.
BBFC:X — *A* — *EN*
Cannon Releasing — *Guild Home Video*
H, P

Beastmaster, The   Fil-Ent '82
Drama/Fantasy
09780   118 mins   C
B, V
Marc Singer, Tanya Roberts, Rip Torn, John Amos, directed by Don Coscarelli
A mystery and magic fantasy set in an enchanted long ago time. The mythical hero uses his astonishing powers to control animals and together they fight the evil powers of darkness.
BBFC:PG — *S,A* — *EN*
A Paul Pepperman; Leisure Investment Co Production — *THORN EMI* **P**
TXA 90 17174/TVA 90 17172

Beat, The   Fil-Ent '83
Music/Video
10021   40 mins   C
B, V
Music video tracks include 'Can't Get Used to Losing You' and 'Mirror in the Bathroom.'
M,A — EN
Unknown — *Palace Video Ltd* **P**
PVC 3004M

Beat in Concert   Fil-Ent '??
Music-Performance
09999   60 mins   C
B, V
This tape features 'The Beat' in concert. It includes such hits as 'Two Swords', 'Doors of Your Heart', 'Get a Job', 'Stand Down Margaret', 'Full Stop', 'Mirror in the Bathroom', 'Hands Off, She's Mine' and 'Jackpot'.
F — EN
Holiday Brothers — *Holiday Brothers Ltd*
P

Beat Street   Fil-Ent '84
Drama/Music
13747   104 mins   C
B, V
Guy Davis, Robert Taylor, Leon Grant, Frank Reyes, John Chardiet, Rae Dawn Chong, directed by Stan Lathan
Set to a background of contemporary music and breakdancing on the streets of New York, this film is about the struggle for survival for the youths with no job or prospects to look forward to.
BBFC:PG — *S,A* — *EN*
Orion Pictures — *Rank Video Library* **H, P**
7016D

Beat the Devil   Fil-Ent '54
Adventure
01048   89 mins   B/W
B, V
Humphrey Bogart, Jennifer Jones, Peter Lorre, Robert Morley, directed by John Huston
Satire about con artists who double-cross one another in their race to a uranium plunder in Africa.
F — EN
Columbia; John Huston — *CBS/Fox Video* **P**
3B-059

Beauty and the Beast   Fil-Ent '??
Romance/Fantasy
06262   86 mins   C
B, V
George C. Scott, Trish Van Devere, Virginia McKenna, Bernard Lee
An adaptation of the classic tale of magical fantasy, tragedy and romance which transforms the legend into an epic.
S,A — EN
Unknown — *VCL Video Services* **P**
P207D

Because He's My Friend   Fil-Ent '78
Drama
09139   91 mins   C

(For Explanation of codes, see USE GUIDE and KEY)

PALADIN VIDEO HOME ENTERTAINMENT GUIDE

V2, B, V

Karen Black, Keir Dullea, Jack Thompson, Tom Oliver, Don Reid, Barbara Stephens, Warwick Poulsen, directed by Ralph Nelson

A young couple have a beautiful but retarded 12-year-old son. The story tells of their sensitive relationships. However, the parents begin to realise that hiding their pain and anger is not what the boy needs. They slowly come to grips with the urgency of admitting that their son is not normal but that they can be a happy family all the same.

S,A — EN

Transatlantic Entprs — *Go Video Ltd* P
PIC 002

Becket   Fil-Ent '64
Drama
13776   149 mins   C
B, V

Richard Burton, Peter O'Toole, Sir John Gielgud, Sian Phillips, Marrita Hunt

This film tells the story of Henry II and Thomas Becket's stormy relationship culminating with the martyrdom of Becket in Canterbury Cathedral.

F — EN

Paramount — *Odyssey Video*   H, P

Bedazzled   Fil-Ent '68
Comedy
07707   103 mins   C
V2, B, V

Peter Cook, Dudley Moore, Eleanor Bron, Raquel Welch, directed by Stanley Donen

A timid Wimpy Bar cook agrees to sell his soul to the devil if he can 'make-it' with the girl of his dreams, the waitress where he works. In exchange for his soul the devil gives him seven wishes.

S,A — EN

Twentieth Century Fox — *CBS/Fox Video* P
1120

Bedknobs and Broomsticks   Fil-Ent '71
Fantasy
08004   97 mins   C
B, V

Angela Lansbury, David Tomlinson, Sam Jaffe, Roddy McDowall, Roy Smart, Bruce Forsyth, Cindy O'Callaghan, directed by Robert Stevenson

This film, set in the year 1940, tells the story of three evacuee children and a kind witch, who ride on a magic bedstead and defeat the invasion of England.

BBFC:U — F — EN

Walt Disney Productions — *Rank Video Library* H
01600

Bedtime with Rosie   Fil-Ent '??
Comedy
05461   70 mins   C
V2, B, V

Una Stubbs, Diana Dors, Ivor Burgoyne, directed by Wolf Rilla

A young pregnant girl plans a new life for herself in Holland. En route she drops in on her Aunt in London after a bed for the night. The Aunt is pleased to see her but is unsure about the reaction of her lodger. He is hostile about sharing his room but during the night their relationship changes and she reconsiders her future.

BBFC:A — S,A — EN

Unknown — *Iver Film Services*   P
151

Beebtots   Chi-Juv '8?
Cartoons/Fantasy
06972   52 mins   C
V2, B, V
Animated

A special compilation for children featuring Noggin the Nog, Clangers, Bagpuss and Ivor the Engine.

PS,M — EN

Oliver Postgate — *BBC Video*   H, P
BBCV 9004

Bees, The   Fil-Ent '78
Horror
06797   93 mins   C
V2, B, V

John Saxon, Angel Tompkins, John Carradine
Giant ravenous bees threaten the existence of mankind when they leave their South American breeding ground and spread over the world.

C,A — EN

New World — *Intervision Video*   H, P
A-A 0331

Beetle Bailey   Fil-Ent '63
Cartoons
09971   73 mins   C
B, V
Animated

Beetle Bailey, Sergeant Snorkle, Zero, General Halftrack and Otto, Snorkle's faithful dog all live in Camp Swampy. Beetle is assigned to messenger duty during a military exercise with

(For Explanation of codes, see USE GUIDE and KEY)

55

PALADIN VIDEO HOME ENTERTAINMENT GUIDE

inevitable chaos. A troop of female soldiers arrive at the camp and although Sergeant Snorkle can't stand the thought he finds the situation has its compensations.
F — EN
King Features — *Select Video Limited* P
3551/43

Beetle Bailey Fil-Ent '63
Cartoons/Comedy
12239 60 mins C
B, V
Animated
Twelve fabulously funny episodes in which the boys get into all kinds of hot water and give the General and Sergeant Snorkle a few more grey hairs.
F — EN
King Features Syndicate — *Select Video Limited* P
3552/43

Beggar's Opera, The Fil-Ent '53
Musical-Drama
01611 90 mins C
B, V
Laurence Olivier, Stanley Holloway, Dorothy Tutin, directed by Peter Brook
Macheath sets the keynote the minute he appears as a shadow riding over the heath. His capture in gaming salons, after a sword-fight all over the green baize, shows the well-choreographed nimbleness of the film's tone. Based on the opera by John Gay.
BBFC:U — F — EN
Herbert Wilcox — *THORN EMI* P
TXB 90 0092 4/TVB 90 0092 2

Beguiled, The Fil-Ent '70
Drama
13326 100 mins C
B, V
Clint Eastwood, Geraldine Page, Pamelyn Ferdin, Elizabeth Hartman, Mae Mercer, directed by Don Siegal
A wounded Union soldier is taken in by a girl's school during the Civil War and as they tend his wounds he plays one off against the other to prevent them handing him over to the Confederates.
BBFC:18 — C,A — EN
Universal — *CIC Video* H, P
BEN 1123/VHN 1123

Behave Yourself Fil-Ent '51
Crime-Drama/Comedy
06195 78 mins B/W
B, V
Shelley Winters, Farley Granger, William Demarest
A newly-wed wife is delighted when her husband brings home a stray dog; little do they know that the dog is a 'courier' in a two million dollar hijack plot, organised by two rival and hostile gangs.
F — EN
RKO — *VCL Video Services* P
X0262

Behind Convent Walls Fil-Ent '??
Drama
07913 91 mins C
V2, B, V
Ligia Branice, Marina Pierrot, Howard Ross, directed by Walerian Borowczyk
This story investigates woman's natural instincts and tells of the life and fantasies of those women who spend their lives in seclusion in convents. Based on Stendhal's 'Roman Walks.'
A — EN
Unknown — *Video Programme Distributors* P
Cannon—001

Being Different Fil-Ent '81
Documentary
07681 90 mins C
B, V
Narrated by Christopher Plummer, directed by Harry Rasky
This film presents in a warm and humourous way the true story of a modern-day Elephant Man. Avoiding sensationalism the film provides an insight into the lives of those described as human oddities or 'freaks'.
S,A — EN
Double S Productions Ltd — *Video Network* P
0013

Being There Fil-Ent '80
Comedy
05303 121 mins C
V2, B, V
Peter Sellers, Melvyn Douglas, Shirley MacLaine
The story of a gardener whose entire knowledge of life comes from watching television. Having been a recluse for most of his life, when he enters the real world he is mistaken for a sex symbol, a presidential candidate and a philosopher.
Academy Award '80: Best Supporting Actor (Douglas). S,A — EN
Andrew Bransberg Prod; Hal Ashby Prod — *MGM/UA Home Video* P
UCB10026/UCV10026

56 (For Explanation of codes, see USE GUIDE and KEY)

PALADIN VIDEO HOME ENTERTAINMENT GUIDE

Belle et la Bete, La Fil-Ent '45
Fairy tales
09774 86 mins B/W
B, V
Jean Marais, Josette Day, directed by Jean Cocteau
In this adaptation of the classic fairy tale Beauty gives herself to the Beast who has kidnapped her father. Through love the monster turns into a handsome prince. Subtitled in English.
BBFC:PG — S,A — EN   FR
CLT — *THORN EMI* P
TXE 90 0848 4/TVE 90 0848 2

Belle Starr Story, The Fil-Ent '7?
Western
07794 95 mins C
V2, B, V
Elsa Martinelli, Robert Wood
This film follows the story of the notorious and deadly Belle Starr and her rise to infamy.
S,A — EN
Unknown — *Fletcher Video* H, P
V107

Belle Stars—Live Signs, Live Times, The Fil-Ent '84
Music-Performance
13135 60 mins C
B, V
Featuring The Belle Stars live at the Marquee '84, the sixteen tracks include 'Sign of the Times,' 'The Clapping Song,' 'Cool Disguise,' 'Burning' and 'Sign of the Times.'
S,A — EN
Unknown — *Polygram Video* P
041 0504/041 0502

Bells Fil-Ent '81
Horror/Suspense
08376 119 mins C
V2, B, V
Richard Chamberlain, John Houseman, Sara Botsford, Gary Reineke
Someone has the ability to turn an ordinary telephone into a death machine. An innocent girl is the first victim, killed when she answers a public telephone. Her former tutor sets out to discover who is behind this horrific plan.
BBFC:X — A — EN
Unknown — *Guild Home Video* H, P, E

Below the Belt Fil-Ent '??
Drama
08854 91 mins C
V2, B, V
Regina Baff, John Becher
A waitress at a hamburger joint in a wrestling stadium has to defend herself against a man. A promoter sees her, and persuades her that she is a 'natural' for the ring.
BBFC:X — A — EN
Unknown — *Video Programme Distributors* P
Inter-Ocean 080

Belstone Fox, The Fil-Ent '72
Drama
04252 99 mins C
B, V
Eric Porter, Dennis Waterman, Bill Travers, Jeremy Kemp, Rachel Roberts, Heather Wright
This animal adventure film stars Eric Porter as a huntsman who unwittingly pits the forces of nature against each other. Tag, an orphaned fox cub, is reared with a litter of hound puppies and through this kindly act comes tragedy for both humans and animals.
BBFC:A — M,A — EN
20th Century Fox — *Rank Video Library*
H, P
0016

Ben Hur Fil-Ent '59
Drama
07725 209 mins C
B, V
Charlton Heston, Jack Hawkins, Haya Harareet, Stephen Boyd, Hugh Griffith, Martha Scott, Sam Jaffe, directed by William Wyler
This is a Biblical drama set in Rome during the early days of Christianity. The story of Judah Ben Hur is best known for the breath-taking chariot race when he emerges as victor over the treacherous Messala. Based on the classic by General Lew Wallce.
Academy Awards '59: Best Actor (Heston); Best Supporting Actor (Griffith); Best Director (Wyler); Best Cinematography.
BBFC:A — S,A — EN
MGM — *MGM/UA Home Video* P
UMB 1000 4/UMV 1000 4

Benatar Fil-Ent '83
Music-Performance
12463 72 mins C
B, V
Pat Benatar
This is the videotape of Grammy Award-winning Pat Benatar's concert at the New Haven Veterans Memorial Coliseum in New Haven, Connecticut during her 50-city world tour, and it features a line-up of her hit tunes, including 'Love Is a Battlefield'.
BBFC:U — F — EN
Unknown — *RCA/Columbia Pictures Video UK*
H, P
10282

(For Explanation of codes, see USE GUIDE and KEY) 57

PALADIN VIDEO HOME ENTERTAINMENT GUIDE

Beneath the Planet of the Apes Fil-Ent '70
Science fiction
01760 95 mins C
B, V
James Franciscus, Kim Hunter, Maurice Evans, Linda Harrison, directed by Ted Post
An astronaut is sent to find a fellow astronaut on the site of New York, 2,000 years after it was destroyed by an atomic blast.
BBFC:A — F — EN
20th Century Fox, Arthur P Jacobs — *CBS/Fox Video* P
3A-003

Benji Chi-Juv '73
Comedy-Drama
12881 87 mins C
B, V
Benji, Peter Brek, Christopher Connelly, Deborah Walley
A warm and amusing story of how a small vagabond dog finds love and a family of his own.
F — EN
Mulberry Square Productions — *Vestron Video International* P
15003

Berenstain Bears Easter Surprise and Comic Valentine, The Chi-Juv '82
Cartoons
12167 50 mins C
V2, B, V
Animated
Two adventures of the Berenstain Bears are featured on this tape, based on the children's story books. This programme is the first of a new series.
PS,I — EN
Joseph Cates — *Embassy Home Entertainment* P
8001

Berenstein Bears, Volume 2, The Chi-Juv '82
Cartoons
12165 50 mins C
V2, B, V
Animated
The second volume in this series contains two more cartoons: 'Play Ball' and 'Meet Big Paw.'
PS,1 — EN
Joseph Cates — *Embassy Home Entertainment* P
8003

Berlin Express/Isle of the Dead Fil-Ent '4?
War-Drama/Horror
05716 152 mins B/W
B, V
Robert Ryan, Merle Oberon, Paul Lukas, Charles Corvin, directed by Jacques Tourneur, Boris Karloff, Ellen Drew, Jason Robards, Alan Napier, directed by Mark Robson
Two films are featured on one cassette. 'Berlin Express' (Black/white, 83 mins, 1949) is set against the background of Cold-War Berlin and the story of a desperate mission to loving a marked man to safety. 'Isle of the Dead' (Black/white, 69 mins, 1946) is set during the Balkan Wars of 1912, a Greek general and his men take refuge on an island and find themselves in the midst of a plague of vampirism. An invalid girl is blamed for the deaths as madness takes over.
S,A — EN
RKO — *Kingston Video* H, P
KV26

Bermuda Triangle, The Fil-Ent '78
Documentary/Mystery
05684 91 mins C
B, V
Narrated by Brad Crandall, directed by Richard Friedenberg
This film explores the history of an area in the Atlantic Ocean, roughly a triangle bounded by Bermuda, Puerto Rico and Miami, Florida. More than five hundred incidents have occured in which ships and planes have mysteriously disappeared.
BBFC:U — F — EN
Sunn Classic Pictures; Charles E Sellier Jr and James L Conway Prods — *Rank Video Library* H, P
2011C

Bert Kaempfert and His Orchestra Fil-Ent '81
Music-Performance
04622 55 mins C
B, V
This programme was recorded live at the Royal Albert Hall, London during one of his rare concert performances. This programme is a tribute to the music of Bert Kaempfert.
F — EN
VCL Video Services Ltd — *VCL Video Services* P

Best Friends Fil-Ent '82
Comedy/Romance
12686 105 mins C
B, V
Goldie Hawn, Burt Reynolds, Keenan Wynn, Jessica Tandy, directed by Norman Jewison

PALADIN VIDEO HOME ENTERTAINMENT GUIDE

Two top Hollywood writers live happily together — but when they decide to get married and go on their honeymoon, their troubles really start!
BBFC:PG — F — EN
Norman Jewison; Patrick Palmer — *Warner Home Video* **P**
61265

Best in Europe 1980, The　　Spo-Lei '80
Football
05917　　60 mins　　C
V
Commentator David Coleman
The film features two British clubs in the European Finals. In the first match Nottingham Forest are defending the trophy against Hamburg in the 1980 Cup Final. In the second match Arsenal face Valencia in the 1980 European Cup Winners Cup Final.
F — EN
Unknown — *JVC* **P**
PRT 46

Best in Europe 1981, The　　Spo-Lei '81
Football
05916　　60 mins　　C
V
Commentator David Coleman
This film sees Liverpool attempt to win their third European Cup Final since 1977. Their opponents are the legendary Real Madrid, the winners of the European Cup six times. Also included are highlights of the 1981 European Cup Winners Cup Final between Dinamo Tblisi and Carl Zeiss Jena.
F — EN
Unknown — *JVC* **P**
PRT 48

Best in Football—Cassette 1, The　　Spo-Lei '??
Football
08609　　50 mins　　C
V2, B, V
George Best, narrated by John Adams
This tape, the first in a series of four, is designed for those wishing to improve their football skills and techniques. In the first part, the accuracy of passing, dribbling, keeping the ball on the move, the 'wall-pass' and tackling procedures are covered.
M,A — I
Unknown — *Hokushin Audio Visual Ltd* **P**
G102

Best in Football—Cassette 2, The　　Spo-Lei '8?
Football
08610　　50 mins　　C
V2, B, V
George Best, narrated by John Adams
This tape, the second in a series of four, is designed for those wishing to improve their football skills and techniques. In this second part the following tactics are covered: taking the pace off the ball, screening, heading at goal, goal-keep distribution and weighting of a pass.
M,A — I
Unknown — *Hokushin Audio Visual Ltd* **P**
G103

Best in Football—Cassette 3, The　　Spo-Lei '8?
Football
08611　　50 mins　　C
V2, B, V
George Best, narrated by John Adams
This tape, the third in a series of four, is designed for those wishing to improve their football skills and techniques. In this third part the following tactics are covered: control with the chest, the chip pass, trapping a moving ball, reverse pass and shooting.
M,A — I
Unknown — *Hokushin Audio Visual Ltd* **P**
G104

Best in Football—Cassette 4, The　　Spo-Lei '8?
Football
08612　　50 mins　　C
V2, B, V
George Best, narrated by John Adams
This tape, the last in a series of four, is designed for those wishing to improve their football skills and techniques. In this final part the following tactics are covered: goal keeping on high crosses, volleying in defense, heading for defenders, swerving the ball and volleying at goal.
M,A — I
Unknown — *Hokushin Audio Visual Ltd* **P**
G 105

Best Little Whorehouse in Texas, The　　Fil-Ent '82
Comedy/Musical
10120　　110 mins　　C
B, V
Burt Reynolds, Dolly Parton, Dom DeLuise, directed by Colin Higgins

(For Explanation of codes, see USE GUIDE and KEY)

PALADIN VIDEO HOME ENTERTAINMENT GUIDE

This is the film of the successful Broadway musical comedy. The peace of a rural bordello is shattered when a crusading TV consumer watchdog decides that it offends public decency and should be closed down.
BBFC:15 — S,A — EN
Universal — CIC Video   H, P
BEA 1072/VHA 1072

Best of Benny Hill Volume 1, The   Fil-Ent '81
Comedy
05903   120 mins   C
V2, B, V
Benny Hill, Henry McGhee, Bob Todd, Jack Wright, Rita Webb
A compilation from the Benny Hill Show television series.
F — EN
Thames Video — THORN EMI   P
TPB 90 6203 3/TXB 90 6203 4/TVB 90 6203 2

Best of Benny Hill Volume 2, The   Fil-Ent '81
Comedy
05904   104 mins   C
B, V
Benny Hill, Henry McGhee, Bob Todd, Jack Knight, Rita Webb
A compilation from the Benny Hill Show television series.
F — EN
Thames Video — THORN EMI   P
TXB 90 0506 4/TVB 90 0506 2

Best of Benny Hill—Volume 3, The   Fil-Ent '82
Comedy
07417   114 mins   C
B, V
Benny Hill, Bob Todd, Henry McGee, Jack Wright, Rita Webb
This tape is a further compilation of the best sketches from the Benny Hill television show.
S,A — EN
Thames Television — THORN EMI   P
TXB 90 0729 4/TVB 90 0729 2

Best of Blondie, The   Fil-Ent '81
Music-Performance
05420   60 mins   C
B, V
Debbie Harry

This film is a visual record of four years of success reached by the group Blondie. It features all their hit singles and combines promotional video film with live footage shot in New York.
F — EN
Chrysalis Group Ltd — Chrysalis Video   P
CVIM BE4/CVIM VH4

Best of Both Worlds   Fil-Ent '8?
Comedy/Romance
12147   87 mins   C
V2, B, V
Sugith Varughese, Gaye Burgess, Malika Mendez, directed by Douglas Williams
The family of a successful young advertising executive of Indian heritage have arranged a marriage for him. His girlfriend is horrified to hear that his proposed fiancee will be bringing a large dowry with her from India. A plan is devised and set into action.
BBFC:A — C,A — EN
Unknown — Intervision Video   H, P
A-A 0487

Best of Friends, The   Fil-Ent '82
Drama/Romance
09343   97 mins   C
B, V
Angela Punch McGregor, Graeme Blundell
This film tells the story of a bachelor, Tom, and Melanie, a television interviewer who has also never been married. They have both been the best of friends since pre-school days but have never been romantically involved. That is until one night after the 30th anniversary of their friendship Melanie seduces Tom, and from here the plot unfolds.
C,A — EN
New South Wales Film Corp.; Friendly Film Co. — Precision Video Ltd   P
BSWPV 2601/VSWPV 2601

Best of George and Mildred, The   Fil-Ent '81
Comedy
05910   104 mins   C
B, V
Yootha Joyce, Brian Murphy, directed by Peter Frazer-Jones
Taken from the television series, this is the story of a couple who move from their familiar environment in central London to the suburban executive belt.
F — EN
Peter Frazer-Jones — THORN EMI   P
TXB 90 0508 4/TVB 90 0508 2

60   (For Explanation of codes, see USE GUIDE and KEY)

PALADIN VIDEO HOME ENTERTAINMENT GUIDE

Best of Little Lulu, The   Fil-Ent '78
Cartoons
12020   86 mins   C
V2, B, V
Animated
Little Lulu and her gang provide more laughter in four episodes entitled 'Little Fireman,' 'The Endurance Test,' 'Good Luck, Guard' and 'Operation Baby-Sitting.'
F — EN
Ziv International — *Videomedia*   P
PVM 2121/BVM 2121/HVM 2121

Best of Reggae Sunsplash-Part One   Fil-Ent '82
Music-Performance
09380   60 mins   C
B, V
Set in Montego Bay, Jamaica, at the World's biggest reggae festival, this tape features live performances from Chalice, Steel Pulse, Eek-A-Mouse, Asward, Burning Spear, Big Youth and The Mighty Diamonds. Recorded in stereo.
F — EN
Unknown — *VCL Video Services*   P
Z336G

Best of Reggae Sunsplash-Part Two   Fil-Ent '82
Music-Performance
09381   60 mins   C
B, V
Live in Montego Bay, Jamaica, 1982, this tape features further performances from Chalice, Yellowman, Denice Williams, Big Youth, Toots and the Maytals, Taj Mahal, Mutabaruka and Twinkle Brothers. Recorded in stereo.
F — EN
Unknown — *VCL Video Services*   P
Z337G

Best of Rising Damp, The   Fil-Ent '8?
Comedy
06167   96 mins   C
V2, B, V
Leonard Rossiter, Richard Beckinsale, Frances de la Tour, Dan Warrington
A cassette, number one in a series, of the best of the television comedy 'Rising Damp,' which tells the story of Rigsby a self-styled aristocrat and landlord in bed-sitter land. He pretends to be unprejudiced but is more or less prejudiced about everyone and everything.
S,A — EN
Ian MacNaughton Prod — *Guild Home Video*
H, P, E

Best of the Badmen/Sealed Cargo   Fil-Ent '52
Western/War-Drama
05665   166 mins   C
B, V
Robert Ryan, Claire Trevor, Bruce Cabot, Robert Preston, Jack Buetel, directed by William D. Russell, Dana Andrews, Claude Rains, Carla Balenda, Philip Dorn, directed by Alfred Werker
Two films are contained on one cassette. 'Best of the Badman' (Colour, 81 mins, 1952) is the story of a U.S. Cavalry officer arrested after the Civil War on a charge of murder. He is innocent and escapes to Badman's territory to organise an army of outlaws to seek revenge. 'Sealed Cargo' (Black/white, 85 mins, 1952) is a suspense thriller involving an abandoned ship and captgain found by fishermen. They tow it to safety and discover it has a cargo of torpedoes; they destroy the ship but the crew are in hiding and plan to take over the whole area.
S,A — EN
RKO — *Kingston Video*   H, P
KV47

Best of the Best 1972/Fast Company 1973   Spo-Lei '73
Automobiles-Racing
04517   55 mins   C
B, V
Emerson Fittipaldi becomes the youngest world driving champion ever at age 25. Defending champion Jackie Stewart is hampered by ill health, accidents, and breakdowns, but is able to overcome them to defend his title gallantly, though in vain. 'Fast Company' recounts Jackie Stewart's final season, ending in a championship.
F — EN
Brunswick Intl — *Quadrant Video*   H, P
M11

Best of the Sandbaggers, The   Fil-Ent '7?
Drama
06142   104 mins   C
B, V
Ray Lonnen, Richard Vernon, Roy Marsden, Jerome Willis, Alan MacNaughton
This film is from the television series 'The Sandbaggers' that tells the stories of the complex world of modern intelligence. Involving politically sensitive tasks, escorting defecting foreigners, the rescue of endangered field agents, the last resort assassinations of those too powerful or too inaccessible to be silenced in any other way.
S,A — EN
Michael Ferguson Prod — *Guild Home Video*
H, P, E

PALADIN VIDEO HOME ENTERTAINMENT GUIDE

Best of Sandbaggers- Fil-Ent '7?
Cassette 2, The
Drama
09424   101 mins   C
V2, B, V

Ray Lonnen, Richard Vernon, Roy Marsden, Jerome Willis, Alan MacNaughtan, directed by Michael Ferguson, Peter Cregeen

This tape contains two further episodes from the Sandbaggers. In 'First Principles', a Norwegian radar surveillance aircraft has crashed onto Russian territory against his better judgement, the Director of Operations for SIS is ordered to assist the Norwegians. In 'It Couldn't Happen Here' and American Senator is mysteriously assassinated.

S,A — EN

Michael Ferguson Prod. — Guild Home Video
H, P, E

Best of the Two Ronnies, Fil-Ent '8?
The
Comedy-Performance
09399   ? mins   C
V2, B, V

Ronnie Barker, Ronnie Corbett

This is a classic collection of some of the well-known duo's most favourite sketches.

F — EN

BBC — BBC Video   H, P
BBCV 7002

Best of the Two Ronnies, Fil-Ent '7?
The
Comedy
12731   45 mins   C
B, V

Ronnie Corbett, Ronnie Barker

This film features a special collection of The Two Ronnies' funniest sketches.
British Academy and Television Arts: Award Winner.   F — EN

Unknown — BBC Video   H, P
7002

Best of Upstairs, Fil-Ent '73
Downstairs—Volume 1,
The
Drama
08423   104 mins   C
B, V

Gordon Jackson, Angela Baddely, Jean Marsh, Simon Williams, Nicola Paget, David Langton, Hannah Gordon, Pauline Collins, John Alderton

Set in Edwardian London, 'Upstairs, Downstairs' follows the life of the Bellamy family and their staff who live below. The Bellamy family is headed by Lord Richard Bellamy, a highly respected government minister. On this cassette are two episodes in the series of fourteen available on seven cassettes.

F — EN

London Weekend Television — THORN EMI
P

TXB 90 0693 4/TVB 90 0693 2

Best of Upstairs, Fil-Ent '73
Downstairs—Volume 2,
The
Drama
08424   104 mins   C
B, V

Gordon Jackson, Angela Baddely, Jean Marsh, Simon Williams, Nicola Paget, David Langton, Hannah Gordon, Pauline Collins, John Alderton

This programme, the second in the series, contains two further episodes of 'Upstairs, Downstairs'.

F — EN

London Weekend Television — THORN EMI
P

TXB 90 0720 4/TVB 90 0720 2

Best of Upstairs, Fil-Ent '73
Downstairs—Volume 4,
The
Drama
08426   103 mins   C
B, V

Gordon Jackson, Angela Baddely, Jean Marsh, Simon Williams, Nicola Paget, David Langton, Hannah Gordon, Pauline Collins, John Alderton

This programme, the fourth in the series, contains two further episodes. 'A Change of Scene': Hudson accompanies James Bellamy to a weekend house party. In 'Desirous of Change' Richard is the object of attention of two women.

F — EN

London Weekend Television — THORN EMI
P

TXB 90 1010 4/TVB 90 1010 2

Best of Upstairs, Fil-Ent '73
Downstairs—Volume 5,
The
Drama
08427   100 mins   C
B, V

Gordon Jackson, Angela Baddely, Jean Marsh, Simon Williams, Nicola Paget, David Langton, Hannah Gordon, Pauline Collins, John Alderton

This programme, the fifth in the series, contains two more episodes of the series. In the first, 'The Bolter', Hazel plays a part in a practical joke which exposes James to ridicule, herself to

PALADIN VIDEO HOME ENTERTAINMENT GUIDE

personal danger, and their marriage in serious doubt. In the second, 'A Perfect Stranger', Rose's relationship with a young man forces her to make a very important decision.
F — EN
London Weekend Television — *THORN EMI*
P
TXB 90 1011 4/TVB 90 1011 2

Best of Upstairs, Downstairs—Volume 6, The
Fil-Ent '73

Drama
08428   102 mins   C
B, V
Gordon Jackson, Angela Baddely, Jean Marsh, Simon Williams, Nicola Paget, David Langton, Hannah Gordon, Pauline Collins, John Alderton
Two further episodes are contained in this sixth volume. In the first, entitled 'The Glorious Dead' both Rose and Hazel receive important news and James returns from the War. In the second, entitled 'Facing Fearful Odds', Richard's help is sought by an old friend to help clear her son of the charge of cowardice.
F — EN
London Weekend Television — *THORN EMI*
P
TXB 90 1012 4/TVB 90 1012 2

Best of Upstairs, Downstairs—Volume 7, The
Fil-Ent '73

Drama
08429   102 mins   C
B, V
Gordon Jackson, Angela Baddely, Jean Marsh, Simon Williams, Nicola Paget, David Langton, Hannah Gordon, Pauline Collins, John Alderton
This programme, the final in this series, contains the last two episodes. 'Wanted, a Good Home' is when the Bellamys are away, and the unpopular Governess takes over the running of the house, managing to upset most people. The last episode, 'An Old Flame', tells of James' indiscretion with the wife of his best friend which nearly ends in a public scandal.
F — EN
London Weekend Television — *THORN EMI*
P
TXB 90 1013 4/TVB 90 1013 2

Best of Upstairs, Downstairs—Volume 3, The
Fil-Ent '73

Drama
08425   99 mins   C
B, V
Gordon Jackson, Angela Baddely, Jean Marsh, Simon Williams, Nicola Paget, David Langton, Hannah Gordon, Pauline Collins, John Alderton
This programme, the third in the series, contains two more episodes. 'Guest of Honour' tells of the arrival of King Edward VII to dinner at Eaton Place. 'A Special Mischief' tells of Elizabeth's involvement with the Suffragette Movement which causes Rose to suffer a shattering experience.
F — EN
London Weekend Television — *THORN EMI*
P
TXB 90 1009 4/TVB 90 1009 2

Best of Walt Disney's True Life Adventures, The
Fil-Ent '??

Adventure/Documentary
05597   85 mins   C
B, V
Directed by James Algar
A true life adventure feature which goes on a world wide journey in search of fascinating wildlife. The often strange and wonderful world of animals is witnessed from the desert and the scorpions courtship dance to the cold world of the polar bear.
F — EN
Walt Disney Productions — *Rank Video Library*
H
04800

Best of Wimbledon, The
Spo-Lei '84

Tennis
12729   90 mins   C
B, V
This is the first in a series that takes a look back at some of the greatest matches and players of all time. It is introduced by John Barrett and features the final sets of the 1972 Men's Final between Stan Smith and Ilie Nastase, and the 1977 semi-final between Bjorn Borg and Vitas Gerulaitis.
F — EN
John Vigar — *BBC Video*   H, P
5020

Betsy, The
Fil-Ent '78

Drama
12682   122 mins   C
B, V
Laurence Olivier, Robert Duvall, Katharine Ross, Tommy Lee Jones, Lesley-Anne Down, directed by Daniel Petrie
A saga of intrigue and power within the automobile industry spanning five decades of a wealthy family dynasty, with all the ingredients of sex, success, money, revenge, blackmail, incest, homosexuality, lust and greed.
BBFC:18 — A — EN
Robert R Weston; Jack Grossberg — *Warner Home Video*   P
99306

(For Explanation of codes, see USE GUIDE and KEY)

PALADIN VIDEO HOME ENTERTAINMENT GUIDE

Better Late Than Never   Fil-Ent '79
Comedy-Drama
09964   90 mins   C
V2, B, V
Harold Gould, Tyne Daly, Strother Martin, Donald Pleasence, Victor Buono, Lou Jacobi, Harry Morgan, Jeanette Nolan, directed by Richard Crenna
A number of senior citizens follow an aging rebel in his plan to escape from a retirement home in order to steal a train and have one last fling at life.
BBFC:U — F — EN
Ten-Four Prods; Gregg Strangis and William Hogan — *Video Unlimited*   **H, P, E**
042

Better Late Than Never   Fil-Ent '82
Comedy-Drama
09462   92 mins   C
V2, B, V
David Niven, Art Carney, Maggie Smith, Catherine Hicks, Lionel Jefferies, Melissa Prophet, Kimberly Partridge, directed by Bryan Forbes
This is David Niven's last film, about two not-so-young men, one British and the other American, together with a 10-year-old girl worth seventy million dollars a year.
BBFC:PG — F — EN
Golden Harvest; Jack Haley; David Niven Prod. — *Guild Home Video*   **H, P, E**

Better Rugby   Spo-Lei '8?
Sports
13539   129 mins   C
B, V
4 pgms
This series of films was produced under the coaching direction of Don Rutherford, RFU Technical Adviser and has a commentary by Bill McLaren.
1.Development of Skill 2.Confidence in Contact 3.Unit Skills 4.The Coach's Programme
F — EN
Unknown — *TFI Leisure Ltd*   **H, P**

Better Tennis   Spo-Lei '80
Tennis
05894   98 mins   C
B, V
Directed by Charles Grinker   2 pgms
In the first programme, eleven top players demonstrate basic strokes and techniques. The second programme gives tips on fitness, preparation and strategy. The two parts are available individually.
F — I
Sanford H Fisher — *THORN EMI*   **P**
TXB 90 4000 4/TVB 90 4000 2; TXB 90 4001 4/TVB 90 4001 2

Beyond, The   Fil-Ent '??
Horror
07937   89 mins   C
V2, B, V
Katherine McColl, David Warbeck, Sarah Keller, Antoine Saint John, Veronica Lazar, directed by Lucio Fulci
A young woman inherits an eerie rundown hotel in Louisiana. She does not know that the hotel was built on the Seven Gates of Hell until it is too late and the zombies rise to claim victims for eternal damnation.
BBFC:X — A — EN
Unknown — *Videomedia*   **P**
PVM 1021/BVM 1021/HVM 1021

Beyond and Back   Fil-Ent '78
Documentary/Occult sciences
05608   93 mins   C
B, V
Richard Cannaday, Elizabeth Grand, Shelly Osterloh
This film explores the possibilities that life exists after death. It illustrates experiences of more than a dozen people and recounts scientific studies by experts, parapsychologists and doctors.
S,A — EN
Schick Sunn Classic Prod — *Home Video Merchandisers*   **H, P**
008

Beyond Atlantis   Fil-Ent '73
Drama
04473   91 mins   C
V2, B, V
Patrick Wayne, John Ashley, Leigh Christian, George Nader, Lenore Stevens
Scientists explore an uncharted island believed to be the lost city of Atlantis.
F — EN
Dimension Pictures — *Intervision Video*
H, P
A-A 0140

Beyond Death's Door   Fil-Ent '??
Drama
07487   96 mins   C
B, V
Tom Hallick, Howard Platt, Joann Harris, directed by Henning Schellerup
This film tells the true stories of people who, through modern lifesaving techniques, have taken a journey into the world beyond. After being revived from temporary death they describe what it is like to die, how it has changed their lives and why they no longer fear the hereafter.
S,A — EN
Unknown — *Quadrant Video*   **H, P**
FF6

PALADIN VIDEO HOME ENTERTAINMENT GUIDE

Beyond Reason
Fil-Ent '??
Drama
09396   ? mins   C
B, V
Telly Savalas
This is the powerful story of a rebel psychiatrist and his battle to treat the criminally insane with dignity and respect.
A — EN
Unknown — *VCL Video Services*   P
P377

Beyond the Poseidon Adventure
Fil-Ent '80
Drama/Adventure
06043   110 mins   C
B, V
Michael Caine, Sally Field, Telly Savalas, directed by Irwin Allen
The 'Poseidon' capsized by a freak wave is still in the Atlantic Ocean. A salvage tug and a yacht arrive both with crews intent on salvaging both jewels and arms from the liner. They find survivors while taking differing routes through the ship; the tug captain abandons his quest for jewels to save the people resulting in a violent confrontation with the arms dealer.
BBFC:A — *S,A — EN*
Warner Bros — *Warner Home Video*   P
WEX1028/WEV1028

Beyond the Valley of the Dolls
Fil-Ent '70
Drama
01288   109 mins   C
B, V
Edy Williams, Dolly Reed, directed by Russ Meyer
Russ Meyer's story of an all-girl rock combo and their search for Hollywood stardom.
BBFC:X — *A — EN*
Twentieth Century Fox — *CBS/Fox Video*   P
3A-079

Bible, The
Fil-Ent '66
Drama
01759   174 mins   C
B, V
Richard Harris, Stephen Boyd, George C. Scott, directed by John Huston
The book of Genesis is dramatised, including the stories of Adam and Eve, Cain and Abel, and Noah and the Flood.
BBFC:U — *F — EN*
20th Century Fox, Dino De Laurentiis — *CBS/Fox Video*   P
4A-029

Bible—In the Beginning, The
Fil-Ent '66
Drama
13677   155 mins   C
B, V
Stephen Boyd, Ava Gardner, Richard Harris, John Huston, Peter O'Toole, Michael Parks, directed by John Huston
This is a biblical epic which spans the Book of Genesis from the creation of the world to the story of Abraham and the sacrifice of Isaac.
BBFC:U — *F — EN*
Dino De Laurentis — *CBS/Fox Video*   P
1020

Bicycle Thieves
Fil-Ent '48
Drama
08667   90 mins   B/W
B, V
Lamberto Maggiorani, Enzo Staiola, directed by Vittorio de Sica
This is the story of a man crushed by years of unemployment. He at last gets a job as a billsticker. On his first day whilst putting up a poster, his bicycle, essential to his job, is stolen. He begins searching the city, but in vain. Finally in desperation he steals another bicycle, only to be caught, and shamed in front of his young son.
Academy Awards '48: Best Foreign Film (Cesare Zavattini).   *S,A — EN*
PDS-ENIC — *Longman Video*   P
LGBE 5005/LGVH 5005

Big Bad Mama
Fil-Ent '74
Crime-Drama
08532   82 mins   C
B, V
William Shatner, Tom Skerritt, Angie Dickinson, Susan Sennett, Robbie Lee, Noble Willingham, directed by Steve Carver
A tough, intelligent mother moves her two teenage daughters out of poverty-stricken Texas in 1932. Accompanied by two men, they embark on a trail of crime including bank robbery and kidnapping.
BBFC:X — *A — EN*
New World Pictures — *THORN EMI*   P
TXC 90 0270 4/TVC 90 0270 2

Big Banana Feet
Fil-Ent '8?
Comedy-Performance/Documentary
07955   77 mins   C
B, V
Billy Connolly

(For Explanation of codes, see USE GUIDE and KEY)

65

PALADIN VIDEO HOME ENTERTAINMENT GUIDE

This tape follows Billy Connolly through a string of shows in Ireland, capturing both the off-stage atmosphere and the hilarious performances by this off-beat Scottish comedian.
S,A — EN
Unknown — *Brent Walker Home Video Ltd*
P

Big Bands of the 30's and 40's—Volume 2, The   Fil-Ent '4?
Music-Performance
09108   100 mins   B/W
B, V
This cassette features a collection of some of the greatest swing and jazz bands of the era. It includes Gene Krupa, Luis Arcaraz, Phil Harris, The Johnny Long Orchestra, Jan August, The Tommy Tucker Orchestra, Enric Madriguera, Cy Coleman Trio with Margaret Phelan, The Dick Stabile Orchestra, Nick Stuart and Stan Kenton.
F — EN
RKO et al — *Kingston Video*   **H, P**
KV 64

Big Bands of the '30s and '40s, The   Fil-Ent '??
Music-Performance
05656   ? mins   B/W
B, V
This cassette features short films of the Big Bands including 'Swing It' with Louis Prima and his band (1937), 'Music will Tell' with Ted Fio Rito and his orchestra (1938), 'So this is Harris' with Phil Harris and his Orchestra (1932), The Jerry Wald Orchestra, 'Carla Comes Calling' with Frankie Carle and his orchestra (1947), 'Mexican Rhythm' with Luis Arcaraz and his Orchestra (1949), 'Knee Deep in Music' with Ruth Etting (1938), 'Piano Rhythm' with Jan August (1949) and Tex Beneke and The Glenn Miller Orchestra (1946).
F — EN
Unknown — *Kingston Video*   **H, P**
KV56

Big Bird Cage, The   Fil-Ent '72
Drama
12495   91 mins   C
B, V
Pam Grier, Anitra Ford, Candice Roman, Carol Speed, directed by Jack Hill
A revolutionary leads a daring escape by women prisoners from a sadistic jail in a corrupt banana republic.
BBFC:18 — *A — EN*
Jane Schaffer — *Warner Home Video*   **P**
74018

Big Boss, The   Fil-Ent '74
Martial arts
06927   95 mins   C
B, V
Bruce Lee, Maria Yi, James Tien
A young man travels to Bangkok to work in an ice factory. He soon discovers that there are sinister activities going on behind the respectable facade of the factory. He is drawn further and further into the evil he has exposed and finds himself fighting for justice and his life.
BBFC:X — *A — EN*
National General — *Rank Video Library*
H, P
0070C

Big Bus, The   Fil-Ent '76
Comedy
13293   86 mins   C
B, V
Joe Bologna, Stockard Channing, Jose Ferrer, Lynn Redgrave, Sally Kellerman, John Beck, Ned Beatty, directed by James Frawley
A band of ill-assorted people come together on the maiden trip of the world's first nuclear-powered bus on its journey from New York to Denver.
BBFC:PG — *S,A — EN*
Paramount — *CIC Video*   **H, P**
BEN 2089/VHN 2089

Big Cat, The   Fil-Ent '49
Western/Adventure
05625   80 mins   C
V2, B, V
Ian McCallister, Peggy Ann Garner, Preston Foster, Forrest Tucker, directed by Phil Karlson
A deadly mountain lion goes on the rampage and terrorises people and livestock on a mountain in Utah. A long standing family feud hampers the fight to find the killer cat as two men filled with hatred, over a woman who is dead, attempt to fight the common foe.
S,A — EN
Eagle Lion — *Go Video Ltd*   **P**
GOK107

Big Chill, The   Fil-Ent '83
Drama
13078   101 mins   C
B, V
Tom Berenger, Glenn Close, Jeff Goldblum, William Hurt, Kevin Kline, Meg Tilly, directed by Laurence Kasdan
A group of friends are reunited at a funeral and find they have a need to return to their college-day relationships. The story has a musical backing which includes songs from The Stones, Marvin Gaye and Procul Harem.

PALADIN VIDEO HOME ENTERTAINMENT GUIDE

C,A — EN
Carson Productions Group Ltd; Michael Shamborg — *RCA/Columbia Pictures Video UK* **H, P**
10299

Big Combo, The Fil-Ent '55
Suspense/Crime-Drama
05638   89 mins   B/W
V2, B, V
Cornel Wilde, Richard Conte, Brian Donlevy, Jean Wallace
A story about the American underworld in which a dedicated detective intent on smashing a crime syndicate has his plans thwarted when a thrill-seeking society girl becomes entangled in the syndicate's web.
S,A — EN
Philip Yordan — *Video Unlimited* **H, P**
004

Big Fish Down Gen-Edu '84
Under—Away From It All
Documentary/Adventure
13565   60 mins   C
B, V
Explaining tackle and equipment Malcolm Florence and Vic McCrystal go fishing on The Great Barrier Reef and sight coral trout, bass, barracuda, sharks and big mackerel. Part 4 of this seven part series.
F — EN
Unknown — *TFI Leisure Ltd* **H, P**

Big Fish Down Gen-Edu '84
Under—Black Marlin
Documentary/Adventure
13567   60 mins   C
B, V
We see the ships of the commercial Japanese longliner fleets while they haul their 50 mile long lines and Malcolm Florence explains his own attitudes to releasing and not killing the giant Black Marlin, in part 6 of this seven part series.
F — EN
Unknown — *TFI Leisure Ltd* **H, P**

Big Fish Down Gen-Edu '84
Under—Island Holiday
Documentary/Adventure
13566   60 mins   C
B, V
Malcolm Florence takes his family camping in the Palm Islands in part 5 of this seven part series. He explains the equipment necessary for a trouble-free boating/camping adventure in the tropics.
F — EN
Unknown — *TFI Leisure Ltd* **H, P**

Big Fish Down Gen-Edu '8?
Under—Professionals at Play
Documentary/Adventure
13568   60 mins   C
B, V
In the last programme of this series, we see Malcolm Florence fishing on the remote, isolated reefs a hundred nautical miles north of the Great Barrier Reef, catching, releasing and feeding fish by hand.
F — EN
Unknown — *TFI Leisure Ltd* **H, P**

Big Fish Down Gen-Edu '8?
Under—Sailfish
Documentary/Adventure
13563   60 mins   C
B, V
This is the story of a fourteen year old's attempt to catch a sailfish, a brilliant acrobatic fish that challenges even the most experienced sportsman. This is part 2 of this seven part series.
F — EN
Unknown — *TFI Leisure Ltd* **H, P**

Big Fish Down Gen-Edu '84
Under—The Beginnings
Documentary/Adventure
13562   60 mins   C
B, V
In part 1 of this Australian series, the Great Barrier Reef and surrounding islands are shown and the start of sport and game fishing is explained.
F — EN
Unknown — *TFI Leisure Ltd* **H, P**

Big Fish Down Gen-Edu '84
Under—The Ribbons
Documentary/Adventure
13564   60 mins   C
B, V
Four experienced tropical sportfishmen set off in the latest twin-hulled gamesfishing machine to fish a remote coral wilderness teeming with large tropical fish in part 3 of this seven part series.
F — EN
Unknown — *TFI Leisure Ltd* **H, P**

Big Fix, The Fil-Ent '78
Drama
12043   103 mins   C
B, V
Richard Dreyfuss, Susan Anspach, directed by Paul Kagan

PALADIN VIDEO HOME ENTERTAINMENT GUIDE

A divorced ex-radical activist is working as a private detective. He is approached by a former girl-friend who enlists his help to find the person responsible for a smear campaign against a candidate running for Governor. His investigations reveal a 1960s radical group of four people.
BBFC:PG — S,A — EN
Universal — CIC Video   H, P
BEL 1089/VHL 1089

Big Land, The/Pioneer Builders   Fil-Ent '??
Western
05764   169 mins   C
B, V
Alan Ladd, Virginia Mayo, Edmond O'Brien, Anthony Caruso, directed by Gordon Douglas, Richard Dix, Ann Harding, Donald Cook, Julie Hayden, Guy Kibbee, directed by William Wellman
Two films are contained on one cassette. 'The Big Land' (colour, 88 mins, 1958) is based on a story by Frank Gouber. A man unites cattlemen and farmers to build a new Kansas town, he finds himself up against a local gang that plunders, burns, and terrorises. 'Pioneer Builders' (black/white, 81 mins, 1933) is also known as 'The Conquerors' and tells the story of a banker who, after a financial crash, moves West with his wife and builds a new future.
S,A — EN
Warner Bros; RKO — Kingston Video   H, P
KV18

Big Meat Eater   Fil-Ent '84
Comedy/Horror
10024   78 mins   C
B, V
George Dawson, Andrew Gillies, Big Miller
A mild-mannered butcher in a small, sleepy town finds himself involved in hilarious situations featuring corpses in his freezer, desperate aliens and a boy genius.
BBFC:15 — S,A — EN
Lawrence Keane — Palace Video Ltd   P
PVC 2059A

Big Red   Fil-Ent '62
Drama/Adventure
13446   88 mins   C
B, V
Walter Pigeon, Gilles Payant
This is the story of a fourteen-year-old French Canadian boy's relationship and adventures with an Irish setter dog.
BBFC:U — F — EN
Walt Disney Productions — Rank Video Library   P
195

Big Red One, The   Fil-Ent '80
War-Drama
05301   109 mins   C
V2, B, V
Lee Marvin, Mark Hamill, Robert Carradine, Bobby DiCicco, directed by Samuel Fuller
A story based on the records kept by Samuel Fuller of his experiences as a rifleman in the U.S. Army's legendary First Infantry Division—The Big Red One—during the Second World War. It follows the epic trail of five fighting men, four of whom were teenagers, exposing the human side of war.
S,A — EN
Lorimar — MGM/UA Home Video   P
UCB10052/UCV10052

Big Risk, The   Fil-Ent '??
Martial arts
08902   90 mins   C
V2, B, V
A secret agent is sent to retrieve some top secret documents. This ordinary assignment becomes increasingly more dangerous when other people become interested in the papers.
BBFC:X — A — EN
Unknown — Video Programme Distributors   P
Inter-Ocean 088

Big Sky, The/Code of the West   Fil-Ent '??
Western
05708   172 mins   B/W
B, V
Kirk Douglas, Dewey Martin, Elizabeth Threatt, Arthur Hunnicutt, Buddy Baer, directed by Howard Hawks, Raymond Burr, James Warren, Debra Alden, directed by William Berke
Two films are featured on one cassette. 'The Big Sky' (Black/White, 117 mins, 1953) is based on the novel by A.B. Guthrie Jr. Two young men join an early pioneering expedition in 1830 up the Missouri River bound for the Blackfoot Indian country. Despite the dangers they rescue an Indian girl along the way in the hope that they can trade with her tribe. 'Code of the West' (Black/White, 55 mins, 1948) is the story of a hero who challenges a badman out to deprive settlers of their claims.
F — EN
RKO — Kingston Video   H, P
KV34

Big Sleep, The   Fil-Ent '78
Crime-Drama/Mystery
05954   95 mins   C
B, V
Robert Mitchum, Sarah Miles, Richard Boone, James Stewart, Oliver Reed, Candy Clark, Joan Collins, Edward Fox, John Mills, directed by Michael Winner

PALADIN VIDEO HOME ENTERTAINMENT GUIDE

The famous fictional detective Philip Marlowe is involved in a world of eccentric, dangerous and evil people—petty criminals, sexually obsessed women and dishonest policemen. In this film he uncovers a pornographic operation and becomes involved with a wealthy family with two beautiful daughters and discovers blackmail and murder. Based on the 1939 novel by Raymond Chandler.
BBFC:AA — S,A — EN
Elliott Kastner; Jerry Bick — *Precision Video Ltd* **P**
BITC 2026/VITC 2026

Big Zapper   Fil-Ent '??
Crime-Drama/Adventure
07685   90 mins   C
B, V
Linda Marlowe, Gary Hope, Sean Hewitt, Michael O'Malley, Jack May, directed by Lindsay Shonteff
A millionaire hires Private Detective Harriet Zapper to rescue his three kidnapped teenage children. One is involved with a gang-land criminal whose two aides, both top Samurai swordsmen, are sent to confront her.
BBFC:X — A — EN
Unknown — *Video Network* **P**
0021

Biggest Battle, The   Fil-Ent '7?
War-Drama
02112   110 mins   C
V2, B, V
Henry Fonda, Samantha Eggar, Helmut Berger, John Huston
A war story tracing the lives, loves, and deaths of a group of international delegates thrown together in 1943 in the ugliest war of all time.
C,A — EN
Unknown — *Hokushin Audio Visual Ltd* **P**
VM-13

Biggin Hill '81   Gen-Edu '81
Aeronautics
06841   58 mins   C   (PAL, NTSC)
V2, B, V
This film, a compilation of two days' flying, looks at the Biggin Hill International Air Fair. Regular circuit pilots and aircraft are seen in action with the Red Arrows closing the display.
S,A — EN
Beattie/Forth Productions — *Beattie-Edwards Aviation Ltd* **P**
BEA 001

Bilitis   Fil-Ent '77
Drama
09011   91 mins   C
V2, B, V
Patti D'Arbanville, Mona Kristensen, Bernard Girandeau, directed by David Hamilton
A young girl from a private girl's school is initiated into the pleasures of sex and unexpected demands of love.
BBFC:X — A — EN
Topar; Slyvio Tabet; Jacques Nahum — *Intervision Video* **H, P**
AA 0465

Bill   Fil-Ent '81
Drama
09445   93 mins   C
B, V
Mickey Rooney, Dennis Quaid, Largo Woodruff
Bill cannot read or write. He is 40 years old, mentally retarded and must learn to survive the harsh realities of New York or be recommitted to an institution forever. With the help of his new-found friends he begins to realise that he does belong.
BBFC:PG — F — EN
Alan Landsburg Prod. — *Guild Home Video* **H, P, E**

Bill of Divorcement, A   Fil-Ent '32
Drama
04185   75 mins   B/W
B, V
John Barrymore, Katharine Hepburn, Billie Burke, David Manners
A girl, hopelessly in love, wants a marriage that cannot be, because of insanity in her family. Hepburn's film debut.
BBFC:A — S,A — EN
Selznick; RKO — *Guild Home Video* **H, P**

Bill on his Own   Fil-Ent '83
Drama
13782   93 mins   C
B, V
Mickey Rooney, Helen Hunt, Teresa Wright, Dennis Quaid, directed by Anthony Page
In this sequel to 'Bill', a film about a long term mental home inmate, we see Bill released from the mental institution trying to understand and come to terms with world about him.
BBFC:PG — S,A — EN
Unknown — *Odyssey Video* **H, P**
6542

Billy Connolly—'Bites Yer Bum'   Fil-Ent '81
Comedy-Performance
05423   105 mins   C
B, V
Billy Connolly

(For Explanation of codes, see USE GUIDE and KEY)

PALADIN VIDEO HOME ENTERTAINMENT GUIDE

This film is a live recording of Billy Connolly in concert at the Apollo Victoria, London in February 1981. It captures the earthy humour which this Scottish comedian is famous for through his stories and songs as presented on stage.
S,A — EN
Chrysalis Group Ltd — *Chrysalis Video* P
CVID BE2/CVID VH2

Billy Idol: Dancing with Myself   Fil-Ent '83
Music/Video
10029   12 mins   C
B, V
Directed by Tobe Hooper
Billy Idol's first video EP includes three tracks: 'Dancing with Myself,' 'White Wedding' and 'Hot in the City.'
M,A — EN
Unknown — *Palace Video Ltd* P
CVIM 9

Billy Jack   Fil-Ent '71
Drama
13171   111 mins   C
B, V
Tom Laughlin, Delores Taylor
An idealistic half-breed Vietnam veteran who, committed to aiding a 'freedom school' resorts to violence following a vicious rape on a teacher at the school.
BBFC:AA — C,A — EN
National Student Film Corp — *Warner Home Video* P
61040

Billy Liar   Fil-Ent '63
Comedy-Drama
01598   96 mins   B/W
B, V
Tom Courtenay, Julie Christie, directed by John Schlesinger
A young man, disillusioned with his love life and a dead-end job, tries to escape by entering a fantasy world of his own making.
BBFC:A — C,A — EN
Joseph Janni — *THORN EMI* P
TXE 90 0091 4/TVE 90 0091 2

Billy Squier—In the Dark   Fil-Ent '82
Music-Performance
08569   64 mins   C
B, V
Billy Squier
This programme features Billy Squier, the rock artist, at the Santa Monica Civic Theatre, California during his 1981 U.S. Tour. It includes songs such as 'In the Dark', 'Rich Kid', 'My Kinda Lover', 'Whadda You Want from Me', 'Lonely Is the Night', 'Young Girls', 'I Need You', 'the Stroke', 'You Should Be High Love', 'Too Deze Gone' and 'The Big Beat'.
S,A — EN
Capitol Records — *THORN EMI* P
TXE 90 0932 4/TVE 90 0932 2

Billy the Kid vs. Dracula   Fil-Ent '65
Horror
10073   80 mins   C
V2, B, V
John Carradine, Chuck Courtney, Melinda Plowman
A mysterious bat comes to terrorize the early pioneers of the West. Dracula has returned. He is determined to make Billy the Kid's bride his own. A deadly fight ensues.
A — EN
Carroll Case — *Embassy Home Entertainment* P
2099

Bim   Fil-Ent '76
Drama
06319   98 mins   C
V2, B, V
Ralph Maharaj, Hamilton Parris, Wilbert Holden, directed by Hugh A Robertson
This film set in Trinidad before 1962 deals with conflict between Asians and blacks. After his father is murdered an Indian boy sinks to the lowest level of society to eventually avenge his father's killing.
S,A — EN
Sharc Prods Ltd — *World of Video 2000*
H, P
GF504

Bird About Town   Gen-Edu '8?
Birds/Wildlife
09100   ? mins   C
B, V
Bill Oddie
Bill Oddie takes a look at birds around town, all of whom share the slightly unusual ability to thrive among the activities of man.
BISFA '80: Gold Award.   F — ED
Royal Society for the Protection of Birds — *Royal Society for the Protection of Birds*   H, P

Bird with the Crystal Plumage, The   Fil-Ent '70
Mystery/Horror
08595   98 mins   C
V2, B, V
Tony Musante, Suzy Kendall, Enrico Maria Salerno, Eva Renzi, Umberto Raho, Ray Valenti, directed by Dario Argento

PALADIN VIDEO HOME ENTERTAINMENT GUIDE

An alleged murderer is cleared when the woman believed to be his next victim is revealed to be a psychopathic killer.
BBFC:X — A — EN
UMC — Videomedia   P
PVM 1028/BVM 1028/HVM 1028

Birds, The　　　　　　　　　　Fil-Ent '63
Horror
07961　119 mins　C
B, V
Rod Taylor, Jessica Tandy, Suzanne Pleshette, Tippi Hedren, directed by Alfred Hitchcock
A small seaside town is terrorised by thousands of birds of all shapes and sizes, as the residents are inexplicably attacked again and again. Based on the story by Daphne du Maurier.
S,A — EN
Universal — CIC Video   **H, P**
BEA1022/VHA1022

Birds of Prey　　　　　　　　Fil-Ent '72
Drama/Suspense
08023　881 mins　C
V2, B, V
David Janssen, Ralph Meeker, Elayne Heilveil, Harry Klekas, Sam Dawson, Don Wilbanks, James Gavin, Directed by William Graham
Whilst on air traffic control duty, a former World War II pilot sees an armed bank robbery and the taking of a hostage. He continues the chase despite warnings from the police captain. The bank robbers switch from car to helicopter and the hunter becomes the hunted.
BBFC:U — F — EN
Tomorrow Entertainment — Iver Film Services
P
165

Birth of a Nation, The　　　　Fil-Ent '15
Drama/Film-History
05838　158 mins　B/W
B, V
Lillian Gish, Mae Marsh, Henry Walthall, Miriam Cooper, Robert Harran, Wallace Reid, Joseph Henaberry, Elmer Clifton, Donald Crisp, Raoul Walsh, Elmo Lincoln, Bessie Love, directed by D. W. Griffith
The dramatization of events leading up to and following the Civil War as seen by two families who became involved in the dramatic events of the war and the difficult days of reconstruction that ensued, including a vivid depiction of the forming of the original Ku Klux Klan. Based on 'The Clansman' by Thomas Dixon.
S,A — EN
Epoch Prods — Polygram Video   **P**
40125/20125

Birthday Party, The　　　　　Fil-Ent '68
Drama
04261　122 mins　C
B, V
Robert Shaw, Dandy Nichols, Moultrie Kelshall, Patrick Magee, Sydney Tafler, Helen Fraser
Film version of Harold Pinter play. This film has been described as a comedy of menace, a dramatic expose of contemporary man's inability to cope with his fears and guilt.
BBFC:A — C,A — EN
Continental; Walter Reade — Rank Video Library   **H, P**
0031

Bisexual　　　　　　　　　　Fil-Ent '72
Fantasy
05691　92 mins　C
B, V
Yves-Marie Maurin, Florence Cayrol, Marion Game, Jenny Avasse
This film exposes the fanatical daydreams of a young computer clerk. He dreams of his fiance and her maid when a soldier intrudes on their 'games.' He also imagines he is a Prince and his fiance is a Lady in turn of the century France.
BBFC:X — A — EN
Unknown — Derann Film Services   **H, P**
GS701B/GS701

Bitch, The　　　　　　　　　Fil-Ent '79
Drama
01266　90 mins　C
B, V
Joan Collins
A continuation of 'The Stud.' A woman faces divorce from her wealthy husband who has discovered her infidelity. She must now support her high-living life-style without the reserve of funds she had enjoyed previously.
BBFC:X — C,A — EN
Brent Walker Film Prods — Brent Walker Home Video Ltd   **P**

Bitter Tears of Petra Von Kant, The　　　　　　　　Fil-Ent '75
Drama
08966　124 mins　C
B, V
Hanna Schygulla, Margit Carstensen, Irm Hermann, directed by Rainer Werner Fassbinder
This tells the story of a woman who has a bizzare sado-masochistic relationship with her 'slave'. Their lesbian affair is interrupted by the

PALADIN VIDEO HOME ENTERTAINMENT GUIDE

arrival of another woman whose uncomplicated attitudes provoke her to outbursts of passion. The 'slave' looks on, despising them both. It is subtitled in English.
Chicago Film Festival '75: Special Jury Prize.
BBFC:X — A — EN
Cinegate — *Palace Video Ltd* P
PVC 2012B

Bittersweet Love Fil-Ent '77
Drama
01005 95 mins C
B, V
Lana Turner, Celeste Holm, Robert Lansing, Meredith Baxter Birney, Robert Alda, Scott Hylands
A young couple meet, fall in love, and marry, not knowing they both have the same father.
A — EN
Avco Embassy — *CBS/Fox Video* P
3C-098

Bizet's Carmen Fil-Ent '80
Dance
04387 50 mins C
B, V
The Mercedes Molina Dance Company is featured in this interpretation of Bizet's classic, 'Carmen.'
F — EN
Unknown — *VCL Video Services* P

Black Arrow, The Fil-Ent '??
Cartoons/Adventure
08798 45 mins C
B, V
Animated
This tells the story of a knight who sets out to find his father's slayer. He meets the beautiful daughter of the man who is supposed to have killed his father. It is based on the novel by Robert Louis Stevenson.
F — EN
Unknown — *VCL Video Services* P
A323B

Black Arrow, The Fil-Ent '84
Drama
13756 90 mins C
B, V
Oliver Reed, Donald Pleasance, Fernando Rey, Benedict Taylor
This is an adventure story based on Robert Louis Stevenson's historical novel of England during the War of the Roses.
BBFC:U — F — EN
Walt Disney Productions — *Rank Video Library* P
709

Black Beard's Ghost Fil-Ent '68
Adventure
07934 102 mins C
B, V
Peter Ustinov, Suzanne Pleshette
In this swashbuckling adventure the ghost of a rascally old buccaneer is conjured up with hilarious consequences.
F — EN
Walt Disney — *Rank Video Library* H
06200

Black Beauty Fil-Ent '70
Adventure
02093 104 mins C
V2, B, V
Mark Lester, Walter Slezak, Ursula Gla
Anna Sewell's classic about a boy and a black horse. A beautiful story for children of all ages.
BBFC:U — F — EN
Paramount — *Hokushin Audio Visual Ltd*
P
VM-15

Black Beauty Fil-Ent '78
Cartoons/Drama
10204 60 mins C
B, V
Animated, voices by David Gregory, Mike Evans, Barbara Stevens
Based on the novel by Anna Sewell, this animated feature tells the story of Black Beauty the horse brought up by his mother to be a friend to man. When his first kind owner is forced to sell him he falls into the hands of Reuben Smith whose cruelty leaves Beauty deformed for life. He is sold to a kind owner who unfortunately dies and once more, in the hands of Reuben Smith, Beauty ends up on the road to the slaughter house. However, at the sale he is spotted by friends of his first owner, who return him to the countryside of his youth.
F — EN
Hanna-Barbera — *Video Form Pictures*
H, P
CLO V12

Black Belt Jones Fil-Ent '74
Martial arts/Drama
13169 83 mins C
B, V
Jim Kelly, Gloria Hendry, directed by Robert Clouse
This is a martial arts movie, dealing with the ensuing conflict when Mafia men plan the requisitioning of a school for self-defence.
BBFC:X — A — EN
Warner Bros — *Warner Home Video* P
61274

(For Explanation of codes, see USE GUIDE and KEY)

PALADIN VIDEO HOME ENTERTAINMENT GUIDE

Black Carrion/A Distant Scream   Fil-Ent '84
Drama/Suspense
13158   150 mins   C
B, V

Season Hubley, Leigh Lawson, directed by John Hough, David Carradine, Stephanie Beacham, directed by John Hough

Two films are contained on one cassette. In 'Black Carrion' a journalist and a photographer are assigned to solve the mystery of two chart-topping pop stars and 'A Distant Scream' features two lovers on holiday in Cornwall whose lives become entwined in mysterious past events.
BBFC:15 — S,A — EN
Hammer Film Prods — *Brent Walker Home Video Ltd*   P
BW 33

Black Cat   Fil-Ent '??
Horror
07813   88 mins   C
B, V

Patrick Magee, Mimsy Farmer, David Warbeck, directed by Lucio Fulci

After a series of bizarre and fatal incidents the only link appears to be the malevolent presence of a supernatural black cat. The cat is either controlled by his master or has an unnatural plan to commit him to madness. Based on the story by Edgar Allan Poe.
S,A — EN
Unknown — *Video Tape Centre*   P
VTC 1018

Black Dragon, The   Fil-Ent '7?
Adventure/Martial arts
04609   90 mins   C
V2, B, V

Mr. Yen, a wealthy kung-fu fanatic, is determined to find the truth behind Bruce Lee's death. He hires martial arts champion Ron Van Cliff to investigate.
C,A — EN
Unknown — *Video Programme Distributors* P
Inter-Ocean—022

Black Emmanuelle, White Emmanuelle   Fil-Ent '76
Drama
02418   90 mins   C
B, V

Laura Gemser, Annie Belle

In her magnificent villa on the banks of the Nile at Assuan, rich divorcee Cristal has gathered around her an extravagant group of expatriates, including her eighteen-year-old daughter and head of staff Ali, when into their lives comes Pia, a strange young student.
A — EN
Unknown — *Derann Film Services*   H, P
DV 117B/DV 117

Black Fox   Fil-Ent '63
Documentary/World War II
05061   85 mins   C
B, V

Narrated by Marlene Dietrich

An account of the rise and fall of Hitler including film of the 1936 Olympic Games in Berlin, and the Nuremburg Rallies. Based in part on 'Reynard the Fox' as adapted by Johann Wolfgang von Goethe.
Academy Award '63: Best Documentary Feature.   F — EN
Jack Le Vien — *THORN EMI*   P
TXD 90 0510 4/TVD 90 0510 2

Black Gestapo   Fil-Ent '??
Crime-Drama
05443   81 mins   C
V2, B, V

Rod Perry, Charles P. Robinson, directed by Lee Frost

A black organization is set up to deal with the problems of the Black Ghetto in opposition to a White Syndicate. When a black nurse is raped and beaten the organization is formed into a security force out for vengeance and power.
BBFC:X — A — EN
Unknown — *Iver Film Services*   P

Black Gold   Fil-Ent '??
Crime-Drama
06084   102 mins   C
V2, B, V

Richard Harrison, Florence Cayrol, Jean Marie Lemaire

This film set in the Middle East is a story of four men and a woman sent by a petrol company to sabotage the wells of an Arab Emirate that does not want to respect a contract. A story of murder, counter-espionage and the fatal charms of a woman.
S,A — EN
Unknown — *Video Programme Distributors* P
Cinehollywood—V1550

Black Hand, The   Fil-Ent '??
Crime-Drama
06083   104 mins   C
V2, B, V

(For Explanation of codes, see USE GUIDE and KEY)

PALADIN VIDEO HOME ENTERTAINMENT GUIDE

Lionel Stander, Philippe Leroy, Rosanna Fratella, Mike Placido

A young immigrant newly arrived in New York finds himself involved, against his will, in the criminal activities of The Black Hand. After an assassination and his arrest he is forced into a bargain if he wants to keep his girlfriend, a bargain that proves hard to keep.

S,A — EN

Unknown — *Video Programme Distributors*
P

Cinehollywood—V1100

Black Hole, The   Fil-Ent '79
Science fiction
05598   94 mins   C
B, V

Maximilian Schell, Anthony Perkins, Robert Forster, Joseph Bottoms, Yvette Mimieux, Ernest Borgnine

A mad scientist is determined to acquire the secrets of the Universe by plunging into a black hole, an empty nothingness where space and time end. His ship the USS Cygnus is perched precariously on the edge manned by robots and humanoids specially manufactured to face the unknown and terrifying power of oblivion.

F — EN

Walt Disney Productions — *Rank Video Library*
H
01100

Black Island/Shooting Star   Chi-Juv '7?
Cartoons/Adventure
02281   80 mins   C
V

Animated

Intrepid boy reporter Tin Tin goes to the aid of a stranded aeroplane and starts an adventure which takes him and Snowy to a hospital, puts him under suspicion as a thief, and causes him to be hotly pursued by detectives to the Highlands of Scotland.

M — EN

Unknown — *JVC*   **P**

PRT 38

Black Marble, The   Fil-Ent '81
Crime-Drama
08329   106 mins   C
V2, B, V

Robert Foxworth, Paula Prentiss, Harry Dean Stanton

This film tells the story of a beautiful policewoman who is paired with a policeman who drinks too much, is divorced and ready to retire. Surrounded by urban craziness and corruption, they eventually fall in love. It is based on the novel by Joseph Wambaugh.

BBFC:U — F — EN

Avco Embassy — *Embassy Home Entertainment*   **P**
1617

Black Panther, The   Fil-Ent '77
Crime-Drama
06808   99 mins   C
V2, B, V

Donald Sumpter, Andrew Burt, Ruth Dunning, Debbie Farrington

A fact-based tale of the notorious British killer/kidnapper, Donald Neilson.

S,A — EN

Ian Merrick; Alpha — *Intervision Video*
H, P
A-AE 0357

Black Pirate, The   Fil-Ent '??
Adventure
05560   103 mins   C
V2, B, V

Terence Hill, Bud Spencer, directed by Vincent Thomas

This is a swashbuckling adventure set on the high seas in which Captain Blackie has incurred the wrath of the Spanish Viceroy of the Caribbean by buying his wife in a slave market. It includes battles with Galleons overflowing with bullion, cutlass fights and bounty hunters seeking treasure troves.

BBFC:U — M,A — EN

Unknown — *Videomedia*   **P**
BVM 2115/HVM 2115

Black Pirate, The   Fil-Ent '26
Adventure/Drama
05839   83 mins   B/W
B, V

Douglas Fairbanks Sr, Billie Dove, Donald Crisp, directed by Albert S. Parker

A nobleman in disguise has to over-come a band of pirates in order to win the hand of a lady. He does this single-handed including swimming hundreds of yards underwater, moving several cannons at once, sliding down a mainsail from the top rigging ultimately capturing a ship single handed.

F — EN

United Artists — *Polygram Video*   **P**
40123/20123

PALADIN VIDEO HOME ENTERTAINMENT GUIDE

Black Room, The　　　　Fil-Ent '8?
Horror
09026　　80 mins　　C
V2, B, V
The lure of the black room has destroyed all those foolish enough to have glimpsed inside.
A — EN
Unknown — *Intervision Video*　　**H, P**
AA 0453

Black Sabbath　　　　Fil-Ent '64
Horror
04117　　99 mins　　C
B, V
Boris Karloff, Mark Damon
Three terrifying tales of the supernatural. In 'A Drop of Water,' a nurse meets with terrible consequences after stealing a diamond ring from an elderly dead woman. 'The Telephone' is a tale about a man who, when betrayed by a 'lady about town,' mistakenly strangles his girlfriend. In 'The Wurdalak,' a nobleman seeks shelter in the home of a man who turns into a vampire.
C,A — EN
American International — *Video Programme Distributors*　　**P**
Inter-Ocean—030

Black Sabbath　　　　Fil-Ent '7?
Music-Performance
01956　　60 mins　　C
B, V
The heavy metal energy of Black Sabbath is captured in a performance from the Hammersmith Odeon.
C,A — EN
Unknown — *VCL Video Services*　　**P**

Black Sabbath/Blue　　Fil-Ent '7?
Oyster Cult
Music-Performance
09886　　80 mins　　C
B, V
Black Sabbath are teamed up here with Blue Oyster Cult in a concert film of the joint tour of these two heavy rock bands. It is filmed at the Nassau Coliseum, Long Island, New York. Recorded in stereo.
F — EN
Unknown — *Polygram Video*　　**H, P**
791 5494/791 5492

Black Stallion Returns,　　Fil-Ent '83
The
Adventure
12674　　99 mins　　C
B, V
Kelly Reno, Teri Garr, Allen Goorwitz, Vincent Spano, directed by Robert Dalva
A sixteen-year-old boy stows away from America to North Africa to rescue his beloved black stallion from the Arab Sheik who kidnapped him.
BBFC:PG — *F — EN*
tom Sternberg; Fred Roos; Doug Claybourne — *Warner Home Video*　　**P**
99391

Black Sunday　　　　Fil-Ent '61
Horror/Drama
08602　　83 mins　　B/W
V2, B, V
John Richardson, Barbara Steele, Ivo Garrani, Andrea Checchi, Arturo Dominici, directed by Mario Bava
This is based on Nikolai Gogol's story about the one day in every century when Satan is allowed to walk freely on Earth.
BBFC:X — *A — EN*
Galatra-Jolly Film Prod — *Videomedia*　　**P**
PVM 1026/BVM 1026 /HVM 1026

Black Torment, The　　Fil-Ent '64
Horror
02580　　85 mins　　C
V2, B, V
John Turner, Heather Sears, Ann Lynn
A British gentleman's first wife kills herself. When he remarries, moving back to his old, eerie mansion, he is confronted by murder, rape, and total insanity.
BBFC:X — *A — EN*
Compton Cameo — *Videomedia*　　**P**

Black Tulip, The　　　Fil-Ent '63
Adventure
07626　　109 mins　　C
B, V
Alain Delon, Virna Lisi, Dawn Addams, Francis Blanche, directed by Christian-Jaque
This swashbuckling adventure is based on the novel by Alexandre Dumas. The film follows the adventures of the Black Tulip. To the tyrannical Marquis he is a close friend, to the chief of Police he's a dangerous villain and to the local people he is a hero. The sabres of good and evil clash in this tale of intrigue, action and adventure.
F — EN
Unknown — *VCL Video Services*　　**P**
P255D

Black Uhuru—Tear It Up　　Fil-Ent '82
Music-Performance
07830　　48 mins　　C
B, V
Directed by Annie Rowe

(For Explanation of codes, see USE GUIDE and KEY)

75

PALADIN VIDEO HOME ENTERTAINMENT GUIDE

This film features the reggae trio, Black Uhuru, recorded live at the Rainbow Theatre, London in 1981. Songs include 'Shine Eye Gal,' 'Plastic Smile,' 'Puff She Puff,' 'I Love King Selassie,' 'Youth of Eglington,' 'Push, Push,' 'General Penitentiary,' 'Happiness,' 'World Is Africa,' 'Sponji Reggae' and 'Sensemilla.'
F — EN
Island Records Inc — *Island Pictures* P
IPV003L

Black Veil for Lisa, A Fil-Ent '69
Suspense/Drama
09202   88 mins   C
B, V
John Mills, Luciana Paluzzi, Robert Hoffman, directed by Massimo Dallamano
The Chief of Hamburg's narcotics squad becomes involved in breaking a known drug ring. However, potential informants are assassinated one after another. His wife gives him further problems when he suspects her unfaithfulness.
S,A — EN
Commonwealth United; Filmes Cinematographics — *Video Form Pictures*
H, P
DIP 8

Blackbeard the Pirate/Fish Feathers/Pal's Adventure/The Fireman Fil-Ent '??
Adventure/Comedy
05657   150 mins   C
B, V
Robert Newton, Linda Darnell, William Bendix, Keith Andes, Richard Egan, Torin Thatcher, Edgar Kennedy, Ted Donaldson, Charlie Chaplin
This cassette features one film and three shorts. 'Blackbeard the Pirate' (Colour, 95 mins, 1952) is a romantic tale of a beautiful girl with a fortune in jewels who finds herself captive of the notorious Blackbeard. She is rescued by a handsome hero. 'Fish Feathers' (Black/white, 17 mins) is a short comedy and 'Pal's Adventure' (black/white) is a dog adventure with 'Flame' the Dog. 'The Fireman' (Black/White, 1916) features Chaplin as a fireman who becomes a hero.
F — EN
RKO et al — *Kingston Video*   H, P
KV55

Blackenstein Fil-Ent '72
Horror
06078   87 mins   C
B, V
John Hart, Ivory Stone, directed by William A. Levy

A man who was the victim of a senseless war has lost all four limbs. Dr Stein operates to restore his arms and legs; however, his assistant changes the daily injections and the man turns into a monster who escapes regularly to kill innocent victims.
S,A — EN
Unknown — *Video Programme Distributors*
P
Media—M130

Blackjack Fil-Ent '??
Music-Performance
06241   30 mins   C
B, V
Blackjack, an excitingly visual new rockband from Germany, are seen here recorded live in Munich, with all-new material from their latest album 'Neon Lover.' Three girls, Meli, Vira and Inge support lead singer George Liszt in a fast moving and visually explosive rock programme backed with technical expertise.
F — EN
Unknown — *VCL Video Services*   P
V115

Blackmail Fil-Ent '29
Mystery
01001   86 mins   B/W
B, V
Anny Ondra, John Longdon, Sara Allgood, Charles Paton, directed by Alfred Hitchcock
Britain's first sound film and an early visualisation of some typical Hitchcockian themes. The story follows the police investigation of a murder, and a detective's attempts to keep his girlfriend from being involved.
BBFC:A — F — EN
British Intl; Wardour — *THORN EMI*   P
TXE 90 0093 4/TVE 90 0093 2

Blackout Fil-Ent '78
Horror
08849   90 mins   C
B, V
Belinda Montgomery, Jean Pierre Aumont, Robert Carradine, Jim Mitchum
A police van has to transfer a group of psychotic killers, but while doing so there is a power cut. The van crashes and the group escapes. They run to a nearby block of flats and work their way through in a sadistic orgy of blood and death.
BBFC:X — A — EN
Dal-Agora-Maki; Sommerhill House — *VCL Video Services*   P
M248D

PALADIN VIDEO HOME ENTERTAINMENT GUIDE

Blackstar Fil-Ent '81
Cartoons/Adventure
09970   63 mins   C
B, V
Animated
Blackstar, with his 'Starsword', leads the forces of good against the powers of evil led by the cruel Overlord with his 'Powersword'. Helped by the Trobbits, friendly dwarfs, and Mara, an enchantress who uses her white magic, he continues the fight of good against evil.
F — EN
Filmation — *Select Video Limited*   P
3606/43

Blade Fil-Ent '72
Drama
04201   91 mins   C
B, V
John Marley, Jon Cypher, Kathryn Walker, William Prince, Keene Curtis
This is the true story of an honest New York detective who wages a one man war against police corruption.
BBFC:X — A — EN
Joseph Green Prods — *Guild Home Video*
H, P

Blade Runner Fil-Ent '82
Science fiction
13048   114 mins   C
B, V
Harrison Ford, Rutger Haver, Sean Young, M Emmet Walsh, Joanne Cassidy, Leo Gorcey Jr
By the year 2020, Earth is a forbidden planet for 'replicants,' a species laboratory bred for menial tasks in Outer Space. Four replicants escape to infiltrate Earth's society and only the incredible Blade Runner can recognize them.
BBFC:AA — C,A — EN
The Blade Runner Partnership — *Warner Home Video*   P
70008

Blame It On Rio Fil-Ent '83
Comedy/Romance
13696   96 mins   C
B, V
Michael Caine, Michelle Johnson, Joseph Bologna, Valerie Harper, Demi Moore, directed by Stanley Donen
A middle-aged man is seduced by his best friend's daughter when his wife goes off on holiday and leaves him on his own.
BBFC:15 — S,A — EN
Stanley Donen — *THORN EMI*   P
90 2777

Blancmange—Hello, Good Evening Fil-Ent '84
Music-Performance
13133   60 mins   C
B, V
This tape features live performances from the Hammersmith Palais and includes 'Blind Vision,' 'Waves,' 'Living on the Ceiling' and 'Don't Tell Me.' It is recorded in stereo hi-fi.
F — EN
Unknown — *Polygram Video*   P
041 0574/041 0572

Blancmange-The Videosingles Fil-Ent '8?
Music-Performance/Video
09878   15 mins   C
B, V
This tape includes the artistic video interpretations of three of the band's most well loved tracks; 'Living on the Ceiling', 'Waves' and 'Blind Vision'.
F — EN
Unknown — *Polygram Video*   H, P
791 5654/791 5652

Blastfighter Fil-Ent '84
Crime-Drama
13737   90 mins   C
V2, B, V
Michael Sopkin, Valerie Blake, George Eastman, Mike Miller, Richard Raymond, directed by John Old Jnr
Having just finished a sentence in gaol an ex-cop finds his daughter and best friend have been murdered so he takes revenge with a revolutionary riot gun.
BBFC:18 — A — EN
Medusa Distribuzione srl — *Medusa Communications Ltd*   H, P
MC 026

Blazing Flowers Fil-Ent '7?
Suspense
04478   90 mins   C
V2, B, V
Suspenseful story revolving around the world of the Mafia.
A — EN
Unknown — *Intervision Video*   H, P
A-AE 0164

Blazing Magnum Fil-Ent '77
Drama
09167   94 mins   C
V
Stuart Whitman, John Saxon, Martin Landau, Tisa Farrow, Gayle Hunnicut

(For Explanation of codes, see USE GUIDE and KEY)

77

PALADIN VIDEO HOME ENTERTAINMENT GUIDE

A detective gets the toughest case of his career, to investigate the murder of his sister. His prime suspect is a doctor in Montreal, who was having an affair with her.
BBFC:X — A — EN
American-International — *Medusa Communications Ltd* **H, P**

Blazing Saddles   Fil-Ent '74
Comedy
01248   90 mins   C
B, V
Cleavon Little, Harvey Korman, Madeleine Kahn, Gene Wilder, Mel Brooks, directed by Mel Brooks
A wild, wacky spoof by Mel Brooks of every cliche in the western film genre, telling the story of a black sheriff who is sent to clean up a frontier town, with unpredictable results.
C,A — EN
Warner Bros — *Warner Home Video*   **P**

Blazing Stewardesses   Fil-Ent '76
Comedy/Adventure
07612   82 mins   C
V2, B, V
Yvonne DeCarlo, Bob Livingston, Don 'Red' Barry, Geoffrey Land, Connie Hoffman, Regina Carrol, T. A. King, Harry Ritz, Jimmy Ritz
A pretty stewardess finds her boyfriend in bed with another girl. Angry and distressed, she leaves and takes up an offer to work a charter flight for a rich promoter. This leads to a sequence of insane events.
BBFC:X — A — EN
Unknown — *Iver Film Services*   **P**

Bless This House   Fil-Ent '73
Comedy
05141   87 mins   C
B, V
Sid James, Terry Scott, Diana Coupland, June Whitfield
A film of the popular television comedy in which Sid James recreates his role as head of the Abbot family.
BBFC:U — F — EN
Rank — *Rank Video Library*   **H, P**
1022

Blind Date   Fil-Ent '84
Drama/Suspense
12949   99 mins   C
V2, B, V
Joseph Bottoms, Keir Dullea, Lana Clarkson, James Daughton

This hi-tech video features a blind man who has been given sight through the eyes of a computer and witnesses a killing and thereby becomes next on the killer's list.
BBFC:18 — C,A — EN
Omega Pictures — *Videomedia*   **P**
0810

Blob, The   Fil-Ent '58
Horror
02459   76 mins   C
B, V
Steve McQueen, Aneta Corseaut, Earl Rowe
Two teenagers notice a shooting star fall to earth. They then confront a man howling with pain from a mass attached to his arm from the fallen meteorite. The 'Blob' continues to grow.
A — EN
Paramount, Jack H Harris — *Mountain Video*   **P**

Blondie—'Eat to the Beat'   Fil-Ent '80
Music-Performance
05421   60 mins   C
B, V
Blondie
This cassette is the video production of the hit album by Blondie. It includes the title track 'Eat to the Beat,' 'Atom' and many others, and was shot entirely on location in New York City.
S,A — EN
Chrysalis Group Ltd — *Chrysalis Video*   **P**
CVIM BE5/CVIM VH5

Blondie Live!   Fil-Ent '84
Music-Performance
13314   53 mins   C
B, V
This concert recording features songs from various stages of Blondie's career including 'Rapture,' 'Dance Way,' 'Heart of Glass' and 'Start Me Up.'
F — EN
Universal — *CIC Video*   **H, P**
BER 1113/VHR 1113

Blood   Fil-Ent '??
Horror
05463   57 mins   C
V2, B, V
Alan Bererdt, Hope Stanburg, Patti Gaul, Michael Pischett
Set in 1883 a doctor and his odd assistants rent an isolated house to grow carnivorous plants who are nurtured on blood. He does this to provide a serum for his wife, the daughter of

(For Explanation of codes, see USE GUIDE and KEY)

PALADIN VIDEO HOME ENTERTAINMENT GUIDE

Count Dracula, who without the serum deteriorates into a faceless old hag. Things get out of hand when, as the plants grow stronger, the two assistants are mutilated.
BBFC:X — A — EN
Unknown — Iver Film Services   **P**
38

Blood and Black Lace   Fil-Ent '65
Drama/Suspense
05473   80 mins   C
V2, B, V
Mary Arden, Carmen Mitchell, Eva Bartok
A model who works for a large fashion house is the first to be murdered. She had been stealing drugs for her lover; suspicion rests with the addict.
BBFC:X — A — EN
Allied Artists; Woolner Bros — Iver Film Services   **P**
63

Blood and Guts   Fil-Ent '82
Drama
12610   95 mins   C
V2, B, V
William Smith, Brian Clarke, Micheline Lanctot
A story of tenderness and turmoil of people in love set against the background of professional wrestling and the corrupt monopoly interests who control it.
BBFC:15 — S,A — EN
Unknown — VideoSpace Ltd   **P**

Blood and Honour   Fil-Ent '82
War-Drama
10184   220 mins   C
B, V
This film follows the story of Hitler's rise to power and the subsequent effect on the lives and the economy of people in Germany. It is set against the life of an ordinary German family from 1933 to 1939. Their son becomes a member of the Hitler youth and by the outbreak of war the torn family do not know whether they have a son or enemy.
S,A — EN
Daniel Wilson Productions — Video Form Pictures   **H, P**
MGX 2

Blood and Sand   Fil-Ent '22
Drama/Romance
01758   80 mins   B/W
B, V
Rudolph Valentino, Nita Naldi

Tragic romance of the rise and fall of a matador and the women in his life.
F — EN
Paramount — CBS/Fox Video   **P**
3A-047

Blood at Sundown   Fil-Ent '72
Western
12837   100 mins   C
V2, B, V
Anthony Steffen, John Garko, Carrol Brown, Jerry Wilson, Frank Farrell, directed by Albert Cardiff
A man returns from twelve years in jail to find himself battling for justice against his own brother who has taken control of the farmers, the town and his girlfriend.
BBFC:18 — A — EN
Marlon Sirko — Video Programme Distributors   **P**
VPD 238

Blood Bath   Fil-Ent '75
Horror
08065   82 mins   C
B, V
Harve Presnell, Curt Dawson, Doris Roberts, Sharon Shayne
As the title suggests, this film is full of macabre killings and gore.
BBFC:X — A — EN
Cannon Releasing — Rank Video Library   **H, P**
2015 C

Blood Beach   Fil-Ent '81
Horror
08885   92 mins   C
V2, B, V
David Huffman, Marianna Hill, John Saxon, Burt Young
A group of teenagers are devoured by menacing sand which keeps people from getting to the water.
BBFC:X — A — EN
Shaw Beckerman Productions — Video Programme Distributors   **P**
Media 164

Blood Beast Terror, The   Fil-Ent '68
Horror
04559   88 mins   C
V2, B, V
Peter Cushing, Robert Flemying, Wanda Ventham

(For Explanation of codes, see USE GUIDE and KEY)

PALADIN VIDEO HOME ENTERTAINMENT GUIDE

When two men die horrible deaths, an inspector finds that they were killed by a girl who has a predatory nature—she can turn herself into a giant death's head moth—and her kiss means instant death.
S,A — EN
Tijon; Pacemaker Pictures — *Videomedia*
P

Blood Feud — Fil-Ent '78
Drama
05385   92 mins   C
B, V
Sophia Loren, Marcello Mastroianni, Giancarlo Giannini, Turi Ferro, directed by Lina Wertmuller
This film is set in Italy during a time of political unrest just before World War II. A beautiful woman is befriended by a lawyer after her husband is gunned down; she also becomes close to her dead husband's cousin, who evokes memories of her lost love. The three are thrown together in the common cause of escape from oppression. This film is subtitled in English.
BBFC:X — A — EN
Unknown — *Precision Video Ltd*   **P**
BITC 2046/VITC 2046

Blood from the Mummy's Tomb — Fil-Ent '71
Horror
07441   90 mins   C
B, V
Valerie Leon, James Villiers, Andrew Keir, Hugh Burden, directed by Seth Holt
An explorer's daughter becomes possessed by the spirit of a dead Egyptian princess. When her tomb is opened, the princess takes revenge on those who have desecrated her grave and her victims find they are terrorised by a variety of cruel and frightening objects including a severed hand and a snake statue.
BBFC:X — A — EN
Hammer Film Productions Ltd — *THORN EMI*
P
TXC 90 0315 4/TVC 90 0315 2

Blood of a Poet — Fil-Ent '30
Film-Avant-garde
10038   63 mins   B/W
B, V
Directed by Jean Cocteau
A surrealistic, evocative non-story film, showing the inner thoughts of a poet while he watches a chimney collapse. Subtitled in English.
A — EN   FR
Vicomte de Noailles — *Palace Video Ltd*
PVC 2039A

Blood on Satan's Claw — Fil-Ent '71
Horror
02437   95 mins   C
B, V
Patrick Wymark, Linda Hayden
Townspeople in an English village circa 1670 find the essence of Satan taking over their children.
BBFC:X — A — EN
Cannon Releasing — *Guild Home Video*
H, P

Blood Orgy of the She-Devils — Fil-Ent '73
Horror
02072   73 mins   C
B, V
Linda Zaborin, Tom Pace, William Bagdad
Mara, sadistic queen of the black witches, and her wolf pack of voluptuous virgins invade Satan's tortured realm of the unknown. A horror classic of our time, the plot deals lavishly with all aspects of demonology, and climaxes in a bizarre orgy of death.
A — EN
Genini — *VCL Video Services*   **P**

Blood Queen — Fil-Ent '??
Drama/Biographical
05723   100 mins   C
V2, B, V
Christine Kruger
This film is based on the life story of Eva Peron tracing her dramatic climb to the top of the government and her tragic death.
S,A — EN
Unknown — *Video Unlimited*   **H, P**

Blood Relations — Fil-Ent '77
Comedy/Horror
05741   97 mins   C
B, V
Sophie Deschamps, Maxim Hemel, directed by Wim Lindner
Set in a provincial French town, a new nurse at a hospital discovers that a doctor is supplying blood to a group of vampires. She decides to destroy them; she brings about an accident which puts the doctor in hospital cutting off the supply. She then injects herself with holy water and offers herself to the vampires; however, she is aneamic and has to be given blood—effectively making her one of them.
BBFC:X — A — EN
Van Rij; Chassel — *Home Video Holdings*
H, P
003

---

80   (For Explanation of codes, see USE GUIDE and KEY)

PALADIN VIDEO HOME ENTERTAINMENT GUIDE

Blood Relatives
Fil-Ent '??
Horror/Crime-Drama
06214   90 mins   C
B, V

Donald Sutherland, David Hemmings, Donald Pleasance
A teenager out alone at night comes across the horribly mutilated body of a young girl. The known sex offender, the girl's cousin, her employer all come under suspicion.
S,A — EN
Heroux/Lepicier Production — VCL Video Services   P
P173D

Blood Song
Fil-Ent '??
Horror
07599   88 mins   C
V2, B, V

Frankie Avalon, Donna Wilkes, Dane Clark, Richard Jaeckel, directed by Alan J. Levi
After brutally murdering an attendant, a deranged mental patient escapes. His only possession is a carved wooden flute. Not far away a high school student sees the murder in a nightmarish vision. She is haunted by the mournful tune of a flute; when she hears it another murder is committed. She finally encounters the killer in the act of burying a victim, she is driven nearly insane when he turns on her.
BBFC:X — A — EN
Unknown — Iver Film Services   P
174

Blood Spattered Bride, The
Fil-Ent '7?
Horror
02584   95 mins   C
B, V

Loathsome creatures demand bridal sacrifices in this gory thriller.
BBFC:X — A — EN
Unknown — Mountain Video   P

Blood Sweat and Tears
Fil-Ent '??
Music-Performance
06292   58 mins   C
V2, B, V

This film features in concert the band Blood, Sweat and Tears, songs include 'Nuclear Blues,' 'Manic Depression,' 'You made me so very happy,' 'Drown in my own tears,' 'Spinning Wheel' and 'What goes up.'
F — EN
Unknown — World of Video 2000   H, P
MV235

Blood Tide
Fil-Ent '80
Horror
09233   97 mins   C
B, V

Jose Ferrer, James Earl Jones
Set on a remote Greek Island, this film tells the story of a man in search of his sister. However, he inexplicably gets involved in a string of bloody deaths and bizarre local mythology.
A — EN
Unknown — Video Form Pictures   H, P
SKY 1

Bloodbath at the House of Death
Fil-Ent '84
Comedy/Horror
12912   88 mins   C
B, V

Kenny Everett, Pamela Stephenson, Vincent Price
A team of scientists encounter some hair-raising experiences when they meet up in a lonely manor house. A horror comedy spoof.
BBFC:18 — A — EN
Ray Cameron — THORN EMI   P
TXA 90 24104/TVA 90 24102

Bloodbeat
Fil-Ent '??
Horror
08863   84 mins   C
V2, B, V

Helen Benton, Terry Brown, Dana Day, Peter Spelson, James Fitzgibbons, Claudia Peyton, directed by Fabrice A. Zaphiratos
Whilst a family gather together to celebrate Christmas in their country house, an evil force descends upon them, with brutal murders as a consequence.
A — EN
Unknown — Video Programme Distributors P
Replay 1019

Bloodline
Fil-Ent '79
Drama/Suspense
13273   112 mins   C
B, V

Audrey Hepburn, James Mason, Michelle Phillips, Romy Schneider, Omar Sharif, directed by Terence Young
When the wealthy head of an international pharmaceutical empire dies the money is left to his daughter who soon becomes prey to the individual self-interests of her family.
BBFC:18 — C,A — EN
Paramount — CIC Video   H, P
BEN 2093/VAN 2093

(For Explanation of codes, see USE GUIDE and KEY)   81

PALADIN VIDEO HOME ENTERTAINMENT GUIDE

Bloodlust   Fil-Ent '76
Horror
05701   86 mins   C
B, V
After horrific experiences in his childhood, that left a sore in his mind, a young man seeks comfort with the dead. He feels that they do not mock him and his craving leads him to the mortuary where his passion for the dead leads to others being committed.
BBFC:X — A — EN
Unknown — *Derann Film Services*   **H, P**
DV130B/DV130

Bloodstained Shadow   Fil-Ent '??
Horror
10185   133 mins   C
B, V
Stefania Casini, Craig Hill
In a little God-fearing Italian village people are being murdered. When a young professor from Venice visits his brother, the village priest, a young woman is brutally murdered. His brother struggles against the evil at work in the village; having witnessed the crime, he is aware that the killer must silence him.
A — EN
Unknown — *Video Form Pictures*   **H, P**
DIP 11

Bloodsuckers   Fil-Ent '65
Horror
06781   76 mins   C
V2, B, V
Patrick Macnee, Peter Cushing
A story of vampires, human sacrifices and perverted rituals set in the lush Mediterranean countryside.
A — EN
Orbita; Tefi — *Intervision Video*   **H, P**
A-A 0012

Bloody Birthday   Fil-Ent '80
Horror
07609   83 mins   C
V2, B, V
Lori Lethin, Melinda Cordell, Julie Brown, Susan Strasberg, Jose Ferrer, directed by Ed Hunt
In Meadowvale, California in June 1970, during a solar eclipse, three women give birth at the same moment. Ten years later a series of cold, calculated murders has the town in the grip of terror and panic.
BBFC:X — A — EN
Unknown — *Iver Film Services*   **P**

Bloody Kids   Fil-Ent '79
Drama
05384   88 mins   C
B, V
Derrick O'Connor, Gary Holton, Richard Thomas, Peter Clark, directed by Stephen Frears
This is a tense urban drama involving two eleven year old boys growing up in a British seaside town. The story covers a childish prank which they became involved in one Saturday afternoon. Amid the conflict and violence of the town, the prank designed by the strongest of the two, to test the police, goes badly wrong.
S,A — EN
Jack Gill; Black Lion Films — *Precision Video Ltd*   **P**
BITC 2050/VITC 2050

Bloody Mary   Fil-Ent '7?
Crime-Drama
07775   93 mins   C
V2, B, V
Carroll Baker, George Hilton
This film follows the intrigue and suspense surrounding the theft of a million dollar diamond.
S,A — EN
Unknown — *Fletcher Video*   **H, P**
V140

Blow Out   Fil-Ent '81
Suspense/Horror
09937   108 mins   C
B, V, LV
John Travolta, Nancy Allen, John Lithgow, Dennis Franz, directed by Brian De Palma
When a leading politician plunges his car into a river, with a pretty girl in the passenger seat, the cover-up begins. However, the accident was recorded by a film sound man working nearby. He is determined to get to the truth, however dangerous it may become.
BBFC:18 — A — EN
Filmways; Cinema 77; Geria — *Rank Video Library*   **H, P**
0161 Y

Blow-Up   Fil-Ent '66
Drama/Mystery
05310   104 mins   C
B, V
Vanessa Redgrave, David Hemmings, Sarah Miles, directed by Michelangelo Antonioni
The story of a young free-living London photographer who takes some pictures of a couple in a park. Later the girl tries to get him to give her the negatives, he refuses and when he blows up the pictures he discovers what looks

PALADIN VIDEO HOME ENTERTAINMENT GUIDE

like a murder involving the couple. The film looks at the underground culture of the sixties from the fashion world and its models to public protests.
S,A — EN
Carlo Ponti; MGM Inc — *MGM/UA Home Video*   **P**
UMB10015/UMV10015

Blue Belle   Fil-Ent '7?
Drama
02406   86 mins   C
B, V
Annie Belle, Felicity Devonshire, directed by Massimo Dellemano
Annie leaves for Hong Kong with her jealous 'father' Michael. She meets a wealthy young woman and her husband, who falls for Annie. When Michael is arrested for currency smuggling, Annie adopted by the couple. Events lead Annie to form a 'menage a trois' with the couple, until one night which changed Annie's life.
A — EN
Unknown — *Derann Film Services*   **H, P**
DV 113B/DV 113

Blue Blood   Fil-Ent '73
Drama
01683   86 mins   C
V2, B, V
Oliver Reed, Fiona Lewis, Anna Gael, Meg Wynn Owen, Derek Jacobi
A man obsessed with increasing his family lineage inherits an estate. A butler, intent on ultimately obtaining the estate, preys on his employer's obsession and finally finds himself in the position to take over completely.
BBFC:X — A — EN
Mallard Impact Quadrant — *Intervision Video*   **H, P**
A-A 0013

Blue Eyes of the Broken Doll, The   Fil-Ent '??
Horror
08859   85 mins   C
V2, B, V
Doama :prus
A beautiful young girl, who lives in a large house with her sisters, gives a job to an ex-convict. On his arrival, horrific murders start in the area.
BBFC:X — A — EN
Unknown — *Video Programme Distributors*   **P**
Canon 003

Blue Fantasies   Fil-Ent '7?
Comedy
02106   72 mins   C
V2, B, V
A group of college students fantasise after reading a batch of letters from fellow pupils describing various and exciting erotic episodes.
BBFC:X — A — EN
Unknown — *Hokushin Audio Visual Ltd*   **P**
VM-12

Blue Fire Lady   Fil-Ent '78
Adventure
06231   90 mins   C
B, V
Cathryn Harrison, Mark Holden
The father of a young girl hates horses and wants her to have nothing to do with them. She runs away from home and gets work in a stables; she becones sickened by the inhumane treatment the horses receive. She is sacked for her views. Against all odds she is able to buy her favorite horse, only after help from an unexpected quarter.
F — EN
Blue Fire Prods Pty Ltd for Australian Intl Film Corp — *VCL Video Services*   **P**
F139

Blue Hawaii   Fil-Ent '62
Musical
01757   101 mins   C
B, V, LV
Elvis Presley, Angela Lansbury, Joan Blackman, Roland Winters
A soldier, returning to his Hawaiian home, takes a job with a tourist agency, against his parents' wishes.
BBFC:U — F — EN
Paramount, Hal Wallis — *CBS/Fox Video*   **P**
3B-004

Blue Jeans and Dynamite   Fil-Ent '8?
Drama/Adventure
09289   89 mins   C
V
Chris Mitchum, Claudine Auger
Set in a sinister South American copper mine where new men are being signed up to work, this film follows the story of a young man trying to survive his dreams.
S,A — EN
Unknown — *Direct Video Services*   **H, P**

Blue Max, The   Fil-Ent '66
Drama
01756   155 mins   C
B, V, LV
George Peppard, James Mason, Ursula Andress

(For Explanation of codes, see USE GUIDE and KEY)   83

PALADIN VIDEO HOME ENTERTAINMENT GUIDE

During World War II, a young German, fresh out of aviation school, competes for the coveted 'Blue Max' flying award with other members of a squadron of seasoned flyers of the aristocratic set. Based on a novel by Jack D. Hunter.
F — EN
20th Century Fox — CBS/Fox Video   **P**
4A-036

Blue Peter Makes...   How-Ins '7?
Handicraft/Hobbies
09403   ? mins   C
V2, B, V
This tape features the Blue Peter team showing the secrets of making everything from a sledge to Baked Bean and Dumpling Soup.
M,S — I
BBC — BBC Video   **H, P**
BBCV 9007

Blue Skies Again   Fil-Ent '83
Comedy/Romance
12061   85 mins   C
V2, B, V
Mimi Rogers, Kenneth McMillan, Dana Elcar, Robyn Barto
This film tells the story of an 18-year-old high school graduate whose one ambition in life is to play for the Denver Devils basketball team.
BBFC:PG — S,A — EN
Lantana Productions — Guild Home Video
H, P, E

Blue Thunder   Fil-Ent '83
Drama/Adventure
12479   101 mins   C
B, V
Roy Schneider, Warren Oates, Malcolm MacDowell
The film portrays the fight for possession of an electronic helicopter that could devastate a large city.
BBFC:15 — S,A — EN
Gordon Carroll — RCA/Columbia Pictures Video UK   **H, P**
10160

Bluebeard   Fil-Ent '72
Horror/Suspense
08480   123 mins   C
B, V
Richard Burton, Raquel Welch, Virna Lisi, Nathalie Delon, Marilu Tolo, Karin Schubert, Agostina Belli, Sybil Danning. Joey Heatherton, directed by Edward Dmytryk
This film tells the story of an Austrian aristocrat living in the Austrian Alps in a castle guarded by three huge dogs. The trouble starts when his most recent wife discovers, in the dark vaults of the castle, seven frozen bodies. He gleefully tells their strange stories, all of them his previous wives, having suffered gruesome deaths.
BBFC:X — A — EN
Cinerama Release — THORN EMI   **P**
TXB 90 12854/TVB 90 1285 2

Blues Brothers, The   Fil-Ent '80
Comedy
05325   133 mins   C
V2, B, V
John Belushi, Dan Aykroyd, James Brown, Cab Calloway, Ray Charles, Carrie Fisher, Aretha Franklin, Henry Gibson
Two hoodlum brothers, who are searching for redemption, set out to find the members of their defunct rhythm and blues band in order to raise some honest money. The members have all got straight jobs and are reluctant to go on the road again but they are convinced by the brothers. But as trouble starts, the brothers return to their original ways.
S,A — EN
Universal — CIC Video   **H, P**
CRA1013/BEA1013/VHA1013

Boardwalk   Fil-Ent '79
Drama
02129   95 mins   C
V2, B, V
Lee Strasberg, Ruth Gordon
A story of love, violence, and survival in present-day Brooklyn.
BBFC:AA — S,A — EN
Gerrald Herrod — Hokushin Audio Visual Ltd
P
VM-41

Boat, The   Fil-Ent '81
War-Drama
13083   138 mins   C
B, V
Jurgen Prochnow, Herbert Gronemeyer, Klaus Wennemann, directed by Wolfgang Petersen
This film follows the adventures of the crew of a German U-boat, one of the Grey Wolves, and it is a graphic account of the horrors of submarine warfare. It is subtitled in English.
BBFC:U — C,A — EN
Guther Rohrbach — RCA/Columbia Pictures Video UK   **H, P**
10229

Boatniks, The   Fil-Ent '70
Comedy/Adventure
12581   95 mins   C
B, V
Robert Morse, Stephanie Powers, Phil Silvers

PALADIN VIDEO HOME ENTERTAINMENT GUIDE

An accident-prone Coast Guard finds it hard enough to stay afloat, let alone tangle with a bunch of crooks.
F — EN
Walt Disney Productions — *Rank Video Library* **H**
125

Bob Marley and The Wailers   Fil-Ent '81
Music-Performance
07469   60 mins   C
B, V
Directed by Don Gazzaniga
This cassette charts one of the last concerts given by Bob Marley and The Wailers recorded live at the Santa Barbara County Bowl. It contains some of his most acclaimed songs including 'Exodus,' 'Stand Up for Your Rights,' and 'Ambush in the Night.'
S,A — EN
Avalon Attractions Inc; Media Aids Ltd — *THORN EMI*   **P**
TXE 90 0 707 4/TVE 90 0707 2

Bob Marley and the Wailers—Live   Fil-Ent '78
Music-Performance
07832   72 mins   C
B, V
This film features Bob Marley and the Wailers recorded live in concert at the Rainbow Theatre, London in the summer of 1977. Songs include 'No Woman No Cry,' 'Jamming,' 'Get Up Stand Up,' 'Exodus,' 'The Heathen,' 'No More Trouble,' 'War,' 'Trenchtown Rock,' 'I Shot the Sheriff,' 'Lively Up,' 'Rebel Music,' 'Them Belly Full,' and others.
F — EN
Blue Mountain Films — *Island Pictures*   **P**
IPV001M

Bobbie Jo and the Outlaw   Fil-Ent '76
Adventure
08310   85 mins   C
B, V
Marjoe Gortner, Lynda Carter, Jesse Vint, directed by Mark L. Lester
This programme looks at a badger family, showing how the mother cares for her young by teaching them to hunt and protect themselves.
C,A — EN
American Int'l; Mark L Lester Prod — *Video Film Organisation*   **P**
0002

Bobby Darin   Fil-Ent '7?
Music-Performance
02074   60 mins   C
B, V
Bobby Darin, Linda Ronstadt, George Burns
Bobby Darin—actor, composer, and musician, is joined by great stars Linda Ronstadt and George Burns in this fabulous music special.
F — EN
Unknown — *VCL Video Services*   **P**

Bobby Deerfield   Fil-Ent '77
Drama
13067   123 mins   C
B, V
Al Pacino, Marthe Keller, Anny Duperey, Romolo Valli, directed by Sydney Pollack
While a Formula One racing champion is visiting an injured colleague in a Swiss clinic he meets and becomes fascinated by an impulsive, capricious girl, and even after returning home to Paris cannot forget her.
BBFC:A — C,A — EN
Columbia Pictures Industries Inc; Warner Bros Inc — *Warner Home Video*   **P**
61126

Body, The   Gen-Edu '7?
Documentary/Anatomy and physiology
01593   108 mins   C
B, V
Various aspects of the body are presented through a montage of images and impressions. Sexuality, childbirth, touching, ageing, and reproduction are all seen and discussed.
BBFC:X — A — ED
Tony Garnett — *THORN EMI*   **P**
TXB 90 0044 4/TVB 90 0044 2

Body and Soul   Fil-Ent '47
Drama
01069   104 mins   B/W
V2, B, V
John Garfield, Lilli Palmer, directed by Robert Rossen
The rigged fights and double-crosses of the boxing world are portrayed in this film.
Academy Awards '47: Best Film Editing.
A — EN
United Artists — *Intervision Video*   **H, P**
A-A 0123

Body and Soul   Fil-Ent '82
Drama
08089   95 mins   C
B, V
Leon Issac Kennedy, Jayne Kennedy, Muhammed Ali, Peter Lawford

(For Explanation of codes, see USE GUIDE and KEY)

PALADIN VIDEO HOME ENTERTAINMENT GUIDE

This film is a remake of the 1947 version. It tells the story of a man torn between success and loyalty to his family, whose ambition is for him to become a doctor. The film continues with him choosing to be a boxer and his climb to the top.
BBFC:X — A — EN
Golan—Globus — *Rank Video Library* **H, P**
0111 C

Body Heat   Fil-Ent '81
Drama/Suspense
13057   113 mins   C
B, V
William Hurt, Kathleen Turner, Richard Crenna, Ted Danson, directed by Lawrence Kasdan
A taut, passionate, steamy thriller which is full of suspense as two lovers plot to kill her husband.
BBFC:X — A — EN
The Ladd Company — *Warner Home Video* **P**
70005

Body Massage   How-Ins '80
Beauty/Massage
02050   50 mins   C
B, V
Jane Leddington
The first in the planned 'Hair Tek Beauty Therapy' series.
C,A — I
Hair Tek Video — *VideoSpace Ltd* **H, P**

Body Music   Fil-Ent '81
Music-Performance
05496   30 mins   C
B, V
Six different girls appear in one of six photo collages set to the evocative music of Chris Rainbow. Sight and sound combine to form the effect of the title.
C,A — EN
Chris Rainbow — *THORN EMI* **P**
TXE 90 0513 4/TVE 90 0513 2

Body Rock   Fil-Ent '84
Musical-Drama
13709   90 mins   C
B, V
Lorenzo Lamas, Vicki Frederick, Ray Sharkey, directed by Marcelo Epstein
A story of street break dancing with a music soundtrack from Ashford and Simpson, Laura Branigan, Julian Lennon and Roberta Flack.
BBFC:15 — S,A — EN
Jeffrey Schechtman — *THORN EMI* **P**
90 2878

Body Stealers, The   Fil-Ent '7?
Science fiction
04202   91 mins   C
B, V
George Sanders, Maurice Evans, Patrick Allen, Hilary Dwyer
A plane comes into sight and three paratroopers jump. For some seconds they fall but there is something horribly wrong. The parachutes flutter to the ground shapeless—the men have disappeared.
BBFC:A — C,A — EN
Unknown — *Guild Home Video* **H, P**

Bogie   Fil-Ent '80
Biographical/Drama
09188   120 mins   C
B, V
Kevin O'Connor, Kathryn Harrold, Ann Wedgeworth, Richard Dysart, Patricia Barry, Donal May, Alfred Ryder, Carol Vogel, directed by Vincent Sherman
Based on the book 'Bogie' by Joe Hyams, this film traces the legendary Humphrey Bogart's career, from the early 1930's as a struggling young actor to his most successful years as a famous Hollywood star.
F — EN
Charles Fries Prods — *Video Form Pictures* **H, P**
MGS 10

Bogus Bandits   Fil-Ent '33
Comedy
06861   74 mins   B/W
V2, B, V
Stan Laurel, Oliver Hardy
Laurel and Hardy end up in some hilarious situations when they travel by mule through the Italian Alps and meet up with a notorious bandit. Original title: 'Fra Diavolo.'
M,A — EN
Hal Roach — *European Video Company* **P**

Boheme, La   Fil-Ent '82
Opera
08474   112 mins   C
B, V
Ileana Cotrubas, Neil Shicoff, Marilyn Zschav, Thomas Allen, John Rawnsley, Gwynne Howell
This is a Giacomo Puccini's tragic love story set in the Latin Quarter of Paris amongst the Bohemian students. Ileana Cotrubas and Neil Shicoff as Mimi and Rodolfo have a love affair which is doomed from the start. The music is conducted by Lamberto Gardelli.
S,A — EN
Covent Garden Video Productions — *THORN EMI* **P**
TXH 90 1320 4/TVH 90 13202

PALADIN VIDEO HOME ENTERTAINMENT GUIDE

Boldest Job in the West   Fil-Ent '72
Western
04319   100 mins   C
V2, B, V
Five professional outlaws attempt to rob a gold deposit.
BBFC:U — F — EN
Promofilm — *Intervision Video*   **H, P**
A-AB 0010

Bolling: Concerto for Classic Guitar and Jazz Piano   Fil-Ent '81
Music-Performance
09777   50 mins   C
B, V
Angel Romero, George Shearing, Shelly Manne, Brian Torff
This tape features pianist George Shearing, classical guitarist Angel Romero, jazz drummer Shelly Manne and bassist Brian Torff performing Claude Bolling's 'Concerto for Classic Guitar and Jazz Piano'. This concert was recorded at the Ambassador Auditorium in Pasadena, California.
F — EN
Myriad Media Productions Inc. — *THORN EMI*
P
TXE 90 1034 4/TVE 90 1034 2

Bomb at 10:10   Fil-Ent '67
War-Drama/Suspense
05694   87 mins   C
B, V
George Montgomery, Rada Popovic, Peter Banicevic, Branko Plesa, directed by Casey Diamond
An American pilot escapes from a famous German camp and works his way through dangerous territory to Belgrade where he contacts the underground movement. He then becomes involved in a dangerous plot to kill a notorious and sadistic SS Colonel which results in the group being relentlessly pursued by the SS.
BBFC:A — S,A — EN
Ika Povic Production — *Derann Film Services*
H, P
GS705B/GS705

Bombay Talkie   Fil-Ent '70
Drama/Comedy
05678   105 mins   C
B, V
Jennifer Kendal, Shashi Kapoor, Aparna Sen, directed by James Ivory
An aging western novelist falls for a young Indian movie idol and leaves his wife. The couple are haunted by a writer who still loves the star. Jealousies, coincidences, confrontations and humiliations abound in this comical pseudo-tragedy.
BBFC:A — S,A — EN
Merchant Ivory Productions — *Home Video Holdings*   **H, P**
022

Bon Voyage, Charlie Brown   Fil-Ent '81
Cartoons
07962   74 mins   C
B, V
Animated, directed by Bill Melendez
Charles M. Schultz's 'Peanuts' gang are chosen to be exchange students for two weeks in France. They are joined by Snoopy and Woodstock in this combination of mystery, intrigue and romance, as Charlie Brown faces the usual complexities that surround him wherever he goes.
F — EN
Paramount — *CIC Video*   **H, P**
BEA2019/VHA2019

Bonditis   Fil-Ent '66
Satire
04334   100 mins   C
V2, B, V
A man can't stop dreaming about spies, guns, and women, and is diagnosed as suffering from 'bonditis.'
A — EN
Turnus Films — *Intervision Video*   **H, P**
A-A 0113

Bonnie & Clyde   Fil-Ent '67
Adventure
13177   109 mins   C
B, V
Warren Beatty, Faye Dunaway, Michael J Pollard, Gene Hackman, Estelle Parsons, directed by Arthur Penn
A car thief and the daughter of his intended victim team up to become America's most feared and ruthless bank robbers in the thirties.
BBFC:X — A — EN
Warner Bros — *Warner Home Video*   **P**
61026

Boomtown Rats Live!   Fil-Ent '??
Music-Performance
08844   50 mins   C
B, V

(For Explanation of codes, see USE GUIDE and KEY)   87

PALADIN VIDEO HOME ENTERTAINMENT GUIDE

This tape features the Boomtown Rats Live in concert and some of their hits such as 'Rat Trap', 'Like Clockwork', 'She's So Modern', 'Joey's On the Street Again' and 'Looking After No. 1'.
C,A — EN
Unknown — *VCL Video Services*   **P**
V005B

Border, The   Fil-Ent '82
Drama
09267   107 mins   C
B, V

Jack Nicholson, Harvey Keitel, Valerie Perrine, Warren Oates, directed by Tony Richardson
A border guard faces corruption and violence within his department and tests his own sense of decency when the infant of a poor Mexican girl is kidnapped.
BBFC:18 — *C,A* — *EN*
Universal — *CIC Video*   **H, P**

Border U.S.A., The   Fil-Ent '??
Crime-Drama
06224   97 mins   C
B, V

Telly Savalas, Eddie Albert, Danny La Paz, Michael Gazzo
A patrolman's task is to protect the arid stretch of sun-baked land separating the USA from Mexico, not only stopping drug trafficking but also the smuggling of cheap Mexican labour. After seeing the corrupt businessmen become richer he decides to take them on.
S,A — EN
Donald Langdon — *VCL Video Services*   **P**
P179D

Borderline   Fil-Ent '80
Drama
07348   106 mins   C
B, V

Charles Bronson, Bruno Kirby, Ed Harris, Bert Remsen
This film follows the task of a U.S. border patrolman along the thousand miles of barbed wire border between Mexico and America. It examines the plight of illegal Mexican immigrants' encounters with the Patrol.
S,A — EN
Associated Film Distributors; James Nelson — *Precision Video Ltd*   **P**
BITC 2074/VITC 2074

Born Again   Fil-Ent '78
Drama
12169   106 mins   C
V2, B, V

Anne Francis, Dean Jones, Jay Robinson, Dana Andrews, Raymond St. Jacques, directed by Irving Rapper
The story of Watergate is detailed in this film, as seen through the eyes and the conscience of Charles Colson, former Nixon aide, and the survival of his public disgrace.
S,A — EN
Frank Capra Jr — *Embassy Home Entertainment*   **P**
2082

Born Beautiful   Fil-Ent '84
Drama
13433   100 mins   C
B, V

Lori Singer, Ed Marinaro, Erin Gray
After ten years in the fashion world a top model is told she's too old for the job and she decides to groom a seventeen-year-old to take her place. Their relationship becomes strained when a news photographer arrives on the scene.
C,A — EN
Proctor and Gamble Prods; Telecom Entertainment — *MGM/UA Home Video*   **P**
10442

Born Losers   Fil-Ent '67
Drama
08347   112 mins   C
V2, B, V

Tom Laughlin, Elizabeth James, Jeremy Slate, William Wellman, Jane Russell
This film, set in a small town, tells of a man who takes the law into his own hands when the town is terrorized by a ruthless motorcycle gang.
BBFC:X — *A* — *EN*
American International Pictures — *Guild Home Video*   **H, P, E**

Born to Be Sold   Fil-Ent '7?
Drama
05630   108 mins   C
V2, B, V

Linda Carter
This film traces the hectic life of an over-worked social worker who gets deeply and emotionally involved with a client who has fallen-foul of a 'baby broker' who makes slaves of young pregnant girls and then sells their babies, at extortionate rates, to childless couples.
S,A — EN
Unknown — *Video Unlimited*   **H, P**

Born To Buck   Fil-Ent '71
Western
01042   93 mins   C
B, V

PALADIN VIDEO HOME ENTERTAINMENT GUIDE

Casey Tibbs, narrated by Henry Fonda
This programme follows the exploits of rodeo champion Casey Tibbs and the extraordinary obstacles he encounters.
F — EN
ENE — *VCL Video Services*   **P**

Born Wild   **Fil-Ent '68**
Drama
12758   94 mins   C
B, V
Tom Nardini, Patty McCormack
A feud between two teenage gangs in a US/Mexican border town escalates into rape and murder.
BBFC:18 — A — EN
American International Pictures — *Rank Video Library*   **H, P**
02001E

Born Winner   **Fil-Ent '??**
Drama
06085   103 mins   C
V2, B, V
Joe Dallesandro, Marisa Mell, Elenora Giorgi
A story of two friends and a great dream: money, women and motorcycles.
S,A — EN
Unknown — *Video Programme Distributors* **P**
Cinehollywood—V190

Borsalino   **Fil-Ent '69**
Suspense/Satire
13638   120 mins   C
B, V
Alain Delon, Jean-Paul Belmondo
Two small time operators in search of big money go adventuring in Marseilles in the early 1930's when the big crime syndicates were starting to evolve.
BBFC:15 — S,A — EN
Pierre Caro — *CIC Video*   **H, P**
2134

Boss, The   **Fil-Ent '??**
Crime-Drama
06086   97 mins   C
V2, B, V
Henry Silva, Richard Conte, Antonia Santilli
The daughter of a boss of the underworld is kidnapped; what follows is a dangerous game involving politicians, mobsters and policemen.
S,A — EN
Unknown — *Video Programme Distributors* **P**
Cinehollywood—V120

Boston Strangler, The   **Fil-Ent '68**
Suspense
01755   116 mins   C
B, V
Tony Curtis, Henry Fonda, George Kennedy, Murray Hamilton, Sally Kellerman, directed by Richard Fleisher
This film is based on Gerold Frank's factual book about the killer who terrorised Boston for a year and a half.
BBFC:X — A — EN
20th Century Fox — *CBS/Fox Video*   **P**
3A-005

Botanic Man Volume 1   **Med-Sci '81**
Ecology and environment
04651   104 mins   C
B, V
Presented by David Bellamy
In his highly original style, David Bellamy takes us around the world as he traces the evolution and adaptation of life on earth. In programmes specially made for television we are made aware of the vital interdependence of all the elements in the environment and Man's responsibility in maintaining that balance. Volume 1 contains four programmes: 'Green Print for Life,' 'The Crucible of Life,' 'Living Water,' and 'Potential Energy.'
F — ED
Thames Video — *THORN EMI*   **H, P**
TXB 90 6201 4/TVB 90 6201 2

Botanic Man Volume 2   **Med-Sci '8?**
Ecology and environment
05064   80 mins   C
B, V
Presented by David Bellamy
The first programme, 'Land of Opportunity,' investigates plant and animal life in New Zealand. 'Latitude Zero' looks at the climatic extremes at the Equator in South America. The third deals with the effects of previous Ice Ages on the earth's surface and is entitled 'White Death: New Life.'
F — ED
Randal Beattie — *THORN EMI*   **P**
TXB 90 6215 4/TVB 90 6215 2

Botanic Man Volume 3   **Med-Sci '8?**
Ecology and environment
05065   80 mins   C
B, V
Presented by David Bellamy

(For Explanation of codes, see USE GUIDE and KEY)

PALADIN VIDEO HOME ENTERTAINMENT GUIDE

The first programme, 'Life on the Limit,' explains how badly modern agriculture has devastated the land. 'Extinction Is Forever' investigates the earth's threatened wildlife. The third shows how man's life-style has affected the natural world and is entitled 'Crackpot Jackpot.'

F — ED

Randal Beattie — *THORN EMI* **P**
TXB 90 6222 4/TVB 90 6222 2

Botham's Ashes: The 1981 Cornhill Test Series Spo-Lei '8?
Sports
06971 109 mins C
B, V

Ian Botham, Richie Benaud

In this programme 1981 BBC TV Sports Personality of the Year Ian Botham and Richie Benaud look back at the highlights of the 1981 Ashes series. They analyse the sequence of test matches and the changes of fortunes that helped to keep the Ashes in England.

S,A — EN

John Vigar; Nick Hunter — *BBC Video* **H, P**
BBCV 5015

Bounty, The Fil-Ent '84
Drama
13684 128 mins C
B, V

Mel Gibson, Anthony Hopkins, Edward Fox, Laurence Olivier, directed by Roger Donaldson

Another retelling of the famous sea mutiny and the story of two good friends who became deadly enemies. The musical score is by Vangelis.

BBFC:15 — *S,A — EN*

Orion Pictures — *THORN EMI* **P**
90 2779

Bounty Killers, The/Macao Fil-Ent '??
Western/Mystery
09113 168 mins C
B, V

Rod Cameron, Dan Duryea, Buster Crabbe, Audrey Dalton; Robert Mitchum, Jane Russell, William Bendix, directed by Joseph Von Sternberg

This tape contains two films. 'The Bounty Killers' (1964, colour, 90 mins.) tells of a mild and gentle-mannered Easterner who is led into a life of violence and bounty killing as he wipes out a whole gang of bandits. 'Macao' (1952, black and white, 78 mins.) tells the story of diamond smuggling, murder and mayhem amongst the seas of Hong Kong.

S,A — EN

Premiere Prods; RKO — *Kingston Video* **H, P**
KV62

Bounty Man, The Fil-Ent '72
Drama
04186 74 mins C
B, V

Clint Walker, Richard Basehart, John Ericson, Margot Kidder

A bounty hunter becomes obsessed with tracking down his wife's killer.

C,A — EN

Aaron Spelling; Leonard Goldberg — *Guild Home Video* **H, P**

Boxcar Bertha Fil-Ent '72
Drama/Mystery
09926 92 mins C
B, V

Barbara Hershey, David Carradine, Barry Primus, John Carradine, directed by Martin Scorsese

This film set in the Depression years of the 30's, tells the story of a girl and three men who plan a train robbery and a kidnapping.

BBFC:18 — *A — EN*

A.I.; Roger Corman — *Rank Video Library* **H, P**
0159 E

Boy and His Dog, A Fil-Ent '??
Science fiction
06079 90 mins C
B, V

Jason Robards, Don Johnson, Susanne Benton, Alvy Moore, Helen Winton, Charles McGraw, directed by L. Q. Jones

A film adaptation of Harlan Ellison's story about a misogynistic society in the post World War IV civilization of 2024.

S,A — EN

Alvy Moore — *Video Programme Distributors* **P**
Media—M104

Boy Named Charlie Brown, A Fil-Ent '69
Cartoons
12091 80 mins C
B, V

Animated, voices of Peter Robbins, Pamelyn Ferdin, Andy Pforsich

(For Explanation of codes, see USE GUIDE and KEY)

PALADIN VIDEO HOME ENTERTAINMENT GUIDE

Poor Charlie Brown gets frustrated when everything he does goes wrong. However, Snoopy and the gang help him out in a school spelling competition.
F — EN
National General Pictures; Cinema Center — *CBS/Fox Video* **P**
7121

Boyfriend, The Fil-Ent '71
Musical
10154   125 mins   C
B, V
Twiggy, Tommy Tune, Barbara Windsor, Glenda Jackson
Taken from the stage musical and set against the music and fashions of the twenties, it tells the story of a shy young backstage helper who is forced to replace the star of the show and play opposite the boy she secretly loves.
F — EN
MGM-Emi Prod; Ken Russell — *MGM/UA Home Video* **P**
UMB 10306/UMV 10306

Boys from Brazil, The Fil-Ent '78
Drama
00832   120 mins   C
B, V
Gregory Peck, James Mason, Sir Laurence Olivier, Lilli Palmer
Incredible plot of human cloning when children formed from Hitler's likeness are used to implement a neo-Nazi takeover.
BBFC:X — *A — EN*
20th Century Fox — *Precision Video Ltd* **P**
BITC 3010/VITC 3010

Boys in Blue, The Fil-Ent '83
Comedy
12760   89 mins   C
B, V, LV
Tommy Cannon, Bobby Ball, Suzanne Danielle, Roy Kinnear, Erik Sykes, Jon Pertwee, Jack Douglas
In order to save the sub-police station from getting the chop, criminal action is taken which starts a hilarious chain of events that culminates in the zaniest of car-chase sequences.
BBFC:PG — *F — EN*
Unknown — *Rank Video Library* **H, P**
1065Y

Boys in Company C, The Fil-Ent '78
War-Drama
06933   121 mins   C
B, V
Stan Shaw, Andrew Stevens, James Canning, Michael Lembeck, Craig Wasson, Scott Hyland, directed by Sidney J. Furie
This film follows the fortunes of five young men from widely differing backgrounds whose lives merge when they find themselves in the same company in the US Marine Corps. The film shows what they go through, the horrors they face and the permanent effect it has on their lives.
BBFC:X — *A — EN*
Columbia Pictures — *Rank Video Library* **H, P**
0074C

Boys in the Band, The Fil-Ent '70
Drama
05308   114 mins   C
B, V
Frederick Combs, Leonard Frey, Cliff Gorman, Reuben Greene, Lawrence Luckinbill, directed by William Friedkin
A group of homosexuals gather to celebrate the birthday of one of their group. A game they play, in which each has to call the one he loves, forces the participants to take a good look at themselves and their way of life. A serious drama exposing the problems of homosexuality based on a Mart Crowley play.
BBFC:X — *A — EN*
National General; Cinema Center Films — *MGM/UA Home Video* **P**
UCB10017/UCV10017

BP Challenge to Youth Gen-Edu '8?
Education
13545   33 mins   C
B, V
Directed by Ian Perry
This film shows how, through a series of competitions involving sport, craft, design and technology, youngsters are given their first link with industry and the world outside school.
M,S — ED
Hamilton Perry Film and Video; BP Oil Limited — *TFI Leisure Ltd* **H, P**

Brahms Double Concerto for Violin and Cello Fin-Art '7?
Music-Performance
02271   70 mins   C
V
Zubin Mehta, musical director of both the Israel and New York Philharmonic Orchestras, conducts Isaac Stern and Leonard Rose in their performance with the Israel Philharmonic Orchestra.
F — EN
Unknown — *JVC* **P**
PRT 36

(For Explanation of codes, see USE GUIDE and KEY)

PALADIN VIDEO HOME ENTERTAINMENT GUIDE

Brainstorm
Fil-Ent '83
Drama
12209   101 mins   C
B, V

Natalie Wood, Christopher Walken
An incredible machine is invented that when linked to the brain can read thought processes and record physical and emotional sensations as they are experienced. The film includes many spectacular special effects.
BBFC:15 — S,A — EN
MGM — *MGM/UA Home Video*   P
10314

Brainwash
Fil-Ent '82
Horror/Suspense
09397   98 mins   C
B, V

Christopher Allport, Yvette Mimieux, Cindy Pickett, John Considine, Walter Olkewicz, directed by Bobby Roth
Based on a true story, this film tells the terrifying story of a man caught up in an organisation where the only way to the top is to take 'The Training'. Using interrogators every deepest secret is exposed, and the only way out is to escape.
A — EN
Unknown — *VCL Video Services*   P
P367D

Brainwashed
Fil-Ent '??
Drama
06199   98 mins   C
B, V

Omar Sharif, Florinda Bolkan
A born leader fighting to defend the weak and underpriviledged is imprisoned on an island for his beliefs and ideals. For years his lover has struggled to obtain a permit to visit him, finally they are able to spend an hour together. They try to build hope but it all goes wrong and events slide to a tragic end.
S,A — EN
Unknown — *VCL Video Services*   P
P135D

Brainwaves
Fil-Ent '82
Drama
09087   100 mins   C
V2, B, V

Keir Dullea, Suzanna Love, Tony Curtis, Vera Miles, directed by Ulli Lommell
A young girl is knocked down by a hit-and-run driver. She is left in a coma. The only way to recovery is by a new process developed by a neuro-scientist. The parents agree to undergo this operation. Although she seems to make a miraculous recovery, a series of nightmares and hallucinations plunge her into a terrifying existence.
C,A — EN
Unknown — *Video Tape Centre*   P
VTC 1081

Brave Bunch, The
Fil-Ent '??
War-Drama
05624   100 mins   C
V2, B, V

John Miller, Maria Xenia, Laurie Stevens, Elsa Linberg, Alex Stewart
Set during the Second World War the Bulgarians allied themselves with the 3rd Reich and invaded the northern part of Greece called Macedonia without resistance, bringing tragedy to unarmed citizens. The film follows the story of the re-birth of a nation with violence, passion, suspense and human drama.
BBFC:X — A — EN
Unknown — *Go Video Ltd*   P
GO105

Breakdance, The Movie
Fil-Ent '84
Drama/Dance
13368   88 mins   C
V2, B, V

Lucinda Dickey, 'Shabba Doo', 'Boogaloo Shrimp', 'Ben Lokey', directed by Joel Silberg
A trio of street breakdancers find themselves up against the world of classical dance when they audition for a Broadway show.
BBFC:PG — M,A — EN
Cannon Films Inc — *Guild Home Video*
H, P, E
8321-8

Breakdance—You Can Do It
Fil-Ent '84
Dance
13142   60 mins   C
B, V

Odis Medley
This video explains the finer points of the Moonwalk, Twistoflex, Sit Spins and other body-popping routines for the beginner and features clips from 'Breakdance—The Movie.'
F — I
Unknown — *Polygram Video*   P
KB 8202/KV 8102

Breaker Morant
Fil-Ent '80
War-Drama
07379   108 mins   C
V2, B, V

(For Explanation of codes, see USE GUIDE and KEY)

PALADIN VIDEO HOME ENTERTAINMENT GUIDE

Edward Woodward, Jack Thompson, John Waters, Bryan Brown, Charles Tingwell, Terence Donovan, Frank Wilson, Ray Meagher, Lewis Fitz-gerald, Rod Mullinar, directed by Bruce Beresford
Set in 1901 during the Boer war, a crack British unit consisting mainly of Australians is established to fight in the war which has deteriorated into bitter guerilla confrontations. Their leader is brutally mutilated in an ambush. Lieutenant Morant leads a revenge attack on a Boer camp where the execution of prisoners, plus the mysterious death of a German missionary leads to him and two officers being court-martialed for murder.
S,A — EN
Matt Carroll; South Australian Film Corp — Guild Home Video   H, P, E

Breakfast at Tiffany's   Fil-Ent '61
Comedy/Romance
13284   109 mins   C
B, V
Audrey Hepburn, George Peppard, Patricia Neal, Mickey Rooney, directed by Blake Edwards
Two residents of a bohemian New York brownstone apartment, though attracted to each other are determined in their search for a rich partner. In the end true love prevails.
BBFC:PG — S,A — EN
Paramount — CIC Video   H, P
BEL 2086/VHL 2086

Breaking Away   Fil-Ent '79
Comedy
01198   100 mins   C
B, V, LV
Dennis Christopher, Dennis Quaid, Daniel Stern, Jackie Earle Haley
A comedy about a high school graduate's addiction to bicycle racing whose dreams are tested against the realities of a crucial race. Shot on location at Indiana University.
Academy Awards '79: Best Original Screenplay.
F — EN
20th Century Fox — CBS/Fox Video   P
3A-099

Breaking Glass   Fil-Ent '80
Musical-Drama
01965   104 mins   C
B, V
Phil Daniels, Hazel Connor, Jon Finch, directed by Brian Gibson
The story of Kate, a New Wave singer who forms her own band, Breaking Glass. The group becomes a success, but Kate finds stardom difficult to handle.
BBFC:X — C,A — EN
GTO Films Ltd — VCL Video Services   P

Breaking Up-Love and Life   Fil-Ent '78
Romance/Drama
12834   100 mins   C
B, V
Lee Remick, Granville Van Dusen, Vicki Dawson, David Stambaugh
In the third film of the 'Love and Life' series a young wife is shattered after fifteen years of marriage by her husband's desire to be free.
C,A — EN
Frederick Brogger; Time Life Television — Video Tape Centre   P
5008

Breakthrough   Fil-Ent '78
War-Drama
08385   111 mins   C
V2, B, V
Richard Burton, Robert Mitchum, Rod Steiger, Helmut Griem, Curt Jurgens, Michael Parks
This is a World War II thriller set in the summer of 1944. It tells of top German Officers who plan to assassinate Adolf Hitler and their desperate mission across enemy lines.
S,D — EN
German — Guild Home Video   H, P, E

Breathless   Fil-Ent '83
Drama/Suspense
13469   98 mins   C
B, V
Richard Gere, Valerie Kaprisky, directed by Jim McBride
Set in California, a loner becomes obsessed with a young French student after shooting a cop when stealing a car, and together they have to run from the law.
BBFC:18 — C,A — EN
Orion Pictures — Rank Video Library   H, P
0200D

Bride to Be   Fil-Ent '8?
Drama
12158   ? mins   C
B, V
Stanley Baker, Sarah Miles, Peter Day, directed by Moreno Alba
Based on a novel by Juan Valera, 'Bride to Be' is a love story set in Spain towards the end of the last century. A beautiful woman is betrothed to a wealthy landowner, but the arrival of his son, a novitiate for the priesthood, forms a triangular relationship.
S,A — EN
Unknown — Precision Video Ltd   P
BITC 2145/VITC 2145

(For Explanation of codes, see USE GUIDE and KEY)

PALADIN VIDEO HOME ENTERTAINMENT GUIDE

Brideshead Revisited—Vol.1 Fil-Ent '81
Drama
09328   120 mins   C
B, V

Jeremy Irons, Anthony Andrews, Diana Quick, Laurence Olivier, Claire Bloom, directed by Charles Sturridge and Michael Lindsay-Hogg
The first episode of the popular series based on the novel by Evelyn Waugh is contained on this tape. Entitled 'Et in Arcadia Ego', this programme introduces Captain Charles Ryder to the aristocratic Marchmain family of Brideshead Castle.
S,A — EN
Granada Television — *Granada Video*   H

Brideshead Revisited—Vol. 2 Fil-Ent '81
Drama
09329   120 mins   C
B, V

Jeremy Irons, Anthony Andrews, Diana Quick, Laurence Olivier, Claire Bloom, directed by Charles Sturridge and Michael Lindsay-Hogg
This tape contains episodes two and three of the series, 'Home and Abroud' and 'The Bleak Light of Day.' After spending a summer at Brideshead, Charles visits Venice with a friend but returns to the Castle in time for Christmas.
S,A — EN
Granada Television — *Granada Video*   H

Brideshead Revisited—Vol. 3 Fil-Ent '81
Drama
09330   120 mins   C
B, V

Jeremy Irons, Anthony Andrews, Diana Quick, Laurence Olivier, Claire Bloom, directed by Charles Sturridge and Michael Lindsay-Hogg
Episodes four and five are contained on this tape, 'Sebastian Against the World' and 'A Blow Upon a Bruise'. As Sebastian's drinking continues, he is forces to leave university. Charles realises he cannot help further and decides to leave Brideshead.
S,A — EN
Granada Television — *Granada Video*   H

Brideshead Revisited—Vol. 4 Fil-Ent '81
Drama
09331   120 mins   C
B, V

Jeremy Irons, Anthony Andrews, Diana Quick, Laurence Olivier, Claire Bloom, directed by Charles Sturridge and Michael Lindsay-Hogg
In episodes six and seven, entitled 'Julia' and 'The Unseen Hook', Lady Marchmain becomes seriously ill and asks for Sebastian, who has disappeared. Charles finds Sebastian in North Africa, but he is too ill to travel.
S,A — EN
Granada Television — *Granada Video*   H

Brideshead Revisited—Vol. 5 Fil-Ent '81
Drama
09332   120 mins   C
B, V

Jeremy Irons, Anthony Andrews, Diana Quick, Laurence Olivier, Claire Bloom, directed by Charles Sturridge and Michael Lindsay-Hogg
Episodes eight and nine, entitled 'Brideshead Deserted' and 'Orphans of the Storm' continue the story of Charles Ryder's relationship with Julia and the Marchmain family and his budding success as a well-known artist.
S,A — EN
Granada Television — *Granada Video*   H

Brideshead Revisited—Vol. 6 Fil-Ent '81
Drama
09333   120 mins   C
B, V

Jeremy Irons, Anthony Andrews, Diana Quick, Laurence Olivier, Claire Bloom, directed by Charles Sturridge and Michael Lindsay-Hogg
Episodes ten and eleven, 'A Twitch Upon the Thread' and 'Brideshead Revisted' conclude the story, as Julia decides at the last minute not to marry Charles, leaving him alone with the memories of his life at Brideshead.
S,A — EN
Granada Television — *Granada Video*   H

Bridge for Beginners How-Ins '81
Games/Hobbies
05432   157 mins   C
B, V

Nico Gardener
This film, with the aid of world champion Nico Gardener, shows the beginner stage by stage how to play bridge and how to develop technique and build a successful game.
F — EN
Videorama Studios — *Videorama Studios Ltd*
P

Bridge Too Far, A Fil-Ent '77
War-Drama
13028   175 mins   C
B, V

PALADIN VIDEO HOME ENTERTAINMENT GUIDE

Dirk Bogarde, Michael Caine, James Caan, Sean Connery, Liv Ullmann, Laurence Olivier, Robert Redford, directed by Richard Attenborough
A screen version of an epic bestseller book title about the ill-fated airborne assault on Arnhem.
BBFC:A — *A* — *EN*
United Artists; Joseph E Levine — *Warner Home Video* **P**
99248

Bridge Too Far, A Fil-Ent '77
War-Drama
01280   175 mins   C
V2, B, V
Dirk Bogarde, James Caan, Michael Caine, Sean Connery, Edward Fox, Elliot Gould, Gene Hackman, Anthony Hopkins, Hardy Kruger, Laurence Olivier, Ryan O'Neal, Maximilian Schell, Liv Ullman?directed by Richard Attenborough
A recreation of Arnhem, one of the most disastrous battles of World War II. It shows how misinformation, adverse conditions, and overconfidence combined to prevent the Allied Forces from capturing six major bridges leading from Holland to the German border.
F — EN
United Artists, Joseph E Levine, Richard P Levine Prods — *Intervision Video* **H**
UA A B 5014

Bridges at Toko-Ri, The Fil-Ent '54
War-Drama
13285   99 mins   C
B, V
William Holden, Grace Kelly, Mickey Rooney, Frederic March, directed by Mark Robson
An American pilot is called to war for the second time in Korea, to fly against the bridges of Toko-Ri, a mission so dangerous that it leaves doubts as to his return.
BBFC:PG — *S,A* — *EN*
Paramount — *CIC Video* **H, P**
BEL 2042/VHL 2042

Brief Encounter Fil-Ent '45
Drama/Romance
01891   86 mins   B/W
B, V
Celia Johnson, Trevor Howard, Stanley Holloway
A sensitive portrayal of what happens when two happily married strangers meet and their acquaintance deepens into affection and then to love. They are helpless in their emotions, but redeemed by their moral courage.
BBFC:A — *C,A* — *EN*
Cineguild — *Rank Video Library* **H, P**
0001

Brief Encounter Fil-Ent '74
Romance/Drama
02041   99 mins   C
B, V
Sophia Loren, Richard Burton, Jack Hedley
A happily married housewife meets a not-so-happily married doctor. After several chance meetings, they begin to arrange when they will see each other.
A — EN
Carlo Ponti, Cecil Clarke — *Precision Video Ltd* **P**
BITC 2032/VITC 2032

Brigadoon Fil-Ent '54
Musical/Fantasy
10176   108 mins   C
B, V
Van Johnson, Gene Kelly, Cyd Charisse
Two Americans on holiday in Scotland arrive in Brigadoon, an enchanted village which only comes alive every hundred years. One of them falls in love with a girl who lives there but unwilling to take part in her life, he returns to New York. Realising how much he loves her he returns to the highlands to search her out again.
BBFC:U — *F — EN*
MGM — *MGM/UA Home Video* **P**
UMB 10040/UMV 10040

Brighton Rock Fil-Ent '48
Drama
04462   89 mins   B/W
B, V
Richard Attenborough, Hermione Baddeley, Carol Marsh, directed by John Boulting
A young man, a contender for gang leadership, hunts down a squealer and executes him. A blowsy music-hall artiste appoints herself as his Nemesis in an effort to see justice done. Based on a novel by Graham Greene.
BBFC:A — *S,A* — *EN*
Mayer Kingsley — *THORN EMI* **P**
TXE 90 0011 4/TVE 90 0011 2

Brimstone and Treacle Fil-Ent '82
Drama
08933   87 mins   C
B, V
Sting, Denholm Elliott, Joan Plowright
A middle-aged couple have a mute, helpless but very beautiful daughter. A mysterious young man forces his way into their lives, claiming to be an old friend, from before her accident. He swiftly charms the mother and reassures the husband and moves into their home, looking

(For Explanation of codes, see USE GUIDE and KEY)

95

PALADIN VIDEO HOME ENTERTAINMENT GUIDE

after their daughter. His ultimate night visit leaves her hysterical but restored. It features music by The Police, and the updated version of 'Spread a Little Happiness'.
BBFC:X — A — EN
United Artists Classics — *Brent Walker Home Video Ltd* P

Bringing Up Baby   Fil-Ent '38
Comedy
05049   98 mins   B/W
B, V
Katharine Hepburn, Cary Grant, directed by Howard Hawks
A romantic comedy in which a spoiled, impetuous heiress and a professor of zoology get involved in looking after a tame leopard.
F — EN
RKO — *THORN EMI*   P
TXC 90 0331 4/TVC 90 0331 2

Bringing Up Baby—The First Year   Gen-Edu '83
Infants
12772   60 mins   C
B, V
A comprehensive companion guide to all mothers, especially first-time mothers, which charts the development of children in the first year of life and gives invaluable help and advice. Written by Penny Junor and presented by Doctor Elizabeth Bryan.
A — I
Unknown — *VideoSpace Ltd*   P

Britain, Kingdom of the Seas   Gen-Edu '8?
National parks and reserves
13578   29 mins   C
V, 3/4U
Certain parts of Britain's coastline from Land's End to the deserted beaches of western Scotland have been photographed from a helicopter to demonstrate the work being done by the National Trust to protect the coastline.
F — ED
Unknown — *TFI Leisure Ltd*   H

Britain's Royal Heritage   Gen-Edu '??
Documentary/Royalty-GB
06349   30 mins   C
V2, B, V

A film portraying the history of Britain's Royal Heritage featuring Royal Homes and Castles. It covers traditional events such as the State Opening of Parliament, The Edinburgh Military Tattoo and many other 'Royal' occasions.
F — EN
Unknown — *Walton Film and Video Ltd*
P
P1152

Britannia Hospital   Fil-Ent '82
Drama/Satire
08527   111 mins   C
B, V
Leonard Rossiter, Graham Crowden, Joan Plowright, Jill Bennett, Marsha Hunt, Malcolm MacDowell, directed by Lindsay Anderson
This tells of the life of an old hospital faced with a threatened strike, demonstrators and an impending Royal visit. Chaos starts with a deranged surgeon endeavouring to create a modern day Frankenstein.
S,A — EN
Unknown — *THORN EMI*   P
TXA 90 1279 4/TVA 90 1279 2

British Open, 1971   Spo-Lei '71
Golf
04494   52 mins   C
B, V
Lee Trevino, Tony Jacklin, Liang Huan Lu
Lee Trevino wins his third major tournament in three weeks at Royal Birkdale, outlasting Tony Jacklin and the Formosan, Liang Huan Lu. 'Mr. Lu' and Trevino provide an unbeatable cross-talk and a slice of golfing drama.
F — EN
Trans World Intl — *Quadrant Video*   H, P
G71

British Open, 1972   Spo-Lei '72
Golf
04493   52 mins   C
B, V
Jack Nicklaus, Lee Trevino, Tony Jacklin
Jack Nicklaus has already won the U.S. Open and Masters. A win at Muirfield would put him only a PGA victory away from being the first man ever to complete the modern grand slam, but Lee Trevino steals Nicklaus' glory with his second consecutive British Open win, after duelling with Tony Jacklin for the title.
F — EN
Trans World Intl — *Quadrant Video*   H, P
G72

British Open, 1973   Spo-Lei '73
Golf
04492   52 mins   C
B, V

(For Explanation of codes, see USE GUIDE and KEY)

PALADIN VIDEO HOME ENTERTAINMENT GUIDE

Arnold Palmer, Gene Sarazen, Jack Nicklaus, Tom Weiskopf, Johnny Miller, Neil Coles
Arnold Palmer returns to Troon. Gene Sarazen scores a hole-in-one at age 71. The golfers battle a rain-soaked course. Jack Nicklaus plays a round of 65, Tom Weiskopf and Johnny Miller play head-to-head for the final 18 holes, and Neil Coles has his finest hour.
F — EN
Trans World Intl — *Quadrant Video*   **H, P**
G73

British Open, 1974   Spo-Lei   '74
Golf
04491   52 mins   C
B, V
Gary Player, Bobby Cole, Peter Oosterhuis, Jack Nicklaus, David Graham
South Africa's Gary Player captures the championship, played at the Royal Latham and St. Anne's. He is challenged by fellow countryman Bobby Cole, Britain's Peter Oosterhuis, and America's Jack Nicklaus. Coverage includes David Graham's hole-in-one.
F — EN
Trans World Intl — *Quadrant Video*   **H, P**
G74

British Open, 1975   Spo-Lei   '75
Golf
04497   52 mins   C
B, V
Narrated by Gordon Jackson and Peter Alliss
This programme contains thrilling coverage of all the challengers including Johnny Miller, Jack Nicklaus, Peter Oosterhuis, Hale Irwin, and Neil Coles. Eventually, America's Tom Watson and Australia's Jack Newton Newton engage in an 18-hold playoff to determine the winner.
F — EN
Trans World Intl — *Quadrant Video*   **H, P**
G75

British Open, 1976   Spo-Lei   '76
Golf
04524   52 mins   C
B, V
Johnny Miller fends off challenges from Jack Nicklaus, Ray Floyd, and Severiano Ballesteros on the final day, to win the British Open championship at Royal Birkdale.
F — EN
Trans World Intl — *Quadrant Video*   **H, P**
G76

British Open, 1977   Spo-Lei   '77
Golf
04523   52 mins   C
B, V
Jack Nicklaus and Masters champion Tom Watson play head-to-head in a virtual match-play situation. A birdie on the final hole provides victory for one.
F — EN
Trans World Intl — *Quadrant Video*   **H, P**
G77

British Open, 1978   Spo-Lei   '78
Golf
04522   52 mins   C
B, V
It's a close contest to the end, between Tom Kit, Ray Floyd, Ben Crenshaw, Simon Owen, and Peter Oosterhuis, but Jack Nicklaus comes brilliantly through as he has done so many times in the past.
F — EN
Trans World Intl — *Quadrant Video*   **H, P**
G78

British Open, 1979   Spo-Lei   '79
Golf
01997   52 mins   C
B, V
At Royal Latham, Severiano Ballesteros misses fairways but makes outstanding recovery shots to outlast Nicklaus, Crenshaw, Watson, and Irwin to become the youngest British Open champion since 1868.
F — EN
Trans World International — *Quadrant Video*
H, P
G79

British Open, 1980   Spo-Lei   '80
Golf
01986   52 mins   C
B, V
After battling poor weather conditions and the challenges of other great golfers, Tom Watson captures his third Open title.
F — EN
Trans World International — *Quadrant Video*
H, P
G80

British Open 1981   Spo-Lei   '81
Golf
07485   52 mins   C
B, V
Narrated by Sean Connery, directed by Phil Pilley
This championship took place at Royal St. George's at Sandwich where James Bond played against Goldfinger. This film is not only narrated by Sean Connery but includes clips from the 007 feature film. This championship,

(For Explanation of codes, see USE GUIDE and KEY)

PALADIN VIDEO HOME ENTERTAINMENT GUIDE

one of the most dramatic yet, includes three holes-in-one, surprisingly high scores, brilliant low ones and an outsider setting a course record.
F — EN
Trans World International — *Quadrant Video* **H, P**
G81

British Open 1982 Spo-Lei '82
Golf
09116   52 mins   C
B, V
This programme continues the series, featuring the 1982 British Open Golf Championship, won once again by Tom Watson.
F — EN
Trans World International — *Quadrant Video* **H, P**
G82

British Open '83 Spo-Lei '84
Golf
12771   60 mins   C
V2, B, V
The 1983 Open Championship was as exciting as any in the 112 year history of the event as right up to the finish there were a dozen man still in contention for the title. The narration is by Frank Windsor and there is a commentary by Peter Alliss.
F — EN
Trans World International — *VideoSpace Ltd* **P**

Broadway Danny Rose Fil-Ent '84
Comedy
13763   82 mins   B/W
B, V
Woody Allen, Mia Farrow, Lou Canova
A group of comedians recount the story, told in flashbacks, of a neurotic Jewish theatrical agent who manages a disastrous group of unbookable vaudeville acts.
BBFC:PG — *S,A — EN*
Unknown — *Rank Video Library* **H, P**
1089D

Broken Promise Fil-Ent '83
Drama
13781   84 mins   C
B, V
Ric Gitlin, Isabel Glasser

This film traces a love affair from its beginnings to the end in a bitter divorce. The backing soundtrack features hits from Carole King, The Monkees, Creedence Clearwater Revival and Graham Parker.
BBFC:15 — *S,A — EN*
Unknown — *Odyssey Video* **H, P**
6428

Broken Sabre, The Fil-Ent '64
Western
07986   79 mins   C
B, V
Chuck Connors, Kamala Devi, Macdonald Carey, John Carradine, Cesar Romero, Wendell Corey, directed by Bernard McEveety
This film tells the story of a man posing as a traitor in a group of Mexican outlaws. His task is to lead them into an ambush, but his mission goes dangerously wrong.
S,A — EN
Andrew J Fenady Prod — *Motion Epics Video Company Ltd* **P**
153

Bronco Billy Fil-Ent '80
Adventure
07857   112 mins   C
B, V
Clint Eastwood, Sondra Locke, directed by Clint Eastwood
This film follows the adventures and rise to fame of a rodeo rider.
BBFC:A — *S,A — EN*
Warner Bros — *Warner Home Video* **P**
WEX 61104/WEV 61104

Bronx Warriors Fil-Ent '83
Adventure
09168   84 mins   C
V
Vic Morrow, Christopher Connolly, Fred Williamson, Mark Gregory
Set in the Bronx during 1987, this film tells of warriors prowling through the streets slaying members of rival gangs, aboard their fantastically outfitted blazing chrome helicopters. The Manhattan National Guardsmen cremate everybody in their path with lethal flamethrowers.
C,A — EN
United Film Distribution — *Entertainment in Video* **H, P**

Bronx Warriors 2-The Battle for Manhattan Fil-Ent '83
Adventure
09901   89 mins   C
B, V

98   (For Explanation of codes, see USE GUIDE and KEY)

PALADIN VIDEO HOME ENTERTAINMENT GUIDE

The Bronx has been bought up in its entirety by a powerful multinational corporation, which sets about constructing 'The City of the Future'. This film continues the story of New York street gangs battling to defend their decaying home.
S,A — EN
United Film Distribution — *Entertainment in Video* **H, P**
EVB 1012/EVV 1012

Brood, The Fil-Ent '79
Horror
06805   93 mins   C
V2, B, V
Oliver Reed, Samantha Eggar, Art Hindle, Cindy Hinds, directed by David Cronenberg
A man begins to question the treatment of his institutionalised wife, but the deeper he prys the more ominous events become.
S,A — EN
New World; Canada — *Intervision Video* **H, P**
A-A 0364

Brotherhood of Death Fil-Ent '76
Drama
09220   82 mins   C
B, V
Roy Jefferson, Mike Thomas
When Kinkaid County comes under the brutal control of the Klu Klux Klan, three young black men form a secret brotherhood and with the violent skills that they learnt in Vietnam, set out to claim vengeance.
C,A — EN
Astral — *Video Form Pictures* **H, P**
MGT 8

Brothers Fil-Ent '7?
Drama
09152   106 mins   C
V
Chard Hayward, Ivar Kants, Margaret Laurence, Jennifer Cluff, Alyson Best
During October 1975 two brothers acting as war photographers become witnesses to the slaughter of an entire native community on the Sunda Islands, Indonesia. After the war the brothers return home, attempting to fit back into their society. However, their divergent reactions to the past leads to both conflict and tragedy.
S,A — EN
Unknown — *Cinema Indoors* **H, P**

Brothers, The Fil-Ent '7?
Martial arts
09867   90 mins   C
B, V

A long-lost son returns to join his brother in the struggle against their power-crazy neighbours. However, the greatest danger they face is the love they share for their enemy's daughter.
S,A — EN
Unknown — *Polygram Video* **H, P**
790 4474/790 4472

Brothers and Sisters Fil-Ent '76
Music-Performance
04401   60 mins   C
B, V
Gladys Knight and the Pips, The Jackson Five, Isaac Hayes, The Temptations, Marvin Gaye, Curtis Mayfield
Gladys Knight and the Pips, The Jackson Five, Isaac Hayes, The Temptations, Marvin Gaye, and Curtis Mayfield highlight this outstanding performance recorded live in Chicago.
F — EN
VCL — *VCL Video Services* **P**

Brothers O'Toole, The Fil-Ent '72
Western/Comedy
06194   91 mins   C
B, V
John Astin, Pat Carrol, Hans Conried, Steve Carlson
When a man is arrested and sentenced to hang for crimes he did not commit, he and his brother know they must track down the real culprit. However, the brothers soon find they have taken on more than they bargained for.
F — EN
Gold Key Entertainments — *VCL Video Services* **P**
X0212

Brubaker Fil-Ent '80
Drama
05651   130 mins   C
V2, B, V
Robert Redford, Yaphet Kott, Jane Alexander, Murray Hamilton, David Keith, Morgan Freeman, Matt Clark, directed by Stuart Rosenburg
Based on true experiences this film is set in a rat infested prison in America's deep south. The staff and governor seem to be bigger crooks than the inmates. A new arrival looks on in horror at the bribery, beatings, rapes and squalor. He takes over as governor and begins reforming under violent opposition. Confessions by an inmate reveal that there are bodies of murdered convicts on the farm. He is told if he stops digging up the bodies there will be no opposition to his reforms; he is forced to make the choice.
A — EN
Twentieth Century Fox — *CBS/Fox Video* **H**

(For Explanation of codes, see USE GUIDE and KEY)

PALADIN VIDEO HOME ENTERTAINMENT GUIDE

Bruce Against Iron Hand Fil-Ent '7?
Adventure/Martial arts
04608   89 mins   C
V2, B, V
Bruce Li, Shao Lung, Bruce Liang
Inspector Bruce Li is called in to investigate the death of two martial arts masters; his only clue is a buddah pendant torn from one of the attackers. Following up this clue he calls on each of the suspects until he faces the final and deadly moment of truth.
C,A — EN
Unknown — *Video Programme Distributors*
P
Inter-Ocean—034

Bruce Davidson's 'Champion's Way With Horses' Spo-Lei '82
Animals
13526   435 mins   C
B, V
7 pgms
This is a seven part series in which each sequence is explained in detail by Bruce Davidson. We see him riding, training and jumping with attention given to the horses' welfare at all times.
1.Dressage 2.Cross Country (part I) 3.Cross Country (part II) 4.Showjumping 5.Gridwork 6.Water Schooling 7.General Horse Management
F — I
Unknown — *TFI Leisure Ltd*   H, P

Bruce Lee Against Supermen Fil-Ent '7?
Adventure/Martial arts
04610   80 mins   C
V2, B, V
Bruce Li
Doctor Ting's secret formula would help to solve the world food crisis. An international organisation attempts to kidnap the Doctor and his daughter but they are rescued by her boyfriend using his kung fu skills. Later the gang imprison all three but the boyfriend sends an S.O.S. to his boss, The Green Hornet, and together they defeat the supermen guards.
C,A — EN
Unknown — *Video Programme Distributors*
P
Inter-Ocean—012

Bruce Lee-Chinese Gods Fil-Ent '??
Cartoons/Martial arts
08633   90 mins   C
V2, B, V
Animated

This film features Bruce Lee, in an animated form, battling against monsters and other enemies, once again to save the day.
S,A — EN
Unknown — *Hokushin Audio Visual Ltd*
P
VM 54

Bruce Lee Story, The Fil-Ent '??
Martial arts/Biographical
06324   80 mins   C
V2, B, V
The story of this film is based on the life story of the King of Kung-fu, whose talent as a martial artist brought him recognition and great wealth in Asia and the West. The film shows the master in action and relates the tale behind his mysterious death.
S,A — EN
Unknown — *World of Video 2000*   H, P
GF501

Bruce Lee: The Man—The Myth Fil-Ent '77
Biographical/Martial arts
02417   91 mins   C
B, V
The life and times of Bruce Lee, from his beginnings in Hong Kong, to his days as a student at the University of Washington, and his eventual move to Los Angeles and his involvement in films.
S,A — EN
Cinema Shares — *Derann Film Services*
H, P
DV 118B/DV 118

Bruce's Fingers Fil-Ent '7?
Adventure/Martial arts
04555   91 mins   C
V2, B, V
Chan Wai Man, Bruce Lee
Huang Hsiao Lung, a disciple of the late superstar Bruce Lee, comes to the United States to inherit a manual on kung fu finger techniques. He is pursued by a kung fu gangster who is after the manual.
C,A — EN
Unknown — *Intervision Video*   H, P
A-AE 0174

Brute, The Fil-Ent '77
Drama
01967   90 mins   C
B, V
Sarah Douglas, Julian Glover, directed by Gerry O'Hara

PALADIN VIDEO HOME ENTERTAINMENT GUIDE

An explicit dramatisation of the problems of marital violence. Diane, a young wife, seeks refuge with friends after she decides to leave her brutal husband.
BBFC:X — A — EN
Trigon Prods — Brent Walker Home Video Ltd
P

Brutes and Savages   Fil-Ent '7?
Documentary/Anthropology
02402   85 mins   C
B, V
Directed by Arthur Davis
This film documents tribal rites, barbaric rituals and nature at its rawest.
A — EN
Unknown — Derann Film Services   H, P
DV 103B/DV 103

Bubblies, Volumes I and II, The   Chi-Juv '7?
Puppets
02221   60 mins   C
V
2 pgms
Two sixty-minute programmes available individually featuring the puppet characters who live in the country village of Bubbledon and perform pop songs.
M — EN
Unknown — JVC   P
PRT 7; PRT 23

Buck Rogers in the 25th Century   Fil-Ent '79
Science fiction/Adventure
05335   89 mins   C
B, V
Gil Gerard, Pamela Hensley, Erin Gray, Tim O'Connor, Henry Silva, directed by Daniel Haller
This film chronicles the futuristic adventures of one of the world's 'superheros.' Buck Rogers, pilot of a spacecraft, is hurtled through space at an unbelievable speed into the 25th century. In this future world of glamour and danger he encounters Draconian spaceships, a princess from another star system, her evil prime minister and a vast city protected by a magnetic dome.
S,A — EN
Universal — CIC Video   H, P
BEA1015/VHA1015

Buckstone County Prison   Fil-Ent '??
Adventure
09014   90 mins   C
V2, B, V
Earl Owensby
Set in North Carolina, this film, based on true events, tells the story of an Indian half-breed. He is sometimes hired by the prison authorities to track down escaped prisoners. However, being hated by the prisoners and the sheriff's deputy, he is arrested and placed amongst the men that hate him most. When a prison-break occurs the authorities grant him a reprieve to help recapture the prisoners. Suspicious of a trap, he prepares for anything.
S,A — EN
Unknown — Intervision Video   H, P
AA 0472

Bud and Lou   Fil-Ent '78
Biographical/Comedy
09212   100 mins   C
B, V
Harvey Korman, Buddy Hackett, Michele Lee, Robert Reed, Arte Johnson, directed by Robert C. Thompson
This is a portrayal of the famous comedy team Abbot and Costello. Despite the laughs and antics, the narrative reveals some of the sadness that went with their success.
F — EN
Bob Banner — Video Form Pictures   H, P
MGD 9

Buddy Greco Show, The   Fil-Ent '7?
Variety
04372   60 mins   C
B, V, PH17, 3/4U
Buddy Greco, Frankie Avalon, Susan Barrett
A variety show with Buddy Greco, Frankie Avalon, and Susan Barrett.
F — EN
Unknown — Vidpics International   P

Buddy Holly Story, The   Fil-Ent '78
Biographical/Music
02113   110 mins   C
V2, B, V
Gary Busey, Don Stroud, Charles Martin Smith
The film biography of a musical genius, this is the reconstructed story of Buddy's early triumphs and untimely death.
BBFC:A — F — EN
Columbia — Hokushin Audio Visual Ltd
P
VM-24

Buddy System, The   Fil-Ent '82
Drama
13264   113 mins   C
B, V
Richard Dreyfuss, Susan Sarandon, Wil Wheaton, Nancy Allen, directed by Glenn Jordan

---

(For Explanation of codes, see USE GUIDE and KEY)   101

PALADIN VIDEO HOME ENTERTAINMENT GUIDE

A single mother strives to bring up her son against a background of genteel poverty, and through him meets the school security guard and a friendship blossoms betweeen the three.
BBFC:PG — S,A — EN
Alain Chammas — CBS/Fox Video   P
1316

Buffalo Bill and the Indians   Fil-Ent '76
Comedy/Western
07464   118 mins   C
B, V
Paul Newman, Burt Lancaster, Geraldine Chaplin, Frank Kaquitts, Will Sampson, directed by Robert Altman
Subtitled 'Sitting Bull's History Lesson' this satirical comedy shows how the history of the Wild West has been re-written for the sake of popular appeal. It follows the capers of a Wild West Show in which all whites are 'goodies' and all redskins 'baddies,' until Sitting Bull, released from prison, appears to play himself in a re-enactment of Custer's Last Stand.
Berlin Film Festival '76: Golden Bear Award.
BBFC:A — S,A — EN
United Artists — THORN EMI   P
TXB 90 0687 4/TVB 90 0687 2

Bug   Fil-Ent '75
Drama/Horror
10102   95 mins   C
B, V
Bradford Dillman, directed by Jeannot Szwarc
After an earth tremor near a small township, large members of cockroach-like creatures begin to emerge. They begin to attack and kill the local inhabitants. The biology professor from the nearby college decides to find out all about these creatures, with frightening consequences.
BBFC:18 — C,A — EN
Universal — CIC Video   H, P
BEL 2061/VHL 2061

Bugs Bunny/Road Runner Movie, The   Fil-Ent '79
Cartoons
06032   86 mins   C
B, V
Animated, directed by Chuck Jones
This is a compilation of Warner Brothers cartoons featuring Bugs Bunny, Daffy Duck, Elmer Fudd, the Road Runner, Wile E. Coyote, Porky Pig and Pepe Le Pew. It contains some all new animated sequences.
BBFC:U — F — EN
Warner Bros — Warner Home Video   P
WEX1003/WEV1003

Bugsy Malone   Fil-Ent '77
Musical-Drama
01899   93 mins   C
B, V, LV
Scott Baio, Florrie Dugger, Jodie Foster, John Cassisi, directed by Alan Parker
New York 1929: The custard pies fly in this takeoff on gangster films with a cast made up entirely of chidren, with musical numbers as well.
BBFC:U — M,A — EN
Paramount — Rank Video Library   H, P
7000

Bulldog Breed/The Square Peg, The   Fil-Ent '58
Comedy
12757   183 mins   B/W
B, V
Norman Wisdom
Two of Norman Wisdom's most popular films are contained on this cassette. In the first, he plays the part of a love-lorn failure who becomes a sailor and in the second he is a clumsy road-mender who ends up in the army.
BBFC:U — F — EN
Lopert Pictures — Rank Video Library   H, P
1079 S

Bulldog Drummond Escapes   Fil-Ent '37
Adventure
07640   65 mins   B/W
B, V
Ray Milland, Guy Standing, Heather Angel, Reginald Denny, Porter Hall, directed by James Hogan
The intrepid hero, Bulldog Drummond, returns to England from abroad piloting his own aircraft. Due to dense fog he has to make a forced landing; a chance encounter leads him to the sinister Greystone Manor. There he succeeds in unmasking an unscrupulous gang of counterfeiters who had taken over the Manor.
F — EN
Paramount — VCL Video Services   P
0233G

Bullet for the General   Fil-Ent '??
Western/Drama
05552   118 mins   C
V2, B, V
Klaus Kinski, Gian Maria Volante, Lou Castel, directed by Damiano Damiani

PALADIN VIDEO HOME ENTERTAINMENT GUIDE

A mysterious stranger tries to infiltrate a gang to gain access to the hideout of a revolutionary General. The stranger is part of a sinister plan that explodes with vicious double-crossings, cruelty and violence.
BBFC:X — A — EN
Unknown — *Videomedia*   **P**
PVM 6105/BVM 6105/HVM 6105

Bullitt   Fil-Ent '68
Crime-Drama
06015   109 mins   C
B, V
Steve McQueen, Robert Vaughn, Jacqueline Bisset, Don Gordon, Robert Duvall, Simon Oakland, Norman Fell, directed by Peter Yates
A hoodlum on the run is pursued by members of an underworld syndicate whom he defrauded. He is promised protection by a politician in return for testifying to a sub-committee. Detective Bullitt is assigned to protect him but gunmen gain access and fatally wound the hoodlum. Bullitt is now a target and while investigating the case he discovers the dead man was in fact a stand-in and the real hoodlum is still free.
BBFC:AA — S,A — EN
Warner Bros; Seven Arts — *Warner Home Video*   **P**
WEX1029/WEV1029

Bullshot   Fil-Ent '81
Comedy
12526   84 mins   C
B, V
Alan Sherman, Diz White, Ron House, Frances Tomelty, Billy Connolly, Mel Smith, directed by Dick Clement
Set in the 1930's this film has everything from a stolen formula, a mad professor, a hapless heroine, a devilish Hun, to last but not least, a First World War air-ace.
BBFC:PG — F — EN
Ian La Frenais — *THORN EMI*   **P**
TXA 90 21974/TVA 90 21972

Bundle of Joy/Montana Belle   Fil-Ent '5?
Musical-Drama/Western
09111   174 mins   C
B, V
Debbie Reynolds, Eddie Fisher, Adolphe Menjou, Tommy Noonan, Nita Talbot, Melville Cooper, Bill Goodwin, directed by Norman Taurog; Jane Russell, Scott Brady, George Brent
This tape contains two films on one cassette. 'Bundle of Joy'(1956, colour, 95 mins.) tells the story of a newly fired salesgirl who saves an abandoned baby, and is mistaken to be the child's mother. Further complications arise when her ex-boss is suspected of being the father. 'Montana Belle' (1952, black and white, 79 mins.) tells of the notorious Belle Star, the outlaw, who joins forces with the even more notorious Dalton Gang.
S,A — EN
U-I; RKO — *Kingston Video*   **H, P**
KV59

Bunker, The   Fil-Ent '80
War-Drama
09177   154 mins   C
B, V
Anthony Hopkins, Richard Jordan, Michael Lonsdale, Cliff Gorman, Susan Blakely, directed by George Schaefer
This film recreates the events that took place in and around Adolph Hitler's bunker during the final harrowing days of the collapse of the Third Reich. It is based on the book by James P. O'Donnell.
S,A — EN
Time-Life TV; Societe Francaise de Production et de Creation Audiovisuelles — *Video Form Pictures*   **H, P**
MGS 2

Burglars, The   Fil-Ent '71
Drama/Adventure
13079   110 mins   C
B, V
Omar Shariff, Dyan Cannon, Jean-Paul Belmondo, directed by Henri Verneuil
A gang of thieves get away with a priceless collection of emeralds but an action packed chase gets under way when they find their ship held in port by the local police inspector.
C,A — EN
Henri Verneuil — *RCA/Columbia Pictures Video UK*   **H, P**
10180

Burning, The   Fil-Ent '82
Horror
08469   87 mins   C
B, V
Jean Ubaud, Michael Cohl, Corky Burger, Brian Mathews, Leah Ayres, Brian Backer, Larry Joshua, Lou David, directed by Tony Maylam
In an American Summer camp, a group of teenagers pull an horrific trick on the bad-tempered caretaker. This has unexpected but disastrous results. Years later when they return to a nearby camp, they become the victims of brutal and sinister attacks. Their caretaker is back to claim revenge.
BBFC:X — A — EN
Miramax Production — *THORN EMI*   **P**
TXA 90 0836 4/TVA 90 0836 2

(For Explanation of codes, see USE GUIDE and KEY)

PALADIN VIDEO HOME ENTERTAINMENT GUIDE

Bury Me An Angel   Fil-Ent '81
Drama
12817   72 mins   C
B, V

Dixie Peabody, Terry Mace, Clyde Ventura, directed by Barbara Peters

A girl vows vengeance on a biker who has killed her boyfriend at a wild party and sets off on a bike with a sawn-off shotgun to gun him down.
BBFC:PG — *C,A* — *EN*
Paul Norbert — *VCL Video Services*   P
670140/670150

Bury Them Deep   Fil-Ent '83
Western
12844   93 mins   C
V2, B, V

Craig Hill, Ken Wood, Jose Greci

A stagecoach laden with gold is stolen by a gang of outlaws and the Government charges a man to bring them to justice.
BBFC:15 — *S,A* — *EN*
Unknown — *Video Programme Distributors*
P
VPD 235

Bus Stop   Fil-Ent '56
Comedy/Romance
05643   90 mins   C
B, V

Marilyn Monroe, Arthur O'Connell, Hope Lange, Don Murray, Hans Conreid, Betty Field, directed by Joshua Logan

An unlikely selection of travelers arrive at some truths about themselves while snowed in at an Arizona bus stop. A sexy entertainer is abducted by a exuberant Montana cowboy. Based on the play by William Inge.
S,A — *EN*
Twentieth Century Fox — *CBS/Fox Video*
P
3A-137

Bushido Blade, The   Fil-Ent '80
Adventure/Suspense
08458   103 mins   C
B, V

Richard Boone, Sonny Chiba, Frank Converse, Laura Gemser, James Earl Jones, Mako, Timothy Murphy, Michael Starr, Tetsura Tamba, directed by Tom Kotani

This film is set in 19th-century Japan. The story follows the quest by the American Captain Hawk to rescue the sacred Bushido Blade. This was stolen by a group of samurai warriors. It tells of the courage of Hawk and his men as they discover the mysterious Japanese world, and their love as they discover the beautiful samurai women.
BBFC:AA — *C,A* — *EN*
Arthur Rankin Jr. — *THORN EMI*   P
TXA 90 0963 4/TVA 90 0963 2

Busting   Fil-Ent '73
Comedy
12504   89 mins   C
B, V

Elliot Gould, Robert Blake, Allen Garfield, directed by Peter Hyams

Two Los Angeles Vice Squad Officers find themselves up against their corrupt superiors when they try and bring a crime boss to justice.
BBFC:18 — *A* — *EN*
Irwin Winkler; Robert Chartoff — *Warner Home Video*   P
99365

Butch and Sundance: The   Fil-Ent '79
Early Days
Western
07704   107 mins   C
V2, B, V

Tom Berenger, William Katt, Jill Eikenberry, Jeff Bridges, Authur Hill, John Schuck, directed by Richard Lester

This 'prequel' relates the events that befell the outlaws before 'Butch Cassidy and The Sundance Kid.' The story follows Butch from his release from Laramie jail and his uneasy partnership with Sundance through their early hold-ups and robberies, including a mercy dash through the snow with a consignment of vaccine for an isolated mine.
S,A — *EN*
Twentieth Century Fox — *CBS/Fox Video*
P
1117

Butch Cassidy and the   Fil-Ent '69
Sundance Kid
Western
01754   110 mins   C
V2, B, V, LV

Paul Newman, Robert Redford, Katherine Ross

A couple of legendary outlaws at the turn of the century roam about the countryside with a beautiful, willing ex-schoolteacher.
Academy Awards '69: Best Song ('Raindrops Keep Falling on My Head').
BBFC:AA — *S,A* — *EN*
20th Century Fox — *CBS/Fox Video*   P
3A-037

(For Explanation of codes, see USE GUIDE and KEY)

PALADIN VIDEO HOME ENTERTAINMENT GUIDE

Butcher, The Fil-Ent '70
Mystery
08810   98 mins   C
B, V
Directed by Claude Chabrol
This is a story about an apparently unprovoked spate of brutal murders of young girls in the peaceful French countryside. The film follows the various attempts to try to solve them.
A — EN
Cinerama Releasing — *VCL Video Services*   P
P306D

Butterflies Fil-Ent '7?
Comedy-Drama
09408   ? mins   C
V2, B, V
Wendy Craig, Geoffrey Palmer
Carla Lane's exquisite comedy of romance.
F — EN
BBC — *BBC Video*   H, P
BBCV 7010

Butterfly Fil-Ent '82
Drama/Suspense
08462   104 mins   C
B, V
Stacy Keach, Orson Welles, Edward ALbert, James Franciscus, Lois Nettleton, Stuart Whitman, Pia Zadora, directed Matt Cimber
Set in the Arizona-Nevada desert in the 1930's this film contains murder, incest and revenge. A young girl turns up a silver mine, and surprises her long lost father. Eventually they both become lovers; however, somebody has been watching them. It ends in a courtroom, with Orson Welles as the Judge. It is based on the novel by James M. Cain.
Golden Globe Awards '82: Newcomer of the Year (Zadora).   BBFC:X — A — EN
Analysis Films — *THORN EMI*   P
TXA 90 0981 4/VA 90 0981 2

Butterfly Ball, The Fil-Ent '76
Fantasy/Musical
07654   85 mins   C
B, V
Twiggy, David Coverdale, Ian Gillan, narrated by Vincent Price
Based on the classic 19th Century novel, this musical journey was filmed at the Albert Hall and the Roman Ruins in Windsor Great Park. This combination of live action, animation and music features music by Roger Glover and animation by Halas and Batchelor.
F — EN
Unknown — *VCL Video Services*   P
P190D

By Design Fil-Ent '82
Comedy
12591   92 mins   C
V2, B, V
Patty Duke Astin, Saul Rubinek, Sara Botsford, directed by Claude Jutra
Two ladies with a very unusual relationship are blissfully happy until one finds out she has aspirations to motherhood and then the search is on for a surrogate father.
BBFC:18 — A — EN
Beryl Fox; Werner Aellen — *Intervision Video*
H, P
6563

By the Sea/The Picnic Fil-Ent '7?
Comedy
12725   80 mins   C
B, V
Ronnie Barker, Ronnie Corbett
This cassette features 'The Two Ronnies' in two hilarious 'silent' films. Ronnie Barker plays a crusty old general and Ronnie Corbett his silly son in the adventures of a faimly of English eccentrics.
F — EN
Michael Hurll; Terry Hughes — *BBC Video*
H, P
7024

C

Cabaret Fil-Ent '72
Musical
05144   120 mins   C
B, V, LV
Liza Minelli, Helmut Griem, Fritz Wepper, Michael York, Joel Grey, Marisa Berenson
Set in pre-war Berlin, 'Cabaret' evokes the desperation and decadence of a Germany mesmerized by the remorseless rise of the Nazis.
Academy Awards '72: Best Actress: (Minelli); Best Supporting Actor (Grey); Best Director (Fosse); Best Art Direction.
BBFC:X — A — EN
Allied Artists; ABC Pictures Corp — *Rank Video Library*   H, P
7009

Cabinet of Dr. Caligari, The Fil-Ent '20
Horror
08550   44 mins   B/W
b, V

(For Explanation of codes, see USE GUIDE and KEY)

PALADIN VIDEO HOME ENTERTAINMENT GUIDE

Werner Krauss, Conrad Veidt, Lil Dagover, Friedrich Feher, Hans Von Twardowski, directed by Robert Wiene
This film set in the Middle Ages tells the eerie horror story of a murderous sleepwalker who prowls the streets at night in search of his victims. Dr. Caligari is believed to be the investigator of the crimes but is later found to be the director of a mental asylum. The film has many meanings.
C,A — EN
Samuel Goldwyn — *THORN EMI*   **P**
TXE 90 08264/TVE 90 08262

Cabo Blanco   Fil-Ent '79
Mystery/Adventure
07384   90 mins   C
V2, B, V
Charles Bronson, Dominique Sandra, Fernando Rey, Jason Robards, J. Lee Thompson, Simon MacCorkindale, Camilla Sparv, Dennis Miller, Clifton James, Gilbert Roland, directed by J. Lee Thompson
This film is set just after the war in a tiny fishing village lost on the sun-beaten coast of Peru where two men have gone to live, seeking oblivion after the horrors of the war. The sudden arrival of a British scientific research ship in the deserted bay disturbs the village calm and its mysterious activities, coupled with the arrival by bus of a beautiful French woman, stirs up hidden secrets and muted hatreds.
S,A — EN
Unknown — *Guild Home Video*   **H, P, E**

Cactus Flower   Fil-Ent '69
Comedy
09277   103 mins   C
B, V
Walter Matthau, Ingrid Bergman, Goldie Hawn, Jack Weston, Rick Lenz, Vito Scotti, Irene Hervey, directed by Gene Saks
An easy-going bachelor dentist has trouble when his romantic set-up begins to crumble. His dizzy blond mistress attempts suicide when he tells her he has a wife and two children. He then asks her to marry him but there are still some unforeseen twists and surprises.
Academy Awards '69: Best Supporting Actress (Hawn).   S,A — EN
Columbia — *RCA/Columbia Pictures Video UK*
H, P

Caddie   Fil-Ent '76
Drama
06962   107 mins   C
B, V
Helen Morse, Jack Thompson, directed by Donald Crombie
This is a true story written by a woman who chose never to reveal her name to the public. Set during the years 1925 to 1932, the film opens with Caddie learning that her husband is having an affair. She confronts him and then does the unthinkable, for that time, and leaves him, taking the children. Her first night is spent in a flea-infested room; she eventually overcomes her problems and begins to find friendships that will last.
BBFC:A — S,A — EN
Anthony Buckley Production — *Home Video Merchandisers*   **H, P**
024

Caddyshack   Fil-Ent '80
Comedy
06013   95 mins   C
B, V
Chevy Chase, Rodney Dangerfield, Ted Knight, Michael O'Keefe, Bill Murray, Sarah Holcomb, Scott Colomby, Cindy Morgan, directed by Harold Ramis
Set in a Country Club, a high school senior is determined to win a special scholarship as the best caddy. He requires the support of the arrogant Judge who runs the club but has an ally in a playboy member; others he encounters on his quest are a property developer, an Irish waitress who needs a husband to stay in the country and a sexy debutante.
BBFC:AA — S,A — EN
Warner Bros; Orion Pictures — *Warner Home Video*   **P**
WEX2005/WEV2005

Caesar and Cleopatra   Fil-Ent '46
Drama
08071   121 mins   C
B, V
Vivien Leigh, Claude Rains, Stewart Granger, Jean Simmonds
This film is George Bernard Shaw's version of the teen-age Egyptian, Cleopatra, who conquered Caesar after having learnt the intrigues of politics and romance.
BBFC:A — S,A — EN
Rank — *Rank Video Library*   **H, P**
0094 C

Cage Aux Folles, La   Fil-Ent '79
Comedy
13203   91 mins   C
B, V
Ugo Tognazzi, Michel Serrault, directed by Edouard Molinaro
A 'gay' couple who have lived together for twenty years have problems when the son of one of them wants to marry the daughter of a cabinet-minister who is eagerly looking forward to meeting the parents.
BBFC:AA — C,A — EN
United Artists — *Warner Home Video*   **P**
99235

PALADIN VIDEO HOME ENTERTAINMENT GUIDE

Caged Heat — Fll-Ent '??
Drama
05487 92 mins C
V2, B, V
Junita Brown, Barbara Steel, Roberta Collins, Erica Gavin, Rainbeaux Smith, Ella Reid
This film is set in a woman's prison at Connorville and exposes scenes of rape, riot, murder and revenge.
BBFC:X — *A* — *EN*
Unknown — *Iver Film Services* P
152

Cahill — Fll-Ent '72
Adventure/Western
13026 97 mins C
B, V
John Wayne, George Kennedy, Neville Brand, Gary Grimes, directed by Andrew V. McLaglen
The story revolves around a U.S. Marshal whose two teenage sons become involved in a bank robbery in which the town sheriff and his deputy are gunned down.
BBFC:AA — *C,A* — *EN*
Warner Bros — *Warner Home Video* P
61281

Calculus Affair, The — Chl-Juv '7?
Cartoons/Adventure
02280 60 mins C
V
Animated
Professor Calculus and his latest invention are kidnapped by Bordurians and taken to the Fortress of Bakhine. Tin Tin, Snowy, and Captain Haddock are soon on this trail.
M — *EN*
Unknown — *JVC* P
PRT 39

Calibre 9 — Fll-Ent '??
Crime-Drama
06087 100 mins C
V2, B, V
Barbara Bouchet, Philippe Leroy, Gastone Moschin
A criminal is released from prison after three years. He is accused of stealing 300,000 dollars from a gang of currency smugglers who desperately want the money back, they will stop at nothing to get it.
S,A — *EN*
Unknown — *Video Programme Distributors* P
Cinehollywood—V110

California Dolls, The — Fll-Ent '81
Drama
08680 113 mins C
B, V
Peter Falk, Vicki Frederick, Laurene Landon, directed by Robert Aldrich
This tells the story of two female wrestlers and their manager whose dream is to make it to the top. The unlikely trio travel around the highways in a beat-up car going from one arena to the next, before they get their chance at the big time. It is the tag-team crown they are after where there are no holds barred.
BBFC:X — *A* — *EN*
Aldrich Company — *MGM/UA Home Video* P
UMB 10112/UMV 10112

California Girls — Fll-Ent '82
Drama
08830 ? mins C
B, V
Al Music, Mary McKinley, Alicia Allen, Lantz Douglas, Barbara Parks, directed by William Webb
To advertise an ailing radio station, a disc jockey invents a competition. Three of California's most gorgeous girls set out to win the cash prize. This film features music by Queen, 10cc, The Police, Kool and the Gang and Blondie.
S,A — *EN*
Unknown — *VCL Video Services* P

California Gold Rush — Fll-Ent '79
Western
08038 96 mins C
B, V
John Denver
This is a film adaptation of Bret Harte's experiences of gold fever in the pioneering West.
BBFC:U — *F* — *EN*
Sunn Classic — *Rank Video Library* H, P
0055 C

Calimero — Chl-Juv '7?
Fantasy/Cartoons
04684 54 mins C
B, V
Animated
13 original cartoon stories. Calimero's impulsive and generous gestures inevitably have disastrous consequences for his friends. His innocent actions, all in good faith, always seem to have unexpected results. Luckily, his friends understand and he usually escapes without punishment.
P,S,I — *EN*
Spectrum — *Polygram Video* P

Calimero and the Wonderful Summer — Chl-Juv '80
Cartoons
05850 55 mins C

(For Explanation of codes, see USE GUIDE and KEY)

107

PALADIN VIDEO HOME ENTERTAINMENT GUIDE

B, V
Animated
This cassette presents thirteen original cartoons featuring Calimero, a little black bird, whose innocent actions done in good faith have disastrous consequences for his friends. Luckily his friends understand and he usually escapes punishment.
PS,M — EN
Inter Cartoon Rever — *Polygram Video*
P
40133/20133

Call Him Mr Shatter   Fil-Ent '74
Adventure/Martial arts
12262   86 mins   C
V2, B, V
Stuart Whitman, Peter Cushing
A contract killer assassinates the head of an African State and has to engage the help of a Kung Fu expert for his own protection.
BBFC:PG — *S,A* — *EN*
Avco Embassy; Hammer Films — *Embassy Home Entertainment*   **P**
2104

Call It Murder   Fil-Ent '34
Crime-Drama
07639   70 mins   B/W
B, V
Humphrey Bogart, Sidney Fox, O. P. Heggie, Henry Hull, Helen Flint, directed by Chester Erskine
The press hold a foreman of a jury responsible for sentencing a woman to death. She killed a man who had betrayed her. When being questioned by the foreman she admitted that she took the man's money after killing him. The foreman insists his verdict would be the same even if someone he loved was involved. However, he finds himself in a moral dilemma when his daughter gets on the wrong side of the law.
F — EN
United International — *VCL Video Services*
P
0237G

Call of the Wild   Fil-Ent '72
Adventure
04203   100 mins   C
B, V
Charlton Heston, Michelle Mercier, Raymond Harmstorf
Remake of the immortal classic novel by Jack London.
BBFC:U — *F — EN*
Intercontinental Releasing Corp — *Guild Home Video*   **H, P**

Call of the Wild, The   Chi-Juv '84
Cartoons
12018   68 mins   C
B, V
Animated
Taken from the book by Jack London, this tells the story of a house dog who longs for the wilderness and his native roots. He still enjoys human company and finds in Alaska he achieves both aims.
BBFC:U — *F — EN*
Unknown — *Precision Video Ltd*   **P**
BTOPV 1150/VTOPV 1150

Call to Glory   Fil-Ent '84
Drama
13615   94 mins   C
B, V
Craig T. Nelson, Cindy Pickett, Elisabeth Shue, David Hollander
This film follows the lives of a U.S. Air Force family in the sixties at a particularly trying time during the Cuban missile crisis. The action is interwoven with actual news footage from these years.
BBFC:PG — *S,A — EN*
Paramount — *CIC Video*   **H, P**
2129

Camberwick Green   Chi-Juv '84
Cartoons
13088   60 mins   C
B, V
Animated
Four delightful adventures with the characters of Camberwick Green including Windy Miller, Mr. Crockett, Peter Hazel and Dr. Mopp.
PS,I — EN
Unknown — *Longman Video*   **P**
5024

Camel—Pressure Points   Fil-Ent '84
Music video
13131   80 mins   C
B, V
This programme features fourteen of Camel's songs including 'Waltzing Frauleins,' 'West Berlin,' 'Lady Fantasy' and 'Cloak and Dagger Man.' It is recorded in stereo hi-fi.
F — EN
Unknown — *Polygram Video*   **P**
041 0584/041 0582

Camelot   Fil-Ent '67
Drama/Musical
07858   166 mins   C
B, V
Richard Harris, Vanessa Redgrave, Franco Nero, David Hemmings, Lionel Jeffries, directed by Joshua Logan

(For Explanation of codes, see USE GUIDE and KEY)

PALADIN VIDEO HOME ENTERTAINMENT GUIDE

All is well at the court of King Arthur until Lancelot arrives and falls in love with Queen Guinevere. She returns the love and the King is forced to fight Lancelot. The system of the Round Table breaks down as the harmony at Camelot is devastated.
BBFC:U — F — EN
Warner Bros — *Warner Home Video*   **P**
WEX 61084/WEV 61084

Can-Can   Fil-Ent '60
Musical
01753   131 mins   C
B, V
Frank Sinatra, Shirley MacLaine, Maurice Chevalier, Louis Jourdan, Juliet Prowse
1890's: Dance hall owner is constantly being raided for performing the illegal Can-Can. Based on Abe Burrows' play. Music by Cole Porter.
F — EN
20th Century Fox — *CBS/Fox Video*   **P**
4A-048

Can I Do It...Till I Need Glasses?   Fil-Ent '80
Comedy
08886   73 mins   C
V2, B, V
Roger Behr, Robin Williams, Debra Klose, Moose Carlson, Walter Olkewicz
This suggestive comedy features outrageous, risqe humour.
BBFC:X — A — EN
Mike Callie — *Video Programme Distributors*   **P**
Media 143

Can She Bake A Cherry Pie?   Fil-Ent '84
Comedy
12951   90 mins   C
B, V
Karen Black, Michael Emil
When a health nut and a distraught, lonely divorcee meet up in New York it makes for a very odd romance.
A — EN
Unknown — *Virgin Video*   **H, P**
VVA 032

Canadian Pacific   Fil-Ent '49
Adventure
01070   81 mins   B/W
V2, B, V
Randolph Scott
Adventure film set in the Canadian Rockies about the coming of the railroad.
M,A — EN
Twentieth Century Fox — *Intervision Video*
H, P
A-A 0148

Candid Camera Classics—Volume 1   Fil-Ent '7?
Comedy
08583   60 mins   C
B, V
Introduced by Peter Dulay, Jonathan Routh
This series is a compilation of moments from the long running television series when the Candid Camera team subjected the unwitting public to various unlikely and crazy situations, secretly filming their reactions with a hidden camera. Volume One features the following extracts: Car Without an Engine, Bowling Alley, Inexperienced Driver, Magnetic Counter, The Birdman, Man in the Middle, Donut Machine, Living Head, Pickpocket, Goldfish, Cable Pulling, Rising Telephone Box, Megaphone, Registry Office.
F — EN
Peter Dulay; Jonathan Routh — *Holiday Brothers Ltd*   **P**

Candid Camera Classics—Volume 2   Fil-Ent '7?
Comedy
08584   60 mins   C
B, V
Introduced by Peter Dulay, Jonathan Routh
This tape, the second in the series, is a further compilation of moments from the long running television series. It includes the following extracts: Holding Up Walls, Sheila's Broom, Genie, Stuck Cup, Thirsty Tulip, Windscreen, Crockery Smashing, Ping Pong Balls, Armchair Antics, Arthur's Alibi, Ladies and Gents, Bil's Three Legs, Wrong Floor, Irresistible Perfume, Radio Robots, Ballet Lessons, Smoking Stove, Follow Me.
F — EN
Peter Dulay; Jonathan Routh — *Holiday Brothers Ltd*   **P**

Candid Camera Classics—Volume 3   Fil-Ent '7?
Comedy
08585   60 mins   C
B, V
Introduced by Peter Dulay and Jonathan Routh
This tape, the third in the series, is a further compilation of moments from the long running television series. It includes the following extracts: Who are You?, Shaking Hands, Dirty Laundry, Cracked Mirror, Flea Circus, Hand in Pillar Box, Typewriter Carriage, Fixed

PALADIN VIDEO HOME ENTERTAINMENT GUIDE

Telephones, Pneumatic Drills, Scandal, Supermarket Dance, Late Home Taxi, Wet Paint, Exposed, Wipe Your Feet, Stuck Phone, Threatening Letter, Naked Secretary, Pavement Offices.
F — EN

Peter Dulay; Jonathan Routh — *Holiday Brothers Ltd* **P**

Candid Camera Classics—Volume 4   Fil-Ent '7?
Comedy
08586   60 mins   C
B, V

Introduced by Peter Dulay, and Jonathan Routh
This tape, the fourth in the series, is a further compilation of moments from the long running television series. It includes the following extracts: Pavement Cafe, Ring for Service, Newspaper Censor, Topless Counter, Skull Phone, Phonebox in Drive, National Car Parking, Twopence for a Cuppa, The Interpreter, Flag Day, Nervous Learner Driver, Gangle Pin, Bournemouth Landlady.
F — EN

Peter Dulay; Jonathan Routh — *Holiday Brothers Ltd* **P**

Candid Camera Classics—Volume 5   Fil-Ent '7?
Comedy
08587   60 mins   C
B, V

Introduced by Peter Dulay and Jonathan Routh
This tape, the fifth in the series, is a further compilation of moments from the long running television series. It includes the following extracts: Soda Syphon, Food Redistribution, Snookered, Exploding Jugs, Marty Wildecats, Invisible Man, Celebrity, Geiger Counter, Change of Name, Goat Milk, Long and Short Shelves, Twin Telephone Boxes.
F — EN

Peter Dulay; Jonathan Routh — *Holiday Brothers Ltd* **P**

Candidate, The   Fil-Ent '72
Drama
06030   106 mins   C
B, V

Robert Redford, Peter Boyld, Don Porter, Allen Garfield, Melvyn Douglas, directed by Michael Ritchie
This film takes a behind the scenes look at a Californian senatorial race between a respectable middle-aged incumbent and a young aggressive lawyer who tries to beat the system with his ideals.

Academy Awards '72: Best Story and Best Screenplay. BBFC:A — *S,A — EN*
Warner Bros; Redford-Ritchie Prod — *Warner Home Video* **P**
WEX1022/WEV1022

Candle for the Devil, A   Fil-Ent '75
Horror
02582   84 mins   C
V2, B, V

Two sisters manage a quaint little hotel in a quiet Spanish village. It sounds like a lovely place to stay, but you can only ring for 'doom service.'
BBFC:X — *A — EN*
Tigon — *Videomedia* **P**

Candleshoe   Fil-Ent '77
Comedy/Adventure
12583   101 mins   C
B, V

David Niven, Jodie Foster, Helen Hayes
A rowdy young street urchin from Los Angeles tries to con an uppercrust English matron into believing she is her long-lost granddaughter.
F — EN
Walt Disney Productions — *Rank Video Library*
H
078

Candy Man, The   Fil-Ent '69
Suspense/Crime-Drama
07490   93 mins   C
B, V

George Sanders, Leslie Parrish, directed by Herbert J. Leder
A young film star arrives in Mexico with an entourage including her daughter. The daughter is kidnapped by a grief-crazed woman whose own child has just died. An LSD dealer decides that this is an easy way to make the 50,000 he needs and through trickery gets a ransom paid. However, things are not so simple when the police become involved and return the child to her mother.
S,A — EN
Sagittarius Productions — *Quadrant Video*
H, P
FF9

Candy Stripe Nurses   Fil-Ent '82
Comedy
09312   76 mins   C
B, V

Candice Rialson, Robin Mattson, Kimberly Hyde

PALADIN VIDEO HOME ENTERTAINMENT GUIDE

Three teenage girls enroll as volunteer nurses at their local hospital. Hilarious adventures ensue, with one girl posing as a sex therapist who practices her 'talents' in the linen cupboard.
BBFC:X — A — EN
Unknown — THORN EMI   P
TXB 90 0969 4/TVB 90 0969 2

Cannibal　　　　　　　　　　　Fil-Ent '77
Horror/Drama
05699　　88 mins　　C
V2, B, V
Massimo Foschi, Me Mehay, directed by Reggero Deodati
This film is based on a terrifying but true experience. A party of three men and a woman arrive in the Philippines on an oil exploration trip. At a deserted base they discover evidence of cannibalism, during the next twenty four hours they lose one of the party and after glimpsing cannibals eating limbs they flee under the threat of capture. The only wafy to escape is to join them.
BBFC:X — A — EN
Unknown — *Derann Film Services*　　H, P
DV133P/DV133B/DV133

Cannibal Ferox　　　　　　　　Fil-Ent '??
Horror
08864　　86 mins　　C
V2, B, V
John Morghen, Brian Redford
Whilst looking for emeralds in the South American jungle, the prospectors discover a lost tribe. However, the natives reveal their primitive cannibal instincts.
BBFC:18 — A — EN
Unknown — *Video Programme Distributors*
P
Replay 1016

Cannibal Man, The　　　　　　Fil-Ent '??
Horror
06790　　98 mins　　C
V2, B, V
Vincente Parra, Emma Cohen
A man who works in a canning plant attached to a slaughter house kills a taxi driver in self-defense, starting a series of horrid crimes committed out of fear.
C,A — EN
Jose Truchado — *Intervision Video*　　H, P
A-A 0348

Cannibals　　　　　　　　　　Fil-Ent '??
Horror
06088　　90 mins　　C
V2, B, V
Al Cliver, Shirley Night, Anthony Mayans, Olivier Mathot

A couple, both doctors, and their young daughter are on their way to a hospital deep in the bush, when they are attacked by cannibals. Only the father survives, and ten years later he convinces a group of friends to join him in a search for his daughter in cannibal country.
S,A — EN
Unknown — *Video Programme Distributors*
P
Cinehollywood—V1000

Can't Stop the Music　　　　　Fil-Ent '80
Musical
04634　　120 mins　　C
B, V
Village People, Valerie Perrine, Bruce Jenner, Steve Guttenberg, Paul Sand
A retired model invites friends from Greenwich Village to a party to help the career of her roommate, an aspiring disco composer. A visiting socialite 'discovers' the singing group, who become overnight stars.
C,A — EN
Associated Film Distributors; Allan Carr; Jacques Morali; Henri Belolo — THORN EMI
H, P
TXA 90 0228 4/TVA 90 0228 2

Capers　　　　　　　　　　　　Fil-Ent '8?
Adventure/Comedy
09133　　90 mins　　C
V2, B, V
Adam Roarke, Larry Bishop, Alexandra Hay
This film tells the story of two film stuntmen, who become disillusioned with their boring life, and go in search of fun. They team up with a girl and plan the caper of a lifetime. This involves impersonating police and border guards in an attempt to smuggle marijuana across the Mexican border. All goes well, until they lose the loot, but they end up with the last laugh.
S,A — EN
Unknown — *Go Video Ltd*　　P
GO 143

Capricorn One　　　　　　　　Fil-Ent '78
Science fiction
00840　　118 mins　　C
B, V, LV
Elliot Gould, James Brolin, Brenda Vaccaro
The whole world is watching America's first manned space flight to Mars. But before the countdown ends three astronauts are plunged into a battle for survival in an incredible cover-up conspiracy.
BBFC:A — C,A — EN
Warner Bros — *Precision Video Ltd*　　P
BITC 3011/VITC 3011

(For Explanation of codes, see USE GUIDE and KEY)

PALADIN VIDEO HOME ENTERTAINMENT GUIDE

Captain America   Fil-Ent '??
Cartoons/Adventure
07411   54 mins   C
V2, B, V
Animated
This tape contains three episodes of the adventures of Captain America. In 1941 Steve Rogers was the super-hero of World War II, then a freak stroke of fate threw him into suspended animation for twenty years. Awake again, he seeks his destiny in this brave new world armed with his miraculous mighty shield.
F — EN
Unknown — *Guild Home Video*   **H, P, E**

Captain   Fil-Ent '??
America—Cassette 2
Cartoons/Adventure
08349   40 mins   C
V2, B, V
Animated
This film features three further episodes of Captain America's adventures. Together with his assistant, Bucky Barnes, they fight to save America from her enemies.
F — EN
Unknown — *Guild Home Video*   **H, P, E**

Captain America in The   Chl-Juv '7?
Super-Adaptoid
Cartoons
13365   54 mins   C
V2, B, V
Animated
Captain America comes face to face with another Captain America in this three episode tape.
PS,M — EN
Marvel Comics — *Guild Home Video*   **H, P, E**

Captain America-The Red   Fil-Ent '??
Skull Lives
Cartoons/Adventure
09468   72 mins   C
V2, B, V
Animated
This tape features the brave Captain America in the Red Skull Lives plus three other exciting episodes each 18 minutes long. Captain America fights his worst enemy, Zemo, saves his pal Bucky from death and tackles the Red Skull.
BBFC:U — *F — EN*
Unknown — *Guild Home Video*   **H, P, E**

Captain Apache   Fil-Ent '72
Western
01043   95 mins   C
B, V
Lee Van Cleef, Carroll Baker, Stuart Whitman
An Apache is assigned by Union intelligence to investigate an Indian commissioner's murder.
BBFC:AA — *A — EN*
Philip Yordan; Official Films — *VCL Video Services*   **P**

Captain Blood   Fil-Ent '35
Adventure
13164   99 mins   B/W
B, V
Errol Flynn, Olivia DeHavilland, Basil Rathbone, J. Carrol Naish, Guy Kibbee
An exhilarating pirate adventure in which a man escapes from servitude and becomes a Caribbean pirate.
BBFC:U — *F — EN*
Warner Bros — *Warner Home Video*   **P**
99236

Captain Harlock   Chl-Juv '7?
Cartoons/Science fiction
02215   60 mins   C
V
Animated
Space Pirate Captain Harlock is earth's last hope against the power of the evil Zetons in this space adventure.
PR — EN
Unknown — *JVC*   **P**
PRT 19

Captain Kronos Vampire   Fil-Ent '74
Hunter
Horror
07602   90 mins   C
V2, B, V
Horst Janson, Caroline Munroe, John Carson, Shane Briant, Ian Hendry, directed by Brian Clemens
Captain Kronos sets out to capture a vampire before more beautiful young girls fall prey to his curse.
BBFC:AA — *S,A — EN*
Hammer Films — *Iver Film Services*   **P**
169

Captain Micron's   Chl-Juv '84
Electronic Comic
Adventure/Cartoons
12614   90 mins   C
V2, B, V

112   (For Explanation of codes, see USE GUIDE and KEY)

PALADIN VIDEO HOME ENTERTAINMENT GUIDE

This cassette contains favourite entertainment from 'Raiders of the Lost Ark,' 'Paul Daniels,' 'The Goodies' wildlife footage and cartoon clips. These are just a few of the features from this ongoing comic with new additions to be released periodically.
I,M — EN
IPC Magazines — *VideoSpace Ltd* **P**

Captain's Table, The   Fil-Ent '60
Comedy-Drama
09929   85 mins   C
B, V
John Gregson, Peggy Cummins, Donald Sinden, Nadia Gray
A new captain of a luxury liner bound for Sydney, Australia desires to have everything run smoothly in order for his promotion to be permanent. However, he discovers that he has to do a lot of compromising.
BBFC:PG — *F — EN*
20th Century-Fox; British — *Rank Video Library*   **H, P**
1056 A

Caravan to Vaccares   Fil-Ent '74
Adventure/Suspense
07334   98 mins   C
V2, B, V
Charlotte Rampling, David Birney, Michel Lonsdale, Marcel Bozzuffi, Manitas De Plata, Michael Bryant, Graham Hill, directed by Geoffrey Reeve
This film centres around a plot to smuggle an Hungarian scientist to the USA. The mastermind behind the plan hires a footloose American and his girlfriend to accompany the scientist. However, there are others who want the scientist and who are prepared to kill anyone in their way. The action is set amidst a huge gipsy festival, the tension of the bull ring and the landscape of the Camargue. Based on the novel by Alistair Maclean.
BBFC:AA — *S,A — EN*
Geoffrey Reeve Prods Ltd; Fox Rank — *Rank Video Library*   **H, P**
0112C

Caravans   Fil-Ent '78
Adventure
08396   129 mins   C
V2, B, V
Anthony Quinn, Michael Sarrazin, Jennifer O'Neill, Behrooz Vosoughi, Jeremey Kemp, Christopher Lee, Joseph Cotton, directed by James Fargo
This film is based on James A. Michener's novel set in 1948. It tells of a man trying to find the daughter of a U.S. Senator, who disappeared in Central Asia. She is found, after having married a colonel, but does not want to return. The film features the song 'Caravans' sung by Barbara Dickson.
BBFC:AA — *C,A — EN*
Universal Pictures; Ibex Films-FIDCI Prod — *Guild Home Video*   **H, P, E**

Carbon Copy   Fil-Ent '81
Comedy-Drama
08370   90 mins   C
V2, B, V
George Segal, Susan St. James, Jack Warden, Paul Winfield, Dick Martin, Vicky Dawson, Tom Poston, directed by Michael Schultz
George Segal stars as a successful, happily married business executive. However, in his student days he had an affair with a black girl. Eighteen years later an Afro-haired lad calls on him, to stay.
BBFC:AA — *C,A — EN*
Fast City — *Guild Home Video*   **H, P, E**

Card, The   Fil-Ent '52
Drama
12745   90 mins   B/W
B, V
Alec Guinness, Glynis Johns, Valerie Hobson, Petula Clark
Arnold Bennett's famous story about the archetypal self-made man from a humble Midlands pottery town.
BBFC:U — *F — EN*
Universal International; J Arthur Rank — *Rank Video Library*   **H, P**
0202E

Care of the Horse   Spo-Lei '8?
Animals
13513   38 mins   C
B, V
The management of horses of all kinds (hacks, ponies, show jumpers, race horses, non-sporting horses) is shown in this cassette, including stable routines, exercising, grooming and general care.
F — I
Unknown — *TFI Leisure Ltd*   **H, P**

Carefree/Easy Living   Fil-Ent '??
Musical/Drama
05663   154 mins   B/W
B, V
Fred Astaire, Ginger Rogers, Ralph Bellamy, Jack Carson, Kay Sutter, directed by Mark Sundrich, Victor Mature, Lucille Ball, Elizabeth Scott, Lloyd Nolan, directed by Jacques Tourneur

(For Explanation of codes, see USE GUIDE and KEY)   113

PALADIN VIDEO HOME ENTERTAINMENT GUIDE

Two films are featured on one cassette. 'Carefree' (Black/white, 80 mins, 1939) is the story of a psychiatrist who hypnotises his best friend's girlfriend with the result that she falls for him instead. It all gets sorted out on the dance floor. 'Easy Living' (Black/white, 74 mins, 1951) is based on the story by Irwin Shaw. It reveals the reaction of a football star and his wife to the news that he has heart trouble. The truth is hard to accept not only by him but his friends and colleagues who all have problems of their own.
F — EN
RKO — Kingston Video   H, P
KV49

Carnal Knowledge   Fil-Ent '71
Drama
01752   96 mins   C
B, V, LV
Jack Nicholson, Candice Bergen, Art Garfunkel, Ann-Margret, Rita Moreno, directed by Mike Nichols
This adult satire takes a look at two young men, from their college days in the 1940's to the 1970's, exploring the way they treat women.
BBFC:X — A — EN
Avco Embassy, Mike Nichols — CBS/Fox Video   P
3C-006

Car-Napping   Fil-Ent '??
Crime-Drama
09960   85 mins   C
V2, B, V
Eddie Constantine, Adolfo Celi
A young motor car designer plots to steal 40 Porsches in one foul swoop.
BBFC:U — F — EN
Unknown — Video Unlimited   H, P, E
076

Carnival '80   Fil-Ent '80
Parades and festivals
02227   60 mins   C
V
The colourful impressions of the world famous 1980 carnival in Rio de Janerio.
F — EN
Unknown — JVC   P
PRT 44

Carp Fishing with Duncan Kaye   Spo-Lei '82
Fishing
13546   58 mins   C
B, V

The characteristics of the three types of fish are explained and bait and landing preparations are shown in this cassette.
S,A — I
Unknown — TFI Leisure Ltd   H, P

Carpathian Eagle/Guardian of the Abyss   Fil-Ent '??
Horror
08755   202 mins   C
V2, B, V
Anthony Valentine, Suzanne Danielle, Sian Phillips, Barry Stanton, Ray Lonnen, Rosalyn Landor, John Carson, Paul Darrow, Barbara Ewing
Two 'Hammer House of Horror' films are contained on one cassette. In the first entitled 'Carpathian Eagle' (101 mins.), one murder victim after another is found with his heart ripped out. In the second 'Guardian of the Abyss', a human sacrifice as part of an ancient rite is the unexpected consequence when an attractive antique dealer buys a mirror with mysterious evil powers.
S,A — EN
Hammer Films — Precision Video Ltd   P
CRITC 2119/BITC 2119/VITC 2119

Carquake   Fil-Ent '76
Adventure/Drama
06247   91 mins   C
B, V
David Carradine, Bill McKinney, Veronica Hamel, Robert Carradine, directed by Paul Bartel
This is a hell-raising story of a road-race across America from the Pacific to Manhattan. It speeds of up to 175 mph the stakes are high, the winner receives $100,000 and the losers are lucky to be alive. Originally released as 'Cannonball.'
S,A — EN
New World Pictures — VCL Video Services   P
P200D

Carrie   Fil-Ent '76
Horror
01279   98 mins   C
V2, B, V
Sissy Spacek, Piper Laurie, John Travolta, Amy Irving, William Katt, directed by Brian de Palma
A shy, withdrawn teenage girl, with a domineering religious freak for a mother, discovers she has supernatural powers. She

PALADIN VIDEO HOME ENTERTAINMENT GUIDE

uses these powers at her senior prom to get back at her fellow classmates who have tormented her. Based on the novel by Stephen King.
BBFC:X — S,A — EN
United Artists; Paul Monash Prod — *Intervision Video* H
UA A B 5006

Carrington, V.C.   Fil-Ent '55
Drama
01946   102 mins   B/W
B, V
David Niven, Margaret Leighton, Clive Morton, Mark Dignam
A British Army Officer is accused of stealing funds from his regiment and being absent without leave. He decides to fight the injustice and wrongful accusations against him.
F — EN
Kingsley Intl — *CBS/Fox Video*   P
3B-060

Carry On Abroad   Fil-Ent '72
Comedy
01888   89 mins   C
B, V
Sidney James, Kenneth Williams, Joan Sims, Charles Hawrrey
The Carry On Gang set out for a paradise island. They find out that everything is not as perfect as the brochure promised.
BBFC:A — C,A — EN
Rank — *Rank Video Library*   H, P
1002

Carry On Again Doctor   Fil-Ent '70
Comedy
12756   88 mins   C
B, V
Sid James, Kenneth Williams, Charles Hawtrey, Jim Dale, Barabara Windsor, Hattie Jacques
The Senior Surgeon sets up a high class slimming clinic, but meanwhile one of his doctors is sent off in disgrace to a remote island where he happens to discover a tribal slimming potion that works like a charm!
BBFC:PG — F — EN
Peter Rodgers Prods — *Rank Video Library*
H, P
1078 X

Carry On Again Doctor   Fil-Ent '72
Comedy
13449   88 mins   C
B, V
Sid James, Jim Dale, Kenneth Williams

Another film in the 'Carry On' series centred round the goings on of the doctors, nurses and patients in a British hospital.
BBFC:A — S,A — EN
American International — *Rank Video Library*
H, P
1078X

Carry On at Your Convenience   Fil-Ent '71
Comedy
05146   88 mins   C
B, V
Sid James, Kenneth Williams, Charles Hawtrey, Hattie Jacques, Bernard Bresslaw
This film finds the Carry On gang working for Messrs W.C. Boggs and Sons—makers of fine toiletware.
BBFC:A — C,A — EN
Governor — *Rank Video Library*   H, P
1023

Carry On Behind   Fil-Ent '75
Comedy
05145   88 mins   C
B, V
Sid James, Kenneth Williams, Elke Sommer, Bernard Bresslaw, Joan Sims, Kenneth Connor
When Professor Crump and his sensational assistant set out for an archaeological dig they find themselves sharing a caravan site with the rest of the gang and a bevvy of beauties.
BBFC:A — C,A — EN
EMI — *Rank Video Library*   H, P
1024

Carry On Camping   Fil-Ent '68
Comedy
05249   86 mins   C
B, V
Sid James, Kenneth Williams, Charles Hawtrey, Joan Sims, Terry Scott, Hattie Jacques, Peter Butterworth, Barbara Windsor, Bernard Bresslaw
Sid and his reluctant mate Bernard Bresslaw hit on the idea of a nudist camp holiday to buck up their irresponsive girl friends.
BBFC:A — C,A — EN
Rank — *Rank Video Library*   H, P
1025

Carry On Cleo   Fil-Ent '65
Comedy
01610   92 mins   C
B, V
Sidney James, Amanda Barrie, Kenneth Williams, Kenneth Connor, Jim Dale, Charles Hawtrey, Joan Sims

(For Explanation of codes, see USE GUIDE and KEY)

PALADIN VIDEO HOME ENTERTAINMENT GUIDE

Marc Anthony joins with Cleopatra in aiding slaves to escape and rejoin their loved ones, and Caesar gets his historic comeuppance on the Ides of March.
BBFC:A — C,A — EN
Peter Rogers — THORN EMI P
TXE 90 0089 4/TVE 90 0089 2

Carry On Cowboy Fil-Ent '66
Comedy/Western
05913 94 mins C
V
Sidney James, Kenneth Williams, Jim Dale, directed by Gerald Thomas
An American girl helps a sanitary engineer thwart the outlaw who shot her father.
F — EN
Anglo-Amalgamated — JVC P
PRT 2

Carry On Dick Fil-Ent '74
Comedy
12742 89 mins C
B, V
Sid James, Barbara Windsor, Kenneth Williams, Hattie Jacques, Joan Sims, Bernard Bresslaw
The well known 'Carry On' team engage in highway ribaldry.
BBFC:A — A — EN
Peter Rodgers — Rank Video Library H, P
1077 E

Carry On Doctor Fil-Ent '72
Comedy
12755 94 mins C
B, V
Kenneth Williams, Frankie Howerd, Hattie Jacques, Barbara Windsor, Joan Sims
Another in the 'Carry On' series as the popular team have fun and laughter with the National Health.
BBFC:PG — F — EN
Peter Rodgers — Rank Video Library H, P
107 E

Carry On Emmannuelle Fil-Ent '??
Comedy
06197 78 mins C
B, V
Kenneth Williams, Joan Simms, Peter Butterworth, Kenneth Connor, Jack Douglas, Beryl Reid, Suzanne Danielle, directed by Gerald Thomas

The wife of a London based diplomat and her 'foreign affairs' make her the talk of the town.
S,A — EN
Peter Roger Prod; Gerlad Thomas Films — VCL Video Services P
P189D

Carry On England Fil-Ent '76
Comedy-Drama
09923 86 mins C
B, V
Kenneth Connor, Windsor Davies, Patrick Mower, Judy Geeson, Joan Sims, Jack Douglas, directed by Gerald Thomas
This takes place in a mixed anti-aircraft battery at the beginning of World War II. The inevitable gags and knockabout situations occur with the 'Carry On' gang.
S,A — EN
Rank Prod. — Rank Video Library H, P

Carry On—Follow That Camel Fil-Ent '68
Comedy
13447 94 mins C
B, V
Phil Silvers, Kenneth Williams, Sid James
The 'Carry-On' team appear once more in this send-up of Beau Geste and the Foreign Legion.
BBFC:U — F — EN
Peter Rogers Prods. — Rank Video Library H, P
1084 X

Carry On Henry Fil-Ent '71
Comedy
05143 88 mins C
B, V
Sid James, Kenneth Williams, Barbara Windsor, Kenneth Connor
'Carry On Henry' is based on a recently discovered manuscript by one William Cobbler which reveals the fact that Henry VIII did in fact have two more wives. The story was originally thought to have come from Cromwell but is now-known to be definitely all Cobbler's.
BBFC:A — C,A — EN
American Intl Pictures — Rank Video Library H, P
1021

Carry On Loving Fil-Ent '70
Comedy
12754 90 mins C
B, V
Sid James, Kenneth Williams, Charles Hawtrey, Joan Sims, Hattie Jacques

116 (For Explanation of codes, see USE GUIDE and KEY)

PALADIN VIDEO HOME ENTERTAINMENT GUIDE

Another in the popular 'Carry On' series, this one is situated around a marriage bureau.
BBFC:A — A — EN
Rank — *Rank Video Library*   **H, P**
1080 E

Carry On Matron   Fil-Ent '72
Comedy
01873   89 mins   C
B, V
Sidney James, Kenneth Williams, Hattie Jacques, Joan Sims, Bernard Bresslaw, Barbara Windsor, Kenneth Connor
A bawdy, saucy comedy set in a maternity hospital.
BBFC:A — C,A — EN
Rank — *Rank Video Library*   **H, P**
1004

Carry On Nurse   Fil-Ent '58
Comedy
01261   84 mins   B/W
B, V
Shirley Eaton, Kenneth Connor, Wilfrid Hyde-White, Hattie Jacques, Kenneth Williams
The men's ward in a British hospital declares war on their nurses and the rest of the hospital. The second of the 'Carry On' series.
BBFC:U — F — EN
Governor Films; Peter Rogers — *THORN EMI* **P**
TXE 90 0014 4/TVE 90 0014 2

Carry On Up the Jungle   Fil-Ent '70
Comedy
05178   87 mins   C
B, V
Frankie Howerd, Kenneth Connor, Sidney James, Bernard Bresslaw, Charles Hawtrey, Jacki Piper, Joan Sims, Reuben Martin, Terry Scott, Valerie Leon, Edwina Carroll
When Professor Inigo Tinkle recalls his adventures in darkest Africa in pursuit of the rare Oozulum bird the 'Carry On Gang' take their cues for an uproarious send-up.
BBFC:A — C,A — EN
Governor — *Rank Video Library*   **H, P**
1006

Carry On Up the Khyber   Fil-Ent '68
Comedy
05142   86 mins   C
B, V
Sid James, Roy Castle, Kenneth Williams, Charles Hawtrey

This is the legendary North West Frontier with a difference—only to be expected when the Carry On Team are involved. Reputations are threatened, stiff upper lips are quivering and the British Raj is on the verge of collapse.
BBFC:A — C,A — EN
Rank; Adder — *Rank Video Library*   **H, P**
1020

Carthage in Flames   Fil-Ent '??
Drama
05557   110 mins   C
V2, B, V
Terence Hill, Anne Heywood, directed by Carmine Gallone
Set in Carthage in 164 BC a doomed city awaits the Roman Empire's final onslaught. The beautiful Fulvia has pledged her destiny to Hiram who saved her from pagan sacrifice; however, she faces many tests, submission to an evil warrior, torture, the loss of her loved one and a final confrontation at the edge of a fiery abyss as Carthage burns.
BBFC:U — F — EN
Unknown — *Videomedia*   **P**
PVM 5102/BVM 5102/HVM 5102

Cartoon Bonanza,   Chi-Juv '85
Volumes 1-3
Cartoons
13761   216 mins   C
B, V
Animated
Three cassettes each containing ten cartoon episodes of fun from all the Disney characters are featured in this series.
BBFC:U — F — EN
Walt Disney Productions — *Rank Video Library* **P**
170B?171B?172B

Cartoon Classics of the   Fil-Ent '3?
1930's
Cartoons
06075   59 mins   C
B, V
Animated
An assortment of colour cartoons featuring: Felix the Cat and The Goose that Laid the Golden Egg, Presto Chango, The Sunshine Makers, The Song of the Birds, The Pincushion Man, Daffy and the Dinosaur, Small Fry and Bold King Cole.
F — EN
RKO — *Video Programme Distributors*   **P**
Media—M305

Cartoon Festival I   Fil-Ent '??
Cartoons
05589   44 mins   C

PALADIN VIDEO HOME ENTERTAINMENT GUIDE

B, V
Animated
A cassette featuring six Walt Disney cartoons showing Mickey Mouse, Donald Duck, Pluto and Chip 'n' Dale. Titles include 'The Band Concert', 'Pluto's Quintuplets', 'Donald's Vacation', 'Corn Chips', 'Camp Dog' and 'Three for Breakfast'.
F — EN
Walt Disney Productions — *Rank Video Library*
H
05900

Cartoon Festival II   Fil-Ent '??
Cartoons
05590   38 mins   C
B, V
Animated
This cassette features six Walt Disney cartoons starring Mickey Mouse, Pluto, Goofy, Chip 'n' Dale, and Donald Duck. Titles include 'Mickey Down Under', 'The Big Wash', 'Cold Storage', 'Chip 'n' Dale', 'Pluto's Blue Note' and 'Dragon Around'.
F — EN
Walt Disney Productions — *Rank Video Library*
H
06000

Cartoon Festival III   Fil-Ent '??
Cartoons
05591   41 mins   C
B, V
Animated
This cassette features six cartoons from Walt Disney starring Pluto, Donald Duck, Goofy, Chip 'n' Dale and Mickey Mouse. Titles include 'Pests of the West', 'Canine Casanova', 'Donald's Cousin Gus', 'Goofy and Wilbur', 'Chips Ahoy' and 'Mickey's Grand Opera'.
F — EN
Walt Disney Productions — *Rank Video Library*
H
06100

Cartoon Hour   Fil-Ent '??
Cartoons
06294   58 mins   C
V2, B, V
Animated
This tape is a compilation of cartoons by some of the best of Americas cartoonists.
F — EN
Unknown — *World of Video 2000*   **H, P**
GF522

Cartoon Show No. 10   Fil-Ent '??
Cartoons
06313   58 mins   C
V2, B, V
Animated
Produced in Eastern Europe, this cassette features five cartoon films, 'How Cossacks Played Football,' 'The Little Cabin,' 'How Cossacks Began Olympics,' 'A Ginger Breadman' and 'How Cossacks Cooked.'
F — EN
Unknown — *World of Video 2000*   **H, P**
GF519

Cartoon Show No. 11   Fil-Ent '??
Cartoons
06314   58 mins   C
V2, B, V
Animated
Produced in Eastern Europe, this cassette features four cartoon films, 'The Kingdom of Mushroom,' 'How the Cossacks Battled Pirates,' 'Animal Days' and 'Wives and Husbands.'
F — EN
Unknown — *World of Video 2000*   **H, P**
GF520

Cartoon Show No. 12   Fil-Ent '??
Cartoons
06315   58 mins   C
V2, B, V
Animated
Produced in Eastern Europe, this cassette features three cartoon films, 'The Labyrinth,' 'Love Works Wonders' and 'Sadko The Rich.'
F — EN
Unknown — *World of Video 2000*   **H, P**
GF521

Cartoon Special   Fil-Ent '??
Cartoons
05628   90 mins   C
V2, B, V
Animated
Three half hour cartoons on one tape. Includes 'Noah's Animals,' a story of the flood seen through the eyes of the animals; 'King of the Beasts,' a story of how the lion came to be king of the animal kingdom; and 'The Last of the Red Hot Dragons,' a story of a flying dragon who rescues his animal friends at the North Pole.
F — EN
Unknown — *Video Unlimited*   **H, P**

Cartoon Wonderland   Fil-Ent '??
Cartoons/Fantasy
05697   56 mins   C
B, V
Animated

PALADIN VIDEO HOME ENTERTAINMENT GUIDE

This cassette presents five animated cartoons of well known fairy tales—'The Boy Who Cried Wolf,' 'Thumbelina,' 'Puss 'n' Boots,' 'Two Little Spoiled Bears' and 'Magic Pony.'
BBFC:U — *F* — *EN*
Unknown — *Derann Film Services* **H, P**
BGS201B/BGS201

Casablanca Fil-Ent '43
Drama
01050   102 mins   B/W
V2, B, V
Humphrey Bogart, Ingrid Bergman, directed by Michael Curtiz
Classic story of an American expatriot who involves himself in romance and espionage in North Africa during World War II.
Academy Awards '43: Best Picture, Best Screenplay; Best Director (Curtiz).
BBFC:U — *F* — *EN*
Warner Bros; Hal Wallis — *Intervision Video* **H**
UA A B 5011

Casanova Fil-Ent '76
Drama
12090   150 mins   C
B, V
Donald Sutherland, directed by Federico Fellini
Casanova spends his time touring the cities of Europe declaring undying love to a succession of women.
A — *EN*
Twentieth Century Fox; PEA — *CBS/Fox Video* **P**
1220

Casey's Shadow Fil-Ent '77
Drama
12475   93 mins   C
B, V
Walter Matthau
A tear-jerking story of an impoverished horse trainer and the attachment between his youngest son, Casey, and a grey-roan colt.
BBFC:PG — *F* — *EN*
Columbia; Ray Stark — *RCA/Columbia Pictures Video UK* **H, P**
10167

Casper and the Angels Chl-Juv '79
Cartoons
08394   74 mins   C
V2, B, V
Animated
Casper, the world's friendliest ghost, teams up with the Angels, Mini and Maxi as they become the first policewomen in outer-space.
PS,M — *EN*
Hanna-Barbera — *Guild Home Video* **H, P, E**

Casper and the Angels- Chl-Juv '79
Cassette 2
Cartoons
09425   74 mins   C
V2, B, V
Animated
Casper, the friendliest ghost, returns with his crime-busting police-women friends, Mini and Maxi. His new heavenly assignment leads him into all kinds of spooky space adventures and cosmic catastrophes, along with his goofy cousin Hairy Scarey who always has a joke up his sleeve.
PS,M — *EN*
Hanna-Barbera — *Guild Home Video* **H, P, E**

Cassandra Crossing, The Fil-Ent '76
Drama
00841   114 mins   C
B, V
Sophia Loren, Richard Harris, Burt Lancaster
Military authorities and passengers of a train struggle to thwart an unknown infectious disease contaminating the train's passengers.
BBFC:A — *C,A* — *EN*
Avco Embassy — *Precision Video Ltd* **P**
BITC 3028/VITC 3028

Castaway Cowboy, The Fil-Ent '??
Adventure
12562   91 mins   C
B, V
James Garner, Robert Culp
A cowboy is castaway on a Hawaiian island in 1850 and is nursed back to health by a family with problems of their own.
F — *EN*
Walt Disney Productions — *Rank Video Library* **H**
190

Castle of Evil Fil-Ent '66
Horror/Adventure
09223   85 mins   C
B, V
Scott Brady, Virginia Mayo, David Brian, Lisa Gaye, Hugh Marlowe

(For Explanation of codes, see USE GUIDE and KEY)

PALADIN VIDEO HOME ENTERTAINMENT GUIDE

When a group of prospective heirs arrive at a castle of horror on an isolated Caribbean island for the 'reading of the will', a sinister and hostile force makes its presence felt, terrorising all who remain.
C,A — EN
World Entertainment — *Video Form Pictures*
H, P
MGD 6

Castles and Concerts: The Polish Chamber Orchestra   Fil-Ent '83
Music-Performance
09815   60 mins   C
B, V
Conducted by Jerzy Maksymiuk
This tape, the first release in the 'Castle and Concerts' series, features the Polish Chamber Orchestra playing Mozart's 'Eine Kleine Nachtmusik' and Haydn's 'Farewell', Symphony No. 45. The music is set to a film of Haydn's picturesque hometown of Eisenstadt with a tour of the spectacular palaces of Vienna. Recorded in stereo.
F — EN
EMI Music Video Prod. — *THORN EMI*   P
TXE 90 1434 4/TVE 90 1434 2

Cat and Mouse   Fil-Ent '73
Drama/Suspense
08531   87 mins   C
B, V
Kirk Douglas, Jean Selberg
This film tells of the change of a timid and unassuming man into a vicious killer. Using his biology instruments as weapons he prowls the streets of Montreal, playing a game of cat and mouse with his wife, the inevitable victim.
C,A — EN
Unknown — *THORN EMI*   P
TXC 90 08624/TVC 90 08622

Cat and the Canary, The   Fil-Ent '78
Mystery
05732   100 mins   C
V2, B, V
Honor Blackman, Michael Callan, Edward Fox, Carol Lynley, Olivia Hussey, Wendy Hillier, Wilfred Hyde-White
A classic suspense tale; seven distant relatives gather in a strange house on a stormy night to hear the reading of a will.
Miami International Film Festival '78: Gold Award.   S,A — EN
Grenadier Films; Avdagon Films; Richard Gordon Prod — *Video Unlimited*   H, P
003

Cat From Outer Space, The   Fil-Ent '78
Science fiction/Adventure
07932   99 mins   C
B, V
Ken Berry, Roddy McDowall, Sandy Duncan, Harry Morgan, McLean Stevenson, Jesse White, Alan Young, Hans Conried, directed by Norman Tokar
This film follows the adventures of an alien in the shape of a superintelligent cat, who is forced to crash land on Earth where he attempts to get his craft repaired.
F — EN
Walt Disney — *Rank Video Library*   H
09700

Cat in the Cage   Fil-Ent '??
Horror
08685   100 mins   C
V2, B, V
Behrooz Vossoughi, Sybil Danning, Colleen Camp, directed by Tony Zarindast
This film tells of the weird exploits amongst the members of a wealthy tycoon's household. The tycoon's son has a strange obsession with his cat. The cat has a vicious hatred of the family nurse, and she herself is plotting a murder.
BBFC:X — A — EN
Unknown — *Derann Film Services*   P
FDV 312

Cat on a Hot Tin Roof   Fil-Ent '58
Drama
10173   108 mins   C
B, V, LV
Elizabeth Taylor, Paul Newman, Burl Ives
An alcoholic husband, unable to face up to responsibility, a fiery and passionate wife, and an autocratic father conflict in this film of tense family life set in the Deep South.
BBFC:X — A — EN
MGM — *MGM/UA Home Video*   P
UMB 10060/UMV 10060/UMLV 10060

Cataclysm   Fil-Ent '??
Horror
07828   94 mins   C
V2, B, V
Cameron Mitchell, Faith Clift
This demonic horror epic interweaves the lives of various characters, building up to a shocking blood curdling finale.
A — EN
Unknown — *Video Unlimited*   H, P
043

Catastrophe   Fil-Ent '77
Drama/Documentary
09346   87 mins   C

(For Explanation of codes, see USE GUIDE and KEY)

PALADIN VIDEO HOME ENTERTAINMENT GUIDE

B, V
Narrated by William Conrad
This film portrays some of the world's most spectacular disasters, from hideous aircrashes to enormous towering infernos. The film includes incredible scenes from the Hindenburg crash, the sinking of the 'Andrea Doria', disasters of the Indianapolis 500 auto race and many more.
S,A — EN
Picturmedia — *Precision Video Ltd*   **P**
BPMPV 2620/VPMPV 2620

Catch Me a Spy   Fil-Ent '71
Drama
08804   91 mins   C
B, V
Kirk Douglas, Trevor Howard, Tom Courtenay, Marlene Jobert, Patrick Mower, Bernadette Lafont, Bernard Blier, directed by Dick Clement
This film tells the story of a British agent who falls in love with the wife of a Russian spy. His mission is to smuggle Russian manuscripts into England.
S,A — EN
Rank; Ludgate; Capitol — *VCL Video Services*   **P**
P271D

Catching Up   Spo-Lei '7?
Motorcycles
02070   60 mins   C
B, V
Breathtaking footage of the greatest motorcycling events in the U.S.A. featuring motocross, the hottest sport in America today, and the most terrifying spectacle in the motorcycling world—Daytona.
S,A — EN
Unknown — *VCL Video Services*   **P**

Cathie's Child   Fil-Ent '77
Drama
06266   89 mins   C
B, V
Directed by Donald Gambie
This is the moving story of a young mother's efforts to get her three-year-old daughter back from Greece where her Greek husband has taken the child. She faces hostility from the Greek community and little help from the law courts so she engages the help of a newspaper reporter to assist her in finding the child.
S,A — EN
C-B Film Production; Australian Film Commission — *Home Video Holdings*   **H, P**
023

Cathy's Curse   Fil-Ent '7?
Horror
06812   ? mins   C
V2, B, V
Alan Scarfe, Beverly Murray, Randi Allen
A little girl terrorises her family in this tale of supernatural power.
S,A — EN
Nicole Mathieu Boiaveri — *Intervision Video*   **H, P**
A-AE 0374

Cattle Annie and Little Britches   Fil-Ent '79
Western
07663   88 mins   C
B, V
Diane Lane, Amanda Plummer, Burt Lancaster, Rod Steiger, John Savage
This western is based on the real life wild west escapades of two female outlaws, the nicest young ladies ever to have robbed banks, ride the range and outwit the Marshal.
S,A — EN
Universal — *VCL Video Services*   **P**
P204D

Catwalk Killer, The   Fil-Ent '80
Drama/Mystery
12851   98 mins   C
V2, B, V
Jessica Walter, Eleanor Parker, Connie Sellecca, directed by Gus Trikonis
A murderer is stalking when a group of fashion critics, top buyers, photographers and glamourous models are trapped in a mountaintop mansion.
BBFC:PG — *C,A — EN*
Unknown — *Video Programme Distributors*   **P**

Caught   Fil-Ent '49
Drama
01071   88 mins   B/W
V2, B, V
James Mason, Barbara Bel Geddes, directed by Max Ophuls
A young girl tries to escape her shallow existence by marrying a millionaire.
BBFC:A — *A — EN*
MGM — *Intervision Video*   **H, P**
A-A 0126

Cauldron of Blood   Fil-Ent '68
Horror
01044   95 mins   C
V2, B, V
Boris Karloff, Viveca Lindfors, Jean Pierre Aumont

(For Explanation of codes, see USE GUIDE and KEY)

PALADIN VIDEO HOME ENTERTAINMENT GUIDE

A blind sculptor models his sculptures on skeletons which his wife murders to obtain.
C,A — EN
PC Hispamer Films; Robert D Weinbach — *Videomedia* **P**

Caveman Fil-Ent '81
Comedy
13035   90 mins   C
B, V
Ringo Starr, Barbara Bach, directed by Carl Gottlieb
In this pre-historic comedy a caveman is banished from his tribe for coveting the girl who belongs to the tribal chief. He and other misfits form their own tribe and make several interesting discoveries, including rock and roll.
BBFC:A — *C,A — EN*
United Artists Corp — *Warner Home Video* **P**
99290

Cavern Deep Fil-Ent '??
Adventure
06162   52 mins   C
B, V
Colin Forsythe, Mark Fidelo, Michele Quinn
This story involves a Canadian journalist exploring the legend of Loch Ness, an old hermit who spends his days staring into the dark waters and three children who came much closer to the monster than anyone has before.
F — EN
Scottish Television — *Guild Home Video*
H, P, E

CB Hustlers Fil-Ent '??
Comedy
07816   77 mins   C
V2, B, V
Edward Roehm, Jake Barnes, Valdesta, John Alderman
American truckers using CB Radio pursue fun and freedom by calling up the girls who run vans called Hot Box and Hot Box 2. However, when they cross into Sheriff Ramsay's territory, they discover the law is strictly upheld in his County.
A — EN
Unknown — *Video Unlimited* **H, P**
044

C.C. and Company Fil-Ent '70
Drama
01008   94 mins   C
B, V
Joe Namath, Ann-Margret, William Smith, Jennifer Billingsley, directed by Seymour Robbie

A young man joins a motorcycle gang, but because he does not adhere to their rules, he becomes the enemy.
C,A — EN
Avco Embassy; Rogallan Production — *CBS/Fox Video* **P**
3C-007

Celebrity Fil-Ent '83
Drama
13425   310 mins   C
B, V
Michael Beck, Joseph Bottoms, Ben Masters, Debbie Allen, Karen Austin, Tess Harper, Ned Beatty, Claude Akins
This programme is contained on two cassettes and tells the story of three inseparable high school friends who share a night of violence and passion that later shatters their enormously successful lives.
BBFC:15 — *S,A — EN*
NBC Prods — *MGM/UA Home Video* **P**
CELI

Cemetery of the Living Dead Fil-Ent '65
Horror
08604   92 mins   B/W
V2, B, V
Barbara Steele, Walter Brandt, Marilyn Mitchell, Alfred Rice, Richard Garret, Alan Collins, directed by Ralph Zucker
This tells the story of Dr. Hauff, a tormented soul, who reaches from the grave to claim revenge on those who are responsible for his death. Only his daughter realizes the strength of his occult powers, but no one believes her.
BBFC:X — *A — EN*
Unknown — *Videomedia* **P**
PVM 1031/BVM 1031/HVM 1031

Cenerentola, La Fin-Art '83
Opera
12893   155 mins   C
B, V
Kathleen Kuhlmann, Marta Taddei, Laura Zannini, Laurence Dale, Roderick Kennedy, directed by John Cox
This production of Rossini's opera by the Glyndebourne Festival Opera tells the story of cinderella and is conducted by Donato Renzetti.
F — EN
RM Arts — *THORN EMI* **P**
TXH 90 26954/TVH 90 26952

Centrefold Girls Fil-Ent '7?
Horror
02495   92 mins   C
V2, B, V

PALADIN VIDEO HOME ENTERTAINMENT GUIDE

Clement is determined to kill the voluptuous girls who have posed nude for the centre pages of 'Bachelor' magazine. Possessed of a clinical but warped mind he sees it as his duty to punish them.
BBFC:X — A — EN
Unknown — *Intervision Video*   H
A-A 0134

Chain Reaction, The   Fil-Ent '80
Fantasy/Science fiction
13053   89 mins   C
B, V
Steve Bisley, Arna-Maria Winchester, directed by Ian Barry
A tense, Australian made film about the ruthless attempts to keep secret facts of a spillage of radioactive material and the security team's search for a contaminated scientist who has escaped to warn the public.
BBFC:AA — C,A — EN
Palm Beach Pictures — *Warner Home Video*   P
61244

Chained Heat   Fil-Ent '83
Drama
12898   92 mins   C
B, V
Linda Blair, directed by Paul Nicholas
A girl finds herself in prison for the first time and meets with brutality, murder and rape, inflicted by inmates and guards alike.
A — EN
Billy Fine — *THORN EMI*   P
TXA 90 25614/TVA 90 25612

Challenge, The   Fin-Art '??
Arts/Artists
07942   90 mins   C
V2, B, V
Narrated by Orson Welles, directed by Herbert Kline
This film illustrates the growth and development of modern art. It covers the works of the great artists of the twentieth century from Picasso, Chagall, Dali, Bacon and Moore to Warhol, Klee and Yoko Ono. This film is suitable for art lovers and initiates alike.
S,A — EN
Unknown — *Videomedia*   P
PVM 9001/BVM 9001/HVM 9001

Challenge, The   Fil-Ent '82
Adventure/Fantasy
12012   112 mins   C
B, V
Scott Glenn, Toshiro Mifune, directed by John Frankenheimer

Set in Japan, an American drifter is drawn into a private feud between two brothers, one which has raged for decades and has its roots in ancient traditions. Magic powers are evoked as old traditions clash with new.
S,A — EN
Unknown — *CBS/Fox Video*   P
7137

Challenge of the McKennas, The   Fil-Ent '??
Western
09376   90 mins   C
B, V
This western tells the tale of Don Diego De Castro, a proud and overbearing man, determined to inflict his will on everyone. One day as he is about to lynch the man who has been pursuing his daughter he is interrupted by a fair-minded saddle tramp. Although he tries to set the peace he fails and heads back for the loneliness of life in the saddle.
S,A — EN
Unknown — *Precision Video Ltd*   P
BWPV 502/VWPV 502

Challenge of the Sky   Gen-Edu '??
Aeronautics/Documentary
06348   60 mins   C
V2, B, V
This film takes a look at the work of the Royal Aircraft Establishment at Farnborough including an especially detailed tour of Concorde. This is followed by coverage of the 1980 24th International Air Show staged at Farnborough featuring Lancasters, Spitfires and Hurricanes.
F — EN
Unknown — *Walton Film and Video Ltd*   P
D1153

Challenge of Young Bruce Lee   Fil-Ent '7?
Martial arts
07919   88 mins   C
V2, B, V
This film follows the early years of Bruce Lee, who was adopted by monks after being abandoned as a baby. After the death of his master, who taught him the art of Kung Fu, Bruce leaves the seclusion of the monastery for a life in the city. He is confused and surprised by the modern life style but soon settles down to fight crime using his skills. This film does not star Bruce Lee himself.
S,A — EN
Unknown — *Video Programme Distributors*   P
Inter-Ocean—078

(For Explanation of codes, see USE GUIDE and KEY)

PALADIN VIDEO HOME ENTERTAINMENT GUIDE

Challenge to Be Free   Fil-Ent '75
Adventure
08873   90 mins   C
V2, B, V

Mike Mazurki, Jimmy Kane, narrated by John McIntire, directed by Tay Garnett
This is a true story of a trapper, who accidentally kills a lawman whilst rescuing a nearly frozen wolf from a trap. He is pursued by men and dogs across 1,000 miles of frozen wilderness, through blizzards, avalanches and frozen rivers in an attempt for him and his wolf companion to be free.
BBFC:U — F — EN
Pacific International Enterprises — *Video Programme Distributors*   P
Media 205

Champ, The   Fil-Ent '79
Drama
05306   117 mins   C
V2, B, V

Jon Voight, Faye Dunaway, Ricky Schroder, Jack Warden, Arthur Hill, Strother Martin, Joan Blondell, directed by Franco Zeffirelli
This film is set against the background of a racetrack, the fashion world and a boxing ring. The happy relationship between a one-time boxing champion and his eight year old son is threatened when his former wife appears on the scene; she had left the boy when he was one and now wants him back. Based on the classic 1931 film.
S,A — EN
United Artists; MGM — *MGM/UA Home Video*   P
UMB10034/UMV10034

Champion   Fil-Ent '49
Drama
04675   98 mins   B/W
B, V

Kirk Douglas, Marilyn Maxwell, Arthur Kennedy
Stanley Kramer's 'Champion' exposes the unscrupulous and corrupt side of the boxing profession, and reveals the intrigues that take place on the 'other side of the ropes.'
C,A — EN
United Artists; Stanley Kramer — *Polygram Video*   P

Champions, The   Fil-Ent '83
Drama
13215   95 mins   C
V2, B, V

John Hurt, Edward Woodward, Jan Francis, Ben Johnson, directed by John Irvin
This is the true story of jockey Bob Champion who discovered he had cancer at the height of his career in 1979 and his courageous fight back to win the most coveted prize of all.
BBFC:PG — S,A — EN
Embassy Pictures — *Embassy Home Entertainment*   P
6000

Chanel Solitaire   Fil-Ent '82
Drama/Biographical
08459   107 mins   C
B, V

Marie-France Pisier, Timothy Dalton, Rutger Hauer, Karen Black, Brigitte Fossey, Leila Frechet, directed by George Kaczender
This film tells the story of Gabrielle Chanel, one of the world's most famous fashion designers. It starts at her orphanage then follows her to her tailor's shop and then to the chateau of the prosperous Etienne de Balsan. She has an affair with a politically ambitious man which ends tragically just as her career and wealth escalate to fantastic heights.
BBFC:AA — C,A — EN
France — *THORN EMI*   P
TXB 90 0837 4/TVB 90 0837 2

Change of Seasons, A   Fil-Ent '80
Comedy/Romance
13204   101 mins   C
B, V

Shirley MacLaine, Bo Derek, Anthony Hopkins, Michael Brandon, Mary Beth Hurt
When a married, respectable college professor has an affair with one of his students, his wife soon finds a lover of her own.
BBFC:AA — C,A — EN
Twentieth Century Fox — *Warner Home Video*   P
61245

Changeling, The   Fil-Ent '80
Horror
09086   114 mins   C
B, V

George C. Scott, Trish Van Devere, Melvyn Douglas, John Russell
A music teacher moves into an old house and discovers that a young boy's ghostly spirit is her housemate.
A — EN
Associated Film Distribution — *Video Tape Centre*   P
VTC 1032

Chant of Jimmie Blacksmith, The   Fil-Ent '77
Drama
07890   121 mins   C

---

124   (For Explanation of codes, see USE GUIDE and KEY)

PALADIN VIDEO HOME ENTERTAINMENT GUIDE

V2, B, V
Tommy Lewis, Freddy Reynolds, Tim Robertson, Jane Harders, Jack Charles, Ray Barrett, Angela Punch, Don Crosby, Elizabeth Alexander, Peter Sumner, Ray Meagher, directed by Fred Schepisi
This film, set in Australia at the turn of the century, tells the poignant story of a young half-blood Aborigine who leaves his tribe to find a place in the white man's world where he seeks acceptance. After a series of tragic events he becomes disillusioned and through no fault of his own he explodes in a fateful 'declaration of war' of revenge and violence against the white man.
S,A — EN
Film House — *Walton Film and Video Ltd*
P

Chant of Jimmie Blacksmith, The   Fil-Ent '75
Drama
13769   89 mins   C
B, V
Directed by Fred Schespi
This is a story of racial bigotry and savage revenge set in Australia during the early 1900s.
BBFC:18 — A — EN
Unknown — *Odyssey Video*   H, P
6431

Chariots of Fire   Fil-Ent '81
Drama
07687   124 mins   C
V2, B, V, LV
Ben Cross, Ian Charleson, Nigel Havers, Cheryl Campbell, Alice Krige, Lindsay Anderson, Dennis Christopher, Nigel Davenport, John Gielgud, Ian Holm, directed by Hugh Hudson
This is the story of the rivalry between two athletes as they prepare for and participate in the 1924 Olympic Games. Each man is spurred on by a personal social handicap. One is the son of a wealthy Jewish money lender and is determined to out-distance those at Cambridge who are racially prejudiced. The other is the son of a Scottish missionary in China and runs for the greater glory of God. Music by Vangelis.
Academy Awards '81: Best Picture.   F — EN
20th Century Fox; Enigma Production — *CBS/Fox Video*   H
1118

Charles and Diana   Fil-Ent '82
Royalty-GB/Documentary
08011   100 mins   C
V2, B, V
David Robb, Caroline Bliss, Christopher Lee, Rod Taylor, Margaret Tyzack, Mona Washbourne, Charles Gray, David Langton, directed by James Goldstone
This film tells the true story of Charles and Diana, the Prince and Princess of Wales. It begins with their meeting and ends with the wedding in St. Paul's Cathedral.
F — EN
St Lorraine Prods; Edward S Feldman — *Iver Film Services*   P
230

Charley-One-Eye   Fil-Ent '73
Western
04322   96 mins   C
V2, B, V
Story of a Negro on the run from the Union Army after killing a white officer.
BBFC:X — A — EN
Paramount — *Intervision Video*   H, P
A-A 0015

Charley's Aunt/Mr Axelford's Angel   Fil-Ent '77
Comedy
06180   118 mins   C
B, V
Eric Sykes, Alvin Lewis, Osmond Bullock, Jimmy Edwards, Julia Foster, Michael Bryant, Katy Wild
Two films contained on one cassette. 'Charley's Aunt' (colour, 66 mins) is a comedy of inept attempts by two 'gentlemen' to be alone with two ladies; their plans go very wrong. 'Mr Axelford's Angel' (colour, 52 mins) is the tale of a successful businessman who employs a disorganised and clumsy temporary secretary resulting in utter chaos.
S,A — EN
Unknown — *Guild Home Video*   H, P, E

Charley's Aunt/Mr. Axelford's Angel   Fil-Ent '??
Comedy-Drama/Drama
09467   118 mins   C
B, V
Eric Sykes, Alun Lewis, Osmond Bullock, Jimmy Edwards, directed by Graeme Muir, Julia Foster, Michael Bryant, directed by John Frankau
Two films are contained on one cassette. In 'Charley's Aunt' (66 minutes) two 'gentlemen' are attempting to be alone with two ladies. In 'Mr. Axelford's Angel' a temporary secretary, although disorganised and clumsy but happy and full of life, arrives late to take up her appointment with her new boss, a successful, organised and very meticulous man.
F — EN
Unknown — *Guild Home Video*   H, P, E

Charlie and the Talking Buzzard   Chl-Juv '82
Adventure

(For Explanation of codes, see USE GUIDE and KEY)

125

PALADIN VIDEO HOME ENTERTAINMENT GUIDE

12195　　81 mins　　C
V2, B, V

Bruce Kemp, Duncan McLeod, Christopher Penn

Charlie and his dog are new to town. Their adventure begins when having made friends with a Buzzard called Clarence they set off in hot pursuit of the mischievous town mayor and his henchmen.
BBFC:U — *F — EN*
Unknown — *Medusa Communications Ltd*
H, P

**Charlie Boy/The　　　　Fil-Ent　'7?
Thirteenth Reunion**
Horror
08756　　202 mins　　C
V2, B, V

Leigh Lawson, Angela Bruce, Marius Goring, Frances Cuka, David Healey; Julia Foster, Dinah Sheridan, Richard Pearson, Norman Bird, Warren Clake, George Innes

Two 'Hammer House of Horror' films are contained on one cassette. In the first entitled 'Charlie Boy' (101 mins.), death stalks six people when a curse is placed on them by the new owner of a Central African fetish, a small but valuable and menacing figure found among an inherited collection of primitive art. In 'The Thirteenth Reunion' a writer is assigned to a series of articles about her experiences of a weight-reducing course. Horror lies ahead, from the moment she enrolls.
S,A — EN
Hammer Films — *Precision Video Ltd*　　**P**
CRITC 2118/BITC 2118/VITC 2118

Charlie Chaplin I　　　　　　Fil-Ent　'1?
Comedy
04463　　50 mins　　B/W
B, V

Charlie Chaplin, Edna Purviance, Eric Campbell, directed by Charles Chaplin

A compilation of three Chaplin classics: 'The Tramp' (1915), 'The Pawnshop' (1916), and 'Easy Street' (1917).
F — EN
Mutual; Essanay — *Polygram Video*　　**P**

Charlie Chaplin II　　　　　　Fil-Ent　'1?
Comedy
04464　　111 mins　　B/W
B, V

Charlie Chaplin, Edna Purviance, Eric Campbell, Ben Turpin, Bud Jamison, directed by Charles Chaplin

A compilation of six silent Chaplin classics: 'The Immigrant' (1917), 'His New Job' (1915), 'The Vagabond' (1916), 'The Champion' (1915), 'Work' (1915), and 'The Adventurer' (1917).
F — EN
Mutual; Essanay — *Polygram Video*　　**P**

Charlie Chaplin III　　　　　Fil-Ent　'1?
Comedy/Film-History
04694　　115 mins　　B/W
B, V

Charlie Chaplin, Henry Lehrman, Alice Davenport, Minta Durfee, Edna Purviance, Charles Insley, Marta Golden, Eric Campbell

The original versions of seven of Chaplin's classic two-reel comedies, produced between 1915 and 1919, are included on this tape: 'Making a Living,' 'A Woman,' 'The Floorwalker,' 'The Fireman,' 'The Count,' 'The Rink,' and 'A Jitney Elopement.'
F — EN
Mutual et al — *Polygram Video*　　**P**

Charlie Chaplin IV　　　　　Fil-Ent　'1?
Comedy/Film-History
04693　　54 mins　　B/W
B, V

Charlie Chaplin, Edna Purviance, Billy Armstrong, Charles Insley, Albert Austin, Ben Turpin, Leo White, Bud Jamieson, Fatty Arbuckle, Charley Chase, Minta Durfee

Four of Chaplin's classic two-reel comedies, produced between 1914 and 1916, are included on this tape in their original versions: 'A Night at the Show,' 'One A.M.,' 'A Night Out,' and 'The Rounders.'
F — EN
Mutual et al — *Polygram Video*　　**P**

**Charlie Chaplin Comedy　　Fil-Ent　'1?
Theatre No. 2, The**
Comedy
09109　　119 mins　　B/W
B, V

Charlie Chaplin

This cassette features further short films of the early 1900's; 'Mabel at the Wheel' (24 mins.), 'Laughs of Yesterday' (90 mins.), 'The Tramp' (23 mins.), 'Flicker Flashback No. 10' (8 mins.) 'The Woman' (23 mins.), 'Flicker Flashback No. 11' (8 mins.) and 'At the Bank' (24 mins.).
F — EN
RKO — *Kingston Video*　　**H, P**
KV 63

**Charlie Chaplin Comedy　　Fil-Ent　'??
Theatre No. 1**
Comedy
05661　　121 mins　　B/W
B, V

PALADIN VIDEO HOME ENTERTAINMENT GUIDE

Charlie Chaplin, Mabel Normand, Blanche Sweet
This cassette features short films of the early 1900's all with Modern sound effects, music and commentary. Including 'His Trysting Place' 1914 (24 mins), 'Movie Memories' consisting of 'The Fortune', 'The Regiments Dog' and 'Death Train' (8 mins), 'Shanghaied' 1915 (23 mins), 'Flicker Flashback No 29' consisting of 'Saved from Himself' and 'Never to Late to Mend' 1909 (9 mins), 'The Rink' 1916 (23 mins), 'Flicker Flashback No 14' consisting of 'The Revolutionist's Revenge' 1905 and 'The Goddess of Sagebrush Gulch' 1908 (7 mins) and 'A Night at the Show' 1916 (24 mins).
F — EN
RKO — *Kingston Video*   **H, P**
KV51

Charles Muffin   Fil-Ent '79
Drama
13702   104 mins   C
B, V
David Hemmings, Sam Wanamaker, Jennie Linden, Pinkas Braun, Ian Richardson, Ralph Richardson, directed by Jack Gold
When the smooth young men of British Intelligence disappear one by one on a secret mission the department is forced to bring in one of their discredited, shabbier counterparts to pull off the espionage coup of the century.
S,A — EN
Thames Video — *THORN EMI*   **P**
90 2587

Charlie Rivel—The Clown   Chl-Juv '79
Circus
04410   30 mins   C
B, V
The world-famous clown is seen in his on-stage acts as an 'acrobat', a 'Chaplin,' and a trapeze artist.
F — EN
Unknown — *VCL Video Services*   **P**

Charlotte's Web   Fil-Ent '72
Fantasy/Musical
05613   94 mins   C
B, V
Animated, voices by Debbie Reynolds, Paul Lynde, Henry Gibson, Agnes Moorehead
The famous story by E B White of Wilbur the pig and his friendship with Charlotte the spider transformed into a cartoon musical by Hanna/Barbera.
F — EN
Paramount — *Home Video Merchandisers* **H, P**
003

Charly   Fil-Ent '68
Drama
04262   103 mins   C
B, V
Cliff Robertson, Lilia Skala, Dick Van Patten, Claire Bloom, Leon Janney, William Dwyer
Charly Gordon is a gentle adult with the mind of a child. Attracted to Charly by his determination to improve, his teacher Alice persuades a group of doctors to undertake experimental neuro-surgery on Charly. The effect is dramatic but with a most unexpected ending.
BBFC:A — *S,A — EN*
Cinerama Releasing — *Rank Video Library*
H, P
0032

Charulata   Fil-Ent '64
Drama/Romance
08669   117 mins   B/W
B, V
Soumitra Chatterjee, Madhabi Mukerjee, Sailen Mukherjee, directed by Satyajit Ray
This film tells the story of the innocent relationship between Charu, the wife of a preoccupied businessman and her husband's cousin. As long as they remain unaware of the storm clouds gathering above them, matters are contained. But when she recognizes and declares her love the storm breaks. It is subtitled.
C,A — EN
R D Bansal Productions — *Longman Video*
P
LGBE 5006/LGVH 5006

Checkmate   Fil-Ent '68
Crime-Drama
09356   92 mins   C
B, V
Patrick McGoohan
This tape contains one episode from the highly successful television series 'The Prisoner.' In this episode the Prisoner stands for election as the new 'Number Two' but finds that even a candidate for this top position has no freedom of speech.
S,A — EN
Patrick McGoohan — *Precision Video Ltd*
P
BITC 2136/VITC 2136

Cheech and Chong's Next Movie   Fil-Ent '80
Comedy
13306   94 mins   C
B, V
Cheech Martin, Thomas Chong, directed by Thomas Chong

(For Explanation of codes, see USE GUIDE and KEY)

PALADIN VIDEO HOME ENTERTAINMENT GUIDE

The comedy pair bring their own type of humour to the screen again in a sequel to 'Up in Smoke' containing a further collection of drug and racial jokes in a round of riotous adventure.
BBFC:18 — A — EN
Howard Brown — *CIC Video*   H, P
BET 1118/VHT 1118

Cheerleaders Beach Party   Fil-Ent '78
Comedy
06937   83 mins   C
B, V
Stephanie Hastings, Linda Jenson, Mary Lou Loredan, Denise Upson, Carole Moore, directed by Alex E. Goiten
A university is in danger of losing its best football players. Their sexy cheerleaders step in to save the day.
BBFC:X — A — EN
Unknown — *Rank Video Library*   H, P
1038C

Cheerleaders' Wild Weekend   Fil-Ent '79
Drama/Comedy
13692   84 mins   C
B, V
Kristine DeBell, Jason Williams, directed by Jeff Werner
Fifteen young and pretty cheerleaders are kidnapped to be held as ransom for an extortion plot but the kidnappers have taken on more than they can handle.
BBFC:18 — A — EN
Chuck Russell — *THORN EMI*   P
90 3087

Cherry Picker, The   Fil-Ent '??
Comedy
05457   79 mins   C
V2, B, V
Lulu, Bob Sherman, Spike Milligan, Wilfrid Hyde White, Patrick Cargill, Terry Thomas, Jack Hulbert, Fiona Curzon
An American VIP finds out that his son is leading a 'sleep-in' at Windsor Castle. He hires a girl and her eccentric father to get him back to work. A task that proves more than difficult, she battles to get him to work and he battles to avoid work and stay in bed. Also involves his father's mistress, a pub landlady and a chatty nymphomaniac.
BBFC:AA — C,A — EN
Unknown — *Iver Film Services*   P
68

CherylLadd-Fascinated   Fil-Ent '82
Music-Performance
08473   50 mins   C
B, V
Cheryl Ladd, directed by John Goodhue
This tape features Cheryl Ladd as a photographer who lives out, in a musical fantasy, the characters she is shooting. Some of the tracks included are 'Fascinated', 'Think It Over', 'Just Like Old Times', 'Lesson from the Leavin'', 'Lady Gray,''Cold as Ice,''It's only Love' 'Try a Smile,' 'The Rose Nobody Knows' and 'Sakura, Sakura.'
S,A — EN
EMI — *THORN EMI*   P
TXE 90 14354/TVE 90 14352

Chess Programme I   Spo-Lei '6?
Games
04357   50 mins   B/W
V2, B, V
Six classic chess games are dramatised or 'played' by animated chess pieces. The games are famous matches dated from 1851 to 1932.
S,A — EN
Unknown — *Intervision Video*   H, P
A-AE 0256

Chess Programme II   Spo-Lei '6?
Games
04358   52 mins   B/W
V2, B, V
Six classic chess games are dramatised or 'played' by animated chess pieces. Games recreated date from 1858 to 1870.
S,A — EN
Unknown — *Intervision Video*
A-AE 0257

Chess Programme III   Spo-Lei '6?
Games
04359   48 mins   B/W
V2, B, V
Five classic chess games are dramatised or 'played' by animated chess pieces. Games recreated date from 1886 to 1895.
S,A — EN
Unknown — *Intervision Video*   H, P
A-AE 0258

Chess Programme IV   Spo-Lei '6?
Games
04360   50 mins   B/W
V2, B, V
Six classic chess games are dramatised or 'played' by animated chess pieces. Games recreated date from 1910 to 1925.
S,A — EN
Unknown — *Intervision Video*   H, P
A-AE 0259

PALADIN VIDEO HOME ENTERTAINMENT GUIDE

Chess Programme V   Spo-Lei '6?
Games
04361   45 mins   B/W
V2, B, V
Five classic chess games are dramatised or recreated by animated chess pieces. Games 'played' date from 1820 to 1941.
S,A — EN
Unknown — *Intervision Video*   **H, P**
A-AE 0260

Chess Programme VI   Spo-Lei '6?
Games
04362   45 mins   B/W
V2, B, V
Six classic chess games are dramatised or 'played' by animated chess pieces. Games recreated date from 1916 to 1948.
S,A — EN
Unknown — *Intervision Video*   **H, P**
A-AE 0261

Chess Programme VII   Spo-Lei '6?
Games
04363   50 mins   B/W
V2, B, V
Six classic chess games are dramatised or 'played' by animated chess pieces. Games recreated date from 1928 to 1950.
S,A — EN
Unknown — *Intervision Video*   **H, P**
A-AE 0262

Chicken Chronicles, The   Fil-Ent '77
Comedy
10064   87 mins   C
V2, B, V
Phil Silvers, Ed Lauter, Steven Guttenburg, Lisa Reeves
This film tells the tale of an all-American teenage boy who's having problems from his Principal at school, his employer, but most of all from his girl-friend. Events take their course up until the night of the senior prom.
S,A — EN
Avco Embassy — *Embassy Home Entertainment*   **P**
2112

Chigley   Chi-Juv '84
Cartoons
13089   60 mins   C
B, V
Animated
This tape shows episodes from the television series, featuring Lord Belborough and Bessie the Engine and the make believe town of Chigley.
PS,I — EN
Unknown — *Longman Video*   **P**
5025

Child, The   Fil-Ent '76
Horror
07671   95 mins   C
B, V
Rosalie Cole
Set in an isolated old farmhouse in the middle of a dark wood, a strange little girl with uncanny mental abilities nightly visits her mother's grave. There she communicates with the ghoul-like creatures that roam the woods.
A — EN
Valient Intl Pictures — *Video Network*   **P**
0002

Child Bride of Short Creek, The   Fil-Ent '81
Drama
09254   120 mins   C
V2, B, V
Christopher Atkins, Diane Lane, Conrad Bain, Kiel Martin, Helen Hunt, directed by Robert Lewis
This film is based on true happenings during July 1953 in a small farming village near the Utah/Arizona border. Two young people fall in love. Because of the strict rules of the community the two are not allowed to marry. They plan to elope, but the Arizona State troops invade the village to put an end to this 'State of Insurrection'.
BBFC:A — *S,A — EN*
Lawrence Schiller Prods — *Iver Film Services*   **P**
210

Child of Love   Fil-Ent '8?
Romance
06904   90 mins   C
V2, B, V
Dyan Cannon, Donald Pilon
This film tells of a tender affectionate chapter of a romantic affair which develops into a realistic story of true sentimental feeling. Two people deeply in love suffer as they are unable to spend their lives together.
BBFC:AA — *S,A — EN*
Unknown — *Temple Enterprises Ltd*   **H, P**

Children of An-Lac, The   Fil-Ent '82
Drama
12852   93 mins   C

(For Explanation of codes, see USE GUIDE and KEY)

PALADIN VIDEO HOME ENTERTAINMENT GUIDE

V2, B, V
Shirley Jones, Ina Balin, Beulah Quo
This film tells the story of the attempted evacuation of orphaned children from South Vietnam, during the final stages of the civil war.
S,A — EN
Charles Fries Productions — *Video Programme Distributors* **P**
217

Children of the Corn   Fil-Ent '84
Horror
12884   88 mins   C
B, V
Peter Horton, Linda Hamilton, directed by Fritz Kiersch
A group of children in a small farming community led by a fanatical boy preacher tyrannise the adult population and slaughter breaks loose as they appease a satanic demon.
BBFC:18 — *A — EN*
New World Pictures — *THORN EMI* **P**
TXA 90 25564/TVA 90 25562

Children of the Full   Fil-Ent '73
Moon/Visitor from the
Grave
Horror
08757   170 mins   C
V2, B, V
Christopher Cazenove, Celia Gregory, Diana Dors, Robert Urquhart;Kathryn Leigh Scott, Simon MacCorkindale, Gareth Thomas, Mia Nadasi
Two 'Hammer House of Horror' films are contained on one cassette. In 'Children of the Full Moon' (90 mins.) a married couple are delighted when a colleague loans them his remote Somerset cottage for a weeks delayed honeymoon. However, their happiness turns distinctly sour after a hair-raising ride, which leaves them stranded miles from anywhere. 'Visitor from the Grave' tells of an intruder in the middle of the night, who after tearing through the cottage, turns his attention on the woman occupant.
S,A — EN
Hammer Films — *Precision Video Ltd* **P**
CRITC 2120/BITC 2120/VITC 2120

Children of the Stones   Fil-Ent '??
Mystery
06160   98 mins   C
B, V
Iain Cuthbertson, Gareth Thomas, Freddie Jones, Veronica Strang, Ruth Dunning, Peter Demin, Katherine Levy
A mysterious story surrounding a village called Milbury that is held under the power of a massive circle of Neolithic stones. At the centre is an astronomy professor who lives in the Manor. Newcomers fall victim to the power; into the village arrive a scientist and his son and an old tramp who owns an ancient amulet—his shield against unseen powers.
F — EN
Unknown — *Guild Home Video* **H, P, E**

Children Shouldn't Play   Fil-Ent '69
with Dead Things
Horror
01680   85 mins   C
V2, B, V
Alan Ormsby, Jane Daly
An acting company goes to an island to shoot a film. They find strange and ghoulish things beginning to happen when they start to dabble in witchcraft.
BBFC:AA — *C,A — EN*
Gemeni Film; Benjamin Clark Prods — *Intervision Video* **H, P**
A-A 0018

Children's Cinema   Fil-Ent '7?
Cartoons
06893   53 mins   C
V2, B, V
Animated
A selection of cartoons featuring the adventures of Dick Tracy, the resourceful detective, Jetstream who helps those in danger with his jet planes, and Kidpower, a clan of children who encounter all kinds of situations. The music and songs of the Osmond Brothers accompanies these amusing adventures.
M,S — EN
Unknown — *European Video Company* **P**

Children's Story, The   Fil-Ent '??
Education/Drama
09859   30 mins   C
B, V
Michaela Ross, Mildred Dunnock
This is a telling exposure of the way modern subversive techniques can be utilised in the classroom. It is written, directed and produced by the novelist James Clavell.
S,A — ED
Unknown — *Polygram Video* **H, P**
791 5384/7915 382

Child's Play/And the Wall   Fil-Ent '83
Came Tumbling Down
Drama/Suspense
13154   150 mins   C
B, V
Mary Crosby, Nicholas Clay, directed by Val Guest, Gareth Hunt, Barbi Benton, Peter Wyngarde, directed by Paul Annett

130   (For Explanation of codes, see USE GUIDE and KEY)

PALADIN VIDEO HOME ENTERTAINMENT GUIDE

Two films are contained on one cassette. 'Child's Play' is a tale about a family caught in a series of supernatural events while 'And the Wall Came Tumbling Down' is a story of black magic spanning several centuries.
BBFC:15 — S,A — EN
Hammer Films Prods — Brent Walker Home Video Ltd   P
BW 38

China Rose   Fil-Ent '83
Drama
10186   ? mins   C
B, V

George C. Scott, Ali MacGraw, Michael Bien, Denis Lill, David Snell, James Hang, Carolyn Levine, John Nisbet, Alice Hall, directed by Robert Day

This film, based on an actual incident, takes place during the recent revolution in China and follows a man's search for his son. Convinced he has been murdered in the uprisings, he hires an interpreter with whom he becomes emotionally involved. Desperate to discover the truth their quest leads them deeper into the underground world of political corruption and the intrigues of the heroin trade.
A — EN
Robert Halmi Inc. — Video Form Pictures
H, P
MGS 31

Chinatown   Gen-Edu '74
Mystery
01210   131 mins   C
B, V

Jack Nicholson, Faye Dunaway, John Huston, Diane Ladd, directed by Roman Polanski

A complex tangled mystery involving Jack Nicholson as a private detective working on a seemingly routine case that mushrooms into more than he bargained for.
Academy Awards '74: Best Original Screenplay (Robert Towne)   C,A — EN
Paramount — CIC Video   H, P

Chinese Hercules   Fil-Ent '??
Martial arts
05471   92 mins   C
V2, B, V

Yang Sze, Chaing Fan, directed by Choy Tak

A gigantic super-villain is hired to destroy the lives of poor Chinese labourers. He is defied by a young girl who is the only one able to stand against him. This film is dubbed in English.
BBFC:X — A — EN
Unknown — Iver Film Services   P
24

Chinese Mechanic   Fil-Ent '??
Martial arts
06857   92 mins   C
V2, B, V
Barry Chan

A young man, who witnessed the power of Kung Fu as a young child, decides to study the art. However, he kills a man and has to go to prison. His father is forced to decide whether to fight the Kung Fu gangs or leave his home. He chooses to fight.
S,A — EN
Unknown — European Video Company
P

Chisholms—Cassette 1, The   Fil-Ent '79
Adventure
08366   150 mins   C
V2, B, V

Robert Preston, Rosemary Harris, Ben Murphy, Brian Kerwin, Jimmy Van Patten, Susan Swift, Stacey Nelkin, Charles Frank, Brian Keith, Glynnis O'Conner

This film tells the tale of a family in Virginia, who leave their home to make a dangerous journey west, to California. The two sons are falsely arrested and the family have to go on without them.
C,A — EN
Alan Landsburg Productions — Guild Home Video   H, P, E

Chisholms—Cassette 2, The   Fil-Ent '79
Adventure
08367   150 mins   C
V2, B, V

Robert Preston, Rosemary Harris, Ben Murphy, Brian Kerwin, Jimmy Van Patten, Stacey Nelkin, Charles Frank, Brian Keith, Sandra Griego Cassidy

This continues the story of the Chisholm family heading west. The youngest daughter is stabbed by an Indian War party. However, they are reunited with their two sons and continue their journey.
C,A — EN
Alan Landsburg Productions — Guild Home Video   H, P, E

Chisum   Fil-Ent '70
Western
06038   110 mins   C
B, V

John Wayne, Forrest Tucker, Geoffrey Devel, Glenn Corbett, Christopher George, Ben Johnson, directed by Andrew V. McLaglen

---

(For Explanation of codes, see USE GUIDE and KEY)   131

PALADIN VIDEO HOME ENTERTAINMENT GUIDE

Set in New Mexico in the 1870's, a cattle baron meets up with Pat Garrett and Billy the Kid; together they fight the town boss and his corrupt law officer who plan on taking over Lincoln County and the cattle ranch.
BBFC:U — F — EN
Warner Bros; Batjac Prod — *Warner Home Video*   P
WEX1089/WEV1089

Chitty Chitty Bang Bang   Fil-Ent '68
Musical/Fantasy
01282   142 mins   C
V2, B, V
Dick Van Dyke, Sally Ann Howes, Lionel Jeffries, Gert Frobe, directed by Ken Hughes
The adventures of a crackpot inventor, his beautiful girlfriend, his two children, and a dilapidated car possessed of magical qualities. Based on a novel by Ian Fleming.
BBFC:U — F — EN
United Artists; Albert R. Broccoli; Warfield Prod — *Intervision Video*   H
UA A B 5013

Chocky   Fil-Ent '84
Science fiction
13693   112 mins   C
B, V
Andrew Ellams, James Hazeldine, Carol Drinkwater, Zoe Hart
A strange, far advanced spirit from a different planet visits a young boy who suddenly discovers he has all kinds of talents that he didn't know he possessed.
M,A — EN
Vic Hughes — *THORN EMI*   P
90 3085

Choice, The   Fil-Ent '81
Drama
12921   96 mins   C
B, V
Susan Clark, Mitchell Ryan, Joanne Nail, Justin Lord, Jennifer Warren, directed by David Greene
A twenty-year-old college student goes to her mother for advice when she discovers she is pregnant and learns that she too had a similar experience and had to make a choice between abortion or keeping the baby.
BBFC:15 — C,A — EN
King Features Entertainment — *Video Form Pictures*   H, P
MGS 52

Choices   Fil-Ent '??
Drama
08618   87 mins   C
V2, B, V
Paul Karajotes, Lelia Goldoni, Victor Trench, Val Avery
This film based on a true story tells the tale of a boy who divides his time between football, playing the violin and chasing girls. After a swimming accident he loses his hearing. He is dropped from the the team and his world seems to fall apart. He begins to mix with the 'drop-outs' narrowly escaping the police after a drug-taking session. However, he shakes himself out of this self-pity and begins to climb back to normality.
C,A — EN
Unknown — *Hokushin Audio Visual Ltd*   P
VM 69

C.H.O.M.P.S   Fil-Ent '79
Comedy-Drama
09454   89 mins   C
V2, B, V
Wesley Eure, Valerie Bertinelli, Conrad Bain, Chuck McCann, Red Buttons
A wave of burglaries has put the small town of Hamilton in deep trouble. The police force are baffled and the normal anti-burglar devices ineffective. A man from one of the two rival security system manufacturers unveils the world's top-secret system, CHOMPS, Canine Home Protection System. CHOMPS only has one flaw, which complicates the lives of everyone concerned.
BBFC:15 — S,A — EN
American International; Hanna-Barbera — *Guild Home Video*   H, P, E

Chosen, The   Fil-Ent '82
Drama
10067   112 mins   C
V2, B, V
Maximilian Schell, Rod Steiger, Robby Benson, Barry Miller
Adapted from Chaim Potok's highly acclaimed novel, this is the story of a friendship between two Jewish boys. Set in New York in the forties, it depicts the world events at that time and the clash of traditions which exist between the two sects within the Jewish faith.
BBFC:PG — S,A — EN
Edie and Ely Landau — *Embassy Home Entertainment*   P
1365

Chris Barber Band, The   Fil-Ent '8?
Music-Performance
08711   105 mins   C
V2, B, V, LV

PALADIN VIDEO HOME ENTERTAINMENT GUIDE

This tape features Chris Barber and his jazz band live in the Assembly Rooms, Derby. Some of the songs included are '(Take Me) Back to New Orleans', 'Goodbye, Goodbye, Goodbye' and 'Mack the Knife.'
F — EN
Ken Griffin; Andy Finney — *BBC Video* **H, P**
BBCV 3018

Chris de Burgh—The Video   Fil-Ent '84
Music-Performance
12184   68 mins   C
B, V
This cassette shows Chris de Burgh in conversation, rehearsal and concert. His tracks include 'Carry On,' 'Waiting for the Hurricane,' 'Spanish Train,' 'A Spaceman Came Travelling,' 'Borderline,' 'The Revolution,' 'A Rainy Night in Paris,' 'Ship to Shore' and 'Patricia the Stripper.' It is recorded in stereo.
F — EN
Unknown — *A&M Sound Pictures*   **P**
825

Christiane F   Fil-Ent '81
Drama
12096   120 mins   C
B, V
Natja Brunkhorst, Thomas Haustein, directed by Ulrich Edel
The story of a fourteen year old's degradation as a victim of big city corruption. Based on an original 'Stern' magazine expose.
A — EN   GE
Maran Film; Popular Film — *Polygram Video* **H, P**
0402684/0402682

Christine   Fil-Ent '83
Horror
12484   110 mins   C
B, V
Keith Gordon, John Stockwell, Alexandra Paul, directed by John Carpenter
This film is shot on location in Southern California and is based on a best selling novel whose plot revolves around a vehicle possessed by evil with the power to seduce those of its choosing and the teenager who becomes the object of its wrath. It has a musical backing of 16 songs.
BBFC:18 — C,A — EN
Columbia Pictures; Richard Kobritz — *RCA/Columbia Pictures Video UK* **H, P**
10292

Christine McVie Concert, The   Fil-Ent '84
Music-Performance
12878   60 mins   C
B, V, CED
This concert taped at Reseda Country Club includes tracks such as 'You Make Loving Fun,' 'Don't Stop' and 'World Turning.' The programme includes footage from her current solo tour and music videos of 'Got a Hold on Me' and 'Love Will Show Us How.'
F — EN
Derek and Kate Burbidge for Zoetrope Ltd — *Vestron Video International*   **P**
11013

Christmas Carol, A   Fil-Ent '??
Cartoons/Christmas
08807   45 mins   C
B, V
Animated
This is an adaptation of Charles Dicken's classic tale, which tells the story of a miserly old man who is changed on Christmas Eve.
F — EN
Movietel — *VCL Video Services*   **P**
A275B

Christmas Carol, A   Fil-Ent '??
Cartoons/Christmas
08388   60 mins   C
V2, B, V
Animated
This animated version of Charles Dickens' classic Christmas story features drawings by John Worsley.
M,S — EN
Anglia Television — *Guild Home Video*
H, P, E

Christmas Carol, A   Fil-Ent '8?
Cartoons
12554   72 mins   C
V2, B, V
Animated
The popular characters of Scrooge and Tiny Tim appear in this adaptation of one of Charles Dickens' most popular novels.
F — EN
Unknown — *RPTA Video Ltd*   **H, P**

Christmas Carols from Cambridge   Fil-Ent '78
Music-Performance
09783   57 mins   C
B, V

(For Explanation of codes, see USE GUIDE and KEY)

PALADIN VIDEO HOME ENTERTAINMENT GUIDE

The traditional festival of nine lessons and carols from King's College, Cambridge. Sir John Gielgud reads the lessons and the camera explores the beautiful chapel.
F — EN
EMI Audio Visual Services Ltd. — THORN EMI   P
TXG 90 0001 4/TVG 90 0001 2

Christmas Evil Fil-Ent '7?
Horror/Suspense
08013   89 mins   C
V2, B, V
Brandon Moggart, Jeffrey de Munn
The story tells of three young children waiting expectantly for Santa Claus, only it is not their father. After an attempted suicide by one of the sons, he keeps a list of all the good girls and all the bad girls. With a psychopathic killer on the loose the bad girls become threatened.
BBFC:X — A — EN
Unknown — Iver Film Services   P
177

Christmas Messenger, The Fil-Ent '75
Cartoons/Christmas
09216   30 mins   C
B, V
Animated, Richard Chamberlain, voices by David Essex, Leo McKern, David Hemmings
Colourful animation is used to portray tales of Christmas, together with film sequences.
F — EN
Potterton Prods — Video Form Pictures
H, P
MGK 3

Christmas Mountain Fil-Ent '81
Adventure/Fantasy
08703   90 mins   C
V2, B, V
Slim Pickens, Mark Miller, Barbara Stanger, Bryan Polman, directed by Jacques Moro
An out-of-luck Texas cowboy is caught in a blizzard, and half frozen he stumbles into a small unfriendly mountain town. He lands up in jail, but to repay his misdeeds is given the task of taking food and clothes to a recently widowed pregnant mother. During the night he is visited by the ghost of his old saddle partner who needs his help in order to get to heaven.
BBFC:U — F — EN
Unknown — Video Unlimited   H, P

Christmas Music from York Minster/Handel's Messiah Fil-Ent '??
Music-Performance
06152   142 mins   C
B, V
Two presentations on one cassette. 'Christmas Music from York Minster' (45 mins) features words and music for Christmas with the King's Singers, The Spinners, Gerald Harper, Moira Anderson, The Archbishop of York, Huddersfield Choral Society, Northern Sinfonia Orchestra and more. 'Handel's Messiah' (97 mins) is performed by the Huddersfield Choral Society and the Northern Sinfonia Orchestra conducted by Owain Arwel Hughes.
F — EN
Max-Wilson Prod — Guild Home Video
H, P, E

Christmas to Remember, A Fil-Ent '78
Drama
09077   95 mins   C
B, V
Jason Robards, Eva-Marie Saint, Joanne Woodward, George Parry, Bryan Englund, Mary Beth Manning
An elderly farm couple's city-bred grandson comes to stay for Christmas, during the bleak period of the Depression in the 1930's. The grandfather is gruff and moody, embittered by the death of his only son in the First World War. However, he gradually opens his heart to the young, lively lad.
F — EN
George Englund Entprs — Video Tape Centre
P
VTC 1041

Christy Minstrels, The Fil-Ent '7?
Variety
04367   60 mins   C
B, V, PH17, 3/4U
Christy Minstrels, Righteous Brothers
A musical variety show with the Christy Minstrels and the Righteous Brothers.
F — EN
Unknown — Vidpics International   P

Churchill's Leopards Fil-Ent '8?
War-Drama
07760   84 mins   C
V2, B, V
Richard Harrison, Klaus Kinski
English saboteurs and resistance fighters join forces to blow up a strategic dam.
S,A — EN
Unknown — Fletcher Video   H, P
V110

Cincinnati Kid, The Fil-Ent '65
Drama
07720   101 mins   C
B, V

---

134   (For Explanation of codes, see USE GUIDE and KEY)

PALADIN VIDEO HOME ENTERTAINMENT GUIDE

Steve McQueen, Edward G. Robinson, Karl Malden, Ann-Margret, Tuesday Weld, Joan Blondell, Rip Torn, Jack Weston, directed by Norman Jewison
Set in New Orleans in the late 1930's, a young expert gambler is determined to take the crown away from the King of stud poker. They arrange a non-stop poker duel-to-the-death to decide who will reign. As the tension mounts before the big day, behind-the-scenes events nearly alter the outcome. Based on a novel by Richard Jessup.
BBFC:AA — S,A — EN
MGM;Filmways — MGM/UA Home Video   P
UMB 10135/UMV 10135

Circus, The/A Day's Pleasure   Fil-Ent '??
Comedy
05844   72 mins   B/W
B, V
Charlie Chaplin, Allan Garcia, Merna Kennedy, Henry Crockford, directed by Charlie Chaplin
This cassette features two Charlie Chaplin films: 'The Circus' (1928), a film of life in a travelling circus and 'A Day's Pleasure' (1919), featuring Chaplin's attempts to enjoy a boating excursion with his wife and little children.
F — EN
United Artists — Polygram Video   P
7901484/7901482

Circus of Horrors   Fil-Ent '60
Horror
09000   87 mins   C
B, V
Anton Diffring, Erika Remberg, Yvonne Monlaur, Jane Hylton, Kenneth Griffith
A former plastic surgeon absconds to France when an operation on his lover goes drastically wrong. He finds haven in a circus, able to continue his career. Eventually a mutilated victim catches up with him.
BBFC:X — A — EN
A I; Julian Wintle-Parkwyn Prods — THORN EMI   P
TXC 90 1547 4/TVC 90 1547 2

Circus World   Fil-Ent '64
Drama
01063   137 mins   C
V2, B, V
John Wayne, Rita Hayworth
American circus owner in Europe searches for aerialist he loved 15 years before and whose daughter he has reared.
BBFC:U — F — EN
Paramount; Samuel Bronston Prod — Intervision Video   P
A-A 0204

Circus World Championships   Fil-Ent '80
Circus
04390   60 mins   C
B, V
This film presents breathtaking displays from the world's greatest circuses as performers compete for the coveted title of 'Circus World Champion.'
F — EN
Unknown — VCL Video Services   P

Citizen Kane   Fil-Ent '41
Drama
04638   120 mins   B/W
B, V
Orson Welles, Joseph Cotten, Agnes Moorehead
'Citizen Kane' is the story of a powerful newspaper publisher, told by those who thought they knew him best.
Academy Awards '41: Best Original Screenplay; New York Film Critics Award '41: Best Motion Picture.   F — EN
RKO — THORN EMI   H, P
TXC 90 0052 4/TVC 90 0052 2

City Lights   Fil-Ent '31
Drama/Comedy
05840   88 mins   B/W
B, V
Charlie Chaplin, Virginia Cherrill, Harry Myers, Henry Bergman, Jean Harlow, directed by Charlie Chaplin
A poignant tale of a little tramp's love for a blind flower girl and his efforts to obtain money for an expensive eye operation.
F — EN
United Artists — Polygram Video   P
7901454/7901452

City of the Dead   Fil-Ent '??
Horror
04340   78 mins   C
V2, B, V
Story of a New England town still practising witchcraft.
BBFC:X — A — EN
Vulcan — Intervision Video   H
A-A 0021

City on Fire   Fil-Ent '79
Drama/Suspense
05241   103 mins   C
B, V, LV
Barry Newman, Shelley Winters, James Franciscus, Susan Clark, Leslie Nielson, Ava Gardner, Henry Fonda

(For Explanation of codes, see USE GUIDE and KEY)

PALADIN VIDEO HOME ENTERTAINMENT GUIDE

A single cigarette end falls on dry grass as gasoline leaks into the city's sewers. The combination is catastrophic.
BBFC:AA — C,A — EN
Unknown — Rank Video Library   H, P
0050

City Under the Sea   Fil-Ent '65
Adventure/Fantasy
08999   80 mins   C
B, V

Vincent Price, David Tomlinson, Susan Hart
Based on story by Edgar Allan Poe, this film tells the story of the disappearance of a beautiful young hotel owner. Her two friends set out to find her, only to find themselves dragged down into a beautiful underwater city, presided over by an awesome Vincent Price.
F — EN
American International — THORN EMI   P
TXC 90 1550 4/TVC 90 1550 2

Clairvoyant, The   Fil-Ent '34
Suspense
09940   77 mins   B/W
B, V

Claude Rains, Fay Wray, Jane Baxter, Mary Clare, Athole Stewart, Ben Field, Felix Aylmer, Donald Calthrop
A music hall memory man is amazed to find he really is psychic after a mysterious girl comes to see his bogus mind-reading act.
BBFC:PG — F — EN
Gainsborough — Rank Video Library   H, P
0162 A

Clash By Night   Fil-Ent '52
Drama
06188   90 mins   B/W
B, V

Marilyn Monroe, Barbara Stanwyck, Robert Ryan, Paul Douglas
A small town drama set in a fishing village. The lives of a fishing boat skipper, his defeated wife and morbid friend are contrasted with the rugged beauty and drabness of the environment.
S,A — EN
RKO — VCL Video Services   P
X0292

Clash Of The Titans   Fil-Ent '81
Fantasy
07731   114 mins   C
V2, B, V

Harry Hamlin, Judi Bowker, Burgess Meredith, Maggie Smith, Ursula Andress, Claire Bloom, Sian Phillips, Flora Robson, Laurence Olivier, directed by Desmond Davis

This film, based on centuries-old Greek and Nordic legends, follows the heroic adventures of Perseus as he battles against magic, monsters and ancient gods to rescue the beautiful Andromeda. The nightmare horrors encountered include a hag whose snake-like hair paralyzes, a two-headed dog whose mouth drips poison and three witches that share a single eye.
BBFC:A — S,A — EN
MGM — MGM/UA Home Video   P
UMR 10074/UMB 10074/UMV 10074

Class   Fil-Ent '83
Comedy/Romance
12761   98 mins   C
B, V

Jacqueline Bisset, Rob Lowe, Andrew McCarthy, Cliff Robertson

A romantic comedy about a college boy who enters an affair only to discover that the woman is his room-mate's mother.
BBFC:15 — C,A — EN
Martin Ransohoff — Rank Video Library
H, P
1081 D

Class of 1984   Fil-Ent '81
Drama
09787   90 mins   C
B, V

Perry King, Merrie Lynn Ross, Timothy Van Patten, Stefan Arngrim, Michael Fox, Roddy McDowall, directed by Mark Lester

A brutal portrait of a savage gang of school bullies who victimise their music teacher and all his nearest and dearest. Featuring the song "I Am the Future" performed by Alice Cooper.
BBFC:18 — C,A — EN
Guerrilla High Productions Ltd. — THORN EMI
P
TXA 90 1732 4/TVA 90 1732 2

Class of '63   Fil-Ent '73
Drama/Romance
09261   72 mins   C
V2, B, V

James Brolin, Joan Hackett, Cliff Gorman, Ed Lauter, Woodrow Chambliss, Gary Barton, directed by John Korty

A college reunion stirs up many old memories, especially old love affairs. A woman realises that she has never stopped loving her former college boyfriend, now married to her ex-

PALADIN VIDEO HOME ENTERTAINMENT GUIDE

classmate, and during the reunion week their love is renewed. However, a friend becomes more aggressive with growing jealousy of this affair.
BBFC:A — *S,A* — *EN*
MPC/Stonehenge — *Iver Film Services*
P
212

Claws
Fil-Ent '77
Horror
07888   93 mins   C
V2, B, V
Jason Evers, Leon Ames
A woodsman takes on the dangerous task of tracking down a monster grizzly bear that has been clawing innocent people to death. Based on an ancient Indian legend about an evil bear-like creature that leaves no tracks behind it.
A — *EN*
Chuck D Kean — *Walton Film and Video Ltd*
P

Cleopatra
Fil-Ent '63
Drama
01751   194 mins   C
B, V
Elizabeth Taylor, Richard Burton, Rex Harrison, Pamela Brown, directed by Joseph L. Mankiewicz
Julius Caesar intervenes in the civil war in Egypt, where he falls in love with Cleopatra. Academy Awards '63: Best Cinematography.
S,A — *EN*
20th Century Fox, Walter Wanger — *CBS/Fox Video*   **P**
4A-038

Cleopatra Jones
Fil-Ent '73
Martial arts/Adventure
13170   88 mins   C
B, V
Tamara Dobson, Bernie Casey, Shelley Winters, directed by Jack Starret
A fast moving story about a special agent in the constant war against drug pushers and in particular those operating in the ghetto.
BBFC:X — *A* — *EN*
Warner Bros Inc — *Warner Home Video*
P
61275

Cliff Richard and The Shadows 'Thank You Very Much'
Fil-Ent '81
Music-Performance
05054   52 mins   C
B, V

This film includes scenes from the 1978 reunion concert at the London Palladium, original footage of 'Oh Boy,' film of early stage performances, and interviews. Songs include 'The Young Ones,' 'Let Me Be the One,' 'Devil Woman.'
F — *EN*
Unknown — *THORN EMI*   **P**
TXE 90 0329 4/TVE 90 0329 2

Cliff Richard-The Video Connection
Fil-Ent '83
Music-Performance
09776   55 mins   C
B, V
Cliff Richard
This tape features Cliff Richard performing some of his best known songs including 'My Kinda Life', 'Wired for Sound', 'A Little in Love', 'Hey Mr Dream Maker', 'Summer Holiday', 'Miss You Nights', 'Devil Woman', 'Baby You're Dynamite', 'Please Don't Fall in Love', 'Never Say Die', 'Carrie', 'The Young Ones', 'Dreamin', 'Daddy's Home' and 'We Don't Talk Any More'.
F — *EN*
EMI Records Ltd — *THORN EMI*   **P**
TXE 90 1960 4/TVE 90 1960 2

Clifton House Mystery, The
Fil-Ent '??
Mystery
06161   150 mins   C
B, V
Ingrid Hafner, Sebastian Breaks, Peter Sallis, Margery Withers, June Barrie, Olga Lowe, Oscar Quitak, Donald Morley, Margot Boyd, Ann Way
A family move into an old house in an historic area of Bristol. They realise that they have inherited more than just bricks and mortar when their children establish a strange and disturbing relationship with certain unwelcome guests. They attempt to rid the house of these ghostly visitations.
F — *EN*
Unknown — *Guild Home Video*   **H, P, E**

Clinic, The
Fil-Ent '82
Comedy
12196   90 mins   C
V2, B, V
Chris Haywood, Simon Burke, Pat Levison
This film tackles in a new way some of society's oldest problems and fears which under normal circumstances would be treated as social taboos.
BBFC:18 — *A* — *EN*
Robert Le Tet; Bob Weis — *Medusa Communications Ltd*   **H, P**

(For Explanation of codes, see USE GUIDE and KEY)

137

PALADIN VIDEO HOME ENTERTAINMENT GUIDE

Cloak and Dagger   Fil-Ent '84
Suspense/Drama
13645   99 mins   C
B, V

Henry Thomas, Dabney Coleman, directed by Richard Franklin
When a highly imaginative youngster known to go into his own dream world of spies and secret missions really does the witness the murder of an FBI agent by a spy ring, no one believes him and he finds he is playing a real-life game this time.
BBFC:PG — *S,A* — *EN*
Universal — *CIC Video*   H, P
1156

Clones, The   Fil-Ent '74
Science fiction/Horror
06793   90 mins   C
V2, B, V

Michael Greene, Gregory Sierra, Otis Young, Susan Hunt
A genetic scientist creates a clone of a noted doctor, intending to have the clone replace the original.
C,A — *EN*
Filmmakers International — *Intervision Video*   H, P
A-AE 0355

Clones of Bruce Lee, The   Fil-Ent '80
Martial arts/Adventure
08640   85 mins   C
V2, B, V

Dragon Lee, Bruce Le, Bruce Lai, Bruce Thai, directed by Joseph Kong
This Kung-Fu fan's delight follows gallant warriors from the Far East who battle to reign supreme over the land of exotic self-defense. A syringe of warm blood is taken from the dead Bruce Lee, to create the clones. Three new Bruce Lees are created; number 1 is sent to uncover a gold smuggling gang, and numbers 2 and 3 to eliminate a mad doctor.
C,A — *EN*
Newport Releasing — *Hokushin Audio Visual Ltd*   P
VM 46

Cloud Dancer   Fil-Ent '80
Adventure/Drama
06147   107 mins   C
V2, B, V

David Carradine, Jennifer O'Neill, Joseph Bottoms
A story centered on the Aerobatic Champion of the World who flies planes in the dangerous and exciting world of competitive flying. The woman who loves him accepts his obsession but they have a volatile relationship; his doctor advises him not to fly, however he accepts a challenge by one of his pupils for supremacy in the sky.
BBFC:AA — *S,A* — *EN*
Melvin Simon Productions — *Guild Home Video*   H, P, E

Clowns—Magic—Sensations Fil-Ent '7?
Circus
02223   60 mins   C
V

The circus is part of the Russian tradition—and here their very best perform, including the great clown Popov.
F — *EN*
Unknown — *JVC*   P
PRT 16

Club, the   Fil-Ent '81
Drama
09141   102 mins   C
B, V

Jack Thompson, Graham Kennedy, Frank Wilson, directed by Bruce Beresford
This film tells the story of an Australian Football Club. It tells of the players, on the pitch and off as they try to escape from the relentless pressures of the game. It describes one man's effort to weld a group of hardened individuals into a successful team.
S,A — *EN*
South Australian Film Corp; New South Wales Film Corp — *Video Brokers*   H, P
003X

Clutch of Power, The   Fil-Ent '79
Adventure/Martial arts
04412   90 mins   C
B, V

The Mongolians attack China's largest cities during the Sundy dynasty in the year 1267. Espionage makes the Chinese defence measures more difficult.
S,A — *EN*
Unknown — *VCL Video Services*   P

Cobra   Fil-Ent '??
Crime-Drama
06215   120 mins   C
B, V

Jean Yanne, Senta Berger
A political campaign leads to urban guerrilla warfare on the streets of Marseilles. A candiate massacres his main opponent and the main

138   (For Explanation of codes, see USE GUIDE and KEY)

PALADIN VIDEO HOME ENTERTAINMENT GUIDE

supporters; as the opposition is eliminated a young girl is accidentally killed. Her father, out for revenge, employs an elite band of Vietnam veterans. War is declared.
S,A — EN
Unknown — *VCL Video Services*   **P**
P146D

Cocaine—One Man's Poison   Fil-Ent '83
Drama/Drugs
12938   90 mins   C
B, V
Karen Grassle, Pamela Bellwood, Dennis Weaver
A real estate salesman faced with business and personal problems resorts to drugs and finds his mind and body are being slowly destroyed.
A — EN
Charles Fries; David Goldsmith — *Video Form Pictures*   **H, P**
MGS 33

Cody   Fil-Ent '??
Adventure
05495   74 mins   C
V2, B, V
Tony Becker, Terry Evans
A father, an ex-rodeo rider, is determined that his twelve year old son learns the harsh realities of life and is intolerant of the boy's childhood dreams. The boy's pet dog is killed and he finds a goose who captures his heart and changes the father's attitude to his son.
BBFC:U — F — EN
Unknown — *Iver Film Services*   **P**
116

Cold River   Fil-Ent '84
Drama/Adventure
13262   94 mins   C
B, V
Suzanne Weber, Pat Petersen, Richard Jaekel, Robert Earl Jones
Two teen-age children are left stranded in the Adirondacks just as winter starts to set in and the lessons they have learnt are put to test when they have to pit their wits against man and beast.
BBFC:PG — F — EN
Fred G Sullivan — *CBS/Fox Video*   **P**
6346

Colditz Story, The   Fil-Ent '55
War-Drama
01599   97 mins   B/W
B, V
John Mills, Eric Portman, Lionel Jeffries, Bryan Forbes, Ian Carmichael, Richard Wattis
Prisoners of war from the Allied countries join together in an attempt to escape from Colditz, a castle-prison deep within the Reich, reputed to be escape-proof.
BBFC:U — C,A — EN
British Lion; Ivan Foxwell — *THORN EMI*   **P**
TXC 90 0094 4/TVC 90 0094 2

College   Fil-Ent '27
Comedy
04680   65 mins   B/W
B, V
Buster Keaton, Ann Cornwall, Snitz Edwards
On a campus teeming with students and faculty, stonefaced Buster Keaton builds this screen comedy by proving himself the most inept of them all—and yet still makes them look silly. This film is colour-tinted.
F — EN
United Artists — *Polygram Video*   **P**

Colonel Culpeper's Flying Circus   Gen-Edu '??
Documentary/Aeronautics
06966   50 mins   C
V2, B, V, LV
This film looks at the work of enthusiasts and veterans who work to keep one of the world's finest collections of historic combat aircraft airborne. Based in southern Texas. The Ghost Squadron of the Confederate Airforce perform spectacular aerobatics and re-enact air battles.
F — EN
Tony Salmon — *BBC Video*   **H, P**
BBCV 6014

Colorado Charlie   Fil-Ent '??
Western
06089   96 mins   C
V2, B, V
Charlie Lawrence, Barbara Hudson
A sheriff tries to retire and take up a peaceful life elsewhere. A gunman causes him to return to his former profession. The sheriff not only has the gunman to contend with but also a peace-loving wife. The future is decided when a chase leads to a final confrontation between him and the gunman.
S,A — EN
Unknown — *Video Programme Distributors*   **P**
Cinehollywood—V1640

Colt Concert   Fil-Ent '??
Western
06090   90 mins   C
V2, B, V
Franco Nero, George Hilton, Lynn Shayne

PALADIN VIDEO HOME ENTERTAINMENT GUIDE

A message is received from Laramie Town which says 'come home soon'. Corbett sets out to unveil the mystery of a series of acts of violence and sadistic cruelty.
S,A — EN
Unknown — *Video Programme Distributors*
P

Cinehollywood—V1030

Coma Fil-Ent '77
Suspense/Drama
05313   104 mins   C
V2, B, V
Genevieve Bujold, Michael Douglas, Richard Widmark, Elizabeth Ashley, Rip Torn, Lois Chiles, Harry Rhodes, directed by Michael Crichton
A resident surgeon at Boston Memorial Hospital undertakes her own investigation into the irreparable brain damage her best friend suffers in the course of a minor operation. She discovers that healthy young people having operations in a particular theatre are all suffering the same fare. She becomes obsessed with proving that the hospital is murdering them. Based on the novel by Robin Cook.
S,A — EN
United Artists; MGM — *MGM/UA Home Video*
P

UMB10013/UMV10013

Combat Killers Fil-Ent '??
War-Drama
07906   91 mins   C
V2, B, V
A group of battle weary soldiers return to their camp to discover they have a new Captain. He is only after personal glory and to this end he sacrifices the lives of his men. A Lieutenant then seizes command of the survivors and leads them on a suicidal mission against the Japanese.
S,A — EN
Unknown — *Video Programme Distributors*
P

Replay—1004

Come Back to the Five and Dime, Jimmy Dean, Jimmy Dean Fil-Ent '82
Drama
12055   105 mins   C
V2, B, V
Sandy Dennis, Karen Black, Cher, directed by Robert Altman

This film examines the lives of former members of James Dean's Fan Club at a reunion some 20 years after his death.
BBFC:18 — S,A — EN
Cinecom International — *Intervision Video*
H, P

A-A 0518

Come Play with Me Fil-Ent '7?
Comedy
02095   93 mins   C
V2, B, V
Harrison Marks, Alfie Bass, Mary Millington
A sex romp about two master counterfeiters who abscond with the plates and take refuge in an exclusive health farm staffed by sex-starved nurses.
BBFC:X — A — EN
Unknown — *Hokushin Audio Visual Ltd*
P

VM-01

Come Play With Me 2 Fil-Ent '??
Drama
08637   80 mins   C
V2, B, V
Simone Sanson, Brigitte Lahaie, Celina Mood
A country villa occupied by three beautiful women, seems a heaven-sent invitation for all the predatory males of the area. The stunning woman and her two delectable nieces begin to weave a web of sexual involvement.
A — EN
Unknown — *Hokushin Audio Visual Ltd*
P

VM 49

Comeback, The Fil-Ent '7?
Horror
02419   100 mins   C
B, V
Jack Jones, Pamela Stephenson, David Doyle, Bill Owen
Nick Cooper (played by Jack Jones) is returning to his singing profession after the trauma of a crumbling marriage. Events turn rather horrifying when Nick wakes night after night hearing the screams of his former wife, and sees the vision of a rotting corpse in a wheelchair.
A — EN
Unknown — *Derann Film Services*   H, P

DV 119B/DV 119

Comeback Fil-Ent '83
Drama/Adventure
13256   96 mins   C
B, V
Michael Landon, Jurgen Prochnow, Edward Woodward, Moira Chen, Priscilla Presley

PALADIN VIDEO HOME ENTERTAINMENT GUIDE

An Australian news photographer is determined to rescue his lover from Laos and risking his life he brings her back to the friendly shores of Thailand.
BBFC:15 — S,A — EN
Hall Bartlett — CBS/Fox Video **P**
1344

Comeback Kid, The Fil-Ent '80
Romance/Comedy
09209   104 mins   C
B, V
John Ritter, Susan Dey, James Gregory, Doug McKeon, Jeremy Licht, Rod Gist, directed by Peter Levin
A minor league baseball player leaves his life of glamour and becomes coach to a gang of tough, mistrusting street kids. He meets a beautiful, career-oriented playground supervisor.
F — EN
ABC Circle Films; Louis Randolph — *Video Form Pictures* **H, P**
DIP 7

Comedy of Errors, The Fil-Ent '74
Comedy-Drama
05391   130 mins   C
B, V
The Royal Shakespeare Company
An adaptation of William Shakespeare's 'The Comedy of Errors' performed by the Royal Shakespeare Company. A complicated story that relies on the twists and turns in the plot and confusion between two masters and two servants, the impossibility of telling twins apart, twice, and two sisters romantically involved in all the events.
S,A — EN
Royal Shakespeare Company Production — *Precision Video Ltd* **P**
BITC 3088/VITC 3088

Comedy of Terrors, The Fil-Ent '63
Comedy/Satire
13475   82 mins   C
B, V
Vincent Price, Boris Karloff, Basil Rathbone, Peter Lorre, directed by Jacques Tourneur
A strange tale of unusual happenings in a firm of undertakers.
BBFC:AA — A — EN
American International Pictures — *Rank Video Library* **H, P**
V 1082

Comes a Horseman Fil-Ent '78
Drama
13069   119 mins   C
B, V
Jane Fonda, James Caan, directed by Alan J. Pakula
In this film, set in Montana 1945, neighbouring ranchers are forced into an alliance to protect their grazing land from ruthless oil barons.
BBFC:AA — C,A — EN
United Artists Corp — *Warner Home Video* **P**
99237

Comfort and Joy Fil-Ent '84
Comedy/Drama
13707   90 mins   C
B, V
Bill Paterson, C.P. Grogan, directed by Bill Forsyth
A Glasgow D.J. stumbles across a furious vendetta between rival Italian ice-cream families and undertakes to settle the dispute himself.
BBFC:PG — F — EN
Davina Belling; Clive Parsons — *THORN EMI* **P**
90 2783

Coming Home Fil-Ent '78
Drama
01061   127 mins   C
V2, B, V
Jane Fonda, Jon Voight, Bruce Dern, directed by Hal Ashby.
Fonda falls in love with paraplegic Voight while her husband is overseas. A look at the effect of the Vietnam War on people.
Academy Awards '78: Best Actor (Voight), Best Actress (Fonda).   BBFC:X — A — EN
Jerome Hellman — *Intervision Video* **H**
UA A B 5005

Coming Out Alive Fil-Ent '73
Drama/Suspense
12081   80 mins   C
V2, B, V
A child is snatched from its mother in what seems to be just another custody fight. A mercenary is employed by the mother and is successful in finding the boy but the implications deepen and a sinister plot is unravelled.
BBFC:15 — S,A — EN
Worldwide Entertainment Corporation — *Intervision Video* **H, P**
A-A 0482

Coming Out of the Ice Fil-Ent '82
Drama
09858   93 mins   C
B, V, LV
John Savage, Willie Nelson, Francesca Annis, Ben Cross

(For Explanation of codes, see USE GUIDE and KEY)

PALADIN VIDEO HOME ENTERTAINMENT GUIDE

Based on a true story, this film concerns an idealistic young American who emigrates to the USSR. He is wrongly arrested for spying and spends some eighteen years in labour camps before his final repatriation to his homeland.
S,A — EN
Frank Konigsberg — *Polygram Video* **H, P**
791 5424/791 5422/791 5421

Coming Soon
Fil-Ent '83
Horror/Documentary
13340   53 mins   C
B, V
Narrated by Jamie Lee Curtis, directed by John Landis
This is a compilation of trailers for horror movies, from the silent era through to the sixties and seventies.
C,A — EN
Mick Garris; Robert B Idels — *CIC Video* **H, P**
BEJ 1109/VHJ 1109

Commando Attack
Fil-Ent '69
War-Drama/Adventure
07974   105 mins   C
B, V
Guy Madison, Helen Chanel
This film is set in the Philippines during the Second World War. It tells of a group of American soldiers, trapped on a small island, recently captured by the Japanese Army. They have their task to complete despite being underarmed and outnumbered.
BBFC:A — S,A — EN
Unknown — *AVI Video Ltd* **P**
006

Commandos
Fil-Ent '72
War-Drama
04204   100 mins   C
V2, B, V
Lee Van Cleef, Jack Kelly, directed by Armando Crispino
Commandos must reach an oasis controlled by the Italians and replace them, keeping hold of the base until the Allied landing.
BBFC:X — A — EN
Sansone and Crosciki — *Guild Home Video* **H, P**

Commodore 64 Introduction to Programming—Level I
Bus-Ind '84
Electronic data processing
13108   30 mins   C
B, V
David Redclift
The fundamentals of the machine, screen and keyboard to the construction of a basic program are covered in this tape.
C,A — I
Holiday Brothers Ltd — *Holiday Brothers Ltd* **P**

Commodore 64 Introduction to Programming—Level 2
Bus-Ind '84
Electronic data processing
13109   30 mins   C
B, V
David Redclift
In the second part of this series, the viewer is introduced to the more advanced aspects of programming.
C,A — I
Holiday Brothers Ltd — *Holiday Brothers Ltd* **P**

Communion
Fil-Ent '77
Horror
07649   103 mins   C
B, V
Brooke Shields, directed by Alfred Sole
As a 12-year-old problem child becomes rejected by everyone she retreats into her private basement playroom. Undisturbed and undetected she performs gothic rituals. At morning Mass her sister prepares for her First Communion but she is brutally murdered by a masked fiend.
A — EN
Allied Artists — *VCL Video Services* **P**
P219D

Commuter Husbands
Fil-Ent '??
Comedy-Drama
08867   83 mins   C
V2, B, V
Gabrielle Drake
This film tells of men on the loose with a natural instinct to hunt, not food but women. The prey exists in abundance and usually enjoys being caught; all he needs is opportunity.
BBFC:X — A — EN
Unknown — *Video Film Organisation* **P**
Replay 1011

Companeros
Fil-Ent '70
Western/Adventure
08018   111 mins   C
V2, B, V
Franco Nero, Jack Palance, Fernando Ray, Thomas Milian, Iris Berben, directed by Sergio Corbucci

PALADIN VIDEO HOME ENTERTAINMENT GUIDE

This film, set in Mexico, tells the complicated story of a young Mexican revolutionary and a Swede. Both men desire the country's wealth. The combination to the city's safe is held by Professor Xantos, who first has to be freed from a Texan prison.
BBFC:A — S,A — EN
Cinerama Releasing — Iver Film Services **P**
185

Compleat Beatles, The   Fil-Ent '82
Music-Performance
12211   114 mins   C
B, V
The Beatles, George Martin, Brian Epstein, Billy Preston, Milt Oken, Bruce Johnson, Mick Jagger
This programme traces the Beatles' career in song through eight years, starting with their early days in the Cavern Club. New interviews are featured as well as vintage studio footage.
F — EN
Delilah Films — MGM/UA Home Video **P**
10166

Complete Dinner Party, A   How-Ins '81
Cookery
05947   150 mins   C
B, V
Helge Rubinstein
This film shows, step by step and in detail, how to prepare an eight course dinner for six. Includes Spinach soup, Smoked fish ramekins, Lemon sorbet, Boeuf Bourguignon, Scalloped potatoes, Salad with French Dressing, Iced liquor mousse, almond biscuits and chocolate truffles. Presented by a well known author and regular cookery column writer.
S,A — I
Unknown — Precision Video Ltd **P**
BOPV 2561/VOPV 2561

Complete Potter, The   Gen-Edu '7?
Arts/Handicraft
07355   168 mins   C
B, V
On this tape the potter Leslie Williams reveals the craft she has studied for over 26 years.
F — ED
Unknown — Precision Video Ltd **P**
BOPV 2563/VOPV 2563

Con Artist, The   Fil-Ent '79
Comedy
05692   89 mins   C
V2, B, V
Anthony Quinn, Corinne Clery, Adriano Celentano, Capucine, directed by Serge Carbucci
An unlikely pair of con artists are thrown together under an odd set of circumstances and decide to work together. They each try to outdo the other until they devise a plan to 'sting' a gang of racketeer hoodlums. Their plan is so successful that even the gang laugh at their own gullibility.
BBFC:A — S,A — EN
Unknown — Derann Film Services   **H, P**
GS702P/GS702B/GS702

Conan the Barbarian   Fil-Ent '82
Adventure
08450   124 mins   C
B, V
Arnold Schwarzenegger, James Earl Jones, Gerry Lopax, Sandahl Bergman, directed by John Milius
This film, set in a mythical prehistoric age, brings to life the cartoon character, Conan. It follows the quest of Conan to learn 'the riddle of steel' and therefore seek revenge on those who had brutally murdered his parents, and retrieve the sword bequeathed to him by his father.
BBFC:X — A — EN
Universal — THORN EMI **P**
TXA 90 1275 4/TVA 90 1275 2

Concert for Bangla Desh, The   Fil-Ent '72
Music-Performance
08460   95 mins   C
B, V
George Harrison, Bob Dylan, Leon Russell, Don Preston, Ravi Shankar, Ringo Starr, Eric Clapton
George Harrison assembled a benefit concert in New York's Madison Square Gardens in 1971. He was joined by Ringo Starr, Eric Clapton, Bob Dylan, Leon Russell, Billy Preston, and Ravi Shankar. It features songs such as 'Mr. Tambourine Man', 'Blowin' in the Wind', 'Something', 'Jumpin' Jack Flash', 'Here Comes the Sun' and 'Youngblood'.
F — EN
20th Century Fox — THORN EMI **P**
TXD 90 0911 4/TVA 90 0911 2

Concorde Affair   Fil-Ent '79
Drama/Suspense
06872   92 mins   C
V2, B, V
James Franciscus, Van Johnson, Mimsy Farmer, Joseph Cotten
In this film a Concorde crashes during a test flight near the island of Martinique. The only survivor, an air hostess, is rescued by two fishermen. When she disappears and the fishermen are killed a reporter becomes

PALADIN VIDEO HOME ENTERTAINMENT GUIDE

suspicious. He discovers that the crash was a result of sabotage and the gang are planning a second attack. However the plane, complete with passengers, has already taken off.
S,A — S,A — EN
Italian — European Video Company   P

Concrete Jungle, The   Fil-Ent '82
Drama
10193   106 mins   C
B, V

Jill St. John, Tracy Bregman, Barbara Luna, directed by Tom De Simone

A young girl is set-up by her boyfriend after a romantic skiing holiday. She is arrested, tried and sentenced to the Woman's Correctional Institute after customs find cocaine inside her skis. She is persuaded to keep silence when her boyfriend says he will secure her release. Terrified at the lesbianism, rape, drugs and strong arm tactics she makes enemies whilst trying to retain her sanity.
BBFC:18 — A — EN
Columbia; Billy Fine — Video Form Pictures
H, P
MGS 27

Condorman   Fil-Ent '81
Comedy
08003   87 mins   C
B, V

Michael Crawford, Oliver Reed, Barbara Carrera, James Hampton, Jean—Pierre Kalfon, directed by Charles Jarrott

This film tells the story of Woody Wilkins, an inventive comic book writer, who adopts the identity of his own character in order to help a beautiful Russian spy escape.
BBFC:U — F — EN
Walt Disney Productions — Rank Video Library
H
06600

Conduct Unbecoming   Fil-Ent '75
Drama
07449   107 mins   C
B, V

Michael York, Richard Attenborough, Trevor Howard, Stacy Keach, Christopher Plummer, Susannah York, directed by Michael Anderson

This film is set in a lonely outpost on the North-West frontier during the last years of the nineteenth century where the Twentieth Indian Light Cavalry are preserving the might of the British Raj. Life moves easily until the arrival of two young subalterns whose actions threaten to destroy the honour of the regiment. A young widow accuses one of them of rape, resulting in an unofficial Court Martial through which they try to avoid a public scandal.
BBFC:A — S,A — EN
Allied Artists — THORN EMI   P
TXB 90 0722 4/TVB 90 0722 2

Confessions from the David Galaxy Affair   Fil-Ent '79
Comedy
02097   95 mins   C
V2, B, V

Diana Dors, Allan Lake, Anthony Booth, Kenny Lynch, Glynn Edwards, Queenie Watts, Milton Reed

Funny sex film for both sexes. Mary Millington meets a super stud in a sexy spectacular.
BBFC:X — A — EN
Roldvale Prods — Hokushin Audio Visual Ltd
P
VM-03

Confessions of a Police Captain   Fil-Ent '72
Crime-Drama
10068   100 mins   C
V2, B, V

Martin Balsam, Franco Nero

A police captain's hatred of a vicious gangster and his somewhat dubious methods of bringing him to justice eventually leads to the Police Captain himself being investigated by a new young district attorney.
C,A — EN
Avco Embassy; Euro International — Embassy Home Entertainment   P
2093

Confessions of a Pop Performer   Fil-Ent '75
Comedy
12483   87 mins   C
B, V

Robin Askwith, Anthony Booth

The accident prone, amorously inclined hero of the Confessions series decides to conquer the pop music scene with many a hilarious mishap.
BBFC:18 — C,A — EN
Unknown — RCA/Columbia Pictures Video UK
H, P
10136

Confessions of the Sex Slaves   Fil-Ent '7?
Drama
02102   70 mins   C
V2, B, V

PALADIN VIDEO HOME ENTERTAINMENT GUIDE

True story of extortion, violence, and drug addiction that leads to prostitution as a World Health Authority investigates the practice of white slavery.
BBFC:X — A — EN
Unknown — Hokushin Audio Visual Ltd
P
VM-08

Connecting Rooms   Fil-Ent '69
Drama
08811   99 mins   C
B, V
Bette Davis, Michael Redgrave, Alexis Kanner, Kay Walsh, Gabrielle Drake, Leo Genn, Olga Georges—Picot, Richard Wyler, Brian Wilde
In this film Michael Redgrave plays a lodger in a seedy Bayswater boarding house. Because of his dark past he is continually pried upon by his landlady.
I,S — EN
Telstar — VCL Video Services   P
P319 D

Conquest   Fil-Ent '84
Science fiction
12252   79 mins   C
B, V
George Rivero, Sabrina Siani, Andrea Occhipinti, directed by Lucio Fulci
A hunt across sinister unknown worlds is on between two rivals in this spectacular space odyssey.
F — EN
Merlin Video; Giovanni Di Clemente — VCL Video Services   P
6662

Conquest of Everest, The   Gen-Edu '??
Mountaineering
05062   76 mins   C
B, V
Directed by Leon Clore
This film shows the preparation of the Hunt Expedition, and reveals the meticulous planning and large-scale operation required to get two men to the top of Everest. The camera-work of Thomas Skobank forms the basis of the film.
F — EN
John Taylor — THORN EMI   P
TXC 90 0244 4/TVC 90 0244 2

Conquest of the Planet of the Apes   Fil-Ent '72
Science fiction/Drama
07691   85 mins   C
V2, B, V
Roddy McDowall, Don Murray, Natalie Trundy, Hari Rhodes, Ricardo Montalban, directed by J. Lee Thompson
This film follows a further futuristic chapter in the history of the earth. After destruction through nuclear warfare the planet is ruled by apes and the humans are savages.
S,A — EN
Twentieth Century Fox — CBS/Fox Video
P
1137

Constantine and the Cross   Fil-Ent '60
Drama
07991   120 mins   C
B, V
Cornel Wilde, Belinda Lee, Christine Kaufmann, directed by Lionello DeFelice
This film set in the year 303 A.D. tells of the declaration of the Edict of Tolerance when Constantine becomes the Emperor of Gaul. He rallies his troops and defeats the Roman Legions, assuring freedom of worship for Christians. It is filmed in Italy and dubbed in English.
S,A — EN
Beaver—Champion; Jonia Films — Motion Epics Video Company Ltd   P
158

Contempt   Fil-Ent '63
Drama
10071   102 mins   C
V2, B, V
Brigitte Bardot, Jack Palance, Fritz Lang, Michel Piccoli, directed by Jean-Luc Godard
This psychological drama set in Rome and on the island of Capri tells the story of a beautiful woman searching for love and fulfillment in Rome's glamorous film colony.
A — EN
Embassy; Carlo Ponti — Embassy Home Entertainment   P
2094

Contes d'Hoffmann, Les   Fil-Ent '81
Opera
08472   150 mins   C
B, V
Placido Domingo, Luciana Serra, Agnes Baltsa, Ileana Cotrubus, Geraint Evans, Sigmund Nimsgern, Nicola Ghivselev, Robert Lloyd
This opera by Jacques Offenbach tells the story of the poet Hoffmann who, seeking to exorcise the failure of his current love affair, tells the tales of his three past loves. Each of them was thwarted by the evil influence of his rival. The music is conducted by Georges Pretre.
S,A — EN
Covent Garden Video Productions Ltd — THORN EMI   P
TXH 90 1321 4/TVH 90 1321 2

(For Explanation of codes, see USE GUIDE and KEY)

PALADIN VIDEO HOME ENTERTAINMENT GUIDE

Continental Divide　　　　Fil-Ent '81
Comedy/Romance
09266　　103 mins　　C
B, V

John Belushi, Blair Brown, Allen Goorwitz, directed by Michael Apted
A hard-nosed political columnist heads for the Colorado Rockies on what he thinks, is a 'cushy' assignment. His job is to interview a reclusive ornithologist—however, he ends up falling in love.
BBFC:PG　— *S,A* — *EN*
Universal — *CIC Video*　　**H, P**

Contract　　　　Fil-Ent '??
Drama
05474　　33 mins　　C
V2, B, V

Kenneth Farrington, directed by Paul Bernard
This is a story of racial conflict, set against the background of a decaying and derelict factory. Two people enact a macabre ritual with a loaded gun; they each represent the extremes of their Black and White groups. They are destructive, on drugs and riddled with hatred, ultimately doomed to lose. They project the society into which they were bred.
BBFC:X — *A* — *EN*
Unknown — *Iver Film Services*　　**P**
72

Control Factor　　　　Fil-Ent '7?
Adventure
09091　　92 mins　　C
B, V

Stephen Boyd, Ray Milland, Cameron Mitchell, France Nuyen, directed by Robert Day
A major scientific research group in America has invented an incredible device, capable of controlling impulses in the human brain. With this, mass populations are able to be controlled from great distances. Foreign powers learn of this device and are prepared to stop at nothing to achieve their aims.
S,A — *EN*
Unknown — *Video Tape Centre*　　**P**
VTC 1091

Conversation Piece　　　　Fil-Ent '75
Drama
12248　　? mins　　C
B, V

Burt Lancaster, Helmut Berger, Silvana Mangano, directed by Luchino Visconti
An isolated, wealthy professor has a collection of priceless paintings and through them becomes involved with an intriguing countess and her lovely daughter.
C,A — *EN*
Giovanni Bertolucci; Gaumont International — *VCL Video Services*　　**P**

Convoy　　　　Fil-Ent '78
Adventure
04635　　106 mins　　C
B, V

Kris Kristofferson, Ali MacGraw, Burt Young, Ernest Borgnine
Based on the hit record, 'Convoy' glorifies the trucker who, in pursuance of a feud with Sheriff Lyle Wallace, unites scores of his fellow-drivers via Citizens Band radio into a gigantic mile-long convoy which rolls along the Arizona highways towards the freedom of the Mexican border.
C,A — *EN*
United Artists; EMI — *THORN EMI*　　**H, P**
TXA 90 0231 4/TVA 90 0231 2

Cooking Around the　　　How-Ins '81
World
Cookery
05415　　60 mins　　C
B, V, FO
Prue Leith
Internationally recognised cookery expert Prue Leith demonstrates some basic cooking techniques from countries like Mexico, France, Spain, India, Greece, China and Italy. She shows how to prepare the dishes and produces three complete menus suitable for home dinner parties.
F — *I*
Michael Barratt Ltd — *Michael Barratt Ltd*
P

Cooking with Microwave　　How-Ins '8?
Cookery
07847　　41 mins　　C
B, V

This tape, full of useful tips, explores the versatility and advantages of Microwave cooking.
S,A — *ED*
Toshiba; Good House Keeping Institute — *Polygram Video*　　**H, P**

Cool Breeze　　　　Fil-Ent '72
Crime-Drama
12231　　97 mins　　B/W
B, V

Thalmus Rasulala, Judy Pace, Jim Watkins, Lincoln Kilpatrick
Based on a true and chilling story, the hustling 'Sidney Lord Jones' finds himself rejected from a promising career in football due to a war injury and gives vent to his frustration by acts of violence.
C,A — *EN*
MGM — *MGM/UA Home Video*　　**P**
10323

146　　(For Explanation of codes, see USE GUIDE and KEY)

PALADIN VIDEO HOME ENTERTAINMENT GUIDE

Cool Cats   Gen-Edu '83
Music
10152   76 mins   C
B, V

Paul Weller, Peter Townsend, Phil Everly, Malcolm Maclaren, directed by Stephanie Bennett

This film describes the fashions and fads of twenty-five years of rock and roll style. It includes talks on the influence of these events, and features songs from this era, including Presley, the Pistols, the Beatles, Bowie.
S,A — EN
Delilah Films — MGM/UA Home Video   P
UMB 10317/UMV 10317

Cool Hand Luke   Fil-Ent '67
Drama
06025   115 mins   C
B, V

Paul Newman, George Kennedy, J. D. Cannon, Jo Van Fleet, Lou Antonio, Richard Davalos, directed by S. Rosenberg

A young man in a chain gang operating in a Southern State defies the tough guards who endeavour to subdue him. Due to his actions he gains the respect of his fellow prisoners as he suffers to retain his individuality. Based on a novel by Don Pearce.
Academy Awards '67: Best Supporting Actor (Kennedy). BBFC:X — A — EN
Warner Bros; 7 Arts; Gordon Carroll; Jahem Prods — Warner Home Video   P
WEX1037/WEV1037

Cop in Blue Jeans   Fil-Ent '76
Crime-Drama/Adventure
09230   100 mins   C
B, V

Jack Palance, Tomas Milian

Set in Rome, this film tells of an undercover policeman, who, when he joins the forces with a gang of small-time crooks in an attempt to stamp out street crime, is led into a web of dishonesty at the highest level.
S,A — EN
Unknown — Video Form Pictures   H, P
CLO2

Copter Kids, The   Chi-Juv '74
Adventure
13451   57 mins   C
B, V

When a helicopter pilot accidentally causes a cattle stampede, his children try to make amends by tracking down a rustler who took advantage of the havoc.
BBFC:U — I,S — EN
Canadian Prods. — Rank Video Library   H, P
3109X

Corbari   Fil-Ent '??
War-Drama
08644   97 mins   C
V2, B, V

Tira Aumont, Guiliano Gemma

This film follows the story of how the dramatic love affair of a young Italian resistance partisan is upset by the Nazi and Fascist violence.
A — EN
Unknown — Fletcher Video   H, P
V171

Cormack   Fil-Ent '??
Crime-Drama/Adventure
07809   ? mins   C
B, V

Lynn Frederick, Lionel Stander

Set in the Canadian Rockies, this film follows the trail of a lawman who is feared by the rugged pioneers. When an outlaw he jailed escapes, the lawman relentlessly pursues him through the wild wastes during the fierce winter.
F — EN
Unknown — Video Tape Centre   P
VTC 1013

Cornered/The Woman on Pier Thirteen   Fil-Ent '51
Drama/Crime-Drama
05673   169 mins   B/W
B, V

Dick Powell, Walter Slezak, Micheline Cheirel, Luther Adler, Morris Carnovsky, directed by Edward Dmytryk, Robert Ryan, John Agar, Laraine Day, directed by Robert Stevenson

Two films are featured on one cassette. 'Cornered' (Black/white, 99 mins, 1946) is the story of a Canadian pilot, released from a prison camp, who travels across the world to find a Nazi war criminal who killed his wife and child. 'The Woman on Pier Thirteen' (Black/white, 70 mins, 1951) is the tale of a business man who is blackmailed by a political group into joining their plan to paralyse shipping. When his brother-in-law is killed he becomes determined to fight back.
S,A — EN
RKO — Kingston Video   H, P
KV39

(For Explanation of codes, see USE GUIDE and KEY)

PALADIN VIDEO HOME ENTERTAINMENT GUIDE

Corpse Grinders, The   Fil-Ent '74
Horror
02077   80 mins   C
B, V
Sean Kenney, Monika Kelley, Sanford Mitchell, J. Byron Foster
Cats suddenly, inexplicably attack their human owners, and the city is plagued by a wave of deaths and mutilations. Could the answer lie in an exotic brand of cat food? What is the secret ingredient?
A — EN
Unknown — VCL Video Services   P

Corridors of Blood   Fil-Ent '60
Horror
05468   83 mins   B/W
V2, B, V
Boris Karloff, Christopher Lee, Beta St John, Finlay Currie
Before the discovery of anaesthetics, patients requiring surgery were held down and suffered amputation while fully conscious. A dedicated surgeon, appalled at the suffering, experiments to find an answer.
BBFC:X — A — EN
MGM — Iver Film Services   P
113

Corrupt Ones, The   Fil-Ent '67
Adventure
12168   87 mins   C
V2, B, V
Robert Stack, Elke Sommer, Nancy Kwan
An innocent photographer finds himself drawn into a web of intrigue and violence when he finds himself in possession of a medallion which holds the key to an ancient treasure.
S,A — EN
Nat Wachsberger — Embassy Home Entertainment   P
1326

Corruption of Chris Miller   Fil-Ent '72
Drama
08707   90 mins   C
V2, B, V
Jean Seberg
A woman lives with her stepdaughter in a secluded villa. Her stepdaughter has just returned from a psychiatric clinic, having had treatment due to being raped by a teacher.
BBFC:AA — C,A — EN
Unknown — Video Unlimited   H, P
082

Cosgrove Hall's Funtime   Chi-Juv '84
Puppets
13714   60 mins   C
B, V

Animated
Three puppet shows are featured on this cassette titled 'Charlton and the Wheelies', 'Robin and Rosie of Cockleshell Bay' and 'Jamie and the Magic Torch'.
BBFC:U — PS,I — EN
Thames Video — THORN EMI   P
90 2877

Cosmic Princess   Fil-Ent '76
Science fiction
08744   95 mins   C
V2, B, V
Martin Landau, Barbara Bain, Catherine Schell, Brian Blessed, Anouska Hempel, Tony Anholt, Nick Tate, Zienia Merton
This film features a beautiful alien princess with the power to change at will into any living creature. She comes to the help of Moonbase Alpha when the runaway space outpost is lured to a deadly planet. Once she joins the Alphans, there are more adventures to come.
S,A — EN
ITC — Precision Video Ltd   P
CRITC 2130/BITC 2130/VITC 2130

Cotter/Island of Lost Women   Fil-Ent '??
Western/Adventure
05714   152 mins   C
B, V
Don Murray, Rip Torn, Carol Lynley, Sherry Jackson, directed by Paul Stanley, Venetia Stevenson, Alan Napier, Jeff Richards, John Smith, Diana Jorgens, directed by Frank Tuttle
Two films are featured on one cassette. 'Cotter' (Colour, 88 mins, 1974) is a modern day western in which a rodeo rider is killed because Cotter, an Indian rodeo clown, is too drunk to rescue him. He then gets into further trouble when a rancher is murdered and the towns folk start a lynching party. 'Island of Lost Women' (Black/white, 64 mins, 1960) features an atomic scientist who lives with his daughters on an island, protecting them from a world he does not trust. One day a plane is forced to land on the island and the girls became aware of men other than their father.
S,A — EN
Gold Key Entertainment; Warner Bros — Kingston Video   H, P
KV28

Count Basie   Fil-Ent '??
Music-Performance
06205   43 mins   C
B, V
One of the world's greatest jazz artists performs at the Hollywood Palladium with his own seventeen-piece band. Soloists include: Eddie

PALADIN VIDEO HOME ENTERTAINMENT GUIDE

'Lockjaw' Davies, Al Grey and Fran Jeffries. Songs include: Get it, Still Swinging, Big Stuff, The Spirit is Willing, Splanky Shiny Stockings, Leroy Brown and many more.
F — EN
Unknown — VCL Video Services P
V187A

Count Dracula's Great Love Fil-Ent '82
Horror
12848   79 mins   C
V2, B, V
Paul Naschy, Ingrid Garbo, Vic Winner, Rossana Yanni, Haydee Politoff, Mirta Miller
A heavy metal box is delivered to a nursing home near to the ruins of Count Dracula's castle just before four young girls arrive seeking shelter.
BBFC:18 — A — EN
Unknown — Video Programme Distributors P
VPD 231

Count of Monte-Cristo, The Fil-Ent '75
Drama
05389   98 mins   C
B, V
Richard Chamberlain, Trevour Howard, Louis Jourdan, Donald Pleasence, Tony Curtis, Kate Nelligan, Taryn Power
An adaptation of the classic tale by Alexander Dumas set in the Napoleonic era, which tells the story of Dantes, a young successful man betrayed by his friends.
S,A — EN
Norman Rosemont Productions — Precision Video Ltd P
BITC 2038/VITC 2038

Countdown Fil-Ent '68
Science fiction/Drama
12980   98 mins   C
B, V
James Caan, Robert Duvall, directed by Robert Altman
This is the story of the race of the astronaut chosen to be the first on the moon and of his tough instructor to make a moon landing before Russia.
BBFC:U — F — EN
Warner Bros — Warner Home Video P
61300

Countdown to Disaster Fil-Ent '68
Science fiction/Puppets
08739   90 mins   C
B, V
This features the 'Thunderbirds', sent by International Rescue, on one of their most dangerous missions. They have to save the Empire State Building from collapsing on New York City and at the same time keep control of a blazing fire in a mid-Atlantic oil station.
F — EN
Gerry Anderson Production — Precision Video Ltd P
BITC 2123/VITC 2123

Countess Dracula Fil-Ent '72
Horror
05147   91 mins   C
B, V
Ingrid Pitt, Sandor Eles, Lesley-Anne Down, Nigel Green, Maurice Denham, Patience Collier
Horrific story surrounding the historically true figure of Countess Elizabeth Bathori and her legendary penchant for bathing in the blood of the 600 virgin peasant girls she is reputed to have murdered.
BBFC:X — A — EN
20th Century Fox; Hammer Prods — Rank Video Library H, P
2009

Country Blue Fil-Ent '8?
Adventure
09058   89 mins   C
V
Dub Taylor, Jack Conrad, Rita George, David Huddleston
Two people decide to rob a bank, only to discover that once you have started there is no turning back. They are caught by the police and escape. A chase follows across the Everglades, with a tragic ending.
S,A — EN
Unknown — Astra Video   H, P

Countryman Fil-Ent '7?
Drama/Adventure
10139   98 mins   C
B, V
Directed by Dickie Jobson
Set in the Caribbean this film is an adventure of good against evil, of power misused and of fear against fate. Soundtrack includes music by Bob Marley and The Wailers, Toots and the Maytals, Steel Pulse, Aswad, Wally Badarou and Dennis Brown.
BBFC:AA — S,A — EN
Unknown — Island Pictures   P
IPV 606CV

Cousins in Love Fil-Ent '??
Drama
12781   90 mins   C
V2, B, V

(For Explanation of codes, see USE GUIDE and KEY)

PALADIN VIDEO HOME ENTERTAINMENT GUIDE

Anja Shute?Thierry Tevini?directed by David Hamilton
BBFC:18 — *A* — *EN*
Unknown — *Intervision Video*   **H, P**
A-A0468

Cover Me Babe   Fil-Ent '8?
Drama
12150   86 mins   C
B, V
Robert Forster, Sondra Locke, Susanne Benton, directed by Noel Black
A film student in Los Angeles plans to shoot a film about the lives of the people he knows. One of them becomes suspicious and obtains a reel of shot film to discover just how bizarre and twisted his ideas are.
A — *EN*
Unknown — *CBS/Fox Video*   **P**
1156

Covergirl   Fil-Ent '83
Drama
13661   92 mins   C
B, V
Jeff Conaway, Cathie Shirriff, Irena Ferris, Roberta Leighton, Deborah Wakenham, Kenneth Welsh, directed by Jean-Claude Lord
This film lays bare the hidden passions, jealousy and ruthless ambition that lies behind the glitter of the world of fashion and is the story of a girl and the man determined she will make it to the top.
BBFC:15 — *S,A* — *EN*
Claude Heroux — *CBS/Fox Video*   **P**
3045

Covert Action   Fil-Ent '78
Crime-Drama
09920   100 mins   C
V2, B, V
David Janssen, Corinne Clery, Arthur Kennedy
A man has a tape containing sensational information about the CIA. A friend of his, with more than a grudge against the CIA, knows he has the tape, but the CIA are tracking him down with ruthless determination.
BBFC:18 — *A* — *EN*
Italian — *Derann Film Services*   **P**
FGS 903

Cox and Box   Fil-Ent '8?
Opera
08929   100 mins   C
B, V
Russell Smythe, John Fryatt, Thomas Lawlor
This opera by Gilbert and Sullivan tells the story of Cox, who works by day and Box, who works by night. Their rascally landlord lets the same room to both of them, thereby doubling his profits. But eventually they meet and discover they are not only involved with the same girl, but are long lost brothers as well. The music is performed by The London Symphony Orchestra with The Ambrosian Opera Chorus.
S,A — *EN*
Brent Walker Prods — *Brent Walker Home Video Ltd*   **P**

Crab with the Golden   Chi-Juv '7?
Claws, The
Cartoons/Adventure
02277   60 mins   C
V
Animated
Tin Tin and Snowy are captured by smugglers but escape and meet the brave Captain Haddock. Together they pursue the gang in an adventure that takes them from the ocean to the desert.
M — *EN*
Unknown — *JVC*   **P**
PRT 21

Crackup/I Walked with a   Fil-Ent '4?
Zombie
Crime-Drama/Horror
05707   156 mins   B/W
B, V
Pat O'Brien, Claire Trevor, Herbert Marshall, Wallace Ford, Ray Collins, directed by Irving Reis, Tom Conway, Frances Dee, James Ellison, Edith Barret, directed by Jacques Tourneur
Two films are featured on one cassette. 'Crackup' (Black/white, 90 mins, 1947) involves an expert who lectures on how to detect a forgery in masterpieces. An international gang decide he knows too much and plan to eliminate him. 'I Walked with a Zombie' (Black/white, 66 mins, 1944) is set on an island of superstition and is said to be haunted. A nurse discovers that one of her mental patients wanders at night, the natives say she is one of the walking dead.
S,A — *EN*
RKO — *Kingston Video*   **H, P**
KV35

Cradle Will Fall, The   Fil-Ent '83
Drama/Suspense
12937   101 mins   C
B, V
Lauren Hutton, Ben Murphy, James Farentino, directed by John Moxey.
A woman patient sees a body being loaded into a car in a hospital and ultimately finds her own life in jeopardy.
BBFC:15 — *S,A* — *EN*
Joseph Cates — *Video Form Pictures*   **H, P**
MGS 044

(For Explanation of codes, see USE GUIDE and KEY)

PALADIN VIDEO HOME ENTERTAINMENT GUIDE

Kid with the 200 I.Q., The Fil-Ent '82
Comedy
12936   96 mins   C
B, V

Gary Coleman, Robert Guillaume, Kari Michaelson, directed by Leslie Martinson

A thirteen-year-old boy genius learns to cope with the japes from the other students at high school with the help of his favourite professor.
BBFC:U — F — EN
Jim Begg — *Video Form Pictures*   **P**
MGD 027

Crash Fil-Ent '76
Horror/Suspense
08796   85 mins   C
B, V

John Carradine, Jose Ferrer, Sue Lyon, John Ericson

An evil spirit in the form of a mysterious trinket causes a trail of destruction. A doctor decides to investigate when one of his patients is nearly killed.
A — EN
Group 1 — *VCL Video Services*   **P**
P327D

Crash of Flight 401, The Fil-Ent '78
Documentary/Drama
09175   101 mins   C
B, V

William Shatner, Adrienne Barbeau, Eddie Albert, Brooke Bundy, Christopher Connelly, Lorraine Gary, Ron Glass, Sharon Gless, George Maharis, Ed Nelson

This recounts the true story of one of the most baffling air disasters on record. En route from New York to Florida, the plane unexpectedly crashes in the Everglades. The Coast Guard mounts a heroic rescue effort that saves the lives of 73 passengers. It is based on the book by Rob and Sarah Elder.
S,A — EN
Charles Fries Prods — *Video Form Pictures*   **H, P**
MGS 12

Craze Fil-Ent '74
Drama/Horror
08307   96 mins   C
B, V

Jack Palance, Trevor Howard, Julie Edge, Suzy Kendall

An owner of an antique shop in London is a believer in witchcraft. He keeps an African Idol in the cellar where his black magic rituals occur. The strange Idol exerts a growing influence on the shop-owner, and after his first accidental sacrifice to the African he is greatly rewarded with gold sovereigns. The killings continue, reaping greater rewards.
BBFC:X — A — EN
Warner Bros; Harbour Prod — *Video Film Organisation*   **P**
0005

Crazed Fil-Ent '??
Horror/Mystery
08032   85 mins   C
V2, B, V

Laslo Papas, Belle Mitchel, Beverley Ross

This tells the horrific story of a woman who finds a flat with an old landlady so there will be privacy. The story continues with tragedy and horrible murders, with the old lady having to climb stairs.
BBFC:X — A — EN
Unknown — *Rank Video Library*   **H, P**
2019 C

Crazies Fil-Ent '74
Horror/Drama
07667   104 mins   C
B, V

Lane Carroll, W. G. McMillan, Harold Wayne Jones, directed by George A. Romero

A military plane carrying a biological warfare virus crashes near a small Pennsylvania town. The virus gets into the town's water supply and slowly begins to drive the inhabitants wild.
S,A — EN
Cambist — *Hello Video Ltd*   **P**
H13

Crazy World of Cars Gen-Edu '??
Automobiles
06059   30 mins   C
V2, B, V

A look at the drivers' love affair with the car, from the spectacular sequences of James Bond's Aston Martin to sports car racing, dune buggies, Hot Rods, daredevil dragster races and featuring the famous '500 mile Race' in the Nevada desert.
F — ED
Unknown — *Video Programme Distributors*   **P**
Cinehollywood—V840

Creature from Black Lake Fil-Ent '75
Horror
07905   93 mins   C
V2, B, V

Jack Elam, Bill Thurman, Dub Taylor, John Carson, Dennis Fimple, directed by Joy Houck Jr

(For Explanation of codes, see USE GUIDE and KEY)

PALADIN VIDEO HOME ENTERTAINMENT GUIDE

Mysterious happenings at Black Lake attract a couple of students laden with scientific equipment. They have heard stories that a creature said to weigh over four hundred pounds, stand eight feet tall and run like a deer has been spotted. The locals are wary but with the help of a trapper they locate the monster, with horrific consequences.
S,A — EN
Howco International — *Video Programme Distributors* P
Replay—1003

Creature from the Black Lagoon, The   Fil-Ent '54
Adventure
12047   79 mins   B/W
B, V
Richard Carlson, Richard Denning, Julia Adams, Whit Bissell, directed by Jack Arnold
An old fossilised hand from a web-fingered skeleton is discovered in the Amazon forest. This awakens the interest of a group of scientists and they set out along the river to find themselves at the tropical Black Lagoon. Unaware that the Gill-Man lives in the depths, they decide to go swimming. The Gill-Man is seen, but he stops at nothing to resist capture.
BBFC:PG — S,A — EN
Universal — *CIC Video*   H, P
BEJ 1085/VHJ 1085

Creeping Flesh, The   Fil-Ent '73
Horror
01151   92 mins   C
V2, B, V
Christopher Lee, Peter Cushing
Nightmarish tale which should discourage people from hanging around graveyards.
M,A — EN
Unknown — *Videomedia*   P

Creepshow   Fil-Ent '82
Horror
09020   119 mins   C
V2, B, V
Hal Holbrook, Adrienne Barbeau, Fritz Weaver, Leslie Nielsen, Carrie Nye, E.G. Marshall, Viveca Lindfors, Ed Harris, Ted Danson, Stephen King
'Creepshow' begins with an irate parent throwing a young boy's new horror comic away. At this point, each page comes to life, introducing a new live-action story. In 'Father's Day' a family are having tea in the drawingroom for a Father's Day celebration very unlike any other. The other stories, 'The Lonesome Death of Jordy Verrill,' 'The Crate,' 'Something to Tide You Over' and 'They're Creeping Up on You' contain some terrifying and unexpected events.
A — EN
Warner Bros — *Intervision Video*   H, P
AA 0462

Cries and Whispers   Fil-Ent '72
Drama
08665   91 mins   C
B, V
Liv Ullman, Harriet Andersson, Ingrid Thulin, Kari Sylwan, directed by Ingmar Bergman
This story is set in an old family mansion. Agnes is terminally ill, and is tended by a devoted maid and her two sisters. One of them despises her husband, and the other, a lazy, shallow but beautiful woman, drove her husband to attempted suicide. When Agnes dies, the two women are momentarily drawn closer together, only later to retreat once more into their solitary torments.
S,A — EN
Cinematograph — *Longman Video*   P
LGBE 7001/LGVH 7001

Crime Story   Fil-Ent '??
Suspense
05728   95 mins   C
V2, B, V
Sten Cooper
Secret service agents, from all over the world fight to obtain the serum which will provide immunity against radiation.
S,A — EN
Unknown — *Video Unlimited*   H, P

Crimebusters   Fil-Ent '??
Crime-Drama
07802   ? mins   C
B, V
Henry Silva
An army officer is asked to take up the case when a consignment of new prototype guns disappears. Forming an unwilling alliance with the police, he foils a kidnap attempt on a child, is badly beaten up, has his girlfriend assaulted, nearly dies in a bloody car chase and survives a bomb attack in his attempt to uncover the sinister mastermind.
S,A — EN
Unknown — *Video Tape Centre*   P
VTC 1009

Crocodile   Fil-Ent '78
Horror
04483   83 mins   C
V2, B, V
Dat Puvanai, Tany Tim

PALADIN VIDEO HOME ENTERTAINMENT GUIDE

A giant mutant crocodile is created through radiation emitted from atomic bomb testing. Two scientists attempt to track down the monstrous creature, which is wreaking havoc and terror throughout the country.
A — EN
Spectacular Trading Co — Intervision Video **H, P**
A-A 0206

Crooked Ditch, A   Gen-Edu '83
History-GB
12371   30 mins   C
B, V, 3/4U
This programme tells, with the help of maps and archive material, the history of the BCN.
M,A — ED
I A Recordings — I.A. Recordings   **P**

Cross Country   Fil-Ent '83
Crime-Drama
12913   90 mins   C
B, V
Richard Beymer, Nina Axelrod, directed by Paul Lynch
A man's girl friend is murdered as he sets off on his holiday and he finds himself pursued as a suspect in the killing.
BBFC:18 — A — EN
A Filmline Ronald I Cohen Prod; Yellowbill Prods — THORN EMI   **P**
TXA 90 24044/TVA 90 24042

Cross Creek   Fil-Ent '83
Drama
12908   119 mins   C
B, V
Mary Steenburgen, Rip Torn, Peter Coyote, Dana Hill, directed by Martin Ritt
The true story of Marjorie Kinnan Rawlings who left her comfortable New York home and her husband in 1928 in order to write a novel in an isolated retreat in Florida.
BBFC:U — F — EN
Universal — THORN EMI   **P**
TXA 90 20064/TVA 90 20062

Cross of Iron   Fil-Ent '76
War-Drama
04663   128 mins   C
B, V
James Coburn, Maximilian Schell, James Mason, David Warner, Senta Berger

Set in 1943, with the German army facing destruction by the Russians, this film focuses on a doomed platoon. It shows a set of complex relationships between officers and other ranks in which the instinct for war proves greater than the instinct for survival.
BBFC:X — A — EN
EMI-Rapid Film; Terra Filmkunst — THORN EMI   **H, P**
TXA 90 0260 4/ TVA 90 0260 2

Crossfire   Fil-Ent '47
Crime-Drama/Suspense
07483   86 mins   B/W
B, V
Robert Young, Gloria Grahame, Robert Ryan, Robert Mitchum, directed by Edward Dmytryk
This film opens with the brutal murder of a man and goes on to expose the callous side of big-city life. Following the theme of anti-Semitism, the film shows us who killed him and why. The suspects include four Army friends on leave and a bar-room floosie and her lover. Finally the police link up with the army to set a trap to catch the killer.
S,A — EN
RKO Radio Pictures — THORN EMI   **P**
TXC 90 2001 4/TVC 90 2001 2

Crosstalk   Fil-Ent '82
Suspense
09347   81 mins   C
V2, B, V
Garry Day, Penny Downie, Kim Deacon, Brian McDermott, Peter Collingwood, John Ewart
While trying to identify the malfunctioning of a new super-computer a man is crippled in a suspicious car crash. Confined by his mysterious employers in a luxury apartment with a beautiful nurse he continues the search, only to find himself wrapped up in a web of technological horror.
S,A — EN
Wall To Wall Pty Ltd — Precision Video Ltd   **P**
CRSWP 2602/BSWPV 2602/VSWPV 2602

Crowning Years, The   Spo-Lei '84
Sports
13394   115 mins   C
B, V
This is a record of the most successful decade in Welsh rugby history, 1969 to 1979, when the team won six Triple Crowns and three Grand Slam titles.
F — EN
Unknown — BBC Video   **H, P**
5024

(For Explanation of codes, see USE GUIDE and KEY)

PALADIN VIDEO HOME ENTERTAINMENT GUIDE

Crucible of Terror   Fil-Ent '72
Horror
08834   95 mins   C
B, V
Mike Raven, James Bolam, Ronald Lacey, Mary Maude, Beth Morris
A mad sculptor covers beautiful models with hot wax, then imprisons them in a mold of bronze.
BBFC:18 — *A* — *EN*
Scotia Barber — *VCL Video Services*   P
P335 D

Cruel Sea, The   Fil-Ent '53
War-Drama
01596   121 mins   B/W
B, V
Jack Hawkins, Stanley Baker, Denholm Elliott, Moira Lister, Virginia McKenna, Donald Sinden
This film tells the story of a Royal Navy corvette on convoy duty in the Atlantic.
BBFC:U — *A* — *EN*
Ealing Studios — *THORN EMI*   P
TXC 90 0041 4/TVC 90 0041 2

Cruising   Fil-Ent '80
Crime-Drama
07730   98 mins   C
B, V
Al Pacino, Paul Sorvino, Karen Allen, directed by William Friedkin
An undercover cop is assigned to penetrate the sadomasochistic, heavy leather gay scene of Manhattan's West Village in search of a psychotic killer.
BBFC:X — *A* — *EN*
Lorimar Distribution Intl — *MGM/UA Home Video*   P
UCB 10029/UCV 10029

Cry Blood Apache   Fil-Ent '72
Western
06091   102 mins   C
V2, B, V
Jody McCrea, Dan Kemp, Jack Starret, Joel McCrea
Five adventurers attack an Indian village and slaughter women and children. A solitary Apache is a witness to the massacre. He sets off on the murderers' trail to carry out a cruel revenge. The love of an Indian woman for a white man proves to be fatal to the lone avenger.
S,A — *EN*
Philip Yordan Productions — *Video Programme Distributors*   P
Cinehollywood—V660

Cry of the Banshee   Fil-Ent '70
Horror
08381   87 mins   C

V2, B, V
Vincent Price, Essy Persson, Hugh Griffith, Hilary Dwyer, Patrick Mower, Elizabeth Bergner, directed by Gordon Hessler
This film is set in the 16th Century. It tells of a high priestess of a heathen cult who vows revenge against Lord Edward Whitman, when he causes the death of two of her children. She sends a devil in the form of a young man to destroy him.
BBFC:U — *S,A* — *EN*
American International Pictures — *Guild Home Video*   H, P, E

Cry of the Innocent   Fil-Ent '80
Drama/Suspense
09395   105 mins   C
B, V
Rod Taylor, Joanna Pettet, Nigel Davenport, Cyril Cusack, Walter Gotell, Jim Norton, Alexander Knox, directed by Michael O'Herlihy
After a tragic accident, an ex-Commando ruthlessly pursues and destroys the terrorists who killed his family. Based on the story by Frederick Forsyth.
S,A — *EN*
Unknown — *VCL Video Services*   P
P383D

Cry Wolf   Chi-Juv '70
Adventure
13450   58 mins   C
B, V
An over-imaginative boy hears of a kidnapping plot but is not believed because of past events.
BBFC:U — *I,S* — *EN*
Damor Leaderfilm Ltd — *Rank Video Library*   H, P
3122X

Crypt of Horror   Fil-Ent '60
Horror
08597   92 mins   B/W
V2, B, V
Chrisopher Lee, Jose Campos, Ursula Davis, directed by Camillo Mastrocinque
In the ancient castle of Karnstein, a Count and his daughter live in mortal fear of an old family curse. Meanwhile in the local village, a series of unexplainable deaths have occured. The daughter finds strange consolation in a friendship with the mysterious Lyuba.
BBFC:X — *A* — *EN*
American International Pictures; British — *Videomedia*   P
PVM 1024/BVM 1024?HVM 1024

Crypt of the Living Dead   Fil-Ent '72
Horror
06794   81 mins   C

154   (For Explanation of codes, see USE GUIDE and KEY)

PALADIN VIDEO HOME ENTERTAINMENT GUIDE

V2, B, V
Andrew Prine, Mark Damon
An anthology of horror tales dealing with vampires, blood lust and the undead.
C,A — EN
Atlas Films — *Intervision Video*   H, P
A-A 0338

Crystal Fist   Fil-Ent '7?
Adventure/Martial arts
04604   85 mins   C
V2, B, V
Billy Chong
Wang, a pupil at the Martial Arts Institute, pays for his tuition by working in a kitchen. He discovers that the cook is a veteran kung-fu fighter and when the Institute is attacked and Wang is beaten up, they join forces. The old man together with his young protege set about bringing the wrongdoers to justice.
C,A — EN
Unknown — *Video Programme Distributors*
P
Inter-Ocean—036

Crystal Voyager   Fil-Ent '80
Documentary/Sports-Water
08024   35 mins   C
V2, B, V
George Greenough, filmed by Albert Falzon, George Greenough
George Greenough, an extraordinary photographer, films himself surfing through the hugh tunnels created by the giant waves of the Pacific Surf. The music provided by Pink Floyd creates the atmosphere for this astounding feat.
BBFC:U — F — EN
David Elfick — *Iver Film Services*   P
204

Cujo   Fil-Ent '83
Drama
13367   87 mins   C
V2, B, V
Dee Wallace, Danny Pintauro, Daniel Hugh-Kelly, Christopher Stone, directed by Lewis Teague
An enormous St. Bernard dog, once lovable and affectionate, is bitten by a bat, and turns into an unrecognisable beast who, maddened with pain, terrorizes a couple who are stranded in their car.
BBFC:18 — A — EN
Sunn Classic Pictures Inc — *Guild Home Video*
H, P, E
8356-0

Cul-de-Sac   Fil-Ent '68
Comedy-Drama
05563   105 mins   B/W
V2, B, V
Donald Pleasence, Francoise Dorleac, Lionel Stander, directed by Roman Polanski
In an old castle on an isolated island a middle aged man and his beautiful young wife change and rechange loyalties when their island is invaded by a couple of wounded gangsters who hold them hostage.
Berlin Film Festival '66: Golden Bear (Best Picture).   BBFC:X — A — EN
Filmways — *Videomedia*   P
PVM 4410/BVM 4410/HVM 4410

Culture Club, A Kiss   Fil-Ent '84
Across the Ocean
Music-Performance
12962   60 mins   C
B, V
Recorded live at the Hammersmith Odeon, Culure Club's tracks include 'I'll Tumble 4 Ya', 'Mister Man', 'Melting Pot', 'Do You Really Want to Hurt Me', 'Karma Chameleon' and 'It's a Miracle'.
F — EN
Keefco Production; Hugh Symmonds — *Virgin Video*   H, P
VVD 029

Cup Final   Spo-Lei '80
Football
01989   60 mins   C
V2, B, V, PH15, PH17
Commentary by Frank McGhee
The British football championship highlights are shown from 1923-1978. The programme contains some black and white sequences.
F — EN
MirrorVision — *VideoSpace Ltd*   P

Curious Female   Fil-Ent '7?
Science fiction
05485   85 mins   C
V2, B, V
Angelique Pettyjon, Charlene Jones, Bunny Allister, Michael Greer, directed by Paul Rapp
This film is set in 2177 AD where living is free, easy, amoral and sterile, controlled by a Master Computer. Love, romance and families are forbidden, but one young girl objects and with a friend screens an old 1969 film called 'The Three Virgins,' and they watch what happens to the 'primitives.'
BBFC:X — A — EN
Unknown — *Iver Film Services*   P
138

Curley and His Gang in   Fil-Ent '47
the Haunted Mansion
Adventure/Comedy
07325   51 mins   C
B, V

(For Explanation of codes, see USE GUIDE and KEY)

PALADIN VIDEO HOME ENTERTAINMENT GUIDE

Larry Olsen, Eileen Janssen, Virginia Grey, George Zucco
This film is one of the few Hal Roach comedies to be produced in colour. A doctor disappears in a strange explosion in a cottage on his gloomy estate and his nurse is charged with her murder. Curley and his gang decided to investigate when one of their friends gets involved. They proceed to the doctor's mansion to face secret passages, underground pits, hidden laboratories and wild animals.
BBFC:U — F — EN
United Artists — *Derann Film Services*   P
BDV 116B/BDV 116

Curse of the Crimson Altar   Fil-Ent '68
Horror
04557   87 mins   C
V2, B, V
Boris Karloff, Christopher Lee, Barbara Steele, Mark Eden, Michael Gough, directed by Vernon Sewell
A young man in search of his brother arrives at Greymarsh Lodge in time for the 'burning' of the black witch.
S,A — EN
American International — *Videomedia*   P

Curse of the Devil   Fil-Ent '??
Horror
12776   85 mins   C
V2, B, V
Paul Naschy, Faye Falcon, directed by Charles Auted
A four hundred year old curse is evoked and people are sucked dry of blood and torn apart by the jaws of a wolf. The only solution is to free the beast from the curse.
BBFC:18 — C,A — EN
Unknown — *Intervision Video*   H, P
A-A0485

Curse of the Pink Panther   Fil-Ent '83
Comedy
12977   106 mins   C
B, V
David Niven, Robert Wagner, Capucine, Herbert Lom, Ted Wass, Joanna Lumley, directed by Blake Edwards
Chaos erupts when the worst detective in the world sets out to find the missing Clouseau after the computer has been sabotaged by his arch enemy Inspector Dreyfuss.
BBFC:PG — A — EN
Blake Edwards; Tony Adams — *Warner Home Video*   P
99429

Curtains   Fil-Ent '83
Horror/Suspense
12620   85 mins   C
V2, B, V
Samantha Eggar, Linda Thorson, John Vernon, Lynne Griffin
Six beautiful young actresses are summoned to a remote country mansion for the casting of a film. They all desperately want the part and one is prepared to kill for it.
BBFC:18 — C,A — EN
Peter and Richard Simpson — *VideoSpace Ltd*   P

Cutter's Way   Fil-Ent '81
Drama
12679   106 mins   C
B, V
Jeff Bridges, John Heard, Lisa Eichhorn, Stephen Elliott, Arthur Rosenberg, directed by Ivan Passer
An emotionally and physically scarred Vietnam veteran decides to revenge himself on the corrupt capitalist society by bringing to justice the local oil tycoon who has been accused of murdering and mutilating a teenage girl.
BBFC:18 — A — EN
Paul R Gurian — *Warner Home Video*   P
99352

Cycles South   Fil-Ent '??
Adventure
08899   88 mins   C
V2, B, V
Vaughan Everly, Bobby Garcia
This film follows the adventures of three young men on their journey from Denver to Panama, across seven countries.
BBFC:U — F — EN
Unknown — *Video Programme Distributors*   P
Inter-Ocean 081

Cyclone   Fil-Ent '78
Drama/Horror
09919   100 mins   C
V2, B, V
Arthur Kennedy, Carrol Baker, Lionel Stander
A furious cyclone hits the coastline, leaving a group of survivors at sea, drifting helplessly, without food and water. As the days pass the injured begin to die, and the survivors begin to realise the horrifying truth, that they cannot afford to bury their dead. More horrors hit them when a rescuing lifeboat capsizes, throwing them into shark infested water. Only a few survive.
BBFC:18 — A — EN
Unknown — *Derann Film Services*   P
FDV 310

PALADIN VIDEO HOME ENTERTAINMENT GUIDE

Cyd Charisse Show, The   Fil-Ent   '7?
Variety

04369   60 mins   C

B, V, PH17, 3/4U

Cyd Charisse, Krofft Puppets

A variety show starring Cyd Charisse and the Krofft Puppets.

F — EN

Unknown — *Vidpics International*   P

Cynic, The Rat and The Fist, The   Fil-Ent   '8?
Crime-Drama

07783   95 mins   C

V2, B, V

John Saxon, Mavrizio Merli

This Mafia crime thriller is based on one man's personal war against protection rackets.

S,A — EN

Unknown — *Fletcher Video*   H, P

V105

Czech Mate/In Possession   Fil-Ent   '84
Drama/Suspense

13157   150 mins   C

B, V

Susan George, Patrick Mower, directed by John Hough, Carol Lynley, Christopher Cazenove, directed by Val Guest

'Czech Mate' is a chilling tale illustrating how far intelligence services are prepared to use ordinary innocent people to further their aims and 'In Possession' finds a couple caught in a time warp and witnesses to a murder.

BBFC:15 — *S,A — EN*

Hammer Film Prods — *Brent Walker Home Video Ltd*   P

BW 36

D

D-Day—The Great Crusade   Gen-Edu   '84
Documentary

12198   112 mins   C

B, V

This cassette tells the story of the storming of the Normandy beaches in 1944. It outlines the planning of the operation, the secret maps stolen by the French Resistance from the Germans, the battle for air supremacy in the skies, the Navy's putting to sea, the German viewpoint as told by a U-boat commander. It also shows the Queen, President Reagan and other world leaders visiting the scene and talking to veterans of the landings.

F — EN

Independent Television News; Granada Video — *Granada Video*   H, P

Daffy Duck's Movie: Fantastic Island   Chi-Juv   '83
Cartoons

12987   76 mins   C

B, V

Animated

Daffy Duck has acquired his very own island in this cartoon and is joined by Bugs Bunny, Foghorn Leghorn and other favourite characters.

BBFC:U — *PS,M — EN*

Warner Bros — *Warner Home Video*   P

61324

Daily Fable   Chi-Juv   '7?
Fairy tales

04683   55 mins   C

B, V

Written by Leen Valkenier, directed by Cocky Andreoli

'Sour Grapes,' 'Stilted Birds,' 'Outfoxed,' 'Fable on Ice,' 'Wolf-Trap,' 'Shelly Hiccups,' 'Wolf Hole,' 'Postman's Knock,' 'Hairy Wolf,' 'Needy Assembly,' 'Beaver Brothers,' 'Down the Drain,' and 'Foxbits' are the fables told in this programme.

PS,I — EN

Spectrum — *Polygram Video*   P

Daily Fable—Miss Ant   Chi-Juv   '80
Cartoons

05849   55 mins   C

B, V

Animated, directed by Cocky Andreoli

(For Explanation of codes, see USE GUIDE and KEY)

PALADIN VIDEO HOME ENTERTAINMENT GUIDE

A compilation of stories and songs especially for children featuring Mis Ant, Mr Owl, Mr Crow, Miss Stork, Boris the Wolf, Uncle Gerald the Pigeon, Mr Cunningham the Fox, Bert and Fred Beaver, Martha and Myra Hampster, Shelley the Tortoise, Zippy the Hare, Milard the Horse, Harold the Bear and Momfer the Mole. Written by Leen Valkenier.

PS,M — EN

MM Chanowski Production — *Polygram Video* **P**

40129/20129

Dain Curse, The   Fil-Ent '80
Drama/Suspense
08332   118 mins   C
V2, B, V, LV

James Coburn, Jean Simmons, Nancy Addison, Hector Elizondo, Jason Miller, Paul Stewart, Beatrice Straight, directed by E. W. Swackhamer

This film, set in 1928, is a complex story of a young woman whose fascination and obession with a family curse brings about mystery and excitement that includes murder, suicide and stolen diamonds.

C,A — EN

Martin Poll Productions — *Embassy Home Entertainment*   **P**
1800

Daleks—Invasion Earth 2150 A.D.   Fil-Ent '66
Science fiction/Adventure
07457   80 mins   C
B, V

Peter Cushing, Bernard Cribbins, Ray Brooks, Jill Curzon, Roberta Tovey, Andrew Keir, directed by Gordon Flemyng

Set in the year 2150, in the deserted ruins of London, Dr Who and his time travellers join with a group of resistance fighters to wage a guerilla war against the Daleks. They look like they are losing the battle, until Dr Who discovers what they want from Earth. With their weakness exposed the Daleks are destroyed.

BBFC:U — F — EN

Aaru Productions Ltd — *THORN EMI*   **P**
TXC 90 0688 4/TVC 90 0688 2

Daley's Decathlon   Spo-Lei '??
Sports
12612   59 mins   C
V2, B, V

Daley Thompson

This is the dramatic story of Daley Thompson's Gold Medal Triumph and his shattering of the world record in Athens. Daley is also seen demonstrating the techniques of the original events against the monuments and temples of ancient Greece.

F — EN

Unknown — *VideoSpace Ltd*   **P**

Dallas—Cassette 1   Fil-Ent '78
Drama
08403   94 mins   C
V2, B, V

Barbara Bel Geddes, Jim Davis, Patrick Duffy, Linda Gray, Larry Hagman, Steve Kanaly, Ken Kercheval, Victoria Principal, Charlene Tilton

In this series, two episodes are contained on one cassette. In the first episode, 'Digger's Daughter,' Bobby brings home his bride, Pamela. In 'Lessons', the second episode, Pamela tries to persuade Lucy to stay at school and out of trouble.

F — EN

Lorimar — *Guild Home Video*   **H, P, E**

Dallas—Cassette 2   Fil-Ent '78
Drama
08404   ? mins   C
V2, B, V

Barbara Bel Geddes, Jim Davis, Patrick Duffy, Linda Gray, Larry Hagman, Steve Kanaly, Ken Kercheval, Victoria Principal, Charlene Tilton

In this series, two episodes are contained on one cassette. In the third episode, 'Spy in the House,' Cliff has proof of a shady deal going on with the Ewings. 'Wings of Vengeance,' the fourth episode, sees J.R. and Ray battling against 'heavies' who invade Southfork.

E — EN

Lorimar — *Guild Home Video*   **H, P, E**

Dallas—Cassette 3   Fil-Ent '78
Drama
08405   ? mins   C
V2, B, V

Barbara Bel Geddes, Jim Davis, Patrick Duffy, Linda Gray, Larry Hagman, Steve Kanaly, Ken Kercheval, Victoria Principal, Charlene Tilton

In 'Barbecue,' Pam is pregnant and is hopeful that the news will reunit Jock and Digger. 'Reunion Part 1,' the sixth episode, Bobby brings home the missing brother, Gary, also Lucy's father.

F — EN

Lorimar — *Guild Home Video*   **H, P, E**

Dallas—Cassette 4   Fil-Ent '78
Drama
08406   ? mins   C
V2, B, V

PALADIN VIDEO HOME ENTERTAINMENT GUIDE

Barbara Bel Geddes, Jim Davis, Patrick Duffy, Linda Gray, Larry Hagman, Steve Kanaly, Ken Kercheval, Victoria Principal, Charlene Tilton
In 'Reunion Part 2,' J.R. tries to make Gary feel wanted. 'Old Acquaintance' sees the return of one of Bobby's old flames, wanting help for her fatherless daughter.
F — EN
Lorimar — Guild Home Video   **H, P, E**

Dallas—Cassette 5   Fil-Ent '78
Drama
08407   ? mins   C
V2, B, V
Barbara Bel Geddes, Jim Davis, Patrick Duffy, Linda Gray, Larry Hagman, Steve Kanaly, Ken Kercheval, Victoria Principal, Charlene Tilton
'Bypass' is the ninth episode in this series. J.R. is blamed for Jock's heart attack because of his fighting with Bobby. Sue Ellen is afraid that Pam will beat her in producing the first Ewing grandchild in 'Black Market Baby'. She resorts to black market adoption.
F — EN
Lorimar — Guild Home Video   **H, P, E**

Dallas—Cassette 6   Fil-Ent '78
Drama
08408   ? mins   C
V2, B, V
Barbara Bel Geddes, Jim Davis, Patrick Duffy, Linda Gray, Larry Hagman, Steve Kanaly, Ken Kercheval, Victoria Principal, Charlene Tilton
In the 11th episode, 'Double Wedding,' a man appears saying he is Pam's first husband. In 'Runaway,' it is not a happy birthday for Lucy when Jock refuses to allow her to invite her mother to the party.
F — EN
Lorimar — Guild Home Video   **H, P, E**

Dallas—Cassette 7   Fil-Ent '78
Drama
08409   ? mins   C
V2, B, V
Barbara Bel Geddes, Jim Davis, Patrick Duffy, Linda Gray, Larry Hagman, Steve Kanaly, Ken Kercheval, Victoria Principal, Charlene Tilton
In the 13th episode, 'Election,' Pamela supports her brother Cliff for state senator, against the Ewing candidate. In 'Survival,' J.R. and Bobby's plane crashes in swampland and everyone tries to keep the news from their father, Jock.
F — EN
Lorimar — Guild Home Video   **H, P, E**

Dallas—Cassette 8   Fil-Ent '79
Drama
08410   91 mins   C
V2, B, V
Barbara Bel Geddes, Jim Davis, Patrick Duffy, Linda Gray, Larry Hagman, Steve Kanaly, Ken Kercheval, Victoria Principal, Charlene Tilton
In 'Act of Love,' while J.R. is away on business, Sue Ellen amuses herself with Cliff Barnes. During the 16th esipsode, 'Triangle', both J.R. and Ray Krebbs fall for the same woman.
F — EN
Lorimar — Guild Home Video   **H, P, E**

Dallas—Cassette 9   Fil-Ent '79
Drama
08411   ? mins   C
V2, B, V
Barbara Bel Geddes, Jim Davis, Patrick Duffy, Linda Gray, Larry Hagman, Steve Kanaly, Ken Kercheval, Victoria Principal, Charlene Tilton
In 'Former Idol,' Bobby paints the town red with an old college friend. 'Kidnapped' sees a plan go wrong. When kidnappers try to grab J.R. they get Bobby instead.
F — EN
Lorimar — Guild Home Video   **H, P, E**

Dallas—Cassette 10   Fil-Ent '79
Drama
08412   ? mins   C
V2, B, V
Barbara Bel Geddes, Jim Davis, Patrick Duffy, Linda Gray, Larry Hagman, Steve Kanaly, Ken Kercheval, Victoria Principal, Charlene Tilton
In 'Home Again,' the 19th episode, Ellie wants Garrison to return to his true inheritance. In 'For Love or Money,' Sue Ellen plans to leave J.R. because she is tired of his playing around.
F — EN
Lorimar — Guild Home Video   **H, P, E**

Dallas—Cassette 11   Fil-Ent '79
Drama
08413   92 mins   C
V2, B, V
Barbara Bel Geddes, Jim Davis, Patrick Duffy, Linda Gray, Larry Hagman, Steve Kanaly, Ken Kercheval, Victoria Principal, Charlene Tilton
'Julie's Return' finds Julie coming to town, and Jock seems smitten. The beans are spilt to Ellie. 'The Red File Part 1' finds Julie angry at being used by J.R., and to repay him tells his secrets to Cliff Barnes.
F — EN
Lorimar — Guild Home Video   **H, P, E**

Dallas—Cassette 12   Fil-Ent '79
Drama
08414   ? mins   C
V2, B, V
Barbara Bel Geddes, Jim Davis, Patrick Duffy, Linda Gray, Larry Hagman, Steve Kanaly, Ken Kercheval, Victoria Principal, Charlene Tilton

PALADIN VIDEO HOME ENTERTAINMENT GUIDE

'The Red File Part 2' shows Pam fleeing Southfork because she believes J.R. has framed her brother, Cliff. While Pam is away Sue Ellen's sister, Kristin, makes a play for Bobby in the episode 'Sue Ellen's Sister.'
F — EN
Lorimar — Guild Home Video   H, P, E

Dallas—Cassette 13   Fil-Ent '79
Drama
08415   ? mins   C
V2, B, V
Barbara Bel Geddes, Jim Davis, Patrick Duffy, Linda Gray, Larry Hagman, Steve Kanaly, Ken Kercheval, Victoria Principal, Charlene Tilton
'Call Girl 20': Pam's new friend gives J.R. enough scandal to ruin two reputations at once. In 'Royal Marriage', the 26th Episode, Lucy falls in love with the heir to a powerful Texas oil family.
F — EN
Lorimar — Guild Home Video   H, P, E

Dallas—Cassette 14   Fil-Ent '79
Drama
08416   138 mins   C
V2, B, V
Barbara Bel Geddes, Jim Davis, Patrick Duffy, Linda Gray, Larry Hagman, Steve Kanaly, Ken Kercheval, Victoria Principal, Charlene Tilton
'The Outsiders': Ray falls for Donna McCullum, although she is already married to a powerful politician. In the last episode of this series, 'John Ewing III Parts 1 and 2,' Lucy is taking pills, Sue Ellen drinks and J.R. has committed her to a sanatorium.
F — EN
Lorimar — Guild Home Video   H, P, E

Dallas—Cassette 14   Fil-Ent '79
Drama
09245   92 mins   C
V2, B, V
Barbara Bel Geddes, Jim Davis, Patrick Duffy, Linda Gray, Larry Hagman, Ken Kercheval, Steve Kanaly, Victoria Principal, Charlene Tilton
'Whatever Happened to Baby John', Parts 1 and 2 are contained on Cassette 14. The happiness of the Ewing family on the birth of J.R. Junior soon dims when Sue Ellen shows a total lack of interest in her child. Cliff Barnes is determined to prove that the child is his. The baby is kidnapped from the hospital. J.R. suspects two of his former business associates.
F — EN
Lorimar — Guild Home Video   H, P, E

Dallas—Cassette 16   Fil-Ent '79
Drama
09246   91 mins   C
V2, B, V
Barbara Bel Geddes, Jim Davis, Patrick Duffy, Linda Gray, Larry Hagman, Ken Kercheval, Steve Kanaly, Victoria Principal, Charlene Tilton
This tape contains two further episodes of 'Dallas'. In the 'Silent Killer' Cliff learns that his father has a serious genetic disorder which has been passed on to both himself and Pam. Meanwhile, Kristin, Sue Ellen's little sister, makes her entrance. In 'Secrets', Lucy's mother reappears in an attempt to establish a closer relationship with her daughter. Pam learns that she is pregnant, and her child will carry her father's disease.
F — EN
Lorimar — Guild Home Video   H, P, E

Dallas-Cassette 17   Fil-Ent '79
Drama
09428   91 mins   C
V2, B, V
Barbara Bel Geddes, Jim Davis, Patrick Duffy, Linda Gray, Larry Hagman, Steve Kanaly, Ken Kercheval, Victoria Principal, Charlene Tilton
This tape contains two further episodes of 'Dallas'. In 'The Kristin Affair', Kristin turns her attentions to J.R. and Bobby discovers Pam's pregnancy. In the 'Dove Hunt' Jock is shot by snipers whilst out on a shooting trip. Believing that he is about to die, he confides a staggering secret to J.R.
F — EN
Lorimar — Guild Home Video   H, P, E

Dallas-Cassette 18   Fil-Ent '79
Drama
09429   92 mins   C
V2, B, V
Barbara Bel Geddes, Mary Crosby, Jim Davis, Patrick Duffy, Linda Gray, Larry Hagman, Steve Kanaly, Ken Kercheval, Victoria Principal
This tape contains two further episodes of 'Dallas'. In 'The Lost Child', Bobby grows too fond of a ranch-hand's child so Pam decides to reveal the danger threatening their expected baby. In 'Rodeo', Sue Ellen falls for one of the cowboys, Dusty Farlow.
F — EN
Lorimar — Guild Home Video   H, P, E

Dam Busters, The   Fil-Ent '55
War-Drama
01600   119 mins   B/W
B, V
Richard Todd, Michael Redgrave

(For Explanation of codes, see USE GUIDE and KEY)

PALADIN VIDEO HOME ENTERTAINMENT GUIDE

In 1942 London, a scientist develops a plan to destroy the German Moehne and Eder dams. The plan is accepted by the Air Ministry, and the scientist wrestles with his conscience while the actual bombing takes place.
BBFC:U — C,A — EN
ABPC, Richard Clark — *THORN EMI*   P
TXC 90 0039 4/TVC 90 0039 2

Damien Omen II   Fil-Ent '78
Horror
07696   103 mins   C
V2, B, V, LV
William Holden, Lee Grant, Lew Ayres, Robert Foxworth, Sylvia Sidney, directed by Don Taylor
In this second instalment in 'The Omen' trilogy, the child anti-Christ continues his horrific progress using his demonic powers to kill those who get in his way.
A — EN
Twentieth Century Fox — *CBS/Fox Video*   H
1087

Damned, The   Fil-Ent '69
Drama
06016   148 mins   C
B, V
Dirk Bogarde, Ingrid Thulin, Helmut Griem, directed by Luchino Visconti
This film probes the German soul on the eve of Nazi power, exposing the emotional lives of members of a powerful munitions empire. A man ruthlessly gains control of the steel industry during Hitler's rise to power; another, a leader in the SA troops, is slaughtered by the SS as a result of his schemes; what develops is a weird power struggle of intrigue and obsessions.
BBFC:X — A — EN
Warner Bros; Seven Arts Inc — *Warner Home Video*   P
WEX1059/WEV1059

Damsel in Distress, A/Old Man Rhythm   Fil-Ent '3?
Musical
05768   158 mins   B/W
B, V
Fred Astaire, George Burns, Gracie Allen, Joan Fontaine, Reginald Gardiner, Ray Noble, directed by George Stevens, Betty Grable, Johnny Mercer, Eric Blore, directed by Edward Ludwig
Two films are contained on one cassette. 'A Damsel in Distress' (black/white, 87 mins, 1938) is a comedy musical involving a British Lady who falls for an American dancer. Based on a story by P.G. Wodehouse with music by George and Ira Gershwin. 'Old Man Rhythm' (black/white, 71 mins, 1936) is a romantic musical in which a talented young man from a wealthy background becomes the target for a gold-digger, his father solves the problem by a starting a rumour that he is broke.
Academy Awards '37: Best Dance Director ('A Damsel in Distress').   S,A — EN
RKO — *Kingston Video*   H, P
KV14

Dance and Music of India—Sanskritik Festival of Arts of India   Fil-Ent '81
Music-Performance/Asia
06902   115 mins   C
B, V
This film features classical and traditional songs, music, dance and drums from India. It features some of India's foremost artists including Darshana Jhaveri, M.V. Narasimhachari, Vasanthalashmi, Ramesh Mishra and Kamal Mallick. Narrated in English.
AM Available   F — EN
Nuchron Ltd — *Nuchron Limited*   P
VS10

Dance Fever   Fil-Ent '83
Dance/Drama
13718   60 mins   C
V2, B, V
Russell Russell, Tom Hooker, Patricia Moore, directed by Richard Sesani
Two young disc jockeys strive to attain their ambition of staging the World's Most Fantastic Disco Show.
BBFC:PG — F — EN
Film Holiday Productions — *Warner Home Video*   H, P

Dance Music   Fil-Ent '83
Dance/Drama
13719   60 mins   C
V2, B, V
Barry Mason, Gary Low, Miguel Brown
A modern day fun-filled story of a young dance group trying to make it to the top with music by Shannon, Brooklyn Express and other performers.
BBFC:15 — S,A — EN
Metro Films International — *Medusa Communications Ltd*   H, P
MC 052

Dance of Love   Fil-Ent '73
Drama
08763   104 mins   C
B, V
Helmut Berger, Maria Schneider, Senta Berger, directed by Otto Schenk

(For Explanation of codes, see USE GUIDE and KEY)

PALADIN VIDEO HOME ENTERTAINMENT GUIDE

Set in Vienna during the year 1900, this film tells of the never ending cricle of love. The wiles of the chambermaid are too much for a young student, whilst the young girl finds that there is an addition to her dessert at the end of her dinner.
BBFC:X — A — EN
Unknown — *Precision Video Ltd* P
BHPV 2569/VHPV 2569

Dance of the Vampires Fil-Ent '67
Comedy
07727   124 mins   C
B, V
Jack MacGowran, Sharon Tate, Alfie Bass, Ferdy Mayne, Terry Downes, directed by Roman Polanski
This film is a send-up of horror movies in which a bumbling team attempt to destroy a family of Slovonic vampires. At the Count's castle they save a beautiful village girl from being the main course at a banquet.
BBFC:A — S,A — EN
Cadre Films; Filmways — *MGM/UA Home Video*   P
UMB 10138/UMV 10138

Dancing Princesses, The Fil-Ent '78
Fantasy
05949   52 mins   C
B, V
Jim Dale, Freddie Jones, Petter Butterworth, Gloria Grahame, Peter Benson, directed by Jon Scoffield
This film is based on a story by The Brothers Grimm. A widower King has six beautiful young daughters who have a habit of wearing out a new pair of dancing slippers every night, so much so that the shoemaker is becoming very rich. So mystified is the King that he offers the hand in marriage of any daughter a suitor desires if the mystery can be solved. Those who fail will be beheaded.
F — EN
Unknown — *Precision Video Ltd*   P
BITC 1090/VITC 1090

Dancing Years, The Fil-Ent '79
Musical
05950   143 mins   C
B, V
Anthony Valentine, Celia Gregory, Susan Skipper, Neville Jason, Vera Jakob, Tim Brierley, Joyce Grant, directed by Richard Bramall
This is a musical play divided into two parts written and composed by Ivor Novello. The first part is set in 1911 when a struggling young composer meets an operatic star for the first time. She buys one of his songs for her show and persuades him to move to Vienna where he falls in love with her. In Part Two, set in 1914, they are now living together, she is no longer accepted by the aristocratic society and is troubled because they are not married.
S,A — EN
Cecil Clarke Production — *Precision Video Ltd* P
BITC 3041/VITC 3041

Danger Is My Business Spo-Lei '??
Sports
06060   102 mins   C
V2, B, V
A collection of the most spectacular scenes of all the adventurous and dangerous activities of man: from bull fighting to parachute acrobatics, from the whale trainer to the speedboat jockey. It explores the fascination of the risks involved in a brush with death.
F — ED
Unknown — *Video Programme Distributors* P
Cinehollywood—V500

Danger Mouse Fil-Ent '??
Cartoons/Adventure
08530   60 mins   C
B, V
Animated voices by David Jason, Terry Scott, Edward Kelsey, Brian Trueman
This programme contains four stories starring the rodent Danger Mouse who is constantly battling to save the world from such threats as Baron Greenback, the world's most villainous frog.
M,A — EN
Thames Video — *THORN EMI*   P
TXE 90 02994/TVE 90 0299 2

Danger Mouse Rides Again Chi-Juv '85
Cartoons
13688   60 mins   C
B, V
Animated
Four more adventures from the mouse secret agent are featured on this cassette titled 'Die Laughing,' 'The Day of the Suds,' '150 Million Years Lost' and 'Rogue Robots.'
BBFC:U — PS,M — EN
Thames Video — *THORN EMI*   P
90 3083

Danger Mouse-Volume 2 Chi-Juv '83
Cartoons
09812   80 mins   C
B, V
Animated

(For Explanation of codes, see USE GUIDE and KEY)

PALADIN VIDEO HOME ENTERTAINMENT GUIDE

Four more adventures from Danger Mouse: 'Who Stole the Bagpipes,' 'The Odd-Ball Run-a-Round,' 'The Return of Count Dracula,' and 'Public Enemy.'
PS,A — EN
Thames Video — *THORN EMI* **P**
TXE 90 1731 4/TVE 90 1731 2

Danger Mouse Volume 3 Chi-Juv '84
Cartoons/Adventure
12511 80 mins C
B, V
Animated
Five more adventures about this ever-popular secret agent entitled Chicken Run, Four Tasks of Danger Mouse, The Ghost Bus, The Planet of the Cats and Dream Machine.
PS,M — EN
Cosgrove Hall Productions — *THORN EMI* **P**
TXE 90 2397 4/TVE 90 2397 2

Dangerous Cargo Fil-Ent '75
Adventure/Suspense
13147 90 mins C
B, V
Nick Nolte, Bo Hopkins, Tim Matheson, Jim Davis, directed by Boris Sagal
This is a spirited tale of highjacking and swindling on the cargo boats of the Mississippi.
BBFC:PG — S,A — EN
Lorimar Productions — *Polygram Video* **P**
040 2354/040 2352

Dangerous Davies Fil-Ent '??
Crime-Drama/Comedy
07361 ? mins C
B, V
This is the story of the man they called 'the last detective' because to send him on an important case every other cop in the Metropolitan Police Force would have to have contracted typhoid fever.
S,A — EN
Unknown — *Precision Video Ltd* **P**
BITC 2114/VITC 2114

Dangerous Mission/Impact Fil-Ent '49
Mystery
09110 167 mins C
B, V
Victor Mature, Vincent Price, William Bendix, Piper Laurie; Brian Donlevy, Ella Raines, Charles Coburn, Anna May Wong
This tape contains two films on one cassette. In 'Dangerous Mission' (1954, colour, 73 mins.), a New York girl is witness to a gangland murder. She flees to the Midwest, pursued by the gunmen and the police. 'Impact' (1949, black and white, 94 mins.) tells of a plot to kill a man by his wife and her lover. He survives, but disappears in order to make his wife stand trial for murder.
S,A — EN
RKO; United Artists — *Kingston Video*
H, P
KV57

Dangerous Summer, A Fil-Ent '82
Adventure
09160 90 mins C
V
Ian Gilmor, Wendy Hughes, James Mason, Tom Skerritt
This film tells the story of the construction of a holiday resort in the Blue Mountains, just outside Sydney. However one of the partners involved in the deal intends to burn down the resort for an even greater profit. However the insurance representative becomes suspicious and decides to investigate.
S,A — EN
McElroy & McElroy Prods — *Medusa Communications Ltd* **H, P**

Dangerous Summer, A Fil-Ent '82
Drama/Suspense
12186 90 mins C
V2, B, V
Ian Gilmor, Wendy Hughes, James Mason, Tom Skerritt
Two former associates team up again to construct a holiday resort in the Blue Mountains. One takes pride in his work, but the other plans to burn down the resort undercover of bushfires. The insurance company becomes suspicious and treachery and murder follow.
BBFC:15 — S,A — EN
James McElroy — *Medusa Communications Ltd* **H, P**

Dangerous Traffic Fil-Ent '83
Drama
12841 93 mins C
V2, B, V
Joe Renteria, Robert Random
A soldier returns from Vietnam and resumes his dangerous occupation of smuggling marijuana out from Mexico under the noses of the border patrols.
BBFC:18 — C,A — EN
Unknown — *Video Tape Centre* **P**
1174

Danny Fil-Ent '7?
Drama
07401 89 mins C
V2, B, V

(For Explanation of codes, see USE GUIDE and KEY) 163

PALADIN VIDEO HOME ENTERTAINMENT GUIDE

Janet Zarish, Gloria Maddox, Rebecca Page, George Luce
This is the heart warming story of a washed-up horse and the determination of a young girl to turn him into a champion jumper. When the owner of the horse plans to sell him because he has become impossible to handle, by a stroke of luck the young girl finds he is hers. After a summer of loving and training him she rides him triumphantly to victory.
BBFC:U — *F* — *EN*
Unknown — *Guild Home Video* **H, P, E**

Danny Travis   Fil-Ent '??
Crime-Drama
07815   105 mins   C
V2, B, V
Richard Harris, Martin Landau, directed by Roy Boulting
This film tells the story of a Los Angeles citizen who wages a one-man war against the law and the corrupt politicians who use every trick, including a crack SWAT team, to destroy him.
S,A — *EN*
Unknown — *Video Unlimited* **H, P**
038

Darby O'Fill and the Little People   Chi-Juv '59
Fantasy/Adventure
13741   87 mins   C
B, V
Sean Connery, Albert Sharpe, Janet Munro, Jimmy O'Dea
A caretaker on an Irish estate falls down a well, meets up with a colony of leprechauns, and is granted three wishes.
BBFC:U — *F* — *EN*
Walt Disney Productions — *Rank Video Library*
P
038B

Daring Game   Fil-Ent '68
Drama/Adventure
05449   79 mins   C
V2, B, V
Lloyd Bridges, Nico Minardos, Michael Ansara, Joan Blackman
An undersea expert searches a Latin American island to find the husband and daughter of a former girlfriend. The film includes action sequences of both sky and scuba-diving.
BBFC:U — *F* — *EN*
Paramount; Ivan Tors — *Iver Film Services*
P
98

Dark, The   Fil-Ent '79
Horror
08400   90 mins   C
V2, B, V
William Devane, Cathy Lee Crosby, Richard Jaeckel, Keenan Wynn, Vivian Blaine
A supernatural beast commits a string of gruesome murders. After the murder of his daughter, the father and a young TV reporter team up to try and track down the murderer.
BBFC:X — *A* — *EN*
Film Ventures International — *Guild Home Video* **H, P, E**

Dark Command   Fil-Ent '40
Western/Drama
06317   59 mins   B/W
V2, B, V
John Wayne, Roy Rogers, Claire Trevor, Gabby Hayes, Walter Pigeon, Marjorie Main
At the end of the American Civil War private armies made up of desperate men marauded the countryside. One such army was the Quantrille Raiders who attempted to take over the whole of Texas. This is the story of one man's fight to save the State.
F — *EN*
Republic Films — *World of Video 2000*
H, P
GF509

Dark Crystal, The   Fil-Ent '83
Cartoons/Fantasy
12482   92 mins   C
B, V
Animated
A visually stunning fantasy adventure from the team who created the Muppets and Fraggles in which the forces of good and evil do battle.
BBFC:PG — *F* — *EN*
Jim Henson — *RCA/Columbia Pictures Video UK* **H, P**
10146

Dark Eyes   Fil-Ent '??
Drama/Suspense
07674   90 mins   C
B, V
Britt Ekland, Lana Wood, Kabir Bedi, Don Galloway, John Carradine, Sherry Scott, Elise-Anne, Tom Hallick, directed by James Polakof
This film follows the fate of a woman who, feeling ignored by her husband, often drifts into fantasy daydreams. Her sensual illusions become so strong that one day she is visited by a lover from the spirit world. She allows the world of the Spirit to take her over. Soon her husband and daughter notice her strange behaviour and are threatened by weird, unexplainable occurrences in the house.
A — *EN*
Unknown — *Video Network* **P**
0016

PALADIN VIDEO HOME ENTERTAINMENT GUIDE

Dark Mirror, The Fil-Ent '46
Drama
01072   85 mins   B/W
V2, B, V
Olivia de Havilland, directed by Robert Siodmak
Drama about two sisters—one a murderess intent on covering her own tracks—even if it means her sister is suspected.
BBFC:A — *A* — *EN*
Universal — *Intervision Video*   H, P
A-A 0122

Dark Night of the Scarecrow Fil-Ent '7?
Suspense/Horror
05629   108 mins   C
V2, B, V
Charles Durning
A vigilante group is mustered to track down the killer of a little girl and their vengance is centred on a severely retarded man. After killing him, he is proved innocent, and a revengeful spirit haunts each of the vigilantes with bizarre consequences.
S,A — *EN*
Unknown — *Video Unlimited*   H, P

Dark of the Sun Fil-Ent '68
Adventure
12227   96 mins   C
B, V
Rod Taylor, Kenneth More, Yvette Mimieux
Set in the 1960s, a group of mercenaries in the Congo set out on a dangerous mission to rescue the inhabitants of a town under attack by rebel forces.
S,A — *EN*
MGM — *MGM/UA Home Video*   P
10309

Dark Ride, The Fil-Ent '??
Crime-Drama
07673   90 mins   C
B, V
James Luisi, Susan Sullivan, John Karlen, Martin Speer, directed by Jeremy Hoenack
The background to this film is drawn from a series of murders in Northern California for which to date no one has been arrested. This film offers a fictional conclusion to the case. A Detective is convinced the murder of six women is the work of a psychopath and meticulously pieces together events to capture the killer as he flaunts yet another murder under their noses.
A — *EN*
Unknown — *Video Network*   P
0010

Dark Star Fil-Ent '74
Science fiction
05454   81 mins   C
V2, B, V
Brian Navelle, Cal Koniholm, Dan O'Bannan, directed by John Carpenter
The story of Dark Star, a spaceship that travels the galaxies seeking and destroying unstable planets. The ship's highly advanced computer bombs have their own complex personalities, the scope of which is seen when one of the bombs sent on a mission of destruction becomes lodged in the ship.
BBFC:U — *F* — *EN*
Bryanston; John Carpenter — *Iver Film Services*   P
2

Darkroom, The Fil-Ent '7?
Drama
09164   96 mins   C
V
Alan Cassell, Svet Kovich, Anna Jemison
This film is a tense psycho-sexual thriller, which reveals what occurs when a psychologically disturbed son becomes obsessed with his father's mistress. As his fantasies turn to destruction the film reaches its terrifying and deadly climax.
C,A — *EN*
Unknown — *Medusa Communications Ltd*   H, P

Darts - The John Lowe Way Spo-Lei '8?
Sports-Minor
09092   90 mins   C
V2, B, V
John Lowe, Ritchie Gardiner, Phil Jones, directed by Jeff Woodbridge
This tape enables the viewer to learn the background and basics of darts. John Lowe, winner of over 1000 tournaments, ex-world champion and current captain of the UK International team with the help of Ritchie Gardiner and referee Phil Jones, describes the rules, methods and styles of the game together with the different types of darts and alternative grips.
F — *I*
Unknown — *Video Tape Centre*   P
XTC 1105

Dash of the Irish 1971, A/Road Time 1973 Spo-Lei '73
Automobiles-Racing
04520   50 mins   C
B, V
The 1971 circuit of Ireland is seen through the eyes of former competitor Paddy Hopkirk, who drives a specially prepared camera car

(For Explanation of codes, see USE GUIDE and KEY)

PALADIN VIDEO HOME ENTERTAINMENT GUIDE

throughout the entire rally, capturing spectacular highlights. The second feature highlights the 1973 challenge of the Monte Carlo Rally.
F — EN
Brunswick Intl — *Quadrant Video*   **H, P**
M20

Fabulous Fantastic Four, The   Fil-Ent '67
Cartoons/Adventure
08383   66 mins   C
V2, B, V
Animated
After being bombarded with cosmic rays in outer space, Reed Richards and his crew all under went transformations. Reed became plastic, able to bend at will, Sue was given the power of invisibility and Ben became fantastically strong. On this cassette, there are three 22-minute episodes.
PS,M — EN
Hanna-Barbera — *Guild Home Video*   **H, P, E**

Dastardly and Muttley—Cassette 1   Fil-Ent '6?
Cartoons/Adventure
09456   68 mins   C
V2, B, V
Animated
This tape tells the adventures of Dick Dastardly and his canine companion Muttley who command the notorious vulture Squadron, a band of flying rascals dedicated to the destruction of Yankee Doodle, the carrier pigeon.
BBFC:U — F — EN
Hanna-Barbera — *Guild Home Video*   **H, P, E**

Dastardly and Muttley—Cassette 2   Fil-Ent '6?
Cartoons/Adventure
09244   60 mins   C
V2, B, V
Animated
This cartoon tells of the further adventures of Dick Dastardly and his faithful doggy deputy, Muttley, as they come flying back with more diabolical doings to outwit their long suffering pigeon pal, Yankee Doodle.
BBFC:U — M,S — EN
Hanna Barbera — *Guild Home Video*   **H, P, E**

Dastardly and Muttley in Home Sweet Homing Pigeon   Chi-Juv '6?
Cartoons
13363   60 mins   C
V2, B, V
Animated
This tape features ten more adventures from the flying-ace villian and his deputy dog.
BBFC:U — PS,M — EN
Hanna-Barbera — *Guild Home Video*   **H, P, E**

Daughter of Emmanuelle   Fil-Ent '78
Romance
02099   84 mins   C
V2, B, V
Laurence Casey, Sarah Crystal
Emmanuelle's daughter follows in her mother's footsteps in this love story involving a twisted fashion designer and an American G.I. with amnesia. Filmed in Paris and Greece.
BBFC:X — A — EN
Titanus Films — *Hokushin Audio Visual Ltd*   **P**
VM-05

Dave Brubeck-A Musical Portrait   Fil-Ent '8?
Music-Performance/Documentary
06969   81 mins   C
V2, B, V
This film provides an insight into the music and life of jazz pianist Dave Brubeck. Extracts of concerts include the 1976 Silver Jubilee Concert in Boston featuring one of the last appearances of saxophonist Paul Desmond. Amongst the hits played by Brubeck and his musicians are 'Take Five', 'Balcony Rock' and 'Three to Get Ready'.
S,A — EN
Jo Austin; Margaret McCall; BBC Video — *BBC Video*   **H, P**
BBCV 3011

David and Goliath   Fil-Ent '60
Drama/Bible
07984   95 mins   C
B, V
Orson Welles, Ivo Payer, Edward Hilton, directed by Richard Potter, Ferdinando Baldi
This tells the story of the battle between the young Israelite David, a shepherd who became a warrior King, and the giant Goliath, leader of the mighty Philistines
F — EN
Allied Artists; Ansa Productions — *Motion Epics Video Company Ltd*   **P**
151

David Bowie Live   Fil-Ent '84
Music-Performance
12926   60 mins   C

---

166   (For Explanation of codes, see USE GUIDE and KEY)

PALADIN VIDEO HOME ENTERTAINMENT GUIDE

B, V
This programme was filmed in Vancouver in 1983 during Bowie's tour and features tracks such as 'Rebel, Rebel', 'Young Americans' and 'Ashes to Ashes', plus an interview.
BBFC:U — F — EN
Concert Productions International — *Video Form Pictures* **H, P**
VFV 18

David Copperfield　　　　　Fil-Ent '8?
Cartoons
12552　72 mins　C
V2, B, V
Animated
An immortal story of the struggles and hardships of David Copperfield set against the background of Victorian England. It is adapted from the novel by Charles Dickens.
F — EN
Unknown — *RPTA Video Ltd*　**H, P**

David Grant　　　　　Fil-Ent '83
Music/Video
10026　12 mins　C
B, V
This video EP includes the tracks 'Stop and Go,' 'Love Will Find a Way' and 'Watching You, Watching Me.'
M,A — EN
Unknown — *Palace Video Ltd*　**P**
CVIM 12

David Soul in Concert　　　　　Fil-Ent '??
Music-Performance
06304　58 mins　C
V2, B, V
David Soul
This is a film of David Soul performing in concert; songs include 'Troubadour,' 'Surrender to me,' 'Dancin' Jones', 'Fool for Love,' 'You're a Woman Now' and 'Don't give up on us.'
F — EN
Unknown — *World of Video 2000*　**H, P**
MV232

Davy Crockett　　　　　Fil-Ent '55
Western/Adventure
05584　88 mins　C
B, V
Fess Parker, Buddy Ebsen
This film relieves the drama, humour and adventure that immortalized the 'wild frontier', It follows the life of Davy Crockett from the Indian Creek Uprising, through his political career as legislator and U.S. Congressman to his heroic death at the Battle of the Alamo.
F — EN
Walt Disney Productions — *Rank Video Library*
H
01400

Dawn of the Mummy　　　　　Fil-Ent '82
Horror
10097　90 mins　C
B, V
A recently disturbed tomb is used as a backdrop for a fashion photosession. An unstoppable 'rise and kill' curse is activated. The four American model girls are threatened by a long-dead Pharaoh and his army of flesh-hungry ghouls. Two of the girls discover a way to destroy them but they have to act fast to avoid being killed.
BBFC:R — A — EN
Frank Agarna; Harmony Gold Prods — *VideoSpace Ltd*　**P**

Day After, The　　　　　Fil-Ent '83
Drama
13660　121 mins　C
B, V
Jason Robards, Jobeth Williams, Steven Guttenberg, John Cullum, John Lithgow, directed by Nicholas Meyer
This film graphically portrays the effects of a nuclear confrontation on a group of unsuspecting American citizens.
BBFC:15 — S,A — EN
Robert Papazian — *CBS/Fox Video*　**P**
8094

Day of the Assassins　　　　　Fil-Ent '81
Crime-Drama/Suspense
07665　96 mins　C
B, V
Chuck Connors, Glenn Ford, Richard Roundtree, Andres Garcia, Susana Dosamantes, Henry Silva, Jorge Rivero
A Shah's fortune becomes the target as assassins gather to do battle for the prize.
S,A — EN
Unknown — *Hello Video Ltd*　**P**
H16

Day of the Cobra　　　　　Fil-Ent '80
Crime-Drama
07774　90 mins　C
V2, B, V
Franco Nero, Sybil Danning

(For Explanation of codes, see USE GUIDE and KEY)

PALADIN VIDEO HOME ENTERTAINMENT GUIDE

This film follows the quest of an ex-narcotic agent to seek revenge on the boss of an enormous crime syndicate.
S,A — EN
Unknown — *Fletcher Video* **H, P**
V150

Day of the Dolphin, The   Fil-Ent '73
Drama
05528   104 mins   C
B, V, LV

George C. Scott, Trish Van Devere, Paul Sorvino, Fritz Weaver, Jan Korkes, Edward Herrman, directed by Mike Nichols

A marine biologist, his wife and some students have discovered a method of teaching dolphins to talk. They agree to give a press conference but en route the dolphins are hi-jacked and it appears that the group financing the research are in fact a Fascist gang out to assassinate the US president. They plan to use the dolphins to attach a bomb to his boat. Based on the novel by Robert Merle.
S,A — EN
Icarus Productions; Avco Embassy — *CBS/Fox Video*   **P**

Day of the Jackal, The   Fil-Ent '73
Drama/Suspense
13287   136 mins   C
B, V

Eric Porter, Edward Fox, Michael Lonsdale, Derek Jacobi, directed by Fred Zinnemann

A ruthless anonymous assassin is hired by an exiled OAS chief to kill General De Gaulle during one of his public appearances for half a million dollars.
BBFC:PG — S,A — EN
Universal — *CIC Video*   **H, P**
BEL 1068/VHL 1068

Day of the Triffids   Fil-Ent '63
Science fiction
01987   89 mins   C
B, V

Howard Keel, Nicole Maurey, Janette Scott

Man eating plants are brought to earth by a meteorite shower, rendering all but a few blind. A professor finally discovers a way to get rid of them.
C,A — EN
Allied Artists — *Quadrant Video*   **H, P**
FF4

Day of the Wolves/Gang Busters   Fil-Ent '??
Crime-Drama
05762   155 mins   C
B, V

Richard Egan, Martha Hyer, Rick Jason, Jan Murray, directed by Ferde Grofe Jr, Myron Healey, Don C Harvey, Sam Edwards, Frank Richards, Allan Ray, directed by Bill Karn

Two films are contained on one cassette. 'Day of the Wolves' (colour, 87 mins, 1972) in which one man prepares to do battle with a team of trained killers whose aim is to ransack an entire town by dynamiting bridges, powerlines, and the phone exchange. 'Gang Busters' (black/white, 68 mins, 1956) is a suspense story about a Public Enemy who escapes from prison with a friend. They are shot at and wounded, when the 'Enemy' loses consciousness his friend buries him but when the police find the grave it is empty.
S,A — EN
Gold Key Entertainment; RKO — *Kingston Video*   **H, P**
KV21

Day of Violence   Fil-Ent '??
Crime-Drama
06092   120 mins   C
V2, B, V

Daria Norman, Mario Antoni, Ely Galleani

Two young delinquents contravene every civil and moral code, raping and killing with a horrific nonchalance. They are hunted by police and abandoned by their friends; they stop at nothing in their desperate flight from justice.
S,A — EN
Unknown — *Video Programme Distributors* **P**
Cinehollywood—V1080

Day the Earth Caught Fire, The   Fil-Ent '62
Science fiction
06772   100 mins   B/W
V2, B, V

Janet Munro, Leo McKern, Edward Judd, directed by Val Guest

Nuclear tests cause the earth to move out of its orbit and began to fall toward the sun.
S,A — EN
Val Guest; Universal — *Intervision Video* **H, P**
A-A 0027

Day the Earth Moved, The   Fil-Ent '74
Suspense/Drama
04187   74 mins   C
B, V

Jackie Cooper, Cleavon Little, Stella Stevens

PALADIN VIDEO HOME ENTERTAINMENT GUIDE

A pilot and a photographer accidentally discover a new method of predicting earthquakes. They try to save a town from being destroyed but no one believes them until the tremors start and the walls begin to collapse.
BBFC:U — F — EN
20th Century Fox — Guild Home Video
H, P

Day the Earth Stood Still, The   Fil-Ent '51
Science fiction
07688   88 mins   B/W
B, V
Michael Rennie, Patricia Neal, Hugh Marlowe, Bobby Gray
This film follows the events that occur when aliens from another world land in Washington D.C. without warning but with peaceful intentions.
S,A — EN
20th Century Fox — CBS/Fox Video   P
1011

Day the Eiffel Tower Ran Away, The   Fil-Ent '??
Cartoons/Fantasy
05567   56 mins   C
V2, B, V
Animated
A fantasy animation film in which the Eiffel Tower, who is feeling lonely, longs to meet Big Ben, the Statue of Liberty and other monuments. He sets off on his travels; while he enters a fishing contest and travels on a subway train Paris is in an uproar. They try to find him to tell him how much he is missed.
BBFC:U — M,A — EN
Films Jean Image Productions — Videomedia
P
BVM 3116/HVM 3116

Day Time Ended, The   Fil-Ent '80
Science fiction
06811   80 mins   C
V2, B, V
Chris Mitchum, Jim Davis, Dorothy Malone, Marcy Lafferty, Scott Kolden, Natasha Ryan
A family tries to survive on earth when past, present, and future collide.
F — EN
Wayne Schmidt; Steve Neill; Paul W Gentry — Intervision Video   H, P
A-A 0378

Daylight Again: Crosby, Stills & Nash   Fil-Ent '84
Music-Performance

10112   108 mins   C
B, V
Directed by Tom Trbovich
This tape recorded from three live performances at the New Universal Amphitheatre in Los Angeles features 21 songs both new and old from Crosby, Stills and Nash. Songs include 'Judy Blue Eyes', 'Love the One You're With', 'Teach Your Children' and 'Wooden Ships'.
BBFC:U — F — EN
Universal — CIC Video   H, P
BER 1074/VHR 1074

Days Of Fury   Fil-Ent '78
Disasters
07676   90 mins   C
B, V
Narrated by Vincent Price, directed by Doro Vlado Hreljanovic and Fred Warshofsky
This film based on the book 'Doomsday: The Science of Catastrophe' by Fred Warshofsky, looks at disasters which destroy the world and many lives. It includes the collapse of a suspension bridge, jet collisions, assassinations, riots, destruction of oil tankers and the effect on ocean life, volcanic eruptions, tidal waves, typhoons, tornadoes, locusts ravaging crops, earthquakes, famines and other disasters both natural and man-made.
S,A — EN
Markwood Productions Ltd — Video Network
P
0007

Days of Heaven   Fil-Ent '79
Drama/Romance
10108   91 mins   C
B, V
Richard Gere, Sam Shephard, Brooke Adams, Linda Manx, directed by Terrence Malick
A Chicago factory worker arrives in the wheatlands of Texas with his sweetheart. She marries a farmer and finds herself torn between the two men. Musical score by Ennio Marricone.
BBFC:PG — S,A — EN
Paramount — CIC Video   H, P
BEA 2055/VHA 2055

Dayton's Devil   Fil-Ent '68
Suspense/Drama
09219   103 mins   C
B, V
Leslie Nielsen, Hans Gudegast, Rory Calhoun, Laurie Kazan

(For Explanation of codes, see USE GUIDE and KEY)

PALADIN VIDEO HOME ENTERTAINMENT GUIDE

A brilliant but evil ex-Air Force Officer trains a group of hand picked individuals into a disciplined military squad in order to steal the two and a half million dollar payroll from the Palomar Air Force Base.
F — EN
Madison Prods — Video Form Pictures **H, P**
DIP 6

Dead and Buried   Fil-Ent '??
Horror
08524   90 mins   C
B, V
James Farentino, Melody Anderson, Jack Albertson
The setting for this film is the misty seaside town of Potters Bluff in California and tells a gruesome tale of bodies returning from the dead. The natives of the town hide this secret; however, a man discovers more than is good for him.
BBFC:X — A — EN
Unknown — THORN EMI   **P**
TXA 90 1286 4/TVA 90 1286 2

Dead End Street   Fil-Ent '83
Drama
12764   86 mins   C
B, V
A TV producer makes a film about a prostitute and becomes so infatuated with his subject that he puts his career on the line to help her find a new life of respectability.
Cannes Film Festival '83: Special Award Winner.   BBFC:18 — A — EN
Unknown — Rank Video Library   **H, P**
0180 E

Dead Kids   Fil-Ent '??
Horror
07604   97 mins   C
V2, B, V
Michael Murphy, Louise Fletcher, Arthur Dignam, Dan Shor, Fiona Lewis, directed by Michael Laughlin
A Mid-Western college town is shattered when a young girl is attacked and her boyfriend killed by a maniac at a fancy dress party. Murders keep occurring and the police believe there is more than one killer. Meanwhile, the police chief's son enrolls as a volunteer for a research programme on auto-suggestion. When a cleaning lady interrupts a session and witnesses a murder, she manages to ring the police before she is killed. The murder hunt nows leads to the psychiatry department.
BBFC:X — A — EN
Unknown — Iver Film Services   **P**
171

Dead Man's Float   Fil-Ent '??
Adventure
08701   70 mins   C
V2, B, V
Sally Boyden, Greg Rowe, Jacqui Gordon, Rick Ireland, Bill Hunter
During the summer days three children and their American friend spend most of their time surfing and playing around in boats. A strange trawler moves into their isolated cove, and one of their surfboards is smashed up by the remote control speedboat they claim to be testing. They are paid off but also warned off. The children intend to find out why.
BBFC:U — F — EN
Unknown — Video Unlimited   **H, P**

Dead Men Don't Wear Plaid   Fil-Ent '82
Comedy
12048   88 mins   B/W
B, V
Steve Martin, Rachel Ward, directed by Carl Reiner
This is a spoof of the 1940's detective movies, with scenes from 'This Gun for Hire,' 'The Big Sleep' and 'Dark Passage' having been intercut by the director.
BBFC:PG — S,A — EN
Universal — CIC Video   **H, P**
BEA 1082/VHA 1082

Dead of Night   Fil-Ent '72
Horror
04345   78 mins   C
V2, B, V
A boy reported dead in combat returns home—but somehow he is different.
BBFC:X — A — EN
Impact Quadrant — Intervision Video   **H**
A-A 0026

Dead Pigeon on Beethoven Street   Fil-Ent '72
Drama
09799   86 mins   C
B, V
Anton Diffring, Glenn Corbett, Christa Lang, Stephane Audran, directed by Samuel Fuller
An American private eye on the trail of an international black mailing gang encounters an atmosphere of sudden death and double dealing. Set in Germany, his greatest threat comes from the gang's seductive lady member.
A — EN
Bavaria Atelier — THORN EMI   **P**
TXB 90 16644/TVB 90 1664 2

PALADIN VIDEO HOME ENTERTAINMENT GUIDE

Dead Zone, The Fil-Ent '83
Suspense/Horror
12910   100 mins   C
B, V

Christopher Walken, Brooke Adams, Tom Skerritt, Herbert Lom, Martin Sheen, directed by David Cronenberg

Based on a novel by Stephen King, a man emerges from a 5 year coma to find he has developed psychic powers and must make a decision that will alter the fate of mankind.
A — EN
Paramount — *THORN EMI*   P
TXA 90 24884/TVA 90 24882

Deadliest Season, The Fil-Ent '77
Drama
10195   98 mins   C
B, V

Michael Moriarty, Meryl Streep, Kevin Conway, Patrick O'Neal, Andrew Duggan

For a husband and wife ice hockey is their life. When he is relegated he fights to make a swift and bloody comeback. He is soon the hero of the crowds-'The Penalty Killer'. However, disaster strikes and he finds himself fighting a very different battle in the big business politics behind the fastest and most physical game in the world.
S,A — EN
Titus Prods — *Video Form Pictures*   H, P
6246

Deadly Blessing Fil-Ent '81
Horror
08987   90 mins   C
V2, B, V

Maren Jensen, Jeff East, Lois Nettleton, Ernest Borgnine, directed by Wes Craven

This film centres on the effects of psychological terror. The story tells of a strange religious cult whose members strive to prevent the outside world from influencing their own closed community. When one of the young men marries an outsider a bizarre string of events take place, leading to a terrifying climax.
A — EN
Poly Gram — *Polygram Video*   P
790 405

Deadly Chase Fil-Ent '??
Crime-Drama
06093   90 mins   C
V2, B, V

Luc Merenda, Janet Agren, Maria Baxa

The story of an offbeat police inspector investigating a series of acts of violence masterminded by an elusive baron.
S,A — EN
Unknown — *Video Programme Distributors*   P
Cinehollywood—V210

Deadly Commando Fil-Ent '7?
War-Drama
09286   96 mins   C
V

Vic Vargas, George Regan, Ray Malonzo

When a high ranking American SEATO officer is taken hostage by rebels, a special unit of the most highly trained and ruthless commandoes is sent in. After parachuting into the mountainous terrain of the Far Eastern province, they face their most dangerous mission yet.
S,A — EN
Unknown — *Direct Video Services*   H, P

Deadly Females, The Fil-Ent '7?
Drama
05483   105 mins   C
V2, B, V

Tracey Reed, Rula Lenska, Jean Rimmer, Roy Purcell, Brian Jackson, Bernard

A bored housewife sets up, and runs from an antique shop in Chelsea, an agency for other housewives, secretaries and actresses. They deal in murder by contract and the hit girls seldom fail, but demand a high price. As the E.C.C. spreads its wings, the 'stepmother' is in danger of a takeover from a larger continental group.
BBFC:X — A — EN
Unknown — *Iver Film Services*   P
102

Deadly Force Fil-Ent '83
Crime-Drama
13211   92 mins   C
V2, B, V

Wings Hauser, Joyce Ingalls, Peter Shenar, directed by Paul Aaron

A mass murderer is on the loose in America and having killed sixteen seemingly unconnected people, a vigilante is called in to protect victim number seventeen in this random trail of death.
BBFC:18 — A — EN
Sandy Howard; Hemdale — *Embassy Home Entertainment*   P
6102

Deadly Games Fil-Ent '7?
Suspense
06817   ? mins   C
V2, B, V

(For Explanation of codes, see USE GUIDE and KEY)

PALADIN VIDEO HOME ENTERTAINMENT GUIDE

Sam Groom, Steve Railsback, Dick Butkus, Jo Ann Harris, Coleen Camp, June Lockhart
An erotic thriller in which a maniac plays deadly games with his victim.
A — EN
Raymond M Dryden — *Intervision Video* **H, P**
A-A 0372

Deadly Harvest   Fil-Ent '77
Science fiction
09144   90 mins   C
B, V
Clint Walker, Mary Davies, David Brown, directed by Timothy Bond
This is the story of an ecological disaster set in the future, when there is a world food shortage. The American Government predicts doom unless desperate measures are taken. However, will the people accept rationing, martial law and no communications?
S,A — EN
Three Star Movies — *Video Brokers* **H, P**
006X

Deadly Hero   Fil-Ent '76
Suspense
01007   102 mins   C
V2, B, V
Don Murray, Diahn Williams, James Earl Jones, Lilia Skala, directed by Ivan Nagy
A psychotic N.Y. City cop terrorises a woman who complains about his violent behaviour in saving her from an assault.
A — EN
Avco Embassy; Thomas J McGrath Prods — *Embassy Home Entertainment* **P**
2024

Deadly Hunt, The   Fil-Ent '71
Suspense/Drama
06256   72 mins   C
B, V
Peter Lawford, Jim Hutton, Tony Franciosa, Tom Hauff, Anjanette Comer
The story of a playboy who is after his wealthy wife's business empire. He hires professional killers to appear as unexpected guests on a second honeymoon. They are to frighten her into jumping off a cliff but raging forest fires ruin the plan.
S,A — EN
Four Star Entertainment — *VCL Video Services* **P**
C153C

Deadly Impact   Fil-Ent '83
Adventure/Suspense
13234   85 mins   C
B, V
Bo Svenson, Fred Williamson, Marcia Clingan, John Morghen, Vincent Conte
A policeman discovers the corpse of a young man who had invented an electronic device and enlists the help of a helicopter pilot to track down the killers.
C,A — EN
Larry Ludman — *Entertainment in Video* **H, P**
EVB 1020/EVV 1020

Deadly Inheritance   Fil-Ent '8?
Crime-Drama
07769   84 mins   C
V2, B, V
Tom Drake, Femi Benussi
Intrigue, murder and suspense follows the publication of the will of a fatal accident victim.
S,A — EN
Unknown — *Fletcher Video* **H, P**
AV601

Deadly Revenge   Fil-Ent '7?
Suspense
04294   90 mins   C
V2, B, V
Van Johnson
Paul Valery is left behind and captured during a daring robbery in Vienna. After being sentenced to a long term in prison, his escape is arranged by 'The Professor' (Van Johnson) and they set out to track down Paul's accomplices and recover the loot.
C,A — EN
Unknown — *Video Programme Distributors* **P**
Inter-Ocean—038

Deadly Trackers, The   Fil-Ent '73
Western/Adventure
13025   101 mins   C
B, V
Richard Harris, Rod Taylor, directed by Barry Shear
A tough western in which a sheriff sets out to avenge the brutal deaths of his wife and son at the hands of outlaws.
BBFC:X — A — EN
Warner Bros — *Warner Home Video* **P**
61282

Deadly Trap, The   Fil-Ent '71
Suspense/Drama
07843   92 mins   C
B, V
Faye Dunaway, Frank Langella, Barbara Parkins, Karen Glangvernon, Maurice Ronet, directed by Rene Clement

PALADIN VIDEO HOME ENTERTAINMENT GUIDE

A brilliant American mathematician goes to France with his wife and two children to write a novel. An organisation of international racketeers contact him to use his mathematical genius for industrial espionage. He refuses, and his children disappear without a trace.
S,A — EN
Les Films Corona — *Polygram Video* **H, P**
791 522

Death at Owell Rock   Fil-Ent '81
Western
12847   85 mins   C
V2, B, V
Mark Damon, Stephen Forsyth, directed by George Lincoln
A small western town is held in the grasp of one family who stop at nothing to get what they want and the return of a major's son unearths old secrets.
BBFC:15 — S,A — EN
Unknown — *Video Programme Distributors* **P**
VPD 232

Death Collector   Fil-Ent '82
Crime-Drama
12829   98 mins   C
B, V
Joseph Cartese, directed by Ralph de Vito
A debt collector is prepared to go to any lengths in a violent and dangerous job for the crime syndicates and finds himself in trouble with the Mafia.
BBFC:18 — A — EN
William M Panzer — *Video Tape Centre* **P**
1173

Death Cruise   Fil-Ent '74
Drama/Suspense
12075   70 mins   C
V2, B, V
Richard Long, Polly Bergen, Edward Albert, Kate Jackson
After winning a pleasure cruise in a contest three couples find that their tickets have guaranteed them a one-way passage to death.
BBFC:PG — S,A — EN
Metromedia Producers; Aaron Spelling — *Guild Home Video* **H, P, E**

Death Dimension   Fil-Ent '7?
Suspense
04479   90 mins   C
V2, B, V
Jim Kelly, Aldo Ray, George Lazenby, Myron Lee

A microdot which can revolutionize warfare is implanted under a woman's skin. She is pursued by agents from several organisations who want to obtain the secret of the microdot.
A — EN
Unknown — *Intervision Video* **H, P**
A-AE 0167

Death Drive   Fil-Ent '76
Suspense/Drama
07331   104 mins   C
B, V
Franco Nero, Corinne Clery, directed by Pasquale Festa Campanile
In this film a young couple, who are tired of their way of life, decide to attempt to save their marriage by going on a long caravan trip through the United States. On the way they pick up a hitch-hiker but realise too late that he is a bank robber on the run. Their journey turns into a nightmare, finally exploding into violence.
BBFC:X — A — EN
Unknown — *Derann Film Services* **P**
FDV 303B/VHS FDV 303

Death Flight   Fil-Ent '77
Drama/Suspense
09196   97 mins   C
B, V
Peter Graves, Lorne Green, Season Hubley, Tina Louise, George Maharis, Burgess Meredith, Doug McClure, Robert Reed, Susan Strasberg, Barbara Anderson
This tells of America's first supersonic transport which is launched from New York with Paris as its destination. However, mechanical problems develop due to sabotage. On board is a doctor who is transporting a highly contagious sample of Senegal flu. When the malfunction causes an explosion, releasing the virulent flu germs, the crew must decide whether to land in London, thereby endangering many lives, or to try to reach an isolated airfield in Senegal.
F — EN
ABC Circle Films — *Video Form Pictures* **H, P**
DD 6

Death Force   Fil-Ent '7?
Crime-Drama/Martial arts
07683   90 mins   C
B, V
James Iglehart, Carmen Argenziano, Leon Isaac, Jayne Kennedy, Roberto Gonzales
Three US soldiers stop off in the Philippines after making money on the Vietnam black market. Two of them decide to do away with the other as he is not interested in making a take over bid for the crime empire in L.A. when they return. His throat is slashed, he is thrown over board but he lives and is nursed back to health by two World War II Japanese stragglers on an

(For Explanation of codes, see USE GUIDE and KEY)   173

PALADIN VIDEO HOME ENTERTAINMENT GUIDE

island, who teach him the art of the Samurai warrior. When he is finally rescued, he begins a violent one man war to destroy the crime empire.
A — EN
Cosa Nueva Productions — Video Network   P
0005

Death Hunt Fil-Ent '81
Drama/Adventure
07700   97 mins   C
V2, B, V
Lee Marvin, Charles Bronson, directed by Peter Hunt
This is the story of a Canadian mountie who attempt to track down a framed trapper across the snowy wastes of the Yukon in the 1930's.
S,A — EN
Twentieth Century Fox — CBS/Fox Video   P
1125

Death in Venice Fil-Ent '71
Drama
06014   125 mins   C
B, V
Dirk Bogarde, Bjorn Andresen, Silvana Mangano, directed by Luchino Visconti
A German composer and conductor on a pleasure trip to Venice idly observes the other guests in the hotel reflecting on his past life. He becomes infatuated with a boy of 14 while there are hushed rumours, denied by the authorities, of an epidemic. The Venetians are unwilling to admit the outbreak due to the importance of tourist income—the composer decides to stay and searches for the boy.
BBFC:AA — S,A — EN
Warner Bros — Warner Home Video   P
WEX1060/WEV1060

Death Line Fil-Ent '75
Mystery/Suspense
06918   84 mins   C
B, V
Donald Pleasance, Christopher Lee, David Ladd, Sharon Gurney
When a couple discover a dying man in their local underground station they start an investigation that reveals a sinister and macabre plot. Prominent people have been disappearing from tube stations and an M15 agent is called in to help solve the mystery of who or what is turning the tunnel into a death line.
BBFC:X — A — EN
American International — Rank Video Library
H, P
0062B

Death of a Centrefold Fil-Ent '81
Drama
13423   95 mins   C
B, V
Jamie Lee Curtis, directed by Gabrielle Beaumont
This is a film about the 'Playboy' girl Dorothy Stratten and the high price she paid for stardom and he involvement on meeting wheeler-dealer Paul Snider.
A — EN
Larry Wilcox Prods. — MGM/UA Home Video   P
10422

Death of a Hooker Fil-Ent '71
Mystery
06727   86 mins   C
V2, B, V
Red Buttons, Sylvia Miles, Alice Playten, Sam Waterston, directed by Ernie Pintoff
Former bantamweight boxing champion decides to solve the murder of an obscure New York streetwalker he never even met. Originally titled 'Who Killed Mary Whats'ername?'
BBFC:AA — A — EN
Cannon Releasing — Intervision Video
H, P
A-A 0120

Death of a Snowman Fil-Ent '7?
Suspense/Crime-Drama
04313   84 mins   C
V2, B, V
A hit man wants a piece of New York's street action, and gets Harlem gangs to help him fight the Mafia.
A — EN
Unknown — Intervision Video   H, P
A-A 0031

Death of Adolf Hitler, The Fil-Ent '73
War-Drama
06279   107 mins   C
B, V
Frank Finlay, Caroline Mortimer, directed by Rex Firkin
This film is a frighteningly realistic portrayal of Adolf Hitler during the last days of his life from his birthday on April 20th 1945, until his suicide ten days later.
Society of Film and TV Arts '73: Best Actor (Finlay).   S,A — EN
London Weekend Television Limited — THORN EMI   P
TXB 90 0701 4/TVB 90 0701 2

Death on the Nile Fil-Ent '78
Mystery
04632   135 mins   C

PALADIN VIDEO HOME ENTERTAINMENT GUIDE

B, V
Peter Ustinov, Jane Birkin, Lois Chiles, Bette Davis, Mia Farrow, Jon Finch, Olivia Hussey, David Niven
Agatha Christie's fictional detective Hercule Poiret is called upon to solve the mystery of who killed an heiress on a steamer cruising down the Nile.
C,A — EN
EMI; John Brabourne; Richard Goodwin — *THORN EMI*   H, P
TXA 90 0226 4/TVA 90 0226 2

Death Promise   FII-Ent '??
Martial arts
06853   90 mins   C
V2, B, V
Charles Bonet
A group of young people living in a New York slum area decide to kill their landlords, if they keep demanding more rent without improving conditions. All the young tenants are Kung Fu or Karate experts.
S,A — EN
Unknown — *European Video Company*
P

Death Race 2000   FII-Ent '75
Science fiction/Adventure
07950   80 mins   C
B, V
David Carradine, Simone Griffeth, Sylvester Stallone, directed by Paul Bartel
Set in the year 2000 this film follows the most popular sport where racing car drivers on a cross country race compete to see how many pedestrians they can kill to score points for the championship.
BBFC:X — A — EN
New World Pictures — *Brent Walker Home Video Ltd*   P

Death Raiders   FII-Ent '83
Adventure/Drama
13686   77 mins   C
B, V
Johnny Wilson, George Pallance, directed by Segundo Ramos
A hand-picked group of commandoes are chosen to free the governor of a province and his daughters when they are kidnapped by raiders and taken to their rebel camp.
BBFC:18 — A — EN
Emperor Films International Inc — *THORN EMI*   P
90 2678

Death Ship   FII-Ent '80
Mystery/Adventure
08529   87 mins   C
B, V
George Kennedy, Richard Crenna, Nick Mancuso, Sally Ann Howes, directed by Alvin Rakoff
A mysterious vessel collides with a cruise ship somewhere in the Caribbean. A few manage to survive by clambering aboard the freighter, only to find themselves prisoners on a former German wartime vessel. As they are taken to an unknown destination they realize that something is intent on destroying each of them.
C,A — EN
Avco Embassy — *THORN EMI*   P
TXA 90 0960 4/TVA 90 09602

Death Sport   FII-Ent '78
Science fiction
07859   87 mins   C
B, V
David Carradine, Claudia Jennings, Richard Lynch, David McLean, Will Walker, directed by Henry Susa and Allan Arkush
This futuristic science fiction gladiator film is set 1,000 years in the future. The good warriors ride horses and carry see-through sabres in their fight against the 'baddies' who drive lethal motorcycles known as 'Death Machines.'
BBFC:X — A — EN
New World Pictures — *Warner Home Video*   P
WEX 74027/WEV 74027

Death Squad   FII-Ent '74
Drama
13346   71 mins   C
V2, B, V
Robert Forster, Melvyn Douglas, Michelle Phillips, Claude Akins, directed by Harry Falk
After a series of gangland-style executions occur a tough ex-cop is taken back on the force to infiltrate renegade elements in the department and expose officers involved.
BBFC:15 — S,A — EN
Spelling-Goldberg Productions — *Guild Home Video*   H, P, E
8407-3

Death Threat   FII-Ent '??
Drama/Suspense
08848   86 mins   C
B, V
William Smith, Jude Farese, Don Stroud
This tells the story of a man, an actor and director whose life is making films. However, his latest film could mean his death.
BBFC:X — A — EN
Unknown — *VCL Video Services*   P
M251D

(For Explanation of codes, see USE GUIDE and KEY)   175

PALADIN VIDEO HOME ENTERTAINMENT GUIDE

Death Trap Fil-Ent '82
Drama/Suspense
13060   113 mins   C
B, V

Michael Caine, Dyan Cannon, Chrisopher Reeve, directed by Sidney Lumet
This is a compelling thriller based on Broadway's longest running mystery play by Ira Levin, which has so many twists it commands total attention.
BBFC:A — C,A — EN
Warner Bros Inc — *Warner Home Video* **P**
61256

Death Valley Fil-Ent '81
Drama/Suspense
09271   90 mins   C
B, V

Paul Le Mat, Catherine Hicks, Peter Billingsley
A trio sets out to drive through Death Valley, a trip which soon becomes a nightmare of danger and insanity.
BBFC:R — A — EN
Universal — *CIC Video*   **H, P**

Death Vengeance Fil-Ent '8?
Crime-Drama
08451   92 mins   C
B, V

Tom Skerritt, Patti LuPone, Michael Sarrazin
This film follows one man's efforts to rid the horrific level of crime from his previously peaceful neighbourhood. He forms the 'People's Neighbourhood Patrol' with the help of the town's residents, their intention being to combat violence with violence. As the patrol are driven to use increasingly more corrupt measures the moral of their ways comes into doubt.
BBFC:X — A — EN
Unknown — *THORN EMI*   **P**
TXA 90 1276 4/TVA 90 1276 2

Death Weekend Fil-Ent '76
Horror
07936   92 mins   C
V2, B, V

Brenda Vaccaro, Don Stroud, Chuck Shamata, Richard Ayres, Kyle Edwards, directed by William Freut
A young couple arrive at a serene and isolated haven for a weekend break. Their weekend turns into a nightmare when they encounter four thugs who are out for sadistic kicks.
BBFC:X — A — EN
Cinepix — *Videomedia*   **P**
PVM 1025/BVM 1025/HVM 1025

Death Wish Fil-Ent '74
Drama
01211   93 mins   C
V2, B, V

Charles Bronson, Vincent Gardenia, William Redfield, Hope Lange, directed by Michael Winner
Charles Bronson turns vigilante after his wife and daughter are violently attacked and raped by a gang of hoodlums. He stalks the streets of New York seeking revenge on other muggers, pimps, and crooks. Music by Herbie Hancock.
A — EN
Paramount — *CIC Video*   **H, P**
CRA 2004/BEA 2004/VHA 2004

Deathcheaters Fil-Ent '76
Adventure
06163   83 mins   C
B, V

John Hargreaves, Noel Ferrier, Margaret Gerard, Grant Page
The plans of two ex-commandos who run a successful stuntman business are interrupted by the Secret Service. They are recruited as agents and get involved in a series of assignments from Australia to the Philippines. This film features many daring stunt scenes.
BBFC:U — F — EN
Trenchard Smith Prod — *Guild Home Video*   **H, P, E**

Deathdream Fil-Ent '??
Horror
06094   98 mins   C
V2, B, V

John Marley, Lynn Carlin, Richard Backus, Henderson Forsyth
When a man, presumed killed in army action, returns home, unexplained murders occur. He is in fact a living Dead Being and his existence depends on his supply of fresh blood.
S,A — EN
Unknown — *Video Programme Distributors* **P**
Cinehollywood—V1750

Deathhead Virgin, The Fil-Ent '74
Horror
02491   90 mins   C
V2, B, V

Jock Gaynor, Larry Ward, Diane McBain
A strange amulet removed from a skeleton at the bottom of the sea releases the bloody curse of the Deathhead Virgin—chained for 100 years in a sunken tomb.
BBFC:X — A — EN
Wargay — *Intervision Video*   **H**
A-A 0160

PALADIN VIDEO HOME ENTERTAINMENT GUIDE

Deathwatch
Fil-Ent '79
Drama/Science fiction
07814 128 mins C
B, V

Harvey Keitel, Romy Schneider, Max Von Sydow, Harry Dean Stanton
Set in the future, where ill-health is conquered by medicine and any old age or an accident causes death, this film follows an advanced society where TV has a strong grasp. A woman, told by doctors that she has only three weeks to live, is pressured into having her last days broadcast on a new programme called 'Deathwatch.'
S,A — EN
Selta Films; Gaumont Prods — *Video Tape Centre* **P**
VTC 1023

Debrief: Apollo 8
Med-Sci '69
Space exploration
01100 28 mins C
B, V, PH15, PH17, 3/4U

Several prominent figures in America give comments on man's first journey in orbit around the moon.
CINE Golden Eagle '69; Atlanta Film Festival '69: Bronze Medal. C,A — ED
NASA — *Istead Audio Visual* **P**
HQ 188

Decade of British Open
Spo-Lei '81
Golf
05050 60 mins C
B, V

A collection of memorable moments from the seventies in the international golf championship, featuring many world-famous golfing personalities.
F — EN
Trans World International — *THORN EMI* **P**
TXE 90 7103 4/TVE 90 7103 2

Decade of Grand Prix/The Frank Williams Story
Spo-Lei '81
Automobiles-Racing
05052 46 mins C
B, V

'Decade of Grand Prix' traces the progress of Formula 1 racing in the seventies. 'The Frank Williams Story' tells of the skills, struggles and dedication which eventually won his team the championship in 1980.
F — EN
Brunswick Films International — *THORN EMI* **P**
TXE 90 7102 4/TVE 90 7102 2

Decade of Wimbledon
Spo-Lei '81
Tennis
05051 60 mins C
B, V

This is a record of matches of the seventies between some of the most famous names in tennis history.
F — EN
Trans World International — *THORN EMI* **P**
TXE 90 7101 4/TVE 90 7101 2

Decameron, The
Fil-Ent '70
Comedy
12503 108 mins C
B, V

Franco Citti, Ninetto Davoli, M. Gabriella Frankel, directed by Pier Paolo Pasolini
Eight tales of love, lust and lechery set in the Middle Ages and based on classic stories by the famed fourteenth century author Giovanni Boccaccio.
BBFC:18 — A — EN
Franco Rossellini — *Warner Home Video* **P**
99366

Deep Jaws
Fil-Ent '??
Comedy
05482 100 mins C
V2, B, V

David Kelly, Anne Gaybis, Gordon Herigstadt, Candy Samples, Sandra Carey, directed by Perry Dell
A family film maker finds his studios are going out of business. Just in time he is given a contract to make a simulated version of the U.S.-Russian outer space link-up. With some of the funds he decides to make a low budget sex movie; problems arise when both films are shot on the same set.
BBFC:X — A — EN
Unknown — *Iver Film Services* **P**

Deep Purple—Concerto for Group and Orchestra
Fil-Ent '84
Music-Performance
13380 51 mins C
B, V

This programme combines the talents of the Deep Purple rock band and the Royal Philharmonic Orchestra in a unique event recorded at the Royal Albert Hall in 1969.
F — EN
Unknown — *BBC Video* **H, P**
3027

(For Explanation of codes, see USE GUIDE and KEY)   177

PALADIN VIDEO HOME ENTERTAINMENT GUIDE

Deep Purple—California Jam April 6th 1974   Fil-Ent '81
Music-Performance
04863   77 mins   C
V2, B, V, LV
This is a special recording of Deep Purple in concert at the Ontario Speedway in California.
F — EN
Andy Finney — *BBC Video*   **H, P**
BBCV 3000

Deep Red   Fil-Ent '75
Drama/Suspense
08648   105 mins   C
V2, B, V
David Hemmings, Daria Nicolodi, Gabriele Lavia, Clara Calamai, directed by Dario Argento
During a parapsychiatrists' conference in Rome a mentalist starts screaming when she gets strange thoughts from a twisted mind. When she is later murdered an English pianist almost gets himself killed when he attempts to track down her killer.
BBFC:R — *A — EN*
Mahler Films — *Fletcher Video*   **H, P**
V188

Deep River Savages   Fil-Ent '??
Adventure
08689   88 mins   C
V2, B, V
Ivan Rassimov, Me Me Lay
This is the story of savagery, tribal torture and one man's fight for survival. It tells of his tragic love for a beautiful native girl.
BBFC:X — *A — EN*
Unknown — *Derann Film Services*   **P**
FDV 305

Deep Sea Fishing   Spo-Lei '82
Fishing
13550   55 mins   C
B, V
Two successful methods of boat angling are shown on this tape, firstly fishing over a sandy bottom whilst at anchor and secondly, fishing over reefs and rough terrain.
S,A — I
Unknown — *TFI Leisure Ltd*   **H, P**

Deer Hunter, The   Fil-Ent '78
Drama
04643   176 mins   C
B, V
Robert De Niro, John Cazale, John Savage, Meryl Streep, Christopher Walken, directed by Michael Cimino
Three friends from a Pennsylvania steel town go to Viet Nam and learn that war is a human roulette game. Their town, their loves and their lives will never again be the same.
Academy Awards '78: Best Picture; Best Director (Cimino).   BBFC:X — *A — EN*
Universal — *THORN EMI*   **H, P**
TXA 90 0230 4/TVA 90 0230 2

Deerslayer, The   Fil-Ent '78
Adventure/Drama
06959   98 mins   C
B, V
Steve Forrest, Ned Romero, John Anderson, Victor Mohica, Joan Prather, Betty Ann Carr, Charles Dierkop, directed by Dick Friedenberg
Set during the French and Indian war, an intrepid frontiersman and his Indian companion set out on a dangerous mission to save a beautiful princess from hostile Indians. Based on the novel by James Fenimore Cooper.
F — EN
Schick Sunn Classic — *Home Video Merchandisers*   **H, P**
034

Deerslayer, The   Fil-Ent '57
Adventure/Drama
07996   77 mins   C
B, V
Lex Barker, Forrest Tucker, Rita Moreno, Carlos Rivas
This film is based on James Fenimore Cooper's classic novel of early American life. It tells of a white man, raised by Mohican Indians, who discovers a white-scalp hunter.
S,A — EN
Twentieth Century—Fox — *Motion Epics Video Company Ltd*   **P**
163

Delia Smith's Home Baking   How-Ins '81
Cookery
04866   105 mins   C
V2, B, V, LV
Delia Smith demonstrates home baking of every kind, from bread to choux pastry. Three accompanying books, 'A Delia Smith Cookery Course,' available from booksellers.
AM Available   *S,A — I*
Erica Griffiths — *BBC Video*   **H, P**
BBCV 1009

Delirium   Fil-Ent '8?
Drama
09072   85 mins   C
B, V
Turk Cekovsky, Dehi Shaney, Terry Ten Brock, Barron Winchester

PALADIN VIDEO HOME ENTERTAINMENT GUIDE

An ex-Vietnam War veteran escapes from a mental institution. He is hired as an assassin by a group headed by an ex-Army Officer, to kill escaped criminals. Unfortunately he gets out of control, killing wherever he finds a victim.
A — EN
Unknown — *Video Tape Centre*   P
VTC 1020

Deliverance   Fll-Ent '72
Drama
07860   100 mins   C
B, V
Burt Reynolds, Jon Voight, Ned Beatty, Ronny Cox, directed by John Boorman
Four men on a weekend camping and canoeing trip on a dangerous stretch of river, deep in a mountain wilderness, find that the real danger to their lives comes from themselves and other humans as their weekend turns into a terrifying nightmare. Based on the novel by James Dickey.
BBFC:X — A — EN
Warner Bros — *Warner Home Video*   P
WEX 61004/WEV 61004

Delta Factor   Fll-Ent '70
Drama
04409   90 mins   C
B, V
Christopher George, Yvette Mimieux, Diane McBain, Ralph Taeger
An escaped prisoner is given the choice of returning to prison or helping a female federal agent rescue a scientist from an impregnable fortress.
F — EN
Continental; Spillane Fellows — *VCL Video Services*   P

Demented   Fll-Ent '??
Horror
07924   92 mins   C
V2, B, V
Sallee Elyse, Bruce Gilchrist, directed by Arthur Jeffreys
A beautiful and talented woman is brutally raped by four men. She takes revenge on the intruders by brutally murdering them, ignoring their pleas for mercy.
S,A — EN
Unknown — *Video Programme Distributors*   P
Media—179

Demon   Fll-Ent '76
Horror/Science fiction
09085   87 mins   C
B, V
Tony Lo Bianco, Sandy Dennis, Deborah Raffin, Sylvia Sidney, Sam Levene
A New York cop, trapped between the choice of wife and mistress is investigating a series of murders. He has to reveal the identity of the figure provoking innocent people to go on the rampage.
A — EN
New World — *Video Tape Centre*   P
VTC 1038

Demon, The   Fll-Ent '81
Horror
12621   94 mins   C
V2, B, V
Cameron Mitchell, Jennifer Holmes
A demon-like maniac attacks a family and takes off with the young daughter. Attempts to find her leave a trail of brutal murders in their wake.
A — EN
Gold Key Entertainment — *VideoSpace Ltd*
P

Demon Seed   Fll-Ent '77
Science fiction/Horror
07724   90 mins   C
B, V
Julie Christie, Fritz Weaver, directed by Donald Cammell
The home of a dedicated scientist and his wife, an experimental psychologist, is controlled by a series of his computers. The ultimate computer is the Proteus IV, a machine with an artificial organic brain capable of holding the world's knowledge. However, it 'kidnaps' his wife, locks her in a room and takes her on a voyage through time and space during which it rapes her and incubates a child.
BBFC:AA — S,A — EN
MGM — *MGM/UA Home Video*   P
UMB 10129/UMV 10129

Demonoid   Fll-Ent '81
Horror
08880   85 mins   C
V2, B, V
Stuart Whitman, Samatha Eggar, Roy Cameron Jenson, Narcisco Dusquets, Erika Carlsson, Lew Saunders
The Demonoid is an evil presence who destroys lives by possessing its victims.
BBFC:X — A — EN
Zach Motion Pictures; Panorama Films — *Video Programme Distributors*
P
Media 201

Demons of the Mind   Fll-Ent '71
Drama/Suspense
08446   85 mins   C

(For Explanation of codes, see USE GUIDE and KEY)

179

PALADIN VIDEO HOME ENTERTAINMENT GUIDE

B, V
Paul Jones, Patrick Magee, Yvonne Mitchell, Robert Hardy, Gillian Hills, Michael Hordern
Set in the 19th century, this film tells the story of a Bavarian count who keeps his children locked away from the outside world, in case they discover a dark family secret.
BBFC:X — A — EN
Hammer Films — *THORN EMI* P
TXC 90 0858 4/TVC 90 0858 2

Deputy Dawg   Fil-Ent '??
Cartoons
01749   30 mins   C
B, V
Animated
Features five Terrytoon cartoons: Deputy Dawg in 'Space Varmint,' Mighty Mouse in 'The Mysterious Package,' Heckle and Jeckle in 'Moose on the Loose,' Little Roquefort in 'Haunted Cat,' and Astronut in 'Space Cowboy.'
BBFC:U — F — EN
Paramount — *CBS/Fox Video*   P
1B-028

Dernier Milliardaire, Le   Fil-Ent '34
Comedy
12510   88 mins   B/W
B, V
Max Dearly, Renee Saint-Cyr, Marthe Mellot, Raymond Cordy, directed by Rene Clair
The queen of a bankrupt kingdom invites a millionaire to marry her daughter. When the girl elopes with a bandleader the queen decides to offer herself instead.
BBFC:U — F — EN
Pathe Natan — *THORN EMI*   P
TXJ 90 2365 4/TVJ 90 2365 2

Desert Chase   Fil-Ent '7?
Drama/Adventure
07977   96 mins   C
B, V
Michael Coby, Michel Constantin, Franco Nero
This story involves a group of oil surveyors who get mixed up in Middle Eastern terrorist activities. When one of the group gets killed, the remainder of the group set out across the desert in an attempt to catch the murderers.
BBFC:AA — C,A — EN
Unknown — *AVI Video Ltd*   P
009

Desert Commando   Fil-Ent '7?
War-Drama
07759   99 mins   C
V2, B, V
Ken Clark, Horst Frank, Jeanne Valerie
This film depicts an attempt by German commandos to assassinate Churchill, Roosevelt and Stalin at the Casablanca Conference.
S,A — EN
Unknown — *Fletcher Video*   H, P
V120

Desert Fox, The   Fil-Ent '51
War-Drama
07702   83 mins   B/W
V2, B, V
James Mason, Sir Cedric Hardwicke, Jessica Tandy, Luther Adler, directed by Henry Hathaway
This film follows the career of Field Marshal Rommel, commander of the Afrikan Korps during World War II. His career was brought to an abrupt close when he was involved in the July 1944 plot to assassinate Hitler.
S,A — EN
Twentieth Century Fox — *CBS/Fox Video* P
1014

Desert Tigers   Fil-Ent '??
War-Drama
08894   83 mins   C
V2, B, V
Gordon Mitchell, Richard Harrison
A daring raid on a German oil depot in North Africa seriously hampers the German Army stationed there. The survivors from the attack are taken to a German concentration camp ruled by a sadistic commander.
BBFC:X — A — EN
Unknown — *Video Programme Distributors*   P
Canon 010

Desert Warrior   Fil-Ent '84
Adventure
13731   90 mins   C
V2, B, V
Mark Harmon
An army column invades a desert camp and kills their honoured guest—a deed that must be avenged by the tribal code.
BBFC:18 — A — EN
SACIS; Medusa Communications — *Medusa Communications Ltd*   H, P
MC 034

Deserter, The   Fil-Ent '70
Drama
13613   96 mins   C
B, V
Bekim Fehmiu, Richard Crenna, Mimmo Palmara, John Huston, directed by Burt Kennedy

(For Explanation of codes, see USE GUIDE and KEY)

PALADIN VIDEO HOME ENTERTAINMENT GUIDE

When a U.S. Army captain finds his wife mutilated by Apaches he deserts and wages a one-man war on all Indians until offered a pardon if he agrees to help with defensive strategy to protect the Cavalry from attack.
BBFC:15 — S,A — EN
Paramount — CIC Video   H, P
2126

Despair   FII-Ent '78
Drama/Suspense
08563   108 mins   C
B, V
Dirk Bogarde, Andrea Ferreol, Klaus Lowitsch, Volker Spengler, Bernhard Wicki, directed by Rainer Werner Fassbinder
Dirk Bogarde plays a bored chocolate manufacturer in Nazi Germany. Whilst making love to his wife he feels that he can step out of his body and watch 'them' from another room. He then meets a tramp who he believes is his double. He plots the murder of this tramp so that he can assume his identity and start a new life.
BBFC:AA — C,A — EN
NF Geria 11 Film GmbH — THORN EMI P
TXB 90 0980 4/TVB 900980 2

Desperate Characters   FII-Ent '71
Drama
07339   91 mins   C
B, V
Shirley MacLaine, Kenneth Mars, Gerald O'Loughlin, Sada Thompson, Jack Somack, Chris Gample, Mary Ellen Hokenson, directed by Frank D. Gilroy
In this film a comfortably middle-class, childless couple are forced to acknowledge that their day-to-day existence is shadowed by fear and disillusionment.
BBFC:X — A — EN
ITC — Precision Video Ltd   P
BITC 2070/VITC 2070

Desperate Intruder   FII-Ent '83
Drama
09955   90 mins   C
V2, B, V
Meg Foster, Nick Mancuso
A handsome escaped convict falls in love with a young blind woman who lives alone in an isolated beach house.
BBFC:A — S,A — EN
Comworld Productions — Video Unlimited
H, P, E
079

Desperate Living   FII-Ent '74
Comedy/Fantasy
08968   90 mins   C
B, V
Mink Stole, Edith Massey, directed by John Waters
This is an adult fairy-tale about a Queen Carlotta who rules the depraved town of Mortville. It involves murder, flight, love, death, wrestling, sex change operations and rabies. The Queen is eventually overthrown by the women of Mortville.
A — EN
New Line Cinema — Palace Video Ltd   P
PVC 2015B

Desperate Ones, The   FII-Ent '68
Adventure
12753   103 mins   C
B, V
Maximilian Schell, Raf Vallone, Irene Papas, directed by Alexander Ramati
Two Polish brothers escape from a Siberian labour camp in 1941 to find that their only hope of freedom is to swim the heavily guarded river that stands between themselves and freedom.
BBFC:15 — C,A — EN
Alexander Ramati — Rank Video Library
H, P
0187Y

Desperate Voyage   FII-Ent '80
Crime-Drama/Suspense
05631   108 mins   C
V2, B, V
Christopher Plummer, Cliff Potts, Christine Belford, Lara Parker, directed by Michael O'Herlihy
This is a tale of crime and murder on a modern day pirate ship in the Gulf of Mexico. The captain and his demented son scour the high seas looking for vessels in distress which they can then raid, ruin and kill any survivors. A young couple on a cruise become involved.
S,A — EN
Barry Weitz Prod — Video Unlimited   H, P

Desperate Women   FII-Ent '78
Adventure/Comedy
12093   97 mins   C
B, V
Susan Saint-James, Dan Haggerty, Ronee Blakely, Ann Dusenberry, Michael Delano, directed by Earl Bellamy
A kindly ex-hired gunslinger helps three women escape from going to prison and finds himself in trouble as he fights off marauding Indians, lecherous miners and an outlaw gang.
F — EN
Lorimar — Polygram Video   H, P
0401354/0401352

(For Explanation of codes, see USE GUIDE and KEY)

PALADIN VIDEO HOME ENTERTAINMENT GUIDE

Destination Inner Space/The Wizard of Mars
Fil-Ent '66
Science fiction
10215　　81 mins　　C
B, V
Scott Brady, Sheree North, Gary Merrill/John Carradine, Roger Gentry, Vic McGee, Jerry Rannow
Two films are contained on one cassette. 'Destination Inner Space' follows the story of a team of marine scientists cut off in their underwater laboratory who battle for survival as creatures from another world attempt to colonise Earth. 'The Wizard of Mars' follows the fate of the first manned flight which is forced to crash-land, in search of oxygen they chance upon an ancient Martian city.
F — EN
Harold Goldman et al — *Video Form Pictures*　**H, P**
MGT B11

Destination Moon
Chl-Juv '7?
Cartoons
02214　　60 mins　　C
V
Animated
Professor Calculus proposes to the amazed Tin Tin, Snowy, and Captain Haddock an expedition to the moon. Sinister forces unsuccessfully try to prevent them from the attempt.
PS,I — EN
Unknown — *JVC*　**P**
PRT 15

Destination Moonbase Alpha
Fil-Ent '7?
Science fiction
00834　　96 mins　　C
B, V
Martin Landau, Barbara Bain
Terrifyingly unexpected space adventure has befallen the personnel of Moonbase Alpha, the scientific space station on the moon. They receive visitors to rescue them and take them back to earth. Only one man sees the visitors for what they really are, Commander Koenig. In his eyes, the visitors are not old friends from earth but hideous aliens. From the 'Space: 1999' series.
A — EN
ITC — *Precision Video Ltd*　**P**
BITC 2019/VITC 2019

Detective, The
Fil-Ent '68
Mystery
01750　　114 mins　　C
B, V
Frank Sinatra, Lee Remick
A beautiful woman requests the services of a detective in order to discover her husband's killer.
F — EN
20th Century Fox — *CBS/Fox Video*　**P**
3A-009

Detroit 9000
Fil-Ent '??
Crime-Drama
05734　　106 mins　　C
V2, B, V
Hain Rhodes, Alex Rocco, Vonetta McGee, Scatman Crothers, Herbert Jefferson Jr, directed by Arthur Marks
A story of murder and racial mayhem that hits Detroit. A black super-policeman leads an action-packed investigation into a violent half million dollar fraud deal.
S,A — EN
General Film Corp — *Video Unlimited*　**H, P**

Devil and Leroy Bassett, The
Fil-Ent '??
Drama
08754　　89 mins　　C
B, V
Cody Bearpaw, John Goff, George Flower, Elliott Lindsey, Dick Winslow, Bobbi Shaw, James Ward
This film tells the story of three brothers who escort a murderer, who is being extradited to his home state. The murderer drives to a secluded mountain cabin where he hides. The cabin is inhabited by a family, and he decides to use them as a cover to get to town.
A — EN
Unknown — *Precision Video Ltd*　**P**
BITC 2567/VITC 2567

Devil and Max Devlin, The
Fil-Ent '81
Comedy/Fantasy
12580　　96 mins　　C
B, V
Elliot Gould, Bill Cosby
A man makes a pact with the Devil after being flattened by a bus.
F — EN
Walt Disney Productions — *Rank Video Library*　**H**
067

Devil Doll/The Curse of Simba
Fil-Ent '6?
Horror/Drama
05761　　156 mins　　B/W
B, V

182　　(For Explanation of codes, see USE GUIDE and KEY)

PALADIN VIDEO HOME ENTERTAINMENT GUIDE

Bryant Halliday, Yvonne Romain, William Sylvester, Sandra Dorne, Francis DeWolff, directed by Lindsay Shonteff, Bryant Halliday, Dennis Price, Lisa Danielly, directed by Lindsay Shonteff
Two films are featured on one cassette. 'Devil Doll' (Black/White, 77 mins, 1965) is a spinechilling story of a ventriloquist's dummy that is locked in a cage every night. It is revealed that the dummy contains the soul of a former performer. A journalist unmasks the ventriloquist in time to save a young girl who is totally under his hypnotic power. 'The Curse of Simba' (Black/white, 79 mins, 1964) is the story of an American who falls foul of an African tribe and is put under a curse. He returns to civilization and tries to find a way to stop the threat of death and the nightmares that haunt him.
F — EN
Gordon Films; Allied Artists — Kingston Video H, P
KV22

Devil Hunter, The   Fil-Ent '??
Horror
06095   94 mins   C
V2, B, V
Al Cliver, Gisela Hahn, Robert Foster
A model on an assignment in South America is kidnapped by a gang and carried off into the jungle. She finds herself in the savage clutches of a primitive and bloodthirsty world. Her rescuers not only have to face this violence but the lust for blood by a primitive and cruel god.
S,A — EN
Unknown — Video Programme Distributors P
Cinehollywood—V1590

Devil in Miss Jones Part   Fil-Ent '7?
II, The
Drama
12149   84 mins   C
B, V
Georgina Ventura, Samantha Fox, Jacqueline Lorians
A woman's spirit is transferred from body to body as the Devil jealously tries to find one in which she cannot sin, but she continues in her pursuit of pleasure.
BBFC:18 — A — EN
Unknown — Entertainment in Video   H, ?
EVB 3000/EVV 3000

Devil Times Five   Fil-Ent '7?
Horror
01681   87 mins   C
B, V, FO
Gene Evans, Sorrel Booke

Six adults and five children became stranded in an isolated mansion. One-by-one, the adults begin losing their lives. Death by hanging, man-eating piranhas, knife, and fire are the methods, but who is doing the killing?
C,A — EN
Unknown — Intervision Video   H, P

Devil with Seven Faces,   Fil-Ent '72
The
Crime-Drama
08651   93 mins   C
V2, B, V
Carroll Baker, George Hilton
This thriller follows the theft of a million dollar diamond and the resulting intrigue.
S,A — EN
Unknown — Fletcher Video   H, P
V140

Devil Within Her, The   Fil-Ent '75
Horror
12825   100 mins   C
B, V
Juliet Mills, Richard Johnson, directed by O. Hellman and R. Barret
A pregnant woman becomes possessed by a demonic force and as the evil foetus grows within her she plans to unleash indescribable terror onto an unsuspecting world.
BBFC:18 — A — EN
Arcade Video — VideoSpace Ltd   P
VS 23

Devils, The   Fil-Ent '71
Drama
13065   105 mins   C
B, V
Oliver Reed, Vanessa Redgrave, directed by Ken Russell
This story is based on the book by Aldous Huxley in which a Mother Superior's sexual obsession with a priest leads to the sensational exorcising of the convent nuns.
BBFC:X — A — EN
Warner Bros Inc — Warner Home Video P
61110

Devil's Advocate, The   Fil-Ent '77
Drama
08534   105 mins   C
B, V
Stephane Audran, Jason Miller, Paola Pitagora, John Mills
This film is based on Morris West's novel and tells the story of a man dying of cancer who accepts from his superiors a final mission. He has to go into one of the wildest parts of Italy

(For Explanation of codes, see USE GUIDE and KEY)

PALADIN VIDEO HOME ENTERTAINMENT GUIDE

and investigate the cult of a local miracle worker. As he unravels the secrets of this legendary figure, he finds his true self for the first time both as a priest and as a man.
C,A — EN
Unknown — THORN EMI   P
TXB 90 1274 4/TVB 90 1274 2

Devils Angels   Fil-Ent '67
Drama
13461   80 mins   C
B, V

John Cassevetes, Beverly Adams, Mimsy Farmer, directed by Daniel Haller

This is the story of two gangs of Hells Angels bikers and their clash with the forces of law and order.
BBFC:18 — A — EN
Orion Pictures — Rank Video Library   H, P
2037

Devil's Canyon/A Cry in the Night   Fil-Ent '5?
Western/Crime-Drama
05672   160 mins   C
B, V

Dale Robertson, Virginia Mayo, Stephen McNally, Arthur Hunnicutt, Robert Keith, directed by Alfred Werker, Raymond Burr, Natalie Wood, Brian Donlevy, Edmond O'Brien, directed by Frank Tuttle

Two films are featured on one cassette. 'Devil's Canyon' (Colour, 88 mins, 1954) in which a young woman stagecoach bandit becomes the only woman imprisoned with 500 men in a notorious prison in Arizona. A U.S. Marshal who killed two men in self defence is sent to join her but becomes an instant murder target. 'A Cry in the Night' (Black/White, 72 mins, 1957) is the story of a homicidal psychopath on the loose who kidnaps the police chief's daughter. A massive hunt is on, the girl unwillingly gets to know her capture and soon realises their problems in many ways are alike.
S,A — EN
RKO; Warner Bros — Kingston Video   H, P
KV40

Devil's Men   Fil-Ent '7?
Horror
01947   93 mins   C
B, V

Donald Pleasence, Peter Cushing

The priest of a small Balkan village searches for devil worshippers, whom he feels are responsible for the horrifying ritualistic murders of many young tourists.
S,A — EN
Unknown — CBS/Fox Video   P
3D-078

Devil's Nightmare   Fil-Ent '72
Horror
05627   90 mins   C
V2, B, V

Erika Blanc, Jean Servais, Daniel Emilfork, directed by Jean Brismee

A strange and horrific film in which the satanic forces clash with virtue in an ancient castle.
BBFC:X — A — EN
AIP — Go Video Ltd   P
A104

Devils of Darkness   Fil-Ent '65
Horror
02396   90 mins   C
B, V

William Sylvester, Hubert Noel, Tracy Reed, directed by Lance Comfort

A young man is forced into the web of black magic as he seeks a band of worshippers. He soon comes face to face with Satan himself.
A — EN
20th Century Fox — Derann Film Services   H, P
DV 102B/DV 102

Devil's Rain, The   Fil-Ent '75
Horror
08311   90 mins   C
B, V

William Shatner, Ernest Borgnine, Keenan Wynn, Tom Skerritt, Eddie Albert, directed by Robert Fuest

This film tells the story of a Satanist who, having been dead for three hundred years, returns to avenge himself on a family, the concealers of the Devil's secret book.
BBFC:X — A — EN
Bryanston Pictures — Video Film Organisation   P
0001

Devil's Widow, The   Fil-Ent '71
Horror
10206   106 mins   C
B, V

Ava Gardner, Ian McShane, Stephanie Beacham, Madeline Smith, Joanna Lumley, Sinead Cusack, directed by Roddy McDowell

PALADIN VIDEO HOME ENTERTAINMENT GUIDE

Every seven years a young man is sacrificed and the 'tithe to hell' is paid. A young man is fated to meet and fall in love with a Vicar's daughter. He visits the Devil's Widow and pleads for his freedom; she gives him a week whilst vowing to hunt him down and kill him.
A — EN
Alan Ladd Jr. — Video Form Pictures   H, P
DIP 10

Devo—'The Men Who Make the Music'   Fil-Ent '79
Music-Performance
07954   55 mins   C
B, V
This tape features a group of musicians 'Devo' who have an eccentric approach to visual programming. This is a collection of live concert recordings linked with promotional film of their songs by original narrative footage expounding their theory of de-evolution.
S,A — EN
Virgin Video — VideoSpace Ltd   P
VV2

Devouring Waves   Fil-Ent '84
Suspense
13715   90 mins   C
V2, B, V
Michael Sopkiw, Lawrence Morgant, Cinthia Stewart, directed by John Old Jnr.
Speculation is rife as to what sort of animal in the sea is savagely attacking boats and killing and mutilating their occupants.
BBFC:18 — A — EN
National Cinematography; Grippon Films — Medusa Communications Ltd   H, P
MC 039

Dial M for Murder   Fil-Ent '54
Suspense
12996   123 mins   C
B, V
Ray Milland, Grace Kelly, Robert Cummings, John Williams, directed by Alfred Hitchcock
This is the story of an unfaithful husband who plots to murder his wife for her money.
C,A — EN
Warner Bros — Warner Home Video   P
61046

Diamond Hunters   Fil-Ent '75
Adventure
08766   95 mins   C
B, V
Hayley Mills, David McCallum, Jon Cypher, directed by Dirk De Villiers
An old man is the head of a diamond empire. A terminal disease forces him to hand over his job, to his three contenders. They are his playboy son, his divorced daughter and his tough, hard working adopted son. The three of them become trapped in a web of intrigue, violence and love. Based on the novel by Wilbur Smith.
S,A — EN
Astral — Precision Video Ltd   P
BAPV 2590/VAPV 2590

Diamonds   Fil-Ent '75
Drama/Suspense
10076   104 mins   C
V2, B, V
Robert Shaw, Richard Roundtree, Barbara Seagull, Shelley Winters
The Israeli Diamond Exchange is the target for a trio of jewel thieves. Between them they manage to turn every trick, confuse every cop and turn every key as they unlock the riches of the world.
C,A — EN
Avco Embassy; Israeli — Embassy Home Entertainment   P
2090

Diamonds Are Forever   Fil-Ent '71
Adventure
13191   119 mins   C
B, V
Sean Connery, Jill St. John, Charles Gray, directed by Guy Hamilton
In a search for a megalomaniac diamond smuggler James Bond visits Amsterdam, Los Angeles, Las Vegas, and a secret and sinister desert establishment.
BBFC:A — C,A — EN
Danjaq SA; United Artists — Warner Home Video   P
99206

Diary of Anne Frank, The   Fil-Ent '59
Drama
01141   150 mins   C
B, V
Millie Perkins, Joseph Schildkraut, Shelley Winters, Richard Beymer, Gusti Huber, Ed Wynn
In June 1945, a liberated Jewish refugee returns to the hidden third floor of an Amsterdam factory where he finds the diary kept by his younger daughter during their years in hiding from the Nazis.
National Board of Review '59: Best Picture; Academy Awards '59: Best Supporting Actress (Winters).   F — EN
20th Century Fox — CBS/Fox Video   P
4A-089

(For Explanation of codes, see USE GUIDE and KEY)

PALADIN VIDEO HOME ENTERTAINMENT GUIDE

Dick Clark Show Music   Fil-Ent '7?
Programme 1
Music-Performance
06754   60 mins   C
V2, B, V
Dick Clark hosts this musical programme featuring Billy Preston, Loggins and Messina, and The Hollies.
F — EN
Dick Clark Productions — *Intervision Video*
H, P
A-AE 0211

Dick Clark Show Music   Fil-Ent '7?
Programme 2
Music-Performance
06753   60 mins   C
V2, B, V
Dick Clark hosts this musical programme featuring B.B. King and The Guess Who.
F — EN
Dick Clark Productions — *Intervision Video*
H, P
A-AE 0212

Dick Clark Show Music   Fil-Ent '7?
Programme 3
Music-Performance
06752   60 mins   C
V2, B, V
Dick Clark hosts this musical programme featuring Bonnie Bramlett and Tower of Power.
F — EN
Dick Clark Productions — *Intervision Video*
H, P
A-AE 0213

Dick Clark Show Music   Fil-Ent '7?
Programme 4
Music-Performance
06761   60 mins   C
V2, B, V
Dick Clark hosts this musical programme featuring Neil Sedaka, Freddy Fender, and the Average White Band.
F — EN
Dick Clark Productions — *Intervision Video*
H, P
A-AE 0214

Dick Clark Show Music   Fil-Ent '7?
Programme 5
Music-Performance
06751   60 mins   C
V2, B, V
Dick Clark hosts this musical programme featuring Bachman Turner Overdrive and the Pointer Sisters.
F — EN
Dick Clark Productions — *Intervision Video*
H, P
A-AE 0215

Dick Clark Show Music   Fil-Ent '7?
Programme 6
Music-Performance
06750   60 mins   C
V2, B, V
Dick Clark hosts this musical programme featuring Jim Stafford and the Sensational Alex Harvey Band.
F — EN
Dick Clark Productions — *Intervision Video*
H, P
A-AE 0216

Dick Clark Show Music   Fil-Ent '7?
Programme 7
Music-Performance
06760   60 mins   C
V2, B, V
Dick Clark hosts this musical programme featuring America, Leo Sayer and Focus.
F — EN
Dick Clark Productions — *Intervision Video*
H, P
A-AE 0217

Dick Clark Show Music   Fil-Ent '7?
Programme 8
Music-Performance
06749   60 mins   C
V2, B, V
Dick Clark hosts this musical programme featuring Jerry Lee Lewis, Freddy Cannon, and Del Shannon.
F — EN
Dick Clark Productions — *Intervision Video*
H, P
A-AE 0218

Dick Clark Show Music   Fil-Ent '7?
Programme 9
Music-Performance
06748   60 mins   C
V2, B, V
Dick Clark hosts this musical programme featuring Roberta Flack, Little Richard, and Stevie Wonder.
F — EN
Dick Clark Productions — *Intervision Video*
H, P
A-AE 0219

PALADIN VIDEO HOME ENTERTAINMENT GUIDE

Dick Clark Show Music Programme 10 Fil-Ent '7?
Music-Performance
06759   60 mins   C
V2, B, V
Dick Clark hosts this musical programme featuring Chuck Berry, Bo Diddley, and Johnny Rivers.
F — EN
dick Clark Productions — *Intervision Video*
H, P
A-AE 0220

Dick Clark Show Music Programme 12 Fil-Ent '7?
Music-Performance
06747   60 mins   C
V2, B, V
Dick Clark hosts this musical programme featuring Steve Miller and the James Calton Blues Band.
F — EN
Dick Clark Productions — *Intervision Video*
H, P
A-AE 0222

Dick Clark Show Music Programme 13 Fil-Ent '7?
Music-Performance
06758   60 mins   C
V2, B, V
Dick Clark hosts this musical programme featuring The Kinks, Brian Ferry and Roxy Music, Blue Swede, and Stevie Marriot and Humble Pie.
F — EN
Dick Clark Productions — *Intervision Video*
H, P
A-AE 0223

Dick Clark Show Music Programme 14 Fil-Ent '7?
Music-Performance
06746   60 mins   C
V2, B, V
Dick Clark hosts this musical programme featuring Crystal Gayle, Andy Gibb, Robert Hedges.
F — EN
Dick Clark Productions — *Intervision Video*
H, P
A-AE 0224

Dick Clark Show Music Programme 15 Fil-Ent '7?
Music-Performance
06757   60 mins   C
V2, B, V
Dick Clark hosts this musical programme featuring Frankie Valli, Donna Summer, Bachman Turner Overdrive, and K.C. and the Sunshine Band.
F — EN
Dick Clark Productions — *Intervision Video*
H, P
A-AE 0225

Dick Clark Show Music Programme 16 Fil-Ent '7?
Music-Performance
06745   60 mins   C
V2, B, V
Dick Clark hosts this musical programme featuring Linda Ronstadt and George Carlin.
F — EN
Dick Clark Productions — *Intervision Video*
H, P
A-AE 0226

Dick Clark Show Music Programme 17 Fil-Ent '7?
Music-Performance
06756   60 mins   C
V2, B, V
Dick Clark hosts this musical programme featuring The Beach Boys, Olivia Newton-John, Chicago, The Doobie Brothers, Herbie Hancock, and Bobby Lamm.
F — EN
Dick Clark Productions — *Intervision Video*
H, P
A-AE 0227

Dick Clark Show Music Programme 19 Fil-Ent '7?
Music-Performance
06744   60 mins   C
V2, B, V
Dick Clark hosts this musical programme featuring The Platters, Chubby Checker, Bobby Rydell, Fats Domino, Creedence Clearwater Revival, Otis Redding, The Supremes, and Connie Francis.
F — EN
Dick Clark Productions — *Intervision Video*
H, P
A-AE 0229

Dick Clark Show Music Programme 20 Fil-Ent '7?
Music-Performance
06755   60 mins   C
V2, B, V

(For Explanation of codes, see USE GUIDE and KEY)

PALADIN VIDEO HOME ENTERTAINMENT GUIDE

Dick Clark hosts this musical programme featuring Ike and Tina Turner, Bobby Blue Band, The Staple Singers, and The Dramatics.
F — EN
Dick Clark Productions — *Intervision Video* **H, P**
A-AE 0230

Dick Deadeye Fil-Ent '75
Cartoons/Adventure
08012   77 mins   C
V2, B, V
Animated, voices by Victor Spinetti, Linda Lewis, Julia McKenzie, Barry Cryer, Miriam Karlin, John Baldry, Peter Reeves
This film tells the story of an able seaman, Deadeye, who has been commanded by Queen Victoria to retrieve the ultimate secret which has been stolen by a wicked sorcerer. Another enemy is also trying to gain the important secret. The music and lyrics are by Gilbert and Sullivan arranged by Jimmy Horowytz.
BBFC:U — *I,M — EN*
Intercontinental Releasing — *Iver Film Services* **P**
205

Die Screaming Marianne Fil-Ent '73
Drama/Horror
09913   99 mins   C
V2, B, V
Susan George, Barry Evans, Christopher Sandford, Judy Huxtable, Leo Genn, directed by Pete Walker
A woman is forced to make a quick escape from her apartment in Spain. She is picked up by a man and returns to England, where a casual romance develops into an even more casual wedding, in which she ends up marrying the best man. Her original boyfriend is furious and vows revenge by revealing her whereabouts to her father, the Judge.
BBFC:18 — *A — EN*
Unknown — *Derann Film Services* **P**
FDV 321

Die Sister, Die Fil-Ent '7?
Horror
09231   82 mins   C
B, V
Jack Ging, Edith Atwater
A man, anxious to be rid of his neurotic sister, hires a maid to encourage her to commit suicide. However, his plans go awry, and the awful family secret is revealed.
C,A — EN
Unknown — *Video Form Pictures* **H, P**
MGT 1

Different Story, A Fil-Ent '78
Comedy/Romance
07806   107 mins   C
B, V
Perry King, Meg Foster, Valerie Curtin, Peter Donat, Richard Bull, directed by Paul Aaron
This film tells the story of Albert, a handsome, charming, intelligent homosexual, and Stella, an attractive real estate agent who has no interest in men. When he loses his job, out of sympathy she offers him a job, but to prevent his deportation they enter into a marriage of convenience only to discover that they are in fact in love.
A — EN
Avco Embassy — *Video Tape Centre* **P**
VTC 1011

Dimension 5 Fil-Ent '67
Suspense/Drama
07997   84 mins   C
B, V
Jeffrey Hunter, France Nuyen, Harold Sakata, Donald Woods
This film tells of a secret agent who discovers that an atomic bomb is to be exploded in Los Angeles. Using a time dimension machine, desperate attempts are used to save millions from this disaster.
S,A — EN
Emerson — *Motion Epics Video Company Ltd* **P**
164

Dinah East Fil-Ent '83
Drama
12619   90 mins   C
V2, B, V
Jeremy Stockwell
This film portrays the story of a young man who masquerades as an actress to realise his career dreams and carries on in this role until his death twenty years later.
BBFC:18 — *A — EN*
Unknown — *VideoSpace Ltd* **P**

Diner Fil-Ent '82
Comedy
10158   86 mins   C
B, V
Steve Guttenberg, Daniel Stern, Mickey Rourke, Kevin Bacon, Timothy Daly, Ellen Barkin, directed by Barry Levinson
A group of friends just out of college, meet up at 'The Diner' which is open all hours. Not wanting to let the past go and apprehensive about

PALADIN VIDEO HOME ENTERTAINMENT GUIDE

embarking on the next step of life, with all the responsibilities that go with it, they are determined to have their fling before they go their separate ways.
BBFC:AA — S,A — EN
MGM — MGM/UA Home Video P
UMB 10164/UMV 10164

Dinner at Seven — How-Ins '??
Cookery
09120 120 mins C
B, V
Countess Maria de Brantes
In this programme four dinner party menus are prepared step by step by the proprietress of New York's famous 'Le Coup de Fusils', Countess Maria de Brantes.
S,A — I
Unknown — *Quadrant Video* H, P
CK1

Dinosaurs—Fun, Fact and Fantasy — Gen-Edu '8?
Dinosaurs
08659 60 mins C
B, V
Animated, narrated by Derek Griffiths
This video combines the reality contained in fossil studies with the fantasy of cinema fiction. It features Dil the crocodile, searching for clues about his ancestors, exploring archaeological parks, museums, dinosaur parks and the murky waters. It shows how to make one's own fossil or build a model of a stegosaurus.
M,A — ED
Picture Palace Productions — *Longman Video* P
LGBE 5003/LGVH 5003

Dinosaurus — Fil-Ent '60
Horror
02457 80 mins C
B, V
Ward Ramsey, Paul Lukather, Kristine Hanson
This is the story of hazards faced by a cave man and two prehistoric monsters who are accidentally unearthed on an isolated tropical island.
A — EN
Jack H Harris — *Mountain Video* P

Dio Live in Concert — Fil-Ent '83
Music-Performance
13144 60 mins C
B, V
This programme features Ronnie Dio's four piece band performing in Holland and includes 'Stand Up and Shout,' 'Straight Through the Heart,' 'Children of the Sea,' 'Holy Diver' and 'Rainbow in the Dark' amongst its tracks. It is recorded in stereo.
F — EN
Unknown — *Polygram Video* P
040 3654/040 3652

Dirt Band-Tonite, The — Fil-Ent '82
Music-Performance
08471 60 mins C
B, V
Directed by Derek Burbidge
This tape was filmed in Denver's Rainbow Music Hall featuring the six-man, multi-instrumental group, Dirt Band. They perform 15 of the hits including 'Mr. Bojangles', 'Rocky Top', 'Will the Circle Be Unbroken,' 'Make a Little Magic,' 'An American Dream', 'Fish Song,' 'Badlands', 'Battle of New Orleans,' 'Jealousy' and 'Fire in the Sky.'
S,A — EN
EMI — *THORN EMI* P
TXE 90 14364/TVE 90 14362

Dirty Deal — Fil-Ent '8?
Drama
09130 90 mins C
V2, B, V
James Mason, Luc Merenda
This film tells the story of the kidnapping of the son of a wealthy industrialist. The thugs show no mercy, murdering his friend to prove that they mean business. The huge ransom paid by the distraught father is recovered by a tenacious young detective. He uses it to bribe his way through the criminal underworld to gain his own brand of rough justice.
S,A — EN
Unknown — *Go Video Ltd* P
GO 124

Dirty Dozen, The — Fil-Ent '67
Adventure/War-Drama
06491 137 mins C
V2, B, V
Lee Marvin, Telly Savalas, Charles Bronson, George Kennedy, Jim Brown
During World War II, twelve convicts serving life sentences are recruited for a difficult commando mission in Germany.
S,A — EN
MGM — *MGM/UA Home Video* P
UMB 10008/UMV 10008

Dirty Harry — Fil-Ent '71
Drama
01250 103 mins C

(For Explanation of codes, see USE GUIDE and KEY) 189

PALADIN VIDEO HOME ENTERTAINMENT GUIDE

B, V
Clint Eastwood, directed by Don Siegel
Clint Eastwood is detective Harry Callahan, who is attempting to track down a psychopathic rooftop killer before a kidnapped girl dies.
C,A — EN
Warner Bros — *Warner Home Video*   P

Dirty Mary, Crazy Larry   Fil-Ent '74
Adventure
01748   92 mins   C
B, V, LV
Peter Fonda, Susan George, Adam Roarke, Vic Morrow, Roddy McDowall
Two stock car racers extort $150,000 from a supermarket in order to buy a first-class racing car. Lawmen in helicopters pursue the pair through a series of escapades around rural California.
F — EN
20th Century Fox — *CBS/Fox Video*   P
3A-049

Dirty Money   Fil-Ent '??
Crime-Drama
07833   92 mins   C
B, V
Ian McShane, Warren Clarke
This film is a dramatization of events which took place in France in 1976 centered on an incredible and daring band raid.
S,A — EN
Unknown — *Precision Video Ltd*   P
BITC 2101/VITC 2101

Dirty Money   Fil-Ent '72
Crime-Drama
07834   95 mins   C
B, V
Alain Delon, Richard Crenna, Catherine Deneuve, Riccardo Cucciola, Michael Conrad, Paul Crauchet, directed by Jean-Pierre Melville
A young police inspector, whose friend runs a nightclub on the borderline of legality, is in pursuit of a drug racket gang who are using the club as a front. His trail leads him across France and a dangerous game of hide-and-seek aboard a hurtling express train. He has no illusions about his task and knows he has to win at any cost, even if it means the life of his friend.
S,A — EN
Les Films Corona — *Polygram Video*   H, P
791 523

Dirty Tricks   Fil-Ent '80
Crime-Drama
07397   90 mins   C

V2, B, V
Elliott Gould, Kate Jackson
A Harvard professor joins forces with a beautiful young reporter to recover a stolen document. They find themselves playing a game of life and death and discover they are losing.
BBFC:AA — S,A — EN
Unknown — *Guild Home Video*   H, P, E

Disappearance, The   Fil-Ent '77
Suspense
02075   90 mins   C
B, V
Donald Sutherland
'The Disappearance' is a story about the no-margins-for-error world of international murder-by-contract. One of the top field specialists, Donald Sutherland, is assigned a contract which conflicts with his own personal life and the disappearance of his wife. An explosive climax and an ingenious revelation are the perfect conclusions to this romantic thriller.
C,A — EN
Canadian — *VCL Video Services*   P

Disco Dynamite   Fil-Ent '7?
Musical-Drama
02107   79 mins   C
V2, B, V
Boney M, Eruption, La Bionda, The Teens
A group of young people's lives, loves, and adventures reach fever pitch along with disco music by top disco stars.
C,A — EN
Unknown — *Hokushin Audio Visual Ltd*   P
VM-19

Disco Fever   Fil-Ent '??
Drama
05460   87 mins   C
V2, B, V
Richie Desmond
A story of an ageing pop idol, a 'has been' who sets out to prove he is now into the music of today and tomorrow. Features music, dance and bike racing.
BBFC:AA — S,A — EN
Unknown — *Iver Film Services*   P
146

Disney Channel, Volume 5, The   Chl-Juv '84
Cartoons
13759   120 mins   C
B, V
Animated

PALADIN VIDEO HOME ENTERTAINMENT GUIDE

This cassette is a mixture of educational entertainment and cartoons featuring all the favourite Disney characters.
BBFC:U — I,M — EN
Walt Disney Productions — Rank Video Library
P
718B

Disney Channel, Volume 4, The   Chl-Juv '84
Cartoons
13757   120 mins   C
B, V
Animated
This cassette is a mixture of educational entertainment and cartoons featuring all the favourite Disney characters.
BBFC:U — I,M — EN
Walt Disney Productions — Rank Video Library
P
717B

Disney Channel, Volume 1, The   Chl-Juv '84
Cartoons
13753   120 mins   C
B, V
Animated
This cassette is a mixture of educational entertainment and cartoons featuring all the favourite Disney characters.
BBFC:U — I,M — EN
Walt Disney Productions — Rank Video Library
P
714B

Disney Channel, Volume 6, The   Chl-Juv '84
Cartoons
13758   120 mins   C
B, V
Animated
This cassette is a mixture of educational entertainment and cartoons featuring all the favourite Disney characters.
BBFC:U — I,M — EN
Walt Disney Productions — Rank Video Library
P
719B

Disney Channel, Volume 3, The   Chl-Juv '84
Cartoons
13755   120 mins   C
B, V

Animated
This cassette is a mixture of educational entertainment and cartoons featuring all the favourite Disney characters.
BBFC:U — I,M — EN
Walt Disney Productions — Rank Video Library
P
716B

Disney Channel, Volume 2, The   Chl-Juv '84
Cartoons
13754   120 mins   C
B, V
Animated
This cassette is a mixture of educational entertainment and cartoons featuring all the favourite Disney characters.
BBFC:U — I,M — EN
Walt Disney Productions — Rank Video Library
P
715B

Disney's Greatest Dog Stars   Chl-Juv '83
Cartoons/Animals
12572   61 mins   C
B, V
Animated
A host of canine celebrities are featured in this cassette including Lady and the Tramp, Goofy and Pluto.
F — EN
Walt Disney Productions — Rank Video Library
H
127

Disney's Greatest Villains   Chl-Juv '83
Cartoons
12571   75 mins   C
B, V
Animated
This film introduces you to a host of villains including Sheer Khan, The Wicked Witch and Captain Hook.
F — EN
Walt Disney Productions — Rank Video Library
H
128

Disney's Scary Tales   Chl-Juv '84
Cartoons
13751   91 mins   C
B, V
Animated

PALADIN VIDEO HOME ENTERTAINMENT GUIDE

A compilation of ghostly happenings in eight cartoons featuring Mickey Mouse, Donald Duck and Pluto.
BBFC:U — F — EN
Walt Disney Productions — *Rank Video Library*
P
221A

Distance Casting Spo-Lei '82
Fishing
13548 52 mins C
B, V

John Holden, the international beach caster, shows how to improve in accuracy and gain greater distance through correct stance and casting a well balanced rod.
S,A — I
Unknown — *TFI Leisure Ltd* **H, P**

Diva Fil-Ent '81
Drama
08969 120 mins C
B, V

Frederic Andrei, Richard Bohringer, Roland Bertin, Gerad Darman, Jacques Fabri, directed by Jean Jacques Beineix

The plot centres on two tapes; one is the recording of an ex-prostitute, which threatens to reveal vast criminal corruption, involving the police force itself, and the other is an illicit recording of the world famous opera singer, Diva, who has refused ever to record. Both tapes are sought after by different parties, whose common link is a post-boy who by chance possesses both. It is subtitled.
C,A — EN
Les Films Galaxie; Greenwich Film Prods — *Palace Video Ltd* **P**
PVC 2013A

Divine Healing Gen-Edu '??
Religion
06283 55 mins B/W
B, V, PH15

In this film Dennis Gault gives testimonies of two healings and answers questions on healing.
S,A — R
Audio Visual Ministries — *Audio Visual Ministries* **H, L, P**
VCC242

Divine Madness Fil-Ent '80
Music-Performance
07861 90 mins C
B, V
Bette Midler

A film featuring the many talents of Bette Midler.
BBFC:AA — S,A — EN
The Ladd Company — *Warner Home Video*
P
WEX 70001/WEV 70001

Diving Spo-Lei '80
Sports-Water
00261 60 mins C
B, V, FO

Nine basic dives and practices are demonstrated in this programme. The dives include: forward dive piked; forward dive straight; back dive piked; reverse dive straight; reverse dive piked; inward dive straight; and forward dive 1/2 twist straight.
F — I
London Video Ltd — *Video Sport for All*
P
1005

Divorce His, Divorce Hers Fil-Ent '72
Drama
12752 143 mins C
B, V
Elizabeth Taylor, Richard Burton

A fascinating story of a divorce—and a surprise reconciliation—told by the two parties involved, against a background of intrigue.
A — EN
John Heyman — *Rank Video Library* **H, P**
0126 C

Dixie Dynamite Fil-Ent '76
Comedy-Drama
09066 89 mins C
V2, B, V

Warren Oates, Jane Anne Johnstone, Kathy McHaley, R.G. Armstrong, Stanley Adams, Christopher George, directed by Lee Frost

A local moonshiner who was cheated out of his property suddenly dies. His two young daughters, enraged by his death, set the whole town in uproar as they become set on revenge. Features music by Duane Eddy, The Mike Curb Congregation and Dorsey Burnette.
S,A — EN
Dimension Pictures — *Temple Enterprises Ltd*
H, P

Django Fil-Ent '68
Western
04119 100 mins C
B, V
Franco Nero, Leredana Nusciak, Angel Alvarez

192 (For Explanation of codes, see USE GUIDE and KEY)

PALADIN VIDEO HOME ENTERTAINMENT GUIDE

A stranger arrives in a Mexican border town where Mexicans and Americans have been fighting. He befriends a woman and kills some Americans, then double-crosses a Mexican general by stealing a goodly sum of gold. Also known as 'The Mercenary.'
C,A — EN
Sergio Corbucci Prods — Video Programme Distributors **P**
Inter-Ocean—013

Django's Cut Price Corpses Fil-Ent '7?
Western
07790   81 mins   C
V2, B, V
Jeff Cameron, John Desmont, Esmeralda Barros, Gengher Gatti, Edilio Kim
This film is set in a small Mexican town and tells the story of a fight to recover stolen 'loot'.
S,A — EN
Unknown — Fletcher Video   **H, P**
AV 603

Doctor at Large Fil-Ent '57
Comedy
12751   102 mins   C
B, V
Dirk Bogarde, Muriel Parlow
Another sequel from the well known 'Doctor' series, in which the young doctor is followed into the maelstrom of General Practice—and back again!
BBFC:U — F — EN
Universal International — Rank Video Library **H, P**
1071 E

Doctor at Sea Fil-Ent '55
Comedy
05179   89 mins   C
B, V
Dirk Bogarde, Brenda de Banzie, Brigitte Bardot, James Robertson Justice
The film version of Richard Gordon's hilarious sequel to 'Doctor in the House.' Once again Dirk Bogarde stars as the now qualified Dr. Simon Sparrow setting out for sunnier climes having signed on as a ship's doctor aboard the SS Lotus.
BBFC:U — F — EN
Republic — Rank Video Library   **H, P**
1007

Dr. Coppelius Fil-Ent '66
Dance
08760   97 mins   C
B, V
Walter Slezak, Claudia Corday, Eileen Elliot, Caj Selling
This is the story of the ballet, enacted and expanded on the screen. It features the Ballet of The Teatro Del Liceo, Barcelone.
F — EN
Childhood Productions — Precision Video Ltd **P**
BARPV 2591/VARPV 2591

Doctor Detroit Fil-Ent '83
Comedy
13603   87 mins   C
B, V
Dan Aykroyd, directed by Michael Pressman
A seemingly meek English professor leads a dual life as a pimp protecting his girls from the organized crime mob but his two worlds meet head-on one night at a faculty dinner.
BBFC:15 — S,A — EN
Universal — CIC Video   **H, P**
1128

Doctor Doolittle Fil-Ent '67
Musical
01020   144 mins   C
B, V
Rex Harrison, Samantha Eggar, Anthony Newley, Richard Attenborough
An adventure about a 19th century English doctor who embarks on linguistic lessons for his animals. Based on Hugh Lofting's stories. Academy Awards '67: Best Song ('Talk To The Animals').   F — EN
20th Century Fox; APJAC — CBS/Fox Video **P**
4A-030

Doctor Faustus Fil-Ent '67
Drama
09932   92 mins   C
B, V
Elizabeth Taylor, Richard Burton, Andreas Teuber
In the 1550's, an aged doctor of alchemy, astrology, and physiology makes a pact with Lucifer's disciple that after 24 years of living life to the full, the devil may have his soul. Elizabeth Taylor appears as Helen of Troy, who fulfills the doctor's lust-crazed fantastic dreams. Based on Christopher Marlowe's play.
BBFC:18 — A — EN
Columbia; A Burtons Prod — Rank Video Library   **H, P**
0182E

Dr. Heckyl and Mr. Hype Fil-Ent '??
Comedy
08095   96 mins   C
B, V
Oliver Reed, Jackie Coogan

(For Explanation of codes, see USE GUIDE and KEY)

PALADIN VIDEO HOME ENTERTAINMENT GUIDE

This film is a naughty and comical version of the Jeckyl and Hyde story. In this story the wrong medicine turns an ugly doctor into a handsome lady killer.
BBFC:X — A — EN
Golan Globus Productions — *Rank Video Library* **H, P**
1043 C

Doctor in Clover Fil-Ent '66
Comedy
13468 99 mins C
B, V
Leslie Phillips, James Robertson Justice
This is the sixth of the Richard Gordon stories and it takes a light-hearted look at life in a British hospital.
BBFC:A — C,A — EN
Betty Box; Ralph Thomas — *Rank Video Library* **H, P**
0204X

Doctor in Distress Fil-Ent '63
Comedy
05148 100 mins C
B, V
Dirk Bogarde, Samantha Eggar, James Robertson Justice, Mylene Demongeot
Simon is deeply concerned by an abrupt change in Sir Lancelot's usually cantankerous character. All is soon revealed—Sir Lancelot is in love!
BBFC:A — C,A — EN
Governor — *Rank Video Library* **H, P**
1026

Doctor in the House Fil-Ent '54
Comedy
01885 92 mins C
B, V
Dirk Bogarde, Muriel Pavlow, Kenneth More, Donald Sinden
Hilarious tale of a young doctor's first five years at St. Swithin's Hospital.
S,A — EN
Rank — *Rank Video Library* **H, P**
1001

Dr. Jekyll and Mr. Hyde Fil-Ent '80
Horror/Musical
02076 90 mins C
B, V
Kirk Douglas, Susan Hampshire, Susan George, Stanley Holloway, Sir Michael Redgrave
Robert Louis Stevenson's classic horror tale is given new dimension and universal appeal in this brilliant musical version.
S,A — EN
Unknown — *VCL Video Services* **P**

Dr. Jekyll and Mr. Hyde Fil-Ent '20
Horror
05837 63 mins B/W
B, V
John Barrymore, Nita Naldi, Louis Wolheim, Martha Mansfield, directed by John S. Robertson
An adaptation of the classic horror tale of split personalities by Robert Louis Stevenson, in which a doctor experiments with the good and evil nature of man. This film provides some gruesome change-over scenes, an apparition appearance as a giant spider and a savage murder sequence. Silent.
S,A — EN
Unknown — *Polygram Video* **P**
40118/20118

Doctor Jekyll and Sister Hyde Fil-Ent '71
Horror/Suspense
07458 94 mins C
B, V
Ralph Bates, Martine Beswick, Gerald Sim, Lewis Fiander, directed by Roy Ward Baker
A young doctor in search of a life-prolonging drug drinks his own potion and becomes a lovely but lethal woman. Jack the Ripper becomes involved when the doctor turns to killing prostitutes in order to obtain corpses for his experiments.
BBFC:X — A — EN
Hammer Film Productions — *THORN EMI* **P**
TXC 90 0276 4/TVC 90 0276 2

Dr Mabuse—The Gambler (Der Spieler) Fil-Ent '22
Crime-Drama
07456 95 mins B/W
B, V
Rudolf Klein-Rogge, Alfred Abel, Gertrude Welcker, Lil Dagover, Paul Richter, directed by Fritz Lang
This silent film with English sub-titles is a classic of the German cinema. The film reflects the break-down of German society after the First World War. Dr Mabuse is the power mad criminal who hypnotises his victims in order to satisfy his passion for wealth.
S,A — EN
Friedrich Wilhelm Murnau Stiftung-Wiesbaden — *THORN EMI* **P**
TXC 90 2002 4/TVC 90 2002 2

Dr. No Fil-Ent '62
Adventure
13185 111 mins C
B, V
Sean Connery, Ursula Andress, Joseph Wiseman, Jack Lord

PALADIN VIDEO HOME ENTERTAINMENT GUIDE

The first of the 'Bond' series, this sets the tone of exotic locales as 007 sets off for the Caribbean to investigate strange happenings.
BBFC:A — C,A — EN
United Artists; Eon Prods — *Warner Home Video* **P**
99210

Dr Seuss Video Festival Chl-Juv '70
Cartoons
10160   49 mins   C
B, V
Animated
Two cartoon fables are contained in this cassette: 'HortOn Hears a Who' narrated by Hans Conreid and 'How The Grinch Stole Christmas' told by Boris Karloff. Horton the elephant, Snoffer Snoof and Reindeer dog parade through the films.
F — EN
MGM — *MGM/UA Home Video* **P**
UMB 10176/UMV 10176

Dr Snuggles Chl-Juv '79
Cartoons
12031   60 mins   C
B, V
Animated
Living in his quaint house on the edge of an enchanted wood, Dr. Snuggles invents a whole variety of contraptions, each one designed to make the lives of children and animals happier.
PS,M — EN
Unknown — *Polygram Video* **H, P**
0403084/0403082

Dr. Who and the Daleks Fil-Ent '65
Science fiction/Adventure
07479   78 mins   C
B, V
Peter Cushing, Roy Castle, Jennie Linden, Robeta Tovey, directed by Gordon Flemyng
With Dr. Who in this adventure through time and space are his two granddaughters and the accident-prone Ian. Ian's clumsiness sends them off to an unknown world devastated by radiation fall-out where they are captured by the mean and murderous Daleks.
BBFC:U — F — EN
Aaru Productions Ltd — *THORN EMI* **P**
TXC 90 0595 4/TVC 90 0595 2

Doctor Who and the Revenge of the Cybermen Fil-Ent '??
Science fiction/Adventure
09407   120 mins   C
V2, B, V
Tom Baker
This tape features one of the time-travelling Doctor's adventures.
F — EN
BBC — *BBC Video* **H, P**
BBCV 2003

Dr. Who, the Brain of Moribus Fil-Ent '84
Science fiction/Adventure
13401   60 mins   C
B, V
Tom Baker
Dr. Who and his assistant find themselves on the planet of Karn and have to prevent the evil Moribus from regaining absolute power.
F — EN
BBC — *BBC Video* **H, P**
2012

Doctor's Wives Fil-Ent '70
Drama
12474   98 mins   C
B, V
Richard Crenna, Janice Rule, Gene Hackman, Dyan Cannon, Diana Sands
An outrageous soap opera which revolves around five Californian doctors, their wives, finances, and sex.
BBFC:18 — A — EN
Columbia — *RCA/Columbia Pictures Video UK* **H, P**
10201

Dog Day Afternoon Fil-Ent '75
Drama
06028   120 mins   C
B, V
Al Pacino, John Cazale, Sully Boyar, Penny Allen, Charles Durning, James Broderick, directed by Sidney Lumet
This film, set in Brooklyn, New York in 1972, tells the true story of the bizarre bank robbery and seige which took place at the Chase Manhattan Bank on a hot day in August.
Academy Awards '75: Best Original Screenplay.
BBFC:X — S,A — EN
Warner Brothers; Artists Entertainment Complex Prod — *Warner Home Video* **P**
WEX1024/WEV1024

Dogpound Shuffle Fil-Ent '75
Drama
05409   93 mins   C
B, V
Ron Moody, David Soul, directed by Jeffrey Bloom
A down and out ex-vaudeville tap dancer has only one friend, his scruffy dancing dog, Spot. The dog goes missing and he discovers that the dogpound have picked him up as a stray and to

(For Explanation of codes, see USE GUIDE and KEY)   195

PALADIN VIDEO HOME ENTERTAINMENT GUIDE

get the dog back he has to pay thirty dollars. He meets a young man, also on the road, who plays the harmonica. They develop an unlikely friendship and work together to get Spot back.
BBFC:A — S,A — EN
Jeffrey Bloom Productions — *Precision Video Ltd*   **P**
BITC 2045/VITC 2045

Dogs, The   Fil-Ent '77
Horror
02393   91 mins   C
B, V

David McCallum, Sandra McCabe, George Wyner, Eric Server, directed by Burt Brinckerhoff
Professor Thompson tries to discover the reason why domestic dogs have suddenly turned on humans.
A — EN
RC Riddell and Associates — *Derann Film Services*   **H, P**
DV 123B/DV 123

Dolemite   Fil-Ent '7?
Martial arts/Crime-Drama
08959   91 mins   C
V2, B, V

Rudy Ray Moore
A nightclub owner stops at nothing in seeking revenge over the gang who put him in prison. His own determination, support of the FBI and his army of beautiful Kung-Fu killer girls assure his victory.
S,A — EN
Unknown — *Walton Film and Video Ltd*   **P**

Doll Squad, The   Fil-Ent '74
Suspense
02085   90 mins   C
B, V

Michael Ansara, Francine York, Anthony Eisley, John Carter, Lisa Garrett
The screen explodes with action as an elite band of female assassins battle in a race against time and death to save the world from a diabolical fate at the hands of a madman.
C,A — EN
Gamini Film — *VCL Video Services*   **P**

Dollmaker, The   Fil-Ent '83
Drama
12033   135 mins   C
B, V

Jane Fonda, Levon Helm, Jason Yearwood, Amanda Plummer, Nikki Creswell, directed by Daniel Petrie

A woman follows her husband to wartime Detroit and is caught up in a situation beyond her control. Faced with family misfortune, she finds solace in her hobby of dollmaking and through her skilled sculpting their fortunes take an unexpected turn.
F — EN
Jane Fonda; Bruce Gilbert — *Polygram Video*   **H, P**
0402624/0402622

Doll's House, A   Fil-Ent '73
Drama
08076   102 mins   C
B, V

Jane Fonda, Edward Fox, Trevor Howard, David Warner, Delphine Seyrig, directed by Joseph Losey
This film tells the story of a beautiful woman who realises that all her life she has been treated like a doll, first by her father and then by her husband. She breaks free to establish herself as an individual. it is based on Henrik Ibsen's classic drama.
S,A — EN
World Film Services; Tomorrow Entertainment — *Rank Video Library*   **H, P**
0131 C

Dolly in London   Fil-Ent '83
Music-Performance
12467   80 mins   C
B, V

Dolly Parton
This video covers a day in Dolly Parton's life and begins with her arrival at London's Heathron Airport to the finish of her concert at The Dominion Theatre, and includes such songs as 'Jolene,' 'Baby, I'm Burning' and 'Coat of Many Colors.'
BBFC:PG — F — EN
Stan Harris; Speckled Bird Inc — *RCA/Columbia Pictures Video UK*   **H, P**
10230

Dominique   Fil-Ent '79
Drama/Mystery
06151   98 mins   C
V2, B, V

Cliff Robertson, Jean Simmons, Jenny Agutter, Simon Ward, Ron Moody, Judy Geeson, Michael Jayston, Flora Robson, David Tomlinson, Jack Warner
A crippled woman cannot believe that the sounds she hears, the body she sees hanging in her conservatory, or the car accident that nearly

PALADIN VIDEO HOME ENTERTAINMENT GUIDE

kills her are all figments of her active imagination. Either her husband is behind these events or the condition that has crippled her body is affecting her mind.
BBFC:AA — S,A — EN
Melvin Simon; Sword and Sorcery Production — Guild Home Video   H, P, E

Domino Killings, The   Fil-Ent '77
Crime-Drama
02044   95 mins   C
B, V
Gene Hackman, Candice Bergen, Richard Widmark, Mickey Rooney, Edward Albert
A convict serving twenty years in prison becomes skeptical when he is taken for a meeting with a prison official.
C,A — EN
Stanley Kramer — Precision Video Ltd   P
BITC 2029/VITC 2029

Don is Dead, The   Fil-Ent '73
Drama
13637   109 mins   C
B, V
Anthony Quinn, Frederic Forrest, Robert Forster, directed by Richard Fleischer
A new Don is selected for a Mafia family but there is a struggle for power and open warfare erupts between different branches of the syndicate.
BBFC:18 — A — EN
Hal B Wallis — CIC Video   H, P
1149

Don Pasquale   Fil-Ent '??
Opera
06143   112 mins   C
B, V
Sir Geraint Evans, Lillian Watson, Ryland Davies, Russell Smythe
An adaptation of the opera by Donnizetti with Sir Geraint Evans as Pasquale, Lillian Watson as Norina, Ryland Davies as Ernesto and Russell Smythe as Dr Malatesta.
S,A — EN
Unknown — Guild Home Video   H, P, E

Donald Duck Goes West   Fil-Ent '83
Cartoons
12589   81 mins   C
B, V
Animated

Donald cavorts through a series of classic tales of the West including 'Don Donald,' 'The Legend of Coyote Rock,' 'Pueblo Pluto' and '2 Gun Goofy.'
F — EN
Walt Disney Productions — Rank Video Library
H
129

Donkeys' Years   Fil-Ent '79
Comedy-Drama
05393   78 mins   C
B, V
Penelope Keith, Colin Blakely, Denholm Elliott, Robert Lang, Timothy Bateson, Christopher Benjamin
A Cabinet Minister, a Hurley Street surgeon, a Civil Servant, a priest and a writer all now in middle age gather for a reunion at one of Oxford University's older colleges. The Master of the College is away lecturing in Canada and his wife, a Lady, is acting as hostess to the graduates. Written by Michael Frayn.
S,A — EN
Unknown — Precision Video Ltd   P
BITC 2089/VITC 2089

Donner Pass   Fil-Ent '78
Drama/Western
06951   92 mins   C
B, V
Robert Fuller, Diane McBain, Andrew Prine, John Anderson, Michael Callan, directed by James L. Conway
This film recreates a grim chapter in American pioneer history. A determined group of settlers struggling against insurmountable odds are trying to reach California but the wagon train becomes racked by internal dissension and is devastated by Indian raids. Finally the fear of starvation forces them to turn against each other.
S,A — EN
Sunn Classic — Home Video Merchandisers
H, P
027

Don's Party   Fil-Ent '78
Comedy
06961   90 mins   C
B, V
John Hargreaves, Graham Kennedy, directed by Bruce Beresford
This is the story of an election victory party in which events take an unexpected turn. Two of the guests are unenthusiastic about having a Labour Government and so cause a hint of friction. A host of tensions surface, long simmering hostilities boil over and flirtations trigger off fights bringing friendships to grief.

(For Explanation of codes, see USE GUIDE and KEY)

PALADIN VIDEO HOME ENTERTAINMENT GUIDE

BBFC:X — A — EN
Double Head Production; Australian Film Commission — *Home Video Merchandisers*
H, P
020

Don't Answer the Phone   Fil-Ent '??
Horror
06311   90 mins   C
V2, B, V
James Westmoreland, Flo Gerrish, Ben Frank, Nicholas Worth, Stan Haze, Gary Allen, Pamela Bryant
A nurse is found strangled and assaulted after answering her phone. Other murders are discovered throughout the town with the same pattern, they are all girls living alone and patients of one particular doctor. The riddle of the telephone murders has to be solved before the killer strikes again.
BBFC:X — A — EN
Unknown — *World of Video 2000*   **H, P**
XF132

Don't Be Afraid of the Dark   Fil-Ent '73
Horror
12095   72 mins   C
B, V
Kim Darby, Jim Hutton, William Demarest, Barbara Anderson, directed by John Newland
A young couple move into an old Victorian house unaware of the strange and evil nocturnal creatures secreted within.
A — EN
Lorimar — *Polygram Video*   **H, P**
0402384/0402382

Don't Call Us   Fil-Ent '??
Comedy
08809   60 mins   C
B, V
This film begins with an advertisement requiring unusual and bizarre visual acts. A compilation of comic acts are assembled, all of them wild and hysterical.
C,A — EN
Unknown — *VCL Video Services*   **P**
P322C

Don't Go in the Woods.....Alone   Fil-Ent '81
Horror
07675   88 mins   C
B, V
Nick McClelland, Mary Galeartz, James P. Hayden, Tom Drury, Ken Carter
Four young campers in the mountains for a relaxing weekend, wander into a forest and before long realise they are lost. They are suddenly attacked by a large form wielding a machete. With one dead the others flee screaming into the forest to spend a terrifying night hiding from the maniac who is in constant pursuit.
A — EN
Double S Productions Ltd — *Video Network*
P
0012

Don't Look in the Basement   Fil-Ent '73
Horror
08684   95 mins   C
V2, B, V
William Bill McGhee, Jessie Lee Fulton, Robert Dracup, Harryette Warren
The story is set in a private sanitorium, where they practice total integration between staff and patients. Just before a new girl starts working there, the Doctor in charge is fatally attacked. Another Doctor takes over intending to restore calm. However, a series of frightening outbursts occur and horrifying attacks have a terrible conclusion.
BBFC:X — A — EN
Unknown — *Derann Film Services*   **P**
FCV 604

Don't Look Now   Fil-Ent '73
Suspense
04461   110 mins   C
B, V
Donald Sutherland, Julie Christie, Hilary Mason, directed by Nicolas Roeg
A young couple whose child recently drowned travels to Venice, where they meet a clairvoyant whose psychic powers entangle them in a series of strange and frightening experiences. Based on a short story by Daphne du Maurier.
BBFC:X — A — EN
Paramount; Peter Katz — *THORN EMI*   **P**
TXB 90 0005 4/TVB 90 0005 2

Don't Open the Door   Fil-Ent '7?
Horror
09232   110 mins   C
B, V
Susan Bracken, Larry O'Dwyer, Gene Ross
A girl re-visits the house in which her mother met her brutal death. A shattering climax is reached, with murder, voodoo and effigies.
A — EN
Unknown — *Video Form Pictures*   **H, P**
MGT 2

Don't Play With Fire   Fil-Ent '8?
Adventure
09023   90 mins   C
V2, B, V

PALADIN VIDEO HOME ENTERTAINMENT GUIDE

Three young men are forced into the terrible experiences of blackmailand gutter violence, which are the hallmarks of Hong Kong's shelterless underworld. The film escalates towards an horrific climax in which the young men fight for lives which are no longer worth living.
C,A — EN
Unknown — *Intervision Video* **H, P**
AA 0452

Doomed to Die Fil-Ent '40
Crime-Drama
07632   65 mins   B/W
B, V
Boris Karloff, Grant Withers, Marjorie Reynolds, directed by William Nigh
A ship containing over a million dollars in bonds is sunk. The shipping magnate who owned the ship is mysteriously murdered. The son of a rival magnate was the last to see him alive and is arrested. A reporter believes he is innocent and enlists the help of Mr. Wong when a murder attempt is made on the son's life.
F — EN
Monogram — *VCL Video Services* **P**
0227G

Doomwatch Fil-Ent '72
Science fiction
04205   92 mins   C
B, V
Ian Bannen, Judy Geeson
A man investigating sea life on a small island discovers that a large chemical company is illegally dumping radioactive materials into the water, causing the inhabitants to look like Neanderthal men.
BBFC:A — S,A — EN
Tigon British Film Prods — *Guild Home Video*
H, P

Dorian Gray Fil-Ent '70
Drama
09201   86 mins   C
B, V
Helmut Berger, Richard Todd, Herbert Lom
A handsome young man agrees to pose for a painter, who is a close friend. He falls in love with a young actress. When the portrait is finished, he observes how strange it is that the painting will retain his youth whereas he, himself will have to wither with age. Overwhelmed with his own beauty, he vows that he would give his soul to reverse the positions.
S,A — EN
Commonwealth United — *Video Form Pictures*
H, P
MGS 7

Dot and Bunny Chl-Juv '7?
Cartoons/Adventure
12067   78 mins   C
V2, B, V
Animated
The little baby kangaroo Joey is still lost and Dot is determined to find him at last and reunite him with his mother. This is the third release in this series.
BBFC:U — PS,M — EN
Satori Productions — *Guild Home Video*
H, P, E

Dot and Santa Claus Chl-Juv '??
Cartoons/Adventure
08382   80 mins   C
V2, B, V
Animated, Drew Forsythe
This is a sequel to 'Dot and the Kangaroo.' Dot meets Santa Claus and tells him of her adventures with the Kangaroo, who had lost her baby. They both set out to find the baby. Features both live action and animation.
PS,S — EN
Satori Productions — *Guild Home Video*
H, P, E

Dot and the Kangaroo Chl-Juv '7?
Adventure/Fantasy
04206   80 mins   C
V2, B, V
This story features cartoon animals against settings shot live in the Australian bush. Artwork by Spike Milligan.
BBFC:U — I,M — EN
Unknown — *Guild Home Video* **H, P**

Double Agent 73 Fil-Ent '74
Comedy/Crime-Drama
07908   77 mins   C
V2, B, V
Chesty Morgan, directed by Doris Wishman
A well endowed, young, blonde international spy is sent on a mission to destroy a heroin ring. With a secret camera implanted in one of her ample breasts she infiltrates the gang. Employing bizarre and devious methods she eliminates the henchmen but falls in love with a man sent to kill her. When the film is developed she realises he is the leader. She has to make the decision whether to complete her mission or not.
S,A — EN
Juri Prods — *Video Programme Distributors*
P
Replay—1006

Double Crossers, The Fil-Ent '75
Crime-Drama
06932   96 mins   C

(For Explanation of codes, see USE GUIDE and KEY)   199

PALADIN VIDEO HOME ENTERTAINMENT GUIDE

B, V
Chen Sing
Set in the Far East, a Singapore police detective is investigating his father's murder. He discovers that his father was a member of a smuggling ring and that his one-time partner is now living the high life in Hong Kong. Set on revenge, the detective and one of his father's friends set a trap for the man on the island of Bali, where an elaborate hoax is designed to kill him.
S,A — EN
Unknown — Rank Video Library   **H, P**
0077C

Double Deal   Fil-Ent '7?
Drama
09161   90 mins   C
V
Louis Jordan, Angela Punch-McGregor, Diane Craig, Warwick Comber
A shrewdly successful head of a vast business empire is married to a young woman, who is bored and sexually frustrated. The story involves a million dollar opal, bank robbery and kidnapping, with unexpected and frightening occurrences.
S,A — EN
Unknown — Medusa Communications Ltd
H, P

Double Exposure   Fil-Ent '8?
Mystery
09025   80 mins   C
V2, B, V
Anoushka Hempel, David Baron, Hazel O'Connor, directed by William Webb
A top photographer foolishly falls for the beautiful mistress of an immensely powerful and wealthy man. Murder, intrigue, jealousy and kidnapping follow.
C,A — EN
Unknown — Intervision Video   **H, P**
AA 0455

Double Exposure   Fil-Ent '82
Mystery/Suspense
12514   91 mins   C
B, V
Michael Callan, Joanna Pettet, James Stacy, directed by William Byron Hillman
In this film a photographer is beset by dreams in which he sees himself murdering beautiful women. When the dreams turn to reality he begins to suspect he may be responsible.
A — EN
Grey Hill Productions — THORN EMI   **P**
TXA 90 2362 4/TVA 90 2362 2

Double Life, A   Fil-Ent '47
Drama
01073   103 mins   B/W
V2, B, V
Ronald Colman, Shelley Winters, directed by George Cukor
Ronald Colman stars as an actor whose stage roles affect his real-life situations.
Academy Awards '47: Best Actor (Colman); Best Music Score.   BBFC:A — S,A — EN
Universal — Intervision Video   **H, P**
A-A 0119

Double Man, The   Fil-Ent '67
Adventure
13198   105 mins   C
B, Vl
Yul Brynner, Britt Ekland, Claire Revill
A CIA Agent flies to the Austrian Tyrol to investigate the death of his son in a so-called skiing 'accident,' but subsequently discovers it was all a trick to get him there.
BBFC:U — F — EN
Albion Film Distributors Ltd — Warner Home Video   **P**
61276

Double Nickles   Fil-Ent '77
Adventure/Comedy-Drama
09860   90 mins   C
B, V
Jack Vacek, Patrice Schubert, Ed Abrams, directed by Jack Vacek
Smokey, the C.B. and speed crazy Highway Patrolman, gets more than he bargained for when he gets involved in a car repossession racket.
F — EN
Smokey Prods; John Vacek Sr — Polygram Video   **H, P**
790 2194/790 2192

Double Possession—The Doctor Cannot Die   Fil-Ent '7?
Horror
02447   75 mins   C
V2, B, V
Gory horror film about a murderous undead doctor who cannot be killed.
BBFC:X — A — EN
Iver Film Services — Iver Film Services
P

Dove, The   Fil-Ent '75
Adventure/Drama
05046   100 mins   C
B, V
Joseph Bottoms, Deborah Raffin, John McLiam, Dabney Coleman, directed by Charles Jarrott

200   (For Explanation of codes, see USE GUIDE and KEY)

PALADIN VIDEO HOME ENTERTAINMENT GUIDE

The true story of Robin Lee Graham, a 16-year-old boy who made a solo voyage round the world in a 24-foot sloop. Based on the book by Robin Lee Graham and Derek Gill.
F — EN
Paramount Pictures; Gregory Peck — THORN EMI P
TXC 90 0257 4/TVC 90 0257 2

Down Memory Lane Fil-Ent '51
Comedy
07641   54 mins   B/W
B, V
Mack Sennett, Bing Crosby, W. C. Fields, Gloria Swanson, TheKeystone Kops, directed by Mack Sennett
Four of Mack Sennett's greatest comedies are woven into a modern story. A television disc-jockey brings in Franklyn Pangborn to interview, he has several reels of film showing sequences from silent comedies. They have trouble identifying some of the actors so they contact Mack Sennett and he arrives at the studio with more films.
F — EN
Eagle Lion — VCL Video Services   P
0228G

Downhill Racer Fil-Ent '69
Drama
13633   101 mins   C
B, V
Robert Redford, Gene Hackman, directed by Michael Ritchie
Many thrilling ski sequences are featured in this film about a self-seeker chosen to compete for the honour of joining the US Olympics ski team and his coach who has the difficult task of curbing his arrogance.
BBFC:PG — F — EN
Richard Gregson — CIC Video   H, P
2131

Dr Syn—Alias the Scarecrow Fil-Ent '62
Adventure
13439   97 mins   C
B, V
Patrick McGoohan, George Cole, Tony Britton, Michael Hordern, Geoffrey Keen
This is the story of the fabled 18th Century smuggler of the Kent coast, who doubled as a defender of the people against injustice.
BBFC:U — F — EN
Walt Disney Productions — Rank Video Library   P
189

Dracula Fil-Ent '79
Horror/Drama
05334   109 mins   C
B, V
Frank Langella, Laurence Olivier, Donald Pleasance, Kate Nelligan, directed by John Badham
An adaptation of the classic gothic horror tale of the count who is one of the 'undead' and needs human blood for survival. He fills the hearts of men with terror and the hearts of women with desire, as he is constantly pursued by a devout vampire hunter.
S,A — EN
Universal — CIC Video   H, P
BEA1011/VHA1011

Dracula Fil-Ent '74
Horror
09137   97 mins   C
V2, B, V
Jack Palance, Simon Ward, Nigel Davenport, Pamela Brown, Fiona Lewis
Set in the 1880's, this is based on Bram Stoker's classic tale of horror about a vampire terrorising the countryside in search of human blood.
C,A — EN
Dan Curtis Prods — Go Video Ltd   P
PIC 004

Dracula Fil-Ent '31
Horror
13290   73 mins   B/W
B, V
Bela Lugosi, David Manners, Helen Chandler, directed by Tod Browning
Based on a story by Bram Stoker, Count Dracula appears in England to terrorize more people in his insatiable thirst for blood.
BBFC:PG — S,A — EN
Universal — CIC Video   H, P
BEJ 1046/VHJ 1046

Dracula Saga, The Fil-Ent '80
Horror
12855   88 mins   C
V2, B, V
Tina Sainz, Tony Isbert, Christina Suriani, Maria Kosti, directed by Leon Klimovsky
The granddaughter of Count Dracula returns to the family castle and strange and evil things start to happen.
A — EN
Unknown — Video Programme Distributors   P
229

(For Explanation of codes, see USE GUIDE and KEY)

PALADIN VIDEO HOME ENTERTAINMENT GUIDE

Dracula's Last Rites   Fil-Ent '??
Horror
06934   84 mins   C
B, V
This is the horrific tale of a family fallen victim to a vampire's insatiable lust for blood.
BBFC:X — A — EN
Unknown — *Rank Video Library*   H, P
2017C

Dracula's Virgin Lovers   Fil-Ent '??
Horror
05464   76 mins   C
V2, B, V
Haydee Politoff
Set in 1870, a mysterious English Doctor hires two hoodlums to carry a heavy metal box into a nursing home situated near the ruins of Dracula's castle. Curious to see if anything worth stealing is in the box they open it and find a coffin and a woman's skeleton. Nearby a coach has an accident and four girls and a young man are forced to spend the night in the home.
BBFC:X — A — EN
Unknown — *Iver Film Services*   P
59

Dragon Dies Hard, The   Fil-Ent '7?
Adventure/Martial arts
04611   90 mins   C
V2, B, V
Bruce Li
Saddened by the death of his friend Bruce Lee, Cheng swears vengeance. An underworld boss tries to cash in on Cheng's remarkable physical resemblance to Bruce; however, Cheng gets involved in a fierce fight when warned to stop prying into Bruce's death.
C,A — EN
Unknown — *Video Programme Distributors*
P
Inter-Ocean—024

Dragon Lives, The   Fil-Ent '80
Adventure/Martial arts
08935   80 mins   C
B, V
Bruce Li
This film tells the story of Bruce Lee—the transition from a gentle philosopher into the most deadly, human fighting machine. In Long Beach, California, he brought a major international Martial Arts Tournament to a shattering climax by demolishing the top contenders.
BBFC:X — A — EN
Unknown — *Brent Walker Home Video Ltd*
P

Dragon Lives Again, The   Fil-Ent '79
Adventure/Martial arts
04416   90 mins   C
B, V
Bruce Leong
A Kung Fu expert wins the respect of an underworld king. When he refuses the King's request that he become his royal guard, the Kung Fu expert is sentenced to hard labour.
S,A — EN
Unknown — *VCL Video Services*   P

Dragon Lord   Fil-Ent '7?
Martial arts
09417   94 mins   C
V2, B, V
Jackie Chan, Chen Hui-Min, Sidney Yim, Whang In-Sik
This film features the master of martial arts and his friend Cowboy in a furious fight to stop Big Boss from selling treasure from the Forbidden City.
BBFC:18 — A — EN
Golden Harvest — *Guild Home Video*   H, P, E

Dragonfly for Each Corpse, A   Fil-Ent '??
Crime-Drama
09950   90 mins   C
V2, B, V
Paul Naschy, Erika Blanc
A police inspector is investigating a case of murders where the only clue in each case is a dragonfly dipped in blood.
BBFC:AA — C,A — EN
Unknown — *Video Unlimited*   H, P, E
087

Dragon's Executioner, The   Fil-Ent '??
Martial arts
06858   90 mins   C
V2, B, V
Barry Chan, Lung Chun Erh, Wei Chin Yun
When Japan occupied part of China they started demanding money from the people. In a small fishing village a headman commits suicide and his daughter is raped and murdered. When his son returns home and discovers what has happened, to take revenge on the Japanese he becomes the Dragon's Executioner.
S,A — EN
Unknown — *European Video Company*
P

Dragon's Teeth   Fil-Ent '??
Adventure/Martial arts
06297   85 mins   C
V2, B, V

PALADIN VIDEO HOME ENTERTAINMENT GUIDE

This film is structured as four tales of the 'Shaolin Temple' placing martial arts in their historical and mythical context through legendary stories.
S,A — ED
Unknown — *World of Video 2000*   **H, P**
GF525

Dragonslayer   Fil-Ent '81
Fantasy/Adventure
12586   106 mins   C
B, V
Peter MacNicol, Caitlin Clarke, Ralph Richardson
Vermithrax is the giant evil dragon who reigns supreme over a frightened medieval kingdom until a brave young sorcerer bursts upon the scene in a whirl of magic.
F — EN
Walt Disney Productions — *Rank Video Library*
H
106

Draughtman's Contract, The   Fil-Ent '82
Drama
12072   102 mins   C
V2, B, V
Anthony Higgins, Janet Suzman, Anne Louise Lambert, Neil Cunningham, Hugh Fraser
This film follows the fortunes of an ambitious young draughtsman who is persuaded to accept a very strange commission—twelve drawings in return for twelve sexual favours.
BBFC:15 — C,A — EN
Peter Greenaway; BFI — *Guild Home Video*
H, P, E

Drawing   Fin-Art '81
Drawing
05428   60 mins   C
B, V
Harold Riley
This cassette is a complete programme in the 'Master Class Painting Course' series led by Harold Riley, the famous artist and lecturer. In this film Harold Riley deals with drawing in the media of pencil, pen and charcoal, examining the relationship an artist is able to form with the medium and the pleasure derived from developing a personal approach.
S,A — I
Harrison Partnership and Holiday Bros Ltd — *Holiday Brothers Ltd*   **P**

Draws   Fil-Ent '??
Comedy
06325   75 mins   C
V2, B, V

The mad story of a search and chase after a mysterious treasure chest involving a gang of greasers, nuns on roller skates, a midget pimp and his girls, and a group of karate experts.
S,A — EN
Unknown — *World of Video 2000*   **H, P**
GF505

Dream for Christmas, A   Fil-Ent '73
Drama
09857   97 mins   C
B, V
Hari Rhodes, George Spell, Beah Richards
This film tells the story of a hard working black family headed by Reverend Douglas, who moves to Los Angeles to take over a dilapidated church and manages, against all odds, to restore both the building and the flagging congregation.
F — EN
Lorimar Prods — *Polygram Video*   **H, P**
040 1394/040 1392

Dream of Passion   Fil-Ent '77
Drama
13146   110 mins   C
B, V
Melina Mercouri, Ellen Burstyn, directed by Jules Dassin
An expatriate Greek actress returns to her homeland to play the lead in a new production and forms an obsessional and fateful relationship with a woman she meets.
BBFC:18 — A — EN
Avco Embassy — *Polygram Video*   **P**
040 2344/040 2342

Dreamer, The   Fil-Ent '70
Drama
08072   83 mins   C
B, V
Leora Rivlin, Tuvia Tavi, Berta Litvina
This film tells the story of a young man who cares for the aged at a rest home in Israel. He develops a special relationship with an old woman who encourages him to become an artist. He is then introduced to a beautiful girl and his attention is drawn away from his responsibility to the old people.
BBFC:X — C,A — EN
Cannon — *Rank Video Library*   **H, P**
0100C

Dreamscape   Fil-Ent '83
Science fiction
13699   95 mins   C
B, V
Dennis Quaid, Max Von Sydow, Christopher Plummer, Eddie Albert, Kate Capshaw, directed by Joe Ruben

---

(For Explanation of codes, see USE GUIDE and KEY)

PALADIN VIDEO HOME ENTERTAINMENT GUIDE

A psychic enters the world of fantasies that haunt the US president and confronts a psychopathic killer in a world where literally anything can happen.
BBFC:15 — S,A — EN
Bruce John Curtis — THORN EMI   P
90 2557

Dressed to Kill   Fil-Ent '80
Crime-Drama
07373   104 mins   C
V2, B, V
Michael Caine, Angie Dickinson, Nancy Allen, Dennis Franz, Keith Gordon, directed by Brian De Palma
A woman is brutally slashed to death. Her son teams up with a prostitute who saw what happened in an attempt to reveal the killer's identity. The trail connects with a successful psychiatrist practising in New York's East Side whose patients include an attractive woman suffering from erotic fantasies so vivid that she has difficulty separating dreams from reality.
BBFC:X — A — EN
George Litto Productions — Guild Home Video
H, P, E

Dribble   Fil-Ent '??
Comedy-Drama
08697   92 mins   C
V2, B, V
Charles Fatone, Freya Crane, Pete Maravich, directed by Michael de Gaetano
This film tells the story of a down and out professional woman's basketball team. Through trying to make it to the top they suffer everyting from broken ankles to broken love affairs. When they finally have to play their big match, their opponents are the men's Army team instead of the women.
BBFC:A — S,A — EN
Unknown — Video Unlimited   H, P
052

Driver   Fil-Ent '78
Drama
04668   88 mins   C
B, V
Ryan O'Neal, Bruce Dern, Isabelle Adjani
'Driver' is the story of a cop, irritated at failing to compel a girl to testify against a man in the bank robbery identity line-up, who uses minor crooks as bait to hook the big one.
C,A — EN
TCF; EMI; Lawrence Gordon — THORN EMI
H, P
TXA 90 0221 4/TVA 90 0221 2

Drop Dead Dearest   Fil-Ent '80
Drama
12933   90 mins   C
B, V
Elke Sommer, Donald Pilon, directed by Murray Markowitz
A courtroom drama, with a man accused of murdering his wife, and a series of flashbacks to his earlier years.
BBFC:18 — A — EN
Unknown — Video Form Pictures   H, P

Drum   Fil-Ent '76
Drama
08354   101 mins   C
V2, B, V
Warren Oates, Isela Vega, Ken Norton, Yaphet Kotto, John Colicos, Pam Grier, Fiona Lewis, Paula Kelly, Brenda Sykes
Drum is the son of a plantation owner's wife and his black slave. When the slaves rise up in violent revolt against their masters, the black and white natures in him are thrown into conflict.
C,A — EN
United Artists — Guild Home Video   H, P, E

Drum, The   Fil-Ent '38
Drama
09862   91 mins   C
B, V
Roger Livesey, Sabu, Desmond Tester, Raymond Massey, Valerie Hobson
Set in the trouble torn northwest frontier of India during the days of the British Raj, this film is the story of two friendships that exist between Captain Carruthers and the Khan, and between the Khan's young son and the British drummer boy.
F — EN
London Films — Polygram Video   H, P
790 2514/790 2512

Drum Beat/To Beat the Band   Fil-Ent '??
Western/Comedy
05715   168 mins   C
B, V
Alan Ladd, Charles Bronson, Marisa Pavan, Audrey Dalton, Anthony Caruso, directed by Delmer Daves, Johnny Mercer, Hugh Herbert, Helen Broderick, Roger Pryor, directed by Ben Stoloff
Two films are featured on one cassette. 'Drum Beat' (Colour, 105 mins, 1955) is a story based on a true incident. An Indian fighter is sent by the President to bring peace to the Modoc tribe, without bloodshed. A renegade causes problems. 'To Beat the Band' (Black/white, 63 mins, 1936) is a comedy musical in which a bachelor inherits a fortune on the condition he

PALADIN VIDEO HOME ENTERTAINMENT GUIDE

marries a widow. A friend offers to marry his girlfriend and make her a widow but the scheme is halted when a real widow appears eager to get hold of the money.
S,A — EN
Warner Bros; RKO — *Kingston Video* **H, P**
KV27

Drummer of Vengeance　　　Fil-Ent　'7?
Western
02407　73 mins　C
B, V
Ty Hardin, Rossano Brazzi, Craig Hill, directed by Robert Paget
British-made western featuring Ty Hardin in various disguises as he takes his revenge on the men who killed his wife and son.
S,A — EN
Unknown — *Derann Film Services*　**H, P**
DV 127B/DV 127

Duchess and the　　　Fil-Ent　'76
Dirtwater Fox, The
Comedy
01747　104 mins　C
B, V
George Segal, Goldie Hawn
A music-hall girl meets a man on the make.
A — EN
20th Century Fox, Melvin Frank — *CBS/Fox Video*　**P**
3A-050

Duck Soup　　　Fil-Ent　'33
Comedy/Satire
12040　70 mins　B/W
B, V
The Marx Brothers, Gloria Teasdale, directed by Leo McCarey
This film is set in the fictitious republic of Freedonia. Groucho plays the president, with Chico and Harpo as his two aides in league against him, working for the neighbouring state of Sylvania.
BBFC:U — F — EN
Universal — *CIC Video*　**H, P**
BEJ 1086/VHJ 1086

Duel in the Sun　　　Fil-Ent　'47
Western/Drama
04188　130 mins　C
B, V
Jennifer Jones, Gregory Peck, Joseph Cotten
Tale of violent love and hate set in Texas, which finds brother against brother and father against son.
BBFC:A — S,A — EN
Selznick — *Guild Home Video*　**H, P**

Duel of Champions　　　Fil-Ent　'61
Drama
05558　105 mins　C
V2, B, V
Alan Ladd, Franca Bettoja, directed by Ferdinando Baldi
A film set in our arena which unfolds a story of lovers, cowardice, monumental battles, jealousy and triumph. The Gods have decreed that an epic battle should be fought between three Roman brothers and three brothers from Alba to call a halt to the deadly rivalry between the two cities.
BBFC:U — F — EN
Medallion — *Videomedia*　**P**
PVM 5101/BVM 5101/HVM 5101

Duellists, The　　　Fil-Ent　'77
Drama
07368　101 mins　C
B, V
Keith Carradine, Harvey Keitel, Edward Fox, Albert Finney, Christina Raines, Robert Stephens, directed by Ridley Scott
This film is the dramatic story of two officers in Napoleon's army who violently confront each other in a series of savage duels. The duels begin as a reaction to a minor incident but become a consuming passion ruling their lives for thirty years until the final unexpected outcome. Based on the story by Joseph Conrad. Cannes Film Festival '77: Best Debut Film.
S,A — EN
Paramount — *CIC Video*　**H, P**
BEA 2021/VHA 2021

Dulux Videoguide to　　　Gen-Edu　'8?
Colouring Your Home,
The
Interior decoration
09907　55 mins　C
B, V
9 pgms
This tape gives practical advice together with lavish illustration. Designers and colour consultants join Johnny Ball to share the secrets of colouring your home both inside and out.
1.Introduction: Johnny Ball 2.Colour As A Language: Dilys Morgan 3.The Cogwheels of Colour: How It Works 4.Journey Through The Rainbow: Red and Orange Interlude 5.Colour Outside: Tom Porter 6.Journey Through The Rainbow: Yellow and Green 7.An Englishman's Home: David Mlinaric 8.Journey Through The Rainbow: Blue and Violet 9.Colour In A Roomscape: Jack Widgery
S,A — I
Michael Barratt Ltd. — *Michael Barratt Ltd*　**P**
MBV 6050683

PALADIN VIDEO HOME ENTERTAINMENT GUIDE

Dumbo   Chi-Juv '41
Cartoons
13740   84 mins   C
B, V
Animated
The classic tale of Dumbo the outcast elephant with gigantic ears who becomes the darling of the circus world when he discovers he can fly.
F — EN
Walt Disney Productions — *Rank Video Library*   **P**
024S

Dune   Fil-Ent '84
Fantasy/Adventure
13689   130 mins   C
B, V
Francesca Annis, Kyle Maclachlan, Sian Phillips, Sting, Max Von Sydow, Jose Ferrer, Linda Hunt, Jurgen Prochnow, Everett McGill, Sean Young, Dean Stockwell, directed by David Lynch
Full of spectacular special effects with music by Toto, this film, based on the novel by Frank Herbert, is set on the planet Dune, and is a battle between good and evil for control of the Universe.
BBFC:PG — *S,A — EN*
Dino De Laurentiis — *THORN EMI*   **P**
90 3025

Dunwich Horror, The   Fil-Ent '70
Horror
07374   86 mins   C
V2, B, V
Sandra Dee, Dean Stockwell, Sam Jaffe, Ed Begley, directed by Daniel Haller
A young man arrives at University from the town of Dunwich which has a history of weird and evil happenings. He persuades a young student to let him see a rare and banned book on the occult. He drugs her into a supernatural trance and makes plans for her to be used as a sacrifice to the devil. A professor discovers that the young man is the great-grandson of a man who was hanged as a demon and rescues the girl in the nick of time.
S,A — EN
American International Pictures — *Guild Home Video*   **H, P, E**

Duran Duran   Fil-Ent '83
Music-Performance
08482   60 mins   C
B, V
Directed by Russell Mulcahy
This tape features many of the videos that helped the group Duran Duran to the top including glimpses of their exotic world tour. Songs include: 'Planet Earth', 'Careless Memories', 'My Own Way', 'Girls on Film', 'The Chauffeur', Hungry Like the Wolf', Save a Prayer', Nightboat', 'Rio', 'Lonely in Your Nightmare' and many others.
S,A — EN
TVD Ltd — *THORN EMI*   **P**
TXE 90 0984 4/TVE 90 0984 2

DUTCH GIRLS   Fil-Ent '85
Comedy/Romance
13695   83 mins   C
B, V
Bill Paterson, Colin Firth, Timothy Spall, directed by Giles Foster
A team of eighteen-year-old boys from a remote Scottish public school are taken to Holland by their coach to play hockey, but the boys have other plans and hockey is the last thing on their minds.
C,A — EN
Sue Birtwistle — *THORN EMI*   **P**
90 3142

Dying Sea, The   Fil-Ent '7?
Horror
02586   44 mins   C
B, V
A scientist explores weird creatures found at the bottom of the sea.
A — EN
Unknown — *Mountain Video*   **P**

Dynamite Brothers, The   Fil-Ent '7?
Adventure/Martial arts
09008   90 mins   C
V2, B, V
Alan Tang, Timothy Brown, Aldo Ray, directed by Al Adamson
Set in the violent world of Los Angeles, this film tells the story of a vicious gang war between rival Chinese factions.
S,A — EN
Unknown — *Intervision Video*   **H, P**
AA 0449

Dynamo   Fil-Ent '80
Adventure/Martial arts
04602   96 mins   C
V2, B, V
Bruce Li
Glamorous advertising executive Mary is in Hong Kong at the time of Bruce Lee's funeral. She notices that her taxi driver Lee bears a striking resemblance to Bruce and induces him to sign an exclusive contract.
C,A — EN
Unknown — *Video Programme Distributors*   **P**
Inter-Ocean—037

PALADIN VIDEO HOME ENTERTAINMENT GUIDE

E

Eagle Has Landed, The　　　Fil-Ent '76
War-Drama
00843　118 mins　C
B, V, LV
Michael Caine, Donald Sutherland, Robert Duvall
German paratroopers stage a dramatic attempt to kidnap Winston Churchill.
BBFC:A — C,A — EN
Columbia — Precision Video Ltd　　P
BITC 3009/VITC 3009

Eagle Has Landed: The　　　Med-Sci '69
Flight of Apollo 11
Space exploration
01225　29 mins　C
B, V, PH15, PH17, 3/4U
The story of the historic first landing on the moon in July, 1969. Highlights of the mission with astronauts Neil Armstrong, Buzz Aldrin, and Mike Collins are seen.
U.S. Industrial Film Festival '69: Gold Camera.
M,A — ED
NASA — Istead Audio Visual　　P
HQ 194

Eagle in a Cage　　　Fil-Ent '71
Drama
12080　98 mins　C
V2, B, V
John Gielgud, Ralph Richardson, Kenneth Haigh, Billie Whitelaw
This historical story traces the last days of Napoleon Bonaparte as a prisoner of the British on the island of St. Helena.
BBFC:PG — S,A — EN
Group W — Intervision Video　　H, P
A-A 0438

Eagles Attack at Dawn　　　Fil-Ent '74
War-Drama/Adventure
08039　101 mins　C
B, V
Rick Jason, Peter Brown, Joseph Shiloal, directed by Menahem Golan
This film is an action packed story of the brave rescue of Israeli prisoners from a Syrian prison. An escaped prisoner returns with a small command force to find and kill the sadistic commander of the prison and release the tortured prisoners
C,A — EN
Globus Productions — Rank Video Library
H, P
0106 C

Eagle's Killer, The　　　Fil-Ent '7?
Martial arts
09820　90 mins　C
B, V
Having joined the 'Dragon Fist', Chou Tai unknowingly puts himself on an assassin's death list. He escapes and becomes a pupil of a professional killer. His admiration for his master turns to contempt and he directs his skills towards vengeance.
S,A — EN
Unknown — Polygram Video　　H, P
790 4484/790 4482

Eagle's Wing　　　Fil-Ent '79
Western
05246　104 mins　C
B, V
Martin Sheen, Sam Waterston, Harvey Keitel, Stephane Audran, Caroline Langrishe
This dramatic western takes as its theme the timeless tragedy of civilisation's clash with the wild.
BBFC:A — C,A — EN
Unknown — Rank Video Library　　H, P
8000

Early Bird, The　　　Fil-Ent '65
Comedy-Drama
09943　94 mins　C
B, V
Norman Wisdom, John Le Mesurier, Bryan Pringle, Frank Thornton, Dandy Nichols, Edward Chapman, Jerry Desmonde, Paddie O'Neil
Norman Wisdom plays a milkman who gets involved in deadly rivalry between a giant milk marketing company and an old-fashioned one horse dairy.
BBFC:U — F — EN
Rank — Rank Video Library　　H, P
1051 A

Early Frost　　　Fil-Ent '8?
Crime-Drama
09156　90 mins　C
V
Daina McClean, Jon Blake, Janet Kingsbury, David Franklin, Daniel Cumerford, Guy Doleman

(For Explanation of codes, see USE GUIDE and KEY)

PALADIN VIDEO HOME ENTERTAINMENT GUIDE

A private detective, while gathering evidence for a divorce, finds a corpse. The death is listed as an accident but he suspects it to be more. The more he investigates, the more complicated and sinister it becomes.
S,A — EN
Unknown — *Medusa Communications Ltd*
H, P

Early One Morning　　　　　Gen-Edu '78
Birds/Wildlife
04278　　24 mins　　C
B, V
The beauty of our countryside and wildlife is still wonderfully rich and varied. Each season has its own special birds...every period of the day, from the first glimmer of dawn, to the darkness of nightfall, has an atmosphere of its own.
British Sponsored Film Festival '78: Bronze Award　　F — ED
Royal Society for the Protection of Birds — *Royal Society for the Protection of Birds*　　**H, P**

Earth-Sun Relationship　　　Med-Sci '74
Astronomy
01102　　6 mins　　C
B, V, PH15, PH17, 3/4U
This programme explains the relationship between the earth and the sun.
S,A — ED
NASA — *Istead Audio Visual*　　**P**
HQ 235

Eartha Kitt Show, The　　　　Fil-Ent '7?
Variety
04380　　60 mins　　C
B, V, PH17, 3/4U
Eartha Kitt, Sergio Mendes and Brazil '66
A musical variety special with Eartha Kitt and Sergio Mendes and Brazil '66.
F — EN
Unknown — *Vidpics International*　　**P**

Earthling, The　　　　　　　Fil-Ent '82
Adventure
13459　　97 mins　　C
B, V
William Holden, Ricky Schroeder
A man and a boy find themselves alone in the vast wilderness of the Australian outback struggling for survival.
BBFC:15 — S,A — EN
Orion Pictures — *Rank Video Library*　　**H, P**
0178

Earthquake Below　　　　　Med-Sci '75
Earthquakes
01128　　14 mins　　C
B, V, PH15, PH17, 3/4U
NASA is studying the earth to predict when earthquakes will occur.
S,A — ED
NASA — *Istead Audio Visual*　　**P**
HQ 248

East of Eden　　　　　　　　Fil-Ent '81
Drama
09179　　250 mins　　C
B, V
Jane Seymour, Timothy Bottoms, Lloyd Bridges, Warren Oates, Anne Baxter, Howard Duff
This film, available in two parts, is based on John Steinbeck's classic novel and recounts a modern version of Cain and Abel, two brothers whose lives are set in opposition to each other by their domineering father. Into their lives, comes Cathy, a beautiful, fascinating woman whose innocent appearance masks her evil nature.
S,A — EN
Mace Neufeld Prods — *Video Form Pictures*
H, P
MGX1

East of Elephant Rock　　　Fil-Ent '76
Drama
05383　　93 mins　　C
B, V
John Hurt, Jeremy Kemp, Judi Bowker, directed by Dan Boyd
This film is set in 1948, a young first secretary of the British Embassy returns from leave in England to a tense atmosphere in a Colony in South East Asia. He has to attend a party at Government House where members of the British community have gathered to honour the new governor. They stolidly refuse to accept that the tension in the countryside could change their comfortable lives.
BBFC:AA — S,A — EN
Unknown — *Precision Video Ltd*　　**P**
BBPV 2559/VBPV 2559

East Side Hustle　　　　　　Fil-Ent '7?
Drama
08994　　86 mins　　C
B, V
Anne Marie Provencher, Alan Moyle, directed by Frank Vitale
A prostitute decides to give up her former life, and aims to persuade the other girls to leave ex-boyfriend 'Campbell's' prostitution racket. One by one the girls begin to leave. However,

PALADIN VIDEO HOME ENTERTAINMENT GUIDE

Campbell responds with explosive violence including abductions, murder and terror leading to a violent showdown on the streets of America.
BBFC:18 — A — EN
Unknown — *Video Programme Distributors*
P
Replay 1021

Easter Parade   Fil-Ent '48
Musical
10169   100 mins   C
B, V, LV
Fred Astaire, Judy Garland, Peter Lawford
When a dancer is jilted by his partner, he makes a bet with a wealthy friend that he can make a star out of any young girl. He finds a singer in a cheap cafe, grooms her, and together they find success. Featuring Irving Berlin's music and lyrics including 'Drum Crazy' and 'We're a Couple of Swells'.
BBFC:U — F — EN
MGM — *MGM/UA Home Video*   **P**
UMB 10256/UMV 10256/UMLV 10256

Eaten Alive   Fil-Ent '76
Horror
07938   85 mins   C
V2, B, V
Robert Kerman, Ivan Rassimov, Janet Agren, Paola Senatore, Mel Ferrer, directed by Umberto Lenzi
A young girl travels to New Guinea to search for her sister who, after joining the Sect of the Purification, disappeared. There are suspicions that the Sect's true purpose, hidden deep inside the jungle, is too horrific to admit.
BBFC:X — A — EN
Virgo International — *Videomedia*   **P**
PVM 1022/BVM 1022/HVM 1022

Eating Raoul   Fil-Ent '82
Comedy
10136   87 mins   C
B, V
Paul Bartel, directed by Paul Bartel
A middle-aged, middle-class couple resort to a career of sexual and murderous antics in order to finance their dream of a country restaurant.
BBFC:18 — A — EN
20th Century Fox Classics; Quartet Films — *Palace Video Ltd*   **P**
VIRV 008A

Echoes   Fil-Ent '80
Drama
09053   87 mins   C
V
Richard Alfiere, Nathalie Nell, Mercedes McCambridge, Ruth Roman, Gale Sondergaard
A man's dreams and his meetings with the psychic lead him to a new realization about his past life. However, it also messes up his present life, losing his girlfriend, and as an artist, has his paintings rejected and becomes alienated from his fellow artists.
C,A — EN
Unknown — *Astra Video*   **H, P**

Eddie Macon's Run   Fil-Ent '83
Crime-Drama
13341   91 mins   C
B, V
Kirk Douglas, John Schneider, Leah Ayres, directed by Jeff Kanew
An innocent man on the run from prison to see his wife and family is pursued relentlessly by a tough cop.
BBFC:15 — C,A — EN
Louis J Stroller — *CIC Video*   **H, P**
BET 1104/VHT 1104

Eddy Grant   Fil-Ent '80
Music-Performance
06237   30 mins   C
B, V
Eddy Grant and his band the Frontline Orchestra perform live at the annual Notting Hill summer carnival. Music includes: Cockney Black, Living on the Frontline, Walking on Sunshine, My Turn to Love You, Neighbour, Neighbour and many more.
F — EN
Mimosa Films — *VCL Video Services*   **P**
V161A

Educating Rita   Fil-Ent '83
Drama/Romance
13463   108 mins   C
B, V
Michael Caine, Julie Walters, Michael Williams, Maureen Lipman, directed by Lewis Gilbert
A married woman enrolls at the Open University and through her tutor's encouragement begins to change radically.
BBFC:15 — S,A — EN
Columbia Pictures — *Rank Video Library*
H, P

Education on Pike Fishing, An   Spo-Lei '82
Fishing
06838   45 mins   C
B, V
Ian Heaps

(For Explanation of codes, see USE GUIDE and KEY)

PALADIN VIDEO HOME ENTERTAINMENT GUIDE

In this film on pike fishing, Ian Heaps, the world champion angler is joined by Pete Morgan of the British Pike Fishing Club. They demonstrate how to read the water, spinning, and how to handle pike before and after capture.
S,A — I
VTR Studios Ltd — *TFI Leisure Ltd* **P**

Education on Pole   Spo-Lei '82
Fishing, An
Fishing
06840   80 mins   C
B, V
Ian Heaps
In this film Ian Heaps, the world champion angler, demonstrates different methods, illustrates conditions of water, assembly of tackle, shotting patterns, ground baiting, float design, and how to fish.
S,A — I
VTR Studios Ltd — *TFI Leisure Ltd* **P**

Education on Stick Float   Spo-Lei '82
Fishing, An
Fishing
06839   40 mins   C
B, V
Ian Heaps
In this film on stick float fishing, Ian Heaps, the world champion angler demonstrates running through and holding back methods. He gives much invaluable, match-winning advice.
S,A — I
VIR Studios Ltd — *TFI Leisure Ltd* **P**

Educational Release No 2   Gen-Edu '84
Birds/Wildlife
13602   62 mins   C
V2, B, V
Topics of migration, Britain's birds of prey and our disappearing wetlands are covered in this cassette.
AM Available   F — ED
Unknown — *Royal Society for the Protection of Birds* **H, P**

Edward and Mrs.   Fil-Ent '79
Simpson Volume 1
Royalty-GB/Documentary
05892   156 mins   C
B, V
Edward Fox, Cynthia Harris, directed by Waris Hussein
In the first programme, 'The Little Prince,' the popular Prince of Wales is introduced to Wallis Simpson. In the second, 'Venus at the Prow,' their friendship causes gossip and scandal. In the third programme, 'The New King,' Edward becomes King on the death of George V, and Ernest Simpson issues an ultimatum.
Emmy Award '80: Best Television Drama
F — EN
Andrew Brown; Thames Television — *THORN EMI* **P**
TXB 90 62144 4/TVB 90 62144 2

Edward and Mrs.   Fil-Ent '79
Simpson Volume 2
Royalty-GB/Documentary
05891   104 mins   C
B, V
Edward Fox, Cynthia Harris, directed by Waris Hussein
In the first programme, 'The Divorce,' criticism and gossip continue, and comments regarding a divorce cannot be suppressed. In the second programme, 'The Decision,' the king receives a letter warning him that Press silence cannot be maintained.
Emmy Award '80: Best Television Drama
F — EN
Andrew Brown; Thames Television — *THORN EMI* **P**
TXB 90 6219 4/TVB 90 6219 2

Edward and Mrs.   Fil-Ent '79
Simpson Volume 3
Royalty-GB/Documentary
05293   104 mins   C
B, V
Edward Fox, Cynthia Harris, directed by Waris Hussein
In the first programme, 'Proposals,' there is mounting controversy over the King's intention to marry Mrs. Simpson. In the second, 'The Abdication,' the instrument of abdication is signed, and the ex-King broadcasts his farewell to the nation.
Emmy Award '80: Best Television Drama
F — EN
Andrew Brown; Thames Television — *THORN EMI* **P**
TXB 90 6220 4/TVB 90 6220 2

Eiger Sanction, The   Fil-Ent '75
Drama/Suspense
13276   113 mins   C
B, V
Clint Eastwood, George Kenndey, Jack Cassidy, directed by Clint Eastwood
A professional government assassin comes out of retirement to avenge the killing of a friend and to do this he has to climb the north face of the Eiger.
BBFC:15 — S,A — EN
Universal — *CIC Video* **H, P**
BEN 1100/VHN 1100

PALADIN VIDEO HOME ENTERTAINMENT GUIDE

80,000 Suspects   Fil-Ent '63
Drama
06915   96 mins   B/W
B, V
Claire Bloom, Richard Johnson, Michael Goodliffe, Yolande Donlan, Cyril Cusack
Two dedicated doctors face not only a possible smallpox epidemic but a crisis that threatens to wreck both their marriages. They are too professional to let personal matters affect their work but one of the wives is convinced her husband is having an affair with the wife of his partner. In the midst of smouldering emotions they fight to save a frightened city.
BBFC:A — S,A — EN
Continental; Walter Reade — *Rank Video Library*   **H, P**
0064C

El Cid   Fil-Ent '61
Adventure
01064   180 mins   C
V2, B, V
Charlton Heston, Sophia Loren
Story of Spain's 11th century Christian hero who freed his country from Moorish invaders.
BBFC:U — F — EN
Allied Artists; Samuel Bronston — *Intervision Video*   **P**
A-A 0202

Electric Light Voyage   Fil-Ent '??
Fantasy
06072   60 mins   C
B, V
Animated
An electronic fantasy with images that explode with colour combined with flowing shapes and rythms.
S,A — EN
Unknown — *Video Programme Distributors* **P**
Media—M307

Electric Horseman   Fil-Ent '79
Drama
01150   120 mins   C
B, V
Robert Redford, Jane Fonda, John Saxon
A newspaper woman seeking a story discovers the reason behind a rodeo star's kidnapping of a prized horse. In the process she falls in love with the rodeo star.
F — EN
Columbia, Ray Stark — *CIC Video*   **H, P**

Electric Light Orchestra   Fil-Ent '78
Music-Performance
05304   58 mins   C
B, V
One of the world's most successful and popular bands filmed in concert and capturing their unique rock-with-strings style. Songs performed include 'Roll Over Beethoven,' 'Do Ya,' 'Living Thing' and 'Evil Woman.'
F — EN
Jet Holdings Inc — *MGM/UA Home Video* **P**
UCB10021/UCV10021

Elephant Boy, The   Fil-Ent '37
Adventure/Drama
09865   76 mins   C
B, V
Sabu, W.E. Holloway, Allan Jeaves
This is based on Kipling's book 'Tomomai of the Elephants', and is the touching story of a boy and his elephant.
F — EN
United Artists — *Polygram Video*   **H, P**
790 2554/790 2552

Elephant Called Slowly, An   Fil-Ent '70
Adventure/Wildlife
08541   86 mins   C
B, V
Bill Travers, Virginia McKenna, George Adamson, directed by James Hill
Virginia McKenna and Bill Travers star as themselves in this safari story set in Kenya. After receiving an invitation to look after a home whilst the owner is away, they travel to East Africa. They encounter many wild animals and visit George Adamson and his well known lions Boy, Girl and Ugas.
BBFC:U — F — EN
Morning Star Prod Ltd — *THORN EMI*   **P**
TXC 90 07554/TVC 90 0755 2

Elephant Man, The   Fil-Ent '80
Drama
05294   119 mins   B/W
B, V
Anthony Hopkins, John Hurt, Anne Bancroft, Sir John Gielgud, Wendy Heller
The true story of a man hideously deformed by disease who is encouraged by a young surgeon to leave his life as a specimen in a travelling circus and to rejoin society.
S,A — EN
Jonathan Sanger — *THORN EMI*   **P**
TXA 90 0301 4/TVA 90 0301 2

Elephant Man, The   Fil-Ent '82
Drama
08745   97 mins   C
B, V
Philip Anglim, Kevin Conway, Penny Fuller

(For Explanation of codes, see USE GUIDE and KEY)

PALADIN VIDEO HOME ENTERTAINMENT GUIDE

This is the television-film version of the life of John Merrick, a young Englishman who suffered from such extreme, grotesque deformities that he was forced to exhibit himself to make a living. It is based on the Broadway production of the film.
S,A — EN
ITC — Precision Video Ltd   P
BITC 2115/VITC 2115

Elephant Parts   Fil-Ent '81
Music/Comedy
08085   30 mins   C
B, V
Michael Nesmith
A video album by Michael Nesmith which contains several amusing comedy sketches and original music by himself.
Grammy Awards '81: Video of the Year Award.
BBFC:A — S,A — EN
Michael Nesmith; Kathryn Nesmith — *Rank Video Library*   **H, P**
7011 A

Eliminator, The   Fil-Ent '80
War-Drama
09186   104 mins   C
B, V
Alain Delon, Curt Jurgens, Natacha Belokhvostikova, directed by Alexandre Alov, Vladimir Naoumov
A crucial meeting is due to take place in Teheran, Iran, 1943. Churchill, Stalin and Roosevelt meet to discuss their operations. However, during this conference the German Secret Services plan an assassination. Thirty-seven years later the documents relating to this conspiracy are found. From the disputes of the papers, the attempted crime of World War II is reconstructed.
S,A — EN
Unknown — *Video Form Pictures*   **H, P**
DD 5

Elmer   Fil-Ent '77
Drama/Adventure
05493   73 mins   C
V2, B, V
Phillip Swanson, directed by Christopher Cain
An old toothless dog who has become a problem to his family is retired to the Grandfather's home in the country. However, on the journey there he slips out of the Station Wagon into the woods and is soon lost. Also lost is a young boy who was blinded in a plane crash; they chance upon each other and develop a mutually dependent relationship.
BBFC:U — F — EN
Mogul Productions — *Iver Film Services*
P

Elmer Gantry   Fil-Ent '60
Drama
12603   142 mins   C
B, V
Burt Lancaster, Jean Simmons, Dean Jagger, Arthur Kennedy, Shirley Jones, directed by Richard Brooks
The story of a bible thumping, immoral, womanising evangelist in the Mid-West in the twenties whose indiscretions lead to a tragedy of epic proportions where only a miracle can save him.
Academy Awards '61: Best Actor (Lancaster); Best Supporting Actress (Jones); Best Screenplay for Writer (Brooks).
BBFC:PG — F — EN
Bernard Smith — *Warner Home Video*   **P**
99358

ELO—Live in Concert   Fil-Ent '??
Music-Performance
06219   60 mins   C
B, V
A record of one of the best-known Electric Light Orchestra concerts where a vast hundred foot spaceship landing in a blaze of laser beams heralds a spectacular event. Songs include: 'Concerto for a Rainy Day,' 'Standin' in the Rain,' 'Wild West Hero,' 'Rockaria,' 'Turn to Stone,' 'Thing,' 'Mr Blue Sky,' 'Rollover Beethoven' and more.
F — EN
Jet Records — *VCL Video Services*   **P**
Z159G

Elton John   Fil-Ent '80
Music-Performance
06255   60 mins   C
B, V
Nine film cameras, including one in a helicopter, and twenty four track sound equipment recorded this Elton John concert live from Central Park, New York. Song titles include: 'Little Jeannie,' 'Benny and the jets,' 'Imagine,' 'Goodbye Yellow Brick Road,' 'Your Song,' 'Bite your Lip,' 'Get Up and Dance' and many others.
F — EN
Danny O'Donnovan — *VCL Video Services*
P
V134

Elton John - The Fox   Fil-Ent '81
Music-Performance
08083   40 mins   C
B, V
Elton John
This video, produced on the west coast of America, features Elton John and his music
F — EN
Independent — *Rank Video Library*   **H, P**
7012 A

PALADIN VIDEO HOME ENTERTAINMENT GUIDE

Elton John-The Videosingles
Fil-Ent '8?
Music-Performance/Video
09877   16 mins   C
B, V
This tape comprises four tracks from two of Elton John's most popular albums; 'I Guess That's Why They Call It the Blues', 'Empty Garden', 'Blue Eyes' and 'I'm Still Standing'. Recorded in stereo.
F — EN
Unknown — Polygram Video   H, P
791 5644/791 5642

Elvis
Fil-Ent '68
Music-Performance
06298   114 mins   C
V2, B, V
Elvis Presley
This film features extracts from shows by Elvis Presley. It includes his 1968 'Special Comeback' show including the number 'Let Yourself Go,' a live concert performance in 1956 and tracks from two 'Elvis in Concert' shows.
F — EN
Unknown — World of Video 2000   H, P
SP1

Elvis in Hawaii
Fil-Ent '73
Music-Performance
02454   56 mins   C
B, V
Elvis sings his popular hits live in concert.
F — EN
Unknown — Mountain Video   P

Elvis on Tour
Fil-Ent '72
Music-Performance
10167   90 mins   C
B, V
Elvis Presley
This film follows Elvis Presley from one concert to another featuring all his smash hits, including 'Love Me Tender' and 'Burning Love'. It details moments from his early career and of his off-stage private life.
BBFC:U — F — EN
MGM — MGM/UA Home Video   P
UMB 10153/UMV 10153

Elvis—That's the Way It Is
Fil-Ent '70
Music-Performance
12228   104 mins   C
B, V
Elvis Presley

This cassette captures 'The King' in spectacular live performances, from the opening night of his first concert tour in 13 years to his triumphant season at the Vegas International Hotel. It includes rare footage of Elvis off stage and takes a fascinating look at Elvis fans.
BBFC:U — F — EN
MGM — MGM/UA Home Video   P
10373

Elvis—The Movie
Fil-Ent '79
Musical-Drama
01966   122 mins   C
B, V
Kurt Russell, Shelley Winters, Pat Hingle, Season Hubley
A dramatisation of Elvis Presley's life from his boyhood through his explosive rise to fame, and ending with his musical rebirth in 1969.
C,A — EN
Dick Clark Prods — VCL Video Services   P

Embassy
Fil-Ent '72
Drama/Adventure
06204   90 mins   C
B, V
Richard Roundtree, Chuck Connors, Marie-Jose Nat, Ray Milland, Broderick Crawford
The American Embassy in Beirut is thrown into confusion by the arrival of a high-ranking Soviet Foreign Ministry official who wants to defect. After interrogation they agree to take him, but first he has to be gotten out of the country alive.
S,A — EN
Hemdale Films; Mel Ferrer — VCL Video Services   P
C191C

Embryo
Fil-Ent '76
Science fiction
09182   110 mins   C
B, V
Rock Hudson, Diane Ladd, Roddy McDowall, Barbara Carrera
This is the story of a foetal research experiment that gets frighteningly out of hand. It tells of a woman who grows from infancy to womanhood in just 4 1/2 weeks. The doctor responsible becomes obsessed with his perfect progeny and forces her to assist in even more terrifying experiments.
C,A — EN
Cine Artists Pictures — Video Form Pictures   H, P
MGS 4

Emerson Lake and Palmer
Fil-Ent '8?
Music-Performance

(For Explanation of codes, see USE GUIDE and KEY)

PALADIN VIDEO HOME ENTERTAINMENT GUIDE

08759   45 mins   C
B, V
This tape features Emerson, Lake and Palmer, recorded live at the London Lyceum. It shows fascinating optical effects which complements their unique musical style.
BBFC:U — F — EN
Unknown — *Precision Video Ltd*   P
BITC 2575/VITC 2575

Emily   Fil-Ent '76
Drama/Romance
09045   90 mins   C
B, V
Koo Stark, Victor Spinetti, Sarah Brackett, Jane Hayden, directed by Henry Herbert
This film follows the poignant story of a young girl's first love. Original music score by American songwriter Rod McKuen.
BBFC:X — A — EN
Emily Productions — *VideoSpace Ltd*   P
VS 8

Emma And Grandpa   Chi-Juv '84
Flowers/Animals
13095   120 mins   C
B, V
Emma Helmer, Alan Mason, Storyteller Thora Hird
A six year old girl, her grandfather and his dog, together share the wonders, pleasures and day-to-day happenings of their country community through the nature cycle of the year.
I, M — EN
Griffin Productions; Longmar Video — *Longman Video*   P

Emmanuelle   Fil-Ent '74
Drama
07953   92 mins   C
B, V
Sylvia Kristel, Alain Cuny, Marika Green
Shot in Bangkok, this film tells the story of a young, beautiful and restless woman who is introduced to an uninhibited world of sexuality where she experiences her wildest dreams.
BBFC:X — A — EN
Columbia — *Brent Walker Home Video Ltd*
P

Emmanuelle 4   Fil-Ent '84
Drama
12909   85 mins   C
B, V
Sylvia Kristel, Mia Nygren, directed by Francis Giacobetti
A new Emmanuelle emerges in the fourth episode of this series.
A — EN
Unknown — *THORN EMI*   P
TXA 90 24094/TVA 90 24092

Emmanuelle—Queen of the Sados   Fil-Ent '??
Drama
08630   93 mins   C
V2, B, V
Laura Gemser, Livia Russo, Gabriele Tinti, Harry Stevens
Emmanuelle's life becomes unbearable when her husband's perverse intentions get worse. As he goes to the extreme of forcing their daughter to be witness to a sadistic ritual, Emmanuelle plots to get rid of him. A killer is hired, his services being paid with sex and money. However, once again she is at the hands of a sex maniac, and is forced to take revenge once again.
A — EN
Unknown — *Hokushin Audio Visual Ltd*
P
VM 57

Emmanuelle 3   Fil-Ent '??
Drama
08636   78 mins   C
V2, B, V
Silva Castell, Brigette Lahaie, Jean-Marie Pallady
This film tells the story of a photographer who is on an assignment with two stunning French models in Bangkok. However, he is actually undertaking a secret mission to search for two missing spies.
BBFC:X — A — EN
Unknown — *Hokushin Audio Visual Ltd*
P
VM 50

Emmanuelle 2   Fil-Ent '75
Drama
07438   76 mins   C
B, V
Sylvia Kristel, Umberto Orsini, Catherine Rivet, Frederic Lagache, Caroline Laurence, Venantino Venantini, directed by Francis Giacobetti
In this film the exotic settings of Hong Kong and Bali provide the backdrop for Emmanuelle's many and varied exploits. She and her husband have what is for them the ideal marriage with complete sexual liberation, yet a deep bond which none are able to come between. Music by Francis Lai.
BBFC:X — A — EN
Trinacra Films — *THORN EMI*   P
TXA 90 0702 4/TVA 90 0702 2

PALADIN VIDEO HOME ENTERTAINMENT GUIDE

Empire Strikes Back, The   Fil-Ent '80
Science fiction/Fantasy
13250   119 mins   C
B, V
Mark Hamill, Harrison Ford, Carrie Fisher, Billy Dee Williams, Anthony Daniels, directed by Irvin Kershner
The battle to save the galaxy from the evil of Darth Vadar rages on starting with a spectacular opening battle and ending with a stunning duel in which Luke learns the secret of his destiny. This is the sequel to 'Star Wars.'
BBFC:U — F — EN
Gary Kurtz; 20th Century Fox — *CBS/Fox Video*   **P**
1425

Enchanted Island/Westward Passage   Fil-Ent '??
Adventure/Romance
05717   160 mins   C
B, V
Dana Andrews, Jane Powell, Arthur Shields, Dan Dubbins, Ted De Corsia, directed by Allan Dwan, Laurence Olivier, Ann Harding, ZaSu Pitts, Irving Pichel, Bonita Granville, directed by Robert Milton
Two films are featured on one cassette. 'Enchanted Island' (Colour, 90 mins, 1959) is based on the novel by Herman Melville. Set in the South Pacific in the 1840's a crew of an American whaling ship meet a tribe of cannibals. A man falls in love with a native girl but rebels against the savage way of life. 'Westward Passage' (Black/white, 70 mins, 1934) portrays a volatile, arrogant husband whose wife discovers that poverty can easily cool a romance. She seeks a divorce, so she can marry a man who offers her mature love and affection.
S,A — EN
Warner Bros; RKO — *Kingston Video*   **H, P**
KV25

Encounter with Disaster   Gen-Edu '79
Documentary/Disasters
08073   89 mins   C
B, V
Narrated by Brad Cradell
This film recounts harrowing disasters and catastrophes over the last fifty years. It includes the 1956 Andrea Doria sinking; the 1937 crash of the Hindenburg; 1964's Hurricane Camille; the 1964 Earthquake that shook Anchorage, Alaska; and the 1974 tornado that demolished Xenia, Ohio
BBFC:U — F — EN
Sunnclassic; Savadore Productions — *Rank Video Library*   **H, P**
0061 B

End, The   Fil-Ent '78
Comedy
12505   96 mins   C
B, V
Burt Reynolds, Dom DeLuise, Sally Field, Joanne Woodward, directed by Burt Reynolds
A man discovers that he is suffering from a fatal illness and decides to kill himself-which is when his troubles really start!
BBFC:15 — C,A — EN
Laurence Gordon — *Warner Home Video*   **P**
99368

End of August, The   Fil-Ent '7?
Drama/Romance
08074   104 mins   C
B, V
Lilia Skala, David Marshall Grant
This film is set in New Orleans in the year 1900. It tells the story of a girl torn between duty to her family and the need for sensual love.
BBFC:A — S,A — EN
Unknown — *Rank Video Library*   **H, P**
0093 C

End of the World   Fil-Ent '77
Science fiction
01155   88 mins   C
V2, B, V
Christopher Lee, Sue Lyon, Lew Ayres, MacDonald Carey
A coffee machine explodes, sending a man flying and screaming through a window and into a neon sign, where he is electrocuted. A haunted priest witnesses this and retreats to a convent where he meets his double and heads for more trouble.
BBFC:A — S,A — EN
Charles Band Prods — *Intervision Video*   **P**
A-A 0291

Endangered Species   Fil-Ent '82
Drama/Horror
10161   93 mins   C
B, V
Robert Urich, Jo Beth Williams
A tough ex-New York detective living in Colorado has to come out of retirement when he discovers local cattle have been mutilated in some sort of a bizarre ritual. He joins forces with the lady County Sheriff and together they try to find an answer to these killings, but they are blocked in their investigations by government intrigue and local superstition.
A — EN
MGM/UA — *MGM/UA Home Video*   **P**
UMB 10217/UMV 10217

(For Explanation of codes, see USE GUIDE and KEY)

PALADIN VIDEO HOME ENTERTAINMENT GUIDE

Endless Love Fll-Ent '81
Romance/Drama
07845   110 mins   C
V2, B, V
Brooke Shields, Martin Hewitt, Shirley Knight, Don Murray, Richard Kiley, Penelope Milford, Beatrice Straight, directed by Franco Zeffirelli
This story centers on the love between Jade, a 15 year-old girl and David, a 17 year-old boy and the effect it has on those that surround them. Their affair is doomed by a series of unfortunate events including a short spell in prison for David, Jade's parents' divorce and the death of her father. They intend to say goodbye at the funeral but realise their love is still strong. Based on the book by Scott Spencer.
BBFC:AA — S,A — EN
Keith Barish-Dyson Lovell Production — *Polygram Video*   **H, P**
790 403

Endless Summer, The Fll-Ent '66
Sports-Water/Travel
12823   90 mins   C
B, V
Directed by Bruce Brown
This film is about two California surfers' world-wide search for the perfect wave which they eventually find on a beach near Durban, South Africa.
BBFC:U — S,A — EN
Pacific Arts; Bruce Brown Films — *VideoSpace Ltd*   **P**
PA2

Enemy Below Fll-Ent '57
War-Drama
07703   98 mins   C
V2, B, V
Robert Mitchum, Curt Jurgens, Kurt Kreuger, Theodore Bikel, Russell Collins, Al Hedison, directed by Dick Powell
The Captain of an American destroyer on anti-submarine patrol in the South Atlantic and the Commander of a German U Boat, both of whom have faced personal tragedy as a result of the war, engage in a duel of bluff and double bluff in the Atlantic.
S,A — EN
Twentieth Century Fox — *CBS/Fox Video*   **P**
1133

Enfants du Paradis, Les Fll-Ent '45
Drama
08549   180 mins   B/W
B, V
Arletty, Jean-Louis Barrault, Pierre Brasseur, Pierre Renoir, Marie Casares, directed by Marcel Carne
This is the original version of the film with English subtitles. It is about the lives and dreams of a small band of Bohemian actors. In the beginning it deals with the poverty and struggle for existence in the slums and then follows the heroine into high society, when she marries a wealthy count.
BBFC:A — S,A — EN
Pathe Cinema — *THORN EMI*   **P**
TXC 90 0825 4/TVC 90 0825 2

Enforcer, The Fll-Ent '76
Drama
06040   93 mins   C
B, V
Clint Eastwood, Harry Guardino, Bradford Dillman, John Mitchum, Tyne Daly, directed by James Fargo
The San Francisco detective 'Dirty Harry' is assigned to deal with enemy agents who successfully steal Army weapons and then proceed to kidnap the mayor of San Francisco.
BBFC:X — A — EN
Warner Bros; Robert Daly Prod — *Warner Home Video*   **P**
WEX1082/WEV1082

England Made Me Fll-Ent '73
Drama
02086   90 mins   C
B, V
Peter Finch, Michael York, Hildegard Neil, Michael Horden
'England Made Me,' adapted from Graham Greene's fourth novel, is set in the late 1930's which are clouded by the depression in England. Filmed on location in Yugoslavia and Germany.
C,A — EN
Cine Globe, Jack Levine Prods — *VCL Video Services*   **P**

England's Year 1979/80 Spo-Lei '8?
Sports
13535   32 mins   C
B, V
2 pgms
Don Rutherford (RFU) and Bill Beaumont discuss England's strategy and comment on excerpts from the international matches.
1.Play from Scrum Ball 2.Play from Line Out Ball.
F — EN
Unknown — *TFI Leisure Ltd*   **H, P**

Enigma Fll-Ent '81
Drama/Suspense
09461   99 mins   C
V2, B, V

216   (For Explanation of codes, see USE GUIDE and KEY)

PALADIN VIDEO HOME ENTERTAINMENT GUIDE

Martin Sheen, Brigette Fossey, Sam Neill, directed by Jeannot Szwarc
Five highly trained KGB assassins are sent on a mission to eliminate five Soviet dissidents. The date of the execution is well known to Western Intelligence but not the names of the victims. The only way to get this information is to steal a coded micro-processor kept under maximum security in Moscow.
BBFC:15 — C,A — EN
Filmcrest Intl Corp.; Peter Shaw Prod. — *Guild Home Video* **H, P, E**

Enigma of Kaspar Hauser, The   Fil-Ent '75
Drama
07741   110 mins   C
B, V
Bruno S, Walter Ladengast, directed by Werner Horzog
Based on a true incident, this film follows the life of a strange, unkempt boy discovered in May 1828 in the townsquare of Nuremberg clutching a prayerbook and a letter. Hardly able to walk, just able to write his name and only able to say 'I want to be a gallant rider like my father was' he spent a period as a circus freak being taught to appreciate the wonders of nature and music. Five years later he is found stabbed to death with a mysterious letter in his hand.
S,A — EN
Cinema 5 — *Palace Video Ltd*   **P**

Enjoy Better Golf: Basic Principles   Spo-Lei '81
Golf
05416   60 mins   C
B, V, FO
Tommy Horton
A programme for golfers of all ability levels in which Tommy Horton, a leading international professional and respected teacher gets down to the basic principles with Michael Barratt. Includes grip, stance, swing, tee and fairway shots, pitching, putting and 'splashing' out of bunkers.
F — I
Commercial Video Ltd; Cognac Courvoisier — *Michael Barratt Ltd*   **P**

Enjoy Better Golf 2: Tips from the Masters   Spo-Lei '82
Golf
09096   30 mins   C
B, V
Tommy Horton
In this programme Tommy Horton and Michael Barratt learn some of the personal secrets of International stars. Fuzzy Zoeller, Hubert Green, Graham Marsh, Des Smyth demonstrate their skills how to tee up, how to stop hooking, hitting out backwards, long grass shots, and many more hints from players at the Dunlop Masters Tournament at St. Pierre.
F — I
Commercial Video Ltd; Cognac Courvoisier — *Michael Barratt Ltd*   **P**

Enola Gay   Fil-Ent '80
War-Drama
09193   156 mins   C
B, V
Patrick Duffy, Gregory Harrison, Kim Darby, directed by David Lowell Rich
Set in August, 1945 this film tells the story of the dropping of the atomic bomb on Hiroshima. It recreates the planning of this top-secret mission, as well as the human drama and romantic attachments experienced by the crew.
S,A — EN
Viacom — *Video Form Pictures*   **H, P**
MGS 5

Ensemble   Gen-Edu '84
Languages-Instruction
13386   120 mins   C
B, V
This programme provides a French instruction course for beginners with the emphasis very much on communication.
AM Available   F — I
Unknown — *BBC Video*   **H, P**
1027

Enter the Devil   Fil-Ent '71
Horror
07892   83 mins   C
V2, B, V
Josh Bryant, Irene Kelly, Dave Cass, directed by Frank Q Dobbs
After a series of strange incidents thought to be accidents, the suspicions of a Sheriff are aroused. Together with a lady professor studying the occult they begin an investigation which leads to them witnessing the sacrifice of a young girl. The satanic worshippers become aware of their presence and give chase.
S,A — EN
Gold Key — *Video Programme Distributors* **P**
Inter-Ocean—059

Enter the Dragon   Fil-Ent '73
Adventure/Martial arts
01249   90 mins   C
B, V
Bruce Lee, John Saxon, Jim Kelly

(For Explanation of codes, see USE GUIDE and KEY)   217

PALADIN VIDEO HOME ENTERTAINMENT GUIDE

Martial arts film starring Bruce Lee, with spectacular fighting sequences featuring karate, judo, tai kwan do, tai chi chuan, and hapkido techniques.
C,A — EN   EL, SP
Warner Bros — *Warner Home Video*   P

Enter the Streetfighter Fil-Ent '7?
Martial arts/Adventure
09076   90 mins   C
B, V
Sonny Chiba, Gerald Yamada, Doris Nakajima, Tony Setera
This film tells of the notorious 'streetfighter' who takes on the government police, Mafia and an international ring of kidnappers aiming to dispossess a beautiful young heiress of her millions, in a bid to conquer corruption and evil.
S,A — EN
Unknown — *Video Tape Centre*   P
VTC 1042

Entertaining Electron, The Gen-Edu '??
Television/Video
09470   52 mins   C
B, V
Frankie Howard
This tape presents a unique and revealing insight into the world of the television programme maker and broadcaster. It also shows how sound and pictures are transmitted all over the world and how video itself works.
S,A — ED
Unknown — *Guild Home Video*   H, P, E

Entertaining Mr Sloane Fil-Ent '70
Comedy-Drama
05437   90 mins   C
B, V
Beryl Reid, Harry Andrews, Peter McEnery, Alan Webb, directed by Douglas Hickox
A black comedy of collision between high-minded appearances and crudely realistic appetites. The story of a brother and sister who take in a lodger and by 'blackmail' persuade him to stay to make up a queer 'menage a trois.' He becomes a prisoner of desire. The film marks the end of the 'anything goes' era of the sixties, written by Joe Orton.
BBFC:X — A — EN
Unknown — *THORN EMI*   P
TXC 90 0246 4/TVC 90 0246 2

Entity, The Fil-Ent '82
Horror
12007   119 mins   C
B, V
Barbara Hershey, directed by Sidney Furie
Based on events which took place in California in 1976, a woman is repeatedly attacked and raped in her own home by a force she cannot see, only feel.
C,A — EN
20th Century Fox — *CBS/Fox Video*   P
1234-40

Equinox Fil-Ent '71
Horror
02461   78 mins   C
B, V
Edward Connell, Barbara Hewitt, directed by Jack Woods
Four teenagers look for a missing archaeologist and instead discover an ancient book on devil worship. The devil himself appears in human form.
A — EN
VIP Distributors — *Mountain Video*   P

Equus Fil-Ent '77
Drama
12598   132 mins   C
B, V
Richard Burton, Peter Firth, Colin Blakely, Joan Plowright, Jenny Agutter, directed by Sidney Lumet
A teenage boy commits a bizarre and shocking crime and is treated by a psychiatrist who starts to question his own sense of vocation.
BBFC:15 — C,A — EN
Lester Persky; Elliot Kastner — *Warner Home Video*   P
99426

Eraserhead Fil-Ent '78
Film-Avant-garde
07737   90 mins   B/W
B, V
Directed by David Lynch
This surrealist film combines both repulsive beauty and grisly comedy as the fuzzy-haired hero ends up with his head being processed and reduced to thousands of tiny erasers for the ends of pencils.
A — EN
Libra Films — *Palace Video Ltd*   P

Eric Fil-Ent '75
Drama
09856   95 mins   C
B, V
John Savage, Mark Hamill, Patricia Neal, Claude Akins

PALADIN VIDEO HOME ENTERTAINMENT GUIDE

This is the story of a young man suffering from a terminal illness and the love and support afforded him by his close-knit family.
F — EN
Lorimar Prods; NBC — Polygram Video
H, P
040 1334/0401332

Eric Clapton, On Whistle Test Fil-Ent '84
Music-Performance
13399 60 mins C
B, V
This concert was recorded during his 1977 tour with a band and singer Yvonne Elliman and the ten numbers include 'Hello Old Friend,' 'I Shot the Sheriff,' 'Sign Language' and 'Badge.'
S,A — EN
Unknown — BBC Video **H, P**

Ernani Fil-Ent '82
Opera
08672 138 mins C
B, V
Placido Domingo, Mirella Freni, Renato Bruson, Nicolai Ghiaurov, directed by Preben Montell
This is Verdi's fifth opera, written in 1844, based on Victor Hugo's play. It is performed in four acts, at La Scala, Milan and conducted by Riccardo Muti. It tells of the suave King Charles of Spain and a proud Spanish grandee whose inplacable sense of humour propels the action to its tragic conclusion.
S,A — EN
Ente Autonomo; National Video Corp Ltd — Longman Video **P**
LGBE 7005/LGVH 7005

Erotic Adventures of Zarro, The Fil-Ent '??
Adventure
08686 84 mins C
V2, B, V
Douglas Frey, Robyn Whitting, Penny Boran, John Alderman, Lynn Harris, Michelle Simon, directed by Col. Robert Freeman
Don Diego, Spain's greatest horseman, swordsman and lover, is summoned to a small quiet town to rid it of its lecherous Mayor and his henchman. During the day he becomes an ordinary townfolk, but by night, he becomes the masked avenger, leaping from roof tops and balconies to bedchambers.
BBFC:X — A — EN
Unknown — Derann Film Services **P**
84

Erotic Inferno Fil-Ent '75
Suspense
02101 82 mins C
V2, B, V
When a businessman disappears, his two sons, his illegitimate son, his all-purpose housekeeper and his eldest son's girlfriend spend a weekend they will never forget, as they wait for the old man's last will. Sexual and mercenary lusts are extended to the full.
BBFC:X — A — EN
English Film Company Prods — Hokushin Audio Visual Ltd **P**
VM-07

Eroticise Fil-Ent '82
Fantasy/Physical fitness
12875 60 mins C
B, V
Directed by Ed Hansen
The voluptuous kitten Natividad has her very own brand of sensual aerobics exercises in this tape.
A — EN
Pisanti Productions — Vestron Video International **P**
13018

Eroticist, The Fil-Ent '80
Drama
12856 85 mins C
V2, B, V
Lionel Stander, Lando Buzzanca, Anita Strindberg, Francis Blanche
A senator who is running for presidency cannot keep his hands off women and is pursuaded to go into a short spiritual retirement in a convent.
BBFC:18 — A — EN
Unknown — Video Programme Distributors
P
228

Escapade in Japan/A Gift for Heidi Fil-Ent '??
Adventure
05765 174 mins C
B, V
Cameron Mitchell, Teresa Wright, Jon Provost, Roger Nakagawa, Philip Ober, directed by Arthur Lubin, Sandy Descher, Douglas Fowley, directed by William Cruikshank
Two films are contained on one cassette. 'Escapade in Japan' (colour, 89 mins, 1958) is an account of a plane crash and its seven year old survivor who believes the police are after him so he runs away with a Japanese boy, his parents desperately try to trace him. Shot on location in Japan. 'A Gift for Heidi' (colour, 75 mins, 1960) in which Heidi receives a gift of a carving depicting Faith, Hope and Charity. She

(For Explanation of codes, see USE GUIDE and KEY)

PALADIN VIDEO HOME ENTERTAINMENT GUIDE

learns the meaning of her gift when she hears a boy singing Ave Maria, encounters a haughty intruder from the city and helps rescue a man from an avalanche.
F — EN
RKO — Kingston Video   H, P
KV17

Escape from Alcatraz   Fil-Ent '79
Drama
05330   112 mins   C
B, V
Clint Eastwood, Patrick McGoohan, directed by Don Siegel
This film shot on location in Alcatraz is the reenactment of the story of the only three men ever to escape from the infamous maximum security prison. The escape was masterminded in fine detail by a bank robber despite the suspicions of one of the wardens. The escape, as far as anyone knows, was successful as the three men were never heard of again.
S,A — EN
Universal — CIC Video   H, P
BEA2015/VHA2015

Escape from Angola   Fil-Ent '7?
Adventure
07992   ? mins   C
B, V
Stan Brock, Anne Collings, Ivan Tors
This is a spectacular adventure story filmed in the vast African veldt. It tells of the trials and triumph of a family in their struggle to survive on one of the world's last frontiers.
S,A — EN
Unknown — Motion Epics Video Company Ltd   P
159

Escape From Cell Block 3   Fil-Ent '7?
Crime-Drama
07973   83 mins   C
B, V
Carolyn Judd, Teri Gusman, Darlene Mattingly, Angel Colbert, Bonita Kalem, directed by Kent Osborne
This film tells the story of five women who break out of a tough jail. It continues with them desperately trying to evade the police, which includes car chases and shoot-outs.
C,A — EN
Unknown — AVI Video Ltd   P
005

Escape from Galaxy III   Fil-Ent '??
Science fiction
07627   85 mins   C
B, V
Cheryl Buchanon, James Milton, Don Powell, directed by Ben Norman
During a cosmic war the beautiful Princess Bellastar and Captain Lithan battle against the evil forces of Ureklon the King of the Night. They crash land on a distant planet inhabited by beautiful people who teach them the joys of love. They almost forget the dark dangers, but Ureklon is hot on their trail.
S,A — EN
Unknown — VCL Video Services   P
P256D

Escape from New York   Fil-Ent '81
Science fiction/Adventure
08337   106 mins   C
V2, B, V, LV
Kurt Russell, Lee Van Cleef, Issac Hayes, Ernest Borgnine, Donald Pleasance, Harry Dean Stanton, Adrienne Barbeu
In 1997, the island of Manhattan has been turned into a maximum security prison inhabited by millions of felons. When the President's plane crashes there, a convicted criminal is sent in to save him.
BBFC:X — A — EN
AVCO Embassy — Embassy Home Entertainment   P
1602

Escape to Athena   Fil-Ent '79
Adventure
02042   115 mins   C
B, V
Roger Moore, Telly Savalas, David Niven, Stephanie Powers, Claudia Cardinale
Specially-assigned POW's dig for Greek art treasures while under the watchful eye of a Greek antique-loving Austrian commandant.
S,A — EN
David Niven Jr, Jack Weiner — Precision Video Ltd   P
BITC 3012/VITC 3012

Escape to the Sun   Fil-Ent '72
Drama/Romance
08053   96 mins   C
B, V
Laurence Harvey, John Ireland, Jack Hawkins, Josephine Chapin, Yuda Barkan, Leila Kedrova, Gila Almagor, Clive Reville, directed by Menahem Golan
This film tells the dramatic story of two young lovers. In an attempt to flee from their communist country they skyjack a plane to try to start a fresh life.
BBFC:AA — S,A — EN
Menahem Golan — Rank Video Library
H, P
0117C

PALADIN VIDEO HOME ENTERTAINMENT GUIDE

Escape to Victory   Fil-Ent '81
War-Drama
07392   116 mins   C
V2, B, V
Sylvester Stallone, Michael Caine, Max Von Sydow, Pele
Set in 1943, a team of Allied prisoners of war are manipulated into playing a propaganda football game against the German National Team. To the Allied team victory is vital.
BBFC:A — S,A — EN
Paramount — Guild Home Video   H, P, E

Escape to Witch Mountain   Fil-Ent '75
Fantasy/Adventure
12576   91 mins   C
B, V
Ray Milland, Donald Pleasance, Kim Richards, Ike Eisenmann, Eddie Albert
Two Young orphans with supernatural powers are adopted by a ruthless millionaire who plans to hold them captive and use their psychic gifts for his own selfish purposes.
F — EN
Walt Disney Productions — Rank Video Library   H
013

Essential Mike Oldfield, The   Fil-Ent '8?
Music-Performance/Documentary
07952   70 mins   C
B, V
This tape features Mike Oldfield live in concert at Knebworth Festival performing some of his most successful compositions, 'Tubular Bells,' 'Ommadawn' and 'Guilty.' He is also interviewed at home in his studio, which offers insight into his life and music.
S,A — EN
Virgin Video — VideoSpace Ltd   P
VVI

Eureka   Fil-Ent '83
Drama
12678   125 mins   C
B, V
Gene Hackman, Rutger Hauer, Jane Lapotaire, Theresa Russell, directed by Nicolas Roeg
The true story of an eccentric millionaire whose obsessive and stormy relationships with the people around him eventually leads to his brutal and bizarre murder and an intriguing court case.
BBFC:18 — A — EN
Jeremy Thomas — Warner Home Video   P
99424

Eureka Stockade   Fil-Ent '83
Adventure
12520   200 mins   C
B, V
Bryan Brown, Carol Burns, Bill Hunter, Amy Madigan, Brett Cullen, Penelope Stewart, directed by Rod Hardy
This is the story of the historic rebellion of the people of the Australian town of Ballarat against the government's restriction on their right to dig for gold.
A — EN
Unknown — THORN EMI   P
TXA 90 2349 4 /TVA 90 23492 2

Europa '80   Spo-Lei '80
Football
06743   50 mins   C
V2, B, V
The official film of the European Football Championship.
F — EN
West Nally-Samuelson — Intervision Video
H, P
A-AE 0350

Europeans, The   Fil-Ent '79
Drama/Romance
05681   92 mins   C
B, V
Lee Remick, Robin Ellis, directed by James Ivory
This film is set in the countryside around Boston in 1850. A Baroness and her brother have come from Europe to seek out wealthy American cousins they had heard of but never met, in an attempt to improve their own fortunes. The film is based on an early novel by Henry James, characteristically it is a story of European experience versus American innocence.
BBFC:A — S,A — EN
Merchant Ivory Productions — Home Video Holdings   H, P
008

Even Better Rugby   Spo-Lei '82
Sports
13540   32 mins   C
B, V
This film shows excerpts from 'Better Rugby' inter-related with material filmed at Twickenham and illustrates how progressive development may be achieved.
F — EN
Unknown — TFI Leisure Ltd   H, P

Evening with Charles Aznavour, An   Fil-Ent '82
Music-Performance
07662   60 mins   C

PALADIN VIDEO HOME ENTERTAINMENT GUIDE

B, V
On this cassette Charles Aznavour performs many of his best-loved songs. Recorded at the Duke of York theatre in London songs include: 'She,' 'Ava Maria,' 'What Makes a Man,' 'The Old-Fashioned Way', 'Yesterday, When I Was Young,' 'We Had It All,' 'Etre,' 'Between Us,' 'Mon Ami, Mon Judas' and many more.
F — EN
VCL Video — *VCL Video Services*   P
Z244G

Evening With Liza Minnelli, An   Fil-Ent '81
Music-Performance/Variety
07450   50 mins   C
B, V
Liza Minnelli, directed by Fred Ebb
This is a film of the live show given by Liza Minnelli in the New Orleans Theater of the Performing Arts in 1980. She performs a blend of song, dance, theatre and comedy. Numbers include 'Keep You From The Rain,' 'Arthur In The Afternoon,' 'City Lights,' 'The Lord Must Be In New York City,' 'Lullaby Of Broadway,' 'New York, New York' and 'Life Is A Cabaret.'
S,A — EN
Artel Home Video — *THORN EMI*   P
TXE 90 0706 4/TVE 90 0706 2

Everly Brothers—Album Flash, The   Fil-Ent '84
Music-Performance
13132   30 mins   C
B, V
This programme features four tracks from the Everly Brothers and includes interviews with them.
F — EN
Unknown — *Polygram Video*   P
041 0614/041 0612

Everly Brothers Reunion Concert, The   Fil-Ent '83
Music-Performance
12217   65 mins   C
B, V
Recorded live at London's Albert Hall, The Everly Brothers are back on stage for the first time in a decade with all their hits including 'Bye Bye Love', 'All I Have to Do Is Dream', 'Be Bop A Lula' and 'Cathys Clown.'
BBFC:U — F — EN
Delilah Films; The Everly Brothers — *MGM/UA Home Video*   P
10331

Every Home Should Have One   Fil-Ent '70
Comedy
07482   90 mins   C
B, V
Marty Feldman, Shelley Berman, Julie Ege, Penelope Keith, directed by Jim Clark
A naive but enthusiastic advertising agent is given the task of providing a new sexy image for a brand of frozen porridge. This satire of the advertising and television industries was written by Marty Feldman, Barry Took and Dennis Norden.
S,A — EN
Unknown — *THORN EMI*   P
TXB 90 0311 4/TVB 90 0311 2

Every Which Way But Loose   Fil-Ent '78
Comedy/Adventure
06044   101 mins   C
B, V
Clint Eastwood, Sondra Locke, Geoffrey Lewis, Bevery D'Angelo, Ruth Gordon, directed by James Fargo
A good natured trucker in love with a lady singer pursues her across the south west. He is also a bar-room brawler and enlists the help of his friends, a fight promoter and an orangutan, to find the girl. However, they are trailed by a disgruntled motorcycle gang and two policemen who have taken a holiday to settle an account with the trucker.
BBFC:AA — S,A — EN
Warner Bros — *Warner Home Video*   P
WEX1028/WEV1028

Everything You Always Wanted to Know About Sex But Were Afraid to Ask   Fil-Ent '72
Comedy
13041   88 mins   C
B, V
Woody Allen, John Carradine, Lou Jacobi, Louise Lasser, Anthony Quayle, Lynn Redgrave, Burt Reynolds, Gene Wilder, directed by Woody Allen
A visual conception of the book by Dr Rueben in which each of the seven episodes depict an aspect of sex.
BBFC:X — A — EN
United Artists Corp — *Warner Home Video*   P
99238

Everything You Always Wanted to Know About Sex (But Were Afraid to Ask)   Fil-Ent '72
Comedy
01270   85 mins   C
V2, B, V

PALADIN VIDEO HOME ENTERTAINMENT GUIDE

Woody Allen, John Carradine, Lou Jacobi, Louise Lasser, Anthony Quayle, Lynn Redgrave, Tony Randall, Burt Reynolds, Gene Wilder, directed by Woody Allen
A series of comical sketches involving sex, such as a timid sperm cell, an oversexed court jester, and a giant disembodied breast.
BBFC:X — A — EN
United Artists — *Intervision Video* **H**
UA A B 5000

Everything You Always Wanted to Know About Computers But Were Afraid to Ask   Fil-Ent '84
Electronic data processing
13424   88 mins   C
B, V
Lewis Grenville, Susan Whitcomb, Patrice Colihan, Elizabeth Zasso, directed by Stephen Mantell
This programme demonstrates, with the help of a typical family group, how to choose a home computer and answers a lot of questions for those who work regularly with computers.
F — ED
Unknown — *MGM/UA Home Video* **P**
10460

Evidence of Power   Fil-Ent '79
Crime-Drama
07891   92 mins   C
V2, B, V
Steve Wayne Carry, Rae LeBlond, James Matz, Gordon Jump, Alan Hale, directed by Vern Piehl
Bizarre deaths and mysterious accidents invade the summer peace of a small town. The police chief and his criminology student son disagree over their investigation and part company. The chief becomes victim number five. The son and an old friend start a relentless search to find the killer, hindered by a patrolman who they suspect. Woken in the night by gun fire, the son runs into the square, only to have his life saved by the patrolman, who shoots the killer.
S,A — EN
Vern Piehl — *Walton Film and Video Ltd* **P**

Evil, The   Fil-Ent '78
Horror
07680   96 mins   C
B, V
Richard Crenna, Joanna Pettit, Andrew Prine, Victor Buono, directed by Gus Trikonis
A group of people led by a psychologist and his wife set out to re-build a long abandoned eerie mansion. In the cellar the doctor manages with great difficulty to open a dust-covered trap door. An all-powerful 'force' rages out, causing a series of unexplainable events, overtaking everyone and causing havoc. After deadly accidents occur, the doctor manages to confront the 'force,' allowing enough time for those left to escape.
A — EN
New World Pictures — *Video Network* **P**
0008

Evil Dead, The   Fil-Ent '82
Horror
08970   90 mins   C
B, V
Bruce Campbell, Ellen Sandweiss, Betsy Baker, Hal Delrich, Sarah York, directed by Sam Raimi
Whilst on holiday in the Tennessee woodlands, five innocent teenagers unknowingly release the spirit of the 'Evil Dead'. This first possesses the trees, and then the bodies of the people themselves. One by one the teenagers fall victim to this evil demon, until there is one left. Alone, he solves the mystery to the horrific terror.
BBFC:X — A — EN
Unknown — *Palace Video Ltd* **P**
PVC 2018A

Evil that Men Do, The   Fil-Ent '84
Drama
13478   86 mins   C
V2, B, V
Charles Bronson, Rene Enriquez, Jorge Luke, Joseph Maher, Raymond St. Jacques, Teresa Saldana, Nicole Thomas, Jose Ferrer
A professional assassin is brought out of retirement in the Caribbean to avenge the murder of one of his friends. He finds he has to dispose of his bodyguards before he can reach him.
BBFC:18 — A — EN
Pancho Kohner — *Precision Video Ltd* **P**
3150

Evil Under the Sun   Fil-Ent '82
Mystery/Suspense
08464   112 mins   C
B, V
Peter Ustinov, Jane Birkin, Colin Blakely, Nicholas Clay, James Mason, Roddy McDowall, Sylvia Miles, Denis Quilley, Diana Rigg, Maggie Smith, directed by Guy Hamilton
Adapted from the novel by Agatha Christie, this film, set at a luxury hotel on an exclusive Mediterranean isle, follows the fortunes of the strange collection of guests. After a girl is strangled on the beach a Belgian detective tries to find out who is the guilty party. However, they all have a motive but an equally good alibi.
BBFC:A — S,A — EN
EMI Films; Titan Productions — *THORN EMI* **P**
TXA 90 07084/TVA 90 0708 2

PALADIN VIDEO HOME ENTERTAINMENT GUIDE

Evilspeak   Fil-Ent '81
Suspense
10096   91 mins   C
B, V
Clint Howard, Don Stark, Lou Gravance, Lauren Lester
Set in a U.S. military academy, the forces of satanic evil are summoned by an unfortunate young student using the school computer. He unleashes a variety of horrors including a herd of razor-tusked wild boars.
BBFC:R — *A* — *EN*
Leisure Investments — *VideoSpace Ltd*
P

Excalibur   Fil-Ent '83
Cartoons/Adventure
09147   60 mins   C
B, V
Animated
In company with Lancelot, Arthur sets out to seek the truth of King Uther's death. They are pursued on their journey by the dreaded Black Knights, but join forces with Sir Tristram and escape. Their exploits lead to the finding of the legendary sword Excalibur and the beginning of further adventures.
F — EN
ZIV International — *Video Brokers*   **H, P**
012C

Excalibur   Fil-Ent '81
Drama/Fantasy
13056   140 mins   C
B, V
Nicol Williamson, Nigel Terry, Helen Mirren, Nicholas Clay, Cherie Lunghi
The Arthurian legend and Camelot are given an intriguing twist in this visually stunning film shot on location in Ireland.
BBFC:AA — *C,A* — *EN*
Orion Pictures Co — *Warner Home Video*
P
72018

Executioner on the High Seas, The   Fil-Ent '77
Adventure
07780   90 mins   C
V2, B, V
Richard Harrison, Michele Mercier
A bloodthirsty, swashbuckling tale of pirates on the high seas.
F — EN
Unknown — *Fletcher Video*   **H, P**
V116

Executioner's Song, The   Fil-Ent '82
Drama
10133   200 mins   C
B, V
Tommy Lee Jones, Rosanna Arquette, Eli Wallach
This film tells the true story of Gary Gilmore, a man who spent most of his life in prison. When he was found guilty of two murders he insisted that the State of Utah execute him by firing squad. The screen-play was written by Norman Mailer based on his Pulitzer Prize winning book.
BBFC:15 — *S,A* — *EN*
Lawrence Schiller — *Palace Video Ltd*   **P**
VIRV 0014A

Existance   Fil-Ent '74
Drama
05494   86 mins   C
V2, B, V
Jack Wild, June Brown, directed by David Hemmings
A story of fourteen children in the East End of London who are left to fend for themselves when their Mother dies. The eldest fights to maintain this down and out family in the Slums, torn between his promise to his dying mother and his inability to provide hope.
BBFC:U — *F — EN*
Unknown — *Iver Film Services*   **P**
41

Exit the Dragon, Enter the Tiger   Fil-Ent '76
Adventure/Martial arts
04121   84 mins   C
B, V
Bruce Li
A martial arts teacher is shocked to learn about the death of his friend, Bruce Lee. He sets out to unravel some of the rumours surrounding his death.
C,A — EN
Dimension — *Video Programme Distributors*
P
Inter-Ocean—005

Exorcism   Fil-Ent '??
Horror
08896   86 mins   C
V2, B, V
Maria Perschy
The beautiful young daughter of an English aristocrat, whilst searching for new kicks, leads herself and her boyfriend into evil, and is nearly killed as a result.
BBFC:X — *A* — *EN*
Unknown — *Video Programme Distributors*
P
Canon 008

(For Explanation of codes, see USE GUIDE and KEY)

PALADIN VIDEO HOME ENTERTAINMENT GUIDE

Exorcist, The   Fil-Ent '73
Drama
01247   120 mins   C
B, V
Ellen Burstyn, Linda Blair, Jason Miller, Max Von Sydow, directed by William Friedkin
A harrowing film based on William Peter Blatty's novel of a young girl who is possessed by a demon, raising havoc with her family and the priests who attempt to exorcise her.
C,A — EN
Warner Bros — *Warner Home Video*   P

Exorcist II—The Heretic   Fil-Ent '77
Drama/Suspense
06029   113 mins   C
B, V
Linda Blair, Richard Burton, Louise Fletcher, Max Von Sydow, Kitty Winn, Paul Heinreid, James Earl Jones, Ned Beatty, directed by John Boorman
This film is the sequel to the 'Exorcist.' Four years have passed and the girl is now a teenager still in the hands of the psychiatrist, who examines what she can remember and how she is still suffering the residual effects of her demonic possession. The evil power is traced to Africa and the cult of the locust.
BBFC:X — S,A — EN
Warner Bros; John Boorman Prod — *Warner Home Video*   P
WEX1023/WEV1023

Explorers on the Moon   Chl-Juv '7?
Cartoons/Adventure
02282   60 mins   C
V
Animated
Professor Calculus, Snowy, Captain Haddock, and Tin Tin land on the moon where evil forces put them in extreme danger.
M — EN
Unknown — *JVC*   P
PRT 5

Exposed   Fil-Ent '83
Drama
12991   96 mins   C
B, V
Nastassia Kinski, Harvey Keitel, Ian McShane, Rudolf Nureyev, directed by James Toback
A young college student finds herself hailed as a top model but is drawn into a web of violence and destruction when she becomes attracted to a mysterious concert violinist.
BBFC:15 — S,A — EN
United Artists — *Warner Home Video*   P
99451

Espresso Bongo   Fil-Ent '59
Musical
12082   100 mins   B/W
V2, B, V
Cliff Richard, Laurence Harvey, Sylvia Syms
Set in London in the 50's, hip coffee bars, beat girls, shady Soho nightclubs, this film shows the rise of a teen-age idol and is based on the real-life story of Tommy Steele. Cliff Richard's songs include 'Love', 'A Voice in the Wilderness' and 'The Shrine on the Second Floor'.
BBFC:A — S,A — EN
British Lion; Continental — *Videomedia*
P
PVM 0808/RVM 0808/HVM 0808

Exterminator, The   Fil-Ent '80
Adventure
06777   99 mins   C
V2, B, V
Christopher George, Samantha Eggar, Robert Ginty, Stan Getz
A Vietnam War veteran decides to avenge a youth gang's attack on his friend.
S,A — EN
Avco Embassy — *Intervision Video*   H, P
A-A 0353

Exterminators of the Year 3000   Fil-Ent '83
Drama/Adventure
12191   90 mins   C
V2, B, V
Alan Collins, Beryl Cunningham, Robert Jannucci, Luca Venantini
In a world devoid of water, small groups of people, desperately attempting to survive, struggle against evil marauding gangs who rape, murder and pillage.
BBFC:18 — A — EN
2T Productions — *Medusa Communications Ltd*   H, P

Extra Girl, The   Fil-Ent '23
Comedy
04677   65 mins   B/W
B, V
Mabel Normand, Ralph Graves, George Nicholls, Max Davidson
Packed with period Americana, this film tells the story of a typical small-town girl who wins a beauty contest through a misunderstanding and goes to Hollywood. This film is colour-tinted.
F — EN
Associated Exhibitors — *Polygram Video*   P

Eye for a Horse, An   Gen-Edu '8?
Animals
13519   35 mins   C

PALADIN VIDEO HOME ENTERTAINMENT GUIDE

B, V
Directed by Bill Latto
This is a film of practical information for all owners who wish to breed from their mares and all those people who are determined to maintain and improve the many breeds of horses and ponies that give such willing service to man.
C,A — I
Town and Country Productions — *TFI Leisure Ltd* **H, P**

Eye for an Eye, An   Fil-Ent '80
Adventure/Martial arts
08333   106 mins   C
V2, B, V, LV
Chuck Norris, Christopher Lee, Richard Roundtree, Matt Clark
This is a story of pursuit and revenge with Chuck Norris as an undercover cop pitted against San Francisco's underworld and high society.
BBFC:X — A — EN
Avco Embassy — *Embassy Home Entertainment*   **P**
1601

Eye of the Needle   Fil-Ent '81
Drama/Suspense
13059   106 mins   C
B, V
Donald Sutherland, Kate Nelligan, directed by Richard Marquand
In this World War II spy thriller set in Britain a top German agent codenamed 'The Needle,' heads for Scotland to rendezvous with a U-boat as British intelligence start to close on him, and then takes refuge on Storm Island.
BBFC:AA — C,A — EN
Juniper Films — *Warner Home Video*   **P**
99275

Eyes Behind the Stars   Fil-Ent '79
Science fiction
04468   90 mins   C
V2, B, V
Robert Hoffman, Nathalie Delon
A fashion photographer and his model are working in a meadow at sunset. Suddenly, an oppressive heaviness stills the air, and the two feel that they are being watched by someone...or something.
F — EN
Arabic — *Intervision Video*   **H**
A-AE 0161

Eyes of the Dragon   Fil-Ent '81
Drama/Suspense
09236   83 mins   C
B, V
Chris Mitchum
A top U.S. agent is assigned to track down a missing Russian scientist who is carrying a formula that could change the balance of world power. Whilst protecting the scientist's daughter he has to fend off both Russian and Chinese efforts to reach him first.
S,A — EN
Jack H Harris Prods — *Home Video Holdings* **H, P**

Eyewitness   Fil-Ent '70
Drama
05955   88 mins   C
B, V
Mark Lester, Lionel Jeffries, Susan George, Peter Vaughan, Tony Banner, Betty Marsden, Jeremy Kemp, directed by John Hough
This thriller is set in a Mediterranean island where a young boy has witnessed an assassination. However, he is not believed because of his day-dreaming habit of relating fanciful adventures. But he did see the assassin and the assassin saw him. The killer and his accomplice set out to silence the only eyewitness. Based on the novel by Mark Hebden.
BBFC:A — S,A — EN
Unknown — *Precision Video Ltd*   **P**
BITC 2051/VITC 2051

F

Fables of the Green Forest   Chi-Juv '7?
Fairy tales
02219   86 mins   C
V
Famous characters created by Thorton W. Burgess come to life in this delightful story.
M — EN
ZIV — *JVC*   **P**
PRT 27

Fabulous Adventures of Baron Munchausen, The   Chi-Juv '79
Fantasy
05568   78 mins   C
V2, B, V
Animated, written by France and Jean Image, music and songs by Michel Legrand, sung by Claude Lemesle
The story of a legendary Baron who invites all his friends to magnificent banquets and tells them amazing stories. He is summoned by the King of Trukesban who sends him on a mission

PALADIN VIDEO HOME ENTERTAINMENT GUIDE

where he meets a flying horse, gets swallowed by a gigantic whale, travels from the heart of a fiery volcano in a balloon and experiences many more fantastical adventures.
Moscow International Film Festival '79: Special Diploma and Prix du Jury   I,M — EN
Films Jean Image Production — *Videomedia*   **P**
BVM 2112/HVM 2112

Fabulous Fantastic Four, Cassette 2, The   Chl-Juv '??
Cartoons
12066   82 mins   C
V2, B, V
Animated
Four episodes are contained in this cassette: 'Medusa and the Inhumans', 'The Diamond of Doom'; 'The Mole Man' and 'The Fabulous Fantastic Four in The Olympics of Space'.
BBFC:U — PS,M — EN
Unknown — *Guild Home Video*   **H, P, E**

Fabulous Fantastic Four in Meet Dr. Doom, The   Fil-Ent '84
Cartoons
13358   66 mins   C
V2, B, V
Animated
When four people are exposed to cosmic rays they are transformed and given strange, fantastic powers. The three episodes on this cassette are titled 'The Phantom of Film City,' 'Meet Dr. Doom' and 'Calamity on the Campus.'
BBFC:U — F — EN
Marvel Comics — *Guild Home Video*   **H, P, E**
8429-3

Fabulous Funnies   Fil-Ent '78
Cartoons/Comedy
12178   55 mins   C
B, V
Animated
Meet the terrible twins Hans and Fritz, Broomhilda the witch and Nancy and Slugger in this terrific cartoon compilation.
F — EN
Filmation Association — *Select Video Limited*   **P**
3616/43

Face of Fu Manchu, The   Fil-Ent '65
Suspense
01595   96 mins   C
B, V
Christopher Lee, Nigel Green, Marion Crawford, directed by Don Sharp
Fu Manchu is suspected to be the instigator of a kidnapping involving a German scientist who has a formula for a deadly poisonous fluid.
BBFC:U — S,A — EN
Harry Alan Towers — *THORN EMI*   **P**
TXB 90 0098 4/TVB 90 0098 2

Face to Face   Fil-Ent '7?
Western
07792   113 mins   C
V2, B, V
Tomas Milian, William Berger
This story traces the transportation of conscience of two dying men, one a professor and the other a notorious bandit.
S,A — EN
Unknown — *Fletcher Video*   **H, P**
V124

Fade to Black   Fil-Ent '80
Horror
07925   100 mins   C
V2, B, V
Dennis Christopher, Tim Thomerson, Norman Burton, Morgan Paull, Gwynne Gilford, Eve Brent Ashe, James Luisi, Linda Kerridge, directed by Vernon Zimmerman
This is the horrifying story of a man who lives for the movies and re-enacts the scenes he watches.
BBFC:X — A — EN
Leisure Investment Co; Movie Ventures Ltd — *Video Programme Distributors*   **P**
Media—154

Fairy Tales   Chl-Juv '8?
Cartoons/Fairy tales
12555   77 mins   C
V2, B, V
Animated
This collection of classic stories brings to life the fairy tale worlds created by Hans Andersen and the Brothers Grimm.
UK Video Awards '82: Winner of Children's Category.   PS,I — EN
Unknown — *RPTA Video Ltd*   **H, P**

Fake Out   Fil-Ent '82
Crime-Drama
08528   89 mins   C
B, V
Pia Zadora, Telly Savalas, Desi Arnaz Jnr.

(For Explanation of codes, see USE GUIDE and KEY)

PALADIN VIDEO HOME ENTERTAINMENT GUIDE

This film tells the story of a girl, under pressure to testify against her gangland lover. Telly Savalas is a tough cop who tries to protect her from gangland corruption, and his partner falls for her.
C,A — EN
Unknown — *THORN EMI* **P**
TXA 90 1277 4 / TVA 90 1277 2

Falklands—Task Force South Gen-Edu '83
Armed Forces-GB/Documentary
08720 120 mins C
V2, B, V, LV
This shows the harrowing and heroic times of Britain's first naval campaign since the Suez crisis. This film portrays the grim reality of modern warfare and was produced in aid of the South Atlantic Fund.
F — ED
Gordon Carr — *BBC Video* **H, P**
BBCV 6016

Fall and Rise of Reginald Perrin, The Fil-Ent '7?
Comedy-Drama
09409 ? mins C
V2, B, V
Leonard Rossiter, Pauline Yates, John Barron
This is the first very popular series of the life of Reginald Perrin.
F — EN
BBC — *BBC Video* **H, P**
BBCV 7012

Fall of the Giants, The Fil-Ent '7?
War-Drama
04290 91 mins C
V2, B, V
Jack Palance
American Major Heston and four officers parachute into Nazi Germany on a secret Commando mission. They are joined by a German officer, Truniger. He visits Rommel with a proposition but he refuses to leave Germany with the Americans. Gestapo Major Wolf, suspecting the anti-Hitler plot, orders their arrest, but the German troops who storm the Americans' outpost are led by Truniger.
C,A — EN
Unknown — *Video Programme Distributors* **P**
Inter-Ocean—023

Fall of the House of Usher, The Fil-Ent '80
Horror
06953 95 mins C
B, V
Martin Landau, Robert Hays, Charlene Tilton, Ray Walston
A young architect visits the House of Usher to make some badly needed repairs. In a secret room he learns the secret of the building's horrific and blood-stained history. Based on the classic tale by Edgar Allen Poe.
S,A — EN
Schick Sunn Classic — *Home Video Merchandisers* **H, P**
028

Fall of the Roman Empire, The Fil-Ent '64
Drama
01688 178 mins C
V2, B, V
Sophia Loren, Stephen Boyd, Alec Guinness, James Mason, Christopher Plummer
The death of Emperor Marcus Aurelius heralds the decline of the mighty empire, for his tyrannical son ascends the throne. His licentious ways lead to civil discord and the abandonment of the virtues that made Rome great.
BBFC:A — S,A — EN
Paramount, Samual Bronston — *Intervision Video* **H, P**
A-A 0203

Fallen Idol Fil-Ent '49
Drama
01002 92 mins B/W
B, V
Sir Ralph Richardson, Bobby Henrey, Michele Morgan, directed by Carol Reed
A young boy wrongly believes that a man he idolises is guilty of murder, so the child tries to influence the police investigation. Screenplay by Graham Greene from his short story, 'The Basement Room.'
BBFC:A — F — EN
Selznick; Carol Reed — *THORN EMI* **P**
TXE 90 0040 4/TVE 90 0040 2

Falling in Love Again Fil-Ent '81
Romance/Drama
07601 95 mins C
V2, B, V
Elliott Gould, Susannah York, Kaye Ballard, Stuart Paul, Michelle Pfeiffer, directed by Steven Paul
A middle-aged dreamer longs for his youth spent in his dream-world of the Bronx. His wife tries to help him recreate those idyllic days but his obsession only serves to highlight the

PALADIN VIDEO HOME ENTERTAINMENT GUIDE

failures of his present existence. His wife decides she has had enough, but a night in New York brings them together again to shape a new future.
BBFC:A — S,A — EN
Unknown — *Iver Film Services* **P**
175

Falling Man, The Fil-Ent '68
Suspense/Drama
05476 86 mins C
V2, B, V
Henry Silva, Keenan Wynne, Beba Loncar
An ex-policeman whose career was ruined by a frame-up sets out to correct the wrong done to him. His family is scattered and the truth he uncovers brings sorrow to him and an ex-colleague who trusted him; before he dies a violent death he finds the murderer of his small son.
BBFC:X — A — EN
Cinegai and Jolly Film — *Iver Film Services* **P**
102

Falstaff Fin-Art '83
Opera
09781 139 mins C
B, V
Renato Bruson, Katia Ricciarelli, Leo Nucci, Barbara Hendricks, Dalmacio Gonzalez, Lucia Valentini-Terrani, Brenda Boozer
This production of Verdi's last opera is conducted by Carlo Maria Giulini after an absence of 14 years. It is based on Shakespeare's 'The Merry Wives of Windsor' and is performed by The Royal Opera at Covent Garden.
F — EN
Covent Garden Video Productions
Ltd. — *THORN EMI* **P**
TXH 90 17042/TVH 90 17042

Fame Fil-Ent '80
Musical/Drama
05302 133 mins C
V2, B, V
Eddie Barth, Irene Cara, Lee Curreri, directed by Alan Parker, choreography by Lewis Folcas
A story that follows the antics and disappointments of eight young and talented teenagers at New York's High School of Performing Arts. It combines drama, pulsating music and dancing; from Forty Second Street to the bright lights of Broadway they live out their dreams of fame.
S,A — EN
MGM — *MGM/UA Home Video* **P**
UMB10027/UMV10027

Family Enforcer Fil-Ent '7?
Drama
04550 81 mins C
V2, B, V
Joseph Cortese, Anne Johns, Lou Criscola, Joseph Pesci, Keith Davis, directed by Ralph DeVito
A young fiery hoodlum is hired by the mob to be a collector. As a self-styled enforcer, he uses any method to get the money. Yet he too may have to pay a price for being mixed up with the 'mob.'
C,A — EN
First American Films Release; John B Kelly
Presentation — *Intervision Video* **H, P**
A-AE 0289

Family Life Fil-Ent '71
Drama
00592 102 mins C
B, V
Sandy Ratcliff
A young girl's mildly irrational behaviour develops into an extreme form of schizophrenia. Her parents, believing they know what is best for her, commit her to a mental hospital where she undergoes two kinds of treatment.
BBFC:AA — C,A — EN
Tony Garnett — *THORN EMI* **P**
TXE 90 0099 4/TVE 90 0099 2

Family Man, The Fil-Ent '82
Drama/Romance
09095 94 mins C
V2, B, V
Edward Asner, Anne Jackson, Meredith Baxter Birney, directed by Glenn Jordan
A happily married man offers an attractive 24-year-old blonde the old chauffeur's quarters on the roof of his New York City garage as a practice room. They are at first only good friends, however, an affair soon develops. His guilty conscience grows, forcing him eventually to make a crucial decision.
S,A — EN
Time-Life Films — *Video Tape Centre* **P**
VTC 1065

Family Plot Fil-Ent '76
Mystery/Drama
13298 115 mins C
B, V
Barbara Harris, Cathleen Nesbitt, William Devane, Karen Black, directed by Alfred Hitchcock
Two underhand couples become involved with a wealthy old lady who is searching for her missing heir in this film of strange coincidences.
BBFC:PG — S,A — EN
Universal — *CIC Video* **H, P**
BEN 1095/VHN 1095

(For Explanation of codes, see USE GUIDE and KEY) **229**

PALADIN VIDEO HOME ENTERTAINMENT GUIDE

Family View Vol. 1 — Fil-Ent '81
Comedy/Fairy tales
08918   122 mins   C
V2
This cassette contains four family favourites: 'The Plank,' 'Rhubarb, Rhubarb,' 'The Pied Piper' and 'Cinderella.'
F — EN
D Kirkland; D Clark; M Hall; B Cosgrove — *THORN EMI*   **P**
TPB 90 0841 3

Famous Five—Five On A Secret Trail — Chi-Juv '84
Adventure
13096   90 mins   C
B, V
Four more stories from the Famous Five are featured on this tape titled 'Five Go On A Secret Trail,' 'Five Go to Billycock Hill', 'Five on Finniston Farm' and 'Five on a Hike Together'.
I,M — EN
Unknown — *Longman Video*   **P**
4013

Fan, The — Fil-Ent '81
Suspense/Drama
09265   95 mins   C
B, V
Lauren Bacall, Maureen Stapleton, James Garner, Hector Eizondo, directed by Edward Bianchi
A Broadway star is threatened by a lovestruck fan who feels he has been personally rejected by his idol.
BBFC:18 — *C,A — EN*
Paramount — *CIC Video*   **H, P**

Fanciulla del West, La — Fin-Art '8?
Opera
12517   130 mins   C
B, V
Puccini's opera is set in a mining town in the height of The Gold Rush. Carol Neblett sings the role of Minnie, Placido Domingo is Dick Johnson and Silvano Carroli is sheriff Jack Rance. It is recorded in stereo with sets by Ken Adam and is conducted by Nello Santi at The Royal Opera House.
F   EN
National Video Corporation Limited — *THORN EMI*   **P**
TXH 90 21984/TVH 90 21982

Fanny by Gaslight — Fil-Ent '44
Drama
13467   106 mins   B/W
B, V
James Mason, Stewart Granger, Phyllis Calvert
This is the famous Victorian melodrama and the story centres around the illegitimate daughter of a prominent politician.
BBFC:A — *C,A — EN*
Gainsborough — *Rank Video Library*   **H, P**
0204X

Fanny Hill — Fil-Ent '83
Drama
09891   87 mins   C
B, V
Lisa Raines, Wilfred Hyde-White, Alfred Marks, Oliver Reed, Shelley Winters
This film version of John Cleland's novel portrays all the eroticism and humour of the well-known 'memoirs of a woman of pleasure'.
BBFC:18 — *A — EN*
F.H. Productions — *Brent Walker Home Video Ltd*   **P**

Fantastic Plastic Machine, The — Fil-Ent '69
Adventure
06053   80 mins   C
B, V
Nat Young, Bob McTavish
An adventure that captures the performances of the world's greatest surfers.
F — EN
Crown Intl — *VCL Video Services*   **P**

Fantastic Voyage — Fil-Ent '66
Science fiction
01014   100 mins   C
B, V
Stephen Boyd, Edmond O'Brien, Raquel Welch, Arthur Kennedy, Donald Pleasence, Arthur O'Connell
A famous scientist, rescued from behind the Iron Curtain, is so severely wounded by enemy agents that surgery is impossible.
Academy Awards '66: Best Art Direction.
F — EN
20th Century Fox; Saul David — *CBS/Fox Video*   **P**
3A 010

Far East & Far Out, Council Meeting in Japan — Fil-Ent '84
Music video
13148   60 mins   C
B, V
The Style Council

PALADIN VIDEO HOME ENTERTAINMENT GUIDE

Shot at a live performance of the band in Japan, the tracks include 'The Big Boss Groove,' 'Here's One that Got Away,' 'It Just Came to Pieces in my Hands,' 'Money Go Round' and 'Speak Like a Child.'
F — EN
Polygram Music Video Ltd — *Polygram Video* **P**
040 3694/040 3692

Far from the Madding Crowd — Fil-Ent '67
Drama
01183   159 mins   C
B, V
Julie Christie, Alan Bates, Terence Stamp, Peter Finch, directed by John Schlesinger
An English farm heiress, courted by three men, marries the wrong man and regrets it when her fortune is almost lost due to his gambling. Based on a novel by Thomas Hardy.
BBFC:U — S,A — EN
MGM; Joseph Janni — *THORN EMI* **P**
TXB 90 0018 4/TVB 90 0018 2

Far Pavilions, The — Fil-Ent '83
Drama/Romance
12901   120 mins   C
B, V
Ben Cross, Amy Irving, Christopher Lee, Benedict Taylor, Omar Sharif, Robert Hardy
Based on the book by M M Kaye, this story is set in the late 19th century India, and portrays love, treachery and intrigue in a war-torn land.
C,A — EN
HBO; Goldcrest Films — *THORN EMI* **P**
TXJ 90 23674/TVJ 90 23672

Farewell My Lovely — Fil-Ent '75
Drama
02040   91 mins   C
B, V
Robert Mitchum, Charlotte Rampling, John Ireland, Sylvia Miles
A very tough private eye meets a very big ex-con who is searching for his old girlfriend whom he hasn't seen in seven years.
C,A — EN
Elliot Kastner — *Precision Video Ltd* **P**
BITC 2031/VITC 2031

Farewell to Arms, A — Fil-Ent '32
War-Drama/Romance
07635   75 mins   B/W
B, V
Gary Cooper, Helen Hayes, Adolphe Menjou, directed by Frank Borzage
An American adventurer joins the Italian Medical Service during the war. He falls in love with an English nurse. When he learns that she is going to have a baby, he deserts to search for her. He finds her too late and she dies in his arms as the Armistice is announced. Based on the novel by Ernest Hemingway.
F — EN
Paramount — *VCL Video Services* **P**
0234G

Farewell to Arms, A — Fil-Ent '57
War-Drama/Romance
07718   146 mins   C
V2, B, V
Rock Hudson, Jennifer Jones, Victorio de Sica, Alberto Sordi, Kurt Kasznar, Mercedes McCambridge, Oscar Homolka, Elaine Stritch, directed by Charles Vidor
Based on the novel by Ernest Hemingway, this is the story of a doomed romance between an American ambulance driver and a British nurse who cares for him when he is wounded. She reveals that she is pregnant and an unhappy incident leads to them deserting to Switzerland. There she dies during childbirth.
S,A — EN
David O. Selznick Productions — *CBS/Fox Video* **P**
1050

Farmer's Daughter, The — Fil-Ent '47
Comedy
04189   97 mins   B/W
B, V
Loretta Young, Joseph Cotten, Ethel Barrymore
A young Swedish servant girl makes a fight for a Congressional seat against a wealthy young Congressman, her boss and the man she loves. Academy Awards '47: Best Actress (Loretta Young).   BBFC:A — S,A — EN
Dore Schary; Selznick — *Guild Home Video* **H, P**

Farnborough International '84 — Gen-Edu '84
Aeronautics/Documentary
13105   40 mins   C
B, V
This programme shows highlights from the air display and features the F20 Tigershark, the Russian MIL helicopter, the Tornado F2 and the Skyship 600 airship.
F — EN
Quadrant Television; Reed Vision — *Quadrant Video* **H, P**

Farnborough International '82 — Gen-Edu '82
Aeronautics/Documentary
09124   49 mins   C
B, V

(For Explanation of codes, see USE GUIDE and KEY)

PALADIN VIDEO HOME ENTERTAINMENT GUIDE

This tape looks at a selection of aeroplanes and helicopters from the wide range of aircraft that took part in the 1982 Farnborough International Airshow.
F — EN
Flight Intl; Plessey Aerospace — *Quadrant Video* **H, P**
AV2

Farriery the Master Craft   How-Ins '83
Occupations/Animals
13514   35 mins   C
B, V
Directed by Bill Latto
The art and science of farriery is examined including all the individual skills of trimming, shoe making, fitting and nailing on. Training at Herefordshire Technical College is also shown.
S,A — V
Town and Country Productions — *TFI Leisure Ltd* **H, P**

Fast Company—Jackie Stewart   Spo-Lei '78
Automobiles-Racing
04418   30 mins   C
B, V
Former world champion racer Jackie Stewart is seen driving with the courage and skill which made him one of the greatest race drivers ever. The Grand Prix tour is followed through four continents.
F — EN
Unknown — *VCL Video Services* **P**

Fast Drive in the Country, A   Spo-Lei '7?
Automobiles-Racing
04533   52 mins   C
B, V
The many chapters in the history of the 24 hours of Le Mans are traced, from the days when ordinary roads of Northern France served as the race course. The money, glory, profits, decline, and worst disaster in motor racing history are covered.
F — EN
Tony Maylam — *Quadrant Video* **H, P**
M16

Fast Kill, The   Fil-Ent '73
Crime-Drama
07679   90 mins   C
B, V
Tom Adams, Susie Hampton, Michael Culver, Patricia Haines, Peter Halliday, Ray Chiarella, directed by Lindsay Shontoff
Six professional thieves become involved in a plot to steal eight million pounds worth of jewelry. After multiple murders, a nightmare dash to an airfield and a series of double crosses, they each meet violent deaths.
S,A — EN
Shanteff Film Prods — *Video Network* **P**
0020

Fast Lady, The   Fil-Ent '62
Comedy
05149   94 mins   C
B, V
James Robertson Justice, Leslie Phillips, Kathleen Harrison, Stanley Baxter, Julie Christie
Cycle-riding civil servant sets out to woo car-mad daughter of belligerent tycoon. The fun starts when he is persuaded to buy a vintage Bentley to assist his courtship.
BBFC:AA — C,A — EN
Julian Wintle — *Rank Video Library* **H, P**
1027

Fast Times at Ridgemont High   Fil-Ent '82
Drama/Musical
12039   89 mins   C
B, V
Sean Penn, Judge Reinhold, Robert Romanus, Ray Walston, directed by Amy Heckerling
This film traces the erratic and often painful course of a group of teenagers through high school. It features a pop soundtrack from artists including the Eagles, Ringo Starr, Todd Rundgren, Stevie Nicks and Bob Seger.
BBFC:18 — S,C — EN
Universal — *CIC Video* **H, P**
BEA 1079/VHA 1079

Fast-Walking   Fil-Ent '81
Drama
08369   116 mins   C
V2, B, V
James Wood, Tim McIntire, Kay Lenz, Robert Hooks, M. Emmet Walsh
This film is set within a prison camp, where an easy-going prison guard discovers that his cousin, a convict, is planning an assassination. The two men are continually trying to outsmart each other.
BBFC:X — A — EN
Lorimar — *Guild Home Video* **H, P, E**

Fastest Man on Earth, The   Spo-Lei '7?
Automobiles-Racing
04534   52 mins   C
B, V

(For Explanation of codes, see USE GUIDE and KEY)

PALADIN VIDEO HOME ENTERTAINMENT GUIDE

A dramatic documentary about man's pursuit of speed on land, from early electric and steam cars, to rocket powered machines of the Seventies.
F — EN
Tony Maylam — *Quadrant Video* **H, P**
M17

Fatal Games Fil-Ent '7?
Drama/Suspense
12242   83 mins   C
B, V
Sally Kirkland, Lynn Banashek, Teal Roberts, Sean Masterson
A new generation of Olympic athletes are being groomed at the Falcon Academy, America, but a desperate killer with a javelin is at large.
BBFC:18 — *C,A — EN*
Christopher Mankiewicz — *VCL Video Services* **P**

Father Brown, Detective Fil-Ent '79
Crime-Drama
05953   94 mins   C
B, V
Barnard Hughes, Kay Lenz, directed by John Moxley
Father Brown is a fictional detective, created in 1911 by G. K. Chesterton. He is an English parish priest whose involvement with crime is through his calling which brings him in contact with every strata of society. In this film he is seen as a modern-day parish priest based in New York City. The film was shot primarily on location in New York.
S,A — EN
Unknown — *Precision Video Ltd* **P**
BITC 2073/VITC 2073

Father Murphy Fil-Ent '83
Western
12179   95 mins   C
B, V
Merlin Olsen, Moses Gunn, Katherine Cannon
This is a story about the gold rush. Two partners strike it rich but a crook and his gang hear about it and set about blowing up the mining camp; a dramatic fight follows.
S,A — EN
NBC International; Starbox Video — *Select Video Limited* **P**
3124/43

Fatty Finn Fil-Ent '??
Comedy
08619   90 mins   C
V2, B, V
Bert Newton, Noni Hazlehurst, Lorraine Bayly, Gerrard Kennedy, Ben Oxenbould

This film, produced in Australia, is based on one of Australia's most popular comic strip characters of the past fifty years. It is set in the Great Depression.
S,A — EN
Unknown — *Hokushin Audio Visual Ltd* **P**
VM 68

Fawlty Towers, Tape 1, The Germans Fil-Ent '84
Comedy
13389   90 mins   C
B, V
John Cleese, Prunella Scales, Andrew Sachs, Connie Booth
The first cassette from this popular television series of hotel life, features 'The Hotel Inspector,' 'A Touch of Class,' and 'The Germans.'
F — EN
BBC Enterprises — *BBC Video* **H, P**
7033

Fawlty Towers, Tape 2, The Psychiatrist Fil-Ent '84
Comedy
13390   98 mins   C
B, V
John Cleese, Prunella Scales, Andrew Sachs, Connie Booth
The second cassette from this popular television series of hotel life features three episodes, 'The Builders,' 'The Wedding Party' and 'The Psychiatrist.'
F — EN
BBC Enterprises — *BBC Video* **H, P**
7029

Fawlty Towers, Tape 3, The Kipper and the Corpse Fil-Ent '84
Comedy
13387   90 mins   C
B, V
John Cleese, Prunella Scales, Andrew Sachs, Connie Booth
This cassette features three more episodes of hotel life from the popular television series titled, 'Waldorf Salad,' 'Gourmet Night' and 'The Kipper and the Corpse.'
F — EN
BBC Enterprises — *BBC Video* **H, P**
7030

Fawlty Towers, Tape 4, Basil the Rat Fil-Ent '84
Comedy
13385   94 mins   C

(For Explanation of codes, see USE GUIDE and KEY)

PALADIN VIDEO HOME ENTERTAINMENT GUIDE

B, V
John Cleese, Prunella Scales, Andrew Sachs, Connie Booth
This cassette features three more episodes of hotel life from the popular television series titled 'Communication Problems,' 'The Anniversary' and 'Basil the Rat.'
F — EN
BBC Enterprises — *BBC Video*   **H, P**
7031

Fear Eats The Soul   Fil-Ent '74
Drama/Romance
08971   93 mins   C
B, V
Brigitte Mira, El Hedi Ben Salem, Barbara Valentin, Irm Hermann, Rainer Werner Fassbinder, directed by Rainer Wrener Fassbinder
A widowed German cleaning lady takes pity on a Moroccan worker when she learns of the overcrowded room in which he lives with other foreign workers. She offers him a bed for the night, and to her surprise shares it with him. After a brief affair, they marry but encounter difficulties with the social prejudice of their friends and family. Subtitled.
BBFC:AA — C,A — EN
Cinegate — *Palace Video Ltd*   **P**
PVC 2022B

Fear in the Night   Fil-Ent '72
Drama/Suspense
07442   86 mins   C
B, V
Judy Geeson, Joan Collins, Ralph Bates, Peter Cushing, directed by Jimmy Sangster
A school master returns during the holidays to his prep school with his new bride who has just recovered from a nervous breakdown. When strange events occur in the deserted corridors of the school she begins to feel instinctively uneasy about the place. The enigmatic Headmaster and his strange wife do little to alleviate her mounting terror and deteriorating mental state.
S,A — EN
Hammer Film Productions Ltd — *THORN EMI* **P**
TXC 90 0743 4/TVC 90 0743 2

Fear Is the Key   Fil-Ent '72
Adventure/Suspense
08558   101 mins   C
B, V
Barry Newman, Suzy Kendall, John Vernon, directed by Michael Tuchner
This is an adaptation of Alistair MacLean's novel about a man trying to escape from his trial for a bar-room brawl. However, it is really part of his ingenious scheme to get revenge on an oil millionaire who is responsible for his wife's death.
BBFC:A — S,A — EN
EMI — *THORN EMI*   **P**
TXB 90 02224/TVB 90 02222

Fear No Evil   Fil-Ent '80
Horror
10069   87 mins   C
V2, B, V
Stefan Arngrim, Elizabeth Hoffman, Kathleen Rowe McAllen
The devil and three arch-angels are re-incarnated as human beings for their final confrontation on earth. The eighteen year old Lucifer summons the walking dead to leave their graves to ravage mankind. This film features music by B-52's, Boomtown Rats, Ramones, Sex Pistols, Patti Smith, Richard Hell, The Rezillos and Talking Heads.
A — EN
Avco Embassy — *Embassy Home Entertainment*   **P**
1612

Fearless Fly in Fly by Might   Chl-Juv '8?
Cartoons
13001   95 mins   C
V2, B, V
Animated
This cassette contains sixteen episodes featuring Fearless Fly in his unending fight against injustice.
BBFC:U — PS,M — EN
Juniper Releasing Inc; Hal Seeger Productions Inc — *Guild Home Video*   **H, P, E**

Fedora   Fil-Ent '78
Drama/Mystery
08562   108 mins   C
B, V
William Holden, Marthe Keller, Henry Fonda, Michael York, Mario Adorf, Jose Ferrer, Stephen Collins, Hans Jaray, directed by Billy Wilder
This film is about a Legendary Hollywood star, Fedora, who has been retired for many years. However, a film producer is trying to find out the reason for her to be kept prisoner on a Greek island by her devoted staff and a doctor. He wants to find the source of her alluring beauty after all the years.
BBFC:A — S,A — EN
NF Geria Films — *THORN EMI*   **P**
TXB 90 0979 4/TVB 90 0979 2

PALADIN VIDEO HOME ENTERTAINMENT GUIDE

Feeling Fit — Spo-Lei '81
Sports
06910   ? mins   C
LV
Susan Hampshire, Anthony Van Laast
On this disc Susan Hampshire and Anthony Van Laast present a complete head-to-toe fitness course for home use with a special section on jogging.
F — I
Unknown — *Rank Video Library*   **H, P**
5024

Felix the Cat—No. 1 — Fil-Ent '60
Cartoons
07882   60 mins   C
V2, B, V
Animated
This is an hour long cassette featuring the adventures of Felix the Cat.
F — EN
Felix the Cat Prods; King Features Syndicate — *Intervision Video*   **H, P**
A-A0386

Felix the Cat—No. 2 — Fil-Ent '60
Cartoons
07883   60 mins   C
V2, B, V
Animated
This is an hour long cassette featuring the adventures of Felix the Cat.
F — EN
Felix the Cat Prods; King Features Syndicate — *Intervision Video*   **H, P**
A-A0387

Felix the Cat—No. 3 — Fil-Ent '60
Cartoons
07884   60 mins   C
V2, B, V
Animated
This is an hour long cassette featuring the adventures of Felix the Cat.
F — EN
Felix the Cat Prods; King Features Syndicate — *Intervision Video*   **H, P**
A-A0388

Felix the Cat—No. 4 — Fil-Ent '60
Cartoons
07885   60 mins   C
V2, B, V
Animated
This is an hour long cassette featuring the adventures of Felix the Cat.
F — EN
Felix the Cat Prods; King Features Syndicate — *Intervision Video*   **H, P**
A-A0389

Felix the Cat—No. 5 — Fil-Ent '60
Cartoons
07886   60 mins   C
V2, B, V
Animated
This is an hour long cassette featuring the adventures of Felix the Cat.
F — EN
Felix the Cat Prods; King Features Syndicate — *Intervision Video*   **H, P**
A-A0421

Felix the Cat—No. 6 — Fil-Ent '60
Cartoons
07887   60 mins   C
V2, B, V
Animated
This is an hour long cassette featuring the adventures of Felix the Cat.
F — EN
Felix the Cat Prods; King Features Syndicate — *Intervision Video*   **H, P**
A-A0422

Female Mud Wrestling — Spo-Lei '81
Sports/Women
06260   82 mins   C
B, V
Introduced by Adam West, Rory Calhoun
This film, shot live in Las Vegas, presents America's newest cult sport from the 1981 International Female Mud-Wrestling Championships. It presents the sport as something new and different looking at the amusing and erotic aspects of the new cult.
S,A — EN
Unknown — *VCL Video Services*   **P**
S176

Female Trouble — Fil-Ent '78
Comedy
08972   90 mins   C
B, V
Divine, David Lochary, Mary Vivian Pearce, Mink Stole, Edith Massey, directed by John Waters
This film chronicles the outrageous life of Dawn Davenport, the transvestite, from teenager to the electric chair
A — EN
Dreamland Prods — *Palace Video Ltd*   **P**
PVC 2009B

(For Explanation of codes, see USE GUIDE and KEY)

PALADIN VIDEO HOME ENTERTAINMENT GUIDE

Femme Est une Femme, Une
Fil-Ent '61
Comedy
05635   80 mins   C
V2, B, V
Anna Karina, Jean-Paul Belmondo
A saucy French comedy—a strip-tease dancer wants a baby, her boyfriend declines to oblige so she decides to ask the first man she meets to be the father. Music by Michel Legrand. The film is in French with English sub-titles.
BBFC:A — S,A — EN   FR
Unknown — *Video Unlimited*   **H, P**
O11

Feria de Abril
Spo-Lei '79
Sports-Minor/Parades and festivals
04419   30 mins   C
B, V
Spain's best bullfighters take part in the April Festival in Seville. Paco Camino, El Vit Curro Romero, and other stars are featured.
F — EN
VCL — *VCL Video Services*   **P**

Ferry to Hong Kong
Fil-Ent '61
Adventure
12750   111 mins   C
B, V
Curt Jergens, Orson Welles, Sylvia Syms
The adventures of an expatriate Austrian layabout condemned to travel indefinitely on the Hong Kong ferry to Macao, because neither port will let him land.
BBFC:PG — F — EN
20th Century Fox; Rank — *Rank Video Library*   **H, P**
0186A

Fi Hob Allah
Gen-Edu '??
Religion/Documentary
08000   180 mins   C
B, V
This programme comes in two parts, each 90 minutes long, and is about the love of God. Produced entirely in Arabic.
F — R   AB
Unknown — *Motion Epics Video Company Ltd*   **P**

Fiction Makers, The
Fil-Ent '67
Mystery/Adventure
07338   104 mins   C
B, V
Roger Moore, Sylvia Simms, Justine Lord, directed by Roy Baker

A travelling adventurer is mistaken for the author of far-fetched thrillers and is trapped into carrying out a robbery of larger-than-life dimensions. Based on the television series 'The Saint.'
S,A — EN
ATV — *Precision Video Ltd*
BITC 2068/VITC 2068

Fiddler on the Roof
Fil-Ent '71
Musical
01208   178 mins   C
V2, B, V
Topol, Norma Crane, Leonard Frey, Molly Picon, directed by Norman Jewison
This film, based on the long-running Broadway musical, is the story of a poor Jewish farmer at the turn of the century in a small Ukranian village, his five dowry-less daughters, his lame horse, his wife, and his companionable relationship with God.
Academy Awards '71: Best Cinematography; Best Adaptation and Original Song Score; Best Sound.   BBFC:U — F — EN
United Artists — *Intervision Video*   **H**
UA A B 5016

Fiend
Fil-Ent '??
Horror
08694   93 mins   C
V2, B, V
Don Leifert, George Stover, Richard Nelson, Elaine White
This film tells the gruesome story of the 'Fiend' who, having risen from the grave, has to drain life from his mortal victims in order to restore his youth.
BBFC:X — A — EN
Unknown — *Video Unlimited*   **H, P**
050

Fiend, The
Fil-Ent '65
Horror
05693   87 mins   C
B, V
Ann Todd, Patrick Magee, Tony Beckley, directed by Robert Hartford-Davis
A story involving a woman and her schizoid son who at night becomes a 'Jack the Ripper' style avenger. They become involved in a religious sect led by an awe-inspiring 'Minister.' A woman writer shows interest and snoops around resulting in an horrific incident with son. When his mother dies his murderous intentions turn towards the 'Minister.'
BBFC:X — A — EN
Unknown — *Derann Film Services*   **H, P**
GS709B/GS709

PALADIN VIDEO HOME ENTERTAINMENT GUIDE

Fiendish Plot of Dr Fu Manchu, The
Fil-Ent '80
Comedy/Adventure
06049   96 mins   C
B, V

Peter Sellers, Helen Mirren, Sid Ceasar, Simon Williams, Steve Franklin, David Tomlinson, directed by Piers Haggard

Until the theft of a rare diamond, the evil Fu Manchu was thought to be dead and his adversary Inspector Naylor Smith suitable for treatment. Russia, owners of the diamond, threaten world war so Inspector Smith is called upon to solve the mystery; being the expert on oriental mayhem he discovers who stole it and why.

BBFC:A — S,A — EN

Warner Bros; Orion Pictures — *Warner Home Video*   **P**
WEX2014/WEV2014

Fifth Dimension with Dionne Warwick and The Carpenters, The
Fil-Ent '7?
Music-Performance
02081   60 mins   C
B, V

Dispelling doom and gloom, the 'travelling sunshine show' is just that—a blend of music and rhythm by the Fifth Dimension. Their sound and heat has total energy and is aided by the music of The Carpenters and Dionne Warwick.

F — EN

VCL Video Services — *VCL Video Services*   **P**

Fifth Musketeer, The
Fil-Ent '77
Drama/Adventure
07390   120 mins   C
V2, B, V

Beau Bridges, Sylvia Kristel, Ursula Andress, Rex Harrison

This is the story of twin brothers born into royalty. One became king and the other disappeared. Years later they meet in a fight for the throne and a bride.

BBFC:X — A — EN

Columbia — *Guild Home Video*   **H, P, E**

Fifth Offensive, The
Fil-Ent '??
War-Drama
07940   105 mins   C
V2, B, V

Richard Burton

This film follows the exploits of the leader of a partisan group who brought his people to victory during World War II when 120,000 German soldiers attacked their strongholds in the Balkan Mountains.

S,A — EN

Unknown — *Videomedia*   **P**
PVM 7102/BVM 7102/HVM 7102

55 Days at Peking
Fil-Ent '63
Drama
01065   150 mins   C
V2, B, V

Charlton Heston, Ava Gardner

The Chinese people's resentment against the infiltration of Western ideas erupts into violence against missionaries and foreigners.

BBFC:U — M,A — EN

Samuel Bronstein Prods — *Intervision Video*   **P**
A-A 0205

Fighting Back
Fil-Ent '80
Drama
09252   100 mins   C
V2, B, V

Lewis Fitz-Gerald, Kris McQuade, Robyn Nevin, Paul Smith, directed by Michael Caulfield

This film tells the story of a 13-year-old boy who has been fighting a losing battle for most of hi slife. It describes a mind in adolescent turmoil, in rebellious conflict with society, unsure of its direction, purpose and future. It is based on the book 'Tom' by John Embling.

BBFC:15 — C,A — EN

Gilson International — *Iver Film Services*   **P**
223

Fighting Fist, The
Fil-Ent '82
Martial arts
12849   83 mins   C
V2, B, V

A young man, proficient in the art of pure Kung fu finds he has a lot to learn from a beautiful young lady and a fortune teller.

BBFC:15 — S,A — EN

Unknown — *Video Programme Distributors*   **P**
VPD 233

Fighting Fists Of Shangai Joe, The
Fil-Ent '8?
Western/Martial arts
07795   94 mins   C
V2, B, V

Chen Lee, Klaus Kinski

(For Explanation of codes, see USE GUIDE and KEY)

237

PALADIN VIDEO HOME ENTERTAINMENT GUIDE

This Kung Fu western follows the adventures of a Samurai warrior in the wild west.
S,A — EN
Unknown — *Fletcher Video* **H, P**
V106

Fille Mal Gardee, La Fil-Ent '81
Dance/Drama
08475   100 mins   C
B, V
Lesley Collier, Michael Coleman, Brian Shaw, Leslie Edwards, Garry Grant, directed by Norman Morrice
This is Frederick Ashton's ballet, set in the English countryside, telling how a young girl manages to win the hand of the man she loves, despite her mother's determination to marry her off to a dimwitted son of a wealthy vineyard owner. The music is composed by Ferdinand Herold and conducted by John Lanchbery.
S,A — EN
Covent Garden Video Productions Ltd — *THORN EMI* **P**
TXH 90 1319 4/TVH 90 13192

Fillmore Rock Festival Fil-Ent '72
Music-Performance
02583   90 mins   C
B, V
Performances from the legendary Fillmore Theater featuring The Grateful Dead, Jefferson Airplane, Santana, and Linda Ronstadt.
C,A — EN
Unknown — *Mountain Video* **P**

Final Assignment Fil-Ent '80
Drama
07398   80 mins   C
V2, B, V
Genevieve Bujold, Michael York, Burgess Meredith, Colleen Dewhurst
A Canadian reporter becomes involved in an attempt to smuggle the young granddaughter of a dissident to the West for vital medical treatment.
BBFC:AA — S,A — EN
Unknown — *Guild Home Video* **H, P, E**

Final Countdown, The Fil-Ent '80
Drama/Science fiction
12989   99 mins   C
B, V
Kirk Douglas, Martin Sheen, Katharine Ross, James Farentino, directed by Don Taylor
The world's largest nuclear-powered aircraft carrier is spirited back to the day before the Japanese attack on Pearl Harbour and its commander is faced with a decision.
BBFC:PG — S,A — EN
United Artists — *Warner Home Video* **P**
99370

Final Exam Fil-Ent '81
Horror/Suspense
08331   90 mins   C
V2, B, V, LV
Cecile Bagdai, Joel Rice
This film tells of a college at examination time. There is a psychotic killer about, and one by one the students are murdered by the knife wielding intruder.
A — EN
John Chambliss — *Embassy Home Entertainment* **P**
1618

Final Hour, The Fil-Ent '??
Horror/Suspense
08793   ? mins   C
B, V
This film tells a brutal story of lust, greed and violence. A young girl is raped by an armed maniac and held to ransom.
A — EN
Unknown — *VCL Video Services* **P**
P342D

Final Mission, The Fil-Ent '84
Adventure/Drama
13711   96 mins   C
B, V
Richard Young, John Dresden, directed by Cirio Santiago
When an ex-Vietnam soldier's family is massacred before his eyes, armed with an MG 82, he becomes a killing machine out for revenge.
A — EN
Anthony Maharaj — *THORN EMI* **P**
90 2874

Final Programme, The Fil-Ent '81
Science fiction/Fantasy
07452   85 mins   C
B, V
Jon Finch, Jenny Runacre, Sterling Hayden, Harry Andrews, Hugh Griffith, Graham Crowden, Julie Ege, Patrick Magee, directed by Robert Fuest
This story concerns the efforts of the free-wheeling, Nobel Prize-winning hero to rescue his sister from their drug-crazed brother together with the microfilm of a plan for world domination. The plan involves a bisexual

---

(For Explanation of codes, see USE GUIDE and KEY)

PALADIN VIDEO HOME ENTERTAINMENT GUIDE

computer-programmer giving birth to an all purpose human being—a self-fertilising, self-regenerating, immortal hermaphrodite. The hero is to be the unwilling father of this new breed which he aims to stop.
BBFC:X — a — EN
EMI Films Ltd — THORN EMI   P
TXC 90 0320 4/TVC 90 0320 2

Final Terror, The   Fil-Ent '83
Horror/Drama
13685   86 mins   C
B, V
Daryl Hannah, Rachel Ward, directed by Andrew Davis
A merciless killer stalks a group of youngsters on an isolated camping trip and tension mounts as they become meshed in his trap.
BBFC:18 — A — EN
Joe Roth — THORN EMI   P
90 1996

Finally Sunday   Fil-Ent '83
Comedy/Drama
12512   107 mins   B/W
B, V
Fanny Ardant, Jean-Louis Trintignant, Phillippe Laudenbach, directed by Francois Truffaut
An estate agent, suspected of murdering his wife and friend, embarks on a personal investigation with the aid of his secretary. This is a French film dubbed into English.
BBFC:PG — S,A — EN
Unknown — THORN EMI   P
TXB 90 23644/TVB 90 23642

Find A Place To Die   Fil-Ent '??
Western
07335   96 mins   C
B, V
Giovanni Pallavicino, Daniela Giordano, directed by Anthony Ascott
A young geologist and his wife, who have discovered gold, are attacked by a ruthless gang of outlaws. They escape by using dynamite, but the young man is injured. His wife goes to get help but discovers that the nearest town is inhabited by thieves, bandits and cut throats. The prospect of gold and her favours tempts an unlikely group of dubious characters to help her.
BBFC:X — A — EN
Unknown — Derann Film Services   P
GS 717B/GS 717

Find the Lady   Fil-Ent '76
Comedy
04305   90 mins   C
V2, B, V
Mickey Rooney, Peter Cook
A comedy of errors about kidnappings, riots, and mistaken identity.
F — EN
Quadrant Films — Intervision Video   H, P
A-A 0090

Finest Hours, The   Fil-Ent '64
Documentary/World War II
05060   111 mins   C
B, V
Narrated by Orson Welles, directed by Peter Baylis
Sir Winston Churchill's own story as told in his memoirs of the Second World War.
F — EN
Columbia; Jack Le Vien — THORN EMI
P
TXB 90 0511 4/TVB 90 0511 2

Fire and Ice   Fil-Ent '82
Cartoons/Adventure
12887   81 mins   C
B, V
Animated
The people of the fortress city of Fire Keep have to defend themselves against annihilation by the glaciers of the evil Lord Nekron in this tale of sword and sorcery.
BBFC:PG — S,A — EN
Unknown — THORN EMI   P
TXA 90 24054/TVA 90 24052

Firefox   Fil-Ent '82
Drama
13168   121 mins   C
B, V
Clint Eastwood, Freddie Jones, David Huffman, Warren Clarke, Ronald Lacey, director Clint Eastwood
A former Vietnam pilot reluctantly accepts the greatest challenge of his career to steal from the Russians the world's most advanced and sophisticated war plane—Codenamed Firefox.
BBFC:AA — C,A — EN
Warner Bros — Warner Home Video   P
61219

Fire Over England   Fil-Ent '37
Drama
07943   91 mins   B/W
V2, B, V
Laurence Olivier, Flora Robson, Vivien Leigh, Raymond Massey, Leslie Banks, James Mason, directed by William K. Howard

---

(For Explanation of codes, see USE GUIDE and KEY)   239

PALADIN VIDEO HOME ENTERTAINMENT GUIDE

This film, set in the 16th century, chronicles events in the court of Queen Elizabeth I during the time when Spain and England were locked in rivalry.
BBFC:U — F — EN
United Artists — *Videomedia* **P**
PVM 4416/BVM 4416/HVM 4416

Firebird 2015 A.D.   Fil-Ent '7?
Adventure
09227   97 mins   C
B, V
Doug McClure, Darren McGavin
This is a futuristic spectacle about two car enthusiasts, and the thrill and conflict involved in driving a vehicle in a world where oil shortages have led to a total ban on the use of automobiles and made driving a capital offence.
S,A — EN
Unknown — *Video Form Pictures* **H, P**
MGD 2

Firechasers, The   Fil-Ent '70
Drama
07336   101 mins   C
B, V
Chad Everett, Anjanette Comer, Keith Barron, Joanne Dainton
Set in England, an insurance investigator sets out to find who is responsible for causing a series of devastating fires.
BBFC:U — F — EN
ITC — *Precision Video Ltd* **P**
BITC 2062/VITC 2062

Firehouse   Fil-Ent '73
Drama
09255   74 mins   C
V2, B, V
Richard Roundtree, Vince Edwards, Andrew Duggan, Richard Jaeckel, Shelia Frazier, directed by Alex March
A tough young trainee fireman joins a team of top fire fighters, Engine Company 33. There is a spate of fatal, deliberate fires in a black area of the city. In addition to fighting these terrifying fires, the new black recruit has to face unrelenting racial intimidation from his fellow fire fighters.
BBFC:A — S,A — EN
Circle Entertainment — *Iver Film Services* **P**
207

Firepower   Fil-Ent '79
Crime-Drama/Suspense
05400   99 mins   C
V2, B, V
Sophia Loren, James Coburn, O. J. Simpson, Eli Wallach, Anthony Franciosa, George Grizzard, Vincent Gardenia, directed by Michael Winner
A millionaire, who is the third richest man in the world, lives in a mansion in the Caribbean. He is guarded, no-one knows what he looks like and he has not been photographed for thirty years. He is wanted by the U.S. Government for fraud, tax evasion and other offences. An illegal attempt is made to return him to American soil.
BBFC:AA — S,A — EN
ITC Entertainment — *Precision Video Ltd* **P**
CRITC 2036/BITC 2036/VITC 2036

Firesign Theatre Presents   Fil-Ent '82
Nick Danger
Comedy
12819   60 mins   C
B, V
Zany comedy fans will enjoy this revolutionary video show from one of America's best loved comedy troupes.
BBFC:15 — S,A — EN
Firesign Theatre; Michael Nesmith; David Bean — *VideoSpace Ltd* **P**
PA 1

Firestarter   Fil-Ent '84
Suspense/Drama
13700   109 mins   C
B, V
Drew Barrymore, Martin Sheen, George C Scott, Louise Fletcher, directed by Mark L Lester
An eight-year-old girl has the power of turning anyone into a human torch and though she may not want this awesome gift a sinister government agency does and are intent on tracking her down.
BBFC:15 — S,A — EN
Dino de Laurentiis — *THORN EMI* **P**
90 2873

First Aid for Horses, Part   How-Ins '8?
1
Animals
13516   32 mins   C
B, V
Veterinary advice is given in this film on the diagnosis and treatment of poisons, digestive orders, colic, laminitus, abrasions, cuts, scratches and leg wounds.
C,A — ED
Unknown — *TFI Leisure Ltd* **H, P**

First Aid for Horses, Part   How-Ins '8?
2
Animals
13517   25 mins   C
B, V

PALADIN VIDEO HOME ENTERTAINMENT GUIDE

Veterinary advice is given in this film on the diagnosis and treatment of arterial bleeding, puncture, wounds of the foot, eye injuries, strains, sprains and bruises.
C,A — ED
Unknown — *TFI Leisure Ltd* **H, P**

First Blood   Fil-Ent '82
Adventure
09315   90 mins   C
B, V
Sylvester Stallone, Richard Crenna, Brian Dennehy
A Vietnam veteran runs afoul of a small-town Southern sheriff. Forced to go on the run, he must call on his old army skills to survive this life-or-death manhunt.
BBFC:AA — *S,A — EN*
Orion Pictures — *THORN EMI*   **P**
TXA 90 1720 4/TVA 90 1720 2

First Chukkas   Spo-Lei '82
Sports
13515   34 mins   C
B, V
Directed by Bill Latto
This film shows how, through progressive coaching methods, the playing of polo can become a real possibility for all young riders and their ponies.
F — I
Town and Country Productions — *TFI Leisure Ltd*   **H, P**

First Deadly Sin, The   Fil-Ent '80
Crime-Drama
12985   108 mins   C
B, V
Frank Sinatra, Faye Dunaway, Brenda Vaccaro, David Dukes, Martin Gabel
A tough homicide detective on the verge of retirement sets out on the trail of a multiple murderer which ends in direct-confrontation.
BBFC:15 — *S,A — EN*
Filmways; Artanis; Cinema Seven — *Warner Home Video*   **P**
61368

First Love   Fil-Ent '70
Romance/Drama
10196   96 mins   C
B, V
Maximillian Schell, Dominique Sanda, John Moulder Brown, Valentina Cortese
Based on the novel by Ivan Turgenev, this film tells the story of a father and son who undergo an emotional battle for the love of a woman.
S,A — EN
U.M.C. — *Video Form Pictures*   **H, P**
MGD 17

First Monday in October   Fil-Ent '81
Drama
12034   99 mins   C
B, V
Jill Clayburgh, Walter Matthau, directed by Ronald Neame
This is a story of two High Court judges, one a man and the other a widow. From the start they are in opposition against each other, but a grudging respect starts to grow. They both become very involved in a particular case, which leads to an unexpected discovery.
BBFC:15 — *S,A — EN*
Paramount — *CIC Video*   **H, P**
BEA 2058/VHA 2058

First of the Few, The   Fil-Ent '42
War-Drama
09373   117 mins   B/W
B, V
Leslie Howard, David Niven, Rosamund John, Roland Culver, David Horne, directed by Leslie Howard
This tells the true story of R.J. Mitchell who saw World War II coming and devised the Spitfire. Set initially in September 1940, the film begins at a fighter station as the pilots await the order to scramble. It flashes back to 1922 to show how Mitchell was inspired with his idea.
BBFC:U — *F — EN*
Melbourne; British Aviation — *Precision Video Ltd*   **P**
BAPV 500/VAPV 500

First Travelling Saleslady,   Fil-Ent '??
The/A Lady Takes a Chance
Comedy-Drama/Western
09112   170 mins   C
B, V
Ginger Rogers, Barry Nelson, Carol Channing, James Arness, David Brian, Clint Eastwood; John Wayne, Jean Arthur, Phil Silvers
This tape contains two films on one cassette. 'The First Travelling Saleslady' (1956, colour, 90 mins.), set in 1897, tells the story of a corset designer who heads west with her secretary, to meet many fascinating characters. 'A Lady

(For Explanation of codes, see USE GUIDE and KEY)

PALADIN VIDEO HOME ENTERTAINMENT GUIDE

Takes a Chance' (1943, black and white, 80 mins.) tells of a working girl with matrimonial ideas, and John Wayne as a rodeo rider, who yearns for wide open spaces.
F — EN
U-1; RKO — Kingston Video   **H, P**
KV60

First Turn-On   Fil-Ent '??
Comedy
12190   85 mins   C
V2, B, V
Michael Sawville, Googy Gress, Jenny Johnson, Heidi Bassett
A comedy film which traces the first sexual experiences of five friends who relate their stories through a series of flashbacks.
BBFC:18 — C,A — EN
Michael Herz Lloyd; Kaufman — Medusa Communications Ltd   **H, P**

Fish That Saved Pittsburgh, The   Fil-Ent '79
Comedy
06169   103 mins   C
V2, B, V
Julius Erving, Jonathan Winters, Jack Kehoe, Kareem Abdul-Jabbar, Margaret Avery, James Bond III, Michael V. Gazzo, Peter Isacksen, Nicholas Pryor, M. Emmet Walsh
After a slump the Pittsburgh Pythons Basketball Team have new members and a new name. The Pittsburgh Pisces include a permanent drunk, a forty year old minister, a black disc jockey who speaks in rhymes and a black man who dresses like an Arab Sheik and believes he is of Royal Egyptian descent. Includes appearances by Meadowlark Lemon from the Harlem Globetrotters, Stockard Channing and Flip Wilson.
BBFC:AA — S,A — EN
Stromberg Production — Guild Home Video
H, P, E

F.I.S.T.   Fil-Ent '78
Drama
13061   133 mins   C
B, V
Sylvester Stallone, Rod Steiger, Peter Boyle, Melinda Dillon, directed by Norman Jewison
An engrossing drama about the rise of a tough resilient worker to prominence and power in the Federation of Interstate Truckers Union.
BBFC:A — C,A — EN
United Artists Corp. — Warner Home Video
P
99291

Fist of Fear, Touch of Death   Fil-Ent '80
Martial arts/Adventure
06963   90 mins   C
B, V
Bruce Lee, Fred Williamson, Ron Van Clief
A compilation adventure film featuring three past-masters of the Martial arts.
S,A — EN
Aquarius Promotions Production — Home Video Merchandisers   **H, P**

Fist of Fury   Fil-Ent '73
Martial arts
06928   100 mins   C
B, V
Bruce Lee, Nora Miao
Set in Shanghai in 1908, a martial arts expert sets out on a one-man vendetta against the gang that kills his kung-fu master and terrorises his former school.
BBFC:X — A — EN
National General — Rank Video Library
H, P
0071C

Fist of Fury II   Fil-Ent '76
Adventure/Martial arts
02091   95 mins   C
V2, B, V
Bruce Li
Ho-Yuan-Cha, one of the Knights of China, is reported to have died from an illness. Chen Chen is suspicious and subsequent investigations involve him in violent adventure.
BBFC:X — A — EN
Unknown — Hokushin Audio Visual Ltd
P
VM-17

Fist of Fury 3   Fil-Ent '??
Martial arts
08627   90 mins   C
V2, B, V
Ho Chung Do, Ngai Pingo, Ku Phong, Tong Yim Chen
After having revenged the death of his brothers, Chen returns home, looking forward to a quiet time with his mother. However, the 'organisation' have other plans and contrive to involve him in a series of crimes. He tries desperately to stay clear, but when a gang beat his mother to death, he has no option but to fight back.
S,A — EN
Unknown — Hokushin Audio Visual Ltd
P
VM 60

PALADIN VIDEO HOME ENTERTAINMENT GUIDE

Fistful of Dollars, A   Fil-Ent '64
Western
13178   96 mins   C
B, V
Clint Eastwood, Gian Maria Volonte, Marianne Koch, directed by Sergio Leone
A first programme in a series in which the star is pitted against a murderous gang, notorious for taking no prisoners.
BBFC:A — C,A — EN
United Artists; Harry Colombo; George Papi — *Warner Home Video*   P
99277

Fistful of Dynamite, A   Fil-Ent '72
Adventure
13160   132 mins   C
B, V
Two men, one a Fugitive IRA revolutionary, the other a brutal bandit, team up to rob a Mexican bank which doubles as a jail for political prisoners, and become heroes of the revolution and the quarry of government troops.
BBFC:X — A — EN
Rafran Cinematografica SpA — *Warner Home Video*   P
99264

Fists of the Double K   Fil-Ent '7?
Martial arts
09938   89 mins   C
B, V
This film features action-packed Kung Fu adventure.
BBFC:18 — A — EN
Unknown — *Rank Video Library*   H, P
0151 A

Fists of Vengeance, The   Fil-Ent '73
Adventure/Martial arts
10065   77 mins   C
V2, B, V
Kung Bun, Tong Chi, Shoji Harada
A young government officer is sent back home to investigate stories of Japanese brutality towards his townfolk in China.
S,A — EN
Unknown — *Embassy Home Entertainment*   P
1366

Fitzcarraldo   Fil-Ent '81
Drama/Adventure
07742   160 mins   C
B, V
Klaus Kinski, Claudia Cardinale, directed by Werner Herzog
Set in the Amazon, this film tells the extraordinary tale of an Irishman who attempts to bring opera to the jungle and manhandle a steam boat across a mountain with the help of local Indians. Hailed as a White God he can do anything he chooses. In the end the boat is destroyed, but there is still the opera to occupy him.
S,A — EN
Unknown — *Palace Video Ltd*   P

Five Bloody Graves   Fil-Ent '70
Horror/Western
07621   81 mins   C
V2, B, V
Robert Dix, Scott Brady
After inhuman rape killings, cruel Indian torture and fights to the death a man survives 'dead inside' to continue his desert ride in a strange and ghostly way.
BBFC:X — A — EN
Independent International — *Iver Film Services*   P

Five Days from Home   Fil-Ent '78
Drama
06154   107 mins   C
V2, B, V
George Peppard, Neville Brand, Savannah Smith, Sherry Boucher, William Larsen, directed by George Peppard
An ex-policeman who killed his wife's lover escapes from prison to fight his way across the American Continent to reach the bedside of his seriously ill son by Christmas eve. He carries a puppy and a gun but is relentlessly pursued by an evil Police Inspector.
BBFC:AA — S,A — EN
Universal — *Guild Home Video*   H, P, E

Five Days One Summer   Fil-Ent '82
Drama/Adventure
13063   105 mins   C
B, V
Sean Connery, Betsy Brantley, Lambert Wilson, directed by Fred Zinnemann
A doctor takes a young girl half his age on holiday in the Swiss Alps. A youthful Alpine guide falls in love with her, and during a tense, dangerous climb, challenges the older man's right to her.
BBFC:A — C,A — EN
Cable and Wireless (Finance) Ltd — *Warner Home Video*   P
70010

Five Desperate Women   Fil-Ent '71
Drama
04190   73 mins   C
B, V
Robert Conrad, Anjanette Comer, Bradford Dillman, Joan Hackett, Denise Nichols, Stephanie Powers, Julie Sommars

(For Explanation of codes, see USE GUIDE and KEY)

PALADIN VIDEO HOME ENTERTAINMENT GUIDE

Five women who were at college together are reunited after 5 years for a weekend in a rented mansion on an isolated island. Trapped, panic-stricken, and desperate, the women fight for their lives.
BBFC:A — C,A — EN
Spelling — *Guild Home Video*   **H, P**

Five Go to Smuggler's Top   Fil-Ent '77
Adventure
10011   75 mins   C
B, V
Written by Enid Blyton
This tape contains two adventures of the Famous Five, 'Five Go to Smuggler's Top' and 'Five Go Off in a Caravan'. In the first episode, the five go to stay with the Lenoir family. They meet the eccentric Mr. Barlow, the mystery begins with excitement in and out of underground passages and on surrounding sea marshes. In the second episode the five go off in two caravans for a holiday.
M,S — EN
Southstar TV — *Longman Video*   **P**
LGBE 4003/LGVH 4003

Five Guns West   Fil-Ent '56
Western
13448   78 mins   C
B, V
John Lund, Dorothy Malone
An action packed film involving robbery, double-crossing and murder.
BBFC:A — C,A — EN
Unknown — *Rank Video Library*   **H, P**
8010 E

Five Kung-Fu Dare Devil Heroes   Fil-Ent '??
Adventure/Martial arts
05722   87 mins   C
V2, B, V
Loli
Five brave young men ride together to secure a supply of ammunition and arms from Russia for the new Chinese leaders. This film is dubbed.
S,A — EN
Unknown — *Video Unlimited*   **H, P**
015

5-Man Army, The   Fil-Ent '70
Adventure/Suspense
12230   101 mins   C
B, V
James Daly, Bud Spencer, Peter Graves

Set in Mexico in the early 1900s 'The 5-Man Army' are already wanted men when they set out to rob a train and divert its shipment of gold into the hands of Mexican revolutionaries.
S,A — EN
MGM — *MGM/UA Home Video*   **P**
10286

Five on Kirrin Island   Fil-Ent '77
Adventure
10012   75 mins   C
B, V
Written by Enid Blyton
This tape contains two adventures of the Famous Five, 'Five on Kirrin Island' and 'Five Go Adventuring Again'. In the first episode Julian and Anne arrive at Kirrin Cottage to stay with their cousin George. They find her upset because her uncle has taken over Kirrin Island for one of his experiments. In the second adventure, Timmy the dog earns his right to be counted as one of the five.
M,S — EN
Southstar TV — *Longman Video*   **P**
LGBE 4002/LGVE 4002

Flame Trees of Thika, The   Fil-Ent '81
Drama
08571   150 mins   C
B, V
Hayley Mills, David Robb, Holly Aird, directed by Roy Ward-Baker
Set in Africa, this film tells the story of a British family who intend to settle and make their fortune planting coffee. They encounter Africa's wildlife roaming the plains in profusion and the native tribes, still following their traditional customs. It is based on Elspeth Huxley's childhood memories.
F — EN
Thames Video — *THORN EMI*   **P**
TXB 90 0728 4/TVB 90 0728 2

Flaming Bullets   Fil-Ent '??
Western
06306   59 mins   B/W
V2, B, V
Tex Ritter
The Texas Rangers led by a western veteran and a songster are given the task of unmasking the identity of a mystery criminal after bounty hunters fail to find him.
F — EN
Unknown — *World of Video 2000*   **H, P**
GF513

Flare-Up   Fil-Ent '70
Drama/Suspense
12229   94 mins   C
B, V

PALADIN VIDEO HOME ENTERTAINMENT GUIDE

Raquel Welch, James Stacy
In exciting Las Vegas locations, a beautiful night club dancer is pursued by a psychopathic killer.
C,A — EN
MGM — *MGM/UA Home Video*   P
10378

Flash Gordon   Fil-Ent '80
Fantasy/Science fiction
05045   109 mins   C
B, V
Sam J Jones, Ornello Muti, Melody Anderson, Max von Sydow, Topol, Timothy Dalton, Brian Blessed, Peter Wyngarde, Mariangela Melato
An evil emperor from another planet sets out to cause havoc on the earth before he ultimately destroys it. Flash Gordon leads the fight to save the earth. This film contains music composed and performed by Queen.
F — EN
Dino de Laurentiis — *THORN EMI*   P
TXA 90 0300 4/TVA 90 0300 2

Flash Gordon   Fil-Ent '??
Cartoons/Adventure
08314   60 mins   C
B, V
Animated
This fully animated cartoon features Flash Gordon on the small planet of Mongo, whose two countries are in continual conflict. It follows the adventures of Flash Gordon, Dora and Dr. Zarkov in five episodes. In 'The Freedom Balloon' they escape from their slavery. 'Flashback' 'Beware of Gifts', 'Deadly Double' and 'The Seed' see them battling against grim odds.
F — EN
King Features Syndicate — *Select Video Limited*   P
3505

Flash Gordon 2-The Big Battle   Fil-Ent '??
Cartoons/Adventure
09980   60 mins   C
B, V
Animated
This tape features five exciting episodes of Flash Gordon and Dale Arden in outer space. Flash makes a new friend when he frees a baby dragon called Gremlin from a tribe of wild men. It then proceeds to follow him everywhere.
F — EN
King Features Syndicate — *Select Video Limited*   P
3508/43

Flashpoint Africa   Fil-Ent '80
Adventure/Drama
12816   99 mins   C
B, V
Gayle Hunnicutt, Trevor Howard, Belinda Mayne, directed by Francis Magahy
This film tells the story of a news hungry team reporting on a terrorist's activities in an African state.
C,A — EN
Barry Saint Clair — *VCL Video Services*   P
277540/277550

Flat Top   Fil-Ent '52
War-Drama/Adventure
07994   89 mins   C
B, V
Sterling Hayden, Richard Carlsen, Keith Larsen, John Bromfield, Phyllis Coates
This film tells the true story of the fight for control of the skies over the Pacific during World War II. In the film actual battle footage from the Navy is used.
S,A — EN
Monogram — *Motion Epics Video Company Ltd*   P
161

Fleetwood Mac   Fil-Ent '81
Music-Performance/Documentary
06048   58 mins   C
B, V
This film looks at the making of Fleetwood Mac's LP 'Tusk' and the tour that followed it. It features live shows recorded at the St Louis Checkerdrome with scenes of the group onstage, in the studio and at home. Songs include 'Sisters of the Moon', 'Walka thinline,' 'Tusk,' 'Angel,' 'Save me a place,' 'The Chain,' 'Go Your Own Way,' 'Sara' and others.
F — EN
Warner Bros — *Warner Home Video*   P
WEX4022/WEV4022

Fleetwood Mac in Concert   Fil-Ent '8?
Music-Performance
09885   80 mins   C
B, V
This features all-time favourites such as 'Gypsy', 'Rhiannon', 'Tusk', 'Go Your Own Way' and 'Eyes of the World'. Fleetwood Mac perform at home in front of several thousand fans at the Los Angeles Forum. Recorded in stereo.
F — EN
Unknown — *Polygram Video*   H, P
790 6494/790 6492

(For Explanation of codes, see USE GUIDE and KEY)

PALADIN VIDEO HOME ENTERTAINMENT GUIDE

Flesh and Blood Show, The
Fil-Ent '7?
Horror
01900   97 mins   C
V2, B, V
Ray Brooks, Jenny Hanley, Luan Peters, Patrick Barr
A group of actors called to an audition for a West End production find themselves fighting for their lives.
A — EN
VideoView — Videomedia   P

Flesh Gordon
Fil-Ent '7?
Science fiction/Comedy
06073   70 mins   C
B, V
Jason Williams, Suzanne Fields, Joseph Hudgins, William Hunt
This film is an adult super-spoof of science fiction, a parody of yesterday's super heros. The Earth is thrown into carnal chaos by a mysterious sex ray. Flesh Gordon and his friends travel to the planet Porno to save the earth.
A — EN
Unknown — Video Programme Distributors
P
Media—M502

Flight 90: Disaster on the Potomac
Fil-Ent '84
Drama
13735   90 mins   C
V2, B, V
Jeanetta Arnett, Barry Corbin, Stephen Macht, Dinah Manoff, Richard Masur, Donnelly Rhodes, Jamie Rose
The true story of the plane that crashed into the icy waters of the Potomac river in January '82 and the rescue operation.
BBFC:PG — S,A — EN
Bill and Pat Finnegan — Medusa Communications Ltd   H, P
MC 027

Flight of Apollo 7, The
Med-Sci '68
Space exploration
04427   14 mins   C
B, V, PH15, PH17, 3/4U
A report on the first manned mission in the Apollo series.
C,A — ED
NASA — Istead Audio Visual   P
HQ 187

Flight of Dragons, The
Fil-Ent '82
Cartoons/Adventure
09855   85 mins   C
B, V

Animated, voices of James Earl Jones, John Ritter, Harry Morgan, Victor Buono, James Gregory, Don McLean
This is a story from mythological times, when knights were bold and dragons stalked the earth.
F — EN
Rankin/Bass — Polygram Video   H, P
791 5634/791 5632

Flight of the Phoenix, The
Fil-Ent '66
Suspense/Drama
12089   149 mins   C
B, V
James Stewart, Richard Attenborough, Peter Finch, Hardy Kruger, Ernest Borgnine, directed by Robert Aldrich
A twin-engined plane crashes in the North African desert. The only hope of survival is to re-build another plane from the wreckage.
S,A — EN
Twentieth Century Fox — CBS/Fox Video
P
1221

Flight to Holocaust
Fil-Ent '77
Adventure
02087   90 mins   C
B, V
Patrick Wayne, Christopher Mitchum, Desi Arnaz Jr, Sid Caesar, Lloyd Nolan
This is the exciting story of one day in the lives of the 'trouble shooter' group. Action-packed, including the rescue of a plane which has crashed into a skyscraper at Los Angeles Airport.
F — EN
Aycee Prods, First Artists, NBC — VCL Video Services   P

Flight to Mars
Fil-Ent '52
Science fiction
09218   75 mins   C
B, V
Cameron Mitchell, Marguerite Chapman, Arthur Franz, William Forrest, Virginia Huston
An expedition crash lands on the red planet and discovers an advanced underground society. Their friendly welcome is marred by just one Martian, who will stop at nothing to prevent them from leaving Mars.
F — EN
Monogram; Walter Mirisch — Video Form Pictures   H, P
MGT 10

Flight to Mars
Fil-Ent '52
Science fiction
10216   75 mins   C
B, V

PALADIN VIDEO HOME ENTERTAINMENT GUIDE

Cameron Mitchell, Marguerite Chapman
Five writers and scientists make a successful landing on Mars although their ship was damaged by meteoric showers. They find that they have been expected. Through super-radio and viewscopes the Martians know most of what is going on in the Universe. Familiar with Earth language and customs they reveal that their race is doomed.
S,A — EN
Monogram; Walter Mirsch — *Video Form Pictures* **H, P**
MGT 10

Florida Connection Fil-Ent '78
Suspense
04480   102 mins   C
V2, B, V
Dan Pastorini, June Wilkinson
Drug smuggling in Florida provides for a lot of action in this fast-paced movie.
S,A — EN
Lone Star Pictures — *Intervision Video* **H, P**
A-AE 0173

Flower Angel, The Fil-Ent '80
Cartoons/Adventure
05959   46 mins   C
B, V
Animated
The Flower Angel and her friends are searching for the Flower of Seven colours. In their travels they help a lonely old man and his daughter find the love they have for each other, and enter into a town's Rose Festival. An evil witch is stalking them trying to get to the Flower of Seven colours first.
BBFC:U — F — EN
ZIV International; Family Home Entertainment — *Home Video Holdings* **H, P**
025

Flower Arranging How-Ins '8?
Flowers/Arts
08082   65 mins   C
B, V
This programme comes in two parts, and describes the preservation of plant material and the ground rule for successful flower arrangements. In the first part (38 minutes) it describes the three fundamental methods for preserving plants. In the second part (27 minutes) it demonstrates how to use simple and inexpensive material for foundations to elaborate flower arrangements
S,A — I
Independent — *Rank Video Library* **H, P**
5022 B

Flower Arranging: Part 1: How-Ins '8?
The Basics
Flowers/Arts
06898   60 mins   C
B, V
Presented by Bill Lomas
On this tape Bill Lomas, the internationally respected flower arranger, shows examples of varying forms of plant material used to make an arrangement and how to use space, form, line and colour to create your own unique effect.
S,A — I
Holiday Brothers Ltd — *Holiday Brothers Ltd*
P

Flower Arranging: Part 2: How-Ins '8?
A Step Further
Flowers/Arts
06899   60 mins   C
B, V
Presented by Bill Lomas
In this second part of the series Bill Lomas, the internationally respected flower arranger, gives practical advice on the techniques of preserving plant material. Success in the art is based on a knowledge of how to help the plants survive, how to choose them, and how to keep them in the right conditions. He also gives further advanced ideas for the design of arrangements.
S,A — I
Holiday Brothers Ltd — *Holiday Brothers Ltd*
P

Flower Arranging with How-Ins '7?
Jean Taylor
Flowers/Handicraft
05242   38 mins   C
B, V
2 pgms
This series describes the preservation of plant material and the ground rules for successful flower arrangements. Part 1 describes the three fundamental methods of preserving plants. Part 2 shows how simple and inexpensive devices are used to provide the foundations for elaborate arrangements.
C,A — I
Unknown — *Rank Video Library* **H, P**
5022; 5023

Flower Out of Place, A Fil-Ent '74
Musical
06076   50 mins   C
B, V
Linda Ronstadt, Johnny Cash, Roy Clark, Foster Brooks, hosted by Glen Sherley
A special concert performed for the 2,000 plus inmates at the Tennessee State Prison. Johnny Cash performs 'Folsom Prison,' 'Orange

---

(For Explanation of codes, see USE GUIDE and KEY)

PALADIN VIDEO HOME ENTERTAINMENT GUIDE

Blossom Special' and 'A Boy Named Sue' among others. Linda Ronstadt sings 'Silver Threads' and 'You're No Good.' They all join together for a finale of 'I Saw The Light.'
F — EN
Unknown — *Video Programme Distributors*
P
Media—M424

Flower Stories Chi-Juv '81
Cartoons/Fantasy
05617   84 mins   C
V2, B, V
Animated
This tape, especially designed for young children, features eight ten minute adventures of a fat black and white cat who lives in an enchanted garden, with his friends Plain Bee, Sad Dragon, Green Elephant, Silk and Lawn and the wicked Black Queen. Titles are 'The Sad Dragon,' 'James the Gardener,' 'The Journey,' 'The Lonely Potted Bush,' 'The Black Queen Returns,' 'The Green Elephant,' 'James and the Yellow Canary' and 'The Vain Rose.'
PS,M — EN
HTV; Taurus Films GMBH — *RPTA Video Ltd*
H, P

Flush Fil-Ent '7?
Comedy/Adventure
09088   75 mins   C
V2, B, V
William Callaway, William Bronder, Jeannie Linero, directed by Andrew J. Kuehn
An eccentric millionaire, shortly before his death, buried six boxes of treasure in different places around the country. Twenty years later after a cesspool blows up, a man is sent to clear up. He finds one of the boxes containing a clue to the whereabouts of the treasure. He embarks on a wild hunt to get his hands on the fortune. However other people have the same idea.
F — EN
Unknown — *Video Tape Centre* **P**
VTC 1058

Fluteman, The Chi-Juv '82
Fantasy
13403   90 mins   C
V2, B, V
John Jarrat, Aileen Britton
This is a modern-day version of the pied piper legend, with the mysterious flute player who offers to end a town's drought—at a price.
BBFC:U — F — EN
Alpha Films — *Intervision Video*   **H, P**
0010

Flyer Flies Faster Spo-Lei '83
Sports-Water
12721   75 mins   C
V2, B, V
This film gives an insight into the intense planning, preparation and attention to detail that sets this Dutch skipper and his crew apart from the rest in the last two Whitbread Round the World Yacht races.
F — EN
Cornelis van Rietschoten — *Quadrant Video*
H, P

Flying Birds/Birds of the Lake/Osprey Watch Gen-Edu '8?
Birds/Wildlife
09104   42 mins   C
B, V
This programme contains three films on one cassette, ideal for classroom use and bird lovers of all ages.
F — ED
Royal Society for the Protection of Birds — *Royal Society for the Protection of Birds*   **H, P**

Flying Deuces, The Fil-Ent '39
Comedy
02455   60 mins   B/W
B, V
Stan Laurel, Oliver Hardy, Jean Parker, Reginald Gardner
Laurel and Hardy join the Foreign Legion.
F — EN
RKO — *Mountain Video*   **P**

Flying Finns 1968, The/The Golden Age of Rallying Spo-Lei '76
Automobiles-Racing
04512   27 mins   C
B, V
Hannu Mikkola and Time Makinen battle fellow Scandinavians in Finland's leading event—the Rally of the Thousand Lakes. The second feature is a history of rallying from 1958-68, covering all the well-known events, personalities, and manufacturers of the era.
F — EN
Ford Motor Company; Castrol — *Quadrant Video*   **H, P**
M18

Flying Leathernecks, The/Beyond a Reasonable Doubt Fil-Ent '5?
War-Drama/Suspense
05774   175 mins   C
B, V

PALADIN VIDEO HOME ENTERTAINMENT GUIDE

John Wayne, Robert Ryan, Janis Carter, directed by Nicholas Ray, Dana Andrews, Joan Fontaine, Sidney Blackmer, directed by Fritz Lang

Two films are contained on one cassette. 'Flying Leathernecks' (colour, 98 minutes, 1952) features a flying squad in action during the war, which is taken over by a tough commander, who leads his team against tremendous odds, controlling the men with an inflexible strength of will. 'Beyond a Reasonable Doubt' (black and white, 77 minutes, 1957) is about a newspaperman who is opposed to capital punishment. He plans a 'murder' that will seem to implicate his son-in-law (who is in on the plan). However it all goes wrong.

S,A — EN

RKO — Kingston Video   **H, P**
KV8

Flying Superboy, The   Fil-Ent '??
Crime-Drama
06859   90 mins   C
V2, B, V

Robert Widmark, Gilshen Bubiko

A likeable adventurer becomes involved in an organisation led by a 'Godfather'. After a series of spell-binding events the adventurer falls in love with a girl who turns out to be the Godfather's daughter. Many misunderstandings occur between the two men until the Godfather becomes a grandfather and his new son-in-law takes over as the Godfather.

S,A — EN

Unknown — European Video Company   **P**

F.O.C.A Start to Finish   Spo-Lei '82
Automobiles-Racing
10156   86 mins   C
B, V

This film contains highlights from the 1981 Grand Prix season. It goes from race to race, recording the accidents survivals, and deaths which took place in this particular year.

S,A — EN

Unknown — MGM/UA Home Video   **P**
UMB 10232/UMV 10232

Focus on Soccer 1-3   Spo-Lei '7?
Soccer
01893   50 mins   C
B, V, LV

Mike Channon, Sir Matt Busby, Ray Clemence, Colin Todd, Trevor Brooking, Gordon Hill, Kevin Keegan   3 pgms

This series of tapes introduces the game of soccer with professional players showing their skills, telling the history of the game and the importance of being part of a team. In three parts.

S,A — I

Rank — Rank Video Library   **H, P**
5014; 5015; 5016

Fog, The   Fil-Ent '78
Horror
07689   87 mins   C
V2, B, V

Adrienne Barbeau, Jamie Lee Curtis, John Houseman, Janet Leigh, directed by John Carpenter

This tale of supernatural horror concerns a ghostly fog that reappears to fulfil a curse. The fog moves counter to the wind, slowly enveloping the town and its victims.

A — EN

Avco Embassy — Embassy Home Entertainment   **P**
2003

Follow That Rainbow   Fil-Ent '7?
Drama
02228   95 mins   C
V

The story of a teenage girl who leaves her Swiss boarding school to track down her father who is a famous pop star.

F — EN

Unknown — JVC   **P**
PRT 47

Food, Wine and Friends: Volume 4   How-Ins '79
Cookery/Alcoholic beverages
08439   94 mins   C
B, V

Jane Seymour, Hugh Johnson, Burgess Meredith, Linn Ullmann, Liv Ullmann, presented by Robert Carrier, directed by Sebastian Robinson

Robert Carrier continues in this fourth programme by introducing some very simple but delicious dishes. A charcoal steak and a grilled veal steak are prepared. He introduces the Chinese tradition of wok cookery. In the wine section a traditional Sancerre is examined at the home of the Chateaubriant and a talk to the Cellar-master of the Chateau Mouton-Rothschild.

S,A — I

HTV; Hemisphere Productions Ltd — THORN EMI   **P**
TXD 90 0756 4/TVD 90 0756 2

(For Explanation of codes, see USE GUIDE and KEY)

PALADIN VIDEO HOME ENTERTAINMENT GUIDE

Food, Wine and Friends: Volume 5
How-Ins '79

Cookery/Alcoholic beverages
08440　　92 mins　　C
B, V

Sally Kellerman, Bianca Jagger, Jean Marsh, Kasper, presented by Robert Carrier, directed by Sebastian Robinson
Robert Carrier continues in his fifth programme of the series with a conducted tour of the 18th century kitchen gardens at Hintlesham Hall. He prepares a courgette frittata, a rich beef stew and turbot in champagne. Henri de Rambuteau of the Chateau des Granges discusses the different types of Beaujolais and the Italian Barolo.
S,A — I
HTV; Hemisphere Productions Ltd — *THORN EMI*　**P**
TXD 90 0852 4/TVD 90 0852 2

Food, Wine and Friends: Volume 6
Gen-Edu '82

Cookery/Alcoholic beverages
09310　　90 mins　　C
B, V

Petula Clark, Virginia McKenna, Maud Adams, presented by Robert Carrier
Robert Carrier, the world's most famous writer on food, introduces more of his favourite recipes, visits the wine country of the Loire and talks with several of his glamorous actress friends.
S,A — EN
HTV; Hemisphere Productions Ltd — *THORN EMI*　**P**
TXD 90 0865 4/TVD 90 0865 2

Food, Wine and Friends: Volume 1
How-Ins '79

Cookery/Alcoholic beverages
07426　　102 mins　　C
B, V

John Cleese, Joanna Lumley, Joseph Cotten, Valentina Cortese, presented by Robert Carrier, directed by Sebastian Robinson
In this series, Robert Carrier, the world famous writer on food introduces a new style of living. Volume 1 contains four programmes in which he demonstrates the art of deep frying, cooking a roast, making pate and preparing au gratin potatoes. He introduces his four guests and his search for the best wines takes him to vineyards in Bordeaux, Beaujolais, Macon and Italy.
S,A — I
HTV; Hemisphere Productions Ltd — *THORN EMI*　**P**
TXC 90 0591 4/TVC 90 0591 2

Food, Wine and Friends: Volume 2
How-Ins '79

Cookery/Alcoholic beverages
07427　　93 mins　　C
B, V

Susannah York, John Schlesinger, Patricia Medina, Michael Broadbent, presented by Robert Carrier, directed by Sebastian Robinson
Robert Carrier continues in this second volume by giving instructions on how to cook with wine and prepares Boeuf Bourguignon. He shows how to steam vegetables, make a Chinese-style chicken dish, variations of Bechamel sauce and baking en papillote. He introduces his four guests and travels to Bordeaux, Brovilly, Beaune and the Cote de Nuits to look for the best wines including an impromptu lesson in wine tasting.
S,A — I
HTV; Hemisphere Productions Ltd — *THORN EMI*　**P**
TXC 90 0714 4/TVC 90 0714 2

Food, Wine and Friends: Volume 3
How-Ins '79

Cookery/Alcoholic beverages
07428　　92 mins　　C
B, V

Jenny Agutter, Michael Winner, Gordon Jackson, Cloris Leachman, presented by Robert Carrier, directed by Sebastian Robinson
Robert Carrier continues in this third programme of the series by introducing two party dishes. The first consists of a whole fresh salmon poached in wine stock with veal steaks and the second an old fashioned chicken soup with fettucine. He introduces his friends and visits an 18th century distillery to taste the cognac and discover what distinguishes a true Chianti. He also visits the cellars of Chateau de Mersault to learn something of the ritual of 'taste vin.'
S,A — I
HTV; Hemisphere Productions Ltd — *THORN EMI*　**P**
TXC 90 0737 4/TVC 90 0737 2

Foolin' Around
Fil-Ent '80

Comedy
08814　　101 mins　　C
B, V

Gary Busey, Annette O'Toole, Eddie Albert
This film tells the story of a college kid. He has been shot through with enough electricity to power several buildings. He falls in love with his lab assistant.
C,A — EN
Columbia — *VCL Video Services*　**P**
P296D

Football
Spo-Lei '80

Football
00264　　105 mins　　B/W

(For Explanation of codes, see USE GUIDE and KEY)

PALADIN VIDEO HOME ENTERTAINMENT GUIDE

B, V, FO
2 pgms
This video cassette adaptation of eleven films produced by the Football Association identifies and explains key factors which determine effective tactics and effective teamwork in Association Football. The matches used for analysis are from the 1966 World Cup Series. The presentation is contained on two video cassettes, each available separately; Part 1 runs 120 minutes and Part 2 runs 90 minutes.
F — I
London Video Ltd — Video Sport for All
P
1004

Footloose   Fil-Ent '84
Musical-Drama
13330   103 mins   C
B, V
Kevin Bacon, Frances Lee McCain, John Lithgow, Lori Singer, Dianne Wiest, Chris Penn, directed by Herbert Ross
When a mother brings her teenage son to a small mid-western town from Chicago, he finds himself faced with prejudice and intolerance. The musical score features songs from Bonnie Tyler, Deniece Williams, Kenny Loggins and other performers.
BBFC:PG — S,A — EN
Paramount — CIC Video   H, P
BER 2098/VHR 2098

Footsteps   Fil-Ent '72
Drama
09260   72 mins   C
V2, B, V
Richard Crenna, Clu Gulager, Joanna Pettet, Forrest Tucker, Ned Beatty, Bill Overton, directed by Paul Wendkos
The tough action and colour of college football provides the background for a grimly realistic look at the American game. The coach will stop at nothing to provide a winning team, inciting hatred and encouraging the use of dirty tactics within the team. However, when the big game comes the team want to win, but win fairly.
BBFC:A — S,A — EN
Metromedia/Stonehenge Prods — Iver Film Services   P
213

Footsteps of Giants   Gen-Edu '7?
Space exploration/Documentary
06954   60 mins   C
B, V

This documentary relives the triumphs and tragedies of American and Russian space exploration. It includes extensive NASA film footage, interviews with scientists and astronauts and finishes with the successful launching of the American space shuttle.
F — ED
Unknown — Home Video Merchandisers
H, P
050

For a Few Dollars More   Fil-Ent '65
Western
13184   133 mins   C
B, V
Clint Eastwood, Lee Van Cleef, directed by Sergio Leone
This is a second film in a series, in which a bounty hunter teams up with another to hunt a drug-addicted murderer known as El Indio.
BBFC:X — A — EN
Sergio Leone; Fulvio Morsell — Warner Home Video   P
99276

For Ladies Only   Fil-Ent '81
Drama
09015   95 mins   C
V2, B, V
Gregory Harrison, Patti Davis, Lee Grant, Marc Singer,
A young actor arrives in New York in search of an acting career. Because of hard times he is persuaded to take a waiter's job at a club open only to ladies, a club where the women are entertained by male strippers. However, he finds that becoming a stripper is not, after all, an advantageous step towards the famous Broadway stage.
A — EN
Film Town — Intervision Video   H, P
AA 0463

For Love of Ivy   Fil-Ent '68
Comedy-Drama/Romance
04191   102 mins   C
B, V
Sidney Poitier, Abbey Lincoln, Beau Bridges, Nan Martin, Lauri Peters
A brother and sister decide to find a man for their maid-housekeeper who is threatening to leave. They find the perfect 'victim,' but they could never have imagined the consequences—embarrassment, intrigue, and light-hearted blackmail.
BBFC:A — S,A — EN
Cinerama — Guild Home Video   H, P

(For Explanation of codes, see USE GUIDE and KEY)

PALADIN VIDEO HOME ENTERTAINMENT GUIDE

For the Love of Ada   Fil-Ent '??
Comedy-Drama
08643   86 mins   C
V2, B, V
Wilfred Pickles, Irene Handl, Jack Smethhurst
A quiet well-organised wedding anniversary party turns out to be a riot, with misunderstandings, accidents, double bookings and arguments.
S,A — EN
Unknown — *Hokushin Audio Visual Ltd*
P
VM 43

For Whom the Bell Tolls   Fil-Ent '43
Drama
13289   128 mins   C
B, V
Ingrid Bergman, Gary Cooper, Katina Paxinov, directed by Sam Wood
Based on Ernest Hemingway's story of the Spanish Civil War, this film tells the story of a soldier of fortune and the brutalized peasant girl he falls in love with.
BBFC:PG — *S,A — EN*
Paramount — *CIC Video*   **H, P**
BEJ 1024/VHJ 1024

For Your Eyes Only   Fil-Ent '81
Adventure
13196   127 mins   C
B, V
Roger Moore, Carole Bouquet, directed by John Glen
A British agent is killed attempting to retrieve a top secret, highly dangerous device from a sunken surveillance vessel off the Greek coast. Bond investigates and encounters a variety of mysterious and ruthless characters in exotic locations.
BBFC:A — *C,A — EN*
Danjaq SA — *Warner Home Video*   **P**
99247

For Your Love Only   Fil-Ent '83
Drama/Romance
09443   99 mins   C
V2, B, V
Nastassia Kinski, Christian Quadflieg, Judy Winter, Klaus Schwarzkopf, directed by Wolfgang Peterson
A 17-year-old schoolgirl has fallen madly in love with her teacher. Despite being a happily married man he returns her passionate infatuation. They are discovered by one of her classmates, a boy who wants her for himself. Their once idyllic world is shattered, becoming a nightmare of blackmail, murder and despair.
BBFC:18 — *A — EN*
NDR/Studio Hamburg — *Guild Home Video*
H, P, E

Forbidden Planet   Fil-Ent '56
Science fiction
06492   98 mins   C
B, V
Leslie Nielsen, Walter Pidgeon, Anne Francis, Robby the Robot
In the year 2200, a space cruiser visits the planet of Altair Four to rescue the survivors of a colony that had lived there peacefully until a mysterious series of killings began to occur.
F — EN
MGM — *MGM/UA Home Video*   **P**
UMB 10041/UMV 10041

Forbidden World   Fil-Ent '82
Science fiction/Horror
12166   77 mins   C
V2, B, V
Jessie Vint, directed by Allan Holzman
Scientists in outer space have developed a new form of food which now threatens their own survival.
BBFC:18 — *C,A — EN*
Roger Corman — *Embassy Home Entertainment*   **P**
4030

Force of One, A   Fil-Ent '79
Crime-Drama/Martial arts
07799   90 mins   C
B, V
Chuck Norris, Jennifer O'Neill, Bill Wallace, Eric Laneuville
The six times undefeated world karate champion is enlisted by a small town Californian police department to help in the investigation of a multi-million dollar drug racket.
S,A — EN
Michael Leone; Alan Belkin — *Video Tape Centre*   **P**
VTC 1002

Forced Impact   Fil-Ent '81
Crime-Drama
12854   86 mins   C
V2, B, V
Richard Conte, John Steiner, Maurizio Merli, Ray Lovelock
A police officer embarks on a personal crusade against crime, hitting out mercilessly without bothering too much about the law but finds he is forced to resign from the force.
BBFC:18 — *A — EN*
Unknown — *Video Programme Distributors*
P
224

Forced Vengeance   Fil-Ent '82
Adventure/Martial arts
10150   87 mins   C

PALADIN VIDEO HOME ENTERTAINMENT GUIDE

B, V
Chuck Norris
Set in Hong Kong's gangland, this tells the story of a one-time Vietnam combat veteran who now works as a casino security chief. He finds himself in the centre of a struggle for power between two different syndicates in a desperate fight for control.
BBFC:PG — S,A — EN
MGM; SLM Entertainment — *MGM/UA Home Video* **P**
VMB 10189/UMV 10189

Forest Feast   Spo-Lei '81
Automobiles-Racing
05603   37 mins   C
B, V
A special sports feature for Car Rally enthusiasts featuring the 1981 Welsh and Scotish Car Rallies.
F — EN
Vintage Television — *Vintage Television Ltd*
H, P, E

Forever Young   Fil-Ent '83
Drama
13708   84 mins   C
B, V
James Aubrey, Nicholas Crecks, Alec McCowen, Karen Archer, Liam Holt, directed by David Drury
Two one-time friends meet up accidentally after twenty years—one has become a priest but the other finds out he does have a certain vulnerability.
BBFC:15 — S,A — EN
David Puttnam — *THORN EMI*   **P**
90 2784

Forgotten Man, The   Fil-Ent '71
Drama
04265   71 mins   C
B, V
Dennis Weaver, Lois Nettleton, Anne Francis, Andrew Duggan
This film tells the story of an American POW who escapes from North Vietnam after five years of captivity only to find that he had been reported killed in action. His wife has re-married, his partner has sold his business, he has ceased to exist.
S,A — EN
Worldvision — *Rank Video Library*   **H, P**
0034

Formula, The   Fil-Ent '80
Drama
06490   117 mins   C
V2, B, V
Marlon Brando, George C. Scott

Despite numerous attempts on his life, a Los Angeles policeman continues to search for the formula that could end America's dependence on foreign oil.
S,A — EN
Steve Shagan; MGM — *MGM/UA Home Video*
P
UMB 10037/UMV 10037

Fort Apache   Fil-Ent '48
Western/Drama
05884   112 mins   B/W
B, V
Henry Fonda, John Wayne, Shirley Temple, directed by John Ford
The story of conflict between the U.S. cavalry and the Indians, also between the colonel and his second-in-command.
F — EN
RKO; John Ford — *THORN EMI*   **P**
TXC 90 0079 4/TVC 90 0079 2

Fort Apache, The Bronx   Fil-Ent '81
Crime-Drama
09067   120 mins   C
B, V
Paul Newman, Edward Asner, Ken Wahl, Danny Aiello, Rachel Ticotin, Pam Grier, Kathleen Beller, directed by Daniel Petrie
This film is a police drama, set in the beleaguered South Bronx of New York City, based on the real-life experiences of two former New York cops who served there.
A — EN
Time-Life Films — *Video Tape Centre*   **P**
VTC 1040

---

48 Hrs.   Fil-Ent '83
Crime-Drama
10106   97 mins   C
B, V
Nick Nolte, Eddie Murphy, Frank McRae, James Remar, David Patrick Kelly, Sonny Landham, directed by Walter Hill
A police detective and a jail-bird join forces in trying to track down a gang of crooks. The detective wants to nail two killers and the jail-bird is after his money.
BBFC:18 — C,A — EN
Paramount — *CIC Video*   **H, P**
BEA 2074/VHA 2074

---

40 Million Bucks on a   Fil-Ent '7?
Dead Man's Chest
Adventure
02416   82 mins   C
B, V
Rod Taylor, Stuart Whitman, Elke Sommer, Jeremy Kemp, directed by Henry Levin

---

(For Explanation of codes, see USE GUIDE and KEY)

PALADIN VIDEO HOME ENTERTAINMENT GUIDE

A chance meeting leads two former college friends into a search for sunken treasure, a search which involves them with the double dealing Landers, supporter of their expedition.
S,A — EN
Unknown — *Derann Film Services*   **H, P**
DV 106B/DV 106

49th Parallel   Fil-Ent '41
Drama
13762   121 mins   B/W
B, V
Eric Portman, Laurence Olivier, Anton Walbrook, Leslie Howard, Raymond Massey
The story of six survivors from a German U-boat sunk off the coast of Canada is protrayed in this cassettee.
BBFC:A — S,A — EN
Unknown — *Rank Video Library*   **H, P**
0207A

4D Man   Fil-Ent '59
Horror
02460   81 mins   C
B, V
Robert Lansing, Lee Meriwether
Brilliant scientist is able to pass his body through any substance. This power transforms him into a robbing, murdering monster.
A — EN
Universal — *Mountain Video*   **P**

Four Feathers, The   Fil-Ent '78
War-Drama/Adventure
08454   100 mins   C
B, V
Simon Ward, Robert Powell, Beau Bridges, Jane Seymour, Harry Andrews, Richard Johnson, directed by Don Sharp
This tells the story of a young man, who on the eve of his engagement receives a telegram summoning him to war in Egypt. He burns this, but on his friends' discovery they send each him a white feather. A fourth white feather, the symbol of cowardice, is sent to him by his fiancee together with his ring. He sets out, disgraced and ashamed, to redeem his honour, and regain his love.
BBFC:U — F — EN
Trident Films Ltd; Norman Rosemount Prod — *THORN EMI*   **P**
TXA 90 09644/TVA 90 0964 2

Four Feathers, The   Fil-Ent '39
Drama/Adventure
09869   109 mins   C
B, V
John Clements, Ralph Richardson, C. Aubrey Smith, June Duprez, directed by Zolton Korda
This film tells the story of a young British officer who fights to preserve his honour after being branded a coward. Based on a novel by A.E.W Mason.
F — EN
United Artists — *Polygram Video*   **H, P**
790 2524/790 2522

Four for All   Fil-Ent '7?
Crime-Drama
07764   90 mins   C
V2, B, V
A man attempts to eliminate all his enemies in order to become the boss of a criminal organisation.
S,A — EN
Unknown — *Fletcher Video*   **H, P**
AV616

Four Musketeers, The   Fil-Ent '75
Adventure/Comedy
08453   102 mins   C
B, V
Oliver Reed, Faye Dunaway, Raquel Welch, Richard Chamberlain, Michael York, Frank Finlay, directed by Richard Lester
In this sequel to 'The Three Musketeers' a trail of cheerful chaos reigns as they attempt to rescue the beautiful Constance from her evil kidnapper Cardinal Richelieu.
BBFC:U — F — EN
20th Century Fox — *THORN EMI*   **P**
TXB 90 1283 4/TVB 90 1283 2

Four Seasons (Antonio Vivaldi), The   Fin-Art '7?
Music-Performance
02263   50 mins   C
V
The different moods of Vivaldi's music are illustrated and enhanced by the settings and costumes of Vivaldi's time. The programme is directed by Pierre Neel and features Roberto Michelluci on violin.
F — EN
Unknown — *JVC*   **P**
PRT 34

Fourth Man, The   Fil-Ent '83
Drama/Suspense
13219   95 mins   C
V2, B, V
Jeroen Crabbe, Rene Soutendjik, Thom Hoffman, directed by Paul Verhoeven

PALADIN VIDEO HOME ENTERTAINMENT GUIDE

A writer becomes involved with a beautiful girl and her lover and enters a wierd and bizarre adventure where he discovers the girl's three previous husbands have died in a series of strange accident's. This film has been dubbed into English.
BBFC:18 — A — EN
Spectra Films — Embassy Home Entertainment P
1378

Fox and His Friends Fil-Ent '75
Drama
08973 123 mins C
B, V
Rainer Werner Fassbinder, Peter Chatel, Karl Heinz Bohm, directed by Rainer Werner Fassbinder
This tells of the lives of homosexuals, their passions, quarrels, enforced pretences and discrimination. It is a German film, subtitled in English.
BBFC:X — A — EN GE
Cinegate — Palace Video Ltd P
PVC 2019B

Fox and the Hare, The Fil-Ent '??
Cartoons/Comedy
06228 60 mins C
B, V
Animated
A nasty scheming fox dreams-up and tries out seven wicked ways to trap the clever hare. Seven complete episodes—A Hunting We Will Go, Duck Soup, The Quiet Life, The Unwelcome Guest, Hurtling Heavens!, Double Cross and Friendly Enemies.
F — EN
Estudios Castilla SL — VCL Video Services P
F122

Fox and the Hare—Part 2, The Fil-Ent '??
Cartoons/Comedy
08839 45 mins C
B, V
Animated
This tape features six more adventures of the sly fox and the clever hare.
F — EN
ESTUDIOS CASTILLA S L — VCL Video Services P
F123B

Foxes Fil-Ent '80
Drama
12973 102 mins C
B, V
Jodie Foster, Sally Kellerman, Adam Faith, Cherie Currie, Kandice Stroh, Marilyn Kagan, Scott Baio, Randy Quaid
The relationship between four adolescent girls with their parents and contemporaries are portrayed in this film set in the seamy jungle of downtown Hollywood.
BBFC:15 — C,A — EN
United Artists; Casablanca — Warner Home Video P
99377

Foxhole in Cairo Fil-Ent '60
Adventure
04330 80 mins C
V2, B, V
James Robertson Justice, Adrian Hoven, Peter Van Eyck
Story about a secret agent in World War II.
BBFC:A — A — EN
Britannia Prods; Paramount — Intervision Video H, P
A-A 0002

Foxy Brown Fil-Ent '74
Crime-Drama
07383 94 mins C
V2, B, V
Pam Grier, Peter Brown, Terry Carter, Kathryn Loder, Harry Holcombe, directed by Jack Hill
A black nurse is out for revenge when mobsters kill her boyfriend, an undercover narcotics investigator. She finds out that the head of the crime ring is a 'madame' and manages to become a call girl in the establishment to learn about the activities of the gang. When she attempts to help one of the girls escape she is imprisoned and tortured.
BBFC:X — A — EN
American International Pictures — Guild Home Video H, P, E

Framed Fil-Ent '74
Crime-Drama
13605 101 mins C
B, V
Joe Don Baker, Conny Van Dyke, Joshua Bryant, John Marley, Brock Peters, directed by Phil Karlson
A nightclub owner who witnesses a shoot-out is framed and sent to prison but on his release starts his own series of investigations which take him into state government circles.
BBFC:18 — C,A — EN
Paramount — CIC Video H, P
2117

Frances Fil-Ent '82
Drama
09790 133 mins C

(For Explanation of codes, see USE GUIDE and KEY)

255

PALADIN VIDEO HOME ENTERTAINMENT GUIDE

B, V
Jessica Lange, Sam Shephard, Kim Stanley, directed by Graeme Clifford
A real life story of a strong minded young girl destined for stardom. Her conflicts against authority and her film studios leads to an eventual breakdown and a period spent in an asylum.
BBFC:15 — *S,A* — *EN*
Brooks films — *THORN EMI* **P**
TXA 90 17084/TVA 90 1708 2

France's Year 1980/81   Spo-Lei '8?
Sports
13537   20 mins   C
B, V
Pierre Villepreux explains aspects of back play in rugby football that are particular to the French.
F — *EN*
Unknown — *TFI Leisure Ltd*   **H, P**

Frankenstein   Fil-Ent '31
Horror
01056   71 mins   B/W
B, V
Boris Karloff, Mae Clark, Colin Clive, John Boles
An adaptation of the Mary Shelley novel about Dr. Henry Frankenstein, the scientist who creates a terrifying yet strangely sympathetic monster.
F — *EN*
Universal — *CIC Video*   **H, P**

Frankenstein's Castle of   Fil-Ent '73
Freaks
Horror
09297   81 mins   C
B, V
Rossano Brazzi, Edmund Purdom
A misguided genius surrounds himself with a bizarre assortment of assistants whilst trying to bring his creation, Goliath, to life by using the brain of a beautiful girl. Hostility from villagers and dissent in his own castle bring death and destruction when Goliath's power is unleashed.
A — *EN*
Unknown — *Abacus Video*   **P**
303

Frankenstein's Island   Fil-Ent '??
Horror
08268   91 mins   C
V2, B, V
John Carradine, Cameron Mitchell, Andrew Ruggan

This film tells the story of four balloonists who come to grief after being caught up in a storm. They drift ashore onto a strange island. They end up as permanent guests of Frankenstein's great-great-granddaughter.
BBFC:X — *A* — *EN*
Unknown — *Rank Video Library*   **H, P**
2020C

Frankie Avalon Show,   Fil-Ent '7?
The
Variety
04371   60 mins   C
B, V, PH17, 3/4U
Frankie Avalon, Buddy Greco, Joanie Summers
A variety show with Frankie Avalon and guests.
F — *EN*
Unknown — *Vidpics International*   **P**

Fraud!   Fil-Ent '74
Drama
12763   89 mins   C
B, V
Brian O'Shaughnessy, Anabel Linder, Michael McCabe
Based on real-life events, this film tells the story of two men who made a killing on the stock exchange by cheating the system.
BBFC:15 — *C,A* — *EN*
Unknown — *Rank Video Library*   **H, P**
0181 E

Frauleins in Uniforms   Fil-Ent '72
War-Drama
05700   97 mins   C
B, V
Brigitte Bergen, Karen Heske, Elizabeth Felchner, directed by Erwin C. Dietrich
During the war Hitler calls for young girls to form a volunteer corp to fight alongside the soldiers. A doctor who is responsible for the examination of the volunteers persuades many of the girls to go home. He is aware of the sexual debasement hidden behind the glamour and has two daughters of his own. For this humane gesture the Gestapo send him to the Russian Front.
BBFC:X — *A* — *EN*
Unknown — *Derann Film Services*   **H, P**
DV131B/DV131

Freaky Friday   Fil-Ent '??
Adventure
05587   94 mins   C
B, V
Jodie Foster, Barbara Harris, John Astin, directed by Gary Nelson
A mother and her daughter constantly disagree, the mother envies the freedom of the daughter and feels overworked, the daughter feels that

PALADIN VIDEO HOME ENTERTAINMENT GUIDE

her mother doesn't understand what it is like to be a teenager. One Friday the thirteenth they both wish they could change places for one day, and their wish is granted.
F — EN
Walt Disney Productions — *Rank Video Library* **H**
05600

Fred Bassett   Chi-Juv '7?
Cartoons
02217   60 mins   C
V
2 pgms
Two untitled sixty minute programmes available individually featuring the cartoon character Fred Bassett, whose view of life is whimsical and amusing and sets the 'human' world into true perspective.
M — EN
Unknown — *JVC*   **P**
PRT 4; PRT 22

Free Wheelin'   Fil-Ent '77
Adventure
05740   76 mins   C
B, V
Directed by Scott Diltrich
A story of a young skateboard enthusiast, his girlfriend and his dream of turning professional. Includes a skateboard 'safari' along the Californian coast and examples of all the many different styles, skills and skateboarding sites.
BBFC:U — F — EN
Scott Diltrich Productions — *Home Video Holdings*   **H, P**
002

Freebie and the Bean   Fil-Ent '73
Comedy
13207   111 mins   C
B, V
Alan Arkin, James Caan, directed by Richard Rush
A pair of incompetent policemen create havoc and chaos in San Francisco as they try to protect a big time mobster, pending his arrest when a key witness arrives.
BBFC:X — C,A — EN
Warner Bros — *Warner Home Video*   **P**
61237

Freedom Afloat   Spo-Lei '8?
Boating
13557   20 mins   C
B, V

This film illustrates the basic work of the Royal Yachting Association and includes shots of children in Optimists and Cadets, Olympic boats in action, ocean racers under spinnaker and catamarans in a Force 6.
F — EN
Unknown — *TFI Leisure Ltd*   **H, P**

Freedom Force, The   Chi-Juv '78
Cartoons/Fantasy
13116   52 mins   C
B, V
Animated
The Freedom Force live in the Valley of Time and use their magical powers and daring in their fight against the evil forces of darkness.
I,M — EN
Filmation Associates — *Select Video Limited* **P**
3630/43

Freedom Road   Fil-Ent '79
Drama
10207   300 mins   C
B, V
Muhammad Ali, Kris Kristofferson, Ron O'Neal, Barbara Jones, Edward Herrman, Fred Covington, Bill Mackey, Sonny Jim Gaines, Joel Avellen
This film is the story of a black man's rise from slave status to a seat in the United States Senate. Based on the novel by Howard Fast.
S,A — EN
Zev Braun TV — *Video Form Pictures*   **H, P**
6225

Freelance   Fil-Ent '7?
Suspense
02412   95 mins   C
B, V
Ian McShane, Gayle Hunnicut, Keith Barron, Alan Lake, directed by Francis Megahy
Small-time crook witnesses a fatal attack on an old man and finds himself number one target on the killer's list.
S,A — EN
Unknown — *Derann Film Services*   **H, P**
DV 105B/DV 105

French Connection, The   Fil-Ent '71
Crime-Drama
01016   102 mins   C
V2, B, V, LV
Gene Hackman, Fernando Rey, Roy Scheider, Tony LoBianco, Marcel Bozzuffi
Two hard-nosed N.Y. narcotics detectives stumble onto what turns out to be the biggest narcotics haul to that time.

PALADIN VIDEO HOME ENTERTAINMENT GUIDE

Academy Awards '71: Best Picture; Best Actor (Hackman); Best Director (William Friedkin).
A — EN
20th Century Fox; Philip D'Antoni — *CBS/Fox Video* **P**
3A-031

French Connection II, The Fil-Ent '75
Crime-Drama
07694 114 mins C
V2, B, V
Gene Hackman, Fernando Rey, Bernard Fresson, Jean-Pierre Castaldi, Charles Millot, directed by John Frankenheimer
In this sequel to the 'French Connection', Popeye Doyle, the New York policeman, arrives in Marseilles where he becomes the pursued instead of the pursuer as he attempts to crack the heroin-smuggling ring.
A — EN
Twentieth Century Fox — *CBS/Fox Video* **H**
1127

French Lieutenant's Woman, The Fil-Ent '81
Drama
13055 121 mins C
B, V
Meryl Streep, Jeremy Irons, directed by Karel Reisz
An adaptation from the book by John Fowles in which a Victorian gentleman becomes intrigued by an enigmatic young woman.
BBFC:AA — *C,A — EN*
Juniper Films — *Warner Home Video* **P**
99246

French Line, The/Texas Tough Guy/Murder in a Flat Fil-Ent '??
Musical/Comedy
05659 145 mins C
B, V
Jane Russell, Gilbert Roland, Arthur Hunnicutt, Craig Stevens, Leon Errol, Skitch Henderson
This cassette features one film and three shorts. 'The French Line' (Colour, 97 mins, 1954) in which a millionairess travels incognito to Paris, posing as a model. A dashing young Frenchman takes command. 'Texas Tough Guy' (Black/White) is a western comedy, 'Murder in A Flat' (Black/White) is a musical mystery and also featured is a musical with Dick Stabile Orchestra and The Sportsmen (15 mins).
S,A — EN
RKO — *Kingston Video* **H, P**
KV53

French Way, The Fil-Ent '??
Drama
07893 100 mins C
V2, B, V
Jane Birkin
This is the story of a crippled unsuccessful novelist who uses his friend, a meek bank clerk, to live his life for him. The clerk is amused by the intrigues at first and then begins to relish each new situation, especially with women. He meets with a beautiful prostitute which sparks off a unique love triangle.
S,A — EN
Unknown — *Video Programme Distributors* **P**
Replay—1008

Friday the 13th Part 2 Fil-Ent '81
Horror
09269 87 mins C
B, V
Amy Steel, John Furer, Adrienne King, Betsy Palmer, directed by Steve Miner
A group of teenager camp counsellors are horrifically murdered by yet another unknown assailant.
BBFC:R — *A — EN*
Paramount — *CIC Video* **H, P**

Friendly Fire Fil-Ent '78
Drama
07343 145 mins C
B, V
Carol Burnett, Ned Beatty, Sam Waterston, Dennis Erdman, Timothy Hutton, Fanny Spiess, Sherry Hursey, directed by David Greene
This is the true story of an American family and their search to find out what really happend to their son whose body was returned to them by the U.S. Army from Vietnam. They are told his death was attributed to 'friendly fire.' Based on the book by C. D. B. Bryans.
S,A — EN
Marble Arch Prods — *Precision Video Ltd* **P**
BITC 3095/VITC 3095

Fright Fil-Ent '71
Drama/Horror
08559 84 mins C
B, V
Susan George, Honor Blackman, Ian Bannen, John Gregson, directed by Peter Collinson
The boy's parents seem anxious to leave him in the hands of Amanda, the babysitter, while they go out for the evening. She claims to be scared

PALADIN VIDEO HOME ENTERTAINMENT GUIDE

of nothing, not even the ghosts that the father jokingly suggests might haunt the isolated country house. However someone is prowling outside, and faces appear at the window.
BBFC:X — A — EN
Fantale Films Ltd — THORN EMI   P
TXC 90 0759 4/TVC 90 0759 2

Frightmare   Fil-Ent '7?
Horror
09918   86 mins   C
V2, B, V
Rupert Davies, Sheila Keith, Paul Greenwood, Deborah Fairfax, Kim Butcher, directed by Peter Walker, Leo Genn
A husband and wife were committed to a mental institution in 1957 for sickening crimes. In the present day a girl confesses to a psychiatrist friend that she is worried about her delinquent sister. At night she delivers mysterious parcels to an isolated farmhouse. The elderly couple that live there have recently been released from an asylum.
BBFC:18 — A — EN
Unknown — Derann Film Services   P
FDV 319

Frisco Kid, The   Fil-Ent '79
Comedy/Western
13210   119 mins   C
B, V
Gene Wilder, Harrison Ford, directed by Robert Aldrich
In the days of the Gold Rush an unlikely duo, a Rabbi and an outlaw, team up to cross America but are soon beset by outrageous adventures.
BBFC:A — C,A — EN
Warner Bros — Warner Home Video   P
61095

Fritz the Cat   Fil-Ent '72
Comedy
12529   78 mins   C
B, V
Animated, directed by Ralph Bakshi
The tale of a raunchy New York tom cat and his encounters with pot, politics and revolution.
BBFC:18 — A — EN
Steve Krantz — THORN EMI   P
TXB 90 2199 4/TVB 90 2199 2

Frogs   Fil-Ent '72
Horror
07382   91 mins   C
V2, B, V
Ray Milland, Sam Elliott, Joan Van Ark, Adam Roarke, directed by George McCowan
A man gathers his entire family at the ancestral mansion on a secluded swamp island to celebrate his birthday and the fourth of July. The traditional reunion is saddened by a feeling of strangeness in the air and tension mounts when the caretaker is found dead in the woods. A series of grisly deaths follow as frogs, snakes, leeches, lizards and alligators engulf the mansion, intent on the destruction of man.
BBFC:AA — S,A — EN
American International Pictures — Guild Home Video   H, P, E

From a Far Country, Pope   Fil-Ent '81
John Paul II
Drama/Biographical
08750   138 mins   C
B, V
Sam Neill, Christopher Cazenove, Lisa Harrow, Maurice Denham, Warren Clarke
The story of Karol Wojtyla is told in this film, who ascended the throne of St. Peter as Pope John Paul II to become the first non-Italian Pope in over 400 years. It also tells of modern Poland, and the struggle for survival of the Catholic faith against repression.
S,A — EN
ITC — Precision Video Ltd   P
BITC 3102/VTC 3102

From Africa with   Gen-Edu '78
Love—Nature Film
Africa/Wildlife
04411   60 mins   C
B, V
This beautiful nature programme takes the viewer to the heart of Africa for an intimate look at the wildlife of the continent.
F — ED
Unknown — VCL Video Services   P

From Corleone to   Fil-Ent '79
Brooklyn/Convoy
Busters
Crime-Drama
08010   181 mins   C
V2, B, V
Maurizio Merli, Mario Merola, Van Johnson, Biagio Pelligra, Venantino Venantini directed by Umberto Lenzi; Maurizio Merli, directed by Stelvio Massi
Two films contained on one cassette: 'From Corleone to Brooklyn' (colour, 93 minutes) features a determined cop and a killer each with their own reason for jailing a gangster. 'Convoy Busters' (colour, 88 minutes) features a tough cop banished to a quiet coastal town where his problems are only just beginning.
BBFC:AA — C,A — EN
Unknown — Iver Film Services   P
179

(For Explanation of codes, see USE GUIDE and KEY)   259

PALADIN VIDEO HOME ENTERTAINMENT GUIDE

From Russia with Love
Fil-Ent '63
Adventure
13186　　118 mins　　C
B, V
Sean Connery, Robert Shaw, Daniela Bianchi, Lotte Lenya
SPECTRE plans to trap James Bond. The bait: a valuable Russian cipher machine which Bond must steal from an embassy in Istanbul.
BBFC:A — C,A — EN
United Artists; Eon; Harry Saltzman; Albert Broccoli — *Warner Home Video*　　**P**
99209

From the Earth to the Moon
Chi-Juv '8?
Cartoons/Adventure
12245　　47 mins　　C
B, V
Animated
Based on Jules Verne's story, this is an account of the very first manned attempt to fly to the moon. It features specially composed music from a thirty piece orchestra.
PS,M — EN
Unknown — *VCL Video Services*　　**P**
A381B

From the Earth to the Moon/Jack and the Beanstalk
Fil-Ent '??
Science fiction/Musical
05776　　169 mins　　C
B, V
Joseph Cotton, George Sanders, Debra Paget, directed by Byron Haskin, Bud Abbott, Lou Costello, Dorothy Ford, directed by Jean Yarbrough
Two films are contained on one cassette. 'From the Earth to the Moon' (colour, 96 minutes, 1959) features an account of Victor Barbicane's invention—a source of infinite energy capable of launching a projectile to the moon. One of his astronauts is a girl, and earthly passions are not easily left behind. 'Jack and the Beanstalk' (black and white, 73 minutes, 1953) features Lou Costello falling asleep whilst babysitting and dreaming he is Jack, complete with magic beans, beanstalk, hen that lays golden eggs, a talking harp and the ferocious giant.
F — EN
Warner Bros — *Kingston Video*　　**H, P**
KV5

From the Life of the Marionettes
Fil-Ent '80
Drama
05386　　99 mins　　C
B, V
Robert Atzorn, Christine Buchegger, Martin Benrath, directed by Ingmar Bergman
This film is a portrayal of events during an encounter between a prostitute and a strange and intense man. As she caressed his face she felt that there was something different about the man, as she forced her attentions on him he became aggressive. Frightened, she runs through the seedy building, hoping she can hide from him.
BBFC:X — A — EN
Personafilm GMBH Munich — *Precision Video Ltd*　　**P**
BITC 2092/VITC 2092

Fruit Is Ripe, The
Fil-Ent '??
Drama
09350　　94 mins　　C
B, V, LV
Betty Verges, Olivia Pascal
The lovely young daughter of a wealthy German industrialist during her yearly vacation becomes very bored. She is picked up by a good looking man in a sports car, who takes her to his country house where he seduces her, only to be disturbed by the sudden appearance of his wife. Not being put off she continues, experiencing things that she has never known.
BBFC:18 — A — EN
Unknown — *Precision Video Ltd*　　**P**
BARPV 2593/VARPV 2593/LVHPV 2593

Fugitive, The
Fil-Ent '67
Crime-Drama
10197　　103 mins　　C
B, V
David Janssen, Barry Morse, Bill Raisch, Jacqueline Scott, Richard Anderson, Diane Brewster, Diane Baker, Michael Constantine, Joseph Campanella, J.D. Cannon, directed by Don Medford
This edition contains the last two episodes of the television series. The Fugitive, who escaped when sentenced to death for the murder of his wife, is closing in on the one-armed criminal responsible. The policeman who had been pursuing the Fugitive for four years is also catching up with him. With his one chance to prove his innocence he has to find the criminal and prove that he killed his wife before he is arrested.
S,A — EN
Quinn Martin Prods — *Video Form Pictures*　　**H, P**
6253-50

Fugitive, The/Follow Me Quietly
Fil-Ent '??
Drama/Suspense
05775　　144 mins　　B/W
B, V
Henry Fonda, Dolores del Rio, Ward Bond, directed by John Ford, William Lundigan, Dorothy Patrick, directed by Richard Fleischer

PALADIN VIDEO HOME ENTERTAINMENT GUIDE

Two films are contained on one cassette. 'The Fugitive' (black and white, 86 minutes, 1948) features clergyman Henry Fonda working among the peasants of Mexico where priests are outlawed. He befriends a man who later betrays him for silver, whilst a political trap closes around him. 'Follow Me Quietly' (black and white, 58 minutes, 1950) features a police lieutenant who trails a psychopathic killer who calls himself a judge, with the aid of a girl crime reporter. The killer becomes obsessed with murder whenever it rains.
S,A — EN
RKO — Kingston Video   H, P
KV7

Fun and Fancy Free   Fil-Ent '47
Cartoons/Adventure
07935   70 mins   C
B, V
Animated, Edgar Bergen
This is a compilation of Walt Disney cartoons presented by the cartoon character Jiminy Cricket. Includes Bongo the Bear, Jack and the Beanstalk and others.
F — EN
Walt Disney — Rank Video Library   H
10100

Fun in Acapulco   Fil-Ent '63
Musical
01746   97 mins   C
B, V
Elvis Presley, Ursula Andress, Elsa Cardenas, Paul Lukas
Elvis romances two beauties and acts as a part-time lifeguard and nightclub entertainer.
BBFC:U — F — EN
Paramount, Hal Wallis — CBS/Fox Video
P
3B-051

Fundamental Frolics   Fil-Ent '8?
Comedy-Performance/Music-Performance
06970   94 mins   C
V2, B, V
Introduced by Alexi Sayle
This film is a record of an outrageous evening when a group of contemporary artists gathered on stage in aid of MENCAP. Comedy by Alexi Sayle, 20th Century Coyote, Chris Langham and The Not the Nine O'Clock Team. Music by Alan Price, Neil Innes, Chas and Dave, Elvis Costello and Ian Drury, with dancing by Hot Gossip, is also included.
S,A — EN
Rick Gardner; Andy Finney — BBC Video
H, P
BBCV 7000

Funeral for an Assassin   Fil-Ent '??
Suspense/Drama
05478   90 mins   C
V2, B, V
Vic Morrow, Peter Dissel, Sam Williams, directed by Ivan Hall
A tough professional assassin is on his biggest assignment, a financed revenge mission in South Africa. He is forced in a unique way to hide his identity from Internal Security but his cleverness is matched by the cunning of the police.
BBFC:AA — S,A — EN
Walter Brough and Ivan Hall Prods — Iver Film Services   P
115

Funhouse, The   Fil-Ent '81
Horror
09264   96 mins   C
B, V
Elizabeth Berridge, Shawn Carson, Cooper Huckabee, Largo Woodruff, Sylvia Miles, directed by Tobe Hooper
Four teenagers spend a night at a carnival funhouse. A crazed father and his son turn their night of fun into an horrific nightmare as one by one they are brutally maimed.
BBFC:18 — S,A — EN
Universal — CIC Video   H, P

Funniest Man in the World, The   Fil-Ent '67
Comedy/Documentary
06770   90 mins   B/W
V2, B, V
Charlie Chaplin, Mabel Normand, Edna Purviance, Mack Swain, Ben Turpin, narrated by Douglas Fairbanks Jr.
A special compilation of great scenes from Chaplin films, including informal off-screen footage.
F — EN
United Artists — Intervision Video   H, P
A-AE 0328

Funny Forest   Chi-Juv '7?
Fantasy
02220   60 mins   C
V
The adventures of four loveable and appealing characters: Bonny the Lion, Guffy the Owl, Toppy the Mouse, and Trickey the Crow.
M — EN
Unknown — JVC   P
PRT 8

Funny Money   Fil-Ent '83
Crime-Drama
09897   92 mins   C

PALADIN VIDEO HOME ENTERTAINMENT GUIDE

B, V
Gregg Henry, Elizabeth Daily, Gareth Hunt, Derren Nesbitt, Annie Ross, directed by James Kenelm Clarke
A girl arrives in London with a stack of stolen credit cards. She looks for Ben Turtle, famed as a credit card king, who she needs as a partner in her credit card swindles.
BBFC:18 — A — EN
Cannon Films; Greg Smith — *Entertainment in Video* **H, P**
EVB 1009/EVV 1009

Further Basic With BBC Micro Computer No. 2   Gen-Edu '8?
Electronic data processing
09990   60 mins   C
B, V
On this tape David Redclift continues the teaching of the skills of computer programming using basics. It follows on from the programme 'Starting Basic with BBC Micro Computer No. 1'.
S,A — I
Holiday Brothers Ltd — *Holiday Brothers Ltd* **P**

Fury, The   Fil-Ent '78
Horror
07690   113 mins   C
V2, B, V
Kirk Douglas, John Cassavetes, Carrie Snodgrass, Andrew Stevens, Amy Irving, Charles Durning, directed by Brian DePalma
The head of a government institute for psychic research attempts to track down his son who has been kidnapped by a corrupt government agent. They plan to use the boy who has psychokinetic powers, for subversive political purposes.
A — EN
Twentieth Century Fox — *CBS/Fox Video* **H**
1097

Fury of the Dragon   Fil-Ent '7?
Martial arts
09896   93 mins   C
B, V
Bruce Lee, Van Williams, directed by William Beaudine
The Green Hornet, by day a publisher and by night a crimebuster, together with Kato his bodyguard, battles relentlessly against the forces of urban evil.
S,A — EN
Unknown — *Entertainment in Video* **H, P**
EVB 1008/EVV 1008

Fury on Wheels   Fil-Ent '77
Adventure
04317   85 mins   C (PAL)
V2, B, V
Story of a young man who leaves college to become a daredevil race driver.
BBFC:A — S,A — EN
USA — *Intervision Video* **H, P**
A-A 0007

Futtock's End   Fil-Ent '70
Comedy
05247   47 mins   C
B, V
Ronnie Barker, Michael Hordern, Roger Livesey
At Futtock's End tradition reigns. Here is being lived out one of England's most cherished and nostalgic myths—the country house weekend.
BBFC:A — C,A — EN
Rank — *Rank Video Library* **H, P**
1016

Futureworld   Fil-Ent '76
Science fiction
07381   104 mins   C
V2, B, V
Peter Fonda, Blythe Danner, Arthur Hill, Stuart Margolin, John Ryan, Yul Brynner, directed by Richard Theffron
After the disaster at 'Westworld' when the robots went out of control the complex was redesigned. Covering the re-opening a commentator and a reporter join a party of world leaders. They become suspicious when they realise that the robots are almost impossible to tell from humans. They discover that clones of world leaders are being made and are taking control. They have to fight replicas of themselves to escape.
BBFC:AA — S,A — EN
American International Pictures — *Guild Home Video* **H, P, E**

Fuzz   Fil-Ent '72
Crime-Drama
12680   91 mins   C
B, V
Burt Reynolds, Jack Weston, Tom Skerritt, Yul Brynner, Raquel Welch
A call threatening the life of the Parks Commissioner unless a ransom is paid is treated as a hoax, but the next day the man is dead. The next person threatened is the deputy mayor and the ransom is ten times as much, and the local force have a problem on their hands.
BBFC:18 — A — EN
Jack Farren — *Warner Home Video* **P**
99298

PALADIN VIDEO HOME ENTERTAINMENT GUIDE

G

Galaxina   Fil-Ent   '81
Science fiction/Comedy
07400   96 mins   C
V2, B, V
Dorothy Stratten, Stephen Macht, Avery Schreiber
In this spoof science fiction tale set in the 31st century, a beautiful robot woman capable of human feelings is created.
BBFC:X — *A* — *EN*
Crown International — *Guild Home Video*   **H, P, E**

Gambler, The   Fil-Ent   '74
Drama
13320   107 mins   C
B, V
James Caan, Lauren Hutton, Paul Sorvino, Jacqueline Brookes, Morris Carnovsky, directed by Karel Reisz
A professor of literature at New York University becomes hooked on gambling and as his luck runs out falls into the hands or organised crime.
BBFC:18 — *C,A* — *EN*
Paramount — *CIC Video*   **H, P**
BEN 2108/VHN 2108

Game for Vultures   Fil-Ent   '81
War-Drama
12473   101 mins   C
B, V
Richard Harris, Richard Roundtree, Ray Milland, Joan Collins
An adventure thriller about African guerrilla warfare with the smuggling of U.S. helicopters into Rhodesia to help fight against the Popular Front.
BBFC:18 — *A* — *EN*
Columbia — *RCA/Columbia Pictures Video UK*   **H, P**
10197

Game of Death   Fil-Ent   '79
Martial arts/Adventure
08058   95 mins   C
V2, B, V
Bruce Lee, Dean Jagger, Colleen Camp
This is Bruce Lee's film about a talented young actor who uses his acting skills to take his own death. This is an attempt to outwit a gang who is threatening his career.
Grammy Awards '81: Video of the Year Award.
BBFC:X — *A* — *EN*
Galaxy Films — *Rank Video Library*   **H/P**
0073

Games of the XXI Olympiad   Spo-Lei   '76
Sports-Winter
01883   119 mins   C
B, V
A moving, spectacular, official film which captures the human side of the Olympic Games.
F — *EN*
Rank — *Rank Video Library*   **H, P**
4000

Games That Lovers Play   Fil-Ent   '7?
Comedy
02078   90 mins   C
B, V
Joanna Lumley, Penny Brahms, Richard Wattis, Jeremy Lloyd
Two of London's most successful Madames compete for the prize of who has the best girls. Beautiful Joanna Lumley and Penny Brahms engage in battle—the result a very funny and bawdy film with music by the New Temperance Seven.
A — *EN*
Unknown — *VCL Video Services*   **P**

Gandhi   Gen-Edu   '63
Documentary/Biographical
09326   36 mins   B/W
B, V
Narrated by James Cameron
This tape from the 'Men of Our Time' series features rare footage of Mahatma Gandhi and personal interviews with those who knew him well.
S,A — *ED*
Granada Television — *Granada Video*   **H, P**

Gandhi   Fil-Ent   '82
Drama
13082   180 mins   C
B, V
Ben Kingsley, Candice Bergen, Edward Fox, John Mills, John Gielgud, Trevor Howard, directed by Sir Richard Attenborough
This film portrays the life story of Gandhi, the man who led 350 million people to independance in India.

(For Explanation of codes, see USE GUIDE and KEY)

PALADIN VIDEO HOME ENTERTAINMENT GUIDE

Academy Awards '82: Best Picture; Best Actor (Kingsley); Best Director (Attenborough).
C,A — EN
Richard Attenborough; Columbia;
Goldcrest — RCA/Columbia Pictures Video
UK   **H, P**
10135

Gangster Wars   Fil-Ent '81
Crime-Drama
12045   103 mins   C
B, V
Michael Nouri, directed by Richard C Sarafian
Three youngsters meet on the streets of New York while stealing from the body of a dead mobster. They are reunited again years later during the prohibition and form a partnership in making bootleg liquor. They start making deals with all the gangland mobs but their operation is becoming too large for the gang's liking.
BBFC:15 — S,A — EN
Universal — CIC Video   **H, P**
BEL 1083/VHL 1083

Gangster Wars II   Fil-Ent '81
Crime-Drama
13623   86 mins   C
B, V
Michael Nouri, Brian Benben, Joe Penny, directed by Richard C Sarafian
Fueding, bootlegging and prohibition in Chicago '31 are all featured in this film that continues the story of three gangsters from the previous film.
BBFC:15 — S,A — EN
Universal — CIC Video   **H, P**
1132

Gangsters   Fil-Ent '??
Crime-Drama
06096   120 mins   C
V2, B, V
Antonio Sabato, Max Delys, Giampiero Albertini
A story of a frightened city in the grip of a ruthless racket. The Special Squad fights against impossible odds.
S,A — EN
Unknown — Video Programme Distributors
P
Cinehollywood—V370

Gappa, The Triphibian Monster   Fil-Ent '63
Science fiction/Adventure
07327   81 mins   C
V2, B, V
Tamio Kawaji, Yoko Yamamoto
During an expedition to a remote island to gather tropical birds, a huge egg is discovered. The egg breaks when an enormous octopus rises from the waters of a subterranean lake. A strange scaly creature emerges. The expedition returns with their prize. Meanwhile, two giant monsters are wreaking havoc, at the loss of their offspring by a fire breathing rage that turns aircraft and tanks to cinders.
BBFC:U — F — EN
American International — Rank Video Library
P
2023 C

Garden and Gardener   Gen-Edu '8?
Gardening/Seasons
13576   63 mins   C
V, 3/4U
This is a progrmame of three films showing some of the gardens of the National Trust in spring, summer and autumn as seen through the eyes of the people who made them and work in them today.
A — ED
Unknown — TFI Leisure Ltd   **H**

Garden of Allah, The   Fil-Ent '36
Drama
04172   85 mins   C
B, V
Marlene Dietrich, Charles Boyer, Basil Rathbone
An alluring Englishwoman in Algiers meets and falls in love with a mysterious man who turns out to be a deserter from a Trappist monastery. One of the very first films made in Technicolour.
BBFC:A — S,A — EN
Selznick — Guild Home Video   **H, P**

Gardenia   Fil-Ent '8?
Crime-Drama
10187   90 mins   C
B, V
Martin Balsam, Franco Califano
A Syndicate sets out to seize control of the city's drug dealings. Only one man stands in their way-the man with a gardenia in his buttonhole. He is threatened, savagely beaten, his friends tortured and killed, his restaurant is bombed, but he still refuses to submit and fights back.
BBFC:18 — A — EN
Unknown — Video Form Pictures   **H, P**
DIP 15

Gardening Calendar—April to June, The   Gen-Edu '82
Gardening
07421   55 mins   C
B, V
Presented by Arthur Billitt, and Don Moss

PALADIN VIDEO HOME ENTERTAINMENT GUIDE

Arthur Billit, in this second programme of the series, gives expert guidance on the jobs that must be done in the garden when the warmer weather arrives. He includes the planting of early vegetables and sowing grass seeds, attending strawberries, vines and tomato plants and propagation of magnolias, camellias and rhododendrons. He also gives a guide to electric, motor, manual and rotary lawn mowers.
S,A — ED
Mike Mansfield Enterprises Ltd — THORN EMI
P
TXE 90 0713 4/TVE 90 0713 2

Gardening Calendar—July to September, The
Gen-Edu '82
Gardening
07422 55 mins C
B, V
Presented by Arthur Billitt, and Don Moss
In this tape, the third in the series, Arthur Billitt shows his garden at its colourful best. He shows what to do with the flowers that have finished, attends the flowers in bloom and cares for the lawn. He attends to the fruit and vegetables in August with many hints for a successful crop and finally moves on to the September harvest.
S,A — ED
Mike Mansfield Enterprises Ltd — THORN EMI
P
TXE 90 0735 4/TVE 90 0735 2

Gardening Calendar—January to March, The
Gen-Edu '81
Gardening
06278 55 mins C
B, V
Presented by Arthur Billitt and Don Moss
In this film Arthur Billitt plays host at Clack's Farm, showing the work that can be done in the garden at this time of year. He not only shows what can be achieved in preparation in a variety of areas but gives his own guide to the best garden tools and equipment and the various types of fertiliser.
S,A — ED
Mike Mansfield Enterprises Ltd — THORN EMI
P
TXE 90 0553 4/TVE 90 0553 2

Gardening Calendar—October to December, The
Gen-Edu '82
Gardening
08436 55 mins C
B, V
Presented by Arthur Billitt and Don Moss

This is the final programme in this gardening series. It covers the late Autumn and Winter months of the gardener's year. Arthur Billitt shows the correct way to store apples, tidy up delphiniums, gladioli and dahlias and tend the lawn. Advice is given on how to protect the garden from frost.
S,A — ED
Mike Mansfield Enterprises Ltd — THORN EMI
P
TXE 90 0763 4/TVE 90 07632

Gardening for Pleasure—Acid Soil and Alpines
How-Ins '81
Gardening/Hobbies
05427 50 mins C
B, V
Mike Long
This cassette is a complete programme in the series 'Master Class Gardening,' presented by the professional gardener Mike Long. In this film he deals with acid soil and plants which grow successfully in it. Different types of Alpines are examined including a visit to a show, and he demonstrates how to create your own Alpine or Rock Garden.
S,A — I
Harrison Partnership and Holiday Bros Ltd — *Holiday Brothers Ltd* P

Gardening for Pleasure—Herbacious Borders
How-Ins '81
Gardening/Hobbies
05426 50 mins C
B, V
Mike Long
This cassette is a complete programme in the series 'Master Class Gardening,' presented by the professional gardener Mike Long. In this film he tells how to develop a flower garden with 48 herbacious plants. He demonstrates that once a border is established by careful selection it can provide flowers practically every month of the year. He explains how to feed them for flower development, steady growth and root action.
S,A — I
Harrison Partnership and Holiday Bros Ltd — *Holiday Brothers Ltd* P

Gardening for Pleasure—Propagation Part I and Hybrid Rhododendrons
How-Ins '81
Gardening/Hobbies
05425 50 mins C
B, V
Mike Long

PALADIN VIDEO HOME ENTERTAINMENT GUIDE

This cassette is a complete programme in the series 'Master Class Gardening,' presented by the professional gardener Mike Long. In this film he covers some techniques of propagation that will enable even the most amateur gardener to make the most of his stock and assist his budget. He then goes on to deal with hybridisations.
S,A — I
Harrison Partnership and Holiday Bros Ltd — *Holiday Brothers Ltd* **P**

Gardening with Wildlife Gen-Edu '8?
Birds/Gardening
09103   28 mins   C
B, V
Tony Soper
This programme demonstrates how to make our gardens more attractive to birds and much more interesting for ourselves.
F — ED
Royal Society for the Protection of Birds — *Royal Society for the Protection of Birds*   **H, P**

Garland Fil-Ent '6?
Music-Performance
06303   112 mins   C
V2, B, V
Judy Garland, Liza Minnelli
This film features extracts from shows by Judy Garland. Includes an original film of 'Judy in Concert 1962' plus out-takes from the never completed Garland version of 'Annie Get Your Gun.' The film also features Judy Garland and her daughter at the Palladium in 1964; songs include 'Over the Rainbow,' 'Just Once in a Lifetime' and others.
F — EN
Unknown — *World of Video 2000*   **H, P**
SP4

Gary Glitter—Live at the Rainbow Fil-Ent '81
Music-Performance
06218   54 mins   C
B, V
Gary Glitter performs some of his greatest hits including: 'Leader of the Gang,' 'I Love You,' 'Love Me Love,' 'Rock 'n' Roll,' and 'Oh Yes! You're Beautiful.'
F — EN
Unknown — *VCL Video Services*   **P**
V157B

Gary Numan—The Touring Principle '79 Fil-Ent '79
Music-Performance
08977   60 mins   C
B, V
Gary Numan
This tape was recorded live at Hammersmith Odeon, London, during his European tour. The tour featured spectacular stage and dramatic lighting effects. The songs included are 'Cars','Me' 'I Disconnect from You', 'M.E.', 'We Are So Fragile', 'Every Day I Die', 'Conversations', 'Remember I Was Vapour', 'On Broadway', 'Down in the Park','My Shadow in Vain', 'Are Friends Electric', and 'Tracks'.
S,A — EN
Warner Bros — *Palace Video Ltd*   **P**
PVC 3002B

Gas Pump Girls Fil-Ent '79
Comedy
06936   98 mins   C
B, V
Kristen Baker, Dennis Bowen, Huntz Hall, Sandy Johnson, Leslie King, Linda Lawrence, Rikki Marin, directed by Joel Bender
When a young girl's uncle is forced to close his petrol station due to a brand new one opening up in competition just down the road, she enlists the help of her girlfriends to attract customers.
BBFC:X — A — EN
Unknown — *Rank Video Library*   **H, P**
1033C

Gator Fil-Ent '76
Comedy-Drama
13175   114 mins   C
B, V
Burt Reynolds, Jerry Reed, Lauren Hutton, directed by Burt Reynolds
A jokey, non-conformist is enlisted by a government agent to help gather evidence against a dangerous political boss, which leads to one hair-raising situation after another.
BBFC:AA — C,A — EN
United Artists — *Warner Home Video*   **P**
99263

Gaugin—The Savage Fil-Ent '82
Drama/Biographical
06900   116 mins   C
V2, B, V
David Carradine, Dame Flora Robson, Lynn Redgrave, Michael Horndern, Ian Richardson, Bernard Fox, Barry Houghton, directed by Fielder Cook
Set in Paris and Tahiti in the late nineteenth century, this film is an expose of the turbulent but short life of Paul Gaugin, the French painter now recognised as one of the fathers of modern art. Gaugin abandoned his wife and children in

PALADIN VIDEO HOME ENTERTAINMENT GUIDE

order to pursue a life of artistic freedom. He fled to Tahiti in search of the primitive sources of art and to protest against what he called the 'disease' of civilization.
S,A — EN
Original Film Prod; Alfred Haber
Corp. — *Channel Video*　　**H, P**

Gauntlet, The　　Fil-Ent　'77
Drama/Adventure
06039　107 mins　C
B, V
Clint Eastwood, Sondra Locke, Pat Hingle, William Prince, Bill McKinney, directed by Clint Eastwood
A slow witted Arizona policeman is elected to go to Las Vegas on a special assignment. He is to escort a prostitute back to Phoenix, who is a key witness in a trial, but she is being pursued by members of the mob who want her dead before she exposes their activities.
BBFC:X — A — EN
Warner Bros; Robert Daly Prod — *Warner Home Video*　　**P**
WEX1083/WEV1083

Gay Deceivers　　Fil-Ent　'??
Comedy
05458　86 mins　C
V2, B, V
Kevin Coughlin, Larry Casey, Michael Greer, Jack Starret, directed by Bruce Kessler
In order not to join the U.S. draft two young men decide to pretend to be gay. They dress the part, talk the part and even live the part until they not only convince the draft board but cause concern with their families and girlfriends.
BBFC:X — A — EN
Unknown — *Iver Film Services*　　**P**
101

General, The　　Fil-Ent　'27
Comedy
05836　76 mins　B/W
B, V
Buster Keaton, Marian Mark, directed by Buster Keaton and Clyde Bruckman
This film is a Civil War espionage spoof in which a confederate soldier almost wins the war himself when he goes behind Northern lines to recover his beloved locomotive. The film includes spectacular battle scenes interspersed with almost pantomime antics as he avidly tries to impress a suitably helpless young girl. Silent.
F — EN
United Artists — *Polygram Video*　　**P**
40117/20117

General, The　　Fil-Ent　'68
Crime-Drama
09357　92 mins　C
B, V
Patrick McGoohan
This tape contains one episode from the highly successful television series 'The Prisoner.' In 'The General' a new method of learning is introduced to the inhabitants of the village. By projecting the information at a speed thousands of times faster than the eye can record, it can be imposed directly on the cortex of the brain.
S,A — EN
Patrick McGoohan — *Precision Video Ltd*　　**P**
BITC 2137/VITC 2137

General Stone　　Fil-Ent　'79
Adventure/Martial arts
04415　90 mins　C
B, V
Two young warriors worship the tomb of the founding Emperor of Tang. The tomb is attacked by rebels who are holding the mother of one of the warriors as a hostage.
S,A — EN
Unknown — *VCL Video Services*　　**P**

Generation, A　　Fil-Ent　'60
Drama
08547　86 mins　B/W
B, V
Directed by Andrzej Wajada
This film, the original version with English subtitles, is part of 'The Wajada Trilogy.' It follows the story of a boy during the time of the German occupation; symbolising an entire generation in revolt. The Polish youth took up the fight with whatever means were at hand including stealing coal from German bound trains, killing members of the Gestapo and encouraging older, professional men to come out of hiding. The other films in the triology are' Kanal and 'Ashes and Diamonds.'
BBFC:A — S,A — EN
Film Polski — *THORN EMI*　　**P**
TXE 90 07344/TVE 90 0734 2

Genesis Flood, The　　Gen-Edu　'??
Religion/Bible
06288　40 mins　B/W
B, V, PH15
In this film, John Gray, a Biology Master gives scientific proof of the reliability of Genesis.
S,A — R
Audio Visual Ministries — *Audio Visual Ministries*　　**H, L, P**
VT85

(For Explanation of codes, see USE GUIDE and KEY)

PALADIN VIDEO HOME ENTERTAINMENT GUIDE

Genesis-Three Sides Live   Fil-Ent '8?
Music-Performance
08536   40 mins   C
B, V
This tape features Genesis with Phil Collins, Tony Banks, Mike Rutherford, playing live and includes interviews with individual members of the band. The songs that are played are 'Do-Do', 'Abacab', 'No Reply at All', 'Whodunnit', 'In the Cage', 'Me and Sarah Jane', 'Man on the Corner', 'Turn It on Again'.
S,A — EN
Unknown — THORN EMI   P
TXE 90 09824/TVE 90 09822

Genevieve   Fil-Ent '53
Comedy
01886   86 mins   C
B, V
Dinah Sheridan, John Gregson, Kay Kendall, Kenneth More
The drama and spectacle of the London to Brighton Commemoration Run provide the background for this delightful comedy of friendly rivalry bewteen two couples.
BBFC:U — F — EN
Rank — Rank Video Library   H, P
1000

Genius of the Place, The   Gen-Edu '8?
Landscaping/National parks and reserves
13577   25 mins   C
V, 3/4U
Stourhead and Petworth are the two great National Trust properties featured in this film about the development in the eighteenth century of the English landscape garden and park.
F — ED
Unknown — TFI Leisure Ltd   H

Gentle Giant   Fil-Ent '67
Adventure
05450   79 mins   C
V2, B, V
Denis Weaver, Vera Miles, Ralph Meeker, Clint Howard
The story of a small boy who befriends a bear cub. The boy's father buys the cub for him but it grows into a six hundred and fifty pound bear and after a run in with an alcoholic bully is forced to be sold to a circus. Later the bear escapes to re-join the boy who is his friend. Based on the novel 'Gentle Ben' by Walt Morey.
BBFC:U — F — EN
Paramount; Ivan Tors — Iver Film Services
P
99

Gentle Savage   Fil-Ent '76
Drama
08054   82 mins   C
B, V
William Smith, Gene Evans, Joe Flynn, Kevin Hagen, Barbara Luna
Set in a small town in Arizona, this film tells the story of an Indian, wrongly accused of rape by a very influential businessman. The peaceful Indian becomes the target of the racist people. He escapes from the jail determined to clear his name and seek revenge.
BBFC:X — A — EN
Unknown — Rank Video Library   H, P
0089 C

Gentle Sinners   Fil-Ent '82
Drama
13255   105 mins   C
B, V
Christopher Earle, Charlene Senuik, Ed McNamara, Jackie Burroughs, directed by Eric Till
Set in the 1950's in rural Manitoba, a boy runs away from his repressive home and his world quickly broadens as he encounters the world of treachery, love, hatred, friendship and genuine affection.
BBFC:15 — S,A — EN
Peter Kelly — CBS/Fox Video   P
3023

Gentleman Bandit   Fil-Ent '81
Drama
09250   96 mins   C
V2, B, V
Ralph Waite, Terry Zaks, Julie Bovasso, Joe Grifasi, Estelle Parsons, directed by Jonathan Kaplan
This film, based on a real-life case, tells the story of a Roman Catholic priest with a busy parish in Delaware. His life is turned upside down when he becomes the main suspect in a series of robberies. However, a Jewish lawyer sets out to help him.
BBFC:A — S,A — EN
Highgate Pictures — Iver Film Services
P
220

Gentleman Tramp, The   Fil-Ent '74
Documentary/Biographical
05841   90 mins   B/W
B, V
Charlie Chaplin, Edna Purviance

PALADIN VIDEO HOME ENTERTAINMENT GUIDE

This film is a documentary on the life and works of Charlie Chaplin, following his rags to riches story from direct poverty to fantastic success. It features a wide variety of film clips and rare behind the scenes footage of his tumultuous private life.
F — EN
rbc films — *Polygram Video* P
7901544/7901542

Gentlemen Prefer Blondes Fil-Ent '53
Comedy
01745   91 mins   C
B, V
Marilyn Monroe, Jane Russell, Charles Coburn, Elliot Reid, directed by Howard Hawks
Two showgirls land in police court while seeking rich husbands or diamonds.
BBFC:A — S,A — EN
20th Century Fox — *CBS/Fox Video* P
3A-039

George Fil-Ent '70
Comedy
06890   81 mins   C
V2, B, V
Marshall Thompson, Jack Mullaney, Inge Schoner
This is the story of a carefree bachelor pilot, his beautiful girlfriend and a 250 lb. St. Bernard he received as a present from his eccentric aunt. Set in the Swiss Alps, George, the dog, upsets everything in the house due to his fear of altitude, and promptly sets out to prove that a St. Bernard isn't always an angel. His owner decides to take him to the monastery to be taught some manners.
M,A — EN
Gold Key Entertainment — *European Video Company* P

George and Mildred Fil-Ent '8?
Comedy
05410   89 mins   C
B, V
Yootha Joyce, Brian Murphy, Stratford Johns, Norman Eshley, Sheila Fearn, Kenneth Cope, David Barry
George and Mildred, a very unlikely couple, leave behind their uppercrust neighbours to explore new and hopefully romantic pastures on their Wedding Anniversary. Mildred is determined to celebrate in style; however, it is an effort for George to remember he is married, let alone celebrate it.
BBFC:A — S,A — EN
Unknown — *Precision Video Ltd* P
BITC 2039/VITC 2039

George Carlin—Live at Carnegie Fil-Ent '80
Comedy
12874   90 mins   C
B, V
George Carlin, the renowned American Late Night TV Host has a reputation for being one of America's most controversial comics and the full range of his powers are seen on this video.
A — EN
Unknown — *Vestron Video International* P

Georgia Fil-Ent '81
Drama
12734   113 mins   C
B, V
Craig Wasson, Jodie Thelen, Michael Huddleston, Jim Metzler, Lois Smith, directed by Arthur Penn
This film tells the story of an immigrant and his three closest friends at a time in all their lives when they are faced with decisions that will affect all their lives.
BBFC:15 — C,A — EN
Michael Tolan; Julia Miles — *Rank Video Library* H, P
0185 Y

Get Fit with the Green Goddess Spo-Lei '84
Physical fitness
13395   60 mins   C
B, V
BBC TV's Green Goddess, Diana Moran from 'Breakfast Time' shows you how to look after your body through gentle, painless exercise and a healthy diet.
A — ED
BBC — *BBC Video* H, P
1028

Get Knighted! Fil-Ent '??
Comedy-Performance
09444   60 mins   C
V2, B, V
Barron Anthony Osmond, Butch Baker, Dave Ballinger, Duke D'Mond, Pete Langford, directed by Mike Hardy
This tape features a live performance from the Barron Knights with side-splitting sketches and the best of their inimitable music.
BBFC:U — F — EN
Unknown — *Guild Home Video* H, P, E

Get Mean Fil-Ent '??
Adventure
09394   90 mins   C
B, V

(For Explanation of codes, see USE GUIDE and KEY)

269

PALADIN VIDEO HOME ENTERTAINMENT GUIDE

Tony Anthony, Lloyd Battista, directed by Ferdinando Baldi
This film features The Stranger, who will go anywhere, do anything and kill anyone for a price. He is hired to stop an army of murdering barbarians with a promise of a treasure in gold as his reward.
A — EN
Unknown — *VCL Video Services*   **P**
P390

Get Rita   Fil-Ent '78
Crime-Drama/Adventure
06906   98 mins   C
V2, B, V
Sophia Loren, Marcello Mastroianni
A Milanese prostitute leads an uncomplicated life until she is forced to become the mistress of a big-time gangster.
S,A — EN
Carlo Ponti — *Fourmatt Video Ltd*   **P**

Get Slim—Stay Slim   Spo-Lei '80
Physical fitness
01992   60 mins   C
V2, B, V, PH15, PH17
Angie Best
Former Hollywood fitness expert Angie Best demonstrates special slimming exercises she used on fitness-mad American show-biz stars.
A — I
MirrorVision — *VideoSpace Ltd*   **P**

Getaway, The   Fil-Ent '72
Adventure
13183   123 mins   C
B, V
Steve McQueen, Ali MacGraw, Ben Johnson, directed by Sam Peckinpah
A convict is broken out of jail by his wife to undertake a robbery after doing a special deal.
BBFC:X — A — EN
National General Pictures Corp; First Artists Prods Co Ltd; Solar Prods; David Foster Prods — *Warner Home Video*   **P**
61304

Getting Down to Basic   Gen-Edu '8?
Electronic data processing
08402   120 mins   C
V2, B, V
Presented by Anna Ford
This film presents in a step by step manner all the main features of BASIC microcomputers. It will enable the user to produce programmers and to solve quite complex problems.
S,A — I
Unknown — *Guild Home Video*   **H, P, E**

Getting It On   Fil-Ent '83
Comedy
13780   94 mins   C
B, V
Two student film makers zoom into the intimate lives of fellow school friends and teachers with a video camera and complications arise when the tapes become mixed up with the school's educational programmes.
BBFC:18 — A — EN
Unknown — *Odyssey Video*   **H, P**
6522

Getting of Wisdom, The   Fil-Ent '80
Drama
04192   100 mins   C
B, V
Susannah Fowle, Barry Humphries, John Waters, Hilary Ryan, directed by Bruce Beresford
The film is a vivid, often abrasive picture of the emergence of a very individualistic woman from an immature girl. Based on Henry Handel Richardson's classic Australian novel.
BBFC:A — C,A — EN
Australian — *Guild Home Video*   **H, P**

Getting Over   Fil-Ent '7?
Musical
06783   107 mins   C
V2, B, V
John Daniels, Gwen Brisco, Buzz Cooper, The Love Machine
A man who wants to make a name for himself battles the record giants in the pop music world.
S,A — EN
John R Daniels — *Intervision Video*   **H, P**
A-AE 0317

Getting to Know Birds   Gen-Edu '84
Birds
13600   20 mins   C
V2, B, V
This video shows our garden birds and common summer visitors and helps the viewer to differentiate between easily confused species.
F — ED
Royal Society for the Protection of Birds — *Royal Society for the Protection of Birds*   **H, P**

Ghost Busters, The   Fil-Ent '83
Comedy
12999   67 mins   C
B, V
Forrest Tucker

PALADIN VIDEO HOME ENTERTAINMENT GUIDE

Taken from the American television series, a trio of incompetents including a gorilla, get involved in the most crazy situations, trying to drive the ghosts away from their haunts.
F — EN
Filmation Associates Inc. — Select Video Limited   P
3622/43

Ghost in the Noonday Sun   Fil-Ent '74
Comedy
12762   90 mins   C
B, V
Peter Sellers, Spike Milligan, Anthony Franciosa, Clive Revill, Rosemary Leach
A rip-roaring pirate yarn featuring a wily Irish cook aboard an Algerian pirate ship, who becomes commander when the ship's captain gets buried with the treasure.
BBFC:U — F — EN
Unknown — Rank Video Library   H, P
1069Y

Ghost Story   Fil-Ent '81
Suspense
09272   110 mins   C
B, V
Fred Astaire, Melvyn Douglas, Douglas Fairbanks Jr., John Houseman, Patricia Neal
Based on the novel by Peter Straub, this film tells the story of four elderly men, members of an informal club called the Chowder Society, who all share a terrible secret buried deep in their pasts.
BBFC:R — A — EN
Universal — CIC Video   H, P

Ghostkeeper   Fil-Ent '??
Horror
06799   ? mins   C
V2, B, V
Riva Spier, Georgie Collins
The Indian legend of the Windigo, a creature that devours human flesh, is the basis of this film, set in the Rocky Mountains.
S,A — EN
Harold J Cole — Intervision Video   H, P
A-A 0373

Ghosts from the Deep   Fil-Ent '75
Cartoons/Adventure
09142   90 mins   C
B, V
Animated
This tells of the adventures of Captain Nemo and his crew. They have heard reports of terrifying ghastly figures that appear every time a fisherman goes near the ruins of Carthage. These ruins, nearly 3,000 years old, contain many treasures. Captain Nemo decides to investigate and solve the mystery of the ghosts from the deep.
F — EN
Rainbow Animation Ltd — Video Brokers
H, P

Ghoul, The   Fil-Ent '75
Horror
05190   75 mins   C
B, V
Peter Cushing, John Hurt, Gwen Watford, Alexandra Bastedo, Veronica Carlson, Don Henderson
Two cars roar away into the darkness from the lights of a noisy party on a race to Land's End. But a few hours later impenetrable fog brings them to a halt on a deserted moorland road, and brings the occupants to the brink of an unspeakable fate. For nearby is a house of horror and death which harbours a terrible creature which feeds on human flesh.
BBFC:X — A — EN
J Arthur Rank — Rank Video Library   H, P
2002

G.I. Blues   Fil-Ent '60
Musical
01011   104 mins   C
B, V
Elvis Presley, Juliet Prowse, Robert Ivers, James Douglas
Three G.I.'s form a musical combo while stationed in Germany.
BBFC:U — F — EN
Paramount; Hal Wallis — CBS/Fox Video   P
3B-011

Giant Ant Invasion, The   Fil-Ent '7?
Horror
02588   44 mins   C
B, V
Huge insect mutations wreak havoc over the countryside.
A — EN
Unknown — Mountain Video   P

Giant Blacks and Great Whites, Part 4   Spo-Lei '83
Fishing/Australia
13572   30 mins   C
B, V

(For Explanation of codes, see USE GUIDE and KEY)

PALADIN VIDEO HOME ENTERTAINMENT GUIDE

The Great White Shark is hunted at a remote islet called Dangerous Reef and is fed by hand from an underwater cage in this programme.
F — EN
Unknown — *TFI Leisure Ltd*   **H, P**

Giant Blacks and Great Whites, Part 1   Spo-Lei '83
Fishing/Australia
13569   30 mins   C
B, V
In the deep transparent waters of the Coral Sea the giant Black Marlins are encountered in a dramatic game of tag and release.
F — EN
Unknown — *TFI Leisure Ltd*   **H, P**

Giant Blacks and Great Whites, Part 2   Spo-Lei '83
Fishing/Australia
13570   30 mins   C
B, V
Fishing off the tiny deserted island of Montagu, a few miles off the Southern New South Wales coast for the yellowfin tuna is shown in this programme.
F — EN
Unknown — *TFI Leisure Ltd*   **H, P**

Giant Blacks and Great Whites, Part 3   Spo-Lei '83
Fishing/Australia
13571   30 mins   C
B, V
Set in the mountains of Tasmania, fly fishing and spinning for the world's biggest brown trout in Lake Pedder is demonstrated in this programme.
F — EN
Unknown — *TFI Leisure Ltd*   **H, P**

Giant Salamander, The   Fil-Ent '7?
Horror
02585   44 mins   C
B, V
Slime creatures from out of a nightmare kill and maim everyone in their sight in this terror classic.
F — EN
Unknown — *Mountain Video*   **P**

Giant Spider Invasion, The   Fil-Ent '77
Science fiction/Horror
06251   73 mins   C
B, V
Steve Brodie, Barbara Hale, Leslie Parrish, Alan Hale, Robert Easton

A freak radiation shower turns harmless spiders into giant, creeping, clawing, crushing monsters. From little eggs the giants explode, creating havoc, death and destruction through a small town in North Wisconsin with horrific results.
S,A — EN
Unknown — *VCL Video Services*   **P**
C203C

Giants of Brazil   Spo-Lei '80
Soccer
04388   52 mins   C
B, V
Colour World Cup footage and vintage black and white newsreels of Brazil's early years in world soccer competition recall over 65 goals made between 1938 and 1970. The skill and imagination of Pele are featured.
F — EN
Unknown — *VCL Video Services*   **P**

Gigi   Fil-Ent '58
Musical
10168   116 mins   C
B, V, LV
Leslie Caron, Maurice Chevalier, Louis Jourdan
The setting is Paris at the turn of the century, and this film tells the story of a tomboy who blossoms into a sophisticated young lady who is courted by a rich and eligible playboy. The musical score includes 'Thank Heaven for Little Girls,' 'The Night They Invented Champagne' and 'I Remember It Well.'
Academy Awards '58: Best Picture.
BBFC:U — F — EN
MGM — *MGM/UA Home Video*   **P**
UMB 10050/UMV 10050/UMLV 10050

Gillette London Marathon, The   Spo-Lei '82
Sports/Running
08716   95 mins   C
B, V
This tape features highlights of the first two years of the London Marathon. It had over 18,000 entrants in 1982, double the number running in 1981. It shows the gruelling 26 mile course lined by thousands of spectators.
F — EN
John Shrewsbury; John Vigar; Mike Brock — *BBC Video*   **H, P**
BBCV 5016

Ginger in the Morning   Fil-Ent '73
Romance
08742   90 mins   C
B, V
Monte Markham, Susan Oliver, Mark Miller, Sissy Spacek, Slim Pickens

PALADIN VIDEO HOME ENTERTAINMENT GUIDE

A bachelor pick up a female hitchhiker. They decide to spend New Year's weekend together at his home. As he is preparing himself for his only amorous adventure since his divorce three months ago, his old friend turns up on the doorstep, drunk. Trying to dispose of his friend he doesn't say the most flattering things about her, and when she hears, she intends to leave.
S,A — EN
National General — Precision Video Ltd
P
BITC 2566/VITC 2566

Girl/Boy   Fil-Ent '72
Comedy
08818   84 mins   C
B, V
Joan Greenwood, Michael Horden, Clive Francis
A school-head and his wife constantly argue about their son. They find nothing pleasing about him, his hair, ideas, dress, and especially his friends.
BBFC:X — A — EN
Hemdale Prod — VCL Video Services   P
P310C

Girl Called Jules, A   Fil-Ent '7?
Drama
09909   81 mins   C
V2, B, V
Silvia Dionisio
This film tells the story of a girl in her teenage years and the advances made to her by her governess. Her many affairs do not satisfy her needs and her search for love leads her from the city of Venice, to the ski slopes of the Alps. She meets a successful artist but this is not to be fate's final twist.
BBFC:18 — A — EN
Unknown — Derann Film Services   P
FGS 907

Girl Groups   Fil-Ent '83
Music-Performance
12212   62 mins   C
B, V
This tape features music from the sixties and includes girl groups such as The Supremes, The Ronettes, Martha and the Vandellas and The Shangri-Las.
F — EN
Delilah Films — MGM/UA Home Video
P
10194

Girl in Every Port,   Fil-Ent '??
A/Return of the Badmen
Comedy/Western
05669   170 mins   B/W
B, V
Groucho Marx, William Bendix, Don Defore, Mavis Wilson, Gene Lockhart, directed by Chester Erskine, Robert Ryan, Randolph Scott, Gabby Hayes, directed by Ray Enright
Two films are featured on one cassette. 'A Girl in Every Port' (Black/White, 84 mins, 1953) in which two sailors are tricked into buying a useless race horse, which they have to conceal aboard their warship while trying for a win with an identical substitute. 'Return of the Badmen' (Black/white, 86 mins, 1949) in which notorious outlaws, the Younger Brothers, the Daltons, Billy the Kid and others are in hiding in Badmans Territory. A legendary lawman appears single handed to deal with them; his gun play is the fastest they have ever known.
F — EN
RKO — Kingston Video   H, P
KV43

Girl Next Door, The   Fil-Ent '8?
Comedy-Drama
09146   90 mins   C
B, V
This film tells of the fun and excitement of the 'girl next door,' who proves that romance isn't dead.
BBFC:AA — C,A — EN
Unknown — Video Brokers   H, P
009X

Girl Who Couldn't Say No,   Fil-Ent '68
The
Comedy/Romance
08836   80 mins   C
B, V
George Segal, Virna Lisi, directed by Franco Brusati
This is a lively comedy about the exploits of a fun-loving and carefree girl.
C,A — EN
20th Century Fox — VCL Video Services
P
P260D

Girl with Green Eyes   Fil-Ent '63
Drama
09802   89 mins   B/W
B, V
Peter Finch, Rita Tushingham, Lynn Redgrave, Joe Lynch, T.P. McKenna, directed by Desmond Davis
Edna O'Brien's classic story of the traumas of first love. An innocent Irish country girl falls in love with a mature English writer, and as their love develops, their differences start to grate.
BBFC:18 — C,A — EN
Woodfall Film Productions Ltd; Samuel Goldwyn — THORN EMI   P
TXJ 90 1627 2/TVJ 90 1627 2

(For Explanation of codes, see USE GUIDE and KEY)

PALADIN VIDEO HOME ENTERTAINMENT GUIDE

Girls, Girls, Girls   Fil-Ent '62
Musical
01744   106 mins   C
B, V
Elvis Presley, Stella Stevens, Laurel Goodwin, Jeremy Slate, Guy Lee
A boy refuses his girlfriend's gift of a boat, but changes his mind when he discovers he has a rival for her affections.
BBFC:U — F — EN
Paramount, Hal Wallis — *CBS/Fox Video* **P**
3B-040

Girls in the Office, The   Fil-Ent '79
Comedy-Drama
10217   97 mins   C
B, V
Barbara Eden, Susan St. James, David Wayne, Penny Peyser, Robin Douglas, Tony Roberts, directed by Ted Post
Three young women travel to Texas to enter the competitive world of business and meet in the employment office of a new department store. It follows the stories of the three, one who is willing to use her mind and her body to make it to the top, one who thinks life should be like a romantic movie and one who is willing to work hard but not to compromise her dignity.
BBFC:15 — S,A — EN
ABC Circle Films — *Video Form Pictures* **H, P**
MGT 19

Girls on the Road   Fil-Ent '??
Adventure/Drama
05480   76 mins   C
V2, B, V
Diane Hull, Michael Ontkean, Kathleen Cody
Two young girls take to the road on America's west coast for a vacation to get away from it all. They pick up a Marine who has just been released from a Psycho Hospital. They join a group of hippies; however, girls are being murdered on the Californian beaches and they suspect the marine.
BBFC:X — A — EN
Unknown — *Iver Film Services* **P**
137

Giselle   Fin-Art '7?
Dance
00845   77 mins   C
B, V
Rudolph Nureyev, Lynn Seymour, Monica Mason
A popular presentation of the ballet 'Giselle.'
F — EN
MGM — *Precision Video Ltd* **P**
BITC 2016/VITC 2016

Giselle   Fin-Art '7?
Dance
02260   85 mins   C
V
The Bolshoi Ballet
The Bolshoi Ballet, the world's greatest ballet theatre, is captured in a stunning performance of the supreme romantic ballet, 'Giselle.'
F — EN
Unknown — *JVC* **P**
PRT 24

Giselle   Fil-Ent '79
Dance
09349   77 mins   C
B, V
Rudolf Nureyev, Lynn Seymour, Monica Mason
An international cast highlights this version of Nureyev's greatest success, produced by Stanley Dorfman for television. It tells the story of a nobleman who falls in love with the beautiful peasant girl, Giselle, who is danced by Lynn Seymour.
F — EN
Lord Lew Grade; ITC Entertainment — *Precision Video Ltd* **P**
BITC 2016/VITC 2016

Giselle   Fil-Ent '??
Dance
10008   105 mins   C
B, V
Conducted by Viktor Fedotov
This ballet is performed by the Kirov Ballet with music by the orchestra of the Kirov Theatre, Leningrad.
F — EN
Unknown — *Longman Video* **P**
LGBE 7011/LGVH 7011

Give Me a Boat   Gen-Edu '84
Handicapped
13534   35 mins   C
B, V
This film shows how it is possible to give disabled people a canal holiday.
C,A — SE
Unknown — *TFI Leisure Ltd* **H, P**

Give Me A Signal   Gen-Edu '79
Ear
13531   35 mins   C
B, V
The testing and hearing of handicapped people is shown in this film.
C,A — SE
Unknown — *TFI Leisure Ltd* **H, P**

(For Explanation of codes, see USE GUIDE and KEY)

PALADIN VIDEO HOME ENTERTAINMENT GUIDE

Give Us The Chance Gen-Edu '82
Learning disabilities
13527   36 mins   C
V
Directed by Bill Latto
This cassette aims to promote some positive ideas and approaches which are being carried out successfully in hospitals, Adult Training Centres, Sheltered Communities, Gateway Clubs etc. to help mentally handicapped people enjoy happier lives.
C,A — SE
Town and Country Productions — *TFI Leisure Ltd*   H, P

Glen and Randa   Fil-Ent '71
Science fiction/Adventure
10208   94 mins   C
B, V
Steven Curry, Shelley Plimpton, Woodrow Chambliss, directed by Jim McBride
Twenty-five years after a nuclear holocaust destroys civilisation two young people set out to search for 'the city'. Inspired by a legend that life exists there as it was and the ramblings of a travelling magician they search for relics from a long-forgotten culture.
BBFC:18 — S,A — EN
Sidney Glazier — *Video Form Pictures*
H, P
6262-50

Glen Campbell Live   Fil-Ent '84
Music-Performance
12940   60 mins   C
B, V
This is a compilation of country classics including 'I'm So Lonesome I Could Cry', 'Milk Cow Blues', 'Phoenix', 'Country Boy', 'Galveston', 'Amazing Grace', and 'Wichita Lineman'.
F — EN
Unknown — *Video Form Pictures*   H, P
VFM 005

Glitter Dome   Fil-Ent '84
Drama
13701   90 mins   C
B, V
James Garner, Margot Kidder, John Lithgow, directed by Stuart Margolin
Two detectives are called in when a Hollywood studio boss is brutally murdered and as they start to expose the grim realities of the case so the destruction and hopelessness start to pervade their own lives.
C,A — EN
Stuart Margolin — *THORN EMI*   P
90 2785

Glittering Crowns, The   Fil-Ent '80
Documentary/History-Modern
05898   60 mins   C
B, V
Narrated by Edward Fox, directed by John Kaplan
A visual record of Monarchy in the Twentieth Century, including Tzar Nicholas II, Queen Victoria's Diamond Jubilee, The Investiture of the Prince of Wales, and the abdication of Edward VIII.
F — EN
Nicholas de Rothschild — *THORN EMI*
P
TXE 90 0330 4/TVE 90 0330 2

Glove, The   Fil-Ent '7?
Adventure/Suspense
06818   ? mins   C
V2, B, V
John Saxon, Rosey Grier, Joanna Cassidy, Joan Blondell, Jack Carter, Aldo Ray, Keenan Wynn
A violent tale about a murderous glove—wanted dead, not alive.
A — EN
Julian Roffman — *Intervision Video*   H, P
A-A 0379

Gnome Mobile, The   Fil-Ent '67
Adventure/Fantasy
07931   81 mins   C
B, V
Walter Brennan, Matthew Garber, Karen Dotrice, Richard Deacon, Sean McClory, Ed Wynn, Jerome Cowan, Charles Lane, directed by Robert Stevenson
This film follows the adventures of a millionaire and his grandchildren who discover two gnomes in a 1930 Rolls-Royce and end up helping a colony of gnomes in a forest.
F — EN
Walt Disney — *Rank Video Library*   H
09500

Go-Between, The   Fil-Ent '71
Romance
01152   116 mins   C
B, V
Julie Christie, Alan Bates, Michael Redgrave
A boy of twelve is used to carry messages between a young heiress and a poor tenant farmer who are deeply in love.
Cannes Film Festival '71: Grand Prix.
BBFC:AA — S,A — EN
Columbia — *THORN EMI*   P
TXB 90 0007 4/TVB 90 0007 2

(For Explanation of codes, see USE GUIDE and KEY)

PALADIN VIDEO HOME ENTERTAINMENT GUIDE

Go Fishing With Jack Charlton—Part 1: River Coarse Fishing
Spo-Lei '82
Fishing
07429 30 mins C
B, V

Jack Charlton, directed by Alan Ravenscroft
In this series, Jack Charlton the footballer, looks at fishing from basic river coarse fishing and sea wreck fishing to salmon fishing. In this first programme he meets the experts on the River Severn with whom he discusses and demonstrates methods of coarse fishing. The use of stick floats, wagglers and swim feeders are demonstrated along with methods of casting and a host of hints and tips to aid both beginners and experts.
F — I
Thorn EMI Video Programmes Ltd — *THORN EMI* **P**
TXF 90 0679 4/TVF 90 0679 2

Go Fishing with Jack Charlton—Part 2: Still Water Coarse Fishing
Spo-Lei '82
Fishing
07430 30 mins C
B, V

Jack Charlton, directed by Alan Ravenscroft
In this programme, the second in the series, Jack Charlton goes to Worsborough Reservoir where he meets two of the country's top anglers who demonstrate different methods of catching bream, roach, perch and tench. Includes ledgering with a swingtip and quivertip, pole fishing and waggler float fishing. Advice is given on the selection of equipment for varying conditions of light and weather and there is a lesson on rearing maggots at home.
F — I
Thorn EMI Video Programmes Ltd — *THORN EMI* **P**
TXF 90 0824 4/TVF 90 0823 2

Go Fishing With Jack Charlton—Part 4: Reservoir Trout Fishing
Spo-Lei '82
Fishing
08438 30 mins C
B, V

Jack Charlton, directed by Alan Ravenscroft
In this programme, the fourth in the series, Jack Charlton goes to Rutland Water in Leicestershire. This man-made water is regularly stocked with both brown and rainbow trout. First they fish at anchor and then drift catching trout on small wet flies in front of the boat.
F — I
Thorn EMI Video Programmes Ltd — *THORN EMI* **P**
TXF 90 0845 4/TVF 90 0845 2

Go Fishing With Jack Charlton—Part 3: Sea Wreck Fishing
Spo-Lei '82
Fishing
08437 30 mins C
B, V

Jack Charlton, directed by Alan Ravenscroft
In this programme, the third in the series, Jack Charlton goes fishing over the torpedoed remains of a wartime wreck in the English Channel. Using mackrel, sandeels and artificial eels as bait the team catch pollack, red bream, ling and conger, all of them deep-sea fish.
F — I
Thorn EMI Video Programmes Ltd — *THORN EMI* **P**
TXF 90 0842 4/TVF 90 0842 2

Go Fishing with Jack Charlton—Part 5: River Trout Fishing
Spo-Lei '82
Fishing
09003 30 mins C
B, V

Jack Charlton, Ray King
In this programme, the fifth in the series, Jack Charlton goes to the West Country, taking his trout tackle to Eggesford on Devon's beautiful River Taw. The local river keeper Ray King is his guide, who demonstrates the art of fly fishing and catches a trout to order.
F — I
Thorn EMI Video Programmes Ltd — *THORN EMI* **P**
TXF 90 0856 4/TVF 90 0856 2

Go Fishing with Jack Charlton-Part 6: Salmon Fishing
Spo-Lei '82
Fishing
09803 30 mins C
B, V

Jack Charlton, directed by Alan Ravenscroft
In this programme, the sixth of the series, Jack Charlton's search for salmon takes him to the river Tay in the Scottish Highlands, where he meets with salmon expert Jeremy Miller.
F — I
Thorn EMI Video Programmes Ltd. — *THORN EMI* **P**
TXF 90 0864 4/TVF 90 0864 2

Go Hog Wild
Fil-Ent '??
Comedy
07898 93 mins C
V2, B, V

Patti D'Arbanville, Michael Biehn, Tony Rosato, directed by Les Rose
This is the bawdy tale of the antics of the 'Rustlers,' a group of young motor cycling hoodlums. A college student takes on the gang

PALADIN VIDEO HOME ENTERTAINMENT GUIDE

because he is unable to back down during an argument and also has his eye on the leader's girlfriend. The film culminates in an outrageous motorcycle race.
S,A — EN
Unknown — *Video Programme Distributors* **P**
Inter-Ocean—061

Go Kill and Come Back!   Fil-Ent '67
Western
04299   96 mins   C
V2, B, V
George Hilton, Edd Byrnes, Gilbert Roland
The stranger witnesses a train robbery in which a strong-box is stolen by the Monetero gang. Pajondo, Monetero's deputy, double crosses his leader and makes off with the stolen gold. The stranger sets up an alliance with Monetero and appears master of the situation, but a surprise awaits them.
C,A — EN
Golden Eagle — *Video Programme Distributors*   **P**
Inter-Ocean—039

God Forgives—I Don't   Fil-Ent '67
Western
07796   108 mins   C
V2, B, V
Terence Hill, Bud Spencer
This film follows two men's revenge on a gang of murderous train robbers.
S,A — EN
Italy — *Fletcher Video*   **H, P**
V101

Godchildren, The   Fil-Ent '??
Crime-Drama
05729   90 mins   C
V2, B, V
Tony Porter, Robert Dalton, Christopher Culhane
After the Godfather dies the family have to keep the business going, especially the dope pushing operation. A double-cross results in a sequence of events that spell disaster for those involved in the half-million dollar drug ring.
S,A — EN
Unknown — *Video Unlimited*   **H, P**

Godfather, The   Fil-Ent '72
Drama
01212   171 mins   C
B, V
Marlon Brando, Al Pacino, James Caan, Robert Duvall, Talia Shire, Diane Keaton, directed by Francis Ford Coppola
Epic portrayal of the Corleone family, and their rise to the top of the criminal world, based on Mario Puzo's novel.
Academy Awards '71: Best Picture; Best Actor (Brando); Best Screenplay (Puzo and Coppola).
A — EN
Paramount — *CIC Video*   **H, P**

Godfather of Hong Kong   Fil-Ent '73
Crime-Drama
04310   89 mins   C
V2, B, V
Hong Kong Mafia is attacked by an army of Kung Fu Karate experts. Very violent.
A — EN
Cannon Films — *Intervision Video*   **H, P**
A-A 0035

Godmothers, The   Fil-Ent '??
Comedy-Drama
06097   97 mins   C
V2, B, V
Mickey Rooney, Jerry Lester, Frank Fontaine
A parody of the American Mafia seen through the eyes of a comedian. Features a prosperous, romantic, spaghetti-loving lady, a gun-happy fiance, an over self-confident dwarf with the gift of the gab, a hard and ruthless but too sentimental Godfather and a band of would-be gangsters.
S,A — EN
Unknown — *Video Programme Distributors*   **P**
Cinehollywood—V1540

God's Little Acre   Fil-Ent '58
Drama
05733   110 mins   B/W
V2, B, V
Robert Ryan, Tina Louise, Aldo Ray, Buddy Hackett, Jack Lord, directed by Anthony Mann
A story of love, violence, jealousy and a mad search for gold set in the American deep south. Portrays one man's desperate struggle to keep the town alive. Based on the novel by Erskine Caldwell, musical score by Elmer Bernstein.
BBFC:A — S,A — EN
UA; Sidney Harmon — *Video Unlimited*   **H, P**
010

Gods Must Be Crazy, The   Fil-Ent '??
Comedy-Drama
08378   108 mins   C
V2, B, V
Marious Weyers, Sandra Prinsloo, Nic De Jager, Michael Thys

(For Explanation of codes, see USE GUIDE and KEY)

PALADIN VIDEO HOME ENTERTAINMENT GUIDE

This film tells the story of a tribe of primitive Bushmen. When a Coca-Cola bottle drops from a passing aeroplane, they believe it to be a treasure from the Gods, and all want to own it.
BBFC:A — S,A — EN
Unknown — Guild Home Video   H, P, E

God's Story   Chl-Juv '??
Cartoons/Religion
06159   100 mins   C
V2, B, V
Animated, narrated by Paul Copley
This cartoon was especially designed to introduce children to the New Testament. It begins with the Christmas story at the start of Christ's life and ends with the Easter Story.
PS,M — EN
Hinkin Prod — Guild Home Video   H, P, E

Godsend, The   Fil-Ent '77
Horror
08066   84 mins   C
B, V
Cyd Hayman, Malcolm Stoddard, Angela Pleasence, Patrick Barr, directed by Gabrielle Beaumont
A strange woman befriends a loving family. She gives birth to a girl, leaves it with them and disappears. Many weird things begin to happen as the child grows up. When their own children die, the husband begins to suspect their adopted child.
BBFC:X — A — EN
Cannon Group — Rank Video Library   H, P
2024 C

Godzilla vs. the Cosmic Monster   Fil-Ent '74
Science fiction
02088   80 mins   C
V2, B, V
Earth is invaded by a team of alien scientists led by a giant cosmic monster, a steel replica of the flesh and blood monster Godzila.
S,A — EN
Japan — Hokushin Audio Visual Ltd   P
VM-36

Goin' All the Way   Fil-Ent '82
Comedy-Drama
09834   82 mins   C
V2, B, V
Dan Waldman, Deborah Van Rhyn, Joshua Cadman

A 17-year-old boy is sex mad and highly frustrated. Almost every pretty girl on the campus wants him except his girlfriend. The hilarious consequences effect almost every relationship in the college.
A — EN
Saturn International — Polygram Video
H, P
791 5395/791 5394/791 5392

Goin' Coconuts   Fil-Ent '78
Musical/Comedy
09224   110 mins   C
B, V
Donny Osmond, Marie Osmond, Kenneth Mars, Herbert Edelman, Ted Cassidy
Donny and Marie Osmond whilst en route to Hawaii for a concert tour, get involved with ruthless gangsters and the underworld.
F — EN
Osmond Distributing — Video Form Pictures
H, P
MGT 9

Goin' South   Fil-Ent '78
Western/Comedy
10121   105 mins   C
B, V
Jack Nicholson, Christopher Lloyd, John Belushi, directed by Jack Nicholson
A saddle-tramp is rescued from the noose by an attractive woman whom he marries. However, it transpires that all she really wants is a slave to work in an old gold mine to find the gold she is sure exists.
BBFC:PG — S,A — EN
Paramount — CIC Video   H, P
BEA 2063/VHA 2063

Going Berserk   Fil-Ent '83
Comedy
13316   82 mins   C
B, V
John Candy, Joe Flaherty, Eugene Levy, directed by David Steinberg
When a part-time night club drummer becomes engaged to marry the daughter of a famous congressman he becomes involved in an assassination plot to kill his future father-in-law.
S,A — EN
Universal — CIC Video   H, P
BET 1111/VHT 1111

Going Steady   Fil-Ent '7?
Comedy
08614   90 mins   C
V2, B, V
Jeremy Katzur, Jonathan Segal, Zachi Noy, Yvonne Michaels

(For Explanation of codes, see USE GUIDE and KEY)

PALADIN VIDEO HOME ENTERTAINMENT GUIDE

This film follows the antics of the 'Lemon Popsicle Boys'. It follows a feud with the local motor-cycle gang, when the boys steal the gang's girlfriends and go for a nude midnight swim. However, when the motor-cyclists return claiming their girlfriends, they leave the three boys having to make their own way home without a stitch of clothing.
C,A — EN
Unknown — Hokushin Audio Visual Ltd
P
VM 73

Going Well Over Sixty   Gen-Edu '80
Physical therapy
13530   30 mins   C
B, V
Through involvement in recreative activity, older people are encouraged to keep active, both physically and mentally.
C,A — ED
Unknown — TFI Leisure Ltd   **H, P**

Gold   Fil-Ent '73
Suspense/Drama
06265   122 mins   C
B, V
Roger Moore, Susannah York, Ray Milland, Sir John Gielgud, Bradford Dillman
The story of a mining engineer who falls in love with his boss's grand-daughter. In his search for gold he become sickened by the brutal way in which the natives are treated. He decides to fight for them but falls foul of the Boers when he exposes a conspiracy of graft, corruption and privilege. Shot entirely on location in South Africa and based on the novel by Wilbur Smith.
S,A — EN
Allied Artists — VCL Video Services   **P**
P180D

Gold Medal Swimming, Part 1   Spo-Lei '82
Sports-Water
13555   30 mins   C
B, V
Duncan Goodhew, Mark Tonelli
Part 1 of this two-part series explains and demonstrates the art of breaststroke and starts and turns.
F — I
Unknown — TFI Leisure Ltd   **H, P**

Gold Medal Swimming, Part 2   Spo-Lei '82
Sports-Water
13556   30 mins   C
B, V
Duncan Goodhew, Mark Tonelli
Part 2 of this two-part series explains and demonstrates the art of backstroke, freestyle and the butterfly stroke.
F — I
Unknown — TFI Leisure Ltd   **H, P**

Gold of the Amazon Women   Fil-Ent '79
Drama/Adventure
08348   90 mins   C
V2, B, V
Bo Stevenson, Anita Ekberg, Donald Pleasance, Richard Romanus, Robert Minor, Bond Gideon, Maggie Jean Smith, directed by Mark Lester
Two explorers, after having found an old map, set off in search of gold, with a rival on their trail. Not only do they find gold, but a tribe of man-hungry female warriors.
S,A — EN
Mi-ka Prod; NBC Entertainment — Guild Home Video   **H, P, E**

Gold Rush, The/Pay Day   Fil-Ent '2?
Comedy
05843   92 mins   B/W
B, V
Charlie Chaplin, Mack Swain, Georgia Hale, Tom Murray
This cassette features two Charlie Chaplin films. 'The Gold Rush' (1925) follows the mis-placed romance of the little tramp during the Klondike Gold Rush. The film was re-issued in 1942, in sound, with Chaplin's narration. 'Pay Day' (1922) features Chaplin as a construction worker contending with a domineering wife and a very unsympathetic boss.
F — EN
United Artists — Polygram Video   **P**
7901444/7901442

Gold Train   Fil-Ent '7?
Western
07979   90 mins   C
B, V
Carlo Mohner, John Heston, Topsy Collins
This film tells the story of a small western town terrorised by bandits. The sheriff cannot cope with the murders and contacts Washington for help. Months later a stranger comes to town. He turns out to be a federal agent and together with the sheriff, they plot to trap the bandits.
S,A — EN
Unknown — AVI Video Ltd   **P**
011

Gold Wing   Chi-Juv '??
Cartoons/Science fiction
09379   90 mins   C
B, V
Animated

(For Explanation of codes, see USE GUIDE and KEY)   **279**

PALADIN VIDEO HOME ENTERTAINMENT GUIDE

Young Jack O'Neil, while riding his motorcycle, witnesses a spaceship destroying a car. Without realising it, he has witnessed a confrontation between the prince of the star system and a master criminal. Jack is drawn into this conflict, taking the Prince's side. As a reward he is given superhuman powers.
BBFC:U — I,M — EN
Unknown — Precision Video Ltd   P
BMMPV 2595/VMMPV 2595

Golden Lady, The   Fil-Ent '74
Crime-Drama
06225   90 mins   C
B, V
Christina World, June Chadwick, Suzanne Danielle, Anika Pavel, Hot Gossip, Blonde on Blonde
'The Golden Lady' lives in the hard, glamorous world of the super-rich where lives are cheap and wealth is everything. She plays out a deadly game for the highest stakes imaginable. Various characters struggle to survive in a blitz of fast cars, motorcycles and helicopters.
S,A — EN
Jean Uband/Keith Cavele Production — VCL Video Services   P
P182D

Golden Needles   Fil-Ent '74
Drama/Suspense
09928   95 mins   C
B, V
Joe Don Baker, Elizabeth Ashley, Ann Sothern, Burgess Meredith, directed by Robert Clouse
This is a suspenseful story of a priceless ancient Chinese statue, pursued halfway across the world. Whoever owns the statue with the golden needles can rule the world, for the needles show the precise places that can make men miraculously virile and awesomely powerful.
BBFC:PG — F — EN
American Int'l — Rank Video Library   H, P
0170 A

Golden Rendezvous   Fil-Ent '77
Adventure/Suspense
08077   98 mins   C
B, V
Richard Harris, David Jansen, Gordon Jackson, Ann Turkel, Robert Beatty, Burgess Meredith, Keith Baxter, directed by Ashley Lazarus
The film starts with murderous mercenaries taking over a freighter. It continues with fast moving action and murder on the high seas.
BBFC:A — S,A — EN
Film Trust — Rank Video Library   H, P
0130 B

Golden Seal, The   Fil-Ent '83
Adventure
12907   90 mins   C
B, V
Steve Railsback, Michael Beck, Penelope Milford, Torquil Campbell, directed by Frank Zuniga
This film tells the story of an extraordinary friendship between a rare and beautiful golden seal and a nine year old boy and of the islanders who want to claim the bounty on the animal's pelt.
I,M — EN
Samuel Goldwyn Jr — THORN EMI   P
TXB 90 24114/TVB 90 24112

Golden Treasury of   Chl-Juv '8?
Classic Fairy Tales, The
Cartoons/Fairy tales
08660   60 mins   C
B, V
Animated, narrated by Sheila Hancock, George Cole
This tells six famous fairy tales from some of the world's great fairy tale story writers, Hans Andersen, the Brothers Grimm and Charles Perrault. They feature kings, queens, heroic and handsome princes and princesses, wicked witches and foolish human beings amongst many others. It contains 'Puss in Boots,' 'Four Musicians,' 'The Princess and the Pea,' 'Rapunzel,' 'Ugly Duckling' and 'The Emperor's New Clothes.'
BBFC:U — I,M — EN
Moo Movies — Longman Video   P
LGBE 5002/LGVH 5002

Golden Triangle, The   Fil-Ent '??
Adventure/Drama
06098   100 mins   C
V2, B, V
Lo Lieh, Sambat Matanee, Tien Nee, Tien Fong
A powerful syndicate which produces 70 percent of the world's opium controls territory on a high secluded area bordered by Laos, Thailand and Burma. Rival gangs struggle with ruthless violence for control over the traffic of the flowers.
S,A — EN
Unknown — Video Programme Distributors   P
Cinehollywood—V180

Goldengirl   Fil-Ent '79
Drama
10075   101 mins   C
V2, B, V, LV
James Coburn, Leslie Caron, Richard Cull, Harry Guardino, Susan Anton

PALADIN VIDEO HOME ENTERTAINMENT GUIDE

A girl athlete has been trained all her life to win the Moscow Olympics in three track events-at all costs. However, for Goldengirl the price may be too high.
S,A — EN
Avco Embassy — *Embassy Home Entertainment*   **P**
2069

Goldfinger   Fil-Ent '64
Adventure
13187   108 mins   C
B, V

Sean Connery, Honor Blackman, Gert Frobe, directed by Guy Hamilton

The evil Goldfinger and his indestructible sidekick Oddjob plan to rob Fort Knox.
BBFC:A — C,A — EN
Danjaq SA; United Artists — *Warner Home Video*   **P**
99205

Goldilocks and the Three Bears   Fil-Ent '84
Fairy tales
13411   48 mins   C
B, V

Tatum O'Neal

Goldilocks finds herself in trouble after eating porridge from the three bears plates and falling asleep in one of their beds.
BBFC:U — F — EN
Shelley Duvall — *MGM/UA Home Video*   **P**
10432

Goldrunner   Fil-Ent '??
Adventure
09954   90 mins   C
V2, B, V

Richard Losee, Kristin Kelly

Wilson Cromwell has executed the perfect plan for revenge against T.R. Stockton, a wealthy ex-business partner. However although Stockton agrees to the insane demands, 5000 ounces of gold is not enough.
BBFC:A — S,A — EN
Unknown — *Video Unlimited*   **H, P, E**
080

Golf   Spo-Lei '80
Golf
00260   120 mins   C
B, V, FO

This programme covers the basic aspects of the game of golf, from equipment to courtesy on the course.
F — I
London Video Ltd — *Video Sport for All*   **P**
1010

Golf: Game of Power and Accuracy   Spo-Lei '82
Golf
09800   93 mins   C
B, V

John Jacobs, Johnny Miller, Beth Daniel, directed by Frank Chirkinian

In this programme top professionals shows beginners and advanced players how to improve and enjoy playing the game of golf. They demonstrate all the shots in the golfing repertoire, reveal tactics and explain how to correct common faults. Advice is also given on the grip and the stance, putting, chipping and driving.
F — I
Players Enterprises Productions and Corporation for Entertainment — *THORN EMI*   **P**
TXE 90 1938 4/TVE 90 1938 2

Goliath and the Barbarians   Fil-Ent '60
Drama
09159   90 mins   C
V

Steve Reeves, Chelo Alonso, Bruce Cabot

After the massacre of his homestead and the brutal murder of his father, Goliath sets out to seek revenge on the Barbarian hoards he knows to be responsible.
S,A — EN
American International — *Medusa Communications Ltd*   **H, P**

Gondoliers, The   Fil-Ent '8?
Opera
08919   100 mins   C
B, V

Keith Michell, Eric Shilling, Francis Egerton, Tom McDonnell, Anne Collins, Nan Christie, Sandra Dugdale, Fiona Kimm, Christopher Booth-Jones, directed by Dave Heather

This opera by Gilbert and Sullivan tells the story of two Venetian Gondoliers, one of whom is the rightful King of Barataria. Since no one knows which of them was abducted from the kingdom as a child, they have a chance to put their

---

(For Explanation of codes, see USE GUIDE and KEY)

PALADIN VIDEO HOME ENTERTAINMENT GUIDE

Republican principles into practice by sharing the throne. The music is played by the London Symphony Orchestra, conducted by Alexander Faris, with the Ambrosian Opera Chorus.
S,A — EN
Brent Walker Prods — *Brent Walker Home Video Ltd* **P**

Gone are the Dayes Fil-Ent '84
Drama/Comedy
13748   87 mins   C
B, V
Harvey Korman, Susan Anspach, Robert Hogan
When a family witnesses a gangland killing while dining in a Japanese restaurant, they are forced to go into hiding until they can testify at the killers' trial.
F — EN
Walt Disney Productions — *Rank Video Library* **P**
704B

Gone in 60 Seconds Fil-Ent '??
Crime-Drama
08862   92 mins   C
V2, B, V
H.B. Halicki, Marion Busia, George Cole, James McIntyre, Jerry DaugirdaParnelli Jones, J.C. Agajanian, directed by H.B. Halicki
This tells the dramatic story of the theft of cars such as Rolls Royces, Cadillacs and other expensive models. To fulfill a huge contract 48 cars have to be stolen and delivered to the docks in five days. However, the last car, a Mustang, proves a problem, and results in car chases, crashes and incredible speeds.
S,A — EN
Unknown — *Video Programme Distributors* **P**
Replay 1020

Gone in 60 Seconds II Fil-Ent '81
Drama
12827   92 mins   C
V2, B, V
Christopher Stone, Susan Shaw
A plan is out to assassinate an auto-junkman millionaire a few days before the premiere if his latest movie, as publicly as possible, and the organization behind it sets about demolishing half the state of Nevada and its cars.
BBFC:PG — S,A — EN
H B Halicki — *Video Tape Centre; Video Programme Distributors* **P**

Gone with the West Fil-Ent '75
Western
02082   90 mins   C
B, V
James Caan, Sammy Davis Jr.

A most unusual western packed with humour and action featuring one of Hollywood's greatest stars, James Caan, and the irrepressible Sammy Davis Jr.
F — EN
Unknown — *VCL Video Services* **P**

Gone with the Wind Fil-Ent '39
Drama
10180   220 mins   C
B, V
Clark Gable, Vivien Leigh, Leslie Howard, Olivia De Havilland, directed by Victor Fleming
This is a love story set against the background of the American Civil War. A beautiful young Southern Belle falls hopelessly in love with her friend's husband. She loses her family and home and marries a dashing adventurer but can never become free.
Academy Awards '39: Best Actress (Leigh); Best Supporting Actress (McDaniel); Best Direction (Fleming); Best Screen Play (Howard); Best Picture.   BBFC:U — F — EN
Selznick International Pictures Inc.;
MGM — *MGM/UA Home Video* **P**
UMB 10284/UMV 10284

Good Die Young, The Fil-Ent '55
Drama
01948   95 mins   B/W
B, V
Richard Basehart, John Ireland, Gloria Grahame, Joan Collins
Four men from widely diverse backgrounds meticulously plan a daring bank robbery. The film's message is in the title.
S,A — EN
United Artists, Romulus — *CBS/Fox Video* **P**
3B-061

Good Guys Wear Black Fil-Ent '78
Adventure
09068   96 mins   C
B, V
Chuck Norris, Anne Archer, James Franciscus
A mild-mannered professor keeps his former life as leader of a Vietnam commando unit under wraps until he discovers that he's number one on the C.I.A. hit list. He has to use all his commando skills to stay alive and get to the only man who can stop the C.I.A.
S,A — EN
Mar Vista — *Video Tape Centre* **P**
VTC 1027

Good Life, The Fil-Ent '7?
Comedy-Drama
09406   ? mins   C
V2, B, V

(For Explanation of codes, see USE GUIDE and KEY)

PALADIN VIDEO HOME ENTERTAINMENT GUIDE

Richard Briers, Felicity Kendal, Penelope Keith, Paul Eddington, Reginald Marsh
This tells the hilarious story of Tom and Barbara's fight for self sufficiency in suburbia.
F — EN
BBC — *BBC Video* **H, P**
BBCV 7007

Good, the Bad, and the Ugly, The   Fil-Ent '68
Western
01281   155 mins   C
V2, B, V
Clint Eastwood, Lee Van Cleef, Eli Wallach, directed by Sergio Leone
A mysterious stranger forms a partnership with a Mexican gunman and a sadistic criminal in search of a hidden cash box containing $200,000 which was stolen and put in an unmarked grave during the Civil War. The double-crossers meet for a blazing shoot out in the middle of the cemetery.
BBFC:X — *C,A* — *EN*
United Artists, Alberto Grimaldi — *Intervision Video* **H**
UA A B 5010

Good Time Outlaws   Fil-Ent '??
Comedy/Adventure
06903   90 mins   C
V2, B, V
Jesse Turner, Dennis Fimple, Slim Pickens, Dianne Sherrill, Marcie Barkin, Hope Summers, Gailard Sartain, Sully Boyer, directed by Alex Grasshoff
Two up and coming Country and Western stars are fired from the ranch where they have been working as hands. They decide to head for Nashville. During the 2000-mile trip, they encounter an amazing variety of troubles, escapades and near disasters when they become involved in a demolition derby, a rodeo, a bullfight and the law. Songs include 'I Made It On My Own' and 'I'd Like to Be in Nashville.'
BBFC:U — *F* — *EN*
Unknown — *Temple Enterprises Ltd* **H, P**

Good Times   Fil-Ent '66
Comedy/Musical
05193   89 mins   C
B, V, PH17
Sonny & Cher, George Sanders, Norman Alden, Larry Duran

Sonny and Cher, the swinging sixties American singing duo, star in this madcap musical comedy in which they create fantasy movies for a lugubrious film tycoon called Mordicus.
BBFC:U — *F* — *EN*
Columbia; Motion Pictures Intl — *Rank Video Library* **H, P**
1013

Good, The Bad and The Ugly, The   Fil-Ent '66
Western
13179   161 mins   C
B, V
Clint Eastwood, directed by Sergio Leone
The last film in a series of three, which is set during the American Civil War and leads to a terrible showdown where good and evil are hardly distinguishable.
BBFC:X — *A* — *EN*
PEA Produzioni Europee Associates — *Warner Home Video* **P**
99225

Goodbye, Bruce Lee   Fil-Ent '7?
Adventure/Martial arts
06802   84 mins   C
V2, B, V
Lee Roy, Ronald Brown, Johnny Floyd, Kareem Abdul Jabbar
A master of Kung Fu is invited to finish the late Bruce Lee's last film.
C,A — EN
Robert Chow; Atlas International — *Intervision Video* **H, P**
A-A 0341

Goodbye Girl, The   Fil-Ent '77
Comedy
13032   110 mins   C
B, V
Richard Dreyfuss, Marsha Mason, Quinn Cummings, directed by Herbert Ross
A Broadway dancer whose affairs usually end with the man leaving her, meets an aspiring actor and wonders once again if she is going to be the Goodbye Girl.
BBFC:A — *C,A* — *EN*
Metro Goldwyn Mayer Inc; Warner Bros Inc — *Warner Home Video* **P**
61185

Goodbye, Norma Jean   Fil-Ent '76
Drama
06775   91 mins   C
V2, B, V
Misty Rowe, Terence Locke

(For Explanation of codes, see USE GUIDE and KEY)

PALADIN VIDEO HOME ENTERTAINMENT GUIDE

The adolescence and early starlet years of Marilyn Monroe are dramatised in this film.
S,A — EN
A Sterling Gold — *Intervision Video* **H, P**
A-AE 0333

Goodbye Paradise Fil-Ent '82
Crime-Drama
09354   121 mins   C
V2, B, V
Ray Barrett, Robyn Nevin, Guy Doleman, Paul Chubb, Lex Marinos, Robert Morton, Kate Fitzpatrick, Janet Scrivener
Set around the shores of Australia's South Pacific, the ex-Deputy Commissioner of Police is attempting to uncover corruption in high places. A candidate running for election loses his daughter and the ex-Commissioner is very quietly asked to find her.
F — EN
Petersham Pictures Pty Ltd — *Precision Video Ltd* **P**
CRSWPV 2600/BSWPV 2600/VSWPV 2600

Goodbye Pork Pie Fil-Ent '81
Adventure
08934   105 mins   C
B, V
Tony Barry, Kelly Johnson, Claire Oberman, Shirley Gruar, directed by Geoff Murphy
This is a film from New Zealand about three very unlikely companions and a stolen Mini. As they hurtle through the beautiful New Zealand landscape, gaining pursuers and losing bits off the Mini, they meet with adventures one after the other.
BBFC:AA — C,A — EN
Pork Pie Productions — *Brent Walker Home Video Ltd* **P**

Goodies, The Fil-Ent '??
Comedy
08572   104 mins   C
B, V
Tim Brooke-Taylor, Graeme Garden, Bill Oddie, directed by Bill Spiers
This tape features four episodes of the trio's adventures. In 'Football Crazy' there is trouble with soccer hooliganism both off and on the pitch. In 'Robot' a Goodie has to be replaced by a foot when expenses exceed profits. In 'Big Foot' they decide to investigate the enigma of Arthur C. Clake. In 'Change of Life' it is Bill's birthday and they are in danger of closing down.
F — EN
London Weekend Television — *THORN EMI* **P**
TXB 90 0694 4/TVB 90 0694 2

Goodies and the Beanstalk, The Fil-Ent '7?
Comedy-Drama/Fairy tales
09400   ? mins   C
V2, B, V
Tim Brooke-Taylor, Graeme Garden, Bill Oddie, Alfie Bass
This features the three Goodies and other guests in their interpretation of the well-known fairy tale.
F — EN
BBC — *BBC Video* **H, P**
BBCV 7008

Goodwind Nine Hours 1955/Final Victory 1959 Spo-Lei '7?
Automobiles-Racing
04507   51 mins   C
B, V
The Aston Martin DB35 of Peter Walker and Dennis Poore wins by a lap over the Titterington/Sanderson Ecurie Ecosse D-type. The second feature pits three Aston Martin DBR1s against eleven Ferraris in the 1959 Le Mans.
F — EN
Aston Martin Lagonda — *Quadrant Video* **H, P**
M4

Goofs from the Cutting Room Floor Fil-Ent '80
Outtakes and bloopers
06907   90 mins   C
V2, B, V
Richard Thomas, Sonny and Cher, Alan Alda, Wayne Rogers, McLean Stevenson, Julie Andrews, Sammy Davis Jr, Carol Burnett
This is a compilation of mistakes and mishaps featuring a variety of stars from various American TV serials. It also includes outtakes from commercials plus actual commercials that appear to be outtakes.
F — EN
Unknown — *Fourmatt Video Ltd* **P**

Goose Boxer Fil-Ent '7?
Martial arts
09823   90 mins   C
B, V
A man makes a living by selling roast goose in the market. After having his stall smashed by thugs, he trains in vain to learn curious 'crane' fighting technique but it proves too difficult. Instead he develops his own devastating style.
S,A — EN
Unknown — *Polygram Video* **H, P**
790 4544/790 4542

PALADIN VIDEO HOME ENTERTAINMENT GUIDE

Gorky Park Fil-Ent '84
Drama/Mystery
13470 124 mins C
B, V
William Hurt, Lee Marvin, Brian Dennehy, Ian Bannen, Joanna Pacula, directed by Michael Apted
When three bodies are discovered in Russia's Gorky Park a group of ill-assorted people become involved with each other in unravelling the mystery.
BBFC:15 — S,A — EN
Orion Pictures — *Rank Video Library* H, P
0213 D

Goshawk Gen-Edu '7?
Birds
04499 52 mins C
B, V
A sensitive look at a man and his training of a bird of prey. Man's love and the stubborn intelligence of a hawk combine to show man's role within the animal kingdom, and the delicate balance of life.
F — EN
David Cobham — *Quadrant Video* H, P
WB3

Got It Made Fil-Ent '83
Drama/Comedy
12592 106 mins C
V2, B, V
Lalla Ward, Michael Latimer, Michael Feast, Fabia Drake, directed by James Kenelm Clarke
This cassette features a 24 minute ski-ing comedy hosted by Frankie Howerd and a trailer and introduction for the next programme by Leslie Crowther. 'Got It Made' tells the story of how a young girls' chance meeting with a rock singer affects her wedding plans.
S,A — EN
James Kenelm Clarke — *Intervision Video* H, P
A-A 0520

Goya Fil-Ent '7?
Drama
09951 90 mins C
V2, B, V
Francisco Rabal
This is a powerful true life study of the famous painter.
BBFC:A — S,A — EN
Unknown — *Video Unlimited* H, P, E
086

Grace Jones: A One Man Show Fil-Ent '82
Music-Performance
10138 45 mins C
B, V
Directed by Jean-Paul Goude
This one man show by Grace Jones is loosely structured around her stage show in London. Tracks include 'Warm Leatherette', 'La vie en rose', 'Pull up to the Bumper', 'My Jamaican Guy' and many more.
F — EN
Unknown — *Island Pictures* P
IPVOO55

Grace Kelly Story, The Fil-Ent '83
Drama
12260 99 mins C
V2, B, V
Cheryl Ladd, Lloyd Bridges, Diane Ladd, Alejandro Rey, Ian McShane
This film traces the film star's rise to fame ending with her untimely, tragic death.
S,A — EN
Talcota Productions; Embassy TV — *Embassy Home Entertainment* P
2044

Graduate, The Fil-Ent '67
Comedy/Drama
13033 105 mins C
B, V
Dustin Hoffman, Anne Bancroft, Katharine Ross, directed by Mike Nichols
The story of a young man's first affair, which happens to be with the wife of one of his parents' long-standing friends.
Academy Awards '67: Best director (Nichols); Film Daily Poll 10 Best Pictures of the Year '67.
BBFC:X — A — EN
Embassy; Lawrence Turman Inc — *Warner Home Video* P
99265

Graduation Day Fil-Ent '7?
Horror
07615 85 mins C
V2, B, V
Christopher George, Patch MacKenzie, Danny Murphy, Michael Pataki, E.J. Peaker
The star of a college track team makes a final appearance before graduation. She wins but then slumps to the floor and dies. Soon afterwards there is a series of murders. Each victim is a member of the track team.
BBFC:X — A — EN
Unknown — *Iver Film Services* P

'Graham Parker Live' Fil-Ent '7?
Music-Performance
12028 60 mins C
B, V

(For Explanation of codes, see USE GUIDE and KEY)

285

PALADIN VIDEO HOME ENTERTAINMENT GUIDE

Shot at the Park West, Chicago, the tracks include 'White Honey,' 'Howling Wind' and 'Heat Treatment.'
F — EN
Jay Dublin — *Polygram Video*   H, P
0402654/0402652

Grand Prix 1978—The Shape of Things to Come/Grand Prix 1979—Car Wars   Spo-Lei '80
Automobiles-Racing
04695   52 mins   C
B, V

An account of the 1978 GP season and the impact of ground effect on racing car design. The second film is an account of the 1979 season and the end of a motor racing era.
F — EN
Brunswick International — *Quadrant Video*
H, P

Grand Prix of the Decade 1970-1979   Spo-Lei '80
Automobiles-Racing
01985   26 mins   C
B, V

An historic documentary of the winner of The World Championships of the Decade.
F — EN
Castrol — *Quadrant Video*   H, P
M25

Grand Prix Trio 1955/Grand Prix d'Europe 1958   Spo-Lei '7?
Automobiles-Racing
04535   56 mins   C
B, V

The Monaco, Dutch, and British Grand Prix are reviewed. The stirring duels between Moss and Fangio are fought under the watchful eye of the legendary Mercedes team manager, Alfred Neubauer. In the second feature, Mike Hawthorn sets a new lap record, but doesn't have enough to outlast Tony Brooks' first Grand Prix victory.
F — EN
Castrol — *Quadrant Video*   H, P
M1

Grand Slam   Fil-Ent '8?
Comedy
10145   60 mins   C
V2, B, V
Hugh Griffith, Windsor Davies

A group of Welsh rugby fanatics descend on Paris with the intention of watching Wales beat France. As to whether they get to the match or even get home again is another matter!
F — EN
BBC — *BBC Video*   H, P
BBCV 2005

Grand Theft Auto   Fil-Ent '77
Comedy
12683   82 mins   C
B, V
Ron Howard, Nancy Morgan, Marion Ross, Peter Isacksen, directed by Ron Howard
This is a car-chase cum car-crash adventure, when a couple elope in a Rolls-Royce and are chased by the girl's father, the mother of her former fiance, a disc-jockey, and a mass pursuit of radio listeners out to claim the reward for the apprehension of the Rolls-Royce.
BBFC:PG — F — EN
Jon Davison — *Warner Home Video*   P
74038

Grange Hill   Fil-Ent '7?
Drama
09405   ? mins   C
V2, B, V
This tape features the everyday occurrences of possibly the most-talked about school in the history of education.
M,C — EN
BBC — *BBC Video*   H, P
BBCV 9012

Graphics and Games for the BBC Micro Computer   Gen-Edu '8?
Electronic data processing/Games
09995   60 mins   C
B, V
This tape includes 3 basic programmes which can be transferred into a computer. In the first session simple game frameworks are constructed including checks in the coding to ensure that the moving shape does not stray off the screen. In the second session multi-coloured shapes are introduced and a new form of keyboard control. In the final session sounds are examined using channel mixing and simple envelope control.
S,A — I
Holiday Brothers Ltd — *Holiday Brothers Ltd*
P

Graphics and Games for the Electron Micro Computer   Gen-Edu '8?
Electronic data processing/Games
09994   60 mins   C
B, V

PALADIN VIDEO HOME ENTERTAINMENT GUIDE

This tape includes 3 basic programmes which can be transferred into a computer with instructions on how to do so. Firstly, the movement of a shape around the screen is examined, using a user-definer character. In the 2nd session multi-coloured shapes are introduced, drawn at the graphics cursor position rather than the text cursor. In the 3rd session, sounds are examined, using tones and noises and simple Envelope control to produce changing pitches without programme intervention.
S,A — I
Holiday Brothers Ltd. — Holiday Brothers Ltd
P

Grass Is Greener, The   Fil-Ent '61
Comedy
08723   105 mins   C
B, V
Cary Grant, Deborah Kerr, Jean Simmons, Robert Mitchum
The Earl and Countess of Rhyall open the gates of their stately home to the public because of financial problems. An American millionaire invades the private part of the mansion and falls in love with the lady of the house. Events follow leading to a duel between himself and the Earl.
F — EN
V-1;British — BBC Video   **H, P**
BBCV 8005

Grave of the Vampire   Fil-Ent '73
Horror
02439   91 mins   C
B, V
William Smith, Michael Pataki, Kitty Vallacher
A girl who has been raped by a vampire gives birth to a bloodthirsty creature.
BBFC:X — A — EN
Entertainment Pyramid — Guild Home Video
H, P

Gray Lady Down   Fil-Ent '78
Drama
10104   103 mins   C
B, V
Charlton Heston, Stacy Keach, David Carradine, Ned Beatty, directed by David Greene
A nuclear submarine collides with a Norwegian freighter and plunges into the depths with a broken stern. This is the story of its rescue using an experimental underwater vessel.
BBFC:PG — S,A — EN
Universal — CIC Video   **H, P**
BEL 1067/VHL 1067

Grayeagle   Fil-Ent '77
Western
07396   104 mins   C
V2, B, V
Ben Johnson, Iron Eyes Cody, Lana Wood, Jack Elam, Paul Fix, Jimmy Clem, Jacob Daniels, Cindy Butler, Charles B. Pierce, Alex Cord
A beautiful young girl is kidnapped from her father's cabin by Grayeagle, a handsome young brave of the Cheyenne tribe. During her stay at the Cheyenne camp she realises that she has fallen in love with Grayeagle and that the old chief is her real father. When they return to the cabin they are attacked and Grayeagle sacrifices his life so the girl can escape back to her father.
BBFC:AA — S,A — EN
American International — Guild Home Video
H, P, E

Grease   Fil-Ent '78
Musical
01241   110 mins   C
V2, B, V
John Travolta, Olivia Newton-John, Stockard Channing, Eve Arden, Sha-Na-Na
Film version of the hit Broadway musical about high school life in America in the 1950's. Songs include 'You're the One That I Love,' 'We Go Together,' and 'Summer Nights.'
F — EN
Paramount — CIC Video   **H, P**
CRA 2003/BEA 2003/VHA 2003

Grease 2   Fil-Ent '82
Musical
10116   111 mins   C
B, V
Maxwell Caulfield, Michelle Pfeiffer, directed by Patricia Birch
Singing, dancing, romancing in an American high school in the sixties. Guest appearances from Eve Arden, Sid Caesar, Tab Hunter and Connie Stevens.
BBFC:PG — F — EN
Paramount — CIC Video   **H, P**
BEA 2066/VHA 2066

Greased Lightning   Fil-Ent '77
Adventure/Automobiles-Racing
12990   94 mins   C
B, V
Richard Pryor, Cleavon Little, Beau Bridges, directed by Michael Schultz
Based on a true-life story and set in the world of stock car racing, this film tells the story of the first black man to win the coveted NASCAR trophy.
BBFC:PG — S,A — EN
Third World Films — Warner Home Video
P
61136

(For Explanation of codes, see USE GUIDE and KEY)

PALADIN VIDEO HOME ENTERTAINMENT GUIDE

Great Alligator, The　　　Fll-Ent '8?
Adventure/Suspense
07778　　90 mins　　C
V2, B, V
Barbara Bach, Mel Ferrer
A violent tale of superstition amoungst natives in the wild.
S,A — EN
Unknown — *Fletcher Video*　　H, P
V119

Great American Traffic Jam, The　　　Fll-Ent '80
Comedy
07848　　110 mins　　C
B, V
Desi Arnaz Jr., Ed McMahon, Vic Tayback, Howard Hesseman, Abe Vigoda, Noah Beery Jr., Phil Foster, James Gregory, directed by James Frawley
This film follows the chaos that hits the tri-level of the L.A. Freeway System when an elderly lady takes her hundreth driving lesson. A mad golfer, racing CB truckers and millions of oranges all help to close down the most complicated highway network in the world.
F — EN
Ten-Four Productions — *Polygram Video*
H, P
791 512

Great Balloon Adventure, The　　　Fll-Ent '78
Adventure
01196　　84 mins　　C
V2, B, V
Katharine Hepburn, Kevin McKenzie, Dennis Dimster
A young boy wants to celebrate his deceased grandfather's birthday in a unique way—by flying the circus balloon that his grandfather used to perform aerial stunts at country fairs. In order to overcome the many obstacles he faces, he enlists the aid of his best friend and an enthusiastic spinster named Miss Pudd.
BBFC:U — F — EN
Sanrio — *Intervision Video*　　H, P
A-AE 0186

Great Caruso, The　　　Fll-Ent '51
Musical
12216　　109 mins　　C
B, V
Mario Lanza, Ann Blyth, Dorothy Kirsten
The story of Caruso's rise to operatic fame, from his childhood in Naples, Italy, to his collapse on the stage of the Metropolitan Opera House, is told in this film.
F — EN
MGM — *MGM/UA Home Video*　　P
10067

Great Comedians of the Silents—Feed of Mud, The　　　Fll-Ent '2?
Comedy
05835　　56 mins　　C
B, V
Mack Swain, Chester Conklin, Ben Turpin, Georgia O'Dell, Helen Gilmore, Jack Lipson, Charlie Murray, Polly Moran, Slim Summerville, Harry Langdon
A cassette featuring four silent films: 'Love, Speed and Thrills' (9 mins) in which a criminal runs off with a young man's girlfriend; he chases them, catches the villain and is reunited with his sweetheart; 'The Eyes Have It' (16 mins) in which a fisherman heads for trouble when he accepts an invitation to dry his clothes at a lady's house; 'Those College Girls' (19 mins), a young man finds out life in a girls college kitchen is not easy; 'Feet of Mud' (12 mins), a man lands in trouble with the police when he chases some litter.
F — EN
Unknown — *Polygram Video*　　P
40130/20130

Great Diamond Robbery, The　　　Fll-Ent '??
Crime-Drama
08856　　101 mins　　C
V2, B, V
Richard Harrison, Margaret Lee
Two men ask an actor to take part in a daring diamond robbery, because of his uncanny likeness to the security chief at the company. His new role goes as far as sharing the security officer's mistress. However, unexpected events lead him into doublecross and murder.
C,A — EN
Unknown — *Video Programme Distributors*
P
Inter-Ocean 085

Great Dictator, The　　　Fll-Ent '40
Comedy/Satire
05846　　128 mins　　B/W
B, V
Charlie Chaplin, Paulette Goddard, Jack Oakie, Billy Gilbert, Reginald Gardner, Henry Daniell
This film, a political satire, is the first talkie produced by Charlie Chaplin and features two new comedy characters. Adenoid Hynkel, the maniacal dictator of Tamania, and his look-alike, a little Jewish barber returning to his beloved country after 20 years hospitalization. They appear in a send up of history's more recent personalities.
F — EN
United Artists — *Polygram Video*　　P
7901474/7901472

PALADIN VIDEO HOME ENTERTAINMENT GUIDE

Great English Garden Party, The   Spo-Lei '7?
Tennis
04525   50 mins   C
B, V
Narrated by Peter Ustinov
Rare footage, interviews with past champions, and exciting action of present stars tell the story of one hundred years at Wimbledon.
F — EN
Trans World Intl — *Quadrant Video*   H, P
W1

Great Escape, The   Fil-Ent '63
Adventure/World War II
13199   170 mins   C
B, V
Steve McQueen, James Garner, Charles Bronson, Richard Attenborough
Action and tension are equally balanced in this exciting film depicting one of the most remarkable incidents of World War II.
BBFC:U — F — EN
Mirischa Alpha — *Warner Home Video*   P
99232

Great Event, The   Spo-Lei '7?
Sports/Documentary
01975   50 mins   C
B, V
A documentary on the Badminton Horse Trials in which the fortunes of two outstanding competitors are followed.
F — EN
Unknown — *Quadrant Video*   H, P
E5

Great Expectations   Fil-Ent '46
Drama
01875   118 mins   B/W
B, V
John Mills, Alec Guiness, Jean Simmons, Bernard Miles, Frances Sullivan
A stylish film presentation of Charles Dickens' heartwarming story of a young boy and an escaped convict and their ensuing friendship.
BBFC:A — S,A — EN
Rank — *Rank Video Library*   H, P
0011

Great Expectations   Fil-Ent '74
Drama
02039   119 mins   C
B, V
Michael York, Sarah Miles, James Morley, Robert Morley
An orphaned boy is taken to the residence of a mysterious old woman, Miss Havisham, who commands him to play with a haughty young girl who looks down on the boy as being common. In time, the boy falls increasingly in love with her. Adapted from the immortal story by Charles Dickens.
F — EN
Robert Fryer — *Precision Video Ltd*   P
BITC 3018/VITC 3018

Great Expectations   Fil-Ent '8?
Cartoons/Adventure
12556   72 mins   C
V2, B, V
Animated
This film is an ideal introduction to the classic rags to riches story from Charles Dickens featuring the orphaned Pip and his friendship with the convict Magwich.
I,M — EN
Unknown — *RPTA Video Ltd*   H, P

Great Gatsby, The   Fil-Ent '74
Drama/Romance
13292   140 mins   C
B, V
Robert Redford, Mia Farrow, Bruce Dern, Sam Waterston, directed by Jack Clayton
Set in the 1920's, this is the story of a love affair between a rich, spoiled girl and the man she jilted, against the backdrop of the super-rich east coast American lifestyle of that time.
BBFC:PG — S,A — EN
Paramount — *CIC Video*   H, P
BEN 2088/VHN 2088

Great Golden Hits of the Monkees, The   Fil-Ent '7?
Music-Performance/Comedy
02083   30 mins   C
B, V
Davy Jones, Mickey Dolenz
Two original members of the Monkees, Davy Jones and Mickey Dolenz, join their songwriters to provide a fast moving show featuring many of the Monkees hits and much of their totally crazy humour. Songs include 'Last Train to Clarkesville,' 'I'm a Believer,' and many more.
F — EN
VCL Video Services — *VCL Video Services*
P

Great Gundown, The   Fil-Ent '75
Western
08846   83 mins   C
B, V
Robert Padilla, Richard Rust, Milila St. David, directed by Paul Hunt

PALADIN VIDEO HOME ENTERTAINMENT GUIDE

This is a violent tale set in the Old West. The peace of the frontier of New Mexico erupts when a half-breed Indian leads a brutal assault on an outlaw stronghold.
A — EN
Unknown — VCL Video Services   **P**
P245D

Great Guy   Fil-Ent '36
Crime-Drama
06886   77 mins   B/W
V2, B, V
James Cagney, Mae Clarke, Ed Brophy
An inspector of weights and measures becomes involved in a scandal. His assistant is called in to take his place. Some very important men attempt to play an extremely nasty trick on him, taking advantage of his inexperience. However, the opportunity arises for the assistant to give them a dose of their own medicine.
S,A — EN
Grand National — European Video Company
P

Great Houdinis, The   Fil-Ent '76
Drama
04173   96 mins   C
B, V
Paul Michael Glaser, Vivian Vance, Maureen O'Sullivan, Ruth Gordon
Inner turmoil of the world-renowned illusionist and escape artist, torn between his mother and his wife, is depicted in this film.
BBFC:U — F — EN
ABC Circle Films — Guild Home Video
H, P

Great Ice Rip-Off, The   Fil-Ent '74
Comedy/Mystery
05189   72 mins   C
B, V
Lee J. Cobb, Gig Young, Grayson Hall, Robert Walden
This comedy-whodunit pits semi-professional jewel thief Harkey Rollins against cantankerous ex-cop Willy Calso. Having heisted the ice (diamonds) of the title, Harkey and his cronies board a passenger bus from Seattle to San Diego—but they reckon without sitting next to inquisitive old charmer Willy.
S,A — EN
ABC Circle Films; Dan Curtis — Rank Video Library   **H, P**
1012

Great Kidnapping, The   Fil-Ent '78
Crime-Drama
12528   91 mins   C
B, V
Lee J. Cobb, Jean Sorel

Set in Italy, This is the story of one man who risks the life of his son in bringing crooks to justice.
A — EN
Unknown — THORN EMI   **P**
TXB 90 1727 4/TVB 90 1727 2

Great Little Trains of Wales, The   Fil-Ent '??
Trains/Wales
07404   104 mins   C
V2, B, V
Narrated by Wynford Vaughan-Thomas
This film takes a look at four different train rides in the beautiful country of Wales.
F — EN
Unknown — Guild Home Video   **H, P, E**

Great McGonagall, The   Fil-Ent '75
Comedy
02577   89 mins   C
V2, B, V
Spike Milligan, Peter Sellers, Julia Foster, John Bluthal, Valentine Dyall, Clifton Jones, Julian Chagrin, Victor Spinetti, Charlie Atom, directed by Joseph McGrath
An unemployed Scottish weaver abandons his trade to become a poet. His three published books of poetry sell more than Burns or Tennyson despite the fact that he is the worst poet in the world. He dreams of becoming a poet laureate to the queen, but continuously meets with misfortune. Peter Sellers plays the part of Queen Victoria.
BBFC:A — S,A — EN
Darlton — Videomedia   **P**
PVM 2310/BVM 2310/HVM 2310

Great Monkey Rip-Off, The   Fil-Ent '7?
Comedy
04490   87 mins   C
V2, B, V
Alan Hale, Robert J. Wilke, Ashay Chtire
An unscrupulous animal trader plans to steal the sacred monkeys who inhabit the temple at Bandapur, but his plans go awry when the reception for a visiting dignitary is turned into a shambles when the temple's overseer disrupts a huge bees' nest.
F — EN
Lone Star Pictures Intl — Intervision Video
H, P
A-AE 0199

Great Muppet Caper, The   Fil-Ent '80
Comedy/Musical
05412   98 mins   C
V2, B, V, LV

(For Explanation of codes, see USE GUIDE and KEY)

PALADIN VIDEO HOME ENTERTAINMENT GUIDE

The Muppets, Diana Rigg, Charles Grodin, John Cleese, Robert Morley, Peter Ustinov, Jack Warden, directed by Jim Henson
Kermit and Fozzie Bear are reporters for a paper with Gonzo as their photographer. For their first big scoop they try to obtain an exclusive interview with a chicken; blissfully unaware of a diamond robbery behind them, they are fired for not reporting the story. To try to get their jobs back the trio attempt to solve the mystery and recover the jewels.
BBFC:U — F — EN
Jim Henson Productions — *Precision Video Ltd* **P**
CRITC 2099/BITC 2099/VITC 2099

Great Night with.....Chas and Dave, A   Fil-Ent '??
Music-Performance
09341   71 mins   C
B, V
Filmed in a pub in North London, this tape features some of Chas and Dave's big hits including 'Strummin', 'Gertcha', 'Wish I Could Write a Love Song', 'Ain't No Pleasing You' and 'Rabbit'. Other songs performed are 'Poor Old Mr Woogie', 'The Sideboard Song', 'Edmonton Green', 'Beer Belly', 'Massage Palour', 'I'm in Trouble', 'Stop Dreaming', 'Musn't Grumble' and 'Scruffy Old Cow'.
BBFC:U — F — EN
Unknown — *Precision Video Ltd* **P**
BTPV 1511/VTPV 1511

Great Race, The   Fil-Ent '65
Comedy
06037   147 mins   C
B, V
Jack Lemmon, Tony Curtis, Natalie Wood, Peter Falk, Keenan Wynn, directed by Blake Edwards
Set in 1908, a storybook hero and a villain are rivals in an automobile race from New York to Paris over three continents. A militant suffragette who wants to be a reporter cons a New York newspaper publisher into allowing her to enter the race and cover it for her paper. She becomes another cause of rivalry for the hero and villain.
BBFC:U — F — EN
Warner Bros; 7 Arts; Martin Jurow — *Warner Home Video* **P**
WEX1091/WEV1091

Great Railways Volume I   Gen-Edu '81
Trains/History
04867   98 mins   C
V2, B, V, LV
Introduced by O S Nock
This programme looks at steam railways past and present.
F — EN
Colin Luke; Tony Wheeler; Roger Brunskill — *BBC Video* **H, P**
BBCV 1008

Great Rock 'n' Roll Swindle, The   Fil-Ent '7?
Musical-Drama/Comedy
10131   ? mins   C
B, V
This film is a dramatised history of the controversial band the Sex Pistols recounted by their manager in ten easy lessons. Features music by the Sex Pistols with guest appearances by Mary Millington, Liz Frazer, Irene Handl, Malcolm Mcharen and The Black Arabs.
BBFC:X — A — EN
Unknown — *Palace Video Ltd* **P**
VIRV 001A

Great Skycopter Rescue, The   Fil-Ent '8?
Comedy/Adventure
09237   74 mins   C
B, V
Two characters, Jimmy Jet and Will Powerski, team up to run a Skycopter business. The ingenious combination of hang-glider and whirlybird is used by the heroes to save their town from the ravages of the local Hell's Angels and the double-dealings of a tycoon searching for oil under the town's streets.
F — EN
Unknown — *Home Video Holdings* **H, P**

Great Smokey Roadblock, The   Fil-Ent '78
Comedy/Adventure
07807   106 mins   C
B, V
Henry Fonda, Eileen Brennan, John Byner, Dub Taylor, Dana House, directed by John Leone
A terminally ill trucker decides to escape from hospital to make one final cross country run. He captures his impounded rig and picks up as his final load the contents and girls from a brothel. They head out for another state pursued by the police; news of their flight is broadcast and soon they have a convoy of cars, trucks and vans all heading for a police roadblock.
S,A — EN
Dimension Pictures — *Video Tape Centre* **P**
VTC 1003

(For Explanation of codes, see USE GUIDE and KEY)

PALADIN VIDEO HOME ENTERTAINMENT GUIDE

Great Stories 1   Fil-Ent '??
Cartoons
07756   48 mins   C
V2, B, V
Animated
This tape comprises five cartoons from a collection by international award winning animators: 'December,' 'Pirate Gold,' 'Hands Up,' 'The Little Balloon' and 'Prelude.'
F — EN
Frekvensia Ge Te AB — *Fletcher Video*
H, P
GS1

Great Stories 2   Fil-Ent '??
Cartoons
07755   50 mins   C
V2, B, V
Animated
This tape comprises five cartoons from a collection by international award winning animators. 'The Rubber Duckling,' 'Comics I and II,' 'The Friends of Gosho the Elephant,' 'Rooster's Coin' and 'Buffosynchronists.'
F — EN
Frekvensia Ge Te AB — *Fletcher Video*
H, P
GS2

Great Stories 3   Fil-Ent '??
Cartoons
07754   53 mins   C
V2, B, V
Animated
This tape comprises six cartoons from a collection by international award winning animators. 'The Little Diver,' 'Adventures in the Forest,' 'At the Movies,' 'The Carbon Paper Pirate,' 'Little Hand Little Glove' and 'The Three Fools and the Tree.'
F — EN
Frekvensia Ge Te AB — *Fletcher Video*
H, P
GS3

Great Stories 4   Fil-Ent '??
Cartoons
07753   49 mins   C
V2, B, V
Animated
This tape comprises seven cartoons from a collection by international award winning animators. 'The Apple,' 'Lightning Rod,' 'The Hit,' 'Symbiosis,' 'Musical Story,' 'February' and 'Ga.'
F — EN
Frekvensia Ge Te AB — *Fletcher Video*
H, P
GS4

Great Stories 5   Fil-Ent '??
Cartoons
07752   50 mins   C
V2, B, V
Animated
This tape comprises six cartoons from a collection by international award winning animators. 'Rhapsody in Motley,' 'The Hole,' 'Heirs,' 'The Electronic Housewife,' 'Passion' and 'The Musical Tree.'
F — EN
Frekvensia Ge Te AB — *Fletcher Video*
H, P
GS5

Great Stories 6   Fil-Ent '??
Cartoons
07751   50 mins   C
V2, B, V
Animated
This tape comprises six cartoons from a collection by international award winning animators. 'Pastoral,' 'Jolly Fellows,' 'De Facto,' 'Happy End,' 'Clever Village' and 'A Lesson of Sociology.'
F — EN
Frekvensia Ge Te AB — *Fletcher Video*
H, P
GS6

Great Stories 7   Fil-Ent '??
Cartoons
07750   51 mins   C
V2, B, V
Animated
This tape comprises seven cartoons from a collection by international award winning animators. 'Prometheus XX,' 'Aquarium,' 'Alternative,' 'Causa, Perduta,' 'To and From,' 'Cavalcade' and 'Hypothesis.'
F — EN
Frekvensia Ge Te AB — *Fletcher Video*
H, P
GS7

Great Stories 8   Fil-Ent '??
Cartoons
07749   54 mins   C
V2, B, V
Animated
This tape comprises five cartoons from a collection by international award winning animators. 'The Three Apples,' 'Setting,' 'Marko Totev Treasure Hunter,' 'Marko Totev Fiance,' and 'The Best Friend of Marko Totev.'
F — EN
Frekvensia Ge Te AB — *Fletcher Video*
H, P
GS8

PALADIN VIDEO HOME ENTERTAINMENT GUIDE

Great Stories 9: The Three Fools   Fil-Ent '??
Cartoons
07748   52 mins   C
V2, B, V
Animated
This tape comprises six cartoons from a collection by international award winning animators. 'The Three Fools,' 'The Three Fools and The Car, 'The Three Fools and The Foolish Woman,' 'The Three Fools and The Cow,' 'The Three Fools Teachers,' 'The Three Fools Hunters.'
F — EN
Frekvensia Ge Te AB — *Fletcher Video*
H, P
GS9

Great Stories 10   Fil-Ent '??
Cartoons
07747   48 mins   C
V2, B, V
Animated
This tape comprises seven cartoons from a collection by international award winning animators. 'Ill Sharo,' 'Stop and Look around,' 'The Two Little Frogs,' 'The Two Little Frogs and the Mouse,' 'The Obstacle' and 'The Daisy.'
F — EN
Frekvensia Ge Te AB — *Fletcher Video*
H, P
GS10

Great Stories 11: The Mouse   Fil-Ent '??
Cartoons
07746   48 mins   C
V2, B, V
Animated
This tape comprises seven cartoons from a collection by international award winning animators. 'Mouse Morning,' 'Mouse Competition,' 'Mouse Festivity,' 'Mouse Symphony,' 'Mouse Journey,' 'Mouse Show' and 'Mouse Work.'
F — EN
Frekvensia Ge Te AB — *Fletcher Video*
H, P
GS11

Great Stories 12: The Dog Sharo   Fil-Ent '??
Cartoons
07745   55 mins   C
V2, B, V
Animated
This tape comprises six cartoons from a collection by international award winning animators. 'Sharo Musician,' 'Sharo the Artist,' 'Sharo The Passenger,' 'A Medal for Sharo,' 'Sharo the Photographer' and 'Sharo the Detective.'
F — EN
Frekvensia Ge Te AB — *Fletcher Video*
H, P
GS12

Great Telephone Robbery, The   Fil-Ent '7?
Crime-Drama
08088   98 mins   C
B, V
Gadi Yagil, Bomba Tzur, Shai Ophir
This film tells the story of a kidnapping of a bank clerk's mother. The film continues with the plans of the son, to pull off an extraordinary bank heist so that he can buy back his mother.
BBFC:U — F — EN
Unknown — *Rank Video Library*   **H, P**
1039 C

Great Texas Dynamite Chase, The   Fil-Ent '75
Crime-Drama
12496   92 mins   C
B, V
Claudia Jennings, Jocelyn Jones, Johnny Crawford, directed by Michael Pressman
Two young women embark, armed with dynamite, on a crime spree in Texas, always one jump ahead of the police.
BBFC:18 — A — EN
David Irving — *Warner Home Video*   **P**
74028

Great Toy Robbery, The   Chl-Juv '??
Cartoons
10002   55 mins   C
B, V
Animated
This tape features six cartoons; 'The Great Toy Robbery' sees Father Christmas held up western style; 'Cinderella' is a funny version of the well-known fairy tale; 'Little Red Riding Hood'; 'The Christmas Feast'-farm animals escape when they discover they are being fattened up for Christmas; 'A Christmas Cracker' and 'The Story of Christmas'.
M,S — EN
Unknown — *Longman Video*   **P**
LGBE 5016/LGVH 5016

Great Train Robbery, The   Fil-Ent '78
Comedy
13031   111 mins   C
B, V

(For Explanation of codes, see USE GUIDE and KEY)

PALADIN VIDEO HOME ENTERTAINMENT GUIDE

Sean Connery, Donald Sutherland, Lesley-Anne Down, directed by Michael Crichton
The story of a great train robbery, set in Victorian times.
BBFC:A — C,A — EN
United Artists; Dino de Laurentis — Warner Home Video P
99226

Great Waldo Pepper, The　　Fil-Ent '75
Drama
13641　　103 mins　　C
B, V
Robert Redford, Bo Svenson, Bo Brundin, directed by George Roy Hill
This film portrays the enthusiasm of the young American pilots of the twenties and features a lot of stunt-flying and dog-flying using antique planes.
BBFC:PG — F — EN
George Roy Hill — CIC Video　　H, P
1143

Greatest Attack, The　　Fil-Ent '7?
War-Drama/Romance
09075　　90 mins　　C
B, V
Alain Delon
This is a dramatic love story between an army doctor and a young nurse. It is set in a hospital camp amidst military conflict and the threat of a Third World War, and describes their own feelings of life, death and hatred intensified by the limited time.
C,A — EN
Unknown — Video Tape Centre　　P
VTC 1047

Greatest Heroes of the Bible　　Fil-Ent '79
Drama/Bible
04283　　55 mins　　C
B, V
John Carradine, Victoria Principal, Robert Culp, Dorothy Malone, Dean Stockwell, Robert Vaughn, Cameron Mitchell, Robert Alda, Richard Basehart, Gene Barry, Lew Ayres
14　pgms
A masterful series of video programmes bringing the drama and majesty of the Bible to life.
1.The Deluge 2.Daniel and the Lion's Den 3.The Ten Commandments 4.David and Goliath 5.Samson and Delilah 6.Joshua at Jericho 7.Moses 8.Joseph and His Brothers 9.Tower of Babel 10.Abraham's Sacrifice 11.The Judgement of Solomon 12.Daniel and Nebuchadnezzer 13.Sodom and Gomorrah 14.The Story of Esther
F — EN
Sunn Classics — VCL Video Services　　P

Greek Tycoon, The　　Fil-Ent '78
Drama
13642　　100 mins　　C
B, V
Anthony Quinn, Camilla Sparv, Edward Albert, Jacqueline Bisset, James Franciscus, Marilu Tolo, Robin Clarke
When an American president is assassinated, his wife flees to the sundrenched shores of Greece to find comfort in the arms of a rich Greek businessman.
BBFC:PG — S, A — EN
Universal — CIC Video　　H, P
1134

Green Berets, The　　Fil-Ent '68
War-Drama
13027　　136 mins　　C
B, V
John Wayne, David Janssen, Jim Hutton, Aldo Rey, George Takei, directed by Richard Attenborough
The story concerns two highly trained Army detachments who are posted to Vietnam and is both violent and controversial.
BBFC:A — A — EN
Warner Bros — Warner Home Video　　P
61002

Green Eyes　　Fil-Ent '76
Drama
09854　　90 mins　　C
B, V
Paul Winfield, Rita Tushingham, Jonathan Lippe, directed by John Erman
This is the story of a young black Vietnam veteran who returns to Saigon in search of the pregnant girl he left behind and the search for the baby bearing an unmistakable and hereditary hallmark, green eyes.
S,A — EN
Lorimar Prods — Polygram Video　　H, P
791 5674/791 5672

Green Grow the Rushes　　Fil-Ent '51
Comedy
07826　　99 mins　　B/W
V2, B, V
Richard Burton, Honor Blackman, Roger Livesey, Geoffrey Keen, Bryan Forbes
This film follows the story of how a small South Coast fishing village, with its own laws, manages to stall the men from the Ministry from discovering their whiskey smuggling activities.
F — EN
Monarch — Video Unlimited　　H, P
045

(For Explanation of codes, see USE GUIDE and KEY)

PALADIN VIDEO HOME ENTERTAINMENT GUIDE

Green Horizon Fil-Ent '81
Drama
09195 97 mins C
B, V
James Stewart, Philip Sayer, Eleonora Vallone
A grandfather and his granddaughter have lived peacefully in the wilderness for many years. One day a plane crashes in the savannah, and a man stumbles from the wreckage. He eventually comes upon the house in the jungle where the old man lives. He chases him away, angered by the intrusion, but the granddaughter finds him later, and nurses him back to health.
F — EN
Unknown — Video Form Pictures H, P
SKY 2

Green Ice Fil-Ent '81
Drama/Adventure
05870 112 mins C
B, V, LV
Ryan O'Neal, Anne Archer, Omar Sharif
A thirty-five year old electronics buff takes off for Mexico to escape a broken marriage and a failed business venture. He meets a beautiful and wealthy woman and becomes involved in a corrupt South American organisation involving large quantities of emeralds. The girl discovers that the organisation are responsible for her sister's death and with the American joins a band of rebels who need the 'green ice' for their cause.
BBFC:AA — S,A — EN
ITC Films International; Jack Weiner — Precision Video Ltd P
BITC 3060/VITC 3060

Gregory's Girl Fil-Ent '82
Drama
08625 91 mins C
V2, B, V
Gordon John Sinclair, Dee Hepburn, Clare Grogan
This tells the story of Gregory, who lives a very comfortable existence in a nice clean new town. Most of his life is taken up with football, until Dorothy arrives.
S,A — EN
Samuel Goldwyn — Hokushin Audio Visual Ltd P
Vm 62

Greystoke—The Legend of Tarzan, Lord of the Apes Fil-Ent '84
Adventure
12970 125 mins C
B, V
Ralph Richardson, Ian Holm, James Fox, Christopher Lambert, Andie MacDowell
The story of John Clayton, who was rescued from a shipwreck by a band of apes and lived with them for years before returning to England to take up his rightful position as the Seventh Earl of Greystoke, is portrayed in this film.
BBFC:PG — S,A — EN
Hugh Hudson; Stanley S Canter — Warner Home Video P
61375

Griffin and Phoenix Fil-Ent '76
Drama/Romance
04268 94 mins C
B, V
Peter Falk, John Lehne, Jill Clayburgh, Dorothy Tristan
A story of two young, terminally ill cancer victims who meet and fall in love, each keeping their illness a secret from the other.
C,A — EN
ABC TV — Rank Video Library H, P
0039

Grip of the Strangler/Fiend Without a Face/Goodness a Ghost Fil-Ent '??
Suspense/Horror
05654 157 mins B/W
B, V
Boris Karloff, Jean Kent, Elizabeth Allen, directed by Robert Day, Marshall Thompson, Kim Parker, Kynaston Reeves, directed by Arthur Crabtree
Two main films and a short on one cassette. 'Grip of the Strangler' (black and white, 70 minutes, 1960) is about the Haymarket Strangler whose case was executed twenty years ago. It is reopened by an inquisitive crime-writer who finds a scalpel in The Strangler's grave. With this in his grasp he is overtaken by a strange power. 'Fiend Without a Face' (Black/white, 71 mins, 1959) is the story of inexplicable killings which are the result of experiments in mental power. Brain damaging parasites lay seige to the house of their originator. 'Goodness a Ghost'(Black/white) is a slapstick Harry Langdon comedy in which he finds himself haunted by a helpful grandad (16 mins).
S,A — EN
MGM et al — Kingston Video H, P
KV6

Grissom Gang, The Fil-Ent '71
Drama
04174 128 mins C
B, V
Kim Darby, Tony Musante, Scott Wilson, Robert Lansing, Connie Stevens, Irene Daily

(For Explanation of codes, see USE GUIDE and KEY)

PALADIN VIDEO HOME ENTERTAINMENT GUIDE

During the Depression, a simple robbery turns into a kidnapping with a psychopathic killer falling for the young heiress.
BBFC:X — A — EN
Cinerama — *Guild Home Video* **H, P**

Groovie Ghouls Fil-Ent '77
Cartoons
09973 55 mins C
B, V
Animated
This tape features Frankie, Drac, Wolfie, Mummy, Hagatha and all their weird and wonderful friends. The gang take a trip to Hollywood to see Frankie's favourite film.
F — EN
Filmation Associates — *Select Video Limited* **P**
3601/43

Ground Zero Fil-Ent '74
Crime-Drama
05689 90 mins C
B, V
Ron Casteel, Melvin Belli, directed by J.T. Flocker
A scientist is kidnapped, at the same time a nuclear bomb is stolen. The radicals threaten to set off the bomb unless they receive a colossal sum of money from the City of San Francisco and the release of two important criminals. The Government Agents also have problems with an obstinate local authority.
BBFC:A — S,A — EN
James Flocker Productions — *Derann Film Services* **H, P**
GS710B/GS710

Grow Your Own Vegetables How-Ins '81
Gardening
07434 60 mins C
B, V
Presented by Arthur Billitt
In this tape Arthur Billitt provides a month-by-month guide to the art of growing vegetables. Working in the greenhouse and vegetable patch, he shows how to nurture runner beans, broad beans, peas, lettuce, cauliflower, tomatoes, onions, beetroot, potatoes, parsnips, cabbages, savoys, leeks and carrots. He gives tips on planning and rotation of crops, coping with problems such as frost and blight, and storing vegetables.
F — I
THORN EMI Video Programmes Ltd — *THORN EMI* **P**
TXE 90 0719 4/TVE 90 0719 2

Guerillas in Pink Lace Fil-Ent '64
War-Drama/Comedy
06193 80 mins C
B, V
George Montgomery, Valerie Vanda, Joan Shawlee
After Pearl Harbour the Japanese marched on Manila. A engages the help of a priest so he can escape. Disguised as a priest he finds he is chaperone to a group of five showgirls. The plane they are in is shot down and they are trapped on a small enemy held island.
F — EN
Gold Key Entertainment — *VCL Video Services* **P**
X0222

Guess Who's Sleeping in My Bed? Fil-Ent '73
Comedy
04175 74 mins C
B, V
Barbara Eden, Dean Jones, Kenneth Mars, Susanne Benton, Todd Lookinland
A charming vagabond shows up at his ex-wife's house with his new wife, their 8 week old baby, and a Great Dane, to bring havoc and hilarity into her life.
BBFC:U — F — EN
ABC Circle Films — *Guild Home Video* **H, P**

Guide for the Married Man, A Fil-Ent '67
Comedy
12253 91 mins C
B, V
Walter Matthau, Robert Morse, Inger Stevens, Sue Ane Langdon, directed by Gene Kelly
A faithful husband and lawyer starts to find himself attracted to other women. A neighbour gives him a series of lessons on how to conduct a liaison. Musical score is by John Williams.
C,A — EN
20th Century Fox — *CBS/Fox Video* **P**
1152

Guinness Video Book, The Marathon Challenge, A Spo-Lei '82
Running
13113 75 mins C
B, V
Leslie Watson, Ian Thompson, JPR Williams, Jane Griffin

PALADIN VIDEO HOME ENTERTAINMENT GUIDE

This is the story of eight people's preparation to meet the marathon challenge and includes their training schedules, diet, hill running, fartlek and timing and advice on health.
F — EN
Evolution — *Holiday Brothers Ltd* **P**

Gulliver's Travels — Fil-Ent '39
Cartoons/Fantasy
06968   74 mins   C
V2, B, V, LV
Animated
In this cartoon feature Jonathan Swift's fable is brought to life. It follows the adventures of Gulliver who is shipwrecked on the shores of Lilliput, the land of the little people, where he is seen at first as a terrifying giant and finally as a gigantic friend.
F — EN
Paramount; Max Fleischer — *BBC Video* **H, P**
BBCV 9002

Gulliver's Travels — Fil-Ent '77
Adventure/Fantasy
08081   78 mins   C
B, V
Richard Harris, Catharine Schell, Norman Shelley, Meredith Edwards, directed by Peter Hunt
This partially animated film re-tells Jonathan Swift's classic story. A young doctor, the sole survivor of a shipwreck, is washed ashore to discover a land of little people.
BBFC:U — F — EN
Sun Classic — *Rank Video Library* **H, P**
3004 B

Gumball Rally — Fil-Ent '76
Comedy
13047   103 mins   C
B, V
Michael Sarrazin, Norman Burton, Gary Busey, Susan Flannery, directed by Chuck Bail
A high energy crash course spectacular about a crazy car race from New York to Long Beach.
BBFC:A — C,A — EN
Warner Bros Inc — *Warner Home Video* **P**
61278

Gun in the House, A — Fil-Ent '81
Suspense/Drama
07842   92 mins   C
B, V
Sally Struthers, David Ackroyd, Dick Anthony Williams, Joel Bailey, Frank Koppala, Jeffrey Tambor, Allan Rich, directed by Ivan Nagy

After a series of brutal rapes and robberies the wife of an airline pilot buys a gun and enrolls in firearm classes in an attempt to protect herself while her husband is away. One night two sadistic rapists enter the house; she shoots one of them dead. The police do not believe her and treat the incident as a lover's tiff resulting in murder. The couple investigate themselves, but the psychopath returns this time armed with a gun.
S,A — EN
Channing-Debin-Locke
Production — *Polygram Video* **H, P**
791 513

Gunfight, A — Fil-Ent '70
Western
06912   87 mins   C
B, V
Kirk Douglas, Johnny Cash, Karen Black, directed by Lamont Johnson
Two legendary gunmen meet for the first time in a small Southwestern town. One lives in the town with his wife and son and the other comes in after an unsuccessful mining expedition. Their presence causes the townsfolk to wager on the result of a gunfight. They don't want to kill or be killed until they realise one could benefit. They sell tickets for a gunfight in a bullring over the Mexican border.
BBFC:A — S,A — EN
Paramount — *Rank Video Library* **H, P**
8007B

Gunfight at the O.K. Corral — Fil-Ent '57
Western
13312   121 mins   C
B, V
Burt Lancaster, Kirk Douglas, Rhonda Fleming, John Ireland, Lyle Battger, directed by John Sturges
Two of the West's most celebrated legends, Wyatt Earp and Doc Holliday, join forces to rid the West of the lawless Clanton gang.
BBFC:PG — S,A — EN
Paramount — *CIC Video* **H, P**
BEN 2070/VHN 2070

Guns and the Fury, The — Fil-Ent '82
Adventure
09248   118 mins   C
V2, B, V
Peter Graves, Cameron Mitchell, Michael Ansara, Albert Salmi, Barry Stokes, Derren Nesbitt, Shaun Curry, Ben Feitelson, Monique Vermeer
Set in the year 1900, this film tells the story of two Americans drilling for oil in the Persian Gulf, who become the innocent victims of persecution and bloodshed when they are trapped between the conflicting armies of the

PALADIN VIDEO HOME ENTERTAINMENT GUIDE

Cossacks, the British and the local Sheikh. When the traditional peaceful life is invaded, the two men are forced to abandon their neutrality, and put their own lives at stake.

BBFC:PG — F — EN

Unknown — *Guild Home Video* **H, P, E**

Guns of the Timberland/Bengazi   Fil-Ent '??

Western/Adventure

05778   165 mins   C

B, V

Alan Ladd, Jeanne Crain, Gilbert Roland, directed by Robert D. Webb, Richard Conte, Richard Carlson, Mala Powers, directed by John Brahm

Two films are contained on one cassette. 'Guns of the Timberland' (colour, 88 minutes, 1961) features a government team who arrive to cut down trees in the Northwestern forests in 1895. Local rancher oppose them, fearing soil damage. 'Bengazi' (black and white, 77 minutes, 1956) is the story of three men who set out from Bengazi city, to search for treasure hidden in a mosque. After a few struggles they are trapped by brutal tribesmen who offer a terrible bargain, their lives in exchange for the treasure.

S,A — EN

Warner Bros; RKO — *Kingston Video*   **H, P**

KV3

Guyana   Fil-Ent '80

Drama

05869   108 mins   C

B, V

Stuart Whitman, Gene Barry, John Ireland, Joseph Cotten, Bradford Dillman, Jennifer Ashley, Yvonne DeCarlo

This film tells the story of Rev. James Jones, who established a Temple in California, where through his personality he gathered together 30,000 followers and all their possessions. He emigrates with his people to Guyana where he set up a commune called 'Jonestown,' in which his law and will were absolute, he promised paradise; however, in late 1978 they committed mass suicide.

BBFC:X — A — EN

Universal; Rene Cardona Jr — *Precision Video Ltd*   **P**

BBPV 2557/VBPV 2557

Guys and Dolls   Fil-Ent '55

Musical

12002   149 mins   C

B, V

Marlon Brando, Jean Simmons, Frank Sinatra, Vivian Blaine, directed by Joseph L Mankiewicz

New York gamblers and their girls are portrayed in this film, featuring an innocent girl from 'Save a Soul Missionary' who falls in love with one of the gamblers.

F — EN

Samuel Goldwyn — *CBS/Fox Video*   **P**

7039

Gwendoline   Fil-Ent '83

Adventure/Fantasy

13216   95 mins   C

V2, B, V

Tawny Kitaen, Brent Huff, Bernadette Lafont, directed by Just Jaeckin

Based on the strip cartoons of John Willie, Gwendoline travels to the Far East in search of her father and gets into all sorts of adventures.

BBFC:18 — A — EN

ParaFrance; Serge Laski; Jean Claude Fleury — *Embassy Home Entertainment* **P**

6103

Gypsy, The   Fil-Ent '??

Crime-Drama

06206   100 mins   C

B, V

Alain Delon, Annie Giradot, Paul Meurisse

When the gypsy retaliates against a society that has given him nothing but hard knocks since childhood, he is cruelly punished and imprisoned. He escapes and takes to a life of crime to avenge his people.

S,A — EN

Lira; Adel Prods; Mondial — *VCL Video Services*   **P**

C136C

PALADIN VIDEO HOME ENTERTAINMENT GUIDE

H

H-Bomb
Crime-Drama
06925　93 mins　C
B, V
Fil-Ent '76

Olivia Hussey, Christopher Mitchum
In an attempt to gain control of South East Asia, a power-mad General steals a US nuclear missile and sets the world's spy network against each other in a battle for its possession. The General calls on the godfather of the Thai underworld to get the missile to Cambodia. With the KGB, the Thai Secret Service and an Asian terrorist group after the missile, the Americans send in a special CIA agent.
S,A — EN
Unknown — *Rank Video Library*　**H, P**
0082C

Hair
Musical
01209　118 mins　C
V2, B, V
Fil-Ent '79

Treat Williams, John Savage, Beverly D'Angelo
Film version of the 1960's Broadway musical about the carefree life of the flower children and the shadow of the Vietnam War that hangs over them.
BBFC:AA — C,A — EN
United Artists — *Intervision Video*　**H**
UA A B 5007

Half a House
Comedy
06022　77 mins　C
B, V
Fil-Ent '??

Anthony Eisley, Pat Delaney
A happily married couple, both with good careers, take pride in their house and decide to have a housewarming. After a wild party that ends in a classic fight, the two separate and comic complications occur.
S,A — EN
First American Films; J B Kelly — *VCL Video Services*　**P**

Halfbreed, The/Walk Softly, Stranger
Western/Mystery
05671　156 mins　C
B, V
Fil-Ent '5?

Robert Young, Janis Carter, Jack Buetel, Reed Hadley, directed by Stuart Gilmore, Joseph Cotten, Alida Valli, Spring Byington, Jeff Donnell, Jack Paar, directed by Robert Stevenson
Two films are featured on one cassette. 'The Halfbreed' (Colour, 78 mins, 1953) is the tale of Apaches on the warpath led by a crook wanting gold that lies on Indian territory. A heroic gambler and his half breed friend are able to earn the respect of the Apaches and attempt to avoid a massacre. 'Walk Softly, Stranger' (Black/white, 78 mins, 1951) in which a stranger arrives in a small town, convinces a woman he was born in her house, meets up with a former accomplice and plans a robbery of a night-club owner.
S,A — EN
RKO — *Kingston Video*　**H, P**
KV41

Hallelujah I'm a Tramp
Musical
01087　77 mins　B/W
V2, B, V
Fil-Ent '33

Al Jolson, Harry Langdon, Frank Morgan, Madge Evans, directed by Lewis Milestone
An unusual Depression-era musical about the leader of a group of Central Park tramps, who falls in love with an amnesiac girl. Most of the dialogue is in rhyme, blending in with the songs by Richard Rodgers and Lorenz Hart. The original American title is 'Hallelujah, I'm a Bum.'
BBFC:U — A — EN
United Artists — *Intervision Video*　**H, P**
A-A 0042

Halloween
Horror
06070　92 mins　C
B, V
Fil-Ent '78

Donald Pleasence, Jamie Lee Curtis, P. J. Soles, Nancy Loomis, directed by John Carpenter
A man escapes from Illinois State Mental Hospital after 15 years treatment for the brutal murder of his sister. He returns home, on Halloween, to relive his crime. What follows is a reign of terror.
S,A — EN
Debra Hill — *Video Programme Distributors*　**P**
Media—M131

Halloween II
Horror
08470　88 mins　C
B, V
Fil-Ent '81

Jamie Lee Curtis, Donald Pleasance, directed by Rick Rosenthal
Set in the small town of Haddonfield, Illinois, this film tells of the murderous exploits of a psychopathic killer on the loose. He pursues a

PALADIN VIDEO HOME ENTERTAINMENT GUIDE

beautiful teenager and satisfies his craze for killings, by the slaughter of a couple, a nurse and a guardsman. There is only one man, a doctor, who is capable of stopping him.
BBFC:X — A — EN
Universal — THORN EMI   P
TXA 90 0926 4/TVA 90 0926 2

Halloween III   Fil-Ent '82
Horror
12537   91 mins   C
B, V
Tom Atkins, Stacey Nelkin, Dan O'Herlihy, directed by Tommy Lee Wallace
This is the story of a doctor's investigation into a series of bizarre and horrifying incidents surrounding All Hallows Eve, a night of ancient sacrifice.
BBFC:15 — S,A — EN
Debra Hill; John Carpenter — THORN EMI   P
TXA 90 1911 4; TVA 90 1911 2

Hamlet   Fil-Ent '48
Drama
01263   142 mins   B/W
B, V
Sir Laurence Olivier, Jean Simmons, Stanley Holloway, Eileen Herlie, Anthony Quayle, Terence Morgan, Peter Cushing, directed by Sir Laurence Olivier
Shakespeare's most famous tragedy about a young prince plagued by murder and madness is brilliantly performed in this film.
Academy Awards '48: Best Production; Best Actor (Olivier); Best Art Design, Black and White; Best Costume Design, Black and White.
BBFC:U — F — EN
Universal; J Arthur Rank — Rank Video Library
H, P
0002

Hammersmith is Out   Fil-Ent '72
Drama/Satire
13150   108 mins   C
B, V
Richard Burton, Elizabeth Taylor, Beau Bridges, Peter Ustinov, directed by Peter Ustinov
In this black comedy, a psychotic master criminal escapes from a US lunatic asylum and uses his deadly powers of persuasion to embark on a rampage of violence and murder.
BBFC:15 — S,A — EN
Cinerama; J Cornellus Crean Films — Brent Walker Home Video Ltd   P
BW 30

Hand Made Bricks   Gen-Edu '83
Industrial arts
12369   13 mins   C
B, V, 3/4U
A look at a brickyard that still employs women hand moulders, following the raw clay through to the finished bricks.
M,A — ED
I A Recordings — I.A. Recordings   P

Hand Rolling of Steel   Gen-Edu '83
Metalwork
12368   13 mins   C
B, V, 3/4U
This programme follows the process from raw material to the final rolled section.
M,A — ED
IA Recordings — I.A. Recordings   P

Handel's Messiah and Christmas Music   Fil-Ent '84
Music-Performance/Christmas
13353   97 mins   C
V2, B, V
The Huddersfield Choral Society and the Northern Sinfonia Orchestra join forces under the baton of Owain Arwel-Hughes to perform a programme of Christmas music in York Minster with other artists.
F — EN
Peter Max Wilson — Guild Home Video
H, P, E
6124

Handgun   Fil-Ent '83
Drama
09788   95 mins   C
B, V
Karen Young, Clayton Day, directed by Tony Garnett
A young girl is raped by her boyfriend. Obsessed with hatred, she sets out to take her revenge.
BBFC:18 — C,A — EN
Kestrel Films; EMI Films — THORN EMI   P
TXA 90 1912 4/TVA 90 1912 2

Hands of the Ripper   Fil-Ent '71
Horror
01871   85 mins   C
B, V, LV
Eric Porter, Angharad Rees, Jane Merrow, Dora Bryan, Derek Godfrey
A trail of atrocity leads from the scene of Jack the Ripper's murder of his wife.
BBFC:X — A — EN
Hammer Films — Rank Video Library   H, P
2000

PALADIN VIDEO HOME ENTERTAINMENT GUIDE

Hands Off!   Gen-Edu '84
Martial arts/Women
13375   60 mins   C
V2, B, V
Robin Webb, Friederike Coopa
Robin Webb gives instruction on self defense for women in martial arts in case they need to protect themselves against attack.
F — I
Top Video; World Karate Council UK — *Guild Home Video*   **H, P, E**
8435

Hang 'Em High   Fil-Ent '68
Western
13180   114 mins   C
B, V
Clint Eastwood, directed by Ted Post
A silent gunman survives a lynching and then seeks retribution on the nine men who strung him up.
BBFC:X — A — EN
Leonard Freeman Productions — *Warner Home Video*   **P**
99214

Hangar 18   Fil-Ent '81
Science fiction
10198   99 mins   C
B, V
Darren McGavin, Robert Vaughn, Gary Collins, James Hampton, Joseph Campanella, directed by James L. Conway
An alien space craft crash lands on earth. The government attempts to cover-up the facts by concealing not only the U.F.O in Hangar 18 but also the bodies of alien astronauts.
S,A — EN
Sunn Classic; Charles E Sellier Jr — *Video Form Pictures*   **H, P**
MGS 22

Hannie Caulder   Fil-Ent '71
Western
02094   85 mins   C
V2, B, V
Raquel Welch, Ernest Borgnine, Robert Culp, Diana Dors, Christopher Lee
Unsuccessful bank robbers arrive at the Caulder's relay station. After killing Jim Caulder, they rape his wife. When she has buried her husband, Hannie Caulder sets out after the Clemens brothers, determined to get her revenge.
BBFC:AA — C,A — EN
Paramount — *Hokushin Audio Visual Ltd*   **P**
VM-14

Hansel and Gretel   Fil-Ent '54
Fairy tales
08876   82 mins   C
V2, B, V
Voices by Anna Russell, Mildred Dunnock
This famed Grimm's fairy tale tells the story of the woodcutter's children who venture into the forest and are caught by a wicked old witch. This film uses puppet animation.
BBFC:U — M,S — EN
Hansel and Gretel Company — *Video Programme Distributors*   **P**
Media 314

Hansel and Gretel   Fil-Ent '84
Fairy tales
13412   48 mins   C
B, V
Joan Collins
An adaptation of the classic story of the brother and sister who become lost in the woods and discover a gingerbread house.
F — EN   DU
Shelley Duvall — *MGM/UA Home Video*   **P**
10435

Happiest Millionaire, The   Fil-Ent '67
Musical/Comedy
13438   155 mins   C
B, V
Tommy Steele, Fred MacMurray, Greer Garson, Geraldine Page, Lesley Ann Warren, John Davidson
A new butler starts to work for a very unusual family in this film set in the high society of Philadelphia, 1916.
BBFC:U — F — EN
Walt Disney Productions — *Rank Video Library*   **P**
181

Happily Ever After—Love and Life   Fil-Ent '78
Romance/Drama
12835   100 mins   C
B, V
Bruce Boxleiter, Suzanne Somers, Eric Braden, John Rubenstein
The first in a series, this is a tale of love rejection and regret, from 'Love and Life.'
C,A — EN
Tri-Media Inc. — *Video Tape Centre*   **P**
5003

Happy Hooker, The   Fil-Ent '75
Comedy
06729   87 mins   C
V2, B, V
Lynn Redgrave

(For Explanation of codes, see USE GUIDE and KEY)

PALADIN VIDEO HOME ENTERTAINMENT GUIDE

Xavier Hollander's memoir of her transition from office girl to 'working girl' has been brought to the screen with a sprightly air of naughtiness.
BBFC:X — A — EN
Cannon Releasing — *Intervision Video*
H, P
A-A 0114

Happy Hooker Goes to Washington, The　　Fil-Ent '77
Comedy
06728　　86 mins　　C
V2, B, V
Joey Heatherton, George Hamilton
Further adventures of the world's most famous Madam find Xavier Hollander the target of a U.S. Senate investigation.
BBFC:X — A — EN
Cannon Releasing — *Intervision Video*
H, P
A-A 0115

Hard Country　　Fil-Ent '81
Drama
07347　　101 mins　　C
B, V
Jan-Michael Vincent, Kim Basinger, Michael Parks, Tanya Tucker
A young woman decides to break away from her boyfriend and her small Texas town, causing him to re-evaluate his life.
BBFC:AA — S,A — EN
ITC — *Precision Video Ltd*　　**P**
BITC 2082/VITC 2082

Hard Day's Night, A　　Fil-Ent '64
Musical/Comedy
12883　　90 mins　　B/W
B, V
Paul McCartney, John Lennon, Ringo Starr, George Harrison, directed by Richard Lester
This film reflects the excitement of the group's earlier days and shows them re-enacting a typical day of their life. Songs include 'Can't Buy Me Love,' 'I'm Happy Just to Dance with You' and 'If I Fell.'
BBFC:U — F — EN
Walter Shenson; United Artists — *Vestron Video International*　　**P**
14118

Hard to Hold　　Fil-Ent '84
Music/Romance
13614　　93 mins　　C
B, V
Patti Hansen, Janet Eilber, Albert Salmi, Rick Springfield, directed by Larry Peerce

Rick Springfield performs seven of his songs in this film about a pop star who is determined to pursue and win a beautiful children's counsellor whom he considers to be out of his class.
BBFC:15 — S,A — EN
Universal — *CIC Video*　　**H, P**
1135

Hard Way, The　　Fil-Ent '79
War-Drama
07364　　? mins　　C
B, V
Patrick McGoohan, Lee Van Cleef
This film follows an intriguing clash of styles in the twilight world of mercenaries.
S,A — EN
Unknown — *Precision Video Ltd*　　**P**
BITC 2111/VITC 2111

Harder They Come, The　　Fil-Ent '73
Musical-Drama
09794　　100 mins　　C
B, V
Jimmy Cliff, directed by Perry Henzell
A rebellious young country boy leaves his home town and sets off for the bright lights in Kingston, Jamaica. He finds his way to success as a singer is blocked by corruption in the music business. Soundtrack features songs by Desmond Dekker, The Maytals and Jimmy Cliff.
BBFC:18 — C,A — EN
International Films Ltd. — *THORN EMI*　　**P**
TXB 90 1281 4/TVB 90 1281 2

Harkness on Roses　　How-Ins '81
Gardening
12766　　55 mins　　C
B, V
Amid the hallowed beds of the Royal National Rose Society's gardens at St. Albans, Hertfordshire and in his own celebrated nurseries, Jack Harkness at his meticulous, patient best shows exactly how to grow beautiful roses.
A — I
Unknown — *VideoSpace Ltd*　　**P**

Harlequin　　Fil-Ent '??
Mystery/Suspense
06246　　90 mins　　C
B, V
Robert Powell, David Hemmings, Carmen Duncan, Broderick Crawford
This film set in Australia is a cult-style murder thriller. The Harlequin, a strange mysterious figure, who comes from nowhere to save the life

302　　(For Explanation of codes, see USE GUIDE and KEY)

PALADIN VIDEO HOME ENTERTAINMENT GUIDE

of an ill child, leaves in his wake a series of puzzling influences. He performs many startling feats leaving people to wonder whether he is a common murderer or a miraculous saint.
S,A — EN
Unknown — VCL Video Services   P
P205D

Harold and Maude   Fil-Ent '71
Comedy
13323   88 mins   C
B, V
Bud Cort, Ruth Gordon, Vivian Pickles, directed by Hal Ashby
This is a black comedy, and tells the story of a bored, very wealthy young man obsessed with death who meets up with an 80-year-old lady with a boundless enthusiasm for all living things.
BBFC:15 — S,A — EN
Paramount — CIC Video   H, P
BEN 2109/VHN 2109

Harold Lloyd 'The Unsinkable'   Fil-Ent '??
Comedy
04692   52 mins   B/W
B, V
Harold Lloyd, Snub Pollard, Bebe Daniels, Mildred Davis, Harry Pollard, Gus Leonhard, Noah Young
Four original classic comedies starring Harold Lloyd, all produced in 1919 and 1920, are contained on this cassette: 'Rooms to Let,' 'The Royal Swindle,' 'Good Neighbors,' and 'Haunted Spooks.'
F — EN
Spectrum — Polygram Video   P

Harrad Experiment, The   Fil-Ent '73
Drama
09059   95 mins   C
V2
James Whitmore, Tippi Hedren, Don Johnson, B. Kirby, Laurie Walters, Victoria Thompson, Elliot Street
This film features an experiment in a co-ed school in New England where relations between students are encouraged. It is based on Robert H. Rimmer's novel.
C,A — EN
Cinerama — Astra Video   H, P

Harry and Son   Fil-Ent '84
Drama
13473   105 mins   C
B, V
Paul Newman, Joanne Woodward, Robby Benson, directed by Paul Newman
The relationship between a widower and his out-of-work son with literary aspirations leads to many tempestuous confrontations but it is his skill with words that finally brings about a reconciliation.
BBFC:15 — F — EN
Orion Pictures — Rank Video Library   H, P
0217

Harry Carpenter's Videobook of Sport—Volume 2   Spo-Lei '81
Sports
08713   112 mins   C
V2, B, V, LV
A collection of sporting events from the worlds of tennis, motor cycling, cricket, ice-skating, table tennis and football, this programme features footage from the 1968 European Cup Final at Wembley: Manchester Utd v. Benfica.
F — EN
John Vigar — BBC Video   H, P
BBCV 5019

Harry Carpenter's Videobook of Sport   Spo-Lei '81
Sports
04860   110 mins   C
V2, B, V, LV
This programme is a collection of memorable moments from rugby, cricket and football, and includes excerpts from the 1966 World Cup Final, the 1973 Barbarians v. All Blades match and the 1975 Prudential Cup final.
F — EN
John Vigar; BBC Video — BBC Video   H, P
BBCV 5011

Harry Tracy—Desperado   Fil-Ent '81
Western
07880   91 mins   C
V2, B, V
Bruce Dern, Helen Shaver, Michael G. Gwynne, Gordon Lightfoot, directed by William A. Graham
This film tells the story of Harry Tracy, one of the West's last folk heroes. He captured the public's imagination as a romantic figure by his daring raids on banks and trains and his uncanny ability to escape.
S,A — EN
Unknown — Intervision Video   H, P
A-A 0243

Harry's Game   Fil-Ent '82
Drama/Suspense
13344   150 mins   C

(For Explanation of codes, see USE GUIDE and KEY)

PALADIN VIDEO HOME ENTERTAINMENT GUIDE

V2, B, V
Ray Lonnen, Derek Thompson, directed by Lawrence Gordon Clark
When a British Cabinet Minister is murdered, a British agent goes undercover to track down an IRA assassin.
C,A — EN
Yorkshire Television Limited — *Guild Home Video* **H, P, E**
8334-2

Haunted Fil-Ent '??
Horror
09962 87 mins C
V2, B, V
Aldo Ray, Virginia Mayo
An actress returns to an old abandoned movie ranch and is thought to be the reincarnation of an evil Indian witch.
BBFC:X — A — EN
Michael DeGaetano; Nicholas Nizich — *Video Unlimited* **H, P, E**
051

Haunted House of Horror, The Fil-Ent '70
Horror
04558 79 mins C
V2, B, V
Frankie Avalon, Jill Haworth, Julian Barnes, Richard O'Sullivan
A group of young people, bored with life, decide to explore a haunted house. They organise a seance and terror and death follow.
S,A — EN
American International — *Videomedia* **P**

Haunted Palace, The Fil-Ent '63
Drama/Horror
09931 85 mins C
B, V
Vincent Price, Debra Paget, Lon Chaney Jr., directed by Roger Corman
This film, based on a poem by Edgar Allan Poe, tells the story of a man and wife. They go to a small New England town to open the husband's ancestral home which was closed in 1765 when his ancestor was burned as a male witch. Vincent Price returns from the grave to avenge himself on the descendants of the New England villagers.
BBFC:18 — A — EN
AIP; Roger Corman — *Rank Video Library*
H, P
2031A

Haunting of Julia, The Fil-Ent '81
Suspense
07921 96 mins C
V2, B, V
Mia Farrow, Jill Bennett, Tom Conti, Keir Dullea, directed by Richard Longcraine
Set in a large London house, this is a tale of revenge and remorse. A woman laden with guilt is trying to recover from the death of her daughter but finds herself getting involved with the ghost of another child long since dead.
S,A — EN
Peter Fetterman — *Video Programme Distributors* **P**
Media—159

Haunting Passion, The Fil-Ent '??
Drama/Romance
09338 93 mins C
B, V
Jane Seymour, Gerald McRaney, Millie Perkins, directed by John Korty
This is a supernatural story of love and death about a woman who lives with her husband in a beautiful house by the sea. She feels unexpected passions in her sleep and one afternoon draws the face of a man she has never seen before. This turns out to be, literally, the man of her dreams.
BBFC:15 — C,A — EN
Unknown — *Precision Video Ltd* **P**
BITC 2141/VITC 2141

Haunts Fil-Ent '76
Suspense/Mystery
07329 85 mins C
B, V
May Britt, Cameron Mitchell, Aldo Ray, directed by Herb Freed
This film is a sensitive portrayal of a desperately lonely woman driven to madness by her own sexuality. The harrowing story unfolds as the peaceful life of a small coastal town is disrupted by the brutal attack and murder of a young girl. Terror grips the townspeople as they search for the killer.
BBFC:AA — S,A — EN
Intercontinental Films — *Derann Film Services*
P
FDV 301B/FDV 301

Having A Baby Gen-Edu '8?
Pregnancy/Childbirth
06965 108 mins C
V2, B, V
This programme is a compilation of highlights from the television series. It explains both the physical and emotional experiences of pregnancy and birth. The nine month period is covered by Claire Woolford, who helps the mother-to-be relax and enjoy her own special miracle.
A — ED
Dick Foster — *BBC Video* **H, P**
BBCV 1012

---

304 (For Explanation of codes, see USE GUIDE and KEY)

PALADIN VIDEO HOME ENTERTAINMENT GUIDE

Having It All Fil-Ent '82
Drama/Comedy
12616 95 mins C
V2, B, V
Dyan Cannon, Hart Bochner, Sylvia Sidney, Melanie Chartroff
A beautiful and successful fashion designer with salons in New York and Los Angeles also has a husband in each of these cities and finds her life becoming very complicated in a desperate attempt to keep the two men apart.
BBFC:PG — F — EN
GTO Films; Jozak Productions — *VideoSpace Ltd* P

Hawk the Slayer Fil-Ent '80
Fantasy/Adventure
05407 90 mins C
V2, B, V, LV
Jack Palance, John Terry, Harry Andrews, Cheryl Campbell, Annette Crosbie, Roy Kinnear, Catriana MacCall, Patrick Magee, Ferdy Mayne, Graham Stark, directed by Terry Marcel
A fantasy tale of the forces of good and evil, in two brothers, who meet for an epic conflict. The youngest, a legend in the land, possesses strength, a sense of honour, duty and justice and surrounds himself with trusted helpers to bring peace. The eldest brings death and destruction to all who stand in his way.
BBFC:A — S,A — EN
Chips Productions; Marcel Robertson Film — *Precision Video Ltd* P
CRITC 2052/BITC 2052/VITC 2052

He-Man and Masters of Fil-Ent '83
the Universe
Cartoons/Adventure
09978 62 mins C
B, V
Animated
When danger threatens, Adam the happy-go-lucky Prince of Eternia becomes HE-MAN, the strongest and bravest man in the universe. In the first episode Skeletor finds the 'diamond of disappearance' which makes people vanish. In the next story, Teela reveals a secret from her past and embarks on a perilous journey. In the final story Skeletor perfects a diabolical invention.
F — EN
Mattel Inc.; Filmation Studios — *Select Video Limited* P
3612/43

He-Man and the Masters Fil-Ent '84
of the Universe
Cartoons/Adventure
12182 62 mins C
B, V
Animated
This tape features three more adventures from He-Man, 'The Time Corridor,' 'The Dragon Invasion' and 'A Friend in Need.'
F — EN
Filmation Associates Inc; Characters Mattel Inc — *Select Video Limited* P
3617/43

Head On Fil-Ent '80
Drama
09253 86 mins C
V2, B, V
Sally Kellerman, Stephen Lack, John Huston, Lawrence Dane, directed by Michael Grant
Two cars are involved in a collision. The drivers argue over the insurance claim. After discovering a common professional bond, their relationship develops rapidly, and before long, the psychiatrist and psychologist are pitting their wits and witticisms against each other. The games they play are full of surprises; however, games can go too far.
BBFC:18 — A — EN
Unknown — *Iver Film Services* P
225

Heading for Glory Spo-Lei '7?
Football
06216 90 mins C
B, V
Cruyff, Beckenbauer, Overath, Neeskens, van Hanagem, Rep, Deyna
This film is the offical FIFA record of the 1974 World Cup in Munich. It follows world-class football from the sixteen top footballing nations including Brazil, Holland, West Germany, Uruguay, Italy and Scotland as they battle through finals and semi-finals for the Jules Rimet Cup.
F — EN
FIFA — *VCL Video Services* P
S118C

Healthy Horse, The How-Ins '82
Animals
13518 33 mins C
V
Directed by Bill Latto
Veterinary advice is given on the welfare of the horse, through balanced feeding, care of the feet, worm control, vaccination against influenza and tetanus.
F — ED
Town and Country Productions — *TFI Leisure Ltd* H, P

Hearse, The Fil-Ent '80
Horror
08882 97 mins C
V2, B, V

(For Explanation of codes, see USE GUIDE and KEY) 305

PALADIN VIDEO HOME ENTERTAINMENT GUIDE

Joseph Cotten, Trish Van Devere
While fighting to maintain her sanity, a schoolteacher finds her life threatened by a sinister black hearse.
BBFC:X — *A* — *EN*
Mark Tenser — *Video Programme Distributors*
P
Media 181

Heart Like a Wheel   Fil-Ent '83
Adventure
13217   112 mins   C
V2, B, V
Bonnie Bedelia, Beau Bridges, directed by Jonathan Kaplan
This is the story of Shirley Muldowney, from her beginning sitting on her father's lap as he raced along country roads to her triple win as the World's Champion hot rod racer.
BBFC:PG — *S,A* — *EN*
Aurora Film Partnership — *Embassy Home Entertainment*   **P**
1373

Heart of a Father   Fil-Ent '??
Crime-Drama
06865   88 mins   C
V2, B, V
George Arkin, Ginette Arkin, Ileana Sandri
A member of a large Mafia organisation is being controlled by the police. When his wife dies while he is in prison, the police chief takes care of his son. The Mafia kidnap the boy to get revenge.
S,A — *EN*
Unknown — *European Video Company*
P

Heartaches   Fil-Ent '81
Drama
08398   98 mins   C
V2, B, V
Margot Kidder, Annie Potts, Robert Carradine, Winston Reikert
This film tells the story of Rita and Bonnie, an ill-matched twosome who set up a home together. It tells of their warm friendships and heartaches.
BBFC:X — *A* — *EN*
Rising Star Films — *Guild Home Video*
H, P, E

Heartbeat   Fil-Ent '80
Drama
13073   105 mins   C
B, V
Sissy Spacek, Nick Nolte, John Heard, Anne Dusenberry, directed by John Byrum

This film portrays the curious triangular relationship between Jack Kerouac, the beat generation writer, and Neal and Carolyn Cassady, as seen through the eyes of Carolyn, and how Kerouac's best selling book affected them.
BBFC:X — *A* — *EN*
Orion Pictures Co — *Warner Home Video*
P
72012

Heartbeeps   Fil-Ent '81
Science fiction/Comedy
09268   79 mins   C
B, V
Andy Kaufman, Bernadette Peters
Set in 1995, this film tells the story of two domestic robots who fall in love and elope for a new life together.
BBFC:U — *F* — *EN*
Universal — *CIC Video*   **H, P**

Heartbreak Kid, The   Fil-Ent '72
Comedy-Drama
07709   100 mins   C
B, V
Charles Grodin, Cybil Shepherd, Jeanie Berlin, Eddie Albert, Audra Lindley, directed by Elaine May
Whilst on their honeymoon the newly-wed wife gets sunburnt on the first day and is confined to bed. Her husband, a New York salesman, meets another girl, promptly divorces his new wife and follows the latest girl home and marries her despite protests from her father.
S,A — *EN*
Twentieth Century Fox — *CBS/Fox Video*
P
1083

Heartbreak Motel   Fil-Ent '??
Drama
05448   75 mins   C
V2, B, V
Slim Pickens, Dub Taylor, Shelley Winters, Ted Cassidy, Leslie Uggams
A world famous singer sets out for a rural holiday alone. Her car breaks down on a lonely country road and she walks to a rundown motel. There she meets a young man who promises to satisfy her romantically if she helps her career.
BBFC:A — *S,A* — *EN*
Unknown — *Iver Film Services*   **P**
96

Heartland   Fil-Ent '81
Drama
08478   95 mins   C
B, V

306   (For Explanation of codes, see USE GUIDE and KEY)

PALADIN VIDEO HOME ENTERTAINMENT GUIDE

Rip Torn, Conchata Ferrell, Barry Primus, Lilia Skala, Megan Folsom, Amy Wright, directed by Richard Pearce
Set in 1910, this film chronicles the true story of one woman's life. She leaves her home in Denver to become housekeeper and later wife to a Scotsman, on his remote ranch in Wyoming. It tells of their hardships and determination in farming the harsh, barren land.
BBFC:A — S,A — EN
Wilderness Women Productions
Ltd — THORN EMI   P
TXB 90 14774/TVB 90 14772

Hearts of the West   Fil-Ent '75
Drama/Comedy
13419   103 mins   C
B, V
Jeff Bridges, Donald Pleasance, Alan Arkin
A naive farming boy travels from the country to Hollywood in the 1930's and almost by accident becomes a star.
S,A — EN
MGM — MGM/UA Home Video   P
10388

Heatwave   Fil-Ent '??
Drama
08361   95 mins   C
V2, B, V
Judy Davis, Richard Moir
This film follows an argument between an architect proposing a newbuilding development, and a defending resident whose home is going to be bulldozed. However, they find themselves coming closing together as mystery and intrigue culminates in a night of terror in Sydney New Year's Eve celebrations in the grip of a heatwave.
BBFC:AA — C,A — EN
Unknown — Guild Home Video   H, P, E

Heaven Can Wait   Fil-Ent '78
Romance/Fantasy
05332   101 mins   C
V2, B, V
Warren Beatty, Julie Christie, James Mason, Charles Grodin, Dyan Cannon, Buck Henry, Vincent Gardenia, Jack Warden, directed by Warren Beatty and Buck Henry
A Los Angeles Rams quarterback is accidentally summoned to Heaven by an over zealous celestial escort. He is returned to earth in the body of a corporate giant. While still practicing for the Rams he has to escape attempts on his life as well as pursuing a beautiful English woman who objects to the destruction of her village by one of his corporations.
S,A — EN
Paramount — CIC Video   H, P
CRA2012/BEA2012/VHA2012

Heaven 17's—Industrial Revolution   Fil-Ent '83
Music video
12964   23 mins   C
B, V
Six performances from Heaven 17 including 'Penthouse and Pavement', 'Temptation' and 'Come Live With Me'.
F — EN
Wiener World — Virgin Video   H, P
VVD 26

Heavenly Body   Fil-Ent '80
Crime-Drama
13462   87 mins   C
B, V
Pam Grier, Yaphet Kotto, Eartha Kitt, Godfrey Cambridge, Ted Lange, Thalmus Rasulala
A girl photographer gets into hot water with organised crime when she finds herself shooting pictures of an attempted assassination plot.
BBFC:18 — A — EN
Orion Pictures — Rank Video Library   H, P
0158

Heavens Above   Fil-Ent '63
Comedy
04640   105 mins   B/W
B, V
Peter Sellers, Cecil Parker, Isabel Jeans, Eric Sykes, Ian Carmichael
Clergy life is satirised in this film in which Sellers plays a quiet, down-to-earth reverend who is appointed to a parish in a snooty neighbourhood.
F — EN
British Lion — THORN EMI   H, P
TXE 90 0248 4/TVE 90 0248 2

Heaven's Gate   Fil-Ent '80
Drama/Western
13064   211 mins   C
B, V
Kris Kristofferson, Christopher Walken, John Hurt, Jeff Bridges, Isabelle Huppert, directed by Michael Cimino
This is a social drama of the American West which is based on a real range war of the 1890's which unfolds with moments of drama and passion.
BBFC:X — A — EN
United Artists Corp — Warner Home Video   P
99284

Heavy Traffic   Fil-Ent '73
Comedy
12524   73 mins   C

(For Explanation of codes, see USE GUIDE and KEY)

PALADIN VIDEO HOME ENTERTAINMENT GUIDE

B, V
Animated, directed by Ralph Bakshi
This adult cartoon tells the story of a fantasized love affair between a Jewish-Italian youth and a black barmaid.
BBFC:18 — *A* — *EN*
American International — *THORN EMI* **P**
TXB 90 2310/TVB 90 2310 2

Heckle and Jeckle   Fil-Ent '??
Cartoons
01743   30 mins   C
B, V
Animated
Feature five Terrytoon cartoons: 'The Stowaways,' Mighty Mouse in 'The Pirates,' Sad Cat in 'Grand Prix Winner,' Dinky Duck in 'Sink or Swim,' Sidney in 'The Littlest Bully.'
BBFC:U — *F* — *EN*
Paramount — *CBS/Fox Video*   **P**
1B-046

Heidi   Fil-Ent '37
Drama
01742   75 mins   B/W
B, V
Shirley Temple, Jean Hersholt, Helen Westley, Arthur Treacher, Pauline Moore, Delmar Watson, Sidney Blackmer, directed by Allan Dwan
The story of a young orphan girl who is sent to live with her crusty old grandfather in the Swiss Alps. Heidi softens the heart of her grandfather, transforming him into a charming man. She is kidnapped by her wicked aunt and is found just in time to prevent her being sold to gypsies. This film is based on the famous children's classic by Johanna Spyri.
BBFC:U — *F* — *EN*
20th Century Fox — *CBS/Fox Video*   **P**
3A-052

Heidi   Fil-Ent '68
Drama
08316   100 mins   C
B, V
Maximilian Schell, Jean Simmons, Sir Michael Redgrave, Walter Slezak, Jenifer Edwards, directed by Delbert Mann
This tells the story of a little orphaned girl who goes to live with her grandfather in the Swiss Alps. He has led a recluse-like life in the mountains but his hard appearance is gradually softened by Heidi's charm. Her rich uncle decides to remove her, to become a playmate to his invalid daughter Klara.
F — *EN*
NBC International — *Select Video Limited*
P
3105

Hell Drivers   Fil-Ent '57
Drama/Suspense
09921   106 mins   B/W
B, V
Sean Connery, Stanley Baker, Patrick McGoohan, Herbert Lom, Peggy Cummins
Recently out of prison, a man gets a job as a 'hell-driver', on a ballast hauling run across dangerous terrain. Soon he is fighting with the jealous top driver, stealing his best friend's girl and then he discovers a management racket for which his bosses are ready to kill to keep the secret.
BBFC:PG — *F* — *EN*
Lopert; J. Arthur Rank — *Rank Video Library*
H, P
0184 A

Hell in the Pacific   Fil-Ent '69
War-Drama
04176   104 mins   C
B, V
Lee Marvin, Toshiro Mifune
Stranded on a Pacific Island during World War II, an American and a Japanese first stalk each other, then join forces to build a raft and escape.
BBFC:U — *F* — *EN*
Cinerama — *Guild Home Video*   **H, P**

Hell Is Empty   Fil-Ent '7?
Crime-Drama
02411   90 mins   C
B, V
Anthony Steele, Shirley-Anne Field, James Robertson Justice, Jess Conrad, directed by John Ainsworth
A daring robbery, in which one of the gang is murdered, causes the others to flee and hide out in an island mansion, and hold its inhabitants hostage. The personalities of the gang members clash with those of the hostages.
S,A — *EN*
Unknown — *Derann Film Services*   **H, P**
DV 104B/DV 104

Hell Night   Fil-Ent '81
Horror
08883   100 mins   C
V2, B, V
Vincent Van Patten, Kevin Brophy, Linda Blair, directed by Tom DeSimone
Three young people must spend the night in a mysterious mansion as part of their initiation into Alpha Sigma Rho fraternity.
BBFC:X — *A* — *EN*
Compass International Pictures — *Video Programme Distributors*   **P**
Media 157

PALADIN VIDEO HOME ENTERTAINMENT GUIDE

Hell on Frisco Bay/The Mad Miss Manton
Fil-Ent '??
Crime-Drama/Mystery
05780 170 mins C
B, V

Alan Ladd, Edward G. Robinson, Joanne Dru, directed by Frank Tuttle, Henry Fonda, Barbara Stanwyck, directed by Leigh Jason

Two films are contained on one cassette. 'Hell on Frisco Bay' (colour, 94 minutes, 1956) features a cop framed for murder and falsely imprisoned who is out for revenge. His trail leads to a waterfront and a speedboat battle. 'The Mad Miss Manton' (black and white, 76 minutes, 1939) features a wealthy young tearaway who finds a body which goes missing. She is not believed and sets out to prove the police wrong.

S,A — EN
Warner Bros; RKO — *Kingston Video* H, P
KV1

Hellbenders, The
Fil-Ent '66
Drama
13212 88 mins C
V2, B, V

Joseph Cotton, directed by Sergio Corbucci

A fanatic ex-Confederate colonel steals over one million dollars and plans to re-group his old 'Hellbenders Regiment' and continue hostilities against the North.

BBFC:18 — C,A — EN
Unknown — *Embassy Home Entertainment* P
2118

Hello, Dolly!
Fil-Ent '69
Musical
01013 146 mins C
B, V, LV

Barbra Streisand, Walter Matthau, Michael Crawford, Louis Armstrong, directed by Gene Kelly

Widow Dolly Levi, while matchmaking for her friends, sets her mind on a Yankee merchant. Based on the stage musical adapted from Thornton Wilder's play 'Matchmaker.'

Academy Awards '69: Best Score of a Musical Picture; Best Art Direction; Best Sound.
F — EN
20th Century Fox; Ernest Leham — *CBS/Fox Video* P

Hello World—Chinese (Mandarin)
Gen-Edu '8?
Languages-Instruction
05571 90 mins C
V2, B, V

A cassette in the 'Hello World' series that takes the learner through ten easy-to-follow lessons, including passport and customs formalities, arriving at the airport, booking in at an hotel, ordering a meal and sightseeing. No previous knowledge of the language is required and a full instructional booklet is enclosed with the cassette.

AM Available S,A — I
Response Language Learning Foundation — *Videomedia* P
BVV 106/HVV 106

Hello World—English
Gen-Edu '8?
Languages-Instruction
05572 90 mins C
V2, B, V

A cassette in the 'Hello World' series that takes the learner through ten easy-to-follow lessons, including passport and customs formalities, arriving at the airport, booking in at an hotel, ordering a meal and sightseeing. No previous knowledge of the language is required and a full instructional booklet is enclosed with cassette.

AM Available S,A — I
Response Language Learning Foundation — *Videomedia* P
BVV 101/HVV 101

Hello World—French
Gen-Edu '8?
Languages-Instruction
05573 90 mins C
V2, B, V

A cassette in the 'Hello World' series that takes the learner through ten easy-to-follow lessons, including passport and customs formalities, arriving at the airport, booking in at an hotel, ordering a meal and sightseeing. No previous knowledge of the language is required and a full instructional booklet is enclosed with the cassette.

AM Available S,A — I
Response Language Learning Foundation — *Videomedia* P
BVV 100/HVV 100

Hello World—German
Gen-Edu '8?
Languages-Instruction
05574 90 mins C
V2, B, V

A cassette in the 'Hello World' series that takes the learner through ten easy-to-follow lessons, including passport and customs formalities, arriving at the airport, booking in at an hotel,

PALADIN VIDEO HOME ENTERTAINMENT GUIDE

ordering a meal and sightseeing. No previous knowledge of the language is required and a full instructional booklet is enclosed with the cassette.
AM Available   S,A — I
Response Language Learning Foundation — *Videomedia*   P
BVV 103/HVV 103

Hello World—Hindi   Gen-Edu '8?
Languages-Instruction
05575   90 mins   C
V2, B, V
A cassette in the 'Hello World' series that takes the learner through ten easy-to-follow lessons, including passport and customs formalities, arriving at the airport, booking in at an hotel, ordering a meal and sightseeing. No previous knowledge of the language is required and a full instructional booklet is enclosed with the cassette.
AM Available   S,A — I
Response Language Learning Foundation — *Videomedia*   P
BVV 107/HVV 107

Hello World—Italian   Gen-Edu '8?
Languages-Instruction
05576   90 mins   C
V2, B, V
A cassette in the 'Hello World' series that takes the learner through ten easy-to-follow lessons, including passport and customs formalities, arriving at the airport, booking in at an hotel, ordering a meal and sightseeing. No previous knowledge of the language is required and a full instructional booklet is enclosed with the cassette.
AM Available   S,A — I
Response Language Learning Foundation — *Videomedia*   P
BVV 104/HVV 104

Hello World—Russian   Gen-Edu '8?
Languages-Instruction
05577   90 mins   C
V2, B, V
A cassette in the 'Hello World' series that takes the learner through ten easy-to-follow lessons, including passport and customs formalities, arriving at the airport, booking in at an hotel, ordering a meal and sightseeing. No previous knowledge of the language is required and a full instructional booklet is enclosed with the cassette.
AM Available   S,A — I
Response Language Learning Foundation — *Videomedia*   P
BVV 105/HVV 105

Hello World—Spanish   Gen-Edu '8?
Languages-Instruction
05578   90 mins   C
V2, B, V
A cassette in the 'Hello World' series that takes the learner through ten easy-to-follow lessons, including passport and customs formalities, arriving at the airport, booking in at an hotel, ordering a meal and sightseeing. No previous knowledge of the language is required and a full instructional booklet is enclosed with the cassette.
AM Available   S,A — I
Response Language Learning Foundation — *Videomedia*   P
BVV 102/HVV 102

Hell's Angels on Wheels   Fil-Ent '67
Drama
05646   95 mins   C
B, V
Adam Roarke, Jack Nicholson, Sabrina Schart, Jana Taylor, directed by Richard Rush
This film tells the story of a young gas station attendant who gives up his job to join a group of Hell's Angels, believing his motorbike to be the path to personal freedom.
S,A — EN
Twentieth Century Fox — *CBS/Fox Video*   P
3B-129

Henderson Monster, The   Fil-Ent '80
Science fiction
09371   99 mins   C
B, V
Jason Miller, Christine Lahti, Stephen Collins, David Spielberg, Larry Gates, Nehemiah Persoff, directed by Waris Hussain
A Nobel Prize-winning scientists' work in attempting to create new life forms in a university laboratory, causes a controversy that affects the individual lives of a whole community. It also threatens a potential life and death crisis for society.
S,A — EN
Herbert Blodkin, Robert Berger — *Precision Video Ltd*   P
BITC 2136/VITC 2136

Henry Cotton Celebrity Golf Lesson, The   Spo-Lei '8?
Golf
12057   60 mins   C
V2, B, V
This cassette features many historic clips of Cotton's unparalleled playing as well as a wealth of tips and hints for the golfer.

PALADIN VIDEO HOME ENTERTAINMENT GUIDE

Showbusiness personalities Suzanne Danielle, Frankie Vaughan, Ed Stewart, Henry Cooper, and Jerry Stevens have a hilarious time improving their golf.
F — I
ON TV Production; Sandy Gall Enterprises Ltd — *Intervision Video* **H, P**
A-A 0490

Henry V   Fil-Ent '45
Drama
01264   137 mins   C
B, V, LV
Laurence Olivier, Robert Newton, Leslie Banks, Leo Genn, Renee Asherton, directed by Laurence Olivier
The first movie version of Shakespeare's great drama, with brilliant dialogue and colour.
BBFC:U — *F — EN*
J Arthur Rank — *Rank Video Library* **H, P**
0010

Henry VIII and His Six Wives   Fil-Ent '73
Biographical/Drama
00591   120 mins   C
B, V
Keith Mitchell, Donald Pleasance, Charlotte Rampling, Jane Asher
Told in flashbacks from his deathbed, Henry VIII's life, loves, triumphs, and disappointments are depicted in this film.
BBFC:A — *S,A — EN*
Roy Baird — *THORN EMI* **P**
TXB 90 0202 4/TVB 90 0202 2

Henry's Cat and Friends, Cassette 1   Chi-Juv '83
Cartoons
13361   45 mins   C
V2, B, V
Animated
Ten exciting adventures from the tubby cat and his friends, Chris Rabbit, Douglas Dog, Ted Tortoise, Denise Duck, to list just a few! British Academy of Film and Television Arts Award '84: Best Cartoon.
BBFC:U — *PS,M — EN*
Bob Godfrey Films Ltd; Stan Hayward — *Guild Home Video* **H, P, E**
8426-2

Her First Affaire   Fil-Ent '32
Romance
07630   65 mins   B/W
B, V
Ida Lupino, George Curzon, Diana Napier, Harry Tate, directed by Alan Dwan
A young girl becomes infatuated with the author of sensational novels, believing that his novels report his own experiences. The author leases a house near her home and the young girl throws herself at him. He decides to teach her a lesson about life. However, his scheme backfires at a fancy dress ball.
F — EN
Unknown — *VCL Video Services* **P**
0226G

Herbie Goes Bananas   Fil-Ent '80
Comedy
08007   90 mins   C
B, V
Cloris Leachman, Charles Martin—Smith
The Volkswagen with a mind of its own causes disorder, south of the border, when he meets with Paco the pickpocket.
BBFC:U — *F — EN*
Walt Disney Productions — *Rank Video Library*
09400

Herbie Hancock and the Rockit Band   Fil-Ent '84
Music-Performance
13261   73 mins   C
B, V
A visual and sound extravaganza recorded live at the Hammersmith Odeon and Camden Palace with breakdance sequences.
F — EN
CBS Video Enterprises — *CBS/Fox Video* **P**
6619

Herbie Rides Again   Fil-Ent '74
Comedy
12561   88 mins   C
B, V
Helen Hayes, Stephanie Powers, Ken Berry, Keenan Wynn
In this film of love, laughter and disaster round the streets of San Francisco, Herbie the lovable VW protects Grandma against an evil property tycoon.
F — EN
Walt Disney Productions — *Rank Video Library* **H**
042

Hercules Challenge   Fil-Ent '63
Drama
04285   95 mins   C
V2, B, V
Alessandra Panaro, Gordon Scott
After the death of the King of the Mycenes, his Queen gives birth to a hideously deformed son, Moloch. He grows up to become a tyrant and

---

(For Explanation of codes, see USE GUIDE and KEY)

PALADIN VIDEO HOME ENTERTAINMENT GUIDE

the people call on Hercules to free them from the terror. Hercules completes the task only after facing many dangers in his bid to save the city.
C,A — EN
Avco Embassy — *Video Programme Distributors* **P**
Inter-Ocean—040

Hercules in New York   Fil-Ent '83
Comedy/Adventure
08995   86 mins   C
B, V
Arnold Schwarzenegger, Arnold Stang, Deborah Loomis, James Karen, Ernest Graves, Fanny McDonald, Howard Burstein, Merwin Goldsmith, George Bartenieff, Erica Fitz
Hercules, bored with life on Mount Olympus, decides to visit Earth, against the wishes of his father, Zeus. Zeus explodes with anger and hurls a thunder bolt at him. He falls into the sea, to be rescued by a freighter bound for New York. He is befriended by a sailor who tries to keep Hercules out of trouble and away from pretty girls.
F — EN
Filmpartners Inc — *Video Programme Distributors* **P**
Replay 1023

Here Comes Noddy Again   Chl-Juv '??
Cartoons
05848   51 mins   C
B, V
Animated, narrated by Richard Briers, directed by Mark Hall
A selection of stories featuring Noddy and Big Ears from Enid Blyton's 'Noddy' books. Includes 'Here Comes Noddy Again' (14 mins), 'Noddy Goes to Sea' (13 mins), 'Look Out Noddy' (11 mins) and 'Noddy Goes to the Fair' (13 mins). With lyrics by Ruth Boswell.
PS,M — EN
Copyright Promotions Ltd; Stop Frame Production — *Polygram Video* **P**
40131/20131

Here Comes the Grump   Chl-Juv '??
Cartoons/Fantasy
06164   85 mins   C
V2, B, V
Animated
A compilation of children's cartoons featuring a dragon who constantly, accidentally sneezes fire on his master—The Grump. The Grump is out to stop a little Princess and her friend from finding the crystal key which will lift the curse of gloom from her land; unfortunately The Grump keeps having accidents.
I,S — EN
DePatie-Freleng Productions — *Guild Home Video*   **H, P, E**

Here Comes the Grump-   Chl-Juv '??
Cassette 2
Cartoons
09448   85 mins   C
V2, B, V
Animated
This tape contains nine more adventures of the five-sneezing dragon and his mean-minded master The Grump.
BBFC:U — I,S — EN
DePatie-Freleng Prod. — *Guild Home Video*
H, P, E

Hero at Large   Fil-Ent '80
Comedy
10151   95 mins   C
B, V
John Ritter
A struggling young actor decked out in a super-hero costume to promote a new film finds that fiction becomes reality when faced with a couple of thugs robbing his local grocery shop. He goes to the rescue and finds, in fact, that he has actually become a hero. Encouraged by this, he sets out to fight crime in the city.
F — EN
United Artists — *MGM/UA Home Video*
P
UMB 10316/UMV 10316

Hero Bunker   Fil-Ent '??
War-Drama
05621   86 mins   C
V2, B, V
John Miller, Maria Xenia, Anna Maggi, F. Bislani, Mario Masters
During the Second World War, a Greek battleship is torpedoed. The Greeks become involved in a bloody conflict and were determined to fight to the last man, eventually forcing the enemy to withdraw into Albania.
BBFC:A — S,A — EN
Unknown — *Go Video Ltd*   **P**
GO111

Heroes of Telemark, The   Fil-Ent '65
War-Drama
06919   126 mins   C
B, V
Kirk Douglas, Richard Harris, Michael Redgrave

PALADIN VIDEO HOME ENTERTAINMENT GUIDE

This is the story of a handful of brave Norwegians who altered the course of the war by destroying the Germans' last hope of atomic supremacy. The resistance workers faced many dangers in a series of daring raids to destroy the Germans' vital source of water from the Norsky Hydro factory in occupied Norway.
BBFC:U — F — EN
Columbia — *Rank Video Library* **H, P**
0068C

Heroes of the Regiment   Fil-Ent '35
Comedy
06862   76 mins   B/W
V2, B, V
Stan Laurel, Oliver Hardy, Jimmy Finlayson, Daphne Pollard
When Laurel and Hardy arrive in Scotland to collect an inheritance things go very wrong. They end up in India with the Scottish Army which they have unintentionally joined. Original title: 'Bonnie Scotland.'
M,A — EN
Hal Roach — *European Video Company*
P

Hey, Good Looking!   Fil-Ent '84
Cartoons
12839   77 mins   C
B, V
Animated
This cartoon by Ralph Bakshi tells the story of gang warfare and has a 50s rock'n'roll musical background.
BBFC:18 — A — EN
Ralph Bakshi — *Video Tape Centre* **P**
1133

Hi-jackers, The/The Night Caller/Echo   Fil-Ent '6?
Crime-Drama/Science fiction
05703   168 mins   B/W
B, V
Anthony Booth, Jacqueline Ellis, Derek Francis, John Saxon, Patricia Haines, Morris Denham
This cassette features two films and a short documentary. 'The Hi-jackers' (black/white, 69 mins, 1963) features a gang of criminals who specialize in stealing the contents of long distant lorries. 'The Night Caller' (black/white, 82 mins, 1965) is a mystery involving a U.F.O., an alien mutation, a laboratory and a missing girl. 'Echo' (colour, 17 mins) is a short documentary about Jersey.
BBFC:X — A — EN
Butcher Films; World Entertainment Corp — *Derann Film Services* **H, P**
DV141B/DV141

Hi-Riders   Fil-Ent '78
Adventure
02444   88 mins   C
V2, B, V
Mel Ferrer, Stephen McNally
An adventure drama about the loves and excitement of men on the race-car circuit.
BBFC:AA — C,A — EN
Dimension Pictures — *Iver Film Services*
P

Hide-Aways, The   Fil-Ent '73
Drama
07821   105 mins   C
V2, B, V
Ingrid Bergman, Sally Prager
A fabled art collector lives in total seclusion until a 12 year-old girl seeks her out to check on the creator of a sculpture in the New York Metropolitan Museum.
S,A — EN
Cinema 5 — *Video Unlimited* **H, P**
039

Hide in Plain Sight   Fil-Ent '80
Drama
07733   92 mins   C
B, V
James Caan, Jill Eikenberry, Robert Viharo, Barbra Rae, Joe Grifast, Kenneth McMillan, Josef Sommer, Danny Aiello, directed by James Caan
This film is based on the true story of an ordinary man who spent eighteen harrowing months searching for his two small children who were 'officially kidnapped' by the U.S. Government.
BBFC:A — S,A — EN
MGM — *MGM/UA Home Video* **P**
UMB 10047/UMV 10047

High and Low   Fil-Ent '63
Suspense
10031   142 mins   B/W
B, V
Toshiro Mifune, Kyoko Kagawa, Tatsuya Nakadai, directed by Akira Kurosawa
A wealthy man receives a ransom note, which says that his son has been kidnapped. As it turns out, the kidnappers erred, snatching the son of a chauffeur by mistake.
S,A — EN
Toho — *Palace Video Ltd* **P**
PVC 2041A

High Crime   Fil-Ent '73
Crime-Drama
09304   97 mins   C
B, V

(For Explanation of codes, see USE GUIDE and KEY)   313

PALADIN VIDEO HOME ENTERTAINMENT GUIDE

Franco Nero, Fernando Rey, James Whitmore, Delia Boccardo
This high-adventure thriller centres around a Mafia inspired uncut heroin smuggling racket. It features high speed car chases and a Police Commissioner intent on smashing the villains at any cost.
BBFC:PG — *S,A* — *EN*
Ambassador Releasing — *Abacus Video*
P

High Ice   Fil-Ent '80
Suspense/Adventure
07837   96 mins   C
B, V
David Janssen, Tony Musante, Madge Sinclair, Dorian Harewood, Allison Argo, James G. Richardson, Gretchen Corbett, directed by Eugene S. Jones
This film tells the story of rescue attempts made to save a group of young mountain climbers trapped on a narrow ledge 4,200 feet up a sheer rock face. A ranger has his authority challenged by a young dynamic lieutenant who resents the climbers who have cost the lives of three helicopter men. They are soon openly at war with each other as to how is the best way to rescue the people.
S,A — *EN*
E.S.J. Production — *Polygram Video*   H, P
791 510

High Noon   Fil-Ent '52
Western
06967   82 mins   B/W
V2, B, V
Gary Cooper, Grace Kelly, directed by Fred Zinnemann
A recently married marshall is torn between love and his duty to an ungrateful town when he has to stand alone against a gang of outlaws who have sworn to kill him.
Academy Awards '52: Best Actor (Cooper); Best Music Score (Tiomkin); Best Song ('High Noon').   *F* — *EN*
UA; Stanley Kramer — *BBC Video*   H, P
BBCV 8000

High Plains Drifter   Fil-Ent '73
Western
05328   105 mins   C
B, V
Clint Eastwood, Verna Bloom, Mariana Hill, Mitchell Ryan, Jack Guig, directed by Clint Eastwood
Set in 1870, a stranger arrives in a frontier town passing the grave of the former sheriff. During a meeting the mine owners and residents hire the stranger to protect them from three gunmen they imprisoned the year before. He agrees as long as he has a free hand. He plans a reception that they will never forget, not only including an ambush but he paints the entire town red and re-names it 'Hell.'
S,A — *EN*
Universal — *CIC Video*   H, P
BEA1021/VHA1021

High Risk   Fil-Ent '80
Drama/Adventure
08353   93 mins   C
V2, B, V
James Coburn, Lindsay Wagner, Ernest Borgnine, James Brolin, Anthony Quinn
James Coburn plays the boss of a vast drug-smuggling group. His life is disrupted when four young men and a girl try to steal his wealth.
BBFC:X — *A* — *EN*
City Films — *Guild Home Video*   H, P, E

High Road To China   Fil-Ent '83
Adventure
13370   90 mins   C
V2, B, V
Tom Selleck, Bess Armstrong, Jack Weston, Wilford Brimley, Robert Morley, Brian Blessed, directed by Brian G Hutton
Set in Istanbul in the 1920's, an American heiress seeks the help of an ex-flying ace to find her father who is lost somewhere in the wilds of Asia.
BBFC:PG — *S,A* — *EN*
Golden Harvest; Jadran Film — *Guild Home Video*   H, P, E
8285-5

High Rolling   Fil-Ent '8?
Drama
08746   85 mins   C
B, V
Joseph Bottoms, Grigor Taylor, Judy Davis, Wendy Hughes, Peter Cummins, Sandra McGregor, directed by Igor Auzins
This films tells the story of two young men, an Australian and an American, who have been traveling around North Queensland. One of them is fighting in a boxing troupe and the other in a shooting gallery. One gets the sack for his advances on a girl, and the other finds a boxing opponent nearly too much to handle. For both of them, it seems time to move on.
S,A — *EN*
Unknown — *Precision Video Ltd*   P
BITC 2573/VITC 2573

High Society   Fil-Ent '56
Musical
10179   107 mins   C
B, V

PALADIN VIDEO HOME ENTERTAINMENT GUIDE

Bing Crosby, Frank Sinatra, Grace Kelly, John Lund, Louis Armstrong

Set in the 1950s in a fashionable holiday resort, a beautiful socialite is preparing to re-marry. Her former husband arrives on the scene the day before her marriage to take part in the Jazz Festival but it's soon obvious he's there to win her back. Music and lyrics are by Cole Porter.

BBFC:U — F — EN
MGM — *MGM/UA Home Video*   **P**
UMB 10292/UMV 10292

High Velocity   Fil-Ent '76
War-Drama
07386   106 mins   C
V2, B, V

Ben Gazzara, Britt Ekland, Paul Winfield, Keenan Wynn, directed by Remi Kramer

Two war veterans, now mercenaries, attempt to rescue a kidnapped executive in a small tropical country and end up becoming involved in triple-cross treachery resulting in the world's bloodiest undeclared war.

BBFC:AA — S,A — EN
Turtle Releasing — *Guild Home Video*   **H, P, E**

Higher and   Fil-Ent '??
Higher/Strictly Dynamite
Musical/Comedy
05664   155 mins   B/W
B, V

Frank Sinatra, Victor Borge, Jack Haley, Michele Morgan, Mel Torna, directed by Tim Whelan, Jimmy Durante, Lupe Velez, William Gargan, Sterling Holloway, Marian Nixon, directed by Elliot Nugent

Two films are featured on one cassette. 'Higher and Higher' (Black and white, 87 mins, 1944) is the story of a bankrupt socialite who is persuaded to rescue his finances by marrying his pretty kitchen-maid to the richest man around; complications occur. 'Strictly Dynamite' (Black/white, 68 mins. 1935) is the tale of a penniless poet who achieves fame when his verses are satirised by a radio team and the public demand more. Success brings many troubles.

F — EN
RKO — *Kingston Video*   **H, P**
KV48

Highpoint   Fil-Ent '79
Drama/Suspense
09016   87 mins   C
V2, B, V

Richard Harris, Christopher Plummer, Beverly D'Angelo

This film tells the story of a British accountant, who is drawn into a web of intrigue, involving the Mafia, the FBI and ten million dollars. The climax to the story is filmed on top of the world's tallest building, 1,150 feet above the streets, on Toronto's CN Tower.

S,A — EN
Unknown — *Intervision Video*   **H, P**
AA 0436

Highway to Hell   Fil-Ent '84
Drama/Romance
12948   90 mins   C
V2, B, V

Monico Carrico, Eric Stoltz

A young girl falls in love with a seventeen-year-old boy who has been convicted of killing his father and they share a desperate and brief romance together.

BBFC:18 — C,A — EN
Mark Griffiths — *Videomedia*   **P**
0809

Hijack   Fil-Ent '73
Crime-Drama
12076   72 mins   C
V2, B, V

David Janssen, Keenan Wynn, Lee Purcell, Jeanette Nolan, William Schallert

Two truckers accept a job to haul a top secret government cargo from L.A. to Houston. What they do not know is that they will be chased, attacked and possibly killed.

BBFC:PG — S,A — EN
Metromedia — *Guild Home Video*   **H, P, E**

Hijack!   Chl-Juv '8?
Adventure
13452   59 mins   C
B, V

A group of children are kidnapped aboard their father's yacht and are forced to sail across to France by a youth who theatens violence if there is any intervention from the authorities.

BBFC:U — I,S — EN
Unknown — *Rank Video Library*   **P**
3111X

Hill's Angels   Fil-Ent '78
Comedy
12582   95 mins   C
B, V

Edward Herrmann, Barbara Harris

(For Explanation of codes, see USE GUIDE and KEY)

PALADIN VIDEO HOME ENTERTAINMENT GUIDE

The new town preacher and six of his female flock get together to form the most unorganised vigilante group ever to fight organised crime. Original title: 'The North Avenue Irregulars.'
F — EN
Walt Disney Productions — *Rank Video Library* **H**
017

Hills Have Eyes, The   Fil-Ent '77
Horror/Drama
06323   86 mins   C
V2, B, V
Susan Lanier, Robert Houston, Martin Speer, John Streadman, James Whitworth, directed by Wes Craven
A family crossing the desert wastes of America heading for California are attacked by savage cannibals. Two members of the family meet grisly deaths, the daughter is raped and her baby taken for food. The remaining family battle for survival, reverting to primitive instincts, eventually turning the tables and destroying the savages.
A — EN
Vanguard — *World of Video 2000*   **H, P**
XF122

Hills Have Eyes, Part 2, The   Fil-Ent '84
Horror
13697   97 mins   C
B, V
Michael Berryman, John Laughlin, Tamara Stafford, directed by Wes Craven
Ignoring all warnings, a group of teenagers set out through the desert in a bus and when it runs out of petrol the crazed mutants reappear, their blood lust unabated.
BBFC:18 — A — EN
Adrienne Fancy and VTC; New Realm Entertainments — *THORN EMI*   **P**
90 2575

Hip-Hop, a Street History   Fil-Ent '84
Dance
13138   60 mins   C
B, V
Afrika Bambaataa, Malcolm McLaren, Jonzun Crew, directed by Dick Fontaine
This film pinpoints the origins of break-dance with its own brand of music. The narration is by Gary Byrd and Mel Brooks is seen doing the 'Hitler Rap.'
F — EN
BBC; Polygram Music Video — *Polygram Video*   **P**
041 0254/041 0252

History of Advertising, The   Gen-Edu '8?
Advertising
13490   44 mins   C
B, V
A comprehensive and sometimes lighthearted look at advertising starting in ancient Pompeii through to modern times including famous campaigns that caught public interest and others that have failed.
S,A — EN
Greenpark Productions — *Greenpark Productions*   **H**

History of Aviation, The   Gen-Edu '??
History/Aeronautics
06131   55 mins   B/W
V2, B, V
This chronological documentary has been compiled from authentic international footage, from the first flight of the Wright brothers to the missile carriers. It describes the evolution of man's mechanical flight in many different countries all over the world.
F — ED
Unknown — *Video Programme Distributors* **P**
Cinehollywood—V720

History of Golf, I, The   Spo-Lei '7?
Golf
04496   60 mins   C
B, V
Narrated by Henry Longhurst
Three absorbing productions, 'The Honourable and Ancient,' 'The Good Old Days,' and 'First Prize' comprise a nostalgic look at a prestigious pastime.
F — EN
Trans World Intl — *Quadrant Video*   **H, P**
G1

History of Golf II, The   Spo-Lei '7?
Golf
04495   51 mins   C
B, V
A look at a grand old golf course and its magic moments—historical and humourous—is provided in 'St. Andrews—Home of Golf.' In 'Ladies of the Links,' the unlikely success story that is women's golf today is traced from its beginnings.
F — EN
Trans World Intl — *Quadrant Video*   **H, P**
G2

History of Rock-Volume 4, The   Fil-Ent '8?
Music-Performance
09770   85 mins   C

PALADIN VIDEO HOME ENTERTAINMENT GUIDE

B, V
This series of music videos charts the trends of the music industry over the past 25 years. This tape, the fourth in the series entitled 'England Rules: The Beat Boom', features The Beatles' invasion of the American charts, The Animals, Manfred Mann and The Rolling Stones.
F — EN
Unknown — *THORN EMI* P
TXE 90 1449 4/TVE 90 1449 2

History of the Conquest of Space, The Gen-Edu '??
Space exploration
06132   105 mins   C
V2, B, V
A complete documentation of man's space exploration using both American and Russian authentic footage and original space dialogue. Includes black and white sequences.
F — ED
Unknown — *Video Programme Distributors* P
Cinehollywood—V730

History of the World Part 1 Fil-Ent '81
Comedy
07705   90 mins   C
V2, B, V, LV
Mel Brooks, Dom DeLuise, Madeline Kahn, Pamela Stephenson, Harvey Korman, Cloris Leachman, Ron Carey, Howard Morris, Sid Caesar, Jackie Mason, directed by Mel Brooks
Mel Brooks gives his own irreverent and lunatic view of the history of the world from the dawn of time to the French Revolution.
A — EN
Brooks Films Ltd — *CBS/Fox Video* H
1114

Hit, The Fil-Ent '83
Crime-Drama
13121   97 mins   C
B, V
John Hurt, Terence Stamp, Tim Roth, Laura del Sol, Bill Hunter, Fernando Rey, directed by Stephen Frears
A gangster informs on his fellow criminals and they get sent down for life but ten years after a hit team arrive at his hideout in Spain to take him to Paris and brutal revenge.
BBFC:18 — A — EN
Zenith Productions; The Recorded Picture Company — *Palace Video Ltd* P
PVC 2079A

Hit Back! How-Ins '??
Safety education/Women
09360   121 mins   C
B, V
In this tape the moves are demonstrated, showing in detail how women can combat sexual attack from the three common positions, standing up, sitting down and lying down. These include attacks from the front, side and behind.
S,A — I
Unknown — *Precision Video Ltd* P
BOPV 2581/VOPV 2581

Hit Lady Fil-Ent '74
Drama
13343   69 mins   C
B, V
Yvette Mimieux, Joseph Campanella, Clu Gulager, Dack Rambo, Keenan Wynn, directed by Tracy Keenan Wynn
A woman's successful career as a professional artist is just a cover for her true occupation as a hit lady for a mob and when she decides to quit, she in turn, becomes the hunted.
BBFC:PG — S,A — EN
Spelling Goldberg Productions — *Guild Home Video*   H, P, E
8430

Hit Man, The Fil-Ent '72
Crime-Drama
10163   87 mins   C
B, V
Bernie Casey, Lisa Moore, Pam Grier
When a Los Angeles street hustler's brother is murdered by one of the crime syndicate, he decides to avenge his death. With the help of a beautiful porno-movie star he turns killer and takes on the gangs of Los Angeles' underworld.
BBFC:X — A — EN
MGM; Gene Corman — *MGM/UA Home Video* P
UMB 10265/UMV 10265

Hitch Hike Fil-Ent '??
Drama
07801   ? mins   C
B, V
Franco Nero, Corrine Clery, David Hess
An Italian reporter and his wife pick up a strange hitchhiker during their second honeymoon in California, an act which leads to murder, theft and rape.
S,A — EN
Unknown — *Video Tape Centre* P
VTC 1007

Hitler—The Last Ten Days Fil-Ent '73
Drama
12749   100 mins   C
B, V
Alec Guinness, Simon Ward, Diane Cilento

(For Explanation of codes, see USE GUIDE and KEY)   317

PALADIN VIDEO HOME ENTERTAINMENT GUIDE

A harrowing account of the final chapter in the life of the most terrifying dictator the world has known.
BBFC:A — A — EN
Paramount — *Rank Video Library* **H, P**
0127B

Hits Video, The   Fil-Ent '85
Music video
13665   90 mins   C
B, V
This video consists of twenty-three tracks from artists including 'Nik Kershaw', 'Wham', 'The Sisters Of Mercy', 'Shakin Stevens', 'The Associates', 'Big Sound Authority', and 'The Stranglers'.
M,A — EN
Unknown — *CBS/Fox Video*   **P**

Hitter, The   Fil-Ent '??
Crime-Drama/Adventure
07668   94 mins   C
B, V
Ron O'Neal, Sheila Frazier, Adolph Caesar, directed by Christopher Leitch
This film follows the adventures of 'The Hitter' in his world of money hungry hustlers, love hungry women and blood hungry crowds.
S,A — EN
Unknown — *Hello Video Ltd*   **P**
H12

HMS Pinafore   Fil-Ent '7?
Opera
02035   78 mins   C
B, V
The D'Oyly Carte Opera Company stars in the Gilbert and Sullivan opera about a naval Captain's daughter who is in love with a young sailor but is pursued by an Admiral with his own intentions.
F — EN
Unknown — *Precision Video Ltd*   **P**
BITC 2021/VITC 2021

H.M.S. PINAFORE   Fil-Ent '8?
Opera
08922   100 mins   C
B, V
Peter Marshall, Frankie Howard, Meryl Drower, Michael Bulman, Delia Jones, Alan Watt, directed by Rodney Greenberg
This opera by Gilbert and Sullivan tells the story of the humble sailor who cannot marry the Captain's daughter because of his lowly rank. The daughter does not love her suitor. They elope, but are betrayed. However, due to a mixup as babies, her father is common and the sailor is of noble birth. They are therefore free to wed. The music is by The London Symphony Orchestra, conducted by Alexander Faris.
S,A — EN
Brent Walker Prods — *Brent Walker Home Video Ltd*   **P**

Hoax, The   Fil-Ent '74
Drama
02079   90 mins   C
B, V
Bill Ewing, Frank Bonner, Jacques Aubuchan
In this light-hearted comedy from California, two young Americans find an H-bomb that the USAF has lost. Seizing their big chance to make a quick million, they hold the city of Los Angeles to ransom threatening to trigger the bomb if its inhabitants don't send a dollar each to a Swiss bank account.
F — EN
Citadel Prods — *VCL Video Services*   **P**

Hobson's Choice   Fil-Ent '54
Comedy
01602   102 mins   B/W
B, V
Charles Laughton, John Mills, Brenda de Banzie, directed by David Lean
A prosperous businessman in the Nineties tries to keep his daughter from marrying, but the strong-willed daughter has other ideas.
British Academy: Best British Film 1954.
BBFC:U — S,A — EN
British Lion — *THORN EMI*   **P**
TXE 90 0203 4/TVE 90 0203 2

Hoffman   Fil-Ent '69
Drama
08561   109 mins   C
B, V
Peter Sellers, Sinead Cusack, directed by Alvin Rakoff
Peter Sellers plays a middle-aged man, secretly in love with a 19-year-old typist. He discovers that her fiance is involved with thieves and uses this information to blackmail her. The price she has to pay is to spend a week with him at his flat.
BBFC:AA — C,A — EN
Longstone Film Productions — *THORN EMI*
P
TXB 90 0273 4/TVB 90 0273 2

Hoffnung   Fil-Ent '??
Music-Performance
09952   90 mins   C
V2, B, V

PALADIN VIDEO HOME ENTERTAINMENT GUIDE

Ralph Gothoni, Louis Michal, Martha Carfi, Annetta Hoffnung, William Rogan, Dominique Goujon
This tape combines symphonic music and humour featuring the Hoffnung Festival Orchestra.
BBFC:U — F — EN
Unknown — *Video Unlimited*   **H, P, E**
096

Hold-Up   Fil-Ent '72
Crime-Drama/Suspense
08801   91 mins   C
B, V
Frederich Stafford, Nathalie Delon, Marcel Bozzuffi, directed by German Lorente
After an armed hold-up a security officer is the only survivor of the unit. When he recovers, his memory slightly blurred, the chase begins.
C,A — EN
Salvatore Gerbino Prod; Midjela Films — *VCL Video Services*   **P**
P265D

Holiday on the Buses   Fil-Ent '73
Comedy
08553   83 mins   C
B, V
Reg Varney, Doris Hare, Bob Grant, Michael Robbins, Anna Karen, Wilfred Brambell, Kate Williams, Stephen Lewis, directed by Bryan Izzard
This film sees the 'On the Buses' Team leaving London to work on a Pontin's Holiday Village in North Wales. The fun begins when Blakey sees more of the resident nurse than is good for him.
BBFC:A — S,A — EN
Hammer Film Prod Ltd — *THORN EMI*   **P**
TXC 90 07524/TVC 90 07522

Hollywood Boulevard   Fil-Ent '76
Drama/Satire
12995   79 mins   C
B, V
Candice Rialson, Mary Woronov, Rita George, Jeffrey Kramer, Dick Miller
A dramatised examination of the strange world of the Hollywood low-budget B-movie with a naive young girl as its heroine.
S,A — EN
New World Pictures — *Warner Home Video*   **P**
24055

Hollywood Cartoon Festival   Fil-Ent '4?
Cartoons
08690   50 mins   C
V2, B, V

Animated
This tape is a collection of Hollywood cartoons from the 1940's. It includes 'The Sheepish Wolf', 'A Kick in Time', directed by Dave Fleischer, 'A Day at the Zoo', 'The Land of the Lost', directed by I. Sparber, 'Volcano' directed by Dave Fleischer and 'Jerky Turkey'.
BBFC:U — F — EN
Famous Studios — *Derann Film Services*   **P**
BCV 400

Hollywood Knight   Fil-Ent '??
Drama/Romance
05442   81 mins   C
V2, B, V
Michael Christian, Josette Banzet, Keenan Wynn, Donna Wilkes, directed by David Worth
The seamier side of Hollywood is contrasted with the beauty and splendor of the countryside when a young man becomes a fugitive in an attempt to escape from a tragic and violent past.
BBFC:A — S,A — EN
John B Kelly Presentation — *Iver Film Services*   **P**

Hollywood on Parade   Fil-Ent '7?
Musical
06820   ? mins   C
V2, B, V
Fred Astaire, Maurice Chevalier, Buster Keaton, Busby Berkeley, James Cagney, Jean Harlow, Joan Crawford, Clark Gable, Bing Crosby
A compilation of musical clips from Hollywood films which also stars Jimmy Durante, Al Jolson, Cary Grant, Mae West, Marx Brothers, Shirley Temple, Ginger Rogers, Mickey Rooney, Roy Rogers and others.
F — EN
Paramount et al — *Intervision Video*   **H, P**
A-AE 0371

Holocaust   Fil-Ent '78
Drama
08352   482 mins   C
V2, B, V
Michael Moriarty, Meryl Streep, Tom Bell, Joseph Bottoms, Marius Goring, Rosemary Harris, Ian Holm, Lee Montague, Deborah Norton, Sam Wanamaker, directed by Marvin Chamsky
This film is available on three separate cassettes. 'Holocaust' is the story of two families, one Jewish and the other German. They are both caught up in Hitler's extermination of six million Jews.
Emmy Awards '78: Outstanding Director; Outstanding Screenplay; Outstanding Film Editing.   C,A — EN
Titus; NBC — *Guild Home Video*   **H, P, E**

(For Explanation of codes, see USE GUIDE and KEY)

PALADIN VIDEO HOME ENTERTAINMENT GUIDE

Hombre
Fil-Ent '67
Western
01017   111 mins   C
B, V
Paul Newman, Fredric March, Richard Boone, Diane Cilento, Cameron Mitchell, Barbara Rush, Martin Balsam
A white man, raised by Apaches, is forced to a showdown. He has to help save the lives of people he loathes.
F — EN
20th Century Fox; Martin Ritt; Irving Ravetch — *CBS/Fox Video*   P
3A-013

Home Before Midnight
Fil-Ent '??
Drama
05606   115 mins   C
B, V
James Aubrey, Alison Elliot, Mark Burns, Richard Todd, Debbie Linden
A young successful song-writer picks up a hitch-hiker on a country road and innocently gets caught in a web of wrong assumptions. The girl is fourteen and still at school, they are in love but the law called it rape and he lands in court charged with assault which results in his ruin.
S,A — EN
Unknown — *Home Video Merchandisers*
H, P
001

Home Body Care Part 1
Spo-Lei '8?
Physical fitness
08762   ? mins   C
B, V
Esme Newton-Dunn, directed by John Schroeder
This programme gives a 'keep-fit' lesson which includes exercises that start off with simple basics and become progressively harder. It illustrates what one puts oneself through in a normal day, and how the body suffers unknowingly with aches and pains caused by the increasing pressures of modern day living.
F — I
Unknown — *Precision Video Ltd*   P
BJSPV 1589/VJSPV 1589

Home First Aid
Med-Sci '84
First aid/Emergencies
13579   37 mins   C
B, V
An introduction to first aid, this programme covers burns and scalds, chemical burns, eyes, nose bleeds, cuts and wounds, fainting, electric shock, choking and cardiac arrest and other emergencies that may be encountered.
A — I
Reference Tapes — *Reference Tapes*   P

Home Movies
Fil-Ent '79
Comedy
06172   93 mins   C
V2, B, V
Nancy Allen, Mary Davenport, Kirk Douglas, Vincent Gardenia, Keith Gordon
A young man is shy and unsure of himself, his mother prefers his older brother and his father is a lecherous doctor with designs on a Swedish nurse. When the young man finds out his mother is divorcing his father he feels he has a chance of helping someone, he decides to get pictures of his father 'in the act' and become a hero.
BBFC:AA — S,A — EN
Brian de Palma Prod — *Guild Home Video*
H, P, E

Home of Rest for Horses
Gen-Edu '8?
Animals
13520   15 mins   C
B, V
This film shows a model establishment which provides ideal accommodation for 150 horses, ponies and donkeys—some retired and others in need of rest.
A — ED
Unknown — *TFI Leisure Ltd*   H, P

Home Sweet Home
Fil-Ent '??
Horror
07922   90 mins   C
V2, B, V
Jake Steinfeld, Sallee Elyse, Peter de Paul, Vanessa Shaw, directed by Nettie Pena
A maniac killer brings horror to an innocent family's Thanksgiving Day gathering.
S,A — EN
Unknown — *Video Programme Distributors*
P
Media—177

Home to Stay
Fil-Ent '79
Drama
09094   48 mins   C
V2, B, V
Henry Fonda
A farmer who has suffered a stroke is fighting off repeated lapses into senility. His son and daughter have conflicting interests as to whether he should be committed to a nursing home.
C,A — EN
David Susskind — *Video Tape Centre*   P

Homebodies
Fil-Ent '74
Suspense/Comedy
12263   94 mins   C
V2, B, V

320   (For Explanation of codes, see USE GUIDE and KEY)

PALADIN VIDEO HOME ENTERTAINMENT GUIDE

Peter Brocco, Frances Fuller, William Hansen, Ruth McDevitt, Paula Trueman

Six elderly people who have lived in an old tenement building for years rebel against society when told it is being pulled down to make way for a new office block.

S,A — EN

Avco Embassy — Embassy Home Entertainment   P
2044

Homework   Fil-Ent '82
Drama
10115   88 mins   C
B, V

Joan Collins, directed by James Beshears

A young 16-year-old finds it difficult to interest girls of his own age, and ends up being seduced by an older woman.

BBFC:18 — C,A — EN

Jensen Farley — CIC Video   H, P
BEA 1073/VHA 1073

Honey   Fil-Ent '83
Drama/Fantasy
13247   89 mins   C
B, V

Clio Goldsmith, Catherine Spaak, Fernando Rey

As a writer's manuscript is read aloud, a unique dreamlike and erotic tour unfolds.

BBFC:18 — A — EN

Gianfranco Angelucci — CBS/Fox Video   P
6678

Honeybaby   Fil-Ent '74
Adventure/Drama
02443   90 mins   C
V2, B, V

Diana Sands, Calvin Lockhart

Set against the seething background of the Middle East, an international soldier of fortune meets up with a beautiful American interpreter.

BBFC:X — A — EN

Iver Film Services — Iver Film Services   P

Honeymoon Horror   Fil-Ent '7?
Horror
07971   90 mins   C
B, V

Cheryl Black, Bob Wagner, directed by Harry Preston

This film tells the story of a couple who move into a lodge on a remote island. Their plan is to open up the holiday cabins to cater for honeymoon couples. This goes drastically wrong when a series of mysterious and brutal murders begin.

A — EN

Unknown — AVI Video Ltd   P
002

Honeymoon Killers, The   Fil-Ent '70
Drama
08974   108 mins   B/W
B, V

Shirley Stoler, Tony Lobianco

This tells the story of a nurse, who after a correspondence friendship falls in love with a New York gigolo. Having confessed his profession, she is fired from the hospital, his letters having been read by the hospital supervisor. They embark on a tour of the USA in search of gullible spinsters' money. However, what begins as a straight fraud ends as brutal murder.

BBFC:X — A — EN

Cinerama Releasing; Roxanne Productions — Palace Video Ltd   P
PVC 2014B

Honky   Fil-Ent '76
Drama
07616   92 mins   C
V2, B, V

Brenda Sykes, John Neilson, William Marshall, directed by William A. Graham

This is the story of Sheila, a cool, common, black girl of seventeen, and Wayne, who thinks he is 'hip.' Together they set out on a senseless mission to triple their money by drug dealing, an act which lands them in trouble.

BBFC:X — A — EN

Jack H Harris — Iver Film Services   P

Honky Tonk Freeway   Fil-Ent '81
Comedy/Adventure
07470   102 mins   C
B, V

Beau Bridges, Hume Cronyn, Beverly D'Angelo, William Devane, George Dzundza, Teri Garr, Joe Grifasi, Howard Hesseman, Paul Jabara, Geraldine Page, Jessica Tandy, directed by John Schlesinger

This film takes a satirical look at the 'car-culture' of contemporary America and includes drive-in banks, drive-in cleaners and even a drive-in mortuary. It follows the adventures of a variety of characters from different areas all heading for Florida. Due to the efforts of the

PALADIN VIDEO HOME ENTERTAINMENT GUIDE

inhabitants of a small town, by-passed by the freeway, all the travellers descend on the town having been re-routed by the mayor who is anxious not to lose the dying tourist trade.
BBFC:AA — S,A — EN
Don Boyd Productions; HTF Company — THORN EMI   P
TXA 90 0683 4/TVA 90 0683 2

Honor Thy Father   Fil-Ent '73
Crime-Drama
08025   97 mins   C
V2, B, V
Raf Vallone, Brenda Vaccaro, Joe Bologna, Richard Castellano, Joe De Santis, directed by Paul Wendkos
This film, set in New York, portrays a family bonded by the tradition of crime, as seen through the eyes of the son of the once head of a powerful underworld gang. It is based on the novel by Gay Talese.
BBFC:AA — C,A — EN
M P C — Iver Film Services   P
183

Honorary Consul, The   Fil-Ent '83
Drama
12885   96 mins   C
B, V
Michael Caine, Richard Gere, Bob Hoskins, directed by John Mackenzie
Based on a novel by Graham Greene, this is the story of an alcoholic British consul who unwittingly becomes involved in a web of betrayal, corruption and intrigue in Argentina.
BBFC:18 — A — EN
Paramount; World Film Services — THORN EMI   P
TXA 90 23664/TVA 90 23662

Hoodwink   Fil-Ent '??
Crime-Drama
08770   93 mins   C
B, V
John Hargreaves, Wendy Hughes, Kim Deacon, Judy Davis, directed by Claude Whatham
After a bank robbery in Sydney, a man makes his getaway to rejoin his girlfriend. She is tired of his criminal life and calls their affair off. He picks up a girl in a bar, but she finds the proceeds of the robbery in his briefcase and betrays him to the police. In prison, he pretends to go blind, in order to get off lightly. He meets a woman, the quiet, religious wife of a lay preacher, and falls in love.
S,A — EN
Unknown — Precision Video Ltd   P
BSWPV 2603/VSWPV 2603

Hooper   Fil-Ent '78
Comedy
01252   90 mins   C
B, V
Burt Reynolds, Jan-Michael Vincent, Robert Klein, directed by Hal Needham
A behind-the-scenes look at the world of movie stuntmen. Burt Reynolds is a top stuntman who becomes involved in a rivalry with an up-and-coming young man out to surpass him.
F — EN
Warner Bros — Warner Home Video   P

Hoppity Goes to Town   Fil-Ent '41
Cartoons
04852   75 mins   C
V2, B, V
Animated
This cartoon, set to Hoagy Carmichael's music, follows the adventures of a little grasshopper in the big city.
F — EN
Max Fleischer — BBC Video   H, P
BBCV 9001

Hopscotch   Fil-Ent '80
Comedy-Drama
08457   100 mins   C
B, V
Walter Matthau, Glenda Jackson, Sam Waterston, Herbert Lom, Ned Beatty, directed by Ronald Neame
This film stars Walter Matthau as a CIA agent who falls foul to his superiors. He disappears and helped by Glenda Jackson, herself a former CIA agent, leads his pursuers on a wild goose chase through Europe. Always one step ahead, and full of surprises and gags Matthau evades his captors, outsmarting them at every turn.
BBFC:AA — C,A — EN
Avco Embassy — THORN EMI   P
TXA 90 0991 4/TVA 90 09912

Horror Hospital   Fil-Ent '75
Horror
05469   86 mins   C
V2, B, V
Michael Gough, Robin Askwith, Dennis Price, directed by Anthony Balch
A classic horror tale which includes a mad scientist, a monster, a laboratory, a haunted castle and the victims. Masquerading as a Health Hotel young people are cured of their hang-ups permanently.
BBFC:X — A — EN
Richard Gordon Prod — Iver Film Services P
132

PALADIN VIDEO HOME ENTERTAINMENT GUIDE

Horror of Frankenstein   Fil-Ent '70
Horror
08554   93 mins   C
B, V

Ralph Bates, Kate O'Mara, Veronica Carlson, Dennis Price, directed by Jimmy Sangster

After the sudden death of his father, young Victor Frankenstein inherits his title of Baron. Whilst being interested in the weird branches of science that his family is known for, his other hobby is philandering. In between his love-making he finds time to create another monster.
BBFC:X — A — EN
EMI Film Productions — *THORN EMI*   P
TXC 90 0277 4/TVC 90 02772

Horse Called Nijinsky, A   Spo-Lei '7?
Horse racing
02463   53 mins   C
B, V

Narrated by Orson Welles

Orson Welles narrates this documentary about the famed racehorse, Nijinsky.
C,A — EN
Unknown — *Mountain Video*   P

Horse Sense and Road Safety   Gen-Edu '8?
Animals
13521   32 mins   C
B, V

Made in cooperation with the Mounted Branch of the London Police, this film looks at the behaviour of the horse when startled in the street and also covers safety precautions needed for riding at night.
S,A — ED
Unknown — *TFI Leisure Ltd*   H, P

Horseback   Spo-Lei '81
Sports
04864   110 mins   C
V2, B, V, LV

Introduced by David Vine

Professional coaches describe the world of horse riding for beginners and beyond.
F — I
John Vigar — *BBC Video*   H, P
BBCV 1011

Hostages, The   Fil-Ent '??
Crime-Drama
06866   91 mins   C
V2, B, V

Stuart Whitman

This film follows the trail of havoc created by a gang of youngsters after a robbery. Three of the youngsters escape the clutches of the police only to take a family as hostages.
S,A — EN
Unknown — *European Video Company*
P

Hot Bubblegum   Fil-Ent '81
Comedy
08068   88 mins   C
B, V, LV

Jonathan Segal, Zachni Noy, Yftach Katzur

The three Lemon Popsicle boys discover sex, the beach, rock 'n roll and drag racing. Benji's gorgeous blonde cousin, Frieda, arrives from Germany.
BBFC:X — C,A — EN
Independent — *Rank Video Library*   H/P
1037 C

Hot Dog—The Movie   Fil-Ent '84
Drama
13232   90 mins   C
B, V

David Naughton, Shannon Tweed, Patrick Houser, Tracy N Smith, John Patrick Reger, directed by Peter Markle

Romance and rivalry abound in this film set on the ski slopes. There is spectacular stunt work and a sound track featuring songs by Duran Duran, Patti Austin and John Stewart.
BBFC:18 — A — EN
Edward S Feldman — *Entertainment in Video*
H, P
EVB 1024/EVV 1024

Hot Gossip   Fil-Ent '81
Music-Performance/Dance
08535   35 mins   C
B, V

Directed by David Mallet

This shows the rock dance group performing some of their routines, the most well-known being in 'Love on the Phone','Houses in Motion,' 'Burn for You' and Press Darlings' from the group's latest album 'Geisha Boys and Temple Boys.'
F — EN
Thorn EMI Video Programmes Ltd — *THORN EMI*   P
TXE 90 05324/TVE 90 05322

Hot Rock, The   Fil-Ent '70
Comedy
01024   97 mins   C
B, V

Robert Redford, George Segal, Ron Leibman, Zero Mostel, Paul Sand, directed by Peter Yates

(For Explanation of codes, see USE GUIDE and KEY)

PALADIN VIDEO HOME ENTERTAINMENT GUIDE

Four unlikely robbers try to steal the world's hottest diamond.
F — EN
20th Century Fox; Hal Landers and Bobby Roberts — CBS/Fox Video   P
3A-032

'Hot Summer Night'—Donna Summer, A   Fil-Ent '8?
Music-Performance
12029   80 mins   C
B, V
Recorded live at the Pacific Amphitheatre, Los Angeles, this programme includes an appearance by Musical Youth, and a selection of Donna Summer's songs, 'She Works Hard for the Money,' 'Unconditional Love,' 'Love Is In Control' and 'Stop In The Name of Love.'
F — EN
Christine Smith for Millaney; Grant; Mallet; Mulcahy — Polygram Video   H, P
0401924/0401922

Hot T-Shirts   Fil-Ent '79
Comedy
06943   84 mins   C
B, V
Ray Holland, Stephanie Lawlor, Pauline Rose, Corinne Alphen
In an attempt to bring new business to a run-down drinks bar, sexy young girls are employed to attract customers by wearing clinging wet t-shirts.
BBFC:X — A — EN
Cannon Films — Rank Video Library   H, P
1036C

Hot Touch, The   Fil-Ent '83
Drama
09853   95 mins   C
B, V
Marie-France Pisier, Wayne Rogers, Samantha Eggar, Melvyn Douglas, Patrick Macnee, directed by Roger Vadim
This light-hearted story set in the international art world, tells of a talented painter who enjoys a remunerative living forging the masters.
F — EN
Astral Films; Trans-Atlantic Enterprises — Polygram Video   H, P
791 5434/791 5432

Hotel New Hampshire, The   Fil-Ent '84
Comedy
13710   103 mins   C
B, V
Jodie Foster, Nastassja Kinski, Beau Bridges, Rob Lowe, directed by Tony Richardson
A black comedy featuring an eccentric family consisting of a performing bear, a flatulent dog, a group of Viennese terrorists and a girl dressed in a bear suit.
BBFC:18 — A — EN
Neil Hartley — THORN EMI   P
90 2780

H.O.T.S.   Fil-Ent '82
Comedy
09306   95 mins   C
V2, B, V
Susan Kiger, Lisa London, Pamela Jean Bryant, Kimberley Cameron
Ex-cons, stolen cash, a grizzly bear, a wet-tee-shirt competition all feature in this light hearted look at the antics of a gang of gorgeous college girls out to prove that they are the best.
S,A — EN
Manson International — ADB Video Distribution   P

Hound of the Baskervilles, The   Fil-Ent '78
Comedy/Crime-Drama
07650   80 mins   C
B, V
Peter Cook, Dudley Moore, Max Wall, Terry Thomas, Roy Kinnear, Kenneth Williams, Irene Handl
The last remaining member of the Baskerville family calls on Sherlock Holmes and Dr. Watson to investigate a family mystery. For many years, the ancient Baskerville family have been haunted by a creature so terrifying, cruel and vicious that its mere bark makes them drop dead with fright.
S,A — EN
Hemdale — VCL Video Services   P
P206D

Hound of the Baskervilles, The   Fil-Ent '83
Drama/Mystery
12264   99 mins   C
V2, B, V
Ian Richardson, Donald Churchill, Denholm Elliott, Brian Blessed, Connie Booth
This film is set on the Devon Moors where Sir Charles Baskerville's dead body is discovered, and closely follows Arthur Conan Doyle's original text.
S,A — EN
National Enterprises — Embassy Home Entertainment   P
1364

PALADIN VIDEO HOME ENTERTAINMENT GUIDE

Houndcats and the   Chi-Juv   '8?
Barkleys, Volume 2, The
Cartoons
13723   83 mins   C
V2, B, V
Animated

A cartoon compilation featuring the Houndcats in 'The Great Golo Train Mission' and 'The Misbehavin "Raven" Mission' and the Barkleys in 'Lib and Let Lib' and 'Half-Pint Hero'.

BBFC:U — *F* — *EN*

DePatie-Freleng — *Medusa Communications Ltd*   **H, P**
MC 057

Houndcats and the   Chi-Juv   '8?
Barkleys, Volume 3, The
Cartoons
13724   83 mins   C
V2, B, V
Animated

A cartoon compilation featuring The Houndcats in 'The Call Me Madam X Mission' and 'There's Snow Biz Like Snow Biz Mission' and the Barkleys in 'For the Love of Money' and 'Keeping Up With The Beagles'.

BBFC:U — *F* — *EN*

DePatie-Freleng — *Medusa Communications Ltd*   **H, P**
MC 058

Houndcats and the   Chi-Juv   '8?
Barkleys, Volume 4, The
Cartoons
13725   83 mins   C
V2, B, V
Animated

A cartoon compilation featuring the Houndcats in 'The Perilous Possibly Pilfered Plans Mission' and 'The Ruckus on the Rails Mission' and the Barkleys in 'No Place for a Lady' and 'Play No Favourites'.

BBFC:U — *F* — *EN*

DePatie-Freleng — *Medusa Communications Ltd*   **H, P**
MC 059

Houndcats and the   Chi-Juv   '8?
Barkleys, Volume 1, The
Cartoons
13722   83 mins   C
V2, B, V
Animated

A cartoon compilation featuring the Houndcats in 'The Over The Waves Mission' and 'The Double Deal Diamond Time Mission' and the Barkleys in 'Match Breaker' and 'Finders Weepers.'

BBFC:U — *F* — *EN*

DePatie-Freleng — *Medusa Communications Ltd*   **H, P**
MC 045

Houndcats and the   Chi-Juv   '8?
Barkleys, Volume 5, The
Cartoons
13726   83 mins   C
V2, B, V
Animated

A cartoon compilation featuring the Houndcats in 'The Who's Who Thats Who Mission' and 'The Strangeless than Fiction Mission' and, the Barkleys in 'Barkley Beware' and 'Law and Misorder'.

BBFC:U — *F* — *EN*

DePatie-Freleng — *Medusa Communications Ltd*   **H, P**
MC 060

Houndcats and the   Chi-Juv   '8?
Barkleys, Volume 6, The
Cartoons
13727   83 mins   C
V2, B, V
Animated

A cartoon compilation featuring the Houndcats in 'The French Collection Mission' and 'Is There a Doctor in the Greenhouse Mission' and The Barkleys in 'The Great Disc Jockey' and 'Arnie Come Clean'.

BBFC:U — *F* — *EN*

DePatie-Freleng — *Medusa Communications Ltd*   **H, P**
MC 061

House by the Cemetery   Fil-Ent   '??
Horror
08600   85 mins   C
V2, B, V
Katherine MacColl, directed by Lucio Fulci

The house by the cemetery has had a gruesome past, having once been owned by Dr. Freudstein, a practitioner in bizarre surgical skills. Many victims fall prey to the demented marauding zombie, who is always seeking freshly severed limbs to keep his corrupt, rotting flesh alive.

BBFC:X — *A* — *EN*

Unknown — *Videomedia*   **P**
PVM 1027/BVM 1027/HVM 1027

(For Explanation of codes, see USE GUIDE and KEY)

PALADIN VIDEO HOME ENTERTAINMENT GUIDE

House of Evil   Fil-Ent '74
Horror/Suspense
12249   92 mins   C
B, V

Kathryn McNeil, Eileen Davidson, directed by Mark Rosman

The action in this film takes place in a New England college where the girls decide to take revenge on their hated house mother.
BBFC:18 — C,A — EN
Merlin Video — *VCL Video Services*   P
6559

House of Exorcism   Fil-Ent '75
Horror
09083   91 mins   C
B, V

Telly Savalas, Elke Sommer

A pleasant sight seeing tour in Spain becomes a terrifying nightmare for a woman, when she becomes possessed by a painting of the Devil. A priest battles with the powers of the Demon, trying to exorcise the devil from within her body.
A — EN

Peppercorn-Wormser — *Video Tape Centre* P

VTC 1021

House of the Long Shadows   Fil-Ent '8?
Horror
09242   97 mins   C
V2, B, V

Vincent Price, Christopher Lee, Peter Cushing, John Carradine, Sheila Keith, Julie Peasgood, Richard Todd, Desi Arnaz Jr

An American author challenges his publisher to write a novel within 24 hours. So that he can be in total solitude, he goes to an isolated house deep in the Welsh countryside which hasn't been lived in since before the war. From the moment he arrives mysterious things start to happen around him.
BBFC:PG — F — EN
Golan Globus Prods — *Guild Home Video*
H, P, E

House of Shadows   Fil-Ent '83
Horror
08881   90 mins   C
V2, B, V

John Gavin, Yvonne De Carlo, Leonor Manso, Robert Airaldi, German Krauss

This tells the story of a woman who witnesses a murder, after hearing a voice pleading for mercy. When the Police arrive the body has disappeared. The murder took place twenty-three years ago.
BBFC:X — A — EN
Darwin Productions — *Video Programme Distributors*   P
Media 176

House of the Living Dead   Fil-Ent '7?
Horror
06798   85 mins   C
V2, B, V

Mark Burns, Shirley Anne Field, David Oxley

Evil feeds and kills in the attic of the House of the Living Dead, where insanity clutches a family on a South African estate.
S,A — EN
Philip N Krasne — *Intervision Video*   H, P
A-AE 0319

House of the Lost Girls   Fil-Ent '??
Crime-Drama
06869   90 mins   C
V2, B, V

Sylvia Solar, Sandra Jullien, Oliver Mathot

In a luxurious villa in a remote area girls are taken against their will to work as prostitutes. A young girl escapes with the aid of a customer and goes directly to the police to relate her story. An inspector issues instructions to help the girl. The hunt that follows leads to important clues found in Rome.
S,A — EN
Unknown — *European Video Company*
P

House of the Seven Corpses, The   Fil-Ent '73
Horror
02408   89 mins   C
B, V

John Ireland, Faith Domergue, John Carradine

A deserted Victorian mansion is being used as a set by a motion picture company. The house has a gory history of violent deaths and there is evidence of witchcraft and black magic having been practiced there. Strange happenings start to occur and disaster hovers over the film-makers.
C,A — EN
Intl Amusements — *Derann Film Services*
H, P
DV 110B/DV 110

House of Wax   Fil-Ent '53
Mystery/Horror
06042   85 mins   C
B, V

PALADIN VIDEO HOME ENTERTAINMENT GUIDE

Vincent Price, Frank Lovejoy, Phyllis Kirk, Paul Picerni, Paul Cavanagh, Charles Bronson, Carolyn Jones
As a result of a museum fire, a handsome young man turns into a human monster. With his work destroyed he steals bodies from a morgue to re-create life like images in wax. His evil ways are exposed when the models are recognised as people who had mysteriously disappeared.
BBFC:X — A — EN
Warner Bros; Bryan Foy — Warner Home Video   P
WEX1054/WEV1054

House of Whipcord   Fil-Ent '77
Suspense/Horror
09911   100 mins   C
V2, B, V
Barbara Markham, Patrick Barr, Ray Brooks, Ann Michelle
A model accepts an invitation from a new boyfriend to visit his parents. She is somewhat surprised on arrival by the two sinister uniformed women who greet her. She realizes that she is in prison, a private institution where she is to be used for modelling in the nude. Having learnt from another inmate of the nightmarish tortures, she vows to escape, although no one yet has succeeded.
BBFC:18 — A — EN
Unknown — Derann Film Services   P
FDV 320

House on Garibaldi Street, The   Fil-Ent '79
Suspense/Drama
09173   98 mins   C
B, V
Topol, Nick Mancuso, Janet Suzman, Martin Balsam, Leo McKern, Alfred Burke, Charles Gray, directed by Peter Collinson
This film is based on the actual events that occurred during the capture of the Nazi War criminal, Adolf Eichmann. It is heard that he is hiding in Argentina. Israeli agents locate him and plan to smuggle him out of the country, to stand trial in Israel for the crimes committed against humanity. They must smuggle him past police and customs, to claim their 15 years of vengeance.
S,A — EN
Charles Fries — Video Form Pictures   H, P
MGS 13

House Plants with Percy Thrower   How-Ins '8?
Plants/Flowers
08607   59 mins   C
V2, B, V
Perry Thrower

In a year, millions of house plants are sold, many of them considered expendable. In this tape it is shown how, with the correct attention, plants can last and be enjoyed for many years. It is shown that light, temperature and correct watering and feeding are all important in keeping them healthy.
S,A — I
Midland Video Services Ltd — Hokushin Audio Visual Ltd   P
G 107

House That Bled to Death, The/Growing Pains   Fil-Ent '??
Horror
08758   202 mins   C
V2, B, V
Nicholas Ball, Rachel Davies, Brian Croucher, Pat Maynard; Barbara Kellerman, Gary Bond, Norman Beaton, Mathew Blackstad
Two 'Hammer House of Horror' films are contained on one cassette. In 'The House That Bled to Death' (10 mins.) the scene is an old house, in a run-down state, unoccupied since it was the setting for a macabre murder. For the new occupants it becomes a house of horror. In 'Growing Pains' an attempt is made to recover from the tragic death of their son, by adopting a young boy. He seems almost unnervingly self-possessed and icily correct with his new parents.
S,A — EN
Hammer Films — Precision Video Ltd   P
CRITC 2121/BITC 2121/VITC 2121

House That Dripped Blood, The   Fil-Ent '70
Horror
12688   97 mins   C
B, V
Christopher Lee, Peter Cushing, Ngree Dawn Porter, Denholm Elliott, Ingrid Pitt, directed by Peter Duffell
Vampires, vixens, voodoo and victims abound in this tale about a strange house with its wierd inhabitants.
BBFC:18 — C,A — EN
Cinerama; Amicus Productions — Brent Walker Home Video Ltd   P
BW 27

House That Wouldn't Die, The   Fil-Ent '70
Horror
02561   90 mins   C
B, V
Barbara Stanwyck, Richard Egan, Michael Anderson Jr, Kitty Winn

(For Explanation of codes, see USE GUIDE and KEY)

PALADIN VIDEO HOME ENTERTAINMENT GUIDE

A tale of witchcraft, black magic, and unpleasant ghosts in an inherited house in the Pennsylvania Amish country.
BBFC:X — A — EN
Aaron Spelling Prods — *Guild Home Video*
H, P

Householder, The   Fll-Ent '63
Romance/Comedy
05749   90 mins   B/W
B, V
Shashi Kapoor, Leela Naidu, Durga Khote, directed by James Ivory
A story told in domestic and affectionate terms of a shy, young underpaid Delhi schoolteacher who marries and then, little by little, gets to know his young wife during their first year together. A story derived from the culture of modern, middle class India but able to transcend national boundaries and relate to problems of young couples everywhere.
BBFC:U — F — EN
Merchant Ivory Production — *Home Video Holdings*   **H, P**
013

Houseplants and Patio   Gen-Edu '8?
Gardening
Gardening/Flowers
08545   55 mins   C
B, V
Presented by Arthur Billitt
Arthur Billitt demonstrates, from his home, Clack's Farm, how to obtain healthy houseplants. He looks at potting, watering, feeding and then growing plants from seeds or cuttings. He then looks at the patio and shows the wide range of plants that may be grown there, from herbs to fruits.
F — I
Thorn EMI Video Programmes Ltd — *THORN EMI*   **P**
TXE 90 07484/TVE 90 07482

Hoverbug   Chl-Juv '8?
Adventure/Comedy
13453   57 mins   C
B, V
A group of youths are involved in racing their home-made 'Hoverbug' machines and two of them enlist an inventor's aid but his patent adhesive has its short-comings too.
BBFC:U — I,S — EN
Unknown — *Rank Video Library*   **H, P**
3107X

How Do I Love Thee   Fll-Ent '70
Comedy
05187   87 mins   C
B, V
Jackie Gleason, Maureen O'Hara, Shelley Winters, Rosemary Forsyth
This rollicking send-up of American religion stars genial Jackie Gleason as the much afflicted atheist father of a college professor.
BBFC:AA — C,A — EN
ABC Pictures Corp; Cinerama Release — *Rank Video Library*   **H, P**
1010

How Sleep The Brave   Fll-Ent '??
War-Drama
07684   90 mins   C
B, V
Lawrence Day, Luis Manuel, Thomas Pollard
An American Captain of a remote Vietnam base sends one of his 'killer units', lead by a ruthless Lieutenant, to destroy an arms cache in a village. After heavy losses they return having found no arms; the Captain sends them back. Surrounded by Viet Cong the platoon fight every inch of the way. They achieve their objective but outnumbered they are forced to fight to the death.
A — EN
Unknown — *Video Network*   **P**
0019

How to Beat Home Video   How-Ins '82
Games-Volume 1
Video/Games
09870   60 mins   C
B, V
Narrated by Philip M. Wiswell
This is the first part in a series of three, guiding the player through games such as Space Invaders, Asteroids, Chopper Command, Frogger and many more.
F — I
Vestron Video — *Polygram Video*   **H, P**
791 5554/791 5552

How to Beat Home Video   How-Ins '82
Games-Volume 2
Video/Games
09871   60 mins   C
B, V
Narrated by Philip M. Wiswell
This is the second part in a series of three featuring twenty of the top video games, includes ET, Raiders of the Lost Ark, Megamania, Demons to Diamonds and many others.
F — I
Vestron Video — *Polygram Video*   **H, P**
791 5564/791 5562

How to Beat Home Video   How-Ins '82
Games-Volume 3
Video/Games

PALADIN VIDEO HOME ENTERTAINMENT GUIDE

09872   60 mins   C
B, V
Narrated by Philip M. Wiswell
This is the third part in a series of three and previews the games systems; The Atari 5200, Colecovision and Vectrex. It includes 20 of the most challenging games for these units including Cosmic Chasm, Donkey Kong, Zaxxon and Galaxian.
F — I
Vestron Video — *Polygram Video*   **H, P**
791 5574/791 5572

How to Beat the High Cost of Living   Fil-Ent '80
Comedy
12738   106 mins   C
B, V
Susan Saint James, Jan Curtis, Jessica Lange, Richard Benjamin, directed by Robert Scheerer
Three girls plan to solve their money problems once and for all by stealing thousands of dollars from the local shopping arcade, but things go badly wrong and one girl finds herself diverting attention by doing a strip while the other two take a swim in the river.
BBFC:15 — C,A — EN
Jerome M Zeitman; Robert Kaufman — *Rank Video Library*   **H, P**
1073 Y

How to Boardsail   How-Ins '82
Sports-Water
07436   50 mins   C
B, V
Dee Caldwell, directed by Doug Smith
This programme is designed in twelve self-contained lessons ideal for beginners and experts who can select the section that corresponds to their own standard. Dee Caldwell, overall European Champion, provides the expert advice and is able to demonstrate even the most complicated manoeuvres in a simple and straightforward way.
1.Before Setting Off 2.Starting Position 3.Sailing Position 4.Steering 5.Tacking and Gybing 6.Beating and Running 7.Mistakes All Beginners Make 8.Rigging our Sailboard 9.Safety Precautions 10.Racing 11.Freestyle 12.Jumping
S,A — ED
Infovision/SLR Production — *THORN EMI*
P
TXE 90 0746 4/TVE 90 0746 2

How to Kill 400 Duponts   Fil-Ent '??
Comedy-Drama
06099   98 mins   C
V2, B, V
Terry Thomas, Johnny Dorelli, Margaret Lee
An elusive character, master of a thousand disguises, a womanizer and a skilful thief, keeps an Inspector guessing with fiendish cunning as he sets out on his latest task to kill 400 people.
S,A — EN
Unknown — *Video Programme Distributors*
P
Cinehollywood—V1580

How to Marry a Millionaire   Fil-Ent '53
Comedy
07710   93 mins   C
V2, B, V
Lauren Bacall, Marilyn Monroe, Betty Grable, William Powell, David Wayne, Rory Calhoun, Cameron Mitchell, directed by Jean Negulesco
This is the story of three models who pool all their money to rent a lavish apartment in an attempt to trap millionaire husbands.
S,A — EN
Twentieth Century Fox — *CBS/Fox Video*
P
1023

How to Pass Your Driving Test with the British School of Motoring   How-Ins '81
Driver instruction
05498   60 mins   C
B, V
The British School of Motoring shows in six parts the standard expected by the Department of Transport to achieve a pass in the driving test.
A — I
Unknown — *THORN EMI*   **P**
TXE 90 0503 4/TVE 90 0503 2

How to Solve the Cube   Spo-Lei '81
Games
06816   ? mins   C
V2, B, V
This programme explains how to solve the Rubik's cube, in easy to follow steps.
F — EN
Alpha Video — *Intervision Video*   **H, P**
A-A 0385

How to Use Your Computer, Starting to Program the Electron—No 1   Bus-Ind '84
Electronic data processing
13110   60 mins   C
B, V
David Redclift

(For Explanation of codes, see USE GUIDE and KEY)

329

PALADIN VIDEO HOME ENTERTAINMENT GUIDE

This is an introduction to computer programming the Electron micro computer in basic, to help you write your own programs and contains programs to transfer to your computer.
C,A — I
Holiday Brothers Ltd — *Holiday Brothers Ltd*
P

How to Use Your   Bus-Ind '84
Computer, Starting Basic
with the BBC Micro
Computer, No 1
Electronic data processing
13112   60 mins   C
B, V
David Redclift
This is an introduction to the skill of computer programming to help you understand the principles of Basic and write your own programmes.
C,A — I
Holiday Brothers Ltd. — *Holiday Brothers Ltd*
P

How to Use Your   Bus-Ind '84
Computer, Further Basic
with the BBC Micro
Computer, No 2
Electronic data processing
13111   60 mins   C
B, V
David Redclift
In the second part of this series, the skills of computer programming using basic are continued.
C,A — I
Holiday Brothers Ltd — *Holiday Brothers Ltd*
P

Howling, The   Fil-Ent '81
Horror
08336   90 mins   C
V2, B, V, LV
Dee Wallace, Patrick Macnee, Denis Dugan, Christopher Stone, BelindaBalaski, Kevin McCarthy, John Carradine, Slim Pickens
This film tells the story of a pretty television reporter who takes a rest at a clinic inhabited by loonies, and located near woods inhabited by werewolves.
C,A — EN
Michael Finell; Jack Conrad — *Embassy Home Entertainment*   P
1615

Howzer   Fil-Ent '72
Drama
13140   80 mins   C
B, V

Peter Desiante, Melissa Stocking, Royal Dano, directed by Ken Laurence
Two teenage boys escape from their Midwest home and their parent's constant bickering to Los Angeles but what they find there dispells their youthful dreams forever.
BBFC:PG — S,A — EN
Unknown — *Polygram Video*   P
041 0274/041 0272

Huckleberry Finn   Fil-Ent '75
Adventure
05250   72 mins   C
B, V
Ron Howard, Sarah Selby, William L Erwin, Frederic Downs
Mark Twain's immortal classic of American literature comes to the screen in a fine production that tells the story of Huck's adventures with Jim the runaway slave as they journey by raft down the treacherous Mississippi River. Country and Western star Roy Clark sings the theme song 'Said the River, I'm Your Friend.'
BBFC:U — F — EN
Unknown — *Rank Video Library*   H, P
3003

Hue and Cry   Fil-Ent '46
Mystery
01604   78 mins   B/W
B, V
Alastair Sim, Jack Warner, Valerie White, directed by Charles Crichton
Boys play hide and seek with criminals in order to help a shy mystery writer.
BBFC:U — S,A — EN
Ealing Studios, Michael Balcon — *THORN EMI*
P
TXE 90 0204 4/TVE 90 0204 2

Hugo the Hippo   Fil-Ent '76
Cartoons
07617   76 mins   C
V2, B, V
Animated, narrated by Burl Ives, voices of Robert Morley, Paul Lynde, Marie Osmond, Jimmy Osmond
The home of the Hippos, Zanzibar, was an idyllic tropical island until the sharks arrived. This is the story of how a family of hippos clear the harbour of sharks and how the lovable Hugo becomes the hero.
BBFC:U — F — EN
20th Century Fox — *Iver Film Services*   P

Hullabaloo Over Georgie   Fil-Ent '78
and Bonnie's Pictures
Drama/Comedy
05680   82 mins   C

(For Explanation of codes, see USE GUIDE and KEY)

PALADIN VIDEO HOME ENTERTAINMENT GUIDE

B, V
Dame Peggy Ashcroft, Saeed Jaffrey, Larry Pine, Victor Banerjee, James Booker, Aparna Sen, directed by James Ivory
A private collector from America and a museum buyer from London engage in a battle of wits in their efforts to secure a unique and precious Indian art collection.
BBFC:A — S,A — EN
Merchant Ivory Production — *Home Video Holdings*   **H, P**
018

Human Duplicators, The   Fil-Ent '65
Science fiction
08639   80 mins   C
V2, B, V
George Nader, Barbara Nichols, George Macready, Dolores Faith
Doctor Kolos arrives on Earth, sent by the masters of the galaxy, to meet a professor. His mission is to help create an android society. A security officer suspects the activities going on in the professor's cellars. However, he is captured, imprisoned and duplicated, with dramatic consequences.
S,A — EN
Allied Artists — *Hokushin Audio Visual Ltd*   **P**
VM 47

Human Factor, The   Fil-Ent '79
Suspense
04248   115 mins   C
B, V
Richard Attenborough, Robert Morley, Nicol Williamson, Sir Jonh Gielgud, Derek Jacobi
Otto Preminger directed and Tom Stoppard wrote the screenplay for this film version of a Graham Greene novel. When a minor leak in a small sub-section of the secret service brings Colonel Daintry to unearth the culprit, pressure is brought to bear on Castle, who has compromised his loyalty for the freedom of his beautiful African wife.
BBFC:AA — C,A — EN
Bryanston — *Rank Video Library*   **H, P**
0029

Human Factor, The   Fil-Ent '75
Drama
04193   91 mins   C
B, V
George Kennedy, John Mills, Rita Tushingham, Raf Vallone
The family of a computer expert is wiped out in Italy. He vows revenge and sets about to hunt down the killers with the aid of his computer.
BBFC:X — A — EN
Bryanston Dist — *Guild Home Video*   **H, P**

Human League-Video Single, The   Fil-Ent '8?
Music-Performance
10132   ? mins   C
B, V
This tape features three hit tracks from the Human League-'Mirror Man', 'Love Action', 'Don't You Want Me'.
S,A — EN
Unknown — *Palace Video Ltd*   **P**
VIRV SINI

Human Vapour, The   Fil-Ent '60
Science fiction
02442   78 mins   C
V2, B, V
Scientists create a weird half-human half-beast creature, and it falls in love with a woman.
BBFC:A — S,A — EN
Brenco; Japanese — *Iver Film Services*   **P**

Humongous   Fil-Ent '81
Suspense
12161   93 mins   C
V2, B, V
David Wallace, John Wildman, Janet Baldwin, Janet Julian
A group of teenagers run aground on a lonely island inhabited by a recluse and a pack of vicious dogs.
BBFC:18 — C,A — EN
Embassy Pictures — *Embassy Home Entertainment*   **P**
1613

Hunchback of Notre Dame, The   Fil-Ent '39
Drama
04639   117 mins   B/W
B, V
Charles Laughton, Maureen O'Hara, Edmond O'Brien
The second film version of Victor Hugo's classic tale of the tortured hunchbacked bellringer of Notre Dame.
F — EN
RKO — *THORN EMI*   **H, P**
TXC 90 0060 4/TVC 90 0060 2

Hunchback of Notre Dame, The   Fil-Ent '23
Drama
04671   93 mins   B/W
B, V
Lon Chaney, Norman Kerry, Patsy Ruth Miller, Raymond Hatton, Ernest Torrence, Brandon Hurst

(For Explanation of codes, see USE GUIDE and KEY)

PALADIN VIDEO HOME ENTERTAINMENT GUIDE

The first film version of Victor Hugo's novel about the tortured hunchback bellringer of Notre Dame. Silent; colour-tinted.
F — EN
Universal — *Polygram Video* **P**

Hundra
Fll-Ent '83
Adventure/Fantasy
12897   95 mins   C
B, V
Laurene Landon, directed by Matt Cimber
When a member of a fierce tribe of warrior women finds her family and fellow tribeswomen slain by male barbarians she takes on a vow of revenge.
BBFC:18 — A — EN
Unknown — *THORN EMI* **P**
TXA 90 25644/TVA 90 25642

Hunger, The
Fll-Ent '83
Drama/Horror
10148   96 mins   C
B, V
David Bowie, Catherine Deneuve, Susan Sarandon, directed by Tony Scott
Two eternally young vampires in human form live in New York. They have to feed regularly from human blood to keep their youth. One of them suddenly ages and the other one has to go and find a cure and discovers a young doctor researching into the ageing process.
BBFC:PG — S,A — EN
MGM/UA — *MGM/UA Home Video* **P**
UMB 10281/UMV 10281

Hunted, The
Fll-Ent '??
Drama/Western
12779   90 mins   C
V2, B, V
A young man is harshly imprisoned by a sheriff for a minor offence. He manages to escape and meets a girl and they live a peaceful existence for a while. It is soon to end as the sheriff's posse closes in.
A — EN
Ascot Video — *Intervision Video* **H, P**
A-A0492

Hunter, The
Fll-Ent '80
Crime-Drama
05326   97 mins   C
B, V
Steve McQueen, Eli Wallach, Kathryn Harrold, LeVar Burton, Ben Johnson, directed by Buzz Kulik
This film is the true story of Ralph 'Papa' Thorson, a modern day bounty hunter. His exploits are detailed as he pursues a number of fugitives who have skipped bail. It is a sad tale of a man born in the wrong age as the chase comes full circle when he becomes the quarry of a vengeful psychopath.
S,A — EN
Paramount — *CIC Video* **H, P**
BEA2017/VHA2017

Hunters of the Golden Cobra
Fll-Ent '8?
Adventure
08958   97 mins   C
V2, B, V
Set during 1945, six months before the end of the war, this film tells of two American Rangers who carry out a daring raid on the command post of General Yamato. However, their plan to capture the priceless Golden Cobra fails and the General escapes with it; his plane is then shot down and lost in the jungle. The adventures to find this lost treasure follow.
S,A — EN
Unknown — *Walton Film and Video Ltd*
P

Hurray for Betty Boop
Fll-Ent '3?
Cartoons
09038   80 mins   C
V2, B, V
Animated
This animated feature follows the sad, happy, clever and amusing adventures of Betty Boop in original cartoons from the 1930's.
F — EN
Fleischer Studios — *Radial Choice Distributors Ltd* **H, P**
PIC 20

Hurricane
Fll-Ent '74
Drama/Suspense
08019   72 mins   C
V2, B, V
Larry Hagman, Martin Milner, Michael Learned, Frank Sutton, Will Gear, directed by Jerry Jameson
A small Gulf Coast town is the scene of a devastating hurricane which sweeps through, destroying everything in its path. It is based on the book 'Hurricane Hunters' by William C. Anderson.
BBFC:U — F — EN
Montagne Productions; M P C — *Iver Film Services* **P**
190

Hurricane Express
Fll-Ent '32
Adventure/Mystery
06327   77 mins   B/W
B, V

PALADIN VIDEO HOME ENTERTAINMENT GUIDE

John Wayne, Shirley Grey, Tully Marshal, Conway Tearle, directed by Armand Schaefer and J.T. McGowan

After his father is killed in a mysterious train crash, a young transport pilot sets out to catch 'The Wrecker,' a fiend who is able to assume the identity of anyone he chooses.

F — EN

Mascot — VCL Video Services   P

0232G

Hustle   Fil-Ent '75
Crime-Drama
13636   116 mins   C
B, V

Burt Reynolds, Catherine Deneuve, directed by Robert Aldrich

Caught in the web of the underground world of Los Angeles an old-fashioned detective tries hard to reconcile his moral values with the ugliness of his job.

BBFC:18 — A — EN

Robert Aldrich — CIC Video   H, P

2130

The Hustler   Fil-Ent '61
Drama
05645   130 mins   B/W
V2, B, V

Paul Newman, Piper Laurie, George C. Scott, Jackie Gleason, Myron McCormick, directed by Robert Rossen

A professional pool player becomes involved with a gambler who indirectly causes his girl to commit suicide. He puts his reputation at risk by challenging but beating the pool champion, thus regaining his self respect. Based on the novel by Walter Tevis.

Academy Awards '61: Best Achievement in Art Direction; Best Cinematography.   S,A — EN

Twentieth Century Fox — CBS/Fox Video   P

4A-130

Hysteria   Fil-Ent '64
Drama/Mystery
07722   72 mins   B/W
B, V

Robert Webber, Lelia Goldoni, Anthony Newlands, Jennifer Jayne, Maurice Denham, Peter Woodhorpe, directed by Freddie Francis

An American in Europe is involved in a car accident, as a result of which he loses his memory. He is informed by the doctor that an unknown benefactor has paid his bills and left a luxury flat at his disposal. The American hires a private detective to discover who the benefactor is in an attempt to regain his memory. A series of mysterious events occur; the American wonders whether he is having hallucinations, losing his mind or the victim of a vicious plot.

BBFC:X — A — EN

MGM; Hammer Films — MGM/UA Home Video   P

UMB 10126/UMV 10126

Hysterical   Fil-Ent '83
Comedy-Drama
09898   86 mins   C
B, V

Richard Kiel, Bud Cort, Julie Newmar, Bill Hudson, Mark Hudson, Brett Hudson

Ghouls, zombies and ghosts invade the tiny seaside town of Hellview, Oregon. A pair of 'detectives' devise a wild scheme to get rid of them in this bizarre spoof on famous films.

BBFC:15 — C,A — EN

Cinema Works — Entertainment in Video   H, P

EVB 1010/EVV 1010

I

I Am a Camera   Fil-Ent '55
Drama
01949   95 mins   B/W
B, V

Laurence Harvey, Julie Harris, Shelley Winters

A film based on Christopher Isherwood's memoirs of life in Berlin, immediately prior to WW II. The political climate of Germany coinciding with Hitler's rise to power is conveyed in the film. The musical 'Cabaret' was later adapted from the same story.

F — EN

DCA — CBS/Fox Video   P

3B-062

I Am a Dancer   Fil-Ent '72
Dance/Biographical
01612   90 mins   C
B, V

Rudolph Nureyev, Margot Fonteyn, Carla Fracci, Lynn Seymour, Deanne Bergsma, directed by Pierre Jourdan

As a pupil, Nureyev attends ballet class; then he shows the dedication and sweat needed to bring the purest of the performing arts up to

PALADIN VIDEO HOME ENTERTAINMENT GUIDE

pitch. It then becomes a record of performances which include 'Field Figures,' 'Marguerite and Armand,' 'La Sylphide,' and the pas de deux from 'The Sleeping Beauty.'
BBFC:U — F — EN
Evdoros Demetriou — *THORN EMI* **P**
TXB 90 0088 4/TVB 90 0088 2

I Drink Your Blood   Fil-Ent '71
Horror
08879   82 mins   C
V2, B, V
Horace Bones, Sue Lin, directed by David Durston
A Satanic cult sets up a camp near a small town. The men are acting like mad dogs and have to be stopped.
BBFC:18 — A — EN
Cinemation — *Video Programme Distributors* **P**
Media 186

I Heard the Owl Call My   Fil-Ent '7?
Name
Drama
13777   75 mins   C
B, V
Tom Courtenay
A young priest is sent to a remote mission in British Columbia and decides to stay with the proud Indian tribe who have become his friends when he discovers he is dying.
F — EN
Unknown — *Odyssey Video*   **H, P**
6250

I, Monster   Fil-Ent '71
Horror
08555   74 mins   C
B, V
Christopher Lee, Peter Cushing, Mike Raven, directed by Stephen Weeks
This Spine-Chilling story is set in the year 1906 and tells of a Victorian doctor who is transformed by his own drug. It has startling effects, turning him to a sadistic brute. Each time he takes the drug it has worse effects and eventually turns him into a crazed fugitive.
BBFC:X — A — EN
Amicus Productions Ltd — *THORN EMI* **P**
TXC 90 0761 4/TVC 90 0761 2

I Never Promised You a   Fil-Ent '77
Rose Garden
Drama
12497   90 mins   C
B, V
Bibi Andersson, Kathleen Quinlan, Sylvia Sidney, Martine Bartlett, directed by Anthony Page
A teenage girl attempts to kill herself and is committed to a psychiatric hospital where a sympathetic doctor tries to bring her back to sanity.
BBFC:18 — A — EN
Edgar J Scherick; Terence F Deane — *Warner Home Video* **P**
74033

I Ought to Be in Pictures   Fil-Ent '82
Comedy
12003   104 mins   C
B, V
Walter Matthau, Ann-Margret, Dinah Manoff, directed by Herbert Ross
An ex-Hollywood writer, divorced from his wife, receives an unexpected visit from his teenage daughter. With the help of his level-headed girlfriend, he sets about rebuilding their relationship.
BBFC:15 — S,A — EN
20th Century Fox — *CBS/Fox Video* **P**
1150

I, The Jury   Fil-Ent '82
Crime-Drama
13029   107 mins   C
B, V
Armand Assante, Barbara Carrera
A private detective pursues his own highly individual code of ethics, so when his best friend is brutally murdered he determines to avenge the killing. Taken from a novel by Mickey Spillane.
BBFC:X — A — EN
20th Century Fox — *Warner Home Video* **P**
61294

I Walk the Line   Fil-Ent '70
Drama/Adventure
09278   95 mins   C
B, V
Gregory Peck, Tuesday Weld, Estelle Parsons, Ralph Meeker, directed by John Frankenheimer
A local sheriff who is obsessed with the beautiful daughter of a small town hoodlum turns a blind eye to her family's illicit activites. When the Federal Inspector visits town it leads to violence, death and ultimate tragedy. Soundtrack includes music by Johnny Cash.
S,A — EN
Columbia — *RCA/Columbia Pictures Video UK*
H, P

334   (For Explanation of codes, see USE GUIDE and KEY)

PALADIN VIDEO HOME ENTERTAINMENT GUIDE

I Will Fight No More Forever
Fil-Ent '75
Drama
04194   105 mins   C
B, V
James Whitmore, Sam Elliott, Ned Romero
The epic story of the legendary Chief Joseph, who led the Nez Perce tribe on an historic 1,600-mile trek in 1877, across the Northwest to Canada in flight from the American Army, is recounted. The Nez Perce were the last American Indians to fight government attempts to force them onto a reservation.
BBFC:AA — C,A — EN
Heritage Enterprises — *Guild Home Video*   H, P

I Wonder Who's Killing Her Now
Fil-Ent '7?
Comedy/Satire
05605   95 mins   C
B, V
This film with a host of characters is a sophisticated satire on affluent life, movies, marriage, murder tales, fat farms, psychiatrists, CIA, insurance companies, attorneys, doctors, funerals, the Mafia, musicians, Bogart, ethnic groups et al. Written by Mickey Rose.
S,A — EN
Dennis Stevens; Cinerama Arts — *Home Video Merchandisers*   H, P
002

Ian Hunter—'Ian Hunter Rocks'
Fil-Ent '82
Music-Performance
06834   60 mins   C
B, V
Ian Hunter
This film features Ian Hunter in concert recorded in New York in 1981. Songs include 'All The Young Dudes,' 'Roll Away the Stone' and 'Just Another Night.'
S,A — EN
Chrysalis Visual Programming — *Chrysalis Video*   P
CVIM BE 7/CVIM VH 7

Ibtisama Wahibda Takfi (One Smile Is Enough)
Fil-Ent '??
Drama/Romance
06735   90 mins   C
V2, B, V
A love story about two young people who want to get married, but must first endure a long period of separation while the man finishes his studies abroad.
C,A — EN   AB
Unknown — *Intervision Video*   H, P
A-C 0152

Ice Cold in Alex
Fil-Ent '60
War-Drama
05040   125 mins   B/W
B, V
John Mills, Sylvia Sims, Anthony Quayle, directed by J Lee-Thompson
A British ambulance commander, crossing the mined desert from Tobruk to Egypt, befriends a German spy who is in his care.
Berlin Festival Award.   F — EN
20th Century Fox; W A Whitaker — *THORN EMI*   P
TXE 90 0259 4/TVE 90 0259 2

Ice Station Zebra
Fil-Ent '68
Drama/Adventure
08678   137 mins   C
B, V
Rock Hudson, Ernest Borgnine, Patrick McGoohan, Jim Brown, Tony Bill, Lloyd Nolan, directed by John Sturges
An atomic-powered U.S. submarine carrying Marine riflemen is sent to retrieve a space capsule that has crashed at the North Pole. Also heading for the same destination is the Russian long-distance jet bomber squadron carrying their crack paratroopers. In this race against time the U.S. commander and crew face the relentless elements, icy seas, glaciers, lichen covered tundra and the ocean's frozen depths. Based on the novel by Alistair Maclean.
BBFC:U — M,A — EN
MGM; Filmways — *MGM/UA Home Video*   P
UMB 10160/UMV 10160

Iceman
Fil-Ent '84
Drama
13624   97 mins   C
B, V
Timothy Hutton, Lindsay Grouse, John Lone, directed by Fred Schepisi
A man is discovered encased in a block of ice, preserved and alive after 40,000 years and is slowly brought into our time.
BBFC:PG — S,A — EN
Universal — *CIC Video*   H, P
1131

Idaho Transfer
Fil-Ent '73
Science fiction
06908   90 mins   C
V2, B, V
Kelly Bohanan, Keith Carradine, Kevin Hearst, directed by Peter Fonda
With the approach of the Third World War a scientist has set up a laboratory in the middle of the Idaho desert. The Government believes he is experimenting with the transference of objects. However, he has been transferring scientists, ecologists and biologists, all under

PALADIN VIDEO HOME ENTERTAINMENT GUIDE

20, 50 years into the future. The bomb has been dropped and the teenagers are the new civilisation. A girl has not 'transferred' well and she is deranged; something goes very wrong.
S,A — EN
Unknown — *Fourmatt Video Ltd*   **P**

Ideal Husband, An   Fil-Ent '39
Drama
09837   91 mins   B/W
B, V
Paulette Goddard, Michael Wilding, Hugh Williams, C. Aubrey Smith, Glynis Johns
This is the film based on the play by Oscar Wilde.
S,A — EN
British Lion; London Films — *Polygram Video*   **H, P**
790 2444/790 2442

Idolmaker, The   Fil-Ent '80
Musical-Drama
12992   115 mins   C
B, V
Ray Sharkey, Paul Land, Peter Gallagher, Tovak Feldshuh, directed by Taylor Hackford
Set in the early 1960's a singer and songwriter turns his talents to creating a pop idol. This film is based on a true-life story and includes a soundtrack of original songs.
BBFC:PG — S,A — EN
United Artists — *Warner Home Video*   **P**
99371

Idomeno   Fin-Art '83
Opera
12891   180 mins   C
B, V
Philip Langridge, Jerry Hadley, Yvonne Kenny, Carol Vaness
Mozart's grand opera based on the story of the legendary King of Crete is performed here in Italian by the Glydebourne Festival Opera. The conductor is Bernard Haitink.
F — EN
RM Arts — *THORN EMI*   **P**
TXH 90 26944/TVH 90 26942

If You Can Dance You Can Do It!   Spo-Lei '82
Physical fitness
12768   60 mins   C
B, V
A programme of disco-dance exercises to pave the way to fitness with Una Stubbs.
F — EN
Unknown — *VideoSpace Ltd*   **P**

If You Don't Stop It... You'll Go Blind   Fil-Ent '74
Comedy
08887   80 mins   C
V2, B, V
George Spencer, Pat Wright, Jane Kellem, Keefe Brasselle
A sex farce containing many comic sketches.
BBFC:X — A — EN
Dauntless Productions — *Video Programme Distributors*   **P**
Media 144

If You're Not Winning, You're Not Trying 1973   Spo-Lei '73
Automobiles-Racing
04506   60 mins   C
B, V
The John Player Team Lotus heads for their fourth World Constructors' Championship in six years. The hard work, tension, concentration and humour behind each Grand Prix is focussed upon.
F — EN
John Player — *Quadrant Video*   **H, P**
M12

I'll Be Seeing You   Fil-Ent '45
Drama
04177   85 mins   B/W
B, V
Ginger Rogers, Joseph Cotten, Shirley Temple
Two lost souls, a girl out of prison and an emotionally upset soldier, find a new lease on life during a ten-day romantic interlude.
BBFC:A — S,A — EN
Selznick — *Guild Home Video*   **H, P**

I'll Die For Vengeance   Fil-Ent '7?
Western
07789   89 mins   C
V2, B, V
Kirk Morris, Larry Ward, Alan Steel
This is a bloodthirsty tale of vengeance after a Mexican gang leader murders the hero's friend.
S,A — EN
Unknown — *Fletcher Video*   **H, P**
AV 605

I'll Get You for This   Fil-Ent '51
Crime-Drama
01950   81 mins   B/W
B, V
George Raft, Colleen Gray

PALADIN VIDEO HOME ENTERTAINMENT GUIDE

London is the setting for this classic-action crime drama, starring George Raft at his meanest. An FBI man and a British Intelligence girl track down an international kidnapping ring.
F — EN
Lippert Prods — CBS/Fox Video **P**
3B-063

I'm All Right Jack   Fil-Ent '59
Comedy
04641   104 mins   B/W
B, V
Peter Sellers, Ian Carmichael, Terry-Thomas
A shop steward is caught between two sides in a crooked financial scam in this satire on labour-management relations.
F — EN
British Lion — THORN EMI   **H, P**
TXE 90 0042 4/TVE 90 0042 2

I'm Dancing As Fast As I Can   Fil-Ent '80
Drama
13322   101 mins   C
B, V
Jill Clayburgh, Nicol Williamson, Geraldine Page, Dianne Wiest, directed by Jack Hofsiss
A successful television documentary career woman decides to give up her dependence on pills and has to re-examine her values of life in a struggle for survival.
C,A — EN
Paramount — CIC Video   **H, P**
BET 2107/VHT 2107

I'm For the Hippopotamus   Fil-Ent '??
Comedy
13720   104 mins   C
V2, B, V
Terence Hill, Bud Spencer, Joe Bugner, Dawn Jurgens, Bel Masinga
A band of people are set to make huge profits by selling hippos to collectors around the world but our two heroes are equally determined to keep them in Africa.
BBFC:PG — F — EN
Denver/Zadar Film Production — Medusa Communications Ltd   **H, P**
MC 042

I'm Going To Be Famous   Fil-Ent '7?
Drama
09018   103 mins   C
V2, B, V
Dick Sargent

This film portrays the means by which Hollywood's desperate would-be stars fight their way to success. This story is set against a backdrop of blackmail, murder, sex and drugs which unfurls as they plot and scheme for roles in a new play.
C,A — EN
Excel — Intervision Video   **H, P**
AA 0457

Image of Bruce Lee   Fil-Ent '??
Martial arts
08901   80 mins   C
V2, B, V
Bruce Li
Martial arts fight scenes prevail in this story to uncover an international forgery network. Bruce has to use all his skills to defend himself and bring the villains to justice.
BBFC:X — A — EN
Unknown — Video Programme Distributors
P
Inter-Ocean 048

Images   Fil-Ent '72
Drama
08847   98 mins   C
B, V
Susannah York, Rene Auberjonais, Marcel Bozzuffi, directed by Robert Altman
This film is about an emotionally disturbed wife who, neglected by her husband, is confronted by the images of her former lovers.
Cannes Film Festival '72: Best Actress (Susannah York).   C,A — EN
Hemdale; Lions Gate — VCL Video Services
P
P210 D

Imagination in Concert   Fil-Ent '8?
Music-Performance
09361   72 mins   C
B, V, LV
This tape features the popular group Imagination in concert and includes their hits 'Body Talk', 'In and Out of Love', 'Flashback', 'Just an Illusion', 'Music and Lights', 'In the Heat of the Night' and 'Changes'.
F — EN
Unknown — Precision Video Ltd   **P**
BRBPV 2592/VRBPV 2592/LVRPV 520

Immoral Tales   Fil-Ent '74
Drama
07468   98 mins   C
B, V
Lise Danvers, Charlotte Alexandra, Paloma Picasso, Florence Bellamy, Fabrice Luchini, directed by Walerian Borowczyk

(For Explanation of codes, see USE GUIDE and KEY)

PALADIN VIDEO HOME ENTERTAINMENT GUIDE

This film consists of four stories, 'The Tide' set in this century, 'Therese the Philosopher,' 'Erzsebet Bathroy,' and 'Lucrezia Borgia' set in the past. Using a combination of mystery, comedy, and imagery in these bawdy tales, director Walerian Borowczyk provides an insight into human behaviour, life, love and womanhood.
BBFC:X — A — EN
Argos Films — *THORN EMI*   **P**
TXB 90 0690 4/TVB 90 06 90 2

Impulsion   Fil-Ent '72
Crime-Drama
06019   85 mins   C
B, V
Alejandro Rey, Katherine Justice
A behind the scenes drama that examines crimes of passion in the glittering world of the international jet set.
S,A — EN
Unknown — *VCL Video Services*   **P**

In Broad Daylight   Fil-Ent '71
Suspense
04178   73 mins   C
B, V
Richard Boone, Suzanne Pleshette, Stella Stevens, John Marley, Fred Beir
A blind actor, aware that his wife is having an affair, plans to kill her, believing that no one would suspect him.
BBFC:A — S,A — EN
Aaron Spelling — *Guild Home Video*   **H, P**

In God We Trust   Fil-Ent '80
Comedy
13310   97 mins   C
B, V
Marty Feldman, Wilfred Hyde-White, Andy Kaufman, Peter Boyle, Richard Pryor, directed by Marty Feldman
A monk attempts to save an order of trappist monks from financial ruin and in doing so meets all sorts of strange characters.
BBFC:15 — S,A — EN
Universal — *CIC Video*   **H, P**
BEN 1122/VHN 1122

In-Laws, The   Fil-Ent '79
Comedy
13206   100 mins   C
B, V
Peter Falk, Alan Arkin, directed by Arthur Hiller

In this comedy, problems arise when the son of a CIA agent decides to marry the daughter of his dentist.
BBFC:A — C,A — EN
Warner Bros — *Warner Home Video*   **P**
61009

In Love With an Older Woman   Fil-Ent '80
Comedy/Romance
12818   30 mins   C
B, V
John Ritter, Robert Mandan
A successful, handsome bachelor finds himself falling in love with a woman nearly a generation older than himself when she is hired by his company to work as his investigator.
BBFC:PG — S,A — EN
Images of Love — *VideoSpace Ltd*   **P**
VX 2

In Search of Dracula   Fil-Ent '75
Horror/Documentary
07904   83 mins   C
V2, B, V
Christopher Lee
This film follows the legend of Count Dracula with clips from the numerous films made. It reveals that the story was based on a real person, a Romanian prince who lived five centuries ago.
S,A — EN
Independent Intl Pictures — *Video Programme Distributors*   **P**
Replay—1002

In Search of Skiing   Spo-Lei '??
Sports-Winter
12014   90 mins   C
B, V
Warren Miller
A collection of the best of Warren Miller's films set in some of the world's most famous ski areas.
F — EN
Unknown — *CBS/Fox Video*   **P**
3703

In the Custody of Strangers   Fil-Ent '82
Crime-Drama
10218   95 mins   C
B, V
Jane Alexander, Martin Sheen, Emilio Estevez
A turbulent relationship with his father triggers the wild behaviour of a young lad as he tries to escape the emotional stress. After yet another argument he goes on a drinking spree and

PALADIN VIDEO HOME ENTERTAINMENT GUIDE

collides with a police car. His father insists that he is locked up for a night. When he becomes the victim of homosexual advances and retaliates he faces further charges for assault.
S,A — EN
Moonlight Prods; Filmways — *Video Form Pictures* **H, P**
MGS 30

In the Heat of the Night   Fil-Ent '67
Drama
13068   109 mins   C
B, V
Sidney Poitier, Rod Steiger, directed by Norman Jewison
A bigoted sheriff is reluctantly forced to accept the help of a black detective in solving a curious murder mystery.
Academy Awards '67: Best Picture; Best Actor (Steiger); Best Screenplay; Best Film Editing; Best Sound.   BBFC:A — C,A — EN
The Mirisch Corporation of Delaware — *Warner Home Video*   **P**
99239

In Which We Serve   Fil-Ent '42
War-Drama
08041   96 mins   B/W
B, V
Noel Coward, John Mills, Bernard Miles, Celia Johnson, directed by Noel Coward, David Lean
This film tells of the war experiences of the Royal Navy destroyer, HMS Torrin. The ship was dive—bombed in the Battle of Crete but survived to the end. The story and music were written by Noel Coward.
Academy Awards '42: Special Award? Outstanding Foreign Production.   F — EN
Rank — *Rank Video Library*   **H, P**
0110 B

In Your Greenhouse with   How-Ins '8?
Percy Thrower
Gardening/Flowers
08613   59 mins   C
V2, B, V
Percy Thrower
In this tape Percy Thrower assists the greenhouse owner with advice from choosing a greenhouse to the types of plants to put in it.
C,A — I
Midland Video Services Ltd — *Hokushin Audio Visual Ltd*   **P**
G 101

Inca Road 1970/Scene   Spo-Lei '72
72, Take 7
Automobiles-Racing
04538   46 mins   C
B, V
The story of the Los Caminos del Inca road race, an eight-day excursion in the high Andes of Peru. The second feature combines highlights from the 1972 seasons of drag racing, autotest, hill climb, autocross, circuit racing, rallypoint, and rallying.
F — EN
Castrol — *Quadrant Video*   **H, P**
M19

Incoming Freshmen   Fil-Ent '79
Comedy/Romance
08069   81 mins   C
B, V
Leslie Blalock, Debralee Scott
This film is about four freshmen, having just begun college. They find men the most interesting subject of all their courses.
BBFC:X — A — EN
Cannon; Hi-Test Film Prod — *Rank Video Library*   **H, P**
1042 C

Incredible Hulk, The   Fil-Ent '77
Adventure/Science fiction
08393   54 mins   C
V2, B, V
Animated
A scientist achieves superhuman strength after he is exposed to a massive dose of gamma rays. In three episodes, the 'Incredible Hulk' proves to be the most powerful creature on earth.
M,S — EN
Marvel Comics — *Guild Home Video*   **H, P, E**

Incredible Hulk-Cassette   Fil-Ent '77
2, The
Cartoons/Adventure
09433   60 mins   C
V2, B, V
Animated
In three episodes, each 20 minutes long, this tape follows the further adventures of Incredible Hulk. The origins of the Hulk are discovered as he battles to stop Captain Thorax and the fearful toadmen from destroying the Earth.
BBFC:U — F — EN
Marvel Comics — *Guild Home Video*   **H, P, E**

Incredible Hulk: Hulk vs   Fil-Ent '7?
The Metal Master, The
Cartoons/Adventure
12064   65 mins   C
V2, B, V
Animated

(For Explanation of codes, see USE GUIDE and KEY)   339

PALADIN VIDEO HOME ENTERTAINMENT GUIDE

Caught in the middle of a nuclear explosion, victim of gamma radiation, Doctor Bruce finds himself transformed into a mighty goliath in times of stress. Four episodes are contained in this cassette.
BBFC:U — F — EN
Marvel Comics — Guild Home Video   **H, P, E**

Incredible Hulk in The Man Called Boomerang, The   Fil-Ent '84
Cartoons
13360 49 mins C
V2, B, V
Animated
Three power-packed episodes from the man who can transform himself into a mighty Goliath.
BBFC:U — F — EN
Marvel Comics — Guild Home Video   **H, P, E**
8427-9

Incredible, Indelible, Magical, Physical, Mystery Trip, The   Med-Sci '8?
Anatomy and physiology/Health education
12668 47 mins C
V2, B, V
Live action and animation combine in a colourful trip through the human body stressing the importance of diet and health.
F — ED
David H DePatie; Fritz Freleng — Videomedia   **P**
3112

Incredible Journey, The   Fil-Ent '63
Adventure
12570 80 mins C
B, V
John Drainie, Emile Genest, Tommy Tweed, Sandra Scott, directed by Fletcher Markle
A bull terrier, a Siamese cat and a Labrador retriever make a 200 mile trek across rugged Canadian terrain in search of home.
F — EN
Walt Disney Productions — Rank Video Library   **H**
147

Incredible Magic of Magic Volumes I and II, The   How-Ins '80
Magic
01202 55 mins C
B, V
Bob Yourburg 2 pgms

This instructional series demonstrates the fundamentals of magic in a highly entertaining manner. Four half-hour programmes on two tapes.
F — I
Viacom Intl — CBS/Fox Video   **P**
2B-070; 2B-071

Incredible Rocky Mountain Race, The   Fil-Ent '77
Comedy/Adventure
08040 94 mins C
B, V
Christopher Connelly, Forrest Tucker, Larry Storch, Jack Kruschen, Mike Mazurki directed by Jim Conway
This is the story of young Mark Twain and his bitterest rival, Mike Fink. They set off on a grudge race from Missouri to California using any means at their disposal. The race tests both men to dangerous levels.
BBFC:U — F — EN
Sunn Classic — Rank Video Library   **H, P**
0056 C

Incredible Voyage of Stingray, The   Fil-Ent '??
Science fiction/Puppets
05404 94 mins C
B, V
The Commander of the sleek underwater craft, Stingray, and the leader of the World Aquanaut Security Patrol battle with an evil Lord who rules an empire under the seas. He plans to take over and enslave the people of the surface. With the help of one of his slave girls Stingray and the crew are able to thwart his plans.
F — EN
Gerry Anderson Productions — Precision Video Ltd   **P**
BITC 2071/VITC 2071

Incubus   Fil-Ent '81
Horror
09082 92 mins C
B, V
John Cassavettes, John Ireland, Helen Hughes
This thriller involving a series of rapes and murders tells of an evil power that returns to a small town. Only one man can discover the form that it has taken. It is based on the novel by Ray Russell.
A — EN
Artists Releasing Corp — Video Tape Centre   **P**
VTC 1028

Indiscreet   Fil-Ent '58
Comedy-Drama/Romance
08721 97 mins C

PALADIN VIDEO HOME ENTERTAINMENT GUIDE

V2, B, V
Cary Grant, Ingrid Bergman, Cecil Parker, Phyllis Calvert, David Kossoff, Megs Jenkins, Oliver Johnston, directed by Norman Kransa
Cary Grant stars as a suave NATO officer who meets a beautiful foreign actress. However, as usual, when he meets a woman he is attracted to, he claims to be married and unable to get a divorce.
S,A — EN
Warner Bros; Grandon Prod — *BBC Video*
H, P
BBCV 8001

Indiscretion of an American Wife Fil-Ent '54
Drama
04179   72 mins   B/W
B, V
Jennifer Jones, Montgomery Clift
A married American woman, alone in Rome, plans to meet her lover for one last rendezvous before she returns to her family.
BBFC:A — S,A — EN
Columbia — *Guild Home Video*   **H, P**

Inferno in Paradise Fil-Ent '74
Drama
08857   90 mins   C
V2, B, V
Jim Davis, Richard Young, Betty Ann Carr, directed by Edward Forsyth
The island of Honolulu is threatened by an arsonist who strikes without any known reason. It is based on true exploits from the files of the Honolulu Fire Department.
BBFC:A — S,A — EN
Frank C Coty; Robert Smith — *Video Programme Distributors*   **P**
Inter-Ocean 079

Inglorious Bastards, The Fil-Ent '7?
War-Drama
02111   87 mins   C
V2, B, V
Bo Svenson, Peter Hooten, Fred Williams, Jackie Basehart
An action-packed film set in the centre of a fierce war. Five Americans due for court martial fail to reach the trial. Their escape and adventures earn them the title of The Inglorious Bastards.
C,A — EN
Unknown — *Hokushin Audio Visual Ltd*
P
VM-18

Initiation, The Fil-Ent '79
Drama/Suspense
13257   95 mins   C

B, V
Vera Miles, Clu Gulager, James Read, directed by Larry Stewart
This is a psychological drama involving a beautiful heiress with recurring nightmares and an escaped madman determined to hunt down her father and friends.
BBFC:18 — A — EN
Scott Winant — *CBS/Fox Video*   **P**
3031

Inn of the Damned Fil-Ent '7?
Suspense/Drama
13733   111 mins   C
V2, B, V
Dame Judith Anderson, Alex Cord, Michael Craig, directed by Terry Bourke
A bounty hunter is sent to investigate the mysterious disappearance of travellers on a lonely road that leads to an inn.
BBFC:15 — S,A — EN
Terry Bourke; Rod Hay — *Medusa Communications Ltd*   **H, P**
MC 023

Innocent Bystanders Fil-Ent '73
Suspense
05612   111 mins   C
B, V
Stanley Baker, Geraldine Chaplin, Donald Pleasance, Dana Andrews, directed by Peter Collinson
An ageing secret agent becomes a decoy in an international manhunt to locate an escaped Russian scientist.
S,A — EN
Sagittarus Prods; George H Brown — *Home Video Merchandisers*   **H, P**
010

Inside Moves Fil-Ent '80
Drama
09017   115 mins   C
V2, B, V
John Savage, Diana Scarwid, David Morse, directed by Richard Donner
This film takes a look at handicapped citizens trying to make it in everyday life, focusing on the relationship between an insecure, failed suicide and a volatile man who is only a knee operation away from a dreamed-about basketball career.
BBFC:AA — C,A — EN
Goodmark Productions — *Intervision Video*
H, P
AA 0461

Inside Out Fil-Ent '75
Adventure
12988   94 mins   C
B, V

(For Explanation of codes, see USE GUIDE and KEY)   341

PALADIN VIDEO HOME ENTERTAINMENT GUIDE

James Mason, Telly Savalas, Robert Culp, directed by Peter Duffell
Thirty-five years after the end of the war, an ex-German officer and a former American prisoner of war unite to try to discover a hidden store of Nazi gold.
BBFC:PG — C,A — EN
Warner Bros — *Warner Home Video*   **P**
61279

Inspector General, The   Fil-Ent '49
Comedy
02591   101 mins   C
B, V
Danny Kaye, Walter Slezak, Elsa Lanchester, Barbara Bates
An elixir salesman with a travelling fair is mistaken for an important inspector general by a group of townspeople.
F — EN
Warner Bros — *Mountain Video*   **P**

Intelligence Men, The   Fil-Ent '65
Comedy
05159   102 mins   C
B, V
Eric Morecambe, Ernie Wise
Eric and Ernie, beset by some of the most beautiful spies in the business, set out to crack a dastardly sabotage ring which aims to disrupt vital trade talks between Britain and the USSR.
BBFC:A — C,A — EN
Rank; Hugh Stewart — *Rank Video Library*   **H, P**
1028

Intermezzo   Fil-Ent '39
Romance/Drama
04180   70 mins   B/W
B, V
Leslie Howard, Ingrid Bergman, directed by Gregory Ratoff
Poignant tale of great romance shadowed by tragedy, in which a famous, married violinist falls in love with his protege. Ingrid Bergman's first American film.
BBFC:U — F — EN
Selznick — *Guild Home Video*   **H, P**

Intermezzo   Fin-Art '83
Opera
12892   150 mins   C
B, V
Felicity Lott, Ian Caley, John Pringle

This opera by Richard Strauss is performed by The Glyndebourne Festival Opera in English and is conducted by Gustav Kuhn. Set in the 1920's it tells the story of a wife's innocent fling with a young baron.
F — EN
RM Arts — *THORN EMI*   **P**
TXH 90 26964/TVH 90 26962

International Gymnastics   Spo-Lei '81
Gymnastics
04648   90 mins   C
B, V
Each year Thames Television in conjunction with the British Amateur Gymnastics Association covers some of the major events in international gymnastics. This cassette covers two such events: the Daily Mirror USSR Gymnastics Display Teams and the Coca-Cola Championships.
F — EN
Thames Video — *THORN EMI*   **H, P**
TXB 90 6209 4/TVB 90 6209 2

International Show Jumping   Spo-Lei '8?
Sports
08714   108 mins   C
V2, B, V
Introduced by Raymond Brooks-Ward
This tape features classic moments from The Royal International Horse Show, The Horse of the Year Show and the Olympia International. It includes the top riders Nick Skelton, Harvey Smith, David Broome and Elizabeth Edgar amongst others.
F — EN
John Vigar — *BBC Video*   **H, P**
BBCV 5014

International 'Supasquash' Championship   Spo-Lei '??
Sports-Minor
09119   98 mins   C
B, V
This championship devised specifically for television employs the 'time-limit' format. It shows edited highlights of the first round matches, and then the complete semi-finals and final.
F — EN
Unknown — *Quadrant Video*   **H, P**
3Q3

International Velvet   Fil-Ent '78
Drama/Adventure
10153   89 mins   C
B, V

---

342   (For Explanation of codes, see USE GUIDE and KEY)

PALADIN VIDEO HOME ENTERTAINMENT GUIDE

Tatum O'Neal, Nanette Newman, Christopher Plummer, Anthony Hopkins, directed by Bryan Forbes

This is the story of a rebellious young orphan girl who is sent to live with her aunt. They are brought together through their mutual love for horses and the girl and her horse are selected for the Olympic Games.
F — EN
MGM; Bryan Forbes — MGM/UA Home Video **P**
UMB 10306/UMV 10306

Intimate Relations   Fil-Ent '??
Romance/Drama
08904   84 mins   C
V2, B, V
Philipe Leroy
A couple recently married live in a cottage in grounds belonging to his parents. The wife's sister is attracted to the husband and gradually suceeds in luring him away.
BBFC:X — A — EN
Unknown — Video Programme Distributors **P**
Inter-Ocean 019

Intolerance   Fil-Ent '16
Drama
04673   113 mins   B/W
B, V
Constance Talmadge, Mae Marsch, Lillian Gish, Robert Harron, Elmo Lincoln, Eugene Pallette, directed by D. W. Griffith
Four stories of bigotry and injustice from four different periods of history. The St. Bartholomew's Day Massacre under Catherine de Medici; the events that led to the Crucifixion of Christ; a modern-day drama of social and legal injustice in America, and the overthrow of Belshazzar's democratic rule in Babylon in 639 B.C. Silent; colour-tinted.
F — EN
Universal — Polygram Video **P**

Intrigue   Fil-Ent '47
Adventure/Mystery
08731   90 mins   B/W
B, V
George Raft, June Havoc, Helena Carter, Tom Tully
A man is dishonorably discharged from his post as an Army pilot when two cunning and beautiful women plot against him for revenge. The film follows his plans to expose the black market ring in Shanghai, to accredit himself.
S,A — EN
United Artists — BBC Video **H, P**
BBCV 8018

Invaders from Mars   Fil-Ent '53
Science fiction
01197   71 mins   C
V2, B, V
Helena Carter, Arthur Franz, Jimmy Hunt, Leif Erickson, directed by William Cameron Menzies
A twelve-year-old boy witnesses the landing of a strange spacecraft, and he and his father set out to investigate. The father becomes possessed by alien entities who threaten to take over the entire world.
BBFC:A — M,A — EN
20th Century Fox — Intervision Video **P**
A-A 0179

Invaders from the Deep   Fil-Ent '??
Cartoons
09358   92 mins   C
B, V, LV
Animated
Captain Troy Tempest and his courageous Stingray crew battle with the evil Lord Titan and his army of aquatic aliens bent on world conquest. Preventing their plans to take over the Earth, Tempest is joined by Marina, an underwater mermaid princess.
F — EN
Unknown — Precision Video Ltd **P**
BITC 2127/VITC 2127/LVITC 0006

Invaders of the Lost Gold   Fil-Ent '81
Adventure
07978   86 mins   C
B, V
Stuart Whitman, Glynis Barber, Edmund Purdom, Woody Strode, Harold Sakata, Laura Gemser, directed by Alan Birkinshaw
During 1945 in the Philippines, a group of Japanese soldiers moved a vast consignment of gold to the coast. In Tokyo, 36 years later, the discovery that ten cases went missing is made. The story tells of the search for this gold and the dangers that the mission involves.
S,A — EN
Unknown — AVI Video Ltd **P**
010

Invasion of the Body Snatchers   Fil-Ent '56
Science fiction
08726   80 mins   B/W
B, V
Kevin McCarthy, Dana Wynter, Carolyn Jones, King Donovan, directed by Don Siegel

(For Explanation of codes, see USE GUIDE and KEY)

PALADIN VIDEO HOME ENTERTAINMENT GUIDE

This is the classic story about the invasion of Southern California by seeds of giant plant pods, which exude blank human forms that drain the emotional life of people and threaten to destroy the world.
F — EN
Walter Wanger; Allied Artists — *BBC Video* **H, P**
BBCV 8007

Invasion: UFO   Fil-Ent '??
Science fiction
05405   95 mins   C
B, V
Ed Bishop, George Sewell, Michael Billington, directed by Gerry Anderson, Dave Lane, David Tomblin
A top secret defence organization, S.H.A.D.O., is established to protect earth from alien attack after Unidentified Flying Objects are finally confirmed. The aliens are from a dying planet and they need human organs to repair their own bodies.
S,A — EN
Gerry Anderson Production — *Precision Video Ltd*   **P**
BITC 2072/VITC 2072

Invincible Barbarian, The   Fil-Ent '81
Adventure
12615   83 mins   C
V2, B, V
Sabrina Siani, Peter Mc Coy
This film is the story of two brothers bent on revenge for the slaughter of their tribe.
BBFC:18 — S,A — EN
Unknown — *VideoSpace Ltd*   **P**

Invincible Iron Man, The   Fil-Ent '??
Cartoons
08384   54 mins   C
V2, B, V
Animated
This cartoon tells the story of an inventor who has made an armoured suit. When he wears it he becomes the Invincible Iron Man. This cassette includes three 18-minute episodes.
M,S — EN
Marvel Comics — *Guild Home Video*   **H, P, E**

Invincible Iron Man, Cassette 2, The   Fil-Ent '84
Cartoons
13376   50 mins   C
V2, B, V
Animated
Three episodes are contained in this cassette titled 'If I Die Let It Be With Honour,' 'The Crimson Dynamo' and 'Double Diaster.'
BBFC:U — F — EN
Unknown — *Guild Home Video*   **H, P, E**
8406-6

Invincible Iron Man in Enter Hawkeye, Cassette 3, The   Fil-Ent '??
Cartoons
13359   66 mins   C
V2, B, V
Animated
Four more thrilling episodes from the armour-clad hero of the free world are contained in this cassette.
BBFC:U — F — EN
Marvel Comics — *Guild Home Video*   **H, P, E**
8428-6

Invincible Super Chan   Fil-Ent '7?
Adventure/Martial arts
04615   90 mins   C
V2, B, V
In the Ming Dynasty there lived a man so deadly and cunning that he was feared by all China—his very presence was always a portent of death. Trained from talents a thousand years old his skills were known only to three men, the monk who reared him, the Samurai who taught him the deadly martial arts and the man he has to kill.
C,A — EN
Unknown — *Video Programme Distributors*   **P**
Inter-Ocean—028

Iolanthe   Fil-Ent '8?
Opera
08920   100 mins   C
B, V
Derek Hammond-Stroud, Richard Van Allen, Alexander Oliver, Kate Flowers, Thomas Hemsley, Anne Collins, Beverley Mills, Sandra Dugdale, Pamela Field
This opera by Gilbert and Sullivan tells the story of the beautiful fairy Iolanthe, banished for twenty-five years for marrying a mortal. On her return her youth and beauty cause problems when her half-mortal son, Strephon, can't convince his fiancee that the girl she discovers him with is really his mother. The music is played by the London Symphony Orchestra, conducted by Alexander Faris.
S,A — EN
Brent Walker Prods — *Brent Walker Home Video Ltd*   **P**

---

344   (For Explanation of codes, see USE GUIDE and KEY)

PALADIN VIDEO HOME ENTERTAINMENT GUIDE

Ipcress File, The Fil-Ent '65
Suspense
01874 108 mins C
B, V, LV

Michael Caine, Guy Doleman, Sue Lloyd, Nigel Green

A tense spy thriller. An ex-army sergeant, Harry Palmer, has been blackmailed into working for the secret service, and finds himself caught in a tangled web of intrigue, murder, and treachery.
BBFC:A — *S,A* — *EN*
Rank, Harry Saltzman — *Rank Video Library* **H, P**
0015

Ireland's Triple Crown Spo-Lei '8?
Sports
08715 96 mins C
V2, B, V

Having been presented with the wooden spoon the previous year, Ireland makes a huge comeback led by their new captain, Ciaran Fitzgerald, beating Wales, England and Scotland at Rugby to re-possess the Triple Crown for the first time since 1949.
F — *EN*
John O'Brien; Bill Taylor; John Vigar — *BBC Video* **H, P**
BBCV 5018

Irishman, The Fil-Ent '77
Drama
07959 90 mins C
B, V

Michael Craig, Simon Burke, Robyn Nevin, Lou Brown

In North Queensland during the 1920's, a proud Irish-American teamster is determined to continue his profession in the face of competition from motorised transport. This decision creates disharmony in his family.
S,A — *EN*
Anthony Buckley Productions — *Home Video Holdings* **H, P**
014

Iron Maiden Fil-Ent '81
Music-Performance
05057 30 mins C
B, V

The record of a concert given at the Rainbow, London, in December 1980. Songs include 'Wrathchild,' 'Killers,' 'Remember Tomorrow,' 'Phantom of the Opera,' 'Transylvania,' and 'Iron Maiden.'
F — *EN*
Unknown — *THORN EMI* **P**
TXE 90 5002 4/TVF 90 5002 2

Iron Maiden, The Beast Over Hammersmith Fil-Ent '82
Music-Performance
08564 55 mins C
B, V

This tape features Iron Maiden live on the stage of London's Hammersmith Odeon. The tracks include 'Murder in the Rue Morgue,' 'Run to the Hills,' 'Children of the Damned,' 'Number of the Beast,' 'Another Life,' '22 Acacia Avenue,' 'Total Eclipse,' 'The Prisoner,' 'Hallowed Be thy Name,' 'Iron Maiden,' 'Sanctuary,' 'Drifter' and 'Running Free.'
S,A — *EN*
Unknown — *THORN EMI* **P**
TXE 90 0905 4/TVE 90 0905 2

Iron Master, The Fil-Ent '7?
Adventure
09163 95 mins C
V

Sam Pasco, George Eastman, Elvire Audrey, William Berger

This film, set when this planet was in its formative stage during prehistoric times, tells of the stone age man who discovers the secret of iron and uses it to make weapons for war, adding further to the ferocity of their tribal battles.
S,A — *EN*
Unknown — *Medusa Communications Ltd* **H, P**

Iron Men and Steel Machines/Flames over the Sahara Spo-Lei '7?
Automobiles-Racing/Aeronautics
02267 60 mins C
V

Two half-hour programmes on one tape; the first is a history of motor racing with a great deal of old and rare film showing some of the world's greatest drivers. 'Flames over the Sahara' is the story of two hot air balloons crossing the Sahara desert.
F — *EN*
Unknown — *JVC* **P**
PRT 11

Island, The Fil-Ent '80
Drama
05319 114 mins C
B, V

Michael Caine, David Warner, directed by Michael Ritchie

A writer for a news magazine relentlessly investigates the disappearance of pleasure craft and passengers in an area of the Caribbean. He discovers that descendants of 17th century

PALADIN VIDEO HOME ENTERTAINMENT GUIDE

buccaneers, trapped in a time warp, are continuing in their marauding ways. He is captured along with his 12 year old son, who, affected by the pirates, turns against his father.
S,A — EN
Universal — CIC Video   **H, P**
BEA1012/VHA1012

Island, The   Spo-Lei '81
Motorcycles
06849   43 mins   C   (PAL, NTSC)
V2, B, V
This film covers the 1980 Isle of Man T.T. Festival Fortnight including motorcycle racing, moto-cross, trials and grass-track.
S,A — EN
CH Wood Ltd — Duke Marketing Limited
P
DM1

Island at the Top of the World, The   Fil-Ent '74
Adventure/Drama
05592   90 mins   C
B, V
Donald Sinden, David Hartman, Jacques Marin, Mako, directed by Robert Stevenson
Set in 1908 a young man has gone missing in the Arctic and a search party leaves Norway in a giant airship. Three of them are captured by a lost colony of Vikings. Condemned to death they are aided by a Viking girl and escape only to face further danger and end up trapped in the Bay of Whales.
F — EN
Walt Disney Productions — Rank Video Library
H
05400

Island of Adventure, The   Fil-Ent '8?
Adventure
09247   82 mins   C
V2, B, V
Norman Bowler, Wilfrid Brambell, Catherine Schell, Eleanor Summerfield, Patrick Field, Chloe Franks, Perry Benson, Daryl Back
This children's adventure story, based on the book by Enid Blyton, tells of four children on holiday in Cornwall. They become caught up in a web of intrigue when they stumble across a gang of ruthless international terrorists, planning to destroy the world's currency balance.
BBFC:U — F — EN
Unknown — Guild Home Video   **H, P, E**

Island of Death   Fil-Ent '75
Horror
02120   90 mins   C
V2, B, V

Young parents to be, Tom and Evelyn, arrive at their favourite Spanish Island for a holiday. There is a sinister calm about the place, and the adult population seems to have disappeared. The remaining children are unfriendly. A horrifying series of events traps the young couple on the island.
C,A — EN
Spanish — Hokushin Audio Visual Ltd   **P**
VM-32

Island of Death   Fil-Ent '7?
Horror
07972   100 mins   C
B, V
Bob Belling, Jane Ryale, Nico Tsachiridi, directed by NICO Mastorakis
This film is set on the Greek Island, Mykonos. A couple arrive on the island for a quiet winter vacation. They are thought of as such a nice handsome couple although this is not so when people begin to be brutally murdered.
A — EN
Unknown — AVI Video Ltd   **P**
003

Island of Dr Moreau, The   Fil-Ent '77
Science fiction
07406   98 mins   C
V2, B, V
Burt Lancaster, Michael York, Nigel Davenport, Barbara Carrera, Richard Basehart, directed by Don Taylor
A man is shipwrecked on a lonely Pacific island where he is attacked by a band of strange looking wild animals. He is rescued and taken to a magnificent house in the jungle where he meets a mysterious doctor. Curious about the doctor's work, he discovers that the doctor has extended his chromosome research to transform animals to humans. Based on the novel by H. G. Wells.
BBFC:A — S,A — EN
American International — Guild Home Video
H, P, E

Island of Terror   Fil-Ent '66
Horror
02415   89 mins   C
V2, B, V
Peter Cushing, Edward Judd, Carole Gray, directed by Terence Fisher
The discovery of a complete boneless body on Petrie Island leads to the arrival of Drs Landers and Stanley to carry out an autopsy. During their investigations, their car is attacked by a glutinous jelly-like horror, the result of an experiment gone wrong.
BBFC:X — A — EN
Universal — Rank Video Library   **H, P**
2022 C

PALADIN VIDEO HOME ENTERTAINMENT GUIDE

Island of the Lost Fil-Ent '68
Adventure
04195 91 mins C
B, V
Richard Greene, Luke Halpin, Mark Hulswit
Anthropologist and his family set sail in search of an unchartered island and are shipwrecked on it.
BBFC:U — F — EN
MGM — Guild Home Video H, P

Israel Philharmonic Orchestra 40th Anniversary Concert Fin-Art '7?
Music-Performance
02261 85 mins C
V
On the occasion of their 40th anniversary, the Israel Philharmonic Orchestra, conducted by Zubin Metha perform excerpts from 'A Midsummer Night's Dream' and other symphonies.
F — EN
Unknown — JVC P
PRT 32

It Came From Hollywood Fil-Ent '82
Comedy/Satire
13640 77 mins C
B, V
Directed by Andrew Solt and Malcolm Leo
An offbeat compilation of some of the worst movies ever made hosted by Dan Aykroyd, John Candy, Cheech and Chong and Gilda Radner.
BBFC:15 — S,A — EN
Susan Strausberg; Jeff Stein — CIC Video H, P
2139

It Came from Outer Space Fil-Ent '53
Science fiction
13288 7 mins B/W
B, V
Richard Carlson, Barbara Rush, Charles Drake, Alan Dexter, directed by Jack Arnold
An alien spacecraft lands on Earth to effect repairs and is greeted with fear and suspicion by the local townsfolk so an amateur astronomer intercedes on its behalf.
BBFC:PG — S,A — EN
Universal — CIC Video H, P
BEJ 1087/VHJ 1087

It Rained All Night The Day I Left Fil-Ent '79
Adventure
09211 100 mins C
B, V
Tony Curtis, Sally Kellerman, Lou Gossett
This film tells the story of two bungling American gunrunners down on their luck, who unwittingly get involved in a private war over desert water rights.
F — EN
Unknown — Video Form Pictures H, P
CLO 5

It Seemed Like a Good Idea at the Time Fil-Ent '75
Drama/Comedy
09153 110 mins C
V
Isaac Hayes, Stefanie Powers, Anthony Newley, Yvonne de Carlo, Lloyd Bochner, Henry Ramer, Lawrence Dane, John Candy, directed by John Trent
This film tells the story of a woman who left her husband, despite still loving him, because he could not afford her. She becomes a society wife to a rich but ruthless man. This situation is interwoven with the woman's determination to save her mother's house from destruction, and her meeting with the chairman of historic buildings.
S,A — EN
Quadrant Film — Cinema Indoors H, P

It Shouldn't Happen to a Vet Fil-Ent '76
Comedy
04658 90 mins C
B, V
John Alderton, Colin Blakely, Lisa Harrow, Bill Maynard
Based on James Herriot's novels, this film follows the adventures of a Yorkshire veterinarian just before World War II.
F — EN
EMI; Talent Associates; Readers Digest — THORN EMI H, P
TXA 90 0234 4/TVA 90 0234 2

It Takes All Kinds Fil-Ent '69
Crime-Drama/Suspense
07995 90 mins C
B, V
Robert Lansing, Vera Miles, Barry Sullivan, Sid Melton
This film set in Australia tells of a beautiful but ruthless woman who frames an innocent seaman into believing he committed murder in order to gain his help in the theft of a priceless relic.
S,A — EN
Goldsworthy Prod — Motion Epics Video Company Ltd P
162

(For Explanation of codes, see USE GUIDE and KEY) 347

PALADIN VIDEO HOME ENTERTAINMENT GUIDE

It's Good to be Alive
Fil-Ent '74
Drama/Biographical
08021   100 mins   C
V2, B, V
Paul Winfield, Ruby Dee, Lou Gossett, directed by Michael Landon
This tells the story of the brilliant Brooklyn Dodger whose playing career was brought to an end by a nearly fatal car crash at the climax of his basebal career. The film goes on to show how human courage can regain the will to live.
F — EN
M P C — Iver Film Services   P
195

Italian Job, The
Fil-Ent '68
Drama/Adventure
13319   96 mins   C
B, V
Michael Caine, Noel Coward, Benny Hill, Lelia Goldoni, directed by Peter Collinson
A crook plans to steal gold bullion on its way out of Turin and brings the city to a standstill while he steals the gold and escapes.
BBFC:U — S,A — EN
Paramount — CIC Video   H, P
BEN 2115/VHN 2115

Italian Stallion
Fil-Ent '7?
Drama
09917   72 mins   C
V2, B, V
Sylvester Stallone, Henrietta Holm, Jodi Van Prang, Nicholas Warren, Frank Micelli, Barbara Strom, Directed by Morton Lewis
Sylvester Stallone bares all to play the part of the Stud, whose world revolves entierly around sex, an interest he shares with some of his way out friends.
BBFC:X — A — EN
Unknown — Derann Film Services   P
FGS 905

It'll Be Alright on the Night 3
Fil-Ent '80
Outtakes and bloopers
06281   45 mins   C
B, V
Introduced by Denis Norden, directed by Paul Smith
This film is an original and funny compilation of 'goofs,' 'fluffs,' and technical mistakes from the world of feature films, television programmes and commercials.
F — EN
London Weekend Television Limited — THORN EMI   P
TXB 90 0694 3/TVB 90 0694 2

It's a Mad, Mad, Mad, Mad World
Fil-Ent '63
Comedy
13046   162 mins   C
B, V
Spencer Tracy, Mickey Rooney, Phil Silvers, Terry Thomas, directed by Stanley Kramer
An oddly assorted group of men vie with each other to locate buried treasure.
BBFC:U — F — EN
Casy Productions Inc; Stanley Kramer; United Artists — Warner Home Video   P
99231

It's My Turn
Fil-Ent '80
Comedy/Romance
12472   87 mins   C
B, V
Jill Clayburgh, Michael Douglas
A humorous love story about a modern woman who wants a classic romance.
BBFC:15 — C,A — EN
Rastar; Martin Elfand — RCA/Columbia Pictures Video UK   H, P
10200

It's Not Impossible
Gen-Edu '8?
Learning disabilities/Animals
13560   16 mins   C
B, V
The Marjory Maclure School show how Jaspar the donkey and his cart play a valuable part helping physically disabled children take part in simple routines.
A — ED
Unknown — TFI Leisure Ltd   H, P

Itzhak Perlman Beethoven Violin Concerto
Fin-Art '81
Music-Performance
05896   45 mins   C
B, V
Outstanding violinist Itzhak Perlman performs the ever-popular Beethoven Violin Concerto.
F — EN
Unknown — THORN EMI   P
TXD 90 0493 4/TVD 90 0493 2

Ivanhoe
Fil-Ent '??
Cartoons/Adventure
08799   45 mins   C
B, V
Animated

---

348   (For Explanation of codes, see USE GUIDE and KEY)

PALADIN VIDEO HOME ENTERTAINMENT GUIDE

This is the legendary story of King Richard's knight, Ivanhoe. It is based on the novel by Sir Walter Scott.
F — EN
Unknown — *VCL Video Services*   P
A320B

Ivanhoe   Fil-Ent '53
Adventure
12208   106 mins   C
B, V
Robert Taylor, Elizabeth Taylor, Joan Fontaine, George Sanders
Sir Walter Scott's classic novel of chivalric romance and courtly intrigue among the knights of medieval England is the basis of this film.
Film Daily Poll '53: Ten Best of Year.
F — EN
MGM — *MGM/UA Home Video*   P
10092

Ivor the Engine and the   Chi-Juv '84
Dragons
Cartoons
13383   59 mins   C
B, V
Animated
Ivor the Engine steams up and down the Welsh valleys and with the help of Jones the steam fights off some fire-breathing dragons.
PS,M — EN
BBC Television — *BBC Video*   H, P
9015

J

Jack and the Beanstalk   Chi-Juv '79
Fairy tales
06765   95 mins   C
V2, B, V
Animated
A cartoon version of the famous fairy tale about Jack and his magic beans.
F — EN
Film Rite Productions — *Intervision Video*
H, P
A-A 0349

Jack and the Beanstalk   Fil-Ent '??
Musical/Fantasy
10188   60 mins   C
B, V
Gene Kelly
This musical is a combination of animation and live action. Set in 1890 a yankee peddler trades his magic beans for Jack's cow. Sceptical about the beans' powers, he is soon surprised to find themselves at the top of the beanstalk and in the Giant's castle. They are pursued by the Giant, get lost in the castle, meet a pair of Woggle Bird guards, a band of friendly Minute Mice, the Golden Goose and the imprisoned Princess.
F — EN
Unknown — *Video Form Pictures*   H, P
CLO V8

Jack and the Beanstalk   Fil-Ent '84
Fairy tales
13415   48 mins   C
B, V
Elliott Gould
In this adaptation of the famous classic children's story, Jack decides to climb up the tall beanstalk that has grown from the magic seed and has to confront the wicked giant in his castle when he reaches the top.
BBFC:U — F — EN
Shelley Duvall — *MGM/UA Home Video*
P
10434

Jack Mack and the Heart   Fil-Ent '83
Attack in Concert
Music-Performance
13354   60 mins   C
V2, B, V
This soul band from Los Angeles has recorded fourteen songs on this cassette including 'Goin' Back to Miami,' 'Can I Get a Witness,' 'Pickpocket,' 'Shake' and 'Funky Broadway.'
S,A — EN
DEJ Productions — *Guild Home Video*
H, P, E
6121-6

Jackie Genova-Work   Spo-Lei '8?
That Body
Physical fitness
10141   45 mins   C
B, V
Jackie Genova, directed by Clive Richardson
Jackie Genova introduces her workout programme which is a combination of aerobics, calisthenics and yoga aiming to transform both your body and attitude to life. Music produced by Joe Blocker.
F — I
Unknown — *Island Pictures*   P
IPV0075

(For Explanation of codes, see USE GUIDE and KEY)

PALADIN VIDEO HOME ENTERTAINMENT GUIDE

Jacklin and Palmer Play the Best 18 in Britain
Spo-Lei '84
Golf
12723   90 mins   C
B, V

This features the unique meeting between Tony Jacklin and Arnold Palmer, two of the great personalities of modern golf, over 18 top holes on Britain's seaside links. The late Henry Longhurst, one of the most famous voices in golf, gives a commentary on the game.
F — EN
John Vigar — *BBC Video*   **H, P**
5023

Jacksons in Concert, The
Fil-Ent '??
Music-Performance
06220   45 mins   C
B, V

The Jacksons performing in concert with non-stop music and dance routines, with solo performances by Michael Jackson. Songs include: 'I'll Be There,' 'Ben,' 'ABC, 123,' 'Rockin' Robin' and many more.
F — EN
Unknown — *VCL Video Services*   **P**
V158B1

Jacqueline Bouvier Kennedy
Fil-Ent '81
Biographical/Drama
09187   122 mins   C
B, V

Rod Taylor, Jaclyn Smith, Stephen Elliott, Donald Moffat, James Franciscus, directed by Steven Gethers

This is the story of a mischevious young girl who becomes an adventurous career woman and eventually the world's most celebrated woman. It traces her life through school to her arrival in Washington as a photographer where she meets a handsome young Congressman, John F. Kennedy.
S,A — EN
ABC Circle Films — *Video Form Pictures*
H, P
MGS 3

Jaguar Lives
Fil-Ent '79
Suspense/Martial arts
05251   88 mins   C
B, V, LV

Christopher Lee, Barbara Bach, Joseph Wiseman, John Huston, Donald Pleasence, Woody Strode, Capucine, Joe Lewis

Joe Lewis plays the Jaguar, a master of martial arts who sets out to avenge the death of a fellow agent and becomes involved in a world wide plot known as The Killing Of The Kings.
BBFC:AA — *C,A — EN*
Unknown — *Rank Video Library*   **H, P**
0048

Jaguar Story, The
Gen-Edu '79
Automobiles
04392   60 mins   C
B, V

A detailed history of the British car company containing interviews with early employees and drivers. Video descriptions of the early cars as they are today and contemporary stills and archive shorts of them in action during their time are also included.
F — EN
Vintage Television — *Vintage Television Ltd*
H, P, E

Jailhouse Rock
Fil-Ent '57
Musical/Drama
05314   92 mins   B/W
B, V

Elvis Presley, Judy Tyler, Mickey Shaughnessy, Dean Jones

The story of a young man sent to prison for accidentally killing a man in a brawl. He is taught by a cellmate to play guitar and sing. A beautiful woman gives him a break and a record is released. He then uses his aggressiveness and talent to succeed in music and movies. Based on the story by Ned Young.
F — EN
MGM; Pandro S Berman — *MGM/UA Home Video*   **P**
UMB10011/UMV10011

Jam, 'Trans-Global Unity Express,' The
Fil-Ent '82
Music-Performance
07836   30 mins   C
B, V

This tape features the rock group The Jam recorded in April 1982 during their concert at the Bingly Hall, Birmingham. The programme consists of nine tracks of their most popular songs.
S,A — EN
Unknown — *Polygram Video*   **H, P**
791 526

Jam-Video Snap, The
Fil-Ent '??
Music-Performance
09884   60 mins   C
B, V

PALADIN VIDEO HOME ENTERTAINMENT GUIDE

This is a rare and unique collection of some of the best footage shot on film and video throughout the Jam's spectacular musical career:
F — EN
Unknown — Polygram Video   H, P
040 1904/040 1902

James Brown Story—Soul Connection, The   Fil-Ent '7?
Music-Performance
02229   60 mins   C
V
James Brown
The energy of James Brown is captured as he performs his hits in Africa, Georgia, the Southern States, and New York.
F — EN
Unknown — JVC   P
PRT 43

James Dean Story, The   Fil-Ent '57
Documentary/Biographical
12820   80 mins   B/W
B, V
James Dean
This film traces the development of Dean's career through his family, girlfriends, fraternity brothers and showbusiness contemporaries and contains rare footage from 'East of Eden' and the premiere of 'Giant.'
BBFC:PG — S,A — EN
Altman/George Productions — VideoSpace Ltd   P
PA 543

James Dean—The First American Teenager   Fil-Ent '75
Documentary
13698   80 mins   C
B, V
Directed by Ray Connolly and narrated by Stacy Keach
James Dean had only completed three major films when he died in 1955 at 24 years of age, already a legend. This film tells the story of his life with film clips and interviews with his friends and fellow actors.
BBFC:AA — S,A — EN
David Puttnam — THORN EMI   P
90 2560

James Galway and Kyung Wah Chung Play Bach   Fin-Art '7?
Music-Performance
02265   70 mins   C
V

This special concert was recorded live at the Concertgebouw in Amsterdam. This programme, under the direction of Derek Bailey, features Phillip Moll and Moray Welsh.
F — EN
Unknown — JVC   P
PRT 31

James Hunt: World Champion/The Phoenix, 1977   Spo-Lei '77
Automobiles-Racing
04519   46 mins   C
B, V
Narrated by Stirling Moss
James Hunt's 1976 championship driving season is highlighted from the early frustration to the final victory. In 'The Phoenix, 1977,' Niki Lauda's incredible comeback from a near-fatal accident and his subsequent championship season are documented.
F — EN
Brunswick Intl — Quadrant Video   H, P
M14

Jane Austen in Manhattan   Fil-Ent '80
Drama
05674   108 mins   C
B, V
Anne Baxter, Robert Powell, directed by James Ivory
A young man acquires a newly discovered play by Jane Austen together with a grant to product it. In fact he uses it as a pretext to assemble together a group of naive, idealistic young people with whom he conducts weird and dangerous experiments. His former teacher, now his opponent, tries to get the play and grant away from him, after he is accused of abducting an actress.
BBFC:A — S,A — EN
Merchant Ivory Production — Home Video Holdings   H, P
015

Jane Doe   Fil-Ent '82
Crime-Drama/Mystery
08769   96 mins   C
B, V
William Devane, Karen Valentine, Eva Marie Saint, David Huffman, Stephen Miller, Jackson Davies, Anthony Holland, directed by Ivan Nagy
William Devane plays a police lieutenant on the trail of a multiple killer, known as The Roadside Strangler. The nude body of an unidentified woman is found in a shallow grave, but she survives. However, physical recovery is accompanied by total loss of memory. The

---

(For Explanation of codes, see USE GUIDE and KEY)

PALADIN VIDEO HOME ENTERTAINMENT GUIDE

lieutenant knows that she is the one person who can help his investigations but when the murderer learns she has survived he will certainly strike again.
C,A — EN
ITC — Precision Video Ltd   P
BITC 2132/VITC 2132

Janitor, The   Fil-Ent '81
Crime-Drama
07697   108 mins   C
V2, B, V
William Hurt, Sigourney Weaver, Christopher Plummer, directed by Peter Yates
The night janitor at an office block develops a crush on a TV reporter and regularly records her appearances. When he discovers the murdered body of a Vietnamese diamond importer the reporter is sent to cover the story. To keep her interested he pretends he knows more than he does and leads both of them into danger.
S,A — EN
Twentieth Century Fox — CBS/Fox Video   H
1116

Japan—Instant Pictures   Fil-Ent '83
Music-Performance
12954   30 mins   C
B, V
David Sylvian, Steve Jansen, Mick Karn, Richard Barbieri, Masami Tsuchiya, Rob Dean
The seven tracks from Japan on this programme include 'Gentleman Take Polaroids', 'Cantonese Boy,' 'Swing,' 'Visions of China' and 'Night Porter' and are a mixture of promos and on-stage footage.
F — EN
Unknown — Virgin Video   H, P
VVC 049

Jasper Carrott Live   Fil-Ent '8?
Comedy
08094   60 mins   C
V2, B, V
Jasper Carrott
This tape was specially recorded for video and includes some of the sketches as seen on television, such as 'The Football Match', 'Zits' and 'America.'
C,A — EN
Independent — Rank Video Library   H, P
1031 A

Jaws   Fil-Ent '75
Suspense
01037   124 mins   C
V2, B, V
Roy Scheider, Robert Shaw, Richard Dreyfuss, Lorraine Gary, directed by Steven Speilberg
A 25-foot long great white shark attacks and terrorises residents of a Long Island beach town. Three men set out on a boat to kill it at any cost. Based on the novel by Peter Benchley.
M,A — EN
Universal; Richard Zanuck — CIC Video
H, P
CRA 1001/BEA 1001/VHA 1001

Jaws II   Fil-Ent '78
Suspense
01038   116 mins   C
B, V
Roy Scheider, Lorraine Gary, Murray Hamilton, directed by Jeannot Szwarc
The sequel to 'Jaws.' It's been four years since the man-eating shark plagued the resort town of Amity. Suddenly a second shark stalks the waters and the terror returns.
M,A — EN
Universal; Richard Zanuck; David Brown — CIC Video   H, P

Jaws of the Dragon   Fil-Ent '76
Adventure/Martial arts
02456   92 mins   C
B, V
James Nam, Johnny Taylor, Jenny Kam
The story of two rival gangs in the Far East.
C,A — EN
Robert Jeffery — Mountain Video   P

Jaws 3   Fil-Ent '83
Suspense/Drama
13283   96 mins   C
B, V
Dennis Quaid, John Putch, Bess Armstrong, Louis Gossett Jr, Simon MacCorkindale, directed by Joe Alves
A great white shark becomes trapped in a fantastic man-made aquatic pleasure park and in its frenzy to escape will devour anything that gets in the way.
BBFC:PG — S,A — EN
Universal — CIC Video   H, P
BER 1103/VHR 1103

Jayne Mansfield Story, The   Fil-Ent '80
Biographical/Drama
08380   97 mins   C
V2, B, V
Loni Anderson, Arnold Schwarzenegger, Raymond Buktenica, Kathleen Lloyd, G.D. Spradlin, directed by Dick Lowry

PALADIN VIDEO HOME ENTERTAINMENT GUIDE

This film tells the story of Jayne Mansfield's rise to stardom in Hollywood and then the decline into exploitation, alcohol and obscurity.
C,A — EN
Alan Landsburg Productions — *Guild Home Video*   H, P, E

Jazz Festival   Fil-Ent '81
Music-Performance
04623   60 mins   C
B, V
Benny Goodman, Gene Kruper, Teddy Wilson, Lionel Hampton, Ella Fitzgerald, Duke Ellington, Count Basie, Dave Brubeck, Joe Williams
An all-star swing festival which includes the all time greats of jazz.
F — EN
VCL Video Services Ltd — *VCL Video Services*
P

Jazz Singer, The   Fil-Ent '81
Musical-Drama
05043   110 mins   C
B, V
Neil Diamond, Laurence Olivier, Lucie Arnaz, Catlin Adams
A cantor's son abandons the synagogue in order to pursue show-business success.
F — EN
Jerry Leider — *THORN EMI*   P
TXA 90 0304 4/TVA 90 0304 2

Jean-Pierre Aumont Show, The   Fil-Ent '7?
Variety
04381   60 mins   C
B, V, PH17, 3/4U
Jean-Pierre Aumont, Marisa Pavan, Roger Williams
A variety show starring Jean-Pierre Aumont and featuring Marisa Pavan and Roger Williams.
F — EN
Unknown — *Vidpics International*   P

Jennifer—A Woman's Story   Fil-Ent '79
Drama
05873   94 mins   C
B, V
Elizabeth Montgomery, Bradford Dillman, Scott Hylands, James Booth, Robin Gammel, Michael Goodwin, Kate Mulgrew, directed by Guy Green
The story of a woman determined to become involved in her husband's successful boat building business; he is against this as he feels her place is at home with the children. However, he suffers a fatal heart attack and she has to prove her capabilities as an executive. In a struggle for control of the company, she has to learn to balance the priorities of her career, family and personal life.
S,A — EN
Marble Arch Prods — *Precision Video Ltd*
P
BITC 2077/VITC 2077

Jenny   Fil-Ent '71
Drama/Romance
04266   90 mins   C
B, V
Marlo Thomas, Marian Hailey, Alan Alda, Elizabeth Wilson
This film is a modern romance set against the moral confusion of young Americans in the closing years of the Vietnam War.
BBFC:AA — A — EN
Cinerama Releasing — *Rank Video Library*
H, P
0035

Jeremiah Johnson   Fil-Ent '72
Drama
13066   104 mins   C
B, V
Robert Redford, Will Geer, directed by Sydney Pollack
A man turns his back on civilisation and learns a new code of survival in the brutal and sometimes beautiful land of the Utah mountains.
BBFC:AA — C,A — EN
Warner Bros Inc; Sanford Productions Inc — *Warner Home Video*   P
61061

Jericho Mile, The   Fil-Ent '79
Drama
10209   97 mins   C
B, V
Peter Strauss, Richard Lawson, Roger E. Mosley, Brian Dennehy, Billy Green Bush, Ed Lauter, Beverly Todd, Miguel Pinero, directed by Michael Mann
A man, sentenced to life in a penal colony, has a burning ambition to break the world olympic record for the standing mile. He is offered the chance to enter the O.A. trials which could lead to the fulfilment of his dream. This is filmed within the confines of a real penal institution and contains both emotional and violent scenes.
BBFC:18 — A — EN
ABC Circle Films — *Video Form Pictures*
H, P
MGS 24

Jerk, The   Fil-Ent '80
Comedy
10122   91 mins   C

(For Explanation of codes, see USE GUIDE and KEY)

353

PALADIN VIDEO HOME ENTERTAINMENT GUIDE

B, V
Steve Martin, Bernadette Peters, directed by Carl Reiner
An appallingly naive white adopted son of a black sharecropper sets out to seek his fortune. True to form he makes a fortune but soon loses it again.
BBFC:PG — *F* — *EN*
Universal — *CIC Video* **H, P**
BEA 1056/VHA 1056

Jerry Lee Lewis   Fll-Ent '??
Music-Performance
06305   58 mins   C
V2, B, V
Jerry Lee Lewis
This film features the rock 'n' roll star Jerry Lee Lewis with hits such as 'Whole Lotta Shakin' Goin' On,' 'Roll over Beethoven' and 'Great Balls of Fire.'
F — *EN*
Unknown — *World of Video 2000* **H, P**
MV233

Jerry Lee Lewis Live   Fll-Ent '83
Music-Performance
12204   66 mins   C
B, V
Jerry Lee Lewis is featured at the Hammersmith Odeon in his first solo appearance in the U.K. His tracks include 'Chantilly Lace', 'Saturday Night', 'Great Balls of Fire', 'Down the Line', 'Whole Lotta Shaking', 'Good Golly Miss Molly' and 'Sweet Georgia Brown'.
F — *EN*
On The Road Again Productions — *CBS/Fox Video* **P**
6340

Jerry Lee Lewis—The   Fll-Ent '83
Killer Performance
Music-Performance
12965   50 mins   C
B, V
A specially filmed performance of fourteen rock'n'roll, classics which include 'Whole Lotta Shakin', 'Great Balls of Fire', 'Down the Line', 'Mona Lisa' and 'Chantilly Lace.'
F — *EN*
Unknown — *Virgin Video* **H, P**
VVD 053

Jesse and Lester: Two   Fll-Ent '??
Brothers in a Place Called Trinity
Western/Comedy

05551   97 mins   C
V2, B, V
Richard Harrison, Donal O'Brien, directed by James London
A man learns that he has inherited a piece of land in a place called Trinity and goes to look for his long lost brother to tell him the news. Problems arise when the man, whose gun fighting and womanizing are legendary, wants to build a brothel but his brother, a morman, wants a church. The plot is further complicated by the fact that gold has been discovered on the property.
A — *EN*
Unknown — *Videomedia* **P**
PVM 6102/BVM 6102/HVM 6102

Jesse James Meets   Fll-Ent '66
Frankenstein's Daughter
Horror
10074   63 mins   C
V2, B, V
John Lupton, Cal Bolder, Narda Onyx
Jesse James battles to save a friend in the clutches of Frankenstein's daughter who is determined to create a world of obedient killer zombies.
A — *EN*
Carroll Case — *Embassy Home Entertainment* **P**
2092

Jesse Owens Story, The   Fll-Ent '84
Drama
13625   158 mins   C
B, V
Dorian Harewood, Barry Corbin, Georg Stanford Brown, George Kennedy, Debbi Morgan, directed by Richard Irving
This is the story of the famous black track star who won four gold medals in the 1936 Olympics, from his record breaking college days through to his battle with the US courts.
BBFC:U — *F* — *EN*
Paramount — *CIC Video* **H, P**
2119

Jessi's Girls   Fll-Ent '7?
Western
04554   86 mins   C
V2, B, V
Sondra Currie, Geoffrey Land, Ben Frank, Regina Carrol, Jennifer Bishop, directed by Al Adamson
A newlywed Mormon couple are en route by covered wagon from Utah to Arizona and are attacked by a gang of hoodlums. They devastate the Mormon's belongings, rape and

PALADIN VIDEO HOME ENTERTAINMENT GUIDE

shoot the wife, and kill the husband. The wife survives, removes the bullet from her wound, and sets out to avenge the death of her husband.
S,A — EN
Michael F Goldman, Al Adamson — *Intervision Video* **H, P**
A-A 0292

Jesus Christ Superstar Fil-Ent '73
Musical-Drama
01039   108 mins   C
B, V
Ted Neeley, Carl Anderson, Yvonne Elliman, directed by Norman Jewison
A rock opera that portrays, in music, the last seven days in the life of Christ.
F — EN
Universal; Norman Jewison, Robert Stigwood — *CIC Video* **H, P**

Jesus of Nazareth Fil-Ent '77
Religion/Drama
00844   100 mins   C
B, V
Robert Powell, Anne Bancroft, Olivia Hussey, Ernest Borgnine, Claudia Cardinale, Anthony Quinn, Laurence Olivier, directed by Franco Zeffirelli   4 pgms
'Jesus of Nazareth' was filmed on location in Morocco and Tunisia. The accent is on realism. The settings are the closest the twentieth-century can come to the time of Christ. Christ is portrayed as a simple man, fighting political intrigue on behalf of a dispossessed nation. His earthly reward was crucifixion but his philosophy has survived. Jesus of Nazareth was a man who lived as he believed and his external message was of love, in place of war.
F — EN
ITC — *Precision Video Ltd* **P**
BITC 2005/VITC 2005; BITC 2006/VITC 2006; BITC 2007/VITC 2007; BITC 2008/VITC 2008

Jesus Trip, The Fil-Ent '7?
Drama
09056   90 mins   C
V
Tippy Walker, Robert Porter, Diana Ivarson
This film tells of a group of motorcycle riders; Waco, the long haired kid and Anna, a beautiful young nun who rides on the back of his bike and a whole load of freaks that follow on behind.
S,A — EN
Unknown — *Astra Video* **H, P**

Jet Lag Fil-Ent '8?
Drama
09235   83 mins   C
B, V
Jeannine Mestre, Norman Brisky
An attractive Spanish academic travels to America in an attempt to rekindle a tempestuous romance. Lost in an emotional vacuum, she discovers that her ex-lover has made a new life for himself. Her hopes turn into an obsessive hatred culminating in a meeting destined to be his 'last'.
S,A — EN
Unknown — *Home Video Holdings* **H, P**

Jethro Tull—Slipstream Fil-Ent '81
Music-Performance
05422   60 mins   C
B, V
Jethro Tull
This film featuring the group Jethro Tull is a concept video including live footage, animation and special effects to present some of their well known songs.
F — EN
Chrysalis Group Ltd — *Chrysalis Video* **P**
CVIM BE1/CVIM VH1

Jim Davidson's Falklands Special Fil-Ent '84
Comedy
13687   90 mins   C
B, V
Directed by Stuart Hall
Jim Davidson, plus four dancers, a singer and film crew are transported to the Falkland Islands to perform thirteen concerts for the troops.
S,A — EN
Thames Video — *THORN EMI* **P**
90 3027

Joan Armatrading-'Track Record' Fil-Ent '8?
Music-Performance
10098   75 mins   C
B, V
Joan Armatrading
This is a film portrait of Joan Armatrading. It includes footage shot on her visit to St. Kitts, the Caribbean island where she was born, extracts from her U.S. tour, it shows her at work in the studio, extracts from promotional videos and ends with a live recording of her performance in Sydney. Songs include 'Heaven', 'Bottom to the Top', 'Down to Zero', 'Drop the Pilot', 'Me Myself I', 'Show Some Emotion', 'Love and Affection', 'Willow', 'Frustration', 'Baby I' and many others.
S,A — EN
A&M Sound Pictures — *VideoSpace Ltd* **P**

PALADIN VIDEO HOME ENTERTAINMENT GUIDE

Joan Collins Video Special, The
Fil-Ent '8?
Biographical/Documentary
09052   54 mins   C
V
Joan Collins
This film looks at the life of Joan Collins. She exposes the secrets of her success, beauty, health and eternal youth.
S,A — EN
Unknown — *Astra Video*   H, P

Joan of Arc
Fil-Ent '48
Drama/Biographical
07983   100 mins   C
B, V
Ingrid Bergman, Jose Ferrer, John Ireland, Leif Ericson, directed by Victor Fleming
This film is the life of Joan of Arc, based on the play by Maxwell Anderson
Academy Awards '48: Best Cinematography, Colour;Best Costume Design   F — EN
RKO; Sierra Pictures — *Motion Epics Video Company Ltd*   P
150

Joan Sutherland—'A Life on the Move'
Fil-Ent '79
Documentary/Music-Performance
05853   80 mins   C
B, V
Joan Sutherland, Richard Bonynge, directed by Brian Adams
This documentary, made over a period of thirteen months, tells the story of Joan Sutherland and her conductor-musician husband. The film goes behind the scenes at the Metropolitan Opera House in New York, the Sydney Opera House, on a tour of Japan and Korea and recording sessions in studios in London. It also visits their home near Lake Geneva. It features personal narration by the couple and excerpts from best loved operas.
F — EN
ABC Australia; RM Productions — *Polygram Video*   P
7901764/7901762

Joan Sutherland in Concert
Fil-Ent '82
Music-Performance/Opera
09340   60 mins   C
B, V
This tape features Joan Sutherland in concert at the Perth Concert Hall in Western Australia, accompanied by pianist, husband and mentor Richard Bonynge. The numbers cover a broad range of the classics: 'Tornami a Vagheggiar' from Handel's 'Alcina'; 'Addio Del Passata' from Verdi's 'La Traviata'; 'A Mezzanotte' by Oanizette; 'Chanson de Zora' from Rossini's 'La Petite Bohemienne' and many more.
BBFC:U — *F — EN*
Unknown — *Precision Video Ltd*   P
BITC 1043/VITC 1043

Joe
Fil-Ent '70
Drama
01283   107 mins   C
V2, B, V
Dennis Patrick, Peter Boyle, Audrey Caire, directed by John G. Avildsen
When a young girl overdoses on drugs her father kills her hippie, drug-dealing boyfriend. In shock, the father goes to a bar where a factory worker is sounding off about hippies ruining the world, saying they should be killed. After finding out that the father just killed one they become friends.
C,A — EN
Cannon Films — *Intervision Video*   H, P
A-A 0131

Joe and the Sleeping Beauty
Chi-Juv '7?
Fantasy
01867   62 mins   C
V2, B, V
Animated, written by France and Jean Image, music by Michel Emer
Little Joe, as heroic as Robin Hood, passes through the Kingdom of Flies and their castle in space to help his friend the beautiful Queen Bee, who has been cursed by the wicked Fly Witch. Joe and his pals journey off to incredible adventures.
I,M — EN
Films Jean Image Production — *Videomedia* P
BVM 3113/HVM 3113

Joe at the Kingdom of Ants
Chi-Juv '7?
Fantasy
01866   62 mins   C
V2, B, V
Animated, written by France and Jean Image
Invited by the Queen of the Ants to visit Antville, Little Joe discovers the marvels of the Ant Micro-Kingdom. With him you will be able to learn the secrets of the ant's life and share his adventures.
I,M — EN
Films Jean Image Production — *Videomedia* P
BVM 3112/HVM 3112

(For Explanation of codes, see USE GUIDE and KEY)

PALADIN VIDEO HOME ENTERTAINMENT GUIDE

Joe at the Kingdom of the Bees   Chi-Juv '7?
Fantasy
05570   60 mins   C
V2, B, V
Animated, written by France and Jean Image
In this film Joe discovers the power to become tiny so he can enter the world of the Bees. He is the guest of honour of the Queen herself. She has her necklace stolen which if not found will bring bad luck to the hive, so Joe follows the quest for the necklace even though he knows they are up against gangster hornets. Joe gets to see just how the bee civilization works.
I,M — EN
Films Jean Image Production — *Videomedia*   P
BVM 3114/HVM 3114

Joe Kidd   Fil-Ent '72
Western
13286   87 mins   C
B, V
Clint Eastwood, Robert Duvall, John Saxon, directed by John Sturges
This film tells the story of a bitter struggle between Mexican natives and powerful American business interests at the turn of the century with a ruthless gunshooter working both sides of the fence.
BBFC:15 — *S,A — EN*
Universal — *CIC Video*   H, P
BEL 1092/VHL 1092

Joe Panther   Fil-Ent '76
Drama
04474   110 mins   C
V2, B, V
Brian Keith, Ricardo Montalban, Alan Feinstein, Cliff Osmond
An Indian boy achieves manhood by fighting alligators. Based on a novel by Zachary Ball.
F — EN
Artists Creation and Assocs — *Intervision Video*   H, P
A-AE 0169

John F Kennedy   Fil-Ent '??
Presidency-US/Biographical
12011   104 mins   C
B, V
The CBS news team explores the life of the youngest elected President, covering the Bay of Pigs invasion, the Cuban Missile Crisis, development of the space programme, the fateful meeting with Krushchev and America's deepening involvement in Vietnam.
F — EN
CBS — *CBS/Fox Video*   P
7030

John Martyn — In Vision 1973-1981   Fil-Ent '82
Music-Performance
08709   100 mins   C
V2, B, V
John Martyn
This tape features a collection of rock artist John Martyn's performances taken from various television shows.
S,A — EN
Andy Finney — *BBC Video*   H, P
BBCV 3013

John McEnroe Story, The   Spo-Lei '81
Tennis
09061   90 mins   C
V
John McEnroe, Bjorn Borg, Jimmy Connors, narrated by Bud Collins
John McEnroe is the subject of this programme, which traces his rise to stardom touching upon his rivalry with players such as Bjorn Borg and Jimmy Connors. It follows John McEnroe from his college days to the finals of the world's most important tournaments.
F — EN
Michael Mattei — *Astra Video*   H, P

John Miles   Fil-Ent '??
Music-Performance
08840   52 mins   C
B, V
This tape features John Miles live in concert at the Royal Albert Hall.
C,A — EN
Unknown — *VCL Video Services*   P
V211B

Johnny and the Wicked Giant   Fil-Ent '??
Cartoons/Fairy tales
12019/77 mins   C
V2, B, V
Animated
Johnny and six friends set out to conquer the wicked giant. When they enter his magic castle, Johnny's friends are captured and he is reduced to the size of an insect. Aided by the bees, he invades the castle and sets his friends free.
F — EN
Unknown — *Videomedia*   P
PVM 2122/BVM 2122/HVM 2122

Johnny Guitar   Fil-Ent '53
Western
08725   110 mins   C
B, V
Sterling Hayden, Joan Crawford, Ernest Borgnine, Mercedes McCambridge, Scott Brady

(For Explanation of codes, see USE GUIDE and KEY)

PALADIN VIDEO HOME ENTERTAINMENT GUIDE

This tells the story of a man who rides into Arizona to take a job in a gambling house. He meets a tough female saloon owner whose determination has established her as a reckonable force.
F — EN
Republic — *BBC Video* **H, P**
BBCV 8006

Johnny Winter Live   Fil-Ent '84
Music-Performance
12928   45 mins   C
B, V
This programme features nine tracks from Johnny Winter with John Paris and Bobby Torello including 'Jumping Jack Flash', 'Highway 61 Revisited' and 'Mean Town Blues' and is directed by Stan Jacobson.
S,A — EN
Concert Productions International — *Video Form Pictures* **H, P**
VFX 14/VFV 14

Jonathan Livingston   Fil-Ent '74
Seagull
Fantasy
10124   96 mins   C
B, V
Directed by Hall Bartlett
Taken from Richard Bach's bestseller, this is the story of a seagull who wants to fly higher and dive deeper than any other seagull. Soundtrack by Neil Diamond.
BBFC:U — F — EN
Paramount — *CIC Video* **H, P**
BER 2077/VHR 2077

Jory   Fil-Ent '75
Western
10080   93 mins   C
V2, B, V
John Marley, B.J. Thomas, Robby Benson
Set in the tough and violent world of the Old West, a fifteen-year-old orphan boy has to find his way to manhood, he turns killer, learns how to handle women, cope with grief, and take a man's revenge.
A — EN
Minsky Kirshner; Joseph E Levine; Avco Embassy — *Embassy Home Entertainment*
P
2097

Joseph Stalin—Leon   Gen-Edu '??
Trotzkij
History-Modern/World War II
06134   30 mins   B/W
V2, B, V
Authentic documentary footage of Stalin and Trotzkij. The film covers the careers of two big personalities, two different ways of considering Socialism and two enemies for life.
S,A — ED
Unknown — *Video Programme Distributors*
P
Cinehollywood—V810

Jour de Fete   Fil-Ent '48
Comedy
05562   80 mins   B/W
V2, B, V
Jacques Tati, directed by Jacques Tati
This is the hilarious story of a village fete and a postman's determined efforts to get the mail through.
BBFC:U — F — EN
Unknown — *Videomedia* **P**
PVM 4411/BVM 4411/HVM 4411

Jour Se Leve, Le   Fil-Ent '39
Drama
10037   93 mins   B/W
B, V
Jean Gabin, Jules Berry, directed by Marcel Carne
A murderer hides from police in an attic room and eventually loses his grip on reality. Subtitled in English.
S,A — EN   FR
Sigma — *Palace Video Ltd* **P**
PVC 2057A

Jour Se Leve, Le   Fil-Ent '39
Drama
13123   93 mins   B/W
B, V
Jean Gabin, Jules Berry, Arletty, Jacqueline Laurent, directed by Marcel Carne
A murderer is besieged by the police in his attic room and remembers his past through the night but has to make a final decision before the morning comes. This film has English subtitles.
BBFC:PG — C,A — EN   FR
Sigma — *Palace Video Ltd* **P**
PVC 2057A

Journalist, The   Fil-Ent '??
Drama
09372   79 mins   C
B, V
Sam Neill, Jack Thompson, Liz Alexander
This film tells the story of a journalist whose private life goes to pieces when he quits his job. His wife wants to divorce him and his girlfriend

---

358   (For Explanation of codes, see USE GUIDE and KEY)

PALADIN VIDEO HOME ENTERTAINMENT GUIDE

discovers she is pregnant. However, a good news story comes his way and he lands himself a highly-paid job with a national magazine. With his new found success comes temptation.
BBFC:15 — C,A — EN
Unknown — *Precision Video Ltd* P
BSWPV 2604/VSWPV 2604

Journey   Fil-Ent '77
Suspense
06183   88 mins   C
B, V
Genevieve Bujold, John Vernon
A violent story of a girl who is rescued from the Sangueney River and falls in love with her rescuer. She remains in the remote pioneer community and brings bad luck and misery to the inhabitants.
S,A — EN
First American Films — *VCL Video Services*
P

Journey Among Women   Fil-Ent '82
Drama
12193   93 mins   C
V2, B, V
Lillian Crombie, Jeyne Pritchard, Martin Phelan
A group of convict women are beaten and sexually abused by Red Coat Soldiers guarding them. During a druken orgy 10 of the women flee into the bush where they are hunted with inevitable savage results.
BBFC:18 — A — EN
John Weiley — *Medusa Communications Ltd*
H, P

Journey into Fear   Fil-Ent '75
Mystery
09027   100 mins   C
V2, B, V
Sam Waterston, Zero Mostel, Yvette Mimieux, Ian McShane, Shelley Winters, Stanley Holloway, Donald Pleasance, Vincent Price, directed by Daniel Mann
Set against the exotic countryside of Turkey, this film tells the story of a geologist who holds secret information on a new resource which is vital to his government after narrowly escaping death, he becomes caught up in a web of intrigue and nightmarish realities. Based on the novel by Eric Ambler.
C,A — EN
New World Pictures — *Intervision Video*
H, P
AAE 0430

Journey to the Centre of the Earth   Fil-Ent '??
Cartoons/Adventure
09393   46 mins   C
B, V
Animated
Professor Lidenbrock goes on an exciting adventure of exploration and danger.
F — EN
Unknown — *VCL Video Services* P
A359B

Journey to the Centre of Time   Fil-Ent '67
Science fiction/Adventure
05519   82 mins   C
B, V
Scott Brady, Gigi Perreau, Anthony Eisley, Abraham Safaer, directed by David L. Hewitt
Scientists eager to prove the validity of their research into time travel cast themselves uncontrollably into the year 5000 AD in the midst of an alien war. In an attempt to correct the fault and to escape they overshoot into 1,000,000 BC and are attacked by prehistoric monsters. Some of the crew are killed and time plays evil tricks on the survivors.
BBFC:U — F — EN
Harold Goldman — *Derann Film Services*
H, P
DV140B/DV140

Joy Ride   Fil-Ent '79
Crime-Drama/Adventure
09392   92 mins   C
B, V
Desi Arnaz Jr, Robert Carradine, Melanie Griffith, Ann Lockhart, Tom Ligon
A group of boys, deciding that they have been ripped off once too often, take the law into their own hands to become the hunters and not the hunted.
C,A — EN
American International — *VCL Video Services*
P
P361D

Joy Sticks   Fil-Ent '83
Comedy
12021   88 mins   C
B, V
Joe Don Baker
A video arcade frequented by the local teenagers is the setting for this film. As the fun and games intensify a local business man comes searching for his daughter. Horrified to find out what goes on there he sets about getting it closed down.
BBFC:18 — C,A — EN
Greydon Clark — *Entertainment in Video*
H, P
EVB 1017/EVV 1017

(For Explanation of codes, see USE GUIDE and KEY)   359

PALADIN VIDEO HOME ENTERTAINMENT GUIDE

Jubilee　　　　　　　　　　Fil-Ent '78
Drama/Musical
07661　　103 mins　　C
B, V

Adam Ant, Toyah Willcox, Jenny Runacre, Little Nell, Jordan, Hermine Demoriane, directed by Derek Jarman

In this film, designed to shock, the Queen is transported by her astrologer into the latter part of the 20th century. Violence is a way of life, the police are a law unto themselves, the Queen has been murdered, Buckingham Palace is a recording studio and sexual roles have been reversed. Features music by Adam and the Ants, Siouxsie and the Banshees and many others.
BBFC:X — A — EN
Megalovision — *VCL Video Services*　　P
P248D

Judie Tzuke in Concert　　　Fil-Ent '8?
Music-Performance
09998　　60 mins　　C
B, V

This tape features Judie Tzuke in concert. It includes such hits as 'China Town', Sukarita', 'Higher and Higher', 'Swimming Pools', 'Black Fur' and 'Sports Car'.
F — EN
Holiday Brothers Ltd. — *Holiday Brothers Ltd*
P

Judo Part 1-Basic　　　　　Spo-Lei '8?
Martial arts
09993　　60 mins　　C
B, V

Richard Barraclough, Honorary National Coach of British Judo Association and 5th Dan, with the help of Steve Pullen, takes the pupil through the first stages of training for the sport of Judo. In this first Judo series falls, throws and holds are clearly demonstrated.
S,A — I
Holiday Brothers Ltd. — *Holiday Brothers Ltd*
P

Julia　　　　　　　　　　　Fil-Ent '77
Drama
07713　　113 mins　　C
V2, B, V

Jane Fonda, Vanessa Redgrave, Jason Robards, Maximilian Schell, Hal Holbrook, Rosemary Murphy, Meryl Streep, directed by Fred Zinnemann

Based on the story 'Pentimento' by Lillian Hellman and retold in flashback, this film centres on the author's long-standing relationship with a childhood friend and her fight against the Nazis in Europe in the 30's. Academy Awards '77: Best Supporting Actor (Robards); Best Supporting Actress (Redgrave).
S,A — EN
Twentieth Century Fox — *CBS/Fox Video*
P
1091

Julie London Show, The　　　Fil-Ent '7?
Variety
04376　　60 mins　　C
B, V, PH17, 3/4U

Julie London

A variety special with Julie London and various guest stars.
F — EN
Unknown — *Vidpics International*　　P

Julius Caesar　　　　　　　Fil-Ent '69
Drama
09197　　117 mins　　C
B, V

Charlton Heston, Richard Chamberlain, Jason Robards, John Gielguld, Diana Rigg, Richard Johnson, Robert Vaughan

This is the third adaptation of Shakespeare's classic historical drama. It tells of the victorious Julius Caesar, returning from battle, where the jealous Brutus and Cassius conspire his assassination.
F — EN
Peter Snell; Commonwealth United — *Video Form Pictures*　　H, P
MGS 9

Jungle Book, The　　　　　Chi-Juv '42
Adventure
13213　　105 mins　　C
V2, B, V

Sabu, directed by Zoltan Korda

Adapted from one of Rudyard Kipling's most famous stories, Mowgli, a young Indian boy, grows up in a wolf pack after wandering off on his own into the jungle and encounters many adventures.
BBFC:U — F — EN
United Artists — *Embassy Home Entertainment*　　P
1324

Jungle Man　　　　　　　　Fil-Ent '41
Adventure
06318　　59 mins　　B/W
V2, B, V

Buster Crabbe, Sheila Darcy

An expedition aims to penetrate the darkest depths of the dangerous African swamps to discover the 'City of the Dead.' They, however, lack a vital medicine to combat a deadly jungle

PALADIN VIDEO HOME ENTERTAINMENT GUIDE

disease; the ship bearing the serum has sunk in shark infested waters. They are also under threat from primitive tribes; one man attempts to recover the drugs to save the party.
F — EN
Producers Releasing Corp — World of Video 2000   H, P
GFS11

Jungle Warriors   Fil-Ent '84
Drama
12924   95 mins   C
B, V
A group of fashion models seeking exotic locations are stranded in the jungle when their plane is shot down by para-military forces.
BBFC:18 — C,A — EN
Unknown — Video Form Pictures   H, P
MIX 006

Junior Bonner   Fil-Ent '72
Western
05150   99 mins   C
B, V
Steve McQueen, Ida Lupino, Joe Don Baker, Robert Preston, Ben Johnson, Barbara Leigh
Plenty of rodeo rough stuff, bar room brawling, family feuding and romance with local siren Charmagne.
BBFC:A — C,A — EN
Cinerama Releasing — Rank Video Library
H, P
8005

Jupiter Menace, The   Fil-Ent '82
Documentary/Science fiction
08479   84 mins   C
B, V
Presented by George Kennedy, directed by Peter Matulavich, Lee Auerbach
George Kennedy presents convincing evidence to suggest that the world is on the brink of catastrophe. He predicts a continuing cycle of unnatural occurrences and disasters ending in the year 2000 with numerous volcanic eruptions and earthquakes. It shows a world having been drastically altered by the melting of the polar ice-cap.
C,A — EN
Jupiter Menace Ltd — THORN EMI   P
TXB 90 1288 4/TVB 90 1288 2

Just a Carrott   Fil-Ent '83
Comedy-Performance
09042   100 mins   C
B, V
Jasper Carrott
This tape is a special edition of two live performances by the Midlands comedian, Jasper Carrott. 'Beat the Carrott' was recorded at the London Palladium and 'The Unrecorded Jasper Carrott' from the Theatre Royal, Drury Lane.
A — EN
Weekend Video — VideoSpace Ltd   P

Just a Gigolo   Fil-Ent '80
Comedy-Drama
04225   90 mins   C
B, V
Marlene Dietrich, David Bowie, Kim Novak, Maria Schell, directed by David Hemmings
A sumptuous recreation of life in 1920's Berlin, this film tells of the post-World War I existence of a young Prussian Army officer who falls in with a decadent crowd. Music by the Pasadena Roof Orchestra and Manhattan Transfer.
S,A — EN
Unknown — VCL Video Services   P

Just So Stories   Fil-Ent '82
Cartoons
08661   60 mins   C
B, V
Animated, narrated by Ronald Pickup, directed by Shelia Graber
This tape contains five of Rudyard Kipling's well-known animal myths 'The Elephant Child,' 'The Cat Who Walked by Himself,' 'How the Rhinoceros Got His Skin,' 'The Beginning of the Armadillos' and 'How the Leopard Got His Spots.'
F — EN
Marble Arch Films Ltd; Interama; Strengolt — Longman Video   P
LGBE 5045/LGVH 5045

Justine   Fil-Ent '68
Drama
07827   104 mins   C
V2, B, V
Jack Palance, Akim Tamiroff, Romina Power, Maria Rohm
This film is based on the story by the Marquis de Sade. It follows the story of two sisters who become involved in a series of macabre encounters including a homosexual Marquis, murder, rape, robbery and a gang of sadistic monks.
BBFC:X — A — EN
Unknown — Video Unlimited   H, P
018

(For Explanation of codes, see USE GUIDE and KEY)   361

PALADIN VIDEO HOME ENTERTAINMENT GUIDE

K

Kagemusha   Fil-Ent '80
War-Drama
07712   153 mins   C
V2, B, V, LV

Tatsuya Nakadai, Tsutomu Yamazaki, Kenichi Hagiwara, Kota Yui, Dausuke Ryu, Tetsuo Yamashita, directed by Akira Kurosawa

Set in the final quarter of the 16th century, this film looks at one of the bloodiest periods in Japanese history with rival warlords fighting for supremacy. It was the custom for rulers to have doubles, a 'Kagemusha,' to impersonate them from time to time in battle. One Kagemusha's warlord dies, an event which is kept a secret, and he, a former thief, takes his place to eventually grow in dignity and stature as he assumes leadership. (English subtitles.)
S,A — EN
Toho/Kurosawa Productions — CBS/Fox Video   **H**
1109

Kaja GooGoo-White Feathers Tour   Fil-Ent '83
Music-Performance
09773   60 mins   C
B, V

Directed by Derek Burbidge

This tape features the band Kaja GooGoo recorded live at the Hammersmith Odeon on 31st of May 1983. Songs include 'Kaja GooGoo', 'Interview Rooms', 'This Car Is Fast', 'Monochromatic', 'Hang on Now', 'Magician Man', 'Take Another View', 'Ooh to Be Ah', 'Over the Top', 'White Feathers', 'Frayo', 'Ergonomics', 'Too Shy', 'Lies and Promises' and 'Hang On Now'.
F — EN
EMI Records Ltd — THORN EMI   **P**
TXE 90 2049 4/TVE 90 2049 2

Kampuchea Express   Fil-Ent '8?
Adventure
12145   90 mins   C
V2, B, V

Robert Walker, Christopher George, Nancy Kwan

This action packed film is set against the background of war and revolution in South East Asia.
BBFC:18 — C,A — EN
Inter Light; MVS Video — Intervision Video   **H, P**
A-A 0478

Kanal   Fil-Ent '58
War-Drama
08448   93 mins   B/W
B, V

Teresa Izewska, Tadeusz Janczar, directed by Andrzej Wajada

This is based on the experiences of Poles during World War II. It describes the last terrible stages of the abortive 1944 uprising in Warsaw. It is the original version of the film subtitled in English. 'Kanal' is part of the 'Wajada Trilogy' which includes 'A Generation' and 'Ashes and Diamonds'.
BBFC:18 — A — EN   PO
Film Poloski — THORN EMI   **P**
TXE 90 0733 4/TVE 90 0733 2

Kansas City Bomber   Fil-Ent '72
Drama
08677   90 mins   C
B, V

Raquel Welch, Kevin McCarthy, Helena Kallianiotes, Norman Alden, directed by Jerrold Freedman

This is the story of a rough, tough and brutal rising Roller Game star who is determined to claw her way to the top of the mile-a-minute American skating circuit. Whilst away from the stadium she finds herself involved in a complicated personal affair with the team manager. The film features action on the fast banked tracks from many of America's top skating teams.
BBFC:AA — S,A — EN
MGM — MGM/UA Home Video   **P**
VMB 10162/VMV 10162

Kansas City Massacre   Fil-Ent '75
Crime-Drama
10199   97 mins   C
B, V

Dale Robertson, Sally Kirkland, Bo Hopkins, Scott Brady, Lyn Loring

As a cool, deliberated investigator comes closer to exposing a nest of corruption involving 'respectable' politicians, the FBI's top sleuth develops a strange relationship with the wildest gangster-'Pretty Boy' Floyd. Set in an era when bank robbers were heros and the whole country watched the G-Men track them down.
S,A — EN
Dan Curtis Prods; ABC Circle Films — Video Form Pictures   **H, P**
MGT B12

Kansas Live   Fil-Ent '83
Music-Performance
12027   60 mins   C
B, V

PALADIN VIDEO HOME ENTERTAINMENT GUIDE

This tape was recorded in the Omaha Civic Auditorium in Nebraska and comprises 16 tracks including Paradox, Diamonds and Pearls, Windows and Down the Road.
F — EN
Unknown — *Polygram Video* **H, P**
0402624/0402622

Karamurat Fil-Ent '7?
Drama
07761 90 mins C
V2, B, V
George Arkin, Daniela Giordano
This historical drama follows the struggle for power in ancient Turkey.
S,A — EN
Unknown — *Fletcher Video* **H, P**
AV 602

Karate Part 1 Spo-Lei '8?
Martial arts
06895 60 mins C
B, V
Presented by Steve Powell
This tape is an introduction to the skills and discipline of karate demonstrated by Steve Powell, 5th Dan blackbelt and world authority on the martial arts. This tape is intended for use alongside practical professional lessons and serves as an introduction to the art.
S,A — I
Holiday Brothers Ltd — *Holiday Brothers Ltd*
P

Karate Part 2 Spo-Lei '8?
Martial arts
09992 60 mins C
B, V
Presented by Steve Powell
This tape extends the course started in Part 1 and shows more complex moves for attack and defence which will improve the pupil's skills.
S,A — I
Holiday Brothers Ltd. — *Holiday Brothers Ltd*
P

Kashmiri Run Fil-Ent '??
Drama/Adventure
05615 96 mins C
B, V
Pernell Roberts, Alexandra Bastedo, Julian Mateos, Gloria Camara
A man escapes from a Chinese Communist detachment with two friends in an attempt to cross Tibet to Kashmir. They discover a doctor on a mystical quest with his daughter. The doctor is killed and the daughter joins the party. Their journey is made difficult not only by the Chinese troops but also by murderous Tibetan bandits.
S,A — EN
Unknown — *Home Video Merchandisers*
H, P
012

Kate Bush Live at the Hammersmith Odeon Fil-Ent '81
Music-Performance
05053 52 mins C
B, V
A record of a concert given in 1979, demonstrating Kate Bush's varied talents as a singer, songwriter, pianist, dancer, choreographer and mime artist. Songs include 'Wuthering Heights,' 'Wow,' 'O England My Lionheart.'
F — EN
Unknown — *THORN EMI* **P**
TXD 90 0503 4/TVD 90 0503 2

Kate Bush-The Single File Fil-Ent '83
Music-Performance
09775 50 mins C
B, V
Kate Bush
This tape features Kate Bush performing some of her well known songs. All artistic concepts and choreography throughout by Kate Bush. Songs include 'Wuthering Heights', 'Man With the Child in His Eyes', 'Hammer Horror', 'Wow', 'Them Heavy People', 'Breathing', 'Babooshka', 'Army Dreamers', 'Sat in Your Lap', 'The Dreaming', 'Suspended in Gaffa', 'There Goes a Tenner'.
F — EN
EMI Records Ltd — *THORN EMI* **P**
TXE 90 1430 4/TVE 90 1430 2

Katy Chi-Juv '84
Cartoons
13244 85 mins C
B, V
Animated
This is the story of Katy, the inquisitive little caterpillar, who sets about discovering the big, wide world.
I,M — EN
Fabian Arnaud — *CBS/Fox Video* **P**
6735

Kay Starr Show, The Fil-Ent '7?
Variety
04383 60 mins C
B, V, PH17, 3/4U

(For Explanation of codes, see USE GUIDE and KEY)

PALADIN VIDEO HOME ENTERTAINMENT GUIDE

Kay Starr, Kids Next Door
A variety show starring Kay Starr, with the Kids Next Door.
F — EN
Unknown — *Vidpics International* **P**

Keep, The   Fil-Ent '83
Horror
13618   92 mins   C
B, V
Jurgen Prochnow, Gabriel Byrne, Robert Prosky, Alberta Watson, Ian McKellen
Two members of the German S.S. accidentally unleash a malevolent force when exploring the fortress they have occupied in Rumania which proceeds to wreak murder and mayhem on the new occupants.
BBFC:18 — A — EN
Paramount — *CIC Video*   **H, P**
2123

Keep in Shape System   Spo-Lei '82
Physical fitness
08546   30 mins   C
B, V
Arlene Phillips, directed by Mike Mansfield
In this programme Arlene Phillips takes you through different movements contrived to make you shaplier, slimmer and fitter. It starts with 'warm up' exercises and goes onto the 'super stretch.' Each exercise is designed to get one's lungs better oxygenated, to increase one's energy level.
F — I
Ferroway Ltd — *THORN EMI*   **P**
TXF 90 0961 4/TVF 90 09612

Keep It Up Jack   Fil-Ent '??
Comedy
07910   85 mins   C
V2, B, V
A young man is fired from his job as a female impersonator only to learn that he has inherited a brothel from his old Aunt. He discovers that the girls do not know about the death. He uses his talents to deceive them and runs into trouble when he has to play the parts of the customers as well.
A — EN
Unknown — *Video Programme Distributors* **P**
Replay—1009

Kelly Monteith-A Yank in London   Fil-Ent '8?
Comedy-Performance/Documentary
09437   60 mins   C
B, V
Kelly Monteith
Kelly Monteith takes a personal look at tourist London, walking through Carnaby Street, King's Road, discotheques and Soho at night. He talks to punks, skinheads, the wealthy and the beautiful to name a few.
F — EN
Julian-Barnett Film Prods. — *Guild Home Video*   **H, P, E**

Kenneth Lo's Chinese Cooking Made Easy   How-Ins '82
Cookery
07435   59 mins   C
B, V
In this programme Kenneth Lo, the well known Chinese food expert, introduces the art of Chinese cooking. He proves that preparing the food is not nearly as complicated as generally believed. Including a demonstration of how to use chopsticks he shows how to prepare various dishes such as red-cooked knuckle of pork, baked trout, quick fried chicken with cashews, French beans in garlic and rice.
S,A — I
Mike Mansfield Enterprises Ltd — *THORN EMI* **P**
TXE 90 0692 4/TVE 90 0692 2

Kenneth Lo's Taste of China   Gen-Edu '8?
Cookery
08449   90 mins   C
B, V
Kenneth Lo
This programme shows Kenneth Lo, an authority on Chinese Cuisine and a famous restaurateur, preparing a variety of dishes. He starts with basic methods of preparing a Chinese family meal, to a more elaborate banquet for special occasions.
S,A — I
Thames Video — *THORN EMI*   **P**
TXE 90 1443 4/TVE 90 1443 2

Kenny Ball and his Jazzmen   Fil-Ent '7?
Music-Performance
02071   30 mins   C
B, V
This programme shows Kenny Ball and his band live in concert, and features great jazz numbers including the million seller 'Midnight in Moscow'.
C,A — EN
VCL Video Services — *VCL Video Services* **P**

Kenny Everett Video Show Volume 1, The   Fil-Ent '77
Comedy
05908   104 mins   C

PALADIN VIDEO HOME ENTERTAINMENT GUIDE

V2, B, V
Directed by David Mallett
A compilation of programmes from the television series, typical examples of Kenny Everett's zany brand of humour.
F — EN
David Mallett — *THORN EMI* P
TPB 90 6207 3/TXB 90 6207 4/TVB 90 6207 2

Kenny Everett Video Show Volume 2, The
Fil-Ent '77
Comedy
05909   104 mins   C
B, V
Directed by David Mallett
A compilation of programmes from the television series, typical examples of Kenny Everett's zany brand of humour.
F — EN
David Mallett — *THORN EMI* P
TXB 90 0505 4/TVB 90 0505 2

Kenny Everett Video Show—Volume 3, The
Fil-Ent '82
Comedy
07416   115 mins   C
B, V
Directed by David Mallett and Royston Mayo
This is the third compilation of sketches from the 'Kenny Everett Video Show' television series which features his zany brand of humour with music supplied by some of the top rock and pop artists and including dance routines by Hot Gossip.
F — EN
Thames Television — *THORN EMI* P
TXB 90 0730 4/TVB 90 0730 2

Kentucky Fried Movie
Fil-Ent '77
Comedy
07928   81 mins   C
V2, B, V
This spoof film features a series of sketches satirising many aspects of contemporary society. Includes films, commercials, T.V. talk shows and a mini-feature called 'A Fistful of Yen' which satirises the martial arts film genre.
S,A — EN
KFM Films Inc — *Video Programme Distributors* P
Replay—1001

Keoma
Fil-Ent '79
Western
06873   97 mins   C
V2, B, V
Franco Nero, Woody Strode
This is the story of Keoma, a halfbreed Indian who returns to his parental home only to learn that the nearby town is infested by the plague. The local tyrant who rules the town prevents all attempts to get help until Keoma intervenes. Keoma is then faced with having to fight not only the tyrant but his own halfbrothers who have always hated him.
S,A — EN
Vadib Productions — *European Video Company* P

Kevin Rowland and Dexy's Midnight Runners—The Bridge
Fil-Ent '8?
Music-Performance
08992   50 mins   C
B;V
Directed by Steven Barron
This tape, recorded at London's Shaftesbury Theatre, features the Dexy's Midnight Runners and some of 1982's best selling singles such as 'Come on Eileen', Jackie Wilson said (I'm in Heaven When You Smile)' and 'The Celtic Soul Brothers.'
F — EN
Unknown — *Polygram Video* P
790 587

KGB Connections, The
Gen-Edu '8?
Documentary/Intelligence service
07645   113 mins   C
B, V
Directed by Martyn Burke
This film follows investigations into Soviet intelligence operations in North America, produced by the Norfolk Investigation team. High ranking officials are named in the film which, using daring surveillance techniques, probes beneath the surface of top-level government operations to reveal the day-to-day dealings of the mysterious and sinister KGB.
S,A — EN
Unknown — *VCL Video Services* P
I217C

Khatiat Mallak (An Angel's Sin)
Fil-Ent '??
Comedy
06740   ? mins   C
V2, B, V
Three angels return to earth disguised as humans and become involved a in series of mishaps and misadventures.
S,A — EN   AB
Unknown — *Intervision Video* H, P
A-C 0143

Kick-Off Europe 1872-1968
Spo-Lei '81
Soccer
12773   55 mins   C

(For Explanation of codes, see USE GUIDE and KEY)

365

PALADIN VIDEO HOME ENTERTAINMENT GUIDE

B, V
Produced from the newsreels of British Movietone this video illustrates the history of England's involvement in European soccer from the first international match in 1872 to Manchester United's European Cup Triumph in 1968. It has an introduction by Frank McGhee.
F — EN
Unknown — *VideoSpace Ltd*   P

Kid Blue   Fil-Ent '73
Western/Comedy
12257   100 mins   C
B, V
Dennis Hopper, Warren Oates, Peter Boyle, Ben Johnson, directed by James Frawley
Set at the turn of the century, a young bank robber finds it difficult to give up his life of crime when faced with the hypocrisy of the local townsfolk.
M,A — EN
Marvin Schwartz; 20th Century Fox — *CBS/Fox Video*   P
1121

Kid Creole and The   Fil-Ent '82
Coconuts
Music-Performance
07829   48 mins   C
B, V
Directed by Jay Dubin
This film is a recording of a 'rap' musical by Kid Creole and The Coconuts performed at The Ritz, New York. Using scene and costume changes the storyline follows the search for a lost lover. Songs include 'Going Places,' 'In the Jungle,' 'Animal Crackers,' 'I am,' 'Schweinere,' 'Gina Gina,' 'Coati Mundi Rap,' 'Latin Music,' 'Table Manners' and 'Dear Addy.'
S,A — EN
Champion Ent. Org; Island Records Ltd — *Island Pictures*   P
IPV004L

Kid Creole and the   Fil-Ent '84
Coconuts—The Lifeboat
Party
Music-Performance
12941   60 mins   C
B, V
Filmed at the Hammersmith Odeon, this tape includes 'Stool Pidgeon', 'Broadway Rhythm', 'Naughty Boy', 'Call Me the Entertainer', 'I'm a Wonderful Thing Baby' and 'Annie, I'm Not Your Daddy'.
F — EN
Unknown — *Video Form Pictures*   H, P
VFM 001

Kid Dynamite   Fil-Ent '43
Comedy/Adventure
06321   59 mins   B/W
V2, B, V
The East Side Kids, Pamela Blake
This film is a situation comedy set in a tough quarter of New York City. A young gang leader has a brush with a group of local crooks and his sister's boyfriend takes his place in a boxing contest. Later at a dance the leader challenges the boyfriend to a fight.
F — EN
Monogram — *World of Video 2000*   H, P
GF512

Kid from Not-So-Big, The   Fil-Ent '??
Western
09423   88 mins   C
V2, B, V
Jennifer McAllister, Robert Viharo, Veronica Cartwright, Paul Tulley, Don Keefer, George 'Buck' Flower, Missy Gold, directed by Bill Crain
Set in the Wild West of 1870, this film tells the story of Jenny, a 12 year old girl who takes over as Editor of the local newspaper. She is soon involved in one of the hottest scandals ever to hit the town of Not-So-Big, with runaway stages, swindling con-men, gun-fighters and wild chases.
BBFC:U — F — EN
Unknown — *Guild Home Video*   H, P, E

Kid, The/The Idle Class   Fil-Ent '21
Comedy
05842   90 mins   B/W
B, V
Charlie Chaplin, Jackie Coogan
This tape features two Charlie Chaplin films. 'The Kid' is the story of a young boy adopted by the famous tramp and the consequences. 'The Idle Class' features Chaplin as both the tramp and a club's wealthy resident boozer in a straight 'send-up' of the 'country club' set.
F — EN
First National — *Polygram Video*   P
7901434/7901432

Kidco   Fil-Ent '83
Comedy
13253   100 mins   C
B, V
Scott Schwartz, Clifton James, directed by Ronald F Maxwell
A family of enterprising youngsters find a novel way for making money and cut through the red tape to get it into the bank.
BBFC:PG — F — EN
Frank Yablans; David Niven Jr — *CBS/Fox Video*   P
1359

PALADIN VIDEO HOME ENTERTAINMENT GUIDE

Kidnapped Fil-Ent '71
Drama
04250 103 mins C
B, V

Michael Caine, Trevor Howard, Jack Hawkins, Donald Pleasence, Gordon Jackson, Vivien Heilbron, Lawrence Douglas, Jack Watson

A fast moving drama set against a dramatic Scottish backdrop in the turbulent times following the fearful battle of Culloden.
BBFC:U — F — EN
American International — Rank Video Library H, P
0017

Kidnapped Fil-Ent "?
Cartoons/Adventure
08797 45 mins C
B, V

Animated

This film is based on Robert Louis Stevenson's classic story. It tells the story of an orphan boy, whos is cheated out of his inheritance by his greedy uncle.
F — EN
Unknown — VCL Video Services P
A326B

Kidnapping of the President, The Fil-Ent '80
Suspense/Drama
06153 113 mins C
V2, B, V

William Shatner, Hal Holbrook, Van Johnson, Ava Gardner, Miguel Fernandes, Cindy Girling, directed by George Mendeluk

This film follows the international crisis that occurs when the President is kidnapped while on a state visit to Canada. A determined terrorist and former member of a Marxist Group incarcerates the President in a truck packed with explosives and demands his ransom; a race against time follows.
BBFC:X — A — EN
Sefel Pictures Intl Prod — Guild Home Video H, P, E

Kids Are Alright, The Fil-Ent '79
Music-Performance/Documentary
07850 91 mins C
V2, B, V

Pete Townshend, Roger Daltrey, Keith Moon, John Entwistle

This is a compilation of television, concert and interview footage following the growth of the group 'The Who' from the early 60's Mod era to their super stardom of the late 1970's. The film culminates with a laser dominated performance of the band in full force.
S,A — EN
Who Films Ltd — Polygram Video H, P
791 514

Kids from Fame, The Fil-Ent '??
Music-Performance/Dance
12214 58 mins C
B, V

Debbie Allen, Gene Anthony Ray, Lee Curreri, Erica Gimpel, Lori Singer, Carlo Imperato

The cast of the TV Show 'Fame' sings and dances in a live sold out performance at the Royal Albert Hall, London.
F — EN
MGM UA — MGM/UA Home Video P
10205

Kill Fil-Ent '8?
Drama/Horror
09138 88 mins C
V2, B, V

After a failed mission in Vietnam, a man and his fellow soldiers are captured by the enemy. They are imprisoned and subjected to degrading confinement. When they are eventually released he returns home, only to discover a horror that awaits him. This horror sends him on a vendetta against one of the world's most feared organisations.
C,A — EN
Unknown — Go Video Ltd P
PIC 003

Kill Fil-Ent '71
Crime-Drama
12533 107 mins C
B, V

Jean Seberg, James Mason, Stephen Boyd, directed by Romain Gary

When an Interpol agent is sent to investigate a drug conspiracy his wife appears on the scene and they find themselves entangled in a web of unexplained murders.
BBFC:18 — A — EN
Pathe Films — THORN EMI P
TXB 90 17104/TVB 90 17102

Kill and Kill Again Fil-Ent '7?
Drama/Martial arts
08360 100 mins C
V2, B, V

James Ryan, Anneline Kriel, Stan Schmidt, Bill Flynn, Norman Robinson, Ken Gampu, John Ramsbottom

(For Explanation of codes, see USE GUIDE and KEY)

PALADIN VIDEO HOME ENTERTAINMENT GUIDE

A martial arts champion attempts to rescue a kidnapped Nobel Prize-winning chemist who has developed a high-yield synthetic fuel.
BBFC:PG — S,A — EN
Igo Kantor — Guild Home Video   H, P, E

Kill the Golden Goose   Fil-Ent '79
Martial arts
05481   91 mins   C
V2, B, V
Ed Parker, Bong Soo Han, directed by Elliott Hang
This story follows the trail of a skillful hired assassin who operates all over the world from his base in the Hawaiian Islands. His methods are ingenious and deadly; he is hired by a conglomerate to eliminate three key witnesses. He locates and kills two of them but the third is being kept well protected with the code name 'Golden Goose.'
BBFC:X — A — EN
Skytrain Kim Films — Iver Film Services
P
142

Killer Elite   Fil-Ent '75
Crime-Drama
13173   122 mins   C
B, V
James Caan, Robert Duvall, directed by Sam Peckinpah
Com Teg is an organisation that handles the jobs the CIA prefers not to do and this movie involves the elements of intrigue, deceit, assassins and duplicity.
BBFC:X — A — EN
Exeter Associates — Warner Home Video
P
99287

Killer Inside Me, The   Fil-Ent '76
Drama
08308   95 mins   C
B, V
Stacey Keach, Keenan Wynn, Susan Tyrrell, Charles McGraw
This film features a Deputy Sheriff who is known, by the people in the small town of Central City, Montana, to be a friend of everyone. However, when a prostitute arrives in town, certain happenings occur causing him to reveal a split personality, changing from his usual good-natured self to a brutal, sadistic killer.
A — EN
Warner Bros — Video Film Organisation
P
0004

Killer Inside Me, The   Fil-Ent '83
Western
12946   95 mins   C
B, V
Stacy Keach, Keenan Wynn, John Carradine, Susan Tyrell, directed by Burt Kennedy
Past memories turn a deceptively mild-mannered sheriff of a town in Montana into a savage killer.
A — EN
Michael W Leighton — Video Form Pictures
H, P
MGS 032

Killer Volcano   Fil-Ent '8?
Drama
09194   97 mins   C
B, V
Art Carney, David Huffman, Cassie Yates
This is a story of devastation, involving fear, greed, panic and the deepest bonds of friendship. After 123 years of silence, the 9,677 foot high Mount St. Helens begins to erupt.
S,A — EN
Unknown — Video Form Pictures   H, P
MGS 20

Killerfish   Fil-Ent '78
Crime-Drama
05871   96 mins   C
B, V
Lee Majors, Karen Black, James Franciscus
After a raid on a mining complex, a box containing priceless emeralds is deposited by the gang in the muddy waters of a Brazilian reservoir. They had planned that after sixty days, if the police activity had cooled, the box would be retrieved and the spoils shared. Some of the gang are impatient and as each one attempts to take the emeralds they die a violent death beneath the water.
BBFC:A — S,A — EN
Unknown — Precision Video Ltd   P
BITC 3085/VITC 3085

Killer's Curse   Fil-Ent '??
Horror
07620   80 mins   C
V2, B, V
A con man and his partner specialise in defrauding the wealthy. After a phony attempt to raise a boy from the dead, he apparently dies. However, his evil lives on in a young nurse.
BBFC:X — A — EN
Unknown — Iver Film Services   P

Killer's Gold   Fil-Ent '7?
Crime-Drama
07770   87 mins   C
V2, B, V

PALADIN VIDEO HOME ENTERTAINMENT GUIDE

Robert Widmark, Dan Forest
A suspenseful tale involving blackmail, robbery, murder and romance.
S,A — EN
Unknown — *Fletcher Video*   **H, P**
AV600

Killer's Moon   Fil-Ent '??
Horror
06067   89 mins   C
V2, B, V

A coach load of school girls are stranded in a remote area and as night approaches they take refuge in a derelict country house. Four criminal psychopaths who have escaped from a nearby hospital subject the girls to an endless night of terror.
BBFC:X — A — EN
Unknown — *Video Programme Distributors* **P**
Inter-Ocean—049

Killing Kind, The   Fil-Ent '7?
Suspense
01682   88 mins   C
V2, B, V

John Savage, Ann Sothern, Ruth Roman
A young man, recently released from a two-year sentence on a rape charge for which he claims to be innocent, returns to seek revenge on those who were responsible for his being sent to prison.
C,A — EN
Unknown — *Intervision Video*   **H, P**
A-A 0284

Killing Machine   Fil-Ent '83
Crime-Drama
13220   95 mins   C
V2, B, V

George Rivero, Margaux Hemingway, Lee Van Cleef, Willie Aames, directed by J. Anthony Loma
Savage violence erupts when an organised crime syndicate declares war on the truckers who haul fruit from Spain across Europe to Germany.
BBFC:18 — A — EN
Esme International — *Embassy Home Entertainment*   **P**
1386

Killing of Angel Street, The   Fil-Ent '8?
Mystery
09140   100 mins   C
B, V

Liz Alexander, John Hargreaves, Reg Lye, David Downer, Brendon Lunney, Caz Lederman, Allen Bickford, Alexander Archdale, directed by Donald Crombie
This film tells the story of Angel Street, where a signal was given for the wrecking crews to move in. The shocked residents protested only to be met with 'unfortunate accidents'. It was ignored by the Police, Government Officials and overlooked by the media. It continues with the struggle of two people to battle against the organisation.
S,A — EN
Forest Home Film; Australian Film Commission — *Video Brokers*   **H, P**
004X

Killing of Sister George, The   Fil-Ent '69
Drama
04247   134 mins   C
B, V

Beryl Reid, Susannah York, Coral Browne, Ronald Fraser
This film stars Beryl Reid as an ageing lesbian actress who plays Sister George—everybody's favorite nurse in a long-running TV soap-opera. This hard hitting film pulls no punches in its frank treatment of lesbianism and Sister George's pitiful decline, stage death and final humiliation.
BBFC:X — A — EN
Cinerama Releasing — *Rank Video Library* **H, P**
0030

Killpoint   Fil-Ent '82
Crime-Drama
12925   92 mins   C
B, V

Richard Roundtree, Cameron Mitchell, directed by Frank Harris
An armoury raid takes place and all the hardware is sold off to the local Chinese, Puerto Rican and black criminals with the proviso that whatever they do there must be no witnesses left.
A — EN
Unknown — *Video Form Pictures*   **H, P**
MGX 005

Kim   Fil-Ent '84
Adventure
13225   141 mins   C
V2, B, V

Peter O'Toole, Bryan Brown, John Rhys-Davies, directed by John Davies

---

(For Explanation of codes, see USE GUIDE and KEY)

PALADIN VIDEO HOME ENTERTAINMENT GUIDE

An orphaned street boy, son of a British soldier, is recruited by a British secret agent and becomes a spy against Russian subversives in the Himalayan foothills.
BBFC:15 — S,A — EN
London Films — Embassy Home Entertainment P
1385

Kim Carnes Voyeur Fil-Ent '82
Music-Performance
08579 60 mins C
B, V
Kim Carnes
This tape features Kim Carnes and songs from her first video album. The tracks included are 'Voyeur,' 'Looker,' 'Say You Don't Know Me,' 'Does It Make You Remember,' 'Breakin' Away from Sanity,' 'Undertow,' 'Merc Man,' 'The Arrangement,' 'Thrill of the Grill,' 'Take It on the Chin.'
S,A — EN
Unknown — THORN EMI P
TXE 90 0906 4/TVE 90 0906 2

Kimba the White Lion- Part 2 Fil-Ent '??
Adventure/Cartoons
09900 90 mins C
B, V
Animated
This is the second full-length adventure of Kimba the White Lion where the hero continues to battle as champion of the defenceless against the powerful. He fights with Speckle Rex, King of the spotted lions, calms furious elephants and saves Big O the baboon from deadly sulphur fumes.
F — EN
Unknown — Entertainment in Video H, P
EVB 2002/EVV 2002

Kimberly Jim Fil-Ent '65
Musical/Comedy
07849 78 mins C
B, V
Jim Reeves, Madeline Usher, Olive Parnell
In this musical two gamblers from Tennessee win a diamond mine in a fixed poker game. They discover that it is barren; after a while, however, it begins to produce and they return it to the rightful owner and his lovely daughter.
F — EN
Avco Embassy — Polygram Video H, P
791 509

Kind Hearts and Coronets Fil-Ent '50
Comedy
01179 102 mins B/W
B, V
Alec Guinness, Dennis Price, Valerie Hobson, Joan Greenwood, directed by Robert Hamer
A tour de force for Alec Guinness, who plays eight different roles in this film. An ambitious young man sets out to murder his relatives one by one in an effort to attain a dukedom.
BBFC:A — S,A — EN
J Arthur Rank — THORN EMI P
TXE 90 0010 4/TVE 90 0010 2

Kind of Loving, A Fil-Ent '62
Drama
00588 107 mins B/W
B, V
Alan Bates, Thora Hird, June Ritchie, directed by John Schlesinger
Set against the background of industrial Northern England, this film tells the story of two people trying to adjust to each other and a new way of life after they are forced into marriage when the girl becomes pregnant.
BBFC:X — A — EN
Joseph Janni — THORN EMI P
TXE 90 0205 4/TVE 90 0205 2

King and I, The Fil-Ent '56
Musical
01741 133 mins C
B, V, LV
Deborah Kerr, Yul Brynner, Rita Moreno, Martin Benson
The story is based on the musical play which was adapted from the biography 'Anna and the King of Siam,' by Margaret Landon.
Academy Awards '56: Best Actor (Yul Brynner); Best Scoring Musical. BBFC:U — F — EN
20th Century Fox — CBS/Fox Video P
4A-022

King Creole Fil-Ent '58
Musical-Drama
01009 115 mins B/W
B, V
Elvis Presley, Carolyn Jones, Walter Matthau, Dean Jagger, Dolores Hart, Vic Morrow
A teenager, involved in holdup, becomes a big hit when he's forced to sing in gangster's nightclub.
F — EN
Paramount — CBS/Fox Video P
3B-068

King Kong Fil-Ent '33
Horror
05048 86 mins B/W
B, V
Fay Wray, Bruce Cabot, Robert Armstrong, directed by Merian C Cooper

PALADIN VIDEO HOME ENTERTAINMENT GUIDE

A giant ape is brought to New York to entertain the civilised world, but instead terrorises the city.
F — EN
RKO — *THORN EMI* P
TXC 90 0063 4/TVC 90 0063 2

King Kong Fil-Ent '76
Fantasy/Adventure
07463 128 mins C
B, V
Jeff Bridges, Charles Grodin, Jessica Lange, directed by John Guillermin
Shot entirely on location on the Hawaiian island of Kauai and in New York, this film is a re-make of the 1933 classic. The explorers, now prospecting for oil, find a giant ape which they capture and take back to New York where it terrorizes the city.
BBFC:A — S,A — EN
Dino De Laurentiis Corporation — *THORN EMI* P
TXB 90 0678 4/TVB 90 0678 2

King of Comedy Fil-Ent '82
Drama/Comedy
12509 105 mins C
B, V
Robert De Niro, Jerry Lewis, directed by Martin Scorsese
This is the story of a man prepared to go to any lengths to achieve his dream of a spot on a top TV show.
BBFC:PG — S,A — EN
Embassy International Pictures — *THORN EMI* P
TXB 90 22004; TVB 90 2200 2

King of Kong Island Fil-Ent '77
Horror
01174 92 mins C
V2, B, V
Brad Harris, Marc Lawrence
Intent on world domination, group of mad scientists implant receptors in the brains of gorillas on Kong Island, and the monster apes run amok.
F — EN
Unknown — *Intervision Video* P
A-AE 0166

King of the Mountain Fil-Ent '81
Adventure
09852 86 mins C
B, V
Harry Hamlin, Joseph Bottoms, Dennis Hopper

This film shows devoted racing enthusiasts pitting their driving expertise and super specification cars against each other on Mulholland Drive, Hollywood, as they fight for the title, King of the Mountain.
F — EN
Universal; Polygram — *Polygram Video*
H, P
790 4804/790 4802

King Solomon's Treasure Fil-Ent '76
Adventure
06776 84 mins C
V2, B, V
David McCallum, John Colicos, Patrick Macnee, Britt Ekland
An expedition faces mystery and death when they enter the forbidden city of King Solomon.
S,A — EN
Filmco Limited; Harry Alan Towers — *Intervision Video* H, P
A-AE 0370

Kingdom of the Spiders Fil-Ent '78
Horror
06792 91 mins C
V2, B, V
William Shatner, Tiffany Bolling, Woody Strode
A desert town is invaded by swarms of killer tarantulas which began to consume the townspeople.
C,A — EN
Arachnid Productions — *Intervision Video*
H, P
A-AE 0318

Kingfisher—Secret Splendour of the Brooks Gen-Edu '8?
Birds
09099 28 mins C
B, V
Directed by Ronald Eastman
This programme shows the splendour of the kingfisher, diving with great accuracy into a stream in search of food.
Berlin Agricultural Film Festival '84: Golden Ear Award BISFA '82: Bronze Award S,A — ED
Royal Society for the Protection of Birds — *Royal Society for the Protection of Birds* H, P

King's Story, A Fil-Ent '80
Royalty-GB/Documentary
05897 96 mins C
B, V
Narrated by Orson Welles

(For Explanation of codes, see USE GUIDE and KEY)

PALADIN VIDEO HOME ENTERTAINMENT GUIDE

The Duke of Windsor tells his own life story, from his Victorian childhood, through his years as Prince of Wales, to the abdication in 1936.
F — EN
Jack Le Vieu — *THORN EMI*   **P**
TXB 90 0512 4/TVB 90 0512 2

Kinky Coaches and the Pom-Pom Pussycats, The   Fil-Ent '81
Comedy
08317   100 mins   C
B, V
John Vernon, Normal Fell, Robert Forster
This film features an American football match. Scoring is as high off the pitch as on, as the female supporters try every trick to win the championship. On the day of the match even the supporters join in.
BBFC:X — A — EN
Crunch Productions — *Nutland Video Ltd*
P

Kiri the Clown   Chi-Juv '7?
Puppets
05569   60 mins   C
V2, B, V
Animated, written by France and Jean Image, music by Fred Freed, sung by Guy Pierrault and Denise Benoit
The story of a clown and his puppet circus as they travel from town to town. His friends include a lovable parrott and a mischievous cat who are always quarrelling and getting themselves into unexpected scrapes.
IM — EN
Films Jean Image Production — *Videomedia*
P
BVM 3115/HVM 3115

Kismet   Fil-Ent '55
Musical
13429   107 mins   C
B, V
Howard Keel, Ann Blyth, Dolores Gray, Vic Damone, Sebastian Cabot, directed by Vincente Minnelli
In this Arabian nights fantasy, an evil wizard attempts to marry the Caliph to a princess but is thwarted by the magic powers of a street beggar. The music is adapted from Borodin, producing standards such as 'Stranger in Paradise,' 'And This is My Beloved' and 'Baubles, Bangles and Beads.'
BBFC:U — F — EN
MGM — *MGM/UA Home Video*   **P**
10130

Kiss Daddy Goodbye   Fil-Ent '8?
Horror
08696   92 mins   C
V2, B, V
Fabian Forte, Marilyn Burns, Jon Cedar, directed by Patrick Regan
Set on the rugged coast of North California, a small seaside town becomes the scene for a series of weird events. Two children had witnessed the murder of their father by a gang of bikers. Having inherited their dead mother's psychic powers, they decide to re-animate him to avenge his own death and look after them.
BBFC:AA — C,A — EN
Unknown — *Video Unlimited*   **H, P**
049

Kiss Me Kate   Fil-Ent '??
Musical/Dance
12218   105 mins   C
B, V
Ann Miller, Kathryn Grayson, Howard Keel, Tommy Rall, Bobby Van, Bob Fosse, directed by George Sidney
An actor and his wife star opposite each other in a musical version of Shakespeare's 'Taming of the Shrew'. The musical score is by Cole Porter and includes 'Saint Love', 'Why Can't You Behave' and 'Wunderbar'.
F — EN
MGM — *MGM/UA Home Video*   **P**
10307

Kiss Me Killer   Fil-Ent '??
Crime-Drama
06868   102 mins   C
V2, B, V
Alice Arno, Gilda Arancio, James Harris, Lina Romay, Olivier Mathot
A gang of criminals arrange to meet in a bar after a robbery on a luxury yacht. A quarrel breaks out and two of the gangsters are shot dead. One of them is the boss of the gang. The others agree to tell his wife that he was shot by the police. However, she does not believe them, so she hires a private detective to investigate what really happened.
S,A — EN
Unknown — *European Video Company*
P

Kiss of the Tarantula   Fil-Ent '72
Horror
08638   84 mins   C
V2, B, V
Eric Mason, Suzanne Ling, Herman Wallner, Patricia Landon

PALADIN VIDEO HOME ENTERTAINMENT GUIDE

A young girl, with a fascination for spiders, overhears her mother's plans to murder her father. She employs a horrific scheme to stop her mother. Years later, now an attractive woman, anyone who threatens her way of life is dealt with in a gruesome way.
A — EN
Unknown — *Hokushin Audio Visual Ltd* **P**
VM 48

Kitty—Return to Auschwitz Gen-Edu '80
Documentary/World War II
07244   90 mins   C
B, V
This programme records Kitty Hart's first journey to Auschwitz since the war. She takes her son with her to try and explain to him the full horror of what she and her mother had seen and experienced while they were prisoners. She gives a detailed account of what took place with a determination that it will never be forgotten. Prix Futura, Berlin '81: Documentary Award; Commonwealth Film and TV Festival, Nicosia '80: Special Award; The Royal Television Society Journalism Awards '80: Best Documentary.   *S,A — ED*
Yorkshire Televsion — *THORN EMI; Concord Film Council Ltd*   **P**
TXD 90 0703 4/TVD 90 0703 2

Klansman, The Fil-Ent '74
Crime-Drama/Suspense
07652   90 mins   C
B, V
Richard Burton, Lee Marvin
Set in the late 1960's in Ellerton, a small town in Alabama, this film follows events after a young girl is raped. All she can say is that her attacker was black. As a result the old secret ways of the South re-emerge, the Ku Klux Klan ride by night and murder follows murder as the community becomes divided.
BBFC:X *— A — EN*
Paramount — *VCL Video Services*   **P**
P218D

Klassic Keystone Komedy Kapers Fil-Ent '7?
Comedy
02222   60 mins   C
V
Arbuckle, Chaplin, and Keaton are among the many stars captured in this hour of hilarity with true greats of the early Hollywood era.
F — EN
Keystone — *JVC*   **P**
PRT 10

Kleinhoff Hotel Fil-Ent '??
Drama/Suspense
07929   92 mins   C
V2, B, V
Corinne Clery, Bruce Robinson, Katya Rupe, Michel Placido
A married woman discovers a new side to herself when she meets a tourist in a hotel. Their short-lived relationship becomes intensely emotional.
S,A — EN
Unknown — *Video Programme Distributors* **P**
Cinehollywood—V1790

Klondike Fever Fil-Ent '79
Adventure
06804   102 mins   C
V2, B, V
Rod Steiger, Angie Dickinson, Lorne Greene, Jeff East, Barry Morse
Based on Jack London's exploits during the Klondike Gold Rush, this film follows the adventures of young London as he encounters the gold-madness around him.
S,A — EN
Gilbert W Taylor — *Intervision Video*   H, **P**
A-AE 0366

Klute Fil-Ent '71
Drama
13071   109 mins   C
B, V
Jane Fonda, Donald Sutherland, directed by Alan J. Pakula
A call girl is threatened, and an investigator goes to her aid and becomes emotionally involved.
BBFC:X *— A — EN*
Warner Bros Inc; GUS Productions Inc — *Warner Home Video*   **P**
61027

Knife for the Ladies Fil-Ent '74
Horror
02441   51 mins   C
V2, B, V
Jack Elam, Ruth Roman, Jeff Cooper
Burns, an investigator from St. Louis is called in to investigate the gruesome murders taking place in the once peaceful town of Mescal.
BBFC:X *— A — EN*
Unknown — *Iver Film Services*   **P**

Knife in the Water Fil-Ent '62
Drama
08551   90 mins   B/W
B, V

(For Explanation of codes, see USE GUIDE and KEY)   373

PALADIN VIDEO HOME ENTERTAINMENT GUIDE

Leon Niemczyk, Jolanta Umecka, Zygmunt Malanowicz, directed by Roman Polanski
An affluent married couple nearly run down a 17-year-old hitchhiker. They pick him up. There is immediate antagonism in the car. They take him sailing and a dangerous game starts involving the boy's prized possession, a knife. This is the original version subtitled in English.
BBFC:X — *A* — EN
Film Polski — *THORN EMI*   **P**
TXE 90 0732 4/TVE 90 07322

Knight Without Armour   Fil-Ent '37
Drama
09863   96 mins   B/W
B, V
Marlene Dietrich, Robert Donat, Basil Gill, John Clements, directed by Jacques Feyder
This film, based on a James Hilton novel, tells the story of a Tsarist minister's daughter caught up in the broil of the Russian Revolution. She falls in love with a young English journalist.
F — *EN*
United Artists — *Polygram Video*   **H, P**
790 2544/790 2542

Knocking at Heaven's Door   Fil-Ent '??
Comedy/Fantasy
07619   94 mins   C
V2, B, V
An underworld syndicate member who was 'bumped off' for his shady activities tries to con his way into heaven. The result is an eventful comedy of errors.
BBFC:U — *F* — EN
Unknown — *Iver Film Services*   **P**

Knowledge, The   Fil-Ent '79
Comedy
13704   79 mins   C
B, V
Nigel Hawthorne, Mick Ford, Kim Taylforth, Maureen Lipman, Michael Elphick, directed by Bob Brooks
This is the story of the trials and tribulations of four men as they struggle to pass their tests to become London taxi drivers.
F — *EN*
Christopher Neame — *THORN EMI*   **P**
90 2588

Kotch   Fil-Ent '71
Comedy-Drama
04181   114 mins   C
V2, B, V
Walter Matthau, Deborah Winters, Felicia Farr, Charles Aidman
A 72-year-old widower, living with his son and daugher-in-law, befriends an unwed pregnant teenager. As an alternative to a home for the aged, he buys a house near Palm Springs, and makes it a home for the girl and her baby also.
BBFC:AA — *C,A* — EN
Cinerama — *Guild Home Video*   **H, P**

Kramer Vs Kramer   Fil-Ent '79
Drama
13084   101 mins   C
B, V
Dustin Hoffman, Meryl Streep, Jane Alexander, Justin Henry, directed by Robert Benton
This film depicts the legal battle between a husband and his wife who left him in charge of their six year old son but returns after a year and wants custody.
Academy Awards '79: Best Picture; Best Director (Benton); Best Actor (Hoffman); Best Supporting Actress (Streep).   *S,A* — *EN*
Stanley Jaffe — *RCA/Columbia Pictures Video UK*   **H, P**
10038

Kublai Khan   Fil-Ent '65
Drama
08826   111 mins   C
B, V
Anthony Quinn, Omar Sharif, Orson Welles, Robert Hossein, Elsa Martinelli, Horst Buchholz, directed by Noel Coward, Denys de la Patelliere
This film tells the story of one of history's most terrible rulers, the Great Mogul and Warlord of Cathay, Kublai Khan. It is based on the true story of a group of explorers led by the legendary Marco Polo.
C,A — *EN*
MGM — *VCL Video Services*   **P**
P280D

Kung Fu Gang Busters   Fil-Ent '7?
Martial arts
07917   90 mins   C
V2, B, V
An organised crime syndicate is destroyed in Kung Fu style by the forces of law and order.
S,A — *EN*
Unknown — *Video Programme Distributors* **P**
Inter-Ocean—072

Kung Fu Girl   Fil-Ent '7?
Martial arts
09945   77 mins   C
B, V
Cheng Pei Pei, Ou Wei, James Tien, Tien Mi, Lo Wei

PALADIN VIDEO HOME ENTERTAINMENT GUIDE

A loyal, militant female sets out to avenge the arrest of a student activist, with the expected devastating results.
BBFC:18 — A — EN
Unknown — Rank Video Library   H, P
0088 A

Kung-Fu Warriors, The Fil-Ent '79
Martial arts
12838   82 mins   C
V2, B, V
Trained in the ever-changing art of Kung-Fu, a young man sets about helping people to straighten out their problems.
BBFC:18 — A — EN
Unknown — Video Programme Distributors
P
VPD 237

Kuroneko Fil-Ent '??
Drama
10022   99 mins   B/W
B, V
Directed by Kaneto Shindo
Two women who were raped and murdered by a band of marauding samurai pledge their souls to the devil in order to take their revenge. Japanese with English subtitles.
A — EN   JA
Japanese — Palace Video Ltd   P
PVC 2046A

Kwaheri Gen-Edu '??
Documentary/Africa
08617   52 mins   C
V2, B, V
Mike Carter
In this programme the habits and rituals of African life are observed. Tribesmen still prepare their poisoned arrows as they have for generations and the elephant is still hunted by spear. Further into the search, a witch doctor is found who performs skull operations.
S,A — EN
David Chudnow — Hokushin Audio Visual Ltd
P
VM 70

Kwaidan Fil-Ent '64
Suspense
10032   164 mins   C
B, V
Rentaro Mikuni, Ganjiro Nakamura, Katsuo Nakamura, directed by Masaki Kobayashi

A trilogy of Japanese ghost stories, all written by Lafcadio Hearn, bring a touch of elegance to the spooky doings.
S,A — EN
Ninjin Club; Bungei — Palace Video Ltd
P
PVC 2047A

L

La Ya Oumi (No, Mother) Fil-Ent '??
Drama
06738   102 mins   C
V2, B, V
A wife's pressure for money drives her husband to drink and a life of crime.
C,A — EN   AB
Unknown — Intervision Video   H, P
A-C 0146

Lacemaker, The Fil-Ent '77
Drama/Romance
08838   100 mins   C
B, V
Isabelle Huppert, Yves Beneyton, Florence Giorgetti, Anne Marie Duringer, directed by Claude Goretta
This film tells the story of an 18-year-old girl, in search of the perfect romance. She becomes ill and withdrawn when her first affair breaks up. It is based on the novel by Pascal Laine.
C,A — EN
Action; FR3; Citel — VCL Video Services
P
P215D

Ladies' Doctor Fil-Ent '??
Drama
08908   80 mins   C
V2, B, V
A successful gynecologist, because of rising debts, disappears to the Caribbean. He leaves his assistant in charge who is very popular with the ladies.
BBFC:X — A — EN
Unknown — Video Programme Distributors
P
Inter-Ocean 014

Lady Caroline Lamb Fil-Ent '72
Drama
00586   118 mins   C
B, V

(For Explanation of codes, see USE GUIDE and KEY)

PALADIN VIDEO HOME ENTERTAINMENT GUIDE

Sarah Miles, Jon Finch, Richard Chamberlain, Margaret Leighton, John Mills, Ralph Richardson, Laurence Olivier
A member of Parliament's wife is involved with Lord Byron to the embarrassment of her family and the jeopardy of her husband's position.
BBFC:A — S,A — EN
Fernando Ghia — THORN EMI   P
TXB 90 0084 4/TVB 90 0084 2

Lady from Yesterday, The   Fil-Ent '84
Drama
13771   92 mins   C
B, V
Wayne Rogers, Bonnie Bedelia, Tina Chen, Bryan Price, directed by Robert Day
A soldier's happy family life is shattered when his Vietnamese ex-lover contacts him and asks him to take care of their child as she is dying.
BBFC:PG — S,A — EN
Comworld Productions; The Houston Lady Company — Odyssey Video   H, P

Lady Grey   Fil-Ent '80
Drama
12143   100 mins   C
V2, B, V
Ginger Alden, David Allen Coe, directed by Worth Keeter
A girl singer realises her wildest dreams when she is hired by a band but her life falls to pieces when she is raped by the bandleader.
BBFC:PG — S,A — EN
Inter Light Video — Intervision Video   H, P
A-A 0479

Lady Hamilton   Fil-Ent '8?
Drama
09129   100 mins   C
V2, B, V
John Mills, Michele Mercier, Richard Johnson
This film tells the classic story of Admiral Nelson who falls passionately in love with Lady Hamilton. Her husband, William Hamilton, is the British Ambassador to the Kingdom of the two Sicilies, who is very rich and nearly 70 years old. It tells the tragic event of Trafalgar, where Nelson faced the French Fleet, and a few minutes before the British won the battle, he was killed.
S,A — EN
Unknown — Go Video Ltd   P
GO 138

Lady of the House   Fil-Ent '78
Drama
08030   90 mins   C
V2, B, V

Dyan Cannon, Armand Assante, Zohra Lampert, Susan Tyrell, directed by Ralph Nelson and Vincent Sherman
This traces the life of Sally Stanford through the thirties and forties. It begins with her as a poor girl through her two years in prison, until she eventually becomes the first mayoress in the world.
BBFC:AA — C,A — EN
William Kayden Productions; M P C — Iver Film Services   P
199

Lady, Stay Dead   Fil-Ent '??
Drama
07879   91 mins   C
V2, B, V
Chard Hayward, Louise Howitt, Deborah Coulls, directed by Terry Bourke
Set in an idyllic Australian beach resort, this is the story of a man's flawed fascination for a beautiful actress-singer. His fascination leads to murder and an ensuing drama that is taut, tense and frightening.
S,A — EN
Unknown — Intervision Video   H, P
A-A0398

Lady Vanishes, The   Fil-Ent '38
Suspense
04258   93 mins   B/W
B, V, LV
Margaret Lockwood, Michael Redgrave, Paul Lucas, Dame May Whitty, Googie Withers, Linden Travers, Cecil Parker, directed by Alfred Hitchcock
When a young lady's traveling companion disappears, she finds that no one believes that the woman ever existed.
BBFC:A — F — EN
Gaumont — Rank Video Library   H, P
0026

Lady Vanishes, The   Fil-Ent '78
Mystery
01881   99 mins   C
B, V, LV
Elliot Gould, Cybill Shepherd, Herbert Lom, Arthur Lowe, Ian Carmichael, Angela Lansbury
Set on a fast-moving train, a man tries solving a mystery, not realising he is in the middle of it. A remake of the 1938 Hitchcock classic.
BBFC:A — S,A — EN
Rank — Rank Video Library   H, P
0009

Lady Whirlwind   Fil-Ent '71
Martial arts
06913   85 mins   C
B, V

---

376   (For Explanation of codes, see USE GUIDE and KEY)

PALADIN VIDEO HOME ENTERTAINMENT GUIDE

Angela Mao, Chang Yi
When a young girl sets out to avenge the death of her sister she is misled into believing that the man she seeks is dead. However, he is in hiding from a deadly female mistress of the martial arts. When the young girl finally catches up with the man they decide to temporarily forget their differences and fight the deadly female together.
S,A — EN
Unknown — *Rank Video Library* **H, P**
0086B

Ladykillers, The Fil-Ent '55
Comedy
01182   87 mins   C
B, V
Alec Guinness, Cecil Parker, Katie Johnson, Herbert Lom, Peter Sellers, directed by Alexander Mackendrick
A gang of bumbling bank robbers is foiled by a little old lady from whom they rent a room. Hilarious antics follow, especially on the part of Guinness, who plays the slightly demented-looking leader of the gang.
British Film Academy '55: Best Screenplay; Best Actress (Johnson).   BBFC:U — *F* — *EN*
Continental, J Arthur Rank — *THORN EMI*
P
TXE 90 0016 4/TVE 90 0016 2

Lama Avenger, The Fil-Ent '7?
Adventure/Martial arts
04603   87 mins   C
V2, B, V
Bruce Li
When Hong defeats some bullies from the local kung-fu school he is forced to leave the village. He opens his own school of martial arts and later becomes a famous film star. He is joined by his friend Mok to successfully defend themselves against the avenging bullies.
C,A — *EN*
Unknown — *Video Programme Distributors*
P
Inter-Ocean-041

Lancaster Gen-Edu '83
Aeronautics/World War II
09791   48 mins   C
B, V
This tells the story of the legendary Avro Lancaster, the mainstay of the British bombing offensive for the last three years of the war. A combination of rarely seen wartime film and animated diagrams.
S,A — *ED*
Thorn EMI Video Limited — *THORN EMI*
P
TXE 90 0857 4/TVE 90 0857 2

Land of No Return, The Fil-Ent '81
Adventure/Suspense
09947   85 mins   C
V2, B, V
William Shatner, Mel Torme
When a private aeroplane crashes high in the frozen wasteland of the Rocky Mountains, the ultimate challenge is to survive.
BBFC:U — *F* — *EN*
International Picture Show — *Video Unlimited*
H, P, E
064

Land of Silence and Gen-Edu '??
Darkness/the Flying
Doctors of East Africa
Documentary
08975   131 mins   C
B, V
Fini Straubinger, Heinrich Fleischmann, Vladimir Kokol
In 'Land of Silence' (colour) the life of Fini Straubinger is observed; she lost her sight at the age of 16 and her hearing two years later. A short description of her life is given and she is then shown looking after fellow sufferers. In the 'Flying Doctors of East Africa' (black and white) the lifestyle of the patients and doctors are observed.
S,A — *EN*
Cine-International — *Palace Video Ltd* **P**
PVC2032A

Land That Time Forgot, Fil-Ent '74
The
Adventure/Fantasy
04653   86 mins   C
B, V
Doug McClure, John McEnery, Susan Penhaligon
The film tells how a German U-Boat is swept under the polar ice to land on the fabled continent of Caprona. Whilst searching for oil to refuel their engines the party are attacked by assorted prehistoric monsters and primitive savages.
BBFC:U — *F* — *EN*
Amicus — *THORN EMI*   **H, P**
TXC 90 0238 4 /TVC 90 0238 2

Landscape Painting Fin-Art '81
Painting
05430   60 mins   C
B, V
Harold Riley
This cassette is a complete programme in the 'Master Class Painting Course' series led by Harold Riley, the famous artist and lecturer. This film is a working conversation with the artist as he paints a landscape in his own style offering

(For Explanation of codes, see USE GUIDE and KEY)

PALADIN VIDEO HOME ENTERTAINMENT GUIDE

first-hand information and inspiration. He discusses technique and colour values along with subjects and materials. Presented for the beginner with useful insight for the professional.
S,A — I
Harrison Partnership and Holiday Bros Ltd — *Holiday Brothers Ltd* P

Language of Birds, The Gen-Edu '79
Birds/Wildlife
04279 27 mins C
B, V
Birds communicate in many different ways. Songs and calls are an obvious part of their language, but they also make use of a complex variety of markings, postures and other signals.
BISFA'80: Bronze Award F — ED
Royal Society for the Protection of Birds — *Royal Society for the Protection of Birds* H, P

Laserblast Fil-Ent '78
Science fiction
01154 87 mins C
V2, B, V
Kim Milford, Cheryl Smith, Keenan Wynn, Roddy McDowall
A frustrated young man finds a powerful and deadly laser which was left near his home by aliens. Upon learning of its devastating capabilities, his personality changes and he seeks revenge against all who have taken advantage of him.
BBFC:A — M,A — EN
Charles Band — *Intervision Video* P
A-A 0286

Lassie Fil-Ent '62
Adventure
06230 90 mins C
B, V
Lassie, Jon Provost, Hugh Reilly
A runaway balloon carries off Lassie and young Timmy; they are stranded in the Canadian wilderness. This is the tale of their adventures and how they survived the ordeal.
F — EN
20th Century Fox; Owner-Wrather Corp — *VCL Video Services* P
F119

Lassie Fil-Ent '74
Cartoons/Adventure
09969 77 mins C
B, V
Animated
Lassie, the famous collie, leads the Rescue Rangers, a special team of animals; Old Toothless the mountain lion, a racoon, an owl, a skunk, a porcupine join forces whenever their help is needed. In one adventure Lassie goes to help Gene Fox, when ruthless land developers try to run him off his land. In the second adventure Doctor Simpson is needed to stop a growing epidemic, but he is imprisoned in a foreign country. In the third adventure there are strange lights and noises on the ranch.
F — EN
Filmation Associates — *Select Video Limited* P
3604/43

Lassie and the Rescue Rangers Fil-Ent '83
Cartoons/Adventure
12173 78 mins C
B, V
Animated
After a big storm a plane carrying two criminals crashes. The plane is loaded with dynamite and the rescue rangers are called in to stop their evil plans.
F — EN
Filmation Associates; Lassie Television Inc — *Select Video Limited* P
3620/43

Lassiter Fil-Ent '84
Suspense
13744 96 mins C
B, V
Tom Selleck, Jane Seymour, Lauren Hutton, Bob Hoskins, directed by Roger Young
When a haul of diamonds are secreted in the German Embassy in pre-war London to fund Nazi espionage, a reluctant cat-burglar is dragooned into stealing them by the FBI and Scotland Yard.
BBFC:18 — C,A — EN
Golden Harvest Films — *Rank Video Library*
H, P

Last American Hero, The Fil-Ent '73
Adventure
12256 95 mins C
B, V
Jeff Bridges, Valerie Perrine, Geraldine Fitzgerald, Ned Beatty, directed by Lamont Johnson
A boy from the back woods has to learn that compromises are needed when participating in stock car racing and living life to the full.
S,A — EN
William Roberts; John Cutts; 20th Century Fox — *CBS/Fox Video* P
1227

Last American Virgin, The Fil-Ent '82
Comedy
08341 92 mins C

PALADIN VIDEO HOME ENTERTAINMENT GUIDE

V2, B, V
Lawrence Monoson, Diane Franklin, Steve Antin, Joe Rubbo, Louisa Moritz
Three boys, good-looking Rick, wealthy David and plain, insecure Gary have got one objective—Karen. The film features top hits by Blondie, The Cars, The Commodores, Devo, U-2, Quincy Jones, The Police, REO Speedwagon and Tommy Tutone.
BBFC:X — A — EN
Golan-Globus Productions — *Guild Home Video* **H, P, E**

Last Chase, The Fil-Ent '80
Adventure
09069   106 mins   C
B, V
Lee Majors, Burgess Meredith, Chris Makepeace
Set during the near future, the day comes when there is no more petrol. All cars are ordered to be turned into the nearest depot. A famous racing car driver can't bring himself to get rid of his car, and so dismantles it, and hides it in his garage. He later reassembles it and flees to the country to join an underground movement.
S,A — EN
Martyn Burke; Fran Rosati — *Video Tape Centre* **P**
VTC 1035

Last Child, The Fil-Ent '73
Drama
04275   71 mins   C
B, V
Michael Cole, Harry Guardino, Van Heflin, Janet Margolin, Edward Asner
A sobering tale of the future. Set in 1994 at a time when overpopulation has forced the US government to limit all parents to one child, 'The Last Child' tells of a young mother whose pregnancy is deemed illegal.
C,A — EN
Worldvision — *Rank Video Library* **H, P**
0036

Last Day of the War, The Fil-Ent '69
War-Drama
05609   95 mins   C
B, V
George Maharis, Maria Perschey, John Clark, Aldo Rey
The story of an American Army platoon searching for a famous German Scientist during the last days of World War II. The SS are also searching but plan to kill him.
S,A — EN
Spanish; Sagittarius Prods — *Home Video Merchandisers* **H, P**
007

Last Days of Pompeii, The/The Mysterious Desperado Fil-Ent '??
Drama/Western
05712   150 mins   B/W
B, V
Preston Foster, Basil Rathbone, Alan Hale, Louis Calhern, Dorothy Wilson, directed by Ernest B. Schoedsack, Tim Holt, Richard Martin, directed by Leslie Selander
Two films featured on one cassette. 'The Last Days of Pompeii' (Black/white, 92 mins, 1936) is the story of a humble gladiator who fights his way to wealth and freedom only to be undermined by his adopted son who rescues slaves from the Romans. As the city is shaken by violent earthquakes he must decide where his loyalties lie. 'The Mysterious Desperado' (Black/white, 58 mins, 1950) is a story in which the hero helps a friend make a rightful claim to his late uncle's estate. The crooks who have taken over frame the heir but justice is done and the villains dealt with.
F — EN
RKO — *Kingston Video* **H, P**
KV30

Last Detail, The Fil-Ent '74
Comedy-Drama
12486   100 mins   C
B, V
Jack Nicholson, Otis Young, Randy Quaid
This hilarious but hard-hitting film is the story of two tough naval petty officers detailed to escort a prisoner from Virginia to Hampshire who decide to teach their previously unenlightened prisoner how to have a good time with drinking, fighting and womanising!
BBFC:18 — C,A — EN
Columbia — *RCA/Columbia Pictures Video UK* **H, P**
10076

Last Embrace Fil-Ent '79
Drama
12498   98 mins   C
B, V
Roy Schneider, Janet Margolin, directed by Jonathon Demme
An American government investigator survives an attempt on his life and has to use all his skills and ingenuity to go on living.
BBFC:18 — A — EN
Michael Taylor; Dan Wigutow — *Warner Home Video* **P**
99356

Last Feelings Fil-Ent '83
Drama
12609   98 mins   C
V2, B, V

(For Explanation of codes, see USE GUIDE and KEY)

PALADIN VIDEO HOME ENTERTAINMENT GUIDE

This is the story of a back-street boy who makes good but whose dream of happiness turns to tragedy.
BBFC:A — F — EN
GTO Films — VideoSpace Ltd   P

Last Fight, The　　　　　　　Fil-Ent　'7?
Drama
08825　　? mins　　C
B, V
Willie Colon, Ruben Blades, Fred Williamson, Joe Spinell
This film tells the story of a man involved with the Mafia. When his father is murdered by the mob, he decides to get even.
BBFC:15 — C,A — EN
Unknown — VCL Video Services　　P
M324 D

Last Flight of Noah's Ark, The　　Fil-Ent　'80
Adventure
12569　　93 mins　　C
B, V
Elliot Gould, Genevieve Bujold
A plane load of farm animals and four people are forced to land on the beach of an unmapped tropical island.
F — EN
Walt Disney Productions — Rank Video Library   H
132

Last Giraffe, The　　　　　　Fil-Ent　'79
Adventure
09851　　90 mins　　C
B, V
Simon Ward, Susan Anspach, Gordon Jackson, John Hallum, Rudolph Walker, Don Harrington, Saif Jeffired, directed by Jack Couffer
This is the true story of a young couple's adventure in raising a young rare Rothchild giraffe in Africa. It is based on a book, 'Raising Daisy Rothchild' by Jock and Betty Leslie-Melville.
F — EN
Westfall Prod; Charles G Mortimer
Jr — Polygram Video   H, P
791 5404/791 5402

Last Gun, The　　　　　　　Fil-Ent　'64
Western
06100　　90 mins　　C
V2, B, V
Cameron Mitchell, Carl Mohner, Kitty Carver
A band of gun-happy outlaws take over a village in the West, ill-treating the inhabitants. Only the Sheriff is brave enough to face-up to the bandits. A mysterious masked rider appears at every crucial moment to aid the Sheriff.
S,A — EN
Unknown — Video Programme Distributors   P
Cinehollywood—V1560

Last Horror Film, The　　　　Fil-Ent　'8?
Horror/Suspense
12146　　82 mins　　C
V2, B, V
Joe Spinell, Caroline Munro
This story was filmed against the background of the 1981 Cannes Film Festival. An international star who has won fame and recognition for her roles in horror pictures becomes in turn the victim of a plot.
BBFC:18 — C,A — EN
Unknown — Intervision Video   H, P
A-A 0469

Last Moments　　　　　　　Fil-Ent　'83
Drama
12608　　100 mins　　C
V2, B, V
A motherless boy is forced to fend for himself in the colourful but often squalid world of small-time showbusiness. Weeks of tiredness and malnutrition weaken him and he collapses and is taken to hospital where he must find the will to survive.
F — EN
GTO Films — VideoSpace Ltd   P

Last of the Badmen　　　　　Fil-Ent　'??
Western
08598　　91 mins　　C
V2, B, V
George Hilton, Frank Wolff, Pamela Tudor, Eduardo Fajardo, Franco Balducci, Femi Benussi, Christina Josani, directed by Nando Cicero
A young cowboy working for Don Jaime Morelos is almost beaten to death under his employer's instructions, having flirted with his frivolous wife. Full of hatred, he leaves the ranch, and begins life as an outlaw. However, trouble begins when his partner, a renowned bandit, starts killing for fun, and he only kills when he has to.
S,A — EN
Pacific Productions — Videomedia   P
PVM 6106/BVM 6106/HVM 6106

Last of the Mohicans, The　　Fil-Ent　'??
Western
06101　　104 mins　　C
V2, B, V

PALADIN VIDEO HOME ENTERTAINMENT GUIDE

Jack Taylor, Barbara Loy, Paul Muller
This film is set in North America at the time of the 7 year war. A Colonel in charge of an English Fort attacked by the French sends a party, including his two daughters, for reinforcements. Their Indian guide betrays them to the Delawares. A Mohican, the last of the tribe, who is in love with one of the daughters, fights to his last breath trying to save them.
S,A — EN
Unknown — *Video Programme Distributors*
P
Cinehollywood—V1010

Last of the Mohicans   Fil-Ent '77
Western/Adventure
08060   94 mins   C
B, V
Steve Forrest, Ned Romero, Don Shanks, Andrew Prine, Jane Ackman, directed by James L. Conway
This film is a remake of the classic 1826 story by James Fenimore Cooper. It tells the story of an American scout and his Indian friend who escort a small British party through hostile territory during the war between the native Indians and the French.
BBFC:U — F — EN
Sunn Classic — *Rank Video Library*   **H, P**
8004 C

Last of the Summer Wine   Fil-Ent '84
Comedy
13392   90 mins   C
B, V
Michael Bates, Bill Owen, Peter Sallis
Taken from the popular television series, three elderly, unemployed eccentrics drift contentedly through the small Yorkshire wool town where they live getting into michief.
F — EN
James Gilbert — *BBC Video*   **H, P**
7028

Last of the Vikings   Fil-Ent '60
Adventure
04287   100 mins   C
V2, B, V
Cameron Mitchell, Edmund Purdom, Isabelle Corey
In 700 A.D. Harald returns home to discover that his father, King of the Vikings, has been slain by Sveno, King of Norway. Harald sets off in pursuit and in disguise enters the Norwegian camp. He is recognised and escapes with his brother, who was being held captive by Sveno.
C,A — EN
Medallion — *Video Programme Distributors*
P
Inter-Ocean—018

Last Of The Wild—Volume 1   Gen-Edu '73
Documentary/Animals
07418   75 mins   C
B, V
Narrated by Ivan Tors
This tape is the first in a six-part series covering the private lives of some of the world's wild animals. Animals featured in Volume 1 include sharks who are photographed in their natural habitat by divers; lions who are observed in a family setting; bears who are watched consuming food during the summer in readiness for hibernation; and the gazelle, whose eternal struggle for survival is witnessed.
F — EN
Heritage Enterprises — *THORN EMI*   **P**
TXE 90 0592 4/TVE 90 0592 2

Last Of The Wild—Volume 2   Gen-Edu '73
Documentary/Animals
07419   77 mins   C
B, V
Narrated by Ivan Tors
This second tape in the series looks at camels not only as a means of transport but also as a source of milk, meat and leather; alligators who are equally at home on land or in water and are superbly equipped to survive; elephants and their lifelong support for members of their herd; and leopards, whose search for food depends on their extraordinary strength and agility.
F — ED
Heritage Enterprises Inc — *THORN EMI*
P
TXE 90 07154/TVE 90 07152

Last Of The Wild—Volume 3   Gen-Edu '73
Documentary/Animals
07420   77 mins   C
B, V
Narrated by Ivan Tors
This third tape in the series looks at lizards, especially the Komodo Dragon, which averages ten feet in length; giraffes who rely on each other for protection; kangaroos whose young are born after only one month's gestation; and buffaloes, who, while appearing passive, are the most aggressive of all the animals who inhabit the African plains.
F — ED
Heritage Enterprises Inc — *THORN EMI*
P
TXE 90 0738 4/TVE 90 0738 2

Last of the Wild—Volume 4   Gen-Edu '73
Documentary/Wildlife
08441   80 mins   C

(For Explanation of codes, see USE GUIDE and KEY)

PALADIN VIDEO HOME ENTERTAINMENT GUIDE

B, V
Narrated by Ivan Tors
This fourth tape in the series looks at venomous snakes which in Southern Africa are the deadliest killers in the bush; crocodiles, the last surviving relatives of dinosaurs; antelopes, which are among the most beautiful creatures of the African landscape; and Indian Elephants where there is a strong bond between members of a herd.
F — ED
Heritage Enterprises Inc — *THORN EMI* **P**
TXE 90 0769 4/TVE 90 0769 2

Last of the Wild—Volume 5   Gen-Edu '73
Documentary/Wildlife
08442   80 mins   C
B, V
Narrated by Ivan Tors
This fifth tape in the series looks at Zebras and wildebeests who live together in one of the most fertile parts of Africa, the Serengeti; dolphins whose intelligence is being used to find objects in the water; tigers, jaguars and pumas who have been so fiercely hunted by man that there are now only a few specimens left; and rhinos where there are now only 800 left of the Indian variety.
F — ED
Heritage Enterprises Inc — *THORN EMI* **P**
TXE 90 0849 4/TVE 90 0849 2

Last of the Wild—Volume 6   Gen-Edu '7?
Documentary/Animals
09004   80 mins   C
B, V
This sixth tape looks at the hippopotamus, sea lion, great apes and cheetah. The camera travels from Africa to the Arctic Ocean to film these animals in their natural habitat, revealing an underwater hippo ballet of surprising grace and a young sea lion pup taking to the water for the first time.
F — ED
Heritage Enterprises — *THORN EMI* **P**
TXE 90 0860 4/TVE 90 0860 2

Last Plane Out   Fil-Ent '7?
Adventure
12241   90 mins   C
B, V
Jan-Michael Vincent, Mary Crosby, David Huffman
An investigative journalist and a camera operator become caught up in a fierce civil war ripping apart Nicaragua and have to get themselves out of the country at all costs.
C,A — EN
Unknown — *VCL Video Services*   **P**
P393D

Last Rebel, The   Fil-Ent '7?
Western
07786   85 mins   C
V2, B, V
This film follows the adventures of two Confederate soldiers who choose to escape rather than surrender.
S,A — EN
Unknown — *Fletcher Video*   **H, P**
AV615

Last Reunion, The   Fil-Ent '78
Adventure
07988   96 mins   C
B, V
Cameron Mitchell, Leo Fong, Chanda Romero
In the year 1945, a young Philippine boy witnessed the brutal killing of his family by six American soldiers. Thirty—three years later the men return to the Philippnes for a reunion, to be faced now with an adult full of revenge for his slaughtered family.
C,A — EN
Pelefilm Productions; Koinonia Films — *Motion Epics Video Company Ltd*   **P**
155

Last Roman, The   Fil-Ent '72
Adventure/Drama
08829   100 mins   C
B, V
Orson Welles, Laurence Harvey, Honor Blackman, Michael Dunn
This film, set in Rome, tells of the attack on the city by Barbarian hordes. Only Cethegus, leader of the Roman aristocracy, can save the city from destruction.
S,A — EN
Constantin Films — *VCL Video Services* **P**
P269D

Last Round, The   Fil-Ent '7?
Crime-Drama
07779   94 mins   C
V2, B, V
Carlos Monzon

PALADIN VIDEO HOME ENTERTAINMENT GUIDE

A crime story involving trade union protection, big time operators and gang warfare.
S,A — EN
Unknown — *Fletcher Video* H, P
V118

Last Snows of Spring   Fil-Ent '82
Drama
12607   93 mins   C
V2, B, V
A motherless boy yearns for his father's affection and sadly they find themselves reunited at a hospital bed.
F — EN
GTO Films — *VideoSpace Ltd* P

Last Song, The   Fil-Ent '80
Suspense/Drama
09210   100 mins   C
B, V
Lynda Carter, Ronny Cox, Charles Aidman, Nicholas Pryar, Paul Rudd, directed by ALan J. Levi
A woman, whilst investigating her husband's murder, is pursued by killers, because she unknowingly holds the key to a plot to cover up a blunder involving deadly industrial waste.
S,A — EN
Motown Pictures Co; Ron Samuels — *Video Form Pictures*   H, P
MGT 4

Last Stone Age Tribes, The   Gen-Edu '??
Anthropology
06057   60 mins   C
V2, B, V
A film that studies the tribal settlements in New Guinea, an historical past away from white man's civilization, including connections with races of Papua, Melanesia and Micronesia, initiation rites, cannibalism, the nomadic life of the Pigmies and the headhunters of Ecuador.
F — ED
Unknown — *Video Programme Distributors* P
Cinehollywood—V540

Last Tango in Paris   Fil-Ent '72
Drama
01052   129 mins   C
V2, B, V
Marlon Brando, Maria Schneider, Jean-Pierre Leaud, directed by Bernardo Bertolucci
Brando plays a middle-aged American who meets a French girl. Many revealing moments follow in their frantic, unlikely, and short-lived affair.
BBFC:X — A — EN
United Artists — *Intervision Video* H
UA A B 5009

Last Tango in Paris   Fil-Ent '72
Drama
13072   129 mins   C
B, V
Marlon Brando, Maria Schneider, Jean Paul Leaud, directed by Bernado Bertolucci
A controversial film about a man and a woman whose special relationship defies social convention.
BBFC:X — A — EN
United Artists Corp — *Warner Home Video* P
99222

Last Train from Gun Hill   Fil-Ent '59
Western
01142   94 mins   C
B, V
Kirk Douglas, Anthony Quinn, Carolyn Jones, Earl Holliman
In 1905, a marshal, seeking an Indian girl's killers, finds one to be the son of old friends and boss of Gun Hill. Alone against the town, he has to fight his way out with a captive.
F — EN
Viacom International — *CBS/Fox Video* P
3B-014

Last Train to Berlin   Fil-Ent '76
War-Drama
05523   86 mins   C
B, V
Ty Hardin, Staltus Giallelis, Georgia Moll
An American commando on a suicide mission joins forces with a resistance fighter to blow up a bridge to prevent the Nazis shipping plundered gold. They are not helped by suspicious local villagers and are under constant threat from a band of bloodthirsty renegade Nazi bandits.
BBFC:A — S,A — EN
Unknown — *Derann Film Services* H, P
DV138B/DV138

Last Tycoon, The   Fil-Ent '76
Drama
10219   130 mins   C
B, V

PALADIN VIDEO HOME ENTERTAINMENT GUIDE

Robert De Niro, Tony Curtis, Robert Mitchum, Jeanne Moreau, Jack Nicholson, Donald Pleasance, Ray Milland, Dana Andrews, Peter Strauss, John Carradine, directed by Elia Kazan
This film based on F. Scott Fitzgerald's last novel is set in Hollywood during the Great Depression when the American dream was filmed and exposed to the world, where play acting became reality, where the women were beautiful and the men dashing. It centres around an ageing actor, a studio head who worries that his empire will be taken away by a younger man, a leading star, a Communist union organizer and an English author.
BBFC:AA — S,A — EN
Paramount; Sam Spiegel — Video Form Pictures   **H, P**
MGX 3

Last Unicorn, The   Chi-Juv   '82
Fairy tales
12015   84 mins   C
B, V
Animated, voices of Alan Arkin, Jeff Bridges, Tammy Grimes, Angela Lansbury, Mia Farrow, Robert Klein, Christopher Lee, Kennan Wynn
One day a unicorn who has lived for centuries in a lilac wood discovers she is the last of her species. She sets out on a search and after a series of adventures is turned into a beautiful woman. The King's son falls in love with her but eventually she must revert to her true form.
BBFC:U — F — EN
ITC Entertainment — Precision Video Ltd
P
BITC 3146/VITC 3146

Last Valley, The   Fil-Ent   '70
Adventure/Drama
04270   122 mins   C
B, V
Michael Caine, Omar Sharif
The Thirty Years War has ravaged Medieval Europe when Vogel, a wanderer, stumbles upon the last valley of the title—an oasis of peace and prosperity in a world of rampant destruction. But the peace of the valley is soon disturbed by the the arrival of The Captain and his band of battle-weary troops.
BBFC:AA — C,A — EN
Cinerama Releasing — Rank Video Library
H, P
0043

Last Victim, The   Fil-Ent   '??
Horror
06791   86 mins   C
V2, B, V
Tanya Roberts, Ron Max, Brian Freilino, Billy Longo
A psychotic killer-rapist stalks his victims in this suspense thriller.
A
Jim Botos — Intervision Video   **H, P**
A-A 0332

Last Video and   Fil-Ent   '84
Testament/The Corvini
Inheritance
Drama/Suspense
13156   150 mins   C
B, V
David Langton, Oliver Tobias, directed by Peter Sasdy, David McCallum, Jan Francis, directed by Gabrielle Beaumont
Two films are contained on one cassette. The first film is about an unfaithful wife and the second about a man obsessed with his neighbour next door and both films feature electronic wizards who use high technology to further their sinister aims.
BBFC:15 — S,A — EN
Hammer Films Prods — Brent Walker Home Video Ltd   **P**
BW 35

Last War, The   Fil-Ent   '7?
Science fiction
02451   76 mins   C
V2, B, V
Precious hours tick away and time runs out as the Engines of War over-run the earth in the final chapter of the human race.
BBFC:A — S,A — EN
Iver Film Services — Iver Film Services
P

Late Great Planet Earth,   Fil-Ent   '78
The
Science fiction
07805   90 mins   C
B, V
Orson Welles, directed by Robert Amram
Using a blend of speculation, illumination, fact, fantasy, prophecy and reality this film tells the story of the end of our world in 1985. The film traces future predictions made by ancient biblical prophets which bear a resemblance to the world of nuclear holocaust, population explosion, low energy supplies, floods, famine and droughts.
S,A — EN
Pacific International Enterprises — Video Tape Centre   **P**
VTC 1004

Laughterhouse   Fil-Ent   '84
Comedy
13124   93 mins   C
B, V

PALADIN VIDEO HOME ENTERTAINMENT GUIDE

Bill Owen, Ian Holm, Penelope Wilton, Richard Hope, Rosemary Martin, Stephanie Tague, directed by Richard Eyre

After a factory accident, a Suffolk farmer is obliged to walk his geese to the Christmas market and his ensuing hundred mile journey is brim full of humorous escapades.

BBFC:PG — F — EN

Ann Scott — *Palace Video Ltd*   **P**
PVC 2074A

Laura   Fil-Ent '44
Drama/Suspense
05642   84 mins   B/W
B, V

Gene Tierney, Dana Andrews, Clifton Webb, Judith Anderson, Vincent Price

An American detective falls madly in love with the portrait of a beautiful woman which has been murdered. She mysteriously reappears and they have to find out who was murdered and why.

S,A — EN

Twentieth Century Fox — *CBS/Fox Video*   **P**
3A-140

Laura   Fil-Ent '??
Drama/Romance
08890   91 mins   C
V2, B, V

Carroll Baker

This film tells the story of Laura, a beautiful, wealthy and happily married woman who seems to her friends to have the perfect life. However, this illusion is shattered when a love triangle develops with her stepson.

BBFC:X — A — EN

Unknown — *Video Programme Distributors*   **P**
Canon 009

Laura—Shadows of Summer   Fil-Ent '79
Drama/Romance
07461   86 mins   C
B, V

Maud Adams, Dawn Dunlap, James Mitchell, directed by David Hamilton

This story involves a young fifteen-year-old ballet student whose loveliness inspires a sculptor who happens to be her mother's lover. Although her mother modelled for her lover, she refuses to let her daughter pose in the nude; instead, she supplies him with photographs. Her daughter, who has fallen in love with him, finds fulfilment when he is temporarily blinded in an accident. She goes to him in secret and lets him sculpt her by touch instead of sight.

BBFC:X — A — EN

Safir Films Ltd; Les Films de L'Alma — *THORN EMI*   **P**
TXB 90 0704 4/TVB 90 0704 2

Laurel and Hardy's Laughing Twenties   Fil-Ent '65
Comedy
13418   90 mins   B/W
B, V

Stan Laurel, Oliver Hardy

Six famous short films are included in this video and a clip from 'Kill or Care' showing Laurel as Charlie Chaplin's understudy.

F — EN

MGM; Robert Youngson — *MGM/UA Home Video*   **P**
10461

Lavender Hill Mob, The   Fil-Ent '51
Comedy
01180   78 mins   B/W
B, V

Alec Guinness, Stanley Holloway, Sidney James, Alfie Bass, directed by Charles Chrichton

An underpaid clerk and a frustrated sculptor steal a million pounds in gold bars from the Bank of England. The gold is made into souvenir models of the Eiffel Tower, and when six of the models are inadvertently sold, an hilarious chase across England and the Continent ensues.

Academy Award '52: Best Story and Screenplay (T.E.B. Clarke).   BBFC:U — F — EN

Universal; Arthur Rank — *THORN EMI*   **P**
TXE 90 0012 4/TVE 90 0012 2

Lawrence Durrell's Greece—'Spirit of the Place'   Fil-Ent '76
Documentary/Europe
05854   73 mins   C
B, V

Lawrence Durrell, directed by Peter Adams

This film combines breathtaking scenery and music from the Greek Islands with Lawrence Durrell's eloquent style to present a journel of discovery through ancient Greece.

F — EN

RM Productions — *Polygram Video*   **P**
7901774/7901772

PALADIN VIDEO HOME ENTERTAINMENT GUIDE

Lawrence of Arabia   Fil-Ent '62
Drama
12481   201 mins   C
B, V
Peter O'Toole, Anthony Quinn, Omar Sharif, Jack Hawkins
This is an epic account of the British Officer who became a legend in his own time through his efforts in uniting the Arab tribes in Arabia against the Turks.
BBFC:PG — *S,A* — *EN*
David Lean — *RCA/Columbia Pictures Video*
UK   H, P
10055

League of Gentlemen, The   Fil-Ent '60
Suspense
04251   112 mins   B/W
B, V
Jack Hawkins, Nigel Patrick, Roger Livesey, Richard Attenborough, Brian Forbes
Ex-Lieutenant Colonel Hyde resents his enforced retirement from the Army after 25 years of unblemished service. Methodically he plans to even the score with the Establishment.
BBFC:A — *C,A* — *EN*
Kingsley International — *Rank Video Library*
H, P
0018

Learn About Yoga   How-Ins '8?
Yoga
07945   54 mins   C
V2, B, V
Directed by John Kaye Cooper
This programme has been specially designed by James Hewitt, an internationally best selling author of two books on yoga, to provide a complete guide on the subject. The programme is accompanied by a comprehensive booklet covering diet and giving hints on practising yoga.
AM Available   *S,A* — *I*
Learnrite Productions — *Videomedia*   P
PVM 9002/BVM 9002/HVM 9002

Learning the Guitar   How-Ins '81
Music
05948   108 mins   C
B, V
Peter Sheridan
This film provides a visual course in learning to play the guitar. It takes the student through all the initial problems connected with the instrument.
F — *I*
Unknown — *Precision Video Ltd*   P
BOPV 2560/VOPV 2560

Learning to Love   Med-Sci '7?
Sexuality
01991   60 mins   C
V2, B, V, PH15, PH17
Marje Proops
This programme attempts to correct ignorance, guilt, embarrassment, and confusion about sex on the part of teenagers.
S,C — *ED*
MirrorVision — *VideoSpace Ltd*   P

Learning to Swim   Spo-Lei '80
Sports-Water
00266   30 mins   C
B, V, FO
This programme has been specially made under the supervision of the Amateur Swimming Association. It shows how progressively and effectively, from a very young age, a child can be introduced to the enjoyment of swimming, and emphasises the very important role parents can play.
F — *I*
London Video Ltd — *Video Sport for All*
P
1008

Leave 'Em Laughing   Fil-Ent '81
Comedy
09214   104 mins   C
B, V
Mickey Rooney, Anne Jackson, Allen Goorwitz, Elisha Cook, Red Buttons, William Windom, directed by Jackie Cooper
Mickey Rooney plays a Chicago clown, a man with a zest for life, an extra-ordinary love of people and a special gift of laughter.
F — *EN*
Julian Fowles Prods — *Video Form Pictures*
H, P
DIP5

Left Hand of the Law, The   Fil-Ent '??
Crime-Drama
06102   97 mins   C
V2, B, V
Leonard Mann, Janet Agren, Stephen Boyd, James Mason, Enrico Maria Salerno
A dedicated police officer is ready to go to the very limits of the law in his struggle against the growing world of crime.
S,A — *EN*
Unknown — *Video Programme Distributors*
P
Cinehollywood—V330

Legacy of Horror   Fil-Ent '78
Horror
07909   77 mins   C
V2, B, V

PALADIN VIDEO HOME ENTERTAINMENT GUIDE

Elaine Boies, Chris Broderik, Marilee Troncone, Jeannie Cusick, directed by Andy Milligan
In order to inherit their father's estate, three sisters must live in harmony for three days and nights in the family mansion on a private island. But something evil is lurking and it stalks the sisters, leaving a trail of mutilation and death as the real truth of the mansion is exposed.
S,A — EN
Ken Lane Films — *Video Programme Distributors* P
Replay—1007

Legacy of Satan Fil-Ent '73
Horror
02450 68 mins C
V2, B, V
Linda Christian, Paul Barry, John Francis
In the 20th century, ordinary people are caught in a tide of witchcraft with disastrous consequences.
BBFC:X — A — EN
Damiano — *Iver Film Services* P

Legend of Alfred Packer, The Fil-Ent '??
Drama
06803 90 mins C
V2, B, V
Patrick Dray, Ron Haines, Bob Damon
Set in Colorado in 1877, this film is based on a true story of survival and cannibalism.
C,A — EN
Mark Webb — *Intervision Video* H, P
A-A 0330

Legend of Blood Castle, The Fil-Ent '72
Horror
08868 87 mins C
V2, B, V
This film, based on a true story, tells of Countess Bathori who, in the 16th Century, bathed in the blood of over six hundred maidens.
BBFC:X — A — EN
20th Century-Fox; Hammer Films — *Video Programme Distributors* P
Replay 1014

Legend of Boggy Creek, The Fil-Ent '72
Documentary/Drama
05492 76 mins C
V2, B, V
Narrated by Vern Stierman, directed by Charles E. Pierce
Over the past decade 'The Fouke Monster' has periodically terrorised the people of a small farming community in Southwest Arkansas. It is reported to be seven feet tall, 250 pounds, smelling like a pigsty, able to walk upright, run fast, scream and has bright red eyes. The film crew with trackers spent months prowling the bottomlands to build a picture of 'The Legend of Boggy Creek.'
BBFC:A — S,A — EN
Howco — *Iver Film Services* P

Legend of Frank Woods, The Fil-Ent '77
Western
09151 107 mins C
V
Brad Stewart, Troy Donahue, Kitty Vallacher, Michael Christian
A gunman takes refuge from an ambush, disguised as a preacher. The following adventure has an unusual and unpredictable climax.
S,A — EN
Unknown — *Cinema Indoors* H, P

Legend of Frenchie King, The Fil-Ent '71
Western
06223 90 mins C
B, V
Brigitte Bardot, Claudia Cardinale, Michael Pollard
Four brothers and their sister have life their own way until the arrival of five lovely sisters. The girls' father, a notorious bandit, was hanged some years before; since then the girls have followed a life of crime, all dressed as men.
S,A — EN
Hemdale Productions — *VCL Video Services* P
P144D

Legend of Loch Ness Fil-Ent '76
Adventure
01045 92 mins C
B, V
The search for the world's most famous monster, brought up-to-the-minute with the aid of advanced technology.
F — EN
Gold Key — *VCL Video Services* P

Legend of the Lone Ranger, The Fil-Ent '81
Western
07346 98 mins C
B, V

(For Explanation of codes, see USE GUIDE and KEY)

387

PALADIN VIDEO HOME ENTERTAINMENT GUIDE

Klinton Spilsbury, Michael Horse, Christopher Lloyd, Jason Robards
This film traces the origins of the fabled Lone Ranger and the story of his first meeting with his Indian companion Tonto.
BBFC:A — S,A — EN
Universal — Precision Video Ltd   P
BITC 2098/VITC 2098

Legend of the Northwest   Fil-Ent '78
Adventure/Drama
05452   80 mins   C
V2, B, V
Marshall Reed, Denver Pyle, directed by Rand Brooks
The story of a dog called Bearheart, showing his loyalty and fierce revenge on a drunken hunter who shot and killed his master and how he manages to find a new home.
BBFC:U — F — EN
G G Communications — Iver Film Services   P
120

Legend of the Werewolf   Fil-Ent '75
Horror
05248   88 mins   C
B, V
Peter Cushing, Ron Moody, Hugh Griffith, Roy Castle, David Rintoul
As a child Etoile had run with the wolves and killed with the wolves. Then he was brought to civilisation and his past was forgotten—except when the moon shone full.
BBFC:X — A — EN
Unknown — Rank Video Library   H, P
2003

Legend of Valentino, The   Fil-Ent '75
Drama
12077   92 mins   C
V2, B, V
Franco Nero, Suzanne Pleshette
In 1920 a screenwriter discovered a struggling Italian immigrant and recognised his potential as an actor. Enlisting the help of a press agent, a star was born to thrill all the women who saw him on the screen.
BBFC:15 — S,A — EN
Metromedia Producers; Aaron Spelling — Guild Home Video   H, P, E

Lemon Popsicle   Fil-Ent '7?
Comedy
02114   95 mins   C
V2, B, V
Three seventeen-year-olds are aided on their way to manhood by a nyphomaniac girl and a sleazy street walker and get more than they bargain for in this hilarious film.
BBFC:X — A — EN
Israel — Hokushin Audio Visual Ltd   P
VM-25

Lemora   Fil-Ent '73
Horror
09149   95 mins   C
B, V
Lesley Gibb, Cheryl Smith, William Whitton, Richard Blackburn
A female vampire captures a notorious gangland figure of the 20's in order to lure his innocent daughter to her. She becomes enmeshed in the evil of this vampire.
S,A — EN
Foreign — Cinema Indoors   H, P

Leningrad Ice Show, The   Spo-Lei '7?
Sports-Winter
02259   60 mins   C
V
Ballet artistry and dazzling ice skating technique are combined in a brilliant display by some of the world's leading skaters.
F — EN
Unknown — JVC   P
PRT 17

Lennon-A Legend   Fil-Ent '75
Music/Biographical
09966   60 mins   C
B, V
This is the first NBC Television tribute to John Lennon, broadcast across America the day after John Lennon was gunned down outside the Dakota building in New York. It is followed by interviews with the last journalist to talk to him, Liza Robinson of the New York Post. It covers his drug conviction, the row over the nude 'Two Virgins' album cover and the 'Bed-In' for peace at the Amsterdam Hilton.
S,A — EN
NBC International — Select Video Limited   P
3113/43

Lenny   Fil-Ent '74
Drama
01271   111 mins   B/W
V2, B, V
Dustin Hoffman, Valerie Perrine, directed by Bob Fosse

PALADIN VIDEO HOME ENTERTAINMENT GUIDE

In a cinema verite style of filmmaking, director Bob Fosse has captured the sardonic wit and tragic streak that followed comedian Lenny Bruce throughout the rise and fall of his short career. Hoffman was nominated for an Academy Award.
BBFC:X — M,A — EN
United Artists — *Intervision Video*   **H**
UA A B 5003

Lenny   Fil-Ent '74
Drama/Biographical
12986   108 mins   C
B, V
Dustin Hoffman, Valerie Perrine, directed by Bob Fosse
The story of Lenny Bruce's rise to fame and notoriety in the American nightclubs in the 1960's as a comedian who was ahead of his time is depicted in this programme.
BBFC:18 — A — EN
United Artists — *Warner Home Video*   **P**
99250

Lenny Bruce Live in Concert   Fil-Ent '75
Comedy-Performance
10135   73 mins   C
B, V
Lenny Bruce
This tape features a complete night club performance by Lenny Bruce, the American satirist, plus an eight minute short entitled 'Thank You Mask Man' featuring his own satire coupled with animation.
A — EN
Columbus Prods — *Palace Video Ltd*   **P**
VIRV 005B

Leopard in the Snow   Fil-Ent '78
Drama
02400   94 mins   C
B, V
Keir Dullea, Susan Penhaligon, Kenneth More, Billie Whitelaw, directed by Gerry O'Hara
The story of an attractive young woman forced to abandon her car during a raging blizzard on the Cumberland Fells in Northern England. A mysterious stranger with a prowling leopard intercepts her and offers her shelter in his remote house.
A — EN
Harlequin Productions — *Derann Film Services*
H, P
DV 124B/DV 124

Leroy Gomez   Fil-Ent '78
Music-Performance
04400   30 mins   C
B, V
Popular disco singer Leroy Gomez and his dancers perform 'Lady Let Me Change Your Mind,' 'Gypsy Women,' 'Spanish Harlem,' and others.
F — EN
VCL — *VCL Video Services*   **P**

Les Girls   Fil-Ent '57
Musical/Comedy
12219   113 mins   C
B, V
Gene Kelly, Ray Kendall, Mitzi Gaynor, Taina Elg, directed by George Cukor
This film follows the exploits of three dancing girls and their impresario in their travels across Europe. The musical score is written by Cole Porter.
F — EN
MGM — *MGM/UA Home Video*   **P**

Les Miserables   Fil-Ent '78
Drama
05390   131 mins   C
B, V
Richard Jordan, Anthony Perkins, Cyril Cusak, Claude Dauphin, John Gielgud, Ian Holm, Celia Johnson, Joyce Redman, Flora Robson, directed by Glenn Jordan
A film of Victor Hugo's classic work set in the French town of Faverolles in 1796 portraying a typical Republic of the times where the poor get poorer and the rich, richer. Punishment for crimes is severe. A young woodcutter steals a loaf of bread to feed his starving sister and her child; he is sentenced to years at the galley.
S,A — EN
Norman Rosemount Productions — *Precision Video Ltd*   **P**
BITC 3040/VITC 3040

Lesley Judd's Allsorts   Chl-Juv '80
Games
04423   60 mins   C
B
Lesley Judd, Jimmy Hill
A programme for children, presented by Lesley Judd, formerly of BBC TV's 'Blue Peter,' including music from 'Nuts and Bolts,' football coaching with Jimmy Hill, caring for pets, simple magic tricks and things to make and do.
PS,M — EN
Michael Barratt; Sony — *Michael Barratt Ltd*
P

Leslie Uggams Show, The   Fil-Ent '7?
Variety
04384   60 mins   C
B, V, PH17, 3/4U

PALADIN VIDEO HOME ENTERTAINMENT GUIDE

Leslie Uggams, Lionel Hampton
A musical variety show starring Leslie Uggams and featuring Lionel Hampton.
F — EN
Unknown — *Vidpics International* **P**

Let George Do It Fil-Ent '40
Comedy
01607 81 mins B/W
B, V
George Formby
An unwitting spy in Norway nearly fouls up British intelligence.
BBFC:U — S,A — EN
Ealing Studios; Michael Balcon — *THORN EMI* **P**
TXE 90 0206 4/TVE 90 0206 2

Let Me Die a Woman Fil-Ent '??
Documentary/Sexuality
08691 72 mins C
V2, B, V
This film takes a look at the transsexual phenomenon. It shows the ways in which men are able to become women, and women to become men.
BBFC:A — A — EN
Unknown — *Derann Film Services* **P**
DV151B/DV151

Let's Break—The Definitive Guide to Break-Dancing Spo-Lei '84
Dance
12994 58 mins C
B, V
New York City break-dancers demonstrate the basic steps of this skill allowing the viewer to learn and practice at his own pace.
S,A — I
Image Magnetic Associates Inc. — *Warner Home Video* **P**
84023

Let's Get Married Fil-Ent '6?
Comedy/Romance
01951 88 mins B/W
B, V
Anthony Newley, Anne Aubrey
An amorous milkman finds that the path to true love is not a smooth one.
S,A — EN
Unknown — *CBS/Fox Video* **P**
3B-064

Let's Make a Dirty Movie Fil-Ent '7?
Comedy
02401 81 mins C
B, V
Claude Brasseur, Robert Castel, Nathalie Courval, Catherine Lachens, Sonia Vareuil, directed by Gerard Pires
A sexy comedy concerning the problems that beset the director of a low-budget movie.
A — EN
Unknown — *Derann Film Services* **H, P**
DV 125B/DV 125

Letter from an Unknown Woman Fil-Ent '48
Romance
01074 90 mins B/W
V2, B, V
Joan Fontaine, directed by Max Ophuls
Tragic love story of a woman's lifelong infatuation with a musician.
BBFC:A — A — EN
Universal — *Intervision Video* **H, P**
A-A 0109

Lianna Fil-Ent '83
Drama
13222 122 mins C
V2, B, V
Linda Griffiths, Jane Halleran, directed by John Sayles
A married woman returns to college to finish her degree and begins a strange love affair which forces her to come to terms with her own sexuality.
BBFC:18 — A — EN
Winwood Company — *Embassy Home Entertainment* **P**

Liar's Moon Fil-Ent '82
Romance/Drama
13774 101 mins C
B, V, LV
Matt Dillon, Cindy Fisher, Broderick Crawford, Hoyt Axton
Set in Texas, a poor country boy elopes with a rich girl who discovers a terrible secret her parents have kept from her when she becomes pregnant.
C,A — EN
Unknown — *Odyssey Video* **H, P**

Licensed to Kill Fil-Ent '65
Suspense
05695 96 mins C
B, V
Tom Adams, Karel Stapanek, Veronica Hurst, directed by Lindsay Shonteff
An amazing discovery is made by a Professor and his associate that puts them under threat. When the professor is murdered a secret agent

is assigned to protect his associate and his beautiful assistant. The agent has his work cut out trying to protect them as desperate attempts are made to capture the pair.
BBFC:A — S,A — EN
Unknown — Derann Film Services   H, P
GS706B/GS706

Lichfield on Photography Part 1   How-Ins '8?
Photography
07839   85 mins   C
B, V
Patrick Lichfield
In this, the first in the series, Patrick Lichfield covers the basics of photography and gives a background to modern camera, film formats and portrait work.
S,A — ED
Unknown — Polygram Video   H, P
791 504

Lichfield on Photography Part 2   How-Ins '8?
Photography
07840   85 mins   C
B, V
Patrick Lichfield
This second part in the series covers the use of light in photography and dark room work.
S,A — ED
Unknown — Polygram Video   H, P
791 504

Lichfield on Photography Part 3   How-Ins '8?
Photography
07841   85 mins   C
B, V
Patrick Lichfield
In this third part Patrick Lichfield demonstrates the use of lenses and filters. He then goes on to cover the photography of children and animals.
S,A — ED
Unknown — Polygram Video   H, P
791 504

Lies   Fil-Ent '83
Suspense/Drama
13405   98 mins   C
V2, B, V
Ann Dusenberry, Gail Strickland, Bruce Davison, Stacy Keach, directed by Ken and Jim Wheat

An actress takes the part of a girl in a film of a true story and finds herself the victim of a family plot to dispose of her.
BBFC:18 — C,A — EN
Alpha Films — Intervision Video   H, P
0012

Life?   Med-Sci '76
Microbiology
01127   21 mins   C
B, V, PH15, PH17, 3/4U
A look at the tiny world of microscopic life, explaining the characteristics of living and non-living micro-organisms. Part of the 'Life Science' series.
S,A — ED
NASA — Istead Audio Visual   P
HQ 261

Life Among the Baboons/Run Cheetah Run   Med-Sci '7?
Wildlife
02275   60 mins   C
V
Two half-hour documentaries on one tape dealing with the fascinating world of the baboon colony and the story of a cheetah named Violet Mary, who raises five cubs and teaches them the basic survival lessons of life in Africa.
F — ED
Unknown — JVC   P
PRT 20

Life and Times of Grizzly Adams, The   Fil-Ent '74
Adventure/Drama
06875   93 mins   C
V2, B, V
Dan Haggerty, Denver Pyle, Don Shanks
A true-life adventure story based on the rugged life-style of the legendary frontiersman and a grizzly bear who are both committed to lives of freedom in the wild. They gain an understanding of each other that leads to a relationship of trust and sharing.
S,A — EN
Gold Key Entertainment — European Video Company   P

Life Is Beautiful   Fil-Ent '8?
Drama
09298   88 mins   C
B, V
A one-time military pilot is asked to leave when he refused to gun down innocent civilians. He is now a taxi driver in Lisbon, devoted to a waitress. The cafe owner asks him to take a

PALADIN VIDEO HOME ENTERTAINMENT GUIDE

friend to the airport. Trouble starts when this 'friend' is arrested as leader of a Portugese resistance group. The driver gets deeper into it when he has to lie to protect his girlfriend.
S,A — EN
Unknown — *Abacus Video*　　**P**
202

Life with Father　　Fil-Ent '47
Comedy-Drama
06891　　115 mins　　C
V2, B, V
William Powell, Elizabeth Taylor, Irene Dunne, Edmund Gwenn, Zasu Pitts
Set in New York City of the 1880's, this film tells the story of a stern but susceptible father who rules over his wife and four young red-headed sons with an iron fist. Based on the long running Broadway play by Howard Lindsay and Russell Crouse.
New York Film Critics Award '47: Best Male Performance (Powell).　　S,A — EN
Warner Bros — *European Video Company*
P

Lifetaker, The　　Fil-Ent '75
Drama
04467　　103 mins　　C
V2, B, V
Terence Morgan, Lea Dregorn, Peter Duncan, directed by Michael Papas
A man, disturbed by the fact that his wife has seduced a young boy, shoots his wife and arranges things to look as if the boy killed her.
BBFC:X — A — EN
Michael Papas; Onyx Film Prods — *Intervision Video*　　**H, P**
A-A 0092

Lift, The　　Fil-Ent '83
Horror/Suspense
12494　　94 mins　　C
B, V
Huub Stapel, Willek Van Ammelrooy, Josine Van Dalsum, directed by Dick Maas
A lift in a tower block develops homicidal tendencies and embarks on a reign of terror and death while a lift mechanic and a journalist try and find its secret.
BBFC:15 — C,A — EN
Matthijs Van Heijningen — *Warner Home Video*　　**P**
61327

Light at the Edge of the World, The　　Fil-Ent '71
Adventure
08533　　95 mins　　C
B, V

Yul Brynner, Kirk Douglas, Samantha Eggar, Jean-Claude Drouot, Fernando Rey, Renato Salvatori, directed by Kevin Billington
On an island near Cape Horn, a pirate, played by Yul Brynner, takes over the lighthouse and intends to lure unsuspecting ships to their fate. A sole survivor of one of these raids sets out to stop this plan; however, the pirate uses a beautiful woman as the bait to prevent him.
S,A — EN
Triumfilm — *THORN EMI*　　**P**

Lightning Wheels　　Spo-Lei '84
Bicycling
12720　　30 mins　　C
B, V
This action packed tape focuses on proper BMX training and safety precautions with all the thrills and skills of Bicycle Moto-cross. Highlights include an exhibition of freestyle by Bob Haro and a look at one of 1983's major indoor championships.
F — EN
Business Press International Ltd — *Quadrant Video*　　**H, P**

Likely Lads, The　　Fil-Ent '76
Comedy
04656　　86 mins　　C
B, V
James Bolam, Rodney Bowes, Brigit Forsyth
This film version of the popular TV series sees Bob and Thelma, together with Terry and his new girlfriend Christina, set off on a touring holiday by caravan with disastrous results.
F — EN
EMI; Aida Young — *THORN EMI*　　**H, P**
TXC 90 0237 4/TVC 90 0237 2

Lilacs in the Spring　　Fil-Ent '54
Musical/Drama
07947　　95 mins　　C
V2, B, V
Anna Neagle, Errol Flynn, Peter Graves, David Farrar, Kathleen Harrison, directed by Herbert Wilcox
During the London blitz a young actress is knocked unconscious. She dreams of herself as Nell Gwyn, Queen Victoria and her own mother before she wakes up and has to deal with her own personal problems.
BBFC:U — F — EN
Republic — *Videomedia*　　**P**
PVM 4414/BVM 4414/HVM 4414

Lili Marleen　　Fil-Ent '80
War-Drama
07876　　116 mins　　C
V2, B, V

PALADIN VIDEO HOME ENTERTAINMENT GUIDE

Hanna Schygulla, Giancarlo Giannini, Mel Ferrer, directed by Rainer Werner Fassbinder
In Zurich in 1938 a young man falls in love with a German singer. His father, head of a Jewish organisation, breaks up the affair. Her singing attracts the attention of a Nazi officer who introduces her to Berlin society. She changes her name to Lilli Marleen and becomes both famous and successful. Whilst on a secret mission she meets her former lover again; as he plans to escape over the Swiss border they realise their love could never be the same.
S,A — EN
Unknown — Intervision Video   H, P
A-A 0397

Limbo Line, The   Fil-Ent '67
Suspense/Drama
09013   99 mins   C
V2, B, V
Craig Stevens, Kate O'Mara, Norman Bird
A secret agent has to use a pretty Russian ballerina as bait in order to discover the means by which the Russians are kidnapping and smuggling defectors back to Russia.
S,A — EN
Group W — Intervision Video   H, P
AA 0439

Limelight   Fil-Ent '52
Comedy-Drama
05847   145 mins   B/W
B, V
Charlie Chaplin, Claire Bloom, Buster Keaton
This is the poignant tale of an elderly music hall star and his band in the rise to fame of a young and beautiful ballerina.
F — EN
United Artists — Polygram Video   P
7901534/7901532

Lincoln Conspiracy, The   Fil-Ent '77
Drama
07491   87 mins   C
B, V
Bradford Dillman, John Dehner, John Anderson, directed by James L. Conway
This true historical drama, based on new evidence, gives a step-by-step account of the conspiracy by high level government officials to forcefully remove President Lincoln from office. The film reveals the truth behind his assassination and subsequent successful cover-up.
S,A — EN
Sunn Classic — Quadrant Video   H, P
FF11

L'Incoronazione   Fin-Art '84
Dance
13694   155 mins   C
B, V
Maria Ewing, Dennis Bailey, Cynthia Clarey, Robert Lloyd, Elizabeth Gale, Dale Duesing, directed by Peter Hall
This production by the Glyndebourne Festival Opera is recorded in stereo, written by Monteverdi, and tells the amoral story of the Roman Emperor Nero's love affair with the scheming Poppea.
F — EN
BBC Television; Glyndebourne in association with RM Arts — THORN EMI   P
90 3129

Linda Lovelace for President   Fil-Ent '75
Comedy
06316   93 mins   C
V2, B, V
Linda Lovelace, Mickey Dolenz, Joey Forman, Fuddly Bagley, Val Bisoglio, Jack de Leon
A satirical spoof of the American political scene. A beautiful, innocent, honest and straight girl from a mining town in the mid-west plunges into a cross-country campaign for president, runs into three super heros and finds herself the target of political assassination.
BBFC:X — A — EN
A J J Ltd Production; General Film Corp — World of Video 2000   H, P
XF135

Linda Ronstadt with Nelson Riddle and his Orchestra in Concert—What's New   Fil-Ent '84
Music-Performance
12877   60 mins   C
B, V, LV, CED
This programme of romantic torch songs and standards includes Linda Ronstadt singing 'I've Got A Crush On You,' 'Someone to Watch Over Me,' 'What'll I Do' and 'Crazy He Calls Me.'
F — EN
Peter Asher — Vestron Video International   P
11012

Line, The   Fil-Ent '82
Drama
09123   95 mins   C
B, V
Directed by Robert J. Siegel
This film, set during the Vietnam War, is based on a true story, and tells of a group of inmates at a US stockade for Army 'malingerers.' A sergeant ensures that life in the prison is as savage and terrifying as the war itself, until one

PALADIN VIDEO HOME ENTERTAINMENT GUIDE

man finds the courage to challenge the brutal regime and steps out of 'the Line.' The soundtrack includes songs by Barry Manilow and Dinah Washington.
BBFC:AA — C,A — EN
Enterprise Pictures — *Quadrant Video*
H, P

Linguaphone-French   Gen-Edu '8?
Languages-Instruction
09984   60 mins   C
B, V
This is the first in a series of language tapes starting with basic French. Each cassette includes a comprehensive book with which the viewer can refer to, during the playback. It is filmed on location in France, in typical situations that the viewer may find himself in.
AM Available   S,A — I
Holiday Brothers Ltd — *Holiday Brothers Ltd*
P

Link, The   Fil-Ent '??
Horror
13732   90 mins   C
V2, B, V
Michael Moriarty, Penelope Milford, Geraldine Fitzgerald, Cameron Mitchell, Sarah Langenfeld, Virginia McKenna
In a strange and bizarre way, a man witnesses a series of horrific killings through the murderer's eyes.
BBFC:18 — A — EN
Zadar Film Production — *Medusa Communications Ltd*   **H, P**
MC 037

Lion in Winter, The   Fil-Ent '68
Drama
05526   134 mins   C
B, V
Peter O'Toole, Katharine Hepburn, Jane Merrow, John Castle, Anthony Hopkins, Nigel Terry, Timothy Dalton, Nigel Stock, directed by Anthony Harvey
King Henry II of England decides it is time to consider the succession. At Christmas he calls his three sons to join him and his mistress. He also invites his Queen, a scheming woman who has been imprisoned for the previous ten years. His Queen, whose capacity for intrigue has not waned in prison, ruins his plans. Based on the day by James Goldman.
Academy Awards '68: Best Actress (Hepburn); Best Screenplay; Best Music Score.
S,A — EN
Haworth Productions — *CBS/Fox Video*
P

Lion of Thebes   Fil-Ent '64
Adventure
07981   89 mins   C
B, V
Mark Forest, Yvonne Furneaux, directed by Richard McNamara
This film tells of Helen of Troy's escape from the blazing city of Troy. Accompanied by her lieutenant, Arion, she makes her way to the Egyptian capital, Thebes. She intends to find help to win back the city of Troy but instead endangers her life even further.
S,A — EN
Avco—Embassy — *AVI Video Ltd*   **P**
013

Lionman   Fil-Ent '8?
War-Drama
09294   109 mins   C
V
Steve Arkin, Barbara Lake, Charles Garrett, Allison Soames
This action film centers around two brothers caught up in a bloody medieval Christian/Islamic war.
A — EN
Unknown — *Rex*   **H, P**

Lions for Breakfast   Fil-Ent '??
Adventure/Comedy
06020   86 mins   C
B, V
Jan Rubes, Jim Henshaw, Danny Forbes, Sue Petrie, Paul Bradley, directed by William Davidson
Two brothers aged ten and twenty two team up with an old drifter and go in search of a better life in the country. Along the way they help each other through a series of comic adventures, building a mutual trust and understanding.
F — EN
John B Kelly Productions — *VCL Video Services*   **P**

Lisbon   Fil-Ent '56
Drama/Adventure
08727   90 mins   C
B, V
Ray Milland, Maureen O'Hara, Claude Rains, Yvonne Furneau
Filmed in Portugal this tells of lust, sadism and greed, the motives behind an attempt to free a millionaire industrialist trapped behind the Iron Curtain. A very special form of reception party is arranged for the unsuspecting tycoon on his return.
S,A — EN
Republic — *BBC Video*   **H, P**
BBCV 8008

PALADIN VIDEO HOME ENTERTAINMENT GUIDE

Little Ark, The — Chi-Juv '??
Adventure
12013   100 mins   C
B, V
Theodore Bikel, Genny Ambas, Philip Frame, directed by James B Clark
Two orphans and their beloved pets wake up one morning to discover themselves marooned in a church bell tower, surrounded by water with only rooftops in sight. They spot an empty houseboat floating by and are able to scramble aboard and so set off.
BBFC:U — F — EN
Unknown — CBS/Fox Video   P
7128

Little Big Man — Fil-Ent '70
Western/Adventure
12088   134 mins   C
B, V
Dustin Hoffman, Martin Balsam, Jeff Corey, Chief Dan George, Faye Dunaway, directed by Arthur Penn
A 121-year-old survivor of Custer's last stand sits in a hospital room telling his life's story to an historian. Beginning in 1859 when he was captured by Indians, the film sweeps across five decades of America's history.
S,A — EN
National General — CBS/Fox Video   P
7130

Little Brown Burro, The — Chi-Juv '??
Cartoons
10086   30 mins   C
V2, B, V
Animated
A Christmas story about a little donkey who makes a very special journey to Bethlehem.
BBFC:U — PS,M — EN
Unknown — Embassy Home Entertainment   P
1347

Little Darlings — Fil-Ent '80
Drama
13321   90 mins   C
B, V
Tatum O'Neal, Kristy McNichol, Matt Dillon, Armand Assante, directed by Ronald F Maxwell
This is a story of love, rivalry and antagonism during a season of a summer camp.
BBFC — S,A — EN
Paramount — CIC Video   H, P
BET 2106/VHT 2106

Little Drummer Boy, The — Chi-Juv '84
Cartoons
12944   24 mins   C
B, V
Animated
A little drummer boy helps a devout man from the Holy Land recapture a set of silver bells from a band of wicked tax collectors. The narration is by Greer Garson.
I,M — EN
Unknown — Video Form Pictures   H, P
MGK 004

Little Godfather from Hong Kong — Fil-Ent '??
Martial arts/Suspense
06064   93 mins   C
V2, B, V
Bruce Liang, Gordon Mitchell
A murder company run by a Mafioso boss and his three sons have been hired by an international drug smuggling ring to eliminate Interpol agents. They are successful everywhere except Hong Kong, where they meet a Kung Fu expert. They lure him to Rome, the tables turn and they are eliminated.
BBFC:X — A — EN
Unknown — Video Programme Distributors   P
Inter-Ocean—054

Little Laura and Big John — Fil-Ent '73
Crime-Drama
06876   82 mins   C
V2, B, V
Karen Black, Fabian Forte
Set in turn of the century Florida, this film follows the true-life exploits of the smalltime Ashley Gang and the 'King' and 'Queen' of the Everglades.
S,A — EN
Gold Key Entertainment — European Video Company   P

Little Lord Fauntleroy — Fil-Ent '80
Drama
08576   90 mins   C
B, V
Ricky Schroder, Alec Guinness, Eric Porter, Colin Blakely, Connie Booth, Rachel Kempson, directed by Jack Gold
This film tells the story of a young lad who travels to England from his poor New York home to prepare to take on the title and duties of his ageing grandfather, the Earl of Dorincourt. It is filmed in Belvoir Castle, one of the finest stately homes and based on the popular Victorian novel by Frances Hodgson Burnett.
BBFC:U — F — EN
Rosemont Productions — THORN EMI   P
TXB 90 1123 4/TVB 90 1123 2

(For Explanation of codes, see USE GUIDE and KEY)   395

PALADIN VIDEO HOME ENTERTAINMENT GUIDE

Little Mermaid, The   Chi-Juv '78
Fairy tales
06766   66 mins   C
V2, B, V
Animated
Based on the tale of Hans Christian Andersen, this is the story of a little mermaid princess who sets out to see human society.
F — EN
GG Communications — *Intervision Video*
H, P
A-AE 0308

Little Miss Trouble and Friends   Chi-Juv '84
Cartoons
13086   60 mins   C
B, V
Animated
Little Miss Trouble, Magic, Naughty, Scatterbrain, Sunshine and Shy feature with their friends Mister Men in six episodes from the television series.
PS,I — EN
Unknown — *Longman Video*   P
5029

Little Nezha Fights Great Dragon Kings   Fil-Ent '??
Cartoons/Adventure
08719   59 mins   C
V2, B, V
Animated
This is the story of Nezha, the child who challenges the mighty, child-eating Dragon king of the Eastern Sea. He is armed with two magical gifts from his protector, a ring of steel and a sash of red silk.
M,S — EN
Liu Guimei — *BBC Video*   H, P
BBCV 9006

Little Night Music, A   Fil-Ent '78
Romance/Musical
07380   84 mins   C
V2, B, V
Elizabeth Taylor, Diana Rigg, Len Cariou, Lesley-Ann Down, Hermione Gingold, Laurence Guittard, Christopher Guard, Lesley Dunlop, directed by Harold Prince
Set in Vienna at the turn of the century, a glamorous actress appears at the local theatre; old passions are rekindled and she finds herself at the centre of attention. At a week-end party on a country estate during the course of a balmy summer's night the three mismatched couples overcome all the romantic complications to find happiness and true love.
BBFC:AA — S,A — EN
New World Pictures — *Guild Home Video*
H, P, E

Little Orbit the Astrodog   Chi-Juv '7?
Cartoons/Science fiction
01868   75 mins   C
V2, B, V
Animated, written by France and Jean Image, music by Fred Freed
After the spaceship Cosmos is attacked, Rubin the Robot floats through space to earth. Here he meets a boy with a passion for space travel. Rubin helps the boy, his girlfriend and his dog Orbit to launch their spaceship. In return, he asks them to help him find the Cosmos.
I,M — EN
Films Jean Image Production — *Videomedia*
P
BVM 2111/HVM 2111

Little Rascals   Fil-Ent '3?
Comedy
06863   55 mins   B/W
V2, B, V
This film is from the 'Our Gang' series, a classical comedy feature of the thirties in which a bunch of kids embark on a series of hilarious adventures.
M,A — EN
Hal Roach — *European Video Company*
P

Little River Band — Live Exposure   Fil-Ent '81
Music-Performance
07477   80 mins   C
B, V
Directed by Derek Burbidge
This film, recorded at The Summit in Houston, Texas in October 1981, features The Little River Band who perform a selection from their six hit albums. Songs include 'It's a Long Way There,' 'Man on the Run,' 'Mistress of Mine Happy Anniversary,' 'Don't Let the Needle Win,' 'Reminiscing,' 'Ballerina' and 'Just Say That You Love Me.'
S,A — EN
Zoetrope Ltd — *THORN EMI*   P
TXE 90 0709 4/TVE 90 0709 2

Little Sex, A   Fil-Ent '82
Comedy/Romance
12058   89 mins   C
V2, B, V
Tim Matheson, Kate Capshaw, Edward Herrmann
A comedy romp featuring Tim Matheson as the man every woman wants to seduce.
BBFC:15 — S,A — EN
MTM Enterprises — *Guild Home Video*
H, P, E

PALADIN VIDEO HOME ENTERTAINMENT GUIDE

Little Steven and the Disciples of Soul Fil-Ent '82
Music-Performance
09321   60 mins   C
B, V
This tape features Steve, lead guitarist with Bruce Springsteen, on his own performing songs from his album 'Men Without Women.' The tracks include 'Lyin' in a Bed of Fire,' 'Save Me,' 'Forever' and 'Inside of Me.'
F — EN
Unknown — THORN EMI   P
TXE 90 1289 4/TVE 90 1289 2

Little Super Man   Fil-Ent '??
Adventure
08914   101 mins   C
V2, B, V
Directed by Woo Se Yeun
A young Chinese secret agent in Hong Kong outwits the might of the Japanese enemy.
C,A — EN
Unknown — Video Programme Distributors   P
Inter-Ocean 090

Little Women   Chi-Juv '84
Cartoons
12016   68 mins   C
B, V
Animated
This film is based on Louisa May Alcott's domestic drama and tells the story of a mother and her four daughters living in Concord, New England, and the tragedies and joys of their lives.
BBFC:U — F — EN
Unknown — Precision Video Ltd   P
BTOPV 1151/VTOPV 1151

Littlest Warrior, The   Fil-Ent '75
Cartoons/Adventure
05754   70 mins   C
B, V
Animated
The story of Zooshio who lives with his family and friends, a dog, a mouse and a bear in the Emperor's forest. A wicked official sets fire to the forest and Zooshio's father is sent to prison. The family are separated but Zooshio is raised by a nobleman and eventually is appointed to his father's former position; he is reunited with his family and rules the forest wisely and well for ever after.
BBFC:U — F — EN
ZIV International; Family Home Entertainment — Home Video Holdings   H, P
028

Live a Little, Steal a Lot   Fil-Ent '81
Crime-Drama/Adventure
13457   101 mins   C
B, V
Robert Conrad, Don Stroud, Donna Mills, Robyn Millan, Luther Adler
This film is a true-life account of the partnership of two Miami beach bums with a hunger for riches and their daring plan to steal the Star of India from New York's Museum of Natural History.
BBFC:15 — S,A — EN
Orion Pictures — Rank Video Library   H, P
0172 A

Live and Let Die   Fil-Ent '73
Adventure
13192   121 mins   C
B, V
Roger Moore, Yaphet Kotto, Jane Seymour, directed by Guy Hamilton
Investigating the deaths of three British agents, 007 is soon enmeshed in the malevolent, mystic world of two men who control a vast criminal network stretching from Harlem to the island of San Monique.
BBFC:A — C,A — EN
United Artists — Warner Home Video   P
99203

Live Today, Die Tomorrow   Fil-Ent '71
Drama
10036   95 mins   C
B, V
Directed by Kaneto Shindo
A young man from the country travels to the big city expecting to find happiness, but meets only misfortune and disillusionment.
S,A — EN
Toho — Palace Video Ltd   P
PVC 2048A

Living Form   Fin-Art '7?
Arts
02084   30 mins   C
B, V
The female form has always retained its beauty and fascination. This programme, specially recorded for video, is no exception to the rule. In 'Living Form,' beautiful women are seen in the traditional and classic poses adopted for artists and sculptors through the ages.
F — EN
VCL Video Services — VCL Video Services   P

(For Explanation of codes, see USE GUIDE and KEY)   397

PALADIN VIDEO HOME ENTERTAINMENT GUIDE

Living Proof   Fil-Ent '83
Drama
13434   120 mins   C
B, V
Richard Thomas
This is the story of Hank Williams, the son of the country music superstar, who was moulded into the image of his father with all its attendant stresses, until he had to find his own identity.
C,A — EN
Proctor and Gamble Prods. — *MGM/UA Home Video*   **P**
10443

Liz Greene's Guide to Astrology   Gen-Edu '7?
Occult sciences
07939   155 mins   C
V2, B, V
Liz Greene
On this tape Liz Greene, the lecturer, broadcaster and writer, provides an insight into the world of Astrology. She provides a stage by stage guide through the Signs of the Zodiac, the Planets, the preparations and computations needed to cast a Horoscope and the Houses of the Aspects. A detailed explanatory booklet and a blank Birth Chart are included with the cassette.
AM Available   S,A — ED
Unknown — *Videomedia*   **P**
PVM 9000/BVM 9000/HVM 9000

Lizzie Webb's Exercise Video   Spo-Lei '8?
Sports
09300   30 mins   C
B, V
Lizzie Webb
On this cassette Lizzie Webb introduces a total body firm-up routine to be used at anytime. She has been training beginners and professionals for 12 years. She includes on this tape six beginners who each have different reasons for joining; their ages vary from 20 to 50. She aims to encourage a daily exercise programme for health and fitness.
F — ED
Unknown — *Abacus Video*   **P**
301

Loaded Guns   Fil-Ent '75
Suspense/Drama
06103   90 mins   C
V2, B, V
Ursula Andress, Woody Strode, Marc Porel
An airline stewardess doubles as a leading female intelligence counter-agent. Her big assignment has just become operational; the plan is to totally immobilize a top drug trafficking ring.
S,A — EN
Picturmedia — *Video Programme Distributors* **P**
Cinehollywood—V220

Local Hero   Fil-Ent '83
Comedy-Drama
09789   107 mins   C
B, V
Burt Lancaster, Peter Riegart, Denis Lawson, Fulton Mackay, directed by Bill Forsyth
Set in a quaint Scottish village, this gentle comedy centres round the efforts of an American oil tycoon to transform the nearby bay into a giant oil producing plant. However, there is one sole dissenter to this plan.
BBFC:PG — S,A — EN
Enigma Production; Celandine Films — *THORN EMI*   **P**
TXA 90 1709 4/TVA 90 1709 2

Loch Ness Horror, The   Fil-Ent '7?
Horror
09234   93 mins   C
B, V
Sandy Kenyon, Miki McKenzie, Barry Buchanan, Eric Scott, Karey Louis Scott, directed by Larry Buchanan
An investigative scuba diver escapes the clutches of Nessie, not only with his life, but with the whole future of the Loch Ness moster contained in an egg.
C,A — EN
Unknown — *Video Form Pictures*   **P**
DIP 3

Logan's Run   Fil-Ent '76
Science fiction
07735   115 mins   C
V2, B, V
Michael York, Jenny Agutter, Richard Jordan, Farrah Fawcett-Majors, Peter Ustinov, directed by Michael Anderson
This film shows what life might be like in America during the 23rd century. It shows a perfect world of total pleasure where the only crime is living over the age of 30. A member of the elite Death Squad, who is nearing his 30th birthday, joins up with a young rebel and they escape from the comfort of the domed city. On the 'outside' they discover an old man living with hundreds of cats in a deserted and derelict Washington D.C.
BBFC:A — S,A — EN
MGM — *MGM/UA Home Video*   **P**
UMR 10082/UMB 10082/UMV 10082

PALADIN VIDEO HOME ENTERTAINMENT GUIDE

London Bridge Special, The   Fil-Ent '7?
Music-Performance/Variety
04626   60 mins   C
B, V
Tom Jones, Kirk Douglas, Rudolph Nureyev, Elliot Gould, The Carpenters
Tom Jones stars in the 'London Bridge Special'—not in London, but at Lake Havasu in California. This musical features Kirk Douglas, The Carpenters, Elliot Gould and the fantastic Rudolph Nureyev.
F — EN
VCL Video Services Ltd — *VCL Video Services*
P

London Conspiracy   Fil-Ent '76
Mystery
05945   98 mins   C
B, V
Tony Curtis, Roger Moore, Arthur Brough
Another adventure involving Lord Brett Sinclair and his friend Danny. An old mansion that has been in the Sinclair family for years has been unoccupied except for an aged butler. Brett discovers it has been restored without his permission. Investigating, they find a letter to a theatrical agency asking for an actor that resembles Brett. He applies and gets the job of impersonating himself.
S,A — EN
Unknown — *Precision Video Ltd*   **P**
BITC 2093/VITC 2093

London Rock 'n' Roll Show, The   Fil-Ent '??
Music-Performance
09362   92 mins   C
B, V
This tape features well known rock 'n' roll groups such as Bo Diddley, Jerry Lee Lewis, Bill Haley and the Comets, Little Richard, Chuck Berry and Music and Lights. It also includes an interview with Mick Jagger.
F — EN
Unknown — *Precision Video Ltd*   **P**
BMMPV 2594/VMMPV 2594

Lone Ranger, The   Fil-Ent '??
Cartoons/Adventure
09967   62 mins   C
B, V
Animated
This tape contains five adventures of the West's most famous crime fighter, his faithful Indian friend Tonto and their stallions Silver and Scout.
F — EN
Unknown — *Select Video Limited*   **P**
3603/43

Lone Wolf Mc Quade   Fil-Ent '83
Adventure/Western
12733   105 mins   C
B, V
Chuck Norris, David Carradine, Barbara Carrera
This is a film about a Westerner who fought hard, drank hard, and when he loved—the women knew it. One day he meets a woman with strong feelings, but of hatred, and she was out for revenge.
BBFC:18 — *A — EN*
Yorman Ben-Ami; Steve Carver — *Rank Video Library*   **H, P**
0197D

Loneliest Runner, The   Fil-Ent '77
Drama
12238   74 mins   C
B, V
Michael Landon, Brian Keith, Lance Kerwin, Melissa Sue Anderson, directed by Michael Landon
This film is the story of an athlete with a will to win with a difference. It follows his fortune and personal determination leading to the ultimate goal, the Olympic Gold Medal.
S,A — EN
NBC International — *Select Video Limited*
P
3110/43

Lonely Guy, The   Fil-Ent '84
Comedy/Romance
13608   91 mins   C
B, V
Steve Martin, Robyn Douglass, Charles Grodin, Judith Ivey, Steve Laurence, directed by Arthur Hiller
A tongue-in-cheek approach to the problem of loneliness, but the character in this film solves his problems by writing a book on the subject which drastically changes his lifestyle.
BBFC:15 — *S,A — EN*
Universal — *CIC Video*   **H, P**
1129

Lonely Hearts   Fil-Ent '82
Comedy-Drama/Romance
10089   95 mins   C
B, V
Norman Kaye, Wendy Hughes
This story follows the unlikely romance between a middle-aged piano tuner with an ill-fitting toupee, a practised shoplifter whose best friend is an elderly dachsund and a shy, virginal bank clerk. They meet at a Lonely Hearts Club after the funeral of his mother and her escape from over-protective parents. Set in Australia.
BBFC:15 — *S,A — EN*
Unknown — *VideoSpace Ltd*   **P**

(For Explanation of codes, see USE GUIDE and KEY)

PALADIN VIDEO HOME ENTERTAINMENT GUIDE

Lonely Hearts
Fil-Ent '80
Romance/Comedy
12822　　95 mins　　C
B, V

Norman Kaye, Wendy Hughes, directed by Paul Cox

Two lonely people are brought together through a marriage bureau and their romance blossoms slowly against all odds.
BBFC:15 — S,A — EN
Film Town Video — *VideoSpace Ltd*　　P
PL 4

Lonely Lady, The
Fil-Ent '83
Drama
12536　　87 mins　　C
B, V

Pia Zadora, Lloyd Bochner, Bibi Besch, Joseph Cali, Jared Martin, Anthony Holland, directed by Peter Sasdy

This is the story of a woman who wanted everything that Hollywood could give. When after many disappointments she is finally recognised as a top writer, she stuns everyone with a shocking revelation.
BBFC:18 — A — EN
Robert R Weston; Universal — *THORN EMI*
P
TXA 90 2183 4; TVA 90 2183 2

Loners, The
Fil-Ent '??
Drama/Suspense
06104　　98 mins　　C
V2, B, V

Dean Stockwell, Scott Brady, Gloria Grahame

An Indian half-breed is running from the law after accidentally killing a policeman. He is joined by a friend and a desperate girl, a runaway. They are soon involved in theft and more murder. The police move in as they flee to freedom.
S,A — EN
Unknown — *Video Programme Distributors*
P
Cinehollywood—V1620

Loners Plus Clipper Cup 'Hawaii 78,' The
Spo-Lei '82
Sports-Water/Documentary
07437　　102 mins　　C
B, V

Dame Naomi James

The first part of this programme is a record of the 1980 Observer Single-Handed Transatlantic Race. Modern technology enabled filming of the hitherto hidden dramas of being one of The Loners. The second part covers the inaugural Pan-Am Clipper Cup in Hawaii during August 1978.
S,A — EN
Westward TV; South Pacific
Television — *THORN EMI*　　P
TXB 90 0725 4/TVB 90 0725 2

Long Arm of the Godfather
Fil-Ent '74
Crime-Drama
09009　　90 mins　　C
V2, B, V

Adolfo Celi, Peter Lee Lawrence, directed by Nat Banomi

A young thug steals a consignment of arms from the Mafia. The film describes how the Mafia reaches all areas of society in the ensuing struggle to regain their stolen arms.
S,A — EN
Joseph Green Pictures — *Intervision Video*
H, P
AA 0464

Long Day of Massacre, The
Fil-Ent '??
Western
05727　　100 mins　　C
V2, B, V

Peter Martell

This western is centred on the Sheriff of Kansas City who has a reputation for killing outlaws he is supposed to arrest.
F — EN
Unknown — *Video Unlimited*　　H, P

Long Day's Journey Into Night
Fil-Ent '62
Drama
04678　　135 mins　　B/W
B, V

Katharine Hepburn, Sir Ralph Richardson, Jason Robards Jr., Dean Stockwell

In his most mercilessly autobiographical play O'Neill gives an account of his explosive home life, fused by a drug-addicted mother, a father who becomes an alcoholic after realising that he is no longer a famous actor and an older brother who is emotionally unstable and a misfit.
C,A — EN
Landau-Unger — *Polygram Video*　　P

Long Day's Journey Into Night
Fil-Ent '72
Drama
05868　　162 mins　　C
B, V

400　　(For Explanation of codes, see USE GUIDE and KEY)

PALADIN VIDEO HOME ENTERTAINMENT GUIDE

Laurence Olivier, Constance Cummings, Ronald Pickup, Denis Quilley, Maureen Lipman, directed by Peter Wood

This is the story of a day in the life of the Tyrone family and their love-hate relationships. The father is a talented but frustrated actor. The mother, through being unable to cope with life and the way it has treated her, is a dope addict. One son is an alcoholic, the other a self-tormented but potentially brilliant dramatist with tuberculosis.

Emmy Award '72.   S,A — EN

National Theatre Production — *Precision Video Ltd*   P

BITC 3048/VITC 3048

Long Good Friday, The   Fil-Ent '80
Crime-Drama
05044   109 mins   C
B, V

Bob Hoskins, Helen Mirren, Dave King, Bryan Marshall, Derek Thompson, Eddie Constantine

The story, set in London's dockland, of how things start to go very wrong for a gang boss.

BBFC:X — C,A — EN

Hand Made Films; Barry Hanson — *THORN EMI*   P

TXA 90 0306 4/TVA 90 0306 2

Long Hot Summer, The   Fil-Ent '58
Drama
12254   118 mins   C
B, V

Paul Newman, Joanne Woodward, Anthony Franciosa, Orson Welles, Lee Remick, directed by Martin Ritt

A rich tyrannical rancher decides that none of his family deserve to inherit his fortune. A handsome young roughneck joins his work force and trouble starts when the rancher begins to regard him as the most likely candidate for his money.

S,A — EN

20th Century Fox — *CBS/Fox Video*   P

1045

Long Live Your Death   Fil-Ent '71
Western/Suspense
01816   98 mins   C
V2, B, V

Franco Nero, Eli Wallach, Lynn Redgrave, Horst Janson, Eduardo Fajardo, Marilu Tolo, directed by Duccio Tessari

This tells the story of an ex-Russian Prince who discovers the secret of buried Mexican treasure. However, before finding the fortune, he has to get the map. Before long he gets mixed up with an escaped bandit, a crooked sheriff and an Irish journalist.

BBFC:A — S,A — EN

Unknown — *Iver Film Services*   P

186

Long Night of Veronique, The   Fil-Ent '7?
Drama/Suspense
07765   80 mins   C
V2, B, V

Alex Morrison, Alba Rigazzi

This film follows the tragic story of two young cousins' love for each other which is strangely relived fifty years later.

S,A — EN

Unknown — *Fletcher Video*   H, P

AV613

Long Ride, The   Fil-Ent '83
War-Drama
12513   90 mins   C
B, V

John Savage, Kelly Reno, directed by Pal Gabor

A heart-rending film about an American pilot's attempt to escape from occupied Hungary aided by an orphan boy and a remarkable horse.

S,A — EN

Robert Halmi Inc; Mafilm Production; Brady Run Associates — *THORN EMI*   P

TXA 90 2363 4/TVA 90 2363 2

Long Riders, The   Fil-Ent '80
Adventure/Western
13020   100 mins   C
B, V

David Carradine, Keith Carradine, James Keach, Stacy Keach, Dennis Quaid, Randy Quaid, directed by Walter Hill

The story of three notorious sets of outlaws the brothers James, Younger and Miller who plan a final bank job in Northfield, Minnesota.

BBFC:X — A — EN

United Artists — *Warner Home Video*   P

99268

Long Way Home, A   Fil-Ent '81
Drama
12073   94 mins   C
V2, B, V

Timothy Hutton, Brenda Vaccaro, Rosanna Arquette

(For Explanation of codes, see USE GUIDE and KEY)

PALADIN VIDEO HOME ENTERTAINMENT GUIDE

A boy was separated from his brother and sister when a child. This is the courageous story of his unrelenting search to be re-united with them again.
BBFC:PG — S,A — EN
Alan Landsburg Productions — *Guild Home Video* H, P, E

Long Weekend   Fil-Ent '80
Horror
05744   97 mins   C
B, V
John Hargreaves, Briany Behets, directed by Colin Eccleston
The story of an unhappy married couple who spend a long weekend in a remote wooded spot by the sea. They become a destructive force culminating in the brutal and thoughtless killing of several animals. Nature fights back and their terror mounts; in panic they are separated and forced to face the darkness alone.
BBFC:AA — S,A — EN
Duging Films — *Home Video Holdings* H, P
011

Longest Day, The   Fil-Ent '62
War-Drama
01740   179 mins   C
V2, B, V, LV
Richard Burton, Peter Lawford, Rod Steiger, John Wayne, Edmond O'Brien
The story of D-Day in World War II, as seen through the eyes of Americans, French, British, and Germans. Cast of forty-two international stars.
F — EN
20th Century Fox, Darryl F Zanuck — *CBS/Fox Video* P
4A-041

Longest Hunt, The   Fil-Ent '68
Western/Adventure
05451   85 mins   C
V2, B, V
Brian Kelly, Keenan Wynn, Erica Blank, Fred Munroe, Folco Lulli, Ronald Austin, Virginia Fields, directed by Billy Michaels
A famous gunfighter is hired by a rich Mexican farmholder to bring back his son who has joined up with a group of American outlaws. Upon completion of his task he discovers his employer is planning to torture the boy who he has discovered is his wife's illegitimate son.
BBFC:AA — S,A — EN
Cemofilm — *Iver Film Services* P
103

Longshot   Fil-Ent '81
Drama
13239   100 mins   C
B, V
Leif Garrett, Linda Manz, Ralph Seymour, Zoe Chauveau, directed by EW Swackhamer
This film centres round the 'Table Football Word Championships' at Caesar's Palace with a fourteen-year-old girl running for the title and a group of kids losing their money at the Casino tables and having a spending spree with their parents' credit cards.
BBFC:PG — S,A — EN
Gary M Goodman; Barry Rosen — *CBS/Fox Video* P
6677

Look Again at Garden Birds/Look Again at Gulls   Gen-Edu '76
Birds
00237   48 mins   C
B, V
Narrated by Eric Thompson and Michael Rodd
Two films are featured on one cassette. 'Look Again at Garden Birds' (24 mins) looks at the birds we are most familiar with, their feeding habits, their lives and how they have learnt to exploit the opportunities provided by man. 'Look Again at Gulls' (24 mins) looks at the way gulls have adapted and can profit from the ways of modern man. It examines and explains the language and behaviour patterns of the different species, adapted to suit their habitats.
British Sponsored Film Festival '74: Silver Award (Look Again at Garden Birds), British Sponsored Film Festival '75: Gold Award (Look Again at Gulls)   M,A — ED
Royal Society for the Protection of Birds — *Royal Society for the Protection of Birds* H, P

Look Back in Anger   Fil-Ent '58
Drama
09801   95 mins   B/W
B, V
Richard Burton, Claire Bloom, Edith Evans, Mary Vre, Gary Raymond, directed by Tony Richardson
A trend-setting 'anti-establishment' hero full of bitterness feels for the injustices of humanity takes his feelings out on his life and those close to him. He abandons his pregnant wife in favour of her best friend, eventually alienating himself from all his friends.
BBFC:18 — C,A — EN
Woodfall Film Productions Ltd; Samuel Goldwyn — *THORN EMI* P
TXE 90 0867 4, TVE 90 0867 2

Lookin' to Get Out   Fil-Ent '82
Comedy-Drama
09460   100 mins   C

402   (For Explanation of codes, see USE GUIDE and KEY)

PALADIN VIDEO HOME ENTERTAINMENT GUIDE

V2, B, V
Jon Voight, Ann-Margret
Two small time hustlers have only 24 hours left to pay their large debts to a New York Mob. They head for Las Vegas determined to break the bank at Caesar's Palace. A series of misadventures follow.
BBFC:15 — *C,A* — *EN*
Lorimar — *Guild Home Video*   **H, P, E**

Looking for Mr. Goodbar   Fil-Ent '78
Drama
07370   136 mins   C
B, V
Diane Keaton, Tuesday Weld, William Atherton, Richard Kiley, Richard Gere, directed by Richard Brooks
This film follows the lifestyle of a young woman trying to escape the claustrophobic atmosphere of her family and search for her own identity. A compassionate teacher of deaf children by day she seeks uninvolved sexual encounters by night. Based on Judith Rossner's novel, the film explores the questions faced by today's women regarding mental and sexual development.
S,A — *EN*
Paramount — *CIC Video*   **H, P**
BEA 2022/VHA 2022

Looking Glass War, The   Fil-Ent '70
Drama
09283   106 mins   C
B, V
Christopher Jones, Pia Degermark, Ralph Richardson, Paul Rogers, directed by Frank R. Pierson
A young Polish refugee is trained in spy technique for admission behind the Iron Curtain. He faces danger, death and deception as he is sent to obtain vital information about a Russian missile site based in East Germany. Based on the novel by John LeCarre.
S,A — *EN*
Columbia — *RCA/Columbia Pictures Video UK*
H, P

Looney, Looney, Looney, Bugs Bunny Movie, The   Fil-Ent '81
Cartoons
12501   77 mins   C
B, V
Animated
This cassette contains a conpendium of vintage cartoons, including Bugs Bunny, Sylvester, Tweetie Pie and Porky Pig.
BBFC:U — *F* — *EN*
Warner Bros — *Warner Home Video*   **P**
61142

Looney Tunes Video Show, Volumes 14-19, The   Chl-Juv '84
Cartoons
12966   68 mins   C
B, V
Animated   6 pgms
Bugs Bunny, Daffy Duck, Road Runner and friends are all set about their hilarious capers in this cartoon compilation of classic shorts from the 1940's and 50's.
1. *The Looney Tunes Video Show, Volume 14*
2. *The Looney Tunes Video Show, Volume 15*
3. *The Looney Tunes Video Show, Volume 16*
4. *The Looney Tunes Video Show, Volume 17*
5. *The Looney Tunes Video Show, Volume 18* 6. *The Looney Tunes Video Show, Volume 19*
PS,M — *EN*
Warner Bros — *Warner Home Video*   **P**
61233; 61243; 61235; 61350; 61351; 61352

Loose Connections   Fil-Ent '84
Drama/Romance
12950   95 mins   C
B, V
Lindsay Duncan, Stephen Rea, directed by Richard Eyre
A battle of the sexes ensues when an attractive middle-class feminist builds her own jeep and is obliged to share a trip across Europe with a male chauvinist with a natural inability at almost everything.
S,A — *EN*
Simon Perry — *Virgin Video*   **H, P**
VVA 034

Loose Shoes   Fil-Ent '??
Comedy
08616   70 mins   C
V2, B, V
Bill Murray, Howard Hesseman, Jaye P. Morgan, Buddy Hackett
This film, a compilation of comical sketches, sends up movies from science fiction to musicals. Nothing is spared as in one sketch an ignited burst of 'wind' blows up a submarine and in another the earth shudders as it is invaded by 'private-part' snatchers.
A — *EN*
Unknown — *Hokushin Audio Visual Ltd*
P
VM71

Loot   Fil-Ent '70
Crime-Drama/Comedy
08581   96 mins   C
B, V
Richard Attenborough, Lee Remick, Hynel Bennet, Milo O'Shea, Roy Holder, directed by Silvio Narizzano

PALADIN VIDEO HOME ENTERTAINMENT GUIDE

This film is about a randy son and his mate who plan a bank raid. Their idea is to use their mother's coffin as a hiding place for the money. A nymphomaniac nurse plans to marry the widowed father which confuses him further. This black comedy is based on the play by Joe Orton.
BBFC:X — A — EN
Performing Arts — *THORN EMI* **P**
TXC 90 0751 4/TVC 90 0751 2

Lord of the Rings Fil-Ent '78
Cartoons/Fantasy
07473   127 mins   C
B, V
Animated, directed by Ralph Bakshi
This film, a translation of the great fantasy saga by J. R. R. Tolkien, is a fairy tale of hobbits, elves, dwarves and the Dark Lord of the Rings. The hobbit hero is the reluctant keeper of a magic ring which gives the wearer power over all living creatures. He sets out on a dangerous journey to cast the ring back into its melting pot on Mount Doom to prevent the Armageddon threatening Middle Earth. Music by Leonard Rosenman, with a large cast of mainly British voices including John Hurt.
BBFC:A — S,A — EN
The Saul Zaentz Production
Company — *THORN EMI* **P**
TXA 90 0691 4/TVA 90 0691 2

Lords of Discipline, The Fil-Ent '83
Drama
10100   103 mins   C
B, V
David Keith, Robert Prosky, G.D. Spradlin, directed by Franc Roddam
This film set at the Carolina Military Academy, tells the story of the first black recruit to enter and of the final-year recruit ordered to ensure his safety.
BBFC:15 — S,A — EN
Paramount — *CIC Video* **H, P**
BEA 2073/VHA 2073

Lords of Flatbush, The Fil-Ent '74
Drama
12471   80 mins   C
B, V
Sylvester Stallone, Henry Winkler
A film about growing up tough in New York and being a teenager in the 1950's.
BBFC:15 — S,C — EN
Columbia — *RCA/Columbia Pictures Video UK* **H, P**
10271

Lords of the New Church Live from London, The Fil-Ent '83
Music-Performance
13143   60 mins   C
B, V
This programme features fifteen tracks by the Lords at the Marquee including 'New Church,' 'Eat Your Heart Out,' 'Russian Roulette,' 'Partners in Crime' and others.
F — EN
Unknown — *Polygram Video* **P**
040 3634/040 3632

Los Angeles Connection, The Fil-Ent '??
Crime-Drama
07915   90 mins   C
V2, B, V
John Ireland, Dorothy Malone
A journalist investigating the mysterious death of a friend discovers that his own life is in danger.
S,A — EN
Unknown — *Video Programme Distributors*
P
Inter-Ocean—071

Losers, The Fil-Ent '70
War-Drama/Adventure
07817   95 mins   C
V2, B, V
William Smith, Bernie Hamilton, Adam Roarke, directed by Jack Starrett
A gang of five evil bike riders are recruited as guerillas to rescue a key U.S. advisor from behind Viet Cong lines. Intent on completing their suicide mission, they roar around Vietnam on their motorbikes, crushing everything in their path.
S,A — EN
Fanfare — *Video Unlimited* **H, P**
047

Losin' It Fil-Ent '84
Comedy/Drama
13407   96 mins   C
V2, B, V
Tom Cruise, Shelley Long, Jackie Earle Haley, John Stockwell, directed by Curtis Hanson
Three high school seniors have their long awaited first fling in a series of adventures south of the border.
BBFC:18 — A — EN
Bryan Gindoff; Hannah
Hempstead — *Intervision Video* **H, P**
6592

Lost and Found Fil-Ent '79
Comedy/Romance
09279   104 mins   C

---

404 (For Explanation of codes, see USE GUIDE and KEY)

PALADIN VIDEO HOME ENTERTAINMENT GUIDE

B, V
Glenda Jackson, George Segal, Maureen Stapleton, Hollis McLaren, John Cunningham, directed by Melvin Frank
In this follow-up to 'Touch of Class' this film follows the romance between a happy-go-lucky American professor of English and an English divorcee whose husband has left her for a younger woman.
S,A — EN
Columbia — *RCA/Columbia Pictures Video UK*
H, P

Lost Moment, The   Fil-Ent '47
Drama
01075   89 mins   B/W
V2, B, V
Robert Cummings, Susan Hayward, Agnes Moorehead
Based on Henry James' 'The Aspern Papers'—a publisher is after some famous love letters, and a neurotic woman he meets claims to have access to them.
BBFC:A — A — EN
Universal — *Intervision Video*   H, P
A-A 0110

Lotte Berk Exercise Class—Get Physical, The   Gen-Edu '82
Physical fitness
08302   ? mins   C
B, V
Lois Kingham
This tape features exercises created by Lotte Berk and performed by Lois Kingham. It explains simply how to do the exercises and explains the benefits of each movement. The exercises are done to music, composed by Roger Webb. It contains a warm up, leg, stomach, thigh and bottom exercises and a section on stretching.
S,A — I
Golden Dawn Productions — *Warwick Video*
P
00004

Lou Rawls   Fil-Ent '81
Music-Performance
04625   60 mins   C
B, V
Lou Rawls, Duke Ellington, Freda Payne
Lou Rawls, like all great performers, relaxes and delights a live audience with his own style of music and song. Featuring Duke Ellington and Freda Payne.
F — EN
VCL Video Services Ltd — *VCL Video Services*
P

Love Among the Ruins   Fil-Ent '74
Drama/Romance
04182   120 mins   C
B, V
Katharine Hepburn, Laurence Olivier
The vivacious Mrs. Jessica Medlicott consults a successful barrister, Sir Arthur Granville-Jones, to represent her in a breach of promise suit.
BBFC:U — F — EN
ABC Circle Films — *Guild Home Video*
H, P

Love and Bullets   Fil-Ent '79
Crime-Drama
02043   99 mins   C
B, V
Charles Bronson, Jill Ireland
A plainclothes police lieutenant is given a mission to nail the powerful leader of an organised crime syndicate.
C,A — EN
Pancho Kohner — *Precision Video Ltd*   P
BITC 2030/VITC 2030

Love and Death   Fil-Ent '75
Comedy
13039   83 mins   C
B, V
Woody Allen, Diane Keaton, directed by Woody Allen
In this hilarious send-up of Russian literature is a sweeping, side-splitting spectacle of Europe at war, of clashing armies, and of a Russian's unsuccessful attempts to remain neutral.
BBFC:A — C,A — EN
Rollins and Joffe Productions — *Warner Home Video*   P
99299

Love and Money   Fil-Ent '80
Romance
08397   95 mins   C
V2, B, V
Ray Sharkey, Ornella Muti, Klaus Kinski, Armand Assante, King Vidor
This film tells of the passion for a beautiful young wife of a millionaire, by a young man. To be near her he allows himself to be manipulated into her husband's web of intrigue and corruption.
BBFC:X — A — EN
Lorimar — *Guild Home Video*   H, P, E

Love at First Bite   Fil-Ent '79
Comedy
06171   96 mins   C
V2, B, V

PALADIN VIDEO HOME ENTERTAINMENT GUIDE

George Hamilton, Susan Saint James, Richard Benjamin, Dick Shawn, Arte Johnson, Sherman Hemsley, Isabel Sanford, directed by Stan Dragoti

After living in his Transylvanian home for 700 years Count Dracula is forced to leave with his cockroach eating manservant when the Government plan to turn the castle into a gymnasium. He takes a plane to New York, in his coffin, where he meets a top model and falls in love. Her psychiatrist boyfriend causes complications as he tries to warn New York that a vampire is haunting the night clubs.

BBFC:AA — S,A — EN

American International; Joel Freeman
Prod — Guild Home Video   H, P, E

Love Bug, The   Fil-Ent '68
Comedy/Fantasy
05579   104 mins   C
B, V

Dean Jones, Michele Lee, David Tomlinson, Buddy Hackett

This is a story of an almost-human car that enters the life of a fading racing car driver. He steers his new owner into romance with a lady mechanic then on to victory in a cross-country race.

F — EN

Walt Disney Productions — Rank Video Library   H
01200

Love Butcher, The   Fil-Ent '7?
Horror
02496   90 mins   C
V2, B, V

Erik Stern, Kay Neer

A series of bizarre murders have completely baffled the police to a point where fear grips the entire neighbourhood. This is a profoundly disturbing film depicting senseless and psychotic violence.

BBFC:X — A — EN

Unknown — Intervision Video   H
A-A 0144

Love by Appointment   Fil-Ent '76
Drama
09071   90 mins   C
B, V

Ernest Borgnine, Francoise Fabian, Corinne Clery

This is the sensual story of three call girls, whose lives revolve around the telephone. One of the girls decides to give up her life on the streets to live with her lover. However she learns of his death in a car accident, and in a state of shock returns to her former life.

A — EN

Italy — Video Tape Centre   P
VTC 1021

Love Hate Love   Fil-Ent '70
Drama
04272   70 mins   C
B, V

Ryan O'Neal, Peter Haskell, Lesley Warren, Henry Jones

A lovely fashion model's whirlwind romance turns into a harrowing nightmare in this chilling psychological drama from the pen of Eric Ambler.

A — EN

ABC Films — Rank Video Library   H, P
0042

Love Is a Splendid Illusion   Fil-Ent '7?
Drama
02498   87 mins   C
V2, B, V

Simon Brent, Andree Flamand, Lisa Collings

The story of a husband and father running from one woman to the other, neglecting both his wife and young son and work. He tries to love them all and loses the only ones he cares for.

BBFC:X — A — EN

Unknown — Intervision Video   H
A-A 0091

Love Letters   Fil-Ent '84
Drama
12869   117 mins   C
B, V

Jamie Lee Curtis, James Keach, directed by Amy Jones.

This is the story of a burning attraction between a single woman and a married man and the ultimate heartbreak it brings.

BBFC:18 — A — EN

New World Pictures — Vestron Video International   P
15051

Love, Lust and Ecstasy   Fil-Ent '??
Drama
06069   79 mins   C
V2, B, V

Ajita Wilson, Mireille Damien

---

406   (For Explanation of codes, see USE GUIDE and KEY)

PALADIN VIDEO HOME ENTERTAINMENT GUIDE

A beautiful girl married to a ship owner gets no satisfaction from their marriage. She has an affair with a young portrait painter; her husband's secretary becomes involved and the triangle leads to murder.
BBFC:X — A — EN
Unknown — *Video Programme Distributors* **P**
Inter-Ocean—052

Love Machine from the U.S.A.   Fil-Ent '79
Music-Performance
04402   30 mins   C
B, V
Seven beautiful girls sing and dance to smash hits such as 'Hound Dog,' 'All Shook Up,' 'Jailhouse Rock,' 'In the Mood,' and 'You Should Be Dancing.'
F — EN
VCL — *VCL Video Services*   **P**

Love Me Deadly   Fil-Ent '7?
Horror
02124   95 mins   C
V2, B, V
A horror story of a beautiful young woman whose traumatic childhood experience has left her unable to find satisfaction in the arms of a living man.
C,A — EN
Unknown — *Hokushin Audio Visual Ltd* **P**
VM-37

Love Story   Fil-Ent '70
Drama
01213   100 mins   C
B, V
Ryan O'Neal, Ali McGraw, Ray Milland, directed by Arthur Hiller
Ryan O'Neal and Ali McGraw achieved stardom in this popular adaptation of Erich Segal's novel, with portrayals of a young couple who cross social barriers to marry.
Academy Awards '70: Best Original Score (Francis Lai). *F — EN*
Paramount — *CIC Video*   **H, P**

Love to Eternity   Fil-Ent '??
Adventure/Romance
06261   100 mins   C
B, V
Catherine Deneuve, Marcello Mastroianni
A man lives alone on an isolated island away from his nagging wife and the pressures of modern life. The rugged splendour of their self-inflicted solitude is broken when a young girl lands on the island, marooned by a passing boat. He resents her presence but when the food runs out they are drawn together by a deep bond of love.
S,A — EN
Unknown — *VCL Video Services*   **P**
P137D

Love War, The   Fil-Ent '69
Science fiction
04183   90 mins   C
B, V
Lloyd Bridges, Angie Dickinson
A nerve tingling science fiction drama where the very future of the world is at stake.
BBFC:AA — *C,A — EN*
Thomas; Spelling — *Guild Home Video*
H, P

Love You Till Tuesday   Fil-Ent '69
Music-Performance
12025   30 mins   C
B, V
This tape contains examples of early David Bowie music, including 'Sell Me a Coat,' 'When I Am Five,' 'Rubber Band,' 'Let Me Sleep Beside You,' 'Ching a Ling,' 'Space Oddity.'
F — EN
Unknown — *Polygram Video*   **H, P**
0403134/0403132

Loveless, The   Fil-Ent '82
Drama
08986   83 mins   C
B, V
Willem Dafoe, Robert Gordon, Martin Kanter, J. Don Ferguson, directed by Monty Montgomery and Kathryn Bigelow
Set in the year 1959, in a small southern town, this psychological drama portrays a tangle of love, the loveless and the depraved. Five bikers and a sixteen year old girl in a whirl of pompadour hairstyles and black leather become involved in incest and murder, leaving the town with memories the residents will never forget.
BBFC:X — *A — EN*
Mainline Pictures — *Palace Video Ltd*   **P**
PVC 2026B

Lover of the Great Bear, The   Fil-Ent '7?
Drama/Adventure
08650   93 mins   C
V2, B, V
Senta Berger

(For Explanation of codes, see USE GUIDE and KEY)

PALADIN VIDEO HOME ENTERTAINMENT GUIDE

This film follows the story of how the Great Bear constellation helps guide a group of contrabandists.
S,A — EN
Unknown — Fletcher Video   H, P
V138

Lovers and Other Strangers   Fil-Ent '69
Drama
04274   91 mins   C
B, V
Gig Young, Bea Arthur, Michael Brandon, Bob Dishy, Cloris Leachman, Bonnie Bedelia, Richard Castellano, Harry Guardino, Diane Keaton
Set in an American small town, this film is a domestic drama in which a young couple approaches marriage, fearing that matrimony will drive the romance out of their relationship.
BBFC:AA — A — EN
Cinerama Releasing — Rank Video Library
H, P
0046

Lovesick   Fil-Ent '83
Comedy/Romance
12596   93 mins   C
B, V
Dudley Moore, Elizabeth McGovern, John Huston, Alec Guiness, directed by Marshall Brickman
A successful, married New York psychiatrist falls in love with a beautiful patient and his obsessive pursuit of her lands him in all kinds of zany situations.
BBFC:15 — C,A — EN
Charles Okun — Warner Home Video   P
70011

Loving Couples   Fil-Ent '80
Comedy
09079   120 mins   C
B, V
Shirley MacLaine, James Coburn, Susan Sarandon, Stephen Collins, Sally Kellerman, directed by Jack Smight
Two happily married couples meet each other after an automobile accident and two new couples emerge, only to collide hilariously at a weekend resort.
S,A — EN
20th Century Fox — Video Tape Centre
P
VTC 1033

Loving You   Fil-Ent '57
Musical
09965   90 mins   C
B, V
Elvis Presley, Lizabeth Scott, Wendell Corey, Dolores Hart
This is the story of an unknown singer and his eventual rise to stardom. He is persuaded to sing at a party being held in a small town, and is watched by a press-agent who helps him to his success. This film includes a host of great hits: 'Let Me Be Your Teddy Bear', 'Got a Lot of Livin' to Do', 'Loving You', 'Lonesome Cowboy', 'Hot Dog', 'Mean Woman Blues' and 'Let's Have a Party'.
F — EN
NBC International — Select Video Limited
P
3106/43

L S Lowry   Fin-Art '8?
Artists
06894   60 mins   C
B, V
Presented by Harold Riley
On this tape Salford artist Harold Riley guides the viewer through the Lowry collection in Salford Art Gallery. Harold Riley is internationally famous not only for his formal portraiture and paintings but for the task he has inherited from Lowry of documenting in paintings, photography and drawings, the City of Salford.
S,A — ED
Holiday Brothers Ltd — Holiday Brothers Ltd
P

Lt. Robin Crusoe U.S.N.   Fil-Ent '67
Adventure
12590   90 mins   C
B, V
Dick Van Dyke, Nancy Kwan
A Navy pilot never had it so good when he is stranded on an exotic desert island and meets a beautiful girl whom he christens 'Wednesday' and a bevy of dusky maidens.
U — EN
Walt Disney Productions — Rank Video Library
H
133

Lucia di Lammermoor   Fin-Art '7?
Opera
02264   60 mins   C
V
Anna Moffo, Kosma Lijas   2 pgms
'Lucia di Lammermoor' by Gaetano Donizetti is based upon a novel by Walter Scott. The opera features the well known Mad Scene with a flute solo. Two tapes, sixty minutes each.
F — EN
Unknown — JVC   P
PRT 35; PRT 35-2

PALADIN VIDEO HOME ENTERTAINMENT GUIDE

Lucifer Complex, The   Fil-Ent '78
Science fiction
06874   91 mins   C
V2, B, V

Robert Vaughn, Keenan Wynn, Merrie Lynn Ross, Aldo Ray

This film, set on a remote South American island, features a mad genius and his plot to terrify the world. He has perfected a method of cloning exact programmed duplicates of world leaders, using women prisoners as the unwilling mothers.
A — EN
Unknown — European Video Company
P

Lucky Jim   Fil-Ent '58
Comedy
01609   91 mins   B/W
B, V

Ian Carmichael, Terry-Thomas, Hugh Griffith, directed by John Boulting

A junior lecturer in history at a redbrick university is anything but lucky. He tries to get himself in good graces with the head of his department, but is doomed from the beginning by doing the wrong thing at the worst possible time.
BBFC:U — S,A — EN
Roy Boulting — THORN EMI   P
TXE 90 0208 4/TVE 90 0208 2

Lucky Jim Fishing Adventures   Spo-Lei '77
Fishing
01088   60 mins   C
V2, B, V

Hosted by Jim Conway   13 pgms

A series of fishing programs shot above and below water level, which are instructive, intriguing, and just plain beautiful.
1. Alaska Kulik/Deschutes River, Oregon
2. Sekiu, Washington/ Willamette River Salmon
3. Panama Reef/Umpqua Stripers 4. Kalama Steelhead/East Lake, Oregon 5. Sam Rayburn Reservoir, Texas/Toledo Bend, Louisiana
6. Kona Coast Hawaii/Panama Marlin
7. Acapulco, Mexico/Lake Mead, Nevada
8. Alaska Grayling and Pike/Clark Lake Raft Trip
9. Glacier Bay/Yes Bay Salmon 10. Hawaii Kauai Surf/San Francisco Stripers 11. Ilwaco Salmon/ Alaska Salmon and Char 12. Cozumel, Mexico/Kaula Rock, Hawaii 13. Yes Bay Trout/Klamath River, California
F — EN
Jim Conway — Intervision Video   H, P
A-AE 0231; A-AE 0232; A-AE 0233; A-AE 0234; A-AE 0235; A-AE 0236; A-AE 0237; A-AE 0238; A-AE 0239; A-AE 0240; A-AE 0241; A-AE 0242; A-AE 0243

Lucky Luciano   Fil-Ent '74
Crime-Drama
07666   112 mins   C
B, V

Rod Steiger, Edmond O'Brien, Gian Maria Volonte, Vincent Gardenia, directed by Francesco Rosi

This film follows the story of the Mafia King of narcotics from his deportation in 1946 to his death from a heart attack while discussing a film of his life.
S,A — EN
Avco Embassy — Hello Video Ltd   P
H15

Lucky Luke   Fil-Ent '??
Cartoons/Adventure
08313   85 mins   C
B, V
Animated

A normally peaceful town, Daisytown, has become the scene for gunfights and murder, until Lucky Luke rides into town. He doesn't take long to clear the town of trouble and retire to the saloon. The dreaded Dalton gang return again and are driven out into the desert after a gun battle. They return with the redskins which threatens trouble for the hero.
F — EN
Les Productions Dargaud — Select Video Limited   P
3003

Lucky Luke and the Dalton Gang   Fil-Ent '??
Cartoons
09979   82 mins   C
B, V
Animated

This tape is the second in the Lucky Luke series. He once again crosses the path of the Dalton Gang, this time to stop them from tracking down a judge and jury, who once tried and sentenced their uncle some years before. On his chases, a train is derailed and he has a helter skelter ride inside a gold mine.
F — EN
Dargaud Films — Select Video Limited   P
3004/43

Lucky Star, The   Fil-Ent '80
Drama
06177   110 mins   C
B, V

Rod Steiger, Louise Fletcher, Lou Jacobi, Brett Marx, Yvon Dufour, Helen Hughes, Isabelle Mejius, directed by Max Fischer

Set in 1940 during the War in Holland, a young Jewish boy flees from Amsterdam after losing his parents. He is taken in and looked after by a

PALADIN VIDEO HOME ENTERTAINMENT GUIDE

rich widow, she provides him with his greatest wish, the setting in which he can act out his western fantasies. He is the sheriff and the Germans are the outlaws.
BBFC:AA — S,A — EN
Leger Prod — Guild Home Video   H, P, E

Lucky the Inscrutable   Fil-Ent '??
Crime-Drama
08652   94 mins   C
V2, B, V
Ray Danton, Beba Loncar
A Secret Agent tracks down and destroys the printing blocks used to forge bills with dramatic consequences.
S,A — EN
Unknown — Fletcher Video   H, P
V139

Lunatic   Fil-Ent '8?
Horror
09172   106 mins   C
B, V
Trevor Howard, Liv Ullman, Max von Sydow
Set in Scandanavia during the winter months, this film tells of an insane man, who escapes from an asylum where he was confined two years earlier for the axe murder of a farmhand. Clothed only in shorts and shoes he steals through the forest, murdering his sister and a farmgirl. The police suspect the brother-in-law, made even greater when his claims that he has seen the madman are proved false, as he returns to the asylum after the killings.
A — EN
Unknown — Video Form Pictures   H, P
MGS 17

Lunch Wagon   Fil-Ent '??
Comedy
07901   84 mins   C
V2, B, V
Rick Podell, Pamela Bryant, Rosanne Katon, directed by Ernest Pintoff
This film follows the havoc caused when three young girls with a lunch wagon, two hapless villains and a 50,000 dollar diamond encounter a variety of rival gangs, a professional hit man and the cops. Set to the music of the new wave band Missing Persons.
S,A — EN
Manson International — Video Programme Distributors   P
Inter-Ocean—065

Lungwei Village   Fil-Ent '7?
Martial arts
09822   90 mins   C

B, V
A village magistrate is struck down by a killer dressed in white. Four warriors arrive on the scene too late to save him. They know one of them had betrayed the magistrate.
S,A — EN
Unknown — Polygram Video   H, P
790 4514/790 4512

Lust for a Vampire   Fil-Ent '70
Horror
07444   85 mins   C
B, V
Ralph Bates, Barbara Jefford, Suzanna Leigh, Michael Johnson, Yutte Stensgaard, directed by Jimmy Sangster
Based on the novel 'Carmilla' by Sheridan le Fanu, the plot revolves around Mircalla, who enrolls as a student at an exclusive finishing school and proceeds to wreak havoc among pupils and teachers alike. An English teacher falls victim to her charms but is reluctantly forced to recognise her guilt when the death toll mounts. When outraged villagers set fire to the school he risks his life in an attempt to save her.
BBFC:X — EN
Hammer Film Production — THORN EMI   P
TXC 90 0275 4/TVC 90 0275 2

Lust for Revenge   Fil-Ent '7?
Drama
02500   85 mins   C
V2, B, V
A story of kidnap, rape and murder. The horror of this sends the victim's mother insane and leads the father to seek out and kill the criminals.
BBFC:X — A — EN
Unknown — Intervision Video   H
A-A 0049

Lusty Men   Fil-Ent '52
Western
06187   90 mins   B/W
B, V
Robert Mitchum, Susan Haywood, Arthur Kennedy
The story of a rodeo champ who falls on hard times and decides to teach a new boy all he knows. He is corrupted by the fame and dazzle of the rodeo star life; his relationship with his wife and friends deteriorates. He has to pull himself from the brink of disaster to save the day.
F — EN
RKO — VCL Video Services   P
X0252

PALADIN VIDEO HOME ENTERTAINMENT GUIDE

Lyn Marshall's Everyday Yoga
How-Ins '83
Physical fitness/Yoga
09319   ? mins   C
V2, B, V
Lyn Marshall demonstrates her own yoga techniques in a complete routine of movements that exercise every part of the body without strain.
S,A — I
Peter Ramsden — BBC Video
BBCV 1021
H, P

M

MacArthur
Fil-Ent '78
War-Drama/Biographical
10126   122 mins   C
B, V
Gregory Peck, Ed Flanders, directed by Joseph Sargent
This film is based on the story of General Douglas MacArthur, the American general who obtained the Japanese surrender in World War II.
BBFC:PG — S,A — EN
Universal — CIC Video   H, P
BEL 1066/VHL 1066

Macbeth
Fil-Ent '48
Drama
01076   107 mins   B/W
V2, B, V
Orson Welles, Jeanette Nolan, directed by Orson Welles
Shakespeare's drama of murder and intrigue within royal circles.
BBFC:U — A — EN
Republic — Intervision Video   H, P
A-A 0187

Macho Callahan
Fil-Ent '70
Western
01157   100 mins   C
B, V
David Janssen, Lee J. Cobb, Jean Seberg
The widow of a Confederate Army Colonel, who was raped by her husband's murderer, offers a bounty for his capture.
A — EN
Avco Embassy — CBS/Fox Video   P
3C-015

Mackintosh & T.J.
Fil-Ent '75
Western
05183   93 mins   C
B, V
Roy Rogers, Clay O'Brien, music by Waylon Jennings
Mackintosh is a drifting ranch hand who, in his travels, teams up with the rebellious young vagrant known as T.J.
C,A — EN
Penland Prods — Rank Video Library   H, P
8004

Macon County Line
Fil-Ent '75
Adventure
08305   90 mins   C
B, V
Alan Vint, Jesse Vint, Cheryl Waters, Max Baer
This is based on a true story of two brothers. On their way to the Army Induction Point they pick up a young girl. By mistake the trio becomes involved in the rape and murder of a policeman's wife. Before the policeman finds out that the real killers have been caught he goes on a manhunt that leads into the swamps, which brings death or madness to all but one of them.
A — EN
American International Pictures — Video Film Organisation   P
0007

Mad Bomber, The
Fil-Ent '72
Suspense/Drama
05524   100 mins   C
B, V
Vince Edwards, Chuck Connors, Neville Brand
A self-righteous psychotic decides to punish society for its sins by starting an horrific series of unrelated bombings. A police inspector attempts to piece together the scanty clues to understand the native which results in a dangerous confrontation.
BBFC:A — S,A — EN
Philip Yordan Productions — Derann Film Services   H, P
DV129B/DV129

Mad Bull
Fil-Ent '77
Drama
10210   96 mins   C
B, V
Alex Karras, Susan Anspach, Nicholas Colsanto, Elisha Cook Jr., Richard Karron, Steve Sandor, Tracy Walter, directed by Walter Doniger and Len Steckler
A 'charade' type wrestling match is watched by a blood-thirsty mob. The 'baddy' team consists of Mad Bull and the Executioner against the White Knight and Mr Clean. A reverse decision is given on a technicality which angers the mob,

PALADIN VIDEO HOME ENTERTAINMENT GUIDE

to appease them a championship match is announced. A punk kid in the crowd however has other ideas on how to do away with Mad Bull.
BBFC:18 — A — EN
Steckler Prods; Filmways — *Video Form Pictures* **H, P**
MGD 15

Mad Dog   Fil-Ent '76
Drama
05394   95 mins   C
B, V
Dennis Hopper, David Gulpil, Jack Thompson, Frank Thring, Michael Pate, directed by Phillippe Mora
A twenty year old youth joins the gold rush in Victoria and New South Wales in 1853. He has little luck and drifts into petty crime; a year later he is caught stealing clothes. A hard judge, who sees criminals as a source of labour, unjustly sentences him to twelve years hard labour in 'Success' prison.
BBFC:X — A — EN
Jeremy Thomas Productions — *Precision Video Ltd*   **P**
·BBPV 2558/VBPV 2558

Mad Foxes, The   Fil-Ent '??
Horror
08851   73 mins   C
B, V
Robert O'Neal, Laura Prenika, Laly Espinet, Ana Roca, directed by Paul Gray
A driver accidentally kills a Hell's Angel. A brutal and bloody revenge is inflicted on him by other members of the gang.
BBFC:X — A — EN
Unknown — *VCL Video Services*   **P**
M249D

Mad, Mad, Monsters   Fil-Ent '8?
Cartoons/Comedy
13772   45 mins   C
B, V
Animated by Rankin and Bass
Everyone's favourite horror characters are made fun of in this cartoon, including Frankenstein, Count Dracula, Wolfman and the Invisible Family.
F — EN
Unknown — *Odyssey Video*   **H, P**
6425

Mad, Mad, Movie Makers   Fil-Ent '7?
Adventure/Comedy
02446   86 mins   C
V2, B, V
Michael Pataki, Jo Anne Meredith, Mike Kellin
A Jewish and a Catholic community get behind a religious film production in Hollywood. The director makes a porno pic instead.
BBFC:AA — C,A — EN
Iver Film Services — *Iver Film Services*
P

Mad Max   Fil-Ent '79
Adventure/Science fiction
13049   88 mins   C
B, V
Mel Gibson, directed by George Miller
Max is a rogue cop dedicated to restoring justice in a nightmare futuristic world destroyed by a nuclear holocaust.
BBFC:X — A — EN
Warner Bros Inc — *Warner Home Video*
P
61170

Mad Max 2   Fil-Ent '81
Adventure/Science fiction
13050   91 mins   C
B, V
Mel Gibson, Bruce Spence, Vernon Wells, directed by George Miller
In the aftermath of global conflict Max joins an idealistic communal group but vicious gangs are on the rampage and Max teams up with the Gyro Captain to defend the community.
BBFC:X — A — EN
Kennedy Miller Entertainment Pty Ltd — *Warner Home Video*   **P**
61181

Mad Mission   Fil-Ent '8?
Adventure
09028   80 mins   C
V2, B, V
This film features the work of Hollywood's top eight stuntmen, in a story of gang warfare, with many extraordinary car chases and wild, fearless stunts. A hoard of diamonds is at stake, nobody wishing to share it out.
F — EN
Unknown — *Intervision Video*   **H, P**
AA 0454

Mad Mission Three   Fil-Ent '84
Suspense/Adventure
12906   87 mins   C
B, V
Peter Graves, Richard Kiel, Samuel Hul, Sylvia Chang, Carl Mak, directed by Tsui Hark

PALADIN VIDEO HOME ENTERTAINMENT GUIDE

Set in Paris and Hong Kong, an innocent man becomes involved with a gang of international crooks. This film is dubbed into English.
S,A — EN
Unknown — THORN EMI   P
TXH

Mad Monster Party Fil-Ent '68
Cartoons/Comedy
10085   90 mins   C
V2, B, V
Animated, voices of Boris Karloff, Ethel Ennis, Phyllis Diller
In his gloomy castle retreat on a Caribbean island Dr Frankenstein, who is nearing retirement, gathers together all the renowned monsters of the world to choose his successor.
F — EN
Avco Embassy — Embassy Home Entertainment   P
2077

Madama Butterfly Fil-Ent '??
Opera
10006   140 mins   C
B, V
Raina Kabaivanska, Nazzareno Antinori, Lorenzo Saccomani
Madama Butterfly's theme of love and heartbreak and its wealth of beautiful melodies make this a very popular opera. The music is by the chorus and orchestra of the Arena di Verona conducted by Maurizio Arena.
F — EN
Unknown — Longman Video   P
LGBE 7010/LGVH 7010

Madame Sin Fil-Ent '71
Drama
05395   86 mins   C
V2, B, V
Bette Davis, Robert Wagner, Denholm Elliott, Gordon Jackson, Dudley Sutton, directed by David Greene
Madame Sin lives in an old castle on a remote Scottish Island. She is the power behind a financial empire responsible for some of the biggest crimes, for arranging revolutions, for tumbling monarchies and for the assassination of public figures.
BBFC:A — S,A — EN
Robert Wagner Productions — Precision Video Ltd   P
CRITC 2034/BITC 2034/VITC 2034

Madhouse Fil-Ent '8?
Drama
09157   90 mins   C
B, V

Trish Beverly, Dennis Robertson, Michael Macrae, Morgan Hart, Richard Baker
This story, based on scientifically proven evidence, tells of the bond between identical twins and the sinister possibilities of that bond. Two twins have not met for seven years, during which time one of them has become hideously deformed. The story tells of her terrorisation of her twin sister.
C,A — EN
Unknown — Medusa Communications Ltd
H, P

Madhur Jaffrey's Indian Cookery How-Ins '18
Cookery
08734   120 mins   C
V2, B, V
Madhur Jaffrey
This tape covers sixteen Indian recipes. It shows very simply how to achieve the subtle oriental flavours.
S,A — I
Jenny Rogers — BBC Video   H, P
BBCV 1017

Madigan's Millions Fil-Ent '67
Suspense
04293   89 mins   C
V2, B, V
Dustin Hoffman, Elsa Martinelli, Cesar Romero
After being deported to Italy, mobster Mike Madigan dies. The U.S. Treasury despatch investigator Jason Fister to recover the million dollars he has stolen.
C,A — EN
American International — Video Programme Distributors   P
Inter-Ocean—042

Madron Fil-Ent '71
Western
06207   77 mins   C
B, V
Richard Boone, Leslie Caron
An Indian hunter discovers a nun, the sole survivor of an Apache massacre of a wagon train of French Canadian Sisters. They are captured by drunken drifters and find they have fallen in love.
S,A — EN
Four Star; Excelsior — VCL Video Services   P
C172C

Mae West Fil-Ent '82
Drama/Biographical
09850   90 mins   C
B, V

(For Explanation of codes, see USE GUIDE and KEY)

413

PALADIN VIDEO HOME ENTERTAINMENT GUIDE

Ann Jillian, James Brolin, Roddy McDowell, Piper Laurie
This is the life story of the silver screen's first sex goddess, who, unlike many of her latter-day counterparts, never swore or appeared nude in front of the camera. The film follows Mae's career from vaudeville, through Broadway to her Hollywood debut and eventual stage comeback and movie debut.
S,A — EN
Hill/Mandelker Films — *Polygram Video*
H, P
791 5664/791 5662

Mafia Warfare   Fil-Ent '??
Crime-Drama
08802   101 mins   C
B, V
Jean-Paul Belmondo, Claudia Cardinale, Michel Constantin, directed by Ralph Baum
This film tells the story of two gangsters who are cheated by the powerful Mafia. They set out in revenge, determined to get their own back.
A — EN
Unknown — *VCL Video Services*   **P**
P160D

Mafu Cage, The   Fil-Ent '79
Horror/Drama
05747   101 mins   C
B, V
Lee Grant, Carol Kane, Will Geer, James Olson, Will Sherwood, directed by Karen Arthur.
A successful solar astronomer lives in a Californian mansion where she looks after her deranged sister, Cissie. Cissie devotes herself to looking after a succession of caged monkeys; upon the death of the last one she is bought an orang-outang instead, she brutally bludgeons it to death. Her derangement degenerates into savage lunacy which sets off a chain of events endangering her sister, a colleague of hers and eventually herself.
BBFC:X — A — EN
Clouds Productions — *Home Video Holdings*
H, P
001

Maggie, The   Fil-Ent '54
Comedy
01603   93 mins   B/W
B, V
Paul Douglas, Hubert Gregg, Geoffrey Keen
An American tycoon and a Scottish sea captain, the owner of a dilapidated cargo ship, become involved in a series of mishaps, misadventures, and misunderstandings.
BBFC:U — F — EN
Ealing Studios; Michael Balcon — *THORN EMI*
P
TXE 90 0085 4/TVE 90 0085 2

Magic Adventure   Fil-Ent '??
Cartoons
08702   65 mins   C
V2, B, V
Animated
This is a tale of fantasy based on the fairy tales of Hans Christian Andersen.
BBFC:U — F — EN
Unknown — *Video Unlimited*   **H, P**

Magic Ball, The   Chi-Juv '8?
Cartoons/Fantasy
09324   60 mins   C
B, V
Animated   5 pgms
These five episodes from the popular series follow the adventure of Sam, whose magic ball bounces him inot many exciting worlds of fantasy and history.
1.The Story of the Princess in the Castle 2.The Story of the Cave Man 3.The Story of the Chimney Sweep 4.The Story of the Six Winged Lions 5.The Story of the Grandfather Clock
PS,M — EN
Granada Television — *Granada Video*   **H, P**

Magic Christian, The   Fil-Ent '70
Comedy
09183   95 mins   C
B, V
Peter Sellers, Ringo Starr, Laurence Harvey, Richard Attenborough, Christopher Lee, Spike Milligan, John Cleese, Raquel Welch, Wilfrid Hyde White, directed by Joseph McGrath
With a host of famous actors and actresses, this film tells the story of the richest man in the world who adopts a vagrant for his son, to prove that any man can be corrupted by money. The music is by Paul McCartney.
S,A — EN
Grand Film; Commonwealth United — *Video Form Pictures*   **H, P**
MGS 8

Magic Curse, The   Fil-Ent '7?
Suspense
02109   90 mins   C
V2, B, V
Handsome Man Ying sets out for Borneo in search of his uncle's missing aircraft laden with jewels. He returns with the magic curse which brings a horrible death to any woman he is in contact with.
C,A — EN
Unknown — *Hokushin Audio Visual Ltd*
P
VM-20

---

414   (For Explanation of codes, see USE GUIDE and KEY)

PALADIN VIDEO HOME ENTERTAINMENT GUIDE

Magic Flute, The   Fil-Ent '??
Opera
10000   130 mins   C
B, V
Conducted by Eric Ericson, directed by Ingmar Bergman
This is Bergman's film of one of Mozart's most famous operas. Set in a magical reconstruction of the 18th century Swedish royal palace theatre, it tells of the romantic but funny story of the struggle between the forces of light and darkness. It is performed with the Swedish Radio Chorus and Symphony Orchestra.
F — EN
Unknown — *Longman Video*   P
LGBE 7012/LGVH 7012

Magic of Coronation Street—Distant Memories 1960-64, The   Fil-Ent '82
Documentary/Drama
09327   172 mins   C
B, V
This tape recaptures the nostalgia of this world's longest running drama serial in six early black-and-white episodes which use colour links to connect these vintage moments in the lives of Elsie Tanner, Len Fairelough, Annie Walker, Ken Barlow and Valerie Tatlock, ending with their Christmas pantomine in 1964.
F — EN
Granada Television — *Granada Video*   H, P

Magic of the Sea, The   Gen-Edu '??
Oceanography/Adventure
06055   60 mins   C
V2, B, V
This film presents the sea as a world of adventure, from big game fishing in the warm waters of California to the tracking down and landing of the giant 350 pound tuna along the coast of Peru. It includes sequences of the H-bomb tests in the South Pacific, a warning to save the underwater kingdom.
F — ED
Unknown — *Video Programme Distributors*   P
Cinehollywood—V470

Magic Roundabout, The   Chi-Juv '84
Puppets
13400   60 mins   C
B, V

This cassette contains thirteen stories set in Mr. Rusty's magic garden with Mr. Zebedee, Florence, Dougal and all the other delightful characters.
I,M — EN
Unknown — *BBC Video*   H, P
9009

Magic Sword, The   Fil-Ent '62
Fantasy
06887   80 mins   C
V2, B, V
Basil Rathbone, Estelle Winwood, Gary Lockwood
A young knight sets out to rescue a beautiful princess held captive by an evil sorcerer and his dragon. The young man is aided by his foster-mother, an absent minded witch, who provides him with an enchanted horse and a magic sword.
M,S — EN
United Artists — *European Video Company*
P

Magical Mystery Trip Through Little Red's Head   Fil-Ent '??
Cartoons/Fantasy
08593   46 mins   C
V2, B, V
Animated
This is an unusual version of the 'Little Red Riding Hood' story, which has been updated to produce a fantastic voyage into the human mind, using live action and animation. The film shows in an imaginative way how to understand and express emotions.
M,A — EN
DePatie-Freleng Production — *Videomedia*
P
PVM 3120/BVM 3120/HVM 3120

Magician of Lublin, The   Fil-Ent '??
Mystery
06941   101 mins   C
B, V
This is a mystifying tale of a talented magician who brings his audiences to their feet but also uses his powers to obtain a hold over women.
BBFC:X — A — EN
Unknown — *Rank Video Library*   H, P
0095C

Magnetic Effects in Space   Med-Sci '7?
Space exploration
04452   14 mins   C
B, V, PH15, PH17, 3/4U

(For Explanation of codes, see USE GUIDE and KEY)

PALADIN VIDEO HOME ENTERTAINMENT GUIDE

A look at the behaviour of magnets in the Skylab orbiting spacecraft.
C,A — ED
NASA — Istead Audio Visual   P
HQa 260F

Magnificent Matador, The　　Fil-Ent '55
Drama
01078　　94 mins　　C
V2, B, V
Anthony Quinn, Maureen O'Hara
A heart-stopping story of passion and honour in the bull rings of Mexico.
BBFC:A — S,A — EN
Twentieth Century Fox — Intervision Video
H, P
A-A 0129

Magnificent Seven, The　　Fil-Ent '60
Adventure
13024　　127 mins　　C
B, V
Yul Brynner, Steve McQueen, Robert Vaughn, James Coburn, Charles Bronson, Eli Wallach, directed by John Sturges
A tense and vibrant film based on the Japanese classic 'Seven Samurai' as villagers under attack seek help from the 'Magnificient Seven.'
BBFC:U — F — EN
United Artists; Walter Mirisch — Warner Home Video　　P
99240

Magnificent 7 Deadly Sins　　Fil-Ent '7?
Comedy
04196　　107 mins　　C
B, V
Bruce Forsyth, Harry Secombe, Leslie Phillips, Julie Ege, Harry H. Corbett, Ian Carmichael
Avarice, Envy, Gluttony, Lust, Pride, Sloth, and Wrath are the ingredients of an hilarious 107-minute escapade.
BBFC:A — C,A — EN
Unknown — Guild Home Video　　H, P

Magnificent Tony Carrera, The　　Fil-Ent '??
Drama/Mystery
08700　　90 mins　　C
V2, B, V
Thomas Hunter, Walter Barnes
This thriller story tells of a jewel theif who has remained anonymous to the police. Having retired with the wealth of his work behind him he goes to live in Italy, where mechanical engineering becomes his new hobby.
BBFC:A — S,A — EN
Unknown — Video Unlimited　　H, P
083

Magnificent Two, The　　Fil-Ent '67
Comedy
05188　　96 mins　　C
B, V
Eric Morecambe, Ernie Wise, Margit Saad
Eric and Ernie's third feature film takes them to Parazuelia in South America on the eve of a coup d'etat. It's not long before toy soldier salesman Eric has been mistaken for the leader of the coup and when finally installed in the palace as president it all begins to go to his head.
BBFC:U — F — EN
Alan Enterprises — Rank Video Library
H, P
1008

Magnum Force　　Fil-Ent '73
Suspense/Crime-Drama
01287　　124 mins　　C
B, V
Clint Eastwood, Hal Holbrook, Mitchell Ryan, David Soul, directed by Ted Post
A San Francisco homicide detective investigating a rash of gangster murders discovers that they are the work of a rookie police assassination squad whose members have been frustrated by red tape and civil liberties. A sequel to 'Dirty Harry.'
C,A — EN
Warner Bros, Robert Daly Prods — Warner Home Video　　P

Magritte　　Fin-Art '7?
Artists
04504　　50 mins　　C
B, V
The major works of this Belgian artist are presented in this programme which will prove of interest and fascination to all art lovers.
S,A — EN
RM Prods — Quadrant Video　　H, P
RM 1

Mahler　　Fil-Ent '74
Biographical/Drama
08368　　115 mins　　C
V2, B, V
Robert Powell, Georgina Hale, Richard Morant, Lee Montague, Miriam Karlin, directed by Ken Russell
This film follows the life and works of one of the world's greatest composers, Gustav Mahler.
BBFC:X — A — EN
Specialty Films — Guild Home Video　　H, P, E

Main Event, The　　Fil-Ent '79
Comedy
13208　　107 mins　　C

PALADIN VIDEO HOME ENTERTAINMENT GUIDE

B, V
Barbra Streisand, Ryan O'Neal, directed by Howard Ziett
A retired prizefighter gets a new manager who desperately needs him to be a success.
BBFC:AA — C,A — EN
Barwood Films; First Artists Prod Co Ltd; Warner Bros — *Warner Home Video* P
61021

Making Michael Jackson's Thriller Fil-Ent '83
Music video
12879   60 mins   C
B, V, LV, CED
Directed by Jerry Kramer
Included in this programme is the 14-minute music movie 'Thriller' selected excerpts from 'Beat It' and 'Can You Feel It', the track 'Billie Jean', and a behind-the-scenes look at the production of the 'Thriller' movie, with an interview with Michael Jackson.
M,A — EN
George Folsey Jr; John Landis; Michael Jackson; Optimum Prods. — *Vestron Video International* P

Making of Star Wars, The Fil-Ent '78
Film making
01028   50 mins   C
V2, B, V
Harrison Ford, Carrie Fisher, Peter Cushing, Alec Guinness
A behind-the-scenes view of personalities, technology, special effects, and problems involved in creating this blockbuster movie.
F — EN
20th Century Fox; Gary Kurtz — *CBS/Fox Video* P
2A-033

Making of Superman—The Movie, The Fil-Ent '80
Film making
08456   88 mins   C
B, V
Narrated by Ernie Anderson, directed Iain Johnstone
This film tells of the making of the 'Superman Movie'. It looks at the assembling of the cast, writing the scripts and designing the sets and special effects. The most important part was trying to make the audience believe that a man could fly.
C,A — EN
D C Comics Inc — *THORN EMI* P
TXB 90 1020 4/TVB 90 1020 2

Making of 2 a.m. Paradise Cafe, The Fil-Ent '84
Music video
13351   55 mins   C
B, V
Barry Manilow is accompanied by an all-star jazz ensemble and sings saloon tunes with the help of Sarah Vaughan and Mel Torme.
F — EN
Stilletto Prods — *Guild Home Video* H, P, E

Making Your Own Home Cozy How-Ins '80
Home improvement
04424   60 mins   C
B
Tony Wilkins, editor of 'Do-It-Yourself' magazine, shows how to retain warmth in the home while saving energy. Includes a lesson in painting and wallpapering.
A — I
Michael Barratt Ltd; Sony — *Michael Barratt Ltd* P

Mako-Jaws of Death Fil-Ent '76
Drama
09345   90 mins   C
B, V
Richard Jaeckel, Jennifer Bishop, Harold Sakata
Filmed with no tricks or deception, this tells the story of a man whose job is to capture alive, deadly Mako sharks for leasing to Florida's Marine Biologists. He prefers the company of these killer fish to that of man, and is able to swim with them and even communicate with them. On the discovery that his favourite sharks have been savagely killed by the biologists, he releases them proving just how vicious the sharks can be, and therefore claiming his revenge.
C,A — EN
Unknown — *Precision Video Ltd* P
BPMPV 2620/VPMPV 2620

Malachi's Cove Fil-Ent '73
Adventure
04326   89 mins   C
V2, B, V
Donald Pleasance
Touching story of a young girl who searches the town for help when her father's body washes up on shore.
BBFC:U — M,A — EN
Artemus Films — *Intervision Video* H, P
A-A 0051

(For Explanation of codes, see USE GUIDE and KEY)   417

PALADIN VIDEO HOME ENTERTAINMENT GUIDE

Malibu High   Fil-Ent '79
Crime-Drama
12593   92 mins   C
V2, B, V
Jill Lansing, Stuart Taylor, directed by Irv Berwick
A pretty schoolgirl is dragged into a life of corruption and criminality culminating in a role somewhat unsuited to a schoolgirl; as a 'hit' girl for the Mafia.
BBFC:18 — *C,A* — *EN*
Crown International — *Intervision Video*   **H, P**
6560

Malibu Hot Summer   Fil-Ent '??
Adventure
07328   82 mins   C
B, V
Terry Congie, Leslie Brander, Roselyn Royce, Robert Acey, James Pascucci, directed by Richard Brander
In this film three young beautiful women meet en route to Los Angeles. They have ambitions to become stars, one in films, one in the music business and the other in athletics. Under the Californian sun they not only find their careers but receive the best offer of their lives.
BBFC:X — *A* — *EN*
Unknown — *Derann Film Services*   **P**
FDV 302B/FDV 302

Malpertuis   Fil-Ent '72
Horror
01066   89 mins   C
V2, B, V
Orson Welles, Susan Hampshire
'Malpertuis' is an evil mansion peopled with strange women, the dying owner, and his weird nephew.
Cannes '72: Prix Edgar Allan Poe.
BBFC:X — *A* — *EN*
Britain — *Intervision Video*   **H, P**
A-A 0054

Mame   Fil-Ent '74
Musical/Comedy
07862   126 mins   C
B, V
Lucille Ball, Robert Preston, Beatrice Arthur, Bruce Davison, Joyce Van Patten, John McGiver, Don Porter, Audrey Christie, directed by Gene Saks
A nine year old boy goes to live with his aunt after his father dies. She is a flamboyant woman and he finds living with her an invigorating experience since she makes living an art.
BBFC:A — *S,A* — *EN*
Warner Bros — *Warner Home Video*   **P**
WEX 61100/WEV 61100

Man, a Woman and a Bank, A   Fil-Ent '79
Comedy
08327   101 mins   C
V2, B, V, LV
Donald Sutherland, Brooke Adams, Paul Mazursky
Two con men plan to rob a bank by posing as workers during the bank's construction. An advertising agency woman snaps their picture for a billboard to show how nice the builders have been, then becomes romantically involved with one of the would-be thieves.
BBFC:U — *S,A* — *EN*
John B Bennett; Peter Samuelson — *Embassy Home Entertainment*   **P**
1616

Man About the House   Fil-Ent '74
Comedy
07451   86 mins   C
B, V
Richard O'Sullivan, Paula Wilcox, Sally Tomsett, Brian Murphy, Yootha Joyce, Doug Fisher, directed by John Robins
This film is based on the television series of the same name, which follows the adventures of a virile young man who shares a flat with two young women. Includes guest appearances by Bill Maynard, Arthur Lowe, Aimi McDonald, Michael Ward, Melvyn Hayes, Bill Pertwee, Spike Milligan and many others.
S,A — *EN*
Hammer Film Productions Ltd — *THORN EMI*   **P**
TXC 90 0312 4/TVC 90 0312 2

Man at the Top   Fil-Ent '73
Drama
07443   95 mins   C
B, V
Kenneth Haigh, Harry Andrews, Nanette Newman, Mary Maude, John Quentin, Charlie Williams, directed by Mike Vardy
In this film Joe Lampton, the anti-hero of John Braine's novel 'Room at the Top,' is now established at the top of a huge multinational conglomerate headed by a ruthless tycoon. Joe is being pursued both by the tycoon's wife and his daughter but he finds himself in a moral dilemma when he discovers that the company is selling an untested drug which makes thousands of third-world women sterile.
BBFC:X — *A* — *EN*
Hammer Film Productions Ltd — *THORN EMI*   **P**
TXC 90 0741 4/TVC 90 0741 2

Man Called Blade, A   Fil-Ent '??
Western
07803   ? mins   C
B, V

PALADIN VIDEO HOME ENTERTAINMENT GUIDE

John Steiner, Sonja Jeannie, Donald O'Brien

This film follows a quest for revenge by a man called Blade whose skill with a lethal throwing axe is faster than any gun. His father died defending his homestead from a ruthless and ambitious man who knew of the silver hidden on the land. When his daughter is kidnapped, Blade, who is biding his time, agrees to track her down.

S,A — EN

Unknown — *Video Tape Centre* P
VTC 1009

Man Called Intrepid, A Fil-Ent '79
Suspense/Drama
09185 130 mins C
B, V

David Niven, Michael York, Barbara Hershey, Flora Robson, Peter Gilmore, Renee Asherson, Nigel Stock, Fredy Mayne, Shirley Steedman, Belinda Mayne, directed by Peter Carter

This film tells the story of British Security Co-ordination, the international allied intelligence agency of World War II. It includes top level accounts of crucial wartime undercover operations including the breaking of the German Enigma code and the race for the atomic bomb. It is based on a book by William Stevenson.

S,A — EN

Lorimar Prods; Astral Bellevue Pathe Ltd — *Video Form Pictures* H, P
MGS 6

Man Called Sledge, A Fil-Ent '70
Western
12477 96 mins C
B, V

James Garner, Dennis Weaver, Claude Akins

A fast moving western with action and adventure when an outlaw and his bandit gang try to steal the gold bullion consignment which is shipped through a small western town each week.

BBFC:15 — F — EN

Columbia — *RCA/Columbia Pictures Video UK*
H, P
10212

Man For All Seasons, A Fil-Ent '66
Drama
12485 120 mins C
B, V

Robert Shaw, Paul Scofield, Orson Welles, Wendy Hiller, Susannah York

In this classic tale Henry VIII asks the Pope for a divorce from his wife Catherine, and is backed by all his government save for Thomas More, who amid the persuasion and bribery and corruption that follows will not be swayed and is eventually be headed for treason.

BBFC:U — F — EN

Columbia — *RCA/Columbia Pictures Video UK*
H, P
10013

Man Friday Fil-Ent '75
Adventure/Drama
05874 104 mins C
B, V

Peter O'Toole, Richard Roundtree, Peter Cellier, Christopher Cabot, directed by Jack Gold

This film retains the basic elements of the book by Daniel Defoe called 'Robinson Crusoe' in which a lonely shipwrecked man discovers a cannibal on the island and calls him Friday. In this story Friday and Crusoe have conflicting views on civilisation and their relationship, with Friday asserting his rights as an equal.

BBFC:A — S,A — EN

Avco Embassy — *Precision Video Ltd* P
BITC 3083/VITC 3083

Man from Atlantis, The Fil-Ent '77
Adventure
10200 105 mins C
B, V

Patrick Duffy, Belinda J. Montgomery, Victor Buono, Art Lund

The man from Atlantis emerges from the sea having been swept onto the beach from his underwater home. Water-breathing, faster than a dolphin and with unmatched underwater endurance, he looks and thinks like a human. Unequipped to survive adequately on land he searches for his lost home.

BBFC:PG — F — EN

Solow Prod. Co.; Taft Broadcasting; NBC-TV — *Video Form Pictures* H, P
6260-50

Man from Button Willow, The Fil-Ent '75
Adventure/Musical
01690 79 mins C
V2, B, V

Animated, voices of Dale Robertson, Edgar Buchanan, Barbara Jean Wong, Howard Keel

This classic animated adventure is the story of Justin Eagle, a man who leads a double life. He is a respected rancher and a shrewd secret agent for the American government, but in 1869

(For Explanation of codes, see USE GUIDE and KEY) 419

PALADIN VIDEO HOME ENTERTAINMENT GUIDE

he suddenly finds himself the guardian of a four-year-old Oriental girl, which leads him into a whole new series of adventures. Music by George Stoll.
F — EN
AFC, David Detiege — *Intervision Video*
H, P
A-A 0208

Man from Chicago, The   Fll-Ent '??
Crime-Drama
06864   88 mins   C
V2, B, V
Jess Hahn, Gordon Mitchell
This film portrays the plight of a man who was so involved in his job that he had no time for his ten year old son. The boy, who adored his father, is kidnapped. One of the kidnappers befriends the boy and ensures he comes to no harm. When the father and the boy's friend meet eye to eye the boy decides to stay with his friend. Eventually they build a cabin in the mountains.
S,A — EN
Unknown — *European Video Company*
P

Man from Clover Grove, The   Fll-Ent '??
Comedy
06074   97 mins   C
B, V
Ron Masak, Cheryl Miller, Jed Allan, Rose Marie
A nutty toy inventor puts the sheriff in a spin, he creates toys for his own enjoyment and for the orphans of Clover Grove. Things get out of control when a professional toy manufacturer sends a secret spy to steal his ideas.
F — EN
Unknown — *Video Programme Distributors*
P
Media—M140

Man from Hong Kong, The   Fll-Ent '75
Crime-Drama/Martial arts
06926   99 mins   C
B, V
Jimmy Wang Yu, George Lazenby
A Chief Inspector of the Hong Kong Special Branch is out to break a massive and sinister drug network. He comes face to face with the leader and becomes determined to smash the empire built on human suffering, callous murder and political payola. An all-out running battle follows, with both men out to destroy each other.
BBFC:X — A — EN
Raymond Chow; John Fraser — *Rank Video Library*   H, P
0076C

Man from Snowy River, A   Fll-Ent '80
Adventure
13271   104 mins   C
B, V
Kirk Douglass, Jack Thompson, directed by George Miller
Set in the Australian wilderness in the 1880's, a mountain boy's love for horses and his passage into manhood is portrayed in this film.
BBFC:PG — S,A — EN
Geoff Burrowes — *CBS/Fox Video*   P
1233

Man Hunt   Fll-Ent '??
Crime-Drama
06105   95 mins   C
V2, B, V
Sylva Koscina, Woody Strode, Henry Silva
A man desperately fights to prove his innocence after drugs worth several million dollars disappear.
S,A — EN
Unknown — *Video Programme Distributors*
P
Cinehollywood—V130

Man in the Iron Mask, The   Fll-Ent '76
Drama
05388   101 mins   C
B, V
Richard Chamberlain, Patrick McGoohan, Louis Jourdan, Jenny Agutter, Ian Holm, Ralph Richardson
A film of Alexander Dumas's story based on a strange legend which prevailed in Europe during the seventeenth and eighteenth centuries of a mysterious political prisoner. Always encased in a hideous mask of iron, never revealed to the public gaze and spirited from prison under close guard, his destiny is to assume the throne in place of the weak Louis.
S,A — EN
Norman Rosemont Productions — *Precision Video Ltd*   P
BITC 2086/VITC 2086

Man in the Steel Mask, The   Fll-Ent '??
Drama/Suspense
06948   87 mins   C
B, V
Elliot Gould, Trevor Howard
A key American physicist is horribly mutilated in a car accident in East Germany. His body is wrecked but his brain continues to function. Using advanced atomic surgery, doctors painstakingly piece him together. Part man, part

PALADIN VIDEO HOME ENTERTAINMENT GUIDE

machine, the German Government allows him home. The Americans, however, are suspicious as they cannot tell if it is really him—perhaps he is a spy or even an atomic device.
S,A — EN
Hemisphere Productions — *Home Video Merchandisers*   **H, P**
049

Man in the White Suit, The   Fll-Ent '51
Comedy
01272   84 mins   B/W
B, V
Alec Guinness, Joan Greenwood, Cecil Parker
A humble laboratory assistant in a textile mill invents a cloth that won't stain, tear, or wear out and causes an industry-wide panic.
BBFC:U — F — EN
Ealing Studios; Michael Balcon — *THORN EMI*
P
TXE 90 0087 4/TVE 90 0087 2

Man of Flowers   Fll-Ent '82
Drama
13118   91 mins   C
B, V
Norman Kaye, Alyson Best, directed by Paul Cox
This is a bizarre story of loneliness and fantasy that leads to a man's eerie revenge.
Chicago Film Festival '83: Grand Jury Prize Winner; Australia Oscar '83: Best Actor (Kaye).
BBFC:18 — A — EN
Jane Ballantyne; Paul Cox — *Palace Video Ltd*
P
PVC 2069A

Man of the East   Fll-Ent '76
Comedy/Western
12507   112 mins   C
B, V
Terence Hill, Gregory Walcott, Harry Carey, Dominic Barbo, Yanbi Somer, directed by E. B. Clucher
An eccentric Englishman is taught the ways of the West and becomes a great gunfighter in this send up of the traditional cowboy film.
BBFC:PG — F — EN
Alberto Grimaldi — *Warner Home Video*
P
99367

Man on the Run   Fll-Ent '72
Crime-Drama
07975   90 mins   C
B, V
Henry Silva, Woody Strode, Cyril Cusack, Silva Koscina
This film is about a six million dollar shipment of drugs which goes missing. The man that gets blamed for it knows nothing about the crime. His only aim is to find the guilty men in order to prove his innocence.
BBFC:X — A — EN
Unknown — *AVI Video Ltd*   **P**
007

Man Outside, The   Fll-Ent '68
Suspense/Drama
09019   97 mins   C
V2, B, V
Peter Vaughan, Van Heflin
This film gives a brief but chilling glimpse of the deadly game of political intrigue and espionage. An ex-C.I.A. agent begins to realise that he is doomed—always to be pursued even though he no longer pursues.
C,A — EN
Allied Artists — *Intervision Video*   **H, P**
AA 0441

Man, Pride, Vengeance   Fll-Ent '??
Western/Drama
05553   99 mins   C
V2, B, V
Franco Nero, Tina Aumont, Klaus Kinski, directed by Luigi Bazzoni
A young officer wanted for being an outlaw, a deserter and a murderer seeks vengeance on a Lieutenant who mocks his love for a traitorous gypsy girl. His plans are altered when the coup he orders fails and ends in a massacre.
BBFC:X — A — EN
Unknown — *Videomedia*   **P**
PVM 6103/BVM 6103/HVM 6103

Man Who Fell to Earth, The   Fll-Ent '76
Science fiction
04636   134 mins   C
B, V
David Bowie, Rip Torn, Candy Clark, Buck Henry
A gentle visitor from a dying planet visits Earth and attempts to colonise it, but his dreams and powers are destroyed and he ends up a broken man.
BBFC:X — A — EN
British Lion — *THORN EMI*   **H, P**
TXA 90 0227 4/TVA 90 0227 2

Man Who Had Power Over Women, The   Fll-Ent '70
Comedy/Romance
05530   89 mins   C
B, V

(For Explanation of codes, see USE GUIDE and KEY)

PALADIN VIDEO HOME ENTERTAINMENT GUIDE

Rod Taylor, Carol White, James Booth, Penelope Horner, Clive Francis, directed by John Krish

Based on the novel by Gordon Williams this film is an expose of the advertising and pop scene in Britian in the late 60's. It involves a Public Relations Executive, the wife about to leave him, an awful French pop-star, a friend killed by falling lavatory pans, a fatal abortion, a relationship with his friend's wife and the jural breakdown of Public Relations.

S,A — EN

Avco Embassy — *CBS/Fox Video*   P

Man Who Haunted Himself, The   Fil-Ent '70

Mystery/Suspense
07459   91 mins   C
B, V

Roger Moore, Hildegarde Neil, Olga Georges-Picot, directed by Basil Dearden

A respectable business man has his life shattered when he is suddenly possessed while driving home. The car skids and crashes; he is taken to hospital for major surgery and barely survives. When he returns home he realises he is being haunted—by himself. The character of this 'ghost' is a total opposite whose unnerving effect devastates his life.

S,A — EN

Associated British Productions Ltd — *THORN EMI*   P

TXC 90 0271 4/TVC 90 0271 2

Man Who Knew Too Much, The   Fil-Ent '56

Suspense/Drama
13616   115 mins   C
B, V

James Stewart, Doris Day, Bernard Miles, Brenda Debanzie, directed by Alfred Hitchcock

A married couple becomes involved in a web of intrigue when a secret agent is stabbed, backing them in an assassination plot which leads to their young son's kidnapping.

BBFC:PG — S,A — EN

Universal — *CIC Video*   H, P

1137

Man Who Loved Bears, The   Fil-Ent '7?

Wildlife/Adventure
02276   60 mins   C
V

Narrated by Henry Fonda

The strange but true story of a man who befriends a grizzly bear. Living in a remote part of the United States, the human and the bear gradually come to terms with each other.

F — EN

Unknown — *JVC*   P

PRT 29

Man Who Loved Cat Dancing, The   Fil-Ent '73

Western/Romance
10165   119 mins   C
B, V

Burt Reynolds, Sarah Miles

An unhappily married woman, running away from her marriage, witnesses a robbery. She is taken as a hostage by the gang, and one of the members, an embittered ex-Army officer, is forced to protect her from the rest. A romance develops during their escape from the husband and the Wells Fargo agent.

BBFC:X — A — EN

MGM — *MGM/UA Home Video*   P

UMB 10263/UMV 10263

Man Who Loved Women, The   Fil-Ent '83

Comedy/Romance
13080   106 mins   C
B, V

Burt Reynolds, Julie Andrews, directed by Blake Edwards

A Los Angeles sculptor with an obsession for women decides to consult a psychiatrist but this leads to another romance when it turns out to be yet another woman.

C,A — EN

Blake Edwards — *RCA/Columbia Pictures Video UK*   H, P

10316

Man Who Saw Tomorrow, The   Fil-Ent '81

Fantasy
13052   87 mins   C
B, V

A film that explores the life and prophesies of 16th century French astrologer and physician Michael Nostradamus. An account is narrated by Orson Welles of a man who, 400 years ago, foresaw so many actual events.

BBFC:AA — C,A — EN

Warner Bros Inc — *Warner Home Video*   P

61246

Man Who Would Not Die, The   Fil-Ent '75

Mystery/Adventure
07622   80 mins   C

(For Explanation of codes, see USE GUIDE and KEY)

PALADIN VIDEO HOME ENTERTAINMENT GUIDE

V2, B, V
Dorothy Malone, Keenan Wynn, Aldo Ray, Alex Sheafe, Joyce Ingalls, directed by Robert Arkless
A skipper picks up a mysterious passenger on his new ketchwhile cruising in the Caribbean. He is innocently drawn into a conspiracyof murder, intrigue and double dealing as he becomes hunted by thepolice, the FBI and a crime syndicate. The passenger dies duringthe voyage and is buried at sea but his identity comes under suspicion.
BBFC:AA — S,A — EN
Dandrea Releasing — *Iver Film Services* **P**

Man with the Golden Gun, The   Fil-Ent '74
Adventure
13193   125 mins   C
B, V
Roger Moore, Christopher Lee, Richard Loo, Britt Ekland, Maud Adams, Herve Villechaize, Clifton James
Threatened by an arch assassin, the man with the golden gun, 007's 'self defense' mission takes him to Beirut, Macao and Hong Kong.
BBFC:A — C,A — EN
United Artists — *Warner Home Video* **P**
99204

Manaos   Fil-Ent '??
Adventure/Suspense
07333   90 mins   C
B, V
Agostina Belli, Fabio Testi, Alberto De Mendoza, directed by Alberto Vanquez-Figueroa
This film is set in the ruthless world of a rubber plantation where the workers are watched over by a sadistic manager. A young man with a vendetta plans to escape with the ill treated mistress of the boss. Their journey down the Curicuriari and the Rio Grande Rivers is full of danger both from natural and human sources and ends in a nightmarish battle at Sierra's 'Fortress.'
S,A — EN
Unknown — *Derann Film Services* **P**
FGS 904B/FGS 904

Manchester United Story, The   Spo-Lei '82
Football/Documentary
09097   60 mins   C
B, V
This tape portrays the magic and emotion behind the world's most famous football club. It includes historic footage of the 1948 FA Cup, 1952 League and the 1968 European Cup, and interviews with Bobby Charlton, Denis Law, George Best and Sir Matt Busby. The tape also covers the tragedy of the Munich plane crash and the team's fight for survival.
F — EN
Michael Barratt Ltd; Manchester United Football Club PLC — *Michael Barratt Ltd* **P**

Mandarin Magician, The   Fil-Ent '??
Martial arts
06855   80 mins   C
V2, B, V
Lichin Kun, Ma Hoi Lun
A reporter working for a Hong Kong newspaper receives a telegram from his Kung Fu teacher to say that he will be stopping off in Hong Kong on his way to Bankok. Whilst they are driving from the airport they are forced to stop and an attempt is made by Japanese fighters to kill the teacher. In hospital the teacher is again challenged to a new fight.
S,A — EN
Unknown — *European Video Company* **P**

Mandingo   Fil-Ent '75
Drama
10113   121 mins   C
B, V
James Mason, Perry King, Susan George, Ken Norton, directed by Richard Fleischer
This drama set in 1840 tells the story of two slaves, one a beautiful girl and the other a proud Mandingo warrior who is trained to become a champion fighter by their owner. It provides a picture of violence and moral corruption in the Deep South.
BBFC:18 — C,A — EN
Paramount — *CIC Video* **H, P**
BEA 2027/VHA 2027

Manions, The   Fil-Ent '81
Drama/Adventure
12833   300 mins   C
B, V
David Soul, Simon MacCorkindale, Anthony Quayle, Kate Mulgrew, Barbara Parkins, Peter Gilmore, Pierce Brosnan, Steve Forrest
3 pgms
Based on the book by Rosemary Anne Sisson, this is the story of a migrant Irish family who depart from their beloved land during the famine of 1845 to seek their fortunes in the new world of America.
1.Rebellion 2.Exile 3.Reunion
BBFC:PG — C,A — EN
Stan Kallis — *Video Tape Centre* **P**
202

(For Explanation of codes, see USE GUIDE and KEY)   423

PALADIN VIDEO HOME ENTERTAINMENT GUIDE

Manipulator, The   Fil-Ent '??
Crime-Drama
06949   95 mins   C
B, V
James Coburn, Lee Grant, Harry Andrews, Ian Hendry, Michael Jayston
A multi-national business tycoon controls a network of spies on which he has built his phenomenal success. A beautiful Washington journalist, however, smells a rat when she is offered a top Government position and threatens to expose their espionage activities.
S,A — EN
Hemisphere Productions — *Home Video Merchandisers*   H, P
048

Manitou, The   Fil-Ent '78
Horror
05525   105 mins   C
V2, B, V
Tony Curtis, Michael Ansara, Susan Strasberg, Stella Stevens, Burgess Meredith, directed by William Girdler
A young woman develops a rapidly growing tumour on her neck; on examination it bears an uncanny resemblance to a foetus. On investigation a tarot card expert reveals that certain ancient witch doctors have powers to reincarnate themselves. Occult interventions hinder surgical progress and the foetus is damaged by an X-ray. The hiedeous deformed thing is born and goes looking for the power of evil. The card reader uses the resources of electronic gadgetry to track the beast.
A — EN
Avco Embassy — *Embassy Home Entertainment*   P
2038

Manon   Fin-Art '82
Dance
09784   113 mins   C
B, V
Jennifer Penney, Anthony Dowell, David Wall, Derek Rencher, directed by Colin Nears
The Royal Ballet performs Kenneth MacMillan's production of the famous tragedy with music by Massenet. The ballet tells the story of an impoverished student who falls under the spell of Manon. Recorded in stereo.
F — EN
Covent Garden Video Productions Ltd. — *THORN EMI*   P
TXH 90 1728 4/TVH 90 1728 2

Manon Lescaut   Fin-Art '8?
Opera
12522   133 mins   C
B, V
Kiri te Kanawa and Placido Domingo star together in Puccini's tale of doomed love. Thomas Allen plays the part of Lescaut. It is recorded at the Royal Opera House in stereo and conducted by Giuseppe Sinopoli.
F — EN
National Video Corporation Limited — *THORN EMI*   P
TXH 90 2201 4/TVH 90 2201 2

Many Adventures of Winnie the Pooh, The   Chi-Juv '76
Cartoons
12563   70 mins   C
B, V
Animated
All the favourites from the Hundred Acre Wood appear in this classic cartoon.
PS,I — EN
Walt Disney Productions — *Rank Video Library*   H
025

Many Happy Returns   Fil-Ent '68
Crime-Drama
07356   90 mins   C
B, V
Patrick McGoohan
This tape contains one episode from the highly successful television series 'The Prisoner.'
S,A — EN
Patrick McGoohan — *Precision Video Ltd*   P
BITC 2109/VITC 2109

Marathon   Fil-Ent '80
Comedy-Drama
09422   92 mins   C
V2, B, V
Bob Newhart, Herb Edelman, Dick Gautier, Anita Gillette, Leigh Taylor-Young, John Hillerman, directed by Jackie Cooper
To cope with the onset of middle-age, Walter takes up running. Entering the local marathon he is deeply smitten by a beautiful young woman runner, and for the first time is tempted to be unfaithful to his wife. In his eagerness to prove that he is not over the hill he then enters the gruelling New York Marathon and as he reaches the finish line, fate takes control of this comical love story.
BBFC:PG — F — EN
Alan Landsburg Prod. — *Guild Home Video*   H, P, E

March of the Wooden Soldiers   Fil-Ent '34
Fantasy
02225   75 mins   C
V

PALADIN VIDEO HOME ENTERTAINMENT GUIDE

Stan Laurel, Oliver Hardy
A holiday spectacular, bringing everyone's childhood favourites to life. The Old Lady Who Lived in a Shoe, Old King Cole, Little Bo Peep, and many more fill the screen, backed by Victor Herbert's score.
F — EN
Hal Roach — *JVC*   **P**
PRT 41

March or Die   Fil-Ent '77
Drama
05398   99 mins   C
V2, B, V
Gene Hackman, Terence Hill, Max Von Sydow, Ian Holm, Catherine Deneuve, directed by Dick Richards
A tough ex-World War I American Major, now in the Foreign Legion, is ordered, with his Legionnaires, to protect an archaeological expedition from the Louvre. They are to excavate a tomb in Morocco but the Major knows that the last expedition was wiped out and is opposed to the project as he believes it to be grave robbing. A powerful Arab chieftain is determined to prevent the removal of the tomb.
BBFC:A — *S,A — EN*
Columbia Pictures; Dick Richards Productions — *Precision Video Ltd*   **P**
CRITC 2044/BITC 2044/VITC 2044

Marciano   Fil-Ent '79
Drama
09198   97 mins   C
B, V
Tony Lo Bianco, Vincent Gardenia
This film tells the story of a boxer, who fought his way from nowhere to become the Heavyweight champion of the world. However the time comes when he has to make a decision, the glory of the boxing ring or the love of a woman.
S,A — EN
ABC Circle Films — *Video Form Pictures*
H, P
MGS 19

Marco Polo   Chi-Juv '8?
Cartoons/Adventure
12246   45 mins   C
B, V
Animated
Marco Polo is asked by his friend Kublai Khan to fulfill three important missions which take him to exciting places all round the world. This film features specially composed music from a thirty piece orchestra.
PS,M — EN
Unknown — *VCL Video Services*   **P**
A392B

Mardi Gras Massacre   Fil-Ent '7?
Crime-Drama
08688   92 mins   C
V2, B, V
Curt Dawson, Gwen Arment, Laura Misch, Cathryn Lacey, Nancy Dancer, Butch Benit
During the Mardi Gras Carnival, there is a sinister murder of a prostitute. The police investigate, but do not prevent the next death similar to the first. They suspect a ritual killer, who has his greatest sacrificial offering yet to come.
BBFC:X — *A — EN*
J Weis — *Derann Film Services*   **P**
FGS 900

Margin For Murder   Fil-Ent '81
Drama/Suspense
13345   90 mins   C
V2, B, V
Kevin Dobson, Donna Dixon, Charles Hallahan, Cindy Pickett, directed by Dan Haller
Taken from one of Mickey Spillane's books, private investigator Mike Hammer battles his way through a world of politics, smuggling and violence to find out who has beaten his closest friend to death.
BBFC:15 — *S,A — EN*
Hammer Limited Productions — *Guild Home Video*   **H, P, E**
8408-0

Marihuana—The Devil's Weed   Fil-Ent '36
Exploitation
07634   54 mins   B/W
B, V
Harley Wood, Hugh McArthur, Pat Carlyle, Paul Ellis, directed by Dwain Esper
Set in the camp '30s, this is a comedy about the 'evils' of smoking cannabis. Concentrating on the wild youth of the time and their shameless parties, the film tells the story of a young girl who becomes pregnant. Her boy friend is killed and she becomes a pusher. She plans to steal her sister's baby, unaware that it is her own, given up for adoption.
S,A — EN
Dwain Esper Productions — *VCL Video Services*   **P**
0241G

Marillion-Recital of the Script   Fil-Ent '83
Music-Performance
09814   55 mins   C
B, V
Directed by Martin Bell

(For Explanation of codes, see USE GUIDE and KEY)

PALADIN VIDEO HOME ENTERTAINMENT GUIDE

This tape features the rock band Marillion live in concert at the Hammersmith Odeon. Songs include 'Script for a Jesters Tear', 'Garden Party', 'Chelsea Monday', 'He Knows You Know', 'Forgotten Sons' and 'Market Square Heroes'.
F — EN
EMI Records Ltd. — *THORN EMI* P
TXE 90 1954 4/TVE 90 1954 2

Mark, I Love You   Fil-Ent '80
Drama
09206   120 mins   C
B, V
James Whitmore, Kevin Dobson, Justin Dana, Cassie Yates, Peggy McKay, directed by Gunnar Hellstrom
Based on a true story, this tells of the problems a man experiences when trying to obtain custody of his only son. After the sudden deaths of his mother and sister the young boy moves in with his grandparents. However, when the father prepares to marry again and take the boy, the struggle begins.
S,A — EN
The Aubrey Co; 'James T Aubrey and Mardi Rustam — *Video Form Pictures*   H, P
MGT 5

Mark I Love You   Fil-Ent '80
Drama
12919   96 mins   C
B, V
Kevin Dobson, James Whitmore, Cassie Yates, Justin Dana, Peggy Mckay, directed by Gunnar Hellstron
When a man's wife and daughter are killed in a road accident he temporarily hands over the care of his son to his in-laws but a bitter legal battle is fought when he wants his son back.
C,A — EN
Telepictures — *Video Form Pictures*   H, P
MGT 05

Mark of the Devil   Fil-Ent '70
Horror
06779   90 mins   C
V2, B, V
Herbert Lom, Olivera Vuco, Udo Kler
A cult of devil worshippers bring death and destruction to the countryside.
A — EN
Hallmark — *Intervision Video*   H, P
A-A 0343

Mark of Zorro, The   Fil-Ent '20
Adventure
04669   82 mins   B/W
B, V
Douglas Fairbanks Sr., Marguerite de la Motte, Noah Beery
Zorro crusades for the rights of oppressed Mexicans. Silent; colour-tinted.
F — EN
United Artists — *Polygram Video*   P

Marlborough Safari Rally   Spo-Lei '81
in Kenya 1981
Automobiles-Racing
02045   52 mins   C
B, V
Africa's greatest rally: a world championship round through the length and breadth of Kenya.
S,A — EN
Vintage Television Ltd — *Vintage Television Ltd*   H, P, E

Marlowe-Private Eye   Fil-Ent '8?
Crime-Drama
10033   180 mins   C
B, V
Powers Boothe   2 pgms
Legendary detective Philip Marlowe comes to life again in this package of short stories based on Raymond Chandler's classic novels.
S,A — EN
Unknown — *Palace Video Ltd*   P
PVC 20060A; PVC 20061A

Maroc 7   Fil-Ent '66
Drama/Adventure
13464   90 mins   C
B, V
Gene Barry, Leslie Phillips, Cyd Charisse, directed by Gerry O'Hara
A secret agent is on the trail of a top fashion editress who uses her job to cover up her more illicit activities in the world of crime.
BBFC:A — C,A — EN
Rank — *Rank Video Library*   H, P
0205 E

Marriage   Gen-Edu '??
Religion/Family
06286   50 mins   B/W
B, V, PH15
6 pgms
In this series of six films, each 50 mins in Black and white, Mr S. Thompson brings a background of Bible and Jewish lessons in life to real problems.
1.The Act of Marriage 2.The Husband's Place 3.Homosexuality 4.Disciplining a Child 5.Family Prayers 6.Abortion
S,A — R
Audio Visual Ministries — *Audio Visual Ministries*   H, L, P

---

426   (For Explanation of codes, see USE GUIDE and KEY)

PALADIN VIDEO HOME ENTERTAINMENT GUIDE

Marriage of Maria Braun   Fil-Ent '79
Drama
08837   116 mins   C
B, V

Hanna Schygulla, Ivan Desay, Klaus Lowitsch, produced and directed by Rainer Werner Fassbinder

This film tells the story of one woman's rise to power and wealth.
S,A — EN

New Yorker Films — *VCL Video Services*
P
P261D

Martial Arts   Spo-Lei '81
Martial arts
12774   55 mins   C
B, V

The dazzling shows of the All-China Martial Arts Champions during their 1981 tour of Britain are highlighted, with slow-motion 'replays' and an expert analysis by John Taylor, who travelled with them.
F — EN

Unknown — *VideoSpace Ltd*   **P**

Martian Chronicles—The Expeditions, The   Fil-Ent '80
Science fiction
09190   100 mins   C
B, V

Rock Hudson, Darren McGavin, Gayle Hunnicutt

This is the first part in a series of three that tells the story of 'The Martian Chronicles'. A colonel, despite two previous attempts, plans to colonise Mars. On his arrival he is amazed to find that Martian civilization has been destroyed by germs unwittingly carried from Earth. It is based on the novel by Ray Bradbury.
F — EN

Charles Fries Prods — *Video Form Pictures*
H, P
MGD 5

Martian Chronicles—The Martians, The   Fil-Ent '80
Science fiction
09192   100 mins   C
B, V

Rock Hudson, Darren McGavin, Gayle Hunnicutt, Roddy McDowell, Jon Finch, Nyree Dawn Porter

This is the final part in a series of three that tells the story of 'The Martian Chronicles'. The Colonel's desire to make contact with Martian civilization is increased, a contact which has a stunning psychological effect.
F — EN

Charles Fries Prods — *Video Form Pictures*
H, P
MGD 10

Martian Chronicles—The Settlers, The   Fil-Ent '80
Science fiction
09191   100 mins   C
B, V

Rock Hudson, Roddy McDowell, Darren McGavin, Gayle Hunnicutt, Jon Finch, Nyree Dawn Porter

This is the second part in a series of three that tells the story of 'The Martian Chronicles'. Many of the settlers arriving from Earth find it difficult to adjust to an alien civilization and return home. However the Colonel is determined to establish contact with Martian life.
F — EN

Charles Fries Prods — *Video Form Pictures*
H, P
MGD 8

Marvin Gaye   Fil-Ent '??
Music-Performance
06300   58 mins   C
V2, B, V

Marvin Gaye

This film features performances by Marvin Gaye, who sings 'Ain't nothing like the real thing baby,' 'I heard it through the grapevine,' 'Ain't no mountain high enough,' 'How sweet it is,' 'Distant lover' and 'Ain't that Peculiar.'
F — EN

Unknown — *World of Video 2000*   **H, P**
MV231

Mary and Joseph   Fil-Ent '79
Drama/Religion
09849   115 mins   C
B, V

Blanche Baker, Jeff East, Colleen Dewhurst, Stephen McHattie, Lloyd Bochner, Shay Duffin, Paul Hecht, Marilyn Lightstone

This is a new and authentic version of the story of the Holy Family made in the Holy Land with many scenes shot close to the places where the original biblical events occurred.
F — EN

Lorimar Prods; Gene Corman — *Polygram Video*   **H, P**
040 1374/040 1374

(For Explanation of codes, see USE GUIDE and KEY)

PALADIN VIDEO HOME ENTERTAINMENT GUIDE

Mary Berry's Country Cookery
How-Ins '83
Cookery
08476   90 mins   C
B, V

Mary Berry, directed by David Bellamy

This programme presented by Mary Berry looks at cookery with an accent on Autumn. It shows, with simple instructions, how to prepare the following 12 recipes; game pate, venison pie, chicken and chestnut roulades, frosted walnut cake, honeydew minted pears, roast pork with pippins, Autumn jelly, blackberry and apple trifle, Brandade en Croute and bramble Ice Cream.
S,A — I
Thames Video — *THORN EMI*   P
TXE 90 1444 4/TVE 90 1444 2

Mary Poppins
Fil-Ent '64
Musical
12579   134 mins   C
B, V

Julie Andrews, Dick Van Dyke, David Tomlinson, Glynis Johns

The magical flying nanny enchants her children in this blend of animation and live action, with a backing of dancing and song.
Academy Awards '64: Best Actress (Andrews); Best Musical Score; Best Film Editing; Best Song ('Chim Chim Cher-ee').   F — EN
Walt Disney Productions — *Rank Video Library*   H
023

Mary Stuart
Fil-Ent '8?
Opera
08657   139 mins   C
B, V

Janet Baker, David Rendall, Rosalind Plowright, Robert Dudley, John Tomlinson, George Talbot, Alan Opie, Angela Bostock, Hannah Kennedy

This opera was recorded at the London Coliseum, and sung in English by the English National Opera. The story of this opera centres upon the fates of Mary, Queen of Scots and Elizabeth I. It is well known that they didn't ever meet in history, but this meeting forms the climax of this plot. It is performed in three acts, and conducted by Charles Mackerras.
S,A — EN
Unknown — *Longman Video*   P
LGBE 7002/LGVH 7002

Mary Wilson and the Supremes
Fil-Ent '77
Music-Performance
04399   30 mins   C
B, V

The prominent female soul group as seen and heard in a London concert.
F — EN
VCL — *VCL Video Services*   P

M*A*S*H
Fil-Ent '70
Comedy
01023   116 mins   C
V2, B, V, LV

Donald Sutherland, Elliot Gould, Tom Skerritt, Sally Kellerman, JoAnn Pflug, Robert Duvall, directed by Robert Altman

A pair of surgeons at a Mobile Army Surgical Hospital in Korea creates havoc with their late-night parties, and their practical jokes pulled on the nurses and other doctors.
A — EN
20th Century Fox; Aspen — *CBS/Fox Video*   P
3A-016

Massacre at Central High
Fil-Ent '80
Horror
08852   84 mins   C
B, V

Andrew Stevens, Robert Carradine, Derrel Maury, Kimberly Beck, Rainbeaux Smith, directed by Renee Daalder.

After nine students are killed, the pupils at Central High begin to wonder who will be next.
BBFC:X — A — EN
Harold Sobel — *VCL Video Services*   P
M252 D

Massacre at Fort Holman
Fil-Ent '73
Western/Drama
06166   91 mins   C
V2, B, V

James Coburn, Telly Savalas, Bud Spencer

This film is set in 1862 when the US Civil War is at its height. Six men about to be hanged are given the chance to 'volunteer' for a dangerous mission that could decide the outcome of the war. They are to take the impregnable Confederate Fort Holman. Five take the offer and set out under the command of a 'Colonel' branded as a coward and traitor.
S,A — EN
Heritage Entprs Prod — *Guild Home Video*
H, P, E

Massacre in Rome
Fil-Ent '??
War-Drama
05447   ? mins   C
V2, B, V

Richard Burton, Marcello Mastroianni

This film is set during World War II. The Allies have landed in Italy and are approaching Rome, where the Nazi Administration is collapsing.

(For Explanation of codes, see USE GUIDE and KEY)

PALADIN VIDEO HOME ENTERTAINMENT GUIDE

German troops are being murdered by Italian Loyalists and Hitler is demanding reprisals in a vain attempt to maintain his army's position in the city.
S,A — EN
Unknown — Iver Film Services   P

Massage Girls in Bangkok   Fil-Ent '7?
Crime-Drama
02103   72 mins   C
V2, B, V
Krish and Cheng are involved in a murder and a relationship with the masseuse girls after a casual visit to a massage parlour in the exotic and erotic area of Bangkok.
BBFC:X — A — EN
Unknown — Hokushin Audio Visual Ltd   P
VM-09

Master Golf   Spo-Lei '77
Golf
05239   26 mins   C
B, V
Neil Coles, Richard O'Sullivan   13 pgms
The series begins by examining, understanding and mastering the fundamentals of the game—the grip and the set up—and by developing these sound principles, goes on to consider each major aspect.
1.'Basics' The Grip and the Set-Up
2.'Swingtime' Backswing and Downswing
3.Rhythm and Balance 4.The Lofted Irons 5.The Irons 6.The Woods 7.Pitch or Chips 8.The Trees, the Rough and the Bogey 9.Bunkers
10.The Wrong Way Round 11.Elementary Golf
12.Forethought 13.Putting It Together
C,A — I
Unknown — Rank Video Library   H, P
5000; 5001; 5002; 5003; 5006; 5007; 5008; 5009; 5017; 5018; 5019; 5020; 5021

Master of the World   Fil-Ent '61
Science fiction
07376   98 mins   C
V2, B, V
Vincent Price, Charles Bronson, Henry Hull
Set in the 18th century, a man in a strange flying vessel seeks to destroy all armaments in the world to gain total power and peace. The vessel 'Albatross' is stationed in an inaccessible mountain crater. A U.S. Government agent asks a local balloonist to fly over the crater to investigate. However, they are captured. Based on the books by Jules Verne.
BBFC:U — F — EN
American International Pictures — Guild Home Video   H, P, E

Master the Computer   Gen-Edu '8?
Electronic data processing
09983   60 mins   C
B, V
David Redclift
This tape is designed to help people understand the basics and learn to master the principles. The qualities of the microcomputer are explained, demonstrating its capabilities and introducing the 'stored-program' principles. The computer programs featured on this tape can be transferred to audio cassette.
S,A — I
Holiday Brothers Ltd — Holiday Brothers Ltd   P

Master With Cracked Fingers   Fil-Ent '??
Martial arts
08900   79 mins   C
V2, B, V
Jacky Chan
Using his hands and feet Jacky Chan sets out to avenge the murder of his father.
BBFC:X — A — EN
Unknown — Video Programme Distributors   P
Inter-Ocean 083

Masterbuilders, The   Gen-Edu '8?
Birds
13601   54 mins   C
V2, B, V
The habits of birds when building nests and laying eggs are demonstrated in this film along with their differing lifestyles.
U.S. Industrial Film Festival '82: Gold Camera Award.   F — ED
Royal Society for the Protection of Birds — Royal Society for the Protection of Birds   H, P

Mastermind   Fil-Ent '69
Comedy/Suspense
05192   92 mins   C
B, V
Zero Mostel, Keiko Kishi, Bradford Dillman, Herbert Berghof
In a crazy plot featuring Israeli secret agents, a mad German scientist, a CIA spook played by Brad Dillman and a midget robot called Schaatzi all let loose on an unsuspecting Japan, Zero Mostel pulls off one of his funniest performances ever as the Mastermind.
BBFC:A — C,A — EN
Malcolm Stuart — Rank Video Library   H, P
1015

(For Explanation of codes, see USE GUIDE and KEY)   429

PALADIN VIDEO HOME ENTERTAINMENT GUIDE

Match of Dragon and Tiger
Fil-Ent '7?
Adventure/Martial arts
04614   87 mins   C
V2, B, V

Ko returns to his hometown to avenge the murder of his parents—a task for which he has prepared himself by a study of martial arts. His resolution wavers when he falls in love with the daughter of the arch criminal.
C,A — EN
Unknown — *Video Programme Distributors*   **P**
Inter-Ocean—020

Match of the Century
Spo-Lei '81
Sports
12770   55 mins   C
B, V

This features the England versus Australia, third Cornhill Test at Headingley in 1981, illustrating England's sensational comeback to floor the Australians and pave the way to an incredible Ashes win. There is a commentary by Trevor McDonald and Mike Brearley.
F — EN
Unknown — *VideoSpace Ltd*   **P**

Matilda
Fil-Ent '78
Comedy
05151   89 mins   C
B, V

Elliot Gould, Harry Guardino, Karen Carlson, Robert Mitchum, Clive Revill, Roy Clark
A small-time New York theatrical agent tricks the world heavyweight title holder into a bout with his latest discovery, Matilda the boxing kangaroo.
BBFC:U — F — EN
American Intl; Albert S Ruddy — *Rank Video Library*   **H, P**
1030

Matter of Time, A
Fil-Ent '76
Drama
12024   99 mins   C
B, V

Ingrid Bergman, Liza Minnelli, Charles Boyer, Fernando Rey, directed by Vincente Minnelli
An eccentric recluse living in a faded hotel in Rome befriends a young maid who arrives there to work. She transforms her into a glittering star and, through her, relives the lifestyle she experienced as a younger woman.
BBFC:PG — S,A — EN
American International Pictures — *Entertainment in Video*   **H, P**
EVB 1018/EVV 1018

Mattie the Gooseboy
Chi-Juv '??
Fantasy/Cartoons
06165   77 mins   C
B, V

Animated
This is an adaptation of a traditional fairy story that brings to life a young hero and his close companion—a goose. The wicked Baron of the village seizes the goose and beats the boy. The fun begins when the boy vows to return the beating, thrice over.
I,S — EN
Pannonia Film Studio Budapest — *Guild Home Video*   **H, P, E**

Maul
Fil-Ent '78
Adventure/Romance
05477   98 mins   C
V2, B, V

Lisa Hartman, Robert Hegyes, Debralee Scott, Ricci Martin, Anne Lockhart, directed by Tony Mondente

This is the story of a young man who attempts to come to terms with life and reality in the surf and on the beaches of the Hawaiian Islands. A young man leaves his job as a supermarket boxboy for the 'good life,' a young girl, who is to change his outlook, attempts to steal his luggage at the airport.
BBFC:A — S,A — EN
Unknown — *Iver Film Services*   **P**
106

Mausoleum
Fil-Ent '83
Horror
12611   96 mins   C
V2, B, V

Bobby Bresee
A thirty-year-old woman finds herself possessed by an ancient and terrible family curse. Her life becomes a nightmare of terror and murder and her husband finds himself confronting the face of hell.
BBFC:18 — A — EN
Jerry Zimmerman; Michael Franzese — *VideoSpace Ltd*   **P**

Max
Chi-Ent '??
Crime-Drama
06232   112 mins   C
B, V

Michel Piccoli, Ramy Schneider, Bernard Fresson, directed by Claude Sautet

PALADIN VIDEO HOME ENTERTAINMENT GUIDE

A tough police inspector has a very personal concept of justice, for years however he has played it by the book, until a big arrest goes wrong and the criminals go free. He takes the law into his own hands. This film is shot on location in Paris.
S,A — EN
Lira/Sanacam S A — *VCL Video Services*
P
C131

Max Dugan Returns   Fil-Ent '82
Comedy
13270   94 mins   C
B, V
Marsha Mason, Jason Robards, Donald Sutherland, directed by Herbert Ross
A father returns to his long lost daughter and grandson with a suitcase full of ill-gotten loot and trys to gain their affection by buying them every gift imaginable.
BBFC:PG — *S,A — EN*
Herbert Ross; Neil Simon — *CBS/Fox Video*
P
1236

Maybe This Time   Fil-Ent '81
Drama/Romance
09344   92 mins   C
B, V
Judy Morris, Bill Hunter, Mike Preston, Jill Perryman, Ken Shorter
This film tells the story of Fran, who grew up in a country town working as a teacher. After taking up a job at a university she moves to the city, where she becomes involved with a married man. Although he talks of leaving his wife, he avoids doing anything about it. Fran drifts into an easy, initially casual affair with her boss, but is then confronted by her now-divorced, previous lover.
BBFC:18 — *A — EN*
New South Wales Film Corp.; Cherrywood Films — *Precision Video Ltd*   P

Mayerling   Fil-Ent '69
Drama
08522   135 mins   C
B, V
Omar Sharif, Catherine Deneuve, James Mason
Set in the year 1888 in Austria, this film tells of the exploits of the rebellious crown Prince Rudolf of the Austro-Hungarian Empire. He is bored with his wife and tormented by his position as heir to the throne. He finds a young girl, Baroness Maria Vetsera and together they go into exile.
C,A — EN
MGM — *THORN EMI*   P
TXB 90 1012 4 / TVB 90 1012 2

Maze   Fil-Ent '81
Music-Performance
08568   60 mins   C
B, V
Maze featuring Frankie Beverly gave two concerts at the Saenger Theatre in New Orleans. The day has now been declared 'Maze Day' by the City of New Orleans. Their songs include 'You,' 'Changing Times,' 'Joy and Pain,' 'Happy Feelin's,' 'Southern Girl,' 'Look at California,' and 'Feel That You're Feelin.'
F — EN
Capitol Records — *THORN EMI*   P
TXE 90 0900 4 / TVE 90 0900 2

Mc Q   Fil-Ent '74
Drama
06033   107 mins   C
B, V
John Wayne, Eddie Albert, Diana Muldaur, Colleen Dewhurst, Clu Gulager, directed by John Sturges
A police Lieutenant resigns from the force to risk double-cross, ambush and murder in an attempt to track down some big dope dealers who were involved in killing a couple of police officers.
BBFC:AA — *S,A — EN*
Warner Bros; Batjac Levy-Gardner Prod — *Warner Home Video*   P
WEX1099 / WEV1099

McMasters, The   Fil-Ent '70
Western
08827   90 mins   C
B, V
Burl Ives, Jack Palance, Brock Peters, David Carradine, Nancy Kwan, John Carradine, L.Q. Jones, Dane Clark, directed by Alf Kjellin
Set in an American Southern state, just after the Civil War, this film tells the story of a man who sells half his ranch to his black adopted son. A feud breaks out between the ranch owners full of prejudice and jealousy.
BBFC:U — *F — EN*
Chevron Pictures; Dimitri de Grunwald Prod — *VCL Video Services*   P
P272D

McVicar   Fil-Ent '80
Drama
09833   98 mins   C
V2, B, V
Roger Daltrey
John McVicar was sentenced to 23 years in a top security prison, for violent robbery. He dreamed only of escape and eventually did. Based on a true story.
C,A — EN
The Who Films — *Polygram Video*   H, P
790 4795 / 790 4794 / 790 4792

(For Explanation of codes, see USE GUIDE and KEY)   431

PALADIN VIDEO HOME ENTERTAINMENT GUIDE

Me and My Car How-Ins '8?
Automobiles
08372 150 mins C
V2, B, V

This is a self-instructional programme. It shows the viewer all aspects of routine servicing and necessary checks before a car goes in for its M.O.T. The programme is presented by Mike Smith, with Alan Blevins of the Automobile Association.
C,A — I
Yorkshire TV — *Guild Home Video* H, P, E

Mean Johnny Barrows Fil-Ent '7?
Suspense
01156 90 mins C
V2, B, V

Fred Williamson, Roddy McDowell, Stuart Whitman, Luther Adler, Elliot Gould

Two Mafia families plunge into treachery and intrigue as they attempt to settle a bitter feud.
S,A — EN
Atlas Films; Fred Williamson — *Intervision Video* H, P
A-AE 0172

Mean Machine ('The Longest Yard') Fil-Ent '75
Comedy-Drama
07369 121 mins C
B, V

Burt Reynolds, Eddie Albert, directed by Robert Aldrich

Filmed on location at the Georgia State Prison, this film covers a ferocious football game between the prisoners and the guards. A sadistic warden is prepared to go to any lengths to get his team into a national championship. A one-time pro quarterback, now behind bars, agrees to organize a prisoner's team. The warden tries to assure that his team only meets passive resistance, but the license to attack hated guards is a big incentive to the inmates.
S,A — EN
Paramount — *CIC Video* H, P
BEA 2020/VHA 2020

Mean Streets Fil-Ent '73
Drama
08615 105 mins C
V2, B, V

Robert De Niro, Harvey Keitel, David Proval, Amy Robinson, Richard Romanus

This film, set on New York's Lower East Side, known as Little Italy, tells of a world full of crime, rackets and gang animosities. It depicts the people's hopes, beliefs and romances as portrayed in this dramatic film.
C,A — EN
Warner Bros — *Hokushin Audio Visual Ltd* P
VM 72

Meatballs Fil-Ent '79
Comedy
13278 89 mins C
B, V

Harvey Atkin, Bill Murray, Kate Lynch, Chris Makepeace, directed by Ivan Reitman

This is the story of a group of youngsters and their counsellor let loose at an American Summer Camp.
BBFC:15 — S,A — EN
Paramount — *CIC Video* H, P
BET 2090/VHT 2090

Meatloaf Fil-Ent '83
Music-Performance
12942 60 mins C
B, V

This tape shows Meatloaf live in concert and features songs such as 'Bat out of Hell', 'Deadringer for Love', 'Promised Land', 'Two Out of Three Ain't Bad' and 'All Revved Up and No Place to Go'.
F — EN
Unknown — *Video Form Pictures* H, P
VFM 002

Meatloaf—Hits Out of Hell Fil-Ent '84
Music video
13236 53 mins C
B, V

This video is a compilation of promos and stage clips from Meatloaf including the following tracks: 'Bat Out of Hell,' 'Read 'Em And Weep,' 'Dead Ringer For Love,' 'Razor's Edge' and 'You Took the Words Right Out of my Mouth.'
S,A — EN
Unknown — *CBS/Fox Video* P
3234

Mechanic, The Fil-Ent '72
Drama
12681 97 mins C
B, V

Charles Bronson, Jan-Michael Vincent, Keenan Wynn, Jill Ireland

PALADIN VIDEO HOME ENTERTAINMENT GUIDE

A highly trained professional assasin, proficient in eliminating his victims in such a way that it looks completely natural, makes his only mistake when he hires as an assistant the son of one of his victims.
BBFC:15 — C,A — EN
Irwin Winkler; Robert Chartoff — Warner Home Video   P
99304

Medusa   Fil-Ent '74
Crime-Drama
07889   103 mins   C
V2, B, V
George Hamilton, Cameron Mitchell, Lucianne Paluzzi, Theodroe Roubanis
This film is set on the Greek Isle of Rhodes in the clubs and yachts of the jet-set. When a revised will robs a playboy of his inherited millions the atmosphere of high living and romance explodes with violent intrigue and death as he endeavours to destroy the will before it is delivered.
S,A — EN
Rossanne Prods — Walton Film and Video Ltd
P

Medusa Touch, The   Fil-Ent '78
Drama/Suspense
05957   104 mins   C
B, V
Richard Burton, Lino Ventura, Lee Remick, Harry Andrews, Alan Badel, Marie-Christine Barrault, Michael Byrne, Robert Lang, directed by Jack Gold
A novelist is attacked by an unknown assailant in his flat and left for dead. A beautiful detective is called in to investigate; her trail leads to his lady psychiatrist who explains that he claims to possess the power to cause catastrophe at will. His telekinetic powers can make a plane crash, ruin a moon-landing or demolish a building. The story is told mainly in flashback as related to his psychiatrist.
BBFC:A — S,A — EN
ITC Entertainment Prods; Lord Lew Grade Prods — Precision Video Ltd   P
BITC 2087/VITC 2087

Meet Captain Kidd/The Three Musketeers   Fil-Ent '??
Comedy/Adventure
05763   160 mins   C
B, V
Abbott and Costello, Charles Laughton, Leif Erickson, Fran Warren, directed by Charles Lamont, Margot Grahame, Ian Keith, Walter Abel, Paul Lukas, directed by Rowland Lee
Two films are contained on one cassette. 'Meet Captain Kidd' (colour, 68 mins, 1953) features songs and comedy as Abbott and Costello find themselves on the high seas in the seventeenth century with pirates and buried treasure. 'The Three Musketeers' (black/white, 92 mins, 1936) is an action adventure as D'Artagnan and his friends oppose Cardinal Richelieu and thwart his plans against the Queen of France.
F — EN
Warner Bros; RKO — Kingston Video   H, P
KV19

Meet Me in St Louis   Fil-Ent '44
Musical
13430   103 mins   C
B, V
Judy Garland, Margaret O'Brien, Mary Astor, Tom Drake, June Lockhart, Harry Davenport, directed by Vincente Minnelli
A St. Louis family are heartbroken to discover they have to leave their friends and move to New York and most of all to miss the opening of the 1903 World Fair. The songs include 'The Trolly Song,' 'The Boy Next Door' and 'Have Yourself a Merry Little Christmas.'
BBFC:U — F — EN
MGM — MGM/UA Home Video   P
10005

Meet Me in St. Louis   Fil-Ent '45
Musical/Comedy
05311   110 mins   C
B, V
Judy Garland, Tom Drake, Margaret O'Brien, Mary Astor, Leon Ames, Marjorie Main, Harry Davenport, Lucille Bremer, June Lockhart, Chill Wills, directed by Vincent Minnelli
This film follows the reactions of a middle class St. Louis family upon discovery that they have to move to New York just when the World's Fair is about to open. Especially seen through the eyes of a young teenager in love. Judy Garland sings 'The Trolley Song,' 'The Boy Next Door' and 'Have Yourself a Merry Little Christmas.' Based on the book by Sally Benson.
F — EN
MGM — MGM/UA Home Video   P
UMB10005/UMV10005

Meeting of the Spirits   Fil-Ent '??
Music-Performance
08842   52 mins   C
B, V
John McLaughlin, Paco De Lucia, Larry Coryell
This tape features three guitarists from Masters of the Flamenco, Contemporary Jazz and Classical Schools, playing live in concert at the Royal Albert Hall.
F — EN
Unknown — VCL Video Services   P
Z253G

(For Explanation of codes, see USE GUIDE and KEY)

PALADIN VIDEO HOME ENTERTAINMENT GUIDE

Megaforce Fil-Ent '82
Science fiction
12059   94 mins   C
V2, B, V
Barry Bostwick, Michael Beck, Persis Khambatta
Fantastic motorcycles, armed with six rockets and 50 caliber machine guns form the most powerful deployment force ever created. The team is recruited for a perilous mission.
BBFC:PG — *F* — *EN*
Golden Harvest — *Guild Home Video* **H, P, E**

Megaforce 7-9 Fil-Ent '8?
Drama
09128   100 mins   C
V2, B, V
Hiroshi Katsuno, Toshiyuki Nagashima, Yumi Takigawa, Kayo Matsuo, directed by Kenjiro Dhmori
Set in Tokyo, the world's largest metropolis, this film tells of a devastating earthquake. With the beginning tremors the foundations of the glass and concrete jungle start to shake and then all hell breaks loose, as the dam bursts, buildings and skyscrapers crumble, factories explode, turning the city into a blazing inferno.
S,A — *EN*
Toho Productions — *Go Video Ltd* **P**
GO 130

Mel Torme Show, The Fil-Ent '7?
Variety
04368   60 mins   C
B, V, PH17, 3/4U
Mel Torme, Stan Kenton and his Orchestra, Susan Barrett
A musical variety show with Mel Torme and guests.
F — *EN*
Unknown — *Vidpics International* **P**

Melanie Fil-Ent '82
Drama/Romance
12618   107 mins   C
V2, B, V
Glynnis O'Connor, Don Johnson, Jamie Dick, Paul Sorvino, Burton Cummings
A mother's young son is stolen away by her husband and in her search for him she finds herself caught up in the easy-living, easy-loving pop music world.
BBFC:15 — *F* — *EN*
Richard and Peter Simpson — *VideoSpace Ltd* **P**

Melody in Love Fil-Ent '??
Drama/Romance
08905   96 mins   C
V2, B, V
Melody O'Brien, Claudine Bird
Melody arrives on an island to visit her cousin. She dicovers that her cousin Rachel and her husband have a 'modern' marriage and each have intimate friends. Problems arise with various partnerships, especially Rachel and her lover.
BBFC:X — *A* — *EN*
Unknown — *Video Programme Distributors* **P**
Inter-Ocean 003

Memoirs of a Survivor Fil-Ent '81
Drama/Science fiction
07467   111 mins   C
B, V
Julie Christie, Christopher Guard, Leonie Mellinger, directed by David Gladwell
Adapted from the novel by Doris Lessing, this film presents a frightening version of the future. Communications have been cut, amenities run down and barbarism has taken over. The story centres on 'D', a housewife who reacts to this breakdown of society by retreating into a civilised dream world, and Emily, a teenage girl billeted on her.
BBFC:X — *A* — *EN*
Memorial Films Productions; EMI Films Ltd — *THORN EMI* **P**
TXB 90 0684 4/TVB 90 0684 2

Memory of Us Fil-Ent '74
Drama
04547   87 mins   C
V2, B, V
Ellen Geer, Jon Cypher, Robert Hogan, Will Geer, Barbara Colby, Rose Marie, Peter Brown, directed by H. Kaye Dyal
A housewife tired of her role leaves home in search for happiness and a new identity.
A — *EN*
Cinema Financial; James P Polakof Prod — *Intervision Video* **H, P**
A-A 0297

Men at Work, Live at San Francisco or Was It Berkeley! Fil-Ent '84
Music-Performance
13245   60 mins   C
B, V
Colin Hays, Ron Stryhert, Jerry Speiser, Greg Ham, John Rees

---

434   (For Explanation of codes, see USE GUIDE and KEY)

PALADIN VIDEO HOME ENTERTAINMENT GUIDE

This live performance is the culmination of the Men's 1983 world tour filmed in the San Francisco bay area and tracks include 'Overkill,' 'Underground,' 'Helpless Automation' and 'Be Good Johnny.'
F — EN
MAW Video Pty Ltd — *CBS/Fox Video*   P
1434

Men in War   Fil-Ent '57
War-Drama
05737   102 mins   B/W
V2, B, V
Robert Ryan, Aldo Ray, Robert Keith, Philip Pine, Vic Morrow, Nehemiah Persoff
A film set during the Korean War. An American infantry platoon surrounded by the enemy fight for their objective. Based on Van Praag's novel with musical score by Elmer Bernstein.
S,A — EN
UA; Security Prod — *Video Unlimited*   H, P
016

Men of Destiny I: World   Fil-Ent '7?
Political Figures
History-Modern
01145   120 mins   B/W
B, V
Authentic newsreels that capture the exact mood and drama of history are presented. This programme records the lives and momentous achievements of over 30 leaders in world history featuring Winston Churchill, Herbert Hoover, Mahatma Gandhi, Charles De Gaulle, and many others.
F — EN
Pathe News — *CBS/Fox Video*   P
3D-074

Men of Destiny II: Artists   Fil-Ent '7?
and Innovators
History-Modern
01146   120 mins   B/W
B, V
Authentic newsreels that capture the exact mood and drama of history are presented. This volume features the achievements of over thirty world-renowned figures including Marie Curie, Thomas Edison, Albert Einstein, Jonas Salk, the Wright Brothers, and Charles Lindbergh.
F — EN
Pathe News — *CBS/Fox Video*   P
3D-075

Mephisto   Fil-Ent '81
Drama
07736   140 mins   C
B, V
This film follows the story of an ambitious provincial actor through the rise of Nazi Germany. Marriage into a leading Jewish family, association with the left wing and a passionate affair with a black dancer all threaten his career. His egotism makes him vital to the Nazi cause, as he turns over his political ideals to Nazism to further his career.
Academy Awards '81: Best Foreign Film.
S,A — EN
New Yorker Films — *Palace Video Ltd*   P

Mephisto Waltz, The   Fil-Ent '71
Horror/Suspense
12255   109 mins   C
B, V
Alan Alda, Jacqueline Bisset, Barbara Parkins, directed by Paul Wendkos
A journalist and his wife are drawn into a web of witchcraft, black magic and evil after an interview with a famous concert pianist.
A — EN
Quinn Martin — *CBS/Fox Video*   P
1200

Merchant of Venice, The   Fil-Ent '7?
Drama
00837   128 mins   C
B, V
Laurence Oliver, Joan Plowright
Adapted from Jonathan Miller's brilliant London stage production, this new, updated interpretation of Shakespeare's masterpiece finds the setting shifted from Elizabethan times to Venice of the 1880's.
C,A — EN
ATV — *Precision Video Ltd*   P
BITC 3017/VITC 3017

Merlin and the Sword   Chi-Juv '8?
Fantasy
12153   90 mins   C
V2, B, V
Malcolm MacDowell, Candice Bergen, Edward Woodward, Dyan Cannon
The wizardry of Merlin and the magic of Camelot come to life again when a 20th-century sorceress travels back 1000 years in time to help the Master Magician re-write a legend.
BBFC:PG — S,A — EN
Martin Poll Prods; Comworld Prods and Jadran Film — *Guild Home Video*   H, P, E

Merry Christmas Mr   Fil-Ent '83
Lawrence
War-Drama
10016   123 mins   C
B, V
David Bowie, Tom Conti, Sakamoto, directed by Nagisa Oshima

(For Explanation of codes, see USE GUIDE and KEY)

PALADIN VIDEO HOME ENTERTAINMENT GUIDE

Set in a Japanese P.O.W. camp on Java in 1942, this film portrays not only the cruelty and bitter misery of camp life, but also the curious bond between the Japanese and their Western prisoners.
BBFC:15 — S,A — EN
Nagisa Oshima; Shochiku Studios — *Palace Video Ltd* **P**
PVC 2058A

Merry Wives of Windsor, The   Fil-Ent '65
Opera
01892   97 mins   C
B, V
Norman Foster, Colette Boky, Mildred Miller, Igor Gorin
Magnificent comic opera based on Shakespeare's famous buffoon Falstaff. A bawdy musical reconstruction of life and love in the Middle Ages.
BBFC:U — F — EN
Rank — *Rank Video Library*   **H, P**
7006

Messiah of Evil   Fil-Ent '??
Horror
06106   90 mins   C
V2, B, V
Michael Greer, Marianna Hill
A group of strange beings need human blood to live; they abduct humans one by one, and no one can escape.
S,A — EN
Unknown — *Video Programme Distributors* **P**

Metal Messiah   Fil-Ent '80
Science fiction/Musical
06236   73 mins   C
B, V
John Paul Young, Richard Allen, David Jensen, directed by Tibor Takacs
The Metal Messiah comes to earth; he glides into a city of neon where people are programmed into a numb oblivion. His power is his guitar and his mission is to save a society that wallows helplessly in drugs, sex and mindless violence. A Rock musical written by Stephen Zoller.
S,A — EN
Stephen Zoller — *VCL Video Services*   **P**
C174C

Metalstorm   Fil-Ent '83
Science fiction
12022   83 mins   C
B, V

Mike Preston, Jeffrey Byron, Tim Thomerson
Two evil men on the desert planet of Lemuria are trying to incite the natives to take part in a Crusade which will plunge them all into chaos. A peace keeping ranger pits his wits against them and pursues them through space warps and parallel dimensions.
BBFC:PG — S,A — EN
Universal — *Entertainment in Video*   **H, P**
EVB 1019/EVV 1019

Meteor   Fil-Ent '79
Drama
13163   105 mins   C
B, V
Sean Connery, Natalie Wood, Henry Fonda, directed by Ronald Neame
A five mile wide meteor, with an impact power greater than 10,000 H bombs, is on a collision course for Earth, and Russia and America are forced to co-operate to deflect the meteor, but fragments start hitting the Earth.
BBFC:A — C,A — EN
American International — *Warner Home Video* **P**
76007

Metro-Land   Fil-Ent '84
Documentary/Trains
13388   50 mins   C
B, V
Sir John Betjeman
Sir John Betjeman takes a ride on the Metropolitan Line, the first steam underground in the world, on a journey of discovery, visiting places of interest along the way.
F — EN
Unknown — *BBC Video*   **H, P**
7032

Metropolis   Fil-Ent '26
Science fiction
07447   115 mins   B/W
B, V
Alfred Abel, Gustav Frolich, Brigitte Helm, Rudolf Klein-Rogge, Fritz Rasp, directed by Fritz Lang
This silent film with English captions is a classic of the German cinema. It contains a vision of the future where above ground there is a modern world of skyscrapers, overhead roads and a Nazi-style sports stadium for the children of the rich, below is an underground city of robot-like worker slaves. A mad inventor sends a life-like robot to lead the workers in revolt.
S,A — EN
Friedrich Wilhelm Murnau Stiftung — *THORN EMI*   **P**
TXC 90 0823 4/TVC 90 0823 2

---

436   (For Explanation of codes, see USE GUIDE and KEY)

PALADIN VIDEO HOME ENTERTAINMENT GUIDE

Michel's Mixed-Up Musical Bird
Fil-Ent '??
Cartoons
08594　44 mins　C
V2, B, V
Animated

This is an animated film based on a true story. A young Parisian music student rescues a baby bird that has fallen out of its nest during a storm.
F — EN
DePatie-Freleng Prod; Ennes Prod — *Videomedia*　**P**
PVM 3121/BVM 3121/HVM 3121

Mickey's Golden Jubilee
Fil-Ent '??
Cartoons
05582　81 mins　C
B, V
Animated

In this compilation of Disney cartoons we see Mickey Mouse and friends in shorts such as 'Lonesome Ghosts', 'Mickey's Delayed Date', 'Pluto's Purchase', 'Mickey and the Beanstalk', and excerpts from 'Fantasia' and other feature length cartoons.
F — EN
Walt Disney Productions — *Rank Video Library*　**H**
05200

Micro Music—Gary Numan
Fil-Ent '8?
Music-Performance
07740　120 mins　C
B, V

This film is a recording of Gary Numan's 'farewell' concert live at Wembley Arena featuring his top hits and numerous special effects. Songs include 'I Die You Die,' 'Are Friends Electric,' 'We Are Glass,' 'Please Push No More,' 'My Shadow in Vain,' 'Down in the Park,' 'Tracks,' 'I'm an Agent,' 'I Dream of Wires,' 'She's Got Claws,' 'Cars' and many others.
F — EN
Unknown — *Palace Video Ltd*　**P**

Microwave Massacre
Fil-Ent '8?
Horror
09062　79 mins　C
V

Jackie Vernon, Claire Ginsberg, Lou Ann Webber, Loren Schein, Al Troupe, John Harmon
This tells the horrific story of a man who, one night when drunk, viciously attacks his wife. Next morning he discovers her severed body and limbs in the microwave oven. He turns on the oven, and that evening hiding the evidence, bites into a piece of the remains. However, this is just the beginning.
C,A — EN
Unknown — *Astra Video*　**H, P**

Midas Run, The
Fil-Ent '69
Adventure/Comedy
12687　102 mins　C
B, V

Richard Grenna, Anne Heywood, Fred Astaire, Sir Ralph Richardson, Cesar Romero, John LeMesurier
A British secret service agent who has been passed over for a knighthood decides to take his revenge by stealing a shipment of Her Majesty's Gold.
BBFC:15 — S,A — EN
Cinerama Releasing — *Brent Walker Home Video Ltd*　**P**
BW 28

Midnight
Fil-Ent '??
Horror
09006　? mins　C
V2, B, V

A young girl innocently decides to hitch hike to her sister's home, but is caught up in genuine terror and psychological torment. She becomes locked in a chain of human sacrifices and black mass murder.
A — EN
Unknown — *Intervision Video*　**H, P**
AA 0451

Midnight Blue
Fil-Ent '??
Drama
06107　90 mins　C
V2, B, V

Michael Coby, Monica Camo, Vincenzo Crocitti
A violent love story set during a long hot summer of sundrenched beaches, blue skies and restless seas.
S,A — EN
Unknown — *Video Programme Distributors*　**P**
Cinehollywood—V300

Midnight Cowboy
Fil-Ent '69
Drama/Comedy
12967　110 mins　C
B, V

Dustin Hoffman, Jon Voight, Brenda Vaccaro, John McGiver, Ruth White, Sylvia Miles, directed by John Schlesinger

(For Explanation of codes, see USE GUIDE and KEY)

PALADIN VIDEO HOME ENTERTAINMENT GUIDE

The relationship between a young Texan hustler and a down and outer in New York is depicted in this film.
BBFC:18 — A — EN
Jerome Hellman Prods; United Artists — Warner Home Video P
99372

Midnite Spares Fil-Ent '8?
Adventure/Comedy
09162   90 mins   C
V
James Laurie, Max Cullen, Bruce Spence, Graeme Brundell
This film involves the investigation of a group of baddies who strip cars for spare parts. The hero finds that this group are involved in the disappearance of his father. He attempts to find their hide-out and when he does all hell breaks loose.
S,A — EN
Unknown — Medusa Communications Ltd
H, P

Midsummer Night's Dream, A Fil-Ent '??
Dance/Comedy-Drama
06201   90 mins   C
B, V
The New York City Ballet
Shakespeare's faerie story and Mendelssohn's magical music sensitively interpreted by the New York City Ballet under the direction of George Balanchine, conducted by Robert Irvine.
F — EN
George Balanchine — VCL Video Services
P
P141D

Midsummer Night's Sex Comedy, A Fil-Ent '82
Comedy
13040   85 mins   C
B, V
Woody Allen, Mia Farrow, directed by Woody Allen
Three ill-assorted couples, each in search of intrigue, spend a country house weekend together in an idyllic setting, but it soon turns into a hectic sexual merry go round.
BBFC:AA — A — EN
Orion Pictures Co — Warner Home Video
P
99307

Mighty Joe Young/Little Orvie Fil-Ent '??
Adventure/Drama
05713   153 mins   B/W
B, V
Ben Johnson, Robert Armstrong, Terry Moore, Frank McHugh, Regis Toomey, directed by Ernest B. Schoedsack, Johnny Sheffield, Ann Todd, Ernest Truex, Dorothy Tree, directed by Ray McCarey
Two films are featured on one cassette. 'Mighty Joe Young' (Black/white, 90 mins, 1950) stars a giant ape captured in Africa who is to be the main attraction at a night club. He is pushed into a destructive rampage and the owners have to prove he is 'safe' before he is returned to them. 'Little Orvie' (Black/white, 63 mins, 1941) is a touching story of a little boy forbidden to keep a puppy, he tries without his parents knowledge, is discovered, and ends up running away with his puppy.
Academy Award '49: Best Special Effects ('Mighty Joe Young').   F — EN
RKO — Kingston Video   H, P
KV29

Mighty Micro, The Gen-Edu '80
Documentary/Science
05402   156 mins   C
B, V
Written and presented by Dr Christopher Evans, directed by Lawrence Moore
This is a series of six half-hour documentary films about the era of the silicon chip and the computer age. Complicated scientific ideas are explained simply and directly to dispell any fears that the 'chip' will have a disastrous impact on mankind, paralleled with the Industrial Revolution and reporting on the future.
F — ED
ATV Productions — Precision Video Ltd
P
BITC 3042/VITC 3042

Mighty Mouse Fil-Ent '6?
Cartoons
01739   30 mins   C
B, V
Animated
Five Terrytoon cartoons are featured: Mighty Mouse in 'Frankenstein's Cat,' Heckle and Jeckle in 'King Tut's Tomb,' Terry Bears in 'Little Problems,' Gandy Goose in 'Aladdin's Lamp,' and Possible Possum in 'Happy Hollow Turkey Shoot.'
BBFC:U — F — EN
Paramount — CBS/Fox Video   P
1B-027

Mighty Thor, The Fil-Ent '??
Cartoons/Adventure
07410   54 mins   C
V2, B, V
Animated
This tape contains three episodes of the adventures of Mighty Thor. He lives on earth in the disguise of meek Dr Blake. When danger

PALADIN VIDEO HOME ENTERTAINMENT GUIDE

threatens, he transforms into his immortal self. He soars through the skies in pursuit of evil, raising terrifying storms and righting wrongs with the help of his powerful enchanted hammer.
F — EN
Unknown — *Guild Home Video* **H, P, E**

Mighty Thor-Cassette 2, The Fil-Ent '??
Cartoons/Adventure
09436   60 mins   C
V2, B, V
Animated
In three episodes, each 20 minutes long, the muscle bound hero fights off an attempt to steal his powerful enchanted hammer; fights against the indestructible metal monster, Destroyer, and travels to the 30th century to save the world from destruction.
BBFC:U — *F — EN*
Marvel Comics — *Guild Home Video* **H, P, E**
8431-0

Mighty Thor in Molto the Lava Man, The Chi-Juv '84
Cartoons
13349   49 mins   C
B, V
Animated
Three episodes from the Norse God superhero are contained in this cassette.
BBFC:U — *F — EN*
Marvel Comics — *Guild Home Video* **H, P, E**
8431-0

Mighty Thor in the Power of Pluto, The Fil-Ent '??
Cartoons/Adventure
12068   65 mins   C
V2, B, V
Animated
When lame doctor Donald Blake strikes his walking stick on the ground, it becomes a mystic hammer and Blake is transformed into a Norse God. Three more action-packed adventures are contained in this cassette.
BBFC:U — *F — EN*
Marvel Comics — *Guild Home Video* **H, P, E**

Mikado, The Fin-Art '67
Opera
01884   122 mins   C
B, V, LV
Donald Adams, Philip Potter, John Reed, Kenneth Sandford, Thomas Lawlor, George Cook, Valerie Masterson, Peggy Ann Jones
Gilbert and Sullivan's uproarious comic operatic satire set at the Mikado of Japan. A tour-de-force of colour, costume, comedy, and song.
BBFC:U — *F — EN*
British Home Entertainment — *Rank Video Library* **H, P**
7005

Mikado, The Fil-Ent '8?
Opera
08923   100 mins   C
B, V
William Conrad, Clive Revill, Stafford Dean, John Stewart, Kate Flowers, Anne Collins, Gordon Sandison, Fiona Dobie, Cynthia Buchan
This opera by Gilbert and Sullivan tells of Mikado, the Emperor of Japan, who wants an execution as his Lord Executioner is desperate for a victim. A complicated set of events follow. The music is performed by The London Symphony Orchestra, conducted by Alexander Faris, with The Ambrosian Opera Chorus.
S,A — EN
Brent Walker Prods — *Brent Walker Home Video Ltd* **P**

Mike Harding Goes Over the Top Fil-Ent '8?
Comedy-Performance
08732   113 mins   C
V2, B, V, LV
Mike Harding
This tape features Mike Harding, the comedian, and some of his sketches not seen on television. He entertains his audience with saucy songs and tawdry tales.
A — EN
Barry Bevins — *BBC Video* **H, P**
BBCV 7001

Milestones of the Century I: The Great Wars Fil-Ent '7?
History-Modern
01143   120 mins   B/W
B, V
This volume of 'Milestones of the Century I' records over 30 momentous events in world history and features: FDR leading the nation; Europe ablaze—1914-1917; Hitler's Germany; Britain's Finest Hour; and the Korean Conflict.
F — EN
Pathe News — *CBS/Fox Video* **P**
3D-072

Milestones of the Century II: 20th Century—Turning Points Fil-Ent '7?
History-Modern
01144   120 mins   B/W

(For Explanation of codes, see USE GUIDE and KEY)   439

PALADIN VIDEO HOME ENTERTAINMENT GUIDE

B, V
This volume of great historic newsreels captures the exact mood and drama of history. Featured are: invention and industry, the era of flight, suffragettes and prohibition, the Russian Revolution, and the post-war world.
F — EN
Pathe News — *CBS/Fox Video* **P**
3D-073

Mill Reef Spo-Lei '7?
Horse racing
01976 52 mins C
B, V
A moving tribute to one of the greatest racehorses ever to run in this century, Mill Reef.
F — EN
Unknown — *Quadrant Video* **H, P**
E4

Million Dollar Duck Fil-Ent '71
Comedy
05588 92 mins C
B, V
Dean Jones, Sandy Duncan
A duck used for research is accidentally exposed to radiation and starts to lay eggs with solid gold yolks. The Professor and his wife cash in on the sudden wealth until the Treasury Department become involved. Just in time the duck stops laying the problem eggs.
F — EN
Walt Disney Productions — *Rank Video Library* **H**
OS700

Million Pound Note, The Fil-Ent '54
Drama
13749 91 mins C
B, V
Gregory Peck
This film is based on a novel by Mark Twain and tells the story of a man who takes up a wager to live on the credit of a million-pound-note.
BBFC:U — F — EN
Rank Films — *Rank Video Library* **H, P**
0195

Milton the Monster Show, The Chi-Juv '??
Cartoons
09469 77 mins C
V2, B, V
Animated

When Professor Weirdo and Count Kook make up their special creation they add to the mixture a little too much of the Tincture of Tenderness. The result-a gentle ghoul with the heart of a kitten.
BBFC:U — I,S — EN
Unknown — *Guild Home Video* **H, P, E**

Mina Live Fil-Ent '81
Music-Performance
04631 45 mins C
B, V
Mina, a top Italian singer and entertainer, sings in a 'special' recorded in 'La Bussola,' a well known night club in Italy. Mina sings an international programme of music.
F — EN
VCL Video Services Ltd — *VCL Video Services* **P**

Minder Fil-Ent '79
Comedy/Drama
13690 104 mins C
B, V
Dennis Waterman, George Cole, directed by Peter Sasdy and Christopher King
Two episodes from the popular television series are contained on this cassette titled 'Gunfight at the OK Launderette' and 'Bury My Half at Waltham Green.'
S,A — EN
Thames Video — *THORN EMI* **P**
90 2910

Mini Rugby—It's the Real Thing Spo-Lei '80
Sports
13536 30 mins C
B, V
Made under the 'Challenge to Youth' Scheme, two nine-a-side teams play a game of mini Rugby on the grounds at Twickenham which is interrupted on four occasions by the coach in order to analyse specific aspects of their game.
M,S — I
Unknown — *TFI Leisure Ltd* **H, P**

Mink De Ville Live at the Savoy Fil-Ent '??
Music-Performance
09883 60 mins C
B, V

PALADIN VIDEO HOME ENTERTAINMENT GUIDE

This tape features Mink De Ville along with his six piece band live at the Savoy in New York. This tape includes their hit singles 'Spanish Stroll,' 'Mixed Up,' 'Shook Up Girl' and 'Cadillac Walk' along with many others. It is recorded live at the Savoy, New York.
F — EN
Unknown — Polygram Video   H, P
791 5534/791 5532

Mintex International Rally 1981   Spo-Lei '81
Automobiles-Racing
02048   52 mins   C
B, V
First round of the 1981 British Open Championship.
S,A — EN
Vintage Television Ltd — Vintage Television Ltd   H, P, E

Miracle of Love   Fil-Ent '82
Drama
12920   96 mins   C
B, V
Stephen Elliot, Henry Olek, Carrie Sherman, Erica Yohn, directed by Glenn Jordan
Based on the book written by Barry Neil Kaufman about his autistic son, this is the true story of the determination of a mother and father who through an intensive programme of care and study are able to bring their child back to normality.
C,A — EN
Filmways International — Video Form Pictures H, P
MGS 51

Miracle of the Bells, The   Fil-Ent '48
Drama
01077   120 mins   B/W
V2, B, V
Fred MacMurray, Frank Sinatra
An agent tries to make an actress' deathbed wish come true by having her final film shown.
BBFC:A — S,A — EN
RKO — Intervision Video   H, P
A-A 0108

Miracle on Ice   Fil-Ent '81
Drama
10220   140 mins   C
B, V
Karl Malden, Andrew Stevens, Steve Guttenberg, directed by Steven Hillard Stern
An unknown college coach is asked to lead the 1980 US Olympic ice hockey team. With this impossible task the only way to succeed is to give it his all. He never lets up, he arranges gruelling matches and keeps pushing and pushing. This hard work is rewarded by a win over the Russians in the semi-finals and a 4-2 win over Finland to win the Gold.
S,A — EN
Moonlight Prods; Filmways — Video Form Pictures   H, P
MGD 012

Mirror Crack'd, The   Fil-Ent '80
Mystery/Crime-Drama
05295   100 mins   C
B, V
Angela Lansbury, Geraldine Chaplin, Tony Curtis, Edward Fox, Rock Hudson, Kim Novak, Elizabeth Taylor
Set in 1953 in rural England, a Hollywood film crew unearth old community conflicts and a body. Chief Inspector Craddock is aided in his murder investigation by Miss Marple. Based on the novel by Agatha Christie.
F — EN
John Brabourne; Richard Goodwin — THORN EMI   P
TXA 90 0302 4/TVA 90 0302 2

Mirror, Mirror—Love and Life   Fil-Ent '79
Romance/Drama
12836   100 mins   C
B, V
Robert Vaughan, Janet Leigh, Lee Meriwether, Peter Bonerz, Loretta Swit
The second film in the 'Love and Life' series is the story of a war of romance fought with the deadly weapon of beauty.
C,A — EN
Christiana Productions — Video Tape Centre P
5001

Mirrors   Fil-Ent '??
Horror/Mystery
06184   86 mins   C
B, V
Kitty Wynn, Peter Donat, William Swetland, Mary-Robin Redd, William Burns, directed by Noel Black
With New Orleans as the setting, both modern and old venues are used to unravel the mystery of reincarnation and supernatural destruction. A young woman has nightmares about mirrors resulting in a series of unexpected and natural deaths.
S,A — EN
First American Films — VCL Video Services P

(For Explanation of codes, see USE GUIDE and KEY)   441

PALADIN VIDEO HOME ENTERTAINMENT GUIDE

Miss Julie
Fil-Ent '7?
Drama
04197   105 mins   C
B, V

Helen Mirren
In this outstanding Royal Shakespeare Company production, the world's most distinguished theatrical company presents Strindberg's classic.
BBFC:AA — C,A — EN
Unknown — *Guild Home Video*   H, P

Miss Nude Pageant, The
Fil-Ent '80
Variety
06905   60 mins   C
V2, B, V

This tape covers the Miss Nude Pageant held outdoors in the grounds of a large hotel in Hockley Hills, Ontario, Canada. The contestants are finalists from all over the world competing for a series of valued prizes.
A — EN
Unknown — *Fourmatt Video Ltd*   P

Missile-X
Fil-Ent '78
War-Drama
08820   95 mins   C
B, V

Curt Jurgens, Peter Graves, Michael Dante
A deadly top-secret weapon with enormous destructive powers is developed. It is captured by an international crime syndicate, able to hold the world at ransom. In this film, Soviet and American spy networks unite in a desperate attempt to trace the deadly weapon.
S,A — EN
Unknown — *VCL Video Services*   P
P281D

Missiles of October, The
Fil-Ent '74
War-Drama
08075   149 mins   C
B, V

William Devane, Martin Sheen, Ralph Bellamy, Howard DaSilva, directed by Anthony Page
This film tells the story of the October 1962 Cuban Missile crisis, a confrontation between the USA and the USSR over the placement of nuclear weapons in Cuba. The film goes on to show how the White House dealt with the impending danger.
BBFC:AA — C,A — EN
Viacom; ABC — *Rank Video Library*   H, P
0091 C

Missing
Fil-Ent '82
Drama
10105   116 mins   C
B, V

Jack Lemmon, Sissy Spacek, directed by Costa-Gauras
This film tells the true story of a young American who disappeared during the 1973 military coup which overthrew the world's first democratically elected Marxist president: Salvador Allende of Chile.
Cannes Film Festival '82: Golden Palm Award (Best Screenplay).   BBFC:15 — S,A — EN
Universal — *CIC Video*   H, P
BEA 1064/VHA 1064

Mission Galactica: The Cylon Attack
Fil-Ent '80
Science fiction
05329   108 mins   C
B, V

Lloyd Bridges, Richard Hatch, Dirk Benedict, Lorne Green, directed by Vince Edwards and Christian I. Nyby II
The mighty Battlestar Galactica stands helpless and in danger of attack from their sub-human enemies. The Commander's son returns to the ship with a long lost legendary hero who plans to attack the Cylons leaving the Galactica open to destruction; the Commander is forced to relieve him of control. Meanwhile, the Cylon leader plans his attack to destroy the last of the human race. The climax to this space epic is the final assault by their bat-winged ships.
S,A — EN
Universal — *CIC Video*   H, P
BEA1020/VHA1020

Mission Mars
Fil-Ent '68
Science fiction
07489   87 mins   C
B, V

Darren McGavin, Nick Adams, George de Vries, Heather Hewitt, directed by Nick Webster
The whole future of space travel comes under question as an American expedition to Mars comes under attack by beings that live under the rays of the sun. The mystery of the Red Planet deepens as the weird, abstract, hostile population battle with the Americans who try to survive against the unknown.
S,A — EN
Sagittarius Productions — *Quadrant Video*   H, P
FF8

Mission: Monte Carlo
Fil-Ent '66
Mystery/Suspense
05946   96 mins   C
B, V

Tony Curtis, Roger Moore
Lord Brett Sinclair and his friend Danny have gone to the French Riviera to enjoy the beautiful girls and champagne night-life. While out water

PALADIN VIDEO HOME ENTERTAINMENT GUIDE

skiing they discover the body of a young girl in the sea. They rule out suicide or an accident as no girl would go swimming with a non-waterproof watch and still wearing a hair piece.
S,A — EN
Unknown — Precision Video Ltd   P
BITC 2065/VITC 2065

Missionary, The   Fil-Ent '83
Comedy-Drama
09816   82 mins   C
B, V
Michael Palin, Maggie Smith, Trevor Howard, Denholm Elliott, Michael Hordern, Graham Crowden, Phoebe Nicholls, directed by Richard Loncraine
Set in Edwardian England, this comedy of sexual misadventure follows the exploits of the Rev. Charles Fortescue upon his return from 10 years in Africa. He is sent to London's East End to run a mission for fallen women. Assisted by an attractive lady philanthropist his ideals of share and share alike take on a new meaning. Written by Michael Palin.
BBFC:15 — S,A — EN
Handmade Films — THORN EMI   P
TXA 90 1721 4/TVA 90 1721 2

Missouri Breaks, The   Fil-Ent '76
Drama/Western
13070   124 mins   C
B, V
Marlon Brando, Jack Nicholson, Randy Quaid, Kathleen Lloyd, directed by Arthur Penn
Set in Montana in the 1880's, wealthy landowners commission protection from marauding rustlers by hiring a killer to exercise control, but one horse thief proves particularly difficult.
BBFC:AA — C,A — EN
United Artists Corp — Warner Home Video   P
99283

Mrs R's Daughter   Fil-Ent '??
Drama
12177   93 mins   C
B, V
Cloris Leachman, John McIntire, Season Hubley
A mother begins a lone battle for justice after her daughter has been brutally raped. At the hearing, whatever the evidence, no one wants to believe it. The trial turns into a nightmare but she is determined to see the guilty man punished.
C,A — EN
NBC International — Select Video Limited   P
3121/43

Mr Billion   Fil-Ent '77
Suspense/Adventure
12259   93 mins   C
B, V
Terence Hill, Valerie Perrine, Jackie Gleason, Slim Pickens, directed by Jonathan Kaplan
A garage mechanic has a deadline to meet in San Francisco in order to collect his inheritance of a billion dollars.
M,A — EN
Steven Bach; Ken Friedman; 20th Century Fox — CBS/Fox Video   P
1198

Mr Blandings Builds His Dream House/Mexican Spitfire at Sea   Fil-Ent '??
Comedy
05670   150 mins   B/W
B, V
Cary Grant, Myrna Loy, Lex Barker, Melvyn Douglas, Reginald Denny, directed by H. C. Potter, Lupe Velez, Leon Errol, Charles Rogers, ZaSu Pitts, directed by Leslie Goodwins
Two films are featured on one cassettte. 'Mr Blandings Builds His Dream House' (Black/White, 90 mins, 1949) is a comedy about a couple who buy a derelict house and attempt to convert it into a dream house; everything goes wrong. 'Mexican Spitfire at Sea' (Black/White, 70 mins, 1943) is a comedy set on a Honolulu bound pleasure cruise. A man tries to strike a business deal with a couple of social climbers; the result is hectic confusion.
F — EN
RKO — Kingston Video   H, P
KV42

Mr Horn   Fil-Ent '8?
Adventure/Western
12152   134 mins   C
B, V
David Carradine, Richard Widmark, Karen Black, directed by Jack Starrett
A civilian joins the American Cavalry in its search for Geronimo. Disenchanted with his superiors, he leaves the army and in the following years establishes himself as a sheriff and detective, but not before making enemies intent on framing him for murder.
S,A — EN
Unknown — Polygram Video   H, P
0402374/0402372

Mr Hulot's Holiday   Fil-Ent '53
Comedy
07946   91 mins   B/W
V2, B, V
Jacques Tati, Natalie Pascaud, Michelle Rolia, directed by Jacques Tati

(For Explanation of codes, see USE GUIDE and KEY)

PALADIN VIDEO HOME ENTERTAINMENT GUIDE

Mr Hulot wreaks havoc in the staid sea-side resort of St. Marc-on-Sea.
BBFC:U — F — EN
GDB International — *Videomedia* P
PVM 4415/BVM 4415/HVM 4415

Mister Jerico Fil-Ent '69
Comedy
07342   85 mins   C
B, V
Patrik Macnee, Connie Stevens, Herbert Lom, Marty Allen
A superb confidence trickster is conned himself when he sets out to bring retribution to a corrupt millionaire.
S,A — EN
ATV — *Precision Video Ltd* P
BITC 2094/VITC 2094

Mr Kingstreet's War/Ghost Ship Fil-Ent '??
Drama
05760   155 mins   C
B, V
John Saxon, Tippi Hedren, Rossano Brazzi, Brian O'Shaughnessy, directed by Percival Rubens, Richard Dix, Lawrence Tierney, Russell Wade, Edith Barrett, directed by Mark Robson
Two films are contained on one cassette. 'Mr Kingstreet's War' (colour, 89 mins, 1971) is set in an African wildlife centre threatened by opposing armies in World War II who need a water supply. The owner fights to preserve his territory. 'Ghost Ship' (black/white, 66 mins, 1944) is a story about a young officer who joins a merchant ship and is disturbed by the captain's odd behaviour. Finally he accuses the captain of murder but he finds himself at night, alone with the killer advancing.
S,A — EN
Gold Key Entertainment; RKO — *Kingston Video* H, P
KV20

Mr. Magoo in Sherwood Forest Fil-Ent '64
Cartoons
09090   83 mins   C
V2, B, V
Animated, voices by Jim Backus, directed by Abe Levitow
Mr. Magoo, along with Robin Hood and his merry band, try to undo the evil exploits of King John and the Sheriff of Nottingham. His nearsightedness, however, gets him into many comic predicaments.
F — EN
UPA — *Video Tape Centre* P
VTC 1076

Mister Men Volume 1 Chi-Juv '81
Cartoons/Fantasy
06045   60 mins   C
B, V
Animated, voices by Arthur Lowe, directed by Trevour Bard and Terry Ward
The mister men live in a world of pure fantasy in this film. Mr Silly has an idea and wins a cup in nonsenseland, Mr Bounce visits the doctor and falls through the ceiling, Mr Jelly meets a tramp, Mr Forgetful forgets what he has to do, Mr Snow enjoys Christmas, Mr Funny cheers up the 300 animals, and Mr Happy meets Mr Miserable with surprise results.
PS,M — EN
Warner Bros — *Warner Home Video* P
WEX93001/WEV93001

Mister Men Volume 2 Chi-Juv '81
Cartoons/Fantasy
06046   60 mins   C
B, V
Animated, voices by Arthur Lowe, directed by Trevour Bard and Terry Ward
The Mister Men live in a land of pure fantasy in this film. Mr Impossible does handstands without hands, Mr Small find his dream job, Mr Daydream goes round the world and is nearly eaten by a crocodile, Mr Messy has visitors and is tidied up, Mr Bump walks into an apple tree, Mr Greedy meets a hungry giant and Mr Tickle causes a riot in town.
PS,M — EN
Warner Bros — *Warner Home Video* P
WEX93002/WEV93002

Mister Men Volume 3 Chi-Juv '81
Cartoons/Fantasy
06047   60 mins   C
B, V
Animated, voices by Arthur Lowe, directed by Trevour Bard and Terry Ward
Further adventures of the Mr Men, in which Mr Muddle is helped to get things right. Mr Topsy-Turvy visits town, Mr Mean has a date with the wizard of Mister-Land, Mr Lazy needs a rest, Mr Land breathes a sigh of relief as Mr Noisy becomes quiet, Mr Chatterbox talks endlessly to the moon, worms, trees and everyone and Mr Nosey is too nosey.
PS,M — EN
Warner Bros — *Warner Home Video* P
WEX93003/WEV93003

Mister Men Volume 4 Chi-Juv '81
Cartoons/Fantasy
07863   60 mins   C
B, V
Animated, voices by Arthur Lowe, directed by Trevour Bard and Terry Ward

PALADIN VIDEO HOME ENTERTAINMENT GUIDE

Seven more adventures featuring the Mister Men, who live in a world of pure fantasy.
PS,M — EN
Warner Bros — *Warner Home Video* P
WEX 93004/WEV 93004

Mr Mum Fil-Ent '83
Comedy
12896 91 mins C
B, V
Michael Keaton, Teri Garr, directed by Stan Dragoti
A married couple swap roles when he receives his redundancy notice and gets more than he bargained for as a house-husband.
BBFC:PG — S,A — EN
Lynn Loring — *THORN EMI* P
TXA 90 25634/TVA 90 25632

Mister Roberts Fil-Ent '55
Comedy
13034 115 mins C
B, V
Henry Fonda, James Cagney, Jack Lemmon, directed by John Ford and Mervyn LeRoy
This wry comedy concerns the bored, restless crew of a cargo ship eager to see a bit of wartime action.
BBFC:U — C,A — EN
Orange Productions Ltd — *Warner Home Video* P
61017

Mr. Robinson Crusoe Fil-Ent '32
Adventure
07628 67 mins B/W
B, V
Douglas Fairbanks Sr, Maria Alba, William Farnum, directed by Edward Sutherland
Aboard a yacht in the Pacific, a rich playboy and his friends are reminded of Robinson Crusoe. His friends bet the playboy that he couldn't survive on the deserted island. He accepts, jumps overboard and swims for the island. Once ashore he meets a girl from a nearby island who is trying to escape from an intertribal marriage. He sets some ingenious traps to protect her from the angry tribe.
F — EN
United Artists — *VCL Video Services* P
0225G

Mr Rossi Looks for Happiness Chi-Juv '??
Cartoons/Fantasy
07944 80 mins C
V2, B, V
Animated by Bruno Bozzetto
This film follows the adventures of Mr Rossi, who, thanks to a golden whistle given to him by Fairy Sicura, can travel here, there and everywhere. He travels from the land of the Dinosaurs to desert islands and from the Wild West to the future.
PS,M — EN
Unknown — *Videomedia* P
PVM 2116/BVM 2116/HVM 2116

Mr. Smith's Flower Garden How-Ins '81
Gardening/Flowers
04856 109 mins C
V2, B, V, LV
Geoffrey Smith demonstrates how to get the best results from any size of flower garden. Accompanying book available from booksellers.
AM Available F — I
Brian Davies; Roger Brunskill — *BBC Video*
H, P
BBCV 1001

Mr. Smith's Indoor Garden How-Ins '81
Gardening
04851 110 mins C
V2, B, V, LV
Geoffrey Smith demonstrates how to choose, care for and arrange indoor plants. Accompanying book available from booksellers.
AM Available F — I
Brian Davies; Andy Finney — *BBC Video*
H, P
BBCV 1002

Mr. Smith's Vegetable Garden How-Ins '81
Gardening
04868 109 mins C
V2, B, V, LV
Geoffrey Smith demonstrates all the processes necessary to produce a successful vegetable crop. Accompanying book available from booksellers.
AM Available F — I
Brian Davies; Roger Brunskill — *BBC Video*
H, P
BBCV 1000

Mr. Sycamore Fil-Ent '75
Fantasy
01190 85 mins C
V2, B, V
Jason Robards, Sandy Dennis, Jean Simmons

(For Explanation of codes, see USE GUIDE and KEY)

PALADIN VIDEO HOME ENTERTAINMENT GUIDE

The strange tale of a man who tries to become a tree.
F — EN
Capricorn Productions — *Intervision Video*
H, P
A-AE 0197

Mistral's Daughter
Fll-Ent '83
Drama
12931 360 mins C
B, V
Stephanie Powers, Lee Remick, Stacy Keach, Robert Urich, Timothy Dalton, Pierre Malet, Ian Richardson, Stephanie Audran, Cotter Smith, Philippe Leroy Beaulieu, Joanna Lumley, Caroline Langrishe
This programme is produced on three separate cassettes and tells the story of three generations of women who are determined to succeed in the world of art and high fashion and whose paths take them across America and war-torn France.
BBFC:15 — S,A — EN
Steve Krantz; RTL Production — *Video Form Pictures*   **H, P**

Mistress, The
Fll-Ent '??
Drama
08910 81 mins C
V2, B, V
Senta Berger, Maurizio Arena, Bruno Zanin, Erika Blanc, directed by Mario Lanfranchi
Having bought an estate of a late count, the new owner discovers that along with the mansion he has acquired the Count's widow and her two beautiful daughters.
BBFC:X — A — EN
Unknown — *Video Programme Distributors*
P
Inter-Ocean 008

Mistress of Paradise
Fll-Ent '81
Drama
09848 95 mins C
B, V
Genevieve Bujold, Chad Everett, Anthony Andrews
This is a passionate story set in America's deep south in the days when gentlemen fought duels on points of honour and the flint-lock pistol had not yet given way to the Colt 45.
S,A — EN
Lorimar Prods — *Polygram Video*   **H, P**
040 1284/040 1282

Misunderstood
Fll-Ent '8?
Drama
10091 97 mins C
B, V
Anthony Quayle

A man, unable to cope with the death of his wife, leaves his two little boys to run wild. Unable to take care of themselves they crave love and attention. Inevitably more tragedy ensues and the man, haunted by guilt and grief, tries desperately to prove his love before it is too late.
S,A — EN
Unknown — *VideoSpace Ltd*   **P**

Moby Dick
Fll-Ent '56
Adventure
00590 110 mins C
B, V
Gregory Peck, Richard Basehart, Orson Welles, directed by John Huston
A nineteenth century whaling skipper journeys across the world's oceans, obsessed with gaining revenge on Moby Dick, the great white whale that took off his leg years before. Adapted for the screen from Herman Melville's classic novel by Ray Bradbury.
BBFC:U — F — EN
Warner Bros — *THORN EMI*   **P**
TXB 90 0046 4/TVB 90 0046 2

Moby Dick
Fll-Ent '??
Cartoons/Adventure
08808 49 mins C
B, V
Animated
This film tells in cartoon form the story of the mad Captain Ahab and his obsessive quest for revenge on a great white whale.
F — EN
Movietel — *VCL Video Services*   **P**
A278B

Modern Times
Fll-Ent '36
Comedy
05845 89 mins B/W
B, V
Charlie Chaplin, Paulette Goddard, Henry Bergman, Chester Conklin, directed by Charlie Chaplin
A factory workman tries to cope with the assembly line and mass production in the Depression years. He battles with a monstrous assembly line feeding machine, amongst other incidents, and mistakenly sniffs a nose full of cocaine with hilarious results. (Silent.)
F — EN
United Artists — *Polygram Video*   **P**
7901464/7901462

Modesty Blaise
Fll-Ent '66
Comedy/Adventure
12087 120 mins C
B, V

PALADIN VIDEO HOME ENTERTAINMENT GUIDE

Monica Vitti, Terence Stamp, Dirk Bogarde, directed by Joseph Losey
The female superspy is hired by the government to protect a shipment of diamonds from being hi-jacked.
S,A — EN
Twentieth Century Fox — CBS/Fox Video
P
1230

Mohawk Fil-Ent '56
Western
01693   80 mins   C
V2, B, V
Scott Brady, Rita Gam
The conflict between pioneers and Indians provides a backdrop for this tale of savage frontier action and forbidden love.
S,A — EN
20th Century Fox — Intervision Video   H,
P
A-A 0141

Moment to Kill, The Fil-Ent '??
Western
08599   89 mins   C
V2, B, V
George Hilton, Walter Barnes, Loni Von Friedel, Renato Romando, directed by Anthony Ascott
Two gunmen are hired by a Judge in a small city in the west to handle a delicate mission. This consists of finding five hundred thousand dollars worth of gold which belongs to the Southern Confederation. It has been hidden in the area, by a Southern Colonel, who died whilst trying to defend it from the Northerners.
S,A — EN
Unknown — Videomedia   P
PVM 6107/BVM 6107/HVM 6107

Mommie Dearest Fil-Ent '81
Drama
10117   124 mins   C
B, V
Faye Dunaway, directed by Frank Parry
An autobiographical account of life with one of the greatest film stars, Joan Crawford. Based on the book written by her adopted daughter, Christina, it is the story of a love-hate relationship.
BBFC:15 — S,A — EN
Paramount — CIC Video   H, P
BEA 2068/VHA 2068

Mon Oncle Fil-Ent '58
Comedy
05564   105 mins   C
V2, B, V
Jacques Tati, Jean Pierre Zola, Adrienne Servantie, Alain Bacourt, directed by Jacques Tati
An accident prone Uncle aids his adoring nephew in a war against the parents modernised twentieth century push-button home. They appear to be unable to win.
Academy Awards '58: Best Foreign Language Picture; Cannes Film Festival '58: Special Jury Award.   BBFC:U — F — EN
Continental Distributing Corp — Videomedia
P
PVM 4412/BVM 4412/HVM 4412

Mondo Erotico Fil-Ent '7?
Nightclub/Comedy
02100   70 mins   C
V2, B, V
Introduced by Laura Gemser
Amusing and titillating international tour around some of the most intriguing night spots.
A — EN
Titanus — Hokushin Audio Visual Ltd   P
VM-06

Money Movers Fil-Ent '78
Suspense/Crime-Drama
06158   95 mins   C
V2, B, V
Terence Donovan, Ed Deveraux, Tony Bonner, Charles Tingwell
An armoured payroll van is attacked in the car park of a suburban tavern, leaving the crew beaten, bound and gagged. At the security firm the robbery news hits hard but is overshadowed by a warning that the firm's Counting House with its multi-million dollar contents is to be the next target.
BBFC:X — A — EN
Matt Carroll Prod — Guild Home Video
H, P, E

Money to Burn Fil-Ent '76
Crime-Drama
08768   80 mins   C
B, V
Jack Kruschen, David Wallace, Meegan King, Phillip Pine, directed by Virginia Lively Stone
This film tells of a plan to relieve a federal reserve bank of fifty million dollars, back on release from custody, by a school counselor and his associates.
S,A — EN
Charles Fries — Precision Video Ltd   P
BSPV 2586/VSPV 2586

Mongrel Fil-Ent '83
Horror/Drama
13409   85 mins   C
V2, B, V

(For Explanation of codes, see USE GUIDE and KEY)   447

PALADIN VIDEO HOME ENTERTAINMENT GUIDE

Aldo Ray, directed by Robert Burns
A practical joke backfires in a seedy boarding house and starts a chain of killings as the sinister mystery unravelles.
BBFC:15 — A — EN
Unknown — *Intervision Video* **H, P**
6737

Monsieur Verdoux Fil-Ent '47
Drama
09864 118 mins B/W
B, V
Charlie Chaplin
Chaplin emerges as a modern Bluebeard who during the 1920's French economic depression turns to supporting his invalid wife and young son by marrying and subsequently murdering a succession of empty-headed women.
F — EN
Charles Chaplin — *Polygram Video* **H, P**
790 1524/790 1522

Monsieur Vincent Fil-Ent '47
Drama/Biographical
10034 118 mins B/W
B, V
Pierre Fresnay, Aime Clairiond, directed by Maurice Cloche
A biography of St. Vincent de Paul, the 17th-century priest who gave up all worldly possessions to work with the poor. Subtitled in English.
S,A — EN FR
EDIC; UGC — *Palace Video Ltd* **P**
PVC 2056A

Monsignor Fil-Ent '82
Drama
12004 118 mins C
B, V
Christopher Reeve, Genevieve Bujold, Fernando Rey, Jason Miller, directed by Frank Perry
Summoned to the Vatican at the end of World War II, a priest is put in charge of sorting out the church's financial crisis. Using his underworld connections, he sets up a lucrative black market in Vatican supplies, but soon finds himself in trouble with the Mafia.
BBFC:15 — S,A — EN
20th Century Fox — *CBS/Fox Video* **P**
1108

Monster, The Fil-Ent '8?
Drama/Horror
08091 91 mins C
B, V
Joan Collins, Ralph Bates
An ex-stripper gives birth to a monstrous baby. The film goes on to show monster on a murderous rampage.
C,A — EN
Unknown — *Rank Video Library* **H, P**
0119 C

Monster Club, The Fil-Ent '80
Horror/Comedy
05872 93 mins C
B, V
Vincent Price, Donald Pleasance, John Carradine, Stuart Whitman, Richard Johnson, Barbara Kellerman, Britt Ekland, Simon Ward, Anthony Valentine, Patrick Magee, directed by Roy Ward Baker
A distinguished horror writer is attacked by a vampire. He is assured that the bite was not deep enough to bring him into the fold. The vampire takes him to the Monster Club. The writer gets plenty of material from the weird creatures enjoying themselves; the vampire explains the rules of Monsterdom by illustrating with three stories. Features music by B.A. Robertson, The Pretty Things, The Viewers, John Williams, UB40 and Expressos.
BBFC:A — S,A — EN
Chips Production; Sword and Sorcery Production — *Precision Video Ltd* **P**
BITC 2061/VITC 2061

Monsters Christmas, The Chi-Juv '84
Adventure/Fantasy
13100 50 mins C
B, V
A little girl is reading a story to her teddy bear on Christmas Eve at bed-time and then travels into a world of make-believe where she meets the Mountain Monster, the Wicked Witch, the Insect Monster and the Mud Monsters.
I,M — EN
Unknown — *Quadrant Video* **H, P**
CH4

Monsters from an Unknown Planet Fil-Ent '7?
Science fiction
02409 80 mins C
B, V
Directed by Ishiro Honda
Aliens plan to destroy the world with the might of Mechagodzilla, the mechanical monster, and Titanosaurus, a huge monster which can create whirlwinds with its tail. Godzilla, the earth's guardian, challenges the evil monsters.
S,A — EN
Japanese — *Derann Film Services* **H, P**
DV 115B/DV 115

PALADIN VIDEO HOME ENTERTAINMENT GUIDE

Monstroid   Fil-Ent '78
Horror
06800   80 mins   C
V2, B, V
John Carradine, Jim Mitchum, Phil Carey, Andrea Hartford, Tony Eisley
A re-enactment of four days of terror that rocked a small village in Columbia.
C,A — EN
Ken Hartford — *Intervision Video*   H, P
A-AE 0369

Montana Trap   Fil-Ent '??
Western
09391   ? mins   C
B, V
Stephen Boyd, Hardy Kruger, Peter Schamoni, directed by Peter Schamoni
This tells the tale of robbery, treachery and murder, set in the wild badlands.
C,A — EN
Unknown — *VCL Video Services*   P
P308

Montenegro   Fil-Ent '81
Drama/Romance
08374   96 mins   C
V2, B, V
Susan Anspach, Erland Josephson, Per Oscarsson
The story of an American housewife living in Sweden who tires of her uncomplicated life as a wife and mother, and promptly flees her home in search of excitement.
BBFC:X — A — EN
Atlantic Releasing — *Guild Home Video*
H, P, E

Month in the Country, A   Fil-Ent '8?
Drama/Romance
08748   90 mins   C
B, V
Susannah York, Ian McShane, Linda Thorson, Elspeth March
This film tells the story of a young woman looking for a passionate involvement. She meets a young tutor. Their relationship provides the central theme, with tragic consequences.
C,A — EN
Unknown — *Precision Video Ltd*   P
BAMPV 2577/VAMPV 2577

Montreal Olympics Equestrian Three-Day Event   Spo-Lei '76
Sports
04502   52 mins   C
B, V
Narrated by Richard Meade
The precision of dressage and the excitement of showjumping from the 1976 Summer Olympics are narrated by 1972 gold medalist in the individual and team events, Richard Meade.
F — EN
Michael Samuelson — *Quadrant Video*
H, P
E1

Montreal Olympics 1976   Spo-Lei '81
Sports
05204   45 mins   C
B, V
2 pgms
These unique films convey all the care, training and patience needed to win through in these events.
1.Dressage 2.Individual and Team Grand Prix Jumping
F — EN
Michael Samuelson — *Quadrant Video*
H, P

Monty Python and the Holy Grail   Fil-Ent '75
Comedy
01969   90 mins   C
B, V
Graham Chapman, John Cleese, Terry Gilliam, Eric Idle, Terry Jones, Michael Palin
Monty Python's absurdist humour rewrites the legend of King Arthur in this wild spoof. The tape includes 24 seconds of previously unseen material, plus the trailer for the film.
BBFC:A — C,A — EN
Python Pictures Ltd — *Brent Walker Home Video Ltd*   P

Monty Python Live at the Hollywood Bowl   Fil-Ent '82
Comedy
08463   78 mins   C
B, V
Graham Chapman, John Cleese, Terry Gilliam, Eric Idle, Terry Jones, Michael Palin, Carol Cleveland, Neil Innes, directed by Terry Hughes
This show was performed live in Los Angeles by the Monty Python team. It contains sketches such as the International Soccer Marth (Germans versus The Ancient Greeks), The Ministry of Silly Walks, a row between the Pope and Michelangelo, one-man wrestling, justices in drag and Che Guevara, Lenin and Marx in a quiz game on English football.
S,A — EN
George Harrison; Handmade Films — *THORN EMI*   P
TXA 90 0912 4/TVA 90 0912 2

(For Explanation of codes, see USE GUIDE and KEY)

PALADIN VIDEO HOME ENTERTAINMENT GUIDE

Monty Python's Life of Brian
Fil-Ent '79
Comedy/Satire
05034   89 mins   C
B, V

Graham Chapman, John Cleese, Eric Idle, Terry Gilliam, Terry Jones, Michael Palin

A typical Monty Python romp, this time through the Holy Land in the year 32 A.D. This is the hilarious story of Brian, a man who was born on the same night as Jesus Christ. Through a series of mishaps and misinterpretations, Brian is proclaimed the Messiah, a role he refuses to accept. Consequently, he spends most of his time running from the adoring multitudes, government officials, and several underground groups.
C,A — EN
Warner Bros; John Goldstone — THORN EMI
P
TXA 90 0305 4/TVA 90 0305 2

Monty Python's The Meaning of Life
Fil-Ent '83
Satire
13296   111 mins   C
B, V

John Cleese, Terry Gilliam, Eric Idle, Graham Chapman, Michael Palin, directed by Terry Jones

The Monty Python team delve into the fundamental purpose of human existence in this film.
BBFC:18 — A — EN
Universal — CIC Video   H, P
BET 1093/VHT 1093

Moon in the Gutter, The
Fil-Ent '84
Drama/Suspense
10019   126 mins   C
B, V

Nastassja Kinski, Gerard Depardieu, Victoria Abril

A young man vows revenge on the rapist who caused his sister to commit suicide.
BBFC:18 — A — EN
Gaumont; TF1 Film Productions — Palace Video Ltd   P
PVC 2063A

Moon Is Blue, The
Fil-Ent '53
Romance/Comedy
05652   97 mins   B/W
B, V

William Holden, David Niven, Maggie McNamara, Tom Tully, Dawn Addams, Fortunio Bonanova, Gregory Ratoff, directed by Otto Preminger

A young actress is picked up on top of the Empire State Building by a successful architect who invites her to dinner. She decides to cook for him. While he is out buying food an ex girlfriend and her womanising father turn up. The two men vie for the affections of the actress resulting in the architect being knocked-out. He realises he wants to marry the girl and they meet once again on top of the Empire State Building.
S,A — EN
Twentieth Century Fox — CBS/Fox Video
P

Moonchild
Fil-Ent '74
Drama/Horror
09135   90 mins   C
V2, B, V

Victor Buono, John Carradine, Janet Landgard, Pat Renella, Mark Travis, directed by Alan Gadney

This film includes exorcism, astrology, alchemy, witchcraft, sorcery and occult powers, when a moonchild is reincarnated for the seventh time, forced to repeat his short life every quarter of a century. He is caught up in a seemingly endless nightmare of demons, satanic soldiers, maddened monks, crazed sorcerers, bizarre monsters and a lusting female ghost.
A — EN
Filmmakers Prods — Go Video Ltd   P
GO 142

Moonraker
Fil-Ent '79
Adventure
13195   126 mins   C
B, V

Roger Moore, Lois Chiles, directed by Lewis Gilbert

Bond investigates the disappearance of a space shuttle—a mission which takes him to California, Venice and Rio.
BBFC:A — C,A — EN
Danjag SA — Warner Home Video   P
99200

Moontrek
Fil-Ent '??
Cartoons/Adventure
09473   80 mins   C
B, V
Animated

Sirius, in the 18th century, having a personal fortune at his disposal, decides to send an expedition to the moon. They discover a mysterious life, Selenites, inhabitants of the moon, who according to the ancient books, held in their possession the talisman of long life, the fountain of youth.
F — EN
Film Jean Image; Films A2 — Guild Home Video   H, P, E

PALADIN VIDEO HOME ENTERTAINMENT GUIDE

More Tales From Trumpton Chi-Juv '84
Cartoons
13087   60 mins   C
B, V
Animated
This programme features four more tales from Trumpton with its popular characters Pugh Pugh, Barney McGrew, Cuthbert, Dibble and Grubb.
PS,I — EN
Unknown — *Longman Video*   **P**
5028

Morecambe & Wise Musical Extravaganzas   Fil-Ent '84
Comedy
13382   60 mins   C
B, V
Morecambe & Wise, Glenda Jackson, Vanessa Redgrave, Cliff Richard, Diana Rigg, Diane Solomon, Angela Rippon
A combination of song, dance and humour with clippings from the 70's series of television's Morecambe & Wise shows.
F — EN
John Hammonds — *BBC Video*   **H, P**
7009

Morgan—A Suitable Case for Treatment   Fil-Ent '66
Comedy
01601   93 mins   B/W
B, V
Vanessa Redgrave, David Warner, Robert Stephens, Irene Handl
A schizophrenic artist refuses to recognise his wife's divorce and interferes with her love affair. Cannes Film Festival: Best Actress (Redgrave).
BBFC:A — *S,A — EN*
British Lion; Quintra — *THORN EMI*   **P**
TXE 90 0045 4/TVE 90 0045 2

Moses the Lawgiver   Fil-Ent '76
Religion/Drama
00838   136 mins   C
B, V, LV
Burt Lancaster
The story of Moses and his struggle to free his people from the tyranny of the Egyptian Empire is told in this epic film.
S,A — EN
ITC — *Precision Video Ltd*   **P**
BITC 3023/VITC 3023

Mother Lode   Fil-Ent '8?
Adventure
08371   106 mins   C
V2, B, V
Charlton Heston, Nick Mancuso, Kim Basinger, John Marley, directed by Charlton Heston
This film is a tale of man's quest for gold. According to a legend, hidden in the great Gassair Mountains is a cavern with its walls and ceiling lined with gold. In this film, five people are seeking this fortune, and it tells of the dangers they encounter in their mission.
BBFC:U — *F — EN*
Unknown — *Guild Home Video*   **H, P, E**

Mother's Hands   Gen-Edu '??
Religion/Puppets
06284   30 mins   B/W
B, V, PH15
In this film Gerald Bean and his puppet Gregory perform a Gospel story to show how Jesus died for us through the story of a Mother saving her child.
M,S — R
Audio Visual Ministries — *Audio Visual Ministries*   **H, L, P**
VT146

Motion Epics Cartoon Show   Fil-Ent '??
Cartoons
07989   ? mins   C
B, V
Animated
This is a collection of cartoons. There are old stories, such as 'Kids in the Shoe', 'Simple Simon', 'Old Mother Hubbard' and new ones such as 'Gabby Goes Fishing' and 'Land of the Lost Jewels'.
F — EN
Unknown — *Motion Epics Video Company Ltd*   **P**
156

Moto-Cross Professionals   Spo-Lei '79
Sports-Minor/Motorcycles
09107   62 mins   C   (PAL,NTSC)
V2, B, V
This contains two films spanning the years 1978/79; the 'Motocross Professionals 1978' and 'Moto-Cross Grand Prix 1979'. A lot of world class moto cross riders are featured, including Noyce, Lackey, Malherbe, Mikkola, de Coster and Wolsink, from a range of locations.
S,A — EN
CH Wood Ltd — *Duke Marketing Limited*
P

Motorhead   Fil-Ent '8?
Music-Performance
09828   32 mins   C
B, V

(For Explanation of codes, see USE GUIDE and KEY)   451

PALADIN VIDEO HOME ENTERTAINMENT GUIDE

This tape features the heavy rock band, Motorhead.
F — EN
Unknown — *Polygram Video*   **H, P**
BVI 4001/BVI 2001

Motorhead, Deaf not Blind   Fil-Ent '84
Music video
12963   60 mins   C
B, V
This video is a compilation of tracks from Motorhead including 'The Ace of Spades', 'Shine', 'One Track Mind', 'Dead Men Tell' and 'Capricorn'.
F — EN
Unknown — *Virgin Video*   **H, P**
VVD 052

Moulin Rouge   Fil-Ent '52
Drama
01955   114 mins   C
B, V
Jose Ferrer, Colette Marchand, Katherine Kath
An account of the life of crippled French artist Toulouse-Lautrec. He is followed from his aristocratic family to the notorious clubs of the Montmartre, where he became a distinguished figure in Paris night life.
S,A — EN
United Artists — *CBS/Fox Video*   **P**
3B-065

Mountain Family Robinson   Fil-Ent '79
Adventure
08872   102 mins   C
V2, B, V
Robert F. Logan, Susan Damante Shaw, William Bryant, Heather Rattray, Ham Larsen, George Flower, directed by John Cotter
Having built a home in the mountain wilderness, the Robinson family are faced with the possibility of losing their land. The film tells of the fight to save their home and their land with the help of an old mountain prospector.
BBFC:U — F — EN
Pacific International Enterprises — *Video Programme Distributors*   **P**
Media 207

Mountain Legend 1965   Spo-Lei '65
Automobiles-Racing
04541   43 mins   C
B, V

The story of the legendary Targa Florio road race, held in the mountains of northwest Sicily each spring until 1973.
F — EN
Castrol — *Quadrant Video*   **H, P**
M7

Mountain Man   Fil-Ent '77
Drama/Adventure
08042   93 mins   C
B, V
Denver Pyle, John Denver, Ken Berry, Cheryl Miller, directed by David O'Malley
This film is a true historical drama set in the 1860's. It tells the story of a miner who has contracted miner's lung disease. His only hope for survival is to live in the wilderness where there is fresh air.
BBFC:U — F — EN
Sunn Classic Productions — *Rank Video Library*   **H, P**
0058 C

Mouse and His Child, The   Chi-Juv '77
Cartoons/Fantasy
12606   80 mins   C
V2, B, V
Animated, voices of Peter Ustinov and Sally Keller
Two toy mice sitting in a smart shop window are plunged into a set of thrilling and dangerous adventures in their quest to become self-winding.
BBFC:U — F — EN
Sanrio Film Distribution — *VideoSpace Ltd*   **P**

Mouse and his Child, The   Chi-Juv '77
Cartoons
13099   80 mins   C
B, V
Animated
A clockwork mouse and his child are plunged into a bewildering world pursued by the evil Manny Rat and become involved in many thrilling adventures in their goal to become self-winding.
PS,M — EN
Sanrio Film Distribution — *Quadrant Video*   **H, P**
FF 15

Mouse and the Woman, The   Fil-Ent '??
Drama
05620   105 mins   C
V2, B, V
Dafydd Hywell, Karen Archer, Patricia Napier, Alan Devlin, Peter Spraule, directed by Kaol Francis

PALADIN VIDEO HOME ENTERTAINMENT GUIDE

Set during the 1914-18 war in the secluded valleys of Wales, this is the story of a man who is as handy with his fists as with his poetic fantasy. His masculinity fascinates Gilda, the wife of the owner of the mine, who is a seductress. Based on the short story by Dylan Thomas.
BBFC:AA — S,A — EN
Unknown — *Go Video Ltd* **P**
GO113

Move   Fil-Ent '70
Comedy
12086   86 mins   C
B, V
Elliot Gould, Paula Prentiss, Genevieve Waite, directed by Stuart Rosenberg
A neurotic writer decides to move into an up-market apartment and acquire a more refined image. The action takes place during the week-end of the move and reality is contrasted against the fantasies of his mind.
C,A — EN
Twentieth Century Fox — *CBS/Fox Video* **P**
1154

Movie Movie   Fil-Ent '78
Comedy
02037   102 mins   C
B, V
George C. Scott, Trish Van Devere, Barbara Harris, Art Carney, Eli Wallach
A nostalgic double feature with Movietone News, trailers and two feature films, 'Dynamite Hands' (black and white), and 'Baxter's Beauties of 1933' (colour).
BBFC:A — F — EN
Stanley Donen — *Precision Video Ltd* **P**
BITC2013/VITC2013

Moving Violation   Fil-Ent '76
Crime-Drama
13650   88 mins   C
B, V
Stephen McHattie, Kay Lenn, Eddie Albert, Lonny Chapman, Will Geer, directed by Charles S Dubin
When a drifter meets up with a local girl they inadvertently witness the killing of a police officer by the sheriff and they can do nothing but run away.
BBFC:15 — S,A — EN
Julie Corman — *CBS/Fox Video* **P**
1147

Mozart   Fil-Ent '7?
Music-Performance
04532   55 mins   C
B, V
Isaac Stern, Jean-Pierre Rampal
Major classical music is performed by international giants. Isaac Stern is the conductor. Jean-Pierre Rampal is featured in two flute concerti.
F — EN
David Cobham — *Quadrant Video* **H, P**
RM2

Mozart in Salzburg   Fil-Ent '81
Music-Performance
09806   102 mins   C
B, V
In this specially staged concert programme the orchestra of the Salzburg Mozarteum, under its principal conductor Ralf Weikert, accompanies such celebrated interpreters of Mozart's music as Walter Klien and Jill Gomez.
F — EN
Profilm — *THORN EMI* **P**
TXE 90 1993 4/TVE 90 1993 2

Mr Majestyk   Fil-Ent '74
Drama
12971   100 mins   C
B, V
Charles Bronson, Al Lettieri, Linda Cristal, Lee Purcell, directed by Richard Fleischer
A tough Colorado melon grower finds himself involved in a deadly game of cat and mouse with the Mafia when he tries to hand one of their organisation over to the police.
BBFC:18 — C,A — EN
United Artists; Walter Mirisch — *Warner Home Video* **P**
99379

Muhammed Ali vs Archie Moore   Spo-Lei '6?
Boxing
02069   60 mins   C
B, V
This programme captures the whole fight of Muhammed Ali (Cassius Clay) when he won the World Heavyweight Boxing Championship for the first time during the early sixties.
S,A — EN
Unknown — *VCL Video Services* **P**

Multiple Maniacs/Cocaine Fiends   Fil-Ent '??
Drama/Exploitation
08967   180 mins   B/W
B, V
David Lochary, Vivian Pearce, Edith Massey, Mink Stole; Louis January, Noel Madison, directed by W.A. Conner
In 'Multiple Maniacs' (1970, 90 mins.) Lady Divine and her boyfriend run a travelling freak show that lures housewives and businessmen

(For Explanation of codes, see USE GUIDE and KEY)   453

PALADIN VIDEO HOME ENTERTAINMENT GUIDE

into a small tent, to gawk at their favourite horrors, only to be robbed and sometimes murdered. These bizarre happenings get worse. 'Cocaine Fiends' (1937, 90 mins.) is a camp classic warning of the evils of cocaine. A brother and sister are led to the depths of degradation upon trying cocaine; heroin addiction, prostitution and suicide are the inevitable results.
A — EN
New Line Cinema et al — Palace Video Ltd   P
PVC 2010B

Munch Bunch and Mumfie, The　　Chi-Juv '??
Cartoons
09370　　126 mins　　C
B, V
Animated
Set in a greengrocer's shop, fruit and vegetables swept into one corner make plans to run away. Mumfie tells the story of the lovable little elephant who lives in Pine Tree Forest.
I,M — EN
Unknown — Precision Video Ltd   P
BITC 1076/VITC 1076

Muppet Movie, The　　Fil-Ent '79
Comedy
04224　　94 mins　　C
B, V, LV
The Muppets, Edgar Bergen, Milton Berle, Mel Brooks, Madeline Kahn, Steve Martin
Kermit the Frog travels cross country with his Muppet friends to Hollywood, where he plans to become a film star. He meets many real life stars along the way.
BBFC:U — F — EN
Jim Henson — Precision Video Ltd   P
BITC 2001/VITC 2001

Murder at Midnight　　Fil-Ent '31
Crime-Drama/Mystery
07636　　63 mins　　C
B, V
Wallace Ford, Gavin Gordon, Sarah Padden, Marian Marsh, Dave O'Brien, directed by Eric C. Kenton
An elderly woman is accused of being insane by her relatives who are after her money and property. She proves her sanity in court and is released. She invites her relatives to her country house for the weekend. When several murders occur a reporter decides to investigate.
F — EN
Tiffany — VCL Video Services   P
0230G

Murder by Decree　　Fil-Ent '79
Drama/Suspense
05531　　112 mins　　C
B, V
Christopher Plummer, James Mason, David Hemmings, Susan Clark, Anthony Quayle, John Gielgud, Frank Finlay, Donald Sutherland, Genevive Bujold, directed by Bob Clark
Sherlock Holmes is called in to track down Jack the Ripper who is busy slaughtering prostitutes. On the trail he becomes involved with anarchists, a medium, a frightened girl who disappears, and are held in a mad house. He discovers the murders are done to silence women who know too much; attempts are made on Holmes' life and it becomes clear that the investigations are being laundered by men in high places.
S,A — EN
Avco Embassy — CBS/Fox Video   P

Murder Gang, The　　Fil-Ent '??
Crime-Drama
05479　　90 mins　　C
V2, B, V
Timothy Brown, Russ Tamblyn, Jana Bellan, Geoffrey Land, directed by Al Adamson
A hard Detroit gang leader takes a trip to Los Angeles to make an important illegal arms deal; sitting in their headquarters in a house of pleasure they are unaware that the deal has been arranged by undercover agents. A shoot-out follows and the gang are destroyed in a plane explosion.
BBFC:X — A — EN
Unknown — Iver Film Services   P
122

Murder in Texas　　Fil-Ent '81
Drama/Suspense
09835　　102 mins　　C
B, V
Sam Elliot, Farrah Fawcett, Andy Griffith, Katherine Ross
After the mysterious death of his first wife, Dr. John Hill re-marries. But his own murder is soon to follow.
A — EN
Dick Clark Prods — Polygram Video   H, P
791 5164/791 5162

Murder on Flight 502　　Fil-Ent '75
Drama/Suspense
12074　　92 mins　　C
V2, B, V
Farrah Fawcett, Robert Stack, Walter Pidgeon, Polly Bergen

PALADIN VIDEO HOME ENTERTAINMENT GUIDE

A 747 takes off from New York to London; on board an unknown psychotic killer is threatening several murders. The killings begin and the pilot and security chief try to discover his identity.

BBFC:PG — S,A — EN

Metromedia Producers; Aaron Spelling — Guild Home Video   H, P, E

Murder on the Orient Express   Fil-Ent '74

Mystery
01214   128 mins   C
B, V

Albert Finney, Jacqueline Bisset, Ingrid Bergman, Lauren Bacall, Sean Connery, Martin Balsam, John Gielgud, Vanessa Redgrave, Wendy Hiller, Anthony Perkins, Rachel Roberts, Richard Widmark, Michael York Jean-Pierre Cassel directed by Sidney Lumet

Agatha Christie's classic whodunit becomes an all-star film, with Albert Finney as Beligan master sleuth Hercule Poirot, who eventually solves the murder puzzle aboard the famed Orient Express.

BBFC:A — F — EN

Paramount — THORN EMI   H, P
TXA 90 0090 4/TVA 90 0090 2

Murderers Row   Fil-Ent '66

Mystery/Adventure
09280   108 mins   C
B, V

Dean Martin, Ann-Margret, Karl Malden, Camilla Sparv, James Gregory, Beverley Adams, directed by Henry Levin

A dare-devil secret agent is recalled from his bachelor paradise to rescue a world famous scientist who has been kidnapped. A super-villain and twelve sexy 'Slaygirls' are sent to distract him as he becomes more and more involved in this 'impossible' mission.

S,A — EN

Columbia — RCA/Columbia Pictures Video UK
H, P

Murders in the Rue Morgue   Fil-Ent '71

Horror
09927   86 mins   C
B, V

Jason Robards, Herbert Lom, Christine Kaufman, Adolfo Celi, Lilli Palmer, Maria Perchy, Michael Dunn, directed by Gordon Hessler

A series of murders are committed in and around a theatre in Rue Morgue, Paris at the turn of the century. All the victims have been associates of the stage producer and evidence indicates that the killer is the producer's former partner believed to be dead for many years. It is based on a book by Edgar Allan Poe.

BBFC:PG — S,A — EN

AIP; Louis M. Heyward — Rank Video Library
H, P
2030 E

Murphy's War   Fil-Ent '71

War-Drama
07625   100 mins   C
B, V

Peter O'Toole, Sian Phillips, Philippe Noiret, Horst Jansen, directed by Peter Yates

An eccentric Irish deckhand is the sole survivor when his ship is attacked by a German U-boat off the coast of Venezuela. Having struggled ashore he is nursed back to health by a beautiful missionary. Something snaps inside him when he sees the carnage after the village is shattered by a marauding U-boat which launches a savage assault, killing many people.

S,A — EN

Paramount — VCL Video Services   P
P202D

Music-Image Odyssey   Fin-Art '81

Music/Video
05203   45 mins   C
B, V

An imaginative union of technology, music and art using computer, video and film techniques.

F — EN

Larry Finley Associated — Quadrant Video
H, P

Music Machine, The   Fil-Ent '7?

Musical-Drama
06784   93 mins   C
V2, B, V

Gerry Sundquist, Patti Boulaye

This musical drama revolves around the lives of the people who frequent a discotheque.

C,A — EN

Brian Smedley-Aston — Intervision Video
H, P
A-A 0361

Mussolini   Fil-Ent '77

War-Drama
09171   132 mins   C
B, V

Rod Steiger, Franco Nero, Lisa Gastoni, Henry Fonda

(For Explanation of codes, see USE GUIDE and KEY)   455

PALADIN VIDEO HOME ENTERTAINMENT GUIDE

Starting on April 25th, 1945, this tells of the plight of Mussolini until the 28th of April, when he and his faithful compatriot, Claretta Petacci, are sentenced to death and killed.
S,A — EN
Unknown — *Video Form Pictures* **H, P**
MGS 15

Mutant **Fil-Ent '84**
Horror
13229 100 mins C
B, V
Wings Hauser, Lee Montgomery, Bo Hopkins, Jennifer Warren, Jody Medford, directed by John 'Bud' Cardos
When a load of toxic waste is dumped on an unsuspecting small southern town in America, a type of mutant evolves which require uncontaminated blood to sustain their vampire cravings.
BBFC:18 — A — EN
Film Ventures International — *Entertainment in Video* **H, P**
EVB 1027/EVV 1027

Muthers, The **Fil-Ent '7?**
Adventure
08960 83 mins C
V2, B, V
This film tells of women mercenaries in South America, struggling to protect their territory against rival gangs. When one of the girls disappears, they have to tolerate a horrific plantation prison camp full of violence, abuse and brutality.
C,A — EN
Unknown — *Walton Film and Video Ltd* **P**

Mutiny at Fort Sharp **Fil-Ent '66**
Western
08795 91 mins C
B, V
Broderick Crawford
Set during the Civil War, a stubborn General holds a front line fort against overwhelming odds—invading Mexicans, raiding Indians and rebelling soldiers.
S,A — EN
Teleworld — *VCL Video Services* **P**
P338D

Mutiny on the Bounty **Fil-Ent '62**
Drama
12210 185 mins C
B, V
Marlon Brando, Trevor Howard, Richard Harris, directed by Lewis Milestone
Based on the novel by Charles Nordhoff and James Norman Hall, this account of the most famous mutiny in history aboard the Bounty in 1789 between Fletcher Christian and Captain Bligh is highlighted by lavish photography.
F — EN
MGM; Aaron Rosenberg — *MGM/UA Home Video* **P**
10031

Mutiny on the Buses **Fil-Ent '72**
Comedy
07439 88 mins C
B, V
Reg Varney, Doris Hare, Bob Grant, Anna Karen, Michael Robbins, Stephen Lewis, directed by Harry Booth
Based on the television series 'On the Buses,' bus driver Stan is now engaged to a sexy young girl but, fearing the loss of his wage packet, his family are not too pleased. To add to his problems his brother-in-law is sacked and to remedy the situation Stan gets him a job on the buses with disastrous results. Stan then transfers to the Special Tour Bus. The trial run to Windsor Safari Park turns to chaos when they are overrun by animals.
BBFC:A — S,A — EN
Hammer Film Productions Ltd — *THORN EMI* **P**
TXC 90 0742 4/TVC 90 0742 2

My Bird to the Rescue **Chi-Juv '7?**
Cartoons
12023 87 mins C
B, V
Animated
Based on the Hans Andersen story 'The Shepherdess and the Chimney Sweep,' a tyrant King falls in love with a shepherdess who in turn loves a chimney sweep. They run away together aided by a mockingbird who helps them in their fight against the King.
BBFC:U — F — EN
Unknown — *Entertainment in Video* **H, P**
EVB 2003/EVV 2033

My Bloody Valentine **Fil-Ent '81**
Horror
09270 91 mins C
B, V
Paul Kelman, Lori Hallier, directed by George Mihalka
A deranged killer stalks a town which has not celebrated Valentine's Day in twenty years, ever since a grisly killing took place.
BBFC:R — A — EN
Paramount — *CIC Video* **H, P**

---

456 (For Explanation of codes, see USE GUIDE and KEY)

PALADIN VIDEO HOME ENTERTAINMENT GUIDE

My Boys Are Good Boys   Fil-Ent '??
Drama
04548   85 mins   C
V2, B, V

Ralph Meeker, Ida Lupino, Lloyd Nolan, David F. Doyle, Sean T. Roche, directed by Bethel Buckalew

Three teenage boys successfully carry out their plan to break out of a maximum security prison, commit an armored truck robbery in broad daylight, and then get back into the prison without being detected.
A — EN
Ralph Meeker — *Intervision Video*   **H, P**
A-AE 0175

My Brilliant Career   Fil-Ent '80
Drama
06181   101 mins   C
V2, B, V

Judy Davis, Sam Neill, directed by Gill Armstrong

This story is set in the 1890's and centres on the life of a teenage girl who is very unhappy with her life. She is invited to live with her grandmother and meets a young man; their lives revolve around their frustrating passion for each other and a conflict of ambitions. Based on the novel by Mites Franklin.
BAFTA '81: Best Actress (Davis).
BBFC:U — *F — EN*
Margaret Fink Prod — *Guild Home Video*
H, P, E

My Champion   Fil-Ent '??
Drama
08704   104 mins   C
V2, B, V

Chris Mitchum, Yoko Shimada

Based on a true story about Miki Gorman, this film tells the story of a woman who faces a conflict between her family life and her will to win the New York Marathon.
BBFC:U — *F — EN*
Unknown — *Video Unlimited*   **H, P**
067

My Fair Lady   Fil-Ent '64
Musical
06495   164 mins   C
B, V

Audrey Hepburn, Rex Harrison, Stanley Holloway, Gladys Cooper, Wilfred Hyde-White, directed by George Cukor

Cockney flower girl Eliza Doolittle falls under the spell of a linguistics professor who plans to train her to pass as a lady. A glowing version of Lerner and Loewe's Broadway and West End success based on Shaw's 'Pygmalion.'
Academy Awards '64: Best Picture; Best Actor (Harrison); Best Director (Cukor).   *F — EN*
MGM — *MGM/UA Home Video*   **P**
UCB 10038/UCV 10038

My Favorite Martians   Fil-Ent '74
Cartoons/Adventure
09981   60 mins   C
B, V
Animated

This tape contains three cartoons. To begin with Uncle Martin and Andy catch a space allergy from meteoric dust, with Andy releasing some gravity defying sneezes before Uncle Martin finds a cure. Miss Casserole, Andy's school teacher, disappears, and finally, Andy misuses his special powers, wreaking havoc on all concerned.
F — EN
Filmation Associates — *Select Video Limited*
P
3615/43

My Favourite Year   Fil-Ent '82
Comedy
10159   88 mins   C
B, V, LV

Peter O'Toole, Mark Linn-Baker, Jessica Harper, directed by Richard Benjamin

This is a story centered around a television studio in the '50s. A legendary movie idol is forced to star in a show in order to pay his debts. As he is a rather unpredictable character, a young writer is assigned to keep him away from drink, girls and trouble. He, in turn, is pursued by an assistant producer.
BBFC:PG — *S,A — EN*
Brooksfilm Limited; Michael Gruskoff — *MGM/UA Home Video*   **P**
UMB 10271/UMV 10271/UMLV 10271

My Learned Friend   Fil-Ent '43
Comedy
01608   74 mins   B/W
B, V

Will Hay, Claude Hulbert, Mervyn Johns, directed by Basil Dearden and Will Hay

Two lawyers are always one jump behind a murderer, until they stop his attempt to blow up the House of Lords.
BBFC:U — *S,A — EN*
Ealing Studios; Michael Balcon — *THORN EMI*
P
TXE 90 0209 4/TVE 90 0209 2

(For Explanation of codes, see USE GUIDE and KEY)

PALADIN VIDEO HOME ENTERTAINMENT GUIDE

My Mother, the General Fil-Ent '79
War-Drama/Comedy
08087   76 mins   C
B, V
Gila Almagor, Zachi Noy
This film tells the story of a big hearted Jewish mother who descends on the Sinai battleground with a tank laden with goodies for her fighting husband and sons. She then encounters an Egyptian mother on a similar mission.
BBFC:A — S,A — EN
Golan—Globus; Noah Films — *Rank Video Library*   **H, P**
1040 C

My Name Is Mallory Fil-Ent '??
Western
06109   90 mins   C
V2, B, V
Robert Wood, Gabriella Giorgelli
A famous gunman plans to retire peacefully on a ranch. He has one more risk to take, to avenge the murder of his friend.
S,A — EN
Unknown — *Video Programme Distributors*   **P**
Cinehollywood—V1700

My Name Is Nobody Fil-Ent '75
Western
12187   115 mins   C
V2, B, V
Henry Fonda, Terence Hill
An aging, legendary gunfighter out to revenge his brother's death teams up with a younger, up and coming gunslinger.
BBFC:15 — S,A — EN
Sergio Leone; Fulvio Norsella — *Medusa Communications Ltd*   **H, P**

My Nights With....Susan, Olga, Julie, Albert, Piet and Sandra Fil-Ent '8?
Drama/Horror
09299   90 mins   C
B, V
Four girls live in a weird community on a farm. They are spied on by a man who lives there but prefers to watch through cracks in the walls. They also accept the village idiot but only one member of the community is sane, and as visitors begin to be murdered their insanity is horribly revealed.
A — EN
Unknown — *Abacus Video*   **P**
203

My Old Man Fil-Ent '83
Drama/Romance
12826   102 mins   C
B, V
Warren Oates, Kristy McNichol, Eileen Brennan, directed by John Erman
Based on an Ernest Hemingway short story, a rather disreputable horse-trainer comes back into the life of his fourteen-year-old daughter. They find affection for each other and romantic involvement outside themselves.
BBFC:PG — F — EN
Arcade Video — *VideoSpace Ltd*   **P**

My Pleasure is My Business Fil-Ent '74
Comedy
08815   96 mins   C
B, V
Xaviera Hollander, Henry Ramer, Kenny Lynch, directed by Albert S. Waxman
The authoress of 'The Happy Hooker' plays a sexy star who lampoons corrupt politics, investigative reporting, undercover detectives and international spies.
BBFC:X — A — EN
Brian Distributing — *VCL Video Services*   **P**
P296D

My Therapist Fil-Ent '8?
Comedy-Drama
10093   90 mins   C
B, V
Marilyn Chambers
Shot on location in California this film follows the adventures of a psychologist who helps men with their sexual problems. A country rock superstar, a construction worker and an unsavoury character with sadistic tendencies are some of her clients, but her enthusiasm for her job causes problems with her boyfriend, an athletic coach.
BBFC:18 — A — EN
Unknown — *VideoSpace Ltd*   **P**

My Tutor Fil-Ent '82
Romance/Comedy
12665   97 mins   C
V2, B, V
Matt Lattanzi, Caren Kaye, directed by George Bowers
When a young man flunks his French final his father hires a French lady tutor and he finds he is learning a lot more than French.
BBFC:18 — C,A — EN
Marilyn J Tenser; Michael D Castle — *Videomedia*   **P**
0804

My Wife Next Door Fil-Ent '84
Comedy-Drama
12728   86 mins   C

(For Explanation of codes, see USE GUIDE and KEY)

PALADIN VIDEO HOME ENTERTAINMENT GUIDE

B, V
John Alderton, Hannah Gordon
A feature length video from the first classic 70's comedy series of a newly separated couple trying to get away from it all, including each other, only to discover they have bought adjoining country cottages.
F — EN
Graeme Muir — *BBC Video*   **H, P**
7027

My Young Man   Fil-Ent '??
Drama
06110   105 mins   C
V2, B, V
Lee J. Cobb, James Whitmore, Marina Malfatti, Cyril Cusac, Adolfo Celi
A moving story of generosity and courage as a little boy desperately strives for love and life.
S,A — EN
Unknown — *Video Programme Distributors*
P
Cinehollywood—V270

Myra Breckenridge   Fil-Ent '70
Comedy
01289   100 mins   C
B, V
Mae West, Raquel Welch, John Huston, Rex Reed, Farrah Fawcett
A no-talent named Myron has a sex change operation and becomes Myra (Mae West). Based on Gore Vidal's book.
BBFC:X *— A — EN*
Twentieth Century Fox — *CBS/Fox Video*
P
3A-080

Mysteries from Beyond Earth   Fil-Ent '75
Parapsychology/Documentary
04389   90 mins   C
B, V
This documentary presents an insight into the bizarre world of the paranormal examined in the light of modern scientific techniques—featuring psychic phenomena, E.S.P., the Bermuda Triangle, witchcraft, and psychic healing.
F — EN
Cine Vue — *VCL Video Services*   **P**

Mysterious Heroes   Fil-Ent '79
Adventure/Martial arts
04413   90 mins   C
B, V
A young man becomes a Kung Fu hero in the tradition of his idol, who had won himself a great name only to be banished to the Wanghouse when his enemies plotted against him.
C,A — EN
Unknown — *VCL Video Services*   **P**

Mysterious Monsters, The   Gen-Edu '84
Documentary
13097   90 mins   C
B, V
This is an investigation into some of the world's elusive giant creatures and includes The Loch Ness Monster and the Abominable Snowman.
F — EN
Unknown — *Quadrant Video*   **H, P**
FF 7

Mysterious Two   Fil-Ent '82
Science fiction
08375   97 mins   C
V2, B, V
John Forsythe, James Stephens, Priscilla Pointer, Robert Pine, Karen Werner, Bruce French, Lauren Frost, Noah Beery, Vic Tayback
This film starts with a glowing pentagram of light landing in a desert outside New Mexico. From it emerges two people, he and she, their mission being to find the chosen people of tomorrow.
C,A — EN
Alan Landsberg Productions — *Guild Home Video*   **H, P, E**

N

Nabucco   Fil-Ent '8?
Opera
08656   145 mins   C
B, V
Renato Bruson, Ghena Dimitrova, Bruna Balgioni, Otavio Garaventa
This is an opera by Giuseppe Verdi recorded at the vast open air Roman Arena at Verona. It tells of the exiled Hebrews, containing the famous chorus Va pensiero, sung on the banks of the Euphrates. It is performed in four acts and conducted by Maurizio Arena.
S,A — EN
Unknown — *Longman Video*   **P**
LGBE 7003/LGVH 7003

Nadia   Fil-Ent '84
Drama
13767   99 mins   C

PALADIN VIDEO HOME ENTERTAINMENT GUIDE

B, V
Talia Balsam, Jonathan Banks, Joe Bennett, Simone Blue, Johann Carlo, Conchata Ferrell, Carrie Snodgrass, Carl Strano
This film is based on the life of Nadia Comaneci, depicting her victory at Montreal in 1976 when she won three gold medals at the Olympics to her years of decline afterwards and her recovery.
BBFC:U — F — EN
Dave Bell Productions; Tribune Entertainment Co; Jadran Film — *Odyssey Video*   **H, P**

Naked and the Dead, The—Target   Fil-Ent '5?
War-Drama/Western
05704   177 mins   C
B, V
Cliff Robertson, Raymond Massey, Aldo Ray, William Campbell, Richard Jaeckel, directed by Raoul Walsh, Tim Holt, Richard Martin, Walter Reed, directed by Stuart Gilmore
Two films are featured on one cassette. 'The Naked and the Dead' (colour, 123 mins, 1959) is set during the Pacific War and involves the lives and deaths of the US Infantry. A platoon led by an idealistic officer and sadistic sergeant go on a dangerous mission behind enemy lines.
'Target' (Black/White, 54 mins, 1953) involves a girl who disguises herself as a masked bandit to outwit a crook who is seizing land to sell to the railroad. She calls for the help of the hero and a friend to ensure justice is done.
S,A — EN
Warner Bros; RKO — *Kingston Video*   **H, P**
KV38

Naked Civil Servant, The   Fil-Ent '75
Drama
04650   88 mins   C
V2, B, V
John Hurt
The film biography of Londoner Quentin Crisp, an effeminate, flamboyant, but outspoken homosexual.
British Academy Awards '75: Best Actor (Hurt).
C,A — EN
Euston Films Production; Thames Video — *THORN EMI*   **H, P**
TPB 90 6206 3/TXB 90 6206 4/TVB 90 6206 2

Naked Exorcism   Fil-Ent '??
Horror
05466   84 mins   C
V2, B, V
Richard Conte
Set in Rome in 1976, a Priest is warning thousands of people that the Devil is amongst them. In a cave, a servant of Satan has enticed a young man to join the circle. He becomes violently ill. His sister, a Nun, calls in an 'exorcist' to rid her ailing brother of the demons. She is relieved when he succeeds but is suddenly aware that she has the dreaded mark of Satan and has to meet her Hell on Earth.
BBFC:X — A — EN
Unknown — *Iver Film Services*   **P**
110

Naked Fist   Fil-Ent '81
Crime-Drama/Martial arts
07677   90 mins   C
B, V
Jillian Kessner, Darby Hinton, Ken Metcalfe, Chanda Romero, Tony Ferrer, Vic Diaz, Reymond King, directed by Cirio H. Santiago
A US martial arts instructor travels to the Orient in search of her missing sister who had been working on a story for a newspaper by photographing suspicious activities at a club owned by gangsters. She uses her skills as an instructor to perform at the club but finds herself in the middle of a contraband operation, and, determined that she will discover no more, they send their own martial expert after her.
S,A — EN
New World Pictures — *Video Network*   **P**
0009

Naked Kiss, The   Fil-Ent '64
Drama
05738   95 mins   B/W
V2, B, V
Anthony Eisley, Constance Towers, Michael Dante
The story of a glamorous prostitute who begins a new life devoting herself to the care of handicapped children. She is jailed for the murder of her wealthy fiance when she discovers him molesting a child. The police persuade the child to reveal the story.
BBFC:A — S,A — EN
Allied Artists — *Video Unlimited*   **H, P**
006

Naked Truth, The   Fil-Ent '7?
Drama
02125   45 mins   C
V2, B, V
Apart from being a tribute to sexuality, this story gives a fascinating insight into the life style of a girl who considered her body beautiful and was happy to share it with the world.
A — EN
Unknown — *Hokushin Audio Visual Ltd*   **P**
VM-38

Naked Truth, The   Fil-Ent '57
Comedy-Drama
09922   92 mins   B/W

PALADIN VIDEO HOME ENTERTAINMENT GUIDE

B, V
Peter Sellers, Terry-Thomas, Peggy Mount, Dennis Price, Shirley Eaton
This is the comic story of the kidnapping and blackmailing of a scandal magazine publisher.
S,A — EN
Rank; Mario Zampi — *Rank Video Library*
H, P

Name for Evil, A   Fil-Ent '8?
Drama/Suspense
09290   100 mins   C
V
Robert Culp, Samantha Eggar, Sheila Sullivan
An architect, in an attempt to break away from the commercial world, takes his wife to an isolated, run-down mansion in the Deep South. The property was left to him by his great-great-grandfather, whose evil ghost still exists. The architect, unable to resolve his problems, is taken over by this spirit which urges him to kill his wife.
A — EN
Unknown — *Direct Video Services*   H, P

Nana   Fil-Ent '8?
Drama
08362   90 mins   C
V2, B, V
Katya Berger, Mandy Rice-Davies, Jean-Pierre Aumont, Debra Berger, Shirin Taylor, Yehuda Efroni, Paul Mueller
This tells the story of Nana, a young, beautiful and sensuous girl who seduces many men until she destroys a once noble and proud family. Based on the classic by Emile Zola.
BBFC:AA — C,A — EN
Golan Globus Production — *Guild Home Video*
H, P, E

Nancy Wilson   Fil-Ent '81
Music-Performance
04629   60 mins   C
B, V
Nancy Wilson performs some of her well known songs before a live audience.
F — EN
VCL Video Services Ltd — *VCL Video Services*
P

Naou Minal Nisaa (A Type   Fil-Ent '??
of Woman)
Drama
06734   102 mins   C
V2, B, V
A successful solicitor who is always broke because of women decides to marry a rich widow.
S,A — EN   AB
Unknown — *Intervision Video*   H, P
A-C 0153

Narrow Edge   Spo-Lei '82
Motorcycles
06846   65 mins   C   (PAL, NTSC)
V2, B, V
This film is the story of a full season of Grand Prix motorcycle racing. Following an introduction by six times world motorcycling champion Geoff Duke, attention is focussed on superstar Giacomo Agostini during 1974 when he switched to riding Yamahas from the Italian MV team. The film also features the impressive first season of Barry Sheene.
S,A — EN
CH Wood Ltd — *Duke Marketing Limited*
P
DM4

Nasser   Gen-Edu '??
Documentary
08001   60 mins   C
B, V
This is a documentary on the first Egyptian President, Gamal Abdel Nasser, and the history of Egypt. Produced entirely in Arabic with an English voice over.
S,A — ED   EL, AB
Unknown — *Motion Epics Video Company Ltd*
P

Natas   Fil-Ent '83
Drama/Horror
13410   90 mins   C
V2, B, V
A newspaper reporter who is obsessed with a nightmare legend, searches for the source of the story and stumbles onto a ghost town full of ghouls.
BBFC:18 — A — EN
Unknown — *Intervision Video*   H, P
0001

National Lampoon's   Fil-Ent '83
Class Reunion
Comedy
12735   84 mins   C
B, V
Directed by Michael Miller

PALADIN VIDEO HOME ENTERTAINMENT GUIDE

A High School reunion party turns into a hilarious send-up of a horror movie with the popular 'National Lampoon' team.
BBFC:18 — A — EN
Matty Simmons — Rank Video Library   **H, P**
1076 Y

National Lampoon's Vacation   Fil-Ent '83
Comedy
12490   95 mins   C
B, V
Beverley D'Angelo, Imogene Coca, Randy Quaid, directed by Harold Ramis
A man driving his wife and two children from Chicago to California to visit a fabulous amuzement park gets involved in a series of misadventures.
BBFC:15 — F — EN
Matty Simmons — Warner Home Video   **P**
61315

Natural, The   Fil-Ent '84
Drama
13659   122 mins   C
B, V
Robert Redford, Robert Duvall, Glenn Close, Kim Bassinger, directed by Barry Levinson
The promising career of an ambitious young baseball player comes to an end after a meeting with a strange woman and a cruel clash with fate but years later he appears again set on making a comeback.
BBFC:PG — S,A — EN
Mark Johnson — CBS/Fox Video   **P**
6732

Natural Enemies   Fil-Ent '79
Drama
08621   100 mins   C
V2, B, V
Hal Holbrook, Louise Fletcher, Jose Fecrer, Viveca Lindfors, Patricia Elliot
This film tells the story of a 48-year-old man, the successful publisher of a respected magazine. He owns a beautiful, old new England house, is apparently happily married with three healty children. However, one day he unsuspectingly plans to kill his family and himself.
S,A — EN
Cinema 5 — Hokushin Audio Visual Ltd   **P**
VM 66

Nazareth—Live   Fil-Ent '??
Music-Performance
08841   58 mins   C
B, V
This tape features the Scottish rock group Nazareth performing live on stage. Some of the tracks included are 'Love Hurts', 'Razamanaz', 'Telegram', 'Hair of the Dog' and 'Expect No Mercy'.
C,A — EN
Unknown — VCL Video Services   **P**
Z254G

Nearly No Christmas   Fil-Ent '7?
Fantasy/Christmas
09051   60 mins   C
V
Michael Haigh, Mildred Woods, John Banas, John Bach
This is a Christmas pantomine which tells the story of one of Santa's Christmases. The boiler Rumbletum which drives the toy machines in the workshop blows a valve just before Christmas. Mrs. Santa and The elves struggle to keep toy production going using a manual generator with the help from the penguin colony, whilst Santa goes off to try and raise the money for a new valve.
F — EN
Unknown — Astra Video   **H, P**

Needles of Death   Fil-Ent '7?
Adventure/Martial arts
04606   89 mins   C
V2, B, V
A poor young man, Hung, takes lessons in the ancient arts with a kung-fu master. He learns quickly and soon develops a new and terrifyingly deadly technique known as 'The Flying Bolt.' He becomes feared and unwanted by all around until he gets the chance to save the community from ruthless smugglers using the feared 'Flying Bolt.'
C,A — EN
Unknown — Video Programme Distributors   **P**
Inter-Ocean—044

Neil Diamond—Love at the Greek   Fil-Ent '76
Music-Performance
12876   52 mins   C
B, V
This recording in stereo from the Los Angeles' Greek Theatre, includes some of Neil Diamond's greatest songs such as 'Sweet Caroline,' 'I Am I Said,' 'Song Sung Blue,' 'Play Me' and 'Holly Holy.'
F — EN
Arch Angel Television Inc — Vestron Video International   **P**
11005

PALADIN VIDEO HOME ENTERTAINMENT GUIDE

Neither the Sea Nor the Sand
Fil-Ent '7?
Romance/Drama
04198   94 mins   C
B, V
Susan Hampshire, Michael Petrovitch
A love story with a difference, which is sinister and macabre and yet beautiful and touching.
BBFC:AA — C,A — EN
Unknown — *Guild Home Video*   **H, P**

Neopolitan Carousel
Fil-Ent '53
Adventure
07763   126 mins   C
V2, B, V
Sophia Loren, Nadia Gray
An entertaining and musical film about Naples, detailing its history of life, drama and comedy through the ages.
S,A — EN
Italy — *Fletcher Video*   **H, P**
V155

Neptune Disaster, The
Fil-Ent '73
Adventure
12258   98 mins   C
B, V
Ben Gazzara, Yvette Mimieux, Walter Pidgeon, Ernest Borgnine, directed by Daniel Petrie
The captain of a deep diving submersible who is sent to the aid of a team of oceanographers who are trapped in a deep underwater cave finds he has to fight his way through a breed of giant sea animals.
M,A — EN
Sanford Howard; 20th Century Fox — *CBS/Fox Video*   **P**
1201

Network
Fil-Ent '76
Drama
01268   121 mins   C
V2, B, V
Faye Dunaway, Peter Finch, William Holden, Robert Duvall, Wesley Addy, Ned Beatty, Beatrice Straight, directed by Sidney Lumet
A satire of television and the men behind the networks.
Academy Awards '76: Best Actor (Finch); Best Actress (Dunaway); Best Supporting Actress (Straight); Best Screenplay Written Directly for the Screen (Chayefsky).
BBFC:AA — S,A — EN
MGM — *Intervision Video*   **H**
UA A B 5018

Never a Dull Moment
Fil-Ent '68
Comedy
12584   87 mins   C
B, V
Dick Van Dyke, Edward G Robinson
A struggling New York actor tries to evade a young hoodlum who mistakes him for a notorious mobster and is then forced to continue playing his role.
F — EN
Walt Disney Productions — *Rank Video Library*   **H**
135

Never Cry Wolf
Fil-Ent '83
Documentary/Wildlife
13442   103 mins   C
B, V
Charlie Martin Smith, directed by Carroll Ballard
The true-life drama of biologist Farley Mowat who lived in the arctic wastes of Northern Canada to study the habits of wolves and finds a deep affinity with the creatures and their environment.
BBFC:PG — S,A — EN
Walt Disney Productions — *Rank Video Library*   **P**
VW 182

Never Say Never Again
Fil-Ent '83
Drama
12677   130 mins   C
B, V
Sean Connery, Klaus Maria Brandauer, Barbara Carrera, Kim Basinger, Edward Fox, directed by Irvin Kershner
Sean Connery is once again James Bond, and looking as suave and courageous as ever, he is forced to use all his initiative to thwart the evil SPECTRE from devastating the world in a nuclear holocaust.
BBFC:PG — F — EN
Jack Schwartzman — *Warner Home Video*   **P**
61337

Never to Love
Fil-Ent '40
Drama
04171   74 mins   B/W
B, V
Maureen O'Hara, Adolphe Menjou
Strange circumstances force a young girl to renounce marriage, while urging her mother to marry the man she loves.
BBFC:A — S,A — EN
Selznick — *Guild Home Video*   **H, P**

Neville Marriner Conducts The Academy of St. Martin in the Fields at Longleat
Fin-Art '83
Music-Performance
09786   55 mins   C

(For Explanation of codes, see USE GUIDE and KEY)   463

PALADIN VIDEO HOME ENTERTAINMENT GUIDE

B, V
Neville Marriner, directed by Dave Heather
The historic home of Longleat is the setting for this programme of popular classics including the works of Greig, Handel, Pachelbel, Mozart, Borodin, Rossini, Bach, and Gluck.
F — EN
EMI Records Ltd — *THORN EMI*   **P**
TXE 90 1962 4/TVE 90 1962 2

New Adventures of Heidi, The   Fil-Ent '78
Musical
12251   100 mins   C
B, V
Burl Ives, Katy Kurtzman
Heidi's life changes drastically when her grandfather is given up for dead in a blizzard and she goes to live with her best friend in the city.
F — EN
Pierre Cossette Enterprises; NBC — *VCL Video Services*   **P**
P371D

New Barbarians, The   Fil-Ent '8?
Science fiction/Horror
09903   91 mins   C
B, V
Timothy Brent, Fred Williamson, George Eastman, Anna Kanakis, Thomas Moore
Civilisation has ended after the Great Nuclear catastrophe, when merciless marauders in motorised metal monsters roam the wastes inflicting a reign of terror.
BBFC:18 — *A — EN*
Unknown — *Entertainment in Video*   **H, P**
EVB 1007/EVV 1007

New Black Emanuelle   Fil-Ent '??
Romance
08903   85 mins   C
V2, B, V
Don Powell, Emanuelle Nera
Having been wounded in the Libyan war, Emanuelle is nursed back to health by a Professor. Problems arise when his drug addicted niece arrives.
BBFC:X — *A — EN*
Unknown — *Video Programme Distributors*
P
Inter-Ocean 015

New Edition-The Videosingles   Fil-Ent '8?
Music-Performance/Video
09876   16 mins   C
B, V
This comprises four tracks from this talented group of school children; 'Candy Girl', 'Popcorn Love', 'She Gives Me a Bang' and 'Is This the End'. Recorded in stereo.
F — EN
Unknown — *Polygram Video*   **H, P**
040 1934/040 1932

New Good Birth Guide, The   Med-Sci '83
Childbirth
10023   120 mins   C
B, V
Sheila Kitzinger
This entertaining and informative programme deals with the many questions that prospective mothers and fathers need answered in order for them to make responsible decisions as to how and where their babies are born.
A — ED
Irving Rappaport — *Palace Video Ltd*   **P**
PVC 2062A

New Life in the Garden   How-Ins '79
Gardening
04425   60 mins   C
B, V
Recorded at Wisley, the Royal Horticultural Society's Garden, director Chris Brickell demonstrates all the major means of propagation, from sowing seeds to taking cuttings and grafting.
A — I
Michael Barratt — *Michael Barratt Ltd*   **P**

New Mafia Boss, The   Fil-Ent '7?
Crime-Drama
13730   90 mins   C
V2, B, V
Telly Savalas, Antonio Sabato, directed by Albert de Martino
A Mafia hitman challenges the head of the organization in his ruthless path to the top and finds himself branded a traitor.
BBFC:15 — *S,A — EN*
Claudia Cinematography — *Medusa Communications Ltd*   **H, P**
MC 043

New View of Space   Med-Sci '72
Space exploration
01112   28 mins   C
B, V, PH15, PH17, 3/4U
A visually dynamic look into the uses of photography in the space programme.
C,A — ED
NASA — *Istead Audio Visual*   **P**
HQ 214

PALADIN VIDEO HOME ENTERTAINMENT GUIDE

New Years Evil
Fil-Ent '81
Mystery/Suspense
06942   86 mins   C
B, V
The tension mounts as a live phone-in TV show tracks the New Year activities of a crazed murderer.
BBFC:X — A — EN
Menahem Golan; Yoram Globus — *Rank Video Library*   **H, P**
2016C

New York After Midnight
Fil-Ent '??
Drama
08682   96 mins   C
V2, B, V
John Ferris
After a brilliant but lonely career, a woman meets and marries a man. Initially they are happy, but after a while she is troubled by flashes in her head. During therapy a strange and recurring nightmare is revealed. She becomes tormented by her husband's frequent absence and refusal to have a child. One night she becomes insane and races through the streets, leaving a trail of horror.
BBFC:X — A — EN
Unknown — *Derann Film Services*   **P**
FCV 600

New York City Ballet, The
Fin-Art '74
Dance
01184   114 mins   C
B, V
New York City Ballet
The New York City Ballet performs three dances choreographed by George Balanchine: Tchaikovsky's 'Serenade for Strings,' Bizet's 'Symphony in C,' and Brahms' 'Liebeslieder Waltzes.'
F — EN
RM Prods — *Polygram Video*   **P**

New York Mystery
Fil-Ent '43
Comedy/Adventure
06308   59 mins   B/W
V2, B, V
The East Side Kids
This film is a situation comedy set in a tough quarter of New York City. The leader of a young gang posing as a junior reporter becomes involved in a murder mystery; a socialite is accused of the killing. With the help of his gang and some hectic car chases they unmask the real culprit.
F — EN
Monogram — *World of Video 2000*   **H, P**
GF514

New York Nights
Fil-Ent '83
Drama
09892   109 mins   C
B, V
This film involves a chain of nine overlapping love affairs, involving rock stars, a photographer, a prostitute and debutantes, all of them glamorously attractive. Filmed in over 40 New York hotspots the film weaves a believable jet set fantasy.
BBFC:18 — A — EN
Unknown — *Brent Walker Home Video Ltd*
P

Newman Numan
Fil-Ent '8?
Music-Performance
08976   45 mins   C
B, V
Gary Numan, Paul Gardiner, Cedric Sharpley, Chris Payne, Russell Bell, Billy Currie, Dennis Haines, Mick Karn, John Webb, Pino Palladino, Chris Slade, Roger Mason
This tape contains the videos of Gary Numan's hits, made for 'Top of the Pops' and similar shows. It includes the following songs: 'The 1930's Rust', 'I Die: You Die', 'Music for Chameleons', 'Cars', 'She's Got Claws', 'We Take Mystery', 'Complex', 'Love Needs No Disguise', 'Down in the Park', 'Are Friends Electric', 'This Wreckage' and 'We Are Glass'.
S,A — EN
Beggars Banquet; Machine Music — *Palace Video Ltd*   **P**
PVC 3003M

Newsfront
Fil-Ent '78
Drama
05746   110 mins   C
B, V
Bill Hunter, Wendy Hughes, Gerard Kennedy, directed by Phil Nayce
A story set during the migration of people to Australia in the 1950s. The film is a blend of fictional and film documentary material; the events of the time are portrayed through the lives of two brothers, one a film cameraman and the other a newspaper boss, combined with actual footage of political, social and sporting events.
BBFC:A — M,A — EN
Palm Beach Pictures; New South Wales Film Corp; Australian Film Comm — *Home Video Holdings*   **H, P**
017

Next Man, The
Fil-Ent '76
Drama/Suspense
08057   104 mins   C
B, V
Sean Connery, Cornelia Sharpe, Albert Paulsen, Adolpho Celi, Charles Cioffi directed by Richard C. Sarafian

---

(For Explanation of codes, see USE GUIDE and KEY)

PALADIN VIDEO HOME ENTERTAINMENT GUIDE

Kalil Abdul Muhsen is the man that holds the power to gain lasting peace in the Middle East. The three men that shared his opinion have all been assassinated. The beautiful young woman, an assassin, has him next on her list.
BBFC:X — A — EN
Allied Artists — Rank Video Library   H, P
0092 C

Next One, The   Fil-Ent '83
Drama/Fantasy
12622   100 mins   C
V2, B, V
Keir Dullea, Adrienne Barbeau
A strange visitor suddenly materialises on a beautiful Greek Island and is taken in by a small boy and his mother. His childlike innocence of daily life contrasts with his wisdom, the wisdom of ancients, but one man sets about to plot his downfall.
BBFC:15 — F — EN
Unknown — VideoSpace Ltd   P

Nicholas Nickelby   Fil-Ent '47
Drama
01004   106 mins   B/W
B, V
Derek Bond, Sir Cedric Hardwicke, Mary Merrall, Sally Ann Howes, Stanley Holloway, Sybil Thorndike
A young man tries to save his family and the girl he loves from the machinations of his evil uncle. Based on the novel by Charles Dickens.
F — EN
Ealing Studios; Michael Balcon — THORN EMI   P
TXE 90 0013 4/TVE 90 0013 2

Nickelodeon   Fil-Ent '76
Comedy
04660   117 mins   C
B, V
Burt Reynolds, Ryan O'Neal, Brian Keith, Tatum O'Neal, directed by Peter Bogdanovich
In 1910, several characters come together to make films, and finally attend the 1915 opening in Hollywood of 'Birth of a Nation.'
F — EN
Columbia; EMI; Chartoff-Winkler — THORN EMI   H, P
TXC 90 0235 4/TVC 90 0235 2

Night at the Opera, A   Fil-Ent '35
Comedy
07957   88 mins   B/W
B, V
The Marx Brothers, Allan Jones, Kitty Carlisle
The Marx Brothers blunder through the world of high society, creating a near riot aboard ship, a scandal in New York and an evening of insanity in a concert hall.
F — EN
MGM — MGM/UA Home Video   P
UMB 10009/UMV 10009

Night Before Christmas, The   Fil-Ent '81
Cartoons/Christmas
08877   30 mins   C
V2, B, V
Animated
This tells the story of the famous visit from St. Nicholas during the night before Christmas.
BBFC:U — F — EN
Bill Turnball; Playhouse Pictures — Video Programme Distributors   P
Media 313

Night Bombers   Fil-Ent '81
World War II/Documentary
05901   60 mins   C
B, V
Directed by Air Cdre H.I. Cozens
Using actual film shots at the time, this is the record of one of the nightly raids made on Germany by the RAF Bomber Command in the winter of 1943-44.
F — EN
EMI — THORN EMI   P
TXC 90 4002 4/TVC 90 4002 2

Night Creature   Fil-Ent '77
Horror
04549   83 mins   C
V2, B, V
Donald Pleasance, Nancy Kwan, Ross Hagen
A renowned writer-philosopher plans to stalk a vicious black leopard. When he comes face to face with the animal he is unable to use his gun and is mauled on the leg. Determined to get over his fear he has the leopard brought to his private estate. While hunting the animal there, his two daughters and granddaughter arrive. One of the daughters and the granddaughter go looking for their dog who has been missing all afternoon. Suddenly the leopard appears. The granddaughter runs and hides but the daughter is terrorised by the leopard—stalking, attacking, letting her go, then attacking again, before finally killing her.
C,A — EN
Lee Madden Assoc Prods — Intervision Video   H, P
A-AE 0285

PALADIN VIDEO HOME ENTERTAINMENT GUIDE

Night Crossing   FII-Ent '81
Adventure/Drama
12578   104 mins   C
B, V
John Hurt, Beau Bridges, Jane Alexander, Glynnis O'Connor
This is the story of two families' flight to freedom in a hand-crafted hot air balloon from East to West Germany.
F — EN
Walt Disney Productions — *Rank Video Library*
H
090

Night God Screamed, The   FII-Ent '??
Horror
06176   85 mins   C
V2, B, V
Jeanne Crain, Alex Nicol, Daniel Spelling, Michael Sugich, Barbara Hancock, Dawn Cleary, Gary Morgan, Stewart Bradley, Corinne Conley
A woman testifies against the leader of an outlaw religious band for hideously killing her husband and he vows vengeance. She is now working for the Judge and reluctantly agrees to look after his three teenage children for the weekend in an isolated country house. The events that follow are horrific; trapped in the house, death seems the only way out.
BBFC:AA — *S,A* — *EN*
Carlin-Lasky Prod — *Guild Home Video*
H, P, E

Night Moves   FII-Ent '75
Mystery
06052   96 mins   C
B, V
Gene Hackman, Susan Clark, Jennifer Warren, Edward Binns, Harris Yilin, Melanie Griffith, directed by Arthur Penn
A Hollywood detective assigned to track down a missing teenager in the Florida Keys area uncovers information about a bizarre smuggling operation.
BBFC:X — *A* — *EN*
Warner Brothers — *Warner Home Video*
P
WEX1102/WEV1102

Night of the Assassin, The   FII-Ent '75
War-Drama
05488   90 mins   C
V2, B, V
Michael Craig, Eva Renzi, Klaus Kinsky, Adolpho Celi, George Sanders, Margaret Lee, directed by Robert McMahon
Set during the height of terrorist activity in Cyprus, the U.N. Secretary is due to arrive to initiate peace talks. A Lieutenant Colonel is captured by the underground movement and is forced to sign a statement that he plotted to kill the U.N. Secretary. He escapes with the leader of the movement who is threatened, and in a shootout they blow-up a guerilla munitions boat. Now a hero, he denounces war and politics, walking out on fame and glory.
BBFC:A — *S,A* — *EN*
Producing Artists — *Iver Film Services*   **P**

Night of the Big Heat   FII-Ent '72
Science fiction
02414   94 mins   C
V2, B, V
Christopher Lee, Peter Cushing, Patrick Allen, directed by Terence Fisher
During November, with the temperature in the nineties and still rising, scientists try to discover the cause as the area is thrown into electrical chaos and telephones fail. An ear-shattering noise fills the air when alien creatures are found that even dynamite cannot stop.
BBFC:X — *A* — *EN*
Maron Films Ltd — *Rank Video Library*
H, P
2021 C

Night of the Bloody Apes   FII-Ent '7?
Horror/Suspense
08029   82 mins   C
V2, B, V
Jose Elias Moreno, Armando Silvestre, Carlos Lopez Moctezuma, Norma Lazareno, Augustin Solares, directed by Rene Cardona
This is the horrific story of an experimental transplant, the donor being an ape, which goes terribly wrong in a desperate attempt to save a boy's life. A mutant, half ape, half man is produced which then escapes and causes havoc in a small town.
BBFC:X — *A* — *EN*
Unknown — *Iver Film Services*   **P**
218

Night of the Demon   FII-Ent '??
Horror
07605   95 mins   C
V2, B, V
Michael J Cutt, Joy Allen, Bob Collins, Jodi Lazarus, Richard Fields, Michael Lang, Melanie Graham, directed by James C Watson
A professor insists that the legend of 'Big Foot' is true after he has been brutally attacked in a forest. Horrific incidents are recalled in flashback: the vicious murder of a fisherman, the mutilation of a couple in a car and the horrendous death of a motorcyclist. A group from the university set out to solve the mystery.

PALADIN VIDEO HOME ENTERTAINMENT GUIDE

They disturb a Black Magic ritual and force the truth from a hermit. She had been raped by the monster and given birth to a mutation. The group are trapped and killed by the demon.
A — EN
Unknown — Iver Film Services   P
173

Night of the Generals   Fil-Ent '66
War-Drama
12470   137 mins   C
B, V
Peter O'Toole, Omar Sharif, Christopher Plummer, Donald Pleasance
The story of a manhunt for a psychopathic sex killer set against a background of the Nazi occupation in Warsaw and Paris during World War II.
BBFC:PG — S,A — EN
Columbia — RCA/Columbia Pictures Video UK
H, P
10199

Night of the Juggler   Fil-Ent '80
Suspense
08853   96 mins   C
B, V
James Brolin, Cliff Gorman, Richard Castellano, Mandy Patinkin, directed by Robert Butler
This film tells the story of a dangerous plan to kidnap the daughter of a wealthy family. This, however, goes wrong, getting the daughter of an ex-policeman instead.
BBFC:X — A — EN
Columbia '— VCL Video Services   P
M262D

Night of the Living Dead   Fil-Ent '68
Horror
06762   91 mins   B/W
V2, B, V
Judith O'Dea, Duane Jones, directed by George A. Romero
Space radiation causes the recently dead to come back to life and there is only one thing that will satisfy their hunger—human flesh.
A — EN
Continental — Intervision Video   H, P
A-A 0356

Night on the Town, A   Fil-Ent '??
Musical
09894   ? mins   C
B, V
Lewis Collins, Eartha Kitt, Ann Reinking, Elaine Paige, Frank Gorshin, Bobby Short
This show is a fantasy journey through the great songs and cities of the 1930's, with the music of Cole Porter, George Gershwin, Noel Coward and Irving Berlin. It features songs such as 'Anything Goes', 'Night and Day', 'Putting on the Ritz' and a special new interpretation of 'An American in Paris'.
F — EN
Unknown — Brent Walker Home Video Ltd
P

Night Partners   Fil-Ent '??
Crime-Drama/Suspense
09367   98 mins   C
B, V
Yvette Mimieux, Diana Canova, Arlen Dean Snyder, Emmet Walsh, Patricia McCormack, Patricia Davis
Based on a true story, this is the suspenseful tale of two housewives who volunteer to help victims of crime in their small California town. Their personal involvement with two rape victims leads them onto the trail of a dangerous criminal who will stop at nothing to protect himself from the law.
BBFC:15 — C,A — EN
Unknown — Precision Video Ltd   P
BITC 2139/VITC 2139

Night Patrol   Fil-Ent '84
Comedy
13652   82 mins   C
B, V
Linda Blair, Pat Paulsen, Jaye P. Morgan, Jack Riley, Billy Barty, Murray Langston, directed by Jackie Kong
A police officer who doubles up as an 'unknown comic' at night is assigned to catch 'The Bagman' thief who robs bars with a paper bag over his head.
BBFC:18 — A — EN
William Osco — CBS/Fox Video   P
3082

Night Stalker, The   Fil-Ent '71
Mystery
04170   73 mins   C
B, V
Darren McGavin, Carol Lynley, Simon Oakland, Ralph Meeker
A Las Vegas newspaperman investigates a series of murders which have baffled the local police.
BBFC:X — A — EN
Aaron Spelling Prods — Guild Home Video
H, P

Night Strangler, The   Fil-Ent '72
Suspense/Drama
04169   90 mins   C
B, V
Darren McGavin, Jo Ann Pflug, Simon Oakland, Wally Cox, Scott Brady, Margaret Hamilton

PALADIN VIDEO HOME ENTERTAINMENT GUIDE

This gripping sequel to 'The Night Stalker' features Carl Kolchak, a crusading newsman, and a 120-year-old killer.
BBFC:A — S,A — EN
Aaron Spelling Dan Curtis Prods — *Guild Home Video* **H, P**

Night The Lights Went Out In Georgia, The Fil-Ent '81
Drama
08338   115 mins   C
V2, B, V, LV
Kristy McNichol, Dennis Quaid, Mark Hamill, Don Stroud
This film is based on the popular hit song. It tells of a brother and sister trying to cash in on the country music scene in Nashville.
BBFC:U — F — EN
Elliot Geisinger; Howard Kuperman; Ronald Saland; Howard Smith — *Embassy Home Entertainment*   **P**
2026

Night the Prowler, The Fil-Ent '??
Drama
09378   92 mins   C
B, V
Written by Patrick White, directed by Jim Sharman
When the strange teenage daughter is interrupted in her sleep by a would-be rapist, she turns the tables on him. Grabbing the man's knife she casually smokes a cigar while forcing him to take a drink, then ejects him from house. It is only then that she cries 'rape'.
BBFC:15 — C,A — EN
Unknown — *Precision Video Ltd*   **P**
BSWPV 2606/VSWPV 2606

Night They Robbed Big Bertha's, The Fil-Ent '??
Comedy/Mystery
06892   85 mins   C
V2, B, V
Robert Nichols, Hetty Galen, Doug Hale, Gary Allen, Bill Moses, Josie Johnson, Frank Natasi, Directed by Peter J. Kares
Set in a small town outside Atlanta City this film revolves around a 'House' run by the Professor and Big Bertha whose good reputation is tarnished when their clients are robbed.
A — EN
Sidney Ginsberg — *European Video Company*   **P**

Night to Remember, A Fil-Ent '58
Drama
01895   123 mins   B/W
B, V
Kenneth More, Honor Blackman, Michael Goodliffe, David McCallum, directed by Roy Baker
In April 1912 the Titanic sank with the loss of 1500 passengers and crew. The film depicts the drama, the heroism, and the horror of the night the unthinkable happened.
BBFC:U — F — EN
Rank — *Rank Video Library*   **H, P**
0003

Night Train Murders Fil-Ent '78
Mystery/Drama
06309   89 mins   C
V2, B, V
This is a thriller involving rape, murder and reprisal set on the famous Trans-Europe Express.
S,A — EN
Unknown — *World of Video 2000*   **H, P**
GFS06

Night with Lou Reed, A Fil-Ent '83
Music-Performance
12468   60 mins   C
B, V
Lou Reed, Fred Maher, Fernando Saunders, Robert Quine
A visual record of Lou Reed's sell-out homecoming concert at The Bottom Line in New York City.
BBFC:PG — F — EN
Bill Boggs; Richard Baker; RCA Video Productions — *RCA/Columbia Pictures Video UK*   **H, P**
10231

Nightcomers, The Fil-Ent '72
Drama/Suspense
08335   96 mins   C
V2, B, V, LV
Marlon Brando, Stephanie Beacham, Harry Andrews, Thora Hird, Directed by Michael Winner
This film tells the story of two orphaned children. They both view death as a reunion of loved ones, which is the reason they have to murder their governess and her loved one.
C,A — EN
AVCO Embassy — *Embassy Home Entertainment*   **P**
2027

Nightingale, the Fil-Ent '??
Drama/Puppets
08543   35 mins   C
B, V
Richard Goolden, Mandy Carlin, John Dalby, directed by Christine Edzard

---

(For Explanation of codes, see USE GUIDE and KEY)

PALADIN VIDEO HOME ENTERTAINMENT GUIDE

This tells the story of the Emperor of China, a Hans Christian Andersen tale. He lives in a beautiful palace with perfect surroundings. It is only the kitchen girl that knows the most beautiful thing is the song of a nightingale. The Emperor prefers a jewel encrusted mechanical imitation. However, on his death-bed the Emperor realises his mistake.
M,A — EN
Unknown — *THORN EMI* P
TXE 90 0847 4/TVE 90 0847 2

Nightingale Sang in Berkeley Square, A   Fil-Ent '8?
Crime-Drama
08988   90 mins   C
B, V
David Niven, Richard Jordan, Elke Sommer, Oliver Tobias
This film gives an exciting and sometimes humorous view of the world of crime.
S,A — EN
Unknown — *Polygram Video* P
791 537

Nightmare City   Fil-Ent '??
Horror
07800   ? mins   C
B, V
An unidentified plane lands at a major airport despite having been refused permission to land. The occupants have been subjected to horrific nuclear contamination causing the flesh to die on their bones. They wreak havoc as they kill to get the plasma to keep them alive. A reporter tries to contain the infection as the mutants advance on the town.
S,A — EN
Unknown — *Video Tape Centre* P
VTC 1006

Nightmares   Fil-Ent '83
Suspense
12044   95 mins   C
B, V
Christina Raines, directed by Joseph Sargent
This film features four stories; the first of a young woman venturing out at night on her own, the second about a computer buff who spends his time in video arcades, the third of a troubled priest who has lost his faith and the fourth is about the occupants of a suburban house troubled by rats.
BBFC:15 — S,A — EN
Universal — *CIC Video*   H, P
BEA 1091/VHA 1091

Nights of Cabiria   Fil-Ent '57
Drama
08560   106 mins   B/W
B, V
Giulietta Masina, Francois Perier, Amedeo Nazzari, directed by Federico Fellini
This film tells the story of a prostitute who dreams of a rich, beautiful life but who constantly meets with disaster. She throws herself into many love affairs in the hope of securing a happy marriage and family. However, many of the men inevitably abuse her.
BBFC:X — A — EN
Famous Films — *THORN EMI*   P
TXB 90 0834 4/TVB 90 0834 2

Nik Kershaw—Single Pictures   Fil-Ent '84
Music video
13329   20 mins   C
B, V
This four track collection features the songs 'Wouldn't It be Good,' 'I Won't Let the Sun Go Down on Me,' 'Dancing Girls' and 'Human Racing' written and performed by Nik Kershaw.
F — EN
Unknown — *CIC Video*   H, P
MCB 101/MCV 101

Nina von Pallandt   Fil-Ent '81
Music-Performance
04630   30 mins   C
B, V
Nina von Pallandt provides a glimpse into her world of song.
F — EN
VCL Video Services Ltd — *VCL Video Services* P

Nine Ages of Nakedness   Fil-Ent '72
Drama
02404   89 mins   C
B, V
Directed by Harrison Marks
Beauties from the Stone Age to the Computer Age reveal their seductive dreams in this story of the 'history of passion.'
A — EN
Charles Band — *Derann Film Services*
H, P
DV 111B/DV 111

Nine Lives of Fritz the Cat, The   Fil-Ent '74
Cartoons
09830   72 mins   C
V2, B, V
Animated

470   (For Explanation of codes, see USE GUIDE and KEY)

PALADIN VIDEO HOME ENTERTAINMENT GUIDE

This adult cartoon follows the coolest cat in the world through drug orgies, race wars and outer space.
BBFC:X — A — EN
Steven Krantz — *Polygram Video* **H, P**
791 5205/791 5204/791 5202

---

9 to 5 Fil-Ent '80
Comedy
07708   105 mins   C
V2, B, V, LV
Jane Fonda, Lily Tomlin, Dolly Parton, Dabney Coleman, Sterling Hayden, Elizabeth Wilson, Henry Jones, Lawrence Pressman, directed by Colin Higgins
A divorcee arrives at Consolidated Companies to take up a new job. She and two other girls dream of what they would do to their tyrannical boss. When she nearly kills him they decide to kidnap him. They manage to take command and make the office a haven for office girl libbers and boost business no end. When the boss escapes he is congratulated, promoted and sent to Brazil. The girls are left in control.
S,A — EN
Twentieth Century Fox — *CBS/Fox Video*
H
1099

1980 1000 Lakes Rally Spo-Lei '80
Automobiles-Racing
05600   30 mins   C
B, V
A special sports feature for Car Rally enthusiasts featuring the 1980 1000 Lakes Car Rally.
F — EN
Salora; Vintage Television — *Vintage Television Ltd*   **H, P, E**

1980 Mintex International Rally Spo-Lei '80
Automobiles-Racing
01273   60 mins   C
B, V
Highlights from twelve different locations of the 1980 Mintex International Rally, featuring the top 20 competitors, are contained in this programme.
F — EN
Vintage Television — *Vintage Television Ltd*
H, P, E

1981 Circuit of Ireland Rally Spo-Lei '81
Automobiles-Racing
05601   37 mins   C
B, V
A special sports feature for Car Rally enthusiasts featuring the 1981 Circuit of Ireland Rally.
F — EN
Vintage Television — *Vintage Television Ltd*
H, P, E

1981 Manx Rally Spo-Lei '81
Automobiles-Racing
05602   35 mins   C
B, V
A special sports feature for Car Rally enthusiasts featuring the 1981 Manx Rally
F — EN
Vintage Television — *Vintage Television Ltd*
H, P, E

1981 Military Musical Pageant, The Fil-Ent '81
Music-Performance/Parades and festivals
06221   90 mins   C
B, V
In the presence of HRH The Prince of Wales and the Lady Diana Spencer, over 1,800 marching bandsmen cram into the huge arena of Wembley Stadium. Forty eight Regimental and Staff bands perform an astonishingly wide repertoire of popular and military music.
F — EN
VCL Production — *VCL Video Services*
P
I196C

1981 1000 Lakes Rally Spo-Lei '81
Automobiles-Racing
05599   40 mins   C
B, V
A special sports feature for Car Rally enthusiasts featuring the 1981 1000 Lakes Car Rally.
F — EN
Vintage Television — *Vintage Television Ltd*
H, P, E

1941 Fil-Ent '79
Comedy/War-Drama
10107   114 mins   C
B, V
John Belushi, Tim Matheson, Nancy Allen, Dan Aykroyd, Toshiro Mifune, Christopher Lee, Murray Hamilton, Ned Beatty, Warren Oates, Robert Stack, Slim Pickens, directed by Steven Spielberg
Los Angeles is thrown into chaos when, six days after Pearl Harbour, a sudden power failure occurs when a Japanese submarine is sighted off the coast. A wealth of eccentrics cause mayhem in just 24 hours. A pilot is determined to destroy the first enemy plane, a tank

(For Explanation of codes, see USE GUIDE and KEY)

PALADIN VIDEO HOME ENTERTAINMENT GUIDE

commander accidentally destroys Hollywood, which is also the aim of the sub commander, and riots break-out as the Americans fight each other.
BBFC:PG — F — EN
Columbia/Universal — CIC Video   **H, P**
BEA 1014?VHA 1014

1978 British Open Squash Championship Spo-Lei '78
Sports-Minor
04516   46 mins   C
B, V
Hunt's stamina and fortitude are stretched to the limit in a match with Mohibullah Khan. One of the most amazing squash matches of the decade.
F — EN
Multisquash Ltd Films — Quadrant Video
H, P
SQ2

1979 Lombard RAC Rally, The Spo-Lei '79
Automobiles-Racing
04393   60 mins   C
B, V
This show follows the four-car team of Group 1 Opel Kadett GTE's taking part in England's most popular motoring event through the forests of Yorkshire, Scotland, the Lake District, and Wales.
F — ED
Vintage Television — Vintage Television Ltd
H, P, E

1976 Irish Masters Squash Championship Spo-Lei '76
Sports-Minor
04515   50 mins   C
B, V
Hunt and Zaman play masterfully. Hunt plays aggressively to offset Zaman's deliberate style, shaking loose from the grip which Zaman had originally taken.
F — EN
Multisquash Ltd Films — Quadrant Video
H, P
SQ1

92 in the Shade Fil-Ent '75
Drama
05944   96 mins   C
B, V
Peter Fonda, Warren Oates, Margot Kidder
This is the story of a drifter, who is trying to find a way to survive, in his home town on the edge of Florida's mangrove swamps. The only opportunity is to become a fishing guide and lead visitors to the more bountiful fishing areas. Two other guides see him as a threat and stop at nothing, even murder, to discourage him.
S,A — EN
United Artists — Precision Video Ltd   **P**
BITC 2064/VITC 2064

Ninth Configuration, The Fil-Ent '81
Drama
06144   108 mins   C
V2, B, V
Stacy Keach, Scott Wilson, Jason Miller, Ed Flanders, Neville Brand, George DiCenzo, Moses Gunn, Robert Loggia, directed by William P. Blatty
Confined in a secluded gothic mansion are high ranking military officers who have all had mental breakdowns, put there by the Pentagon to find out the reasons for their potentially embarrassing mental malfunctions. A unorthodox psychiatrist has been bought in to psycho-analyse this eccentric group. The film traces his unusual methods of correcting the madnesses.
BBFC:X — A — EN
William Blatty Prod — Guild Home Video
H, P, E

No Deposit, No Return Fil-Ent '76
Comedy/Adventure
12574   106 mins   C
B, V
David Niven, Darren McGavin
This is the story of two children who decide to fake their own kidnapping.
F — EN
Walt Disney Productions — Rank Video Library
H
136

No Drums, No Bugles Fil-Ent '71
War-Drama
09307   90 mins   C
V2, B, V
Martin Sheen
Filmed on location in the beautiful Virginian countryside, this film tells the true story of personal courage. A young man who stood alone against war survived for more than three years in a backwoods less than two miles from all he cherished. Surrounded by the devastation of war he fought deprivation, nature, the elements and his own mental agonies.
S,A — EN
Cinerama — ADB Video Distribution   **P**

No Mercy Man, The Fil-Ent '73
Adventure
04315   91 mins   C

PALADIN VIDEO HOME ENTERTAINMENT GUIDE

V2, B, V
An ex-Vietnam veteran rekindles his violent, war-time attitude when his town is terrorised by a gang of toughs.
BBFC:X — *A* — *EN*
John Proffit Films — *Intervision Video* H, P
A-A 0005

No One Would Believe Her Fil-Ent '77
Suspense/Horror
13268 99 mins C
B, V
Laurence Harvey, Joanne Pettet, Meg Foster, directed by Laurence Harvey
A series of young girls disappear after being invited into the home of an aristocratic war veteran.
BBFC:18 — *A* — *EN*
Jack Cushingham — *CBS/Fox Video* P
5008

No Place to Hide Fil-Ent '74
War-Drama
08622 86 mins C
V2, B, V
Sylvester Stallone, Antony Page
An anti-militarist resistance movement plans the bombing of the Park Avenue Headquarters of the international military contractors. However, all does not go to plan.
S,A — *EN*
Unknown — *Hokushin Audio Visual Ltd* P
VM 65

No Place to Hide Fil-Ent '81
Suspense/Drama
09257 120 mins C
V2, B, V
Kathleen Beller, Mariette Hartley, Arlen Dean Snyder, Gary Graham, Keir Dullea, Sandy McPeak, directed by John Llewellyn Moxey
A young woman for unknown reasons is followed by a mysterious man who threatens to kill her. However, she can produce no evidence or witness, and no one believes her. She goes to stay with her stepmother in a lakeside cabin. One night when she is alone, the telephone and power lines are cut, and the mysterious man appears.
BBFC:A — *S,A* — *EN*
MPC; Robert D. Wood — *Iver Film Services* P
209

Noah's Animals Fil-Ent '??
Cartoons
07824 90 mins C
V2, B, V
Animated
Three half hour cartoons on one tape. 'Noah's Animals' tells the story of the Great Flood through the eyes of the animals. 'King of the Beasts' explains how the lion came to be crowned as the leader of the animal kingdom. 'The Last of The Red Hot Dragons' tells the story of a flying dragon who uses his talent for providing fire to rescue his animal friends at the North Pole.
F — *EN*
Unknown — *Video Unlimited* H, P
036

Nobody Runs Forever Fil-Ent '68
Suspense
04253 97 mins C
B, V
Rod Taylor, Lilli Palmer, Christopher Plummer, Camilla Sparv, Daliah Lavi
Scobie Malone, a detective sergeant from the outback, is chosen to arrest the Australian High Commissioner in London on a murder charge, in this film version of a Jon Cleary novel. Scobie finds the job distasteful and dangerous.
BBFC:A — *S,A* — *EN*
Cinerama Releasing — *Rank Video Library* H, P
0019

Nobody's Boy Fil-Ent '7?
Fantasy/Cartoons
02587 82 mins C
B, V
Animated
A full-length animated film about an orphan's adventures with his dog.
F — *EN*
Unknown — *Mountain Video* P

Noddy Goes to Toyland Chl-Juv '7?
Fantasy
04686 55 mins C
B, V
Narrated by Richard Briers
Noddy is a little wooden fellow who runs away from his father, a wood-carver, and goes to Toyland. Noddy finds a home there and lots of adventures.
PS,I — *EN*
Spectrum — *Polygram Video* P

Norma Rae Fil-Ent '79
Drama
01199 114 mins C
B, V
Sally Field, Ron Leibman, Beau Bridges

(For Explanation of codes, see USE GUIDE and KEY)

PALADIN VIDEO HOME ENTERTAINMENT GUIDE

Sally Field portrays a textile worker who joins forces with a New York labour organiser to unionise a Southern mill.
Academy Awards '79: Best Actress (Field), Best Song ('It Goes Like It Goes'). M,A — EN
20th Century Fox — *CBS/Fox Video* **P**
3A-111

Norman Conquests: FII-Ent '77
Table Manners
Comedy-Drama
04645   108 mins   C
B, V
Richard Briers, Penelope Keith, Tom Conti
'Table Manners' is the first part of Alan Ayckbourn's comedy trilogy 'The Norman Conquests.'
F — EN
Thames Video — *THORN EMI*   **H, P**
TXB 90 6202 4/TVB 90 6202 2

Norman Conquests: FII-Ent '77
Living Together, The
Comedy-Drama
05413   93 mins   C
B, V
Richard Briers, Penelope Keith, Tom Conti, directed by Herbert Wise
The second part in a trilogy written by Alan Ayckbourn, originally a West End hit. The play follows the unfortunate Norman through a disastrous weekend as he tries to seduce first his sister-in-law, his brother-in-law's wife and then his own wife. He brings chaos to the weekend family gathering in a country house. The three parts view events from different angles; this part reveals what happens in the living room.
S,A — EN
Thames Television — *THORN EMI*   **P**
TXB 9005224/TVB 9005222

Norman Conquests: FII-Ent '77
Round and Round the Garden, The
Comedy-Drama
05414   106 mins   C
B, V
Richard Briers, Penelope Keith, Tom Conti, directed by Herbert Wise
The last play in the trilogy by Alan Ayckbourn. Each play is complete in itself yet follows the events in the other two. In this final part the unfortunate Norman, who according to his wife has 'three emotions for every occasion,' makes his first furtive appearance in the garden which suggests that the weekend is going to misfire.
S,A — EN
Thames Television — *THORN EMI*   **P**
TXB 9005234/TVB 9005232

North by Northwest   FII-Ent '59
Drama/Suspense
10174   136 mins   C
B, V
Cary Grant, Eva Marie Saint
In a case of mistaken identity a man's life is threatened, he's drugged and later discovered standing over a body with a blood-stained knife. He is helped to escape by a beautiful blond, who helps him to prove his innocence.
BBFC:U — S,A — EN
MGM — *MGM/UA Home Video*   **P**
UMB 10104/UMV 10104

North Country   FII-Ent '69
Adventure
06878   94 mins   C
V2, B, V
This film uses the mountain country and barren ice packs of Alaska to illustrate the lives of two men living off the land. The film follows the woodsmen who have chosen their solitary life for the love of nature and the Eskimo born to the life of a lonely hunter and how they face danger and adventure with little help from modern technology.
S,A — EN
Gold Key Entertainment — *European Video Company*   **P**

North Dallas Forty   FII-Ent '79
Drama
13311   114 mins   C
B, V
Nick Nolte, Mac Davis, Charles Durning, Dayle Haddon, directed by Ted Kotcheff
A veteran professional footballer who has made the game his whole life, finds he has to make a choice when a woman shows him a more attractive, different way of life away from the violence of the field.
BBFC:18 — C,A — EN
Paramount — *CIC Video*   **H, P**
BEN 2114/VHN 2114

North-East of Seoul   FII-Ent '72
Adventure/Drama
05698   91 mins   C
B, V
Anita Ekberg, John Ireland, Victor Buono
A famous ancient jewelled sword has disappeared from a museum. In the heart of Korea an American travel guide, a dealer in ancient weapons and a woman get caught up in a million-dollar caper.
BBFC:U — F — EN
Philip Yordan Productions — *Derann Film Services*   **H, P**
DV128B/DV128

PALADIN VIDEO HOME ENTERTAINMENT GUIDE

North Sea Hijack Fll-Ent '79
Drama
07371   99 mins   C
B, V
Roger Moore, James Mason, Anthony Perkins, directed by Andrew V. McLagen
This is the story of the hijack of an oil rig supply vessel and the holding to ransom of a mammoth platform and the seven hundred men aboard. The ruthless leader of the gang, a wanted man, faces an eccentric underwater sabotage expert called in by Lloyds, the insurers, to remedy the situation. A tense count-down of bluff and counter bluff follows with hundreds of human lives, billions of oil dollars and the security of the nation at stake.
S,A — EN
Universal — CIC Video   **H, P**
BEA 1026/VHA 1026

Northville Cemetery Massacre, The Fll-Ent '79
Drama
04552   86 mins   C
V2, B, V
David Hyry, Craig Collicott
A group of young motorcyclists run into trouble with local country residents. One of the girl motorcyclists is raped by a policeman and her father is told by the police that a motorcyclist is to blame. This leads to a massacre of all the motorcyclists.
C,A — EN
Cannon Group — Intervision Video   **H, P**
A-A 0117

Northwest Frontier Fll-Ent '59
Western
01890   87 mins   C
B, V
Kenneth More, Lauren Bacall, Herbert Lom
A turn of the century drama set in the savage mountains of the Indian Northwest Frontier. An epic tale of courage and heroism against terrible odds.
BBFC:U — F — EN
Rank; Marcel Hellman — Rank Video Library
H, P
0004

Northwest Stampede Fll-Ent '49
Western
01079   76 mins   C
V2, B, V
Jack Oakie
Friction between a ranch owner's son and his female foreman results in a rodeo where both are determined to win.
BBFC:U — F — EN
Eagle Lion — Intervision Video   **H, P**
A-A 0180

Nosferatu: A Symphony of Horror Fll-Ent '22
Horror
08548   63 mins   B/W
B, V
Max Schreck, Gustav von Wangenheim, Greta Schroeder, Alexander Granach
This film is set in Bremen in the 1830's. It tells one of the first accounts of the Vampire, Count Dracula. A man is clerk to a mysterious house agent who has just leased one of his properties to the Count. This house happens to be opposite his home, where he lives with his beautiful wife. It is a silent film with English captions.
BBFC:A — C,A — EN
Friedrich Wilhelm Murnau Stiftung — THORN EMI   **P**
TXC 90 08304/TVC 90 08302

Not For Publication Fll-Ent '84
Comedy
13682   83 mins   C
B, V
Nancy Allen, David Naughton, Laurence Luckinbill, directed by Paul Bartel
A girl reporter who campaigns for the Mayor of New York for re-election on an anti-vice ticket discovers more than she bargains for when asked to cover an orgy for her newspaper.
BBFC:15 — S,A — EN
Anne Kimmel — THORN EMI   **P**
90 2781

Not Just a Spectator Gen-Edu '8?
Learning disabilities
13528   35 mins   C
B, V
Physical activities and recreation for disabled people, including climbing, sailing, basket ball, wheelchair dancing and many other leisure pursuits are shown in this film.
C,A — SE
Unknown — TFI Leisure Ltd   **H, P**

Not Just Another Affair Fll-Ent '8?
Romance
08031   120 mins   C
V2, B, V
Victoria Principal, Gil Gerard, Robert Webber, Barbara Barrie, Richard Kilne, Albert Hague, directed by Steven Stern
This is the story of a very handsome, successful young man chasing a beautiful woman who is not so sure she wants to be involved. The story follows the ups and downs, of which at times is a one-sided romance.
BBFC:U — F — EN
Unknown — Iver Film Services   **P**
219

(For Explanation of codes, see USE GUIDE and KEY)   475

PALADIN VIDEO HOME ENTERTAINMENT GUIDE

Not Now, Darling — Fil-Ent '73
Comedy
04199   93 mins   C
B, V

Leslie Phillips, Julie Ege, Barbara Windsor, Moira Lister, Joan Sims, Bill Fraser
A West End furrier's large appetite for charming girls makes him try to sell an expensive mink at a cheap price to the husband of his prospective mistress.
BBFC:A — S,A — EN
LMG; Sedgemore; Not Now Film Prods — Guild Home Video   **H, P**

Not Tonight Darling — Fil-Ent '??
Comedy
05459   91 mins   C
V2, B, V

Edwige Fenech, Alberto Lionello, Aldo Maccione
A wife, whose husband plays around, plans a vacation for revenge to boost her ego. However, she cannot bring herself to be unfaithful. Meanwhile, the husband tries frantically to find his wife and gets involved in a series of comic events. The injured wife eventually gives in to a gigolo, despite the guilt, and the husband appears to become involved in an eternal triangle.
BBFC:X — A — EN
Unknown — Iver Film Services   **P**
105

Nothing But the Night — Fil-Ent '72
Horror
05152   88 mins   C
B, V

Christopher Lee, Peter Cushing, Diana Dors, Georgia Brown
Special branch man and pathologist pursue violent ex-prostitute who is out to find the child she claims has been abducted to a sinister orphanage on a remote Scottish island.
BBFC:AA — C,A — EN
J Arthur Rank — Rank Video Library   **H, P**
0047

Notorious — Fil-Ent '46
Suspense/Drama
04168   103 mins   B/W
B, V

Cary Grant, Ingrid Bergman, Claude Rains, Louis Calhern, directed by Alfred Hitchcock
A government agent and a girl, whose father was convicted of treason, undertake a dangerous mission to Brazil.
BBFC:A — S,A — EN
Selznick — Guild Home Video   **H, P**

Now and Forever — Fil-Ent '82
Romance
12613   90 mins   C
V2, B, V

Cheryl Ladd, Robert Coleby
Based on Danielle Steel's novel, this is the story of a perfect happy marriage until one experiences an afternoon's casual faithlessness and they find their lesson of love only just beginning.
C,A — EN
Interplanetary Pictures — VideoSpace Ltd   **P**

Now Voyager — Fil-Ent '84
Music-Performance/Fantasy
13128   60 mins   C
B, V

Barry Gibb, Sir Michael Hordern, directed by Storm Thorgerson
A musician is plummeted into a series of strange encounters with a mysterious stranger. Eleven tracks are featured including 'Driver,' 'Fine Line,' 'She Says,' 'Temptation' and 'Stay Along.'
F — EN
Unknown — Polygram Video   **P**
041 0524/041 0522

Nowhere to Hide — Fil-Ent '77
Drama/Suspense
09229   74 mins   C
B, V

Lee Van Cleef
A former hit-man is about to testify for the state, against his former gangland boss. However, with a contract out on his life, it is disputable whether he will make the trial.
S,A — EN
Unknown — Video Form Pictures   **H, P**
MGD 4

Nuclear Countdown — Fil-Ent '77
Crime-Drama
07624   118 mins   C
B, V

Burt Lancaster, Richard Widmark, Joseph Cotten, Melvyn Douglas, Richard Jaeckel, Leif Erickson, directed by Robert Aldrich
A band of escaped convicts led by a renegade General capture a missile site. The missiles are armed and ready to fire. The White House has just 90 minutes to meet their demands and decide the fate of the World.
S,A — EN
Lorimar — VCL Video Services   **P**
P250D

No. 1—Licensed to Love and Kill — Fil-Ent '77
Suspense

476   (For Explanation of codes, see USE GUIDE and KEY)

PALADIN VIDEO HOME ENTERTAINMENT GUIDE

04488 92 mins C
V2, B, V
Gareth Hunt, Nick Tate, Fiona Curzon, Geoffrey Keen, Gary Hope
Charles Bind, the 'number one' agent of the British Intelligence Service, is sent to the U.S. to find a missing diplomat. In the process he encounters the diplomat's beautiful daughter, and evil senator, and the ultimate psychopath, who makes exploding people and turns strong men into beautiful women.
A — EN
Lindsay Shonteff — *Intervision Video* H, P
A-A 0191

No. 1 of the Secret Service   Fil-Ent '77
Suspense
04489 91 mins C
V2, B, V
Nicky Henson, Richard Todd, Aimi Mac Donald
British intelligence agent No. 1 and a beautiful female agent named Anna are assigned to a case involving the murder of several men in high finance. They must pit their skill, luck, and wits against a diabolical villain in order to stop him.
BBFC:AA — *S,A — EN*
Lindsay Shonteff — *Intervision Video* H, P
A-A 0188

Nurburgring 100 KMS 1956/Monaco Grand Prix 1957   Spo-Lei '7?
Automobiles-Racing
04536 60 mins C
B, V
The race-long duel between the Moss/Behra Maserati and the Fangio/Castelotti Ferrari is highlighted. In 'Monaco Grand Prix 1957,' Fangio is victorious in a race from which Moss, Collins, and Hawthorn are eliminated because of a dramatic accident.
F — EN
Castrol — *Quadrant Video* H, P
M2

Nursery Rhymes   Chl-Juv '8?
Cartoons
09334 60 mins C
B, V
Animated, voices by Isla St. Clair, Floella Benjamin, Martin Carthy, Valentine Dyall, Mike Berry
Seventy of the best known and well loved nursery rhymes are featured on this tape. 'Humpty Dumpty' topples off his wall, a real sheep sings 'Baa Baa Black Sheep' and the merry Morris men dance 'Over the Hills and Far away.' Also included are 'Georgie Porgie,' 'Wee Willie Winkie,' 'Hey Diddle Diddle' and 'Old King Cole.'
PS,M — EN
AB&C — *Longman Video* P
LGBE 5001/LGVH 5001

Nutcase   Chl-Juv '7?
Comedy-Drama
09873 50 mins C
B, V
Melissa Donaldson, Peter Shand, Aaron Donaldson
Daring youngsters foil the baddies on this madcap kid's comedy.
M,S — EN
Unknown — *Polygram Video* H, P
791 1494/791 1492

Nutcracker, The   Fil-Ent '78
Dance
05300 86 mins C
B, V
Bolshoi Ballet Company
The most popular Christmas ballet, with music by Tchaikovsky, performed by the Bolshoi Ballet Company. From a Yuletide party and an eccentric toymaker this fantasy leads to a world of mice and toy soldiers, a snow forest and a kingdom of sweets.
F — EN
Lothar Bock Assoc; GMBH — *MGM/UA Home Video*
UCB10024/UCV10024

Nutcracker, The   Fil-Ent '74
Musical
05240 29 mins C
B, V
Animated
This animated cartoon is taken from the Hoffman version of the tale and set to the music of Tchaikovsky's 'Nutcracker Suite.'
BBFC:U — *F — EN*
Unknown — *Rank Video Library* H, P
9000

Nutcracker Fantasy   Fil-Ent '8?
Puppets/Fantasy
10090 81 mins C
B, V
Voices by Christopher Lee, Roddy McDowall, Melissa Gilbert, Eva Gabor, Jo-Anne Worley
This puppet animation film is based on E.T.A. Hoffman's classic tale 'The Nutcracker and the Mouseking' and incorporates Tchaikovsky's music. A little girl who lives with her Uncle and Aunt falls asleep one night while waiting for her cousin to come home. She dreams that her

PALADIN VIDEO HOME ENTERTAINMENT GUIDE

nutcracker doll is stolen by an army of wicked mice. She joins forces with King Goodwin and his Captain in their battles against the mice and their evil Queen.

F — EN

Unknown — *VideoSpace Ltd* **P**

Nutcracker Fantasy   Chl-Juv '84

Puppets

13098   81 mins   C

B, V

Animated with the voices of Christopher Lee, Roddy McDowall, Eva Gabor and Jo Anne Worley

This films portrays E.T.A. Hoffman's classical story 'The Nutcracker and the Mouseking' with the soundtrack by Tchaikovsky.

PS,M — EN

Unknown — *Quadrant Video*   **H, P**

FF 18

Nutcracker, The   Fin-Art '7?

Dance

02262   85 mins   C

V

A live recording of the world's most popular ballet from the stage of the Bolshoi theatre in Moscow, featuring Valdimir Vasiliev and Ekaterina Maximova in the first act, and Vyacheslav Gordeyev and Nadia Pavolva in the second.

F — EN

Unknown — *JVC*   **P**

PRT 33

Nuts in May   Fil-Ent '84

Comedy/Drama

13397   82 mins   C

B, V

Alison Steadman, Roger Sloman, directed by Mike Leigh

A trendy couple embark on a camping holiday in Dorset all set to obey the country code and find that their tolerance is stretched to its limits.

F — EN

Unknown — *BBC Video*   **H, P**

2013

O

077 Fury in Istanbul   Fil-Ent '??

Crime-Drama/Adventure

07920   88 mins   C

V2, B, V

Ken Clark

A special agent is sent to investigate the death of a Professor who was found by his secretary whilst they were on a trip to Istanbul. The agent discovers that the secretary is a member of a lethal gang who faked the Professor's death. The Professor is being forced to perfect the 'Beta Ray' weapon which is capable of destruction on a vast scale. The agent has his work cut out to save the world.

S,A — EN

Unknown — *Video Programme Distributors* **P**

Inter-Ocean—077

Observer Guide to   How-Ins '82
European Cookery, The

Cookery/Alcoholic beverages

06960   60 mins   C

B, V

Presented by Jane Grigson

In this film Jane Grigson, the cookery writer, uses selected recipes to give an informed and interesting course through the cookery books of Italy, Spain, Austria, Hungary, France, Germany, Portugal, Scandinavia, Greece, Russia and Britain. There are also hints on wine and where special ingredients can be bought in this country to produce good results.

S,A — I

Home Video Productions; Observer — *Home Video Merchandisers*   **H, P**

056

Obsessive Love   Fil-Ent '84

Drama

13479   92 mins   C

V2, B, V

Yvette Mimieux, Simon MacCorkindale, Constance McCashin, Lainie Kazan, Jill Jacobson, Louise Latham

A lonely woman becomes obsessive over an actor and sets out to meet him. When a relationship develops between them he realizes she is unstable and decides to break free.

BBFC:PG — *C,A — EN*

Moonlight Productions — *Precision Video Ltd* **P**

2148

(For Explanation of codes, see USE GUIDE and KEY)

PALADIN VIDEO HOME ENTERTAINMENT GUIDE

Ocean World — Gen-Edu '??
Oceanography/Sports-Water
06139   60 mins   C
V2, B, V

An underwater cameraman shows coral gardens, kelp forests, scuba diving and big game hunting with cannons and the harpooning of a ninety foot whale. This is followed by speed boat racing, surfing, fancy diving and other sports of the sea.
F — ED
Unknown — *Video Programme Distributors*
P
Cinehollywood—V480

Ocean's Eleven — Fil-Ent '60
Comedy
13036   127 mins   C
B, V

Frank Sinatra, Peter Lawford, Sammy Davis Jr, Dean Martin, Angie Dickinson
A gang of eleven plan to rob Las Vegas Casinos in a meticulously planned operation.
BBFC:A — C,A — EN
Dorchester Productions Inc — *Warner Home Video*   P
61177

Octagon, The — Fil-Ent '80
Suspense/Martial arts
07798   103 mins   C
B, V

Chuck Norris, Karen Carlson, Lee Van Cleef, Tadashi Yamashita
A martial arts chanpion out to revenge the death of his girlfriend at the hands of a band of lethal Ninja killers discovers 'The Octagon,' a sinister training centre run by international extremists.
S,A — EN
Joel Freeman — *Video Tape Centre*   P
VTC 1001

Octaman — Fil-Ent '71
Science fiction
05455   76 mins   C
V2, B, V

Kerwin Matthews, Pier Angeli, Jeff Morrow, Harry Guardino
A creature from outer space lands on earth after the discovery of a small squid-like mutant in the tropics of South America. This half man, half octopus is a great threat to the continent.
BBFC:A — S,A — EN
Filmers Guild — *Iver Film Services*   P
94

October Man, The — Fil-Ent '47
Drama
13766   94 mins   B/W
B, V

John Mills
A man, shattered by guilt after blaming himself for the dealth of a girl in a car crash, has a nervous breakdown and after release from hospital, is accused of murdering a fashion model.
BBFC:PG — S,A — EN
Eric Ambler — *Rank Video Library*   H, P
0209E

Octopussy — Fil-Ent '83
Drama/Suspense
12685   127 mins   C
B, V

Roger Moore, Maud Adams, Louis Jourdan, Kristina Wayborn, Kabir Bedi, directed by John Glen
The auction of a Faberge egg results in a trip to India for Bond and in a race against time to stop a renegade Russian general from blowing up half of West Germany with a nuclear bomb. He encounters the inevitable opposition in the guise of the beautiful Octopussy.
BBFC:PG — F — EN
Albert R Broccoli — *Warner Home Video*   P
99212

Odd Angry Shot, The — Fil-Ent '79
War-Drama
06146   92 mins   C
V2, B, V

Graham Kennedy, John Hargreaves, John Jarrat, Bryan Brown, Graeme Blundell
The story of four S.A.S. soldiers from Australia's toughest army unit who are sent to Vietnam for twelve months active service. They believe they can deal with any situation after their training but in truth they are unprepared for the harsh realities of war. The behaviour of the men in the face of armed combat becomes increasingly outrageous.
BBFC:X — A — EN
Australian Film Commission; The New South Wales Film Corp — *Guild Home Video*   H, P, E

Odd Man Out — Fil-Ent '47
Drama
04249   113 mins   B/W
B, V

James Mason, F.J. McCormick, Kathleen Ryan, Elwyn Brook-Jones, Robert Newton, William Hartnell, Denis O'Dea, Maureen Delaney, Cyril Cusack, Fay Compton

(For Explanation of codes, see USE GUIDE and KEY)

PALADIN VIDEO HOME ENTERTAINMENT GUIDE

Set in the bleak winter streets of an Irish city the story follows Johnny, a wounded rebel, as he stumbles from pillar to post in search of the ship that will take him to freedom.
BBFC:A — C,A — EN
Universal — *Rank Video Library* **H, P**
0020

Odds and Evens Fil-Ent '78
Comedy
12466   111 mins   C
B, V
Terence Hill, Bud Spencer
In this hilarious comedy the crazy Lieutenant duo Johnny and Charlie Firpo are chosen to take action to rid Miami of its gambling and bookmaking fraternity.
BBFC:PG — F — EN
Columbia; EMI; Warner — *RCA/Columbia Pictures Video UK* **H, P**
10166

Of Mice and Men Fil-Ent '81
Drama
09259   116 mins   C
V2, B, V
Robert Blake, Randy Quaid, Mitchell Ryan, Lew Ayres, Ted Neeley, Cassie Yates, Pat Hingle, Whitman Mayo, directed by Reza Badiyi
Adapted from John Steinbeck's classic novel, this film tells the story of the lives of two itinerant ranch hands. Lenny is physically strong but pathetically retarded; his lifelong friend has committed himself to protecting him from his innocent but often near-tragic failings. They struggle along together encountering many difficulties and hardships.
BBFC:A — S,A — EN
NBC — *Iver Film Services* **P**
214

Off on a Comet Fil-Ent '??
Cartoons/Adventure
08800   45 mins   C
B, V
Animated
This film tells of a voyage of discovery and adventure, based on the novel by Jules Verne.
M,A — EN
Unknown — *VCL Video Services* **P**
A321B

Off Road Action Spo-Lei '81
Motorcycles
06847   64 mins   C   (PAL, NTSC)
V2, B, V
This treble feature covers three different aspects of off-road motorcycle sports. 'The Chairman' features the European sidecar motorcross championships with commentary by Stuart Hall. 'Enduro du Touquet' is about a French race held on sand dunes attracting over 1,000 competitors with music by The Police. 'Trials Superstars' features the world's top trials aces competing over very demanding Yorkshire Terrain.
S,A — EN
CH Wood Ltd — *Duke Marketing Limited*
P
DM3

Off the Wall Fil-Ent '82
Comedy
10094   90 mins   C
B, V
Paul Sorvino, Rosanna Arquette
This film follows the adventures of a rich runaway and a streetwise kid who get sentenced to Snake Canyon jail. The Warden is crazed, their cellmate keeps breaking out, there is a Birdman and the wrestling champion has a crush on the kid. When persuaded to enter the wrestling match the kid wins singlehanded, pandemonium ensues as the boys are helped to escape by a wild and crazy lady.
BBFC:15 — S,A — EN
Unknown — *VideoSpace Ltd* **P**

Officer and a Gentleman, An Fil-Ent '81
Drama
12050   126 mins   C
B, V
Richard Gere, Louis Gossett Jr, David Keith, Debra Winger, Lisa Blount, directed by Taylor Hackford
A group of Naval Aviation Officer Candidates are subjected to three months rigorous training by a drill inspector determined to weed out the weak ones. This film tells the story of two of this group who form a friendship together, of the victimisation of one of them by the drill inspector and of the two girls in their lives.
Academy Awards '82: Best Supporting Actor (Gossett); Best Original Song ('Up Where We Belong'). BBFC:15 — S,A — EN
Paramount — *CIC Video* **H, P**
BER 2085/VHR 2085

Oh! Calcutta! Fil-Ent '71
Comedy
02090   95 mins   C
V2, B, V
Bill Macy, Mark Dempsey
This is the original American stage version filmed in America; funny, erotic, sometimes shocking.
BBFC:X — C,A — EN
Cinemation — *Hokushin Audio Visual Ltd*
P
VM-22

---

480   (For Explanation of codes, see USE GUIDE and KEY)

PALADIN VIDEO HOME ENTERTAINMENT GUIDE

Oh God!   Fil-Ent '79
Comedy
13042   99 mins   C
B, V
George Burns, John Denver, directed by Carl Reiner
An assistant supermarket manager is chosen by him to spread the word, which leads to all sorts of confusion.
BBFC:A — C,A — EN
Warner Bros Inc — *Warner Home Video*   P
61010

Oh God! Book II   Fil-Ent '80
Comedy
13043   90 mins   C
B, V
George Burns, directed by Gilbert Cates
In this sequel, God meets a young girl who promises to help him regain some of his lost popularity by writing an advertising slogan and spreading the word.
BBFC:A — C,A — EN
Warner Bros Inc — *Warner Home Video*   P
61044

077 Mission Bloody Mary   Fil-Ent '7?
Suspense
04295   99 mins   C
V2, B, V
C.I.A. agent 077 Dick Malloy is sent to track down an atom bomb 'Bloody Mary' believed to have fallen into the hands of the 'Black Lily' spy ring.
C,A — EN
Unknown — *Video Programme Distributors*   P
Inter-Ocean—043

Oh! What a Lovely War   Fil-Ent '69
War-Drama/Satire
13621   132 mins   C
B, V
Dirk Bogarde, John Geilgud, Laurence Olivier, John Mills, Vanessa Redgrave, Susannah York, directed by Richard Attenborough
This is an anti-war film set against the everyday life of an Edwardian seaside pier and portrays the folly and the tragedy of the disastrous 1914-18 war with songs, jokes, and battle scenes.
BBFC:PG — S,A — EN
Paramount — *CIC Video*   H, P
2121

O'Hara'a Wife   Fil-Ent '81
Comedy
12032   87 mins   C
B, V
Edward Asner, Mariette Hartley, Jodie Foster, directed by William Bartman
A successful partner in a law firm has his cherished dream of a holiday of a life time shattered by his wife's untimely death. He soon finds out she is not as far away as he thought and can conjure her up at will.
S,A — EN
Davis Panzer — *Polygram Video*   H, P
0402324/0402322

Oil   Fil-Ent '77
Drama
01189   95 mins   C
V2, B, V
Stuart Whitman, Ray Milland, Woody Strode, William Berger, Tony Kendall, George Dinica
When the powerful owner of one of the world's largest oil fields refuses to cooperate in oil price negotiations, his oil field is sabotaged. The explosion and consequent fire threaten to destroy much of the country; seven brave firefighters are called in to battle the blaze.
M,A — EN
Italian — *Intervision Video*   H
A-AE 0165

Oklahoma!   Fil-Ent '55
Musical
06494   140 mins   C
B, V
Gordon MacRae, Shirley Jones, Rod Steiger, Charlotte Greenwood, Gloria Grahame, Eddie Albert, Gene Nelson, directed by Fred Zinneman
Film version of Rodgers and Hammerstein's musical classic about a cowboy's on-again off-again romance with his girl, in the Oklahoma Territory of 1907. Songs include 'Oh, What a Beautiful Morning' and 'The Surrey with the Fringe on Top.'
F — EN
Todd-AO — *MGM/UA Home Video*   P
UCB 10020/UCV 10020

Old Boyfriends   Fil-Ent '79
Drama
08738   103 mins   C
B, V
Talia Shire, Richard Jordan, John Belushi, Keith Carradine, Buck Henry, John Houseman
This film tells the story of a woman whose marriage is broken. She becomes obsessed with memories of the past, and decides to revisit her former lover. In Denver she finds a man she almost married. Although he is at first hesitant,

PALADIN VIDEO HOME ENTERTAINMENT GUIDE

she seduces him and once again he falls in love with her. Without warning she leaves town. Next she takes revenge on a boyfriend who humiliated her, and then continues Eastward.
BBFC:X — A — EN
Avco Embassy — *Precision Video Ltd*   **P**
BITC 2579/VITC 2579

Old Man Who Cried Wolf, The   Fil-Ent '70
Mystery
04167   74 mins   C
B, V
Edward G. Robinson, Martin Balsam, Diane Baker, Percy Rodriguez, Ruth Roman
A man who saw his old friend beaten to death sets out to find the truth after the police claim the dead man died of a heart attack.
BBFC:A — S,A — EN
Spelling — *Guild Home Video*   **H, P**

Old Yeller   Fil-Ent '57
Adventure/Drama
12566   83 mins   C
B, V
Dorothy McGuire, Fess Parker
The family who took in a stray dog finds he proves his worth in their fight against the elements in the American West.
F — EN
Walt Disney Productions — *Rank Video Library* **H**
037

Oliver Twist   Fil-Ent '48
Drama
05686   112 mins   B/W
B, V
Robert Newton, John Howard Davies, Alec Guinness, Francis L. Sullivan, Anthony Newley, directed by David Lean
An adaptation of Charles Dickens' classic story about a workhouse orphan who is forced into criminal company.
Venice Festival 1948: Best Sets.
BBFC:U — F — EN
Cineguild — *Rank Video Library*   **H, P**

Oliver Twist   Fil-Ent '8?
Cartoons/Adventure
12557   72 mins   C
V2, B, V
Animated
An adaptation of one of Charles Dickens' most popular novels, with appearances from Fagin, The Artful Dodger and Bill Sykes.
I,M — EN
Unknown — *RPTA Video Ltd*   **H, P**

Oliver Twist   Fil-Ent '82
Drama
13773   98 mins   C
B, V
George C. Scott, Tim Curry, Sir Michael Hordern, Richard Charles, directed by Clive Donner
Set in gloomy Victorian London and adapted from Charles Dickens' novel, this tells the story of a poor orphan boy who discovers his true identity and claims his inhertance.
F — EN
Grafton Films — *Odyssey Video*   **H, P**
6427

Olivia Newton-John: Live   Fil-Ent '8?
Music-Performance
08324   90 mins   C
V2, B, V, LV
Olivia Newton-John
This features Olivia Newton-John Live in concert during her tour of America. It includes songs such as 'Jolene' 'Xanadu', 'Little More Love,' You're The One That I Want' and 'Physical'.
F — EN
Unknown — *Embassy Home Entertainment*
P
1241

Olivia Newton-John—Physical   Fil-Ent '81
Music-Performance
05497   60 mins   C
B, V
Olivia Newton-John
A film shot especially for video in studios in London and Los Angeles. It features tracks from the album 'Physical' and other hits including 'Hopelessly devoted to you', 'A little more love' and 'Magic'.
F — EN
EMI Music — *THORN EMI*   **P**
TXD 90 0531 4/TVD 90 0531 2

Omen, The   Fil-Ent '76
Horror
01260   111 mins   C
V2, B, V, LV
Gregory Peck, Lee Remick, Billie Whitelaw, David Warner, directed by Richard Donner
'The Omen' is an effective horror piece on the coming of the 'anti-Christ,' personified in a young boy.
BBFC:X — A — EN
20th Century Fox — *CBS/Fox Video*   **P**
3A-096

PALADIN VIDEO HOME ENTERTAINMENT GUIDE

On Any Sunday   Spo-Lei '71
Motorcycles
02089   79 mins   C
V2, B, V
Steve McQueen
The story of men who love motorcycles and racing. Join Bruce Brown as he follows competitors across the USA in races over frozen lakes and deserts.
BBFC:U — F — EN
Cinema Five — Hokushin Audio Visual Ltd   P
VM-30

On Golden Pond   Fil-Ent '81
Drama
08740   105 mins   C
V2, B, V, LV
Henry Fonda, Jane Fonda, Katharine Hepburn, Dabney Coleman, Doug McKeon, William Lanteau
This is the story of three generations coming to grips with life, mortality and their own emotional distance, set at a summer home in New England.
Academy Awards '81: Best Actor (Fonda); Best Actress (Hepburn); Best Screenplay Adaptation (Ernest Thompson).   BBFC:A — S,A — EN
ITC; IPC Films — Precision Video Ltd   P
Critic 3107/BITC 3107/VITC 3107/LVITC 0014

On Her Majesty's Secret Service   Fil-Ent '69
Adventure
13190   130 mins   C
B, V
George Lazenby, directed by Peter Hunt
007 flies to Switzerland when it is discovered that innocent young girls are being used as a means of conquering the world.
BBFC:A — C,A — EN
Danjaq SA — Warner Home Video   P
99211

On the Buses   Fil-Ent '71
Comedy
07445   88 mins   C
B, V
Reg Varney, Doris Hare, Stephen Lewis, Bob Grant, Anna Karen, Michael Robbins, directed by Harry Booth
Based on the television series, this comedy features the antics of a bus driver and his lecherous conductor. They get their come-uppance when their tormented inspector brings in women drivers to put an end to their cocky certainty that shortage of staff means he can't sack them. All seems lost until the inspector is forced to admit that he's made an error, again.
BBFC:A — S,A — EN
Hammer Film Productions Ltd — THORN EMI   P
TXC 90 07234/TVC 90 07232

On the Nickel   Fil-Ent '80
Drama
08027   96 mins   C
V2, B, V
Donald Moffat, Penelope Allen, Ralph Waite, Hal Williams, James Gammon, Bert Conway, Jack Kehoe, directed by Ralph Waite
This film is set in downtown Los Angeles and portrays the moving story of alcoholics, their friendships, hardships and the contrasts between the other society. The conformist society often seems uncaring in its attitude towards these people.
BBFC:AA — C,A — EN
Ralph Waite — Iver Film Services   P
188

On the Town   Fil-Ent '49
Musical-Drama
10172   98 mins   C
B, V, LV
Frank Sinatra, Gene Kelly, Betty Garett, Ann Miller, Jules Munskin, Vera-Ellen
The story of two sailor friends on a 24-hour leave in New York. One of them falls in love with a picture of 'Miss Turnstiles' and sets out to find her. There are many song and dance routines including 'New York New York', 'Come Up to My Place', and 'We're Going to Town'.
Academy Awards '49: Best Film Score (Bernstein).   BBFC:U — F — EN
MGM — MGM/UA Home Video   P
UMB 10057/UMV 10057/UMLV 10057

Once Upon a Brothers Grimm   Fil-Ent '77
Fairy tales
02067   90 mins   C
B, V
Dean Jones, Paul Sand, Arte Johnson, Chita Rivera
An enchanting forest provides the setting for the meeting between the creators of Hansel and Gretel, Little Red Riding Hood, and the Sleeping Beauty—Jacob and Wilhelm Grimm—and some of their most famous characters.
F — EN
Rothman and Wahl; Vidtronics Company — VCL Video Services   P

PALADIN VIDEO HOME ENTERTAINMENT GUIDE

Once Upon a Girl   Fil-Ent '7?
Satire/Cartoons
08891   80 mins   C
V2, B, V
Richmond Johnson, Carol Pacente
This is a compilation of fairy stories for adults only. It is both animated and live action.
BBFC:X — A — EN
Unknown — *Video Programme Distributors*   P
Media 520

Once Upon a Scoundrel   Fil-Ent '73
Drama
09355   92 mins   C
B, V
Zero Mostel, Katy Jurado
Set in a small town in Mexico, a wicked mayor sentences a young villager to jail for the 'crime' of being kind to an animal. The townspeople decide that it is time to teach the mayor a lesson. Through an elaborate scheme designed to trick the mayor into thinking he has died and returned as a ghost, the townspeople cause him to repent his evil ways.
F — EN
Carlyle Films — *Precision Video Ltd*   P
BPMPV 2623/VPMPV 2623

Once Upon a Time in America   Fil-Ent '84
Drama
13683   219 mins   C
B, V
Robert De Niro, James Woods, Elizabeth McGovern, Tuesday Weld, directed by Sergio Leone
This gangster movie spans several decades and traces the destinies of four friends from childhood in the Jewish quarter of New York to their maturity as notorious gangsters.
British Academy Awards '84: Best Score (Morricone); Best Costume Design (Pascucci).
BBFC:18 — C,A — EN
Arnon Milchan — *THORN EMI*   P
90 2778

Once Upon a Wheel   Spo-Lei '7?
Automobiles-Racing
01149   53 mins   C
B, V
Hosted by Paul Newman
A journey through motor racing history with Paul Newman. A racing driver himself, Newman takes a look behind the scenes at the Indianapolis 500 and the stock car circuit.
F — EN
Unknown — *VCL Video Services*   P

One Armed Boxer   Fil-Ent '74
Martial arts
06911   76 mins   C
B, V
Wang Yu, Tang Shin, Tien Yeh, Lung Fei
A young student loses an arm in the fierce fighting which ensues when a vicious gang attacks his boxing school, killing the other students and his teacher. While being nursed back to health by the daughter of a boxing expert, he learns enough about one-armed combat not only to defend himself but wreak vengeance on the entire gang. Features Thai Boxing, Judo, Karate and Taikwando.
BBFC:X — A — EN
Unknown — *Rank Video Library*   H, P
0083B

One Away   Fil-Ent '??
Drama/Suspense
09958   96 mins   C
V2, B, V
Patrick Mower
This is a story of escape from a South African hard labour camp.
BBFC:AA — C,A — EN
Unknown — *Video Unlimited*   H, P, E
053

One Blow Too Many   Fil-Ent '84
Drama
13251   96 mins   C
B, V
James Cagney, Art Carney, Ellen Barkin, Peter Gallagher, directed by Joseph Sargent
An elderly retired boxing champion is pleased to be reconciled with his granddaughter after fifteen years of absence but is unaware of the real reason behind her re-appearance.
BBFC:PG — S,A — EN
Robert Halmi — *CBS/Fox Video*   P
2527

One Brief Summer   Fil-Ent '72
Drama
09369   87 mins   C
B, V
Clifford Evans, Jennifer Hilary, Peter Egan, Felicity Gibson, directed by John MacKenzie
Set in the Kent countryside this film begins with an invitation to Susan Long to spend the summer at the home of a wealthy divorced financier and his daughter, Jennifer. The two soon become involved despite Jennifer's intervention. However, on their wedding night events take an unexpected turn.
BBFC:PG — F — EN
20th Century-Fox; Twickenham Film Assocs — *Precision Video Ltd*   P
BARPV 2597/VARPV 2597

PALADIN VIDEO HOME ENTERTAINMENT GUIDE

One Down, Two To Go   Fil-Ent '82
Martial arts/Suspense
09847   87 mins   C
B, V

Fred Williamson, Jim Kelly, Jim Brown

A fight promoter takes on the 'mob' to rid pro-karate of match-fixing and intimidation.
S,A — EN
Bay Prods; Camelot Films — *Polygram Video*   **H, P**
791 5464/791 5462

One-Eyed Soldiers, The   Fil-Ent '68
Adventure/Drama
05522   89 mins   C
B, V

Dale Robertson, Luciana Paluzzi, Guy Deghy, Andrew Faulds, directed by Jean Christophe

A police chief arrives at the scene of an 'accident' in time to hear the last words of the dying man; he is unaware that he has heard a clue to the location of a hoard of treasure. However, the inspector is not the only one to have heard the words. The man's daughter enlists the help of a newspaper reporter to find out why her father died and the meaning of the words.
BBFC:A — S,A — EN
Avala-BACO; British-Yugoslavia Prod — *Derann Film Services*   **H, P**
DV122B/DV122

One Flew Over the Cuckoo's Nest   Fil-Ent '75
Drama
04633   129 mins   C
B, V

Jack Nicholson, Louise Fletcher, William Redfield, directed by Milos Forman

A man committed to a mental institution suffers all the indignities the system can deal out, but in between he leads his fellow inmates into several adventures designed to infuriate the sadistic Nurse Ratched.

Academy Awards '75: Best Picture; Best Actor (Nicholson); Best Actress (Fletcher); Best Director (Forman); British Academy Award '76: Best Film.   BBFC:X — A — EN
United Artists; Fantasy Films — *THORN EMI*   **H, P**
TXA 90 0280 4/TVA 90 0280 2

---

147 Break   Spo-Lei '82
Sports/Documentary
09323   58 mins   C
B, V

Steve Davis

This programme follows the 1982 Lader Classic snooker tournament in which Steve Davis made snooker history by becoming the first man to pot 15 reds, 15 blacks and all the colours in sequence to obtain a maximum break of 147.
F — EN
Granada Television — *Granada Video*   **H, P**

---

100 Rifles   Fil-Ent '69
Western
01767   110 mins   C
B, V

Jim Brown, Raquel Welch, Burt Reynolds, Fernando Lamas

An Indian bank robber and a black American lawman join up with a female Mexican revolutionary to help save the Mexican Indians from annihilation by a despotic military governor.
A — EN
20th Century Fox — *CBS/Fox Video*   **P**
3A-042

One Is a Lonely Number   Fil-Ent '72
Drama
12232   93 mins   C
B, V

Trish Van Devere, Monte Markham, Janet Leigh, Melvyn Douglas

A young wife finds comfort and encouragement from a compassionate old man after being rejected by her husband.
C,A — EN
MGM — *MGM/UA Home Video*   **P**
10377

One Just Man   Fil-Ent '7?
Crime-Drama
07784   90 mins   C
V2, B, V

Joseph Cotton, Tomas Milian

This film follows one man's fight against crime in a world of violence.
S,A — EN
Unknown — *Fletcher Video*   **H, P**
V104

One Little Indian   Fil-Ent '73
Adventure/Western
12565   91 mins   C
B, V

James Garner, Vera Miles

(For Explanation of codes, see USE GUIDE and KEY)

PALADIN VIDEO HOME ENTERTAINMENT GUIDE

A US Cavalryman escapes from jail and heads out into The Mexican desert on a camel, pursued by the camel's offspring and a small Indian runaway boy.
F — EN
Walt Disney Productions — *Rank Video Library*
H
138

One-Man Jury   Fil-Ent '78
Crime-Drama
06771   95 mins   C
V2, B, V
Jack Palance, Christopher Mitchum, Pamela Shoop, Angel Tompkins
A vengeful policeman turns vigilante in order to apprehend a psychotic murderer.
S,A — EN
Broadwood Productions — *Intervision Video*
H, P
A-A 0377

One Million Years B.C.   Fil-Ent '66
Drama
04665   96 mins   C
B, V
Raquel Welch, John Richardson
Two young people from warring Stone Age tribes fall in love, and they must face prehistoric monsters and other obstacles before they can fulfill their love.
C,A — EN
Hammer; Michael Carreras — *THORN EMI*
H, P
EVX 40240/EVH 20240

One More Chance   Fil-Ent '??
Drama
06935   86 mins   C
B, V
John Lamotta, Kirstie Aley, Logan Clarke
This is the heartrending drama of an ex-con's pathetic attempts to re-integrate into society.
S,A — EN
Unknown — *Rank Video Library*
H, P
0096C

One Night.....Only   Fil-Ent '84
Drama
13674   86 mins   C
B, V
Lenore Zann, Geoffrey Mackay, Helen Udy, Tarorah Johnson, directed by Timothy Bond

---

A girl overhears a conversation to stage a party for a male hockey team and a crowd of girls and decides to cut herself in by making the arrangements and so earning $50,000.
BBFC:18 — *A — EN*
Robert Lantos; Stephen J Roth — *CBS/Fox Video*   **P**
6812

One of Our Aircraft Is Missing   Fil-Ent '41
War-Drama
08728   98 mins   B/W
B, V
Godfrey Tearle, Eric Portman, Hugh Williams, Bernard Miles, Hugh Burden, Emrys Jones
An aircraft fails in mid-air and ploughs headlong into electricity pylon. There is a blinding flash and explosions. However, the six-man crew had been forced to bail out over occupied Holland. This film follows the efforts of the crew to get back to England.
S,A — EN
United Artists; British — *BBC Video*   **H, P**
BBCV 8009

One of Our Dinosaurs Is Missing   Fil-Ent '74
Adventure/Comedy
12588   90 mins   C
B, V
Peter Ustinov, Helen Hayes
A Chinese intelligence agency discovers that a secret micro film is hidden in the skeleton of a museum dinosaur and there follows a chase across London as it is pursued by a band of outrageous British nannies.
F — EN
Walt Disney Productions — *Rank Video Library*
H
137

One on Top of the Other   Fil-Ent '70
Drama
04296   99 mins   C
V2, B, V
Elsa Martinelli, Marisa Mell, Jean Sorel
On the death of his wife Susan, a young American doctor, George, receives a large amount of insurance. He is later arrested when traces of poison are found in her body. Whilst he is under sentence of death his friends Jane and Larry begin an investigation to prove his innocence.
C,A — EN
GGP Releasing — *Video Programme Distributors*   **P**
Inter-Ocean—045

---

486   (For Explanation of codes, see USE GUIDE and KEY)

PALADIN VIDEO HOME ENTERTAINMENT GUIDE

One Show Makes It Murder   Fil-Ent '82
Crime-Drama
09846   90 mins   C
B, V, LV
Robert Mitchum, Angie Dickinson, Mel Ferrer
This is the story of the undercover world of a private investigator attempting to solve a mysterious suicide, or was it murder?
S,A — EN
Fellows-Keegan Co.; Lorimar Prods — *Polygram Video*   **H, P**
791 5504/791 5502

One Silver Dollar   Fil-Ent '7?
Western
04298   90 mins   C
V2, B, V
After the Civil War, Gary and wife Judy follow his brother Phil out West. A reward is offered to Gary to capture the notorious Black Eye, who turns out to be Phil. Lured into a trap he is murdered and Gary sets out to avenge his death. Joining up with a band of outlaws who discover he is a spy, they torture him; but his wife informs the Sheriff.
C,A — EN
Unknown — *Video Programme Distributors* **P**
Inter-Ocean—021

1001 Rabbit Tales   Chi-Juv '82
Cartoons
12979   71 mins   C
B, V
Animated
Bugs Bunny is joined by Daffy Duck, Sylvester and Tweety, Speedy Gonzales and other favourite characters in a hilarious romp through the classic fairy tales, adapted from the popular Warner Bros. cartoons of the 1940's and 50's.
BBFC:U — F — EN
Warner Bros — *Warner Home Video*   **P**
61303

One Touch of Venus   Fil-Ent '48
Comedy/Romance
01284   82 mins   B/W
V2, B, V
Robert Walker, Ava Gardner, Dick Haymes, directed by William A. Seiter
A Greek statue of Venus comes to life in a department store, charms a modest window trimmer, and causes romance and misunderstandings. Based on the Broadway musical.
F — EN
Universal — *Intervision Video*   **H, P**
A-A 0287

One Two Two   Fil-Ent '??
Drama
12780   85 mins   C
V2, B, V
Nicole Calfan, Francis Huster
A story of two people who meet in a bordello and fall in love. Set in pre-war Paris against the changing political scene as Hitler rises to power.
BBFC:18 — A — EN
Abacus Video — *Intervision Video*   **H, P**
A-A 0511

Oni Baba   Fil-Ent '64
Drama
10035   104 mins   B/W
B, V
Nobuko Otowa, Jitsuko Yoshimura, Kei Sato, directed by Kaneto Shindo
A mother and daughter earn a living in sixteenth-century Japan by killing stray soldiers and selling their armour.
S,A — EN
Kindai Elga Kyokai; Tokyo Elga — *Palace Video Ltd*   **P**
PVC 2045A

Onibaba   Fil-Ent '63
Horror
06773   105 mins   B/W
V2, B, V
Nobuko Otowa, Jitsuko Yoshimura
A horror film which deals with the feudal past of Japan, an era filled with bestial killings and primitive sexuality.
A — EN
Kindai Eiga Kyokai — *Intervision Video*
H, P
A-A 0056

Onion Field, The   Fil-Ent '79
Crime-Drama
07695   123 mins   C
V2, B, V, LV
John Savage, James Woods, Franklyn Seales, Ted Danson, Ronny Cox, David Huffman, directed by Harold Becker
A policeman's partner is shot to death in an onion patch near Bakersfield, California in 1963. The criminals are apprehended and are sent to trial where they admit the murder but disagree on who committed it. Based on a true incident.
A — EN
Avco Embassy — *Embassy Home Entertainment*   **P**
2034

Only Once in a Lifetime   Fil-Ent '??
Drama
09963   90 mins   C
V2, B, V

PALADIN VIDEO HOME ENTERTAINMENT GUIDE

Miguel Robelo, Frank Whiteman
This is a humourous and quizzical love story about an immigrant artist in California that loses his wife. He gets by on growing corn and breeding canaries.
BBFC:U — *F* — *EN*
Unknown — *Video Unlimited* H, P, E
021

Only One Winner Fil-Ent '83
Drama
13238 99 mins C
B, V
Richard Chamberlain, Rod Steiger, directed by Robert Day
The true story of two courageous men who together and then separately make the historic and dangerous trek to the North Pole.
BBFC:PG — *S,A* — *EN*
Robert Halmi Junior — *CBS/Fox Video* P
2528

Only Two Can Play Fil-Ent '62
Comedy
01606 101 mins B/W
B, V
Peter Sellers, Mai Zetterling, Virginia Maskell, Richard Attenborough
A librarian embarks on a series of amorous escapades with a board member's wife. Learning that a poet is courting his wife brings him to his senses; he returns home a wiser, happier man.
BBFC:X — *A* — *EN*
Leslie Gilliat — *THORN EMI* P
TXE 90 0210 4/TVE 90 0210 2

Only Way, The Fil-Ent '??
War-Drama
08698 86 mins C
V2, B, V
Martin Potter, Jane Seymour
This film tells the story of one of the greatest heroic episodes of World War II. It depicts the true story of how the Danish people saved the Danish Jews from the Nazis.
BBFC:A — *C,A* — *EN*
Hemisphere Productions — *Video Unlimited*
H, P
078

Only Way to Spy, The Fil-Ent '??
Comedy/Adventure
06111 108 mins C
V2, B, V
Mike Paris, Pamela Palm, Rusty Blitz, Andrea Adler

A farce on the Secret Service. The nose cone from a deadly missile disappears; a group of secret agents are called to locate its whereabouts and who is behind it.
S,A — *EN*
Unknown — *Video Programme Distributors*
P
Cinehollywood—V360

Ooh.....You Are Awful Fil-Ent '72
Comedy
07440 97 mins C
B, V
Dick Emery, Derren Nesbitt, Ronald Fraser, Pat Coombs, William Franklyn, directed by Cliff Owen
The plot of this comedy enables Dick Emery, the impersonator, to star in many of his favourite guises. He plays the principal character of Charlie the con man, who, just released from jail, attempts to collect the money he conned from a wealthy family. Unfortunately, the Mafia also have an interest in retrieving it, which leads to a series of hair-raising escapades.
BBFC:A — *S,A* — *EN*
British Lion — *THORN EMI* P
TXC 90 0740 4/TVC 90 0740 2

Open All Hours Fil-Ent '8?
Comedy
10144 90 mins C
V2, B, V
Ronnie Barker, David Jason, Lynda Baron
This programme follows the adventures of the shopkeeper Arkwright whose passion for money is second only to his lust for Nurse Gladys Emanuel.
S,A — *EN*
BBC — *BBC Video* H, P
BBC 7017

Operation Amsterdam Fil-Ent '58
War-Drama
06916 98 mins B/W
B, V
Peter Finch, Eva Bartock, Tony Britton, Alexander Knox
In 1940 in Amsterdam as German troops are advancing, three men and a girl have fourteen hours to beat the Nazis to a multi-million pound cache of diamonds. Dodging bombs and shellfire they reach the city to find that the vaults are closed. They must blow the massive safes and snatch the diamonds before the enemy arrives. Based on a true story.
BBFC:U — *F* — *EN*
20th Century Fox — *Rank Video Library*
H, P
0063C

PALADIN VIDEO HOME ENTERTAINMENT GUIDE

Operation Black September
Fil-Ent '??
Crime-Drama
07657 84 mins C
B, V

Oshir Levy, Tamar Spivac, Esther Katz

Based on a true story, this film tells of the boarding by 10 Palestinians on a Sabena Airlines flight bound for Israel. They demand the release of convicted terrorists or they will take the lives of the passengers and crew. Meanwhile, crack Israeli security forces prepare to storm the aircraft.

S,A — EN

Unknown — VCL Video Services P
C214C

Operation Thunderbolt
Fil-Ent '77
Drama
08044 119 mins C
B, V

Yehoram Gaon, Klaus Kinski, Assaf Dayan, Dri Levy, Arik Lavi, directed by Menahem Golanm

This film re-tells the fantastic rescue operation by Israeli commandoes of the hostage Jews in Entebbe.

BBFC:AA — S,A — EN

G S Films — Rank Video Library H, P
0118 C

Optimists of Nine Elms, The
Fil-Ent '73
Comedy-Drama
05614 110 mins C
B, V

Peter Sellers, Donna Mullane, John Chaffey, David Daker, directed by Anthony Simmons

A story of an ex-vaudeville performer who has hit hard times and develops a relationship with two South London children. Featuring Lionel Bart's songs and music.

F — EN

Paramount; Adrian Gaye and Victor Lyndon Prods — Home Video Merchandisers H, P
005

Orca...Killer Whale
Fil-Ent '77
Adventure/Suspense
07462 88 mins C
B, V

Richard Harris, Charlotte Rampling, Will Sampson, Bo Derek, directed by Michael Anderson

While searching for sharks off the coast of Newfoundland a deep sea fisherman witnesses an attack by a 40 foot Orca whale. He sets out to catch one despite the anger of a marine biologist; by mistake he wounds a pregnant female. He realises too late that the Orca mates for life. The male Orca drives the fisherman's boat further north until he is forced to accept the Orca's challenge of a duel to the death.

BBFC:A — S,A — EN

Famous Films; Dino De Laurentiis — THORN EMI P
TXB 90 0686 4/TVB 90 0686 2

Orchestral Manoeuvres in the Dark Live
Fil-Ent '8?
Music-Performance
09041 52 mins C
B, V

This tape is a video souvenir of a sell out concert by one of Europe's top bands, recorded live at the Theatre Royal, Drury Lane and contains all of their hit songs.

F — EN

Virgin Video — VideoSpace Ltd P
VV003C

Ordeal, The
Fil-Ent '83
Drama
13402 90 mins C
V2, B, V

George Lazenby, Diane Craig

A policeman comes out of retirement to track down the criminals who drove his friend to commit suicide and brings them to justice.

BBFC:15 — S,A — EN

Alpha Films — Intervision Video H, P
0011

Ordeal of Bill Carney, The
Fil-Ent '81
Drama
09956 90 mins C
V2, B, V

Richard Crenna, Ray Sharkey, Betty Buckley

Based on a true story, this film tells the case of a father of two small boys who lost custody because he was disabled.

BBFC:U — F — EN

The Belle Company; Comworld Prods — Video Unlimited H, P, E
088

Ordeal of Dr. Mudd, The
Fil-Ent '80
Drama
07345 150 mins C
B, V

Dennis Weaver, Susan Sullivan, Richard Dysart, Michael McGuire, Nigel Davenport, Arthur Hill, directed by Paul Wendkos

(For Explanation of codes, see USE GUIDE and KEY)

PALADIN VIDEO HOME ENTERTAINMENT GUIDE

This film tells the story of Dr Samuel Mudd, the Maryland physician who unwittingly aided in the escape of Abraham Lincoln's assassin by setting his broken leg. The doctor became the subject of one of the country's most infamous trials.
S,A — EN
Marble Arch Prods — *Precision Video Ltd*
P
BITC 2112/VITC 2112

Ordeal of Patty Hearst, The   Fil-Ent '79
Crime-Drama
10211   138 mins   C
B, V
Dennis Weaver, Liza Gilbacher, Stephen Elliott, Dolores Sutton, directed by Paul Wendkos
This film tells the true story of the kidnapping of Patty Hearst as seen through the eyes of FBI Special Agent Charles Bates. He was assigned to the case after her abduction by terrorists in May 1974 and remained in change until her capture nineteen months later.
S,A — EN
David Paradine TV; Marvin Minoff — *Video Form Pictures*   **H, P**
6226-50

Order of Death   Fil-Ent '84
Drama/Suspense
12957   100 mins   C
B, V
Harvey Keitel, John Lydon, Nicole Garcia, Leonard Mann, Sylvia Sidney, directed by Carla Romanelli
A cop-killer is at loose and when a strange youth gives himself up there follows a struggle for dominance against a background of torture, guilt and corruption
BBFC:18 — A — EN
Jean Vigo RL; Aura Film — *Virgin Video*
H, P
VVA 031

Orders Are Orders   Fil-Ent '57
Comedy
05521   78 mins   B/W
B, V
Peter Sellers, Terry Hancock, Brian Reece, Margret Grahame, Raymond Huntley, Sidney James
The Adjutant of a barracks has a few friends to visit; they turn out to be an entire American film crew. Chaos ensues when the General arrives for a surprise inspection and enters through the gymnasium doors into a 'film' set and finds himself surrounded by female Martian invaders.
BBFC:U — F — EN
DCA — *Derann Film Services*   **H, P**
DV137B/DV137

Orphan, The   Fil-Ent '??
Horror
07669   100 mins   C
B, V
Peggy Fevry, Joanna Miles, Donn Whyte, Mark Owens, Stanley Church, Ed Foreman, Jim Broder, directed by John Ballard
This psychological thriller follows the path of devastation caused by an orphan who takes revenge on those who took away everything he ever loved and cared for.
A — EN
Unknown — *Hello Video Ltd*   **P**
H11

Orphee   Fil-Ent '49
Fantasy
09001   90 mins   B/W
B, V
Jean Marais, Maria Casares, Francois Perier, Marie Dea, directed by Jean Cocteau
This is a modernised version of Orpheus' trip to the Underworld to reclaim his wife Eurydice. It is subtitled in English.
Grand Prix De La Critique International '49; Venice Film Festival '49; British Film Academy Award '49.   F — EN
Andre Paulve Films du Palais Royal — *THORN EMI*   **P**
TXE 90 1623 4/TVE 90 16232

Orpheus in the Underworld   Fil-Ent '??
Musical/Opera
09893   118 mins   C
B, V
Dennis Quilley, Honour Blackman, Christopher Gable
'Orpheus in the Underworld', an operetta by Offenbach, is set between Napoleon the Third's France and Ancient Greece. It contains everything from laurel wreathes to the Can-Can. This production has a new translation which emphasises the fun of the piece.
F — EN
Unknown — *Brent Walker Home Video Ltd*
P

Oshkosh Down Under '81   Gen-Edu '81
Aeronautics
06843   118 mins   C   (PAL, NTSC)
V2, B, V
This film takes a look at the seven day EAA convention which continues to be the world's biggest aviation event. The event attracted 500,000 visitors and 10,000 aircraft. The film includes footage of many rare aircraft.
S,A — EN
Beattie/Forth Productions — *Beattie-Edwards Aviation Ltd*   **P**
BEA 012

PALADIN VIDEO HOME ENTERTAINMENT GUIDE

Osibisa—Live at the Rainbow   Fil-Ent '??
Music-Performance
06257   51 mins   C
B, V

This film features a non-stop performance by Osibisa, the Afro-Rock group. Songs include 'Dawn,' 'Fatima,' 'Bassa Bassa,' 'Meeting Point,' 'Pata Pata,' 'Kelee Celebration' and many others.
F — EN
Unknown — VCL Video Services   P
V199B

Osmond Brothers Special/Tom Jones at Knott's   Fil-Ent '7?
Music-Performance/Variety
02226   80 mins   C
V

The Osmond Brothers, Ann-Margret, Kris Kristofferson, Rita Coolidge, Tom Jones, Tanya Tucker

The four Osmond Brothers are featured in their own variety special with guest stars. This tape also features Tom Jones appearing at Knott's Berry Farm with his guests Tanya Tucker, Evelyn 'Champagne' King and the Knott's Berry Farm Ice Spectacular.
F — EN
Unknown — JVC   P
PRT 42

Osmonds, The   Fil-Ent '80
Music-Performance
06227   60 mins   C
B, V

This concert was filmed in the Osmonds' home state of Utah. Spectacular visual effects add to the magic of the performance including the songs: 'Crazy Horses,' 'Once, Twice, Three Times a Lady,' 'Isn't She Lovely,' 'Boogie Wonderland,' 'Singin' in the Rain,' 'Cabaret' and many others.
F — EN
Osmond Production — VCL Video Services
P
V116

Osterman Weekend, The   Fil-Ent '83
Suspense
12895   102 mins   C
B, V

Burt Lancaster, John Hurt, Rutger Haver, Craig T. Nelson, Dennis Hopper

A TV personality is looking forward to a weekend reunion with his friends when he is warned by the CIA that they are all Soviet agents and he and his family are at risk.
BBFC:18 — C,A — EN
Peter S Davis; William N Panzer — THORN EMI   P
TXA 90 24074/TVA 90 24072

Otello   Fil-Ent '82
Opera
08664   143 mins   C
B, V

Vladimir Atlantov, Piero Cappuccilli, Kiri te Kanawa

This is an opera by Giuseppe Verdi filmed in 1982 in Verona. It is performed in four acts and conducted by Zoltan Pesko.
S,A — EN
Unknown — Longman Video   P
LGBE 7004/LGVH 7004

Othello   Fil-Ent '64
Drama
01876   170 mins   C
B, V

Laurence Olivier, Maggie Smith, Robert Lang, Frank Finlay, Joyce Redman

A masterful production of one of Shakespeare's most popular pieces. Magnificent dialogue, colourful costumes—a screen classic.
BBFC:U — C,A — EN
British Home Entertainment — Rank Video Library   H, P
0006

Other Side of Madness, The   Fil-Ent '??
Drama
10018   80 mins   C
B, V

With stark realism, this film portrays the brutal, horrific murders committed by Charles Manson and his 'family.'
A — EN
Unknown — Palace Video Ltd   P
WW 993

Other Side of Midnight, The   Fil-Ent '77
Drama
07716   159 mins   C
V2, B, V

Marie-France Pisier, John Beck, Susan Sarandon, Raf Vallone, Clu Gulager, Michael Lerner, Sorrel Booke, directed by Charles Jarrott

Based on the novel by Sidney Sheldon, this film follows the story of a poor Marseilles girl. Set during and after the second World War she was

PALADIN VIDEO HOME ENTERTAINMENT GUIDE

abandoned, having been seduced by a Canadian airman, and went on to sleep her way to fame, fortune and the position of mistress to an internationally powerful shipping tycoon.
A — EN
Twentieth Century Fox — *CBS/Fox Video*
P
1135

Other Side of Nashville, The
Fil-Ent '84
Music-Performance
13432 112 mins C
B, V

A compilation of country music and a comprehensive insight into all aspects of the music, the people and the city are provided by this programme. The artists presented include Kenny Rogers, Johnny Cash, Kris Kristofferson, Emmylou Harris, Carl Perkins, Hank Williams, Jr., and Terry Gibbs on a stereo soundtrack.
F — EN
Transfilm Productions — *MGM/UA Home Video*   P
10351

Our Animals
Gen-Edu '??
Animals/Europe
06140 30 mins C
V2, B, V

A documentary of the multitude of animals and flowers that populate the mountains and rivers, marshes and woods of Europe. The little known world of water birds, chamois and many other animals are captured.
F — ED
Unknown — *Video Programme Distributors*
P
Cinehollywood—V950

Our Man Flint
Fil-Ent '66
Suspense/Adventure
07701 108 mins C
V2, B, V

James Coburn, Lee J. Cobb, Gila Golan, Edward Mulhare
An American super-agent living a life of luxurious bliss is hired by the Pentagon to put an end to the activities of an organisation called Galaxy. They plan to take over the world by controlling the weather.
S,A — EN
Twentieth Century Fox — *CBS/Fox Video*
P
1131

Out of Season
Fil-Ent '75
Drama/Romance
05436 87 mins C
B, V

Vanessa Redgrave, Cliff Robertson, Susan George, directed by Alan Bridges
Set in an English sea-side town during the bleak off season, this is the story of a mother and her daughter who run a small hotel. The mother's ex-lover from twenty years ago reappears to attempt to rekindle the relationship with the result that both the women become rivals for his affections.
BBFC:X — A — EN
Executive Action Enterprises — *THORN EMI*
P
TXC 90 0253 4/TVC 90 0253 2

Out of the Past/Hell's Highway
Fil-Ent '??
Crime-Drama/Drama
05705 152 mins B/W
B, V

Kirk Douglas, Robert Mitchum, Rhonda Fleming, Jane Greer, Steve Brodie, directed by Jacques Tourneur, Richard Dix, Tom Brown, Louise Carter, Rochelle Hudson, directed by Rowland Brown
Two films are contained on one cassette. 'Out of the Past' (Black/white, 93 mins, 1948) tells the story of a private detective who is hired by a man to find a girl who claims shot him and escaped with a large sum of money. The detective traces her to a New Mexico but becomes sure that she is innocent. 'Hell's Highway' (Black/white, 59 mins, 1933) is set in 1930 and draws attention to the appalling prison conditions of the time, a story involving chain gang fights and feuds with brutal prison guards.
S,A — EN
RKO — *Kingston Video*   H, P
KV37

Outback
Fil-Ent '71
Drama
09024 99 mins C
V2, B, V

Donald Pleasence, Gary Bond
A naive young teacher struggles against the harsh realities of the Australian outback, whilst an alcoholic dropout is determined to ram home some unbearably humiliating truths.
S,A — EN
United Artists — *Intervision Video*   H, P
AA0443

Outland
Fil-Ent '81
Science fiction
13054 109 mins C
B, V

Sean Connery, Peter Boyle, Frances Sternhagen, James B Sikking, directed by Peter Hyams

PALADIN VIDEO HOME ENTERTAINMENT GUIDE

A science fiction adventure in which a Marshall is detailed to unravel the mystery behind a spate of attempted suicides and psychotic attacks among the workers on the planet Lo, third moon of Jupiter.
BBFC:AA — C,A — EN
Outland Productions — *Warner Home Video* **P**
70002

Outlaw Blues
Fil-Ent '77
Comedy-Drama
13174   97 mins   C
B, V

Susan Saint James, directed by Richard T. Heffron

A prisoner on parole discovers that a country and western star has stolen his song and fights to get his due royalties, and at the same time gets involved in an accidental shooting.
BBFC:AA — C,A — EN
Warner Bros — *Warner Home Video* **P**
61146

Outlaw Josey Wales, The
Fil-Ent '76
Western
07864   130 mins   C
B, V

Clint Eastwood, Chief Dan George, Sondra Locke, Bill McKinney, John Vernon, directed by Clint Eastwood

An ex-Confederate soldier sets out to seek vengeance when his wife, family and home are destroyed during the Kansas-Missouri border wars. Based on a novel by Forrest Carter.
BBFC:AA — S,A — EN
Warner Bros — *Warner Home Video* **P**
WEX 61125/WEV 61125

Outlaw, The/Law of the Underworld
Fil-Ent '??
Western/Crime-Drama
05766   170 mins   B/W
B, V

Jane Russell, Walter Huston, Jack Buetel, Thomas Mitchell, directed by Howard Hughes, Anne Shirley, Chester Morris, Eduardo Cianelli, Jack Carson, directed by Lew Landers

Two films are contained on one cassette. 'The Outlaw' (black/white, 111 mins, 1944) is an adaptation of the Billy the Kid story. Billy and his girlfriend have a romantic interlude before the final showdown with Pat Garrett. 'Law of the Underworld' (black/white, 59 mins, 1939) is the story of two young lovers who are mugged and in an attempt to recover their life savings confront the leader of the gang. He uses them as part of a jewel raid and they are accused of robbery and murder.
S,A — EN
Howard Hughes; RKO — *Kingston Video* **H, P**
KV16

Outlaws Live in Concert, The
Fil-Ent '83
Music-Performance
12026   80 mins   C
B, V

This tape comprises 11 tracks, including 'Ghost Riders' and 'There Goes Another Love Song.' Recorded at the Tower Theatre in Philadelphia.
F — EN
Unknown — *Polygram Video* **H, P**
0402634/0402632

Outrage
Fil-Ent '73
Drama
04166   77 mins   C
B, V

Robert Culp, Marlyn Mason, Beah Richards, Jacqueline Scott, Ramon Bieri

Terrorism shows its ugly face in this story, based on reported incidents on the west coast of America.
BBFC:U — F — EN
ABC Circle Films — *Guild Home Video* **H, P**

Outsiders, The
Fil-Ent '83
Drama
12981   89 mins   C
B, V

Matt Dillon, Tom Cruise, Ralph Macchio, C. Thomas Howell, Dianne Lane, directed by Francis Ford Coppola

Based on the novel by S.E. Hinton, two teenage gangs, the rich kids and the boys from the wrong side of the tracks, wage war in Tulsa, Oklahoma
BBFC:PG — S,A — EN
Fred Roos; Grey Fredrickson — *Warner Home Video* **P**
61310

Over the Edge
Fil-Ent '83
Drama
13249   95 mins   C
B, V

Michael Kramer, Matt Dillon, Pamela Ludwig, directed by Jonathan Kaplan

---

(For Explanation of codes, see USE GUIDE and KEY)

PALADIN VIDEO HOME ENTERTAINMENT GUIDE

A band of teenage kids, bored by everyday life, turn against society and go on a rampage of sabotage and violence.
BBFC:18 — A — EN
George Litto — *CBS/Fox Video*   **P**
6618

Overlord   Fil-Ent '75
War-Drama
05885   85 mins   C
B, V
Brian Stirner, Davyd Harries, Nicholas Ball, Julie Neesam, directed by Stuart Cooper
Incorporating genuine newsreel footage, this is the story of one young man from his call-up to his death during the Normandy invasion in June 1944.
A — EN
James Quinn — *THORN EMI*   **P**
TXC 90 0223 4/TVC 90 0223 2

P

Pacific Inferno   Fil-Ent '??
Drama/Adventure
05559   90 mins   C
V2, B, V
Jim Brown, Wilma Reading, Richard Jaeckel, directed by Rolf Bayer
This film is the true story of the recovery of 16,000,000 dollars worth of silver pesos dumped into Manila Bay during the second World War. The pesos were ordered to be dumped to prevent their capture and use by the invading Japanese army. This film was shot on location where the incident took place.
BBFC:A — S,A — EN
Unknown — *Videomedia*   **P**
PVM 7100/BVM 7100/HVM 7100

Package Tour   Fil-Ent '??
Comedy-Drama
09465   84 mins   C
V2, B, V
Lasse Alberg
A man decides to escape the gloomy Swedish winter by going on holiday to the Canary Islands. Afraid of flying he visits a popular clinic where a doctor not only cures him, but makes him an innocent victim of a plot to smuggle money out of the country.
BBFC:PG — F — EN
Unknown — *Guild Home Video*   **H, P, E**

Paco de Lucia   Fil-Ent '7?
Music-Performance
04403   30 mins   C
B, V
The programme showcases the famous classical Spanish guitarist, Paco de Lucia.
F — EN
VCL — *VCL Video Services*   **P**

Paddington Goes to the Movies   Chl-Juv '8?
Fantasy
09811   42 mins   C
B, V
Narrated by Sir Michael Hordern, directed by Barry Leith
Paddington stars in five adventures from the award-winning 'Anywhere' TV shows. Also, a 20 minute special 'Paddington Visits the Cinema', and stars in his own special song and dance act.
F — EN
Film Fair Ltd. — *THORN EMI*   **P**
TXE 90 0867 4/TVE 90 0867 2

Paddington's First 'Anywhen' T.V. Show   Chl-Juv '77
Fantasy
01185   25 mins   C
B, V
The Paddington Bear appears in five separate stories on one videocassette: 'Please Look After This Bear,' 'A Bear in Hot Water,' 'Paddington Goes Underground,' 'A Shopping Expedition,' and 'Paddington and the Old Master.'
BBFC:U — F — EN
FilmFair — *THORN EMI*   **P**
TXF 90 0032 4/TVF 90 0032 2

Paddington's Second 'Anywhen' T.V. Show   Chl-Juv '77
Fantasy
05039   25 mins   C
B, V
Five separate Paddington Bear stories on one cassette: 'Mr. Amber's Mystery Tour,' 'A Family Group,' 'A Spot of Decorating,' 'Paddington Turns Detective' and 'Trouble at Number Thirty-Two.'
BBFC:U — F — EN
Film Fair — *THORN EMI*   **P**
TXF 90 0033 4/TVF 90 0033 2

Paddington's Third 'Anywhen' T.V. Show   Chl-Juv '77
Fantasy
01186   25 mins   C
B, V

PALADIN VIDEO HOME ENTERTAINMENT GUIDE

That lovable little character, Paddington Bear, appears in five misadventures: 'Paddington and the Christmas Shopping,' 'Christmas,' 'Too Much Off the Top,' 'A Visit to the Dentist,' and 'Do-It-Yourself.'
BBFC:U — F — EN
FilmFair — THORN EMI P
TXF 90 0034 4/TVF 90 0034 2

Paddington's Fourth 'Anywhen' T.V. Show
Chl-Juv '77
Fantasy
05036   25 mins   C
B, V
Five Paddington Bear stories on one cassette: 'A Disappearing Trick,' 'Paddington and the Cold Snap,' 'Paddington Makes a Clean Sweep,' 'An Unexpected Party' and 'Paddington Hits the Jackpot.'
BBFC:U — F — EN
Film Fair — THORN EMI P
TXF 90 0035 4/TVF 90 0035 2

Paddington's Fifth 'Anywhen' T.V. Show
Chl-Juv '77
Fantasy
01187   25 mins   C
B, V
Five further misadventures of Paddington Bear: 'A Sticky Time,' 'Paddington Hits Out,' 'A Visit to the Hospital,' 'Paddington Makes a Bid,' and 'Paddington Recommended.'
BBFC:U — F — EN
FilmFair — THORN EMI P
TXF 90 0036 4/TVF 90 0036 2

Paddington's Sixth 'Anywhen' T.V. Show
Chl-Juv '79
Fantasy
05438   25 mins   C
B, V
Narrated by Michael Harden, directed by Ivor Wood
Five more Paddington stories—'Something Nasty in the Kitchen,' 'Trouble at the Launderette,' 'Paddington Cleans Up,' 'Mr. Curry Takes a Bath' and 'Fortune Telling.'
BBFC:U — F — EN
Film Fair — THORN EMI P
TXF 90 0037 4/TVF 90 0037 2

Paddington's Seventh 'Anywhen' T.V. Show
Chl-Juv '82
Fantasy
08434   25 mins   C
B, V
Narrated by Michael Hordern, directed by Ivor Wood

Five more adventures with Paddington Bear: 'Paddington Clears the Coach', 'Trouble on the Beach', 'Paddington in the Hot Seat', 'Paddington Weighs In', and 'Paddington In Touch'.
BBFC:U — F — EN
FilmFair — THORN EMI P
TXF 90 0750 4/TVF 90 0750 2

Paddington's Eighth 'Anywhen' T.V. Show
Chl-Juv '79
Fantasy
08435   25 mins   C
B, V
Narrated by Michael Hordern, directed by Ivor Wood
Five more Paddington Bear Stories entitled 'Paddington in Court,' 'In and Out of Trouble,' 'Paddington and the Mystery Box,' 'Paddington Buys a Share' and 'Paddington Dines Out!'
BBFC:U — F — EN
FilmFair — THORN EMI P
TXF 90 0762 4/TVF 90 0762 2

Paddington's Ninth 'Anywhen' T.V. Show
Chl-Juv '82
Fantasy
09317   50 mins   C
B, V
Ten Paddington stories are included in this volume, among them 'A Picnic on the River', 'Trouble in the Bargain Basement' and 'Paddington Takes the Stage'.
F — EN
FilmFair — THORN EMI P
TXE 90 0855 4/TVE 90 0855 2

Paid In Blood
Fil-Ent '7?
Western
07787   88 mins   C
V2, B, V
Jeff Cameron, Donald O'Brian, Christa Nell, Alfredo Rizzo, Edilio Kim
This is the story of a man's quest to find the murderers of his brother.
S,A — EN
Unknown — Fletcher Video H, P
AV 614

Paint!
Fin-Art '8?
Painting
08735   100 mins   C
V2, B, V, LV
John FitzMaurice Mills
This tape introduces the pleasures of painting. It demonstrates basic techniques and approaches. Using the examples of landscape

PALADIN VIDEO HOME ENTERTAINMENT GUIDE

and still-life it shows how to create a good composition, the influence of light on a picture and how to build up major lines and shapes, and assess tone values.
S,A — I
Dick Foster — *BBC Video* **H, P**
BBCV 1016

Paint Me a Murder/The Late Nancy Irving   Fil-Ent '84
Drama/Suspense
13159   150 mins   C
B, V
Michelle Phillips, James Laurensen, David Robb, directed by Alan Cooke, Christina Raines, Marius Goring, Simon Williams, directed by Peter Sasdy
Two films are contained on one cassette. In 'Paint Me a Murder' an artist fakes his own death in order to push up the price of his paintings and 'The Late Nancy Irving' features a famous golfer who is kidnapped and realises she is to be killed.
BBFC:15 — S,A — EN
Hammer Film Prods — *Brent Walker Home Video Ltd* **P**
BW 34

Painting for Pleasure   Gen-Edu '8?
Painting
08761   157 mins   C
B, V
Duncan Killen
The tape is designed to introduce the beginner to an understanding of the use of artistic materials. Starting with charcoal and pencil a landscape develops into a water colour and an oil painting. It shows how the same landscape can become stylized, abstracted and made into a work of fantasy.
S,A — I
OVS Production — *Precision Video Ltd* **P**
VITC 2565/BITC 2565

Pam's Party   Fil-Ent '81
Comedy-Performance
06254   50 mins   C
B, V
Pam Ayres
A children's entertainment programme with the topical poetess Pam Ayres. She is seen with children playing games and reading selections of her rhymes in her unique style. The 'party' includes a day out at Crystal Palace Park where Pam and the children investigate the famous dinosaurs and the children's zoo.
F — EN
VCL; John Drury Associates — *VCL Video Services* **P**
F206C

Pancho Villa   Fil-Ent '72
Drama
01003   92 mins   C
B, V
Telly Savalas, Clint Walker, Chuck Connors, Anne Francis
Legendary bandit-hero becomes the symbol for freedom, as well as savagery, during revolt and war.
F — EN
Scotia Intl; Gene Martin — *VCL Video Services* **P**

Panda and the Magic Serpent   Fil-Ent '75
Cartoons/Adventure
05756   78 mins   C
B, V
Animated
An ancient Chinese legend tells of a little boy who found a white snake in his garden; he was not able to keep it for a pet. When he grew up and lived with a Panda and a Raccoon he still thought about the snake. It had grown into a beautiful maiden with magical powers; an evil magician kills the boy and she brings him back to life to end happily ever after.
BBFC:U — F — EN
ZIV International; Family Home Entertainment — *Home Video Holdings* **H, P**
026

Panic City   Fil-Ent '74
Suspense
04476   92 mins   C
V2, B, V
Austin Stoker, James Pickett, Hugh Smith, D'Urville Martin
A wily killer eludes homicide detectives, while the witness who can help them capture remains unconscious.
BBFC:X — A — EN
Essaness Pictures Corp — *Intervision Video* **H, P**
A-AE 0139

Panic in Echo Park   Fil-Ent '77
Drama
06955   75 mins   C
B, V
Dorian Harewood, Catlin Adams, Robin Gammell, Norman Bartold, directed by John Llewellyn Moxey
A doctor discovers that those suffering from a mysterious illness all live in the same apartment building in a minority community. He becomes determined to fight the hospital authorities and

PALADIN VIDEO HOME ENTERTAINMENT GUIDE

government officials to uncover the sinister causes of the epidemic. As the illness claims more victims he is accused of causing an unnecessary panic.
S,A — EN
Edgar J Scherick Associates — *Home Video Merchandisers* **H, P**
024

Panic in Needle Park   Fil-Ent '71
Drama
05641   106 mins   C
B, V

Al Pacino, Kitty Winn, Richard Bright, directed by Jerry Schatzberg

An innocent girl from Indiana falls in love with a New York heroin addict and becomes addicted herself. In this pathetic world they become involved in robbery pushing and prostitution to support their need. Based on a James Mills novel.
Cannes Film Festival '71: Best Actress (Winn).
S,A — EN
Twentieth Century Fox — *CBS/Fox Video*
P
3A-140

Panic in the City   Fil-Ent '68
Science fiction/Suspense
10201   96 mins   C
B, V

Howard Duff, Linda Cristal, Stephen McNally

An unidentified man is admitted to Los Angeles' General Hospital. His body is giving off enough radiation to infect everyone. A National Bureau of Investigation agent is brought in, and after the man's death it is discovered he was a noted European scientist. An atomic bomb has been activated within the city limits. The agent sacrifices his life by calling in a helicopter in a desperate attempt to deactivate the device.
BBFC:PG — S,A — EN
Harold Goldman; Feature Film Corp — *Video Form Pictures* **H, P**
DIP 17

Paper Chase, The   Fil-Ent '73
Drama
07715   107 mins   C
B, V

Timothy Bottoms, Lindsay Wagner, John Houseman, Graham Beckel, directed by James Bridges

A Harvard law student discovers that the going is tough during his first year but finds it even tougher when he falls in love with the attractive daughter of his tyrannical tutor.

Academy Awards '73: Best Supporting Actor (Houseman).   S,A — EN
Twentieth Century Fox — *CBS/Fox Video*
P
1046

Paper Tiger   Fil-Ent '75
Drama
08093   96 mins   C
B, V

David Niven, Toshiro Mifune, Hardy Kruger, Ivan Desny, Irene Tsu, Miiko Taka, Ronald Fraser, Jeff Corey, Directed by Ken Annakin

This film tells the story of an aging Englishman who becomes a tutor to the son of the Japanese Ambassador in a Pacific state. He regales his charge with brilliant, but false, accounts of his war exploits and then has to live up to these heroic fantasies when they are both abducted by terrorists.
BBFC:A — S,A — EN
Maclean and Company — *Rank Video Library*
H, P
0137 C

Paradine Case, The   Fil-Ent '48
Drama
04165   116 mins   B/W
B, V

Gregory Peck, Ann Todd, Charles Laughton, directed by Alfred Hitchcock

Legal battery engaged in defense and prosecution of woman accused of murdering her husband; the lady's attorney falls in love with her.
BBFC:A — S,A — EN
Selznick — *Guild Home Video*   **H, P**

Paradise   Fil-Ent '82
Adventure/Romance
10062   102 mins   C
V2, B, V, LV

Willie Aames, Phoebe Cates

A caravan travelling from Baghdad and Damascus is massacred by a slave trader called 'The Jackal'. Only two survive and they are pursued across the land by him until they came to an oasis. There they survive and learn to love.
S,A — EN
Robert Lantos; Stephen J Ross — *Embassy Home Entertainment*   **P**
1603

Paradise Alley   Fil-Ent '78
Drama
13297   105 mins   C
B, V

Sylvester Stallone, Armand Assante, Kevin Conway, Terry Funk, directed by Sylvester Stallone

(For Explanation of codes, see USE GUIDE and KEY)

PALADIN VIDEO HOME ENTERTAINMENT GUIDE

Three brothers set out to make some money out of wrestling in down town New York City.
BBFC:PG — S,A — EN
Universal — CIC Video   **H, P**
BEN 1096/VHN 1096

Paradise, Hawaiian Style   Fil-Ent '66
Musical
01012   91 mins   C   (PAL, NTSC)
B, V
Elvis Presley, Suzanna Leigh, James Shigeta
Out-of-work pilot returns to Hawaii, where he and a buddy start a charter service with two helicopters.
BBFC:U — F — EN   EL, SP
Paramount; Hal Wallis — CBS/Fox Video **P**
3B-069

Paraffin and Parafango Waxing   How-Ins '80
Beauty
02049   50 mins   C
B, V
Grace Andrews
The first in the planned 'Advanced Hair Tek Beauty Therapy' series.
C,A — I
Hair Tek Video — VideoSpace Ltd   **H, P**

Paranoia   Fil-Ent '69
Drama
09203   94 mins   C
B, V
Carroll Baker, Lou Castel, Colette Descombes
This film tells of a beautiful widow who meets, at her Roman villa, a college student, who seduces her. She becomes imprisoned by her own paranoia, as the people she had once trusted conspire to betray and blackmail her.
BBFC:X — A — EN
Commonwealth United; Titanius Films — Video Form Pictures   **H, P**
MGD 7

Parasite   Fil-Ent '8?
Horror
09169   80 mins   C
V
Robert Glaudini, Denis Moore, Buca Bercovici, James Davidson, Al Fann, Tom Villard, Cherie Currie, Vivian Blaine
Set in the year 1992, this film tells of the nightmarish creation of a squirming parasite, a deadly demon designed to decimate a panicked population. It feeds on flesh and blood, with rows of razor sharp teeth.
C,A — EN
Unknown — Entertainment in Video   **H, P**

Paris, Texas   Fil-Ent '84
Drama
13119   144 mins   C
B, V
Harry Dean Stanton, Dean Stockwell, Nastassja Kinski, directed by Wim Wenders
An emaciated man comes staggering out of the Texas badlands where he has been lost for four years and after being re-united with his small son, begins a search for his wife.
Cannes Grand Prix '84.
BBFC:15 — S,A — EN
Road Movies; Argos Films; Project Film — Palace Video Ltd   **P**
PVC 2078A

Partners   Fil-Ent '82
Comedy/Suspense
13315   90 mins   C
B, V
Kenneth McMillian, Ryan O'Neal, Joseph R Sicari, John Hurt, directed by James Burrows
Two Los Angeles cops set up together to infiltrate the gay community in order to get a lead on a homosexual murder.
BBFC:15 — S,A — EN
Paramount — CIC Video   **H, P**
BET 2102/VHT 2102

Passage, The   Fil-Ent '??
War-Drama
06210   98 mins   C
B, V
Patricia Neal, Malcolm McDowell, Anthony Quinn, James Mason, Christopher Lee
For an escaping scientist there is only one way out; he must cross the perilous mountain passage separating occupied France from Spain. His shepherd guide is unaware that the fugitive intends to take his family with him. They are pursued by a brutal S.S. officer.
S,A — EN
Goldsmith/Binder Production — VCL Video Services   **P**
P188D

Passione d'Amore   Fil-Ent '81
Drama
12870   88 mins   C
B, V
Valeria D'Obici, Bernard Giraudeau, Laura Antonelli, directed by Ettore Scola
A sensual drama in which a man has to choose between a woman who lived for his love and the other who would die for it. Musical score played by Benny Goodman.
Cannes Film Festival: Special Award
BBFC:18 — A — EN
Warner International — Vestron Video International   **P**
14026

PALADIN VIDEO HOME ENTERTAINMENT GUIDE

Pat Garrett and Billy the Kid
Fil-Ent '73
Western
08675   102 mins   C
B, V

James Coburn, Kris Kristofferson, Bob Dylan, Jason Robards, Rita Coolidge, directed by Sam Peckinpah
This film tells the story of an aging outlaw who, whilst trying to come to terms with the end of the 'wild west, turns into a lawman. An old sidekick finds himself on the run from his friend, a chase which takes the pair deep into New Mexico where it leads to the inevitable tragic climax.
BBFC:X — A — EN
MGM — *MGM/UA Home Video*   P
UMB10159/UMV 10159

Pathfinders—Code Name 'Gomorrah'
Fil-Ent '7?
War-Drama
05507   53 mins   C
B, V

Jack Watling, Robert Urquhart, Paul Massie, Mike Pratt, Bernard Lee
This film is an episode in the 'Pathfinder' series centred round an elite squadron of Lancaster bombers. Each episode is a complete story and is based on actual events. In 'Code Name 'Gomorrah'' the squadron together with scientists and a Belgian Resistance group are involved with the first operational trial of a revolutionary blind-bombing radar aid.
S,A — EN
Unknown — *Derann Film Services*   H, P
BDV106B/BDV106

Pathfinders—Fly There—Walk Back
Fil-Ent '7?
War-Drama
05504   53 mins   C
B, V

Jack Watling, Robert Urquhart, Michael Coles, Jane Seymore
This film is an episode in the 'Pathfinder' series centred round an elite squadron of Lancaster bombers. Each episode is a complete story and is based on actual events. 'Fly There—Walk Back' is an escape drama in which three crew members of a bomber make their way through Germany and France with the help of the Resistance.
S,A — EN
Unknown — *Derann Film Services*   H, P
BDV103B/BDV103

Pathfinders—Fog
Fil-Ent '7?
War-Drama
05503   53 mins   C
B, V

Jack Watling, Robert Urquhart, Christopher Casenove, Kate O'Mara, Jack May, William Marlowe
This film is an episode in the 'Pathfinder' series centred round an elite squadron of Lancaster bombers. Each episode is a complete story and is based on actual events. 'Fog' follows a hazardous low-level mine laying operation against a heavily defended naval base. There is also a personal drama involving two of the pilots and a W.A.A.F. officer.
S,A — EN
Unknown — *Derann Film Services*   H, P
BDV102B/BDV102

Pathfinders—For Better, For Worse
Fil-Ent '7?
War-Drama
05505   53 mins   C
B, V

Jack Watling, Robert Urquhart, Jennifer Clulaw, Peter Armitage
This film is an episode in the 'Pathfinder' series centred round an elite squadron of Lancaster bombers. Each episode is a complete story and is based on actual events. 'For Better, For Worse' follows the squadron's co-operation with a Commando force and a civilian 'boffin' to try to capture vital enemy radar personnel and equipment from occupied Europe.
S,A — EN
Unknown — *Derann Film Services*   H, P
BDV105B/BDV105

Pathfinders—In the Face of the Enemy
Fil-Ent '7?
War-Drama
05513   53 mins   C
B, V

Jack Watling, Robert Urquhart, Dennis Waterman
This film is an episode in the 'Pathfinder' series centred round an elite squadron of Lancaster bombers. Each episode is a complete story and is based on actual events. 'In the Face of the Enemy' involves two crew members of a Lancaster, recently wounded in action who come face to face with the enemy in a hospital ward.
S,A — EN
Unknown — *Derann Film Services*   H, P
BDV111B/BDV111

Pathfinders—Into the Fire
Fil-Ent '7?
War-Drama
05502   53 mins   C
B, V

Jack May, Jonathan Sweet, David Ashford, Robert Urquhart, Jack Watling

PALADIN VIDEO HOME ENTERTAINMENT GUIDE

This film is an episode in the 'Pathfinder' series centred round an elite squadron of Lancaster bombers. Each episode is a complete story and is based on actual events. 'Into the Fire' follows the squadron through the various hazards of their operation. Their task is to lead bombing raids, flying without fighting escort, before the main force to place flares and markers on the target.
S,A — EN
Unknown — *Derann Film Services* H, P
BDV101B/BDV101

Pathfinders—Jonah Man   Fil-Ent '7?
War-Drama
05508   53 mins   C
B, V

Jack Watling, Robert Urquhart, Julian Orchard, Eric Flynn, Colin Campbell
This film is an episode in the 'Pathfinder' series centred round an elite squadron of Lancaster bombers. Each episode is a complete story and is based on actual events. 'Jonah Man' follows an air raid during which at a most critical point a crew are forced to ditch their aircraft in the sea.
S,A — EN
Unknown — *Derann Film Services* H, P
BDV107B/BDV107

Pathfinders—Nightmare   Fil-Ent '7?
War-Drama
05514   53 mins   C
B, V

Jack Watling, Robert Urquhart, John Bluthal, Paul Shelley, Ian Stirling
This film is an episode in the 'Pathfinder' series centred round an elite squadron of Lancaster bombers. Each episode is a complete story and is based on actual events. In 'Nightmare' a Lancaster has to force-land at its base with a live bomb aboard. This story pays particular tribute to the ground crew of the R.A.F.
S,A — EN
Unknown — *Derann Film Services* H, P
BDV112B/BDV112

Pathfinders—One Man's   Fil-Ent '7?
Lancaster
War-Drama
05506   53 mins   C
B, V

Jack Watling, Anthony Valentine
This film is an episode in the 'Pathfinder' series centred round an elite squadron of Lancaster bombers. Each episode is a complete story and is based on actual events. 'One Man's Lancaster' concerns a clash of personalities between two pilots with differing temperaments leading to an attempt by one of them to fly his crewless Lancaster back from a raid on an Italian target.
S,A — EN
Unknown — *Derann Film Services* H, P
BDV105B/BDV105

Pathfinders—Operation   Fil-Ent '7?
Pickpocket
War-Drama
05511   53 mins   C
B, V

Jack Watling, Robert Urquhart, Richard Franklin, Mark Eden
This film is an episode in the 'Pathfinder' series centred round an elite squadron of Lancaster bombers. Each episode is a complete story and is based on actual events. 'Operation Pickpocket' is a prisoner of war story in which the navigator of a shot-down Lancaster tries to prevent the Germans from gaining the secret of a new target finding device the aircraft was carrying.
S,A — EN
Unknown — *Derann Film Services* H, P
BDV109B/BDV109

Pathfinders—Our   Fil-Ent '7?
Daffodils Are Better Than
Your Daffodils
War-Drama
05510   53 mins   C
B, V

Jack Watling, Robert Urquhart, Christopher Timothy, John Levene
This film is an episode in the 'Pathfinder' series centred round an elite squadron of Lancaster bombers. Each episode is a complete story and is based on actual events. 'Our Daffodils Are Better Than Your Daffodils' is a light hearted romp in which two airmen are commissioned to pick up a member of the resistance in France. After befriending a German sergeant they return to England taking him along and end up in trouble with the C.O.
S,A — EN
Unknown — *Derann Film Services* H, P
BDV113B/BDV113

Pathfinders—Sitting   Fil-Ent '7?
Ducks
War-Drama
05509   53 mins   C
B, V

Jack Watling, Robert Urquhart, Johnny Wade, Richard Shaw, Julian Orchard
This film is an episode in the 'Pathfinder' series centred round an elite squadron of Lancaster bombers. Each episode is a complete story and is based on actual events. In 'Sitting Ducks'

PALADIN VIDEO HOME ENTERTAINMENT GUIDE

German Night Fighters have gained temporary control over Bomber Command but the Lancaster squadron with the Dutch Resistance soon rectify the situation.
S,A — EN
Unknown — *Derann Film Services* H, P
BDV108B/BDV108

Pathfinders—Sweets from a Stranger   Fil-Ent '7?
War-Drama
05512   53 mins   C
B, V
Jack Watling, Robert Urquhart, Johnny Briggs, Christopher Cazenove, Linda Marlow
This film is an episode in the 'Pathfinder' series centred round an elite squadron of Lancaster bombers. Each episode is a complete story and is based on actual events. 'Sweets from a Stranger' involves a small boy who becomes an unusual ally of the crew of a Lancaster in their attempts to delay the growing menace of the German Fighters.
S,A — EN
Unknown — *Derann Film Services* H, P
BDV110B/BDV110

Patience   Fil-Ent '8?
Opera
08924   100 mins   C
B, V
Donald Adams, Roderick Kennedy, Terry Jenkins, Derek Hammond-Stroud, John Fryatt, Shirley Chapman, Shelagh Squires, Patricia Hay, Anne Collins
This opera by Gilbert and Sullivan tells of a world gone mad, with languid ladies and affected gentlemen. Reginald Bunthorne falls in love with the village milkmaid, who doesn't like poetry, nor understand love. When she finally discovers, it is Reginald's rival that she decides to marry. The music is performed by The London Symphony Orchestra, conducted by Alexander Faris with The Ambrosian Opera Chorus.
S,A — EN
Brent Walker Prods — *Brent Walker Home Video Ltd*   P

Patrick   Fil-Ent '78
Suspense
06238   104 mins   C
B, V
Susan Penhaligon, Robert Helpmann, Rod Mullinar
A young man has suffered an electrical 'accident' and is in a coma. In a seedy hospital he develops unusual powers which enable him to influence the lives of people around him, his powers develop and strengthen.
S,A — EN
Anthony I Ginnane — *VCL Video Services*   P
C154C

Patti Page Show, The   Fil-Ent '7?
Variety
04375   60 mins   C
B, V, PH17, 3/4U
Patti Page, International Children's Choir
A variety show starring Patti Page, with the International Children's Choir.
F — EN
Unknown — *Vidpics International*   P

Patton   Fil-Ent '70
War-Drama
01738   171 mins   C
V2, B, V
George C. Scott, Karl Malden, Stephen Young, directed by Franklin J. Schaffner
World War II: General Patton and his battles in North Africa, Sicily, and with the War Department.
Academy Awards '70: Best Picture; Best Actor (Scott); Best Director.   BBFC:A — *F — EN*
20th Century Fox — *CBS/Fox Video*   P
4A-017

Paul Anka Show, The   Fil-Ent '7?
Variety
04370   60 mins   C
B, V, PH17, 3/4U
Paul Anka, Hannah Ahroni
A variety show with Paul Anka and Hannah Ahroni.
F — EN
Unknown — *Vidpics International*   P

Paul Daniels—'Now You See It'   Fil-Ent '82
Magic
06835   60 mins   C
B, V
Paul Daniels
In this programme Paul Daniels, Britain's most popular magician, runs through 22 routines. He spends the first half performing the tricks and the second half revealing how to do them. He demonstrates how to achieve magical illusion with such simple props as rope, dice, cups, rice

PALADIN VIDEO HOME ENTERTAINMENT GUIDE

and even a telephone. He ends the show with a series of baffling card shuffles showing how progress can be made once the basics are mastered.
S,A — EN
Chrysalis Visual Programming — *Chrysalis Video* **P**
CVIM BE 6/CVIM VH 6

Paul McCartney and Wings Rockshow   Fil-Ent '81
Music-Performance
05297   102 mins   C
B, V
A record of the concert given by Wings at the King Dome in Seattle in front of 67,000 fans. It features twenty-three songs, including 'Yesterday,' 'Band on the Run,' 'Maybe I'm Amazed,' 'Jet,' and 'Venus and Mars.'
F — EN
MPL Communications — *THORN EMI* **P**
TXD 90 0512 4/TVD 90 0512 2

Paul Simon in Concert   Fil-Ent '81
Music-Performance
07865   60 mins   C
B, V
This is a record of a concert given by singer, song writer and guitarist Paul Simon at the Tower Theatre in Philadelphia. It features songs including 'Me and Julio', 'Fifty Ways to Leave Your Lover,' 'Sounds of Silence,' 'Late in the Evening' and 'One Trick Pony.'
S,A — EN
Michael Tannen; Phil Ramone; Peregrine Inc — *Warner Home Video* **P**
WEX 84005/WEV 84005

Paul Young—The Video Singles   Fil-Ent '85
Music video
13666   30 mins   C
B, V
Paul Young sings five songs on this cassette titled 'Wherever I Lay My Head', 'Come Back And Stay', 'Tear Your Playhouse Down', 'Everything Must Change' and 'Everytime You Go Away'.
M,A — EN
Unknown — *CBS/Fox Video* **P**

Pavarotti   Fil-Ent '??
Music-Performance/Opera
09882   60 mins   C
B, V, LV
This tape features one of the world's greatest tenors, Luciano Pavarotti, accompanied by the Royal Philharmonic Orchestra at the Royal Albert Hall in the presence of HM the Queen Mother. Recorded in stereo.
F — EN
Unknown — *Polygram Video*   **H, P**
790 5884/790 5882/790 5881

Pawnbroker, The   Fil-Ent '65
Drama
04679   109 mins   B/W
B, V
Rod Steiger, Brock Peters, Jaime Sanchez, Geraldine Fitzgerald
The key figure is a survivor from a Nazi extermination camp and the film deals with his attempts to live cloistered in the midst of modern life.
Berlin Film Festival '64: Best Actor (Steiger).
F — EN
Landau-Unger — *Polygram Video* **P**

PayDay   Fil-Ent '72
Drama
05433   98 mins   C
B, V
Rip Torn, Ahna Capri, Michael C. Gwynne, Jeff Morris, Cliff Emmich, Elayne Heilveil, directed by Daryl Duke
The story of a Country and Western singer who, despite having all the trappings of a star, is disillusioned with his far from glamorous existance. His mother will not feed his dog, his wife and three children have become millstones, his mistresses are boring; the only person he can turn to is his driver-cum-bodyguard. The film exposes the sleazy world of life 'on the road.'
A — EN
Saul Zaentz Company — *THORN EMI* **P**
TXB 90 0324 4/TVB 90 0324 2

Pearl Bailey Show, The   Fil-Ent '71
Variety
04366   60 mins   C
B, V, PH17, 3/4U
Pearl Bailey, Krofft Puppets, Ethel Waters
A musical variety show with Pearl Bailey and an assortment of celebrity guest stars.
F — EN
Unknown — *Vidpics International* **P**

Pearls—The Video   Fil-Ent '82
Music-Performance
09335   90 mins   C
B, V
Elkie Brooks, directed by Derek Burbridge
This tape features live performances by Elkie Brooks filmed during her 1982 UK tour when she played 64 sold-out concerts in 61 days.

PALADIN VIDEO HOME ENTERTAINMENT GUIDE

Songs include tracks from her 'Pearls' album plus some that have not been released on record. All her hit songs are featured—'Lilac Wine,' 'Nights in White Satin,' 'Pearl's a Singer,' and 'Fool.'
F — EN
A&M Sound Pictures; Zeotrope Ltd — *A&M Sound Pictures* **P**

Peeper Fil-Ent '75
Comedy/Drama
12085   87 mins   C
B, V
Michael Caine, Natalie Wood, directed by Peter Hyams
Two girls run off with their gangster father's ill-gotten gains. A private eye is hired to find them and bring back the money.
S,A — EN
Twentieth Century Fox — *CBS/Fox Video* **P**
1222

Peggy Lee Show, The Fil-Ent '7?
Variety
04374   60 mins   C
B, V, PH17, 3/4U
Peggy Lee   2 pgms
Two separate musical variety shows starring Peggy Lee, with various guest stars.
F — EN
Unknown — *Vidpics International* **P**

Peking Blond Fil-Ent '67
Suspense
06192   78 mins   C
B, V
Edward G. Robinson, Mireille Darc, Claude Brook
American, Russian and Chinese Secret Services tangle in a web of world-wide espionage. A young girl suffering from amnesia gets caught in the snare; she is recognised as the mistress of a top scientist. The CIA and KGB close in but find she does not possess stolen secrets but a priceless black pearl.
F — EN
Ben Barry Associates — *VCL Video Services* **P**
X028Z

Pele Spo-Lei '79
Football
01995   69 mins   C
B, V
Commentary by Martin Tyler
The story of the world's greatest footballer is told from Pele's unheralded triumph as a 17-year-old in Sweden in 1958, through four World Championships and over 1,000 goals. Pele also passes on his skills to aspiring young football players.
F — EN
Brazil — *Quadrant Video* **H, P**

Pele Spo-Lei '80
Football
05890   60 mins   C
B, V
The film traces the progress of the Brazilian footballer, from his success as a 17 year-old in Sweden in 1958, to Brazil's World Cup victory in Mexico in 1970. Pele also demonstrates his talent and skills in his role as a coach.
F — EN
TV Globo Limitado — *THORN EMI* **P**
TXE 90 7100 4/TVE 90 7100 2

Pele: The Master and His Method Fil-Ent '??
Football/Documentary
05653   60 mins   C
B, V
The Brazilian soccer star is seen instructing children, at practice and in highlights from his most famous matches. It covers his career until he retired in 1971. He demonstrates his skill and the film covers technical aspects of the game from ball juggling to conditioning.
F — EN
Unknown — *CBS/Fox Video* **P**

Penitentiary Fil-Ent '81
Drama
05419   99 mins   C
V2, B, V
This is the compelling and harrowing story of a man, wrongly convicted of murder, who struggles to transcend the brutality of prison life by becoming a boxer.
C,A — EN
Unknown — *Videomedia* **P**
PVM 1030/BVM 1030/HVM 1030

Penitentiary II Fil-Ent '82
Drama
08605   108 mins   C
V2, B, V
Leon Isaac Kennedy
This film is the sequel to 'Penitentiary' and tells the rough and bitter story of Two Sweet, who fought his way to freedom from the State

(For Explanation of codes, see USE GUIDE and KEY)   503

PALADIN VIDEO HOME ENTERTAINMENT GUIDE

Penitentiary. It retraces the vendetta between him and his rival who has sworn to kill him. He enters the boxing ring with the aim of winning the biggest prize in the world.
BBFC:X — A — EN
MGM/UA — *Videomedia* **P**
PVM 0100/BVM 0100/HVM 0100

People, The   Fil-Ent '71
Science fiction
08020   74 mins   C
V2, B, V
William Shatner, Kim Darby, Diane Varsi, produced by Francis Ford Coppola, directed by John Corty
The film is set in a small, secluded, rural village. Two outsiders enter the community to discover to their amazement that the pupils have telepathic powers.
S,A — EN
M P C — *Iver Film Services* **P**
182

People's Champion, The   Spo-Lei '82
Sports-Minor
08717   150 mins   C
B, V
This tape features the 1982 Embassy World Professional Snooker Championships. It begins with Steve Davis defending the coveted world title and ends with the triumphant success for Alex 'Hurricane' Higgins, the eventual winner of the series.
F — EN
Nick Hunter; John Vigar; Mike Brock — *BBC Video*   **H, P**
BBCV 5017

Percy   Fil-Ent '71
Comedy
05035   97 mins   C
B, V
Hywel Bennett, Elke Sommer, Denholm Elliott, Britt Ekland, directed by Ralph Thomas
Hywel Bennett plays a suave antique dealer who has an unfortunate accident which results in him having to have a penis transplant.
BBFC:X — A — EN
Betty Box — *THORN EMI* **P**
TXB 90 0310 4/TVB 90 0310 2

Percy's Progress   Fil-Ent '74
Comedy
08552   109 mins   C
B, V
Leigh Lawson, Elke Sommer, Denholm Elliot, Judy Geeson, Harry H. Corbett, Vincent Price, Barry Humphries, Anthony Andrews, directed by Ralph Thomas

This film continues the story of Perry who now finds himself the only man who possesses a Percy not made lifeless by polluted drinking water. Before he can take advantage of all the frantic women he is taken into custody until he is needed to serve the needs of the lovely winners of a contest.
BBFC:X — A — EN
Welbeck Films — *THORN EMI* **P**
TXB 90 0766 4/TVB 90 07762

Perfect Crime, The   Fil-Ent '??
Crime-Drama
06112   105 mins   C
V2, B, V
Gloria Guida, Anthony Steel, Leonard Mann, Adolfo Celi
A President of a world trust is killed in an explosion when his jet is sabotaged; his three remaining vice-presidents all die atrocious deaths in rapid succession. Millions of dollars are tied up in the murders; Scotland Yard have the task of solving the crimes.
S,A — EN
Unknown — *Video Programme Distributors* **P**
Cinehollywood—V1090

Perfect Friday   Fil-Ent '70
Crime-Drama/Comedy
08822   92 mins   C
B, V
Ursula Andress, Stanley Baker, David Warner, Patience Collier, directed by Peter Hall
An assistant bank manager, tired of his ordinary London life, plans to rob his bank. He finds an aristocratic but near bankrupt couple to assist him in his perfect robbery.
BBFC:X — A — EN
Chevron; Dimitri de Grunwald Prod — *VCL Video Services* **P**
P273D

Perfect Killer, The   Fil-Ent '77
Crime-Drama
07682   90 mins   C
B, V
Lee Van Cleef, Tita Barker, John Ireland, Robert Widmark
A man manages to avoid serving his prison sentence by working as a hired killer for the Syndicate. He becomes tired of violence and wants to live in peace. Before beginning a new life, he sets out to seek revenge on two people who doublecrossed him, but the Syndicate have sent a sadistic young killer to eliminate him.
S,A — EN
A.J.P.T and Metheus Film Production — *Video Network* **P**
0014

---

504   (For Explanation of codes, see USE GUIDE and KEY)

PALADIN VIDEO HOME ENTERTAINMENT GUIDE

Performance   Fil-Ent '70
Drama
07866   101 mins   C
B, V

Mick Jagger, James Fox, Anita Pallenberg, Michele Breton, directed by Donald Cammell and Nicholas Roeg

A vicious strong-arm man finds himself in trouble when he oversteps his bosses. In need of a change of identity and a hideout, he moves into the apartment of a temporarily retired rock star.
BBFC:X — *A* — *EN*
Warner Bros — *Warner Home Video*   P
WEX 61131/WEV 61131

Perils of Pauline, The   Fil-Ent '47
Musical/Comedy
06880   93 mins   C
V2, B, V

Betty Hutton, John Lund, Billy DeWolfe, Directed by George Marshall

This film portrays the life story of Pearl White, the queen of the silent movies. From humble beginnings the film traces her romantic ups and downs to the movie debut that made her top-of-the-bill at the Folies Bergere. Songs by Frank Loesser include 'I Wish I Didn't Love You So.'
S,A — *EN*
Paramount — *European Video Company*
P

Persecution   Fil-Ent '74
Horror
05177   93 mins   C
B, V

Lana Turner, Ralph Bates, Trevor Howard, Olga Georges-Picot

David Masters is dominated by his rich, bitter and crippled mother. As a child he was tormented and terrified by her in a series of bizarre incidents. Now aged twenty four, with a wife and baby he is still subject to his mother's evil influence. When she is involved in two dramatic deaths, David's mind snaps with horrifying and tragic results.
BBFC:AA — *C,A* — *EN*
Fanfare — *Rank Video Library*   H, P
2001

Perversion Story   Fil-Ent '??
Drama
08909   91 mins   C
V2, B, V

Brett Halsey, Romina Power

A man sets out to discover the reason for his sister's suicide. He eventually finds a conspiracy of corruption, perversion and drugs.
BBFC:X — *A* — *EN*
Unknown — *Video Programme Distributors*
P
Inter-Ocean 032

Peter Cook and Co   Fil-Ent '81
Comedy-Performance
06280   52 mins   C
B, V

Peter Cook, Rowan Atkinson, John Cleese, Terry Jones, Robert Langdon, Beryl Reid, Paula Wilcox, Body Language

This film is a comedy special written by and starring Peter Cook in a series of new sketches and characteristics. Sketches include John Cleese as Neville Chamberlain, Rowan Atkinson interviewing the world's authority on ants, a tale in the series 'Tales of the Much Expected,' the soap opera 'The Amnesiacs' and many others featuring a host of new characters.
International Film and TV Festival '81: Gold Award for Comedy.   *S,A* — *EN*
London Weekend Television Limited — *THORN EMI*   P
TXB 90 0744 4/TVB 90 0744 2

Peter Grimes   Fin-Art '81
Opera
09798   153 mins   C
B, V

Jon Vickers, Heather Harper, Norman Bailey, directed by John Vernon

This opera, the work of Benjamin Britten, was first performed in 1945. It is acknowledged as one of the twentieth century's finest operas. Set in a small fishing village on the east coast of England, it tells of the conflict between an individual and the outside world, ending in tragedy.
F — *EN*
Covert Garden Video Productions Ltd. — *THORN EMI*   P
TXH 90 1712 4/TVH 90 1712 2

Peter-No-Tail   Fil-Ent '83
Cartoons/Fantasy
12669   81 mins   C
V2, B, V
Animated

This is a film telling the adventures of a host of colourful cats called Mons, Silly Billy, Stupid Bull and Peter-No-Tail.
F — *EN*
The Swedish Film Institute — *Videomedia*
P
2119

(For Explanation of codes, see USE GUIDE and KEY)

PALADIN VIDEO HOME ENTERTAINMENT GUIDE

Peter Ustinov Tells   Chl-Juv   '7?
Stories from Hans
Christian Andersen
Fairy tales
04681   45 mins   C
B, V
Narrated by Peter Ustinov
'The Ugly Duckling,' 'The Swineherd' and 'The Steadfast Tin Soldier' are the famous fairy tales related in this programme.
PS,I — EN
Spectrum   —   *Polygram Video*   **P**

Petersfinger Cuckoos,   Gen-Edu   '8?
The
Birds/Wildlife
09098   ? mins   C
B, V
Directed by Ted Channell
This programme vividly depicts the unusual lifestyle of the cuckoo. It shows an actual filming of a parent bird laying an egg in a reed warbler's nest.
F — ED
Royal Society for the Protection of Birds — *Royal Society for the Protection of Birds*   **H, P**

Pete's Dragon   Fil-Ent   '77
Fantasy/Musical
05583   102 mins   C
B, V
Helen Reddy, Jim Dale, Mickey Rooney, Red Buttons, Shelley Winters
This film blends animation with live-action in a musical about a Dragon called Elliott. He helps his orphan friend run away from a mean foster family to live in a New England lighthouse. However, the villains are on their trail.
F — EN
Walt Disney Productions — *Rank Video Library*   **H**
01000

Phantasm   Fil-Ent   '79
Horror
01962   90 mins   C
B, V
Michael Baldwin, Bill Thornbury
Two brothers discover the startling secret of the living dead when their friend is murdered.
BBFC:X — *C,A — EN*
Avco Embassy — *VCL Video Services*   **P**

Phantom of the Opera,   Fil-Ent   '25
The
Horror
04672   74 mins   B/W
B, V
Lon Chaney, Norman Kerry, Mary Philbin
An unknown entity terrorises a Paris Opera House. Silent; colour-tinted.
F — EN
Universal — *Polygram Video*   **P**

Phantom of the Opera   Fil-Ent   '83
Horror
10221   120 mins   C
B, V
Maximillian Schell, Jane Seymour, Michael York, Jeremy Kemp, Diana Quick, Phillip Stone, Paul Brooke, directed by Robert Markowitz
Set in Budapest before World War I. A rising opera star commits suicide after a Baron, whose affections she had spurned, bribes a critic to print poor reviews. Her husband confronts him; during the struggle the critic is killed and the husband is badly burned. He retreats to the sewers hiding his madness behind a deathlike mask. Four years later he returns to destroy the Baron and avenge his wife's death in a final performance.
BBFC:18 — *A — EN*
Robert Halmi — *Video Form Pictures*   **H, P**
MGS 34

Philadelphia Experiment,   Fil-Ent   '84
The
Science fiction
13706   96 mins   C
B, V
Michael Pare, Nancy Allen, directed by Stewart Raffill
Two young seamen are accidentally projected through a time warp forty years ahead of time to 1984 and as they try to return catastrophe threatens the world.
BBFC:PG — *F — EN*
Joel B Michaels; Douglas Curtis — *THORN EMI*   **P**
90 2782

Phillip the Evangelist   Gen-Edu   '??
Religion/Bible
06287   43 mins   B/W
B, V, PH15
In this film Mr. W. Turner gives an exposition of Evangelism on New Testament lines and how a person may believe today.
S,A — R
Audio Visual Ministries — *Audio Visual Ministries*   **H, L, P**
VT143

Phobia   Fil-Ent   '80
Drama
09808   85 mins   C
B, V

PALADIN VIDEO HOME ENTERTAINMENT GUIDE

Paul Michael Glaser, Susan Hogan, John Colicos, directed by John Huston
A psychological thriller which centres round five phobia victims, all convicted murderers, who become guinea pigs in medical experiments to cure them of their illness.
BBFC:18 — C,A — EN
Borough Park Productions — THORN EMI P
TXB 90 08504/TVB 90 08502

Photographer, The   Fil-Ent '75
Crime-Drama/Suspense
10066   93 mins   C
V2, B, V
Michael Callan, Spencer Milligan, Harold J. Stone, Edward Andrews, Jed Allan, Barbara Nichols
A trendy photographer, filled with a passionate hatred for his mother, sets out to take his revenge on all the women who find him attractive. One by one they die in bizarre circumstances. Comic relief is provided by two detectives whose main obsession is food.
C,A — EN
Unknown — Embassy Home Entertainment P
2088

Physical Assault   Fil-Ent '??
War-Drama
05472   82 mins   C
V2, B, V
Peter Hooten, Maleo, directed by W. H. Bushnell
A group of G.I.'s capture a Vietcong spy during the war in Vietnam. The G.I.'s are not the same again after the spy is subjected to merciless torture and as a result dies.
BBFC:X — A — EN
Unknown — Iver Film Services P
61

Piaf   Fil-Ent '82
Drama/Biographical
09043   102 mins   C
B, V
Brigitte Ariel
Set in the 1930's, this film portrays the life of the legendary French singer, Edith Piaf, from her birth in a Paris gutter, through the scandals and setbacks on her way to her fight for recognition. The soundtrack includes many of the great singer's most popular recordings.
BBFC:PG — S,A — EN
Moritz-Weissman — VideoSpace Ltd P

Picnic at Hanging Rock   Fil-Ent '75
Mystery/Drama
05745   115 mins   C
B, V
Rachel Roberts, Dominic Guard, Helen Morse, Jack Weaver, directed by Peter Weir
This film is based on a true incident that occurred in Australia on St. Valentine's Day 1900 and which has remained unsolved to this day. A party of schoolgirls, a french teacher and a maths teacher arrange a picnic at a local beauty spot. A strange eerie incident occurs and they return without three girls and a teacher; only one girl is found, who remembers nothing.
BBFC:A — M,A — EN
Picnic Productions Pty Ltd — Home Video Holdings   H, P
010

Picture Music   Fil-Ent '81
Music-Performance
05318   80 mins   C
B, V
A compilation of the original videos made initially for promotional purposes of contemporary hits. Features Kate Bush, Duran Duran, Toyah, Depeche Mode, Gary Numan, Kim Carnes, Genesis, Classix Noveaux, The Tubes, Bill Wyman, Bad Manners, John Watts, UB40, The Undertones, The Stranglers, Dr Feelgood, Bow Wow Wow, The Vapours, Peter Gabriel and Thomas Dolby.
F — EN
EMI Music — THORN EMI P
TXE90 0555 4/TVE 90 0555 2

Picture Show Man, The   Fil-Ent '77
Comedy
04157   99 mins   C
B, V
John Mellion, Rod Taylor, John Ewart, Harold Hopkins, Patrick Cargill
A father and son team Australia putting on picture shows. All is well until a rival starts poaching their territory.
BBFC:U — F — EN
Australian — Guild Home Video   H, P

Pied Piper, The   Fil-Ent '72
Fantasy/Musical
05610   90 mins   C
B, V
Donovan, Donald Pleasance, Jack Wild, Diana Dors, directed by Jacques Demy
This film is based on the immortal fourteenth century legend of the Pied Piper of Hamelin brought to life as a parable for modern times.
S,A — EN
Paramount; Sagittarius Prod — Home Video Merchandisers   H, P
004

(For Explanation of codes, see USE GUIDE and KEY)

PALADIN VIDEO HOME ENTERTAINMENT GUIDE

Pied Piper/Cinderella   Chi-Juv '81
Fairy tales/Puppets
05902   70 mins   C
B, V
Directed by Mark Hall
Two puppet films made at Thames Television's animation theatre. 'The Pied Piper' is set in the 11th Century. In 'Cinderella,' the story is told entirely by the music.
F — EN
Mark Hall; Brian Cosgrove — *THORN EMI*
P
TXE 90 0509 4/TVE 90 0509 2

Pigmies of the Rain   Gen-Edu '??
Forest, The
Anthropology
06058   60 mins   C
V2, B, V
A glimpse into a primal world unchanged for the last 6000 years: the everyday life of the Mbuti tribe who live in isolation in the rain forest, including sequences of a bull elephant chase in the Ituri forest, one of the world's least known regions.
F — ED
Unknown — *Video Programme Distributors*
P
Cinehollywood—V530

Pigs   Fil-Ent '7?
Horror
08022   81 mins   C
V2, B, V
Jessie Vint, Jim Antonio, Marc Lawrence, Walter Barnes, Erik Holland, Toni Larence, directed by Marc Lawrence
A deranged girl, suffering from the memory of her father's attempted rape, escapes from a mental hospital. Although she had killed her father she cannot be convinced that he is dead. She comes across a farm where the pigs have tasted human blood, and the horror begins.
BBFC:X — A — EN
Unknown — *Iver Film Services*   P
176

Pigs Versus the Freaks,   Fil-Ent '80
The
Comedy
06946   120 mins   C
B, V
Eugene Roche, Tony Randall, Grant Goodeve
This comedy centres on the mid-60's tensions between young American hippies and the police. The local police chief decides to ease the situation by arranging a football game between the 'Pigs and Freaks' with all proceeds going to charity. The game, however, takes second place.
S,A — EN
Ten-Four Productions — *Home Video Merchandisers*   H, P
054

Pilgrimage to the Holy   Fil-Ent '??
Land
Documentary/Religion
06150   108 mins   C
B, V
A programme offering a glimpse of the Holyland and the way of life of the bible. Includes visits to Jerusalem—the Holy city, the Cenacle—the room of the Last Supper, Qumran—where the dead sea scrolls were discovered, Galilee—the scene of the miracle of the loaves and fishes and Nazareth where Jesus lived. Also a look at the lifestyle of the people today.
F — EN
Ogwen-Williams Prod — *Guild Home Video*
H, P, E

Pilot, The   Fil-Ent '79
Drama
05687   91 mins   C
B, V
Cliff Robertson, Frank Converse, Diana Baker
This story centres around an international airline pilot and his drink problem. A delayed flight coupled with a change of destination through bad weather causes a near disaster when the pilot, who is out of drink, makes for a distant airport where he knows he can get alcohol without being discovered. He realises the dangers and ties to break his habit but suspicions are aroused as he battles for his future and the lives of 200 passengers.
BBFC:AA — S,A — EN
Unknown — *Derann Film Services*   H, P
GS704B/GS704

Pimpernel Smith   Fil-Ent '42
War-Drama/Suspense
08729   116 mins   B/W
B, V
Leslie Howard, Mary Morris, Francis Sullivan, Hugh McDermott
The enraged Gestapo are trying to work out how so many prisoners have escaped. An absent minded professor, working on archaeological excavations, is actually an undercover agent, hiding people from the Gestapo. However, they hold the final word, as they have the woman he loves.
S,A — EN
Anglo-American — *BBC Video*   H, P
BBCV 8010

---

508   (For Explanation of codes, see USE GUIDE and KEY)

PALADIN VIDEO HOME ENTERTAINMENT GUIDE

Pinball Summer Fil-Ent '8?
Drama
09158   90 mins   C
V
Karen Stephen, Joey McNamara, Robert Maze
This film features a group of teenagers who live for girls, money, prestige and more girls. A pinball competition is held, the prize being a date with the pinball queen.
S,A — EN
Unknown — *Medusa Communications Ltd*
P

Pink Flamingos Fil-Ent '73
Comedy
07738   95 mins   C
B, V
Divine, David Lochary, Mink Stole, Mary Vivian Pearce, Edith Massey, directed by John Waters
This film follows two groups of outcasts vying for the title of 'The Filthiest People Alive.' On one side there is the Queen of Sleaze with her family: a demented hill-billy-hippy son, a bleach-blonde voyeur companion and a 250 pound senior citizen who sits in a playpen. The challengers are a publicity-hungry couple with pre-punk coloured hair who are kidnapped by the Sleaze Queen's family.
A — EN
Saliva Films — *Palace Video Ltd*   **P**

Pink Floyd at Pompeii Fil-Ent '72
Music-Performance
05855   62 mins   C
B, V
David Gilmour, Roger Waters, Richard Wright, Nick Mason
A performance by Pink Floyd recorded in an ancient amphitheatre among the ruins of old Pompeii, using the coliseum by day and the eerily lit scene by night, produced especially for video. The set includes 'Careful with That Axe, Eugene,' 'Sauceful of Secrets,' 'Set the Controls for the Heart of the Sun' and 'Echoes I and II.'
F — EN
RM Productions — *Polygram Video*   **P**
7901824/7901822

Pink Panther, The Fil-Ent '63
Comedy
13044   113 mins   C
B, V
Peter Sellers, Robert Wagner, Claudia Cardinale, David Niven, directed by Blake Edwards
The very first movie from the enduring series about the bungling, incompetent Police Inspector Clouseau. Music by Henry Mancini.
BBFC:A — C,A — EN
Mirisch G & E Productions — *Warner Home Video*   **P**
99242

Pink Panther Strikes Again, The Fil-Ent '76
Comedy
13045   110 mins   C
B, V
Peter Sellers, Lesley-Anne Down, Herbert Lom, directed by Blake Edwards
Clouseau's superior, the Chief Inspector, having been driven into a mental institute by his bungling subordinate, escapes and goes to elaborate lengths to plan Clouseau's death.
BBFC:U — F — EN
United Artists Corp — *Warner Home Video*
P
99255

Pink Panther Strikes Again, The Fil-Ent '76
Comedy
01277   103 mins   C
V2, B, V
Peter Sellers, Herbert Lom, Colin Blakely, Leonard Rossiter, directed by Blake Edwards
Inspector Clouseau finally drives his chief, Dreyfus, to the point of insanity. Dreyfus forces a scientist to develop a special ray gun. Clouseau must outwit a number of assassins to get to Dreyfus before he causes further damage.
BBFC:U — F — EN
United Artists, Blake Edwards Prod — *Intervision Video*   **H**
UA A B 5017

Pink Panther, Volume I, The Fil-Ent '7?
Cartoons
13420   57 mins   C
B, V
Animated
A compilation of cartoons including 'Slink Pink,' 'Pink a Boo,' 'Smile Pretty, Say Pink' and 'Pink Aye.'
BBFC:U — F — EN
David H DePatie; Friz Freleng — *MGM/UA Home Video*   **P**
10481

Pinocchio Fil-Ent '76
Fairy tales/Musical
02066   76 mins   C

(For Explanation of codes, see USE GUIDE and KEY)

PALADIN VIDEO HOME ENTERTAINMENT GUIDE

B, V
Danny Kaye, Sandy Duncan, Flip Wilson, Liz Torres, Clive Revill
A feature length musical motion picture of the classic tale about the puppet who becomes a real boy. Danny Kaye plays Gepetto, the wood carver, and Sandy Duncan plays Pinocchio, the irrepressible puppet.
F — EN
Rothman and Wahl, Vidtronics Company — *VCL Video Services*   **P**

Pinocchio   Chl-Juv '84
Fantasy
13417   57 mins   C
B, V
Carl Reiner, Lainie Kazan, Paul Reubens, James Coburn
Carlo Collodi's folk tale about a wooden boy who is bestowed with the gift of life by a kind fairy warned that if he ever tells a lie his nose will grow.
F — EN
Shelley Duvall — *MGM/UA Home Video*   **P**
10465

Pinocchio in Outer Space   Chl-Juv '64
Cartoons
12060   64 mins   C
V2, B, V
Animated
Pinocchio zooms off into outer space to capture Astro the flying Whale which is terrorising space craft throughout the galaxies.
BBFC:U — *PS,M — EN*
SFM Entertainment — *Guild Home Video*
H, P, E

Pinocchio's Storybook Adventures   Chl-Juv '7?
Fairy tales
06767   80 mins   C
V2, B, V
John Fields, Armand MacKinnon, Owen Edward
Combining live action and animation, this film presents Pinocchio in a new series of adventures revolving around his efforts to put on a puppet show.
F — EN
John B Kelly; First American Films — *Intervision Video*   **H, P**
A-AE 207

Pipe Dreams   Fil-Ent '76
Drama
08752   90 mins   C
B, V
Gladys Knight, Barry Hankerson
Set in the freezing wastes of Alaska, this film tells the story of a woman who arrives to start a new job. Her real reason for moving to such a desolate place is to confront her ex-husband and tell him that he has a daughter. She soon finds that life is not so easy, especially being surrounded by frustrated men.
C,A — EN
LGN Prods.; Verona Enterprises; Avco Embassy — *Precision Video Ltd*   **P**
BITC 2574/VITC 2574

Pippin   Fil-Ent '81
Musical
06964   120 mins   C
B, V
Ben Vereen, William Katt, Martha Raye, Chita Rivera, directed by Kathryn Doby
This musical extravaganza portrays a young man's search for meaning and truth. This is a video production of Bob Fosse's original Broadway stage show, choreographed by Kathryn Doby with music and lyrics by Stephen Schwartz.
S,A — EN
Sheehan Elkins Video Venture Ltd — *Home Video Merchandisers*   **H, P**

Piranha   Fil-Ent '78
Horror
13030   95 mins   C
B, V
Bradford Dillman, Heather Menzies, Kevin McCarthy, directed by Joe Dante
At a holiday camp and beach resort, visitors are terrorised when they realize that the waters in which they swim are infested with mutant piranha fish.
BBFC:X — *A — EN*
New World Pictures — *Warner Home Video*   **P**
99281

Piranha, Piranha   Fil-Ent '72
Adventure/Drama
06189   86 mins   C
B, V
Peter Brown, William Smith, Ahna Capri
A young photographer, her brother and their guide journey on motorcycles along the uncharted banks of the Amazon River. They meet and are taken to a compound by a sadistic hunter known for his cruelty. They learn they are to be victims of the most dangerous game, a manhunt; they are forced to use primitive animal instincts to survive.
F — EN
Gold Key Entertainment — *VCL Video Services*   **P**
X0232

PALADIN VIDEO HOME ENTERTAINMENT GUIDE

Pirate, The   Fil-Ent '48
Musical
13428   97 mins   C
B, V
Judy Garland, Gene Kelly, Walter Slezak, Gladys Cooper, George Zucco, directed by Vincente Minnelli
Set to a musical score by Cole Porter, a young girl dreams of a romance with Macoco, the legendary pirate, and her dreams seem to have been answered when she meets him.
BBFC:U — F — EN
MGM; Arthur Freed — MGM/UA Home Video   P
10101

Pirate Movie, The   Fil-Ent '82
Adventure/Musical
12200   98 mins   C
V2, B, V
Kristy McNichol, Christopher Atkins, Ted Hamilton, Bill Kerr, Garry McDonald, directed by Ken Annakin
A young girl dreams herself into the 19th century and finds herself romantically involved with a handsome adventurer. This romance leads to a dangerous revenge, a pirate battle and the discovery of a stolen fortune under the sea bed.
F — EN
20th Century Fox — CBS/Fox Video   P
1185

Pirates of Penzance, The   Fil-Ent '8?
Opera
08921   100 mins   C
B, V
Peter Allen, Keith Michell, Alexander Oliver, Janis Kelly, Gillian Knight, Paul Hudson, Kate Flowers, Jenny Wren, directed by Rodney Greenberg
This opera by Gilbert and Sullivan tells the story of the apprentice pirate Frederic. He is finally twenty-one and free to marry Mabel. However, he was born on a leap year, and is still only five. He must now rescue the pirates that he has betrayed to the police. The music is performed by the London Symphony Orchestra, conducted by Alexander Faris.
S,A — EN
Brent Walker Prods — Brent Walker Home Video Ltd   P

Pirates of Penzance, The   Fil-Ent '82
Musical
12041   107 mins   C
B, V
Rex Smith, Angela Lansbury, Linda Ronstadt, George Rose, Kevin Kline, directed by Wilford D Leach
A member of a pirate band decides to abandon his wicked ways and lead an honest life. This Gilbert and Sullivan story is an adaptation of the American stage production and includes their songs.
BBFC:U — F — EN
Universal — CIC Video   H, P
BEA 1080/VHA 1080

Pit and the Pendulum, The   Fil-Ent '61
Horror
08399   85 mins   C
V2, B, V
Vincent Price, John Kerr, Barbara Steele, Luana Anders, directed by Roger Corman
A woman and her lover plan to drive her brother mad, and he responds by locking them in his torture chamber. It is based on Edgar Allan Poe's story.
BBFC:X — A — EN
American International Pictures — Guild Home Video   H, P, E

Pixote   Fil-Ent '80
Drama
08978   125 mins   C
B, V
Fernando Ramos De Silva, Marilia Pera, Jorge Juliao, directed by Hector Babenco
Pixote is a ten-year-old street kid in Sao Paolo, Brazil. When he is sent to a juvenile detention centre, he and his companions become hardened to criminal life. It is subtitled in English.
BBFC:18 — A — EN
Unifilm-Embrafilme — Palace Video Ltd   P
PVC 2021A

Place in Hell, A   Fil-Ent '65
War-Drama
06113   105 mins   C
V2, B, V
Guy Madison, Monty Greenwood, Lillice Neying, Fabio Testi, Helen Chanel, directed by Joseph Warren
This film chronicles the true story of a group of American soldiers in the Philippines. Their enemies are the fierce nationalist Japanese struggling to reverse the destiny of the war in the Pacific.
S,A — EN
Unknown — Video Programme Distributors   P
Cinehollywood—V1040

Plague Dogs, The   Fil-Ent '82
Adventure
09771   99 mins   C

(For Explanation of codes, see USE GUIDE and KEY)

PALADIN VIDEO HOME ENTERTAINMENT GUIDE

B, V
Animated, directed by Martin Rosen
Based on the novel by Richard Adams, this film tells the story of two dogs who succeed in escaping from an animal research station. Wild and free they attempt to survive on the rugged fells of the Lake District. However, they have to run for their lives when it is rumored that they are plague carriers. Animated by the team responsible for 'Watership Down', including a song by Alan Price.
F — EN
Rowf Films Ltd; Nepenthe Productions — *THORN EMI* **P**
TXA 90 1707 4/TVA 90 1707 2

Plan 9 from Outer Space   Fil-Ent '56
Science fiction/Horror
08979   79 mins   B/W
B, V
Bela Lugosi, Tor Johnson, Lyle Talbot, Vampira, Gregory Walcott, Mona McKinnon, Tom Keene, Dudley Manlove, Joanna Lee, John Breckinridge
UFO's containing strange inhabitants from an unknown planet invade the earth.
Golden Turkey Award: Worst Film of All Time.
F — EN
DCA — *Palace Video Ltd*   **P**
PVC 2020A

Planet of the Apes   Fil-Ent '68
Science fiction
01737   112 mins   C
B, V
Charlton Heston, Roddy McDowall, Kim Hunter, directed by Franklin J. Schaffner
Four American astronauts are hurtled 2,000 years through time and space, and crash land in the wilderness of a strange planet dominated by apes.
BBFC:U — *F — EN*
20th Century Fox — *CBS/Fox Video*   **P**
3A-054

Planet of the Dinosaurs   Fil-Ent '??
Science fiction
05456   82 mins   C
V2, B, V
James Witworth, Pamela Bottaro, Louie Lawless, Harvey Shain, Charlotte Speer, Chuck Pennington, directed by Jim K. Shea
An out of control spaceship with survivors aboard hurtles towards an unknown planet, inhabited by the once extinct mammoth reptiles—dinosaurs. Reduced to making their own primitive weapons the party gradually learn to fight back at the dangers of the unknown.
BBFC:A — *S,A — EN*
Unknown — *Iver Film Services*   **P**
129

Plank, The/Rhubarb, Rhubarb   Fil-Ent '81
Comedy
05911   52 mins   C
B, V
Eric Sykes, Frankie Howerd, Diana Dors, Bernard Cribbins, Jimmy Edwards, Hattie Jacques, Beryl Reid
Two films without dialogue. The first is about two builders who find that they are missing a floorboard. The second is about a game of golf between a Police Inspector and a Vicar.
F — EN
Denis Kirkland; David Clark — *THORN EMI* **P**
TXE 90 6223 4/TVE 90 6223 2

Play Better Snooker   Spo-Lei '??
Sports-Minor
09353   54 mins   C
B, V
Terry Griffiths, John Pullman
This tape covers every part of snooker technique from the elements of the basic stance, aim and cueing to the finer tactics of the game. It is directed at learners as well as regular players who need to improve their game.
S,A — I
Unknown — *Precision Video Ltd*   **P**
BDPV 1596/VDPV 1596

Play-Box 1   Chi-Juv '80
Variety/Fantasy
01970   102 mins   C
V2, B, V
Animated, introduced by Brian Rix
An anthology of children's programmes specially selected for video, including animated stories, puppets, and mime. Includes 'The Enchanted House' (two 12-minute stories), 'Jungle Ted the Lacybuttonpoppers' (three 5-minute stories), 'Mr Eppynt and Klara the Cow' (two 6-minute stories) and 'Up and Down Man' (two 12-minute stories), featuring mime artist Ben Benison.
AM Available   *PS,M — EN*
Mary Plumbly; HTV/Taurus Films; Lacybuttonpoppers Ltd; Caricature Theatre; Radius Films — *RPTA Video Ltd*   **H, P**

Play-Box 2   Chi-Juv '81
Variety/Fantasy
05616   102 mins   C
V2, B, V
Animated
This tape, a compilation of children's programmes, is the second in the Play Box series and features five further adventures in the series entitled 'The Enchanged House' (two 12 min stories), 'Flower Stories' (two 12 min

(For Explanation of codes, see USE GUIDE and KEY)

PALADIN VIDEO HOME ENTERTAINMENT GUIDE

stores), 'Jungle Ted and the Laceybuttonpoppers' (three 5 min stories), 'Mr Eppynt and Klara the Cow' (two 6 min stories) and 'Up and Down Man' (two 12 min stories).
PS,M — EN
Mary Plumbly; HTV/Taurus Films; Lacybuttonpoppers Ltd; Caricature Theatre; Radius Films — *RPTA Video Ltd* **H, P**

Play Dead Fil-Ent '??
Drama
08309   90 mins   C
B, V
Yvonne De Carlo, Stephanie Dunham, David Cullinane
This tells the story of a woman whose only love left her to marry her sister. After both her sister's and her former lover's death she sets out to claim her revenge by eliminating the two children of the union. Her weapon of death is a dog, a seemingly gentle pet, totally unsuspected of being capable of killing.
C,A — EN
Unknown — *Video Film Organisation* **P**
0003

Play Golf Spo-Lei '81
Golf
04870   108 mins   C
V2, B, V, LV
Peter Alliss presents all the basics of golf, assisted by top players.
F — I
Gordon Menzies; John Vigar — *BBC Video* **H, P**
BBCV 1004

Play It Again, Sam Fil-Ent '72
Comedy
10103   82 mins   C
B, V
Woody Allen, Susan Anspach, Tony Roberts, Diane Keaton, directed by Herbert Ross
Woody Allen plays the part of an obsessive film buff who is haunted by the ghost of Humphrey Bogart who offers him advice on how to deal with women. The closing scene is a parody of the airport scene in 'Casablanca'.
BBFC:15 — S,A — EN
Paramount — *CIC Video* **H, P**
BEL 2064/VHL 2064

Play School Chi-Juv '8?
Education/Games
10147   60 mins   C
V2, B, V

This compilation of the television series for young children features all the fun of the four seasons with songs, dances and things to make and do.
PS,M — EN
BBC — *BBC Video* **H, P**
BBCV 9011

Play Tennis Spo-Lei '81
Tennis
04865   110 mins   C
V2, B, V, LV
Presented by Derek Horwood
This programme takes the viewer through individual strokes step-by-step. An accompanying book is available from booksellers.
AM Available   F — I
Peter Ramsden — *BBC Video* **H, P**
BBCV 1010

Playbirds, The Fil-Ent '78
Drama
02096   94 mins   C
V2, B, V
Mary Millington
A policewoman is assigned as an undercover agent to investigate the deaths of beautiful nude models. She reveals all and succumbs to the desire of the chief suspect to obtain vital information.
BBFC:X — C,A — EN
Roldvale Prods — *Hokushin Audio Visual Ltd* **P**
VM-02

Playboy of the Western World Fil-Ent '62
Comedy
05440   96 mins   C
B, V
Siobhan McKenna, Gerry Raymond, directed by Brian Desmond Hurst
Set in Ireland, a young playboy enters the lives of the inhabitants of a County Mayo village and triggers off a series of unbelievable events. An innkeeper's daughter falls in love with him and persuades her father to give him a job. Naturally she believes his story that he killed his father with a spade, until the father shows up. Based on the play by J. M. Synge.
S,A — EN
4 Provinces Films Ltd — *THORN EMI* **P**
TXC 90 0251 4/TVC 90 0251 2

Playing Better Tennis Spo-Lei '80
Tennis
01979   25 mins   C
B, V

(For Explanation of codes, see USE GUIDE and KEY) 513

PALADIN VIDEO HOME ENTERTAINMENT GUIDE

America's top tennis pros combine playing and coaching skills to help viewers improve their own tennis game.
F — I
Unknown — *Quadrant Video* **H, P**

Playing with Fire   Fil-Ent '84
Drama/Suspense
13241   96 mins   C
B, V
Sybil Danning, Eric Brown, directed by Howard Avedis
A young student becomes involved with his teacher and finds himself the prime suspect of a plot to gain money unlawfully with a psychopathic killer at large.
BBFC:18 — A — EN
Howard Avedis; Marlene Schmidt — *CBS/Fox Video* **P**
3032

Playtime   Fil-Ent '68
Comedy
08601   115 mins   C
V2, B, V
Jacques Tati
This film is another Jacques Tati classic. He traces the ways in which man's attempts to organise himself misfire.
BBFC:U — F — EN
Continental — *Videomedia* **P**
PVM 4419/BVM 4419/HVM 4419

Plaza Suite   Fil-Ent '70
Drama/Comedy
13281   109 mins   C
B, V
Walter Matthau, Barbara Harris, Lee Grant, Jennie Sullivan, directed by Arthur Hiller
This film consists of three sketches set in a single hotel suite with Walter Matthau taking the part of a fretful businessman, a lecherous film producer and an anxious father-of-the-bride.
BBFC:PG — S,A — EN
Paramount — *CIC Video* **H, P**
BEN 2092/VHN 2092

Please Sir   Fil-Ent '71
Comedy
01870   101 mins   C
B, V
John Alderton, Derek Guyler, Joan Sanderson, Noel Howlett
The masters and pupils of Fenn Street School go on an annual camp. A big-screen version of the television series.
BBFC:U — F — EN
Rank — *Rank Video Library* **H, P**
1005

Pleasure Palace   Fil-Ent '80
Drama
05396   92 mins   C
B, V
Omar Sharif, Victoria Principal, J. D. Cannon, Gerald S. O'Loughlin, Jose Ferrer
This is a story of gambling, the excitement of the gambling tables and the behind-the-scenes power games for control. The gamblers are called 'high rollers' who win or lose a fortune at one sitting. One is called upon to play Baccarat for the ownership of a famous hotel-casino in Las Vegas as he vies for the affections of two beautiful women.
S,A — EN
Norman Rosemount Prod; Marble Arch Prods — *Precision Video Ltd* **P**
BITC 2080/VITC 2080

Ploughman's Lunch, The   Fil-Ent '83
Drama
10134   100 mins   C
B, V
Jonathan Pryce, Tim Curry, Rosemary Harris, Frank Finlay, Charlie Dore, directed by Richard Eyre
This film explores the drama of public and private deceit, exploitation and betrayal.
A — EN
Greenpoint Films — *Palace Video Ltd* **P**
VIRV 0015A

Pocket Money   Fil-Ent '72
Western
09474   102 mins   C
B, V
Paul Newman, Lee Marvin, Strother Martin, Hector Elizondo
Based on the novel 'Jim Kane' by J.P.S. Brown, this tells the story of a Texas cowboy, good natured, none too smart, who owes money to his ex-wife and the bank and has a perfect knack for making bad bargains. Lee Marvin plays his old Mexican hand buddy, who drinks himself oblivious while planning outrageous schemes to get rich quick.
F — EN
First Artists — *Guild Home Video* **H, P, E**

Poco   Fil-Ent '77
Drama/Adventure
05491   87 mins   C
V2, B, V
Chill Wills, Michelle Ashburn, Clint Ritchie, Sherry Bain, John Steadman, Tom Rovhowe, directed by Dwight Brooks
After a car accident, the only passenger not hurt, the small family dog, runs away confused into the desert. His 12 year old mistress, recovering from a broken leg, feels it is her fault

PALADIN VIDEO HOME ENTERTAINMENT GUIDE

and will not leave hospital until the dog returns. Meanwhile, the little dog begins his amazing journey home coping with all the dangers. Shot in Yosemite National Park.
BBFC:U — F — EN
Cinema Shares — *Iver Film Services*   **P**

Point Blank   Fil-Ent '67
Crime-Drama
10155   88 mins   C
B, V
Lee Marvin, Angie Dickinson
After being cheated by his wife and left for dead by his partner, a man is out for revenge. He takes on one of the crime syndicates, leaving a trail of corpses behind him, in his efforts to regain the fortune that was taken from him.
S,A — EN
MGM; Judd Bernard-Irwin Windler Prod — *MGM/UA Home Video*   **P**
UMB 10278/UMV 10278

Pole Position   Gen-Edu '7?
Documentary/Automobiles-Racing
07797   100 mins   C
V2, B, V
The film provides an insight into the world of motor racing detailing spectacular scenes and horrific crashes.
S,A — EN
Unknown — *Fletcher Video*   **H, P**
V158

Police Around the World   Fil-Ent '81
Music-Performance
08452   75 mins   C
B, V
Andy Summers, Stewart Copeland, Sting
This tape features 'The Police' filmed on their world-wide tour of 1980-81. They are seen performing in many exotic locations including Hong Kong, Australia, India, Egypt, and South America. 'Walking on the Moon', 'So Lonely', 'Roxanne', 'Don't Stand So Close to Me', and 'Message in a Bottle' are some of the 18 tracks contained on this cassette.
S,A — EN
Unknown — *THORN EMI*   **P**
TXE 90 1302 4/TVE 90 1302 2

Police Trap   Fil-Ent '72
Crime-Drama
07976   98 mins   C
B, V
Dean Stockwell, Scott Brady, Gloria Grahame

This film is about a man wrongly accused of the murder of a policeman. He is being chased by the dead policeman's partner. The more he tries to escape, the deeper the trouble he forces himself into.
BBFC:X — A — EN
Fanfare — *AVI Video Ltd*   **P**
008

Policewoman Centrefold   Fil-Ent '8?
Drama
12159   96 mins   C
B, V
Melody Anderson, Ed Marinaro, Donna Pescow
A young policewoman sends some candid photographs of herself to a magazine. Threatened with expulsion from the force, she is torn between her profession and her femininity. Based on a true story when a policewoman in Ohio appeared in the Playboy magazine.
BBFC:15 — S,A — EN
Unknown — *Precision Video Ltd*   **P**
BITC 2143/VITC 2143

Polyester   Fil-Ent '82
Comedy
09046   86 mins   C
B, V
Divine, Tab Hunter, directed by John Waters
This 'trash' classic features Divine, a twenty-one stone transvestite, as Francine Fishpaw, an all-American housewife with a problem family—a pornographer husband, nymphette daughter and a glue-sniffing son. Her over-developed sense of smell causes difficulties.
BBFC:X — A — EN
New Line Cinema — *VideoSpace Ltd*   **P**

Pom Pom Girls, The   Fil-Ent '76
Comedy
12054   90 mins   C
V2, B, V
Jennifer Ashley, Robert Carradine, Lisa Reeves
A portrait of American teenage life with two High Schools in fierce competition against each other is shown in this film.
BBFC:15 — S,A — EN
Crown International — *Intervision Video*
H, P
A-A 0517

Poor Albert, Little Annie   Fil-Ent '73
Drama
04475   82 mins   C
V2, B, V
Zooey Hall, Geri Reischl

(For Explanation of codes, see USE GUIDE and KEY)

PALADIN VIDEO HOME ENTERTAINMENT GUIDE

A seriously mentally disturbed young man believes all women are evil and ritualistically murders them.
A — EN
Romal Films — Intervision Video   H, P
A-A 0154

Poor Glassblower, The   Chi-Juv '79
Fairy tales
01094   24 mins   C
B, V
Based on the Grimm Brothers' story 'The Fisherman's Wife,' concerning a poor glassblower who lived with his wife and two daughters in the far, far north.
PS,I — ED
Carousel Films — VCL Video Services   P

Poor White Trash   Fil-Ent '7?
Horror
09007   90 mins   C
V2, B, V
Gene Ross, Ann Stafford, Norma Moore, Camilla Carr, Charlie Dell, Hugh Feagin, Joel Colodner
This is a Gothic horror story. A couple start their summer holiday in a tranquil remote cabin. All is idyllic until the man is found with an axe in his chest.
A — EN
Unknown — Intervision Video   H, P
A-A 0481

Pope in the Park, The   Gen-Edu '8?
Documentary/Religion
08588   60 mins   C
B, V
This programme, produced by the Salford artist Harold Riley, follows the visit of Pope John Paul to Heaton Park in Manchester. Included on this original cassette are some of the 1,000 photographs and drawings by Harold Riley made on the day which complement the live footage.
F — EN
Holiday Brothers — Holiday Brothers Ltd
P

Pope Joan   Fil-Ent '72
Drama
07387   111 mins   C
V2, B, V
Olivia DeHavilland, Lesley-Anne Downe, Trevor Howard, Patrick Magee, directed by Michael Anderson
This film is based on the 19th century legend about a young German girl, a semi-prostitute, who discovered she had a vocation to preach.

Disguised as a monk for a number of years she was eventually elected Pope. Her secret, however, when revealed brought her to an horrific end.
BBFC:AA — S,A — EN
Big City Productions — Guild Home Video
H, P, E

Pope John Paul II in   Gen-Edu '79
Ireland
Religion/Documentary
01877   168 mins   C
B, V
Narrated by Brian Farrell, Reverend Romuald Dodd
A pilgrimage with the new pope on his first visit to Ireland. A compilation of his visits, including the liturgy, the music, and the sermons.
F — ED
Rank — Rank Video Library   H, P
9002

Popeye   Fil-Ent '80
Adventure/Comedy
07933   92 mins   C
B, V
Robin Williams, Shelley Duvall, Ray Walston, Paul Dooley, directed by Robert Altman
The cartoon seaman is bought to life and arrives in the village of Sweethaven to find his long lost father, meets Olive Oyl and discovers little Sweet Pea. Music by Harry Nilsson.
F — EN
Walt Disney — Rank Video Library   H
09300

Popeye and Friends at   Fil-Ent '??
Sea
Cartoons/Adventure
09977   60 mins   C
B, V
Animated
This film, the third in the series, sees Popeye tussling with underwater pirates, the Sea Witch, an irate pirate and the Voice from the Deep. Snuffy Smith and Loweezy lose their bearings on a sea trip and Beetle Bailey gets an underwater assignment he should never have had.
F — EN
King Features Syndicate — Select Video Limited   P
3503/43

Popeye and Friends,   Fil-Ent '84
Days Gone By
Cartoons
13000   60 mins   C
B, V
Animated

---

516   (For Explanation of codes, see USE GUIDE and KEY)

PALADIN VIDEO HOME ENTERTAINMENT GUIDE

P video compilation of cartoons from Popeye, Krazy Kat, Ignaz the Mouse, Snuffy Smith and Beetle Bailey.
F — EN
King Features Syndicate — *Select Video Limited* **P**
3506/43

Popeye and Friends in Outer Space Fil-Ent '??
Cartoons/Adventure
09976 60 mins C
B, V
Animated
This tape features more adventures of Popeye and his friends. The Professor sends Popeye into space using his time machine, which is the beginning of more adventures. Olive Oyl meets a space man for a boyfriend.
F — EN
King Features Syndicate — *Select Video Limited* **P**
3502/43

Popeye and Friends-No Fun Like Snow Fun Fil-Ent '??
Cartoons
09975 60 mins C
B, V
Animated
On this tape Popeye attempts to capture the Abominable Snowman and battles with the Sea Witch who has kidnapped Santa Claus. Popeye gets the chance to demonstrate the amazing powers of Spinach in a fight with his arch-rival Brutus.
F — EN
King Features Syndicate — *Select Video Limited* **P**
3507/43

Popeye And Superman Fil-Ent '4?
Cartoons
06884 56 mins C
V2, B, V
Animated
This tape is a series of colour cartoons featuring the adventures of Bugs Bunny, Popeye and Superman.
M,A — EN
Max Fleischer; Warner Bros — *European Video Company* **P**

Popeye Globetrotting Fil-Ent '8?
Cartoons/Adventure
12180 60 mins C
B, V
Animated
More adventures of Popeye and his friends in excitement all over the world.
F — EN
King Features Syndicate — *Select Video Limited* **P**
3505/43

Popeye in the Wild West Fil-Ent '??
Cartoons/Adventure
08312 60 mins C
B, V
Animated
This tape features the spinach-swallowing Popeye, Brutus the Bully, Wimpy the Scrounger, Swee'Pea and Olive Oyl. Popeye is out to clean up the Wild West and rid it of such villains as Krazy Kat, Snuffy Smith and Beetle Bailey before he can be reunited with Olive.
F — EN
King Features Syndicate — *Select Video Limited* **P**
3501

Poppies Are Also Flowers Fil-Ent '66
Adventure
08340 85 mins C
V2, B, V
Yul Brynner, Omar Sharif, Angie Dickinson, Trevor Howard, Anthony Quayle, Rita Hayworth, Stephen Boyd, Jack Hawkins, Trini Lopez, Senta Berger
This film, based on an idea by the thriller writer Ian Fleming, follows the illegal world of drug trafficking. Intrigue, murder and exotic locations follow the demise of the poppies as they are converted into heroin and shipped to the United States.
C,A — EN
Terence Young — *Embassy Home Entertainment* **P**
1301

Porgy and Blue/High Island Pollack Spo-Lei '7?
Fishing
02270 52 mins C
V
Bernard Cribbins
The sea off the coast of Southern Ireland is the setting for this instructional film on sea fishing. Bernard Cribbins and a group of experts chase after a blue shark in 'Porgy and Blue.' In 'High Island Pollack' they hunt for a variety of fish and discuss some of the finer points of sea angling.
S,A — I
Unknown — *JVC* **P**
PRT 18

(For Explanation of codes, see USE GUIDE and KEY) 517

PALADIN VIDEO HOME ENTERTAINMENT GUIDE

Porky's
Fil-Ent '82
Comedy
12009   94 mins   C
B, V

Dan Monahan, Wyatt Knight, Tony Ganios, Mark Herrier, Cyril O'Reilly, Roger Wilson

This film follows the adventures of six frantic youths from Angel Beach High School who are drawn to the notorious night club 'Porky's' to prove their manhood.
S,A — EN
Melvin Simon Productions; Astral Bellevue
Pathe — *CBS/Fox Video*   **P**
1149

Porridge
Fil-Ent '79
Comedy
00833   79 mins   C
B, V

Ronnie Barker, Richard Beckinsale, Fulton Mackay

Habitual prisoner Norman Stanley Fletcher is doing porridge again, detained at Her Majesty's pleasure at Slade Prison. During the course of the story, Fletcher and Godber find themselves unexpectedly free—and their problem is breaking into jail.
BBFC:A — F — EN
Witzend Prods — *Precision Video Ltd*   **P**
BITC 2014/VITC 2014

Portes de la Nuit, Les
Fil-Ent '46
Drama
09807   99 mins   B/W
B, V

Pierre Brasseur, Serge Reggiani, Yves Montand, Nathalie Nattier, Saturnin Fabre

The malaise of a city recovering from the occupation is passionately captured in this film, which records the events of a single night in a dingy suburb of Paris. Subtitled in English.
BBFC:PG — A — EN   FR
Pathe-Cinema — *THORN EMI*   **P**
TXE 90 1703 4/TVE 90 1703 2

Portnoy's Complaint
Fil-Ent '72
Comedy-Drama
13202   101 mins   C
B, V

Richard Benjamin, Karen Black, Lee Grant, directed by Ernest Lehman

A Jewish boy with sexual hang-ups and suffocating parents can't make a relationship with a girl until he meets his dream girl and they embark on a torrid affair.
BBFC:X — A — EN
Warner Bros — *Warner Home Video*   **P**
61166

Portrait of a Great Lady
Gen-Edu '80
Royalty-GB/Documentary
01988   60 mins   C
V2, B, V, PH15, PH17
Commentary by David Niven

The life of the Queen Mother and the dramatic years through which she was the Grande Dame of the British Empire are documented.
F — ED
MirrorVision — *VideoSpace Ltd*   **P**

Portrait of a Showgirl
Fil-Ent '82
Drama
09256   120 mins   C
V2, B, V

Lesley Ann Warren, Tony Curtis, Rita Moreno, Dianne Kaye, Barry Primus, directed by Steven H. Stern

The beautiful Jillian arrives from New York to work in the show at Caesar's Palace. Her talent and beauty combine to alienate her from her fellow dancers. It seems that everyone she meets has a problem and somehow she is able to sort them out.
BBFC:A — S,A — EN
Hamner Prods — *Iver Film Services*   **P**
208

Portrait of a Stripper
Fil-Ent '79
Drama
10212   97 mins   C
B, V

Lesley Ann Warren, Ed Herrmann, Vic Tayback, Alan Miller, Sheree North, Walt Sterling, K.C. Martel, directed by John A. Alonzo

A young mother arrives in Los Angeles with her son after the death of her husband. She is being secretly followed and photographed by a second rate detective hired by her father in law who wants to gain custody of the boy by proving she is an unfit mother. By day she is a serious dance student; at night she dances at club trying to bring back clean burlesque. However the owner sells out to a chain of hard core strip joints. To earn a living she now has to strip.
BBFC:18 — A — EN
Moonlight Prods; Filmways — *Video Form Pictures*   **H, P**
MGD 14

Portrait of Jennie
Fil-Ent '48
Drama
04164   86 mins   B/W
B, V

Jennifer Jones, Joseph Cotten, Ethel Barrymore, Lillian Gish, Cecil Kellaway, David Wayne

PALADIN VIDEO HOME ENTERTAINMENT GUIDE

An artist meets a strange girl in Central Park who inspires him to paint her portrait.
Academy Awards '48: Best Special Effects.
BBFC:U — F — EN
Selznick — *Guild Home Video* **H, P**

Portrait Painting Fin-Art '81
Painting
05429 60 mins C
B, V
Harold Riley
This cassette is a complete programme in the 'Master Class Painting Course' series led by Harold Riley, the famous artist and lecturer. In this film he examines the method, the materials and the objective approach of a master towards portrait painting. This dialogue with Mr. Riley provides an insight to the more serious painter and information for those with a more academic interest.
S,A — I
Harrison Partnership and Holiday Bros Ltd — *Holiday Brothers Ltd* **P**

Poseidon Adventure, The Fil-Ent '72
Adventure
01736 117 mins C
V2, B, V, LV
Gene Hackman, Ernest Borgnine, Shelley Winters, Red Buttons, Jack Albertson, Carol Lynley
The S.S. Poseidon, on her last voyage from New York to Athens, is capsized by a tidal wave on New Year's Eve.
Academy Awards '72: Best Song ('The Morning After'); Special Effects. F — EN
20th Century Fox, Irwin Allen Prod — *CBS/Fox Video* **P**
3A-043

Possession Fil-Ent '74
Horror
09081 87 mins C
B, V
Isabelle Adjani, Sam Neill, Heinz Bennett
A marital crisis leads to increasingly bizarre exploits, from murder, adultery and corruption to the eventual incarnation of a hideous, slimy monster.
A — EN
ATV — *Video Tape Centre* **P**
VTC 1031

Possession of Joel Delaney, The Fil-Ent '71
Drama
05956 104 mins C
B, V
Shirley Maclaine, Miriam Colon, Michael Hordern

A wealthy divorcee, bringing up her two children on a good allowance and earnings from novel writing, leads an uneventful life until her brother is suspected of murder. An unknown killer has brutally decapitated several girls. She believes he is innocent as he was not in the country at the time of one of the murders; she discovers, however, that a possible witness has the same address as her brother.
S,A — EN
Unknown — *Precision Video Ltd* **P**
BITC 2049/VITC 2049

Postman Always Rings Twice, The Fil-Ent '81
Drama
06179 122 mins C
V2, B, V, LV
Jack Nicholson, Jessica Lange, John Colicos, directed by Bob Rafelson
The story of a couple who become lovers with a savage intensity whose passions they cannot control or understand. With no other solution they plot to kill the woman's husband. This film, although erotic, places its emphasis on people, their feelings, their ambitions and their conflicts.
BBFC:X — A — EN
Andrew Braunsberg Production — *Guild Home Video* **H, P, E**

Postman Pat Chi-Juv '82
Puppets/Adventure
08662 55 mins C
B, V
Animated
This tape contains four tales featuring the jovial Postman Pat, his black and white cat and his friends who live in Greendale: 'Pat's Rainy Day', 'The Sheep in the Clover Field,' Pat's Tractor Express' and Pat's Thirsty Day.'
M,S — EN
Woodland Animations Ltd — *Longman Video*
P
LGBE 5011/LGVH 5011

Postman Pat 2 Chi-Juv '82
Puppets/Adventure
10009 60 mins C
B, V
Animated
This tape contains four more adventures of Postman Pat and his black and white cat. The people of Greendale are in all sorts of trouble when the snowfalls, Pat gets lost in the fog and there is an exciting van, bicycle and roller skate chase.
A — EN
Woodland Animations Ltd. — *Longman Video*
LGBE 5019/LGVH 5019

PALADIN VIDEO HOME ENTERTAINMENT GUIDE

Powderkeg   Fil-Ent '70
Drama
05444   100 mins   C
V2, B, V
Rod Taylor, Dennis Cole, Michael Ansara, Fernando Lamas, Tisha Sterling
A pair of tough trouble-shooting investigators in the South West during the 1914 era are called in to help get a train back which has been hijacked with seventy-five civilians aboard, who are being held hostage for the release of a Bandit leader.
BBFC:U — F — EN
Filmways — Iver Film Services   P

Power of Football—World Cup 1978, The   Spo-Lei '78
Football
06742   87 mins   C
V2, B, V
This sports spectacular features highlights of the 1978 World Cup.
S,A — EN
Unknown — Intervision Video   H, P
A-AE 0283

Power Play   Fil-Ent '78
Suspense/Drama
04254   98 mins   C
B, V
Peter O'Toole, Barry Morse, Donald Pleasence, David Hemmings, Marcella Saint-Amant
In this film David Hemmings plays the part of a loyal army colonel in a country blighted with cruelty, corruption and fascism. Much against his will but inspired by dissident intellectual Dr. Rousseau (Barry Morse) Hemmings foments a plot to topple the government.
BBFC:A — S,A — EN
Canadian — Rank Video Library   H, P
0021

Powers of Evil   Fil-Ent '84
Mystery
13406   80 mins   C
V2, B, V
Terence Stamp, Jane Fonda, Peter Fonda, James Robertson Justice, directed by Roger Vadim and Federico Fellini
Three tales of the macabre and supernatural are featured on this cassette by author Edgar Allen Poe.
BBFC:15 — S,A — EN
Alpha Films — Intervision Video   H, P
001

Pranks   Fil-Ent '??
Drama/Horror
08893   83 mins   C
V2, B, V
Directed by Jeffrey Obrow
A derelict building is waiting to be bulldozed. A group of young students volunteer over the Christmas holidays to clear it of its remaining furniture. However, the job isn't as pleasant as it appears, because an insane killer in the building has other ideas.
BBFC:X — A — EN
Unknown — Video Programme Distributors   P
Canon 002

Preacherman   Fil-Ent '??
Drama
09957   90 mins   C
V2, B, V
Amos Huxley
Amos Huxley is supposed to be a man of God and his mission to the people of Whiteoak County is to give them a 'House of Lord'. However, his passion for money and pretty young women makes him a wanted man.
BBFC:A — S,A — EN
Unknown — Video Unlimited   H, P, E
092

Predators, The   Gen-Edu '7?
Wildlife
02272   60 mins   C
V
A study of predators all over America, from the snowy peaks of Alaska through the rugged areas of the west to the sanctuary swamps of Louisiana.
F — ED
Unknown — JVC   P
PRT 30

Premature Burial, The   Fil-Ent '62
Horror
09457   81 mins   C
V2, B, V
Ray Milland, directed by Roger Corman
A man is so obsessed with the fear of being buried alive that he constructs himself a special tomb fitted with every possible escape device. However events take a horrific turn and his worst fear becomes a reality.
BBFC:18 — A — EN
American International; Roger Corman — Guild Home Video   H, P, E

Premonition   Fil-Ent '8?
Drama
09301   90 mins   C
B, V
A young man, whilst working as a driver and guide for an alcoholic anthropology professor, witnesses the discovery, intact, of an ancient skeleton in the Mexican desert. Instead of

PALADIN VIDEO HOME ENTERTAINMENT GUIDE

seeing a 200 year old cranium he saw a man whose skull had been cracked open and whose eyes clung to life. He now wanders, coming from nowhere with no place to go, not sure his past existed, carrying the 'premonition' with him.
A — EN
Unknown — Abacus Video   P
101

Premonition   Fil-Ent '75
Drama/Suspense
09291   91 mins   C
V2, B, V
Sharon Farrell, Richard Lynch, Jeff Corey, Ellen Barber, directed by Robert Allan Schnitzer
When their five-year-old adopted daughter disappears, a couple are led into a strange and sinister world of psychic phenomena when they consult a parapsychologist in an attempt to find her. Beyond exorcism and science they discover a world of terror with two damned souls and a trapped spirit.
A — EN
Avco Embassy — Embassy Home Entertainment   P
2079

President's Mistress, The   Fil-Ent '78
Drama/Suspense
09070   97 mins   C
B, V
Larry Hagman, Beau Bridges, Karen Grassle, Susan Blanchard, Joel Fabiani, Don Porter, Gail Strickland, Titos Vandis, Thalmus Rasulala
This film tells the story of a man who is caught in a deadly cover-up, but determined to uncover the truth about the murder of his former girlfriend. Each time he gets a clue, he is put off the scent, and his enquiries seem to lead to the Oval Office itself. Based on a novel by Patrick Anderson.
S,A — EN
Kings Road Prods — Video Tape Centre   P
VTC 1021

Press For Time   Fil-Ent '66
Comedy
13750   94 mins   C
B, V
Norman Wisdom
Norman Wisdom stars in a double role as the Prime Minister and his embarrassing grandson, with one chaotic mix-up following another.
BBFC:U — F — EN
Rank Films — Rank Video Library   H, P
1086

Pretty Baby   Fil-Ent '79
Drama
05327   106 mins   C
B, V
Brooke Shields, Keith Carradine, Susan Sarandon, directed by Louis Malle
This film, set in 1917, centres around a photographer who is obsessed with the prostitutes in New Orleans' red-light district. He is bewitched by a young child prostitute who captivates him with her curious naive coquettishness.
S,A — EN
Paramount — CIC Video   H, P
BEA2014/VHA2014

Pretty Poison   Fil-Ent '68
Drama/Suspense
12084   85 mins   C
B, V
Anthony Perkins, Tuesday Weld, directed by Noel Black
A psychotic is released from prison and teams up with a young girl high school student. Together they plan to sabotage a chemical factory, but things start to go wrong when the night watchman is murdered by the girl.
C,A — EN
Twentieth Century Fox — CBS/Fox Video   P
1223

Prey   Fil-Ent '77
Horror
02576   85 mins   C
V2, B, V
A young alien stranger turns nightmares into tragic realities, as he reveals that man, the hunter for millions of years, is now the prey. This film contains many graphic cannibalistic scenes.
BBFC:X — A — EN
Tymar — Videomedia   P

Price of Death, The   Fil-Ent '??
Western
06114   102 mins   C
V2, B, V
Klaus Kinski, John Garko
A highly paid hired killer discovers other dirty goings-on in a respectable Texas village when he is on the trail of the killer of a girl and a barman. Before he finally springs his deadly trap others meet their death.
S,A — EN
Unknown — Video Programme Distributors   P
Cinehollywood—V1600

(For Explanation of codes, see USE GUIDE and KEY)   521

PALADIN VIDEO HOME ENTERTAINMENT GUIDE

Price of Power, The Fil-Ent '??
Drama
05549   118 mins   C
V2, B, V
Van Johnson, Fernando Rey, Giuliano Gemma, directed by Tonino Valerii
Set in Texas in 1880, the President is murdered while leaving Dallas. A man is accused of being an accomplice and killed. To clear his name a friend sets out to unravel the plot laying his trust in the only law he knows, that of the gun.
BBFC:X — A — EN
Unknown — Videomedia   P
RVM 6104/BVM 6104/HVM 6104

Pride of Jesse Hallam, The Fil-Ent '81
Drama
06944   120 mins   C
B, V
Johnny Cash, Brenda Vaccaro, Eli Wallach, Ben Marley, Crystal Smith
This is the story of a 45-year-old widowed Kentucky farmer struggling to bring up his two children in the unfamiliar surroundings of a big city.
S,A — EN
Konigsberg Co — Home Video Merchandisers   H, P
051

Priest of Love Fil-Ent '82
Drama/Biographical
06957   120 mins   C
B, V
Ian McKellan, Janet Suzman, Ava Gardner, Penelope Keith, Jorge Rivero
This story centres on the life and loves of D. H. Lawrence, said to be 'the greatest imaginative novelist of our generation.' The novelist and his wife shared a relationship punctuated by violent quarrels and tender reconciliations.
S,A — EN
Unknown — Home Video Merchandisers   H, P
035

Prime of Miss Jean Brodie-Cassette 1, The Fil-Ent '??
Drama
09416   99 mins   C
V2, B, V
John Castle, Robert Urquhart, Geraldine McEwan
Based on the novel by Muriel Spark, this film tells the story of a school-teacher whose liberal attitude towards the education of her young ladies is ahead of its time.
S,A — EN
Unknown — Guild Home Video   H, P, E

Prince Arthur Emerges Fil-Ent '83
Cartoons/Adventure
09148   60 mins   C
B, V
Animated
Arthur, a natural leader, travels adventurously through life in the company of Lancelot, Guinevere and the magical Merlin. He sets out on a knightly errand to help clear his father's name of the crime of murder.
F — EN
ZIV International — Video Brokers   H, P
011C

Prince Charles: A Royal Portrait Fil-Ent '81
Royalty-GB/Documentary
05058   25 mins   C
B, V
An informal record of the life of Prince Charles, including scenes from his childhood, state occasions, and an interview with the Prince and Lady Diana at the time of their engagement.
F — EN
UPITN; Michael Berry — THORN EMI   P
TXE 90 2000 4/TVE 90 2000 2

Prince of the City Fil-Ent '81
Drama
13058   162 mins   C
B, V
Treat Williams, Jerry Orbach, directed by Sidney Lumet
A detective who enjoys a luxurious life-style, the fruits of a corrupt department, becomes troubled by his conscience, and agrees to co-operate in an investigation of police methods, but finds himself lured into a web of betrayal.
BBFC:X — A — EN
Orion Pictures; Warner Bros Inc — Warner Home Video   P
72021

Princes and Princesses Fil-Ent '??
Cartoons/Fairy tales
10001   60 mins   C
B, V
Animated
This tape features five stories of adventure and romance; 'The Princess and the Goat Boy', 'The Warrior Maiden', 'Aucassin and Nicolletle', 'The Bag of Winds' and 'The Lady of the Apple'.
F — EN
Unknown — Longman Video   P
LGBE 5017/LGVH 5017

Princess Gen-Edu '82
Documentary/Biographical
06909   60 mins   C
V2, B, V

PALADIN VIDEO HOME ENTERTAINMENT GUIDE

Narrated by Robert Lacey
This film, exclusively about Diana, Princess of Wales, gives a revealing insight into the young girl who has sprung from relative obscurity to the most talked about and photographed woman in the world. This film is narrated by Robert Lacey, the author of the book of the same name.
F — EN
Michael Barratt Limited — *Michael Barratt Ltd*
P

Princess and the Magic Frog, The   Chi-Juv '7?
Fairy tales
02065   90 mins   C
B, V
An Irish lad lost in a forest on his way home and the strange adventures that befall him unfold into an enchanting story packed with magic and adventure, leprechauns and wicked wizards, talking signposts, gallant knights, beautiful princesses, and genies.
F — EN
Unknown — *VCL Video Services*   **P**

Princess and the Pea, The   Fil-Ent '84
Fairy tales
13414   50 mins   C
B, V
Liza Minnelli, Tom Conti
An adaptation of the well known classic story of the princess who is unable to sleep because she can feel the pea that has been placed under several layers of mattresses.
BBFC:U — *F — EN*
Shelley Duvall — *MGM/UA Home Video*
P
10436

Princess and the People   Gen-Edu '84
Documentary
12722   51 mins   C
B, V
This is a profile of Diana, Princess of Wales, filmed during her overseas tours of Australia, New Zealand and Canada, and her visits within the United Kingdom, and traces her development into the leading world figure she is today. Narrated by Richard Whitmore.
F — EN
Gordon Carr — *BBC Video*   **H, P**
6019

Princess Daisy   Fil-Ent '83
Drama
12939   180 mins   C
B, V
Merete Van Kamp, Stacy Keach, Rupert Everett, Robert Urich, Lindsay Wagner, Paul Michael Glaser, Claudia Cardinale
This is a glittering and international saga of a beautiful and spirited daughter of an American movie star and a Russian prince who, after a childhood marked by tragedy, carves herself a place in the world of commercial advertising.
C,A — EN
Steve Krantz Productions; NBC — *Video Form Pictures*   **H, P**

Princess Ida   Fil-Ent '8?
Opera
08926   100 mins   C
B, V
Frank Gorshin, Neil Howlett, Laurence Dale, Bernard Dickenson, Richard Jackson, Tano Rea, Peter Savidge, Christopher Booth-Jones, Nan Christie, Anne Collins, Claire Powell, Jenny Wren
This opera by Gilbert and Sullivan tells the story of the Princess, betrothed as a baby to Prince Hilarion. With her father tortured, and her brothers defeated in a fight, she agrees to subordinate herself to Hilarion. The music is performed by The London Symphony Orchestra conducted by Alexander Faris, with The Ambrosian Opera Chorus.
S,A — EN
Brent Walker Prods — *Brent Walker Home Video*   **P**

Prisoner of Second Avenue, The   Fil-Ent '75
Comedy-Drama
06026   101 mins   C
B, V
Jack Lemmon, Anne Bancroft, Gene Saks, Elizabeth Wilson, Florence Stanley, directed by Melvin Frank
A New Yorker in his late 40's is facing the mid life crisis without a job or any confidence in his ability. He tries to face up to the future with the help of his understanding wife. Based on the Broadway play by Neil Simon.
BBFC:A — *S,A — EN*
Warner Bros — *Warner Home Video*   **P**
WEX1035/WEV1035

Prisoner of the Cannibal God   Fil-Ent '7?
Horror
02116   96 mins   C
V2, B, V
Ursula Andress, Stacy Keach

PALADIN VIDEO HOME ENTERTAINMENT GUIDE

Primitive tribes and a trail of death follow Professor Stevenson's wife when she sets out in the jungle to find him after his disappearance from his jungle base.
C,A — EN
Unknown — Hokushin Audio Visual Ltd
P
VM-27

Prisoner Without a Name, Cell Without a Number
Fil-Ent '83
War-Drama
10092   90 mins   C
B, V
Roy Scheider, Liv Ullman, directed by Linda Yellen
This film is set in Argentina amid the horror and brutality of the military junta. A newspaper editor is imprisoned and tortured for daring to question his country's dictators. Based on the true story of editor Jacobo Timerman.
BBFC:15 — S,A — EN
Chrysalis/Yellen — VideoSpace Ltd   P
FT6

Private Benjamin
Fil-Ent '80
Comedy
07867   106 mins   C
B, V
Goldie Hawn, Eileen Brennan, Armand Assante
This film follows the hilarious adventures of a girl who joins the army after her husband dies on her wedding night.
BBFC:AA — S,A — EN
Warner Bros — Warner Home Video   P
WEX 61075/WEV 61075

Private Eyes, The
Fil-Ent '80
Comedy
09078   91 mins   C
B, V
Don Knotts, Tim Conway, Trisha Noble, Bernard Fox
Two bungling sleuths are engaged to investigate two deaths and are led on a merry chase through secret passages, past exploding bombs and finally to a meeting with a ghostly adversary.
F — EN
Lang Elliot; Wanda Dell; TriStar Pictures — Video Tape Centre   P
VTC 1043

Private Life of Adolf Hitler, The/The Public Life of Adolf Hitler
Fil-Ent '46
Documentary
06312   91 mins   B/W
V2, B, V

Two films involving the life of Adolf Hitler on one cassette. 'The Private Life of Adolf Hitler' reveals actual interviews and sequences from film taken privately by Hitler and the few survivors of the Berlin Bunker. 'The Public Life of Adolf Hiter' reveals the politics, strategy and ambitions of Hitler the Dictator.
S,A — EN
Unknown — World of Video 2000   H, P
GF517

Private Life of Sherlock Holmes, The
Fil-Ent '70
Comedy/Mystery
12493   125 mins   C
B, V
Robert Stephens, Colin Blakely, directed by Billy Wilder
The great detective Sherlock Holmes tackles his most baffling case which involves him with a beautiful and treacherous woman, spies and the Loch Ness monster.
BBFC:PG — F — EN
Billy Wilder; United Artists — Warner Home Video   P
99361

Private Nurse
Fil-Ent '78
Comedy
02117   75 mins   C
V2, B, V
Charles Lambert's family all hope his health will deteriorate, but from the moment Angel, his private nurse, strips and changes into her uniform in front of him, Charles begins to rally. Angel is propositioned by each member of the family in turn.
BBFC:X — A — EN
France — Hokushin Audio Visual Ltd   P
VM-28

Private Parts
Fil-Ent '72
Drama/Suspense
10157   83 mins   C
B, V
Cheryl Stratton, Lucille Benson
A teenage girl goes to stay with her aunt in a seedy Los Angeles hotel and is caught up in a series of bizarre events, which start when she is caught spying on a kinky photographer.
A — EN
Premier Prods (MGM) — MGM/UA Home Video   P
UMB 10279/UMV 10279

Private Popsicle
Fil-Ent '7?
Comedy
09421   96 mins   C
V2, B, V

PALADIN VIDEO HOME ENTERTAINMENT GUIDE

Yftach Katzur, Zachi Noy, Jonathan Segall, Sonja Martin
The mischievous trio, Benji, Bobby and Huey return in a followup to 'Lemon Popsicle'. After signing up with the Army for three years the boys find the discipline of Army life not to their liking and contrive every means possible to outsmart, confuse and bamboozle their superior officers, with total havoc as a result.
BBFC:18 — A — EN
Golan-Globus — Guild Home Video   H, P, E

Private Right, The   Fil-Ent '66
Suspense
04471   81 mins   C
V2, B, V
Dimitris Andreas, George Kafkaris, directed by Micael Papas
A Cypriot guerilla leader is betrayed by one of the group and later tortured. Bent on revenge, he follows the man to London after the independence of Cyprus, where he finally catches and executes his betrayer.
BBFC:X — A — EN
Michael Papas — Intervision Video   H, P
A-A 0094

Private School   Fil-Ent '83
Comedy/Romance
13309   86 mins   C
B, V
Phoebe Cates, Betsy Russell, Sylvia Kristel, Michael Zorek, Kathleen Wilhoite, Kari Lizer
Fun and pranks abound when the girls from Cherryvale Academy get together with the boys from neighbouring Freemount.
BBFC:18 — C,A — EN
Universal — CIC Video   H, P
BET 1100/VHT 1100

Privates on Parade   Fil-Ent '83
Comedy
09779   107 mins   C
B, V
John Cleese, Denis Quilley, Michael Elflick, Simon Jones, Joe Melia, John Standing, Nicola Pagett, directed by Michael Blakemore
A film adaptation of an award winning West end stage production. The plot centers round the antics of an army song-and-dance unit in the late 1960's. But behind the force and the fun, lies the reality of war, which cannot be put aside.
BBFC:15 — S,A — EN
HandMade Films — THORN EMI   P
TXA 90 1698 4/TVA 90 1698 2

Prize Fighter, The   Fil-Ent '79
Comedy-Drama
08878   99 mins   C
V2, B, V
Tim Conway, Don Knotts, David Wayne, Robin Clarke, John Myhers
This story tells of an out of luck and money boxer and his trainer. They meet a gangster who promises to arrange some big fights for them. They prepare for the fight which has the audience laughing and cheering.
S,A — EN
New World Pictures — Video Programme Distributors   P
Media 211

Prize of Peril, The   Fil-Ent '84
Suspense/Drama
12689   88 mins   C
B, V
Gerard Lanvin, Marie France Pisier, directed by Yves Boisset
This is the story of the ultimate TV Game Show where the contestants have to stay alive to win a million dollars and failure means death.
BBFC:18 — C,A — EN
Unknown — Brent Walker Home Video Ltd   P
BW25

Probability Zero   Fil-Ent '??
War-Drama/Adventure
06950   95 mins   C
B, V
Henry Silva
In this World War II drama, an English plane installed with a new radar system is attacked by German fighters. There follows a daring commando raid involving five brave men whose objective is to destroy the radar equipment. The probability of a successful mission, against such overwhelming odds, is zero.
S,A — EN
Unknown — Home Video Merchandisers   H, P
023

Producers, The   Fil-Ent '68
Comedy
07706   84 mins   C
B, V, LV
Zero Mostel, Gene Wilder, Dick Shawn, Kenneth Mars, Estelle Winwood, directed by Mel Brooks
A has-been theatrical producer and his accountant figure out how they can make money from producing a flop musical 'Springtime for Hitler.' They conspire to raise more money than they need from rich, flighty old ladies and run off with the proceeds.
S,A — EN
Avco Embassy — CBS/Fox Video   P
4058

PALADIN VIDEO HOME ENTERTAINMENT GUIDE

Professionals, The Fil-Ent '7?
Crime-Drama/Adventure
06145 100 mins C
V2, B, V

Gordon Jackson, Martin Shaw, Lewis Collins
This cassette features two episodes from the television series 'The Professionals.' 'The Female Factor' (50 mins) in which the Prime Minister's private line number is found on a pad in a prostitute's flat, she is then found naked, wet and dead. The K.G.B. become involved. 'Where the Jungle Ends' (50 mins) involves a group of greedy mercenaries who plan and execute a ruthless bank robbery in London.
S,A — EN
Fennell and Clemens Prod — *Guild Home Video* **H, P, E**

Professionals, The Fil-Ent '7?
Crime-Drama/Adventure
06148 100 mins C
B, V

Gordon Jackson, Martin Shaw, Lewis Collins
Two episodes on one cassette from the television series 'The Professionals.' 'Close Quarters' (50 mins) finds Bodie holding a dangerous terrorist on his own in a beseiged vicarage with gunmen moving in. 'Heros' (50 mins) involves innocent members of the public being killed off one by one after a fake bullion raid.
S,A — EN
Fennell and Clemens Prod — *Guild Home Video* **H, P, E**

Professionals III, The Fil-Ent '7?
Crime-Drama/Adventure
07389 100 mins C
V2, B, V

Gordon Jackson, Martin Shaw, Lewis Collins
Two episodes on one cassette from the television series 'The Professionals,' 'Old Dog New Tricks' (50 mins) and 'When the Heat Cools Off' (50 mins).
S,A — EN
Fennell and Clemens Prods — *Guild Home Video* **H, P, E**

Professionals IV, The Fil-Ent '??
Crime-Drama
09449 102 mins C
V2, B, V

Gordon Jackson, Martin Shaw, Lewis Collins
This tape contains two further encounters with C15. In 'The Killer With a Long Arm' an unusually powerful rifle is found in an abandoned car and reports come in of an unknown man carrying out firing practice with a long range gun. In 'Everest Was Also Conquered' a senior security officer confesses on his death bed that he was involved in a murder. When Cowley and his men investigate, they unleash a spate of murders.
S,A — EN
Fennelland Clemens Prod. — *Guild Home Video* **H, P, E**

Projected Man, The/Guns Don't Argue Fil-Ent '??
Horror/Crime-Drama
05658 173 mins C
B, V

Mary Peach, Bryant Halliday, Norman Wooland, Ronald Allen, Derek Fass, Tracey Crisp, Myron Healey, Jean Harvey, Richard Crane, Jim Davis
This cassette features two films. 'The Projected Man' (Colour, 86 mins, 1967) tells the story of a laboratory experiment which goes wrong, turning a scientist into a madman with the power to kill in one-hand, which contains death dealing high voltage. 'Guns Don't Argue' (Black/white, 87 mins, 1958) is a re-enacted documentary on the lives of public enemies John Dillinger, Ma Barker, Pretty Boy Floyd and others. It concentrates on their fate at the hands of the 'G' men.
S,A — EN
Universal; Visual Drama Inc — *Kingston Video* **H, P**
KV54

Prom Night Fil-Ent '79
Horror
08339 87 mins C
V2, B, V, LV

Leslie Nielsen, Jamie Lee Curtis, Casey Steven, Eddie Benton, Antoinette Bower
A masked killer stalks four high school senior girls during their senior prom, as a revenge for a murder that took place six years ago.
BBFC:X — A — EN
AVCO Embassy — *Embassy Home Entertainment* **P**
2049

Prophecy Fil-Ent '79
Horror
05320 102 mins C
B, V

Talia Shire, Robert Foxworth, Armand Assante, Richard Dysart, Victoria Racimo, directed by John Frankenheimer
An idealistic doctor and his wife, at the request of a friend, travel to Maine to research into the impact of the lumber industry on the local environment. They begin to investigate a series of horrific events including ecological freaks of

PALADIN VIDEO HOME ENTERTAINMENT GUIDE

nature and the grisly deaths that have occurred. The film, through the story, comments on the deadly forces that result from the pollution of the environment.
S,A — EN
Paramount — *CIC Video* **H, P**
BEA2016/VHA2016

Proud and Damned, The Fil-Ent '72
Western
06190   93 mins   C
B, V
Chuck Connors, Cesar Romero, Jose Greco, Aron Kincaid
Five veterans form a mercenary outfit after the American Civil War. Led by their former sergeant they trail blaze through Latin America hiring their services to the highest bidder. They accidentally meet up with a mad Dictator who forces them to embark on a mission from which they may never return.
S,A
Gold Key Entertainment — *VCL Video Services* **P**
X0272

Psalm 23 Gen-Edu '??
Religion/Bible
06291   45 mins   B/W
B, V, PH15
In this film Sandy Thompson, a missionary in Israel, relates Bible truth to local customs.
S,A — R
Audio Visual Ministries — *Audio Visual Ministries* **H, L, P**
VT65

Psycho Fil-Ent '60
Suspense
01040   109 mins   B/W
B, V
Anthony Perkins, Janet Leigh, Vera Miles, John Gavin, Martin Balsam, directed by Alfred Hitchcock
A young woman steals a fortune and encounters a young peculiar man and his mysterious mother.
A — EN
Paramount — *CIC Video* **H, P**

Psycho II Fil-Ent '83
Suspense
12036   109 mins   C
B, V
Anthony Perkins, Vera Miles, Meg Tilley, Robert Loggia

A psychopathic killer is released after forty years in prison and goes back to the scene of the murders. A series of disappearances takes place and the finger of suspicion is once again pointed at him.
BBFC:15 — S,A — EN
Universal — *CIC Video* **H, P**
BEA 1090/VHA 1090

Psychomania Fil-Ent '73
Horror
09390   90 mins   C
B, V
George Sanders, Beryl Reid, Nicky Henson, Mary Larkin, Roy Holder, directed by Don Sharp
This is a story of the supernatural, the occult and the violence which lies just beyond the conventions of society for a gang of Hells Angels.
BBFC:18 — A — EN
Unknown — *VCL Video Services* **P**
P364D

Psychopath Fil-Ent '74
Horror/Drama
05518   93 mins   C
B, V
Tom Basham, Gene Carlson, Barbara Graner, directed by Larry Brown
This film centers on the young, well liked, host of a children's television show who, unknown to anyone, sees himself as a judge, jury and executioner with a duty to seek out and murder parents who abuse children.
BBFC:X — A — EN
Larry Brown Prod — *Derann Film Services* **H, P**
DV143B/DV143

P'tang Yang, Kipperbang Fil-Ent '82
Comedy
12899   77 mins   C
B, V
John Albasiny, Alison Steadman, Garry Cooper, directed by Michael Apted
A fourteen year old schoolboy's dreams come true when he is cast-opposite his classmate in the school play and has the chance of a stage kiss.
BBFC:PG — S,A — EN
Unknown — *THORN EMI* **P**
IXB 90 23684/TVB 90 23682

Puberty Blues Fil-Ent '82
Comedy-Drama
08526   85 mins   C
B, V
Nell Schofield, Jad Capelja, directed by Bruce Beresford

(For Explanation of codes, see USE GUIDE and KEY)

PALADIN VIDEO HOME ENTERTAINMENT GUIDE

This film follows the exploits of two 17-year-old girls, who try desperately to lose their viginity in an attempt to gain acceptance to the elite Australian beach crowd.
A — EN
Unknown — THORN EMI   P
TXA 90 1280 4/TVA 90 1280 2

Pugwash Chi-Juv '87
Cartoons
12559   80 mins   C
V2, B, V
This cassette contains eighteen swashbuckling adventures featuring Captain Horatio Pugwash, Tom the Cabin Boy and arch-adversary, Cut-Throa: Jake.
PS,I — EN
Unknown — RPTA Video Ltd   H, P

Puma Man, The Fil-Ent '??
Science fiction
06871   93 mins   C
V2, B, V
Donald Pleasence, Walter George Alton, Sydney Rome, Miguel Angel Fuentes
A madman seeking the power to conquer the world obtains an ancient mask which has the power to make people obey the user. However the mask belongs to an alien race who want it back. The Puma Man, whose powers come from a magic belt, and the Inca priest, who gave him the belt, offer to help. They eventually acquire the mask and return it to the rightful owners.
S,A — EN
Unknown — European Video Company
P

Pumping Iron Spo-Lei '77
Documentary/Physical fitness
08445   81 mins   C
B, V
Arnold Schwarzenegger, Mike Katz, Franco Columbo, Lou Ferrigno, directed by George Butler
This film takes a documentary look at the sport of body-building, following the behind-the-scenes action surrounding the competition for the 'Mr. Olympia' title. The grueling training ritual and the constant striving for perfection are all explored.
BBFC:A — S,A — EN
Cinema 5 — THORN EMI   P
TXB 90 1544 4/TVB 90 1544 2

Punch and Jody Fil-Ent '74
Drama
09258   72 mins   C
V2, B, V
Glenn Ford, Pam Griffin, Ruth Roman, Kathleen Widdoes, Billy Barty, Patty Maloney

An executive drop-out achieves a boyhood dream by joining a small, struggling, travelling circus. He is soon made manager, which means he becomes book-keeper, ticket taker, canvas boss, advance man, East-Indian knife thrower, elephant trainer and clown. However, one day he discovers that his wife has died and that he has a 15-year-old daughter, who intends to spend her vacations with him. He soon discovers that parent-hood and the circus do not mix.
BBFC:A — S,A — EN
MPC/Stonehenge — Iver Film Services
P
211

Puppet on a Chain Fil-Ent '72
Crime-Drama
07377   98 mins   C
V2, B, V
Sven-Bertil Taube, Barbara Parkins, Alexander Knox, directed by Geoffrey Reeve
An undercover agent from Interpol's Narcotics Bureau flies to Amsterdam to track down an international drug ring. On arrival he becomes the chief target for bizarre and vicious killers. As his investigations lead him closer to the heart of the ring more people die violently. Eventually he discovers a police inspector and his niece are the leaders. Based on the novel by Alistair Maclean.
BBFC:AA — S,A — EN
Cinerama — Guild Home Video   H, P, E

Purple Plain, The Fil-Ent '55
War-Drama
09930   98 mins   C
B, V
Gregory Peck, Maurice Denham, Win Min Than, Bernard Lee, Brenda De Banzie
A Canadian flyer serving with the RAF in Burma struggles to hold on to his courage and keep his sanity after losing his wife in an air raid. Filmed in Burma, this is based on the H.E. Bates novel.
BBFC:PG — S,A — EN
U.A.; J. Arthur Rank — Rank Video Library
H, P
0163 A

Purple Taxi, The Fil-Ent '77
Drama/Mystery
07608   98 mins   C
V2, B, V
Fred Astaire, Charlotte Rampling, Phillippe Noiret, Peter Ustinov, directed by Yves Boisset
A country doctor in southern Irelands uses a purple taxi to make his rounds, to the consternation of his patients
BBFC:AA — S,A — EN
Parafrance Films; Sofracima Rizzoli
Film — Iver Film Services   P

PALADIN VIDEO HOME ENTERTAINMENT GUIDE

Pushing Up Daisies   Fil-Ent '??

Western/Crime-Drama

07985   85 mins   C

B, V

Ross Hagen, Kelly Thordsen, Christopher George

This film tells of the plight of four criminals, who after a daring bank raid, head across the Mexican border leaving behind a trail of dead and wounded deputies. In revenge a sheriff sets out after them.

C,A — EN

Unknown — *Motion Epics Video Company Ltd*   **P**

152

Puzzle   Fil-Ent '78

Mystery

09134   91 mins   C

V2, B, V

James Franciscus, Wendy Hughes

A woman becomes involved in action and excitement when she is determined to find a cache of gold bars. They had been hidden away by her crooked husband whilst playing a dangerous game of duplicity and deceit.

S,A — EN

Transalantic Entprs — *Go Video Ltd*   **P**

PIC 001

Pyx, The   Fil-Ent '70

Drama/Suspense

13153   107 mins   C

B, V

Karen Black, Christopher Plummer

A dead prostitute is found clutching a sacred object and sets off a chain of bizarre events.

BBFC:18 — C,A — EN

Cinerama; Host Robar Productions — *Brent Walker Home Video Ltd*   **P**

BW 29

Q

Quackser Fortune Has a Cousin in the Bronx   Fil-Ent '70

Drama/Comedy

09178   88 mins   C

B, V

Gene Wilder, Margot Kidder

An Irish fertilizer salesman meets an exchange student from the United States, who finds herself attracted to this unlearned but not unknowing man.

C,A — EN

John H Cunningham; Mel Howard — *Video Form Pictures*   **H, P**

MGS 16

Quadrophenia   Fil-Ent '79

Musical-Drama

05857   115 mins   C

V2, B, V

Phil Daniels, Mark Wingett, Philip Davis, Leslie Ash, Garry Cooper, Toyah Wilcox, Trevor Laird, Kate Williams, Michael Elphick, Kim Neve, Gary Shail, directed by Franc Roddam

This film captures in accurate detail the excitement and aggression of the Mods and Rockers of the 'Swinging 60's.' The clubs, the drugs, the music and the girls are all portrayed climaxing with the bloody Bank Holiday battles at Brighton.

BBFC:X — A — EN

Who Films; Curbishley Baird Production — *Polygram Video*   **P**

7901865/7901864/7901862

Quartet   Fil-Ent '81

Drama

07714   96 mins   C

V2, B, V

Isabelle Adjani, Alan Bates, Maggie Smith

This film looks at the lives of four expatriates whose paths entwine in Paris in the late 1920s.

S,A — EN

Twentieth Century Fox — *CBS/Fox Video*   **P**

1142

Quartet   Fil-Ent '48

Drama

12748   118 mins   B/W

B, V

Dirk Bogarde, Honor Blackman, Basil Radford, George Cole, Hermione Baddeley, Cecil Parker

(For Explanation of codes, see USE GUIDE and KEY)

PALADIN VIDEO HOME ENTERTAINMENT GUIDE

The dramatization of four Somerset Maugham short stories—'The Facts of Life,' 'The Alien Corn,' 'The Kite' and 'The Colonel's Lady' are featured in this film.
BBFC:A — A — EN
J. Arthur Rank; Eagle-Lion — *Rank Video Library* **H, P**
0203 E

Quatermass Fil-Ent '79
Science fiction
13713   105 mins   C
B, V
John Mills, Simon MacCorkindale, Barbara Kellerman, directed by Piers Haggard
Once again Professor Quatermass must meet an evil force and destroy it before it succeeds in terminating a society which is bent on destroying itself.
BBFC:15 — S,A — EN
Thames Video — *THORN EMI*   **P**
90 2589

Queen for Caesar, A Fil-Ent '62
Drama
04289   95 mins   C
V2, B, V
Pascale Petit, Gordon Scott, Akim Tamiroff
Cleopatra and her brother Ptolemy jointly rule Egypt, but each desires to rule alone. Cleopatra promises to marry Theodotus if he will betray the imprisoned Ptolemy; instead he sets him free. Condemned to death Cleopatra flees to Syria where she plots the defeat of Caesar's occupying army and her triumphant return to Egypt.
C,A — EN
Commonwealth United TV — *Video Programme Distributors*   **P**
Inter-Ocean—029

Queen: Greatest Flix Fil-Ent '81
Music-Performance
05056   60 mins   C
B, V
A compilation of original films made to accompany Queen's hit records, forming an audio-visual biography of the group. Songs include 'Killer Queen,' 'Bohemian Rhapsody,' 'Somebody to Love,' 'We Are the Champions,' 'Flasti.'
F — EN
Unknown — *THORN EMI*   **P**
TXD 90 0504 4/TVD 90 0504 2

Queen in Arabia, The Gen-Edu '79
Royalty-GB
13488   60 mins   C
B, V
A film of the Queen's historic journey to the Middle East in 1979 from her arrival by Concorde in Kuwait and her 15 day tour of Bahrain, Saudi Arabia, Qatar, The United Arab Emirates and Oman.
F — EN   AB
Greenpark Productions — *Greenpark Productions*   **P**

Queen of Spades, The Fil-Ent '48
Drama
00589   92 mins   C
B, V
Anton Walbrook, Edith Evans, Yvonne Mitchell
A poor Russian Army officer tries to obtain the secret of winning at cards, even though it costs him his soul.
C,A — EN
Anatole de Grunwald — *THORN EMI*   **P**
TXE 90 0211 4/TVE 90 0211 2

Queen of the Blues Fil-Ent '79
Crime-Drama
02098   62 mins   C
V2, B, V
Mary Millington
Mike and Tony are threatened by protection racketeers when they convert a staid gentleman's club into a successful strip club starring the 'Queen of the Blues.'
BBFC:X — C,A — EN
Roldvale Prods — *Hokushin Audio Visual Ltd*
P
VM-04

Queen—We Will Rock You Fil-Ent '82
Music-Performance
13357   90 mins   C
V2, B, V
Twenty one of Queen's tracks are recorded in stereo on this cassette including 'Another One Bites the Dust,' 'Keep Yourself Alive,' 'Under Pressure,' 'Play the Game' and 'Love of My Life.'
S,A — EN
Queen Films Ltd — *Guild Home Video*   **H, P, E**
6122-3

Queen's Birthday Parade, The Fil-Ent '81
Royalty-GB/Documentary
04861   88 mins   C
V2, B, V, LV

530 (For Explanation of codes, see USE GUIDE and KEY)

PALADIN VIDEO HOME ENTERTAINMENT GUIDE

This record of 'Trooping the Colour,' with its military bands and ceremonial, features the detailed planning and hard work involved in the staging of the parade. It also includes one of Lord Louis Mountbatten's last public appearances.
F — EN
Michael Begg; Ian Smith — *BBC Video* **H, P**
BBCV 5000

Queen's Ransom, A Fil-Ent '77
Crime-Drama/Suspense
08045   87 mins   C
B, V
George Lazenby, Judith Brown, Jimmy Wang Yu
This film tells of the plans of a daring terror squad, which involve blowing up Hong Kong's harbour tunnel, assassinating the Queen of England and seizing a cache of gold.
C,A — EN
Unknown — *Rank Video Library* **H, P**
0075 B

Querelle Fil-Ent '82
Drama
10020   106 mins   C
B, V
Brad Davis, directed by Rainer Werner Fassbinder
A surreal world of passion and sexuality is the setting of one of Fassbinder's finest films, in this story of a sexually ambiguous sailor who becomes the toast of the French waterfront denizens.
A — EN
Gaumont — *Palace Video Ltd* **P**
PVC 2067A

Quest for Love Fil-Ent '71
Drama/Romance
08092   87 mins   C
B, V
Joan Collins, Tom Bell, Denholm Elliot, directed by Ralph Thomas
This film tells the story of a scientist whose life is altered when an experiment goes wrong. He lives two existences in different times, putting one experience to advantage in the other.
BBFC:A — S,A — EN
Rank — *Rank Video Library* **H, P**
0122 C

Question of Love Fil-Ent '78
Drama
06958   60 mins   C
B, V
Gena Rowlands, Jane Alexander, Ned Beatty, Clu Gulager, Bonnie Bedelia, Keith Mitchell, directed by Jerry Thorpe
Based on actual events, this film tells the story of a mother's struggle to keep her young son when a suit is brought by her ex-husband seeking custody of the child because the mother is a lesbian. The film highlights the conflict between cultural morality and individual love and affection.
S,A — EN
Viacom Prods — *Home Video Merchandisers* **H, P**
032

Quick Dog Training with Barbara Woodhouse How-Ins '83
Animals
12164   88 mins   C
V2, B, V
Barbara Woodhouse
This well known dog trainer takes several owners and their dogs through some of the most important elements of dog training.
F — I
Bruce D Stout — *Embassy Home Entertainment* **P**
1108

Quiller Memorandum, The Fil-Ent '67
Suspense
04245   99 mins   C
B, V
George Segal, Alec Guinness, Max Von Sydow, Senta Berger, George Sanders, Robert Helpmann
Berlin, spy capital of Europe. British Intelligence has been suffering some personnel losses in the effort to track down a neo-Nazi hideaway somewhere in the city. Enter Quiller, a maverick with his own way of operating.
BBFC:A — C,A — EN
20th Century Fox — *Rank Video Library* **H, P**
0022

Quinns, The Fil-Ent '77
Drama
07488   74 mins   C
B, V
This film covers the story of the Quinns, four generations of an Irish-American family. This is a character study of the Quinn household and how they react to people in their lives and the changing world they live in. They are a family in conflict, of fierce loyalty and strong tradition and a family in transition.
S,A — EN
Unknown — *Quadrant Video* **H, P**
FF7

(For Explanation of codes, see USE GUIDE and KEY)   531

PALADIN VIDEO HOME ENTERTAINMENT GUIDE

Quo Vadis   Fil-Ent '51
Adventure/Drama
12222   168 mins   C
B, V
Robert Taylor, Deborah Kerr, Peter Ustinov
The savagery and splendour of ancient Rome is depicted in this film when a triumphant warrior returns to the city and falls in love with a beautiful slave.
F — EN
MGM — *MGM/UA Home Video*   P
10276

R

Rabbit Test   Fil-Ent '78
Comedy
10079   84 mins   C
V2, B, V
Billy Crystal, Joan Prather, Alex Rocco, Doris Roberts, directed by Joan Rivers
A comedy about the world's first pregnant man. At first he is horrified but once he gets used to the idea he is overjoyed at the thought of fatherhood and decides to keep his baby.
C,A — EN
Avco Embassy — *Embassy Home Entertainment*   P
2100

Rabid   Fil-Ent '77
Horror
06764   95 mins   C
V2, B, V
Marilyn Chambers, Joe Silver, Howard Ryshpan, Patricia Cage
A young girl undergoes radical surgery and develops an strange and unexplained lesion in her armpit—along with a craving for human blood.
A — EN
New World; Canada — *Intervision Video*
H, P
A-A 0354

Raccoons and the Lost Star, The   Chi-Juv '82
Cartoons
10082   60 mins   C
V2, B, V
Animated
On a far-away planet, the evil Cyril Sneer plots his take-over of Earth. The raccoons and friends save the earth from his evil clutches.
BBFC:U — *PS,M — EN*
Kevin Gillis; Sheldon S Wiseman — *Embassy Home Entertainment*   P
1352

Raccoons on Ice/The Christmas Raccoons   Fil-Ent '82
Cartoons
08325   50 mins   C
V2, B, V, LV
Animated, narrated by Rich Little
This tape contains two 25 minute cartoons. In 'Raccoons on Ice' three raccoons, a dog and a mystery player compete against the evil Cyril Sneer and his team of bears in an ice hockey game. In 'The Christmas Raccoons' Cyril Sneer is trying to cut down all the trees and has to be stopped. Includes songs by Rita Coolidge, Leo Sayer and Rupert Holmes.
BBFC:U — *I,M — EN*
Kevin Gillis; Sheldon S Wiseman — *Embassy Home Entertainment*   P
1350

Race for the Championship, The   Spo-Lei '84
Football
12916   90 mins   C
B, V
This video portrays the 1983/84 season of the Canon League.
F — EN
Derek Sando — *THORN EMI*   P
TXE 90 25504/TVE 90 25502

Race for the Yankee Zephyr   Fil-Ent '81
Crime-Drama/Adventure
08477   111 mins   C
B, V
Donald Pleasance, George Peppard, Ken Wahl, Lesley Ann Warren, directed by David Hemmings
This film tells the story of a deerhunter who discovers an old U.S. cargo plane which went missing with a cargo of gold over New Zealand in 1944. A group of villainous criminals are also after this valuable cargo and the race begins to see who can salvage it first.
BBFC:A — *S,A — EN*
Hemdale; Pact Productions — *THORN EMI*
P
TXB 90 1543 4/TVB 90 1543 2

Race to the Top   Spo-Lei '82
Motorcycles
06845   65 mins   C   (PAL, NTSC)

PALADIN VIDEO HOME ENTERTAINMENT GUIDE

V2, B, V
This film is a double feature about up-and-coming privateers trying to establish themselves. 'Assen' is a documentary about the 1977 Dutch Grand Prix with Tom Herron and Kork Ballington. 'Mallory Magic' features the 1981 Race of the Year and Pro-Am Race showing Barry Sheene, Randy Mamola, Graeme Crosby and Kork Ballington in action. Introduced by world champion Geoff Duke.
S,A — EN
CH Wood Ltd — *Duke Marketing Limited*
P
DM5

Racecraft 1973/Collision Course 1976   Spo-Lei '7?
Automobiles-Racing
04505   44 mins   C
B, V
The versatile and successful Frank Gardner shows what it takes to handle and win with the mighty Camaro. In 'Collision Course 1976,' the story of the memorable Daytona 500 is told and the famous last-lap crash of Richard Petty and David Pearson is relived.
F — EN
STP — *Quadrant Video*   **H, P**
M15

Rachel's Man   Fil-Ent '74
Drama/Romance
06259   87 mins   C
B, V
Mickey Rooney, Rita Tushingham, Michael Bat-Adam, Leonard Whiting, directed by Moshe Mizrahi
Based on Old Testament writings, this film tells the story of Rachel and Jacob and their love for each other, their tenderness and their sensuousness. A story fraught with emotional violence and frustration shot entirely on location in and around Israel.
S,A — EN
Michael Klinger Production — *VCL Video Services*   **P**
C185C

Racing Game, The   Fil-Ent '7?
Drama
06155   64 mins   C
V2, B, V
Mike Gwilym, Mick Ford
A story of the world of horse racing, the series is based on the works of ex National Hint jockey and author Dick Francis, and goes behind the scenes to look at the real business of racing and its shadowy and criminal underside. A jockey no longer racing after a cruel injury investigates the various forms of corruption. Cassette No. 1 in the series.
S,A — EN
Stoller Prod — *Guild Home Video*   **H, P, E**

Racing with the Moon   Fil-Ent '84
Drama
13617   103 mins   C
B, V
Sean Penn, Nicholas Cage, Suzanne Adkinson, Julie Phillips, directed by Richard Benjamin
This film traces the story of two childhood friends from diverse backgrounds and the strains placed on their relationship as they enlist in the marines as World War II enters its second year.
BBFC:15 — S,A — EN
Paramount — *CIC Video*   **H, P**
2124

Racquet   Fil-Ent '79
Drama
07399   91 mins   C
V2, B, V
Bert Convy, Lynda Day George, Susan Tyrell, Edie Adams, Phil Silvers, Bjorn Borg, Bobby Riggs, directed by David Winters
A former Wimbledon champion turned instructor is now afraid of losing his status as a 'heart-throb.' He embarks on a search for the perfect girl, one with enough money to buy him his own tennis club.
BBFC:X — A — EN
Creswin Release — *Guild Home Video*
H, P, E

Ragan   Fil-Ent '68
Adventure
13484   84 mins   C
B, V
Ty Hardin, Antonella Lualdi, Gustavo Rojo, Jack Stewart
This is the story of a daring aircraft rescue attempt to free a general from his mountain prison in a counrty under military control.
BBFC:15 — S,A — EN
Orion Entertainment — *Precision Video Ltd*
P
514

Rage   Fil-Ent '80
Drama
09184   98 mins   C
B, V
David Soul, James Whitmore, Yaphet Kotto, Caroline McWilliams, Vic Tayback, Craig T. Nelson, directed by William Graham

---

(For Explanation of codes, see USE GUIDE and KEY)

PALADIN VIDEO HOME ENTERTAINMENT GUIDE

A man accused of rape, despite pleas of his innocence, is sentenced to prison. He has to attend intensive group therapy for sex offenders, the object being rehabilitation. Despite the disapproval of the family and friends, his wife stays faithfully in touch, and eventually provides the key to his recovery.
S,A — EN
Diane Silver; Charles Fries — *Video Form Pictures*   **H, P**
DIP 9

Ragewar Fll-Ent '84
Adventure/Science fiction
13231   85 mins   C
B, V
Jeffrey Byron, Leslie Wing, Richard Moll, directed by Charles Brand
In this battle of electronic magic against old-fashioned wizardry, a computer expert is whisked away to put his wits against the evil Mestrema in a series of bizarre jousts.
S,A — EN
Empire Pictures; Charles Band — *Entertainment in Video*   **H, P**
EVB 1025/EVV 1025

Raggedy Man Fll-Ent '81
Drama
09273   94 mins   C
B, V
Sissy Spacek, Eric Roberts, Sam Shepard, directed by Jack Fisk
This tells the poignant story of a woman raising two sons alone in a small Texas town during World War II and the sailor who enters her lonely life.
BBFC:PG — S,A — EN
Universal — *CIC Video*   **H, P**

Raging Moon, The Fll-Ent '70
Drama/Romance
08582   107 mins   C
B, V
Malcolm MacDowell, Nanette Newman, Georgia Brown, directed by Bryan Forbes
A young working-class man is suddenly confined to a wheelchair after a crippling disease. He is taken to a home for the disabled, but his bitterness of his fate and his dislike of the rules only help to make him more withdrawn. Then a fellow inmate, a victim of polio, helps him through his troubles.
BBFC:A — C,A — EN
EMI Film Productions Ltd — *THORN EMI*   **P**
TXC 90 0272 4/TVC 90 0272 2

Ragnarok Fll-Ent '83
Cartoons/Science fiction
08319   90 mins   C
B, V
Animated, Voices by David Tate, Jon Glover, Norma Ronald
This tape features three stories of science fiction adventure set many years in the future. Earth is a wasteland after a vicious intergalactic war. The only law left is Ragnarok and his alien friend, Smith, who travel the Universe trying to keep order. 'The Shattered World', 'Gates of Hell' and 'Sacrifice' tell of Ragnarok's adventures.
F — EN
Nutland Video Ltd — *Nutland Video Ltd*
P

Ragtime Fll-Ent '81
Drama
08467   149 mins   C
B, V
James Cagney, Brad Dourif, Moses Gunn, Elizabeth McGovern, Kennet McMillan, Pat O'Brien, Donald O'Connor, James Olson, Mandy Patinkin, directed by Milos Forman
Set in the early years of the century in America, this film mixes fact and fiction to tell the real-life scandal of a chorus girl. Her crazy, rich husband shot her former lover in public. It follows the crusade for justice by a black piano player for damage to his car. Based on the novel 'Ragtime' by E.L. Doctorow. The music in the film is by Randy Newman.
BBFC:AA — C,A — EN
Paramount — *THORN EMI*   **P**
TXA 90 0962 4/TVA 90 0962 2

Raid on Entebbe Fll-Ent '76
Adventure/Drama
07465   113 mins   C
B, V
Peter Finch, Charles Bronson, Yaphet Kotto, Martin Balsam, Horst Buchholtz, John Saxon, Sylvia Sidney, Jack Warden, directed by Irvin Kershner
This film relates the true story of the highjack of a passenger airliner by terrorists in June 1976. The plane carrying 244 passengers and 12 crew was forced to land at Uganda's Entebbe airport. The Jewish passengers were held in a transit lounge and threatened with death unless Palestinian prisoners were released. The film shows the daring rescue attempt of the Israeli task force.
BBFC:A — S,A — EN
Edgar J Scherick Associates — *THORN EMI*
P
TXB 90 0689 4/TV 90 0689 2

PALADIN VIDEO HOME ENTERTAINMENT GUIDE

Raiders of the Lost Ark — Fil-Ent '81
Adventure
10111   115 mins   C
B, V
Harrison Ford, Karen Allen, Denholm Elliott, Ronald Lacey, John Rhys-Davies, directed by Steven Spielberg
According to legend, The Ark of the Covenant disappeared from ancient Jerusalem and lies hidden beneath the sands of Tunis. The Nazis are close to finding it and our hero is involved in a series of hair-raising escapades to beat them to it.
BBFC:U — F — EN
Paramount — *CIC Video*   H, P
BER 2076/VHR 2076

Raiders of the Treasures of Tayopa — Fil-Ent '8?
Western
09136   90 mins   C
V2, B, V
Rena Winters, Bob Corrigan, Frank Hernandez, directed by Bob Cawley
This film is set in the American West, tells of a savage land, pillaged by treasure seekers, desperate men and women as ruthless as the land itself. Into this area rides two men and women, battling with the elements urged on by lust for hidden gold and treasures.
S,A — EN
Unknown — *Go Video Ltd*   P
GO 141

Railway Children, The — Fil-Ent '71
Comedy-Drama
01041   106 mins   C
B, V
Dinah Sheridan, Bernard Cribbins, Jenny Agutter, directed by Lionel Jeffries
Based on E. Nesbit's novel, this is the story of three children whose father is put in prison and must move from city to the country. Their cottage is near a railway line, which becomes the children's road to adventure.
BBFC:U — F — EN
Universal; EMJ Prods — *THORN EMI*   P
TXB 90 0017 4/TVB 90 0017 2

Rainbow — Chi-Juv '84
Language arts
12890   60 mins   C
B, V
Presented by Geoffrey Hayes
This cassette uses films, animation, puppets, songs and stories to help children understand the world about them and develop an appreciation of language and numbers.
PS — ED
Thames Video — *THORN EMI*   P
TXE 90 17304/TVE 90 173042

Rainbow—Live Between the Eyes — Fil-Ent '8?
Music-Performance
08993   75 mins   C
B, V
Directed by Nigel Gordon
This tape, filmed at the San Antonio Stadium in Texas, features the rock group Rainbow. Amongst eleven of the songs performed are 'It Can't Happen Here', 'Smoke on the Water' and 'Stone Cold'.
F — EN
Unknown — *Polygram Video*   P
790 587

Raise the Titanic — Fil-Ent '80
Drama
05399   110 mins   C
V2, B, V, LV
Jason Robards, Richard Jordan, David Selby, Anne Archer, Alec Guinness, directed by Jerry Jameson
Seventy years after the Titanic collided with an iceberg on her maiden voyage and sank, it is believed that the world's supply of byzanium, a vital ingredient for a nuclear deterrent, is on board. The winner in the arms race will be the one who has the new system. The superpowers vie to locate the byzanium, and the President orders that the Titanic be raised.
BBFC:A — S,A — EN
Martin Starger Production — *Precision Video Ltd*   P
CRITC 3027/BITC 3027/VITC 3027

Rajab Faouka Safih Sakhen (Rajab on a Hot Tin Roof) — Fil-Ent '??
Comedy
06739   120 mins   C
V2, B, V
A farmer visits the big city for the first time.
S,A — EN   AB
Unknown — *Intervision Video*   H, P
A-C 0145

Raks Shabi — Fil-Ent '??
Dance/Documentary
08002   120 mins   C
B, V
This is an Arabic film about Egyptian local dance.
F — EN   AB
Unknown — *Motion Epics Video Company Ltd*
P

Randy Crawford — Fil-Ent '8?
Music-Performance
07868   60 mins   C

PALADIN VIDEO HOME ENTERTAINMENT GUIDE

B, V
This tape features Randy Crawford live in concert at the Theatre Royal, Drury Lane, London.
S,A — EN
Warner Bros — *Warner Home Video*   P
WEX 93005/WEV 93005

Randy Edelman   Fil-Ent '7?
Music-Performance
02080   30 mins   C
B, V
Randy Edelman
Randy Edelman, one of America's most respected songwriters, performing his own material to an invited audience in one of London's leading nightspots. Conquering his natural shyness, Randy achieved instant success as a solo artist. This film provides an opportunity to watch a fascinating and rarely seen talent in concert.
F — EN
VCL Video Services — *VCL Video Services*
P

Ransom   Fil-Ent '77
Drama/Suspense
06156   84 mins   C
V2, B, V
Oliver Reed, Deborah Raffin, Stuart Whitman, Jim Mitchum, John Ireland, Paul Kaslo
A sinister reign of terror is aimed against a whole town. Deadly arrows cut down the police force and its influential citizens to set the scene for a ransom demand of five million dollars. The wealthy residents hire a tough and ruthless ex-detective to fight for them against the cold, calculating killer.
BBFC:AA — S,A — EN
Jim V Hart Prod — *Guild Home Video*   H, P, E

Ransom   Fil-Ent '74
Crime-Drama/Suspense
07446   97 mins   C
B, V
Sean Connery, Ian McShane, directed by Casper Wrede
An ailing British ambassador in Scandinavia is kidnapped by a terrorist who demands the release of six of his associates from a British prison and an aircraft to take them to an undisclosed dropping zone. The head of Norwegian National Security is against meeting the demands but things become complicated when a hijacked plane approaches, the criminals threaten to kill all aboard if the terrorist is not allowed to join them.
S,A — EN
British Lion Films Ltd — *THORN EMI*   P
TXB 90 0256 4/TVB 90 0256 2

Rape Because of the Cats, The   Fil-Ent '73
Crime-Drama
08765   96 mins   C
B, V
Bryan Marshall, Alexandra Stewart, Sylvia Kristel, Sebastian Graham Jones, Ida Goemans
The Amsterdam Police are baffled by a series of destructive burglaries. The wife of a rich jeweler is then brutally raped by six men in the presence of her husband. The inspector's first clue leads him to a rich suburb of Amsterdam, where he is confronted by the impenetrable attitude of a group of youngsters who call themselves The Ravens.
BBFC:X — A — EN
Fons Rademakers — *Precision Video Ltd*
P
BHPV 2570/VHPV 2570

Rape of the Third Reich   Fil-Ent '72
Drama
12240   90 mins   C
B, V
Peter Finch, Michael York
Based on Graham Greene's novel 'England Made Me' this film is set in the depression of the 30's and centres round the business activities of a ruthless German financier.
C,A — EN
Hemdale; Atlantic — *VCL Video Services*
P
P079D

Raquel   Fil-Ent '??
Music-Performance
06240   60 mins   C
B, V
Raquel Welch, John Wayne, Tom Jones
A musical special with guest stars John Wayne and Tom Jones, that emphasises the unique talents of Raquel Welch.
F — EN
Unknown — *VCL Video Services*   P
V062

Raquel—Total Beauty and Fitness   Spo-Lei '84
Physical fitness
12900   60 mins   C
B, V
Raquel Welch
Raquel Welch demonstrates the fitness programme she has developed and followed during the last eight years in this video.
C,A — I
Thorn EMI — *THORN EMI*   P
TXE 90 25734/TVE 90 25732

PALADIN VIDEO HOME ENTERTAINMENT GUIDE

Rascals and Robbers   Fil-Ent '81
Comedy
13678   97 mins   C
B, V
Patrick Creadon, Anthony Michael Hall, Anthony James, Allyn Ann McLerie, directed by Dick Lowry
A couple of boys overhear a crooks' plot and when discovered are chased miles down the river and have to find their way home in a series of escapades.
BBFC:U — F — EN
Hunt Lowry — *CBS/Fox Video*   **P**
7160

Rats, The   Fil-Ent '82
Horror
09464   83 mins   C
V2, B, V
Sam Groom, Sara Botsford
Based on the book by James Herbert, this film tells the frightening story of how one of the world's greatest cities becomes a battleground in man's fight for survival against a deadly force of evil, the rats.
BBFC:18 — A — EN
Northshore Investments Ltd — *Guild Home Video*   **H, P, E**

Rattle of a Simple Man   Fil-Ent '64
Comedy-Drama
04661   91 mins   B/W
B, V
Harry H. Corbett, Diane Cilento, Michael Medwin, Thora Hird
A shy football supporter in London spends the night with a prostitute in order to win a bet.
BBFC:X — A — EN
Sydney Box — *THORN EMI*   **H, P**
TXE 90 0254 4/TVE 90 0254 2

Rattlers   Fil-Ent '??
Drama
09845   80 mins   C
B, V
Sam Chew, Elizabeth Chauvet, Dan Priest, Ron Gold, Tony Ballen
This is the story of mysterious unprovoked snake attacks that result in an investigation which uncovers the insidious use of nerve gas by the military.
S,A — EN
Unknown — *Polygram Video*   **H, P**
040 1094/040 1092

Ravagers, The   Fil-Ent '78
Horror/Drama
09281   103 mins   C
B, V
Richard Harris, Ernest Borgnine, Anne Turkel, Art Carney, directed by Richard Compton
In the aftermath of a nuclear holocaust, a man sees his wife brutally murdered by animal-like humans called Ravagers. They terrorise the few remaining civilised inhabitants of the earth as they try to set up a vigilante group in a desperate quest for a place to live in peace.
S,A — EN
Columbia — *RCA/Columbia Pictures Video UK*   **H, P**

Ravine, The   Fil-Ent '69
Drama
09022   97 mins   C
V2, B, V
David McCallum, Nicoletta Machiavelli, Johnny Crawford
Set in World War 11, a young German soldier is sent to capture a Yugoslavian sniper. However, he makes the tragic mistake of falling in love with her.
C,A — EN
United Artists — *Intervision Video*   **H, P**
AA 0444

Raw Deal   Fil-Ent '48
Crime-Drama
04158   94 mins   C
B, V
Dennis O'Keefe, Claire Trevor, John Ireland, Raymond Burr
Convict escapes jail and seeks revenge on the gang that sent him up. T-Men get involved.
BBFC:AA — C,A — EN
Edward Small Prods — *Guild Home Video*   **H, P**

Reach for the Sky   Fil-Ent '56
War-Drama
01889   136 mins   B/W
B, V
Kenneth More, Muriel Pavlow
A true story based on the war experiences of Douglas Bader, depicting one man's indomitable courage and endurance after losing both legs in a flying accident. He not only overcomes his disability but goes on to become a Battle of Britain ace.
BBFC:U — C,A — EN
Rank — *Rank Video Library*   **H, P**
0005

Reaching for the Moon   Fil-Ent '31
Romance
07629   64 mins   B/W
B, V
Douglas Fairbanks Sr., Bebe Daniels, Bing Crosby, directed by Edmund Golding

---

(For Explanation of codes, see USE GUIDE and KEY)

PALADIN VIDEO HOME ENTERTAINMENT GUIDE

A Wall Street finance wizard tells a young girl that he is not interested in women. She pretends to fall for him until he changes his mind. They book separate state-rooms on a luxury liner and she continues to lead him on. Eventually he proposes to her. Unknown to him, an audience of her friends is watching. Unamused, he plans a novel revenge.
F — EN
Artcinema — VCL Video Services   P
0222G

Ready Steady Go!- Volume One   Fil-Ent '83
Music-Performance
09785   ? mins   B/W
B, V
Original performances from the classic TV show of the sixties including The Beatles, Dusty Springfield, The Animals, Cilla Black, Billy Fury, Them, Lulu, Sandie Shaw, The Searchers, The Rolling Stones, The Who, Gerry and the Pacemakers, Georgie Fame, Peter Cook and Dudley Moore.
F — EN
EMI Records Ltd. — THORN EMI   P
TXE 90 1959 4/TVE 90 1959 2

Real Bruce Lee, The   Fil-Ent '80
Adventure/Martial arts
01692   120 mins   C
V2, B, V
Bruce Lee, Dragon Lee, Bruce Li
This is an early Bruce Lee film that was once feared lost, but was recently found in the Chinese archives. Bruce Lee, Dragon Lee, and Bruce Li compete in fast-paced martial arts action.
A — EN
Serafim Karalexis — Intervision Video   H, P
A-AE 0176

Real Life   Fil-Ent '84
Drama
13233   93 mins   C
B, V
Katy Rabett, Rupert Everett, Christina Raines, directed by Francis Megahy
A young man meets a beautiful woman on the run from her estranged husband and his involvement with her triggers off a chain of events leading to the arrest of a dangerous criminal.
BBFC:PG — S,A — EN
Bedford Productions — Entertainment in Video   H, P
EVB 1023/EVV 1023

Rear Window   Fil-Ent '54
Suspense
13307   107 mins   C
B, V
James Stewart, Grace Kelly, Raymond Burr, Irene Winston, Thelma Ritter, directed by Alfred Hitchcock
A photographer immobilized in his wheelchair amuses himself by spying on his neighbours through their open blinds during the hot weather and after hearing a scream one night becomes convinced a murder has taken place.
BBFC:PG — S,A — EN
Alfred Hitchcock — CIC Video   H, P
BET 1126/VHT 1126

Reardon on Snooker   Spo-Lei '7?
Sports-Minor
09471   80 mins   C
B, V
Ray Reardon, introduced by Clive Everton
Ray Reardon, World Professional Snooker Champion in 1970, 1973 to 1976 and 1978 shows how to play the game, from the basic shots right through to the trick shots which have proved so appealing to players and spectators.
S,A — I
Unknown — Guild Home Video   H, P, E

Rebecca   Fil-Ent '40
Drama
04163   130 mins   B/W
B, V
Laurence Olivier, Joan Fontaine, George Sanders, Judith Anderson, directed by Alfred Hitchcock
Film adaptation of Daphne du Maurier's classic novel about dark secrets at the country estate of Manderley.
Academy Awards 1940: Best Picture; Best Cinematography Black and White (George Barnes).   BBFC:A — S,A — EN
Selznick — Guild Home Video   H, P

Rebecca of Sunnybrook Farm   Fil-Ent '38
Drama
05650   83 mins   B/W
B, V
Shirley Temple, Randolph Scott, Jack Haley, Gloria Stuart, Phyllis Brooks, Helen Westley, Slim Summerville, directed by Allan Dwain
A radio presenter is seeking a child singer to launch his new show; he finds one but loses her due to an administrative error. She has been sent to her Aunt's farm, which just happens to be next door to the presenter. While preparing to launch the new star and courting her cousin

PALADIN VIDEO HOME ENTERTAINMENT GUIDE

he is confronted by a rival arranged by the scheming father. The little girl loses her voice until the radio presenter regains the right to star her, and she recovers just in time.
F — EN
Twentieth Century Fox — *CBS/Fox Video*
P

Recommendation for Mercy   Fil-Ent '??
Crime-Drama
08865   81 mins   C
V2, B, V
Andrew Skido, Karen Martin, Robb Judd
This film tells the true story of the brutal murder of a 13-year-old girl. John, a 14-year-old, is arrested for the killing but maintains his innocence.
BBFC:X — A — EN
Unknown — *Video Programme Distributors*
P
Replay 1018

Red Arrows—Gnats and Hawks, The   Spo-Lei '80
Sports/Aeronautics
09313   30 mins   C
B, V
Two exciting displays by the RAF aerobatic team in action are included on this tape. The first, made in 1968, features the Red Arrows flying Gnats and the second, filmed in 1980, shows them in Hawks.
F — EN
Unknown — *THORN EMI*   P
TXF 90 1718 4/TVF 90 1718 2

Red Baron, The   Fil-Ent '7?
Cartoons
13779   45 mins   C
B, V
Animated by Rankin and Bass
All time flying ace 'The Red Baron' takes to the air in battle to save the beautiful Princess Sophie who has been kidnapped by his arch enemy, the evil cat Putzi.
F — EN
Unknown — *Odyssey Video*   H, P
6424

Red Berets, The   Fil-Ent '82
Adventure/Suspense
12671   100 mins   C
V2, B, V
Ivan Rassimov, Priscilla Drake, Sieghardt Rupp, Kirk Morris, directed by Mario Siciliano

A team of fighting men are sent deep into the heart of the African Congo to wrest secret documents from the hands of nationalist guerillas.
S,A — EN
Mario Siciliano — *Videomedia*   P
7104

Red Flag   Fil-Ent '81
War-Drama
09364   92 mins   C
B, V
Barry Bostwick, Joan Van Ark, Fred McCarren, Debra Feuer, George Coe
During training exercises an aircraft is shot down by the 'aggressor' squadron. A personal vendetta now exists and another confrontation takes place, only this time the plane crashes and the crew is killed. The pilot feels responsible and plans to resign from the Air Force. However, he soon realizes his skills can be used for a positive purpose, to save the lives of other pilots.
F — EN
Marble Arch Prods — *Precision Video Ltd*
P
BITC 2104/VITC 2104

Red Light in the White House   Fil-Ent '??
Drama/Mystery
07825   90 mins   C
V2, B, V
Karin Mary Shea, Frank Whiteman
The widow of a former Senator from California decides to run for his vacant seat. As she is leading in the polls, a high powered investigative reporter is hired to delve into her past. There are rumours that she was once a high-class prostitute.
S,A — EN
Unknown — *Video Unlimited*   H, P

Red Light Sting, The   Fil-Ent '84
Crime-Drama
13325   92 mins   C
B, V
Beau Bridges, Farrah Fawcett, Harold Gould, directed by Rod Holcomb
A government department takes over the running of a brothel in an effort to trap a notorious local drug racketeer.
BBFC:15 — C,A — EN
Universal — *CIC Video*   H, P
BET 1124/VHT 1124

Red Nights of the Gestapo, The   Fil-Ent '??
War-Drama
08817   100 mins   C

(For Explanation of codes, see USE GUIDE and KEY)

PALADIN VIDEO HOME ENTERTAINMENT GUIDE

B, V
Enzo Miani, Fred Williams, Mike Morris, directed by Fabio De Agostini
A plan is uncovered by the Gestapo to kill Hitler. An Elite Squad of SS officers is formed to prevent the mission. They have orders to use any means at their disposal to execute the conspirators.
BBFC:X — A — EN
Unknown — VCL Video Services   **P**
P236D

Red Pony, The   Fil-Ent '49
Adventure
08730   89 mins   C
B, V
Myrna Loy, Robert Mitchum, Louis Calhern
A sensitive boy has one great love, his pony. When it tragically dies, his passion turns to violence at the apparent injustice of this fate. It is based on the book by John Steinbeck.
S,A — EN
Republic — BBC Video   **H, P**
BBCV 8011

Red Rackham's Treasure   Chl-Juv '7?
Cartoons/Adventure
02278   60 mins   C
V
Animated
Tin Tin and his friends set out to find the long lost treasure of Red Rackham, the pirate.
M — EN
Unknown — JVC   **P**
PRT 25

Red Shoes, The   Fil-Ent '48
Dance/Fairy tales
05158   132 mins   C
B, V
Marius Goring, Moira Shearer, Leonide Massine, Ludmilla Tcherina, Albert Basserman, Anton Walbrook, Esmond Knight, Robert Helpmann
Sir Thomas Beecham conducts the Royal Philharmonic Orchestra in this timeless presentation of Hans Christian Andersen's fairy tale. Robert Helpmann choreographed this triple Academy Award winning production of the enchanting ballet.
BBFC:U — F — EN
GFD — Rank Video Library   **H, P**
7010

Red Sun   Fil-Ent '71
Western
07844   103 mins   C
V2, B, V
Charles Bronson, Ursula Andress, Toshiro Mifune, Alain Delon, directed by Terence Young
Set in the year 1871 the Emperor of Japan decides to make a gift of a priceless Samurai sword to the President of the United States. En route the sword and a bullion shipment are stolen. A desperado and a Samurai team up to reclaim the goods.
S,A — EN
Les Films Corona — Polygram Video   **H, P**
791 515

Redeemer, The   Fil-Ent '7?
Mystery
02399   83 mins   C
B, V
Damien Knight, Jeanetta Arnette, directed by Constantine Gochis
Six people with guilty consciences arrive at a class reunion and are surprised to find that they are the only ones in the school. One by one they are singled out to meet their death at the hands of a sinister stranger in a weird disguise.
A — EN
Unknown — Derann Film Services   **H, P**
DV 120B/DV 120

Redneck   Fil-Ent '73
Drama
09844   94 mins   C
B, V
Telly Savalas, Franco Nero, Mark Lester
This is the story of a sadistic killer caught up in a jewel robbery. He and his partner-in-crime take a teenage boy as a hostage, blasting their way out of one desperate situation after another.
S,A — EN
Int'l Amusement Corp — Polygram Video   **H, P**
790 4234/790 4232

Reds   Fil-Ent '81
Drama
10118   188 mins   C
B, V
Warren Beatty, Diane Keaton, Edward Herrmann, Jack Nicholson, Maureen Stapleton, directed by Warren Beatty
This film tells the true story of John Reed, an American who witnessed the Russian Revolution at first hand and wrote the book. 'Ten Days That Shook the World.' The drama is interspersed with interviews with people who actually knew Reed, thus giving the film a 'documentary' flavour.
Academy Awards '82: Best Director (Beatty); Best Supporting Actress (Stapleton); Best Cinematography (Storaro).
BBFC:15 — S,A — EN
Paramount — CIC Video   **H, P**
BEA 2067/VHA 2067

PALADIN VIDEO HOME ENTERTAINMENT GUIDE

Reflection of Fear, A — Fil-Ent '73
Horror/Suspense
09282   90 mins   C
B, V

Robert Shaw, Sally Kellerman, Mary Ure, Sondra Locke, directed by William A. Fraker

A shy retarded teenage girl who is kept secluded from the outside world by her mother and grandmother develops an extreme hatred for them when her father returns after 10 years. One night she diguises herself as a man and brutally murders them.
S,A — EN
Columbia — RCA/Columbia Pictures Video UK   H, P

Reggae Sunsplash — Fil-Ent '7?
Music-Performance
06860   105 mins   C
V2, B, V

Bob Marley, Peter Tosh, Third World, Burning Spear

This tape features some of the top reggae groups in concert. Bob Marley songs include, 'No Woman No Cry,' 'Lively Up,' 'Get Up, Stand Up,' and 'Exodus.' Peter Tosh songs include 'Mystic Man,' 'Legalize It' and 'Buck in Ham Palace.' Songs from Third World include 'Talk To Me' and 'Third World Man' and songs from Burning Spear include 'Man in the Hills' and 'Healing.'
M,A — EN
Unknown — European Video Company   P

Regle du Jeu, La — Fil-Ent '38
Drama/Satire
08666   110 mins   B/W
B, V

Marcel Dalio, Nora Gregor, Mila Parely, Jean Renoir, directed by Jean Renoir

This film, subtitled in English is set during a weekend chateau party. It involves adultery, mistaken identities and a crime passionel. The film is a satire on love and morals.
C,A — EN
La Nouvelle Edition Francaise — Longman Video   P
LGBE 50071 LGVH 5007

Reilly—Ace of Spies — Fil-Ent '83
Drama/Adventure
12915   80 mins   C
B, V

Sam Neill, Leo McKern, Tom Bell, directed by Jim Goddard and Martin Campbell

This is the true life story about a spy, born in 1874, who lived on his wits and thrived on danger, ruthlessly killing when necessary.
S,A — EN
Euston Films — THORN EMI   P
TXJ 90 24864/TVJ 90 24862

Reluctant Heroes, The — Fil-Ent '71
War-Drama
04162   80 mins   C
B, V

Ken Berry, Cameron Mitchell, Warren Oates, Jim Hutton, Don Marshall, Ralph Meeker

A Lieutenant, the regiment historian, is chosen to lead a motley crew on a non-strategic hill during the Korean War. When they are faced with a regiment of advancing enemy soldiers, only through his knowledge of history is the Lieutenant able to save his platoon.
BBFC:U — F — EN
Spelling — Guild Home Video   H, P

Remarkable Rocket — Chl-Juv '7?
Cartoons/Adventure
09226   30 mins   C
B, V

Animated, narrated by David Niven, voices by Graham Stark

This tells the story of the Remarkable Rocket and his fellow fireworks as they prepare themselves to be set off at a Royal Celebration. It is adapted from a story by Orson Welles.
M,S — EN
Unknown — Video Form Pictures   H, P
MGK2

Rentadick — Fil-Ent '72
Comedy
13466   94 mins   C
B, V

James Booth, Richard Briers, directed by Jim Clark

Written by John Cleese and Graham Chapman, this film centres round the misadventures of a firm of private detectives.
BBFC:A — C,A — EN
Rank — Rank Video Library   H, P
1063 E

Repo Man — Fil-Ent '84
Drama/Science fiction
13647   89 mins   C
B, V

Emilio Estevez, Harry Dean Stanton, Olivia Barash, Fox Harris, directed by Alex Cox

(For Explanation of codes, see USE GUIDE and KEY)

PALADIN VIDEO HOME ENTERTAINMENT GUIDE

A lobotomised nuclear scientist with a deadly secret in the boot of his car is desperately chased by the car repossession men, a variety of ruthless goverment agents and some murderous thugs.
BBFC:18 — C,A — EN
Universal — CIC Video   H, P
1147

Repulsion   Fil-Ent '65
Horror
02579   104 mins   B/W
V2, B, V
Catherine Deneuve, Ian Hendry, John Fraser, directed by Roman Polanski
A Belgian manicurist in London is driven to psychotic madness by outside pressures. She is terrified by sex most of all. When her boyfriend and landlord approach her in the apartment she has secluded herself in, she murders them.
Berlin Festival: Silver Bear Special Jury Award.
BBFC:X — A — EN
Compton, Tekli — Videomedia   P

Restless Breed, The   Fil-Ent '56
Western
01081   81 mins   C
V2, B, V
Scott Brady, Anne Bancroft
The story of a lawyer in the Old West.
BBFC:U — F — EN
Twentieth Century Fox — Intervision Video
P, E
A-A 0125

Resurrection, The   Gen-Edu '??
Religion/Bible
06290   30 mins   B/W
B, V, PH15
In this film Roger Forster provides evidence that the Bible is accurate.
S,A — R
Audio Visual Ministries — Audio Visual Ministries   H, L, P
VT88

Return, The   Fil-Ent '7?
Science fiction
05726   108 mins   C
V2, B, V
Raymond Burr, Cybil Shepherd, Martin Landau, Jan-Michael Vincent
A space craft soars through deep space, past our sun to break into the earth's atmosphere and come to rest over a deserted street in a small town in New Mexico. Two children witness the event and are engulfed in light. Twenty five years later a flaw is noticed in a satellite picture; scientists are sent to investigate.
F — EN
Unknown — Video Unlimited   H, P
002

Return Engagement   Fil-Ent '78
Drama/Romance
09089   72 mins   C
V2, B, V
Elizabeth Taylor, Joseph Bottoms, Allyn Ann McLerie, Peter Donat, James Ray, directed by Joseph Hardy
An ex-show biz performer and now a divorcee and a professor teaching history refuses all invitations designed for her to meet eligible men. She instead becomes intrigued by one of her pupils, which eventually leads to an affair.
C,A — EN
The Production Co; Mike Wise and Franklin R Levy Prods — Video Tape Centre   P
VTC 1074

Return from Witch Mountain   Fil-Ent '78
Fantasy/Adventure
12575   89 mins   C
B, V
Bette Davis, Christopher Lee, Ike Eisenmann, Kim Richards
In this sequel to 'Escape from Witch Mountain,' cars mysteriously fly and human beings float as a group of criminals manipulate a boy's supernatural powers for their own devious gain.
F — EN
Walt Disney Productions — Rank Video Library
H
148

Return of a Man Called Horse, The   Fil-Ent '76
Adventure/Western
12601   121 mins   C
B, V
Richard Harris, Gale Sondergaard, Geoffrey Lewis, directed by Irvin Kershner
An Englishman who had once been adopted by the Yellowhand Indian tribe in America returns after ten years to find the tribe has been killed or sold into slavery, and sets out to restore the courage, lightning spirit and pride into the few survivors hiding in the hills.
BBFC:15 — C,A — EN
Terry Morse Sr — Warner Home Video   P
99300

PALADIN VIDEO HOME ENTERTAINMENT GUIDE

Return of Martin Guerre, The   Fil-Ent '84
Romance/Suspense
13117   110 mins   C
B, V
Gerard Depardieu, Nathalie Baye, directed by Daniel Vigne
Set in rural France in 1542, a man returns home from the war after eight years absence to his wife but doubts grow as to whether he is the man he claims to be.
BBFC:15 — *C,A* — *EN*
Societe Francaise de Production Cinematographique Societe de Production de Films; Marcel Dassault — *Palace Video Ltd* **P**
PVC 2070A

Return of the Dinosaurs   Chi-Juv '83
Cartoons
12189   82 mins   C
V2, B, V
Animated
The gravitational pull of a mysterious comet barely missing a collision with earth causes havoc. Up from the depths come creatures of another time. An all nation Dinosaur Patrol is formed to capture and protect them.
BBFC:U — *F* — *EN*
Mark Cohen; Sid Caplan — *Medusa Communications Ltd*   **H, P**

Return of the Dragon   Fil-Ent '72
Adventure/Martial arts
04118   91 mins   C
B, V
Bruce Lee, Chuck Norris, Nora Miao
When enemy agents seek to put an end to a rehabilitation clinic for victims of Japanese dope and gambling rings, the students use their martial arts expertise to defeat the evil ones and keep their school open.
C,A — *EN*
Bryanston Pictures — *Video Programme Distributors*   **P**
Inter-Ocean—017

Return of the Evil Dead   Fil-Ent '80
Horror
13487   83 mins   C
B, V
Tony Kendall, Esther Roy, Fernando Sancho
An evil religious sect which flourished in the Middle Ages in a small Portugese town, returns from the dead to wreak carnage on the population again.
BBFC:18 — *A* — *EN*
New Line Cinema — *Precision Video Ltd* **P**
2640

Return of the Pink Panther, The   Fil-Ent '75
Comedy
00842   108 mins   C
B, V
Peter Sellers, Christopher Plummer, Catherine Schell, directed by Blake Edwards
Inspector Clouseau is called upon to rescue the Pink Panther diamond stolen from a museum.
BBFC:U — *F* — *EN*
United Artists — *Precision Video Ltd*   **P**
BITC 2002/VITC 2002

Return of the Soldier, The   Fil-Ent '83
Drama
09420   100 mins   C
V2, B, V
Glenda Jackson, Julie Christie, Alan Bates, Ann-Margret, Ian Holm, Frank Finlay, Jeremy Kemp
A captain returns home from the war without any memory of the last fifteen years. His beautiful wife is a total stranger and the dowdy middle-aged Margaret is again the youthful lover he can remember from long ago. However, she holds the key that can return him to the present.
BBFC:15 — *C,A* — *EN*
Brent Walker, Barry R. Cooper, Skreba Films — *Guild Home Video*   **H, P, E**

Return of the Tiger   Fil-Ent '??
Martial arts/Suspense
06063   95 mins   C
V2, B, V
Bruce Li, Paul Smith
American and Chinese rivals head a narcotics smuggling operation in Bangkok. The Chinese head plots to eliminate the American, a night club owner. A Kung-Fu expert is employed as an under-cover agent.
BBFC:X — *A* — *EN*
Unknown — *Video Programme Distributors* **P**
Inter-Ocean—055

Return to Boggy Creek   Fil-Ent '77
Adventure/Suspense
12006   80 mins   C
B, V
Dawn Wells, Dana Plato, directed by Tom Moore
The story of a shadowy legendary creature that dwells in a swamp near a small isolated fishing village is told in this film.
BBFC:PG — *S,A* — *EN*
Bayou Productions — *CBS/Fox Video*   **P**
7147

Return to Oz   Chi-Juv '8?
Cartoons
13775   60 mins   C

PALADIN VIDEO HOME ENTERTAINMENT GUIDE

B, V
Animated
Featuring the characters and nine songs from the original 'The Wizard of Oz', the story tells how Dorothy and friends trip back to Oz in search of the Wizard.
PS,I — EN
Unknown — *Odyssey Video* **H, P**
6305

Revenge Fil-Ent '71
Drama/Suspense
04161   90 mins   C
B, V
Shelley Winters, Carol Rossen, Bradford Dillman, Stuart Whitman
A man is caged in a house by an old woman seeking revenge.
BBFC:A — *C,A — EN*
Spelling — *Guild Home Video* **H, P**

Revenge of the Barbarians Fil-Ent '??
Adventure
06065   99 mins   C
V2, B, V
Anthony Steel, Daniela Rocca
The sister of the Roman Emperor is captured by barbarians. Her lover fights in vain to secure her release; however, she decides to marry her former enemy, the chief of the barbarians.
BBFC:U — *F — EN*
Unknown — *Video Programme Distributors* **P**
Inter-Ocean—053

Revenge of the Mysterons from Mars Fil-Ent '??
Science fiction/Puppets
07350   ? mins   C
B, V
In this marionette production Earth is at war with a bizarre alien enemy, the Mysterons. Only Captain Scarlet can stop the intergalactic war. Based on an original format by Gerry and Sylvia Anderson.
F — EN
Gerry and Sylvia Anderson — *Precision Video Ltd* **P**
BITC 2097/VITC 2097

Revenge of the Ninja Fil-Ent '83
Martial arts
12062   86 mins   C
V2, B, V
Sho Kosugi, Arthur Roberts, Keith Vitali
This cassette is part two of a trilogy and tells the story of a brilliant martial arts star who meets his match in a battle from which only one can survive.
BBFC:18 — *C,A — EN*
Golan Globus Production — *Guild Home Video*
H, P, E

Revenge of the Pink Panther Fil-Ent '78
Comedy
01276   99 mins   C
V2, B, V
Peter Sellers, Herbert Lom, Dyan Cannon, Robert Webber, Burt Kwouk, Robert Loggia, Paul Stewart, directed by Blake Edwards
Inspector Clouseau travels all over the world tracking down an international drug ring.
BBFC:A — *F — EN*
United Artists; Blake Edwards
Prod — *Intervision Video* **H**
UA A B 5015

Revenge of the Pink Panther Fil-Ent '78
Comedy
13012   99 mins   C
B, V
Peter Sellers, Herbert Lom, Dyan Cannon, Robert Webber, directed by Blake Edwards
An attempt on the life of Inspector Clousea gets the wrong man, and as France mourns the passing of the famous detective, Clouseau is busy with disguises and tracking down the criminals.
BBFC:U — *C,A — EN*
United Artists Corp — *Warner Home Video* **P**
99251

Rewind: Volume 3 Fil-Ent '82
Music-Performance/Comedy-Performance
07480   60 mins   C
V
This three hour tape consists of 60 minutes of 'video magazine' and two hours of blank tape for personal use. The pre-recorded section is a compilation of hilarious snippets, stories, interviews and crazy advertisements. Billy Connolly and Kenny Everett provide the comedy with musical entertainment from the Hee Bee Gee Bees, Pamela Stephenson, Landscape, M and Ultravox.
S,A — EN
Unknown — *THORN EMI* **P**
TVX 90 0559 2

Rhinestone Fil-Ent '84
Drama/Comedy
13663   111 mins   C

PALADIN VIDEO HOME ENTERTAINMENT GUIDE

B, V
Sylvester Stallone, Dolly Parton, Richard Fransworth, Ron Liebman, directed by Bob Clarke
When a New York driver's cab is written off in a smash-up he has to turn to his dancing and teams up with a girl singer to get together some money for a new cab.
BBFC:PG — S,A — EN
Howard Smith; Marvin Worth — *CBS/Fox Video* **P**
1438

Rich and Famous Fil-Ent '81
Drama
08676   113 mins   C
V2, B, V
Jacqueline Bisset, Candice Bergen, David Selby, Hart Bochner, directed by George Cukor
This film tells the poignant story of two young women, friends from college days, who desire to live each other's lives. Liz is a serious highminded writer and Merry a delightful free spirit. Torrents of rage and jealousy threaten their relationship when Merry tries her hand at writing and becomes an instant hit on the literary scene.
BBFC:X — A — EN
Jacquet-William Allyn Production — *MGM/UA Home Video* **P**
UMR 10111/UMB 10111/UMV 10111.

Richard Pryor Live in Concert Fil-Ent '8?
Comedy-Performance
09040   78 mins   C
B, V
Richard Pryor
On this tape, Richard Pryor, star of 'Stir Crazy', shows how funny he can be as a solo performer when he tackles taboo subjects with hilarious accuracy.
BBFC:X — A — EN
Virgin Video — *VideoSpace Ltd* **P**
VV004A

Riddle of the Sands, The Fil-Ent '79
Mystery/Drama
01880   102 mins   C
B, V, LV
Michael York, Simon MacCorkindale, Jenny Agutter
Set in 1901. Englishman Arthur Davies is enjoying a single-handed sailing holiday when a series of events finds him wrapped up in a mystery not to his liking.
BBFC:U — F — EN
Rank — *Rank Video Library* **H, P**
0007

Ride Spo-Lei '??
Sports-Minor
09118   72 mins   C
B, V
Presented by David Broome and Steve Hadly
This film follows all that a new horse rider needs to know.
S,A — I
Unknown — *Quadrant Video* **H, P**
E7

Ride in a Pink Car Fil-Ent '74
Drama/Adventure
09295   80 mins   C
B, V
Glenn Corbett, Morgan Woodward, Ivy Jones, Big John Hamilton
A man returns to his hometown after Vietnam but soon discovers that everyone thinks he was dead. His fiancee had married his brother which makes him determined to claim what is rightfully his. His actions result in murder and the town erupts when he kidnaps his fiancee and escapes in a pink car. A deadly posse is gathered to bring him back.
S,A — EN
Clarion Pictures — *Abacus Video* **P**
201

Ride the Hot Wind Fil-Ent '??
Adventure
09959   85 mins   C
V2, B, V
Tom Kirk, Duke Kelly
Having been disgraced by a Vietnam massacre, an Army Captain desperately struggles to re-build his life after prison.
BBFC:X — A — EN
Unknown — *Video Unlimited* **H, P, E**
054

Ride the Tiger Fil-Ent '71
Crime-Drama/Adventure
09287   97 mins   C
V
George Montgomery, Marshall Thompson, Victoria Shaw, Andre Marquis
This is a story of murder and intrigue centered around the Club Crystal in Manila Bay. The double dealing starts in the Philippines and moves rapidly from Hong Kong, to Borneo, Zamboanga and back to Manila.
S,A — EN
Gold Key Entertainment — *Direct Video Services* **H, P**

Ride to Glory Fil-Ent '64
Western
07990   97 mins   C
B, V

(For Explanation of codes, see USE GUIDE and KEY)

PALADIN VIDEO HOME ENTERTAINMENT GUIDE

Chuck Connors, Robert Lansing, Burt Reynolds, Jim Davis, Lee Van Cleef, Kathie Brown, David Brian, Greg Morris, directed by Bernard McEveety

This film is set just after the Civil War. It tells of the battles between the red and the white, the United States cavalry and the Indians. A major in the army sets out to kill an Indian chief and an ex-army captain, thought of as a coward intervenes.

S,A — EN
Andrew J Fenady Prods — Motion Epics Video Company Ltd   P
157

Rider on the Rain   Fil-Ent '70
Crime-Drama
10081   113 mins   C
V2, B, V
Charles Bronson, Jill Ireland, Marlene Jobert
A young girl shoots the man who rapes her and disposes of his body, telling no-one. A man appears on the scene, apparently aware of her crime. A tale of mystery and intrigue follows.
A — EN
Avco Embassy — Embassy Home Entertainment   P
2043

Riding High   Fil-Ent '??
Adventure
06212   92 mins   C
B, V
Eddie Kidd, music by Dire Straits, Boomtown Rats, Pretenders, Cliff Richard, Sky, Squeeze, Police, Lene Lovich, Madness, Gary Numan, Emerson Lake & Palmer, Joe Jackson?Jerry Lee Lewis
A young motorcycle fanatic is offered the chance to turn fantasy into fact. If he can fly across Devil's Leap and beat the World Stunt Champion, he can win a gold-plated dream machine.
F — EN
Klinger Production — VCL Video Services   P
P181D

'Riding That Train'   Fil-Ent '7?
Music-Performance
12717   60 mins   C
B, V
This tape features some of the West Coast bands at the height of their careers including Grateful Dead, Beach Boys, Santana, Boz Skaggs and Jefferson Airplane.
F — EN
Unknown — Mountain Video   P
FOJ1

Riding to Win   Spo-Lei '80
Horse racing
01990   60 mins   C
V2, B, V, PH15, PH17
Champion jockey Willie Carson shows Noel Whitcomb what it takes to be first past the post.
F — EN
MirrorVision — VideoSpace Ltd   P

Riding Towards Freedom   Gen-Edu '8?
Learning disabilities
13524   35 mins   C
B, V
How riding can help to overcome some of the limitations and frustrations of disabilities is shown in this film and a riding holiday in Windsor Park attended by HRH The Princess Anne, is also seen.
A — SE
Unknown — TFI Leisure Ltd   H, P

Right Stuff, The   Fil-Ent '84
Adventure
12982   185 mins   C
B, V
Sam Shepard, Scott Glenn, Dennis Quaid, Charles Frank, Fred Ward, Ed Harris, Lance Henrikson, Scott Paulin, directed by Philip Kaufman
This is the story of American space travel, from the breaking of the sound barrier in 1953 to John Glenn's historic orbit of the earth nine years later, outlining the rigorous selection and training and taking a look into the private lives of the astronauts.
BBFC:15 — S,A — EN
Irwin Winkler; Robert Chartoff — Warner Home Video   P
70014

Right to Choose, The   Gen-Edu '8?
Learning disabilities
13532   35 mins   C
B, V
This film shows individual adult riders who, despite severe physical damage, have learned to ride with varying degrees of independence and accomplishment.
C,A — SE
Unknown — TFI Leisure Ltd   H, P

Rigoletto   Fin-Art '82
Opera
12894   140 mins   C
B, V
John Rawnsley, Marie McLaughlin, Arthur Davies, John Tomlinson

PALADIN VIDEO HOME ENTERTAINMENT GUIDE

This recording of Verdi's tragic opera in English by the English National Opera at The Coliseum is brought forward from 16th century Mantua to Mafia-controlled Manhattan in the 1950's.
SWET '82: Best Opera   F — EN
Jonathan Miller — THORN EMI   **P**
TXH 90 25904/TVH 90 25902

Ring of Bright Water   Fil-Ent '69
Adventure
04160   109 mins   C
V2, B, V, LV
Bill Travers, Virginia McKenna, Mij the Otter
A London clerk takes a pet otter with him to the Scottish highlands where he intends to become a writer. When the otter is killed, his offspring turns up to renew the writer's inspiration.
BBFC:U — F — EN
Cinerama — Guild Home Video   **H, P**

Ringmasters 1967, The/Pause for Nostalgia   Spo-Lei '6?
Automobiles-Racing
04539   57 mins   C
B, V
A report of the 1967 German Grand Prix and the seventeen men who took part. 'Pause for Nostalgia' presents recorded highlights from the 1951 Grand Prix d'Europe, Monaco 1952, Monaco Grand Prix 1957, and the 1959 East African Safari Rally, to name a few.
F — EN
Castrol — Quadrant Video   **H, P**
M8

Ringo's World   Fil-Ent '??
Animals/Documentary
06056   53 mins   C
V2, B, V
A feature film telling the story of a raccoon, Ringo, who wanders away from the cave where he was born, making the inevitable journey from innocence to maturity.
F — ED
Unknown — Video Programme Distributors
P
Cinehollywood—V830

Rings of Fear   Fil-Ent '??
Mystery
09126   90 mins   C
V
A young police detective is investigating the discovery of the body of a 16-year-old girl, found mutilated and sexually assaulted on the outskirts of the city. His investigations lead him to a luxury villa, where wealthy businessmen enjoy themselves with the murdered girl's schoolfriends.
C,A — EN
Unknown — Video Film Promotions   **H, P**

Rio Bravo   Fil-Ent '59
Western
06023   135 mins   C
B, V
John Wayne, Dean Martin, Ricky Nelson, Angie Dickinson, Ward Bond, Walter Brennan, Claude Akins, John Russell, directed by Howard Hawks
A sheriff and his posse that consists of an old cripple, an ex-deputy turned drunk, a youth who is too fast with his guns and a girl outsmart a powerful rancher who wants to get his killer brother released from prison. Based on the short story by B. H. McCampbell.
BBFC:U — F — EN
Warner Brothers; Howard Hawks — Warner Home Video   **P**
WEX1050/WEV1050

Rio Lobo   Fil-Ent '70
Western
06493   103 mins   C
B, V
John Wayne, Jennifer O'Neill, Jack Elam, Chris Mitchum, directed by Howard Hawks
A gunfighter tracks two traitors responsible for the death of his best friend to the town of Rio Lobo, Texas.
S,A — EN
Cinema Center — MGM/UA Home Video
P
UCB 10016/UCV 10016

Rip Van Winkle   Fil-Ent '??
Fantasy
04337   70 mins   C
V2, B, V
A full-length version of Washington Irving's classic tale about a man who sleeps for twenty years.
F — EN
Unknown — Intervision Video   **H, P**
A-AE 0100

Ripping Yarns   Fil-Ent '7?
Comedy
09404   ? mins   C
V2, B, V
Michael Palin

PALADIN VIDEO HOME ENTERTAINMENT GUIDE

This tape contains three classic stories written by Michael Palin and Terry Jones, combining schooldays, the Great War and football.
F — EN
BBC — *BBC Video* **H, P**
BBCV 7013

Rise and Rise of Casanova, The   Fil-Ent '78
Adventure/Comedy
05875   101 mins   C
B, V

Tony Curtis, Marisa Berenson, Marisa Mell, Jean Lefebvre, Andrea Ferreole, Silva Koscina, Victor Spinetti, Umberto Orsini, Hugh Griffith, Britt Ekland, directed by Francois Legrand

Set in eighteenth century Venice, a Senator has the task of persuading a Caliph to sign a roseoil contract. He arrives with his exotic Caliph and an extensive entourage in a myriad of Gondolas to the Doge's Palace. The Caliph will not allow the contract to be signed until she is satisfied, she is sure this cannot be done, but Casanova is called upon and on delivery to her bedchamber the contract will be signed.

BBFC:X — *A — EN*
Delta Films; Panther Films — *Precision Video Ltd*   **P**
BBPV 2556/VBPV 2556

Rising Damp   Fil-Ent '80
Comedy
05411   94 mins   C
V2, B, V

Leonard Rossiter, Frances de la Tour, Don Warrington, Christopher Strauli, Denholm Elliott, directed by Joe McGrath

Rigsby owns a seedy boardinghouse in London. One of the tenants, a quiet black medical student, he has a grudging respect for because he boasts he is a son of a Chieftain and has twelve wives back 'home.' Another is a spinster in her thirties; Rigsby attempts to woo her but discovers she is directing her attentions on the unwilling student.

New Standard British Film Awards '80: Best Comedy.   BBFC:A — *S,A — EN*
Cinema Arts International Production — *Precision Video Ltd*   **P**
CRITC 2035/BITC 2035/VITC 2035

Risky Business   Fil-Ent '83
Comedy
12969   96 mins   C
B, V

Tom Cruise, Rebecca DeMornay, directed by Paul Brickman

When a young college student is left alone in the house for a weekend he turns the family home into a brothel for one night and makes himself a pile of money.
BBFC:18 — *A — EN*
Steve Tisch; Jon Avent — *Warner Home Video*   **P**
61323

Rituals   Fil-Ent '78
Horror
06115   96 mins   C
V2, B, V

Hal Holbrook, Lawrence Dane, Robin Gammell, Ken James, directed by Peter Carter

Five doctors, all old friends, make their annual trip to the forest for a camping trip. They fall prey to evil lurking, turning their vacation into a desperate fight for survival.
S,A — EN
Lawrence Dane Productions — *Video Programme Distributors*   **P**
Cinehollywood—V320

Ritz, The   Fil-Ent '76
Comedy
12975   88 mins   C
B, V

Rita Moreno, Jack Weston, Jerry Stiller, Kaye Ballard, Bessie Love, directed by Richard Lester

In an attempt to evade his brother-in-law who has sworn to kill him that night, a middle-aged business man checks into a New York bath house of dubious repute with uproarious consequences.
BBFC:18 — *A — EN*
Warner Bros — *Warner Home Video*   **P**
61356

Rivals   Fil-Ent '72
Drama
08620   101 mins   C
V2, B, V

Joan Hackett, Robert Klein, Scott Jacoby

This film tells the story of a boy, who at the age of six had an IQ of 143. At ten he shows alarming adult perception of life. He adores his mother, who marries an easy going bachelor. Jamie desperately resents him, and sets in motion a campaign of pyschological warfare. However, his plans go grotesquely wrong.
C,A — EN
Avco Embassy — *Hokushin Audio Visual Ltd*   **P**
VM 67

Rivals of the Dragon   Fil-Ent '7?
Adventure/Martial arts
05731   80 mins   C
V2, B, V

---

548   (For Explanation of codes, see USE GUIDE and KEY)

PALADIN VIDEO HOME ENTERTAINMENT GUIDE

Jeffrey Chan
A young man banned from a Kung-Fu school because of his criminal activities becomes a fatal victim of a gang seeking information connected with drug smuggling. Information is 'planted' on the master of the school, a trap is set, and he is brought face to face with the bandits.
S,A — EN
Unknown — Video Unlimited **H, P**
012

Rivkin: Bounty Hunter Fil-Ent '80
Crime-Drama
06945   114 mins   C
B, V

Ron Leibman, Bo Rucker, Harry Morgan, Glen Scarpelli
This is the true story of an ex-marine and modern-day bounty hunter who captures criminals who have jumped bail in the state of New York. He meets his match when a multiple felon and bail skipper becomes determined not to be tracked down.
S,A — EN
Ten-Four Productions — Home Video Merchandisers **H, P**
053

Road Games Fil-Ent '81
Drama/Horror
08330   87 mins   C
V2, B, V, LV

Stacy Keach, Jamie Lee Curtis
This film is about a truck driver who suspects the murder of a young hitch hiker. He plays a game of cat and mouse with the vicious killer.
C,A — EN
Avco Embassy; Richard Franklin — Embassy Home Entertainment **P**
2016

Road Hustlers Fil-Ent '69
Drama
07993   96 mins   C
B, V

Jim Davis, Scott Brady, Andy Device, Bruce Yarnell, Bob Dix, Victoria Carroll, directed by Larry E. Jackson
This film tells of the fight of a father and his three sons for their survival against the evil ambitions of a gangland chief. It includes car chases, battles and explosions.
S,A — EN
American International — Motion Epics Video Company Ltd **P**
160

Road to Utopia Fil-Ent '46
Comedy
13274   86 mins   B/W
B, V

Bob Hope, Bing Crosby, Dorothy Lamour, Douglass Dumbrille, directed by Hal Walker
A pair of card sharpers and a girl singer set out to locate an old Alaskan goldmine, hotly pursued by villains.
BBFC:PG — S,A — EN
Paramount — CIC Video **H, P**
BEJ 1088/VHJ 1088

Roar Fil-Ent '81
Adventure
09010   90 mins   C
V2, B, V

Tippi Hedren, Noel Marshall, Melänie Griffith, John Marshall, Jerry Marshall, Kyalo Mativo, directed by Noel Marshall
Set in the bush country of East Africa, this film tells the story of an energetic scientist. He has built a fine house in a beautiful setting and filled the valley with wild animals. Then one day, things start to go terribly wrong. The rest of his family arrive, only to be scared away by the big cats.
F — EN
Filmways Australasian Distributors — Intervision Video
AA 0467

Robbers of the Sacred Mountain Fil-Ent '8?
Adventure
12156   90 mins   C
V2, B, V

John Marley, Simon MacCorkindale, Louise Vallance
Legend has it that one of the Church's most sacred treasures is buried in a holy mountain. An archaeologist and a reporter set off to find it, unaware that their beautiful guide is a spy.
BBFC:15 — S,A — EN
Unknown — Guild Home Video **H, P, E**

Robbery Fil-Ent '67
Crime-Drama/Suspense
05529   114 mins   C
B, V

Stanley Baker, James Booth, Frank Finlay, Joanna Pettet, directed by Peter Yates
This film is based on the real-life Great Train Robbery. A young man whose ambition is to rob the night mail train from Glasgow gets a group of criminals together to fulfil his dream. A diamond robbery done to raise the money, but

(For Explanation of codes, see USE GUIDE and KEY)

PALADIN VIDEO HOME ENTERTAINMENT GUIDE

after the hi-jacking a member of the group phones his wife. They are all caught except the man who hatched the scheme; he leaves the country with all the money to start a new life.
S,A — EN
Avco Embassy — *CBS/Fox Video* P

Robbery Fil-Ent '67
Crime-Drama
12266 97 mins C
V2, B, V
Stanley Baker, Frank Finlay, James Booth, Barry Foster
This film tells the true-life story of Britain's first mail train robbery in over a century.
S,A — EN
Avco Embassy — *Embassy Home Entertainment* P
2033

Robe, The Fil-Ent '53
Drama
01735 133 mins C
B, V
Richard Burton, Jean Simmons, Victor Mature, Michael Rennie
The chronicle of the life of a drunken, dissolute Roman tribune, Marcellus, after he wins the robe of Christ in a dice game.
BBFC:U — F — EN
20th Century Fox — *CBS/Fox Video* P
4A-018

Robin Hood Fil-Ent '??
Cartoons/Adventure
08806 44 mins C
B, V
Animated
This tells of the adventures of Robin Hood, the outlaw of Sherwood Forest, and his Merry Men. It follows their exploits as they stole from the rich to give to the poor.
F — EN
Unknown — *VCL Video Services* P
A277B

Robinson Crusoe Fil-Ent '??
Cartoons/Adventure
09389 44 mins C
B, V
Animated
This cartoon tells the story of Robinson Crusoe, the Shipwrecked Mariner and Man Friday, his native friend.
F — EN
Unknown — *VCL Video Services* P
A360B

Rock and Roll Revival Fil-Ent '81
Music-Performance
04620 60 mins C
B, V
Exciting live concert from the Capital Centre in Washington featuring some of the greatest Rock and Roll music in the world. See the urgency of a live performance, the enthusiastic fans, top artists giving themselves to the finest of all Rock and Roll Revivals.
F — EN
VCL Video Services Ltd — *VCL Video Services* P

Rock Cocktail Fil-Ent '84
Music-Performance/Music video
13259 36 mins C
B, V
This is a compilation of rock music featuring tracks from Chain Reaction, The Romantic, Bonnie Tyler, Down Under and Toto.
F — EN
Unknown — *CBS/Fox Video* P
7111

Rock Gala Fil-Ent '82
Music-Performance
12215 58 mins C
B, V
Recorded at the Dominion Theatre, London, July 1982, this tape features rock and pop groups including Wacky Madness and Robert Plant.
F — EN
Unknown — *MGM/UA Home Video* P
10179

Rock Guitar—A Guide from the Greats Fil-Ent '8?
Music-Performance
08663 60 mins C
B, V
Jimi Hendrix, Ron Wood, Joni Mitchell, Michael Schenker, Richard Thompson, John Wilson
This tape, full of live action on film, form Jimi Hendrix and Joni Mitchell, amongs many others, demonstrates the gimmicks, tricks and genius required to be a true rock professional. It includes a discussion on all aspects of the guitar, including the choice of your guitar, finger picking, plectrums, chord shapes and inversions.
S,A — EN
Premier Programming — *Longman Video* P
LGBE 5004/LGVH 5004

Rock 'n' Roll High School Fil-Ent '79
Musical-Drama/Comedy
12684 91 mins C

PALADIN VIDEO HOME ENTERTAINMENT GUIDE

B, V
P.J. Soles, Vincent Van Patten, Clint Howard, Dey Young, The Ramones, directed by Allan Arkush
This is the story of the conflict between the efforts of the school's dictatorial administration to stamp out rock 'n' roll and the determination of the number one fan of The Ramones to counteract them. The soundtrack features tracks from The Ramones, Paul McCartney and Wings and Fleetwood Mac.
BBFC:15 — *S,A* — *EN*
Michael Finnell — *Warner Home Video*   **P**
74054

Rock 'n' Soul Live   Fil-Ent '83
Music-Performance
12469   91 mins   C
B, V
Daryl Hall, John Oates, G E Smith, directed by Marty Callner
This is a video album of the singer/songwriter duo Daryl Hall and Hall and John Oates at their concert in Montreal's 'Forum' arena during the critically acclaimed 1983 'H2O' tour, and features all their biggest hits.
BBFC:U — *F* — *EN*
RCA — *RCA/Columbia Pictures Video UK*
H, P
10232

Rock Revolution, The   Fil-Ent '84
Music-Performance
13355   60 mins   C
V2, B, V
This is a compilation of major artists of the last decade and features the Clash, Bob Marley and The Waiters, Graham Parker, The Ramones and Sex Pistols amongst others.
S,A — *EN*
deJ Music Productions — *Guild Home Video*
H, P, E
6123-0

Rock, Rock, Rock!   Fil-Ent '56
Musical-Drama/Documentary
07332   84 mins   B/W
B, V
Alan Freed, Frankie Lymon and the Teen-Agers, LaVern Baker, Chuck Berry, Jimmy Cavallo, The Moonglows, Connie Francis, Tuesday Weld
This film was made at the height of Alan Freed's career and is almost a musical documentary of the 'Fabulous 50's,' the nostalgic era of black leather jackets, poodle skirts, cheerleaders and prom queens. The story centres on a young girl whose father insists she earn enough money to buy a new gown for the senior prom.
BBFC:U — *F* — *EN*
DCA — *Derann Film Services*   **P**
BGS 203B/BGS 203

Rockers   Fil-Ent '79
Drama/Musical
07831   100 mins   C
B, V
Leroy Wallace, Richard Hall, Jack Ruby, Peter Honiball, Majorie Norman, directed by Theodoros Bafaloukos
This film follows the adventures of an impoverished Rasta musician whose attempts to enter the Jamaican music business bring him up against the more unsavoury elements in the industry. Features music by Inner Circle, Jacob Miller, Junior Murvin, Peter Tosh, Third World and Burning Spear.
S,A — *EN*
Rockers Film Corp — *Island Pictures*   **P**
IPV002H

Rocky   Fil-Ent '76
Drama
01206   119 mins   C
V2, B, V
Sylvester Stallone, Talia Shire, Burgess Meredith, directed by John G. Avildsen
A young man from the slums of Philadelphia pursues his dream of becoming a boxing champion.
Academy Awards '76: Best Picture; Best Director (Avildsen); Best Achievement in Film Editing.   BBFC:A — *M,A* — *EN*
United Artists — *Intervision Video*   **H**
UA A B 5002

Rocky   Fil-Ent '76
Drama
13010   121 mins   C
B, V
Slyvester Stallone, directed by John G Avildsen
A fading, small time boxer is suddenly given the chance to regain some confidence and self respect by going in the ring for the world heavyweight championship.
BBFC:A — *C,A* — *EN*
United Artists — *Warner Home Video*   **P**
99216

Rocky II   Fil-Ent '79
Drama
13021   117 mins   C
B, V
Sylvester Stallone, Talia Shire, Burt Young, directed by Sylvester Stallone
The sequel to the overwhelmingly successful film 'Rocky'' about a heavyweight boxer who tries for a comeback.
BBFC:A — *C,A* — *EN*
United Artists; Irwin Winkler; Robert Chartoff — *Warner Home Video*   **P**
99229

(For Explanation of codes, see USE GUIDE and KEY)

PALADIN VIDEO HOME ENTERTAINMENT GUIDE

Rocky III
Fil-Ent '82
Drama
13005   97 mins   C
B, V
Sylvester Stallone, directed by Sylvester Stallone
Third in the 'Rocky' series; the heavyweight boxer has to come to terms not only with a fearsome new challenger, but other personal and professional problems.
BBFC:A — C,A — EN
United Artists — *Warner Home Video*   **P**
99301

Rocky Horror Picture Show, The
Fil-Ent '75
Comedy/Musical
13265   96 mins   C
B, V
Tim Curry, Susan Sarandon, Barry Bostwick, Meatloaf, Patricia Quinn, Richard O'Brien
A young couple seek shelter from a storm in an old castle where they meet up with a band of freaks and oddities of mankind.
BBFC:18 — A — EN
Michael White — *CBS/Fox Video*   **P**
1424

Rocky II
Fil-Ent '79
Drama
01278   119 mins   C
V2, B, V
Sylvester Stallone, Talia Shire, Burt Young, Carl Weathers, Burgess Meredith, directed by Sylvester Stallone
Rocky goes back to the ring for a return match with Apollo Creed for the World Heavyweight title.
BBFC:A — F — EN
United Artists, Robert Chartoff and Irwin Winkler Prod — *Intervision Video*   **H**
UA A B 5019

Rod Stewart: Tonight He's Yours
Fil-Ent '82
Music-Performance
08326   90 mins   C
V2, B, V, LV
Rod Stewart
This features Rod Stewart recorded live at the Forum in Los Angeles, with Tina Turner. It includes some of his new and old hits such as 'You're in My Heart,' 'Young Turks,' 'Maggie May' and 'Do Ya Think I'm Sexy.'
F — EN
Unknown — *Embassy Home Entertainment*   **P**
1211

Rodeo Girl
Fil-Ent '80
Western/Drama
07340   100 mins   C
B, V
Katherine Ross, Bo Hopkins, Candy Clark, Wilfred Brimley, Jacqueline Brooks, directed by Jackie Cooper
Inspired by the true story of Sue Pirtle, a seven-time women's world rodeo champion, this film tells the story of a young woman who rides to fame on the all-women rodeo circuit in the face of adversity, and the threat of losing her husband.
S,A — EN
Marble Arch Prods — *Precision Video Ltd*   **P**
BITC 2078/VITC 2078

Roger Daltrey—Ride A Rock Horse
Fil-Ent '7?
Music-Performance
02073   30 mins   C
B, V
A most unusual and atmospheric film of the popular star of 'Tommy' and 'Mahler.' This programme also contains some brilliant full animation sequences.
S,A — EN
Video Tape Network — *VCL Video Services*   **P**

Rogue Lion
Fil-Ent '75
Adventure
01046   95 mins   C
B, V
Larry Seymour, Alec Dudley
Lion roaming outside the border of Africa's great Ekoluleni Game Reserve, sets in motion events pitting the reserve's warden against local landowners.
F — EN
Stanley Norman — *VCL Video Services*   **P**

Roland Rat Roadshow, The
Chi-Juv '84
Fantasy
12914   60 mins   C
B, V
This special rat was born in the depths beneath King's Cross station and rises to the heights of an international celebrity.
PS,I — EN
Unknown — *THORN EMI*   **P**
TXE 90 24874/TVE 90 24872

Roller Boogie
Fil-Ent '??
Musical-Drama
06071   103 mins   C
B, V

552   (For Explanation of codes, see USE GUIDE and KEY)

PALADIN VIDEO HOME ENTERTAINMENT GUIDE

Linda Blair, Beverly Garland, Jimmy Van Patten, Roger Perry, Kimberly Beck, Sean McClary, Jim Bray, directed by Mark Lester
A young girl, a musical prodigy, has been accepted to study classical flute in Venice. She feels alienated from her neglectful parents and becomes involved with the young people in Venice where roller skating and boogie music have become a way of life.
S,A — EN
Unknown — Video Programme Distributors P
Media—M141

Rollerball Fil-Ent '75
Science fiction
01053 V 119 mins C
V2, B, V
James Caan, John Houseman, Maud Adams, Moses Gunn, directed by Norman Jewison
In the year 2018 there is rollerball, a brutal sport combining the violence of all other sports.
BBFC:X — A — EN
United Artists — Intervision Video H
UA A B 5004

Rollermania Fil-Ent '71
Drama/Sports
04617 90 mins C
B, V
This film is Rollermania—real pros skating at their peak. Experience the drama, grace and high excitement of freewheeling including Roller Disco, world champion skaters, and the famous Los Angeles Thunderbirds Roller Derby team.
F — EN
Cinerama Releasing — VCL Video Services P

Rolling Man Fil-Ent '70
Drama
04276 71 mins C
B, V
Dennis Weaver, Donna Mills, Don Stroud, Slim Pickens
This film is about a man convicted for the attempted murder of the driver who caused the death of his wife. When released from prison his precious sons are nowhere to be found. He sets out across America to search for the missing boys.
BBFC:AA — C,A — EN
Aaron Spelling — Rank Video Library H, P
0044

Rolling Stones; Let's Spend the Night Together, The Fil-Ent '82
Music-Performance
09796 90 mins C
B, V
Mick Jagger, Keith Richards, Charlie Watts, Ron Wood, Bill Wyman, directed by Hal Ashby
This tape features twenty-five songs from the Rolling Stones spanning 20 years of their career in the Rock 'n' Roll world. Footage is also included of their 1981 American tour.
BBFC:PG — F — EN
Raindrop Films Inc. — THORN EMI P
TXA 90 1724 4/TVA 90 1724 2

Rolling Thunder Fil-Ent '78
Drama
13743 97 mins C
B, V
William Devane, Tommy Lee Jones, Linda Haynes
A serviceman returns home after seven years of torture in a Hanoi prison to see his wife and son murdered by a gang of thugs. He recovers, tracks the hoodlums down, and avenges the killings.
BBFC:X — A — EN
Orion Pictures — Rank Video Library H, P
2038D

Rollover Fil-Ent '81
Drama/Romance
12499 112 mins C
B, V
Jane Fonda, Kris Kristofferson, directed by Alan J. Pakula
The investigation of the murder of a big business tycoon by his wife and a financial wizard uncovers a sinister plot to destroy the financial structure of the Western world.
BBFC:15 — C,A — EN
Bruce Gilbert; Orion; Warner Bros — Warner Home Video P
72022

Romance with a Double Bass Fil-Ent '74
Comedy/Romance
13308 40 mins C
B, V
John Cleese, Connie Booth, Dennis Damsdon, directed by Robert Young
On a hot summer's day in Russia around a hundred years ago, a princess and a musician meet while swimming in the river and have to find their way back to the palace naked when their clothes are stolen.
BBFC:PG — S,A — EN
Anton Films — CIC Video H, P
BEJ 3003/VHJ 3003

PALADIN VIDEO HOME ENTERTAINMENT GUIDE

Romancing The Stone   Fil-Ent '84
Adventure
13664   102 mins   C
B, V

Michael Douglas, Kathleen Turner, Danny DeVito, Alfonso Arau, Manuel Ojeda, directed by Robert Zemeckis
A mercenary and a sophisticated New York girl team up through the jungle pursued by crooks, con-men and crocodiles in a mad chase to find the girl's sister and a brilliant, priceless emerald.
BBFC:PG — *F* — *EN*
Michael Douglas — *CBS/Fox Video*   **P**
1358

Romantic Englishwoman, The   Fil-Ent '??
Drama/Romance
06222   112 mins   C
B, V

Glenda Jackson, Michael Caine, Helmut Berger
A successful novelist's wife takes a holiday in a German Spa; she meets a handsome young gigolo and falls in love. The roots to her marriage, however, are far more complex than she thought and a three-way relationship develops with extraordinary consequences.
S,A — *EN*
Daniel Angel — *VCL Video Services*   **P**
P168D

Rome Express   Fil-Ent '32
Suspense
04255   91 mins   B/W
B, V

Esther Ralston, Joan Barry, Gordon Harker, Donald Calthrop, Frank Vosper, Eliot Makenham, Conrad Veidt, Harold Huth, Cedric Hardwicke, Hugh Williams, Muriel Aked, Finlay Currie
From the moment the steam enshrouded loco pulls out Esther Ralston and Conrad Veidt become involved in an absorbing tale of robbery, murder and intrigue.
BBFC:A — *S,A* — *EN*
Gaumont — *Rank Video Library*   **H, P**
0023

Rome 2033   Fil-Ent '83
Science fiction/Adventure
12192   90 mins   C
V2, B, V

Janeo Martin, Fred Williamson, Howard Ross
Set in the future, Drake, the greatest gladiator to wield a lazer, is forcibly returned to Rome from a distant galaxy to take part in the Gladiator Games, a fight to the death for all but the final victor.
BBFC:18 — *C,A* — *EN*
Regency Productions — *Medusa Communications Ltd*   **H, P**

Romeo and Juliet   Fil-Ent '66
Dance
09348   125 mins   C
B, V

Rudolf Nureyev, Carla Fracci, Margot Fonteyn
This new production of the ballet based on Shakespeare's 'Romeo and Juliet' stars Rudolf Nureyev as Romeo, Carla Fracci as Juliet and Dame Margot Fonteyn as Lady Capulet. The story of ill fated love of a boy and girl for each other is told, produced for television by Patricia Foy and directed by Nureyev with the cast from his La Scala, Milan, production and the company's corps de ballet and orchestra.
F — *EN*
Paul Czinner; British — *Precision Video Ltd*   **P**

BITC 2122/VITC 2122

Ronde, La   Fil-Ent '50
Drama/Romance
08671   93 mins   B/W
B, V

Simone Signoret, Serge Reggiani, Danielle Darrieux, Jean-Louis Barrault, Fernand Gravey, Odette Joyeux, directed by Max Ophuls
This film, set in the year 1900 in Vienna, shows that love is a merry-go-round. A prostitute meets a soldier who then meets a housemaid. She then meets a master, who meets a married woman who meets a midinette and so on until an officer meets a prostitute who meets a soldier. It is subtitled in English.
A — *EN*
Franscope — *Longman Video*   **P**
LGBE 5008/LGHV 5008

Ronde Infernale 1969, La   Spo-Lei '69
Automobiles-Racing
04540   39 mins   C
B, V

The story of the tremendous battle in the 1969 24 hours of Le Mans, in which Ford defeated Porsche by a mere two seconds.
F — *EN*
Castrol — *Quadrant Video*   **H, P**
M9

Ronnie Lane Appeal for ARMS, The Royal Albert Hall Concert, Tape Two   Fil-Ent '84
Music video/Music-Performance
12929   60 mins   C
B, V

(For Explanation of codes, see USE GUIDE and KEY)

PALADIN VIDEO HOME ENTERTAINMENT GUIDE

This recording of the charity appeal concert features many rock'n'roll artists including Eric Clapton, Steve Winwood, Rolling Stones, Bill Wyman and Charile Watts, Led Zeppelin's Jimmy Page, Kenney Jones of 'The Who' and many others.
S,A — EN
Ronnie Lane; Glyn Jones — Video Form Pictures **H, P**
VFX 17/VFV 17

Ronnie Lane Appeal for   Fil-Ent '84
ARMS, The Royal Albert-
Hall Concert, Tape One
Music video/Music-Performance
12930   60 mins   C
B, V
This recording of the charity appeal concert features many rock'n' roll artists including Eric Clapton, Steve Winwood, Rolling Stones, Bill Wyman and Charlie Watts, Led Zeppelin's Jimmy Page, Kenney Jones of 'The Who' and many others.
S,A — EN
Ronnie Lane; Glyn Jones — Video Form Pictures **H, P**
VFX 16/VFV 16

Roobarb and More   Chi-Juv '8?
Roobarb
Cartoons
12558   67 mins   C
V2, B, V
Animated, narrated by Richard Briers
15 pgms
There are fifteen separate cassettes in this series and each episode features the escapades of the trouble-prone mongrel Roobarb and his cunning cat-pal Custard. Each cassette is approximately 67 minutes long.
PS,I — EN
Unknown — RPTA Video Ltd   **H, P**

Room at the Top   Fil-Ent '59
Drama
01176   117 mins   B/W
B, V
Laurence Harvey, Simone Signoret
An ambitious young man struggles to reach the top of the financial ladder by encouraging a romance with the daughter of a local industrialist.
Academy Award '59: Best Actress (Signoret); Best Screenplay (Neil Paterson).
BBFC:U — S,A — EN
Continental, Walter Reade — CBS/Fox Video
P
3B-066

Rose, The   Fil-Ent '80
Musical-Drama
05644   129 mins   C
V2, B, V, LV
Bette Midler, Alan Bates
The story of a rock-singer hellbent on self-destruction, a heroine in her time whose fans love it the wilder she gets. On stage she is alive but faced with reality her heartbreak becomes the story of her generation.
A — EN
Twentieth Century Fox — CBS/Fox Video
H
4A-123

Rose Marie   Fil-Ent '54
Musical
13431   97 mins   C
B, V
Ann Blyth, Howard Keel, Bert Lahr, Marjorie Main, Fernando Lamas
Set against the sweeping background of The Rockies, a Mountie is attracted to the wild daughter of a trapper but meets the beautiful daughter of an Indian Chief and falls in love with her. The dance routines are by Busby Berkeley.
BBFC:U — F — EN
Ronald Miller — MGM/UA Home Video
P
10374

Roseland   Fil-Ent '77
Drama
05750   103 mins   C
B, V
Geraldine Chaplin, Joan Copeland, Dan De Natale, Helen Gallagher, Lou Jacobi, Conrad Janis, Lilia Skala, David Thomas, Christopher Walken, Tersea Wright, directed by James Ivory
Filmed at the New York Ballroom, 'Roseland' is divided into three segments, each a microcosmic view of life set against the background of a different dance and involving a central paradox. 'The Waltz'—a genteel widow meets an unpolished widower; 'The Hustle'—a romantic triangle; and 'The Peabody'—an old couple attempt to win the trophy again.
BBFC:A — M,A — EN
Merchant Ivory — Home Video Holdings
H, P
012

Rosemary's Baby   Fil-Ent '68
Horror
13622   129 mins   C
B, V
Mia Farrow, John Cassavetes, Ruth Gordon, directed by Roman Polanski

---

(For Explanation of codes, see USE GUIDE and KEY)

PALADIN VIDEO HOME ENTERTAINMENT GUIDE

When a pregnant woman moves into her new flat sinister things start to occur. Her neighbors have diabolical designs on her infant and her husband also comes under suspicion.
BBFC:18 — *A* — *EN*
Paramount — *CIC Video* **H, P**
2122

Rosemary's Killer
Fil-Ent '8?
Horror
09904   87 mins   C
B, V
Farley Granger, Vicky Dawson, Christopher Goutman, Cindy Weintraub, directed by Joseph Zito
Years ago Rosemary and her lover were butchered by a G.I. killer in combat garb. He returns again to slaughter with merciless ferocity.
BBFC:18 — *A* — *EN*
Unknown — *Entertainment in Video* **H, P**
EVB 1006/EVV 1006

Roses
How-Ins '82
Gardening/Flowers
07433   60 mins   C
B, V
Presented by Arthur Billit
In this film Arthur Billit, one of Britain's most enthusiastic rose gardeners, shows how, with the right methods, to achieve show-standard blooms. He starts from scratch in January and gives advice for each stage of cultivation. He introduces some of the many varieties at the St. Albans gardens of the National Rose Society and demonstrates how new varieties are created.
S,A — *I*
Mike Mansfield Enterprises Ltd — *THORN EMI* **P**
TXE 90 0680 4/TVE 90 0680 2

Rostropovich
Fil-Ent '82
Music-Performance
08566   65 mins   C
B, A
Mstisiav Rostropovich
This programme includes the 'Dvorak Cello Concerto in B Minor' and 'Saint-Saens Cello Concerto No 1. in a Minor, OP.33.' They are both performed by the famous cellist Mstislav Rostropovich, with the London Philharmonic Orchestra, conducted by Carlo Maria Giulini.
F — *EN*
EMI — *THORN EMI* **P**
TXE 90 07474/TVE 90074 72

Rottweiler—The Dogs of Hell
Fil-Ent '84
Horror
12917   93 mins   C
B, V
Earl Owensby, directed by Worth Keeter III
A pack of vicious dogs trained to kill by the US government escape from a truck and terrorize a quiet mountain resort.
BBFC:18 — *A* — *EN*
Unknown — *THORN EMI* **P**
TXA 90 24424/TVA 90 24422

Rouen Round 1962/Brands Hatch Beat 1964
Spo-Lei '6?
Automobiles-Racing
04537   55 mins   C
B, V
Jim Clark, Graham Hill, and Bruce McLaren head the lineup of star drivers in the 1962 World Racing Drivers' Championship but Dan Gurney wins it in his Porsche. The second feature is the story of the 1964 RAC European and British Grand Prix, set to music.
F — *EN*
Castrol — *Quadrant Video* **H, P**
M6

Roughnecks
Fil-Ent '8?
Adventure
12154   179 mins   C
V2, B, V
Cathy Lee Crosby, Sam Melville, Vera Miles, Harry Morgan
The story of the tough, determined lives of a group of men who work in the outfields, and play with the same wild energy when they are off duty, is told in this film.
BBFC:15 — *S,A* — *EN*
Metromedia Producers Corporation — *Guild Home Video* **H, P, E**

Round Robin
Gen-Edu '78
Birds/Wildlife
04282   30 mins   C
B, V
Bernard Cribbins
The robin is better known as a carrier of Christmas greetings than as a wild bird, but dispensing peace and goodwill is certainly not part of the robin's private life. Bernard Cribbins gives a robin's-eye view of man in this programme.
U.S. Industrial Film Festival '78: Silver Screen Award *F* — *ED*
Royal Society for the Protection of Birds — *Royal Society for the Protection of Birds* **H, P**

Roustabout
Fil-Ent '64
Musical-Drama
01010   101 mins   C

PALADIN VIDEO HOME ENTERTAINMENT GUIDE

B, V
Elvis Presley, Barbara Stanwyck, Joan Freeman, Leif Erickson, Sue Ann Landon
A roving, reckless singer joins a carnival and romances the owner's daughter.
F — EN
Paramount; Hal Wallis — *CBS/Fox Video* **P**
3B-034

Rover, The   Fil-Ent '66
Adventure
08895   107 mins   C
V2, B, V
Anthony Quinn, Richard Johnson, Rosanna Schiaffino, Rita Hayworth, directed by Terence Young
During the French Revolution, an ageing adventurer is suspected of being a spy when he outwits the English guarding the harbour of Toulon. Based on the novel by Joseph Conrad.
C, A — EN
S J Seligman Prod — *Video Programme Distributors* **P**
Canon 007

Roxy Music—The High Road   Fil-Ent '8?
Music-Performance
08991   75 mins   C
B, V
Bryan Ferry
This tape features twelve of Roxy Music's popular songs such as 'Both Ends Burning', 'Love is the Drug', 'Dance Away' and 'Jealous Guy.' These were recorded at a concert the group gave in France.
F — EN
Unknown — *Polygram Video* **P**
790 585

Royal Four in Hand   Spo-Lei '82
Animals
13522   52 mins   C
B, V
An exposition of the exciting and fast growing sport of competition carriage driving, featuring and presented by His Royal Highness, the Duke of Edinburgh.
F — EN
Unknown — *TFI Leisure Ltd* **H, P**

Royal Jordan   Gen-Edu '84
Royalty-GB
13489   60 mins   C
B, V
This is a record of the State Visit of Queen Elizabeth II and the Duke of Edinburgh to Jordan in March '84 and shows Her Majesty viewing the new hospitals and visiting the Royal Stud. It is narrated by H.R.H. Princess Alia.
F — EN   AB
Greenpark Productions — *Greenpark Productions* **P**

Royal Philharmonic Orchestra Plays Queen, The   Fil-Ent '81
Music-Performance
08580   60 mins   C
B, V
This programme staged in the Royal Albert Hall features the Royal Philharmonic Orchestra and the Royal Choral Society performing some of the best known songs from the rock group Queen. The songs included are 'Flash,' 'You're My Best Friend,' 'Don't Stop Me Now,' 'Love of My Life,' 'Another One Bites the Dust,' 'Bohemian Rhapsody' and 'Imagine.'
F — EN
CTV Ltd — *THORN EMI* **P**
TXE 90 0839 4/TVE 90 0839 2

Royal Wedding, The   Gen-Edu '81
Documentary/Royalty-GB
05153   30 mins   C
B, V
A compilation of the highlights of the Royal Wedding produced by Movietone News.
F — EN
Movietone News — *Rank Video Library*
H, P

Royal Wedding, The   Gen-Edu '81
Documentary/Royalty-GB
04858   115 mins   C
V2, B, V, LV
This programme features the events of the Royal Wedding Day, including the procession, the Marriage Service and the Balcony Appearances.
F — EN
Michael Lumley — *BBC Video*   **H, P**
BBCV 5013

Royal Wedding, The   Gen-Edu '81
Documentary/Royalty-GB
05063   60 mins   C
B, V
Introduced by Ronald Allison

PALADIN VIDEO HOME ENTERTAINMENT GUIDE

This programme recounts the events of the Royal Wedding Day, and includes an interview with the Royal Couple and selected highlights of the Wedding's Eve celebrations.
F — EN
Jim Pople — *THORN EMI* **P**
TXE 90 6218 4/TVE 90 6218 2

Royal Wedding, The Gen-Edu '81
Documentary/Royalty-GB
08917 120 mins C
V2
This cassette contains highlights of the Royal Wedding plus 60 minutes of blank tape for personal home recording.
F — EN
Jim Pople — *THORN EMI* **P**
TPB 90 0841 3

Ruby Fil-Ent '77
Horror
08937 80 mins C
B, V
Roger Davis, Stuart Whitman, Piper Laurie, Janit Baldwin, Crystin Sinclaire, Paul Kent, Len Lesser, Jack Perkins, Edward Donno, Rory Stevens
A 16-year-old deaf mute is being sent away from home as a result of strange and destructive behaviour. Her threatened departure coincides with an outbreak of even greater violence.
BBFC:X — A — EN
Dimension Pictures — *Brent Walker Home Video Ltd* **P**

Ruby and Oswald Fil-Ent '78
Drama/Documentary
09447 96 mins C
B, V
Michael Lerner, Frederic Forrest, Doris Roberts, Lou Frizzell, Bruce French, Sandy McPeak, Lanna Saunders, Sandy Ward, directed by Mel Stuart
This is the story of the four days that shook the world in November, 1963 before Lee Harvey Oswald shot President John F. Kennedy on the streets of Dallas on 22nd of November, in full view of nearly one million television viewers.
BBFC:U — F — EN
EMI Film Dist.; Alan Landsburg Prod. — *Guild Home Video* **H, P, E**

Ruby Gentry Fil-Ent '52
Drama
04159 82 mins B/W
B, V
Jennifer Jones, Charlton Heston, Karl Malden

Girl from the wrong side of the tracks, cast aside by the man she loves, marries town's wealthy businessman and sets out to destroy all who snubbed her.
BBFC:A — S,A — EN
Selznick — *Guild Home Video* **H, P**

Ruckus Fil-Ent '81
Adventure
08741 97 mins C
B, V
Dirk Benedict, Linda Blair, Richard Farnsworth, Matt Clark, Jon Van Ness, Ben Johnson, Taylor Lacher.
An army vet uses his training to defend himself when he runs into trouble in a small town.
S,A — EN
International Vision — *Precision Video Ltd* **P**
BSPV 2585/VSPV 2585

Ruddigore Fil-Ent '8?
Opera
08927 100 mins C
B, V
Vincent Price, Keith Michell, John Treleaven, Donald Adams, Paul Hudson, Norma Burrowes, Ann Howard, Johanna Peters, Beryl Korman, Elise McDougall
This opera, by Gilbert and Sullivan, tells of Sir Despard Murgatroyd who is bound by an ancient curse to commit a crime every day. He is greatly relieved to learn that the shy Robin Oakapple is the rightful Lord and therefore the victim of the curse. The music is performed by The London Symphony Orchestra, conducted by Alexander Faris, with The Ambrosian Opera Chorus.
S,A — EN
Brent Walker Prods — *Brent Walker Home Video Ltd* **P**

Rugby—A Game for Everyone Spo-Lei '8?
Sports
13538 45 mins C
B, V
Pierre Villepreux suggests some new and successful coaching techniques, with particular reference to junior players.
F — ED
Unknown — *TFI Leisure Ltd* **H, P**

Rugby—It's Childs Play Spo-Lei '8?
Sports
13544 28 mins C
B, V
Directed by Andrew Davie
Made with the support of the 'Challenge to Youth' Scheme, The Welsh Rugby Union has devised a Bronze, Silver and Gold Proficiency

(For Explanation of codes, see USE GUIDE and KEY)

PALADIN VIDEO HOME ENTERTAINMENT GUIDE

Award to encourage youngsters to achieve their maximum potential commensurate with age and this programme shows them practicing for their tests.
M,S — I
Town and Country Productions — *TFI Leisure Ltd* **H, P**

Rugby—Treatment of a Neck Injury Spo-Lei '8?
Sports
13542 18 mins C
B, V
The Irish Casualty Surgeons Association and the Irish Rugby Football Union deal with the management of injuries in the match situation.
C,A — ED
Unknown — *TFI Leisure Ltd* **H, P**

Rulers of the City Fil-Ent '??
Crime-Drama
06116 96 mins C
V2, B, V
Jack Palance, Gisela Hahn, Edmund Purdom, Vittorio Caprioli
The boss of a big gambling circle sets out to punish those who dared to cheat him of a substantial amount of money. However, his opponents are more difficult to deal with than he imagined.
S,A — EN
Unknown — *Video Programme Distributors* **P**
Cinehollywood—V250

Rumble Fish Fil-Ent '83
Drama
13339 91 mins B/W
B, V
Matt Dillon, Glenn Withrow, Mickey Rourke, Dennis Hopper, Vincent Spano, Tom Waits, Diana Scarwid, directed by Francis Ford Coppola
Set in a decaying city some time in the future, this film of S.E. Hinton's novel is about two brothers' desire to break out of their urban trap.
BBFC:18 — A — EN
Fred Roos; Doug Claybourne — *CIC Video* **H, P**
BET 1105/VHT 1105

Run, Angel, Run Fil-Ent '69
Drama/Adventure
05484 80 mins C
V2, B, V
William Smith, Valerie Starrett, Gene Shane, Lee De Broux, directed by Jack Starrett
A young man hunting for freedom and love is being hunted himself by a bike gang of which he was a former member. He exposed them in a magazine article and is now running from them with his girlfriend.
BBFC:AA — S,A — EN
Fanfare Films — *Iver Film Services* **P**
144

Run For The Roses Fil-Ent '78
Adventure
07808 93 mins C
B, V
Vera Miles, Stuart Whitman, Panchito Gomez
A foal, born lame to a thoroughbred, is saved by a little Mexican boy before the owners have it put down. The boy, with the help of his stepfather, works hard to earn money for an operation to heal the foal's injury. It succeeds and together they train and enter the horse in the famed Kentucky Derby.
F — EN
Kodiak Films;Pan-American Film Prods — *Video Tape Centre* **P**
VTC 1005

Run for Your Life Fil-Ent '7?
Drama/Suspense
09285 93 mins C
B, V
Dennis Safren, Lang Jeffries
This is the story of an American G.I. who decides that fighting in Vietnam is pointless. For his refusal to obey orders, he is court-martialled and sentenced to ten years in prison. Whilst in transit he and his guards are attacked by the Viet Cong. With the guards dead, he runs—his only aim is to survive.
BBFC:AA — S,A — EN
Unknown — *AVI Video Ltd* **P**
015

Run, Man, Run Fil-Ent '??
Western
06117 90 mins C
V2, B, V
Thomas Milian, John Ireland
A clandestine organization preparing for a Mexican revolution needs money to fight against repression and poverty. A treasure hunt for three million dollars sees many competitors, all determined to get their hands on the money by fair means or love.
S,A — EN
Unknown — *Video Programme Distributors* **P**
Cinehollywood—V1020

(For Explanation of codes, see USE GUIDE and KEY)

PALADIN VIDEO HOME ENTERTAINMENT GUIDE

Run of the Arrow/Cry Danger
Fil-Ent '5?
Western/Crime-Drama
05772   158 mins   C
B, V

Rod Steiger, Charles Bronson, Brian Keith, directed by Samuel Fuller, Dick Powell, Rhonda Fleming, Richard Erdman, directed by Robert Parrish

Two films are contained on one cassette. 'Run of the Arrow' (colour, 83 minutes, 1958) is set after the Civil War in America. A Southern soldier is captured by the Sioux, and is forced into a survival race against the tribe's fiercest warriors. If he lasts the course, a Sioux wife is waiting; but the Union Army is also advancing to wipe out the Indians. 'Cry Danger' (black and white, 75 minutes, 1952) stars Dick Powell as an innocent ex-bookie intent on clearing his name. Closely trailed by the detective who arrested him, he hunts down the real crook.
S,A — EN
Universal; RKO — *Kingston Video*   H, P
KV10

Runner Stumbles, The
Fil-Ent '80
Drama/Mystery
06178   88 mins   C
B, V

Dick Van Dyke, Kathleen Quinlan, Maureen Stapleton, Ray Bolger, Tammy Grimes, Beau Bridges

The story of a relationship between a nun and a priest which brings their natural emotions and needs into conflict with their vows of chastity. The story takes an unexpected turn when the priest is accused of murder.
BBFC:A — S,A — EN
Stanley Kramer Production — *Guild Home Video*   H, P, E

Runners
Fil-Ent '83
Adventure/Suspense
09388   110 mins   C
B, V

James Fox, Jane Asher

This film tells the story of a man desperate to find his daughter, combing the underworld to find out if she is dead or has joined 'The Runners'.
C,A — EN
Hanstoll Production — *VCL Video Services*
P

Running
Fil-Ent '79
Drama
07603   98 mins   C
V2, B, V

Michael Douglas, Susan Anspach, Lawrence Dane, Eugene Levy, Charles Shamata, Philip Akin, directed by Steven Stern

A long distance runner who has never won, who dropped out of law school, who has had countless jobs and two failed businesses is now being divorced by his wife. She loves him but having kept him for 14 years she feels that it is time for him to make his own life. In a rough hotel he decides to enter the Olympic Marathon with the chance to win self-respect, his wife and his children. He faces ridicule as he runs and runs through the New York streets, until at last he is entered in the Marathon.
BBFC:A — S,A — EN
Universal — *Iver Film Services*   P
170

Running Brave/The Story of Zola Budd
Fil-Ent '83
Drama
13141   114 mins   C
B, V

Robby Benson, Claudia Cron, directed by D.S. Everett

Two films are contained on one cassette. 'Running Brave' (102 minutes, 1983) portrays the story of Billy Mills, an American Red Indian, who had to overcome racial prejudice before running in the 1964 Olympics and 'The Story of Zola Budd' (12 minutes, 1984), tells of the controversy surrounding her 1984 Olympic run.
F — EN
Buena Vista — *Polygram Video*   P
041 0264/041 0262

Running Scared
Fil-Ent '7?
Suspense
09189   98 mins   C
B, V

John Saxon, Bradford Dillman, Annie McEnroe, Judge Renhold, Kin Wahl

In April, 1961 two men return home from military service in the Panama Canal Zone. The plane they are travelling in makes an unexpected supply drop at a secret military base. One of them innocently takes a photograph, and when an intelligence agent learns of this, assumes they are spies. The chase begins.
S,A — EN
Unknown — *Video Form Pictures*   H, P
MGS 18

Rush-Exit Stage Left
Fil-Ent '81
Music-Performance
09881   60 mins   C
B, V

560   (For Explanation of codes, see USE GUIDE and KEY)

PALADIN VIDEO HOME ENTERTAINMENT GUIDE

This features Canada's best known exports live at the Montreal Forum during the band's world tour in 1981. There are ten songs and a medley of four on this cassette including 'Limelight', 'Tom Sawyer' and 'YYZ'. Recorded in stereo.
F — EN

Polygram Records; Moon Video
Production — *Polygram Video* **H, P**
791 5584/791 5582

Rush the Assassin Fil-Ent '84
Drama/Adventure
13494   90 mins   C
B, V

Conrad Nichols, Laura Trotter, Gordon Mitchell, directed by Anthony Richmond

This film takes place in a post-holocaust world where one man holds sway over the remains of civilization and another challenges him for liberty.
BBFC:18 — *A — EN*

Biro Cinematografica — *Capricorn Entertainments* **P**
104

Russian Roulette Fil-Ent '75
Drama
05397   87 mins   C
B, V

George Segal, Christina Raines, Bo Brindin, Denholm Elliott, Richard Romanus, Gordon Jackson, Peter Donat, directed by Lou Lombardo

A story of a race against time to prevent the assassination of the Russian Premier during his visit to Vancouver. Only one man knows what is happening and he is being held a prisoner. A human bomb is about to be launched into the Premier's motorcade. The story is based on the novel 'Kosygin Is Coming' by Tom Ardes.
BBFC:A — *S,A — EN*

Avco Embassy — *Precision Video Ltd* **P**
BITC 2084/VITC 2084

Rust Never Sleeps Fil-Ent '79
Music-Performance
09080   111 mins   C
B, V

Neil Young

This tape features Neil Young performing all the songs that made him a star. These include 'My, My, Hey, Hey (Out of the Blue)', 'Sugar Mountain', 'Comes a Time', 'Cinnamon Girl', 'I am a Child','Hurricane', 'Thrasher' and many other contemporary classics.
S,A — EN

LA Johnson — *Video Tape Centre* **P**
VTC 1034

Ruthless Fil-Ent '47
Drama
01082   104 mins   B/W
V2, B, V

Zachary Scott

A power-crazed, wealthy businessman alienates all those who are close to him.
BBFC:A — *A — EN*

Eagle Lion — *Intervision Video* **H, P**
A-A 0111

Rutles, The: All You Need Is Cash Fil-Ent '78
Musical/Comedy
10025   74 mins   C
B, V

Eric Idle, Neil Innes, Rikki Fataar, John Halsey, Mick Jagger, Paul Simon, George Harrison, Dan Aykroyd, Bianca Jagger, Gilda Radner

A satirical pseudo-documentary about the career of the "Pre-Fab Four," whose history bears a suspicious resemblance to the Beatles. Written and directed by Eric Idle.
F — EN

Gary Weiss; Craig Kellem; Rutles
Corp — *Palace Video Ltd* **P**
PVC 2065A

Ryan's Daughter Fil-Ent '70
Drama
08679   186 mins   C
B, V

Robert Mitchum, Trevor Howard, Sarah Miles, Christopher Jones, John Mills, Leo McKern, directed by David Lean

Set in the 1900's on the barren Atlantic coast of Ireland, this film tells the story of a rural school master, who on his return from the Easter Rising against the British, falls in love and marries one of his ex-pupils. His happiness is shattered when a Major, who has come to take command of the British Army Garrison, is drawn to the young bride, further complicated by the village freak, a disfigured and twisted man, concealing an unrequited love for her.

Academy Awards '70: Best Supporting Actor (John Mills); Best Cinematography.
BBFC:AA — *S,A — EN*

MGM — *MGM/UA Home Video* **P**
UMB 10163/UMV 10163

PALADIN VIDEO HOME ENTERTAINMENT GUIDE

S

Sabotage   Fil-Ent '36
Suspense
04259   73 mins   B/W
B, V

Sylvia Sydney, Desmond Tester, Joyce Barbow, Oscar Homolka, John Loder, Matthew Boulton, directed by Alfred Hitchcock

A young London wife discovers that her husband is a saboteur in the employ of a foreign power.
BBFC:A — F — EN
Gaumont — *Rank Video Library*   H, P
0028

Sad Cafe   Fil-Ent '81
Music-Performance
04624   52 mins   C
B, V

This film shows Sad Cafe playing their own unique brand of music at London's Victoria Palace and confirming their reputation for giving the ultimate in 'live' performances.
F — EN
VCL Video Services Ltd — *VCL Video Services*
P

Safari Rally   Fil-Ent '??
Drama/Adventure
06119   90 mins   C
V2, B, V

Joe Dallesandro, Marcel Bozzuffi, Olga Bisera, Eleonora Giorgi

Rivalry and jealousy explode during an African rally. A series of dramatic adventures involve two pilots, their loves and their lives.
S,A — EN
Unknown — *Video Programme Distributors*
P
Cinehollywood—V170

Safe Gun   Spo-Lei '84
Gun control/Safety education
13580   35 mins   C
B, V

This programme covers different aspects of gun safety, then goes on to show shooting style and accuracy and gives a demonstration of rough and driven shooting on estates in Norfolk and Wales, plus clay and pigeon shooting.
A — I
Reference Tapes — *Reference Tapes*   P

Sahara   Fil-Ent '84
Adventure/Romance
13362   106 mins   C
V2, B, V

Brooke Shields, Sir John Mills, Lambert Wilson, Horst Buchholz, John Rhys-Davies, directed by Andrew McLaglen

A beautiful heiress disguises herself as a man to enter the gruelling Sahara motor rally but she becomes the prize for which two warring Arab tribes are prepared to fight.
BBFC:PG — S,A — EN
Golan-Globus Production — *Guild Home Video*
H, P, E
8242-2

Sahara Cross   Fil-Ent '??
Adventure/Drama
06118   96 mins   C
V2, B, V

Franco Nero, Michael Coby, Michel Constantin

When research is started on behalf of a Petrol Company in the Sahara a member of the team is killed by saboteurs. His friends set off in pursuit; they are held to ranson by the saboteurs and events take an unexpected turn.
S,A — EN
Unknown — *Video Programme Distributors*
P
Cinehollywood—V1630

Saigon—Year of the Cat   Fil-Ent '83
Drama/Romance
13705   104 mins   C
B, V

Judi Dench, Frederic Forrest, directed by Stephen Frears

The developing relationship between a middle-aged bank official and a young CIA man is played out against the backdrop of Saigon 1974-75.
BAFTA Awards '84: Best Music   S,A — EN
Thames Video — *THORN EMI*   P
90 2684

Sailing—The RYA Method, Part 1   Spo-Lei '8?
Boating
13553   28 mins   C
B, V

Part 1 of this two-part series demonstrates sailing techniques including simple rowing instructions, rigging a boat, reefing, launching, control of boat by sail and rudder and The Glybe: land drill and in practice.
S,A — I
Unknown — *TFI Leisure Ltd*   H, P

PALADIN VIDEO HOME ENTERTAINMENT GUIDE

Sailing—The RYA Method, Part 2
Spo-Lei '8?
Boating
13549   20 mins   C
B, V
Part 2 of this two-part series demonstrates sailing techniques including launching from a lee shore, hove to: jib aback, simple meteorology and tides, sailing a figure of 8 course, a triangular course and a circular course, and capsize drill.
S,A — I
Unknown — *TFI Leisure Ltd*   **H, P**

Sailor Who Fell from Grace with the Sea, The
Fil-Ent '76
Drama
07698   103 mins   C
V2, B, V, LV
Sarah Miles, Kris Kristofferson, Jonathan Kahn, Margo Cunningham, directed by Lewis John Carlino
A 13 year old boy tries to understand his widowed mother's affair with a disillusioned sailor. Under the influence of a gang of sadistic schoolboys he is convinced that the man should be ritually murdered with knives, ropes and surgical instruments. Based on the novel by Yukio Mishima.
S,A — EN
Avco Embassy — *CBS/Fox Video*   **P**
4012

Salahdin Al Ayoobi
Fil-Ent '??
Drama
06741   90 mins   C
V2, B, V
The kings of England, France and Austria unite to attack Sultan Salahdin in this historical epic set in thirteenth-century Palestine.
S,A — EN   AB
Unknown — *Intervision Video*   **H, P**
A-C 0142

Salamander, The
Fil-Ent '81
Drama/Mystery
09363   97 mins   C
V2, B, V, LV
Franco Nero, Anthony Quinn, Martin Balsam, Sybil Danning, Christopher Lee, Cleavon Little, Paul Smith, John Steiner
Set against a background of high society, politics and finance in modern Italy, Rome, Milan and Venice, the mysterious death of General Pantaleone, an aristocratic neo-facist, sets off a remarkable chain of events. Intelligence experts are called in to investigate, given a small clue, a visiting card bearing the crest of a Salamander.
S,A — EN
ITC, William R. Foreman — *Precision Video Ltd*
P
CRITC 3130/BITC 3130/VITC 3130/LVITC 0016

Sally of the Sawdust
Fil-Ent '25
Comedy
04674   86 mins   B/W
B, V
W C Fields, Alfred Lunt, Carol Dempster, directed by D. W. Griffith
This recently rediscovered classic is W. C. Field's first and most famous silent feature film. Colour-tinted.
F — EN
United Artists — *Polygram Video*   **P**

Salmo the Leaper
Spo-Lei '8?
Fishing
13552   55 mins   C
B, V
A beautifully photographed film about the life cycle of the salmon and sea trout narrated by Hugh Falkus.
F — EN
Unknown — *TFI Leisure Ltd*   **H**

Salome—Where She Danced
Fil-Ent '45
Drama
07782   86 mins   C
V2, B, V
Yvonne de Carlo, Rod Cameron, Albert Dekker, David Bruce, Walter Slezak, Marjorie Rainbeau, directed by Charles Lamont.
Set during the Austro-Prussian war, a dancer is suspected of being a spy and escapes to Arizona where she affects the lives of all the people.
S,A — EN
Universal — *Fletcher Video*   **H, P**
V113

Saludos Amigos
Fil-Ent '??
Cartoons/Adventure
05585   40 mins   C
B, V
Animated
This film is a combination cartoon including both animation and live-action. Set in South America, Donald Duck stars as a tourist who is exploring

(For Explanation of codes, see USE GUIDE and KEY)

PALADIN VIDEO HOME ENTERTAINMENT GUIDE

in the Andes and meets Pedro a plucky mail plane, Goofy a gaucho on the pampas and Joe Carioca who introduces Donald to the night life of Rio.
F — EN
Walt Disney Productions — *Rank Video Library*   **H**
05100

Salute to the Edinburgh Tattoo   Fil-Ent '81
Parades and festivals/Armed Forces-GB
04859   108 mins   C
V2, B, V
This programme is a collection of highlights from the Edinburgh Military Tattoo from 1975 to 1980, with commentary by Tom Fleming.
F — EN
Charles Clifford; Jo Austin; Ian Christie — *BBC Video*   **H, P**
aBBCV 5012

Salvatore Giuliano   Fil-Ent '80
Drama
13120   123 mins   C
B, V
This is the story of a Sicilian bandit who terrorized the country for seven years and whose crimes cost him a 1,300 year jail sentence.
BBFC:18 — A — EN
Unknown — *Palace Video Ltd*   **P**
PVC 2054A

Samson and Delilah   Fil-Ent '83
Drama/Adventure
13248   93 mins   C
B, V
Antony Hamilton, Belinda Bauer, Max Von Sydow, directed by Lee Philips
In this biblical story, Samson, the strongest man in the world, is seduced and betrayed by Delilah as he fights for the future of his people.
BBFC:PG — S,A — EN
George Litto — *CBS/Fox Video*   **P**
6745

Samson and Delilah   Fil-Ent '49
Drama
13612   120 mins   C
B, V
Victor Mature, Hedy Lamarr, Angela Lansbury, George Sanders, directed by Cecil B. DeMille
The biblical story of Samson who had his strength sapped by Delilah when she cut off his hair but still managed to bring down the Philistines' temple onto the heads of his disbelieving enemies.
BBFC:U — F — EN
Paramount — *CIC Video*   **H, P**
2127

Samson et Dalila   Fin-Art '81
Opera
12516   133 mins   C
B, V
Saint-Saens' opera is recorded in stereo at The Royal Opera House and has Shirley Verrett and Jon Vickers in the title roles. It is conducted by Colin Davis and the designs are by Sidney Nolan.
F — EN
National Video Corporation Ltd — *THORN EMI*   **P**
TXH 90 2202 4/TVH 90 2202 4

Samurai   Fil-Ent '74
Western/Comedy
08028   107 mins   C
V2, B, V
Eli Wallach, Giuliano Gemma, Tomas Milian
A sheriff is robbed by a bandit who escapes on a train. On this train is a Holy Japanese pony escorted by a samurai warrior and his servant. The train is raided by Indians who capture the pony. The sheriff, bandit and the samurai servant join forces to try and recapture the pony.
BBFC:A — F — EN
Unknown — *Iver Film Services*   **P**
216

Sand Pebbles, The   Fil-Ent '66
Drama
01021   195 mins   C
B, V
Steve McQueen, Richard Crenna, Richard Attenborough, Candice Bergen, Larry Gates
An American expatriate, transferred to a gunboat on the Yangtze River in 1926, falls in love with a missionary teacher.
F — EN
20th Century Fox; Robert Wise — *CBS/Fox Video*   **P**
3A-090

Sandpiper, The   Fil-Ent '65
Drama
12225   112 mins   C
B, V
Richard Burton, Elizabeth Taylor, Charles Bronson, Eva Marie Saint

PALADIN VIDEO HOME ENTERTAINMENT GUIDE

The eternal triangle is represented in this love story, with a respected member of the community falling for another woman.
C,A — EN
MGM — *MGM/UA Home Video* **P**
10277

Sanjuro　　　　　　　　　　Fil-Ent '62
Adventure
10030　96 mins　B/W
B, V
Toshiro Mifune, Tatsuya Nakadai, directed by Akira Kurosawa
In nineteenth-century Japan, a shabby samurai volunteers to help a noble family and protects them with superlative swordplay.
S,A — EN
Toho — *Palace Video Ltd* **P**
PVC 2040A

Santa and the Three Bears　　　　Chl-Juv '70
Fantasy
04470　63 mins　C
V2, B, V
Animated
The enchanting tale of three hibernating bears and how they discover the magic and wonder of Christmas.
F — EN
RVS Enterprises — *Intervision Video* **H, P**
A-A 0155

Santa and The Three Bears　　　　Chl-Juv '80
Cartoons
13404　45 mins　C
V2, B, V
Animated
This is a story about a family of bear cubs who meet Santa and learn all about Christmas.
F — EN
Alpha Films — *Intervision Video* **H, P**
0018

Santa Claus Conquers the Martians　　Chl-Juv '64
Fantasy
10084　78 mins　C
V2, B, V
John Call, Leonard Hicks, Pia Zadora
Santa Claus is kidnapped and sent up to Mars when their leader realizes that the Martian children have become far too listless and solemn.
BBFC:U — PS,M — EN
Paul L Jacobson; Jalor Prods — *Embassy Home Entertainment* **P**
2105

Santana and Taj Mahal Live　　　　Fil-Ent '??
Music-Performance
08845　40 mins　C
B, V
This tape features Santana and Taj Mahal live in concert.
S,A — EN
Unknown — *VCL Video Services* **P**
V076B

Sara Dane　　　　　　　　Fil-Ent '81
Drama/Romance
12821　300 mins　C
B, V
Based on a novel by Catherine Graskin and produced on two separate cassettes, this is the story of a woman who starts her life on a prison ship bound for Australia and through two marriages becomes the richest and most powerful woman in Sydney.
C,A — EN
Filmtown; Images of Love — *VideoSpace Ltd* **P**

Sartana　　　　　　　　　Fil-Ent '??
Western
07804　? mins　C
B, V
John Garko, Klaus Kinski
When a gang of villains successfully raid a main bank they lay the blame on Sartana, a man of mystery whose speed with a gun has made him a legend. He ruthlessly pursues the villains bringing death to those who dare obstruct his path.
S,A — EN
Unknown — *Video Tape Centre* **P**
VTC 1008

Sartana　　　　　　　　　Fil-Ent '8?
Adventure
13483　91 mins　C
B, V
John Garko, William Berger, Sidney Chaplin, Klaus Kinski, directed by Frank Kramer

---

(For Explanation of codes, see USE GUIDE and KEY)

565

PALADIN VIDEO HOME ENTERTAINMENT GUIDE

Two bankers hatch a devious plan to steal gold from a stagecoach, but a mysterious stranger gets there first and eliminates the gang.
BBFC:15 — S,A — EN
Unknown — Precision Video Ltd   **P**
513

Satan's Brew   Fil-Ent '76
Comedy
08980   100 mins   C
B, V
Kurt Raab, Margit Carstensen, Ingrid Caven, directed by Rainer Werner Fassbinder
This film tells the story of an unproductive poet, who is having trouble over advances with his publishers. He tries various methods of earning money, and various members of the household move in and out of his life, forming a weird comedy. It is subtitled in English.
A — EN
Trio-Film; Albartos Prods — Palace Video Ltd   **P**
PVC 2017B

Satan's Cheerleaders   Fil-Ent '??
Horror
05465   88 mins   C
V2, B, V
John Ireland, Yvonne de Carlo, Sydney Chaplin, Jack Kruschen, John Carradine, Kerry Sherman, Hillary Horan, Alisa Powell, Sherry Marks, Lane Caudell, Jacqulin Cole
A story of witchcraft involving a janitor at a high school who is initiated at a satanic altar by a ritual of a cult led by a High Priest, High Priestess and a Monk. When the school's cheerleaders' car has engine trouble on the way to a football game, the janitor takes them to the satanic altar.
BBFC:X — A — EN
World Amusement Co Release; Greydon Clark Prod — Iver Film Services   **P**
91

Satan's Slave   Fil-Ent '76
Horror
04342   87 mins   C
V2, B, V
A young girl falls in with witches.
BBFC:X — A — EN
Monumental Pictures — Intervision Video   **H**
A-A 0065

Satan's Slave   Fil-Ent '8?
Horror
08936   86 mins   C
B, V

Michael Gough, Barbara Kellerman, Candace Glen Denning, Martin Potter, Gloria Walker, James Bree, Celia Hewitt, directed by Norman J. Warren
Set in an isolated country mansion, this film tells of unexplainable accidents, witchcraft and reincarnation rituals. Brutal murders follow brutal murders, bringing in strange hooded figures, beautiful girls in danger and lots of bodies.
BBFC:X — A — EN
Unknown — Brent Walker Home Video Ltd   **P**

Saturday Night at the Baths   Fil-Ent '74
Drama
04422   81 mins   C
V2, B, V
A tender, double love story which explores and gains new insights into the topic of bisexuality and its liberation.
BBFC:X — A — EN
Buckley Brothers — Intervision Video   **H, P**
A-A 0189

Saturday Night Fever   Fil-Ent '77
Musical-Drama
01259   118 mins   C
B, V
John Travolta, Karen Gorney, Donna Pescow
A Brooklyn teenager who is king of the local disco begins to question his narrow view of life. Acclaimed for its disco dance sequences, with music by the Bee Gees.
F — EN
Paramount — CIC Video   **H, P**

Saturday the 14th   Fil-Ent '81
Comedy/Horror
12261   74 mins   C
V2, B, V
Richard Benjamin, Paula Prentiss, Kevin Brando, Kari Michaelsen, Jeffrey Tambar, Nancy Lee Andrews
A family of four are bequeathed a haunted house and unwittingly unleash all types of monsters and vampires bent on destruction.
S,A — EN
New World Pictures — Embassy Home Entertainment   **P**
4004

Saturn 3   Fil-Ent '80
Science fiction
00835   95 mins   C
B, V, LV
Farrah Fawcett, Kirk Douglas, Harvey Keitel

PALADIN VIDEO HOME ENTERTAINMENT GUIDE

Two research scientists create a futuristic Garden of Eden in an isolated sector of our solar system, but love story turns to horror story when a killer robot arrives.
A — EN
ITC — Precision Video Ltd   P
BITC 2003/VITC 2003

Savage Bees, The   Fil-Ent '76
Drama
08444   94 mins   C
B, V

Ben Johnson, Michael Parks, Paul Hecht, Gretchen Gorbett, Horst Bucholz, directed by Bruce Geller
Set in New Orleans during the carnival celebrations, Mardi Gras, this films tells of the arrival of a plagued South American Cargo ship which unleashes a swarm of millions of deadly African killer bees.
BBFC:15 — C,A — EN
Alan Landsburg Productions — THORN EMI   P
TXB 90 1544 4/TVB 90 1544 2

Savage Encounter   Fil-Ent '7?
Drama
09916   80 mins   C
V2, B, V

John Parsonson, Lieb Bester, Tessa Marie Ziegler, Marcel Van Heerden, directed by Bernard Buys
Set in the wild countryside of South Africa, a man and a woman set out for a new life out of the city. One night they are attacked in their home and the woman is raped. The man sets out on his trail of revenge.
BBFC:X — A — EN
Unknown — Derann Film Services   P
FGS 909

Savage Innocents, The   Fil-Ent '61
Drama/Adventure
08046   107 mins   C
B, V

Anthony Quinn, Yoko Tani, Peter O'Toole, Anna May Wong, directed by Nicholas Ray
This film is set in the Arctic and tells the story of an Eskimo. In great anger he unintentionally kills a missionary. He flees with his wife to the Arctic wastes, but two Canadian policemen catch up with him, with the intention of bringing him to justice. It is based on the novel 'On Top of the World' by Hans Reusch.
BBFC:A — S,A — EN
Paramount — Rank Video Library   H, P
0114 C

Savage Is Loose, The   Fil-Ent '74
Drama
06947   114 mins   C
B, V

George C. Scott, John Carson, Trish Van Devere, Lee H. Montgomery, directed by George C. Scott
A scientist, his wife and son who are marooned on a desert island have managed to survive for 20 years. However, as the son grows, so his inner loneliness and bitterness increase until the relationship with his parents reaches a breaking point.
A — EN
Campbell Devon Prods — Home Video Merchandisers   H, P
052

Savage Islands   Fil-Ent '83
Drama/Adventure
13305   96 mins   C
B, V

Tommy Lee Jones, Max Phipps, Jenny Seagrove, Michael O'Keefe, Grant Tilly, directed by Ferdinand Fairfax
Set in the Pacific in the 1880's, this is a swashbuckling tale of rivalry between a slave trader and an adventurer who goes to the rescue of a girl who has been kidnapped during her wedding ceremony by her enemy.
BBFC:PG — S,A — EN
Paramount — CIC Video   H, P
BET 2110/VHT 2110

Savage Sisters   Fil-Ent '81
Drama/Adventure
13458   89 mins   C
B, V

Gloria Hendry, Cheri Caffaro, Rosanna Ortiz, Sid Haig, John Ashley, directed by Eddie Romero
Three alluring girls become involved in an island revolution, a million dollar robbery and a spectacular jailbreak in this rip-roaring adventure film.
BBFC:18 — C,A — EN
Orion Pictures — Rank Video Library   H, P
0172 A

Savage Weekend   Fil-Ent '78
Horror
02115   76 mins   C
V2, B, V

(For Explanation of codes, see USE GUIDE and KEY)

PALADIN VIDEO HOME ENTERTAINMENT GUIDE

When a group of New Yorkers go forth for a weekend they meet a sinister rural hostility. A dead bat nailed to the door of their weekend retreat heralds the start of violence and macabre killings.
BBFC:X — C,A — EN
Unknown — Hokushin Audio Visual Ltd **P**
VM-26

Savages   Fil-Ent '72
Drama
05683   108 mins   C
B, V

Susan Blakely, Sam Waterston, directed by James Ivory
A disturbing story that centres around the Mud People, a primitive tribe, who are distracted from a human sacrifice by the mysterious appearance of a croquet ball. They trace its origin to an abandoned mansion. The house and its contents have a civilising effect on them and for a while they take on the identities of typical twentieth century socialities—until everything changes.
BBFC:AA — S,A — EN
Merchant Ivory Production; Angelika — *Home Video Holdings*   **H, P**
016

Savages   Fil-Ent '75
Adventure/Suspense
12078   71 mins   C
V2, B, V

Andy Griffith, Sam Bottoms, Noah Beery, Randy Boone
A hunting expedition is arranged in an isolated desert. The young boy hired as a guide discovers that the target is man, not beast.
BBFC:PG — S,A — EN
Aaron Spelling Productions — *Guild Home Video*   **H, P, E**

Savannah Smiles   Fil-Ent '82
Comedy
12594   105 mins   C
V2, B, V

Donovan Scott, Mark Miller, Peter Graves, Brigitte Andersen, directed by Pierre de Moro
A six year old daughter of wealthy Southern parents decides to run away from home and hides herself in the back of a car driven by two inept criminals. Upon discovery she cannot be persuaded to leave her new found friends.
BBFC:PG — F — EN
Clark L Paylow — *Intervision Video*   **H, P**
6653

Say Hello to Yesterday   Fil-Ent '70
Drama/Romance
13152   87 mins   C
B, V

Jean Simmons, Leonard Whiting, directed by Arvin Rakoff
The film tells the story of a tender love affair between a young boy and an experienced married woman.
BBFC:15 — A — EN
Cinerama; Joseph Shaftel — *Brent Walker Home Video Ltd*   **P**
BW 31

Sayonara   Fil-Ent '57
Drama
12005   141 mins   C
B, V

Marlon Brando, James Garner, Patricia Owens, Red Buttons, Ricardo Montalban, Miyoshi Umeki
A portrait of the loves and lives of American servicemen in Japan. These cross-cultural romances are equally scorned by both Japanese and Americans if couples declare their love openly.
Academy Awards '57: Best Supporting Actor (Buttons); Best Supporting Actress (Umeki); Best Art Direction; Best Sound.
BBFC:15 — S,A — EN
Warner Bros — *CBS/Fox Video*   **P**
7146

Scandalous   Fil-Ent '82
Adventure/Comedy
13369   88 mins   C
V2, B, V

Robert Hays, John Gielgud, Pamela Stephenson, Jim Dale, directed by Rob Cohen
When an attractive TV reporter sees an exotic beauty indulging in what seems to be industrial espionage he thinks he has a good news story on his hands and gets involved in a network of intrigue.
BBFC:15 — S,A — EN
Angeles Entertainment Group — *Guild Home Video*   **H, P, E**
8351-7

Scanners   Fil-Ent '81
Horror/Science fiction
06175   103 mins   C
V2, B, V, LV

Patrick McGoohan, Jennifer O'Neill, Stephen Lack, directed by David Cronenberg
The Scanners are a unique breed of people of which there are 237 in the world and they are winning with the aid of the most terrifying

PALADIN VIDEO HOME ENTERTAINMENT GUIDE

powers ever created. Their thoughts alone can kill, they can bend, twist, mutilate and explode other human beings using only the power of their minds.
BBFC:X — A — EN
Claude Heraux Prod — Guild Home Video
H, P, E

Scarecrow, The   Fil-Ent '82
Mystery/Suspense
06901   97 mins   C
V2, B, V
John Carradine, Tracy Mann, Jonathan Smith, directed by Sam Pillsbury
Set in the fictitious New Zealand small town of Klynham in the early 1950's, where the trivial everyday events mask the truth, this film tells the story of the survival of a young boy and his beautiful sister. The town, unable to recognise evil and the significance of events, watches as the boy grapples with manhood, morality and the consequences of chicken stealing while his sister is pursued by the Scarecrow, a magician, murderer, hypnotist and sex maniac.
S,A — EN
New Zealand Film Commission; Oasis Films — Channel Video   **H, P**

Scarecrow   Fil-Ent '73
Drama
13006   112 mins   C
B, V
Al Pacino, Gene Hackman, directed by Jerry Schatzberg
A couple of drifters hitch from Detroit by means of freight trains and open trucks to start a new life in California.
BBFC:X — A — EN
Warner Bros — Warner Home Video   **P**
61098

Scared Straight-Another Story   Fil-Ent '80
Drama
09843   96 mins   C
B, V
Cliff De Young, Stan Shaw
This film, set in a prison, looks at whether hardened criminals can save juvenile delinquents from lives of crime. But when young offenders are exposed to a taste of prison life, the confrontation between the delinquents and the hardened inmates can sometimes go horribly wrong.
C,A — EN
Golden West TV — Polygram Video   **H, P**
791 5524/791 5522

Scared to Death   Fil-Ent '47
Horror
05626   66 mins   C
B, V
Bela Lugosi, Joyce Compton, George Zucco, Douglas Fowley, Nat Pendleton, directed by Christy Cabane
A woman is driven insane by terror and dies of fright when shown the death mask of the man she framed.
A — EN
Robert L Lippert Prod — VCL Video Services   **P**
0229G

Scarface   Fil-Ent '32
Crime-Drama
13334   86 mins   B/W
B, V
Paul Muni, George Raft, Boris Karloff, Osgood Perkins, directed by Howard Hawks
One of the old time classic gangster films, this is the story of organized crime's pinch on the city of Chicago during the prohibition.
BBFC:PG — C,A — EN
Universal — CIC Video   **H, P**
BEJ 1108/VHJ 1108

Scarface   Fil-Ent '83
Crime-Drama
13327   163 mins   C
B, V
Al Pacino, Steven Bauer, Michelle Pfeiffer, Robert Loggia, directed by Brian De Palma
This film follows the story of a small-town Cuban refugee hoodlum who guns his way to the top of Miami's cocaine empire.
BBFC:18 — A — EN
Universal — CIC Video   **H, P**
BEA 1114/VHA 1114

Scarlet and the Black, The   Fil-Ent '83
War-Drama
09366   137 mins   C
V2, B, V
Gregory Peck, Christopher Plummer, John Gielgud
Set in Rome during the German occupation of 1943, this film tells of one man who is known to flaunt the ruthless rule of the Gestapo. He has founded an organisation to help escaping Allied prisoners-of-war and others fleeing from persecution. Attached to the Vatican, this man, an Irish priest, has become adept at vanishing before the Gestapo's very eyes.
F — EN
Bill McCutchen Prods; Marble Arch Prods — Precision Video Ltd   **P**
CRITC 3133/BITC 3133/VITC 3133

(For Explanation of codes, see USE GUIDE and KEY)

PALADIN VIDEO HOME ENTERTAINMENT GUIDE

Scarlet Pimpernel, The   Fil-Ent '35
Adventure/Drama
09866   93 mins   B/W
B, V
Leslie Howard, Merle Oberon, Raymond Massey, Anthony Bushell, John Gardener, directed by Harold Young
This is a tale of heroism and adventure as the 'Scarlet Pimpernel' snatches French aristocrats from certain death under the guillotine during the bloody French Revolution.
F — EN
U.A.; Alexander Korda — *Polygram Video*   **H, P**
790 2494/790 2492

Scarlet Woman, The   Fil-Ent '68
Drama
07777   83 mins   C
V2, B, V
Monica Vitti, Maurice Ronet, Robert Hossein
This film follows the story of the decline of a wealthy woman and her bid to seek revenge on her lover by murdering him.
S,A — EN
France — *Fletcher Video*   **H, P**
V123

Scars of Dracula   Fil-Ent '70
Horror
07460   92 mins   C
B, V
Christopher Lee, Dennis Waterman, Jenny Hanley, Christopher Matthews, directed by Roy Ward Baker
When a young girl is found dead with two fang marks on her neck and a young man on the run finds himself a guest at the famous castle, a couple searching for him and the local farmers decide once and for all that Dracula must meet his end.
BBFC:X — A — EN
Hammer Productions — *THORN EMI*   **P**
TXC 90 0278 4/TVC 90 0278 2

Scavenger Hunt   Fil-Ent '79
Comedy
06170   116 mins   C
V2, B, V
Richard Benjamin, James Coco, Scatman Crothers, Ruth Gordon, Cloris Leachman, Cleavon Little, Roddy McDowall, Robert Morley, Richard Mulligan, Tony Randall, Dirk Benedict, directed by Michael Schultz
A lawyer has the difficult task of executing the will of an eccentric millionaire 'games' inventor. He realised that death was imminent and devised a massive Scavenger Hunt in which the winner takes all. His greedy heirs to the two hundred million dollar fortune are a crotchety sister, a shyster lawyer and his son-in-law. Special appearances by Meat Loaf, Pat McCormick, Vincent Price, Avery Schreiber, Liz Torres, Carol Wayne and Arnold Schwarzenegger.
BBFC:AA — S,A — EN
Melvin Simon Productions — *Guild Home Video*   **H, P, E**

Scavengers, The   Fil-Ent '??
Adventure
08683   85 mins   C
V2, B, V
Jonathan Bliss, Maria Lease
After the war between the North and South was over, a band of renegade soldiers were still full of hatred and murderous lust, instilled into them by their Captain. They enter a town where they find out that a shipment of gold is passing through. They set up an ambush that leads to murder and torture and a fight for survival between black and white.
BBFC:X — A — EN
Unknown — *Derann Film Services*   **P**
FDV 314

Scenes from a Marriage   Fil-Ent '73
Drama
10014   168 mins   C
B, V
Liv Ullman, Erland Josephson, Bibi Anderson, Jan Balm, Anita Wall, directed by Ingmar Bergman
This is the touching and sensitive story of the love relationship of a man and women. Subtitled in English.
National Society of Film Critics Award '74: Best Picture; Best Actress (Liv Ullman); Best Supporting Actress (Bibi Anderson); Best Screenplay. F — EN
MGM-TV; Norman Felton and Stanley Rubin — *Longman Video*   **P**
LGBE 6002/LGVE 6002

Schizo   Fil-Ent '77
Horror
12984   103 mins   C
B, V
Jack Watson, Lynne Frederick, John Leyton, Stephanie Beachan, John Fraser, directed by Peter Walker
A chilling story about a couple who become involved in a series of gruesome murders.
BBFC:18 — A — EN
Peter Walker — *Warner Home Video*   **P**
61328

Schizoid   Fil-Ent '80
Horror/Mystery
06939   85 mins   C
B, V

PALADIN VIDEO HOME ENTERTAINMENT GUIDE

Klaus Kinski, Mariana Hill, Craig Wasson, directed by David Paulsen
An agony columnist receives a series of threatening letters. Meanwhile, a crazed murderer is attacking his women victims with a pair of scissors. This causes the columnist to wonder whether a psychiatrist is killing off his own patients.
BBFC:X — A — EN
Golan Globus Productions — *Rank Video Library* **H, P**
2014C

Schlock Fil-Ent '76
Horror/Comedy
09065   78 mins   C
V
Eliza Garrett, Saul Kahan, directed by John Landis
This is an updated version of the classic story of Beauty and the Beast. It tells of the adventures of a pre-historic ape-man who comes to life in modern California.
S,A — EN
Jack H Harris Enterprises — *Astra Video* **P**

School's Out at Sunset Cove Fil-Ent '8?
Drama
09145   90 mins   C
B, V
A group of beautiful girls cause absolute pandemonium on the beach, to try and show their disapproval towards property developers who want to build there.
BBFC:AA — C,A — EN
Unknown — *Video Brokers* **H, P**
010X

Scooby and Scrappy-Doo—Cassette 1 Chl-Juv '79
Cartoons
08364   80 mins   C
V2, B, V, LV
Animated
Scooby and his energetic nephew pup, Scrappy-Doo, sniff out mysteries with their detective friends, Fred, Velma, Daphne and Shaggy.
PS,S — EN
Hanna-Barbera — *Guild Home Video* **H, P, E**

Scooby and Scrappy-Doo—Cassette 2 Chl-Juv '79
Cartoons
08365   77 mins   C
V2, B, V, LV
Animated
This is the continuing adventures of Scooby and his nephew searching out more spooks help by their friends Fred, Velma, Daphne and Shaggy.
PS,S — EN
Hanna-Barbera — *Guild Home Video* **H, P, E**

Scooby and Scrappy-Doo-Cassette 3 Chl-Juv '79
Cartoons
09426   79 mins   C
V2, B, V
Animated
This tape follows the further adventures of the dectective hound and his pint-sized canine nephew Scrappy-Doo, sniffing out more puzzling mysteries.
BBFC:U — PS,S — EN
Hanna-Barbera — *Guild Home Video* **H, P, E**

Scotland's Grand Slam Spo-Lei '84
Sports
12732   60 mins   C
B, V
A record of 1984—the greatest year in the history of Scottish rugby since 1925—for it was the year they won the Grand Slam!
F — EN
Bill Malcolm;Dewi Griffiths;John D O'Brien — *BBC Video* **H, P**
5021

Scott of the Antarctic Fil-Ent '48
Biographical/Adventure
00587   105 mins   C
B, V
John Mills, Derek Bond, Harold Warrender, James Robertson Justice, Reginald Beckwith
This film is accurately based on one of the most heroic exploits in British history; it is the story of Captain Scott's doomed expedition to the South Pole in 1912.
S,A — EN
Ealing Studios, Michael Balcon — *THORN EMI* **P**
TXB 90 0212 4/TVB 90 0212 2

Scottish International Rally 1980 Spo-Lei '80
Automobiles-Racing
02047   46 mins   C
B, V

PALADIN VIDEO HOME ENTERTAINMENT GUIDE

This programme features Alan Carter in the fast-paced and action-packed 1980 Scottish International Rally.
S,A — EN
Vintage Television Ltd — *Vintage Television Ltd* **H, P, E**

Scottish Rally 1973/12 Hours in Argyll 1974   Spo-Lei '74
Automobiles-Racing
04511   40 mins   C
B, V

Two thousand miles of tough racing separates the men from the boys. In the second feature, the Burmah Rally of 1974 is fought to a dramatic climax among the hills and forests of Argyll.
F — EN
Ford Motor Company; Castrol — *Quadrant Video*   **H, P**
M21

Scouts Honour   Fil-Ent '80
Adventure
12840   100 mins   C
B, V

Gary Coleman, Pat O'Brien, Harry Morgan
A boy scout's skills at survival are severely tested when he and his pack become trapped in a life and death situation.
BBFC:PG — F — EN
Zephyr Productions — *Video Tape Centre* **P**
1170

Scratch Harry   Fil-Ent '69
Adventure
04316   94 mins   C
V2, B, V

Harry's trust of his instincts gets him into big trouble.
BBFC:X — A — EN
Cannon Prods — *Intervision Video*   **H, P**
A-A 0335

Scream .... and Die   Fil-Ent '69
Horror
07911   85 mins   C
V2, B, V

Andrea Allan, Karl Lanchbury, Joseph Larraz
A young model involved with a petty thief witnesses a sadistic murder whilst on a burglary. After a series of horrific incidents her flat mate is murdered. Scared, she gladly accepts an invitation from a man she hardly knows to stay in his country home. During the night she finds the mutilated body of the petty thief. She realises her mistake too late.
A — EN
Hallmark — *Video Programme Distributors* **P**
Replay—1010

Scream Bloody Murder   Fil-Ent '??
Horror/Suspense
06021   83 mins   C
B, V

Fred Holbert, Leigh Mitchell, Robert Knox, Ron Bastone, Suzette Hamilton, directed by Marc B. Ray.
A young boy grinds his father to death with a tractor but mangles his own hand trying to jump off. At nineteen, after receiving a steel claw and release from a mental institution, he continues his murderous ways in and around his home town.
S,A — EN
First American Films — *VCL Video Services* **P**

Scream for Vengeance   Fil-Ent '??
Crime-Drama
06788   ? mins   C
V2, B, V

Sally Lockett, Nicholas Jacquez, Bob Elliot
Robbery, murder, rape and kidnapping abound in this crime thriller.
C,A — EN
Unknown — *Intervision Video*   **H, P**
A-A 0376

Screamtime   Fil-Ent '82
Horror/Comedy
12197   91 mins   C
V2, B, V

Jean Anderson, Robin Bailey, Dora Bryan, Ann Lynn, Yvonne Nicholson, Ian Saynor, David Van Day
A horror video freak becomes totally oblivious to his everyday surroundings and experiences real terror when corpses and other objects come alive.
BBFC:18 — C,A — EN
Al Bereford — *Medusa Communications Ltd* **H, P**

Scrubbers   Fil-Ent '82
Drama
08443   86 mins   C
B, V

Amanda York, Chrissie Cotterill, Elizabeth Edmonds, Kate Ingram, directed by Mai Zetterling

PALADIN VIDEO HOME ENTERTAINMENT GUIDE

This film tells the story of two teenage girls who, having been put in the borstal system, have to try and survive.
BBFC:AA — C,A — EN
Unknown — THORN EMI **P**
TXA 90 1622 4/TVA 90 1622 2

Scum Fil-Ent '79
Drama
01963 96 mins C
B, V
Directed by Alan Clarke
Originally produced as a TV play for the BBC, this tough drama about life in a British Borstal was banned. The plot follows the mean existence of one of the inmates in his struggle for survival.
BBFC:X — A — EN
GTO Films Ltd — VCL Video Services **P**

Sea Birds, The Gen-Edu '??
Birds
05720 27 mins C
B, V
This film is a detailed account of our sea birds showing how, by their adaptation, they are attuned to and in harmony with their marine environment. It also covers the effects on the birds when the balance is altered through man's activities and how they remain under threat unless there is immediate action and long term planning. Photographed by Dr David Urry.
U.S. Industrial Film Festival '82: Gold Camera Award BISFA '81: Gold Award S,A — ED
Royal Society for the Protection of Birds — Royal Society for the Protection of Birds **H, P**

Sea Quest Fil-Ent '7?
Adventure
12243 ? mins C
B, V
Hardy Kruger, Greg Howe
A father and son, totally different in every way, are forced to unite in their fight against the sea.
F — EN
Unknown — VCL Video Services **P**

Sea Wolves, The Fil-Ent '80
War-Drama
05253 117 mins C
B, V, LV
Gregory Peck, Roger Moore, David Niven, Trevor Howard, Barbara Kellerman, Patrick Macnee

---

The true story of one of the most closely guarded and courageous secret missions of World War Two.
BBFC:A — C,A — EN
Unknown — Rank Video Library **H, P**
0049

Sealab 2020 Fil-Ent '72
Cartoons/Science fiction
08390 84 mins C
V2, B, V
Animated
In the year 2020 the population of the submarine city sealab are exploring the oceans. It gives a futuristic view of what life could be like beneath the sea in years to come.
M,S — EN
Hanna-Barbera — Guild Home Video **H, P, E**

Sealab 2020, Cassette 2 Fil-Ent '72
Cartoons/Science fiction
12071 81 mins C
V2, B, V
Animated
Part 2 of the series which contains four adventure stories featuring the futuristic underwater research laboratory and its crew, including 'Battle with the Sharks.'
BBFC:U — M,S — EN
Hanna Barbera — Guild Home Video **H, P, E**

Seapower Gen-Edu '81
Documentary
04855 109 mins C
V2, B, V, LV
Introduced by Lord Hill-Norton
This programme traces the development of naval power during the twentieth century, and includes archive film and new film of modern warships in action.
F — ED
John Dekker; Bill Jones — BBC Video **H, P**
BBCV 6011

Search and Destroy Fil-Ent '81
War-Drama/Suspense
08048 89 mins C
B, V
Perry King, George Kennedy, Don Stroud, Tisa Farrow

(For Explanation of codes, see USE GUIDE and KEY)

PALADIN VIDEO HOME ENTERTAINMENT GUIDE

This film tells the story of an American war veteran returning to the Niagara Falls. The war that he thought had ended begins again when he finds himself stalked by a maniacal Vietnamese Officer out for revenge.
BBFC:AA — C,A — EN
Unknown — Rank Video Library   **H, P**
0090 C

Season for Assassins   Fil-Ent '76
Drama
08913   104 mins   C
V2, B, V
Martin Balsam, Rossano Brazzi
A group of violent teenagers terrorize the town in which they live. To get their kicks they steal cars, rob and fight.
A — EN
Unknown — Video Programme Distributors   **P**
Inter-Ocean 092

Season of the Witch   Fil-Ent '76
Horror
09064   89 mins   C
V
Jan White, Ray Liane, Joedda McClain, Bill Thunhurst, Ann Muffly, Ginger Greewald
A suburban housewife who dabbles in the black arts finds herself becoming a full-fledged witch.
A — EN
Jack H Harris Enterprises — Astra Video
H, P

Sebastiane   Fil-Ent '84
Drama
12956   96 mins   C
B, V
Leonardo Treviglio, Richard Warwick, Barney James, directed by Derek Jarman and Paul Humphress
Set in the time of the Emperor Diocletian's last great purge against the Christians, this film explores love, violence, sensuality and martyrdom amongst the Roman soldiers in Sardinia. Subtitled in English with music by Brian Eno.
BBFC:18 — A — EN
Unknown — Virgin Video   **H, P**
VVA 030

Second Chance/Great Day in the Morning   Fil-Ent '5?
Suspense/Drama
05767   169 mins   C
B, V
Robert Mitchum, Jack Palance, Linda Darnell, Milburn Stone, directed by Rudolph Mate, Robert Stack, Raymond Burr, Virgina Mayo, Ruth Roman, Alex Nicol, directed by Jacques Tourner
Two films are contained on one cassette. 'Second Chance' (colour, 80 mins, 1954) features a girl hunted by a killer who finds the support of a tough boxer. The killer catches up with them and the final confrontation takes place in a disabled cable car. 'Great Day in the Morning' (colour, 89 mins, 1957) involves the arrival of a Southerner in a Northern city, he wins a saloon by gambling and gets involved with a group running gold to buy guns, when the soldiers arrive a desperate chase begins heralding the start of the Civil War.
S,A — EN
RKO — Kingston Video   **H, P**
KV15

Second Chorus   Fil-Ent '40
Musical
02592   81 mins   B/W
B, V
Fred Astaire, Paulette Goddard, Burgess Meredith, Artie Shaw and his Orchestra
Two trumpeters compete for the same girl and for a job with Artie Shaw's Orchestra. Songs include 'I Ain't Hep to That Step but I'll Dig It,' 'Love of My Life,' and 'Concerto for Clarinet,' composed by Artie Shaw and Johnny Mercer.
F — EN
Paramount — VCL Video Services   **P**
0236G

Second Hand Hearts   Fil-Ent '79
Drama
07393   97 mins   C
V2, B, V
Robert Blake, Barbara Harris, Bert Remsen, Shirley Stoller, Sandra Blake, Collin Boone, directed by Hal Ashby
A man sobers up after a wild party to find that he has not only lost his job but also acquired a wife. Before arranging a divorce, he agrees to drive to California to collect her three children. He has not the faintest idea that this will be the strangest journey of his life.
BBFC:X — A — EN
United Artists; Lorimar — Guild Home Video
H, P, E

Second Thoughts   Fil-Ent '83
Comedy-Drama
12535   93 mins   C
B, V
Lucie Arnaz, Craig Wasson, Ken Howard

(For Explanation of codes, see USE GUIDE and KEY)

PALADIN VIDEO HOME ENTERTAINMENT GUIDE

This is a story about modern relationships; a single mother-to-be is wooed by her ex-husband and kidnapped by her lover.
BBFC:15 — S,A — EN
Lawrence Turman; EMI Films;
Universal — THORN EMI   P
TXA 90 1997 4/TVA 90 1997 2

Second Wind   Fil-Ent '76
Drama
08743   92 mins   C
B, V

James Naughton, Lindsay Wagner, Ken Pogue, Tedde Moore, Tom Harvey, Louis Del Grande, directed by Don Shebib

This film tells the story of a young couple, who to the world around them seem to have everything one could wish for. However, they soon discover that the things that are difficult to come by are more worthwhile.
S,A — EN
Olympic Films — Precision Video Ltd   P
BAMPV 2571/VAMPV 2571

Secret Beyond the Door   Fil-Ent '48
Drama
01083   79 mins   B/W
V2, B, V

Joan Bennett, Michael Redgrave, directed by Fritz Lang

A young wife comes to believe that her husband is a fiendish murderer.
BBFC:A — A — EN
Universal — Intervision Video   H, P
A-A 0124

Secret Garden, The   Chi-Juv '84
Fantasy
13384   107 mins   C
B, V

A spoilt little orphan girl from India comes to live in her uncle's lonely house in Yorkshire and finds new friends and happiness in the hidden, overgrown magical garden.
I,M — EN
BBC Enterprises — BBC Video   H, P
9014

Secret of Seagull Island, The   Fil-Ent '??
Suspense
08753   103 mins   C
B, V

Jeremy Brett, Nicky Henson, Prunella Ransom, Pamela Salem, Gabrille Tinti, Fabrizio Iovine, Vassili Karamensinis, directed by Nestore Ungaro

This thriller story begins with the disappearance of an attractive blind girl, and the search leads to the foreboding Seagull Island.
C,A — EN
Unknown — Precision Video Ltd   P
BITC 2125/VITC 2125

Secret Places   Fil-Ent '84
Drama
13746   97 mins   C
B, V

Jenny Agutter, Marie-Theres Relin, Tara MacGowran

A German schoolgirl-refugee who has fled to London to escape the Nazis is sent to a boarding school where she encounters different prejudices but also comfort and friendship.
BBFC:15 — S,A — EN
Unknown — Rank Video Library   H, P
0216D

Secret Policeman's Ball, The   Fil-Ent '79
Comedy-Performance/Music-Performance
08641   95 mins   C
V2, B, V

John Cleese, Peter Cook, Billy Connolly, Rowan Atkinson, Michael Palin, Terry Jones, Pete Townshend, John Williams, Tom Robinson, Clive James

This tape features a live stage performance by a host of stars from rock musicians to comedians. This performance was specifically staged in aid of Amnesty International.
S,A — EN
Document Films; Amnesty International — Hokushin Audio Visual Ltd   P
VM45

Secret Policeman's Other Ball, The   Fil-Ent '82
Music-Performance/Comedy-Performance
09044   90 mins   C
B, V

Rowan Atkinson, Alan Bennett, John Bird, Tim Brooke-Taylor, Jasper Carrott, Graham Chapman, John Cleese, John Fortune, Barry Humphries, Griff Rhys Jones, Alexei Sayle, Victoria Wood, John Wells

This fund-raising comedy gala organized for Amnesty International by John Cleese featured stars from Monty Python, The Goodies, Not the Nine O'Clock News and Beyond the Fringe. Musical interludes were provided by Sting, Jeff Beck, Eric Clapton, Bob Geldof, Johnny

---

(For Explanation of codes, see USE GUIDE and KEY)

PALADIN VIDEO HOME ENTERTAINMENT GUIDE

Fingers, Phil Collins and Donovan. The entire cast joined together as the Secret Police for Amnesy's unofficial anthem, 'I Shall Be Released' for the grand finale.
BBFC:X — A — EN
Amnesty International — *VideoSpace Ltd*
P

Secret Reeds, The   Gen-Edu '82
Birds/Ecology and environment
05719   27 mins   C
B, V
This film explores the ecology and management of the transitory habitat of reed beds and looks at some of its rarer birds. The Royal Society for the Protection of Birds have reserves which include major reed beds that support half the country's bitterns and a third of its bearded tits. The film examines the short life of reed beds as they give way to scrub and woodland.
U.S. Industrial Film Festival '81: Gold Camera Award   S,A — ED
Royal Society for the Protection of Birds — *Royal Society for the Protection of Birds*   **H, P**

Secret Squirrel   Chl-Juv '65
Cartoons
08395   84 mins   C
V2, B, V
Animated
These are the adventures with the secret agent squirrel and his underground assistant Morocco Mole. It also features Squiddly Diddly and Winsome Witch.
PS,M — EN
Hanna-Barbera — *Guild Home Video*   **H, P, E**

Secret Squirrel-Cassette 2   Chl-Juv '??
Cartoons
09431   78 mins   C
V2, B, V
Animated
This tape follows the further adventures of Secret Squirrel and his favourite crime busters, Morocco Mole, Winsome Witch and Squiddly Diddly.
BBFC:U — PS,M — EN
Hanna-Barbera — *Guild Home Video*   **H, P, E**

Secret Squirrel-Cassette 3   Chl-Juv '84
Cartoons
13373   76 mins   C
V2, B, V
Animated
Twelve more adventures from this super-sleuth secret agent are featured in this tape.
F — EN
Hanna Barbera — *Guild Home Video*   **H, P, E**
8424-8

Secrets   Fil-Ent '78
Drama/Romance
06731   81 mins   C
V2, B, V
Jacqueline Bisset, Robert Powell
A beautiful, sensual, taken-for-granted wife, has a brief afternoon of love with a charming stranger and leaves with a secret gift.
BBFC:X — A — EN
Lone Star Pictures Intl — *Intervision Video*   **H, P**
A-AE 0200

Secrets of the All Blacks   Spo-Lei '7?
Sports
01983   48 mins   C
B, V
The powerful New Zealand rugby team demonstrates rugby skills, methods, and recommended practice skills. Action clips from international games are included.
F — I
Unknown — *Quadrant Video*   **H, P**

Secrets of the All Blacks II   Spo-Lei '80
Sports
01984   48 mins   C
B, V
A programme for rugby enthusiasts in which the powerful New Zealand squad demonstrates rugby essentials and strategies, including 'close contact stuff,' and 'scrummaging.'
F — I
Unknown — *Quadrant Video*   **H, P**

Seduced   Fil-Ent '84
Crime-Drama
13681   94 mins   C
B, V
Gregory Harrison, Cybill Shepherd, Jose Ferrer, directed by Jerrold Freedman
A sensual drama set against a background of big business and high finance which leads to murder.
BBFC:18 — A — EN
Franklin R Levy — *CBS/Fox Video*   **P**
3053

PALADIN VIDEO HOME ENTERTAINMENT GUIDE

Seducer, The — Fil-Ent '8?
Drama
08833　? mins　C
B, V
Romy Schneider, Jane Birkin, directed by Michel Deville
This film tells the story of a man whose desire is to become rich and powerful. His asset is that women find him attractive.
A — EN
Unknown — VCL Video Services　P
P334D

Seduction of Joe Tynan, The — Fil-Ent '79
Drama
07372　107 mins　C
B, V
Alan Alda, Barbara Harris, Meryl Streep, Rip Torn, Melvyn Douglas
This film follows the story of a senator whose presidential ambitions and his job in Washington keep him away from his wife and family. He is torn between his political career and his personal life when he has an affair with a civil rights activist. This film was written by, directed by and stars Alan Alda.
S,A — EN
Universal — CIC Video　H, P
BEA 1025/VHA 1025

See How She Runs — Fil-Ent '78
Drama
13491　90 mins　C
B, V
Joanne Woodward, Bernard Hughes, John Considine, directed by Richard Heffron
A very much put upon divorced mother of two teenage daughters decides to take up jogging and her family find they have to fend for themselves when she enters the 26-mile Boston Marathon.
BBFC:PG — F — EN
George Englund — Capricorn Entertainments　P
105

Seed of Innocence — Fil-Ent '7?
Drama/Romance
08090　86 mins　C
B,V
Tim Wead, Mary Cannon
This film tells of the poignant love story of two teenagers. They have a baby and keep it despite their parents' objections. They run from their small home town to try to live in the slums.
BBFC:X — A — EN
Unknown — Rank Video Library　H, P
0115C

Seeds of Evil — Fil-Ent '??
Drama
12778　115 mins　C
V2, B, V
Dominique Sanda, Robert Powell, Erland Josephson, Verna Lisi, directed by Liliana Cavani
Set in the nineteenth century, this film traces the story of Friedrich Nietzsche, a man who challenged the sexual and aesthetic mores of his time and was partly held responsible for the doctrine adopted by Nazi Germany.
BBFC:18 — C,A — EN
Abacus Video — Intervision Video　H, P
A-A0507

Seizure — Fil-Ent '8?
Horror
09060　96 mins　C
V
Jonathan Frid, Martine Beswick, Joe Sirola, Troy Donahue, Herve Villechaize, Roger DeKoven
This is the story of a man, haunted at first by his own dreams and then by three characters of his own creation; the dwarf, the executioner and the Queen of Evil. The creatures descend upon him and his weekend guests, turning it into a deadly weekend and a macabre game of survival.
GA — EN
Unknown — Astra Video　H, P

Self Defence — How-Ins '8?
Martial arts/Safety education
06897　60 mins　C
B, V
Presented by Steve Powell
In this film international martial arts expert Steve Powell gives advice on how to defend yourself. He gives instruction on how to use your body to discover your attacker's weak points and your own strong ones, and includes exercises for home practise.
S,A — I
Holiday Brothers Ltd — Holiday Brothers Ltd　P

Self Defence for Women — How-Ins '8?
Martial arts/Safety education
06896　60 mins　C
B, V
Presented by Steve Powell
In this film international martial arts expert Steve Powell gives advice on how to defend yourself. He shows how to discover your attacker's weak points and your own strong ones in a practical illustration of self defence specifically for women.
S,A — I
Holiday Brothers Ltd — Holiday Brothers Ltd　P

(For Explanation of codes, see USE GUIDE and KEY)

PALADIN VIDEO HOME ENTERTAINMENT GUIDE

Selfish Giant, The Happy Prince, The Little Mermaid, The   Fil-Ent '??
Cartoons
10189   90 mins   C
B, V
Animated
This tape contains a trilogy of animated fairy tales. 'The Selfish Giant' by Oscar Wilde tells of a bad tempered giant who builds a wall round his castle to stop the local children playing in his grounds. 'The Happy Prince' also by Oscar Wilde tells of a swallow who befriends a royal statue. 'The Little Mermaid' by Hans Christian Andersen tells the story of a mermaid who falls in love with a handsome prince.
F — EN
Unknown — *Video Form Pictures*   **H, P**
DIP 13

Sellout, The   Fil-Ent '76
Adventure
13018   100 mins   C
B, V
Richard Widmark, Oliver Reed, Gayle Hunnicut
Two former CIA agents, one of whom has defected to Russia, agree to team up again when one of them becomes the target of a contract killer.
BBFC:AA — C,A — EN
Warner Bros Inc — *Warner Home Video*   **P**
61287

Semi-Tough   Fil-Ent '77
Comedy
01049   107 mins   C
V2, B, V
Burt Reynolds, Kris Kristofferson, Jill Clayburgh, directed by Michael Ritchie
Social satire involving a couple of pro-football buddies and the team owner's daughter.
BBFC:AA — A — EN
United Artists; David Merrick — *Intervision Video*   **H**
UA A B 5008

Semi-Tough   Fil-Ent '77
Comedy
12492   105 mins   C
B, V
Burt Reynolds, Kris Kristofferson, Jill Clayburgh, directed by Michael Ritchie
Two American professional footballers both chase after a millionaire's daughter.
BBFC:15 — C,A — EN
David Merrick — *Warner Home Video*   **P**
99314

Sender, The   Fil-Ent '82
Horror
13324   89 mins   C
B, V
Kathryn Harrold, Shirley Knight, Zeljko Ivanek, directed by Roger Christian
A suicidal mental patient turns his horrific nightmares into reality by choosing receivers for his demented thoughts from the local hospital.
BBFC:18 — A — EN
Paramount — *CIC Video*   **H, P**
BET 2083/VHT 2083

Seniors   Fil-Ent '78
Comedy/Adventure
07610   86 mins   C
V2, B, V
Jeffrey Byron, Gary Imhoff
This satire on students, sex and society involves four students who devise a scheme to avoid the working world. However, they become millionaires and part of the establishment.
BBFC:X — A — EN
Unknown — *Iver Film Services*   **P**

Sense of Freedom, A   Fil-Ent '84
Drama
13712   85 mins   C
B, V
David Hayman, directed by John Mackenzie
This is the true life story of Glasgow's villain, Jimmy Boyle, who was sentenced to life imprisonment for murder, and constantly rebelled against the prison officers until he was sent to a gaol with a completely different approach to their inmates.
BBFC:18 — A — EN
Hand Made Films — *THORN EMI*   **P**
90 2875

Sensuous Nurse, The   Fil-Ent '76
Comedy-Drama
09948   85 mins   C
V2, B, V
Jack Palance, Ursula Andress
The greedy relatives of an ailing rich man hire a registered nurse to make sexual advances to him, in the hope that he will die of a heart attack and his vast fortune will be theirs.
BBFC:X — A — EN
National Centre for Cinema Arts — *Video Unlimited*   **H, P, E**
071

Sentinel, The   Fil-Ent '77
Drama/Horror
09263   88 mins   C
B, V

PALADIN VIDEO HOME ENTERTAINMENT GUIDE

Cristina Raines, Chris Sarandon, Burgess Meredith, Sylvia Miles, Beverly D'Angelo, Ava Gardner, John Carradine
A beautiful model moves into an old apartment block and finds that the inhabitants are not what they seem. The building turns out to be a gateway to another world.
BBFC:18 — A — EN
Universal — CIC Video   H, P
BEA 1063/VHA 1063

Separate Tables   Fil-Ent '83
Drama/Romance
13422   112 mins   C
B, V
Julie Christie, Alan Bates, Clare Bloom, directed by John Schlesinger
Adapted from the Terence Rattigan play and set in a Bournemouth hotel in 1954, two separate stories are played out against this background.
C,A — EN
Edie and Ely Landau — MGM/UA Home Video   P
10427

Separate Ways   Fil-Ent '??
Drama
09342   92 mins   C
B, V
karen Black, Tony Lo Bianco
A husband and wife live with their son in upper middle class suburban comfort. They have all the possessions necessary for the 'good life'. However, discontentment is obvious, which could lead them go to their separate ways.
BBFC:X — A — EN
Unknown — Precision Video Ltd   P
BAMPV 2572/VAMPV 2572

Sergeant Klems   Fil-Ent '??
War-Drama
06120   96 mins   C
V2, B, V
Peter Strauss, Howard Ross, Tina Aumont, Luciana Paluzzi
A conflict of conscience and the 'advances' of a homosexual corporal drive Sergeant Klems to escape from the Foreign Legion. As a deserter he fights innumerable difficulties, alone under the searching sun of the Moroccan desert.
S,A — EN
Unknown — Video Programme Distributors   P
Cinehollywood—V990

Sgt. Pepper's Lonely Hearts Club Band   Fil-Ent '79
Musical/Comedy
13304   108 mins   C
B, V
Peter Frampton, The Bee Gees, George Burns, Frankie Howard, Billy Preston, Alice Cooper, Earth, Wind and Fire
The Lonely Hearts Club Band became America's secret weapon when the enemy laid down their arms on hearing them play and when their hometown Heartland decided to honour the bandleader it was discovered that each of the musical instruments had the power to make dreams come true. Music and lyrics by Lennon and McCartney.
BBFC:PG — S,A — EN
Universal — CIC Video   H, P
BET 1121/VHT 1121

Serial   Fil-Ent '80
Drama/Comedy
13337   87 mins   C
B, V
Martin Mull, Tuesday Weld, Sally Kellerman, Christopher Lee, directed by Bill Persky
Based on Cyra McFadden's satiric novel, this film portrays the lifestyle of the residents of an affluent suburb in smart Marin County, California, and their feverish search for new trends and experiences.
BBFC:18 — C,A — EN
Sidney Beckerman — CIC Video   H, P
BET 2094/VHT 2094

Serpent, The   Fil-Ent '72
Drama/Suspense
08892   117 mins   C
V2, B, V
Yul Brynner, Henry Fonda, Dirk Bogarde, Robert Alda, Michel Bouquet, Farley Granger, Virna Lisi, Philippe Noiret
A top KGB official defects to the West, unfurls a spy thriller. It is based on the novel 'The 13th Suicide' by Pierre Nord.
BBFC:A — S,A — EN
Films La Boetie — Video Programme Distributors   P
Canon 006

Serpico   Fil-Ent '74
Drama/Suspense
10129   125 mins   C
B, V
Al Pacino, John Randolph, Jack Kehoe, directed by Sidney Lumet
Based on a true story of a New York policeman who discovers that honesty is not expected to be part of his job. He decides to put his case to the New York Times and the newspaper's ensuing report causes a national sensation.
BBFC:18 — C,A — EN
Paramount — CIC Video   H, P
BEA 2060/VHA 2060

PALADIN VIDEO HOME ENTERTAINMENT GUIDE

Servant, The — Fil-Ent '64
Drama
01178 112 mins B/W
B, V

Dirk Bogarde, James Fox, Sarah Miles, Wendy Craig, directed by Joseph Losey

British class hypocrisy is starkly portrayed in this story of a spoiled young gentleman's ruin by his socially inferior but crafty and ambitious manservant. From the Harold Pinter story.
British Film Academy: Best Actor (Bogarde); Best Photography (Black and White); Most Promising Newcomer (Fox).
BBFC:X — S,A — EN
Springbok Prod; Landau Unger — *THORN EMI* **P**
TXE 90 0009 4/TVE 90 0009 2

SEVEN — Fil-Ent '79
Crime-Drama
08049 102 mins C
B, V

William Smith, Guich Kook, Barbara Leigh, Art Metrano

This film, set in Hawaii, tells of seven independent crime bosses negotiating a union that could be fatal. The intelligence sources in Washington learn of this and send in a man to deal with it, in any way he likes.
BBFC:X — A — EN
Unknown — *Rank Video Library* **H, P**
0103 C

Seven Alone — Fil-Ent '74
Adventure
08824 95 mins C
B, V

Dewey Martin, Aldo Ray, Anne Collings, Dean Smith, Stewart Petersen, directed by Earl Bellamy

This tells the true story of seven orphaned children. Led by the oldest boy they travel a hazardous 2000 miles from Missouri to Oregon after their parents' death. It is based on the book 'On to Oregon' by Monroe Morrow.
S,A — EN
Doty-Dayton Prods. — *VCL Video Services* **P**
P327D

Seven Brides for Seven Brothers — Fil-Ent '54
Musical-Drama
10177 104 mins C
B, V

Jane Powell, Howard Keel

A young girl gets married and receives a shock when she finds out that her husband has six giant brothers and she is expected to look after them. The husband decides he must marry them off and proceeds to kidnap six girls.
BBFC:U — F — EN
MGM — *MGM/UA Home Video* **P**
UMB 10091/UMV 10091

Seven Crystal Balls/Prisoners of the Sun — Chl-Juv '7?
Cartoons/Adventure
02279 80 mins C
V

Animated

Tin Tin and Captain Haddock become involved in the mysterious deaths of seven explorers who returned from Peru with the Mummy of Rascar Capac, looted from an Inca tomb.
M — EN
Unknown — *JVC* **P**
PRT 37

Seven Golden Men — Fil-Ent '65
Suspense
04292 90 mins C
V2, B, V

Rossana Podesta, Philippe Leroy

Workmen digging up a street in Geneva close to one of the city's biggest banks are being directed, via walkie talkies, by Albert from a nearby flat. He is joined by Giorgia just as workers break through into the vaults and remove gold ingots. Albert has alerted the police with the intention of sharing the reward with Giorgia; however, she has her own plans.
C,A — EN
Warner Bros — *Video Programme Distributors* **P**
Inter-Ocean—025

Seven Golden Men Strike Again — Fil-Ent '??
Adventure
08858 103 mins C
V2, B, V

Philippe Leroy, Rossana Podesta, Gastone Moschin, Enrico Salerno, directed by Marco Vicario

The professor and his gang of professional thieves kidnap a South American dictator and plan to use his atomic submarine to steal a shipload of Russian gold bars.
S,A — EN
Atlantic Cinematographics — *Video Programme Distributors* **P**
Inter-Ocean 087

PALADIN VIDEO HOME ENTERTAINMENT GUIDE

Seven Nights in Japan   Fil-Ent '76
Adventure/Romance
08447   100 mins   C
B, V
Michael York, Hidemi Aoki, directed by Lewis Gilbert
The film tells the story of Prince George, heir to the British throne who arrives in Japan Whilst on leave from the destroyer on which he is serving as a lieutenant. Here, he meets and falls in love with a beautiful Japanese tourist guide. Their elopement causes panic, as a group of men intend to assassinate him. However he knows he must return because of his title.
BBFC:A — S,A — EN
Anglo-EMI Prod Ltd; Marianne Prods S
A — *THORN EMI*   P
TXC 90 0863 4/TVC 90 0863 2

Seven Per Cent Solution, The   Fil-Ent '76
Mystery/Comedy
13291   110 mins   C
B, V
Robert Duvall, Nicol Williamson, Laurence Olivier, Samantha Eggar, Alan Arkin, Vanessa Redgrave, Jeremy Kemp, directed by Herbert Ross
Sherlock Holmes is in the throes of a serious addiction to cocaine and is persuaded by Watson to go to Vienna for treatment where he becomes enmeshed with a scheming count and a femme fatale, in this spoof of a Sir Arthur Conan Doyle story.
BBFC:15 — S,A — EN
Universal — *CIC Video*   H, P
BEN 1097/VHN 1097

Seven x Dead   Fil-Ent '73
Mystery/Horror
08318   90 mins   C
B, V
John Ireland, Faith Domergue, John Carradine
A film crew and actors are re-enacting the horrifying deaths of the Beale family that occured a century ago. Suddenly they become caught up in Black Magic, in the same house where the incidents had happened.
A — EN
Television Corp of America — *Nutland Video Ltd*   P

7 Winchesters for a Massacre   Fil-Ent '7?
Western
07785   86 mins   C
V2, B, V
Ed Byrnes, Louise Barrett
A bloodthirsty western adventure set on the Texan/Mexican border.
S,A — EN
Unknown — *Fletcher Video*   H, P
V160

Seven Year Itch, The   Fil-Ent '55
Comedy
01025   105 mins   C
B, V
Marilyn Monroe, Tom Ewell, Evelyn Keyes, Sonny Tufts, Robert Strauss, Oscar Homolka, directed by Billy Wilder
After a man sees his wife and son off to the country for the summer, he returns home to find that a lovely blonde has sublet the apartment above his.
F — EN
20th Century Fox; Charles K Feldman and Billy Wilder — *CBS/Fox Video*   P
3A-019

Seventh Veil, The   Fil-Ent '45
Drama
09374   94 mins   B/W
B, V
James Mason, Herbert Lom, Ann Todd, Hugh McDermott
This film tells the story of Francesca Cunningham, who is discovered struggling in the Thames in an attempt to drown herself. She is rescued and put in the charge of a psychiatrist. He uses hypnosis in order to discover the reason for her suicide attempt.
BBFC:A — C,A — EN
Theatrecraft; Sydney Box — *Precision Video Ltd*   P
BAPV 501/VAPV 501

Severed Arm, The   Fil-Ent '73
Drama
05475   85 mins   C
V2, B, V
Deborah Walley, Paul Carr, Marvin Kaplan, David Cannon, John Crawford, Vincent Martorano
The story of six amateur explorers who become trapped underground and are starving. Five of them cut off the arm of their companion for food just before they are rescued. They save themselves but the victim seeks revenge.
BBFC:A — S,A — EN
Unknown — *Iver Film Services*   P
95

Sew Into Fashion   How-Ins '??
Sewing
07402   90 mins   C
V2, B, V
Betty Foster

(For Explanation of codes, see USE GUIDE and KEY)

PALADIN VIDEO HOME ENTERTAINMENT GUIDE

On this tape Betty Foster shows how to follow a pattern and provides tips on sewing. The pattern demonstrated is available with the video cassette.
F — I
Unknown — Guild Home Video   H, P, E

Sewers of Paradise, The   Fil-Ent '??
Crime-Drama
07658   107 mins   C
B, V
Francis Huster, Lila Kedrova, Jean-Francois Balmer
A criminal used to danger and adventure grows depressed in his semi-retirement, but the arrival of an old gun-running friend soon alters that. They plan the crime of the century, enlisting the help of some of the top criminal elite. Their target is the biggest bank in Nice and they plan to tunnel through the sewers to get to the largest haul ever.
S,A — EN
Unknown — VCL Video Services   P
C213C

Sex Connection, The   Fil-Ent '69
Comedy
05516   82 mins   C
B, V
Joanna Jung, Alfred Bettner, directed by Werner Kunz
A story of three girls and two boys who pool all their money to buy an old bus to tour Europe. They soon run out of money and their troubles begin with an over zealous policeman, a hitch-hiker and a fake marriage guidance computer.
BBFC:X — A — EN
Unknown — Derann Film Services   H, P
DV132B/DV132

Sex Diary   Fil-Ent '7?
Drama
02118   75 mins   C
V2, B, V
Luca Reali's amourous escapades arouse envy in his friends but upset the pillars of the village community.
BBFC:X — A — EN
Unknown — Hokushin Audio Visual Ltd   P
VM-29

Sex Madness/Mondo Trasho   Fil-Ent '??
Exploitation/Drama
08981   180 mins   B/W
B, V
Divine, David Lochary, Mink Stole, Mary Vivian Pearce, directed by John Waters
'Sex Madness' (1937, 90 mins.) is a camp melodrama about the evils of lechery, lust and passion. 'Mondo Trasho' (1969, 90 mins.) is about a young fashion fanatic and her various exploits.
A — EN
New Line International et al — Palace Video Ltd   P
PVC 2016B

Sex with a Smile   Fil-Ent '76
Comedy
09213   112 mins   C
B, V
Marty Feldman, Barbara Bouchet, Tomas Milian, Edvice Finich, Giovanni Ralli, Enrico Monterrano, directed by Sergio Martino
This is a compilation of five slapstick episodes by five different directors using sexual satire pointed at religion and politics in Italy.
BBFC:X — A — EN
Surrogate — Video Form Pictures   H, P
CLO 1

Sex With the Stars   Fil-Ent '??
Drama
08629   87 mins   C
V2, B, V
Martin Burrows, Thick Wilson, Janey Love, Susie Sylvie
When a new publisher takes over a mild-mannered woman's magazine everyone is told to up-date it. Peter, who runs the astrological column has to change his entry. From then on it has to be called 'Sex With the Stars.' When he protests a lack of knowledge, he is told to go out and research it. His first article is given by the secretary.
A — EN
Unknown — Hokushin Audio Visual Ltd   P
VM 58

Sextette   Fil-Ent '78
Musical/Comedy
08874   91 mins   C
V2, B, V
Mae West, Timothy Dalton, Ringo Starr, George Hamilton, Dom De Luise, Tony Curtis, Alice Cooper, Keith Moon, George Raft
This is a lavish musical about an elderly star, who is constantly interrupted by former spouses and well-wishers while on a honeymoon with her sixth husband.
C,A — EN
Daniel Briggs; Robert Sullivan — Video Programme Distributors   P
Media 188

PALADIN VIDEO HOME ENTERTAINMENT GUIDE

Sexy Dozen, The   Fil-Ent '7?
Drama/Comedy
02413   90 mins   C
B, V

Barbro Hedstom, Vincent Gautier, directed by Norbert Terry

A mother sends her daughter off to finishing school in the Swiss Alps after discovering her making love on the drawing room carpet with her boy friend. However the boy friend is smuggled into school dressed up as a girl.
A — EN
Unknown — *Derann Film Services*   **H, P**
DV 114B/DV 114

Sez Les   Fil-Ent '8?
Comedy
06168   96 mins   C
B, V

Les Dawson, John Cleese

A compilation of the best of Les Dawson, the master of disaster, the mournful misogynist and don of doom who presents jokes and sketches with many guest stars including John Cleese.
S,A — EN
Mallet Prod — *Guild Home Video*   **H, P, E**

Shadow of Chikara, The   Fil-Ent '77
Western
08634   94 mins   C
V2, B, V

Slim Pickens, Sondra Locke, Joe-Don Baker

This film, set in the post Civil War era, tells of an ex-confederate army captain who leads a party in search of hidden treasure on the wild unexplored Buffalo River. However, they cross the path of the chilling Indian legend of Chikara and the mountain demons.
S,A — EN
Unknown — *Hokushin Audio Visual Ltd*
P
VM 53

Shadow of the Tiger   Fil-Ent '81
Martial arts/Drama
12850   93 mins   C
V2, B, V

Cliff Lok, Ka Sa Fa, Chio Chi Ling, Lam Man Wei, directed by Yeung Kuen

Nine of the world's top karate and kung-fu experts are featured in this film about a villainous fighter who usurps control of a Shaolin Kung-fu school.
BBFC:15 — S,A — EN
Unknown — *Video Programme Distributors*
P
202

Shaft   Fil-Ent '71
Crime-Drama
07726   96 mins   C
B, V

Richard Roundtree, Moses Gunn, directed by Gordon Parks

A black detective becomes caught up in an underworld struggle for power and ends up fighting for his life amongst the gangleaders who run rackets in New York's Harlem. The soundtrack features music by Isaac Hayes.
BBFC:X — A — EN
MGM — *MGM/UA Home Video*   **P**
UMB 10149/UMV 10149

Shake Out with Mad Lizzie   Spo-Lei '8?
Physical fitness/Dance
12527   30 mins   C
B, V

This programme demonstrates energetic warm-up routines and disco dance numbers.
F — EN
Unknown — *THORN EMI*   **P**
TXE 90 2194 4 / TVE 90 2194 2

Shakespeare Wallah   Fil-Ent '65
Romance
05682   115 mins   B/W
B, V

Felicity Kendall, Shashi Kapoor, Madhur Jaffrey, directed by James Ivory

An English troupe of Shakespearean actors are touring India and performing wherever they can struggle to keep going. The film tells the story of a sudden but brief romance between an English actress and an Indian playboy.
BBFC:A — S,A — EN
Merchant Ivory Production — *Home Video Holdings*   **H, P**
009

Shalako   Fil-Ent '68
Western/Adventure
05912   116 mins   C
V

Sean Connery, Brigitte Bardot, Stephen Boyd, Jack Hawkins, directed by Edward Dmytryk

Titled European aristocrats, on a hunting tour of the west, have a run in with the Apaches. Rugged loner goes for help and wins a fight with the Apache chief's son. Apaches leave and the aristocrats are saved.
F — EN
Cinerama Release; Palomar Pictures — *JVC*
P
PRT 1

(For Explanation of codes, see USE GUIDE and KEY)   **583**

PALADIN VIDEO HOME ENTERTAINMENT GUIDE

Shalimar
Fil-Ent '79
Crime-Drama
02126   85 mins   C
V2, B, V
Rex Harrison, Sylvia Miles, John Saxon
The story of wild desperados in an enthralling death-hunt for a fabulous gem.
S,A — EN
Judson Prods — Hokushin Audio Visual Ltd   P
VM-42

Shall We Dance
Fil-Ent '37
Musical
05042   116 mins   B/W
B, V
Fred Astaire, Ginger Rogers, Edward Everett Horton, Eric Blore
Set to Gershwin score, famous ballet dancer and performer pretend they are married. Then they make it come true.
F — EN
RKO; Pandro S. Berman — THORN EMI   P
TXC 90 0072 4/TVC 90 0072 2

Shame, Shame on the Bixby Boys
Fil-Ent '82
Comedy/Western
12828   86 mins   C
B, V
A loony gang of cattle rustlers hit town to avenge the shooting of their dad's best friend.
BBFC:PG — *S,A — EN*
Unknown — Video Tape Centre   P
1159

Shamwari
Fil-Ent '??
War-Drama
09387   99 mins   C
B, V
Ian Yule, Ken Gampu, Tamara Franke, directed by Clive Harding
Set in Rhodesia during the brutal war, this film tells the story of two convicts, who amidst the fighting manage to escape when their prison van is ambushed. One being white, one being black, there is hatred between them, but these must be forgotten in order to survive.
A — EN
Unknown — VCL Video Services   P
P310D

Shane
Fil-Ent '53
Western
05336   117 mins   C
B, V
Alan Ladd, Jean Arthur, Van Heflin, Jack Palance, directed by George Stevens
A drifter and retired gunfighter goes to the aid of a homestead family terrorised by an ageing cattleman and his hired gun. In fighting the last decisive battle he sees the end of his own way of life. Based on the novel by Jack Shaeffer.
Academy Awards '53: Best Cinematography—Colour.   *S,A — EN*
Paramount — CIC Video   H, P
BEA2013/VHA2013

Shaolin Iron Finger
Fil-Ent '7?
Adventure/Martial arts
05637   84 mins   C
V2, B, V
Huang Chiu Daa
A brilliant exponent of Kung-Fu crusades against evil Chinese Warlords. This film is dubbed.
S,A — EN
Unknown — Video Unlimited   H, P
013

Shaolin Master and the Kid
Fil-Ent '7?
Adventure/Martial arts
05636   87 mins   C
V2, B, V
Chen Sheng
Set in the early times of the Republic of China, Warlord Chang Hsun plots to bring power back to the former Emperor. By disguising as an Opera Troupe, they succeed in capturing arms and begin a successful history-making revolution. The film is dubbed.
S,A — EN
Unknown — Video Unlimited   H, P
014

Shape of Things to Come, The
Fil-Ent '79
Science fiction
06782   94 mins   C
V2, B, V
Jack Palance, Carol Lynley, Barry Morse, John Ireland
A space colony on the moon contains the only survivors of earth's civilisation after a nuclear holocaust. When an evil scientist tries to appoint himself as dictator, the moon colonists retaliate.
S,A — EN
Film Ventures Intl; CFI Investments — Intervision Video   H, P
A-AE 0365

Sharaz
Fil-Ent '??
Fantasy
09377   ? mins   C
B, V
Luciana Paluzzi, Jeff Cooper

PALADIN VIDEO HOME ENTERTAINMENT GUIDE

In this film all the adventures of Sinbad and the magic of the Arabian Knights are blended together. Omar, returning after a long voyage, finds that there has been a revolution and his kingdom is now ruled by the evil Hixem. Together with the help of Sharaz and his magic powers Omar plots to overthrow the evil tyrant.
F — EN
Unknown — *Precision Video Ltd*   **P**
BWPV 503/VWPV 503

Shark   Fil-Ent '68
Adventure
02449   88 mins   C
V2, B, V
Burt Reynolds, Barry Sullivan, Arthur Kennedy
Burt Reynolds stars in this action feature about gun runners and intrigue in Africa.
BBFC:AA — C,A — EN
Unknown — *Iver Film Services*   **P**

Shark Hunter, The   Fil-Ent '80
Drama/Adventure
07771   95 mins   C
V2, B, V
Franco Nero, Werner Pochat, Mike Forrest, Mirta Miler
This film follows a bid to rescue ten million dollars from plane wreckage deep in shark infested waters.
S,A — EN
Unknown — *Fletcher Video*   **H, P**
V153

Shark's Cave   Fil-Ent '78
Mystery
02105   83 mins   C
V2, B, V
Arthur Kennedy
A professional skin diver is taken from the sea, suffering from amnesia, six months after his ship and crew mysteriously disappeared in the strange and beautiful area known as the Bermuda Triangle. A sinister adventure with overtones of the occult.
C,A — EN
Italy — *Hokushin Audio Visual Ltd*   **P**
VM-11

Sharks' Treasure   Fil-Ent '74
Adventure
12600   92 mins   C
B, V
Cornel Wilde, Yaphet Kotto
Four men sail the Caribbean in search of a fortune in gold located in a sunken Spanish treasure fleet and dangerously encounter man-eating sharks before being captured by five desperate escaped convicts.
BBFC:A — A — EN
Cornel Wilde — *Warner Home Video*   **P**
99403

Sharky's Machine   Fil-Ent '81
Crime-Drama
13017   118 mins   C
B, V
Burt Reynolds, Rachel Ward, Brien Keith, directed by Burt Reynolds
In Atlanta, Georgia, a new king pin known as 'The Ace' has taken over the underworld of drugs, call-girls and political pay-offs, so Sharky organizes his crew of vice cops into a personal 'machine' to flushout 'The Ace.'
BBFC:X — A — EN
Orion; Warner Bros — *Warner Home Video*   **P**
72024

Shatter   Fil-Ent '76
Drama
08306   90 mins   C
B, V
Stuart Whitman, Peter Cushing
This film tells the story of an international killer, who is assigned to assassinate an East African President. In doing so he also kills the President's aide. He goes to Hong Kong to collect his fee where he is shot at. The bullet narrowly misses him. He finds that his own life is now threatened.
C,A — EN
AVCO Embassy — *Video Film Organisation*   **P**
0006

Shave and Face Massage, The   How-Ins '80
Beauty
02053   50 mins   C
B, V
Trevor R. B. Leddington
This programme is the second in the planned 'Hair Tek Barbershop' series.
C,A — I
Hair Tek Video — *VideoSpace Ltd*   **H, P**

Shazam   Fil-Ent '83
Cartoons/Adventure
12174   73 mins   C
B, V
Animated

(For Explanation of codes, see USE GUIDE and KEY)

PALADIN VIDEO HOME ENTERTAINMENT GUIDE

When Billy and his sister Mary say 'Shazam' they turn into Captain and Mary Marvel. With their friend Freddy, they make a team determined to fight villainy anywhere in the world.
F — EN
Filmation Associates — Select Video Limited **P**
3626/43

S*H*E   Fil-Ent '80
Crime-Drama/Adventure
07606   93 mins   C
V2, B, V
Omar Sharif, Cornelia Sharpe, Robert Lansing, William Traylor, Isabella Rye, Anita Ekberg, Fabio Testi, directed by Robert Lewis
A beautiful and sensuous woman is a Security Hazards expert out to do battle with an international crime organisation. The two men at the head of the organisation spend much of their time competing for her affections while plotting to sabotage the world's oil supply by demanding a huge annual ransom from the United Nations. With the help of the Italian Secret Service the net closes on the saboteurs.
BBFC:A — S,A — EN
Seven Arts-Hammer Prods — Iver Film Services   **P**
172

She Came to the Valley   Fil-Ent '??
Drama
08747   90 mins   C
B, V
Ronee Blakley, Dean Stockwell, Scott Glenn, Freddy Fender, directed by Albert Band
This tells the story of a woman who used her love as a weapon to change the course of history.
C,A — EN
Unknown — Precision Video Ltd   **P**
BITC 2578/VITC 2578

Sheena Easton Live at   Fil-Ent '82
the Palace
Music-Performance
08570   60 mins   C
B, V
Sheena Easton
This tape features Sheena Easton Live at 'The Palace' in Hollywood, and includes some of her songs, such as 'Nine to Five,' 'Modern Girl,' 'Raised on Robbery,' 'For Your Eyes Only,' 'Prisoner,' and tracks from her latest album 'Madness, Money and Music.'
F — EN
EMI Records Ltd — THORN EMI   **P**
TXE 90 1273 4/TVE 90 1273 2

She'll Follow You   Fil-Ent '7?
Anywhere
Comedy
04327   98 mins   C
V2, B, V
Two perfumers discover a scent that drives women wild.
A — EN
Unknown — Intervision Video   **H, P**
A-A 0096

Shenandoah   Fil-Ent '65
War-Drama/Western
13338   100 mins   C
B, V
James Stewart, Doug McClure, George Kennedy, Phillip Alford, Eugene Jackson Jr, directed by Andrew V. McLaglen
This film depicts the dilemma of a man opposed to war but is forced to take sides when he goes to search for his soldier son when he is taken prisoner.
BBFC:U — F — EN
Robert Arthur — CIC Video   **H, P**
BEN 1106/VHN 1106

Sheriff and the Satellite   Fil-Ent '8?
Kid, The
Drama/Comedy
13729   90 mins   C
V2, B, V
Bud Spencer, Cary Guffey, Joe Bugner, Raimund Harmstorf
A sheriff has to deal with a visitor from outer space, the town hooligan and a small boy who says his name is 'H7-25'.
BBFC:PG — F — EN
Elio Scardamaglia — Medusa Communications Ltd   **H, P**
MC 029

Sherlock Holmes and the   Fil-Ent '8?
Baskerville Curse
Cartoons
12553   67 mins   C
V2, B, V
Animated
In this adaptation of one of Conan-Doyle's classic stories, the detective and his companion Dr. Watson investigate their most famous and dangerous mystery.
F — EN
Unknown — RPTA Video Ltd   **H, P**

Sherlock Holmes and the   Fil-Ent '45
Woman in Green
Crime-Drama
07637   66 mins   B/W
B, V

PALADIN VIDEO HOME ENTERTAINMENT GUIDE

Basil Rathbone, Nigel Bruce, Hillary Brooke, Henry Danell, Paul Cavendish, Mathew Boulton, Eve Amber, Mary Gordon, directed by Roy William Neill

When a series of bizarre murders take place, Holmes and Watson are called in to assist the baffled police. The victims are all attractive women found with their right forefinger missing. Rich people are also being hypnotised into believing that they have committed the murders. Holmes discovers that the man behind the plot is his deadly adversary—Moriarty.

F — EN

United International — *VCL Video Services* **P**

0235G

Sherlock Holmes Double Feature   Fil-Ent '??
Mystery
05298   147 mins   B/W
B, V

Basil Rathbone, Ida Lupino, Nigel Bruce, Evelyn Anker, Thomas Gomez, directed by Alfred Werker

This cassette features two films: 'Adventures of Sherlock Holmes' (82 mins, 1939) where Holmes is called in on a case when a plot to steal the Crown Jewels is covered up by an attempted murder of a young lady; 'Voice of Terror' (65 mins, 1942) where Holmes steps in after saboteurs carry out their threats of destruction via radio. Based on Sir Arthur Conan Doyle's story 'His Last Bow.'

F — EN

20th Century Fox; Universal International; Howard Benedict — *MGM/UA Home Video* **P**

UCB10046/UCV10046

Shillingbury Blowers, The   Fil-Ent '79
Comedy
07365   ? mins   C
B, V

Trevor Howard, Robin Nedwell

Two men combine to bring total catastrophe to a quaint old English village.

S,A — EN

Unknown — *Precision Video Ltd* **P**

BITC 2110/VITC 2110

Shinbone Alley   Fil-Ent '70
Cartoons/Musical
06248   76 mins   C
B, V

Animated, voices by Carol Channing and Eddie Bracken, directed by John D Wilson

This film, an animated musical is based on the 'Archy and Mehitabel' stories by Don Marquis. It features a cockroach and an alley cat who get together to form a song writing team.

F — EN

Fine Art Films — *VCL Video Services* **P**

F208C

Shining, The   Fil-Ent '80
Horror
07869   143 mins   C
B, V

Jack Nicholson, Shelley Duvall, Danny Lloyd

A caretaker of a hotel soon realises that the building has its own guardians who had been there a long time. A discovery with horrific consequences. Based on the novel by Stephen King.

BBFC:X — A — EN

Warner Bros; The Producer Circle Company — *Warner Home Video* **P**

WEX 61079/WEV 61079

Shivers   Fil-Ent '75
Science fiction
06763   85 mins   C
V2, B, V

Paul Hampton, Lyn Lowry, Alan Migicovsky, Susan Petrie, Barbara Steele

A giant parasite spreads through an apartment complex, causing violent sexual behaviour in its victims.

A — EN

Dal Productions — *Intervision Video* **H, P**

A-A 0326

Shock   Fil-Ent '79
Horror
02581   87 mins   C
V2, B, V

Directed by Mario Bava

A young woman is driven to the edge of insanity as she tries to reconstruct her past. Hidden meanings are contained in her bizarre and violent dreams.

BBFC:X — A — EN

Titanus — *Videomedia* **P**

Shock Corridor   Fil-Ent '63
Drama/Suspense
05721   95 mins   B/W
V2, B, V

Peter Breck, Constance Towers, Gene Evans, James Best

(For Explanation of codes, see USE GUIDE and KEY)

PALADIN VIDEO HOME ENTERTAINMENT GUIDE

A reporter feigns madness to get himself committed to a mental hospital to find out the truth and write about an unsolved murder. He endures beatings and shock to end up as a schizophrenic Pulitzer Prize winner. The film is black and white with colour sequences.
BBFC:X — A — EN
Allied Artists; Samuel Fuller — *Video Unlimited*
H, P
008

Shock Treatment
Horror
08803   86 mins   C
B, V
Annie Girardot, Alain Delon, Robert Hirsch, directed by Alain Belmondo
This film tells of disappearing people and bodies drained of blood. After recovering in a sanitarium a woman decides to investigate the mystery.
A — EN
Unknown — *VCL Video Services*   **P**
P268D

Fil-Ent '72

Shock Waves
Drama/Mystery
07395   90 mins   C
V2, B, V
Peter Cushing, Brooke Adams, Fred Buch, Jack Davidson, Luke Halpin, D. J. Sidney, Don Stout, John Carradine, directed by Ken Weiderhorn
A group of tourists, cruising in the Caribbean are forced to land on a remote island whose only occupant is a former SS Officer living in the abandoned hotel. He carries the grim secret that beneath the water lies a ship with a sinister cargo of experimental, mutant soldiers that are neither dead or alive.
BBFC:AA — S,A — EN
Joseph Brenner — *Guild Home Video*   **H, P, E**

Fil-Ent '77

Shoestring
Crime-Drama
10143   105 mins   C
V2, B, V
Trevor Eve
Private investigator Eddie Shoestring deals with a dead prostitute, a missing beauty queen and a crazed punk guitarist.
S,A — EN
BBC — *BBC Video*   **H, P**
BBCV 2009

Fil-Ent '8?

Shoot
Drama
06956   90 mins   C
B, V
Cliff Robertson, Ernest Borgnine, James Blendick, Larry Reynolds, Gloria Shetwynd, Henry Silva
Five combat veterans who set out for a weekend's deer hunting find themselves in a senseless and violent confrontation with another party of hunters; one of them is wounded and another killed. Instead of reporting to the police the two groups decide to have another final confrontation and return to the scene to fight it out.
S,A — EN
Avco Embassy — *Home Video Merchandisers*
H, P
025

Fil-Ent '76

Shoot the Sun Down
Western
07672   90 mins   C
B, V
Margot Kidder, Geoffrey Lewis, Bo Brundin, A. Martinez, Christopher Walken, directed by David Leeds
Set in 1836 in Santa Fe, this film follows the fortunes of four unusual characters thrown together by gold lust, adventure and circumstance: a samurai-like loner, a vicious scalphunter, a retired sea captain with a treasure map and a beautiful girl apprentice.
A — EN
Baytide Films — *Video Network*   **P**
0015

Fil-Ent '80

Short Back and Sides, The
Beauty
02054   50 mins   C
B, V
Trevor R. B. Leddington
This programme is the first in the planned 'Hair Tek Barbershop' series.
C,A — I
Hair Tek Video — *VideoSpace Ltd*   **H, P**

How-Ins '80

Short-Eared Owl
Birds
09102   26 mins   C
B, V
Narrated by Andrew Sachs
This programme studies the life and habits of Britain's only daylight hunting owl, whose breeding success depends much on the short-tailed vole population.
F — ED
Royal Society for the Protection of Birds — *Royal Society for the Protection of Birds*   **H, P**

Gen-Edu '8?

---

588   (For Explanation of codes, see USE GUIDE and KEY)

PALADIN VIDEO HOME ENTERTAINMENT GUIDE

Short Films 1 — Fil-Ent '7?
Documentary/Biographical
05676   110 mins   C
B, V

Directed by James Ivory

Three films are contained on one cassette. 'Helen Queen of the Natch Girls' (1973, 30 mins, Black/white) is a documentary about Helen the busiest star of the Great Indian Dream Machine, she has starred in over 500 films since 1957. 'Mahatma and the Mad Boy' (1974, 26 mins, Colour) is a portrait of Indian life, showing the diverse social structure and offering a message based on Gandhi's teachings. 'Adventures of a Brown Man in Search of Civilization' (1971, 54 mins. Colour) is a film profile of the author Nirad Chaudhuri, a critic of Hindu life, who was largely self-taught.
S,A — EN

Merchant Ivory Productions — *Home Video Holdings*   **H, P**
021

Short Films 2 — Fil-Ent '??
Documentary
05677   92 mins   C
B, V

Directed by James Ivory

Three films are contained on one cassette. 'The Delhi Way' (1964, 40 mins, Colour) looks at the streets of Delhi, both past and present and exposes the richly varied life that can be seen there. 'The Sword and the Flute' (1959, 24 mins, Colour) looks at the world of miniature painting. 'Sweet Sounds' (1977, 28 mins, Colour) looks at ten five year old children in a pre-school class at New York's Mannes College of Music Preparatory School and explores the good teacher-student relationship they enjoy.
S,A — EN

Merchant Ivory Productions — *Home Video Holdings*   **H, P**
033

Shout, The — Fil-Ent '78
Drama
04244   83 mins   C
B, V

Alan Bates, Tim Curry, Robert Stephens, John Hurt, Susannah York, Julian Hough

Alan Bates delivers a superb and disturbing performance as Crossley, the asylum inmate whose claims to ancient aboriginal powers include the ability to kill with a shout and to possess the souls of others.
Cannes Jury Prize '78.
BBFC:A — C,A — EN
Rank — *Rank Video Library*   **H, P**
0014

Shout at the Devil — Fil-Ent '76
War-Drama
05565   108 mins   C
V2, B, V

Lee Marvin, Roger Moore, Barbara Parkins, Ian Holm, directed by Peter Hunt

A story based on an actual World War I incident involving the destruction of a German battleship on a river in Africa in 1913. Based on the book by Wilbur Smith.
BBFC:A — S,A — EN
American Intl; Michael Klingers Production of a Peter Hunt Film — *Videomedia*   **P**
PVM 7101/BVM 7101/HVM 7101

Showbiz — Fil-Ent '8?
Drama/Television
09832   90 mins   C
V2, B, V

This is the second annual television guide featuring the best from a year's television. Clips include 'Dallas,' 'Soap,' 'Mash' and 'Lou Grant.' It also includes the five alternatives to 'Who Shot JR'.
F — EN
Unknown — *Polygram Video*   **H, P**
791 5414/791 5412

Showboat — Fil-Ent '58
Musical
10171   104 mins   C
B, V, LV

Ava Gardner, Howard Keel, Kathryn Grayson

The story of the lives of a group of people who find themselves thrown together on a riverboat cruising down the Mississippi in the early 1900s. The songs include 'Can't Help Lovin' That Man', 'Make Believe', 'You Are Love' and 'Ol Man River'.
BBFC:U — F — EN
MGM — *MGM/UA Home Video*   **P**
UMB 10167/UMV 10167/UMLV 10167

Shriek of the Mutilated — Fil-Ent '74
Horror
07618   81 mins   C
V2, B, V

Alan Brock, Michael Harris, Jennifer Stock, directed by Michael Findlay

Four college students set out to capture a live Yeti. They head for an island where the creature has been spotted. On the first night, one of the students is clawed to death. Their search sends them on the road to mystery, bloodshed and death.
BBFC:X — A — EN
American Films Ltd — *Iver Film Services*
P

PALADIN VIDEO HOME ENTERTAINMENT GUIDE

Shrubs, Trees and Hedges with Percy Thrower
How-Ins '8?
Gardening
08608   59 mins   C
V2, B, V

Percy Thrower

This tape shows how to make a garden colorful and interesting, yet needing the minimum amount of maintenance. This means permanent planting with trees, shrubs, roses and hardy border plants with ground cover plants to prevent weeds from growing.
S,A — I
Midland Video Services Ltd — *Hokushin Audio Visual Ltd*   P
G 106

Sicilian Connection
Fil-Ent '74
Crime-Drama
10202   98 mins   C
B, V

Ben Gazzara, Silvia Monti

An undercover agent is instructed to take on the world's most ruthless underworld organization to break-up their heroin operation in Sicily.
S,A — EN
P.A.C.; Atlas (Rome); Byre (Paris) — *Video Form Pictures*   H, P
MGD 13

Sicilian Cross
Fil-Ent '76
Crime-Drama
06870   100 mins   C
V2, B, V

Roger Moore, Stacy Keach

The Mafia are outraged when their priceless gift of a beautiful Sicilian Cross to the fishermen of San Francisco is used to smuggle in a million dollars worth of heroin. They decide the culprit must die. A Mafia lawyer and his partner are engaged to track down and execute those involved.
S,A — EN
American International — *European Video Company*   P

Side Kicks The Movie
Fil-Ent '83
Music-Performance
09813   60 mins   C
B, V

Directed by Derek Burbridge

This tape recorded live at Liverpool Royal Court features the Thompson Twins in concert. Songs include 'Kamikaze', 'Love Lies Bleeding', 'Judy Do', 'Tears', 'Watching', 'If You Were Here', 'All Fall Out', 'Lucky Day', 'Lies', 'Detectives', 'In the Name of Love', 'Beach Culture' and 'Love on Your Side'.
F — EN
EMI Records Limited — *THORN EMI*   P
TXE 90 1955 4/TVE 90 1955 2

Siege
Fil-Ent '76
Drama/Horror
12530   80 mins   C
B, V

Tom Nardini, Brenda Bazinet, Darel Haeny, Jeff Pustil, directed by Paul Donovan and Maura O'Connell

This is the story of the massacre, by a self appointed vigilante group, of all but one of the clientele of a gay bar. A hunt for the lone survivor follows.
BBFC:18 — A — EN
Unknown — *THORN EMI*   P
TXA 90 1995 4; TVA 90 1995 2

Sign of Four, The
Fil-Ent '83
Mystery/Adventure
13223   100 mins   C
V2, B, V

Ian Richardson, David Healy, directed by Desmond Davies

When a beautiful woman receives a strange letter and the second largest diamond in the world, Holmes and Watson are called in to investigate.
BBFC:PG — S,A — EN
Mapleton Films — *Embassy Home Entertainment*   P
1865

Silence est D'Or, Le
Fil-Ent '??
Comedy-Drama
09809   87 mins   B/W
B, V

Maurice Chevalier, Francais Perier, Marcelle Derrier

A middle-aged movie director falls in love with an innocent young girl. A French comedy classic, with English sub-titles.
BBFC:PG — S,A — EN   FR
Pathe Cinema — *THORN EMI*   P
TXE 90 0829 4/TVE 90 0829 2

Silence in the North
Fil-Ent '81
Adventure
12049   90 mins   C
B, V

Tom Skerritt, Ellen Burstyn, directed by Allan Winton King

PALADIN VIDEO HOME ENTERTAINMENT GUIDE

Set in rural Canada after the First World War, this is based on true life memoirs and tells the story of a young woman and her fight against hardship and the bitter elements of the North.
BBFC:PG — S,A — EN
Universal — CIC Video **H, P**
BEA 1081/VHA 1081

Silence the Witness — Fil-Ent '74
Drama
06121 100 mins C
V2, B, V
Bekim Fehmiu, Rosanna Schiaffino, Aldo Guiffre
When a doctor witnesses a fatal car accident he goes for help and returns with the police to find the car, but the injured man and the corpse have disappeared. In an attempt to disclose the mystery he is plagued by numerous humiliations and obscure threats.
S,A — EN
Unknown — Video Programme Distributors **P**
Cinehollywood—V140

Silent Clowns: Big Moments from Little Pictures — Fil-Ent '23
Comedy
04691 77 mins B/W
B, V
Will Rogers, Harold Lloyd, Charlie Chaplin, Buster Keaton
Four classic comedies are contained on this cassette in their original versions: 'Big Moments from Little Pictures,' 'Haunted Spooks,' 'The Rink,' and 'The Blacksmith.'
F — EN
Spectrum — Polygram Video **P**

Silent Clowns: Saturday Afternoon — Fil-Ent '??
Comedy
04690 80 mins B/W
B, V
Harry Langdon, Charlie Chaplin, Roscoe Arbuckle, Al St John, Buster Keaton
Four classic comedies, produced between 1914 and 1920, are shown here in their original versions: 'Saturday Afternoon,' 'The Cure,' 'The Waiter's Ball,' and 'One Week.'
F — EN
Spectrum — Polygram Video **P**

Silent Movie, The — Fil-Ent '76
Comedy
13246 83 mins C
B, V
Mel Brooks, Paul Newman, James Caan, Burt Reynolds, Liza Minelli, Anne Bancroft, directed by Mel Brooks
A contemporary director decides to make a silent movie as he feels this will stop his company from being taken over by a conglomerate. Silent with music score.
BBFC:PG — S,A — EN
Michael Hertzberg; 20th Century
Fox — CBS/Fox Video **P**
1437

Silent Night — Fil-Ent '??
Cartoons/Christmas
05751 30 mins C
B, V
Animated
This film tells how 'Silent Night' came to be written in Oberndorf, Germany in the late 19th century. As Christmas approaches, the village organist seeks a replacement part for the church organ which cannot be repaired. Deep snow closes all passes and the organist is forced to improvise; the result is the haunting melody of the Boy's Choir.
BBFC:U — F — EN
ZIV International; Family Home Entertainment — Home Video Holdings **H, P**
031

Silent Night Bloody Night — Fil-Ent '72
Horror
04551 84 mins C
V2, B, V
Patrick O'Neal, James Paterson, John Carradine
Townspeople attempt to buy an old mansion belonging to a family in which incest and insanity abound.
C,A — EN
Cannon Releasing; Ami Artzi — Intervision Video **H, P**
A-A 0006

Silent Partner, The — Fil-Ent '78
Drama
01994 105 mins C
B, V
Elliot Gould, Susannah York, Christopher Plummer
A dull Toronto bank teller is interested only in his tropical fish and lovely co-worker. When a man dressed in a Santa Claus suit robs the bank, a battle of wits is staged between the teller and the bandit.
S,A — EN
EMC Film Corp — Quadrant Video **H, P**
FF 3

(For Explanation of codes, see USE GUIDE and KEY)

PALADIN VIDEO HOME ENTERTAINMENT GUIDE

Silent Running Fil-Ent '72
Science fiction
10127   86 mins   C
B, V
Bruce Dern, directed by Douglas Trumbull
A botanist is detailed to care for the last existing samples of vegetation which once grew on Earth, aided in his horticulture by two robots. When the order comes to abandon the project he rebels and pilots his freighter away to Saturn.
BBFC:U — F — EN
Universal — CIC Video   **H, P**
BEL 1069/VHL 1069

Silent Wilderness Fil-Ent '76
Adventure/Documentary
06243   90 mins   C
B, V
An exploration of the wilderness of Alaska featuring the awesome landscape and fascinating creatures that inhabit these northern wastes. Dr Roger Latham acts as a guide.
F — EN
Ted Leverfech — VCL Video Services   **P**
F039

Silk Stockings Fil-Ent '57
Musical/Satire
10175   116 mins   C
B, V
Cyd Charisse, Fred Astaire, Janis Paige, Peter Lorre
A serious young Russian girl arrives in Paris to persuade Russia's most famous composer to return home. However the attentions of a young film producer distract her from her mission. Featuring songs from Cole Porter including 'Parris Loves Lovers' and 'Silk Stockings'.
BBFC:U — F — EN
MGM — MGM/UA Home Video   **P**
UMB 10051/UMV 10051

Silkwood Fil-Ent '83
Drama
13465   128 mins   C
B, V
Meryl Streep, Kurt Russell, Cher, directed by Mike Nichols
This film is based on the true-life story of Karen Silkwood, a plutonium plant worker, who died in her car one night on her way to give evidence to a journalist about the irresponsible handling of radioactive material at the plant.
BBFC:15 — S,A — EN
ABC Circle Films — Rank Video Library
H, P

Silver Bears, The Fil-Ent '77
Comedy/Suspense
07484   109 mins   C
B, V
Michael Caine, Cybill Shepherd, Louis Jourdan, Stephane Audran, David Warner, Tom Smothers, Martin Balsam, directed by Ivan Passer
Filmed on location in Switzerland and Morocco, the complex plot of this comedy-thriller centres around a Swiss bank where the dealings and double-dealings involve the Mafia and large amounts of silver. Adapted from the novel by one-time president of a Swiss bank, Paul Erdman.
S,A — EN
Raleigh Film Production Ltd — THORN EMI
P
TXB 90 0318 4/TVB 90 0318 2

Silver Dream Racer Fil-Ent '80
Drama/Motorcycles
05252   109 mins   C
B, V, LV
David Essex, Cristina Raines, Beau Bridges
A tale of ambition, love, jealousy, defeat and victory set against the danger and the din of bike racing at Donnington, Brands Hatch and Silverstone.
BBFC:AA — C,A — EN
Unknown — Rank Video Library   **H, P**
0052

Silver Streak Fil-Ent '77
Comedy-Drama
05647   108 mins   C
V2, B, V, LV
Gene Wilder, Jill Clayburgh, Richard Pryor, Patrick McGoohan, Ned Beatty, Scatman Crothers, directed by Arthur Hillier
A young man boards a train in Los Angeles bound for Chicago; aboard he gets involved in art forgery, a young sexy blonde and gets repeatedly thrown off the train. As bullets fly disaster awaits at the end of the line.
S,A — EN
Twentieth Century Fox — CBS/Fox Video
P
3A-091

Simba Fil-Ent '55
Drama
08047   94 mins   C
B, V
Dirk Bogarde, Donald Sinden, Virginia McKenna, Orlando Martins, Basil Sydney, Marie Ney, directed by Brian Desmond Hurst

592 (For Explanation of codes, see USE GUIDE and KEY)

PALADIN VIDEO HOME ENTERTAINMENT GUIDE

A man arrives in Kenya to work on his brother's ranch, to be met with the news of his murder by the Mau Mau. The film goes on to show him staying with his loved one and trying to achieve peace between the people.
BBFC:A — S,A — EN
Rank — *Rank Video Library*   H, P
0121C

Simon   Fil-Ent '80
Comedy
13205   100 mins   C
B, V
Alan Arkin, Madeline Kahn, directed by Marshall Brickman
A university professor is selected by the Institute of Advanced Concepts as the subject of their ultimate project, which involves him becoming an extra-terrestrial being.
BBFC:A — C,A — EN
Orion Pictures — *Warner Home Video*   P
72007

Simon Bolivar   Fil-Ent '??
Drama
09953   90 mins   C
V2, B, V
Maximilian Schell, Francisco Rabal, Rosanna Schiaffino
Set in Venezuela, 1817, this film tells the story of Simon Bolivar who unites various groups of revolutionaries under his command and in a series of fierce battles defeats the Spanish army. He rides into Caracas to proclaim his country's freedom.
BBFC:A — S,A — EN
Unknown — *Video Unlimited*   H, P, E
085

Simon, King of Witches   Fil-Ent '??
Horror
05467   84 mins   C
V2, B, V
Andrew Prine, Brenda Scott, directed by Bruce Kessler
A warlock wants to become a God; he can tell fortunes, make your dreams come true, lay curses and kill. With the aid of a magic mirror energised by his body, he attempts with the aid of a young lady to achieve his dream but loses his body in a fantasy. A yound man has to enter the mirror at the right time to release the warlock so he can rule all spirits.
BBFC:X — A — EN
Unknown — *Iver Film Services*   P
112

Simon Simon   Fil-Ent '??
Comedy
04207   30 mins   C
B, V
Graham Stark, Norman Rossington, Julia Faster, John Junkin
A series of comic mime situations involving two Council workers.
BBFC:U — F — EN
Unknown — *Guild Home Video*   H, P

Simple Multicellular Animals: Sponges, Coelenterates and Flatworms   Med-Sci '85
Biology
13558   20 mins   C
V2, B, V
This film provides the O-level biology student with a clear illustration of the structure and behavior of, and the difference between two-layered (diploblastic) and three-layered (triploblastic) animals.
— C, A — I
Boulton Hawker Films Ltd — *Boulton Hawker Films Ltd*   P

Sin   Fil-Ent '7?
Drama
01677   93 mins   C
V2, B, V
Raquel Welch, Richard Johnson, Dame Flora Robson, Jack Hawkins
The traditions, taboos, and beliefs of the inhabitants of a Mediterranean island combine together to cause the destruction of the secret yet forbidden love of a man and a woman.
BBFC:X — A — EN
Unknown — *Intervision Video*   H, P
A-A 0062

Sinatra   Fil-Ent '??
Music-Performance
06302   97 mins   C
V2, B, V
Frank Sinatra
This film features Sinatra singing some of his greatest hits from the 40's, 50's and 60's. Includes 'Too marvellous for Words,' 'Them there Eyes,' 'Get Happy,' 'All of Me,' 'My Kind of Town,' 'Without a Song.'
F — EN
Unknown — *World of Video 2000*   H, P
SP2

Sinbad the Sailor/The Adventurer/An Apple in His Eye/Pal Fugitive Dog   Fil-Ent '??
Adventure/Comedy
09114   168 mins   C
B, V

(For Explanation of codes, see USE GUIDE and KEY)   593

PALADIN VIDEO HOME ENTERTAINMENT GUIDE

Douglas Fairbanks Jr., Maureen O'Hara, Anthony Quinn, Walter Slezak; Charlie Chaplin; Edgar Kennedy

This tape contains four films on one cassette. 'Sinbad the Sailor' (1947, colour, 112 mins.) tells of the adventures of Sinbad and his motley crew who sail to an island of gold, closely pursued by the greedy King of Baghdad. 'The Adventurer' (1917, Black and White, 24 mins.) features Charlie Chaplin as an escaped convict. He is invited as a house guest by two women who believe he is a gallant sportsman. 'An Apple in His Eye' (Black and White, 14 mins.) is a slapstick comedy. 'Pal Fugitive Dog' (Black and White, 18 mins.) features 'Flame' the dog.

F — EN

RKO; Mutual; et al — *Kingston Video*   **H, P**

KV 61

Since You Went Away   Fil-Ent '44
Drama
04208   172 mins   B/W
B, V

Claudette Colbert, Jennifer Jones, Joseph Cotten, Shirley Temple, Monty Wooley, Lionel Barrymore

Romance, pathos, and drama in the lives of a typical American family during World War II.

Academy Awards '44: Best Scoring, Drama (Max Steiner).   BBFC:U — *F — EN*

Selznick — *Guild Home Video*   **H, P**

Sinclair ZX Spectrum Introduction to Programming—Level I   Bus-Ind '84
Electronic data processing
13106   30 mins   C
B, V

David Redclift

The viewer is introduced to basic programming and it is shown how data entered at the keyboard can be translated into text and graphics on the screen.

C,A — I

Holiday Brothers Ltd. — *Holiday Brothers Ltd*   **P**

Sinclair ZX Spectrum Introduction to Programming—Level 2   Bus-Ind '84
Electronic data processing
13107   30 mins   C
B, V

David Redclift

In the second part of this series, the viewer is introduced to the more advanced aspects of programming including Array Handling, String Slicing and Animation.

C,A — I

Holiday Brothers Ltd — *Holiday Brothers Ltd*   **P**

Singalongamax; The Video   Fil-Ent '84
Music video
13352   55 mins   C
B, V

Max Bygraves

Max Bygraves sings twenty songs on this cassette including 'Write Myself a Letter,' 'Underneath the Arches,' 'It Had to be You' and a Beatles Medley.

F — EN

Unknown — *Guild Home Video*   **H, P, E**

Singer Not the Song, The   Fil-Ent '61
Drama
09925   133 mins   C
B, V

Dirk Bogarde, John Mills, Mylene Demongeot, Laurence Naismith

This film tells of the conflict between churchman and bandits in an isolated Mexican town. The love of a local girl for the priest creates a moral dilemma.

C,A — EN

Rank; Roy Baker — *Rank Video Library*
H, P

Singin' in the Rain   Fil-Ent '52
Musical
10178   102 mins   C
B, V

Gene Kelly, Donald O'Connor, Debbie Rynolds, Jean Hagen

Two friends arrive in Hollywood in the 1920s to make their way in show business. They make the transition from silent movies to sound and start their rise to fame. Many song and dance routines including 'You Were Meant for Me' and 'Singin' in the Rain'.

BBFC:U — *F — EN*

MGM — *MGM/UA Home Video*   **P**

UMB 10185/UMV 10185

Single Room Furnished   Fil-Ent '67
Drama
06018   85 mins   C
B, V

Jayne Mansfield, Dorothy Keller

594   (For Explanation of codes, see USE GUIDE and KEY)

PALADIN VIDEO HOME ENTERTAINMENT GUIDE

The story of three stages in the life of a prostitute, featuring Jayne Mansfield in her last film.
S,A — EN
Michael Musto — *VCL Video Services* **P**

Sins of Dorian Gray, The   Fil-Ent '80
Drama
09842   91 mins   C
B, V
Belinda Bauer, Anthony Perkins, Joseph Bottoms
This is an updated version of the famous Oscar Wilde novel, where Dorian Gray is a beautiful and fiercely ambitious photographic model whose secret is held in the frames of a film where her image receives the punishment for her sins.
S,A — EN
Arthur Rankin Jr., Jules Bass — *Polygram Video*   **H, P**
040 1624/040 1622

Siouxsie and the Banshees-Nocturne (Live)   Fil-Ent '??
Music-Performance
09880   60 mins   C
B, V
This is a live show by the band, at the Royal Albert Hall. It contains 12 tracks including such hits as 'Israel', 'Spellbound', 'Helter Skelter' and 'Voodoo Dolly'. Recorded in stereo.
F — EN
Unknown — *Polygram Video*   **H, P**
040 1914/040 1912

Siouxsie and the Banshees-Once Upon a Time   Fil-Ent '??
Music-Performance
09836   30 mins   C
B, V
Siouxsie and the Banshees present the very best of their single successes. It features such tracks as 'Hong Kong Garden', Playground Twist' and 'Happy House'.
F — EN
Unknown — *Polygram Video*   **H, P**
791 5064/791 5062

Sir Prancelot   Chi-Juv '8?
Cartoons
12560   94 mins   C
V2, B, V
Animated
The heroic Sir Prancelot, inventor extraordinary, sets forth on a Crusade to the Holy Land, supported by his motley household and harrassed by his vast wife Lady Hysteria.
PS,I — EN
Unknown — *RPTA Video Ltd*   **H, P**

Sisters   Fil-Ent '73
Horror/Suspense
09841   90 mins   C
B, V, LV
Margot Kidder, Jennifer Salt, Charles Durning
This film tells the story of Siamese twins, separated at birth, one of whom is gentle and the other a homicidal maniac. The wrong one is arrested after numerous complications.
A — EN
American International Pictures — *Polygram Video*   **H, P**
790 5904/790 5902

Sisters of Death   Fil-Ent '77
Horror
06796   87 mins   C
V2, B, V
Arthur Franz, Claudia Jennings, Cherie Howell, Sherry Boucher
Five former members of a high school sorority are invited to a reunion years later. When they arrive, terror and death begin.
C,A — EN
John B Kelly — *Intervision Video*   **H, P**
A-AE 0320

Six Directions Boxing, The   Fil-Ent '7?
Martial arts
09824   90 mins   C
B, V
A police superintendent finally succeeds in capturing an arms smuggler, using everything at his disposal including his super-intelligent dog and monkey.
S,A — EN
Unknown — *Polygram Video*   **H, P**
790 4524/790 4522

Six Pack   Fil-Ent '82
Adventure/Comedy
12206   108 mins   C
V2, B, V
Kenny Rogers, Diane Lane, Erin Gray, directed by Daniel Petrie

---

(For Explanation of codes, see USE GUIDE and KEY)

PALADIN VIDEO HOME ENTERTAINMENT GUIDE

A stock car racer makes a comeback to the circuit with the help of six personable youths with criminal tendencies as his pit crew.
S,A — EN
Kenny Loggins Productions — *CBS/Fox Video*   **P**
1183

---

16 Candles   Fil-Ent '84
Comedy
13632   93 mins   C
B, V
Molly Ringwald, Paul Dooley, Justin Henry, directed by John Hughes
A sixteen-year-old girl does not quite get the birthday she expected when no one remembers and she has to put up with a lot of embarrassing incidents.
BBFC:15 — F — EN
Hilton Green — *CIC Video*   **H, P**
1141

---

67 Days   Fil-Ent '??
War-Drama
08812   114 mins   C
B, V
Set in the year 1941 this film tells of the German victory over Yugoslavia. Once the army had surrendered the victory was only a formality. However the Partisans of the 'Uzice Republic' heroically resisted for sixty-seven days. It tells of the terrifying struggles and human conflict against the vastly superior German forces.
BBFC:AA — C,A — EN
Unknown — *VCL Video Services*   **P**
M317D

Skag   Fil-Ent '79
Drama
09840   120 mins   C
B, V
Karl Malden, Piper Laurie, Craig Wasson, George Voskovec, Kathryn Holcomb, Peter Gallagher, directed by Frank Perry
This is a family melodrama concerning the inner turmoils experienced by Skag, a hard working labourer, when he finds himself hospitalised with time on his hands to contemplate his own mortality.
S,A — EN
Abby Mann Prod; Lorimar Prods — *Polygram Video*   **H, P**
040 1584/040 1582

Skeezer   Fil-Ent '82
Drama
08771   91 mins   C
B, V
Karen Valentine, Leighton Greer, Tom Atkins
A caseworker in a hospital for emotionally disturbed children acquires a loveable mongrel puppy called Skeezer. After Skeezer nearly destroys her home when left alone for the day, she takes him into work. The children adore the pet, but the Director of the Institute feels that he will upset the children. However, this does not deter her, and the 'experiment' is far from over.
S,A — EN
ITC — *Precision Video Ltd*   **P**
BITC 2075/VITC 2075

Sketches of a Strangler   Fil-Ent '??
Crime-Drama/Suspense
07819   90 mins   C
V2, B, V
Allen Goorwitz, Meredith MacRae, Frank Whiteman, Jennifer Rhodes, Clayton Wilcox, Marlene Tracy, Tanya George, Michael Andres, Bea Busch, directed by Paul Leder
A disturbed art student uses his desire to paint women as a guise to get them alone. The women, prostitutes and dancers, become his victims. After an unsolved string of eight murders, the twin sister of one of the girls, a demure school teacher, teams up with an ex-cop in an attempt to find the killer. She poses as her sister to lure him into the open.
S,A — EN
Unknown — *Video Unlimited*   **H, P**
027

Ski Bum, The   Fil-Ent '70
Crime-Drama
12265   94 mins   C
V2, B, V
Charlotte Rampling, Zalman King
A ruthless girl wants to gain control of a Colorado ski resort and coerces a naive ski bum into helping her.
S,A — EN
Avco Embassy — *Embassy Home Entertainment*   **P**
2095

Skokie   Fil-Ent '81
Drama
12935   122 mins   C
B, V
Danny Kaye, directed by Herbert Wise
This film covers events that took place in 1977 in the Chicago suburb of Skokie when a court decision was upheld that the Nazis could hold a political rally.
BBFC:PG — S,A — EN
Robert Berger — *Video Form Pictures*   **H, P**
MGD 026

(For Explanation of codes, see USE GUIDE and KEY)

PALADIN VIDEO HOME ENTERTAINMENT GUIDE

Sky at Westminster Abbey Fil-Ent '8?
Music-Performance
08710   85 mins   C
V2, B, V, LV
In February 1981, Westminster Abbey became the venue for the musical group, Sky. This band has successfully achieved a blend of classical instruments with the electronic sounds of the 80's.
F — EN
Ken Griffin; Andy Finney — BBC Video
H, P
BBCV 3017

Sky Rider Attack Fil-Ent '??
War-Drama
10190   90 mins   C
B, V
Horst Buchholz, Sylvia Koscina
Set on the island of Crete in 1943 the Axis Forces are planning a raid on the British refineries of the Persian Gulf. The success of their raid depends on a Spanish-born Italian agent whose job it is to get fuel to an Arabian Desert rendezvous as their bombers cannot reach the target without refuelling. But the British are on to him, two men pit their wits and training against each other in a race against time across the desert.
BBFC:PG — S,A — EN
Unknown — Video Form Pictures H, P
DIP 14

Sky Riders Fil-Ent '76
Drama
01734   91 mins   C
B, V
James Coburn, Susannah York, Robert Culp
A group of hang-gliding daredevils ride out like giant birds to rescue a mother and her two children kidnapped by terrorists in Greece.
F — EN
20th Century Fox — CBS/Fox Video   P
3A-044

Sky West and Crooked Fil-Ent '65
Drama/Romance
12744   101 mins   C
B, V
Hayley Mills, Ian McShane
A beautiful but mentally retarded girl runs off into the night into the arms of the gypsy boy they say killed her friend. Fearing for her safety the village comes looking for her, but she has fallen in love, and the caravans are moving on.
BBFC:PG — F — EN
Continental Rank — Rank Video Library
H, P
0198X

Sky West and Crooked Fil-Ent '65
Drama/Romance
13472   101 mins   C
B, V
Hayley Mills, Ian McShane, Laurence Naismith
This is the story of the flowering of teenage love set against a difficult psychological background.
BBFC:A — C,A — EN
Rank — Rank Video Library   H, P
0198X

Skyjacked Fil-Ent '72
Drama/Suspense
12226   97 mins   C
B, V
Charlton Heston, Yvette Mimieux, James Brolin, Walter Pidgeon
A routine airflight turns into a nightmare when it is discovered that a bomb has been placed somewhere aboard the plane.
S,A — EN
MGM — MGM/UA Home Video   P
10290

Sky's the Limit, The/Step Lively Fil-Ent '4?
Musical
05709   172 mins   B/W
B, V
Fred Astaire, Robert Ryan, Joan Leslie, Robert Benchley, directed by Edward Griffiths, Frank Sinatra, Ann Jeffries, George Murphy, Gloria de Haven, directed by Tim Whelan
Two films featured on one cassette. 'The Sky's the Limit' (Black/White, 87 mins, 1944) stars a war hero who spends his ten days leave in New York City and falls in love with a young girl. Includes dance routines with songs by Johnny Mercer. 'Step Lively' (Black/White, 85 mins, 1945) is based on the play and film 'Room Service'. When a cheque arrives out of the blue, a group of hard-up performers are able to open their show.
F — EN
RKO — Kingston Video   H, P
KV33

Slapstick Of Another Kind Fil-Ent '84
Comedy
12958   85 mins   C
B, V
Jerry Lewis, Madeline Kahn, Marty Feldman, Jim Backus, John Abbott, directed by Steven Paul

---

(For Explanation of codes, see USE GUIDE and KEY)

PALADIN VIDEO HOME ENTERTAINMENT GUIDE

Based on the novel by Kurt Vonnegut, a couple of zany misplaced aliens, a brother and sister who, when together, hold the secrets of the universe, are pursued retentlessly by the Government.
C,A — EN
Steven Paul — *Virgin Video* **H, P**
VVA 041

Slaughter Fil-Ent '72
Crime-Drama
07375　90 mins　C
V2, B, V
Jim Brown, Stella Stevens, Cameron Mitchell, Rip Torn, Don Gordon, directed by Jack Starrett
A proud, arrogant, black Vietnam veteran learns that his parents have been murdered by a car bomb. He suspects that the underworld syndicate that his father worked for is responsible. After killing two of the members he is taken in by the police and is offered the choice by a Federal Agent of either being charged for the murders or helping them find the nerve centre of the syndicate.
BBFC:X — *A — EN*
American International Pictures — *Guild Home Video* **H, P, E**

Slaughter in San Francisco Fil-Ent '73
Crime-Drama/Martial arts
08062　84 mins　C
B, V
Chuck Norris
This film tells the story of an American Cop in the San Francisco Police Department who is wrongly dismissed for killing the attacker of a fellow cop. The story follows with him trying to expose the crooked policemen and arresting the mobs in order to regain his credibility in the force.
S,A — EN
Unknown — *Rank Video Library* **H, P**
0079 C

Slaughterhouse Five Fil-Ent '72
Drama
13634　100 mins　C
B, V
Michael Sacks, Ron Leibman, Eugene Roche, Valerie Perrine, directed by George Roy Hill
An American POW comes home with mental illness and living in surburbia combines his experience of being held prisoner by the Nazis with fantasies of life on another planet.
BBFC:18 — *A — EN*
Paul Monash — *CIC Video* **H, P**
1144

Slavers Fil-Ent '77
Adventure
06809　100 mins　C
V2, B, V
Trevor Howard, Britt Ekland, Ron Ely, Jurgen Goslar, Cameron Mitchell, Ray Milland
A tale of inscrupulous slave hunter in 1884 Africa.
S,A — EN
Jurgen Goslar — *Intervision Video* **H, P**
A-A 0304

Slayground Fil-Ent '80
Drama/Suspense
12525　85 mins　C
B, V
Peter Coyote, Mel Smith, Billie Whitelaw, directed by Terry Bedford
The story of a professional criminal whose getaway car kills a nine year old girl. Her father has only one thought in mind, to seek revenge.
BBFC:18 — *A — EN*
John Dark; Gower Frost — *THORN EMI* **P**
TXA 2203 4 / TVA 90 2203 2

Sleeping Beauty, The Fil-Ent '83
Dance/Music
08673　175 mins　C
B, V
Irina Kolpakova, Sergei Berezhnoi, Lubov Kunakova, Vladimir Lopukhov, directed by Elena Macheret
This is Tchaikovsky's ballet based on the fairy tale, Sleeping by Charles Perrault, danced by the Leningrad State Kirov Ballet. Leading the cast in Irina Kolpkova, with the orchestra of the Leningrad Theatre of Opera and Ballet conducted by Viktor Fedotov. It is performed in a prologue and three acts.
S,A — EN
USSR Gosteleradio; National Video Corp Ltd — *Longman Video* **P**
LGBE 7006/LGVH 7006

Sleeping Beauty Fil-Ent '84
Fairy tales
13413　58 mins　C
B, V
Christopher Reeve, Bernadette Peters
An adaptation of the well known classic story of the princess who is awakened from her deep sleep by the kiss of the prince.
BBFC:U — *F — EN*
Shelley Duvall — *MGM/UA Home Video* **P**
10433

PALADIN VIDEO HOME ENTERTAINMENT GUIDE

Sleeping Dogs
Fil-Ent '77
Drama
07486   97 mins   C
B, V

Sam Neil, Ian Mune, Nevan Rowe, Warren Oates, directed by Roger Donaldson
This film is set in New Zealand, where a state of political unrest prevails with strikes, riots and rationing. The Prime Minister has set up an anti-terrorist force of 'specials' supposedly to restore law and order. A man on the run from a broken marriage becomes caught between a repressive Government and a violent resistance movement. He is a hunted man driven by the will to survive.
S,A — EN
Aardvark Films; Roger Donaldson — *Quadrant Video*   H, P
FF5

Sleuth
Fil-Ent '72
Suspense
01200   138 mins   C
B, V

Sir Laurence Olivier, Michael Caine
A mystery novelist takes his work to the limits by playing diabolical and deadly tricks on his guest.
M,A — EN
20th Century Fox — *CBS/Fox Video*   P
4A-097

Slightly Pregnant Man, The
Fil-Ent '73
Comedy
08823   92 mins   C
B, V

Marcello Mastroianni, Catherine Deneuve, Mirelle Mathieu
This film follows an unusual event. A man is sick every morning, and goes to see his doctor. Despite science, he is pregnant.
S,A — EN
Unknown — *VCL Video Services*   P
P162D

Slipper and the Rose, The
Fil-Ent '76
Fairy tales/Musical
05445   136 mins   C
V2, B, V

Richard Chamberlain, Gemma Craven, Annette Crosbie, Edith Evans, Christopher Gablle, Kenneth More, Michael Hordern, Margaret Lockwood, directed by Bryan Forbes
An updated version of the classic fairy tale of Cinderella and Prince Charming. Features music and lyrics by Richard and Robert Sherman.
BBFC:U — F — EN
Universal; Paradine Co-Prods Ltd — *Iver Film Services*   P
27

Slithis
Fil-Ent '79
Science fiction/Horror
06077   86 mins   C
B, V

Alan Blanchard, Judy Motulsky, Mello Alexandria, directed by Stephen Traxler
From the pollution of our nuclear waste comes the killer that cannot be destroyed. Starring a terrifying scaly monster—Slithis.
S,A — EN
Dick Davis — *Video Programme Distributors*   P
Media—M138

Sloane
Fil-Ent '84
Adventure/Suspense
13716   90 mins   C
V2, B, V

Robert Resnik, Debra Blee, Paul Aragon, Ann Milhench, Carissa Carlos
An ex-police officer sets out to rescue a past girlfriend after her husband was murdered and she was assaulted and kidnapped.
BBFC:18 — A — EN
Venture International Pictures; Skouras Pictures — *Medusa Communications Ltd*   H, P
MC 054

Slumber Party '57
Fil-Ent '76
Musical
01084   83 mins   C
V2, B, V

The Platters, Jerry Lee Lewis, Big Bopper, Crewcuts, Paul and Paula
A group of girls get together for a slumber party and exchange stories of their first loves, which turn out to be more fiction than fact. Early rock n' roll music highlights the film.
BBFC:X — A — EN
Unknown — *Intervision Video*   H, P
A-A 0118

Small One, The
Fil-Ent '??
Cartoons/Christmas
08005   71 mins   C
B, V

Animated
This animated Christmas programme includes the story of the donkey who carried Mary to Bethlehem.
BBFC:U — F — EN
Walt Disney Productions — *Rank Video Library*   H
06500

Smash Palace
Fil-Ent '81
Drama
13242   108 mins   C
B, V

(For Explanation of codes, see USE GUIDE and KEY)

PALADIN VIDEO HOME ENTERTAINMENT GUIDE

Bruno Lawrence, Anna Jemison, directed by Roger Donaldson
An ex-racing car driver and his French wife settle in a remote country town but when his wife becomes bored she turns to his best friend for excitement which leads the husband to react with desperate violence.
BBFC:18 — *A* — *EN*
Roger Donaldson — *CBS/Fox Video* **P**
1339

Smirnoff Masters Squash   Spo-Lei '81
1981
Sports
06836   105 mins   C
B, V
Introduced by Jonah Barrington
This film looks at the Masters Squash Championships when the top 64 players in the world met. The film exposes the triumphs, disappointments, courage and lack of courage showing, in action, Ahmed Zaman, Hunt, Awad and Khan.
S,A
VTR Studios Ltd — *TFI Leisure Ltd*   **P**

Smithereens   Fil-Ent '??
Drama
08831   ? mins   C
B, V
Susan Berman, Richard Hell, Brad Rinn
This tells the story of a young girl seeking fame and fortune in New York.
BBFC:15 — *A* — *EN*
Unknown — *VCL Video Services*   **P**
M332D

Smoke On Go! The Red   Gen-Edu '84
Arrows
Aeronautics
12719   55 mins   C
B, V
This film gives an insight into private lives of 'The Red Arrows' as well as showing the professional preparation for the hundred or so air displays carried out each year. Included in the programme is unique footage from the 1983 US tour.
F — *EN*
Unknown — *Quadrant Video*   **H, P**
AV3

Smokey and the Bandit   Fil-Ent '77
Comedy
01054   97 mins   C
B, V
Burt Reynolds, Sally Field, Jackie Gleason, Jerry Reed, Mike Henry, directed by Hal Needham
A legendary truck driver and CB radio fanatic gives a lift to a female hitchhiker and sets off a crazy chain of events climaxing in a wild car chase.
A,F — *EN*
Universal; Mort Engleberg — *CIC Video*
H, P

Smokey and the   Fil-Ent '83
Bandit—Part 3
Adventure/Comedy
13295   84 mins   C
B, V
Jackie Gleason, Pat McCormick, Paul Williams, Jerry Reid, directed by Dick Lowry
There are plenty of hilarious stunts in this film about transporting a fish from Miami to Austin, Texas in a race against time.
S,A — *EN*
Universal — *CIC Video*   **H, P**
BET 1094/VHT 1094

Smokey and the Hotwire   Fil-Ent '7?
Gang
Adventure
02589   81 mins   C
B, V
Auto chases and thrills and spills galore in this madcap adventure film.
C,A — *EN*
Unknown — *Mountain Video*   **P**

Smokey Bites the Dust   Fil-Ent '81
Comedy/Adventure
07951   94 mins   C
B, V
Jimmy McNichol, directed by Roger Corman and Chuck Griffith
A young girl is kidnapped by a charming and reckless young man. The town sheriff, who just happens to be her father, sets off with a posse in hot pursuit. Features spectacular car chase sequences.
S,A — *EN*
Roger Corman — *Brent Walker Home Video Ltd*   **P**

Smurfs and the Magic   Chl-Juv '81
Flute
Fantasy/Musical
06801   73 mins   C
V2, B, V
Animated, music by Michel Legrand
The Smurfs star in this delightful musical tale about a flute with magical powers.
F — *EN*
Unknown — *Intervision Video*   **H, P**
A-A 0360

---

600   (For Explanation of codes, see USE GUIDE and KEY)

PALADIN VIDEO HOME ENTERTAINMENT GUIDE

Snake in the Monkey's Shadow Fil-Ent '7?
Adventure/Martial arts
04613   85 mins   C
V2, B, V
Evil Shao San, exponent of Snake Kung-fu, swears vengeance when defeated in a tournament by Khoo using the Monkey style.
C,A — EN
Alex Gouw — *Video Programme Distributors*
P
Inter-Ocean—009

Snapshot Fil-Ent '??
Comedy
06017   82 mins   C
B, V
Jim Henshaw, Susan Petrie
The story of the adventures of an accident prone hyper-active sports photographer who finds himself in the most unexpected situations.
F — EN
John B Kelly Prods — *VCL Video Services*
P

Snapshot—Australian Style Fil-Ent '78
Suspense
06239   90 mins   C
B, V
Chantal Contouri, Robert Brunning, Sigrid Thornton, Hugh Keays-Byrne
A young girl wanting to become a model is forced to pose nude, her confidence is betrayed and her photographs appear widely in the media. Disowned by her family she has no job or home, she goes to live in a strange commune. Frightening events occur and sinister implications abound.
S,A — EN
Anthony I Ginnane — *VCL Video Services*
P
C140C

Sneakers Fil-Ent '81
Drama
12151   105 mins   C
B, V
Carl Marotte, Charlaine Woodward, Lisa Langlois, directed by Daryl Duke
A story of the lives and loves of teenagers set in the 1960's.
S,A — EN
Unknown — *Polygram Video* **H, P**
040 2334/040 2332

Snooker Century Breakers Spo-Lei '84
Games
12724   90 mins   C
B, V
Many sensational century breaks are shown, mainly taken from the Embassy World Professional Snooker Championships from 1979-1983, but also including the first century break ever recorded on TV by Joe Davis. Other century breakers featured are Fred Davis, Steve Davis, Alex Higgins.
F — EN
John Vigar — *BBC Video* **H, P**
5022

Snooker—Reardon Master Series, No 1 Spo-Lei '84
Games
13103   28 mins   C
B, V
Ray Reardon
This tape is aimed at the novice and is an introduction to the basic skills of snooker incorporating grip, stance, the striking and first stages of potting the ball from different angles.
S,A — I
Unknown — *Quadrant Video* **H, P**
SN1

Snooker—Reardon Master Series, No 2 Spo-Lei '84
Games
13102   28 mins   C
B, V
Ray Reardon
This tape is aimed at the player at intermediate stage who wishes to increase game satisfaction by acquiring technique and skills to enhance break power.
S,A — I
Unknown — *Quadrant Video* **H, P**
SN2

Snooker—Reardon Master Series, No 3 Spo-Lei '84
Games
13101   28 mins   C
B, V
Ray Reardon
This tape concentrates on the strategy of the game, outlining how a champion thinks: planning ahead; exploiting opportunities; using specialist shots and so dominating the table.
S,A — I
Unknown — *Quadrant Video* **H, P**
SN3

Snow Treasure Fil-Ent '67
War-Drama/Adventure
05607   95 mins   C
B, V

(For Explanation of codes, see USE GUIDE and KEY)

PALADIN VIDEO HOME ENTERTAINMENT GUIDE

James Franciscus, directed by Irving Jacoby
This film is set in Norway in the early 1940's and tells the story of a resistance group who are prevented from shipping out gold by a sudden German takeover. A German officer in love with a school teacher permits the gold to be smuggled out by schoolchildren but dies for his efforts.
S,A — EN
Sagittarus Prods; Irving Jacoby — *Home Video Merchandisers* **H, P**
011

Snow White and the Seven Dwarfs   Fil-Ent '84
Fairy tales
13436   57 mins   C
B, V
Vanessa Redgrave, Vincent Price, Rex Smith
In this adaptation of the Brothers Grimm fairy tale, the talking mirror tells the evil Queen that Snow White is more beautiful than her and she sets out to destroy her.
F — EN
Shelley Duvall — *MGM/UA Home Video* **P**
10463

Snowball Express   Fil-Ent '72
Adventure
12567   93 mins   C
B, V
Dean Jones, Nancy Olson
This is the story of a family who uproot themselves from the city and take over a run down hotel high up in the snowy Rockies.
F — EN
Walt Disney Productions — *Rank Video Library* **H**
012

Snowballing   Fil-Ent '84
Drama
13669   96 mins   C
B, V
Alan Seus, Mary McDonough, Jill Carroll, P.R. Paul, directed by Charles E Sellier
Park City, Utah, is the scene for the Junior Ski Championships. The kids from Monroe High School find themselves up against a crooked sheriff intent on ripping them off and decide to turn the tables on him.
BBFC:18 — C,A — EN
Charles E Sellier — *CBS/Fox Video* **P**
7038

Snowman, The   Chl-Juv '82
Cartoons/Fantasy
13122   58 mins   C
B, V
Animated
This programme is introduced by David Bowie and is based on the book by Raymond Briggs about a special snowman who comes to life at midnight. Four supporting cartoons are also included.
F — EN
Snowman Enterprises Ltd — *Palace Video Ltd* **P**
PVC 2073A

So Fine   Fil-Ent '81
Comedy
13209   89 mins   C
B, V
Ryan O'Neal, Jack Warden, Mariangela Melato, Richard Kiel, directed by Andrew Bergman
A timid professor is roped in to save his father's fashion firm which owes money to a mobster and discovers an unusual way to save his father's business, but also gets entangled with the mobster's sex-hungry wife.
BBFC:AA — C,A — EN
Warner Bros — *Warner Home Video* **P**
61143

So Long at the Fair   Fil-Ent '50
Drama
13739   85 mins   B/W
B, V
Jean Simmons, Dirk Bogarde
A brother and a sister become enmeshed in a missing-person mystery during a visit to the Paris World's Fair of 1889.
BBFC:U — F — EN
Rank Films — *Rank Video Library* **H, P**
0198A

So Sweet, So Dead   Fil-Ent '??
Crime-Drama
06122   95 mins   C
V2, B, V
Farley Granger, Sylva Koscina, Susan Scott
The police are faced with a series of savage and motiveless murders. All the victims are young, beautiful women, all having affairs, all had their throats cut before being assaulted. The Police Commissioner discovers the truth through an unexpected and unwelcome revelation.
S,A — EN
Unknown — *Video Programme Distributors* **P**
Cinehollywood—V980

So You Want to Be a Glamour Photographer   How-Ins '8?
Photography
09988   90 mins   C
B, V

PALADIN VIDEO HOME ENTERTAINMENT GUIDE

This tape features Jon Gray, one of Britain's top glamour photographers working with Page Three girls. It shows the viewer how to set up the subject and how to use the camera.
C,A — I
Holiday Brothers Ltd — Holiday Brothers Ltd
P

So You Want to Stop Smoking Gen-Edu '84
Smoking
12726   56 mins   C
B, V
This step-by-step programme is an individual aid to all those who want to give up the habit, with answers to your questions, advice, and most of all, support. Dr. Miriam Stoppard gives her help.
A — I
Anna Jackson — BBC Video   H, P
1018

S.O.B. Fil-Ent '81
Comedy
07391   120 mins   C
V2, B, V
Julie Andrews, William Holden, Richard Mulligan, Robert Preston, Shelley Winters, Robert Webber, Marisa Berenson, Robert Vaughan, Larry Hagman
In this irreverent and zany send-up of the Hollywood film industry a multi-million dollar picture is a box-office flop. The director turns suicidal until he envisages reshooting the entire film with an X rated scene starring his wife, a star who, up until now enjoyed an untainted image.
BBFC:AA — S,A — EN
Blake Edwards Prods — Guild Home Video
H, P, E

Soccer Is Fun Spo-Lei '8?
Football
08589   60 mins   C
B, V
Bobby Charlton
In this programme, the first of a series, Bobby Charlton deals with the basics of Kit, Attitude and the fundamental skill required to get enjoyment and fun out of playing football.
M,S — I
Holiday Brothers — Holiday Brothers Ltd
P

Soccer: Tactics and Skills Spo-Lei '81
Football
05915   50 mins   C
V

Kevin Keegan, Ray Wilkins, Trevour Brooking, Ron Greenwood, Dave Sexton, Terry Venables, Geoff Hurst, Peter Shilton, Bobby Robson, Don Howe   7 pgms
A comprehensive set of soccer training films providing an invaluable aid to football players. Features the F.A. Assistant Director of Coaching, Charles Hughes. Commentary by John Matson, Barry Davies and Bob Wilson. Book available from book sellers.
1.Creating Space 2.Passing and Support 3.Attacking in the Attacking Third of the Field 4.Shooting 5.Goalkeeping 6.Defending 7.Defending and Attacking from Free Kicks and Corners
AM Available   F — I
JVC; Football Association — JVC   P
PRT 50; PRT 51; PRT 52; PRT 53; PRT 54; PRT 55; PRT 56

Soccer: The Game of the Century: Part 2 Spo-Lei '8?
Soccer/Documentary
07835   119 mins   C
B, V
Narrated by Robert Powell, directed by Derek Conrad
This review looks at the people and personalities behind soccer today. Using match footage they meet the superstars, provide an in-depth profile of Maradona and those devoted to developing the game abroad. Shot on location in England, West Germany, Spain, Cameroon, Australia, Canada, U.S.A., Hong Kong, Singapore and Japan.
F — EN
Spectrum — Polygram Video   H, P
791 525

Soccer: The Game of the Century Spo-Lei '78
Soccer
04466   53 mins   C
B, V
This programme provides a comprehensive look at the history of soccer and shows excerpts from World Cup Tournaments from 1920-1978. Also included are portraits of and interviews with soccer stars Pele, Beckenbauer, and Cruyff.
F — EN
Spectrum — Polygram Video   P

Soft Beds, Hard Battles Fil-Ent '73
Comedy
05180   94 mins   C
B, V
Peter Sellers, Lila Kedrova, Curt Jurgens, Beatrice Romand

(For Explanation of codes, see USE GUIDE and KEY)   603

PALADIN VIDEO HOME ENTERTAINMENT GUIDE

Peter Sellers plays no less than six roles as varied as an elderly French general, Hitler and a Japanese prince in this saucy spy spoof set in a Parisian bordello in World War II.
BBFC:X — A — EN
United Artists — *Rank Video Library* H, P
1009

Soft Cell   Fil-Ent '82
Music-Performance
08481   55 mins   C
B, V
Directed by Tim Pope
This tape features Soft Cell and some of their hits from '81 and '82, in a 'Non-Stop Video Show' it includes 'Say Hello Wave Goodbye' with a visit to the Pink Flamingo Jazz Cellar; 'Frustration' where Dave gets buried alive; 'Seedy Films' and visits to various parts of Soho; 'Bedsitter' and life between four walls; 'Tainted Love', 'Memorabilia', 'Secret Life', 'Youth', 'Sex Dwarf', and 'What'.
S,A — EN
GLO; Some Bizzare — *THORN EMI*   P
TXE 90 1478 4/TVE 90 1478 2

Soggy Bottom USA   Fil-Ent '??
Comedy
07388   97 mins   C
V2, B, V
Ben Johnson, Ann Wedgeworth, Lois Nettleton
The depression affected everyone except Soggy Bottom USA, where it was business, plus fighting, bank robbing and car chasing as usual.
BBFC:AA — S,A — EN
Unknown — *Guild Home Video*   H, P, E

Soldier Blue   Fil-Ent '70
Western
01733   109 mins   C
V2, B, V, LV
Candice Bergen, Peter Strauss, Donald Pleasance, Dana Elcar, directed by Ralph Nelson
A western adventure about a U.S. Cavalry unit escorting gold across Cheyenne territory.
BBFC:X — A — EN
Avco Embassy — *CBS/Fox Video*   P
3C-021

Sole Survivor   Fil-Ent '8?
Horror
12144   102 mins   C
V2, B, V
Anita Skinner, Kurt Johnson, Caren Larkey, Robin Davidson, directed by Thom Eberhardt

A girl survives a plane crash only to find she is being watched and terrorised by people she doesn't know. As murder after murder takes place she realises that her time is running out.
BBFC:18 — C,A — EN
Unknown — *Intervision Video*   H, P
A-A 0498

Some Girls Do   Fil-Ent '71
Suspense/Adventure
09924   91 mins   C
B, V
Richard Johnson, Daliah Lavi, Bebi Loncar, James Villiers, Sydney Rome, Robert Morley, Maurice Denham
A famed detective, Bulldog Drummond, is hired to investigate a series of bizarre accidents hampering Britain's supersonic aircraft programme.
S,A — EN
United Artists; Betty E. Box — *Rank Video Library*   H, P

Some Kind of Hero   Fil-Ent '81
Drama
12042   93 mins   C
B, V
Richard Pryor, Lynne Moody, Margot Kidder, directed by Michael
A soldier from Vietnam returns home after five years of imprisonment to find his life completely shattered. Emotionally shocked, he fights back for a place in civilian life.
BBFC:15 — S,A — EN
Paramount — *CIC Video*   H, P
BEA 2080/VHA 2080

Somebody Killed Her Husband   Fil-Ent '78
Comedy/Mystery
06182   96 mins   C
V2, B, V
Farrah Fawcett-Majors, Jeff Bridges, John Wood, Tammy Grimes, John Glover, directed by Lamont Johnson
The story of a young man, a would-be children's writer, who is working in a major New York department store, his mind rarely on his job. He meets an unhappily married woman and one Sunday in her apartment they hear her husband enter, they decide to face him but find his body slumped over the kitchen table with a knife in his back. The young man is suspected.
BBFC:AA — S,A — EN
Columbia Pictures; Markin Poll — *Guild Home Video*   H, P, E

Somebody's Stolen Our Russian Spy   Fil-Ent '??
Suspense/Adventure

PALADIN VIDEO HOME ENTERTAINMENT GUIDE

06307　　77 mins　　C
V2, B, V
A top British Agent is assigned to a dangerous mission: he must rescue a Russian Colonel abducted by the Chinese and Albanians. The Agent not only succeeds but wins the affections of a young lady in the process.
S,A — EN
Unknown — World of Video 2000　　H, P
GFS02

Someone Behind the Door　　Fil-Ent '71
Suspense/Drama
06233　　90 mins　　C
B, V
Charles Bronson, Anthony Perkins, Jill Ireland, directed by Nicholas Gessner
A brain surgeon takes a psychopathic amnesiac patient home. Capitalising on his blank mind the doctor plants suggestions that lead to the murder of the lover of his unfaithful wife.
S,A — EN
Avco Embassy Corp; GSF Prods — VCL Video Services　　P
C130

Someone Is Bleeding　　Fil-Ent '??
Suspense/Drama
06200　　120 mins　　C
B, V
Alain Delon, Mireille Darc, Claude Brasseur
The simplicity of a relationship is confused by the complexities which surround the woman. She lives in an isolated villa looked after by a disturbed caretaker; when the caretaker is murdered her lover discovers that she was acquitted of her husband's killing two years before.
S,A — EN
Unknown — VCL Video Services　　P
P167D

Something Short of Paradise　　Fil-Ent '79
Romance/Drama
09936　　91 mins　　C
B, V
Susan Sarandon, David Steinberg, Jean-Pierre Aumont, Marilyn Sokol
It's love at first sight when a man meets a girl at a party. After spending an idyllic weekend together, everything is ruined by a proposal. It seems the girl is not ready for that kind of commitment, having been hurt before. The unhappy lovers return to New York only to be brought together again in an unexpected way.
BBFC:15 — C,A — EN
American-International — Rank Video Library
H, P
1066 Y

Something to Hide　　Fil-Ent '??
Suspense
06198　　92 mins　　C
B, V
Peter Finch, Shelley Winters, Colin Blakely, John Stride, Linda Hayden
A man gives a forlorn hitch-hiker a lift. He becomes helplessly entangled in a set of circumstances beyond his control, struggling against an impending doom. Based on the novel by Nicholas Monsarrat, music by Roy Budd.
S,A — EN
Unknown — VCL Video Services　　P
P142D

Something to Sing About　　Fil-Ent '37
Musical-Drama
07643　　88 mins　　B/W
B, V
James Cagney, William Frawley, Evelyn Daw, directed by Victor Schertsinger
A Manhattan band leader, when called to Hollywood to star in a musical, is convinced by a scheming producer that his career is a flop. So he marries his former soloist and they go off to the South Seas. When he returns he signs a seven year contract that requires him to fake bachelorhood. His wife leaves him and returns to New York; finally he follows her and they return to the band and freedom.
F — EN
Victor Schertsinger — VCL Video Services
P
0224G

Something Wicked This Way Comes　　Fil-Ent '82
Drama/Fantasy
13437　　93 mins　　C
B, V
Jason Robards, Jonathan Price, Pam Grier, Dianne Ladd, Royal Dano
This film is based on Ray Bradbury's story of good versus evil, as embodied in the mysterious dark carnival which arrives in Green Town, Illinois.
BBFC:PG — S,A — EN
Walt Disney Productions — Rank Video Library
P
166

Son of Kong/You'll Find Out　　Fil-Ent '??
Horror/Comedy
05718　　158 mins　　B/W
B, V
Robert Armstrong, Helen Mack, directed by Ernest Schoedsack, Boris Karloff, Bela Lugosi, Peter Lorre, Kay Kyser, Helen Parrish, directed by David Butler

(For Explanation of codes, see USE GUIDE and KEY)

PALADIN VIDEO HOME ENTERTAINMENT GUIDE

Two films are featured on one cassette. In 'Son of Kong' (66 minutes, 1935), King Kong Junior is discovered on Skull Island, which is inhabited by prehistoric creatures. 'You'll Find Out' (92 minutes, 1941) is a musical comedy complete with a lady in distress, sinister seances, secret passages and skullduggery.

S,A — EN

RKO — *Kingston Video*   **H, P**
KV24

Son of Sinbad/Cyclone on Horseback/Pal's Return   Fil-Ent '??
Adventure/Western
05660   166 mins   C
B, V

Dale Robertson, Vincent Price, Sally Price, Lili St. Cyr, Mari Blanchard, Tim Holt, Marjorie Reynolds, Ray Whitley, Ted Donaldson

This cassette features two films plus one short. 'Son of Sinbad' (Colour, 88 mins. 1955) in which Sinbad is captured by the Khalif of Bagdad and must bring him the secret of Greek Fire to gain his freedom and free the city from the mighty Tamarlane. 'Cyclone on Horseback' (Black/white, 57 mins, 1941) is a story of the hazards of linking the West with the East by telephone. 'Pal's Return' (Black/white, 20 mins) is a short dog adventure starring 'Flame' the dog.

F — EN

RKO — *Kingston Video*   **H, P**
KV52

Son of the Sheik, The   Fil-Ent '26
Romance
04676   64 mins   B/W
B, V

Rudolph Valentino, Vilma Banky, Agnes Ayres

Ahmed, a desert sheik, believes himself betrayed by a dancing girl, whereupon he abducts her and exacts his own form of revenge. Silent; colour-tinted.

F — EN

First National — *Polygram Video*   **P**

Song and Dance   Fil-Ent '84
Musical
13074   100 mins   C
B, V

Sara Brightman, Wayne Sleep, directed by Tom Gutteridge

This video is a compilation of song and dance routines from the original production at the Palace Theatre, London. The music is composed by Andrew Lloyd Webber with lyrics by Don Black and choreography is by Anthony van Laast.

F — EN

Really Useful Theatre Company — *RCA/Columbia Pictures Video UK*
H, P

Song of Norway   Fil-Ent '70
Musical/Biographical
04277   138 mins   C
B, V

Toralv Maurstad, Christina Schollin, Harry Secombe, Florence Henderson, Frank Porretta, Robert Morley, Edward G. Robinson

The music of the London Symphony Orchestra fills this movie with all the dramatic force of Edward Grieg's struggle to create music of genius for an indifferent Norwegian public who believed that fine music could only emanate from Rome or Berlin.

BBFC:U — F — EN

Cinerama Releasing — *Rank Video Library*
H, P
7008

Song of the South   Fil-Ent '??
Musical/Cartoons
12585   91 mins   C
B, V

Lucile Watson, Ruth Warrick, James Baskett, Bobby Driscoll, Luana Patten

This musical tale is a blend of live action and animation and features Brer Rabbit, Brer Fox and Brer Bear, along with the Academy Award-winning song, 'Zip-A-Dee-Doo-Dah.'

F — EN

Walt Disney Productions — *Rank Video Library*
H
102

Songs of Praise   Fil-Ent '84
Music
13391   60 mins   C
B, V

Taken from the popular television religious programme, this video features hymns from all the major Christian festivals sung in churches and cathedrals throughout the United Kingdom.

F — EN

BBC Television — *BBC Video*   **H, P**
8500

Sonny and Cher   Fil-Ent '7?
Music-Performance
04628   60 mins   C
B, V

PALADIN VIDEO HOME ENTERTAINMENT GUIDE

Sonny and Cher bring their special form of entertainment to the screen in this musical variety show.
F — EN
VCL Video Services Ltd — VCL Video Services P

Sons of the Musketeers/The Mysterians Fil-Ent '??
Adventure/Science fiction
05771   162 mins   C
B, V
Maureen O'Hara, Cornel Wilde, Alan Hale, directed by Lewis Allen, Kenji Sahara, directed by Inoshiro Honda
Two films are contained on one cassette. 'Sons of the Musketeers' (colour, 80 minutes, 1953) is based on one of Alexandre Dumas' novels. D'Artagnan Jr, leads one other sons of the original quartet on a romantic quest. The Queen of France enlists their aid to protect life and reputation. 'The Mysterians' (colour, 82 minutes, 1960) is a Japanese film dubbed in English. Alien invaders, their own planet destroyed by an atomic disaster, land in Japan and set out to conquer the Earth, enslave its men, and mate with its women.
S,A — EN
RKO; Japanese — Kingston Video   H, P
KV11

Sooty Video Show, The Fil-Ent '??
Puppets/Comedy
08303   60 mins   C
B, V
Mathew Corbett
This tape features Mathew Corbett and the well-known puppets, Sooty, Sweep, and Soo, up to their usual amusing tricks.
F — EN
Golden Dawn Production — Warwick Video P
003

Sooty's Adventures Chi-Juv '81
Puppets
12904   60 mins   C
B, V
Matthew Corbett, directed by John Woods
Sooty appears in his own show with Sweep the Spaniel and his Panda girlfriend Soo.
F — EN
Unknown — THORN EMI   P
TXE 90 17294/TVE 90 17292

Sophie's Choice Fil-Ent '83
Drama/Romance
09274   140 mins   C
V2, B, V, LV
Meryl Streep, directed by Alan J. Pakula
Set in 1947 this film tells the story of Stingo, a young would-be novelist who moves into a low rent district of Brooklyn. He soon finds that his work is disturbed by the noisy love-making of the couple upstairs. She is a Polish immigrant and he a Jewish intellectual. Stingo becomes involved in their lives, especially when he falls in love with Sophie. Based on the book by William Styron. Academy Awards '83: Best Actress (Streep).
S,A — EN
Universal — Precision Video Ltd   P
CRITC 3135/BITC 3135/VITC 3135/LVITC 0017

Sorcerer Fil-Ent '8?
Opera
08928   100 mins   C
B, V
Clive Revill, Donald Adams, Nuala Willis, Nan Christie, Enid Hartle, Janis Kelly
This opera by Gilbert and Sullivan tells the story of Alexis, who in order to celebrate his forthcoming marriage arranges for a reputable sorcerer to provide a love potion for the whole village. However, this gets slightly out of hand as his father falls for a woman of a lower station and his bride-to-be falls in love with the local vicar. The sorcerer has to sacrifice his soul to remove the spell. The music is by The London Symphony Orchestra, conducted by Alexander Faris.
S,A — EN
Brent Walker Prods — Brent Walker Home Video Ltd   P

Sorcerers, The Fil-Ent '67
Horror/Drama
06351   86 mins   C
V2, B, V
Boris Karloff, Catherine Lacey, Ian Ogilvy, Victor Henry
An impoverished professor and his wife concoct and perfect a 'thought' machine that places other people under their control. They become involved with a mod youth and his friends resulting in a string of horrific activities.
S,A — EN
Allied Artists; Patrick Curtis and Tony Tenser; Tigon-Curtwel-Global Prods — Walton Film and Video Ltd   P
G49

Sorcerer's Apprentice, The Fil-Ent '??
Cartoons/Fairy tales
09225   26 mins   C
B, V
Animated, narrated by Vincent Price

(For Explanation of codes, see USE GUIDE and KEY)

PALADIN VIDEO HOME ENTERTAINMENT GUIDE

This tells, in animated form, the story of the sinister sorcerer, his apprentice Hans and the peasant girl Greta in this imaginative version of the classic tale of Brothers' Grimm.
F — EN
Unknown — *Video Form Pictures* **H, P**
MGK 1

S.O.S Pacific — Fil-Ent '59
Adventure
04335 91 mins B/W
V2, B, V
A sea-plane full of passengers is forced down in the Pacific—right in the middle of a nuclear bomb test zone.
BBFC:A — C,A — EN
Sidney Box — *Intervision Video* **H, P**
A-A 0001

S.O.S. Titanic — Fil-Ent '79
Drama
04667 98 mins C
B, V
David Janssen, Cloris Leachman, Susan Saint James, David Warner, Ian Holm, Helen Mirren
This film tells the story of the disaster completely and in detail, exactly as it happened. The story focuses on the courage and the horror that accompanied the sinking of the 'unsinkable' Titanic.
F — EN
EMI; Argonaut Films — *THORN EMI* **H, P**
TXC 90 0225 4/TVC 90 0225 2

Sound of Music, The — Fil-Ent '65
Musical-Drama
01732 174 mins C
V2, B, V, LV
Julie Andrews, Christopher Plummer, directed by Robert Wise
A true story of the Von Trapp family of Austria prior to World War II, based on Rodgers and Hammerstein's Broadway musical.
Academy Awards '65: Best Picture; Film Daily Poll Ten Best Pictures of Year '65.
BBFC:U — F — EN
20th Century Fox; Robert Wise — *CBS/Fox Video* **P**
4A-020

Sounder — Fil-Ent '72
Drama
09839 95 mins C
B, V
Cicely Tyson, Paul Winfield, Kevin Hooks, Carmen Mathews, James Best, Janet MacLachlan, directed by Martin Ritt
Set in Louisiana, 1930's, this film tells the story of a boy, his dog Sounder, and his family's black sharecroppers. Although very poor and oppressed, with hardships imposed on them by an unjust society, they survive on their love for one another.
F — EN
20th Century Fox; Robert Radnitz — *Polygram Video* **H, P**
791 5454/791 5452

Sounds of the Seventies — Fil-Ent '7?
Music-Performance
04621 52 mins C
B, V
A film featuring one of the world's greatest guitarists—Carlos Santana. Taj Mahal and many superb musicians accompany Santana in this electrifying programme.
F — EN
VCL Video Services Ltd — *VCL Video Services* **P**

South Hell Mountain — Fil-Ent '7?
Crime-Drama
08043 89 mins C
B, V
Anna Stewart, Martin Kelley
This film tells the story of a kidnapping. The unusual occurrence is that the young girl falls hopelessly in love with one of her captors. This relieves the horror that had sent her insane.
C,A — EN
Unknown — *Rank Video Library* **H, P**
0107C

South Pacific — Fil-Ent '58
Musical-Drama
13651 163 mins C
B, V
Rossano Brazzi, Mitzi Gaynor, John Kerr, Ray Walston, Juanita Hall, directed by Joshua Logan
A Rogers and Hammerstein musical set in Hawaii, full of romance, and featuring such songs as 'Happy Talk,' 'Some Enchanted Evening,' 'A Cockeyed Optimist,' 'There Is Nothing Like A Dame' and 'I'm In Love With A Wonderful Guy.'
BBFC:U — F — EN
Buddy Adler — *CBS/Fox Video* **P**
7045

Southern Comfort — Fil-Ent '81
Adventure
08465 99 mins C
B, V
Keith Carradine, Powers Boothe, Fred Ward, T.K. Carter, Franklyn Seales, directed by Walter Hill

PALADIN VIDEO HOME ENTERTAINMENT GUIDE

Set in the swamplands of Louisiana, this film tells the story of a platoon of National Guardsmen on a training exercise. Having thoughtlessly antagonised the native Cajun people, they take revenge. One by one the men are brutally murdered and their battle for victory becomes a struggle for survival.

BBFC:X — A — EN

20th Century Fox — *THORN EMI* P
TXA 90 0838 4/TVA 90 0838 2

Souvenir Video Guide to Royal London 1981   Fil-Ent '81

Documentary

06296   30 mins   C

V2, B, V

This cassette designed to commemorate the Royal Wedding contains well-known places of interest and landmarks including little known places of historical interest presented in a useful, interesting and amusing way with many anecdotes.

F — EN

Unknown — *World of Video 2000*   H, P
GF523

Soylent Green   Fil-Ent '73

Science fiction

07732   94 mins   C

B, V

Charlton Heston, Leigh Taylor-Young, Edward G. Robinson, Chuck Connors, Joseph Cotten, Brock Peters, Paula Kelly, directed by Richard Fleischer

This film is set in the 21st century when the potential of our daily destruction of the earth's natural resources is horrifically realised, when the enormous population of New York exists in perpetual heat and everyone lives on synthetic food. A police inspector investigating a murder discovers what Soylent Green, the staple diet, is made of. Based on the novel by Harry Harrison.

BBFC:AA — S,A — EN

MGM — *MGM/UA Home Video*   P
UMB 10070/UMV 10070

Space Academy   Fil-Ent '73

Science fiction

12175   82 mins   C

B, V

Jonathan Harris, Pamelyn Ferdin, Ric Carrot, Ty Henderson, Maggie Cooper, Brian Tochi, Eric Greene

A gigantic space station glides through the solar system, founded in the star year 3372. Its purpose is to train young astronauts for the exploration of space and to overcome the terrifying problems of the unknown.

F — EN

Filmation Associates — *Select Video Limited*   P
3607/43

Space Bandit   Fil-Ent '??

Cartoons/Science fiction

06249   30 mins   C

B, V

Animated

This film features the comic adventures of the Space Bandit as he is relentlessly pursued from one end of the galaxy to the other and how Intergalactic goodies battle with the Cosmic baddies.

F — EN

Unknown — *VCL Video Services*   P
F125A

Space Cruiser   Fil-Ent '77

Science fiction

02394   91 mins   C

B, V

Animated

Earth is near destruction under attack by the evil Gorgons, but an offer of help is made by the Queen of Iscandar, a planet thousands of light years away. The Space Cruiser is secretly equipped for the journey and sets its course through uncharted space dominated by the Gorgons.

F — EN

Enterprise Pictures — *Derann Film Services*   H, P
DV 121B/DV 121

Space Firebird   Fil-Ent '8?

Cartoons/Science fiction

12715   116 mins   C

B, V

Animated

Set in the year 2776, Godoh is a space pilot trained by robots and computers whose mission is to save the Earth from extinction.

M,S — EN

Unknown — *Mountain/Graphic*   P
MGV 2002

Space Hijack   Fil-Ent '64

Cartoons/Adventure

09143   90 mins   C

B, V

Animated

(For Explanation of codes, see USE GUIDE and KEY)   609

PALADIN VIDEO HOME ENTERTAINMENT GUIDE

This film features the heroic Commander Scott. Having returned from a recent mission, he learns that he must immediately blast off again into space in a desperate attempt to ensure food supplies for mankind. The ingenious device that makes food grow on dead and dying planets has been hijacked, and the crew have to confront the evil queen and her major.
F — EN
TV Comics — Video Brokers **H, P**

Space Riders   Fil-Ent '83
Drama/Adventure
12888   97 mins   C
B, V
Barry Sheene, Gavin O'Herlihy, Toshiya Ito, Stephanie McLean, directed by Joe Massot
This is the story of a team's bid to win the world motorcycle championship. The theme music is performed by Fashion and tracks by other artists are included in the backing.
BBFC:PG — S,A — EN
Unknown — THORN EMI   **P**
TXA 90 23614/TVA 90 23612

Space Sentinels   Chi-Juv '77
Cartoons/Science fiction
13002   62 mins   C
B, V
Animated
A spaceship that lies deep in the heart of an extinct volcano manned by three sentinels and a robot is brought into action to keep the planet Earth safe from its invaders.
PS,M — EN
Filmation Associates — Select Video Limited
P
3629/43

Spacehunter   Fil-Ent '83
Science fiction/Drama
12487   154 mins   C
B, V
Peter Strauss, Molly Ringwald, directed by Lamont Johnson
This is the story of Wolff, a pilot of a salvage space craft who responds to a galactic distress signal and during his search for three lovely space maidens marooned on a plague-infested planet encounters many deadly adversaries in the Forbidden Zone.
BBFC:15 — F — EN
Don Carmody — RCA/Columbia Pictures Video UK   **H, P**
10275

Spaceman and King Arthur, The   Fil-Ent '83
Adventure
12568   93 mins   C
B, V
Kenneth More, Dennis Dugan
Two less than willing travellers find themselves time warped back to the days of King Arthur and become knights in shining space suits.
F — EN
Walt Disney Productions — Rank Video Library
H
160

Spaceship   Fil-Ent '80
Science fiction/Comedy
13235   82 mins   C
B, V
Cindy Williams, Leslie Nielson, Patrick Macnee, Gerrit Graham, Bruce Kimmel, directed by Bruce Kimmel
Alien and man meet face to face aboard the U.S.S. Vertigo and it is a race for survival on both sides.
S,A — EN
Mark Haggard — Entertainment in Video
H, P
EVB 1021/EVV 1021

Spacewatch   Gen-Edu '8?
Astronomy
10010   60 mins   C
B, V
Animated
This is a young person's guide to space and astronomy, the planets, the stars, comets, and meteors. It mixes animation, the latest photographs and images collected by the world's most powerful telescopes.
M,S — ED
Longman Video; TV-am — Longman Video
P
LGBE 5018/LGVH 5018

Spandau Ballet: Live Over Britain   Fil-Ent '83
Music-Performance
10027   60 mins   C
B, V
Filmed live at Sadlers Wells Theatre in London, this music video includes 'Gold,' 'Lifeline,' 'Chant No. 1,' 'Instinction' and 'True.'
M,A — EN
Unknown — Palace Video Ltd   **P**
CVIM 11

Spanish Main/Motor Maniacs/My Pal/Who's Zoo in Africa, The   Fil-Ent '??
Adventure/Comedy
05662   146 mins   C
B, V

610   (For Explanation of codes, see USE GUIDE and KEY)

PALADIN VIDEO HOME ENTERTAINMENT GUIDE

Maureen O'Hara, Paul Henreid, Walter Slezak, Nancy Gates, directed by Frank Borzage, Edgar Kennedy, Ted Donaldson, Sharyn Moffat, James Finlayson

This cassette includes one film and three shorts. 'The Spanish Main' (Colour, 95 mins, 1946) is a film of piracy on the high seas in the 17th Century. An evil pirate is out for revenge on a cruel Spanish Governor. He captures the Governor's fiancee and forces her to marry him; she protests but soon sees the advantage of her new position. 'Motor Maniacs' (Black/White 17 mins, 1947) features a man having trouble with a runaway outboard motor; 'My Pal' (Black/White, 17 mins, 1948) is the tale of a boy and a dog who face separation when his rfeal owner turns up. 'Who's Zoo in Africa' (Black/white, 17 mins 1934) is a comedy in which a jungle safari searches for Tarzan but find something more exotic.

F — EN

RKO et al — Kingston Video   H, P
KV50

Spare Parts   Fil-Ent '8?
Horror
09288   108 mins   C
V

Jutta Spiedel, Wolf Roth, Herbert Herrman, Charlotte Kerr, Christoph Lindert

A small motel in the New Mexico desert called 'Honeymoon Inn' is the setting for a bizarre operation. Young and healthy visitors are abducted at night by ambulance and driven to an Air Force Base Hospital. All vital organs are carefully removed and sold to organ banks; what remains is meticulously incinerated.

A — EN

Unknown — Direct Video Services   H, P

Spasmo   Fil-Ent '75
Adventure
09228   120 mins   C
B, V

Robert Hoffman, Suzy Kendall

When a young playboy meets a charming independent English girl, it seems a perfect love match. Then an unknown man is killed in their bathroom, and when they escape to find out the truth, their nightmare begins.

C,A — EN

Libra Films — Video Form Pictures   H, P
DIP 2

Special Cop in Action   Fil-Ent '76
Crime-Drama
02110   100 mins   C
V2, B, V

Commissioner Bett wages a ferocious war against the underworld after a bank robbery and the kidnapping of some children in a school bus.

C,A — EN

Italy — Hokushin Audio Visual Ltd   P
VM-23

Special Train for Hitler   Fil-Ent '??
War-Drama
06123   90 mins   C
V2, B, V

Monika Swinn, Erik Muller, Claudine Beccarie

This film is set in Berlin during World War II. A dedicated Nazi leaves her cabaret act to lead a group of young girls destined to entertain the soldiers at the Front. The convoy is joined by a group of female prisoners and gets involved in enemy action.

S,A — EN

Unknown — Video Programme Distributors P
Cinehollywood—V990

Specialist, The   Fil-Ent '76
Adventure
09217   90 mins   C
B, V

Franco Gasparri, John Saxon, John Steiner

This film tells a spy story about a secret agent who infiltrates a terrorist movement on behalf of the CIA. However, after an attempt on his life he realises that there is no-one that he can trust.

S,A — EN

Italy — Video Form Pictures   H, P
CLO 4

Spectre of Edgar Allan Poe, The   Fil-Ent '72
Horror
09309   90 mins   C
V2, B, V

Robert Walker Jr, Cesar Romero, Tom Drake, Carole Ohmart

This is an attempt to find out what drove the author of 'The Fall of the House of Usher,' 'The Raven,' 'The Pit and the Pendulum' into the bizarre world of madness and murder.

A — EN

Cinerama — ADB Video Distribution   P

Spectreman   Fil-Ent '6?
Science fiction/Cartoons
04338   60 mins   C
V2, B, V
Animated   12 pgms

Spectreman is endowed with immortal powers to defend Earth against Dr. Gori's prehistoric monsters. Twenty-four untitled half-hour episodes are available on twelve tapes.

PALADIN VIDEO HOME ENTERTAINMENT GUIDE

F — EN
Fuji Studios — *Intervision Video*   **H, P**
A-AE 0244; A-AE 0245; A-AE 0246; A-AE 0247;
A-AE 0248; A-AE 0249; A-AE 0250; A-AE 0251;
A-AE 0252; A-AE 0253; A-AE 0254; A-AE 0255

Speed Fever   Spo-Lei '7?
Automobiles-Racing
09166   96 mins   C
V
This film shows the real-life spills and thrills of the racing circuit, including the dramatic and exciting experience of some of the world's top racing drivers.
F — EN
Unknown — *Medusa Communications Ltd*
H, P

Speedtrap/Carquake   Fil-Ent '78
Crime-Drama/Adventure
08819   180 mins   C
B, V
Joe Don Baker, Tyne Daly, Richard Jaeckel, Robert Loggia, Morgan Woodward, Lana Wood, Directed by Earl Bellamy; David Carradine
Two films are contained on one cassette. In 'Speedtrap' a group of insurance companies hire a private investigator to catch the thief commiting the car thefts that have been occuring. In 'Carquake' one of the most dangerous races in America is featured.
BBFC:A — S,A — EN
First Artist-Intermar Prod — *VCL Video Services*   **P**
P300D

Speedway   Spo-Lei '81
Automobiles-Racing
12769   55 mins   C
B, V
This features the World Individual Final 1981 with action and interviews, starring Bruce Penhall, Ole Olsen, Tommy Knudsen, Kenny Carter, Michael Lee, Eric Gundersen.
F — EN
Unknown — *VideoSpace Ltd*   **P**

Spellbound   Fil-Ent '45
Drama
04209   111 mins   B/W
B, V
Ingrid Bergman, Gregory Peck, directed by Alfred Hitchcock
A young man, suffering from amnesia and accused of murder, is helped by a female psychiatrist who loves him.
BBFC:A — S,A — EN
Selznick — *Guild Home Video*   **H, P**

Spetters   Fil-Ent '80
Drama
10087   110 mins   C
V2, B, V
Toon Agterberg, Maarten Spanjer, Hans von Tongeren, Renee Soutendijk, directed by Paul Verhoeven
This story centres round three youths living in a small town in Holland who dream of success on the international motorcross circuit. They meet up with a restless young girl and each one has to face the truth about himself.
BBFC:18 — A — EN
Joop Van Der Ende — *Embassy Home Entertainment*   **P**
3016

Sphinx   Fil-Ent '80
Drama/Suspense
13167   118 mins   C
B, V
Lesley-Anne Downe, Frank Langella, John Gielgud, directed by Franklin J Schaffner
While holidaying in Cairo, a young Egyptologist finds herself the victim of a vicious gang who are plundering a mysterious tomb, and depends for her survival on locating its secret.
BBFC:AA — C,A — EN
Orion Pictures — *Warner Home Video*   **P**
72015

Spider-Man and The Dragon's Challenge   Fil-Ent '80
Adventure/Fantasy
13077   93 mins   C
B, V
Spider-Man goes into action again to help protect a Chinese official falsely accused of selling military secrets and aids him in proving his innocence.
M,A — EN
Lionel E. Siegel — *RCA/Columbia Pictures Video UK*   **H, P**
10293

Spider-Woman   Fil-Ent '82
Cartoons/Adventure
08389   112 mins   C
V2, B, V
Animated
When Jessica Drew, more commonly known as Spider-Woman, visited her father in his laboratory she was bitten by a poisonous spider. To save her life, Dr. Drew had to inject her with some untested serum. This gave her spider-like powers which she uses to fight off evil.
I,S — EN
Marvel Comics Group — *Guild Home Video*
H, P, E

---

612   (For Explanation of codes, see USE GUIDE and KEY)

PALADIN VIDEO HOME ENTERTAINMENT GUIDE

Spider-Woman-Cassette 2 — Fil-Ent '82
Cartoons/Adventure
09439   60 mins   C
B, V
Animated
This tape contains three further adventures of Jessica Drew, a magazine reporter who is transformed into Spider-Woman whenever evil threatens; The Amazon Adventure, The Kingpin Strikes Again and the Lost Continent.
BBFC:U — F — EN
Marvel Comics — *Guild Home Video*   H, P, E

Spider-Woman in Dracula's Revenge — Fil-Ent '84
Adventure
13372   80 mins   C
V2, B, V
Jessica Drew
Spider-Woman is working as a magazine reporter in four more episodes titled 'Dracula's Revenge,' 'Games of Doom,' 'Spider-Woman and the Fly' and 'The Kongo Spider.'
BBFC:U — F — EN
Unknown — *Guild Home Video*   H, P, E

Spiral Staircase, The — Fil-Ent '46
Suspense/Drama
04210   83 mins   B/W
B, V
Dorothy McGuire, George Brent, Ethel Barrymore
A young mute girl exposes a mysterious killer who can accept no physical defect in a human being.
BBFC:A — S,A — EN
Selznick — *Guild Home Video*   H, P

Spirit of the Wind — Fil-Ent '79
Adventure
10095   98 mins   C
B, V
Slim Pickens, Chief Dan George, Pius Savage
Set in the late 1940's this film tells the true story of a young Eskimo boy who has to leave his family to go into hospital. When he returns he finds the traditional lifestyle constricting. Torn between two cultures he finds the solution by becoming a champion dog-sled racer despite his crippling bone disease.
BBFC:PG — M,A — EN
Unknown — *VideoSpace Ltd*   P

Spirits of Bruce Lee — Fil-Ent '8?
Martial arts
09821   90 mins   C
B, V
Set on the Burma-Thailand border, a young Kung-Fu expert is attacked by bandits. He is rescued by a lonesome traveller in search of his brother. The two become friends but a dangerous journey awaits them.
S,A — EN
Unknown — *Polygram Video*   H, P
790 4504/790 4502

Spitfire — Gen-Edu '82
Documentary/Aeronautics
09311   59 mins   C
B, V
This documentary about the Spitfire fighter plane contains rare archival footage of combat sequences, as well as new colour footage of surviving Spitfires in flight. Some black and white sequences.
S,A — EN
Unknown — *THORN EMI*   P
TXE 90 0844 4/TVE 90 0844 2

Splash — Fil-Ent '84
Romance/Fantasy
13742   105 mins   C
B, V
Daryl Hannah, Eugene Levy, John Candy, Tom Hanks, directed by Ron Howard
A mermaid falls in love with a man she rescues from drowning and follows him to New York where she swaps her tail for a pair of legs and pursues him relentlessly.
BBFC:PG — F — EN
Walt Disney Productions — *Rank Video Library*   P
213

Split Enz — Fil-Ent '83
Music-Performance
13137   54 mins   C
B, V
Neil Finn, Tim Finn, Noel Crombie, Nigel Grigg, Eddie Rayner
This New Zealand group is recorded live at the Hamilton Place, Ontario, and includes their tracks 'Six Months in a Leaky Boat,' 'I Got You,' 'Giant Heartbeat' in the programme and is recorded in stereo.
F — EN
Unknown — *Polygram Video*   P
040 2664/040 2662

Split Image — Fil-Ent '82
Drama
13127   107 mins   C
B, V
Michael O'Keefe, Karen Allen, Peter Fonda, James Woods, directed by Ted Kotcheff

(For Explanation of codes, see USE GUIDE and KEY)

PALADIN VIDEO HOME ENTERTAINMENT GUIDE

Distraught parents seek assistance when their college student son is drawn into an insidious religious sect after becoming attracted by one of its followers.
BBFC:15 — S,A — EN
Orion Pictures; Polygram Pictures — *Polygram Video* **P**
041 0454/041 0452

Sporting Chance   Fil-Ent '72
Crime-Drama/Adventure
07358   60 mins   C
B, V
Tony Curtis, Roger Moore
This is one of a series of adventures featuring the American millionaire and English aristocrat who were born to flirt, especially with danger.
S,A — EN
ITC — *Precision Video Ltd*   **P**
BITC 2066/VITC 2066

Spring Fever   Fil-Ent '82
Drama
13783   95 mins   C
B, V
Susan Anton, Frank Converse, Jessica Walter, directed by Joseph L. Scanlan
Set during the competitive heat of the Junior Tennis Finals in Florida, this is the story of the rivalry between two precocious young girls who will stop at nothing to get ahead in the tournaments.
BBFC:15 — S,A — EN
Manson International Release — *Odyssey Video*   **H, P**
6540

Spy Killer, The   Fil-Ent '69
Suspense
04264   72 mins   C
B, V
Robert Horton, Jill St. John, Sebastian Cabot
Counter espionage, political intrigue and blackmail are the pieces in a puzzle that threatens the life of former secret-agent John Smith in this taut thriller set in London's corridors of power.
C,A — EN
ABC Films — *Rank Video Library*   **H, P**
0033

Spy Story   Fil-Ent '76
Suspense
01195   92 mins   C
V2, B, V

Len Deighton's bespectacled, wisecracking intelligence agent, Harry Palmer, returns to the screen for more action-packed and suspenseful adventures—but this time he uses a different name, Patrick Armstrong.
S,A — EN
Lindsay Shontoff — *Intervision Video*   **H, P**
A-A 0190

Spy Who Loved Me, The   Fil-Ent '77
Adventure
13194   125 mins   C
B, V
Roger Moore, directed by Lewis Gilbert
When British and Russian submarines vanish mysteriously 007 joins forces with a beautiful Soviet spy, and their investigations lead to a megalomaniac shipping magnate and a seven foot, steel toothed giant called Jaws!
BBFC:A — C,A — EN
United Artists — *Warner Home Video*   **P**
99201

S*P*Y*S   Fil-Ent '74
Comedy
04659   100 mins   C
B, V
Donald Sutherland, Elliott Gould
Two rather clumsy CIA agents discover a list of KGB agents in China.
F — EN
Dymphana; C-W; American Film Properties — *THORN EMI*   **H, P**
TXC 90 0236 4/TVC 90 0236 2

Squash Coaching for School and Clubs   Spo-Lei '8?
Sports
13543   25 mins   C
B, V
Directed by Richard Hackett
Basic teaching methods of squash are demonstrated in this film which is made under the 'Challenge to Youth' scheme and highlights from a National Under 16 Championship are shown.
M,S — I
A Gerard Holdsworth Production — *TFI Leisure Ltd*   **H, P**

Squash Part 1   Spo-Lei '80
Sports-Minor
00262   60 mins   C
B, V, FO

614   (For Explanation of codes, see USE GUIDE and KEY)

PALADIN VIDEO HOME ENTERTAINMENT GUIDE

This programme introduces the game and the two fundamental shots, the forehand and backhand drives. This programme has been made on behalf of the Sports Council of Great Britain in association with, and endorsed by, the Squash Rackets Association.
F — I
London Video Ltd — *Video Sport for All*
P
1006

Squash Part 1- Elementary   Spo-Lei '8?
Sports-Minor
09987   60 mins   C
B, V
Introduced by Stephen Alcock
This tape clearly explains and demonstrates the fundamental but important aspects of the game.
S,A — I
Holiday Brothers Ltd — *Holiday Brothers Ltd*
P

Squash Part 2   Spo-Lei '80
Sports-Minor
00263   60 mins   C
B, V, FO
In this second programme, more sophisticated shots are introduced, as well as rules and tactics. This programme has been made on behalf of the Sports Council of Great Britain in association with, and endorsed by the Squash Rackets Association.
F — I
London Video Ltd — *Video Sport for All*
P
1007

Squash Part 2- Intermediate   Spo-Lei '8?
Sports-Minor
09986   60 mins   C
B, V
In this second tape a close look is made of the more advanced attacking and defensive shots. Let and Stroke situations are explained in detail.
S,A — I
Holiday Brothers Ltd — *Holiday Brothers Ltd*
P

Squash Part 3-Advanced   Spo-Lei '8?
Sports-Minor
09985   60 mins   C
B, V
This final tape is aimed at the more competitive player showing advanced techniques.
S,A — I
Holiday Brothers Ltd — *Holiday Brothers Ltd*
P

Squash Rackets 1   Spo-Lei '7?
Sports-Minor
01897   26 mins   C
B, V, LV
The first of two basic films introducing the game of squash which takes players by carefully graded stages and onto a level of match play and tactics.
C,A — I
Rank — *Rank Video Library*   H, P
5004

Squash Rackets 2   Spo-Lei '7?
Sports-Minor
01898   26 mins   C
B, V
Anthony Swift
Second in the series of two squash instruction films. Part two covers more sophisticated shots as well as rules and tactics for the serious match play competitor.
C,A — I
Rank — *Rank Video Library*   H, P
5005

Squeeze, The   Fil-Ent '77
Crime-Drama
12676   102 mins   C
B, V
Stacy Keach, David Hemmings, Edward Fox, Stephen Boyd, Carol White, Freddie Star, directed by Michael Apted
An ex-police inspector who lost his job through alcoholism takes on the vicious gangsters who have kidnapped his ex-wife and his daughter and are holding them hostage to pull off a $1 million robbery.
BBFC:18 — *A — EN*
Stanley OToole — *Warner Home Video*
P
61145

Squeeze a Flower   Fil-Ent '70
Comedy
12142   105 mins   C
V2, B, V
Dave Allen, Walter Chiari, Jack Albertson
A wily monk arrives in Australia with his secret formula for a liquer which was his monastery's main source of income in Italy. He starts to manufacture it under an assumed name, but the local owner of the wine shop and his son-in-law try to outsmart him.
BBFC:U — *F — EN*
NTL Group W Films — *Intervision Video*
H, P
A-A0445

(For Explanation of codes, see USE GUIDE and KEY)

PALADIN VIDEO HOME ENTERTAINMENT GUIDE

Squirm
Fil-Ent '76
Horror
09934 91 mins C
B, V

Don Scardino, Patricia Pearcy, R.A. Dow, Jean Sullivan

This is a horrifying story of a community besieged by bait worms that become charged with electrical energy when a freak storm brings down power cables.
BBFC:18 — A — EN
American International — Rank Video Library
H, P
2028 Y

Squirm
Fil-Ent '76
Horror
13454 91 mins C
B, V

Don Scarding, Patricia Pearcy, R A Dow, Jean Sullivan

This is the story of a community besieged by bait worms who have been charged with electrical energy when a freak storm brings down the power lines.
BBFC:18 — A — EN
Orion Pictures — Rank Video Library
H, P
2028 Y

SS Girls
Fil-Ent '78
War-Drama
08888 82 mins C
V2, B, V

Gabriele Carrara, Marina Davnia, Vassilli Karis, Macha Magal, Thomas Rudy, Lucic Bogoljub Benny, Ivano Staccioli

After the attack of July 1944, Hitler does not trust the Wermacht and extends the power of the SS over Germany. General Berger entrusts Hans Schillemberg to recruit a specially chosen group of prostitutes to test the fighting spirit and loyalty of the Generals.
BBFC:X — A — EN
Topar Films — Video Programme Distributors
P
Media 518

S.T.A.B
Fil-Ent '76
Crime-Drama
06929 96 mins C
B, V

Greg Morris, Tham Thuy Hang

During the Vietnam war a drug syndicate sends a plane-load of gold bars to buy the entire opium harvest of Southeast Asia's Golden Triangle. An international narcotics bureau is after the gold and so are the Vietcong, who skyjack the gold and take it to a stronghold in Laos. Only one man can retrieve the gold, the leader of the mercenary group S.T.A.B. His fee is five million dollars.
BBFC:X — A — EN
Paragon Films — Rank Video Library
H, P
0081C

Stacey!
Fil-Ent '??
Adventure
08687 83 mins C
V2, B, V

Anne Randall, Alan Landers, Marjorie Bennett, Anitra Ford, directed by Andy Sidaris

A female 'private-eye' is hired by a wealthy woman to check out the heirs to her fortune. Her investigations lead her to blackmail and murder with the discovery of vital photographs. She is cornered in a race track gunbattle but escapes in a racing car, pursued by a helicopter.
BBFC:X — A — EN
Unknown — Derann Film Services
P
FDV313

Stage Struck/The Girl Most Likely
Fil-Ent '??
Drama/Musical
05777 180 mins C
B, V

Henry Fonda, Susan Strasberg, Christopher Plummer, directed by Sydney Lumet, Jane Powell, Cliff Robertson, directed by Mitchell Leisen

Two films are contained on one cassette. 'Stage Struck' (colour, 91 minutes, 1949) is about a would-be actress, who climbs to Broadway success with the help of worldly and world-weary producer. 'The Girl Most Likely' (colour, 89 minutes, 1958) is a musical comedy about a girl who dreams of marrying a millionaire, but is about to settle for less when a real one comes along and her troubles begin.
S,A — EN
Buena Vista; Universal; RKO — Kingston Video
H, P
KV4

Stagecoach/Deadline at Dawn
Fil-Ent '4?
Western/Mystery
05667 172 mins B/W
B, V

John Wayne, Claire Trevour, John Carradine, Thomas Mitchell, Andy Devine, directed by John Ford, Susan Hayward, Paul Lukas, Bill Williams, directed by Harold Clurman

Two films are featured on one cassette. 'Stagecoach' (Black/white, 92 mins, 1940) is the story of a man who rides shotgun for a motley group travelling West. He becomes involved with their fears and squabbles when a

616 (For Explanation of codes, see USE GUIDE and KEY)

PALADIN VIDEO HOME ENTERTAINMENT GUIDE

lady shows an interest in him. 'Deadline at Dawn' (Black/white, 80 mins, 1947) is the story of a sailor on leave in New York who is rescued by a girl and a taxi driver when he becomes involved in murder, they help him solve it, but one of them may be the killer.
Academy Award '39: Best Supporting Actor (Mitchell) ('Stagecoach'). *F — EN*
United Artists; RKO — *Kingston Video*
H, P
KV45

Stages to Victory 1976   Spo-Lei '76
Automobiles-Racing
04508   40 mins   C
B, V
The story of the 1976 Castrol/Autosport Rally Championship which was fought over ten rounds with the issue undecided until the very end.
F — EN
Avon Tyre — *Quadrant Video*   **H, P**
M23

Stalag 17   Fil-Ent '52
War-Drama
13332   92 mins   B/W
B, V
William Holden, Don Taylor, Otto Preminger, Peter Graves, Jay Lawrence, Richard Erdman, directed by Billy Wilder
A group of GI's in a German P.O.W. Camp spend their time plotting different ways to escape but when two of them are shot it becomes clear that there is an informer amongst them.
Academy Awards '53: Best Actor (Holden).
BBFC:PG — *S,A — EN*
Paramount — *CIC Video*   **H, P**
BEJ 2096/VHJ 2096

Stamping Ground   Fil-Ent '70
Music-Performance
06785   91 mins   C
V2, B, V
Pink Floyd, Santana, Jefferson Airplane, Canned Heat, the Byrds
This concert was filmed live at the Holland Music Festival before an audience of 300,000 cheering fans.
S,A — EN
Atlas — *Intervision Video*   **H, P**
A-A 0337

Stanley Baxter Picture Show—Part 3, The   Fil-Ent '??
Comedy-Performance
08573   51 mins   C
B, V
Stanley Baxter, directed by Jon Scoffield
Stanley Baxter presents a series of impersonations from the world of film and television. He gives his own version of a 'Warner Sisters' musical production. Other features include an unusual version of 'I've Grown Accustomed to Her Face,' an 'Offer You Can't Refuse' in a party political broadcast and some views from the Vatican.
S,A — EN
London Weekend Television Limited — *THORN EMI*   **P**
TXB 90 1008 4/TVB 90 10082

Stanley Baxter's Moving Picture Show   Fil-Ent '74
Comedy-Performance
06282   51 mins   C
B, V
Stanley Baxter, directed by David Bell
In this film, Stanley Baxter, through his uncannily accurate impersonations, gives a show of a compilation of parody and pastiche on famous personalities from the world of film and television. It includes 'Upstage Downstage,' 'Thumpalong with Reg Varnish' and '2001—a Royal Wedding Odyssey' amongst others.
Society of Film and TV Arts '74: Best Light Entertainment Programme and Performance.
S,A — EN
London Weekend Television Limited — *THORN EMI*   **P**
TXB 90 0695 4/TVB 90 0695 2

Star Chamber, The   Fil-Ent '83
Crime-Drama
13258   104 mins   C
B, V
Michael Douglas, Hal Holbrook, Haphet Rotto, Sharon Gless, directed by Peter Hyams
A young lawyer horrified by vicious criminals who are allowed to get off scot-free joins a secret court who mete out their own brand of justice to these people.
BBFC:15 — *C,A — EN*
Frank Yablans — *CBS/Fox Video*   **P**
1295

Star 80   Fil-Ent '83
Drama/Biographical
12974   100 mins   C
B, V
Mariel Hemingway, Eric Roberts, Cliff Robertson, Carroll Baker, directed by Bob Fosse

---

(For Explanation of codes, see USE GUIDE and KEY)

PALADIN VIDEO HOME ENTERTAINMENT GUIDE

Based on the true story of Dorothy Stratten who was discovered at 17 and groomed to stardom and success in the Playboy magazine to be brutally murdered by her psychopathic husband.
BBFC:18 — A — EN
Wolfgang Glattes; Kenneth Utt — *Warner Home Video* **P**
70013

Star Fleet Chl-Juv '82
Science fiction
09314 48 mins C
B, V
Two programs from television's popular 'Star Fleet' series, featuring the action-packed adventures of the crew of the Star Fleet.
PS,M — EN
Unknown — *THORN EMI* **P**
TXE 90 1663 4/TVE 90 1663 2

Star Is Born, A Fll-Ent '37
Musical-Drama
06882 110 mins C
V2, B, V
Janet Gaynor, Fredric March, Adolphe Menjou, May Robson, Andy Devine, Directed by William Wellman
This film traces the rise to stardom of a stage-struck girl who is helped in her career by an established actor. When her career begins to take-off they decide to marry, but his alcoholism brings tragedy.
S,A — EN
United Artists — *European Video Company* **P**

Star Is Born, A Fll-Ent '76
Musical-Drama/Romance
07870 135 mins C
B, V
Barbra Streisand, Kris Kristofferson, Paul Mazursky, Gary Busey, Oliver Clark, directed by Frank Pierson
This story follows the rise to stardom of an unknown but talented singer whose career is boosted by an established rock star. As their stormy relationship deepens they marry, but as she goes on to become successful and his career wanes, tragedy strikes.
BBFC:AA — S,A — EN
Warner Bros; Barwood/Jon Peters Prods — *Warner Home Video* **P**
WEX 61020/WEV 61020

Star Pilot Fll-Ent '70
Science fiction
08649 78 mins C
V2, B, V
Kirk Morris, Gordon Mitchell

A small space craft bound for the planet Hydra in a distant galaxy is captured by space invaders. The Professor and his assistants are diverted to an unknown planet with frightening results.
S,A — EN
Unknown — *Fletcher Video* **H, P**
V178

Star Trek II: The Wrath of Khan Fll-Ent '82
Science fiction
10119 109 mins C
B, V
William Shatner, Leonard Nimoy, DeForest Kelly, James Doohan, Ricardo Montalban, directed by Nicholas Meyer
The Enterprise team beam down to the swirling desert and find they have to pit their wits against a long-ago enemy out to take revenge.
BBFC:PG — F — EN
Paramount — *CIC Video* **H, P**
BEA 2062/VHA 2062

Star Trek—Menagerie Fll-Ent '67
Science fiction
06879 90 mins C
V2, B, V
William Shatner, Leonard Nimoy, DeForest Kelly, Jeffrey Hunter, Susan Oliver, Majel Barrett
The original 'Star Trek' TV pilot film, starring Jeffrey Hunter as Captain Pike, was incorporated into this two-part episode. Mr. Spock is put on trial for kidnapping Captain Pike and the Enterprise to return to planet Talos 4, the scene of a mystery from years past.
M,A — EN
NBC — *European Video Company* **P**

Star Trek—Shore Leave Fll-Ent '67
Science fiction
02453 49 mins C
B, V
William Shatner, Leonard Nimoy
The crew of the Enterprise lands on a planet that is a giant amusement park.
F — EN
NBC — *Mountain Video* **P**

Star Trek: The Empath/Miri Fll-Ent '6?
Science fiction
10128 96 mins C
B, V
Directed by John Erman and Vincent McEveety
Two films are contained on one cassette. 'The Empath' (1968): The crew of the Enterprise investigate the disappearance of two Federation

PALADIN VIDEO HOME ENTERTAINMENT GUIDE

doctors and come across a strange young woman with healing powers. 'Miri' (1966): The bizarre tale of an alien race consisting of 'children' who are hundreds of years old.
BBFC:U — F — EN
Paramount — CIC Video   **H, P**
BEL 2075/VHL 2075

Star Trek—The Motion Picture   Fil-Ent '79
Science fiction/Adventure
05333   130 mins   C
V2, B, V
William Shatner, Leonard Nimoy, DeForest Kelley, directed by Robert Wise
When an unidentified alien destroys three powerful Klingon cruisers, Captain James T. Kirk returns to the newly-transformed refurbished U.S.S. Enterprise to resume command. He is joined on this heroic mission by his former crew including Mr. Spock and 'Bones.' Based on the 'Star Trek' television series.
F — EN
Paramount — CIC Video   **H, P**
CRA2011/BEA2011/VHA2011

Star Trek III: The Search for Spock   Fil-Ent '84
Science fiction
13628   100 mins   C
B, V
William Shatner, Mark Lenard, Leonard Nimoy, DeForest Kelley, Robin Curtis, Christopher Lloyd, directed by Leonard Nimoy
Mr. Spock's body and soul have become separated by millions of miles and his father asks Kirk to find his son's body and return it to the planet Vulcan and the Enterprise sets out on another mission.
BBFC:PG — S,A — EN
Paramount — CIC Video   **H, P**
2118

Star Trek: Whom Gods Destroy/Plato's Stepchildren   Fil-Ent '69
Science fiction/Adventure
13282   97 mins   C
B, V
William Shatner, Leonard Nimoy, DeForest Kelley, Nichelle Nichols
Two films are contained on one cassette. In 'Whom Gods Destroy' (1969). Captain Kirk Co have to deal with a shape—changing lunatic and in 'Plato's Stepchildren' (1968) they are enslaved by beings with strange mental powers.
F — EN
Paramount — CIC Video   **H, P**
BEN 2084/VHN 2084

Star Wars   Fil-Ent '77
Science fiction
07686   116 mins   C
V2, B, V
Mark Hamill, Harrison Ford, Carrie Fisher, Sir Alec Guinness, Peter Cushing, directed by George Lucas
This epic space adventure features the fearless adventurer Luke Skywalker, the mercenary space pilot Han Solo, the Princess Leia and the robots C-3PO and R2-D2 in the age-old fight against evil. Special effects are used to create wondrous monsters, 'The Force' and the space battles including the death duel between Ben Obi-Wan Kenobi and Darth Vadar.
F — EN
Lucasfilm Ltd; 20th Century Fox — CBS/Fox Video   **P**
1052

Starbird and Sweet William   Fil-Ent '74
Adventure/Drama
02064   90 mins   C
B, V
A heartwarming story of a young American Indian stranded by a plane crash and fighting for survival in the wild. Befriended by an orphaned grizzly bear cub and a lovable raccoon, he fights his way back to civilization.
F — EN
Dick Alexander — VCL Video Services   **P**

Stardust   Fil-Ent '74
Musical-Drama
00584   108 mins   C
B, V
David Essex, Adam Faith, Larry Hagman
A young man goes off to join The Stray Cats rock group. They make the big time, but the sweet taste of success begins to turn sour.
BBFC:AA — C,A — EN
David Puttnam; Sanford Lieberson — THORN EMI   **P**
TXB 90 0213 4/TVB 90 0213 2

Stardust Memories   Fil-Ent '80
Comedy-Drama
12597   85 mins   C
B, V
Woody Allen, Charlotte Rampling, Jessica Harper, Marie-Christine Barrautt, directed by Woody Allen
A famous film-maker faces a crisis in his life and career when he attends a festival of his films where he is hounded by the women in his life, fans, critics, studio executives and groupies.
BBFC:15 — C,A — EN
Robert Greenhut — Warner Home Video
P
99363

(For Explanation of codes, see USE GUIDE and KEY)

PALADIN VIDEO HOME ENTERTAINMENT GUIDE

Starfire
Fil-Ent '77
Music-Performance
04406   60 mins   C
B, V
A performance by the versatile California group recorded live in Helsinki during a European tour. Four very attractive and talented girls sing and dance to 'Everlasting Love,' 'Love Will Keep Us Together,' 'You Sexy Thing,' and 'Full of Fire.'
F — EN
VCL — VCL Video Services   P

Starflight One
Fil-Ent '83
Science fiction/Adventure
09942   114 mins   C
B, V, LV
Lee Majors, Hal Linden, Lauren Hutton, directed by Jerry Jameson
A hypersonic plan is blasted into sub-orbital space after a near collision with an unauthorised missile carrying a pirate communications satellite. This plane, never meant for space travel, fights for survival 87 miles above the earth.
BBFC:PG — F — EN
Orgolini-Nelson Prod. — Rank Video Library   H, P
0175 4

Starhops
Fil-Ent '80
Comedy
12595   82 mins   C
V2, B, V
Dorothy Buhrman, Sterling Frazier, Jillian Kesner, directed by Barbara Peeters
Two young waitresses working in a hamburger joint decide to pitch their savings together and seize their opportunity to become businesswomen.
BBFC:15 — F — EN
John B Kelly; Robert D Krintzman — Intervision Video   H, P
6616

Starlet
Fil-Ent '8?
Drama
09292   99 mins   C
V
Shari Mann, Deidre Nelson, Stuart Lancaster, John Alderman, Chris Mathis
This film follows the sometimes sordid, sometimes sad and sometimes funny story of the path to success of three movie 'hopefuls'.
A — EN
Unknown — Rex   H, P

Stars on 45
Fil-Ent '84
Music-Performance
13313   68 mins   C
B, V

A cast of 22 singers, dancers and musicians perform the top songs of the last 30 years in the styles of the artists who made them famous.
F — EN
Universal — CIC Video   H, P
BER 1112/VHR 1112

Starship Invasions
Fil-Ent '78
Science fiction
12079   88 mins   C
V2, B, V
Robert Vaughan, Christopher Lee
Alien starships are looking for a new planet to conquer and Earth is their choice. It is up to the League of Races to protect the world and they engage the help of a computer expert after one of their saucers are damaged in a skirmish.
F — EN
Warner Bros — Intervision Video   H, P
A-A 7001

Starstruck
Fil-Ent '82
Drama
09902   95 mins   C
B, V
Jo Kennedy, Ross O'Donovan
This film tells the story of a girl whose ambition is to become a singing star. She is working as a barmaid at her family's pub where business is going downhill fast. She is assisted in her attempts by her eccentric young cousin. She is soon a celebrity but cannot ignore the fact that her family is in trouble. The music is supplied by The Swingers, led by former Split Enz member, Phil Judd.
S,A — EN
Cinecom International Films — Entertainment in Video   H, P
EVB 1014/EVV 1014

Starting Basic with BBC Micro Computer No. 1
Gen-Edu '8?
Electronic data processing
09991   60 mins   C
B, V
This is an introduction to the skills of computer programming to help one understand the principles of Basic and writing one's own programmes.
S,A — I
Holiday Brothers Ltd — Holiday Brothers Ltd   P

Status Quo-Live in Concert at the N.E.C. Birmingham
Fil-Ent '??
Music-Performance
09879   80 mins   C
B, V, LV

PALADIN VIDEO HOME ENTERTAINMENT GUIDE

This features one of the world's most established rock bands and includes fourteen of their most well-known tracks. Recorded in stereo.
F — EN
Unknown — Polygram Video H, P
790 6884/790 6882/790 6881

Status Quo—Off the Road Fil-Ent '81
Music-Performance/Sports
04627   30 mins   C
B, V
Sample the skill and pitfalls of a spectacular new motor sport—Off Roading. Featuring the music of Status Quo with sequences of the band in concert.
F — EN
VCL Video Services Ltd — VCL Video Services P

Stay Hungry Fil-Ent '76
Comedy-Drama
12604   99 mins   C
B, V
Jeff Bridges, Sally Field, Arnold Schwarzenegger, directed by Bob Rafelson
A wealthy young man refuses to go into the family business and instead agrees to help shady developers buy up a health club whose site they want to develop, but he falls for the club receptionist and decides to double cross the developers.
BBFC:18 — A — EN
Harold Schneider; Bob Rafelson — Warner Home Video P
99357

Staying Alive Fil-Ent '83
Musical-Drama
13299   94 mins   C
B, V
John Travolta, Cynthia Rhodes, Finola Hughes, Julie Bovasso, directed by Sylvester Stallone.
A young jazz dance class teacher sets out to conquer Broadway and discovers that getting involved with his leading lady gets him into trouble with his girlfriend. The soundtrack is by the Bee Gees.
BBFC:PG — S,A — EN
Paramount — CIC Video H, P
BER 2099/VHR 2099

Steelyard Blues Fil-Ent '73
Comedy/Adventure
07871   89 mins   C
B, V
Jane Fonda, Donald Sutherland, Peter Boyle, Roger Bowen, Garry Goodrow, Howard Hesseman, John Savage, directed by Alan Myerson
An ex-con and his call-girl girlfriend are an embarrassment to his DA brother, especially when they set out to buck the establishment by stealing an old World War II plane and attempting to make it flightworthy.
BBFC:X — A — EN
Warner Bros — Warner Home Video P
WEX 61096/WEV 61096

Stepford Wives, The Fil-Ent '75
Horror
09386   115 mins   C
B, V
Katherine Ross, Paula Prentiss, Peter Masterson, Nanette Newman, Patrick O'Neal, directed by Bryan Forbes
Set in the quiet town of Stepford, this film tells of mysterious happenings during the hours of darkness. Based on the novel by Ira Levin.
BBFC:15 — C,A — EN
Columbia Pictures — VCL Video Services P
P381D

Steps Fil-Ent '76
Drama
13477   91 mins   C
B, V
Irene Papas, Umberto Orsini
A Greek survivor of Nazi terrorism is obsessed by the need to discover whether any others of her family survived the war.
BBFC:PG — S,A — EN
Satorini Prods. — Precision Video Ltd P
2622

Steptoe and Son Fil-Ent '72
Comedy
04655   93 mins   C
B, V
Wilfrid Brambell, Harry H. Corbett, Carolyn Seymour
This lively comedy is the first of the Steptoe films, containing the same ingredients as the popular TV series.
F — EN
EMI; Associated London Films — THORN EMI H, P
TXB 90 0233 4/TVB 90 0233 2

Steve Davis' World of Snooker Volume 1 Spo-Lei '82
Sports
07881   42 mins   C
V2, B, V
Alex Higgins, Steve Davis

(For Explanation of codes, see USE GUIDE and KEY)   621

PALADIN VIDEO HOME ENTERTAINMENT GUIDE

This tape features Alex 'Hurricane' Higgins and Steve Davis in a practice match during which they explain their most spectacular shots and their strategy. They demonstrate their skill with unique shots in slow-motion, 'the machine gun', 'the Steeplechase shot' and 'the cue rampshot' providing the novice player with useful tips. Also features veteran player John Pulman.

F — EN

Unknown — *Intervision Video* **H, P**
A-AE0400

Steve Miller Band Live   Fil-Ent '83
Music-Performance
09772   60 mins   C
B, V

This tape features the Steve Miller Band recorded live in concert. Songs include 'Macho City', 'Gangster of Love', 'Rock'n Me', 'Living in the USA', 'Fly Like an Eagle', 'Jungle Love', 'The Joker', 'Heart Like a Wheel', 'Mercury Blues', 'Take the Money and Run', 'Abracadabra', 'Jet Airliner' and 'Buffalo's Serenade'. Produced by Steve Miller.

F — EN

Sailor Records — *THORN EMI*   **P**
TXE 90 2050 4/TVE 90 2050 2

Stevie   Fil-Ent '78
Biographical/Drama
05757   102 mins   C
B, V

Glenda Jackson, Mona Washbourne, Trevor Howard, Alec McCowan, directed by Robert Enders

The true story of the obscure English poetess and novelist, Stevie Smith, who died in 1971 aged 69. An outwardly conventional woman but with a deep-seated fear of middle-class institutions like marriage and religion, she won the Queen's gold medal for poetry. Written by Hugh Whitemore after two years of intensive research. Photography by Freddie Young.

BBFC:AA — S,A — EN

Bowden; First Artists; Grand Metropolitan — *Home Video Holdings*   **H, P**
006

Stevie Nicks Live in Concert   Fil-Ent '82
Music-Performance
12203   58 mins   C
B, V

This tape contains a selection of Stevie Nicks' songs, including 'Gold Dust Woman', 'Golden Braid', 'I Need To Know', 'Stop Draggin' My Heart', 'Sara', 'Edge of Seventeen', 'Outside The Rain' and 'Rhiannon'.

F — EN

Welsh Witch Inc — *CBS/Fox Video*   **P**
7136

Stiletto   Fil-Ent '69
Crime-Drama
01731   101 mins   C
B, V

Alex Cord, Britt Ekland, Patrick O'Neal, Joseph Wiseman, Barbara McNair, Roy Scheider

A young man is rescued from a mob by a Mafia gang leader after raping a young girl. Based on a novel by Harold Robbins.

A — EN

Avco Embassy; Norman Rosemont — *CBS/Fox Video*   **P**
3C-045

Still of the Night   Fil-Ent '82
Drama/Suspense
13008   88 mins   C
B, V

Roy Scheider, Meryl Streep, directed by Robert Benton

A compulsively neat psychiatrist, a beautiful rich and talented woman, and a murder victim closely connected with both of them is the background for this 'whodunnit.'

BBFC:AA — C,A — EN

United Artists — *Warner Home Video*   **P**
99313

Still Smokin'   Fil-Ent '83
Comedy
13630   92 mins   C
B, V

Cheech Martin, Thomas Chong, directed by Thomas Chong

Cheech and Chong playing all their favorite zonked-out characters and crazy routines are featured on this cassette.

BBFC:18 — A — EN

Peter Macgregor-Scott — *CIC Video*   **H, P**
2128

Stillwater Trout Fishing from a Boat   Spo-Lei '82
Fishing
13547   42 mins   C
B, V

PALADIN VIDEO HOME ENTERTAINMENT GUIDE

Bob Church, international trout angler, explains how weather and time of day affect the feeding patterns of fish and how this influences the choice of fishing methods for the brown and rainbow trout.
S,A — I
Unknown — *TFI Leisure Ltd*   H, P

Sting, The   Fil-Ent '73
Comedy-Drama
01055   129 mins   C
B, V
Paul Newman, Robert Redford, Robert Shaw, Charles Durning, Eileen Brennan, directed by George Roy Hill
A pair of con-artists in Chicago of the 1930's set out to fleece a big time racketeer, pitting brain against brawn and pistol.
Academy Awards '73: Best Picture; Best Story and Screenplay; Best Art Direction; Best Set Decoration.   A,F — EN
Universal; Richard D Zanuck — *CIC Video*
H, P

Sting II, The   Fil-Ent '83
Comedy-Drama
12035   98 mins   C
B, V
Jackie Gleason, Mac Davis, Karl Malden, directed by Paul Kagan
Set in New York in 1940, this film tells the story of two con men, one fresh out of prison, who set about arranging an elaborate hoax. As it unfolds, more and more people become involved as each one in turn tries to pull the wool over the other one's eyes.
BBFC:PG — S,A — EN
Universal — *CIC Video*   H, P
BEA 1078/VHA 1078

Stingiest Man in Town, The   Fil-Ent '84
Cartoons
12945   51 mins   C
B, V
Animated
This is a musical presentation of the classic story of Scrooge with the narration by Walter Matthau.
F — EN
Skyline — *Video Form Pictures*   H, P
CLO 11

Stingray   Fil-Ent '78
Adventure
09249   95 mins   C
V2, B, V
Christopher Mitchum, Les Lannom, Sherry Jackson, directed by Richard Taylor
Set in and around the city of St. Louis, USA, this is a fast-moving story of two men, who unsuspectingly drive off with a fortune in cash and drugs hidden in their red 'Stingray'. The pace quickens when the gangsters arrive to retrieve the loot.
BBFC:PG — F — EN
Avco Embassy — *Iver Film Services*   P
224

Stoner   Fil-Ent '76
Crime-Drama
06931   95 mins   C
B, V
George Lazenby, Angela Mao
A narcotics agent sets out to nail a gang of drug smugglers. His interest is not only professional as they have also killed his fiancee. His trail leads to Hong Kong and the gang's underground headquarters. He also finds he is not alone in his search; a woman agent tells him that she has enough evidence to put them behind bars. Together they storm the gang's stronghold, but the evil boss has other plans for them.
BBFC:X — A — EN
Unknown — *Rank Video Library*   H, P
0078C

Stones in the Park, The   Fil-Ent '69
Music-Performance
09325   53 mins   C
B, V
The Rolling Stones
A video of the classic Stones concert in Hyde Park on 5th July 1969, taking place shortly after the death of Brian Jones.
F — EN
Granada Television — *Granada Video*   H, P

Stop Smoking   Med-Sci '84
Smoking
13115   60 mins   C
B, V
Alf Fowles
This video combines soothing deep relaxation with visual messages aimed below the level of conscious perception to help the viewer to stop smoking
A — I
Holiday Brothers Ltd — *Holiday Brothers Ltd*   P

Stories from a Flying Trunk   Fil-Ent '79
Dance/Fantasy
08542   84 mins   C
B, V
Directed by Christine Edzard

(For Explanation of codes, see USE GUIDE and KEY)

PALADIN VIDEO HOME ENTERTAINMENT GUIDE

This features three of Hans Christian Andersen's fairy tales, 'The Little Match Girl', 'The Kitchen', and 'Little Ida', performed by members of the Royal Ballet, including Lesley Collier, Graham Fletcher, and Denise Nunn.
BBFC:U — F — EN
EMI Film Prod Ltd — THORN EMI   P
TXD 90 07604/TVD 90 07602

Storm Boy   Fil-Ent '79
Drama
04211   89 mins   C
B, V
Peter Cummings, Greg Rowe, David Gulpilil
This film presents the tale of Storm Boy and his tame pelican, Mr. Percival.
BBFC:U — F — EN
Matt Carroll — Guild Home Video   H, P

Storm Over the Nile   Fil-Ent '56
Adventure
01952   111 mins   C
B, V
Laurence Harvey, Anthony Steel, Mary Ure
A young man is accused of cowardice when he resigns from his Army commission, as his fellow officers leave to fight the Dervishes in the Sudan. The film is a remake of 'Four Feathers.'
F — EN
Columbia — CBS/Fox Video   P
3B-067

Story of English Furniture, The   Gen-Edu '81
Antiques
04869   108 mins   C
V2, B, V, LV
2 pgms
A series in two parts on the history of English furniture. An accompanying book entitled 'The Story of English Furniture' by Bernard Price can be obtained from booksellers. Vol 1 gives an account from the Middle Ages to the Eighteenth Century lasting 108 mins. Vol 2 covers the late Eighteeth Century to the present day lasting 107 mins.
AM Available   S,A — ED
Robin Drake; Paul Smith; John Vigar — BBC Video   H, P
BBCV 1006; BBCV 1007

Story of Jesus, The   Fil-Ent '81
Drama/Christianity
05899   110 mins   C
B, V
Brian Deacon
A deliberately matter-of-fact portrayal of the life of Jesus, based on St. Luke's gospel.
F — EN
The Genesis Project; John Heyman — THORN EMI   P
TXB 90 0307 4/TVB 90 0307 2

Story of O   Fil-Ent '75
Drama
06733   93 mins   C
V2, B, V
Corrine Clery, Udo Kier, Anthony Steel, directed by Just Jaeckin
This film based on the novel by Pauline Reage, deals with a unique love involving the willing surrender and eventual deliverance of one's body and soul to a lover.
BBFC:X — A — EN
Allied Artists — Intervision Video   H, P
A-A 0352

Story of Prince Charles and Lady Diana, The   Fil-Ent '81
Royalty-GB/Documentary
05418   60 mins   C
B, V, FO
Narrated by Sir Huw Wheldon
This film tells the parallel stories of Prince Charles and Lady Diana Spencer up to the day of their engagement. Original film material traces historic events in the Prince's life from his birth at Buckingham Palace in 1948. Lady Diana's life story includes new exclusive contributions from people who have been important in her life, including teachers at her boarding school.
F — EN
Michael Barratt Ltd; Radio Rentals — Michael Barratt Ltd   P

Straight Time   Fil-Ent '78
Drama
13004   114 mins   C
B, V
Dustin Hoffman, Harry Dean Stranton, Gary Busey, Theresa Russell, M Emmet Walsh, directed by Ulu Grosbard
An acid, downbeat film about the hopelessness of an ex-con unable to go straight and ensnared by his situation.
BBFC:X — A — EN
Production Co; Warner Bros — Warner Home Video   P
61124

Strange Brew   Fil-Ent '83
Adventure/Comedy
12234   88 mins   C
B, V
Dave Thomas, Rick Moranis

PALADIN VIDEO HOME ENTERTAINMENT GUIDE

A couple of beer-swilling brothers and their beer-powered bionic dog get into all sorts of scrapes in this film with their insatiable desire for beer.
S,A — EN
MGM — MGM/UA Home Video P
10322

Strange Invaders　　　　Fil-Ent　'83
Science fiction
12521　　90 mins　　C
B, V
Paul le Mat, Nancy Allen, Diana Scarwid, Michael Lerner, Louise Fletcher, directed by Michael Laughlin
An eerie blue light over a mid-west town in the mid-fifties heralded the disappearance of its towns-people. Now thirty years later an investigator finds more than he ever bargained for.
BBFC:PG — S,A — EN
EMI Films Inc; Orion Pictures Corporation — THORN EMI P
TXA 90 2348 4; TVA 90 2348 2

Stranger and the Gunfighter, The　　　　Fil-Ent　'76
Adventure/Comedy
05446　　96 mins　　C
V2, B, V
Lee Van Cleef, Lo Lieh, Patty Shepard, Julian Ugarte, directed by Anthony Dawson
A western gunfighter and an Oriental youth, master of martial arts, team up to find a stolen Chinese fortune. Where the fortune is supposed to be are the pictures of four girls, the clues to the whereabouts of the treasure are tatooed on their posteriors; a hunt for the girls follows.
BBFC:AA — S,A — EN
Columbia Pictures; Harbor Prods and Shaw Bros Ltd; Carlo Ponti — Iver Film Services P
118

Stranger from Shaolin　　　　Fil-Ent　'7?
Martial arts
07980　　94 mins　　C
B, V
Wong Hang Sav, Thomson Kao Kan, directed by Loo Chun
This is an Oriental adventure which tells of a young girl's revenge for the murder of her entire family. With no knowledge of the art of Kung Fu, she sets out to learn all that she will need in order to achieve this.
S,A — EN
IMLMPWM — AVI Video Ltd P
012

Stranger in Sacramento　　　　Fil-Ent　'7?
Western/Drama
05555　　100 mins　　C
V2, B, V
Mickey Hargitay, Barbara Frey, directed by Serge Bergon
A man's family is killed and his herd of cattle rustled when a once peaceful valley is taken over by a depraved killer. To seek his revenge he has to convince the frightened townspeople and the Sheriff of the killer's guilt. On the way to the final shootout he faces ambush, a woman and the threat of the gallows.
BBFC:X — A — EN
Unknown — Videomedia P
PVM 6100/BVM 6100/HVM 6100

Stranger in the House　　　　Fil-Ent　'7?
Drama
09132　　90 mins　　C
V2, B, V
This film tells the story of a dangerous kind of loving. He wanted her only for her body, but she in return wanted his love. Inevitably they both get caught up in a web of intrigue and jealousy, which leads to a tragic conclusion.
C,A — EN
Unknown — Go Video Ltd P
GO 140

Stranger Is Watching, A　　　　Fil-Ent　'82
Crime-Drama
10166　　88 mins　　C
B, V
Rip Torn, Kate Mulgrew, James Naughton, Caitlin O'Hearey, Shawn Von Schreiber
A psychotic murderer is at large and is holding two hostages, one young girl who saw her mother killed, the other a female TV newscaster, in the catacombs beneath New York's Grand Central Station.
BBFC:X — A — EN
MGM — MGM/UA Home Video P
UMB 10144/UMV 10144

Strangers Kiss　　　　Fil-Ent　'80
Drama/Romance
13221　　96 mins　　C
V2, B, V
Peter Coyote, Victoria Tennant, Blaine Novak, Dan Shore, Richard Romanus, Linda Kerridge
A real-life romance is played out on a movie set between an ex-boxer turned actor and his leading lady whose gangster boyfriend has financed the film.
A — EN
Douglas Dilge — Embassy Home Entertainment P
1367

(For Explanation of codes, see USE GUIDE and KEY)

PALADIN VIDEO HOME ENTERTAINMENT GUIDE

Strangler of Vienna   Fil-Ent '72
Mystery/Horror
08596   84 mins   C
V2, B, V
Victor Buono
Set in Vienna, 1934, this film tells of the mysterious disappearance of beautiful young girls. The police are totally baffled. However, a man has recently opened a butcher's shop, and his sausages are rapidly becoming famous. It could be that he has discovered a secret ingredient.
BBFC:X — *A* — *EN*
Unknown — *Videomedia*   P
PVM 1023/BVM 1023/HVM 1023

Stranglers Video Collection 1977-82, The   Fil-Ent '82
Music-Performance
08575   58 mins   C
B, V
This tape features The Stranglers and some of their hits including '(Get a) Grip (On Yourself),' 'Something Better Change,' 'Peaches,' 'Hanging Around,' 'Straighten Out,' 'Five Minutes,' 'No More Heroes,' 'Nice 'N' Sleazy,' 'Duchess,' 'Nuclear Device,' 'Golden Brown' and 'Strange Little Girl.'
S,A — *EN*
Liberty-United Records — *THORN EMI*
P
TXE 90 1032 4/TVE 90 1032 2

Strauss Family—Part One, The   Fil-Ent '??
Drama/Biographical
07352   ? mins   C
B, V
Stuart Wilson, Anne Stallybrass, Nikolas Simmonds, Tony Anholt
This dramatization traces the progress of the world's most popular family of composers. Features music played by the London Symphony Orchestra, music direction by Cyril Ornadel.
S,A — *EN*
Unknown — *Precision Video Ltd*   P
BITC 3105/VITC 3105

Strauss Family—Part Two, The   Fil-Ent '??
Drama/Biographical
07353   ? mins   C
B, V
Stuart Wilson, Anne Stallybrass, Nikolas Simmonds, Tony Anholt
This second part in the series continues to trace the progress of the world's most popular family of composers. Features music played by the London Symphony Orchestra, music direction by Cyril Ornadel.
S,A — *EN*
Unknown — *Precision Video Ltd*   P
BITC 3106/VITC 3106

Straw Dogs   Fil-Ent '72
Drama
04212   113 mins   C
V2, B, V
Dustin Hoffman, Susan George
An American mathematician, disturbed by the predominance of violence in American society moves with his British wife to an isolated Cornish village. He discovers that beneath the peaceful surface lies a primitive savagery which destroys his hopes for an idyllic life.
BBFC:X — *A* — *EN*
Cinerama — *Guild Home Video*   H, P

Street Fleet   Fil-Ent '83
Comedy
13631   100 mins   C
B, V
Mr T, Adam Baldwin, Irene Cara, Charlie Barnett, directed by Joel Schumacher
An optimistic youth decides to turn the fortunes of a down-at-heel cab fleet and tries to win round the drivers in a series of comic capers.
BBFC:15 — *F* — *EN*
Topper Carew — *CIC Video*   H, P
1142

Street Killers   Fil-Ent '81
Adventure/Horror
09063   100 mins   C
V
Helmut Berger, Marisa Mell, Richard Harrison
Four dangerous prisoners escape from a high security prison, led by a sadistic homicidal maniac. They go on a rampage of revenge, murder and terror.
A — *EN*
Unknown — *Astra Video*   P

Street of the Damned   Fil-Ent '83
Drama/Suspense
13226   95 mins   C
V2, B, V
Two men come into conflict again after many years when one of them befriend's a young Chinese girl that the other has brutally raped.
BBFC:18 — *A* — *EN*
Parafrance — *Embassy Home Entertainment*
P
6101

PALADIN VIDEO HOME ENTERTAINMENT GUIDE

Streetcar Named Desire, A Fil-Ent '84
Drama
13214   115 mins   C
V2, B, V
Ann-Margret, Treat Williams, Beverly D'Angelo, Randy Quaid, directed by John Erman
A faded southern belle is forced to seek refuge in her sister's home and thinks she will find happiness with the couple's friend but her dreams are shattered when her brother-in-law discovers her sordid past. Based on Tennessee William's play.
BBFC:15 — C,A — EN
Keith Barish Productions — Embassy Home Entertainment   **P**
6105

Streethawk   Fil-Ent '84
Crime-Drama
13277   90 mins   C
B, V
Rex Smith, Joe Regalbuto, directed by Vigil W Vogel
A motorcycle officer and a superbike with a laser weapon and a vertical air lift system join forces to combat crime on the streets.
S,A — EN
Universal — CIC Video   **H, P**
BET 1120/VHT 1120

Streets of Fire   Fil-Ent '84
Drama
13648   90 mins   C
B, V
Diane Lane, William Dafoe, Amy Madigan, Michael Pare, directed by Walter Hill
Set in a gritty urban scenario to a musical backing, two rival gangs battle over a kidnapped girl. This is a fast moving story full of vengeance and confrontation.
BBFC:15 — S,A — EN
Universal — CIC Video   **H, P**
1136

Streets of Fire, The Music Video   Fil-Ent '84
Music video
13272   25 mins   C
V
This video takes a look at the making of the film 'Streets of Fire,' and includes three songs 'Tonight is What It Means To Be Young,' 'Nowhere Fast' and 'I Can Dream About You.' The first two songs are written by Jim Steinman and performed by Fire Inc; the last is written and performed by Dan Hartman.
BBFC:15 — S,A — EN
MCA Home Video — CIC Video   **H, P**
FIREVH 1

Streisand   Fil-Ent '6?
Music-Performance
06299   102 mins   C
V2, B, V
Barbara Streisand
This cassette features two shows performed by Barabara Streisnd—'My Name Is Barbara' her 1965 television special and 'Colour Me Barbara' from 1966.
F — EN
Unknown — World of Video 2000   **H, P**
SP3

Strike Back   Fil-Ent '7?
Crime-Drama
09296   87 mins   C
B, V
A young man takes the rap for a gang of motorbike thieves and ends up in jail, all for the love of his beautiful girlfriend. When he is refused parole and nearly goes insane with frustration, he makes a violent escape in order to strike back.
S,A — EN
Unknown — Abacus Video   **P**
302

Striptease   Fil-Ent '76
Drama
07812   108 mins   C
B, V
Terence Stamp, Corrine Clery, Fernando Rey
A film director with one successful film behind him is under pressure to repeat the success. In a night club near his villa in the Canary Islands he meets the queen of the strippers. He becomes fascinated by her beauty and her life; her story gives him inspiration for a new film. But his attraction turns to love and then to obsession with tragic consequences.
S,A — EN
Unknown — Video Tape Centre   **P**
VTC 1016

Stroker Ace   Fil-Ent '83
Comedy
13646   90 mins   C
B, V
Burt Reynolds, Ned Beatty, Jim Nabors, Loni Anderson, directed by Hal Needham
A high spirited stock car racer falls into the clutches of a greedy fried-chicken magnate who signs him up on a deal that turns out to be the world's most demanding, unbreakable contract.
BBFC:PG — S,A — EN
Universal — CIC Video   **H, P**
1158

(For Explanation of codes, see USE GUIDE and KEY)

PALADIN VIDEO HOME ENTERTAINMENT GUIDE

Stromboli/While the City Sleeps   Fil-Ent '5?
Drama/Mystery
09115   176 mins   B/W
B, V
Ingrid Bergman, Mario Vitale, Renzo Cesana, Mario Sponza; Dana Andrews, George Sanders, Vincent Price, Rhonda Fleming, directed by Fritz Lang
This tape contains two films on one cassette. 'Stromboli' (1950, black and white, 79 mins.), set at the end of the second World War, tells of a homeless girl who marries an Italian soldier. They return to his primitive island, where things are not quite what she had hoped. 'While the City Sleeps' (1956, black and white, 97 mins.) tells of a psychopathic killer on the loose, terrorising the city. A cynical newspaper tycoon pits his three chiefs against each other in a bid to crack the case.
S,A — EN
Roberto Rossellini; Italian; RKO — *Kingston Video*   **H, P**
KV58

Stroszek   Fil-Ent '76
Drama
07743   107 mins   C
B, V
Bruno S, Eva Maltes, Clemens Scheitz, directed by Werner Herzog
Set in the present day this film follows the fortunes of three misfits: a young man, his girlfriend and a neighbour. They are convinced by the dismal aspects of Berlin that they should seek their fortunes in America. The young man, unable to come to terms with his new routine in a strange country, is forced to find his own grim solution.
A — EN
New Yorker Films — *Palace Video Ltd*   **P**

Stryker   Fil-Ent '83
Science fiction
12531   83 mins   C
B, V
Steve Sandor, Andria Savio, William Ostrander, Julie Gray, Monique St Pierre, directed by Cirio H Santiago
Gangs of survivors from a nuclear holocaust roam the arid wasteland looking for the one precious commodity essential for their needs—water.
BBFC:18 — A — EN
Cirio H Santiago — *THORN EMI*   **P**
TXA 90 2204 4/TVA 90 2204 2

Stuck on You   Fil-Ent '82
Comedy
13149   88 mins   C
B, V
Irwin Corey, Virginia Penta, Mark Mikulski, directed by Michael Herz and Samuel Weil
This bawdy romp tells the story of lovers down the ages, calling up such examples as Adam and Eve, Napoleon and Josephine, and Columbus and Isabella, to try and resolve the problems between a pair of modern-day lovers.
BBFC:18 — A — EN
Troma — *Polygram Video*   **P**
040 3296/040 3292

Stud, The   Fil-Ent '79
Drama
01265   90 mins   C
B, V
Oliver Tobias, Joan Collins
An ambitious young man meets a beautiful, rich woman. He manages her fashionable disco and manages to have an affair with her at the same time. International intrigue and high living heighten the story, until the young man realizes he has hit the depths of corruption.
BBFC:X — C,A — EN
Brent Walker Film Prods — *Brent Walker Home Video Ltd*   **P**

Student Bodies   Fil-Ent '81
Comedy/Horror
10114   83 mins   C
B, V
Richard Brando, directed by Mickey Rose
A teenage horror spoof, set in a high school, in which a mysterious Heavy Breather stalks all young couples found kissing and cuddling.
BBFC:15 — S,A — EN
Paramount — *CIC Video*   **H, P**
BEA 2069/VHA 2069

Study in Terror, A   Fil-Ent '65
Horror/Mystery
02578   95 mins   C
V2, B, V
John Neville, Donald Houston, Robert Morley, Cecil Parker, Anthony Quayle
Jack the Ripper is murdering prostitutes in 1880 London. He sends a box of surgical instruments to the home of Sherlock Holmes. The scalpel is missing from the set. Holmes and Dr. Watson search the seedy backstreets and dark alleys of the city and come across a startling revelation.
BBFC:X — A — EN
Compton; Tekli; Sir Nigel — *Videomedia*   **P**

Stunt Man, The   Fil-Ent '80
Drama/Adventure
06157   129 mins   C
V2, B, V, LV

(For Explanation of codes, see USE GUIDE and KEY)

PALADIN VIDEO HOME ENTERTAINMENT GUIDE

Peter O'Toole, Steve Railsback, Barbara Hershey, Allen Goorwitz, Alex Rocco, Adam Roarke, Sharon Farrell, Philip Burns, Clock Bail, directed by Richard Rush

This film is the story of a fugitive on the run from the police who stumbles onto a movie location and is offered a disguise as a stunt man. The director exploits him making him perform dangerous feats pushing him to the limit of human survival. He finds that the biggest stunt is just being able to stay alive; he has nothing to lose but his life.

BBFC:X — A — EN

Melvin Simon Productions — *Guild Home Video*   **H, P, E**

Stunt Squad   Fil-Ent '7?
Crime-Drama
08017   90 mins   C
V2, B, V

Marcel Bozuffi, Ricardo Salvino, Vittorio Mezzagiorno, directed by Domenico Paolella.

When a town's crime level rises to a terrifying level, the police chief forms a special stunt squad to try to clean up the city. It becomes a personal vendetta when the killings involve his own family.

BBFC:AA — C,A — EN

Unknown — *Iver Film Services*   **P**
178

Stunts, the Deadly Game   Fil-Ent '78
Adventure/Drama
05696   89 mins   C
V2, B, V

Robert Foster, Fiona Lewis, directed by Mark L. Lester

A story involving a group of top stunt men who are engaged in making a feature film. Fatal 'accidents' occur on the set which leads to general suspicion that there is a murderer amongst the crew. The film features exciting stunt scenes involving cars, cannons, dangling from helicopters, falling from 100 ft crane elevators and incineration in an exploding house.

BBFC:AA — S,A — EN

Unknown — *Rank Video Library*   **H, P**
0133C

Style Council-The Videosingles, The   Fil-Ent '8?
Music-Performance/Video
09875   16 mins   C
B, V

This tape features four top selling single releases; 'Speak Like A Child', 'Money Go Round', 'Long Hot Summer' and 'A Solid Bond in Your Heart'. Recorded in stereo.
F — EN

Unknown — *Polygram Video*   **H, P**
040 1894/040 1892

Styx—Caught in the Act—Live   Fil-Ent '84
Music-Performance
12185   90 mins   C
B, V

Directed by Jerry Kramer

This video rock show contains live footage and ties in a science fiction spectacular based around the 'Kilroy Was Here' L.P. The song tracks include 'The Roboto,' 'Rockin' the Paradise,' 'Snowblind,' 'Heavy Metal Poisoning,' 'Cold War,' 'Best of Times,' 'Renegade' and 'Come Sail Away.'
F — EN

Jerry Kramer and Associates; Front Line Management — *A&M Sound Pictures*   **P**
824

Sub-Mariner, The   Fil-Ent '??
Cartoons/Adventure
07408   54 mins   C
V2, B, V
Animated

This tape contains three episodes of the adventures of Prince Namor, the son of Neptune. Half human and half Atlantian, he is as strong as a whale underwater and stronger than any man on land. Tiny wings on his ankles enable him to fly with the speed of a bird.
F — EN

Unknown — *Guild Home Video*   **H, P, E**

Sub-Mariner-Cassette 2, The   Fil-Ent '??
Cartoons/Adventure
09440   51 mins   C
B, V
Animated

This tape continues the adventures of the half human and half Atlantian, Prince Namor in three further episodes; To Conquer a Crown, A Ship of Doom and Peril in the Surface World.
BBFC:U — F — EN

Marvel Comics — *Guild Home Video*   **H, P, E**

Suburban Wives   Fil-Ent '72
Comedy
07912   82 mins   C
V2, B, V

Eva Whishaw, Maggie Wright, Peter May

(For Explanation of codes, see USE GUIDE and KEY)

PALADIN VIDEO HOME ENTERTAINMENT GUIDE

A young woman working for a local paper and intent on making it to Fleet Street and fame starts to look for the ultimate story on suburbia. At a coffee morning it is suggested that she write a story on the suburban wife, the nine to five widow. She discovers that they fill the hours in various ways, with wild and hilarious results.
A — EN
Scotia International — *Video Programme Distributors*   P
Replay—1012

Suburbia   Fil-Ent '83
Drama
12871   99 mins   C
B, V
Chris Pedersen, Bill Coyne, Jennifer Clay, Andrew Pece, directed by Penelope Spheeris
When a group of punk teenagers take over an abandoned suburb dwelling, the local town folk start to make trouble.
BBFC:18 — C,A — EN
Bert Dragin; New World Pictures; Roger Corman — *Vestron Video International*   P
14141

Sudden Death   Fil-Ent '77
Adventure
08889   84 mins   C
V2, B, V
Robert Conrad, Felton Perry
Two professional violence merchants put themselves up for hire. Murder, mystery and suspense are daily occurrences for these assassins.
BBFC:X — A — EN
Topar Films — *Video Programme Distributors*   P
Media 152

Sudden Impact   Fil-Ent '83
Crime-Drama
12976   113 mins   C
B, V
Clint Eastwood, Sondra Locke, Pat Hingle, Bradford Dillman, directed by Clint Eastwood
In this sequel to 'Dirty Harry', the tough gun-packing policeman finds himself packed off to a small California town to keep out of trouble but meets up with a beautiful woman who is bent on killing off the gang of men who raped her ten years previously.
BBFC:18 — A — EN
Clint Eastwood — *Warner Home Video*   P
61341

Suddenly Single   Fil-Ent '71
Comedy/Drama
05181   71 mins   C
B, V
Hal Holbrook, Barbara Rush, Margot Kidder, Agnes Moorehead, Cloris Leachman
In this film Hal Holbrook plays a newly divorced man in his late 30's who exploits his new found 'freedom' by plunging into singles society but is quickly repelled by the bizarre people he meets in this swinging world.
A — EN
Chris Rose Prods — *Rank Video Library*
H, P
1014

Sugar Cookies   Fil-Ent '77
Drama
09385   90 mins   C
B, V
Mary Woronov
This is an erotic love story in which young women play out a bizarre game of vengeance, love and death.
A — EN
Unknown — *VCL Video Services*   P
P375

Sugarland Express   Fil-Ent '74
Drama/Comedy
13336   105 mins   C
B, V
Goldie Hawn, Ben Johnson, William Atherton, Micheal Sacks, directed by Steven Spielberg
A well-meaning escaped convict and his scatterbrained wife kidnap a state trooper so they can bargain for the right to keep their infant son who's about to be put up for adoption.
BBFC:PG — S,A — EN
Richard Zanuck; David Brown — *CIC Video*
H, P
BEN 1102/VHN 1102

Suicide Commando   Fil-Ent '68
War-Drama
06952   90 mins   C
B, V
Aldo Ray, Hugh Fangar-Smith, directed by Camillo Bazzoni
Based on the novel 'Commando 44' by Piet Legay which takes a look at the bravery of the red berets and the brutality of war this film tells the story of one secret mission. Parachuted in behind the German lines on the eve of the Normandy invasion, their mission is to destroy an air base used by the Germans to protect their industrial zone.
S,A — EN
Estela Films — *Home Video Merchandisers*
H, P
021

PALADIN VIDEO HOME ENTERTAINMENT GUIDE

Suicide Mission Fil-Ent '83
War-Drama
12845   79 mins   C
V2, B, V
A group of American marines are sent to Germany to capture Rommel but their mission backfires and they are used in a counter-plot to kill Eisenhower.
BBFC:15 — S,A — EN
Unknown — *Video Programme Distributors*
P

Suicide's Wife, The Fil-Ent '79
Drama
09205   120 mins   C
B, V
Angie Dickinson, Gordon Pinsent, Zohla Lampert, Todd LookinLand, Peter Donat, directed by John Newland
After a college English professor kills himself, leaving no explanation, his wife tries to determine the reasons. Underlying her grief is a feeling that she in some way may be the cause, or that she may have been able to prevent it. Her son blames her for his father's death.
S,A — EN
Factor-Newland Prods — *Video Form Pictures*
H, P
MGT 6

Summer Festival Gen-Edu '82
Documentary/Parades and festivals
13573   25 mins   C
V, 3/4U
This film shows the National Trust's first summer festival of 1982 including masquerades, son et lumieres and a theatrical garden party at Cliveden House.
F — EN
Unknown — *TFI Leisure Ltd*   H

Summer Holiday Fil-Ent '62
Musical-Drama/Romance
12523   88 mins   C
B, V
Cliff Richard, Lauri Peters, The Shadows
This is a sixties classic combining fun, drama and dance and a catalogue of hit songs, including 'Bachelor Boy,' 'Dancing Shoes,' 'Foot Tapper' and 'The Next Time.'
BBFC:U — F — EN
ABP — *THORN EMI*   P
TXJ 90 2205 4; TVJ 90 2205 2

Summer Lovers Fil-Ent '82
Romance/Drama
09941   98 mins   C
B, V
Peter Gallaher, Daryl Hannah, Valerie Quennessen, Barbara Rush, John Carradine
Set on a Greek island, Michael and Cathy meet a French girl, which is the beginning of a three-way love affair.
BBFC:15 — C,A — EN
Filmways — *Rank Video Library*   H, P
0169 Y

Summer Night Fever Fil-Ent '??
Adventure/Romance
08764   96 mins   C
B, V
Stephanie Hillel, Olivia Pascal, Claus Obalski, Betty Verges
This film is set on the beaches of Monte Carlo, St. Tropez and Ibiza and describes a vacation with a difference. Two young men head for the French Riviera in their convertible car with sun and plenty of girls in mind. With hot days and even hotter nights they find action packed escapades, exceeding all their expectations.
BBFC:X — A — EN
Unknown — *Precision Video Ltd*   P
BHPV 2568/VHPV 2568

Summer of Fear Fil-Ent '80
Drama/Suspense
08932   93 mins   C
B, V
Linda Blair, Lee Purcell
A young, innocent girl loses the affections of first her boyfriend, then her father and brother, to her mysterious cousin. Her power to attract is an embodiment of evil. The girl's accusations are only dismissed as jealousy. Her only ally is an expert in the occult, whose untimely and mysterious death leaves her to face the horrors of the unknown alone.
BBFC:X — A — EN
Finnegan Associates — *Brent Walker Home Video Ltd*   P

Summer Of My German Soldier Fil-Ent '78
Drama
09251   98 mins   C
V2, B, V
Kristy McNichol, Bruce Davidson, Esther Rolle, Michael Constantine, Barbara Barrie, directed by Michael Tuchner
A young Jewish girl befriends an escaped German prisoner of war in a small southern town during World War II. This moving story is based on the book by Bette Greene.
BBFC:A — S,A — EN
Highgate Pictures; NBC — *Iver Film Services*
P
215

(For Explanation of codes, see USE GUIDE and KEY)

PALADIN VIDEO HOME ENTERTAINMENT GUIDE

Summer of Steam Gen-Edu '79
Automobiles
04391　60 mins　C
B, V
Old steam wagons are featured in this nostalgia-filled programme which shows the historic commercial vehicle runs from London to Brighton, Manchester, and Harrogate. Original motorcar owners reminisce as well.
F — EN
Vintage Television — *Vintage Television Ltd*
H, P, E

Summer With Monika Fil-Ent '53
Drama/Romance
10013　97 mins　B/W
B, V
Harriet Andersson, Lars Ekborg, John Harryson, directed by Ingmar Bergman
A wild, restless girl defies her parents and goes off with her boyfriend for an island holiday. Her subsequent pregnancy and motherhood don't suit her and her father is left with the baby. Subtitled in English.
F — EN
Svenska Filmindustri — *Longman Video*
P
LGBE 5013/LGVH 5013

Summerdog Fil-Ent '79
Adventure
06768　85 mins　C
V2, B, V
James Congdon, Elizabeth Eisenman
Hobo, an abandoned dog, is adopted by a family on summer holiday.
F — EN
GG Communications — *Intervision Video*
H, P
A-AE 0307

Sun Dragon Fil-Ent '7?
Adventure/Martial arts
04605　92 mins　C
V2, B, V
Billy Chong
When a rancher is killed for refusing to sell his property to three hoodlums, his young son escapes. Adopted by a Chinese family he is taught the art of kung-fu. Later as an accomplished fighter he sets out to wreak revenge on the hoodlums, who are eliminated after a ferocious encounter.
C,A — EN
Unknown — *Video Programme Distributors*
P
Inter-Ocean—046

Sunburn Fil-Ent '79
Comedy/Mystery
07656　98 mins　C
B, V
Farrah Fawcett, Joan Collins, Art Carney, Charles Grodin
Set in Acapulco, this thriller is about an insurance fraud. A resourceful and unorthodox investigator is hired to probe a dubious five million dollar claim, aided by a beautiful but accident prone model. They soon discover that they have uncovered more than an insurance swindle.
S,A — EN
Paramount — *VCL Video Services*　**P**
P149D

Sunburst Fil-Ent '7?
Drama
04472　76 mins　C
V2, B, V
Peter Hosten, Katherine Baumann, Peter Brown, Rudy Vallee
This adult love drama involves the problems of a group of young people.
A — EN
CFA; Ronald L Peck — *Intervision Video*
H, P
A-A 0151

Sunday in the Country Fil-Ent '75
Adventure
04314　89 mins　C
V2, B, V
Ernest Borgnine, Michael J. Pollard
Three bank robbers are on the run from police, and hide out with a farm family. Very violent.
BBFC:X — *A — EN*
Quadrant Films — *Intervision Video*　**H, P**
A-A 0063

Sunset Boulevard Fil-Ent '50
Drama
13335　89 mins　B/W
B, V
William Holden, Gloria Swanson, Eric Von Stronheim, Cecil B. BeMille, Nance Olson, directed by Billy Wilder
An aging silent movie queen befriends a struggling writer but their partnership leads to tragedy in this indictment of the darker side of the Hollywood movie world.
BBFC:PG — *C,A — EN*
Paramount — *CIC Video*　**H, P**
BEJ 2097/VHJ 2097

Sunset Limousine Fil-Ent '??
Comedy-Drama
09337　92 mins　C
B, V

632　(For Explanation of codes, see USE GUIDE and KEY)

PALADIN VIDEO HOME ENTERTAINMENT GUIDE

John Ritter
This film tells the amusing story of a stand-up comedian, by day he is a chauffeur, but by night he is a popular comedy act at a local club. He finds himself the unwitting target of criminals. A chase follows after which he ends up in a police station, but luckily his girlfriend is able to come to the rescue.
BBFC:U — F — EN
Unknown — *Precision Video Ltd*   **P**
BITC 2142/VITC 2142

Sunshine on the Skin   Fil-Ent '??
Drama/Romance
08647   88 mins   C
V2, B, V
Ornella Muti
This film tells the romantic tale of two lovers on a desert island. A story with a tragic ending.
S,A — EN
Unknown — *Fletcher Video*   **H, P**
V167

Sunshine Run   Fil-Ent '76
Adventure
09054   109 mins   C
V
Chris Robinson, Ted Cassidy, Robert Leslie, Phyllis Robinson
Set in Florida, during the year 1859 this film tells of a chase, driven by greed, honour and love of freedom, into an untamed world of awesome beauty and danger.
S,A — EN
John B Kelly; First American Films — *Astra Video*   **H, P**

Super Cartoon Show   Fil-Ent '6?
Cartoons
06888   57 mins   C
V2, B, V
Animated
A selection of cartoons featuring Dick Tracy, the master detective in his fight against crime, and Roger Ramsjet who, together with his jet planes, involves himself in difficult tasks for the government.
M,S — EN
UPA — *European Video Company*   **P**

Super Dragon   Fil-Ent '74
Adventure/Martial arts
02119   90 mins   C
V2, B, V
Ray Danton, Marisa Mell
Mung displays his talents for Kung-fu and attracts the attention of the harbour boss.
S,A — EN
United Screen — *Hokushin Audio Visual Ltd*   **P**
VM-31

Super Seal   Fil-Ent '7?
Comedy/Adventure
06769   80 mins   C
V2, B, V
Foster Brooks, Sterling Holloway, Sarah Brown, Bob Sheperd
A young girl and her grandfather adopt a wounded seal pup.
F — EN
Victor Lundin — *Intervision Video*   **H, P**
A-AE 0306

Superbike 6   Spo-Lei '??
Motorcycles
06352   60 mins   C
V2, B, V
This film covers the biggest contest ever staged to find the best all-round motorcycle sportsman in Britain.
F — EN
Unknown — *Walton Film and Video Ltd*   **P**
H368

Superdad   Fil-Ent '75
Comedy
13760   94 mins   C
B, V
Bob Crane, Kurt Russell, Barbara Rush
A father's attempts to bridge the generation gap between himself and his daughter lead to his being arrested as a 'Peeping Tom' and becoming involved with picketing students.
BBFC:U — F — EN
Walt Disney Productions — *Rank Video Library*   **P**
149B

Superfly   Fil-Ent '72
Crime-Drama
13172   90 mins   C
B, V
Ron O'Neal, Carl Lee, Sheila Frazier, directed by Gordon Parks
Set amongst the cocaine peddlers in New York's black ghettos, this is the story of a hip and glamorous dealer who plans one last sale before he retires on the profits.
BBFC:X — A — EN
Warner Bros — *Warner Home Video*   **P**
61138

(For Explanation of codes, see USE GUIDE and KEY)   633

PALADIN VIDEO HOME ENTERTAINMENT GUIDE

Superknights Fil-Ent '72
Comedy
06732   100 mins   C
V2, B, V
Corey Fischer
The amorous escapades of Don Quixote and his sidekick who travel through 17th century Spain in a series of sexual mishaps.
BBFC:X — *A* — *EN*
Burbank Intl Pictures — *Intervision Video*   **H, P**
A-AE 0183

Superman Fil-Ent '4?
Adventure/Cartoons
02465   49 mins   C
B, V
Animated
Cartoon spectacular featuring some of the best Superman cartoons of the 1940's.
F — *EN*
Paramount — *Mountain Video*   **P**

Superman III Fil-Ent '83
Adventure
12532   120 mins   C
B, V
Christopher Reeve, Richard Pryor, Jackie Cooper, Margot Kidder, Marc McClure, Annette O'Toole, directed by Richard Lester
The caped crusader is back again and in order to rescue the world from total domination by his evil adversary he has to battle against an insane computer and a diabolical psychotic force.
BBFC:PG — *F* — *EN*
Pierre Spengler — *THORN EMI*   **P**
TXA 90 19944/TVA 90 19942

Superman—The Movie Fil-Ent '78
Fantasy/Adventure
06031   143 mins   C
B, V
Christopher Reeve, Margot Kidder, Marlon Brando, Gene Hackman, Glenn Ford, directed by Richard Donner
A retelling of the Superman legend from his birth and flight from his home planet of Krypton to his becoming Earth's protector from the villain Lex Luthor.
BBFC:A — *F* — *EN*
Warner Bros — *Warner Home Video*   **P**
WEX1013/WEV1013

Superman—The Musical Fil-Ent '7?
Musical
04616   90 mins   C
B, V
Lesley Warren, David Wayne, Loretta Swit, David Wilson
An adaptation of Hal Prince's hit Broadway musical of Superman. From comics to radio, from TV to the movies, the adventures of the Man of Steel have excited audiences of all ages the world over. The show is a broadly played spoof in story and song, featuring the music and lyrics of Charles Strouse and Lee Adams.
F — *EN*
Unknown — *VCL Video Services*   **P**

Supermen Fil-Ent '76
Fantasy/Adventure
05520   97 mins   C
B, V
George Martin, Brad Harris, Sal Borges, directed by Bitto Albertini
The three supermen leave for an assignment in Africa to purchase an Uranium mine before the Russians. They are captured by a tribe of Amazon girls and the queen decides to marry one of them, meanwhile the Russians believe they have brought the mine. What follows is a series of double dealing thefts, countertheft and swindling.
BBFC:U — *F* — *EN*
Unknown — *Derann Film Services*   **H, P**
DV112B/DV112

Superpower Fil-Ent '??
Adventure/Martial arts
06062   89 mins   C
V2, B, V
Bill Chang
An Imperial Minister's son plots revenge on the Kung-Fu fighters for inflicting defeat on the Manchu Boxers. Only one man can stop them; using new techniques he is able to defeat the son and his henchmen forever.
BBFC:X — *A* — *EN*
Unknown — *Video Programme Distributors*
P
Inter-Ocean—056

Supersnooper Fil-Ent '81
Comedy
13015   92 mins   C
B, V
Terence Hill, Ernest Borgnine, directed by Sergio Corbucci
This is a light-hearted adventure set in Miami in which a policeman accidentally exposed to radiation develops amazing powers and can see a round corners, move a driverless truck and fall from a skyscraper without injury.
BBFC:A — *C,A* — *EN*
Warner Bros Inc — *Warner Home Video*
P
61234

(For Explanation of codes, see USE GUIDE and KEY)

PALADIN VIDEO HOME ENTERTAINMENT GUIDE

Supersonic Man   Fil-Ent '7?
Science fiction
04284   90 mins   C
V2, B, V
Michael Coby, Cameron Mitchell
Supersonic Man KRONOS is sent to Earth to investigate the disappearance of shipments of highly radioactive Iridium.
C,A — EN
Unknown — *Video Programme Distributors*   P
Inter-Ocean—001

Superstar Goofy   Fil-Ent '??
Cartoons
05581   71 mins   C
B, V
Animated
In this film Goofy is featured as the ultimate sportsman. He tries everything from Golf and Boxing to all track and field events in an attempt to become Superstar Champion of the World.
F — EN
Walt Disney Productions — *Rank Video Library*   H
05500

Superstars   Fil-Ent '78
Music-Performance
06226   50 mins   C
B, V
Hosted by Bob Hope, Dan Rowan, Cheryl Tiegs
A film of the Annual Ohio State Fair which is a Rodeo, a variety spectacular, a cattle market and a monster fun-fair rolled into one. Stars include: The Osmonds, Sha Na Na, Tavares, Pat Boone, Kenny Rogers, Eddie Rabbit and many others.
F — EN
Osmond Production; Walter C Miller — *VCL Video Services*   P
V117B

Superstition   Fil-Ent '7?
Horror
09084   95 mins   C
B, V
James Houghton, Albert Salmi, Lynn Carlin, Larry Pennell
Two hundred years ago a witch was supposed to have been sentenced to death by crucifixion. However as she was Satan's daughter, her evil spirit was not destroyed and lurked in the lake. In the present, 1984, a series of bizarre killings begin.
A — EN
Unknown — *Video Tape Centre*   P
VTC 1036

SuperTed-Cassette 1   Chi-Juv '??
Cartoons/Adventure
09455   48 mins   C
V2, B, V
Voices by Derek Griffiths, Peter Hawkins, Melvyn Hayes, Roy Kinnear, Jon Pertwee, Victor Spinnetti, Shiela Steafel, directed by David Edwards
This tape features six episodes of SuperTed, the ordinary teddy bear with a secret, magic word. No adventure is too dangerous.
BBFC:U — F — EN
Unknown — *Guild Home Video*   H, P, E

SuperTed—Cassette 2   Chi-Juv '84
Cartoons
13371   44 mins   C
V2, B, V
Animated
More adventures from the ordinary, furry teddy-bear with the magic word and his enemies Bulk and Skeleton.
BBFC:U — PS,M — EN
S4TV — *Guild Home Video*   H, P, E
8425-5

Supertrain   Fil-Ent '79
Drama/Suspense
12237   92 mins   C
B, V
Steve Lawrence, Keenan Wynn, Don Meredith
Inside an atomic powered luxury train, travelling at 200 mph, a brief-case suddenly explodes and panic spreads amongst the passengers. There is a murder on board, and the journey turns into a race against death.
S,A — EN
NBC International — *Select Video Limited*   P
3109/43

Suppose I Break Your Neck   Fil-Ent '7?
Crime-Drama
07776   90 mins   C
V2, B, V
Frederick Stafford, Silvia Monti
An adventure following the hair-raising activities of blackmail, extortion and the Mafia.
S,A — EN
Unknown — *Fletcher Video*   H, P
V137

Suppose They Gave a War and Nobody Came?   Fil-Ent '70
Comedy
04213   113 mins   C
B, V

PALADIN VIDEO HOME ENTERTAINMENT GUIDE

Tony Curtis, Ernest Borgnine, Brian Keith, Suzanne Pleshette, Tom Ewell, Bradford Dillman
When the sheriff of a small southern town arrests a sergeant for romancing a waitress all hell breaks loose.
BBFC:AA — C,A — EN
Cinerama — Guild Home Video   **H, P**

Surabaya Conspiracy, The   Fil-Ent '6?
Suspense
04619   90 mins   C
B, V
Michael Rennie, Barbara Bouchet, Mike Preston, Richard Jaeckel
A fast moving thriller, a true adventure of guns and gold, torn from the pages of World War II. Locations of Manila and Java set the scene for a film about the ruthless world of the munitions racket.
C,A — EN
Unknown — VCL Video Services   **P**

Surf II   Fil-Ent '84
Comedy
13768   89 mins   C
B, V
Lyle Waggoner, Ruth Buzzi, Eddie Deezon, Cleavon Little, Linda Kerridge
An American beach comedy with a musical soundtrack, in which a mad genius who has a violent dislike of surfers finds a peculiar way to get them off the beach.
BBFC:18 — C,A — EN
Unknown — Odyssey Video   **H, P**
3026

Surfacing   Fil-Ent '81
Drama
08751   88 mins   C
B, V
Joseph Bottoms, Kathleen Beller, R.H. Thompson, Margaret Dragu
This film begins with the news that a girl's father is missing from his North Woods home, and is believed to be dead. She and her lover go in search of him, together with his brother and his wife. The tension quickly mounts, as the foursome are dangerously mismatched.
BBFC:X — A — EN
Pan-Canadian — Precision Video Ltd   **P**
BAMPV 2576/VAMPV 2576

Surprise Attack   Fil-Ent '??
War-Drama
08699   90 mins   C
V2, B, V
Simon Andrew, Danny Martin

This film is set on the battle front on the river Ebro during the year of 1938. One morning a surprise attack is launched, but put down by the enemy fire. It becomes a dangerous situation.
BBFC:AA — C,A — EN
Unknown — Video Unlimited   **H, P**
084

Survival Run   Fil-Ent '78
War-Drama
06922   116 mins   C
B, V
Edward Fox, Susan Penhaligon
This story is based on the true life adventures of Erik Hazelhoff, one of Holland's world war heros. Having reacted to the outbreak of war with apathy, when the Nazis invaded his country his apathy turned to action. He became a fighter in the Resistance, wanted by the Gestapo and eventually escaped to England where Queen Wilhelmina assigned him to a deadly wartime mission.
BBFC:AA — S,A — EN
Unknown — Rank Video Library   **H, P**
0066C

Survival Run   Fil-Ent '??
Adventure
08624   90 mins   C
V2, B, V
Peter Graves, Ray Milland, Vincent Van Patten
An international narcotics group prepare to travel to a secret rendezvous point, where a huge drug deal is to be made. At the same time, however, six teenagers are making their way to the Arizona desert for the weekend. Their van is destroyed in a terrible accident and the six youths prepare to walk back to civilaztion.
S,A — EN
Film Ventures International — Hokushin Audio Visual Ltd   **P**
VM 63

Survive!   Fil-Ent '76
Drama
08998   120 mins   C
B, V
Pablo Ferrel, Hugo Stiglitz, Luz Maria Aguilar, directed by Rene Cardona
In 1972 a chartered plane carrying 45 passengers, most of them members of a young Uruguayan rugby team, crashed into the Andes. This film recounts the story of the 16 young men who managed to survive for 72 days without food or shelter in the world's most inhospitable mountains.
A — EN
Paramount; Robert Stigwood/Allan Carr Prods — THORN EMI   **P**
TXA 90 1545 4/TVA 90 1545 2

PALADIN VIDEO HOME ENTERTAINMENT GUIDE

Survivor, The Fil-Ent '81
Horror/Suspense
07949   93 mins   C
B, V
Robert Powell, Jenny Agutter, Angela Punch-McGregor, Peter Sumner, directed by David Hemmings
This film, based on the novel by James Herbert, is an eerie and frightening tale of the supernatural.
S,A — EN
Tuesday Films — *VideoSpace Ltd*   P
V56

Susan George—Naturally Fil-Ent '7?
Music-Performance
01960   28 mins   C
B, V
Actress Susan George extends herself into the world of music.
F — EN
Unknown — *VCL Video Services*   P

Suspicion of Murder Fil-Ent '73
Mystery
08813   96 mins   C
B, V
Alain Delon, Simone Signoret, Catherine Allegret, directed by Ralph Baum, Suzanne Wiesenfeld
This film, set in a remote, snowbound farmhouse, tells of the discovery of a body, found stabbed to death nearby. An intense investigation follows and everyone comes under suspicion. As the investigation proceeds, deep-rooted family secrets, and finally the truth are revealed.
C,A — EN
France — *VCL Video Services*   P
P293D

Suspiria Fil-Ent '79
Horror
05893   93 mins   C
B, V
Jessica Harper, Stefania Casini, directed by Dario Argento
A young American girl arrives at a German ballet school, and discovers vampires, witches, maggots, bats and blood.
BBFC:X — *A — EN*
Claudio Argento — *THORN EMI*   P
TXB 90 0265 4/TVB 90 0265 2

Svengali Fil-Ent '83
Drama
10222   120 mins   C
B, V
Peter O'Toole, Jodie Foster, Elizabeth Ashley, Larry Joshua, Pamela Blair, Barbara Bryne, Ronald Weyand, Robin Thomas, Brian Carney, directed by Anthony Harvey
This film tells the story of a dictatorial voice teacher who takes professional command of a young rock singer's training and career. His ability is legendary and highly respected, she endures his tyrannical supervision as her rise to fame is successfully sustained. At the peak of her career as she becomes cut off from all close to her his total domination threatens to destroy both of them.
BBFC:18 — *A — EN*
Robert Halmi — *Video Form Pictures*   H, P
MGS 029

Swallows and Amazons Fil-Ent '74
Adventure
01181   88 mins   C
B, V
Virginia McKenna, Ronald Fraser, Simon West, Kit Seymour, directed by Claude Whatham
Four children on holiday in the Lake District in 1929 strike up a friendship with two tomboys. They learn self-reliance through their many adventures. Based on a children's novel by Arthur Ransome.
BBFC:U — *F — EN*
EMI — *THORN EMI*   P
TXB 90 0015 4/TVB 90 0015 2

Swan Lake Fil-Ent '80
Dance
04649   125 mins   C
V2, B, V
This production by the Royal Ballet is descended almost directly from the original St. Petersburg production with addition of choreography by Ninette de Valois, Rudolf Nureyev and Sir Frederick Ashton.
F — EN
Thames Video — *THORN EMI*   H, P
TPB 90 6204 3/TXB 90 6204 4/TVB 90 6204 2

Swan Lake Fil-Ent '7?
Cartoons/Fantasy
07948   75 mins   C
V2, B, V
Animated
This cartoon retells the legend of Swan Lake. Princess Odett waits for her true love Prince Siegfried to rescue her from the spell of the evil magician Roetbert. Music by the Vienna Symphony Orchestra.
F — EN
Unknown — *Videomedia*   P
PVM 2117/BVM 2117/HVM 2117

(For Explanation of codes, see USE GUIDE and KEY)

PALADIN VIDEO HOME ENTERTAINMENT GUIDE

Swan's Way—History and Image
Fil-Ent '84
Music-Performance
13130   50 mins   C
B, V

This video is recorded live at the Astoria, Charing Cross Road, and features eleven tracks from the band including 'The Blade,' 'When the Wild Calls,' 'Stay' and 'Illuminations.' It is recorded in stereo hi-fi.
F — EN
Unknown — *Guild Home Video*   **P**
041 0594/041 0592

Swap, The
Fil-Ent '80
Mystery/Suspense
08056   86 mins   C
B, V

Robert De Niro, Jennifer Warren

This tells the story of a man trying to avenge his brother's death. However, it turns out to be more dangerous than he had expected; his brother had captured the wrong people.
BBFC:X — *A — EN*
Unknown — *Rank Video Library*   **H, P**
0116 C

Swarm, The
Fil-Ent '78
Drama
06035   111 mins   C
B, V

Michael Caine, Katherine Ross, Richard Widmark, Richard Chamberlain, Olivia de Havilland, Ben Johnson, Lee Grant, Jose Ferrer, Patty Duke Astin, Slim Pickens, Bradford Dillman, Fred MacMurray, Henry Fonda?Cameron Mitchell?directed by Irwin Allen

A scientist and military officers have to deal with a swarm of killer bees after the discovery of dead personnel on a government base. They died as a result of a vicious attack by the bees. Based on the novel by Arthur Herzog.
BBFC:A — *S,A — EN*
Warner Bros; Irwin Allen Prod — *Warner Home Video*   **P**
WEX1094/WEV1094

Sweatergirls
Fil-Ent '??
Comedy-Drama
08304   85 mins   C
B, V

Julie Parsons, Meegan King, Noel North

A group of girls throw a party for themselves at one of their grandmother's house. Meanwhile their boyfriends go out on a drinking binge and eventually get to the party. The grandmother's house becomes the scene for misadventure and hysterical fun.
A — EN
Unknown — *Video Film Organisation*   **P**
0008

Swedish Confessions
Fil-Ent '??
Crime-Drama/Romance
07330   90 mins   C
B, V

Barbara Scott, Jack Frank, Anne Von Lindberger, directed by Andrew Whyte

This film is loosely based on an art theft by a gang of international crooks. It centres on a passionate affair between the gang leader's assistant and the beautiful wife of a wealthy banker. Complications occur when her daughter falls in love with him.
BBFC:X — *A — EN*
Unknown — *Derann Film Services*   **P**
DV 146B/DV 146

Swedish Rally 1981
Spo-Lei '81
Automobiles-Racing
02046   52 mins   C
B, V

This programme shows the most important winter rally on the International Calendar. High speeds on snow and ice are depicted.
S,A — EN
Vintage Television Ltd — *Vintage Television Ltd*   **H, P, E**

Sweeney!
Fil-Ent '76
Drama
04666   94 mins   C
B, V

John Thaw, Dennis Waterman

This film from the popular T.V. series deals with the convoluted plotting made by the sophisticated agents of a multinational oil cartel, who shrink from neither murder nor the blackmailing of Britain's Minister for Energy to gain their ends.
BBFC:X — *A — EN*
EMI; Euston Films — *THORN EMI*   **H, P**
TXC 90 0239 4/TVC 90 0239 2

Sweeney 2
Fil-Ent '78
Crime-Drama
05958   103 mins   C
B, V

John Thaw, Dennis Waterman, Denholm Elliott, Ken Hutchison

PALADIN VIDEO HOME ENTERTAINMENT GUIDE

The Flying Squad's temperamental new chief demands instant results after an attempt to catch a gang of bank robbers fails.
S,A — EN
Ted Childs — *THORN EMI*   **P**
TXB 90 0335 4/TVB 90 0335 2

Sweet Creek County War, The   Fil-Ent '78
Western
08767   96 mins   C
B, V
Richard Egan, Albert Salmi, Nita Talbot, Slim Pickens, Robert Wilke, Joe Orton, Ray Cardi, Tom Jackman, directed by Frank James
This film tells the story of an upright lawman and a renegade outlaw. They become joined in a very uneasy alliance, and their homestead is surrounded by a horde of cowboys for the most bizarre siege imaginable.
S,A — EN
Imagery Films — *Precision Video Ltd*   **P**
BSPV 2587/VSPV 2587

Sweet Dreams-The Video Album   Fil-Ent '83
Music-Performance
12465   63 mins   C
B, V
Eurythmics
This video features in-concert performances, conceptual video clips, and animation woven together to create an 'album' including such songs as 'Sweet Dreams,' 'Love Is a Stranger' and 'This Is the House.'
BBFC:U — F — EN
Jon Roseman — *RCA/Columbia Pictures Video UK*   **H, P**
10233

Sweet Revenge   Fil-Ent '77
Drama
12233   85 mins   C
B, V
Stockard Channing, Sam Waterson, Franklin
An off-beat car thief bets a friend that within a month she'll be able to steal and sell enough cars to buy herself the car of her dreams.
S,A — EN
MGM — *MGM/UA Home Video*   **P**
10320

Sweet Scent of Death/Mark of the Devil, The   Fil-Ent '84
Drama/Suspense
13155   150 mins   C
B, V
Dean Stockwell, Shirley Knight, directed by Peter Sadsy, Dirk Benedict, Jenny Seagrove, directed by Val Guest
Two films are contained on one cassette. The first is about a successful American couple who come to live in London but the wife finds her past career as a lawyer begins to haunt her and the second film tells the story of a strange Chinese curse cast upon a murderer.
BBFC:15 — S,A — EN
Hammer Films Prods — *Brent Walker Home Video Ltd*   **P**
BW 37

Sweet Sins of Sexy Susan, The   Fil-Ent '8?
Comedy-Drama
09293   87 mins   C
V
Mike Marshall, Pascale Petit, Terry Torday
This film, set at the beginning of the last century during the French occupation of Germany, follows the adventures of the women of Giessen, Westphalia who are cunning enough to find weapons of their own to overcome French domination.
A — EN
Unknown — *Rex*   **H, P**

Sweet, Sweet Rachel   Fil-Ent '71
Suspense
04263   71 mins   C
B, V
Alex Dreier, Pat Hingle, Stefanie Powers, Louise Latham
A horrifying race against time in which an expert in extra sensory perception tries to identify a person with miraculous telepathic powers which have led one man to his death and driven his beautiful wife to the brink of insanity.
BBFC:A — S,A — EN
ABC Films — *Rank Video Library*   **H, P**
2005

Sweet William   Fil-Ent '79
Drama
02122   88 mins   C
V2, B, V
Sweet William is a philanderer whom women find irresistible, and he seduces them at every opportunity.
BBFC:AA — A — EN
Kendon Films — *Hokushin Audio Visual Ltd*   **P**
VM-34

Sweeten Your Swing   Spo-Lei '80
Golf
01978   26 mins   C

PALADIN VIDEO HOME ENTERTAINMENT GUIDE

B, V
A golf instructional programme for golfers seriously interested in improving their game.
C,A — I
Unknown — *Quadrant Video*   **H, P**

Swim Team   Fil-Ent '79
Comedy
07900   78 mins   C
V2, B, V
James Daughton, Stephen Furst, directed by James Polakof
The 'Whalers' swimming team have not won a swimming meeting in seven years, preferring to cause havoc on land by holding wild parties, tossing sharks into the pool and jet ski racing. When their new coach arrives they prove they can win and still have fun.
S,A — EN
Manson International — *Video Programme Distributors*   **P**
Inter-Ocean—060

Swimming for Disabled People   Spo-Lei '8?
Handicapped
13559   60 mins   C
B, V
This programme for disabled people covers their position and balance in the water, movement in the water and activities and formations.
AM Available   A — I
Unknown — *TFI Leisure Ltd*   **P**

Swimming Strokes   Spo-Lei '80
Sports-Water
00265   90 mins   C
B, V, FO
This programme looks at four strokes: frontcrawl, backcrawl, breast stroke, and butterfly. Specially made under the supervision of the Amateur Swimming Association.
F — I
London Video Ltd — *Video Sport for All*   **P**
1009

Swing High-Swing Low   Fil-Ent '37
Musical-Drama
07642   93 mins   B/W
B, V
Carole Lombard, Fred MacMurray, Dorothy Lamour, Jean Dixon, Charles Butterworth, directed by Mitchell Leisen
A singer meets a soldier in the Panama and discovers that he is a good trumpet player. She gives him the chance to perform professionally. Soon he becomes a success and marries the singer. But as he makes it to the top of the jazz world and success starts to go to his head, he has to fight to save both his marriage and his career.
F — EN
United International — *VCL Video Services*   **P**
0239G

Swingin' Summer   Fil-Ent '65
Musical/Adventure
06191   75 mins   C
B, V
Raquel Welch, James Stacey, Allan Jones
Set in California this film is a light musical with 'fun in the sun' as its theme.
F — EN
United Screen Arts — *VCL Video Services*   **P**
X0242

Swinging Cheerleaders, The   Fil-Ent '??
Comedy
07613   88 mins   C
V2, B, V
Jo Johnston, Rainbeaux Smith, Colleen Camp, Rosanne Katon, Jack Denton
This film takes a look at life on an American campus and the adventures of two girls and the college football team.
BBFC:X — A — EN
Unknown — *Iver Film Services*   **P**

Swiss Family Robinson   Fil-Ent '60
Adventure/Drama
05594   126 mins   C
B, V
John Mills, Dorothy McGuire, Cecil Parker, Janet Munro, directed by Ken Annakin
The story of a family shipwrecked on a tropical island. After salvaging useful supplies, domestic animals and firearms they build a home. The two eldest boys stumble upon pirates holding a sea captain and grandson captive; they are rescued and the grandson turns out to be a girl. The family fortify themselves against attack but during a party the pirates return.
F — EN
Walt Disney Productions — *Rank Video Library*   **H**
05300

Swiss Family Robinson   Fil-Ent '??
Cartoons/Adventure
08805   46 mins   C
B, V
Animated

PALADIN VIDEO HOME ENTERTAINMENT GUIDE

This film tells the story of a family, ship-wrecked on a desert island off the coast of Africa.
F — EN
Movietel — VCL Video Services P
A276B

Switch, The Fil-Ent '72
Crime-Drama/Adventure
07359   60 mins   C
B, V
Tony Curtis, Roger Moore
This is one of a series of wild adventures featuring the American millionaire and English aristocrat who were born to flirt, especially with danger.
S,A — EN
ITC — Precision Video Ltd P
BITC 2067/VITC 2067

Switch, The Fil-Ent '??
Comedy
06854   92 mins   C
V2, B, V
Veronica Parrish, Sonny Landham
A university professor discovers a potion to make people more daring. She decides to experiment on herself as she is in love with her male colleague who, up until now, has taken little notice of her. The change lands the couple in numerous hilarious situations.
A — EN
Unknown — European Video Company P

Switchblade Sisters, The Fil-Ent '??
Drama/Horror
07614   88 mins   C
V2, B, V
Robbie Lee
This film follows the wild adventures of a teenage gang of girls involved in gang warfare, prostitution, protection rackets, rape, street battles and mass murder.
BBFC:X — A — EN
Unknown — Iver Film Services P

Sword and the Sorcerer, The Fil-Ent '82
Fantasy/Adventure
12765   95 mins   C
B, V, LV
Lee Hovsley, Kathleen Beller, Simon MacCorkindale
A stunning medieval fantasy adventure about a sleeping sorcerer awakened to unleash a savage orgy of brutality and destruction.
BBFC:AA — S,A — EN
Group I — Rank Video Library H, P
0124D

Sword of Monte Cristo Fil-Ent '51
Adventure
04324   88 mins   C
V2, B, V
George Montgomery
A swashbuckling adventure about a masked female cavalier, set in 19th century France.
BBFC:U — F — EN
Twentieth Century Fox — Intervision Video
H, P
A-A 0121

Sword of the Barbarians Fil-Ent '7?
Adventure/Fantasy
09127   90 mins   C
V
Peter MacCoy, Margareta Range, Yvonne Fraschetti, Antony Freeman, Sabrina Siani
This is the story of Thor, a young chieftain, and his legendary exploits against the evil Nantuk and his witch guardian Rani. A beautiful girl has been slain by the evil man and Thor undertakes a perilous journey to see if he can bring her back to life. He encounters a ferocious race of lizard men, quicksand and assaults by monkey men.
S,A — EN
Unknown — Video Film Promotions H, P

Swordkill Fil-Ent '84
Fantasy/Adventure
13227   81 mins   C
B, V
An ancient Japanese warrior is brought back to life when his body is discovered frozen in a lake and after fleeing his captors, has to survive on the streets of Los Angeles '84 in the only way he knows.
BBFC:15 — S,A — EN
Albert Band; Swordkill Productions — Entertainment in Video
H, P
EVB 1028/EVV 1028

Sykes Fil-Ent '84
Comedy
13381   88 mins   C
B, V
Eric Sykes, Hattie Jacques, Peter Sellers, Richard Wattis, Derek Guyler
This programme features three stories from the television series about the kindly downtrodden bachelor and his larger than life sister and they are titled 'Golf,' 'Stranger' and 'Squatters.'
F — EN
Roger Race — BBC Video H, P
7021

(For Explanation of codes, see USE GUIDE and KEY)   641

PALADIN VIDEO HOME ENTERTAINMENT GUIDE

T

Table Tennis with Les Gresswell
Spo-Lei '7?
Sports-Minor
05243   25 mins   C
B, V
2 pgms
This is a series of two films made in collaboration with The English Table Tennis Association. Ten of the country's top players demonstrate the basic principles of the game leading up to the finer points of competitive play. Use is made of freeze frame and slow motion techniques to provide detailed demonstrations and analysis of all the most important strokes in the game.
C,A — I
Unknown — Rank Video Library   H, P
5010; 5011

Taboo Island
Fil-Ent '76
Adventure/Romance
09351   90 mins   C
B, V
Laura Gemser, Arthur Kennedy
A young man finds himself adrift at sea in his speedboat after being unconscious. Days pass until, seemingly out of nowhere, an island appears. Thinking he was alone he sets out to explore the island. To his amazement he stumbles upon the most beautiful girl he has ever seen.
BBFC:18 — A — EN
Oscar Dimartino Mansi — Precision Video Ltd
P
BPMPV 2621/VPMPV 2621

Tag the Intrepid Fox
Fil-Ent '??
Cartoons
09475   74 mins   C
B, V
Animated
This tells the story of Tag, the clumsy and carefree cub, and his friends, Arthur and Bertie, the gormless guard dogs, Slivver the Snake, Marty the Rooster, Gus and Gandy, two giggly geese with a drink problem.
F — EN
Unknown — Guild Home Video   H, P, E

Take, The
Fil-Ent '74
Mystery/Drama
09933   92 mins   C
B, V
Billy Dee Williams, Eddie Albert, Frankie Avalon, Tracy Reed, Sorrell Brooke, Albert Salmi, Vic Morrow, directed by Robert Hartford-Davis
A detective looks up to his crime-busting superior until he discovers the truth. He is accepting bribes from the drug syndicate they have been sent to smash. The inevitable showdown will be dangerous and violent. It is based on the novel 'Sir You Bastard' by G.F. Newman.
BBFC:18 — A — EN
World Film Services; Columbia Pictures — Rank Video Library   H, P
0183 Y

Take an Easy Ride
Fil-Ent '??
Drama
05486   40 mins   C
V2, B, V
This film exposes the dangers of hitching a ride and gives a vivid account of rape, theft and murder. It includes short interviews with hitchhikers giving their views and experiences and reconstructs scenes not only of what can happen to those hitching but to those giving the ride.
BBFC:X — A — EN
Unknown — Iver Film Services   P
149

Take Down
Fil-Ent '83
Drama/Sports
12842   107 mins   C
V2, B, V
Edward Herrmann, Lorenzo Lamas, Kathleen Lloyd, Maureen McCormick, directed by Keith Merrill
Mingo Junction High has an appalling record at sport but this year's graduating class decide to put their all into one last concerted effort to win at wrestling.
BBFC:PG — S,A — EN
Keith Merrill — Video Programme Distributors
P
VPD 234

Take Hart
Fil-Ent '8?
Arts
08718   91 mins   C
V2, B, V
Tony Hart
Tony Hart takes a look at a different world of art using odds and ends such as jam jars, cotton wool, salt, paint and wallpaper paste. It also features the plasticine character Morph.
F — EN
Christopher Pilkington — BBC Video   H, P
BBCV 9003

(For Explanation of codes, see USE GUIDE and KEY)

PALADIN VIDEO HOME ENTERTAINMENT GUIDE

Take the Money and Run   Fil-Ent '68
Comedy
05182   83 mins   C
B, V

Woody Allen, Janet Margolin, directed by Woody Allen

Woody Allen stars as Virgil Starkwell in this zany tale of a be-spectacled innocent embroiled in a life of bizarre crimes such as looting gum-ball machines.
BBFC:A — C,A — EN
Palomar Pictures Intl — Rank Video Library   **H, P**
1011

Take This Job and Shove It!   Fil-Ent '81
Comedy-Drama
12162   98 mins   C
V2, B, V

David Keith, Tim Thomerson

A young executive is sent back to his home town to oversee the takeover of the old-town brewery. There are plenty of adventures and the soundtrack features country and western songs, including the voices of Johnny Paycheck, Charlie Pride and Wildman Bobby Bare.
S,A — EN
Avco Embassy — Embassy Home Entertainment   **P**
2082

Taking of Pelham 123, The   Fil-Ent '74
Adventure/Suspense
13176   104 mins   C
B, V

Walter Matthau, Robert Shaw, Martin Balsam, Hector Elizondo, James Broderick, directed by Joseph Sargent

A terrorist leads a cold-blooded quartet who hi-jack a New York subway train and hold the city to ransom.
BBFC:AA — C,A — EN
United Artists — Warner Home Video   **P**
99243

Taking Up the Reins, Parts 1-4   Spo-Lei '8?
Animals
13525   85 mins   C
B, V
4 pgms

Made under the "Challenge to Youth" scheme, this series gives instruction for the rider of the horse on the lunge.

1.Equipment and Technique 2.Cooperation in the School 3.Elements of Jumping 4.Bringing on the Young Horse.
M,S — I
Unknown — TFI Leisure Ltd   **H, P**

Tale of the Frog Prince, The   Chl-Juv '84
Fantasy
13416   57 mins   C
B, V

Robin Williams, Terry Garr, directed by Eric Idle

Adapted from the famous Brothers Grimm fairy story, a prince is turned into frog form but is brought back from his watery home by a princess' kiss.
F — EN
Shelley Duvall — MGM/UA Home Video   **P**
10464

Tale of Three Rallies   Spo-Lei '82
Automobiles-Racing
06844   65 mins   C   (PAL, NTSC)
V2, B, V

Narrated by Stuart Hall

This treble feature is based on feature and documentary material of the following classic car rally events—the 1978 Rally of the Danube, 1979 San Remo Rally and the 1979 Lombard RAC Rally featuring the very best drivers and cars over varied terrain.
S,A — EN
CH Wood Ltd — Duke Marketing Limited   **P**
DM6

Tale of Two Cities, A   Fil-Ent '58
Drama
04260   112 mins   B/W
B, V

Dirk Bogarde, Stephen Murray, Marie Versini, Ernest Clark, Duncan Lamont, Donald Pleasence, Dorothy Tutin, Christopher Lee

Dickens' epic tale follows the fortunes of a disillusioned English lawyer, Sidney Carton, whose solace is drink and who bears an uncanny resemblance to a young French aristocrat named Darnay.
BBFC:U — F — EN
J Arthur Rank — Rank Video Library   **H, P**
0024

Tale of Two Cities, A   Fil-Ent '81
Drama
07360   ? mins   C
B, V

Peter Cushing, Kenneth More, Flora Robson, Billie Whitelaw

(For Explanation of codes, see USE GUIDE and KEY)

PALADIN VIDEO HOME ENTERTAINMENT GUIDE

This is an adaptation of the classic novel by Charles Dickens. A story of man's basest and noblest passions.
S,A — EN
Unknown — *Precision Video Ltd* **P**
BITC 2112/VITC 2112

Tales from the Animal World   Fil-Ent '??
Cartoons/Animals
07655   30 mins   C
B, V
Animated
Each one of these six colour cartoon-features tells the story of one African animal, about its life-style, its friends, its enemies and what it eats. Animals featured are the lion, the leopard, the pelican, the jerboa, the indicator bird and the chimpanzee.
F — EN
Unknown — *VCL Video Services* **P**
F121B

Tales From The Crypt/Vault Of Horror   Fil-Ent '??
Horror
13668   178 mins   C
B, V
Joan Collins, Peter Cushing, Sir Ralph Richardson, directed by Freddie Francis, Daniel Massey, Anna Massey, Curt Jurgens, Tom Baker, Denholm Elliott, directed by Roy Ward Baker
Two films are contained on one cassette. 'Tales From The Crypt (92 minutes, 1972)' finds five tourists exploring the catacombs of ancient martyrs and 'Vault Of Horror (86 minutes, 1973)' features five tales of terror from an underground vault.
BBFC:18 — *A — EN*
Max J Rosenberg; Milton Subotsky — *CBS/Fox Video* **P**
6786

Tales of Beatrix Potter   Fil-Ent '71
Dance/Fairy tales
04242   90 mins   C
B, V
The Royal Ballet
The Royal Ballet of Covent Garden perform a selection of Beatrix Potter's beloved stories. Choreographed by Frederick Ashton.
BBFC:U — *F — EN*
Richard Goodwin — *THORN EMI* **P**
TXB 90 0038 4/TVB 90 0038 2

Tales of Bobby Brewster and More Adventures of Gumdrop   Chi-Juv '??
Cartoons
08321   60 mins   C
B, V
Animated, voices by David Tate, Peter Hawkins
This tape features four tales of Bobby Brewster; 'The Sick Cow' (1974), 'King of Beasts' (1979), 'The Roundabout Horse' (1978), 'George, The Fire Engine' (1976) and a folk tale also by HE. Todd, 'Jungle Silver.' Further adventures of Gumdrop, the trusty old car include 'Gumdrop Gets His Wings' (1979), and 'Gumdrop on the Brighton Run' (1976), by Val Biro.
M,S — EN
Val Biro; Nutland Video — *Nutland Video Ltd* **P**

Tales of Hoffnung   Fil-Ent '??
Cartoons
05851   60 mins   C
B, V
Animated
This film features six animated stories based on the cartoons of Gerard Hoffnung with Donald Adams singing baritone and Maria Korchinska on harp. The tales featured are 'The Symphony Orchestra,' 'The Vacuum Cleaner,' 'The Maestro,' 'The Music Academy,' 'Professor Ya Ya's Memiors' and 'The Palm Court Orchestra.'
F — EN
Halas and Batchelor — *Polygram Video* **P**
7901494/7901492

Tales of Magic   Chi-Juv '7?
Fairy tales
02224   60 mins   C
V
Animated
A beautifully animated, enchanting selection of the world's most loved fairy tales and children's stories including 'The Wild Swan,' 'Cinderella,' 'Gulliver's Travels,' 'The Three Whales,' and 'The Clever Turtle.'
F — EN
Unknown — *JVC* **P**
PRT 9

Tales of Magic   Fil-Ent '??
Cartoons/Magic
05517   56 mins   C
V2, B, V
Animated
This programme contains five tales from around the world—'Lake of Rainbows', 'The Wolf and the Seven Kids', 'Twelve Months', 'White Browed Dog' and 'The Ant and the Grasshopper'.
BBFC:U — *F — EN*
Unknown — *Derann Film Services* **H, P**
BDV114P/BDV114B/BDV114

PALADIN VIDEO HOME ENTERTAINMENT GUIDE

Tales of Ordinary Madness
Fil-Ent '83
Drama/Romance
09384 97 mins C
B, V

Ben Gazzara, Ornella Muti, Tanya Lopert, Susan Tyrrel

This film tells of the fantasies of a tough Los Angeles poet who desires only drink and women. Often explicit, it tells of his sexual adventures which form a mixture of tragedy and farce.
BBFC:18 — A — EN
Miracle — VCL Video Services P
M339D

Tales of Terror
Fil-Ent '62
Horror
08345 90 mins C
V2, B, V

Vincent Price, Peter Lorre, Basil Rathbone, Debra Paget, directed by Roger Corman

This cassette includes three tales of terror; 'Morella,' 'The Black Cat,' and 'The Case of M. Valdemar.' They are based on stories by Edgar Allen Poe.
C,A — EN
American International Pictures — Guild Home Video H, P, E

Tales of the Unexpected—Cassette 1
Fil-Ent '77
Mystery/Suspense
08344 78 mins C
V2, B, V

P. Firth, M. Davies; Jessie Matthews, Bill Maynard, Michael Troughton, Peter Sallis; Siobhan McKenna, Patrick Field

This cassette features three episodes from the 'Tales of the Unexpected' series, each with their own mysteries and twists. 'Man at the Top' features an out of luck seaman caught up in a dockland murder. 'Picture of a Place' is about an eccentric widow and an antique dealer, having found a picture in the attic. 'Vicious Circle' finds an old woman surprising a burglar.
C,A — EN
Quinn Martin — Guild Home Video H, P, E

Tales of the Unexpected-Cassette 2
Fil-Ent '77
Mystery/Suspense
09453 78 mins C
V2, B, V

Warren Oates, Susan Strasburg, Richard Dow

This tape contains three more intriguing mysteries, each of 26 minutes long; 'Nothin' Short of Highway Robbery'; 'On the Cards'; 'The Open Window'.
S,A — EN
Quinn Martin — Guild Home Video H, P, E

Tales of Washington Irving
Fil-Ent '??
Cartoons
09383 43 mins C
B, V
Animated

This tape tells two stories written by Irving during his stay in England; Rip Van Winkle and Sleepy Hollow.
F — EN
Unknown — VCL Video Services P
A314B

Tales that Witness Madness
Fil-Ent '73
Horror
12743 87 mins C
B, V

Donald Pleasence, Joan Collins, Georgia Brown, Kim Novak, directed by Freddie Francis

Four bizarre tales from a clinical casebook are the sinister thread in this shocking account of the mental aberrations that bring people into institutions. However, these tales are nothing to the horrors that lurk in the doctor's own laboratory.
BBFC:18 — A — EN
Norman Prigeen — Rank Video Library H, P
2035

Tall Story
Fil-Ent '60
Comedy
13201 91 mins C
B, V

Jane Fonda, Anthony Perkins, directed by Joshua Logan

A typical American campus comedy involving a baseball team being bribed to lose a vital match against the Russians.
BBFC:U — S,C — EN
Warner Bros — Warner Home Video P
11236

Tamarind Seed, The
Fil-Ent '74
Drama/Suspense
05401 119 mins C
V2, B, V

Julie Andrews, Omar Sharif, Anthony Quayle, Daniel O'Herlihy; Sylvia Syms, Oscar Homolka, directed by Blake Edwards

---

(For Explanation of codes, see USE GUIDE and KEY)

PALADIN VIDEO HOME ENTERTAINMENT GUIDE

A military attache with the Russian Embassy in Paris, who uses this position to conceal the fact that he is second-in-command of the K.G.B., has an innocent meeting in Barbados with a girl who works for the British Foreign Office handling classified information. They are unaware that the heads of both British and Russian intelligence think their meeting was pre-arranged.
BBFC:A — S,A — EN
ITC Entertainment — Precision Video Ltd
P
CRITC 3037/BITC 3037/VITC 3037

Tangier Fll-Ent '82
Drama/Suspense
08674   95 mins   C
V2, B, V
Ronny Cox, Billie Whitelaw, Ronald Lacey, Oscar Quitak, Jack Watson, Glynis Barber, Ronald Fraser, Adel Fredj, Ben Feitelson, Peter Arne, David Collings, directed by Michael E. Briant
Callum, a legendary hell-raiser who made a fortune running guns and contraband in Tangier, is urgently required by British Intelligence. However he has been dead for seven years. An embittered, bankrupt CIA agent who was double-crossed and discharged from the service is blackmailed into becoming Callum's double. He travels to Tangier, treading the path of another man's past, to keep a rendezvous with a man intent on vengeance. Based on the novel by Nicholas Luard.
D,A — EN
Linked Ring Television Film Productions Ltd — *Linked Ring Television Film Productions*
P

Tank Fll-Ent '84
Drama
13629   113 mins   C
B, V
James Garner, G.D. Spradlin, Jennilee Harrison, Shirley Jones, directed by Marvin J. Chomsky
An army officer opposes the local sheriff of a small town and finds his son put in gaol on a false dope charge so goes into action with a fully operational World War II Sherman tank.
BBFC:15 — S,A — EN
Universal — *CIC Video*   **H, P**
1140

Tarantulas Fll-Ent '77
Suspense/Drama
05702   90 mins   C
B, V
Claude Atkins, Charles Frank, Deborah Winters, Sandy McPeak, Bert Remsen, Pat Hingle, Tom Atkins, directed by Stuart Hagman

A plane with a cargo of coffee beans crashes into a field near a small sleepy town in California. The plane explodes and hundreds of tarantulas, that had infested the cargo, escape and scatter into the unknowing town causing mass panic and total chaos.
BBFC:A — S,A — EN
Alan Lansburg Productions — *Derann Film Services*   **P**
TXB 90 15464/TVB 90 15462

Target Fll-Ent '??
Crime-Drama
06867   91 mins   C
V2, B, V
Luc Merenda, Gabriella Giorgelli
Set in Istanbul, this film follows an Interpol chief in his mission to catch a gang of smugglers and drug traffickers. The gang leader attempts to eliminate the investigator but fails. The investigator obtains the services of a local shooting champion, resulting in a long gun battle as they engage the gang one by one.
S,A — EN
Unknown — *European Video Company*
P

Target Eagle Fll-Ent '??
Adventure
08681   98 mins   C
V2, B, V
George Peppard, Maud Adams, Max Von Sydow, George Rivero, Chuck Conners, Susana Dosmantes
Set on the Mediterranean coastline of Africa and Spain, this tells the story of smuggling by a group of free fall parachutists. The smugglers, police and undercover agents, due to their respective interests, become involved in murder, car chases, free fall parachuting and hang-gliding escapades. The agents infiltrate the ring, until their cover is blown and the chase is on again.
BBFC:A — S,A — EN
Unknown — *Derann Film Services*   **P**
FDV 316

Target: Harry Fll-Ent '79
Adventure/Suspense
04269   83 mins   C
B, V
Vic Morrow, Victor Buono, Stanley Holloway, Suzanne Pleshette, Cesar Romero, Charlotte Rampling
Soldier-of-fortune and seaplane owner Harry Black is hired to fly stolen banknote plates to a rendezvous with an oriental buyer in Istanbul.
BBFC:A — C,A — EN
Unknown — *Rank Video Library*   **H, P**
0040

PALADIN VIDEO HOME ENTERTAINMENT GUIDE

Target/Shipment Fil-Ent '??
Crime-Drama
09401 ? mins C
V2, B, V
Patrick Mower
This tape features a 'tip-off' worth half a million, and a murder which brings Hackett, a tough mean cop, back into action.
S,A — EN
BBC — *BBC Video* H, P
BBCV 2004

Tarka the Otter Fil-Ent '79
Adventure
01879 91 mins C
B, V, LV
Narrated by Peter Ustinov
A wildlife adventure film with breathtaking sequences of play, tragedy, and encounters with humans—which lead the otter on to further adventures.
BBFC:A — F — EN
Rank — *Rank Video Library* H, P
0008

Tarzan the Ape Man Fil-Ent '81
Adventure
07719 112 mins C
V2, B, V
Bo Derek, Richard Harris
Based on the original 1932 classic, this new version retells Jane's story of adventure and romance in the African jungle. Jane travels by steamboat, tramp steamer and on foot to find her father. When she locates him they set off on an expedition to find the elephant graveyard, encountering dangerous plants and animals, escaping from tribesmen and lions to eventually meet up with Tarzan.
BBFC:A — S,A — EN
MGM — *MGM/UA Home Video* P
UMR 10109/UMB 10109/UMV 10109

Taste of Evil, A Fil-Ent '71
Drama/Suspense
04214 90 mins C
B, V
Barbara Stanwyck, Barbara Parkins, William Windom, Arthur O'Connell, Roddy McDowell
A young woman returns to a Victorian mansion she will inherit on her 21st birthday after spending seven years in a mental institution. There she finds her mother remarried and mysterious forces plotting to drive her mad again.
BBFC:A — C,A — EN
Spelling — *Guild Home Video* H, P

Taste of Hell, A Fil-Ent '??
War-Drama
07894 86 mins C
V2, B, V
John Garwood, William Smith, Lisa Lorena, directed by Neil Yarema, Basil Bradbury
Two American Army officers trapped in the Philippines by the invasion of the Japanese army join a Filipino Guerilla outfit. They split up to lead separate missions; one of them returns horribly disfigured. He sets out to wage a personal vendetta of revenge on the enemy.
S,A — EN
Unknown — *Video Programme Distributors*
P
Inter-Ocean—066

Tatters Gen-Edu '??
Documentary/Animals
06353 60 mins C
V2, B, V
This film tells the story of a young lion cub found in the bush by an archaeologist. The cub is reared to adulthood but must eventually be returned to the wild.
F — EN
Unknown — *Walton Film and Video Ltd*
P
H283

Tattoo Fil-Ent '81
Drama
08461 99 mins C
B, V
Bruce Dern, Maud Adams, directed by Bob Brooks
A tattoo artist falls in love with a cover-girl. He eventually meets her through a magazine assignment. Although there is a spell of mutual attraction she does not spend long with him. Feeling rejected, and tormented by her beauty he kidnaps her and uses his art to make her his own. It is not long before she starts her sudden and violent revenge.
BBFC:X — A — EN
20th Century Fox — *THORN EMI* P
TXA 90 0835 4 /TVA 90 08352

Taxi Zum Klo Fil-Ent '81
Drama
08984 92 mins C
B, V
Frank Ripplon, Bernd Broderup, Magdalena Montezum, directed by Frank Ripplon

(For Explanation of codes, see USE GUIDE and KEY) 647

PALADIN VIDEO HOME ENTERTAINMENT GUIDE

This tells the story of a man, who by day is a Berlin schoolteacher, and who by night frequents the city's gay bars and public lavatories. It is an explicit story of homosexual life, with English subtitles.
A — EN
Other Cinema — *Palace Video Ltd*   P
PVC 2028B

Te Deum   Fil-Ent '73
Drama/Adventure
08645   93 mins   C
V2, B, V

Jack Palance, Timothy Brent

Te Deum and his family try to off-load their inherited rundown goldmine only to find that it is in fact worth a fortune.
S,A — EN
Unknown — *Fletcher Video*   H, P
V169

Team-Mates   Fil-Ent '??
Adventure
05453   77 mins   C
V2, B, V

Karen Corrado, Max Goff, Christopher Seppe, Ivy Sinclair, directed by Steven Jacobson

A story of American High School life featuring drag racing, football and car chases. Two College football teams set out to prove themselves against each other.
BBFC:X — A — EN
Unknown — *Iver Film Services*   P

Teardrop Explodes in Concert   Fil-Ent '8?
Music-Performance
09997   60 mins   C
B, V

This tape features Teardrop Explodes in concert. It includes such hits as 'Books', 'Passionate Friends', 'Ha Ha I'm Drowning', 'Just Like Hela Khaled Said', 'Poppys in the Field','Suffocate' and 'Treason'.
F — EN
Holiday Brothers Ltd. — *Holiday Brothers Ltd*   P

Tears for Fears—In My Mind's Eye   Fil-Ent '84
Music-Performance
13136   60 mins   C
B, V

Taken from the band's concert appearance at the Hammersmith Odeon, the thirteen tracks include 'Start of the Breakdown,' 'Mother's Talk,' 'Mad World,' 'We Are Broken' and 'Memories Fade.' This programme is recorded in Hi-Fi.
S,A — EN
Unknown — *Polygram Video*   P
040 3494/040 3492

Tears for Fears-The Videosingles   Fil-Ent '8?
Music-Performance/Video
09874   15 mins   C
B, V

This tape comprises the creative videos of 'Mad World', 'Change' and 'Pale Shelter' which were all top five singles. All the tracks are from Tears for Fears first album, 'The Hurting' which entered the British charts at No. 1 and earned the band their first gold disc.
F — EN
Unknown — *Polygram Video*   H, P
791 5604/791 5602

Teddy Pendergrass Live in London   Fil-Ent '82
Music-Performance
12205   75 mins   C
B, V

Filmed at the Hammersmith Odeon this tape features a lot of Teddy Pendergrass' most popular songs, including 'Close the Door', 'Turn off the Lights', 'You're My Latest My Greatest Inspiration', and 'Come Go With Me'.
F — EN
Home Video Premiere Productions — *CBS/Fox Video*   P
7135

Tee to Green   Spo-Lei '80
Golf
06061   120 mins   C
V2, B, V

Vivien Saunders M.Sc., directed by Jane Thorburn

A complete course on golf from the basics to advanced techniques. Contains: the grip, the set-up, the simple golf swing, developing the backswing, down and through ball, wedge to driver, sloping lies, long game faults, short game techniques and taking the fear out of bunkers.
F — I
Genevieve Promotions Ltd — *Video Programme Distributors*   P
T.T.G.

Telefon   Fil-Ent '77
Crime-Drama
07729   99 mins   C

648   (For Explanation of codes, see USE GUIDE and KEY)

PALADIN VIDEO HOME ENTERTAINMENT GUIDE

B, V

Charles Bronson, Lee Remick, Tyne Daly, Alan Badel, Patrick Magee, Donald Pleasance, directed by Don Siegel

Set in the winter of 1977, a Russian defector is moving swiftly across the USA leaving a trail of sabotage and destruction. In pursuit is a Russian secret agent despatched by the KGB in a race against time to prevent the two Super Powers from the ultimate conflict.

BBFC:A — *S,A* — *EN*

United ARtists — *MGM/UA Home Video*

P

UMB 10127/UMV 10127

Telford's Last Canal   Gen-Edu '83
Building
12370   30 mins   C
B, V, 3/4U

This programme describes the building of Thomas Telford's Birmingham & Liverpool Junction Canal and the enormous difficulties he encountered.

M,A — *ED*

IA Recordings — *I.A. Recordings*   P

Tell Them Willie Boy Is Here   Fil-Ent '70
Western
13620   96 mins   C
B, V

Robert Redford, Katherine Ross, Robert Blake, Mikel Angel, directed by Abraham Polonsky

Based on a real life incident, this is the story of a Paiute Indian who kills the father of the girl he wants to marry and is forced to run from the white posse sent to capture him.

BBFC:15 — *S,A* — *EN*

Universal — *CIC Video*   H, P

1133

Tempest, The   Fil-Ent '80
Drama/Fantasy
08983   95 mins   C
B, V

Toyah Willcox, Heathcote Williams, Karl Johnson, Ken Campbell, Elisabeth Welch, directed by Derek Jarman

This is Jarman's adaptation of the well-known Shakespeare play. He concentrates on an atmosphere of wonderment and hallucination.

BBFC:AA — *C,A* — *EN*

Osprey Films Ltd — *Palace Video Ltd*   P

PVC 2027A

Tempest, The   Fil-Ent '82
Drama
12464   136 mins   C

B, V

John Cassavettes, Gena Rowlands, Susan Sarandon, Vittorio Gassman, Raul Julia

The story of a man who flees a stormy Manhattan marriage for a deserted Greek Island only to have the illusion of paradise shattered when a storm begins to rage.

BBFC:15 — *S,A* — *EN*

Columbia — *RCA/Columbia Pictures Video UK*   H, P

10143

Tempter, The   Fil-Ent '76
Horror
07877   100 mins   C
V2, B, V

Carla Gravina, Mel Ferrer, Arthur Kennedy, directed by Alberto De Martino

The daughter of a wealthy Italian family is paralysed by a psychic trauma after a car accident caused by her father kills her mother. The despair of the family manifests itself by weird and frightening events. Under hypnosis, now possessed, she reveals the presence of a spirit that had been burnt at the stake. After a priest fails to exorcise her, demonic powers take over as she runs away to kill herself. Her father follows, attempting to save her in time.

A — *EN*

Joseph E. Levine — *Intervision Video*   H, P

A-A0392

"10"   Fil-Ent '79
Comedy/Romance
06050   118 mins   C
B, V

Dudley Moore, Julie Andrews, Bo Derek, directed by Blake Edwards

A successful song writer with everything going for him feels that his life is incomplete. He searches and finds the girl of his dreams, he rates as the ultimate on the popular girl-watching scale. He pursues her, determined to overcome any obstacles, with unpredictable results. Music by Henry Mancini, features Ravel's 'Bolero.'

BBFC:X — *A* — *EN*

Warner Bros; Orion Pictures — *Warner Home Video*   P

WEX2002/WEV2002

Ten Brothers of Shao Lin   Fil-Ent '7?
Martial arts
09827   90 mins   C
B, V

(For Explanation of codes, see USE GUIDE and KEY)

PALADIN VIDEO HOME ENTERTAINMENT GUIDE

While the Governor's most skilful fighting guards hunt him, Chu hides in a Shao Lin monastery, where he meets a beautiful girl. With ten Shao Lin monks, Chu and Shao set out to restore the Ming Dynasty.
S,A — EN
Unknown — Polygram Video   H, P
790 4564/790 4562

---

10 cc Live at the International Music Show   Fil-Ent '82
Music-Performance
08401   54 mins   C
V2, B, V
This video was filmed live at the International Music Show in March 1982. It celebrates 10 cc's 10th anniversary. It features some of their best known songs such as 'The Wall Street Shuffle', 'Donna', 'Rubber Bullets' and 'Dreadlock Holiday'.
S,A — EN
Unknown — Guild Home Video   H, P, E

10cc Live in Concert   Fil-Ent '??
Music-Performance
08843   60 mins   C
B, V
This tape features 10cc live in concert. It includes their songs 'Things We Do for Love', 'Wall Street Shuffle', amongst many others.
C,A — EN
Unknown — VCL Video Services   P
V065B

Ten Commandments, The   Fil-Ent '56
Drama
01215   219 mins   C
B, V
Charlton Heston, Yul Brynner, Anne Baxter, Yvonne DeCarlo, directed by Cecil B. DeMille
Lavish Biblical epic that tells the life story of Moses (Charlton Heston) who turned his back on a privileged life to lead his people to freedom.
Academy Awards '56: Best Special Effects.
F — EN
Paramount — CIC Video   H, P

Ten Fingers of Steel   Fil-Ent '68
Martial arts/Adventure
05515   95 mins   C
B, V
Wang Yu, Chang Chin Chin, Kan Kai, directed by Kien Lun

A young man returns to Japan to find the leder of a bandit gang who raped his sister when their village was attacked. He encounters many obstacles, but saves the life of a traveller who reveals the identity of the man he is looking for.
BBFC:X — A — EN
Unknown — Derann Film Services   H, P
DV139B/DV139

Ten Violent Women   Fil-Ent '??
Adventure/Drama
06124   105 mins   C
V2, B, V
Sherry Vernon, Dixie Lauren, Sally A Gamble
Ten girls, tired of office work, join together to rob a million dollars in jewels. Their adventures involve a sheik, drugs, police and a luxury yacht in the Mediterranean.
S,A — EN
Unknown — Video Programme Distributors   P
Cinehollywood—V390

Tender Loving Care   Fil-Ent '??
Drama
07927   86 mins   C
V2, B, V
Donna Desmond
This story revolves around the lives of three young nurses working in a large city hospital. They take it upon themselves to get the most out of life but get involved in a web of drugs, blackmail and murder.
BBFC:X — A — EN
Unknown — Video Programme Distributors   P
Inter-Ocean—075

Tender Mercies   Fil-Ent '82
Drama
09805   87 mins   C
B, V
Robert Duvall, directed by Bruce Beresford
A down and out country-and-western singer meets a young widow and learns to appreciate for the first time the healing powers of love.
BBFC:PG — F — EN
EMI Films Inc. — THORN EMI   P
TXA 90 16994/TVA 90 1699 2

Tenebrae   Fil-Ent '80
Horror
12672   101 mins   C
V2, B, V
Anthony Franciosa, John Saxon, directed by Dario Argento

PALADIN VIDEO HOME ENTERTAINMENT GUIDE

This film will take you on a bizarre voyage into a psycho-sexual world.
BBFC:18 — A — EN
Unknown — Videomedia   **P**
1032

Tennis   Spo-Lei '78
Tennis
04417   60 mins   C
B, V
Highlights of the Commercial Union Masters Tennis Tournament, featuring top stars such as Bjorn Borg, Jimmy Connors, Ilie Nastase, and Manuel Orantes.
F — EN
Unknown — VCL Video Services   **P**

Tennis with Mark Cox 1 and 2   Spo-Lei '7?
Tennis
01894   28 mins   C
B, V
Mark Cox   2 pgms
The first tennis programme deals with the layout of the court and reviews the equipment especially for the beginner. The second part progresses to actual play and tactics. Also demonstrated are the service, lob volley and smash.
S,A — I
Rank — Rank Video Library   **H, P**
5012; 5013

Tension at Table Rock/Revenge Is My Destiny   Fil-Ent '??
Western/Suspense
05779   175 mins   C
B, V
Richard Egan, Dorothy Malone, Angie Dickinson, directed by Charles Marquis Warren, Chris Robinson, Sidney Blackmer, directed by Joseph Adler
Two films are contained on one cassette. 'Tension at Table Rock' (colour, 89 minutes, 1957). A gun slinger becomes guardian to an orphan boy whose uncle is sheriff in lawless Table Rock. The local gang boss sends for a professional killer to back him up in preparation for a shoot-out. 'Revenge is my Destiny' (colour, 86 minutes, 1972) features an ex-Vietnamese soldier running for his missing wife in Miami. She reappears then vanishes again, he untangles a web of intrigue leading to a former Nazi mastermind leading a crime wave.
S,A — EN
Universal; Gold Key Entertainment — Kingston Video   **H, P**
KV2

Terminal Choice   Fil-Ent '84
Drama
13672   94 mins   C
B, V
Joe Spano, David McCallum, Diane Venora, directed by Sheldon Larry
Set in a high-tec clinic of the near future, a doctor is trying to clear his name and uncovers a nightmare of corruption which ends in a fight between man and machine.
BBFC:18 — A — EN
Gary Magder — CBS/Fox Video   **P**
3076

Terminate with Extreme Prejudice   Fil-Ent '8?
Crime-Drama/Suspense
09905   95 mins   C
B, V
Miles O'Keefe
This is a spy-thriller about the exploits of glamorous Prince Malko, an undercover CIA man sent to track down a renegade agent in steamy San Salvador.
A — EN
Unknown — Entertainment in Video   **H, P**
EVB 1015/EVV 1015

Terms of Endearment   Fil-Ent '83
Drama
13331   126 mins   C
B, V
Debra Winger, Shirley MacLaine, Jeff Daniels, Jack Nicholson, Danny DeVito, John Lithgow, directed by James L. Brooks
This is the story of the lives, loves and tragedy which surround a mother and her daughter. Academy Awards '84: Best Actress (MacLaine); Best Supporting Actor: (Nicholson); Best Screenplay: (Brooks); Best Director: (Brooks).
BBFC:15 — S,A — EN
Paramount — CIC Video   **H, P**
BER 2105/VHR 2105

Terrahawks 6: Zero Strikes Back   Chl-Juv '8?
Science fiction/Puppets
13481   86 mins   C
V2, B, V
Zelda plans to destroy a freighter laden with gold which is on its way to Earth in this episode.
BBFC:U — F — EN
ITC — Precision Video Ltd   **P**
2635

Terrahawks   Fil-Ent '8?
Science fiction/Cartoons
09339   92 mins   C
B, V

(For Explanation of codes, see USE GUIDE and KEY)

PALADIN VIDEO HOME ENTERTAINMENT GUIDE

Animated
Set on Earth in the year 2020, an alien spacecraft is approaching the NASA base on Mars. Led by the witch-like Zelda, the aliens destroy the base and set up their own. Zelda sets about plotting the invasion of Earth and the destruction of the human race. However the home planet is defended by an international fighting force.
BBFC:U — *F* — *EN*
Unknown — *Precision Video Ltd*   **P**
BABPV 2630/VABPV 2630

Terrahawks 2: The Menace from Mars   Fil-Ent '8?
Science fiction/Cartoons
09336   92 mins   C
B, V
Animated
This continues the space-age battle of Zelda, Imperial Queen of the Planet Guk, to conquer the world. She arranges peace talks with Ninestein who discovers that peace is the last thing she has in mind, and her plan is thwarted. Furious, and encouraged by a crew of repellent relatives, Zelda unleashes from cryogenic slumber the fearful Sporilla.
BBFC:U — *F* — *EN*
Unknown — *Precision Video Ltd*   **P**
BABPV 2631/VABPV 2631

Terrahawks 3: Terror from Mars   Chi-Juv '??
Science fiction/Cartoons
12017   86 mins   C
B, V
Animated
Back in action the fabulous Terrahawks pit their wits against one of Zelda's most powerful monsters, Moid, the master of Infinite Disguise.
BBFC:U — *F* — *EN*
Unknown — *Precision Video Ltd*   **P**
BABPV 2632/VABPV 2632

Terrahawks 4: Hostages of Mars   Chi-Juv '8?
Science fiction/Puppets
13482   92 mins   C
V2, B, V
More adventures in outer space from the aircraft vigilantes.
BBFC:U — *F* — *EN*
ITC — *Precision Video Ltd*   **P**
2633

Terrahawks 5: Flaming Thunderbolts   Chi-Juv '8?
Science fiction/Puppets
13480   86 mins   C
V2, B, V
Another compilation of episodes from The Terrahawks and their enemies in outer space.
BBFC:U — *F* — *EN*
ITC — *Precision Video Ltd*   **P**
2634

Terror   Fil-Ent '??
Drama
06125   102 mins   C
V2, B, V
Florinda Bolkan, Ray Lovelock
Seven women are kept prisoner by three killers who brutalize, rape and humiliate them. Terror and hatred invoke the formation of a diabolical plan in the mind of the 'seventh woman.'
S,A — *EN*
Unknown — *Video Programme Distributors*   **P**
Cinehollywood—V260

Terror   Fil-Ent '79
Horror
08635   84 mins   C
V2, B, V
John Nolan, Carolyn Courage, James Aubrey
Supernatural forces and the shocking effect their mysterious powers have on the life of a young girl are depicted in this weird and terrifying tale.
A — *EN*
Independent — *Hokushin Audio Visual Ltd*   **P**
VM51

Terror at Red Wolf Inn   Fil-Ent '??
Horror
07678   90 mins   C
B, V
Linda Gillin, Arthur Space, John Nielson, Mary Jackson, directed by Bud Townsend
Q young college student wins a two week all expenses paid vacation at the Red Wolf Inn. The charming old place is run by a warm and friendly elderly couple and their grandson. The vacation turns into more than she bargained for.
A — *EN*
Unknown — *Video Network*   **P**
0006

Terror Express   Fil-Ent '7?
Horror/Suspense
07773   85 mins   C
V2, B, V
Silvia Dionisio, Werner Pochath

PALADIN VIDEO HOME ENTERTAINMENT GUIDE

An horrific story of an innocent train journey that explodes into a nightmare for the unsuspecting passengers.
S,A — EN
Unknown — Fletcher Video H, P
V151

Terror Eyes Fil-Ent '8?
Horror/Suspense
08342 90 mins C
V2, B, V
Leonard Mann, Rachel Ward, Drew Snyder, Joe Sicari
Young women attending a Boston night school begin to be terrorised by a mysterious killer. Each of his victims are decapitated. All the evidence points to one of the teachers.
BBFC:X — A — EN
Lorimar — Guild Home Video H, P, E

Terror from the Sky Fil-Ent '79
Suspense/Drama
05500 85 mins C
V2, B, V
Efrem Zimbalist Jr
A doctor and his assistant who work at the national bee centre in New Orleans discover several dead bees at hive '112'. Shortly afterwards a keeper is killed when the bees swarm, stinging him to death. In the laboratory they discover that a strange strain of bees have entered the hive and are taking over everything.
BBFC:A — S,A — EN
Unknown — Derann Film Services H, P
DV136P/DV136B/DV136

Terror of Dr. Hitchcock, The Fil-Ent '62
Horror
08603 84 mins C
V2, B, V
Barbara Steele, Robert Flemyng, Tessa Fitzgerald, directed by Robert Hampton
This is a horrific story of the bizarre killing of a man's first wife. His beautiful second wife then enters his web of dark perversions and unrelenting horror. She finds herself part of his fiendish experiments to rejuvenate his dead wife.
BBFC:X — A — EN
Sigma III — Videomedia P
PVM 1029/BVM 1029/HVM 1029

Terror on Tour Fil-Ent '82
Horror
08997 90 mins C
B, V
Dave Galluzzo, Richard Styles, Rick Pemberton, Chip Greeman, J. Kelly, directed by Don Edmunds
This film tells the story of a rock group,'The Clowns'. Their incredible stage performance delves into sadistic multilating theatrics. Eventually real murders begin and the group become prime suspects.
BBFC:18 — A — EN
IWDC — Video Programme Distributors P
Media 215

Terror Out of the Sky Fil-Ent '78
Horror
09316 81 mins C
B, V
Efrem Zimbalist Jr., Tovah Feldshuh, Dan Haggerty
The queen bee of a savage strain of killer bees infiltrates a hive in New Orleans, causing thousands of newly-hatched bees to terrorize the city.
S,A — EN
Alan Landsburg Prods — THORN EMI P
TXB 90 1549 4/TVB 90 1549 2

Terry Toons Chi-Juv '5?
Cartoons
13435 58 mins C
B, V
Animated
A compilation of cartoons from Luno the magical horse, The Terry Bears, Gandy Goose, Little Roquefort and Sydney the elephant.
F — EN
Paul Terry — MGM/UA Home Video P

Terrytoons, Volume 1 Chi-Juv '6?
Cartoons
12998 58 mins C
B, V
Animated
A festival of cartoons featuring The Terry Bears, Little Roquefort, Luno the Magic Horse, Sydney the lovable elephant and Gandy Goose.
BBFC:U — PS,M — EN
Paul Terry — Warner Home Video P
10479

Tess Fil-Ent '80
Drama
08468 164 mins C
B, V
Nastassia Kinski, Peter Firth, Leigh Lawson, directed by Roman Polanski
This film, set in the countryside of Northern Brittany, is based on the book 'Tess of the d'Urbevilles' by Thomas Hardy. It tells the tragic tale of a young girl from her ravishment by the wealthy Alec d'Urbeville to her short lived marriage to another man.

(For Explanation of codes, see USE GUIDE and KEY) 653

PALADIN VIDEO HOME ENTERTAINMENT GUIDE

Academy Awards '80: Best Cinematography; Best Art Direction; Best Costume Design.
BBFC:A — S,A — EN
Claude Beri; Renn Productions; Burrill Productions — *THORN EMI* **P**
TXA 90 1002 4/TVA 90 1002 2

Test Dept.—Program for Progress Fil-Ent '83
Music video
13145 43 mins C
B, V
Angus Farquhar, Paul Jamrozy, Toby Burdon, Graham Cunnington
This programme stars a new band, Test Dept, and fuses music and video sequences in an innovative manner.
S,A — EN
Unknown — *Polygram Video* **P**
040 3124/040 3122

Testament Fil-Ent '83
Drama
13626 86 mins C
B, V
Jane Alexander, William Devane, Ross Harris, Roxana Zal, directed by Lynne Littman
Based on a short story, this is an account of a mother who strives to protect herself and her children from the creeping radioactive fallout after San Francisco has been flattened by a nuclear explosion.
BBFC:PG — S,A — EN
Paramount — *CIC Video* **H, P**
2120

Testament d'Orphee Fil-Ent '59
Film-Avant-garde
10039 83 mins B/W
B, V
Jean Cocteau, Edouard Dermithe, Yul Brynner, Daniel Gelin, Jean Marais, directed by Jean Cocteau
Cocteau's last film is a surreal voyage through a dream world of life's enigmas and searches. Subtitled in English.
C,A   FR
Editions Cinegraphiques — *Palace Video Ltd* **P**
PVC 2039A

Texas Across the River Fil-Ent '66
Western/Comedy
13610 97 mins C
B, V
Rosemary Forsyth, Peter Graves, Andrew Prine, Dean Martin, Tina Marquand, directed by Michael Gordon
A couple of adventurers are engaged in agreeable rivalry when one of them falls for the other's bride-to-be in the oil-rich state of Texas.
BBFC:U — F — EN
Universal — *CIC Video* **H, P**
1139

Texas Adios Fil-Ent '77
Western
04120 85 mins C
B, V
Franco Nero
A Texas sheriff leaves for Mexico to pursue the man who killed his father. In the process, he learns something about his family, which is directly related to the task he must perform.
C,A — EN
Italian — *Video Programme Distributors* **P**
Inter-Ocean—011

Texas Chainsaw Massacre, The Fil-Ent '??
Horror/Suspense
05462 80 mins C
V2, B, V
Marilyn Burns, Gunnar Hansen, directed by Tobe Hooper
This film based on a true incident is an account of a tragedy which befell a group of five youngsters. An afternoon's drive on a summer's day became a nightmare when they were exposed to an insane and macabre family of chainsaw killers. With his friends brutally butchered, a youth makes a frantic bid to escape.
A — EN
Unknown — *Iver Film Services* **P**
22

Texersize Spo-Lei '83
Physical fitness
12160 35 mins C
V2, B, V
Irlene Mandrell
This programme introduces a new approach to work-outs for men and women in the country way. A complete cardiovascular work-out is achieved in 30 minutes.
A — I
Panda Productions; Highland Productions — *Embassy Home Entertainment* **P**
1111

That Championship Season Fil-Ent '83
Drama
09442 106 mins C
V2, B, V

---

654 (For Explanation of codes, see USE GUIDE and KEY)

PALADIN VIDEO HOME ENTERTAINMENT GUIDE

Robert Mitchum, Martin Sheen, Paul Sorvino, Stacey Keach, Bruce Dern
Five men get together for the 24th annual reunion of their moment of glory as Pennsylvania's State Basketball Champions. The evening is shattered by a violent eruption of personal jealousies, disillusionment and the revelation of a bitter secret.
BBFC:PG — F — EN
Golan-Globus Prod. — Guild Home Video
H, P, E

That Darn Cat · Fil-Ent '65
Comedy/Adventure
05586   112 mins   C
B, V
Hayley Mills, Dean Jones, Dorothy Provine, Roddy McDowell, directed by Robert Stevenson
When a troublesome cat strays from home into the hideout of two bank robbers the fun starts. Their hostage scratches 'Help' on her wristwatch and places it around the cat's neck. On his return everyone becomes involved—the FBI, two sisters and their boyfriends and nosey neighbour.
F — EN
Walt Disney Productions — Rank Video Library
H
OS800

That Lucky Touch · Fil-Ent '75
Comedy
08821   90 mins   C
B, V
Roger Moore, Shelley Winters, Lee J. Cobb, Susannah York
This tells the story of a smooth talking arms dealer who gets involved with a journalist who is covering the NATO war games.
C,A — EN
Gloria Films; Rank Films — VCL Video Services   **P**
P274D

That Man Bolt · Fil-Ent '73
Drama/Martial arts
13279   103 mins   C
B, V
Fred Williamson, Vassili Lambrinos, Teresa Graves, directed by Henry Levin and David Lowell Rich
A courier is hired to convey an attache case containing a million dollars to Mexico City and becomes involved in a series of martial arts confrontations in his efforts to stave off a gang of thieves.
BBFC:18 — C,A — EN
Universal — CIC Video   **H, P**
BET 1098/VHT 1098

That Riviera Touch · Fil-Ent '66
Comedy
05157   96 mins   C
B, V
Eric Morecambe, Ernie Wise
When traffic wardens Eric and Ernie illadvisedly slap a ticket on a royal Rolls Royce they flee the country for the French Riviera.
BBFC:U — F — EN
Continental; Walter Reade — Rank Video Library   **H, P**
1029

That Touch of Mink · Fil-Ent '62
Comedy-Drama/Romance
08733   95 mins   C
B, V
Cary Grant, Doris Day, Gig Young, Audrey Meadows, Dick Sargent, John Astin
A handsome and wealthy New York business tycoon is shocked to find himself smitten by a naive beautiful girl from out of town. Their seemingly ill-matched affair transforms into a true romance as they find themselves at the altar.
C,A — EN
Universal — BBC Video   **H, P**
BBCV 8012

That'll Be the Day · Fil-Ent '73
Musical-Drama
00585   86 mins   C
B, V
David Essex, Rosemary Leach, Ringo Starr
A probe into a young man's torment in finding himself with lost jobs, gained and lost friendships, first love, and rock music.
BBFC:AA — C,A — EN
David Puttnam; Sanford Lieberson — THORN EMI   **P**
TXB 90 0214 4/TVB 90 0214 2

That's Carry On · Fil-Ent '78
Comedy
01887   95 mins   C
B, V
Hattie Jacques, Kenneth Williams, Jim Dale, Barbara Windsor, Sidney James
A feature length compilation combining the most hilarious moments from 20 years of 'Carry On' films. Some sequences are in black and white.
BBFC:A — S,A — EN
Rank — Rank Video Library   **H, P**
1003

That's Entertainment · Fil-Ent '74
Musical/Documentary
05309   123 mins   C
B, V

(For Explanation of codes, see USE GUIDE and KEY)

PALADIN VIDEO HOME ENTERTAINMENT GUIDE

Fred Astaire, Bing Crosby, Gene Kelly, Peter Lawford, Liza Minelli, Donald O'Connor, Debbie Reynolds, Mickey Rooney, Frank Sinatra, James Stewart, Elizabeth Taylor, directed by Jack Haley Jr
An anthology of scenes from the classic MGM musicals and dramas to mark their fiftieth anniversary of film making. Nearly a hundred features provided the source for the film extending from 'The Broadway Melody' produced in 1929 to 'Gigi' in 1958.
F — EN
United Artists; Jack Haley Jr — *MGM/UA Home Video*   **P**
UMB10007/UMV10007

That's Entertainment: Part 2   Fil-Ent '76
Musical/Documentary
07734   121 mins   C
B, V
Narrated by Fred Astaire and Gene Kelly
This sequel to Thats Entertainment is a further compilation of classic moments from the archives of MGM. It spotlights performances by John Barrymore, Clark Gable, Greta Garbo, The Marx Brothers, W.C. Fields, Bing Crosby, Judy Holliday, Judy Garland, and Frank Sinatra, with music by Gershwin, Kern, Hammerstein and others.
BBFC:U — F — EN
MGM — *MGM/UA Home Video*   **P**
UMB 10075/UMV 10075

That's Magic   Fil-Ent '82
Magic
08539   100 mins   C
B, V
John Salisse, Ali Bongo, David Beckley, Alan Shaxon, directed by Kevin Marsland
Four of the world's most well-known magicians perform perplexing feats such as 'The Lady Sawn in Half,' 'Appearing Bank Notes,' 'The Vanishing Lady,' and 'The Jumping Banana'. At the end of each show the performer tells the secrets of the illusions and shows how the feat is accomplished.
F — EN
Unknown — *THORN EMI*   **P**
TXE 90 08514/TVE 90 08512

Theodora Queen of Byzantium   Fil-Ent '54
Drama/Adventure
05550   ? mins   C
V2, B, V
Irene Papas, George Marchal

This is the ruthless, violent and bloody story of how Theodora, a slave Empress, rose to supreme power.
BBFC:X — A — EN
Unknown — *Videomedia*   **P**
PVM 5104/BVM 5104/HVM 5104

There Goes the Bride   Fil-Ent '79
Comedy
05758   90 mins   C
B, V
Tom Smothers, Twiggy, Martin Balsam, Sylvia Syms, Michael Whitney, Geoffrey Sumner, Graham Stark, directed by Terence Marcel
The story of the crazy and chaotic events that befall a neurotic advertising executive on the day of his daughter's wedding. He finds coping with life's problems enough but having to organise a slogan for a bra company, fetching in-laws and preparing for the wedding prove all too much; accidental blows to the head cause him to hallucinate and cause mayhem.
BBFC:A — M,A — EN
Lonsdale Productions Ltd — *Home Video Holdings*   **H, P**
007

There Was A Crooked Man   Fil-Ent '70
Comedy
13013   125 mins   C
B, V
Kirk Douglas, Henry Fonda, directed by Joseph L. Manciewicz
A conniving convict tries to bribe a prison warden for a chance to escape.
BBFC:AA — C,A — EN
Warner Bros; Seven Arts Inc — *Warner Home Video*   **P**
11270

There's No Business Like Show Business   Fil-Ent '54
Musical
01201   117 mins   C
B, V
Ethel Merman, Donald O'Connor, Marilyn Monroe, Dan Dailey, Johnny Ray, Mitzi Gaynor
A top husband and wife vaudeville team return to the stage with their three children, who are now also in the act. Includes 24 songs by Irving Berlin.
F — EN
20th Century Fox — *CBS/Fox Video*   **P**
3A-076

They All Laughed   Fil-Ent '81
Comedy
09093   115 mins   C
V2, B, V

PALADIN VIDEO HOME ENTERTAINMENT GUIDE

Ben Gazzara, John Ritter, Audrey Hepburn, Colleen Camp, Patti Hansen, Dorothy Stratten, directed by Peter Bogdonovich
A madcap private eye caper involving a team of detectives who are both following and being followed by a bevy of dazzling women.
S,A — EN
PSO; Moon Pictures — *Video Tape Centre*
P

They Call Me Bruce — Fil-Ent '83
Comedy-Drama
09899   90 mins   C
B, V
Johnny Yune, Margaux Hemingway
Bruce is a humble cook who does not realise that he is working for the Mafia. On one of his jobs, delivering 'Chinese flour' all across the United States, he is pursued by Texan sheriffs, whores from Las Vegas, mobsters, Kung-Fu exponents and many more.
C,A — EN
Elliot Hong — *Entertainment in Video*   H,
P
EVB 1013/EVV 1013

They Call Me Hallelujah — Fil-Ent '78
Comedy/Western
09302   96 mins   C
B, V
George Hilton
'Hallelujah' leads a motley crew of freedom fighters dedicated to the overthrow of the corrupt Mexican Government. They are searching for a fortune in jewels to pay for arms. The jewels are found but turn out to be fakes resulting in a series of deals and double crosses.
BBFC:U — F — EN
United Pools and Products — *Abacus Video*
P

They Call Me Lucky — Fil-Ent '7?
Drama
02123   103 mins   C
V2, B, V
When his wife is killed by a stray silver bullet from a Mexican pistolero, Juan swears to avenge her death. This is the story of the tragic aftermath of his hatred and revenge.
C,A — EN
Unknown — *Hokushin Audio Visual Ltd*
P
VM-35

They Call Me Trinity — Fil-Ent '72
Western/Comedy
08328   105 mins   C
V2, B, V, LV
Terence Hill, Bud Spencer, Farley Granger, Steffen Zacharias, directed by E.B. Clucher
This film is about a lazy drifter-gunslinger and his outlaw brother who join forces with Mormon farmers to rout bullying outlaws.
BBFC:U — F — EN
AVCO Embassy; West Film Productions — *Embassy Home Entertainment*
P
2020

They Call That an Accident — Fil-Ent '82
Drama
10140   90 mins   C
B, V
Nathalie Delon, Patrick Norbert, Gilles Segai, Jean-Pierre Bagot, Robert Benoit, Monique Melinand, directed by Nathalie Delon
When a young boy dies during a routine appendectomy the clinic insist it was an accident. His mother plots vengeance against the three surgeons including her husband. Convinced it was murder, she threatens their lives and reputations with the help of a young musician. Subtitled in English. Soundtrack features music by Steve Winwood, U2, Marianne Faithfull, Wally Badarou, Jess Roden, and Peter Wood and the Compass Point All Stars.
BBFC:15 — S,A — EN   FR
Goldeneye Productions — *Island Pictures*
P
IPV 014C

They called him Amen — Fil-Ent '??
Western
08912   89 mins   C
V2, B, V
Sydne Rome
This film is full of gunfights, saloon room brawls, hard living and hard loving.
C,A — EN
Unknown — *Video Programme Distributors*
P
Inter-Ocean 091

They Made Me a Criminal — Fil-Ent '39
Crime-Drama
07638   70 mins   B/W
B, V
John Garfield, Claude Rains, Ann Sheridan, Billy Haisp, Huntz Hall, Leo Gorcey, May Robson, Ward Bond, directed by Busby Berkeley
A boxer falsely accused of murder after a drunken brawl is forced to travel west and hide in a deserted ranch. The ranch is run by two

PALADIN VIDEO HOME ENTERTAINMENT GUIDE

women and six New York ruffians. The boxer falls in love with one of the women. Things become complicated when he agrees to enter a prize fight to raise money to save the ranch.
F — EN
Warner Bros — VCL Video Services P
0238G

They Paid With Bullets Fil-Ent '68
Crime-Drama
04308 85 mins C
V2, B, V
Directed by Guilio Diemante
Fast-moving action film set in Chicago during the Roaring Twenties. Contains some extremely violent scenes.
BBFC:X — A — EN
Nike; Copercines — Intervision Video H, P
A-A 0082

They Shoot Horses, Don't They? Fil-Ent '69
Drama
04246 108 mins C
B, V
Jane Fonda, Michael Sarrazin, Susannah York, Gig Young, Red Buttons
The year is 1932, the place California. The Depression is in full swing. Poor and jobless drifters both young and old enter a dance marathon compered by ruthless promoter Rocky.
BBFC:AA — C,A — EN
Cinerama Releasing — Rank Video Library H, P
0041

They're a Weird Mob Fil-Ent '66
Comedy
12736 112 mins C
B, V
Walter Chiari, Clare Dunne, Chips Rafferty, directed by Michael Powell
An Italian arrives in Sydney, Australia to find his cousin has left, leaving behind a pile of debts and an angry, but attractive, landlord. He sets out to pay her back, win her affection and get to grips with the Australians.
BBFC:U — F — EN
Michael Powell — Rank Video Library H, P
1074 E

Thief Fil-Ent '71
Crime-Drama/Suspense
08026 72 mins C
V2, B, V
Richard Crenna, Angie Dickinson, Cameron Mitchell, directed by William Graham
To most people Neal Wilkerson appears as a successful business executive, engaged to a beautiful woman. Only to his close friend, a lawyer, is it known that Neal was a jewel thief now on parole. When gambling leads him into serious debt, his criminal activities increase in order to maintain his comfortable existence.
BBFC:A — S,A — EN
Metromedia — Iver Film Services P
222

Thief of Bagdad, The Fil-Ent '24
Adventure
04670 137 mins B/W
B, V
Douglas Fairbanks Sr., Julanne Johnson, Anna Wong
A notorious thief reforms when he falls in love with a princess. In order to prove himself worthy, he undergoes a series of hazardous adventures. Silent; colour-tinted.
F — EN
United Artists — Polygram Video P

Thief of Bagdad Fil-Ent '??
Cartoons/Fantasy
06301 65 mins C
V2, B, V
Animated
A full length animated musical of the famous fairy tale about a genie, a prince, beautiful maidens, a thief and magic featuring the singing voice of Julie Andrews.
F — EN
Unknown — World of Video 2000 H, P
GF526

Thief of Bagdad, The Fil-Ent '40
Adventure/Fantasy
09818 100 mins C
B, V
Sabu, Conrad Veidt, June Duprez, John Justin
This film tells of the magic, romance and fantasy of the Arabian Knights, together with flying horses, magic carpets, mystical cities and terrifying giants.
F — EN
London Films — Polygram Video H, P
790 2564/790 2562

Thief Who Came to Dinner, The Fil-Ent '73
Comedy-Drama
06034 109 mins C
B, V
Ryan O'Neal, Jacqueline Bisset, Warren Oates, Jill Clayburgh, directed by Bud Yorkin
A chess playing computer analyst gives up the straight life to become a jewel thief. He begins by falling in love with a society girl, continues by

PALADIN VIDEO HOME ENTERTAINMENT GUIDE

causing the town's chess editor to have a nervous breakdown and finally befriends an insurance investigator who finds him so lovable that he cannot turn him in even when he catches him red handed.
BBFC:A — S,A — EN
Warner Bros — *Warner Home Video* **P**
WEX1097/WEV1097

Thin Lizzy Fil-Ent '7?
Music-Performance
01958   50 mins   C
B, V
The Irish rock band plays to an ecstatic audience at the Rainbow Theatre in London.
C,A — EN
Unknown — *VCL Video Services* **P**

Thing, The Fil-Ent '82
Horror
09262   107 mins   C
B, V
Kurt Russell, directed by John Carpenter
This film tells the gruesome, terrifying tale of what happens when an alien capable of imitating the form of any living thing is reawakened after millions of years.
BBFC:18 — A — EN
Universal — *CIC Video* **H, P**
BEA 1062/VHA 1062

Thing from Another Fil-Ent '??
World, The/Stranger on the Third Floor
Science fiction/Crime-Drama
05710   145 mins   B/W
B, V
Kenneth Tobey, James Arness, Margaret Sheridan, Dewey Martin, directed by Christian Nyby, Peter Lorre, John McGuire, Margaret Tallicher, Elisha Cook Jr, directed by Boris Ingster
Two films are featured on one cassette. 'The Thing from Another World' (Black/white, 83 mins, 1952) is the story of a flying saucer that crashes in the Arctic. The alien survivor has an appetite for blood and terrorises the scientists and airmen marooned with it in the icy wastes. 'Stranger on the Third Floor' (Black/white, 62 mins, 1941) is the story of a homicidal maniac. A reporter is convinced a condemned man is innocent when the same pattern of crime repeats itself.
S,A — EN
RKO — *Kingston Video* **H, P**
KV32

Things to Come Fil-Ent '36
Science fiction
09868   108 mins   B/W
B, V
Raymond Massey, Ralph Richardson, Cedric Hardwicke, Margaretta Scott, Ann Tod, directed by William Cameron Menzies
Based on H.G. Wells story 'Shape of things to come', this film depicts the future of mankind, set in fictional 'Everytown', a fantastic city of the future, destined to capture everyone's imagination.
F — EN
London Films; Alexander Korda — *Polygram Video* **H, P**
790 2454/790 2452

Think Ahead with Jackie Gen-Edu '80
Stewart
Safety education
13523   18 mins   C
B, V
Jackie Stewart, World Motor Racing Champion, uses his knowledge as a driver to act as a link and inform horse rider and driver alike on road safety skills.
F — ED
Unknown — *TFI Leisure Ltd* **H**

Third Man, The Fil-Ent '49
Mystery
01030   105 mins   B/W
B, V
Orson Welles, Joseph Cotten, Alida Valli, directed by Sir Carol Reed
An American writer arrives in Vienna to take a job with an old friend whom he finds has been murdered. Based on Graham Greene's mystery. Academy Awards '50: Best Cinematography.
BBFC:A — S,A — EN
Selznick Releasing Organization — *THORN EMI* **P**
TXB 90 0008 4/TVB 90 0008 2

Thirst Fil-Ent '79
Horror
06252   90 mins   C
B, V
David Hemmings, Henry Silva, Chantal Contouri, Shirley Cameron, Ras Mulligan, Rod Mullinar, directed by Rod Hardy
This is a macabre story of psychological conditioning and the bizarre. A secret society attempt to brainwash a beautiful career woman into believing she is the heir to their ghoulish traditions.
S,A — EN
Unknown — *VCL Video Services* **P**
C155C

Thirsty Dead, The Fil-Ent '75
Horror
02420   82 mins   C

(For Explanation of codes, see USE GUIDE and KEY)   659

PALADIN VIDEO HOME ENTERTAINMENT GUIDE

B, V
John Considine, Jennifer Billingsley, directed by Terry Becker
A horror story in the Dracula vein.
A — EN
Wesley E DePue Productions — *Derann Film Services* **H, P**
DV 109B/DV 109

Thirty-Nine Steps, The Fil-Ent '35
Suspense
04257 78 mins B/W
B, V, LV
Madeleine Carroll, Robert Donat, Lucy Mannheim, Godfrey Tearle, Peggy Ashcroft, directed by Alfred Hitchcock
An innocent man is accused of the murder of a young lady found in his apartment. He embarks on a countrywide search for the secret society responsible for her death.
BBFC:A — F — EN
Gaumont — *Rank Video Library* **H, P**
0025

Thirty Nine Steps, The Fil-Ent '78
Suspense
01896 102 mins C
B, V
Robert Powell, David Warner, Eric Porter, Karen Dotrice, John Mills
Richard Hannay is on the run from the law for a murder he didn't commit in this third cinematic version of John Buchan's novel. A new twist finds Hannay dangling from Big Ben at the film's climax.
BBFC:A — S,A — EN
Rank — *Rank Video Library* **H, P**
0000

This Happy Breed Fil-Ent '44
Drama
13745 120 mins C
B, V
Robert Newton, Celia Johnson, John Mills, Stanley Holloway, Laurence Olivier
Set in the years during World War II, this film depicts the lives of a group of ordinary people facing all sorts of domestic drama, and their will to survive at all costs int he shadow of the conflict of war.
BBFC:U — F — EN
Noel Coward — *Rank Video Library* **H, P**
0210E

This Is Callan Fil-Ent '8?
Drama/Suspense
08989 90 mins C
B, V
Edward Woodward, Eric Porter, Carl Mohner, Catherine Schell, Peter Egan, Russell Hunter
This is a film based on the television series, which tells of a killer agent working for British Intelligence who is ordered to assassinate a seemingly charming German businessman, later exposed as a gunrunner. The events lead to a shattering climax.
S,A — EN
Unknown — *Polygram Video* **P**
791519

This Is London Gen-Edu '??
Documentary/Cities and towns
06350 30 mins C
V2, B, V
A film of London that captures both the old and new, its colour, its pageantry and its traditions. It presents the Capitol especially with the 'tourist' in mind.
F — EN
Unknown — *Walton Film and Video Ltd* **P**
P773

This Is Sailing I Spo-Lei '7?
Boating
04514 58 mins C
B, V
'Introduction to a Boat' and 'First Essential Skills' enable the viewer to experience a thorough introduction to handling a modern contreboard dinghy.
F — EN
Nautical Publishing Company. — *Quadrant Video* **H, P**
S1

This Is Sailing II Spo-Lei '7?
Boating
04513 29 mins C
B, V
Advanced sailing techniques, including planing, spilling wind, reefing, and shortening sail, are demonstrated. Right and wrong capsize drills and the trapeze are splendidly demonstrated.
F — EN
Nautical Publishing Company — *Quadrant Video* **H, P**
S2

This Sporting Life Fil-Ent '63
Drama
06921 129 mins B/W
B, V
Richard Harris, Rachel Roberts, directed by Lindsay Anderson
This is the story of a professional rugby player who carries the violence of the football field into every area of his life and his joyless affair with a

PALADIN VIDEO HOME ENTERTAINMENT GUIDE

frigid and withdrawn woman with whom he lodges. Based on the novel by David Storey about violence and its effect on the quality of life.
BBFC:X — A — EN
Continental Distributors — Rank Video Library
H, P
0065C

This, That and the Other!   Fil-Ent '7?
Comedy
06819   ? mins   C
V2, B, V
Dennis Waterman, Victor Spinetti, John Bird
An erotic fantasy.
BBFC:X — A — EN
Stanley Long — Intervision Video   **H, P**
A-A 0384

This Year 1980   Fil-Ent '80
Documentary
06242   120 mins   C
B, V
All the highlights of a memorable year of Independant Television News coverage. Presented by News at Ten's Martyn Lewis, Thames TV's Joan Shenton, and with the year of sport brought to you by Dickie Davies. Includes interviews with the people who made the news in 1980.
F — EN
ITN; Sunday Times — VCL Video Services
P
A113

This Year 1981   Fil-Ent '82
Documentary/History-Modern
07659   120 mins   C
B, V
Presented by Martyn Lewis, Selina Scott and Tony Francis
This is a round-up of a year's news coverage compiled from the archives of ITN. It includes all the headline stories from world affairs, politics, sport, science, the arts and the Royal Wedding. The film includes interviews with many top people.
F — EN
ITN; Times Newspapers — VCL Video Services   **P**
A220

Thomas Crown Affair, The   Fil-Ent '68
Adventure
13182   102 mins   C
B, V
Steve McQueen, Faye Dunaway, directed by Norman Jewison

A bored tycoon seeks intellectual challenge first in arranging a bank robbery then in a duel of wits with the insurance investigator.
BBFC:A — C,A — EN
Mirisch Simkoe Solar Productions — Warner Home Video   **P**
99241

Thompson Twins—Into the Gap Live   Fil-Ent '84
Music-Performance
12955   80 mins   C
B, V
Recorded in stereo at the Del Mar Race Track, California, the thirteen tracks include 'The Gap', 'In the Name of Love', 'Hold Me Now', 'Love on Your Side' and 'Doctor! Doctor!'.
F — EN
Arista Records Ltd. — Virgin Video   **H, P**
VVD 056

Those Calloways   Fil-Ent '65
Adventure/Drama
13445   129 mins   C
B, V
Brian Keith, Vera Miles, Brandon De Wilde
A New England family strive to establish a sanctuary for migrating geese in the face of opposition from those who want to use the same lake to host shooting parties for their own gain.
BBFC:U — F — EN
Walt Disney Productions — Rank Video Library
P
234

Those Magnificent Men in Their Flying Machines   Fil-Ent '65
Comedy
01022   138 mins   C
V2, B, V, LV
Stuart Whitman, Sarah Miles, Robert Morley, Albert Sordi, James Fox, Gert Frobe
In 1910 a wealthy British newspaper publisher is persuaded to sponsor an air race from London to Paris. Contestants from all over the world come.
F — EN
20th Century Fox — CBS/Fox Video   **P**
4A-023

Three Cheers for Us   Fil-Ent '??
Drama
05561   90 mins   C
V2, B, V
Pier Paolo Capponi, Maria Venier, Angela Goodwin

(For Explanation of codes, see USE GUIDE and KEY)   661

PALADIN VIDEO HOME ENTERTAINMENT GUIDE

Written by Luigi Mancini, this film is the moving story of a boy who joins a secret society and how his new found friends help him to come to terms with his father's death and a near fatal illness.
M,A — EN
Unknown — *Videomedia* P
BVM 2114/HVM 2114

Three Guys Strike Again, The   Fil-Ent '7?
Crime-Drama
07768   85 mins   C
V2, B, V
Robert Widmark, Jim Gordon
This film follows an exhilarating chase by three ex-convicts to retrieve stolen money.
S,A — EN
Unknown — *Fletcher Video*   H, P
AV608

---

300 Miles for Stephanie   Fil-Ent '81
Drama
07822   100 mins   C
V2, B, V
Tony Orlando, P.J. Oliveras, Julie Carmen, directed by Clyde Ware
Based on a true story this film tells of the fight by a Mexican-American police officer from San Antonio, Texas to save his daughter who is suffering from a terminal illness. He decides as an offering, if God will let her live longer, to make a personal pilgrimage and run the 320 miles to the 'Church of Miracles' in Texas. He will make the run in five days, one for each year of her life.
S,A — EN
Edward S Feldman — *Video Unlimited*
H, P
040

---

300 Year Weekend, The   Fil-Ent '77
Drama
04267   80 mins   C
B, V
William Devane, Sharon Laughlin, Michael Tolan, Roy Cooper
A gripping drama based on a true life encounter marathon in which ten troubled people with a text book full of hang-ups from sex and drugs to drink and broken marriage seek help in a group therapy session.
A — EN
Victor Stoloff — *Rank Video Library*   H, P
0037

Three Immoral Women   Fil-Ent '7?
Drama
08957   89 mins   C
V2, B, V

Directed by Walerian Borowczyk
This film tells the story of three women, who each in their own compelling and disturbing ways to bring together images of sensuality and violence.
A — EN
Unknown — *Walton Film and Video Ltd*
P

Three in the Attic   Fil-Ent '68
Comedy
07407   90 mins   C
V2, B, V
Yvette Mimieux, Christopher Jones, Judy Page, Maggie Thrett, Nan Martin
A college casanova has three girlfriends and finds it difficult to keep them from finding out about each other. When they do find out, they dream up the perfect revenge. They lock him in an attic room and take turns to go and see him until he is totally exhausted.
BBFC:X — A — EN
American International — *Guild Home Video*
H, P, E

Three in the Cellar   Fil-Ent '70
Comedy-Drama
09935   94 mins   C
B, V
Larry Hagman, Joan Collins, Wes Stern, Judy Pace, David Arkin, Nira Barab
When a college student is kicked out, he moves into a friend's cellar and gets his own back on the principal who refused to reinstate him, by systematically seducing the three women in his life, his secretary, his wife and his daughter.
BBFC:18 — A — EN
Unknown — *Rank Video Library*   H, P
1060 A

Three Musketeers, The   Fil-Ent '73
Comedy-Drama/Adventure
08455   102 mins   C
B, V
Oliver Reed, Raquel Welch, Richard Chamberlain, Michael York, Frank Finlay, Christopher Lee, Geraldine Chaplin, Simon Ward, Faye Dunaway, Charlton Heston
Set in Paris in the 17th century, this film tells of the adventures of D'Artagnan, a young swordsman, and his companions, the three Musketeers. At the court of Louis XIII, a powerful Cardinal intends to withdraw the power from the weak King. D'Artagnan is involved, by foiling a plot to steal the Queen's diamond necklace.
BBFC:U — F — EN
Film Trust SA; Panama — *THORN EMI*
P
TXB 90 1019 4/TVB 90 1019 2

(For Explanation of codes, see USE GUIDE and KEY)

PALADIN VIDEO HOME ENTERTAINMENT GUIDE

Three of a Kind Fil-Ent '84
Comedy
13393   90 mins   C
B, V
Lenny Henry, Tracey Ullman, David Copperfield
This video is a compilation of humourous sketches, all mined from the contributors' award-winning television series.
F — EN
Paul Jackson — *BBC Video*   **H, P**
7033

Three Sisters, The Fil-Ent '70
Drama
04234   158 mins   C
B, V
Alan Bates, Laurence Olivier, Joan Plowright, directed by Laurence Olivier
A film version of Anton Chekhov's classic play about three sisters who live in a Russian provincial household at the end of the last century, bound together by melancholy feelings of empty days, endless longing, and unrequited love for officers from the town's Army barracks.
BBFC:U — S,A — EN
Laurence Olivier — *THORN EMI*   **P**
TXB 90 0215 4/TVB 90 0215 2

Three Superguys, The Fil-Ent '7?
Crime-Drama
07767   89 mins   C
V2, B, V
Robert Widmark, Bob Goldan
This film follows the dire consequences when three mad fools agree to collect a valuable gold statue for a friend.
S,A — EN
Unknown — *Fletcher Video*   **H, P**
AV609

Three Superguys in the Snow, The Fil-Ent '7?
Crime-Drama
07766   95 mins   C
V2, B, V
Robert Widmark, Jim Gordon
The three heroes in this film attempt to rob a fraudulent cashier of his ill-gotten gains.
S,A — EN
Unknown — *Fletcher Video*   **H, P**
AV610

3 Terrytoons Fil-Ent '6?
Cartoons
01954   90 mins   C
B, V
Animated
Dinky Duck, Terry Bears, and Sidney the Elephant are featured together in an hour and a half of cartoon fun for children of all ages.
F — EN
Terrytoons — *CBS/Fox Video*   **P**
3B-095

Three Warriors Fil-Ent '77
Drama
05886   100 mins   C
B, V
Charles White Eagle, Lois Red Elk, McKee 'Kiko' Red Wing, Christopher Lloyd, Randy Quaid
The story of the conflict a teenage American Indian boy experiences between life on the reservation and in the modern commercial world.
F — EN
Saul Zaentz; Sy Gomberg — *THORN EMI*
P
TXB 90 0325 4/TVB 90 0325 2

Threshold Fil-Ent '83
Drama
09459   92 mins   C
V2, B, V
Donald Sutherland, John Marley, Sharon Acker, Mare Winningham, Jeff Goldblum, Michael Lerner, directed by Richard Pearce
This film tells the story of Dr. Thomas Vrain, a brilliant and influential Chief of cardiac surgery at a Los Angeles Hospital. Having saved many lives with his skilful open heart operations and transplants, he faces the supreme challenge and the greatest moral decision of his career.
BBFC:15 — C,A — EN
Jon Slan, Michael Burns — *Guild Home Video*
H, P, E

Thrillkill Fil-Ent '83
Crime-Drama
13237   87 mins   C
B, V
Robin Ward, Gina Massay, directed by Anthony Kramreither and Anthony D'Andrea
A computer operator is murdered with the secret location of a vast amount of money programmed into it and the race is on between the murderers and the operator's sister to find the code and the money first.
BBFC:15 — S,A — EN
Anthony Kramreither — *CBS/Fox Video*
P
6780

Thumbtripping Fil-Ent '72
Adventure
10063   94 mins   C
V2, B, V

(For Explanation of codes, see USE GUIDE and KEY)

PALADIN VIDEO HOME ENTERTAINMENT GUIDE

Michael Burns, Meg Foster, Mariana Hill, Bruce Dern, Mike Conrad, Joyce Van Patten
The story of restless experience-hungry youths who spend their summers hitch-hiking up and down the highways of America. Adapted from the novel by Don Mitchell, who wrote the book based on his own experiences. Filmed in Northern California.
C,A — EN
Avco Embassy — *Embassy Home Entertainment* **P**
2111

Thunder Fil-Ent '8?
Adventure
12148 83 mins C
B, V
Mark Gregory, Bo Svenson, Raymond Harmstorf, directed by Larry Ludman
An ancient Indian burial ground is turned into a building site and a young Indian is prepared to stop at nothing to take his revenge.
BBFC:18 — S,A — EN
Unknown — *Entertainment in Video* **H, P**
EVB 1016/EVV 1016

Thunder and Lightning Fil-Ent '77
Adventure
13662 94 mins C
B, V
David Carradine, Kate Jackson, directed by Corey Allen
Mud-skipping chases across the Everglades, bottle smashing brawls and alligators abound in this action film set in Florida, with two rival groups of moonshiners brewing up illicit liquor.
BBFC:18 — C,A — EN
Roger Corman — *CBS/Fox Video* **P**
1452

Thunderball Fil-Ent '65
Adventure
13188 128 mins C
B, V
Sean Connery, Adolfo Celi, Claudine Auger, directed by Terence Young
In a beautiful Bahamas setting the sinister organisation SPECTRE rears its head to demand $100 million ransom from the West against the threat of atomic devastation.
BBFC:A — C,A — EN
Danjaq SA — *Warner Home Video* **P**
99208

Thunderbirds in Outer Space Fil-Ent '68
Science fiction/Puppets
08737 90 mins C
B, V, LV

A daring mission is planned to launch a super spaceship that will orbit the sun. However, the mission appears to be doomed as the ship's control system fails. The three men aboard face certain death as they are uncontrollably hurtled towards the burning rays of the sun.
F — EN
Gerry Anderson Production — *Precision Video Ltd* **P**
BITC 2128/VITC 2128

Thunderbirds to the Rescue Fil-Ent '??
Science fiction/Puppets
05403 88 mins C
V2, B, V
A new satellite has been launched which is permanently manned to aid humanity, to spot trouble, receive distress signals and set in motion the secret organisation International Rescue. From top secret headquarters somewhere in the Pacific International Rescue run by an astronaut and his five sons, are called upon to help the world.
F — EN
Gerry Anderson Productions — *Precision Video Ltd* **P**
CRITC 2053/BITC 2053/VITC 2053

Thunderbolt and Lightfoot Fil-Ent '74
Adventure
13181 115 mins C
B, V
Clint Eastwood, Jeff Bridges, directed by Michael Cimino
A film with both extreme violence and humour involving a car chase through Montana and a robbery.
BBFC:X — A — EN
The Malpaso Co — *Warner Home Video* **P**
99279

Thursday's Child Fil-Ent '82
Drama
13492 90 mins C
B, V
Gena Rowlands, Don Murray, Jessica Walter, Rob Loroe, directed by David Lowell Rich
A boy returns home from college and begins to feel abnormally tired. It is then discovered that he has an enlarged heart and the whole family unite in their efforts to save him.
S,A — EN
Peter Katz — *Capricorn Entertainments* **P**
101

PALADIN VIDEO HOME ENTERTAINMENT GUIDE

Thursday's Game   Fil-Ent '71
Drama
10213   97 mins   C
B, V

Gene Wilder, Ellen Burstyn, Bob Newhart, Cloris Leachman

Two friends, Harry and Marvin, decide not to tell their wives when their regular Thursday night card game breaks up. They decide to spend Thursdays out on the town. Harry loves his wife but has lost his job, Marvin is very successful but hates his wife. Harry in a depressed state has an affair which fails and his wife leaves him- unemployed and unloved he helps Marvin find the perfect lie to help him escape from his wife and fulfil an ambition to tour Europe footloose and fancy free.
S,A — EN
Spelling-Goldberg — *Video Form Pictures*
H, P
6247-50

THX 1138   Fil-Ent '71
Science fiction
07872   92 mins   C
B, V

Robert Duvall, Donald Pleasence, Maggie McOmie, Don Pedro Colley, Ian Wolfe, Sid Haig, directed by George Lucas

In this dehumanized look at the future, men are reduced by drugs to unfeeling automatons. People are numbered, everyone is watched and love is forbidden. A computer-matched couple discover love, the ultimate offense to the state. She dies and the man escapes to become one man against the whole world.
BBFC:X — A — EN
Warner Bros — *Warner Home Video*   P
WEX 61162/WEV 61162

Tiara Tahiti   Fil-Ent '63
Drama
12747   90 mins   C
B, V

James Mason, John Mills

Two ex-army officers, social classes apart, meet by accident on the paradise island of Tahiti, and a cauldron of conflict erupts between them.
BBFC:PG — F — EN
Zenith International — *Rank Video Library*
H, P
018 E

Ticket to Heaven   Fil-Ent '81
Drama
08816   107 mins   C
B, V

Nick Mancuso, Meg Foster, Kim Cattrail, Saul Rubinek

This film is a thriller dealing with the cult religions in California. A school teacher gradually falls under the influence of this cult, conditioned to lie, cheat and work 24 hours a day.
A — EN
Stalker Productions — *VCL Video Services*
P
P295D

Tiffany Jones   Fil-Ent '74
Comedy-Drama
08033   90 mins   C
V2, B, V

Anouska Hempel, Ray Brooks, Eric Pohlmann, Martin Benson, directed by Pete Walker

In this film the Daily Mail strip cartoon adventures of Tiffany Jones are brought to life. She leads a fast life, wanted by presidents and sought by revolutionaries.
BBFC:X — A — EN
Pete Walker — *Rank Video Library*   H, P
1041C

Tiger and the Flame, The   Fil-Ent '50
Adventure
04325   92 mins   C
V2, B, V
Heroine fights side by side with men to keep her country free.
A — EN
United Artists; Modi Films; Indian — *Intervision Video*   H, P
A-A 0162

Tiger Bay   Fil-Ent '59
Drama
12746   105 mins   B/W
B, V

John Mills, Hayley Mills

A tense murder drama set against the moody background of Cardiff's dockland when a young tomboy befriends a murderer and nearly becomes his second victim.
BBFC:PG — F — EN
Assoc British Pathe Ltd — *Rank Video Library*
H, P
0194 E

Tiger Strikes Again, The   Fil-Ent '7?
Adventure/Martial arts
04612   88 mins   C
V2, B, V

Bruce Li

Three refugees are rescued by a fishing boat and taken to Hong Kong, where they settle down. Wong and Lee practise Kung-fu and

(For Explanation of codes, see USE GUIDE and KEY)

PALADIN VIDEO HOME ENTERTAINMENT GUIDE

when they see two strangers bullying an old man they go to his aid. One of the strangers later asks an underworld gang boss to take revenge.
C,A — EN
Unknown — Video Programme Distributors
P
Inter-Ocean—002

Tiger Town Fil-Ent '84
Drama
13444   90 mins   C
B, V
Roy Scheider, Justin Henry
This is the story of a faded baseball star who is driven on to new triumphs by the devotion of a small boy fan.
S,A — EN
Walt Disney Productions — Rank Video Library
P
VW 191

Tigers Don't Cry Fil-Ent '76
Adventure/Suspense
08078   98 mins   C
B, V
Anthony Quinn, John Phillip Law, Ken Gampu, Sandra Prinsloo, directed by Peter Collinson
This film tells the story of a Third World president who risks his life to get medical treatment. In doing so, a political thriller unfolds. The story is based on the book 'Running Scared'.
BBFC:A — S,A — EN
Unknown — Rank Video Library   H, P
0136 C

Till Death Fil-Ent '76
Horror
09221   96 mins   C
B, V
Keith Atkinson, Belinda Balaski, Burt Freed
After taking their vows, a newly married couple meet a tragic end. In a car accident, having been forced off the road, the wife is killed and the husband seriously injured. The groom is later reunited with his wife at her graveside. This starts a bizarre and violent chain of events.
A — EN
Pamstock — Video Form Pictures   H, P
MGT 3

Till Death Us Do Part Fil-Ent '69
Comedy
04657   99 mins   C
B, V
Warren Mitchell, Dandy Nichols, Anthony Booth, Una Stubbs
This black comedy began as a highly popular and long running television series before making the transfer to the big screen. The films spans some thirty years, from pre-war Britain to post-war Britain and the wedding of Alf's daughter to a man who not only supports the wrong political party but the wrong football team as well!
F — EN
British Lion; Associated London Films — THORN EMI   H, P
TXB 90 0232 4/TVB 90 0232 2

Till the Clouds Roll By Fil-Ent '46
Musical
02590   137 mins   C
B, V
Robert Walker, Judy Garland, Lucille Bremer, Dinah Shore, Van Johnson, Lena Horne, June Allyson
A musical biography of songwriter Jerome Kern, featuring performances of his many classic songs, including 'The Last Time I Saw Paris,' 'Old Man River,' 'Who,' 'Look for the Silver Lining,' 'Make Believe,' and 'Cleopatterer.'
F — EN
MGM; Arthur Freed — Mountain Video   P

Till Tomorrow Fil-Ent '7?
Music-Performance
07607   53 mins   C
V2, B, V
Don Maclean
On this cassette the legendary American singer Don Maclean performs in front of a college audience. Songs featured include 'American Pie' and 'Vincent.'
F — EN
Unknown — Iver Film Services   P

Tilt Fil-Ent '79
Drama
08050   107 mins   C
B, V
Brooke Shields, Ken Marshall, Charles Durning
In this film, Brooke Shields stars as a fourteen year old genius at pinball. She teams up with a rocksinger. Their adventures take them far and wide, their earnings mounting all the time, until eventually it all comes to an end.
BBFC:A — S,A — EN
Warner Bros — Rank Video Library   H, P
0102 C

Time After Time Fil-Ent '79
Drama/Adventure
07873   108 mins   C
B, V
Malcolm McDowell, David Warner, Mary Steenburgen, Patti D'Arbanville, directed by Nicholas Meyer

(For Explanation of codes, see USE GUIDE and KEY)

PALADIN VIDEO HOME ENTERTAINMENT GUIDE

In this film H. G. Wells and Jack the Ripper leave London aboard Wells' famous time machine in 1893 and arrive in San Francisco in 1979.
BBFC:AA — S,A — EN
Orion Pictures; Warner Bros — *Warner Home Video*   **P**
WEX 72017/WEV 72017

Time Bandits   Fil-Ent '81
Fantasy/Comedy
07475   105 mins   C
B, V
John Cleese, Sean Connery, Shelley Duvall, Katherine Helmond, Ian Holm, Michail Palin, Ralph Richardson, Peter Vaughan, Craig Warnock, David Rappaport, directed by Terry Gilliam
The 11 year-old hero of this film dreams of an invasion of amiable dwarves who are absconding employees of the Supreme Being. The dwarves take the boy on a journey through time and space where they meet the giants of history and legend who turn out to be engaging eccentrics. Songs by George Harrison.
BBFC:A — S,A — EN
The Hand Made Film Partnership — *THORN EMI*   **P**
TXA 90 06814/TVA 90 06812

Time Bomb   Fil-Ent '84
Adventure
13619   91 mins   C
B, V
Billy Dee Williams, Merlin Olsen, Joseph Bottoms, Morgan Fairchild, directed by Paul Krasny
A group of malcontents, headed by a female terrorist, seize a nuclear device and a high-tech security team is sent to retrieve it.
BBFC:PG — S,A — EN
Universal — *CIC Video*   **H, P**
1127

Time Machine, The   Fil-Ent '60
Adventure/Fantasy
12207   103 mins   C
B, V
Rod Taylor, Yvette Mimieux, Alan Young, directed by George Pal
H.G. Wells' classic story of a time traveller who journeys through time from 1899 to 802,701 AD is told in this film.
F — EN
MGM — *MGM/UA Home Video*   **P**
10152

Time of Apollo, The   Med-Sci '76
Space exploration
01220   28 mins   C
B, V, PH15, PH17, 3/4U
A tribute of the historical accomplishments and era of Project Apollo in the 1960's.
Festival of the Americas '76: Silver Medal.
M,A — ED
NASA — *Istead Audio Visual*   **P**
HQ 229

Time of Change 1976/Appointment at Penha 1977   Spo-Lei '77
Automobiles-Racing
04509   52 mins   C
B, V
Action sequences from the Mintex, Scottish, and RAC rallies note the impact of Scandinavian drivers during the 1976 British rally season. In the second feature, Fiat, Ford, and Toyota struggle for honours in the mountains of northern Portugal during the 1977 Rally de Portugal.
F — EN
Avon Tyres; Castrol — *Quadrant Video*
H, P
M24

Time Slip   Fil-Ent '8?
Science fiction/Martial arts
09055   100 mins   C
V
Sonny Chiba, Isao Natsuki, Tsunehiko Watase, Raita Ryu, Miyuki Ono, Jun Eto, Hiroko Yakushimaru, Masoa Kusakari
An army unit, whilst on an exercise with the latest military weapons, get caught in cosmic magnetic turbulence and travel back in time 400 years into the 16th century. They enter confrontations with Samurai armies against their modern army with tanks, helicopters and machine guns.
S,A — EN
Japan — *Astra Video*   **H, P**

Time Walker   Fil-Ent '83
Science fiction
09450   83 mins   C
B, V
Ben Murphy, Nina Axelrod, Kevin Brophy, James Karen
A violent earthquake uncovers the coffin of Ankh-Venharis, 'The Noble Traveller', having been trapped in Tutankhamun's tomb. The coffin is shipped to the California Institute but the next day is found empty. After centuries the Time Walker is free again.
BBFC:15 — C,A — EN
New World Pictures — *Guild Home Video*
H, P, E

(For Explanation of codes, see USE GUIDE and KEY)

PALADIN VIDEO HOME ENTERTAINMENT GUIDE

Timerider — Fil-Ent '82
Science fiction
09795   89 mins   C
B, V

Belinda Bauer, Peter Coyote, Ed Lauter, Fred Ward, directed by William Dear

A motor cycling champion travels back in time to 1877. Having frightened an old herder and his mate by suddenly appearing on his motor bike, clad in racing attire, he goes on to experience many adventures including a gunpoint encounter with his great-great-grandmama. Music by Mike Nesmith.
BBFC:15 — S,A — EN
Zoomo Productions Ltd — THORN EMI   P
TXA 90 1956 4/TVA 90 1956 2

Times Square — Fil-Ent '80
Drama/Music-Performance
07471   106 mins   C
B, V

Tim Curry, Trini Alvarado, Robin Johnson, Peter Coffield, Herbert Berghof, directed by Alan Moyle

This is the story of two teenage girls who meet in hospital and decide to run away. Made on location in the tough areas of New York, the girls scratch a living while being sought by social workers and police. Only a radio DJ sympathises with them, helping them to form their own rock band. The film includes performances by Suzi Quatro, XTC, The Pretenders, Joe Jackson and Talking Heads.
BBFC:AA — S,A — EN
EMI Films Ltd — THORN EMI   P
TXA 90 0685 4/TVA 90 0685 2

Tina Turner — Fil-Ent '79
Music-Performance
04398   30 mins   C
B, V

Tina Turner

The sensual singer performs 'You Don't Send Me Flowers Any More,' 'Honky Tonk Woman,' 'Proud Mary,' 'Nut Bush City Limit,' and several others. Taped at London's Apollo Theater.
S,A — EN
VCL — VCL Video Services   P

Tina Turner Nice 'N Rough — Fil-Ent '82
Music-Performance
08565   55 mins   C
B, V

Directed by David Mallet

This tape records Tina Turner live at concert she gave at Hammersmith. She performs twelve of her songs including 'Nutbush City Limits,' 'Proud Mary,' 'Honky Tonk Woman,' 'Hollywood Nights,' 'Giving It Up for Your Love,' 'Acid Queen,' 'Jumping Jack Flash,' 'Tonights the Night' and 'It's Only Rock 'N Roll.'
C,A — EN
Millaney Grant Mallet Mulcahy Prod — THORN EMI   P
TXE 90 0986 4/TVE 90 0986 2

Tintorera — Fil-Ent '??
Suspense
06202   86 mins   C
B, V

Susan George, Fiona Lewis, Jennifer Ashley, Hugo Stiglitz

Set in a small lush tropical island, a retreat from reality, a haven for the rich and spiritually lost, this story involves two men, a woman and their bizarre relationship. A deadly tiger shark appears to cause havoc on the island.
S,A — EN
Gerald Green Production — VCL Video Services   P
C151C

Titfield Thunderbolt, The — Fil-Ent '53
Comedy
01605   82 mins   C
B, V

Stanley Holloway, George Relph, directed by Charles Crichton

Eccentric villagers resurrect a defunct railroad and operate it themselves.
BBFC:U — S,A — EN
Ealing Studios; Michael Balcon — THORN EMI   P
TXE 90 0216 4/TVE 90 0216 2

Title Shot — Fil-Ent '80
Crime-Drama
08623   88 mins   C
V2, B, V

Tony Curtis, Richard Gabourie

This film tells the story of a charming but cunning underworld man, who uses his computer systems to predict the outcome of sporting events. A heavyweight fight promises a large reward, and he makes a deal. When the night arrives, he is til confident, especially with the back-up of a rooftop sniper.
S,A — EN
Title Shot Productions; Regenthall Films — Hokushin Audio Visual Ltd   P
VM 64

To All a Goodnight — Fil-Ent '??
Horror
07923   90 mins   C
V2, B, V

PALADIN VIDEO HOME ENTERTAINMENT GUIDE

Jennifer Runyon, Forrest Swanson, Linda Gentle, William Lauer
Five young girls at a Finishing School innocently smuggle their boyfriends into the building for a party during the Christmas holidays. They disappear one by one as hideous murders are discovered, until there are only two of them left.
S,A — EN
Unknown — Video Programme Distributors
P
Media—178

To Be Or Not To Be   Fil-Ent '83
Comedy
13673   103 mins   C
B, V
Mel Brooks, Anne Bancroft, Tim Matheson, Charles Durning, Jose Ferrer, directed by Alan Johnson
Two actors get caught up in Hitler's invasion of Poland and become involved in a plot to leak top secret information and so thwart the Nazis.
BBFC:PG — S,A — EN
Mel Brooks — CBS/Fox Video   P
1336

To Be Twenty   Fil-Ent '??
Adventure
07930   90 mins   C
V2, B, V
Gloria Guida, Lilli Carati, Ray Lovelock
This is the story of two young girls and their adventures whilst hitch-hiking along the Italian peninsula.
S,A — EN
Unknown — Video Programme Distributors
P
Cinehollywood—V290

To Build a Fire   Fil-Ent '7?
Adventure
04531   52 mins   C
B, V
Narrated by Orson Welles
A newcomer to the frozen Klondike of northwest Canada decides to visit friends in a nearby mining camp. At eighty below zero, it is a particularly dangerous journey, and only his husky dog, Pepper, knows instinctively what to do in such savage conditions. Based on the Jack London short story.
F — EN
David Cobham — Quadrant Video   H, P
D1

To Kill a Stranger   Fil-Ent '83
Suspense/Horror
12815   90 mins   C
B, V

Donald Pleasance, Dean Stockwell, Aldo Ray, Angelica Maria
A girl is forced off the road during a heavy storm and is taken to the home of a respected war hero where she finds herself face to face with an evil rapist and mad killer.
A — EN
J Lopez-Moctesuma — VCL Video Services
P
277440/277650

To Race the Wind   Fil-Ent '79
Drama
09895   97 mins   C
B, V
Steve Guttenberg, Randy Quaid
This is the true story of Harold Krents, a clever, independent boy who goes blind. He is, however, determined not to give up. He goes to Harvard, and takes on student life in all its forms, football, dating women and social rituals, forming an often funny and moving story.
BBFC:PG — F — EN
Walter Grauman Prods; Viacom — Brent Walker Home Video Ltd   P

To Russia...with Elton   Fil-Ent '7?
Music-Performance
00839   74 mins   C
B, V, LV
Elton John
Elton John performs some of his most popular songs in concert.
F — EN
Witzend Prods — Precision Video Ltd   P
BITC 2015/VITC 2015

To See Such Fun   Fil-Ent '80
Film-History/Comedy
01971   91 mins   C
V2, B, V
Hosted by Frank Muir, directed by Jon Scoffield
A compilation of some of the most hilarious and best loved moments from 50 years of British film comedy. There are sequences in colour and black/white. Stars featured include: Peter Sellers, Tony Hancock, Sid James, Margaret Rutherford, Joyce Grenfell, Frankie Howerd, Norman Wisdom, George Formby, Dick Emery, Hattie Jacques, Arthur Lowe, Max Wall, Ronnie Barker, Jimmy Edwards, Benny Hill, Kenneth Williams, Marty Feldman, Harry Secombe, Eric Idle, Barbara Windsor, Spike Milligan, Sylvia Simms, Stanley Baxter, Thora Hird, Bernard Cribbins, Charlie Drake, Ted Ray, Leslie Phillips, Irene Handl and many others.
F — EN
Herbert Wilcox and Michael Grade — RPTA Video Ltd   H, P

(For Explanation of codes, see USE GUIDE and KEY)

PALADIN VIDEO HOME ENTERTAINMENT GUIDE

To the Devil...a Daughter   Fil-Ent '76
Horror
07454   90 mins   C
B, V
Richard Widmark, Christopher Lee, Honor Blackman, Denholm Elliot, Nastassia Kinski
This film, based on the novel by Dennis Wheatley, concerns the struggle for a young girl between the forces of Darkness and Light. An unfrocked priest and his Satanist devotees have the girl 'promised' to them. The girl's lover and her father ask an occult novelist to take care of her. In a climax of immense occult forces the novelist contrives to turn the summoned powers against the Satanists.
BBFC:X — A — EN
Hammer Film Productions Ltd — *THORN EMI*   P
TXC 90 0224 4/TVC 90 0224 2

Tobruk   Fil-Ent '67
War-Drama
13318   105 mins   C
B, V
Rock Hudson, George Peppard, Nigel Green, directed by Arthur Hiller
This is the story of a special attack unit with instructions to destroy Rommel's fuel supply at the port of Tobruk.
BBFC:PG — S,A — EN
Universal — *CIC Video*   H, P
BEN 1099/VHN 1099

Todd Killings, The   Fil-Ent '71
Horror
12673   93 mins   C
V2, B, V
Richard Thomas, Barbara Bel Geddes, Robert F Lyons, directed by Barry Shear
A bisexual youth goes on a rampage of rape and murder in a small American town, leaving a terrible trail of destruction behind him.
BBFC:18 — A — EN
National General Pictures — *Videomedia*   P
1033

Together   Fil-Ent '80
Drama
13266   86 mins   C
B, V
Jacqueline Bisset, Maximilian Schell, Terence Stamp, Monica Guerritore, directed by Armenia Balducci
This is the story of a sensual and intimate relationship between two lovers which unfolds over one weekend.
BBFC:18 — A — EN
Gianni Bozzacchi; Valerio de Paolis — *CBS/Fox Video*   P
6610

Tom and Jerry   Fil-Ent '67
Cartoons/Comedy
05305   56 mins   C
B, V
Animated
A collection of cartoon capers and adventures featuring the famous cat and mouse team. Includes classics like 'The Flying Cat,' 'Dr Jekyll and Mr Mouse,' 'The Cat and the Mermouse' and 'The Cat Concerto.'
F — EN
MGM — *MGM/UA Home Video*   P
UMB10019/UMV10019

Tom and Jerry II   Fil-Ent '5?
Cartoons
07728   56 mins   C
B, V
Animated
A further compilation of cartoon adventures featuring the famous cat and mouse team. Includes 'Cat Napping,' 'His Cup Pup,' 'The Invisible Mouse,' 'Jerry and the Lion,' 'Mouse in Manhattan,' 'Mouse Trouble,' 'Saturday Evening Puss' and 'Milky Waif.'
BBFC:U — F — EN
MGM — *MGM/UA Home Video*   P
UMB 10146/UMV 10146

Tom and Jerry III   Fil-Ent '4?
Cartoons
12213   57 mins   C
B, V
Animated
The famous cat and mouse team continue their adventures in the third volume of this series.
F — EN
MGM — *MGM/UA Home Video*   P
10298

Tom Horn   Fil-Ent '80
Western
07874   93 mins   C
B, V
Steve McQueen, Linda Evans, Richard Farnsworth, Billy Green Bush, Slim Pickens, directed by William Ward
This is the true story of an Old West gunman who by the age of 40 had already been a western railroad worker, stagecoach driver, U.S. Cavalry scout, silver miner, Teddy Roosevelt Rough Rider and a Pinkerton Detective. He has now been invited by a Wyoming ranch to stop cattle rustling. Whilst there he not only completes the task but also falls in love.
BBFC:AA — S,A — EN
Warner Bros — *Warner Home Video*   P
WEX 61042/WEV 61042

(For Explanation of codes, see USE GUIDE and KEY)

PALADIN VIDEO HOME ENTERTAINMENT GUIDE

Tom Jones   Fil-Ent '63
Comedy
08525   122 mins   C
B, V
Albert Finney, Susannah York, Hugh Griffith, Edith Evans, David Tomilson, Joan Greenwood, Diane Cilento, directed by Tony Richardson
This is a comedy based on Henry Fielding's novel about a rustic playboy's wild life in eighteenth-century London with brigands, beauties and scoundrels. His lusty adventures almost lead him to the gallows.
Academy Award '63: Best Picture; Best Director (Richardson); Best Screenplay (John Osborne); Best Original Score (John Addison).
C,A — EN
Woodfall Film Productions — *THORN EMI*
P
TXA 90 1282 4/TVA 90 1282 2

Tom Robinson 2-4-6-8   Fil-Ent '84
Music-Performance
13398   60 mins   C
B, V
This programme features the music of Tom Robinson songwriter and singer, and includes 'Grey Crotina,' 'Glad to be Gay,' 'Martin,' 'Too Good to be True,' 'Night Tide' and 'Never Gonna Fall in Love Again.'
S,A — EN
Unknown — *BBC Video*   H, P
3026

Tombs of the Blind Dead   Fil-Ent '74
Horror
13486   81 mins   C
B, V
Cesar Burner, Lone Fleming, Helen Harp, Joseph Thelman
The long-dead Knights Templar who were executed at the time of the Crusades for devil worship, emerge from their tombs bent on killing all the villagers.
BBFC:18 — A — EN
Contel Prods. — *Precision Video Ltd*   **P**
2641

Tommy   Fil-Ent '75
Musical-Drama/Fantasy
07474   108 mins   C
B, V
Oliver Reed, Ann-Margret, Roger Daltrey, Elton John, Eric Clapton, John Entwistle, Keith Moon, Paul Nicholas, Jack Nicholson, Robert Powell, Pete Townshend, Tina Turner, directed by Ken Russell
This is the story of a deaf, dumb and blind boy, his growing up and the amazing events in his life which follow a series of so-called miracle cures. He becomes Pinball Champion of the World and finally turns into the Superstar Messiah. Based on the rock opera by Pete Townshend, featuring The Who and songs including 'Acid Queen,' 'Tommy, Can You Hear Me?' and 'Pinball Wizard.'
BBFC:AA — S,A — EN
The J Robert Stigwood Organisation Ltd — *THORN EMI*   **P**
TXA 90 0779 4/TVA 90 0779 2

Tomorrow Man, The   Fil-Ent '80
Drama/Science fiction
06235   70 mins   C
B, V
Don Francks, Stephen Markle, Gail Dahms
The story of prisoner 984, a man with no name, no hope, no future with only robots to hear his screams. Imprisoned with no trial or reason, tortured and beaten he is trying to survive as he is innocent. A nightmare glimpse of an electronic future.
S,A — EN
Mega Media Communications; Norfolk Communications — *VCL Video Services*
P
C132

Tomorrow Never Comes   Fil-Ent '77
Crime-Drama
07646   86 mins   C
B, V
Oliver Reed, Susan George, Raymond Burr, John Osborne, Donald Pleasance
A lieutenant in a corrupt police force, wearied and revolted by violence and brutality, decides to return to his hometown. However, his last day turns into a nightmare as he is the only man who can prevent the small town erupting into violence. He has to resolve a major scandal involving an influential citizen without outrage and bloodshed.
S,A — EN
Rank; Classic — *VCL Video Services*   **P**
P129D

Tomorrow Never Comes   Fil-Ent '77
Crime-Drama
12244   86 mins   C
B, V
Oliver Reed, Donald Pleasance, Raymond Burr, Susan George
A police lieutenant in a corrupt resort town finds his last day in the force turns into a nightmare as he tries to resolve a scandal concerning one of the town's most influential citizens.
C,A — EN
Unknown — *VCL Video Services*   **P**
P129D

(For Explanation of codes, see USE GUIDE and KEY)

PALADIN VIDEO HOME ENTERTAINMENT GUIDE

Toni Basil—Word of Mouth   Fil-Ent '81
Music-Performance
05431   30 mins   C
B, V
Toni Basil
This video film is Toni Basil's debut album and as a purely visual artist she presents herself as an accomplished singer, dancer and choreographer after working with some of the biggest names in the rock world. Tracks include 'Mickey,' 'Nobody,' 'My Little Red Book,' 'Time After Time,' 'Be Stiff,' 'Space Girls' and 'Problem.'
F — EN
Radical Choice — *Radial Choice Distributors Ltd*   **P**
BAS C1

Tony Martin Show, The   Fil-Ent '7?
Variety
04379   60 mins   C
B, V, PH17, 3/4U
Tony Martin
A variety show with Tony Martin.
F — EN
Unknown — *Vidpics International*   **P**

Tony Soper's Birdquiz   Gen-Edu '84
Birds
13599   15 mins   C
V2, B, V
This film is a test of skill in identifying birds and is intended to be fun as well as educational.
F — ED
Royal Society for the Protection of Birds — *Royal Society for the Protection of Birds*   **H, P**

Too Hot To Handle   Fil-Ent '80
Crime-Drama
07903   84 mins   C
V2, B, V
Cheri Caffaro, Aharon Ipale, directed by Don Schain
A professional hit woman hears that a detective has decided to investigate her latest victim's sudden death. His trail leads him through intrigue, corruption and more violent murders. His enquiries increasingly point to the hit woman and a mutual admiration develops between them.
BBFC:X — A — EN
New World — *Video Programme Distributors*
P
Inter-Ocean—063

Too Late the Hero   Fil-Ent '70
Drama
04215   133 mins   C
B, V
Michael Caine, Cliff Robertson, Henry Fonda, directed by Robert Aldrich
British combat patrol, sent to destroy a Japanese radio site, finds a large cache of enemy planes. The Japanese chase them through the jungle with messages via loud speakers that they will be spared if they surrender.
BBFC:AA — C,A — EN
Cinerama — *Guild Home Video*   **H, P**

Too Much Gold For One Gringo   Fil-Ent '7?
Western
07793   98 mins   C
V2, B, V
Anthony Steffen, Fernando Sancho
A gang's search for the buried proceeds of a robbery coincides with a bloodthirsty bandit's desire to seize the statue of a Mexican village's patron saint.
S,A — EN
Unknown — *Fletcher Video*   **H, P**
V122

Toolbox Murders, The   Fil-Ent '77
Crime-Drama/Horror
08626   93 mins   C
V2, B, V
Cameron Mitchell, Pamelyn Ferdin
This story involves the murder of three attractive girls in the same apartment building. One was killed with a battery-powered hand drill, one beaten to death with a claw hammer, and the final stabbed with a screwdriver. The police have no information. That night the apartment of a would-be stripper is broken into, the girl raped before being brutally murdered by nails propelled from a nailgun.
C,A — EN
Tony Didio; Cal-Am — *Hokushin Audio Visual Ltd*   **P**
VM 61

Tootsie   Fil-Ent '82
Comedy
13075   112 mins   C
B, V
Dustin Hoffman, Teri Garr, Bill Murray, Jessica Lange, directed by Sydney Pollack
An out of work actor dresses himself up as a woman and lands the lead role in a play and all goes well until he falls in love with one of the actresses in the show but can't do a thing about it.
C,A — EN
Sydney Pollack — *RCA/Columbia Pictures Video UK*   **H, P**
10142

PALADIN VIDEO HOME ENTERTAINMENT GUIDE

Tom and Jerry, Volume IV   Fil-Ent '6?
Cartoons
13421   58 mins   C
B, V
Animated
More fights and chases, scratches and bumps are shown in this cassette from the famous duo.
BBFC:U — F — EN
Hanna Barbera — *MGM/UA Home Video*
P
10478

Top Cat   Fil-Ent '62
Cartoons/Comedy
08392   70 mins   C
V2, B, V
Animated
This film tells of the antics of the New York feline together with Benny the Ball, Choo Choo and Officer Dibble.
PS,M — EN
Hanna-Barbera — *Guild Home Video*   H, P, E

Top Cat—Cassette 2   Fil-Ent '6?
Cartoons/Comedy
09243   70 mins   C
V2, B, V
Animated
Top Cat and his gang of street-wise alley cats are up to some further outrageous antics, driving Officer Dibble crazy at the same time.
BBFC:U — F — EN
Hanna Barbera — *Guild Home Video*   H, P, E

Top Cat Falls in Love   Chl-Juv '84
Cartoons
13378   71 mins   C
V2, B, V
Animated
Top Cat is smitten by the beautiful feline nurse La Rue in this cassette which contains three adventures from this chief of chuckles.
BBFC:U — F — EN
Hanna Barbera — *Guild Home Video*   H, P, E
8396-4

Top Cat: The Great Alley Clean-Up Caper   Chl-Juv '84
Cartoons
13350   69 mins   C
B, V
Animated
Three comedy adventures with Top Cat and his feline chums are contained in this cassette.
BBFC:U — F — EN
Hanna Barbera — *Guild Home Video*   H, P, E
8434-1

Top Hat   Fil-Ent '35
Musical/Romance
04637   97 mins   B/W
B, V
Fred Astaire, Ginger Rogers
Music by Irving Berlin sets the scene as two young people fall in love.
F — EN
RKO; Pandro S Berman — *THORN EMI*   H, P
TXC 90 0077 4/TVC 90 0077 2

Top of the Pops   Fil-Ent '7?
Music-Performance
09402   ? mins   C
V2, B, V
This tape features many bands, including Haircut 100, Duran Duran and The Jam performing on the popular television programme, Top of the Pops.
F — EN
BBC — *BBC Video*   H, P
BBCV 3023

Tor—Mighty Warrior   Fil-Ent '83
Adventure/Fantasy
12853   93 mins   C
V2, B, V
Joe Robinson, Bella Cortez, Harry Baird
Set in the year 15 BC, the peaceful people are attacked by the savage Kicsos and the warrior Tor uses his power to free his people.
BBFC:PG — S,A — EN
Unknown — *Video Programme Distributors*
P
221

Tora! Tora! Tora!   Fil-Ent '70
War-Drama
01018   144 mins   C
V2, B, V
Martin Balsam, Soh Yomamura, Joseph Cotten, E. G. Marshall, Jason Robards, directed by Richard Fleisher
The story of Decembesr 7, 1941 is told from both Japanese and American viewpoints in this large-scale production.
F — EN
20th Century Fox; Elmo Williams — *CBS/Fox Video*   P
4A-092

(For Explanation of codes, see USE GUIDE and KEY)

PALADIN VIDEO HOME ENTERTAINMENT GUIDE

Torn Allegiance   Fil-Ent '83
War-Drama
13721   90 mins   C
V2, B, V

Jonathan Morris, Marius Weyers, Shelagh Holliday, Trevyn McDowell, directed by Alan Nathanson

A story set during the Boer War, showing four days of conflict and families split apart by divided loyalties.
BBFC:15 — S,A — EN
SABC; Mandalay Progear — *Medusa Communications Ltd*   **H, P**
MC 036

Torn Between Two Lovers   Fil-Ent '79
Drama/Romance
08343   97 mins   C
V2, B, V

Lee Remick, Joe Bologna, George Peppard, Derick Jones, Murphy Cross, directed by Delbert Mann

Dianne Conti was a happily married woman, devoted to her husband and her teenage son. Then one day, whilst stranded at an airport because of a blizzard, she meets a young charming and sophisticated man. She continues to see him, until the day she eventually has to make the choice between the life of glamour and her family.
BBFC:A — S,A — EN
Alan Landsburg — *Guild Home Video*   **H, P, E**

Tornado Strike Force   Fil-Ent '84
War-Drama
13734   93 mins   C
V2, B, V

Timothy Brent, Tony Marsina, Alan Collins, directed by Anthony M. Dawson

This is the story of one of the battalions of the Vietnam war, troop-carrying gun ships, one man's fight for survival and helicopters.
BBFC:18 — A — EN
Cico Cinematography — *Medusa Communications Ltd*   **H, P**
MC 028

Torso   Fil-Ent '??
Horror
05489   86 mins   C
V2, B, V

Suzy Kendall, Tina Aumont, Luc Meranda, John Richardson, Roberto Bisacco

A story of bloody, unexplained murder in which six girls are separated piece by piece with a variety of saws. There are no clues as to who is behind the atrocities and the motive remains elusive until the end. This film is dubbed in English.
BBFC:X — A — EN
Unknown — *Iver Film Services*   **P**

Torso   Fil-Ent '73
Horror
07600   86 mins   C
V2, B, V

Suzy Kendall, Tina Aumont, Luc Meranda, John Richardson, Roberto Bisacco, directed by Sergio Martino

Six beautiful girls meet their deaths in this film set in the Italian mountains. Their bodies have been dissected by a saw in a cool and calculated manner so the bloody evidence can be destroyed. The only link is the appearance in each case of a Victorian doll.
BBFC:X — A — EN
Carlo Ponti Production — *Iver Film Services*   **P**
158

Torvil and Dean—Path to Perfection   Spo-Lei '84
Sports-Winter
12538   52 mins   C
B, V

This film chronicles Torvil and Dean's rise to fame and includes interviews with those who knew and helped them on the road to success. Eight whole dance routines are included in the programme featuring the World Championships 1980, 1982 and 1983.
F — EN
Thames Television; National Skating Association — *THORN EMI*   **P**
TXE 90 23144/TVE 90 23142

Touch, The   Fil-Ent '71
Romance/Drama
04216   112 mins   C
B, V

Elliott Gould, Bibi Anderson, Max von Sydow, directed by Ingmar Bergman

This is the story of two people, each married to others, who fall in love and the problems they face—pretence, frustration, confusion.
BBFC:X — A — EN
Cinerama Release; ABC Pictures — *Guild Home Video*   **H, P**

Touch and Go   Fil-Ent '84
Drama
13736   92 mins   C
V2, B, V

PALADIN VIDEO HOME ENTERTAINMENT GUIDE

Wendy Hughes, Chantal Contouri, Carmen Duncan, Jeanie Drynan, Liddy Clark, directed by Peter Maxwell
Six girls have problems keeping their favourite charity solvent so they turn their wits to crime and prove to be the most talented villains in the country.
BBFC:15 — S,A — EN
John Pellatt — *Medusa Communications Ltd*   **H, P**
MC 020

Touch-Me-Not   Fil-Ent '7?
Drama
04481   82 mins   C
V2, B, V
Lee Remick, Michael Hinz, Ivan Desny, Ingrid Garbo
A man involved in industrial espionage for a rival electronics firm feigns interest in the president's secretary in order to gain access to company secrets.
S,A — EN
Unknown — *Intervision Video*   **H, P**
A-AE 0181

Touch of Satan, The   Fil-Ent '74
Horror
02395   87 mins   C
B, V
Michael Berry, Emby Mellay, Lee Amber, directed by Don Henderson
A breakdown whilst on a motoring holiday leads Jodie to Melissa's home, where he senses the growing feeling of evil, but cannot escape the horrors of the powers of darkness and the supernatural.
A — EN
George E Carey — *Derann Film Services*   **H, P**
DV 108B/DV 108

Touched   Fil-Ent '83
Drama/Romance
10088   89 mins   C
B, V
Robert Hays, Ned Beatty, Kathleen Beller
An inmate at a psychiatric hospital refuses to take drugs or be written off by the authorities. Finding comfort and strength from a beautiful young girl he makes an escape, promising to return for her. Having found a job in a fairground he proves to be one of the saner members of society. He sets up a home, returns for the girl and their relationship blossoms.
A — EN
Lorimar — *VideoSpace Ltd*   **P**

Touched by Love   Fil-Ent '80
Drama
08632   93 mins   C
V2, B, V
Deborah Raffin, Diana Lane, Michael Learned
This tells the story of a woman who begins her first job as a nurse at a home for abandoned and disabled children. She becomes captivated by a young girl, suffering from cerebral palsy, who refuses to communicate. For many weeks, her hard work is unrewarding but finally she unlocks the key to the mind that holds her prisoner.
S,A — EN
Columbia — *Hokushin Audio Visual Ltd*   **P**
VM 55

Tough Enough   Fil-Ent '83
Comedy/Music
13676   107 mins   C
B, V
Dennis Quaid, Stan Shaw, Charlene Watkins, Pam Grier, Warren Oates, directed by Richard O. Flesher
A singer-songwriter, frustrated at getting nowhere, puts on boxing gloves and wins the regional finals and has to decide whether the bruises are worth a larger purse of money.
BBFC:PG — S,A — EN
William Gilmore — *CBS/Fox Video*   **P**
1292

Toughest Man In The World   Fil-Ent '84
Crime-Drama
13670   96 mins   C
B, V
Mr T, Dennis Dugan, John P Navin, Peggy Pope, directed by Dick Lowry
A tough guy, with a heart of gold, takes on the local crime syndicate when the centre he runs for troubled kids is threatened with closure.
BBFC:PG — S,A — EN
John Cutts — *CBS/Fox Video*   **P**
6846

Tourist Trap   Fil-Ent '79
Horror
06795   90 mins   C
V2, B, V
Chuck Connors
A group of young people are trapped at a rundown desert gas station by gruesome living mannequins.
C,A — EN
J Larry Carroll — *Intervision Video*   **H, P**
A-A 0339

(For Explanation of codes, see USE GUIDE and KEY)

675

PALADIN VIDEO HOME ENTERTAINMENT GUIDE

Tower of Evil   Fil-Ent '72
Horror
05470   85 mins   C
V2, B, V
Jill Haworth, Bryant Haliday, Anthony Valentine, Jack Watson, Anna Palk, Robin Asquith, directed by Jim O'Connolly
A group of archaeologists suspect that a treasure is hidden in caves below an abandoned old light house on Snape Island, which is said to be infested with ghosts, corpses and eerie sounds. A hideously disfigured being is on the prowl and a crazed girl murders her four companions.
BBFC:X — A — EN
Grenadier Films Ltd; Fanfare Film Corp — *Iver Film Services*   **P**
135

Towering Inferno, The   Fil-Ent '74
Drama/Suspense
13162   165 mins   C
B, V
Steve McQueen, Paul Newman, William Holden, Faye Dunaway, Fred Astaire, directed by Irwin Allen
An inaugural party for the opening of the world's tallest building ends with hundreds being trapped on the top floor as fire spreads from below.
BBFC:A — C,A — EN
20th Century Fox — *Warner Home Video*   **P**
61253

Town Called Bastard, A   Fil-Ent '72
Western/Adventure
10203   97 mins   C
B, V
Robert Shaw, Stella Stevens, Telly Savalas, Martin Landau, Michael Craig, directed by Robert Parrish
A beautiful young widow arrives in a small Mexican town accompanied by a stranger driving a hearse carrying an empty coffin. She offers a reward of gold to anyone who can find her husband's killer. A Mexican colonel and a company of government troops begin hanging suspects but a priest stands in their way.
S,A — EN
Philip Yordan — *Video Form Pictures*   **H, P**
6228-40

Town Like Alice, A   Fil-Ent '56
War-Drama
09939   112 mins   B/W
B, V
Peter Finch, Virginia McKenna, Marie Lohr, Renee Houston, Jean Anderson, directed by Jack Lee
Based on a novel by Nevil Shute, this film follows a small band of women forced by the Japanese to trek through the Malaysian jungle during the second world war. A tough and sentimental Australian prisoner of war befriends them all and falls in love with one of them.
BBFC:PG — F — EN
Rank; Vic Films — *Rank Video Library*   **H, P**
0148 A

Town That Dreaded Sundown, The   Fil-Ent '77
Western
07405   90 mins   C
V2, B, V
Ben Johnson, Andrew Prine, Dawn Wells, Jimmy Clem, Charles B. Pierce, Cindy Butler, Earl E. Smith, Christine Ellsworth
Based on a true story, five citizens of a border town have been murdered and three brutally attacked by a masked madman who is still at large despite the efforts of law enforcement agencies. A series of bizarre and gruesome events turn the town into an armed camp where old friends suspect one another and everyone carries a lethal weapon.
BBFC:X — A — EN
American International — *Guild Home Video*   **H, P, E**

Towser   Fil-Ent '84
Cartoons
13094   60 mins   C
B, V
Animated
Twelve tales from Howser the hippiest hound in town featuring Goblin Gobble, Sadie the sex kitten and other friends.
F — EN
King Rollo Films — *Longman Video*   **P**
5027

Toy, The   Fil-Ent '83
Comedy
12480   97 mins   C
B, V
Richard Pryor, Jackie Gleason
A millionaire department store owner takes his son to the toy department and says he can take home anything he wants. The kid chooses the out of work journalist who is employed there because he makes him laugh.
BBFC:PG — F — EN
Columbia — *RCA/Columbia Pictures Video UK*   **H, P**
10159

(For Explanation of codes, see USE GUIDE and KEY)

PALADIN VIDEO HOME ENTERTAINMENT GUIDE

Toy Soldiers
Fil-Ent '83
War-Drama
12832   30 mins   C
B, V

Jason Miller, Cleavon Little, Rodolfo De Anda, directed by David Fisher

A band of raw, untrained soldiers headed by an ex-marine commander go to the aid of four of their friends who have been captured and held hostage by a terrorist death squad.
BBFC:18 — A — EN
Unknown — *Video Tape Centre*   **P**
1160

Toy Soldiers
Fil-Ent '84
Drama
13658   92 mins   C
B, V

Jason Miller, Cleavon Little, Rodolfo De Anda, Terri Garber, directed by David Fisher

A group of college students on a pleasure cruise off the coast of Central America are kidnapped by a band of guerrillas and a battle for survival between the terrorists and the kids breaks out.
BBFC:18 — C,A — EN
E Darrell Hallenbeck — *CBS/Fox Video*   **P**
3046

Toyah at the Rainbow
Fil-Ent '81
Music-Performance
04862   55 mins   C
V2, B, V, LV

This programme demonstrates the energy and style of actress and rock singer Toyah Willcox, and her group 'Toyah,' in concert.
F — EN
Anthony Edwards; John Craig; Andy Finney — *BBC Video*   **H, P**
BBCV 3012

Toyah—Good Morning Universe
Fil-Ent '82
Music-Performance
08712   57 mins   C
V2, B, V

Toyah Wilcox

This is a spectacular recording of the Old Grey Whistle Test, Christmas 1981 concert. Amongst the songs performed are Toyah's hit records 'I Want to Be Free,' 'It's a Mystery' and 'Thunder in the Mountains.' This live recording of Toyah was filmed at Theatre Royal, Drury Lane.
S,A — EN
Michael Appleton; Jeff Griffin; Andy Finney — *BBC Video*   **H, P**
BBCV 3019

Toyah! Toyah! Toyah!
Fil-Ent '8?
Music-Performance
12775   20 mins   C
B, V

This programme features four of Toyah's best videos, 'I Want To Be Free,' 'Thunder In The Mountains,' 'Brave New World' and 'Rebel Run' plus 'It's A Mystery,' shot at London's Rainbow Theatre.
F — EN
Unknown — *Polygram Video*   **P**
8081

Toytown Series No. 1
Fil-Ent '??
Puppets/Cartoons
06066   54 mins   C
V2, B, V
Animated

Series number one features Larry the Lamb and other Toytown characters in five stories. 'The Tale of the Magician,' 'Larry the Plumber,' 'The Toytown Treasure,' 'The Theatre Royal' and 'Mr Noah's Holiday.'
PS,M — EN
Unknown — *Video Programme Distributors*   **P**
Inter-Ocean—050

Toytown Series No. 2
Chi-Juv '??
Puppets/Cartoons
07895   54 mins   C
V2, B, V
Animated

This programme, the second in the series, features Mr. Mayor and other Toytown characters in five stories. 'The Mayor's Sea Voyage,' 'A Portrait of the Mayor,' 'The Toytown Mystery,' 'Tea for two' and 'How Wireless Came to Toytown.'
PS,M — EN
Unknown — *Video Programme Distributors*   **P**
Inter-Ocean—057

Toytown Series No. 3
Chi-Juv '??
Puppets/Cartoons
07896   54 mins   C
V2, B, V
Animated

This programme, the third in the series, features Ernest the Policeman and other Toytown characters in five stories. 'The Arkville Dragon,' 'The Extraordinary Affair,' 'The Brave Deed of Ernest,' 'The Tale of Ernest the Policeman' and 'Pistols for Two.'
PS,M — EN
Unknown — *Video Programme Distributors*   **P**
Inter-Ocean—058

(For Explanation of codes, see USE GUIDE and KEY)

PALADIN VIDEO HOME ENTERTAINMENT GUIDE

Toytown Series No. 4   Chl-Juv '??
Puppets/Cartoons
07897   54 mins   C
V2, B, V
Animated
This programme, the fourth in the series, features Dennis the Dachshund and other Toytown characters in five stories. 'The Enchanted Ark,' 'Mr Growser Moves,' 'Captain Brass; The Pirate,' 'The Great Toytown War,' 'The Disgraceful Business at Mrs. Goose's'.
PS,M — EN
Unknown — *Video Programme Distributors*
P
Inter-Ocean—076

Toytown Series No. 5   Chl-Juv '??
Puppets/Cartoons
08898   65 mins   C
V2, B, V
Animated
This programme, the fifth in the series, features the Inventor and other Toytown characters in six stories: 'Toytown Goes West', 'Golf', 'Tale of the Inventor', 'Dreadful Doings in Ark Street', 'Dirty Work at the Dog and Whistle', 'Showing-Up of Larry the Lamb'.
PS,M — EN
Unknown — *Video Programme Distributors*
P
Inter-Ocean 082

Track of the Moonbeast   Fil-Ent '76
Horror
09222   93 mins   C
B, V
Chase Cordell, Donna Leigh Drake
When a meteorite particle hits a man, he begins to lead a double life. By day he is a normal person but at night, when the particle reacts to the moon, he becomes a vile reptilian beast with an insatiable appetite for murder.
A — EN
Derio Prods — *Video Form Pictures*   **H, P**
MGT 17

Trackers, The   Fil-Ent '71
Western
05185   71 mins   C
B, V
Sammy Davis Jr, Ernest Borgnine
A full blooded Western adventure starring Sammy Davis Jr. as a singleminded frontier scout enlisted to help Sam Paxton track down his kidnapped daughter.
C,A — EN
Aaron Spelling — *Rank Video Library*   **H, P**
8001

Trader Hornee   Fil-Ent '8?
Comedy-Drama
09910   82 mins   C
V2, B, V
Buddy Pantsari, Christine Murray, Elisabeth Monica, John Alderman, Lisa Grant, Sir Brandon Duffy, Deek Sills
Hamilton Hornee, a private detective, is commissioned to establish whether a 21-year-old multi-million heiress, missing in the jungle since she was six, is still alive. On the expedition are a couple of villainous relatives who inherit the money if the girl is not found.
BBFC:18 — A — EN
Unknown — *Derann Film Services*   **P**
CV 608

Trading Places   Fil-Ent '83
Comedy
13328   112 mins   C
B, V
Dan Aykroyd, Eddie Murphy, Jamie Lee Curtis, Don Ameche, Denholm Elliott, directed by John Landis
Two conniving brothers in an investment firm engineer a change of roles between a rich young investment broker and a poor black street hustler, simply to prove a point.
BBFC:15 — S,A — EN
Paramount — *CIC Video*   **H, P**
BER 2101/VHR 2101

Traffic   Fil-Ent '70
Comedy
07851   97 mins   C
B, V
Jacques Tati, directed by Jacques Tati with Bert Haanstra
In this French comedy, the hero, Monsieur Hulot decides to drive his revolutionary new motor vehicle to an Auto Show, a journey with hilarious consequences.
S,A — EN
Corona — *Polygram Video*   **H, P**
791 511

Trail of the Pink Panther   Fil-Ent '82
Comedy
12491   94 mins   C
B, V
David Niven, Richard Mulligan, Herbert Lom, Peter Sellers, Joanna Lumley, directed by Blake Edwards
The bumbling Inspector Clouseau vanishes while on the trail of the stolen Pink Panther diamond and a lovely TV news reporter investigates the mystery.
BBFC:PG — F — EN
Blake Edwards; Tony Adams — *Warner Home Video*   **P**
99416

PALADIN VIDEO HOME ENTERTAINMENT GUIDE

Train Killer, The   Fil-Ent '81
Drama/Suspense
12911   87 mins   C
B, V
Michael Sarrazin
This film tells the true story of a Hungarian terrorist who, in 1931, sent the Orient Express crashing into a ravine with a barrage of explosives.
C,A — EN
Unknown — *THORN EMI*   **P**
TXA 90 24434/TVA 90 24432

Train Ride to Hollywood, A   Fil-Ent '??
Musical/Comedy
09039   90 mins   C
V2, B, V
In this musical comedy 'Humphrey Bogart', 'Clark Gable', 'Marlon Brando', 'Count Dracula' and other 'stars' join together for madness, masquerade and murder.
S,A — EN
Unknown — *Radial Choice Distributors Ltd*
H, P
PIC 21

Train Robbers, The   Fil-Ent '73
Western
06036   88 mins   C
B, V
John Wayne, Ann Margret, Rod Taylor, Ben Johnson, Christopher George, Ricardo Montalban, directed by Burt Kennedy
A voluptuous, hard drinking but virtuous widow joins forces with two cowboys to recover gold stolen by her dead husband in order to clear her son's name. They are pursued by a gang who also want the gold for themselves.
BBFC:U — F — EN
Warner Brothers — *Warner Home Video*
P
WEX1093/WEV1093

Training Dogs the Woodhouse Way   How-Ins '81
Pets
04871   104 mins   C
V2, B, V, LV
Barbara Woodhouse demonstrates how quickly basic obedience can be taught to previously untrained dogs.
F — I
Peter Riding; Roger Brunskill — *BBC Video*
H, P
BBCV 1003

Training for Ministry   Gen-Edu '??
Religion/Bible
06289   45 mins   B/W
B, V, PH15
In this film Roger Forster provides a practical approach to the Bible method of training in counselling and ministry.
S,A — R
Audio Visual Ministries — *Audio Visual Ministries*   **H, L, P**
VT89

Trap on Cougar Mountain   Fil-Ent '7?
Adventure
07914   93 mins   C
V2, B, V
Erik Larsen, Keith Larsen, Karen Steele
This film tells the story of a boy, his cougar and their adventures together.
F — EN
Sun International Productions — *Video Programme Distributors*   **P**
Inter-Ocean—067

Trapped Beneath the Sea   Fil-Ent '74
Drama
04217   96 mins   C
B, V
Lee J. Cobb, Paul Michael Glaser, Martin Balsam
True story of four men trapped off the Florida coast in a disabled mini-sub with their oxygen running out and the nation waiting in anguish for their rescue.
BBFC:U — F — EN
ABC Circle Films — *Guild Home Video*
H, P

Travelling Executioner, The   Fil-Ent '71
Drama
12224   94 mins   C
B, V
Stacy Keach, Mariana Hill, Bud Cort
An ex-carnival showman decides to make a living by travelling across America in 1918 with his portable electric chair, making a charge for each execution.
S,A — EN
MGM — *MGM/UA Home Video*   **P**
10324

Traviata, La   Fin-Art '??
Opera
01872   113 mins   C
B, V
Anna Moffo, Gino Bechi, Franco Bonisolli, Mafalda Micheluzzi, Afro Poli

PALADIN VIDEO HOME ENTERTAINMENT GUIDE

The first and most magnificent film production of Verdi's sensational tragic opera.
BBFC:U — F — EN
Rank — *Rank Video Library* H, P
7007

Traviata, La Fil-Ent '83
Opera
12824 110 mins C
B, V
Placido Domingo, Teresa Stratas, Cornell MacNeil, directed by Franco Zeffirelli
Verdi's tragic and passionate love story with the Metropolitan Opera Orchestra conducted by James Levine and recorded in stereo.
BBFC:U — F — EN
Unknown — *VideoSpace Ltd* P
VS 22

Treasure Island Fil-Ent '74
Adventure
04218 84 mins C
B, V
Orson Welles, Kim Burfield, Lionel Stander, Walter Slezak
A new version of the Robert Louis Stevenson swashbuckler with an international cast.
BBFC:U — F — EN
Harry Alan Towers Prods — *Guild Home Video*
H, P

Treasure Island Fil-Ent '??
Adventure
01689 64 mins C
V2, B, V
Suspense, pirates, and a search for hidden treasure combine to make an exciting tale of adventure.
BBFC:U — F — EN
Unknown — *Intervision Video* H, P
A-AE 0072

Treasure Island Fil-Ent '50
Adventure/Drama
05595 96 mins C
B, V
Bobby Driscoll, Robert Newton, Basil Sydney, Walter Fitzgerald, Finlay Currie, directed by Byron Haskin
An adaptation of the classic Robert Louis Stevenson tale of pirates and buried treasure. Long John Silver, the one legged rogue leads the pirates on their evil missions, only to have his heart stolen by a young boy's courage.
F — EN
Walt Disney Productions — *Rank Video Library* H
04100

Treasure Island Fil-Ent '8?
Musical
08931 100 mins C
B, V
Christopher Casenove, Piers Eady, Roderick Horne, Harold Innocent, Godfrey Jackman, John Judd, David Kernan, Bernard Miles, Norman Rossington
Adapted from the novel 'Treasure Island' by Robert Louis Stevenson this is a musical version of the classic story. The music is performed by The Royal Philharmonic Orchestra, conducted by Alexander Faris.
F — EN
Brent Walker Prods — *Brent Walker Home Video Ltd* P

Treasure Island Fil-Ent '??
Cartoons/Adventure
09382 44 mins C
B, V
Animated
Adopted from the book by Robert Louis Stevenson, this tells the pirate tale about Long John Silver and young Jim Hawkins.
F — EN
Unknown — *VCL Video Services* P
A313B

Treasure of Jamaica Reef Fil-Ent '74
Adventure
09914 105 mins C
V2, B, V
Stephen Boyd, David Ladd, Cheryl Stoppelmoor, Chuck Woolery, Rosie Grier, Darby Hinton
This adventure story includes a search for underwater treasure, baddies and goodies fighting it out, an unusual car chase, hurricanes and explosions.
BBFC:U — F — EN
Treasure of Jamaica Reef Inc. — *Derann Film Services* P
FCV 601

Treasure of Pancho Villa, The Fil-Ent '55
Western/Adventure
06054 90 mins C
B, V
Rory Calhoun, Shelley Winters, Gilbert Rowland
A story of gold, greed, lust and treachery. An American adventurer and a colonel serving under Pancho Villa rob a federal gold train.
S,A — EN
RKO — *VCL Video Services* P

Treasure of the Four Crowns Fil-Ent '83
Adventure

PALADIN VIDEO HOME ENTERTAINMENT GUIDE

09451 95 mins C
V2, B, V
Tony Anthony, Ana Obregon
In Spanish legend it is said that in the year 700 Visigoth Kings built four crowns to protect the mystical powers of four supernatural gold balls containing the essence of good and evil. In this film five daring heroes, against all odds, set out on a dangerous mission to capture this great treasure.
BBFC:PG — *F* — *EN*
M.T.G.; Lotus Films S.A. — *Guild Home Video*
H, P, E

Treasures of the British   Gen-Edu '81
Crown
Arts/Royalty-GB
04857 100 mins C
V2, B, V, LV
Sir Huw Wheldon presents this private view of one of the world's richest art collections, with the Queen and members of the Royal Family acting as guides to the Royal Collection. Accompanying book available.
AM Available *F* — *EN*
Michael Gill — *BBC Video*   **H, P**
BBCV 6000

Tree Top Tales   Chl-Juv '7?
Fairy tales
01972 15 mins C
B, V
4 pgms
Four untitled stories about the adventurous existence of a group of woodland animals.
PS,M — EN
Unknown — *Quadrant Video*   **H, P**

Trenchcoat   Fil-Ent '83
Drama/Comedy
13752 90 mins C
B, V
Margot Kidder, Robert Hays
A female writer accidentally becomes the possessor of a map and finds herself pursued by a gang of ruthless international terrorists.
BBFC:PG — *S,A* — *EN*
Walt Disney Productions — *Rank Video Library*
P
163A

Trespasser, The   Fil-Ent '??
Romance/Drama
07660 90 mins C
B, V
Alan Bates, Pauline Moran
Based on the novel by D.H. Lawrence, this is the story of a music teacher who enjoys a brief respite from his domestic troubles in an idyllic and fleeting affair with one of his pupils. For five days he escapes to the sunny South Coast where they revel in each other's company, knowing they share a love with no future.
S,A — EN
Unknown — *VCL Video Services*   **P**
P171D

Trial by Jury   Fil-Ent '8?
Opera
08930 100 mins C
B, V
Frankie Howard, Kate Flowers, Ryland Davies, Tom McDonnell, Roger Bryson, Brian Donlan, Elsie McDougall
This opera by Gilbert and Sullivan tells of a court case investigating a breach of promise. The judge is somewhat smitten by the pretty plaintiff's charms, and to solve the case he marries her himself. The music is performed by The London Symphony Orchestra, conducted by Alexander Faris, with The Ambrosian Opera Chorus.
S,A — EN
Brent Walker Prods — *Brent Walker Home Video Ltd*   **P**

Trial by Terror   Fil-Ent '83
Suspense/Drama
13655 90 mins C
B, V
Kay Lenz, Wayne Crawford, Martin Landau, Colleen Camp, Allen Goorwitz, directed by Hildy Brooks
A married couple experience a series of terrifying attacks on their home and a nightmare begins when the husband shoots a stalking intruder.
BBFC:15 — *C,A* — *EN*
Wayne Crawford; Andrew Lane — *CBS/Fox Video*   **P**
6788

Triangle Factory Fire   Fil-Ent '78
Scandal, The
Drama
13347 97 mins C
V2, B, V
David Dukes, Tovah Feldshuh, Lauren Frost, Janet Margolin, Stephanie Zimbalist, Tom Bosley, directed by Mel Stuart
This is the story of the true happening at one of the notorious sweatshops of New York, 1911, when 146 young women were trapped in a factory fire and died.
BBFC:PG — *S,A* — *EN*
Alan Landsberg Productions Inc; Don Kirshner Productions Inc — *Guild Home Video*   **H, P, E**
8273-8

(For Explanation of codes, see USE GUIDE and KEY)

PALADIN VIDEO HOME ENTERTAINMENT GUIDE

Triangle Factory Fire Scandal, The   Fil-Ent '78
Drama
08355   97 mins   C
V2, B, V
David Dukes, Tovah Feldshuh, Lauren Frost, Janet Margolin, Stacey Nelkin, Ted Wass, Stephanie Zimbalist, Tom Bosley
In March 1911, a tragic fire broke out at a small factory, killing 146 young women. This film, based on fact, tells the story of four of the women, the courage they showed and the tragedies they met.
BBFC:X — A — EN
Alan Landsburg Productions — *Guild Home Video*   H, P, E

Triangle of Suspense   Spo-Lei '??
Sports-Minor
05724   90 mins   C
V2, B, V
This tape offers three films in one. 'North Face Air Race', a film showing sky diving on the north face of the Eiger. 'On the Bridge', a short classic and 'Give Me a Ring Sometime'.
F — EN
Unknown — *Video Unlimited*   H, P

Tribute   Fil-Ent '80
Drama
09073   123 mins   C
B, V
Jack Lemmon, Robby Benson, Lee Remick, directed by Bob Clark
This is Bernard Slade's play, brought to the screen, about Scotty Templeton, a dying man determined to achieve a reconciliation with his son. The tense conflict between father and son plays out against Scotty's fight for life, weaving moments of high comedy into the drama.
S,A — EN
20th Century Fox — *Video Tape Centre*   P
VTC 1026

Tricks of the Trade   Fil-Ent '??
Comedy
08705   55 mins   C
V2, B, V
Gloria Le Roy, Patty Kotero
This film tells of the exploits of the 'intrepid heroes' as they sample what is offered in the 'house of ill repute'.
BBFC:X — A — EN
Unknown — *Video Unlimited*   H, P
077

Trip to Kill   Fil-Ent '71
Crime-Drama
07648   89 mins   C
B, V
Telly Savalas, Robert Vaughn, John Marley, Burgess Meredith, directed by Tom Stern
This film tells the story of an ex-Vietnam war hero who is set-up by the FBI. Opening with scenes of the war, he returns to civilian life only to become disillusioned and depressed. He finds comfort amongst the hippy underground but unknown to him he is being used by the FBI to break open a Mafia controlled drug ring. He becomes a target for the Mafia.
S,A — EN
MGM; Tracom Productions — *VCL Video Services*   P
P221D

Triple Cross   Fil-Ent '67
War-Drama
07664   117 mins   C
B, V
Christopher Plummer, Yul Brynner, Romy Schneider, Gert Froebe, Trevor Howard, Claudine Auger, Jean Claudio, directed by Terence Young
An English safecracker captured by the Nazis exploits his criminal ingenuity to become a daring double agent. Based on a true story, the safecracker sells himself to both the Germans and the British, is decorated by both governments and comes out of the war as a hero for the Allies.
S,A — EN
Cineurup Prods — *VCL Video Services*   P
P234D

Triple Echo, The   Fil-Ent '??
War-Drama/Romance
06264   93 mins   C
B, V
Glenda Jackson, Oliver Reed, Brian Deacon
Set in England in 1942, a soldier's wife hides a young deserter and a romance develops. To escape detection she disguises him as her 'sister.' A brutal Military Police Sergeant takes an interest in 'her' and after an attempted rape discovers the truth with sudden, vicious and tragic results.
S,A — EN
Unknown — *VCL Video Services*   P
P143D

Trittico, Il   Fil-Ent '??
Opera
10007   160 mins   C
B, V
Piero Cappucilli, Rosalind Plowright, Juan Pons

PALADIN VIDEO HOME ENTERTAINMENT GUIDE

This is Puccini's triptych of three one-act operas, skilfully contrasted with each other, including 'Il Tabarro', 'Suor Angelica' and 'Gianni Schicchi'. The chorus and orchestra of La Scala, Milan is conducted by Gianandrea Garazzeni
F — EN
Unknown — *Longman Video* **P**
LGBE 7009/LGVH 7009

Trojan War, The Fil-Ent '61
Drama
04286 100 mins C
V2, B, V
Steve Reeves, Juliette Mayniel, John Drew Barrymore, Hedy Vessel, Lydia Alfonso
For ten years the Greeks have laid siege to the heavily fortified city of Troy. The Greek leader Ulysses hatches a cunning plot, withdrawing his army and leaving only an enormous wooden horse. The unsuspecting Trojans drag the trophy of war into their city where at night Greek warriors, secreted in the horse, open the city gates and signal the Greek army to return.
C,A — EN
Colorama Features — *Video Programme Distributors* **P**
Inter-Ocean—047

Tron Fil-Ent '82
Science fiction
12573 94 mins C
B, V
Jeff Bridges, Bruce Boxleitner, David Warner
The viewer is catapulted inside a computer and the eye is tricked into believing the unbelievable. High-tech warriors battle in video games that can only end in death.
F — EN
Walt Disney Productions — *Rank Video Library* **H**
122

Trouble in store/On the Beat Fil-Ent '??
Comedy-Drama
08086 184 mins C
B, V
Norman Wisdom, Margaret Rutherford, Moira Lister;Norman Wisdom, Jennifer Jayne
This tape contains two Norman Wisdom films. 'Trouble in Store' (82 minutes, 1956) features him as a department store employee, his efforts being continually thwarted by his misguided chivalry. On the Beat' (102 minutes, 1962) features his efforts to become a policeman, only he is 12 inches too short.
BBFC:U — F — EN
Republic; United Artists — *Rank Video Library* **H, P**
1044 C

Trouble With Harry, The Fil-Ent '??
Drama/Comedy
13649 92 mins C
B, V
Shirely MacLaine, John Forsythe, Edmund Gwenn, Jerry Mathers, directed by Alfred Hitchcock
A corpse is discovered in the woods and three people blame themselves for the death until the real cause is revealed.
BBFC:PG — S,A — EN
Universal — *CIC Video* **H, P**
1146

Truck Stop Women Fil-Ent '74
Drama
07902 84 mins C
V2, B, V
Claudia Jennings
This film follows the exploits of a gang of girls whose success at hijacking gets them involved in intrigue, revenge and murder.
S,A — EN
American International — *Video Programme Distributors* **P**
Inter-Ocean—068

True Confessions Fil-Ent '81
Drama
13007 106 mins C
B, V
Robert de Niro, Robert Duvall, directed by Ulu Grosbard
This is a drama set in the late 1940's in California in which an ambitious priest, whose shady business contacts are implicated in the murder of a prostitute, is under suspicion when his own policeman brother investigates the killing.
BBFC:AA — C,A — EN
United Artists — *Warner Home Video* **P**
99288

True Grit Fil-Ent '69
Western
01217 128 mins C
B, V
John Wayne, Glen Campbell, Kim Darby, Robert Duvall, directed by Henry Hathaway
John Wayne portrays U.S. Marshal Rooster Cogburn, who is hired by a young girl to find her father's killer, in this popular film that won Wayne his only Oscar.
Academy Awards '69: Best Actor (Wayne).
F — EN
Paramount — *CIC Video* **H, P**

T. T. Tribute Spo-Lei '81
Motorcycles
06848 69 mins C (PAL, NTSC)

(For Explanation of codes, see USE GUIDE and KEY)

PALADIN VIDEO HOME ENTERTAINMENT GUIDE

V2, B, V
Mike Hailwood
This double feature covers the racing career of the late great Mike Hailwood. 'Diamond Senior' shows Hailwood in pitch battle with Agostini during the 1967 TT races. 'Winning Formula' includes his fairy-tale comeback to racing by winning the 1979 Senior TT.
S,A — EN
CH Wood Ltd — *Duke Marketing Limited*
P
DM2

Tubby the Tuba   Chi-Juv '8?
Cartoons
12880   92 mins   C
B, V
Animated
The voices of Dick Van Dyke, Pearl Bailey, Jack Gilford and Hermoine Gingold are heard in this stereo video about Tubby in search for a melody of his own.
PS,M — EN
Unknown — *Vestron Video International*
P
12502

Tubes Video, The   Fil-Ent '81
Music-Performance
05055   53 mins   C
B, V
This film shows The Tubes performing their album 'The Completion Backward Principle' and other music, together with some previously unreleased material. Songs include 'Matter of Price,' 'Sports Fans,' 'Tube Talk,' and 'Sushi Girl.'
F — EN
Unknown — *THORN EMI*   P
TXD 90 5005 4/TVD 90 5005 2

Tukiki and His Search for a Merry Christmas   Chi-Juv '??
Cartoons
10083   30 mins   C
V2, B, V
Animated
An adventure story about a young Eskimo boy who sets out to discover the meaning of Christmas. He visits many countries and learns about the traditions of each Christmas.
BBFC:U — PS,M — EN
Unknown — *Embassy Home Entertainment*
P
1348

Tulips   Fil-Ent '80
Comedy
10070   89 mins   C
V2, B, V
Gabe Kaplan, Bernadette Peters
A successful young executive is knocked down by a lovely young girl while he is contemplating his 85th suicide attempt. They discover they have much in common, and fall in love through many shared adventures.
F — EN
Astral Bellevue Pathe Prods — *Embassy Home Entertainment*   P
2004

Turandot   Fil-Ent '??
Opera
10005   120 mins   C
B, V
Ghena Dimitrova, Nicola Martinucci, Cecilia Gasdia, Ivo Vinco
Set at the open-air arena in Verona, an important part of this opera, the music is performed by the chorus and orchestra of the Arena di Verona conducted by Maurizio Arena.
F — EN
Unknown — *Longman Video*   P
LGBE 7008/LGVH 7008

Turning Point, The   Fil-Ent '79
Drama
01269   119 mins   C
B, V
Shirley MacLaine, Anne Bancroft, Mikhail Baryshnikov, Leslie Browne, directed by Herbert Ross
A woman who gave up ballet for motherhood must come to terms with herself as her daughter's ballet career is launched.
M,A — EN
20th Century Fox — *CBS/Fox Video*   P
3A-112

Twas the Night Before Christmas   Chi-Juv '84
Cartoons
12943   25 mins   C
B, V
Animated
Based on the famous poem by Clement Moore, this is the timeless story of the town which is not going to be visited by Father Christmas.
I,M — EN
Unknown — *Video Form Pictures*   H, P
MGK 005

Twelfth Night   Fil-Ent '81
Comedy-Drama
05392   103 mins   C
B, V
Sir Alec Guinness, Tommy Steele, Sir Ralph Richardson, Joan Plowright, Adrienne Corri, Gary Raymond, John Moffatt, Sheila Reid

PALADIN VIDEO HOME ENTERTAINMENT GUIDE

An adaptation of William Shakespeare's comedy 'Twelfth Night' done especially for television. Sir Alec Guinness plays Malvolio, Sir Ralph Richardson plays Sir Toby Belch, Tommy Steele as the clown, Feste, and Joan Plowright stars as Viola.
S,A — EN
John Dexter Production — *Precision Video Ltd*
P
BITC 2047/VITC 2047

Twelve O'Clock High Fil-Ent '49
War-Drama
01147   132 mins   B/W
B, V
Gregory Peck, Hugh Marlowe, Gary Merrill, Millard Mitchell, Dean Jagger
An epic drama about the heroic 8th Air Force. Peck, as a bomber-group commander, is forced to drive his men to the breaking point in the fury of battle.
Academy Awards '49: Best Supporting Actor (Jagger).   F — EN
20th Century Fox — *CBS/Fox Video*   P
4A-093

Twelve Tasks of Asterix, The Chi-Juv '84
Cartoons
13003   84 mins   C
B, V
Animated
Julius Caesar is determined to conquer the little village of Armorica and sets the inhabitants twelve Herculean tasks to see if these last remaining Gouls are really Gods.
PS,M — EN
Les Productions Dargaud — *Select Video Limited*   P
3005/43

28 Minutes for 3 Million Dollars Fil-Ent '??
Comedy-Drama
06108   99 mins   C
V2, B, V
Richard Harrison, Claudio Biava, Ferruccio Viotti
A famous diamond is stolen by a group of experts on the payroll of a millionaire diamond collector. But his butler, too, proves to be an equally efficient thief.
S,A — EN
Unknown — *Video Programme Distributors*
P
Cinehollywood—V1780

25 Years Impressions Fil-Ent '77
Royalty-GB
05914   74 mins   C
V

Directed by Peter Morley
A comprehensive documentary on the Queen's reign, to mark the occasion of the Silver Jubilee.
F — EN
Unknown — *JVC*   P
PRT 3

21 Hours at Munich Fil-Ent '76
Drama
10223   101 mins   C
B, V
William Holden, Shirley Knight, Franco Nero, Anthony Quayle, Richard Basehart
This film is a dramatisation of the real events leading up to the capture of eleven Israeli athletes and their coaches by the PLO during the Autumn of 1972. The film exposes the plot to capture them by a surprise attack in their own quarter at the Munich Games Olympic Village and the physical and mental brutality suffered by the hostages.
BBFC:18 — A — EN
Filmways Prods — *Video Form Pictures*
H, P
MGS 26

21 Hours at Munich Fil-Ent '76
Drama
12923   101 mins   C
B, V
William Holden, Shirley Knight, Franco Nero, Anthony Quayle, Richard Basehart, directed by William A Graham
This is based on the incident that took place at the Munich Olympics '72, when a group of PLO terrorists held eleven Israeli athletes and their coaches hostage to bargain for the release of their comrades.
BBFC:15 — S,A — EN
Moonlight Productions; Filmways — *Video Form Pictures*   H, P
MGD 029

20,000 Leagues Under the Sea Fil-Ent '54
Adventure/Drama
05593   122 mins   C
B, V
Kirk Douglas, James Mason, Peter Lorre
The story of an atomic-powered submarine commanded by the mysterious Captain Nemo, who guides his prisoner-guests on a spectacular voyage below the seas. They encounter an attack by a gigantic squid, the destruction of a nitrate ship and final atomic blast.
Academy Awards '54: Best Special Effects; Best Art Decoration; Best Set Decoration.
F — EN
Walt Disney Productions — *Rank Video Library*
H
01500

(For Explanation of codes, see USE GUIDE and KEY)   685

PALADIN VIDEO HOME ENTERTAINMENT GUIDE

Twice a Woman   Fil-Ent '79
Drama/Romance
08706   90 mins   C
V2, B, V
Anthony Perkins, Bibi Anderson, Sandra Dumas
This is a story of erotic love, loneliness and fulfillment which are all involved in the tangled web of passions that in the end define the meaning of love itself.
BBFC:X — A — EN
William Howerd/M G S; Actueel Films — *Video Unlimited*   **H, P**
074

Twice and Future King   Spo-Lei '75
1974, The/A Special Breed 1975
Automobiles-Racing
04518   52 mins   C
B, V
In one of the most competitive seasons in Formula One motor racing history, the driving championship is not decided until Emerson Fittipaldi secures it on the last lap of the last race. In 'A Special Breed,' the McLaren team of Emerson Fittipaldi and Jochen Mass are followed through a season of racing with its successes, failures, and mechanical problems.
F — EN
Brunswick Intl — *Quadrant Video*   **H, P**
M13

Twilight Zone, The   Fil-Ent '83
Horror/Fantasy
12605   98 mins   C
B, V
Dan Aykroyd, Albert Brooks, Scatman Crothers, John Lithgow, Vic Morrow, Kathleen Quinlan
This tape contains four tales for ghost lovers and is based on the classic television series.
BBFC:15 — C,A — EN
Warner Bros Inc — *Warner Home Video*   **P**
6134

Twinky   Fil-Ent '69
Drama/Romance
08070   94 mins   C
B, V
Charles Bronson, Susan George, Jack Hawkins, Trevor Howard, Robert Morley, Honor Blackman
This film tells of the ups and downs of the marriage between a mature teenage girl and an older man.
BBFC:A — S,A — EN
American International — *Rank Video Library*   **H, P**
0120 C

Twins of Evil   Fil-Ent '71
Horror
05154   86 mins   C
B, V
Peter Cushing, Mary Collinson, Dennis Price, Madeleine Collinson, Kathleen Byron, Damien Thomas, David Warbook
Full bodied gothic horror film in which glamorous identical twins fall into the hands of an Austrian Count with a vampire kiss.
BBFC:X — A — EN
Universal; Hammer; Rank — *Rank Video Library*   **H, P**
2006

Twisted Nerve   Fil-Ent '68
Drama/Horror
08556   113 mins   C
B, V
Hayley Mills, Hywel Bennet, Billie Whitelaw, Phyllis Calvert, Barry Foster, Frank Finlay
In this film Hywel Bennet plays a psychopath, an intelligent man who is able to use his good looks to manipulate those he comes in contact with. He takes a room at a lodging house, where he is able to control the whole house-hold, playing ruthlessly on the pity of those around him.
BBFC:X — A — EN
Charter Film Productions — *THORN EMI*   **P**
TXC 90 0753 4/TVC 90 0763 2

Twisted Sister, Stay Hungry   Fil-Ent '84
Music-Performance
12961   60 mins   C
B, V
This video features eleven tracks from Twisted Sister including 'The Kids Are Back', 'We're Not Gonna Take It', 'S.M.F.', 'I Wanna Rock', 'Burnin Hell' and 'Stay Hungry'.
F — EN
Marty Callner — *Virgin Video*   **H, P**
VVD 050

Two Faces of Evil, The/Rude Awakening   Fil-Ent '??
Horror
07363   202 mins   C
V2, B, V
Anna Calder-Marshall, Gary Raymond, Pauline Delany, Philip Latham, Jenny Laird, Denholm Elliott, James Lavrenson, Pat Heywood, Lury Gutteridge, Elanor Summerfield
Two 'Hammer House of Horror' films are contained on one cassette. The first entitled 'The Two Faces of Evil' (101 mins.) tells of a family setting off on their holiday. As a storm rages during their journey, the father sees a shadowy figure and almost knocks him down. In the second 'Rude Awakening' (101 mins.) it tells of an estate agent, trapped in a loveless

PALADIN VIDEO HOME ENTERTAINMENT GUIDE

marriage, who dreams of marrying his secretary. Whilst visiting an old property, for sale he hears a disembodied voice saying, 'You shouldn't have killed your wife.'
S,A — EN
Hammer Films — Precision Video Ltd   **P**
CRITC 2117/BITC 2117/VITC 2117

Two Female Spies with Flowered Panties   Fil-Ent '??
Crime-Drama
06850   90 mins   C
V2, B, V
Nadine Pascale, Joelle Leclaire, Candy Coster
A senator in charge of an investigation on some missing V.I.P.'s decides to get two girls out of prison to work as undercover agents. The girls are allowed to go where they want after the job has been done. However, when they discover the names of the members of the organisation, the mission becomes very dangerous.
S,A — EN
Unknown — European Video Company
P

240 Robert   Fil-Ent '79
Adventure
12932   73 mins   C
B, V
Joanna Cassidy, Mark Harmon, John Bennett Perry, directed by Paul Krasny
A helicopter patrols the California beaches rescuing anyone or anything that gets into difficulties.
BBFC:U — F — EN
Unknown — Video Form Pictures   **H, P**
DIP 009

Two in Black Belt   Fil-Ent '79
Adventure/Martial arts
04414   90 mins   C
B, V
An athlete returns home and finds his mother brutally murdered and his blind sister raped. He and a friend set out with anger and fury to find the murderer.
S,A — EN
Unknown — VCL Video Services   **P**

Two of a Kind   Fil-Ent '83
Romance/Fantasy
13243   84 mins   C
B, V
John Travolta, Olivia Newton-John, Charles Durning, Oliver Reed, directed by John Herzfield
When an extremely selfish inventor and a boorish aspiring actress get together the gods above decide to play a trick or two on them to make them nicer people.
BBFC:PG — S,A — EN
Roger M. Rothstein; Joe Wizan — CBS/Fox Video   **P**
1339

2001: A Space Odyssey   Fil-Ent '68
Science fiction/Drama
05299   134 mins   C
V2, B, V
Keir Dullea, Gary Lockwood, William Sylvester, Douglas Rain, directed by Stanley Kubrick
A manned space venture on its way to Jupiter is turned into chaos when a computer, Hal 9000, takes over resulting in the loss of one astronaut in space and the death of several others. The sole survivor dismantles Hal 9000 and encounters a monolithic slot in space. The film examines man's conflict with machines and penetrates man's inner destiny through special effects.
Academy Award '68: Best Visual Effects.
S,A — EN
Stanley Kubrick; MGM — MGM/UA Home Video   **P**
UMB10002/UMV10002

Two-Way Stretch   Fil-Ent '60
Comedy
04654   84 mins   B/W
B, V
Peter Sellers, Wilfrid Hyde-White, David Lodge, Bernard Cribbins
A trio of convicts enjoy a perfect holiday atmosphere—breakfast in bed, a radio, daily deliveries of the milk and the papers with wine stocked in the cupboard. This is the punishment handed three of the inmates of Huntleigh Prison under the benign jurisdiction of Commander Bennett.
F — EN
British Lion — THORN EMI   **H, P**
TXE 90 0249 4/TVE 90 0249 2

Tycoon/Six Gun Gold   Fil-Ent '4?
Adventure/Western
05655   178 mins   C
B, V
John Wayne, Anthony Quinn, Laraine Day, Judith Anderson, Sir Cedric Hardwicke, directed by Richard Wallace, Tim Holt, Lane Chandler, Ray Whitby, LeRoy Mason, Jan Clayton, directed by David Howard
Two films are featured on one cassette.
'Tycoon' (colour, 123 mins, 1948) is the story of two rugged men, a construction engineer and a ruthless tycoon, who battle with each other, with their team, their equipment and the elements to drive a tunnel through a vast expanse of rock in

PALADIN VIDEO HOME ENTERTAINMENT GUIDE

the Andes. 'Six Gun Gold' (Black/white, 55 mins, 1942) features a fake marshal who heads a gang in pursuit of a gold shipment. A man's brother is kidnapped by the gang to get him out of the way; the man tries to rescue his brother in time.
S,A — EN
RKO — *Kingston Video*   **H, P**
KV23

U

UB 40 Live   Fil-Ent '83
Music-Performance
12953   60 mins   C
B, V
Recorded live at the Hammersmith Odeon, the tracks on this programme include 'Nkomo A Go Go', 'One in Ten', 'Cherry Oh Baby', 'Red Red Wine' and 'Sweet Sensation'.
F — EN
Hugh Simmon — *Virgin Video*   **H, P**
VVD 25

UB 40—Labour of Love   Fil-Ent '84
Music-Performance
12952   31 mins   C
B, V
Nine tracks from the Birmingham reggae band including 'Sweet Sensation', 'Please Don't Make Me Cry', 'Johnny Too Bad' and 'Red Red Wine'.
F — EN
Unknown — *Virgin Video*   **H, P**
VVC 051

UFO Journals   Fil-Ent '75
Adventure/Documentary
01047   92 mins   C
B, V
This documentary explores the UFO phenomenon, offering both insights and information.
F — EN
Richard Martin Prods — *VCL Video Services*
P

Ugly Dachshund, The   Fil-Ent '66
Comedy-Drama
08006   90 mins   C
B, V
Dean Jones, Suzanne Pleshette, Charlie Ruggles, Kelly Thordsen, directed by Norman Tokar

This film tells the story of a family and a pet dachshund, who turns out to be a Great Dane.
BBFC:U — *F — EN*
Walt Disney Productions — *Rank Video Library*
H
09900

Ultimate Thrill, The   Fil-Ent '7?
Suspense
04219   84 mins   C
B, V
Britt Ekland, Barry Brown, Eric Braeden, Michael Blodgett
A brilliant, wealthy, powerful industrialist, who demands and gets the best of everything, loses his grip on reality. Life, romance, and business become a deadly game to him, a game where losing is not possible.
BBFC:AA — *C,A — EN*
Unknown — *Guild Home Video*   **H, P**

Ultimate Warrior, The   Fil-Ent '75
Science fiction
13009   94 mins   C
B, V
Yul Brynner, directed by Robert Clouse
A futuristic drama set in the year 2012 when a major plague has struck the earth, destroying virtually all plant life, and survivors huddle together for mutual protection against a group of aggressors.
BBFC:AA — *C,A — EN*
Warner Bros — *Warner Home Video*   **P**
61165

Ultravox: Monument   Fil-Ent '83
Music-Performance
10028   55 mins   C
B, V
This music video contains excerpts from the Quartet concert, including 'Monument,' 'Reap the Wild Wind,' 'The Voice,' 'Vienna,' 'Mine for Life' and 'Hymn.'
M,A — EN
Unknown — *Palace Video Ltd*   **P**
CVIM 10

Ultravox 'The Collection'   Fil-Ent '85
Music video
13125   55 mins   C
B, V
This video combines live and promotional footage and includes all Ultravox's major hits, 'Passing Strangers,' 'The Voice,' 'The Thin Wall,' 'Hymn,' 'Reap the Wild Wind' and others.
F — EN
Unknown — *Palace Video Ltd*   **P**
CVIM 14

PALADIN VIDEO HOME ENTERTAINMENT GUIDE

Ulysses   Fil-Ent '55
Drama/Adventure
05566   118 mins   C
V2, B, V
Kirk Douglas, Anthony Quinn, Silvana Mangano, Rosanna Podesta, directed by Mario Camerini
A version of Homer's epic 'The Odyssey' covering the adventures of the King of Ithaca and his warriors during the Trojan Wars while his wife and son fend off greedy suitors at home. Ulysses' return home from the war is also seen.
BBFC:U — F — EN
Paramount; Dino de Laurentiis and Carlo Ponti — *Videomedia*   **P**
PVM 5100/BVM 5100/HVM

Uncanny, The   Fil-Ent '77
Horror
05155   84 mins   C
B, V
Peter Cushing, Joan Greenwood, Donald Pleasence, Ray Milland, Chloe Franks, Samantha Eggar
Eccentric author tells his publisher three fables of feline vengeance. Gruesome yarns with a nasty twist for the publisher.
BBFC:X — A — EN
Astral Films — *Rank Video Library*   **H, P**
2007

Uncommon Valour   Fil-Ent '83
War-Drama
13317   100 mins   C
B, V
Gene Hackman, Reb Brown, Robert Stack, Harold Sylvester, Patrick Swayze, directed by Ted Kotcheff
A group of Vietnam war veterans team up again to search for one of their battalion who was listed as missing ten years previously.
BBFC:18 — A — EN
Paramount — *CIC Video*   **H, P**
BET 2103/VHT 2103

Uncrowned Champions   Spo-Lei '71
1970/House of Stewart 1971
Automobiles-Racing
04521   56 mins   C
B, V
Highlights of the thirteen events in the 1970 World Championship Grand Prix season. The winner was Jochen Rindt, who was killed at Monza with three races left in circuit. He was awarded the championship posthumously. 'House of Stewart' follows Jackie Stewart through his championship season.
F — EN
Brunswick Intl — *Quadrant Video*   **H, P**
M10

Undefeated, The   Fil-Ent '70
Western
01765   119 mins   C
B, V
John Wayne, Rock Hudson, Bruce Cabot, Roman Gabriel, Lee Meriwether
A Union Army officer leads his war-weary, straggly band of men to a bloody victory, only to find that a peace treaty had been signed three days before.
F — EN
20th Century Fox — *CBS/Fox Video*   **P**
3A-055

Under California Skies   Fil-Ent '48
Western
06881   75 mins   C
V2, B, V
Roy Rogers, Trigger
This film, one of Roy Rogers' few colour films, involves a boy who is not allowed to keep his dog, sending Roy on the trail of a gang of horse thieves in California.
M,A — EN
Republic — *European Video Company*   **P**

Under Capricorn   Fil-Ent '49
Mystery/Suspense
07987   117 mins   C
B, V
Ingrid Bergman, Joseph Cotten, Michael Wilding, Margaret Leighton, directed by Alfred Hitchcock
This film is set in Australia in the year of 1830. It is a dark tale of love and sensitivity, frustration and terror, headed by an all-star cast.
F — EN
Warner Bros — *Motion Epics Video Company Ltd*   **P**
254

Under Fire   Fil-Ent '82
War-Drama
13471   123 mins   C
B, V
Nick Nolte, Gene Hackman, Joanne Cassidy
Three American photo-journalists become involved in the civil war in Nicaragua.
BBFC:15 — S,A — EN
Orion Pictures — *Rank Video Library*   **H, P**
0211

Under Kilimanjaro   Gen-Edu '7?
Wildlife/Africa
02273   26 mins   C
V

(For Explanation of codes, see USE GUIDE and KEY)

PALADIN VIDEO HOME ENTERTAINMENT GUIDE

A look at the wildlife found in the plains surrounding Africa's highest mountain, Kilimanjaro.
F — ED
Unknown — *JVC* **P**
PRT 14

Under Milk Wood   Fil-Ent '71
Drama
01953   87 mins   C
B, V
Richard Burton, Elizabeth Taylor, Peter O'Toole
A film based on Dylan Thomas' classic account of a day in the life of a Welsh village—a kaleidoscope of all human life.
F — EN
Altura Films Intl; Black and Hugh French Prods — *CBS/Fox Video*   **P**
3D-081

Under the Cover Cops   Fil-Ent '??
Comedy
08897   92 mins   C
V2, B, V
A new captain arrives in a town, determined to clean up the area. The town has the lowest number of arrests until he starts.
C,A — EN
Unknown — *Video Programme Distributors* **P**
Inter-Ocean 073

Under the Volcano   Fil-Ent '84
Drama
13671   107 mins   C
B, V
Albert Finney, Jacqueline Bisset, Anthony Andrews, directed by John Huston
A strange trio are brought together during the Day of the Dead festivities in Mexico '38 consisting os a retired British consul, his estranged wife and her former lover and old wounds come to the surface once more. Based on the Malcolm Lowery novel.
BBFC:18 — *A — EN*
Montz Borman; Wieland Schulz-Keil — *CBS/Fox Video*   **P**
6593

Undersea Adventures of   Chi-Juv '7?
Captain Nemo
Cartoons/Adventure
02216   60 mins   C
V
Animated   2 pgms

Two untitled sixty minute programmes available individually featuring Captain Nemo. He encounters many friends and foes, both of human and animal kind, in his journeys on his quest to explore the mysteries of the deep.
M — EN
Unknown — *JVC* **P**
PRT 26; PRT 40

Underwater/The Big   Fil-Ent '5?
Steal
Drama/Crime-Drama
05711   103 mins   C
B, V
Richard Egan, Jane Russell, Gilbert Roland, Lori Nelson, Robert Keith, directed by John Sturges, Robert Mitchum, William Bendix, Jane Greer, Patric Knowles, directed by Don Siegal
Two films are featured on one cassette. 'Underwater' (Colour, 95 mins, 1956) features a trio of skin-divers who are hunting for a sunken galleon in the Caribbean. They find the ship on the edge of a shark-infested ravine and also have to contend with gunmen who move in on the surface. 'The Big Steal' (Black/white, 68 mins, 1950) is the story of a stolen army payroll. A man is wrongly blamed and goes on the trail of the real criminal through Mexico. His journey is both mysterious and dangerous.
F — EN
RKO — *Kingston Video*   **H, P**
KV31

Unfaithfully Yours   Fil-Ent '83
Romance/Comedy
13653   92 mins   C
B, V
Dudley Moore, Nastassja Kinski, Armand Assante, Cassie Yates, Richard Libertini, Albert Brooks, directed by Howard Zieff
Believing his gorgeous, starlet wife is having an affair with his handsome protege, a respected symphony conductor desperately and insanely plots revenge.
BBFC:15 — *S,A — EN*
Marvin Worth; Joe Wizan — *CBS/Fox Video* **P**
1249

Unico   Chi-Juv '8?
Cartoons
12716   90 mins   C
B, V
Animated
Unico is an enchanting unicorn blessed with the gift of spreading happiness wherever he goes.
I,M — EN
Graphic Video — *Mountain/Graphic*   **P**
TGV 1001

PALADIN VIDEO HOME ENTERTAINMENT GUIDE

Union City — Fil-Ent '80
Suspense/Drama
06778   82 mins   C
V2, B, V

Deborah Harry, Pat Benatar, Dennis Lipscomb

An accidental murderer runs from the law. Based on Cornell Woolrich's story 'The Corpse Next Door.'

S,A — EN

Daltyn Film Works; Kinesis Ltd — *Intervision Video*   **H, P**
A-A 0368

Universal Soldier — Fil-Ent '??
War-Drama
06211   98 mins   C
B, V

George Lazenby, Germaine Greer, Robin Hunter, Ben Carruthers

The Universal Soldier is a life-long organiser of mercenaries his business is weapons and he has served a dozen masters. He has come out of a two year retirement and a trivial incident sparks off trouble resulting in his return to the world of war.

S,A — EN

Frederick J Schwartz — *VCL Video Services*   **P**
C183C

Unknown Chaplin — Fil-Ent '83
Film-History/Documentary
09782   156 mins   B/W
B, V

Charles Chaplin

This presentation of a documentary trilogy contains footage of unique Chaplin film reels preserved by his business manager. With an introduction by Geraldine Chaplin, it will be enjoyed by lovers of the silent screen and comedy.

F — EN

Thames Television — *THORN EMI*   **P**
TXH 90 1715 4/TVH 90 1715 2

Unknown Powers — Fil-Ent '79
Documentary/Parapsychology
01686   86 mins   C
V2, B, V

This film probes extrasensory occurrences such as stigmata, psychokinesis, and ectoplasm, as well as the psychic powers that allow people such as Jim Jones of the People's Temple to control the minds of other human beings.

S,A — EN

Don Como — *Intervision Video*   **H, P**
A-AE 0193

Unknown World — Fil-Ent '51
Science fiction
05639   73 mins   B/W
V2, B, V

Victor Kilian, Bruce Kellogg, Marilyn Nash, Jim Bannon

A science fiction thriller involving six men and one woman who embark upon a dangerous journey down the inside of an extinct volcano in Alaska, overcoming various natural disasters to finally reach a strange tropical island.

S,A — EN

Philip Yordan — *Video Unlimited*   **H, P**
009

Unmarried Woman, An — Fil-Ent '78
Drama
05648   119 mins   C
B, V

Jill Clayburgh, Alan Bates, Michael Murphy, Cliff Gorman, Pat Quinn, Kelly Bishop, Lisa Lucas, Linda Miller, directed by Paul Mazursky

This is the poignant story of a woman who believes she has a successful marriage but is devastated when her husband announces that he is in love with another woman and intends to leave. She picks up the pieces and rebuilds her life.

A — EN

Twentieth Century Fox — *CBS/Fox Video*   **P**
3A-136

Unseen, The — Fil-Ent '80
Horror
08884   91 mins   C
V2, B, V

Barbara Bach, Sydney Lassick, Stephen Furst

Three young women from a TV station are covering a story in a remote area of California. Before nightfall, two are horribly killed, leaving the third to come face to face with the terror.

BBFC:X — A — EN

Triune Films — *Video Programme Distributors*   **P**
Media 180

Unsuitable Job for a Woman, An — Fil-Ent '??
Suspense/Drama
07744   90 mins   C
B, V

Billie Whitelaw, Paul Freeman, Pippa Guard, directed by Chris Pettit

---

(For Explanation of codes, see USE GUIDE and KEY)

PALADIN VIDEO HOME ENTERTAINMENT GUIDE

The boss of a seedy London Detective Agency dies and his young secretary takes over only to find herself investigating the very mysterious death of the son of a wealthy businessman. She becomes involved in a web of sexuality and horror.
A — EN
unknown — Palace Video Ltd   P

Untamed Wheels—Agostini   Spo-Lei '80
Motorcycles
04420   30 mins   C
B, V
This show highlights the thrills and spills of the twelve-time world motorcycling champion.
F — EN
Unknown — VCL Video Services   P

Up a Tree   Fil-Ent '??
Comedy-Drama
06234   87 mins   C
B, V
Geraldine Chaplin, Louis de Funes, directed by Serge Korber
A couple driving along a cliff-top road at night hit a curve, by accident the accelerator is activated instead of the brake, the car hurtles down a steep drop. At sunrise the predicament is clear, the car is perched above a 300 ft drop in a tree top and out of sight of the road, the slightest movement is dangerous.
S,A — EN
Lira/Societe Novelle de Cinematographie — VCL Video Services   P
C133

Up in Smoke   Fil-Ent '82
Comedy
12052   86 mins   C
B, V
Cheech Marin, Tommy Chong, Stacy Keach, directed by Lou Adler
The story of two dope-taking hippies and their journey overland in a van made entirely from marijuana, followed by narcotic detectives and smugglers, is hilariously chronicled.
BBFC:18 — A — EN
Paramount — CIC Video   H, P
BEA 2081/VHA 2081

Up Pompeii   Fil-Ent '71
Comedy
04642   90 mins   C
B, V
Frankie Howerd, Patrick Cargill

A servant accidentally gains possession of a scroll containing a plot against Emperor Nero. The conspirators try every means possible to recover the scroll.
A — EN
EMI; Associated London Films — THORN EMI
H, P
TXC 90 0241 4/TVC 90 0241 2

Up the Sandbox   Fil-Ent '72
Comedy/Fantasy
12667   97 mins   C
V2, B, V
Barbra Streisand, Barbara Hershey, Cliff Richard, directed by Irvin Kershner
A bored and pregnant Manhattan housewife fantasises herself into a series of unlikely situations in this film.
BBFC:AA — C,A — EN
Warner Bros — Videomedia   P
0806

Uptown Saturday Night   Fil-Ent '74
Comedy
13014   100 mins   C
B, V
Bill Cosby, Harry Belafonte, directed by Sidney Poitier
Two men decide to go after some crooks themselves after having been ripped-off, which leads them into a succession of dangerous and often lunatic situations.
BBFC:AA — C,A — EN
Vernon Prods Inc; The First Artists Prod Co Ltd; Warner Bros Inc — Warner Home Video   P
61101

Uranium Conspiracy, The   Fil-Ent '78
Mystery/Adventure
06203   100 mins   C
B, V
Asaff Dayan, Janet Agren, Fabio Testi, Sigfried Rauch, directed by Menahem Golam
A story of the Atomic age. In 1968 a ship carrying 506 barrels of uranium disappears without trace; the world's leading nations keep strangely quiet, the consignment was enough to build thirty atomic bombs. In 1977 Secret Service heads gather for a hush-hush meeting, reports are coming in of an atomic reactor being built in the Sahara. The hunt for the truth and the uranium follows.
S,A — EN
Francesco Conti and Menahem Golam Prods — VCL Video Services   P
P201D

(For Explanation of codes, see USE GUIDE and KEY)

PALADIN VIDEO HOME ENTERTAINMENT GUIDE

Urban Cowboy   Fil-Ent '80
Drama
10109   125 mins   C
B, V

John Travolta, Debra Winger, Scott Glen, Madolyn Smith, directed by James Bridges
This film tells the story of the aspirations of a young man from the grasslands of West Texas who tries to maintain the traditions of the West in modern Houston.
BBFC:15 — *S,A* — *EN*
Paramount — *CIC Video*   **H, P**
BEA 2032/VHA 2032

Urgh! A Music War   Fil-Ent '8?
Music-Performance
07378   124 mins   C
V2, B, V, LV

This is a compilation of 34 bands performing live in concert including outrageous Punk, futuristic and modern Pop, Reggae and more. Filmed on location in London, New York, California and the south of France it features bands such as The Police, Toyah, Echo and the Bunnymen, John Otway, Gary Numan, XTC, Steel Pulse, Devo and UB40s.
F — *EN*
Unknown — *Guild Home Video*   **H, P, E**

US Golf on Video   Spo-Lei '84
Golf
12718   70 mins   C
B, V
4 pgms

There are four cassettes in this series. The first is a historical record tracing the tournament from 1895 to 1982, the remaining three concentrate on the US Opens from 1978/79, 1980/81 and 1982/83 respectively.
F — *EN*
Unknown — *Quadrant Video*   **H, P**
G5/GU1/GU2/GU3

Utopia   Fil-Ent '52
Comedy
06889   57 mins   B/W
V2, B, V

Stan Laurel, Oliver Hardy
In this film Stan and Ollie inherit a yacht and an island in the Pacific. They go and live there accompanied by a stateless refugee and young lady on the run from a jealous lover. They settle down to form their own republic; however, their Utopia soon falls to pieces when uranium is found. Original title: 'Atoll K.'
S,A — *EN*
Exploitation Films; Franco London Films — *European Video Company*   **P**

U2 'Under A Blood Red Sky'   Fil-Ent '83
Music-Performance
12960   61 mins   C
B, V

Recorded live at Red Rocks, the twelve tracks include 'Surrender', 'Sunday, Bloody Sunday', 'October', 'New Year's Day' and 'Party Girl'. The soundtrack is in stereo.
F — *EN*
Rick Wurpel; Doug Stewart — *Virgin Video*   **H, P**
VVD 045

V

Valachi Papers, The   Fil-Ent '72
Crime-Drama
07466   129 mins   C
B, V

Charles Bronson, Lino Ventura, Joseph Wiseman, Jill Ireland, Walter Chiari, Gerard O'Loughlin, Amedeo Nazzari, directed by Terence Young
This film is an explicit and bloody account of thirty years of gangland violence in America. Based on the life of Joseph Valachi as told to writer Peter Maas, it begins in the twenties with petty silk stealing and ends with heroin pushing in the sixties and his 'talking' before a crime commission, resulting in a 'contract' on his life. The film exposes the treachery, murder and revenge of big-time crime.
BBFC:X — *A* — *EN*
Dino De Laurentiis; Columbia Pictures — *THORN EMI*   **P**
TXB 90 0594 4/TVB 90 0594 2

Valdez the Half-Breed   Fil-Ent '73
Western
07455   94 mins   C
B, V

Charles Bronson, Marcel Bozzuffi, Jill Ireland, Fausto Tozzi, Melissa Chimenti, Eltore Manni, Vincent Van Patten, directed by John Sturges
In this film Valdez, a half-caste, is both despised and feared by white settlers who look for any excuse to gang up on him. His ambition is to gain respect by breeding the finest strain of horses. In spite of troubles with the sheriff and a Spanish rancher all seems well until the half-sister of his most dangerous enemy appears on the scene.
BBFC:A — *S,A* — *EN*
Dino De Laurentiis Corporation — *THORN EMI* **P**
TXB 90 0717 4/TVB 90 0717 2

(For Explanation of codes, see USE GUIDE and KEY)

PALADIN VIDEO HOME ENTERTAINMENT GUIDE

Valley of the Dolls   Fil-Ent '67
Drama
01764   122 mins   C
B, V
Barbara Perkins, Patty Duke, Sharon Tate, Susan Hayward, Lee Grant, Paul Burke, Martin Milner
The inside story of the Hollywood glamour set, based on Jacqueline Susann's novel.
BBFC:X — A — EN
20th Century Fox — *CBS/Fox Video*   **P**
3A-056

Vals, The   Fil-Ent '83
Comedy
10099   ? mins   C
B, V
Four Vals, suburban California kids, decide to raise money to save a boy's home using the most unconventional methods. After an attempt to win a Dino Ferrari on a horserace bet they try to rip-off the dope dealers. Enlisting their boyfriends as fake police squad officers who make a complete mess of it, they all end up being arrested by the real police.
BBFC:15 — S,A — EN
Unknown — *VideoSpace Ltd*   **P**

Vampira   Fil-Ent '74
Comedy-Drama
09944   84 mins   C
B, V
David Niven, Teresa Graves, Peter Bayliss, Jennie Linden, Linda Hayden, Nicky Henson, Bernard Bresslaw, Veronica Carlson
A vampire lures beauty contest winners to his castle, where their blood is urgently needed to revive his comatose countess.
BBFC:PG — F — EN
Columbia — *Rank Video Library*   **H, P**
2025 E

Vampire Bat   Fil-Ent '33
Horror
07631   60 mins   B/W
B, V
Melvyn Douglas, Fay Wray, Lionel Atwill, directed by Frank Strayer
A remote Bavarian village is terrorised by a series of mysterious murders. As all the victims are drained of blood the villagers kill a helpless village idiot who they think is responsible. However, the head of police is not convinced and, determined to catch the fiend, he sets himself up as bait.
S,A — EN
Majestic — *VCL Video Services*   **P**
0223G

Vampire Circus   Fil-Ent '71
Horror
05156   85 mins   C
B, V
Adrienne Corri, Thorley Walters, Laurence Payne, Elizabeth Seal
More macabre magic from Hammer as two young innocents walk into the world of a travelling circus in a 19th century Transylvanian style village.
BBFC:X — A — EN
Hammer Horror; 20th Century Fox — *Rank Video Library*   **H, P**
2010

Vampire Hookers   Fil-Ent '78
Comedy/Horror
09303   78 mins   C
B, V
John Carradine
In the graveyard of an exotic oriental port a group of vampire 'ladies' get their kicks from luring unsuspecting men into their clutches. After 137 years of celibacy they kill their victims with love. When three American Navy ratings stumble into this den of iniquity all hell breaks loose.
BBFC:18 — S,A — EN
Caprican Three — *Abacus Video*   **P**

Vampyres   Fil-Ent '76
Horror
05245   82 mins   C
B, V
Marianne Morris, Murray Brown, Sally Faulker, Anulka, Brian Deacon, Michael Byrne, Karl Lanchbury
Two lesbians are brutally slain, only to return from the grave as avenging dracularettes. With wine and sex they lure unsuspecting men to the lonely house in the woods where their murder took place.
BBFC:X — A — EN
Cambist — *Rank Video Library*   **H, P**
2008

Van Morrison in Ireland   Fil-Ent '??
Music-Performance
10137   60 mins   C
B, V
Van Morrison
This tape features one hour of Van Morrison performing his songs in his native Ireland. Songs include 'Moondance', 'Check It Out', 'Moonshine Whiskey', 'Tupelo Honey', 'Wavelength', 'Saint Dominic's Preview', 'Don't Look Back', 'I Been Working So Hard', 'Gloria' and 'Cyprus Avenue'.
S,A — EN
Unknown — *Palace Video Ltd*   **P**
NCI

PALADIN VIDEO HOME ENTERTAINMENT GUIDE

Vanishing Point   Fil-Ent '71
Drama
01763   98 mins   C
V2, B, V
Barry Newman, Cleavon Little, Gilda Texler, Dean Jagger
Ex-racer and former U.S. Marine sets out to deliver a supercharged car. Along the way, he eludes police, meets up with various characters, and finally faces a roadblock.
BBFC:AA — C,A — EN
20th Century Fox; Cupid Prod — *CBS/Fox Video*   **P**
3A-025

Vaulting Horse, The   Gen-Edu '8?
Learning disabilities/Animals
13561   20 mins   C
B, V
The physically disabled are shown how to vault on and off a horse on the lunge, a therapeutic exercise which requires a lot of determination.
A — I
Unknown — *TFI Leisure Ltd*   **H, P**

Velvet House, The   Fil-Ent '69
Horror
04346   91 mins   C
V2, B, V
A mother and daughter plot to kill the father.
BBFC:X — A — EN
London Cannon; Abacus — *Intervision Video*   **H**
A-A 0107

Velvet Smooth   Fil-Ent '??
Martial arts
06852   88 mins   C
V2, B, V
Johnnie Hill, Emerson Boozer
This film follows the adventures of a group of young ladies who are working together in a fight against crime. Not only do they know how to look after themselves, but they are all experts in Kung Fu and Karate.
S,A — EN
Unknown — *European Video Company*   **P**

Vendetta for the Saint   Fil-Ent '68
Crime-Drama
05952   94 mins   C
B, V
Roger Moore, Ian Hendry, Rosemary Dexter, George Pastell, directed by James O'Connolly
The Saint becomes involved with the Mafia after running into a man who claims to be a wealthy aristocrat. The Saint believes him to be a clerk who has been reported dead. The Police chief has asked The Saint to investigate Mafia activities as their leader is dying and a successor will be appointed. He befriends the 'aristocrat's' girlfriend, sister and niece, much to the impostor's annoyance. An attempt is made, and fails, on The Saint's life; the girlfriend warns him of more to come.
S,A — EN
ATV; ITC Entertainment — *Precision Video Ltd*   **P**
BITC 2069/VITC 2069

Vengeance   Fil-Ent '77
Drama
13408   105 mins   C
V2, B, V
Jason Miller, Lea Massari
A prisoner is on the run after seven years of unjust captivity. He is pursued by a guard and his dog and on the death of the guard, there follows a battle to the death between the dog and the man.
BBFC:18 — A — EN
Deva Cinematografica — *Intervision Video*   **H, P**
6550

Vengeance Is Mine   Fil-Ent '7?
Drama
09150   87 mins   C
V
Mickey Dolenz, James Ralston, Michael Anthony, Susan McCullough
Set in New Orleans, where the conflict between black and white, rich and poor are only just hidden, this film tells the story of family tension. The conflict comes out in the open leading to uncontrolled jealousy, love and hatred leading to violence and revenge.
S,A — EN
Unknown — *Cinema Indoors*   **H, P**

Vengeance of the Barbarians   Fil-Ent '76
Adventure/Drama
05688   89 mins   C
B, V
Tony Anthony, Lloyd Battista, directed by Ferdinando Baldi
Barbarian hoards have taken over a small Spanish Kingdom and overthrown the Princess. She persuades an American mercenary to help her regain her crown. His task is not an easy one but a renegade who is tortured and escapes returns as a one man army to wreak revenge on the Barbarians.
BBFC:A — S,A — EN
Unknown — *Derann Film Services*   **H, P**
GS711B/GS711

PALADIN VIDEO HOME ENTERTAINMENT GUIDE

Vengeance of the Zombies
Fil-Ent '??
Horror
08860　　84 mins　C
V2, B, V
Vic Winner, Mirta Miller
This film tells the story of a beautiful young woman. Her sister had died the previous day. In the small village where she had been buried, the grave was robbed, but the robbers meet their death, as a horrific shadow lurks near the grave.
BBFC:X — A — EN
Unknown — *Video Programme Distributors*　P
Canon 004

Vengeance with a Gun
Fil-Ent '7?
Western
07788　　85 mins　C
V2, B, V
Jim Reed, Martha Dovan
This is the tale of a man's vendetta against a town that wrongfully sent him to prison for murder.
S,A — EN
Unknown — *Fletcher Video*　H, P
AV611

Venom
Fil-Ent '74
Horror/Mystery
07598　　84 mins　C
V2, B, V
Simon Brent, Neda Aneric, Sheila Allen, Derek Newark, directed by Peter Sykes
While on a working holiday in the Tyrol an artist encounters a waif-like girl roaming the forest alone carrying a scar in the shape of a spider on her back. The mystery deepens when a mill owner is found dead in his own circular saw after setting a gang of thugs on the artist. The girl and the artist are chased into the forest where they meet her father, who has been experimenting with nerve gas on animals.
BBFC:X — A — EN
New Line Cinema — *Iver Film Services*　P
145

Venom
Fil-Ent '81
Drama/Suspense
08466　　89 mins　C
B, V
Sterling Hayden, Oliver Reed, Klaus Kinski, Sarah Miles, Nicol Williamson, Cornelia Sharpe, Susan George, Lance Holcomb
This film features the most deadliest snake in the world, a black mamba. It has been given to a young boy, the son of a big game hunter, instead of the harmless snake he was expecting. A group of men plan to kidnap the boy and in doing so the snake escapes. The snake begins to claim his victims in savage and unprovoked attacks.
BBFC:AA — C,A — EN
Martin Bregman Productions — *THORN EMI*　P
TXA 90 0846 4/TVA 90 0846 2

Venom—The Seventh Gate of Hell
Fil-Ent '84
Music-Performance
13129　　60 mins　C
B, V
This heavy metal band is recorded live from the Odeon, Hammersmith, and the tracks include 'Leave Me In Hell,' 'Countess Bathory,' 'In Nomine Stainus' and 'Bloodlust.' The recording is in stereo hi-fi.
S,A — EN
Unknown — *Guild Home Video*　P
041 0514/041 0512

Vertigo
Fil-Ent '58
Suspense/Drama
13627　　120 mins　C
B, V
James Stewart, Kim Novak, Tom Hellmore, directed by Alfred Hitchcock
This is thought to be one of Hitchcock's most brilliant films and centres around an ex-cop turned detective who is afraid of heights and is assigned to trail his friend's wife who is convinced she is about to commit suicide.
BBFC:PG — S,A — EN
Paramount — *CIC Video*　H, P
1130

Very Important Person
Fil-Ent '7?
Comedy
13738　　98 mins　B/W
B, V
James Robertson Justice, Leslie Philips, Stanley Baxter, Eric Sykes, Richard Nattis
When a VIP is shot down over Nazi-Germany during World War II a rescue plan is put into operation so that his true identity will not be revealed.
F — EN
Rank Films — *Rank Video Library*　H, P
1087A

Very Like a Whale
Fil-Ent '80
Drama
08749　　82 mins　C
B, V
Alan Bates, Gemma Jones, Ann Bell, Anna Cropper, Ian Hogg, Leslie Sands, directed by Alan Bridges

PALADIN VIDEO HOME ENTERTAINMENT GUIDE

A leading industrialist, recently knighted, has all the appearances of an international success, a luxurious apartment, a chauffeur-driven Rolls-Royce, a beautiful wife and a young daughter. However, it is not at all as it seems, as he suffers from a gross disillusionment with himself and is a very lonely man.
C,A — EN
Can-Am — *Precision Video Ltd* **P**
BITC2113/VITC2113

Vic Damone Show, The   Fil-Ent '7?
Variety
04373   60 mins   C
B, V, PH17, 3/4U
Vic Damone, Serendipity Singers
A musical variety show starring Vic Damone and featuring the Serendipity Singers.
F — EN
Unknown — *Vidpics International* **P**

Vice Squad   Fil-Ent '81
Crime-Drama
10078   95 mins   C
V2, B, V, LV
Season Hubley, Gary Swanson, Wings Houser
A story set in the city streets alive with hookers, pimps and hustlers with undercover vice cops patrolling their beat. This film explores the emotions of three people caught up in this corrupt jungle.
A — EN
Sandy Howard; Frank Capra Jr. — *Embassy Home Entertainment* **P**
2015

Victim   Fil-Ent '62
Crime-Drama
06917   96 mins   B/W
B, V
Dirk Bogarde, Sylvia Syms, Dennis Price
An eminent barrister puts a happy marriage and a brilliant career at risk by revealing his homosexual past. He does it to thwart blackmailers who have already caused the death of a friend. His quest to locate the vicious criminals leads him into the twilight world of well-known actors, hairdressers, photographers and the aristocracy.
BBFC:X — A — EN
Allied Film Makers — *Rank Video Library*
H, P
0069C

Victim, The   Fil-Ent '7?
Martial arts
09825   92 mins   C
B, V
A Kung Fu master finds himself threatened by the evil Lee Cho Wong. He is forced to break his oath never to fight Lee, or sacrifice his life. A devoted pupil, however, has another solution.
S,A — EN
Unknown — *Polygram Video* **H, P**
790 4554/790 4552

Victims   Fil-Ent '82
Suspense/Horror
09949   86 mins   C
V2, B, V
Lois Adams, Brandy Carson, Jerome Guardino
This is the horrific story of a psychopathic killer who, seeking help and unaware as to the roots of his compulsions, relives the traumas of his childhood and the unconscious memories of the past.
BBFC:X — A — EN
Unknown — *Video Unlimited* **H, P, E**
091

Victor and Maria   Chi-Juv '81
Cartoons
10003   60 mins   C
B, V
Animated, narrated by Una Stubbs
This tape features twelve adventures of Maria and her friendly bear Victor. He goes shopping for a new coat, goes rock climbing the hard way. He also sings, dances and juggles with his cousin Otto for Maria and her friend Matilda.
M,S — EN
King Rollo Films — *Longman Video* **P**
LGBE 5014/LGVH 5014

Video Cartoon Comic   Fil-Ent '??
Cartoons
05618   56 mins   C
V2, B, V
Animated
A compilation of cartoons including Popeye in 'Headless Horseman' and 'Little Black Sambo,' with 'Music Memories,' featuring 'Aladdin and the Wonderful Lamp' and 'Felix the Cat.'
F — EN
Unknown — *Go Video Ltd* **P**
GOK108

Video Comic   Chi-Juv '??
Variety/Cartoons
05619   60 mins   C
V2, B, V
Animated, Sylvia Bansor

(For Explanation of codes, see USE GUIDE and KEY)

PALADIN VIDEO HOME ENTERTAINMENT GUIDE

A compilation of animation, stories and songs for children. Includes music and songs with Charlie the Crow and Sam the Singer, quiz time with Doggerty the Dog, antics by Alphonse the Horse, stories read by Sylvia Bansor and a film 'The Boy and His Kite.'
PS,M — EN
Unknown — *Go Video Ltd*   **P**
GOK106

Video Rewind—The   Fil-Ent '84
Rolling Stones, Great
Video Hits
Music-Performance/Music video
12873   60 mins   C
B, V, LV
This tape features a collection of video clips including 'Undercover of the Night,' 'Too Much Blood,' 'Neighbours' and 'Brown Sugar,' with vintage Rolling Stones concert and interview footage.
BBFC:18 — *C,A — EN*
Unknown — *Vestron Video International*
P
11016

Video Rock Attack   Fil-Ent '8?
Music-Performance
09829   60 mins   C
B, V
This tape is a compilation of bands featuring Roxy Music, Dire Straits, Soft Cell, Dexy's Midnight Runners, Junior, Shakatak, Level 42, Steve Miller, Rainbow, King Crimson, Tears for Fears, Trio and Golden Earring.
F — EN
Unknown — *Polygram Video*   **H, P**
790 5334/790 5332

Videobook of British   Gen-Edu '81
Garden Birds
Birds/Documentary
04850   72 mins   C
V2, B, V, LV
In this programme David Attenborough looks at over seventy species of British garden birds.
F — ED
Keith Hopkins; Andy Finney — *BBC Video*
H, P
BBCV 1005

Videodrome   Fil-Ent '82
Drama
12038   90 mins   C
B, V
James Woods, Peter Dvorsky, Deborah Harry, Les Carlson, directed by David Cronenberg
This film is set in the near future when the technology of television has gone out of control. A series of sinister happenings occur at a cable television station which are investigated by a director and a lady radio personality.
BBFC:18 — *C,A — EN*
Universal — *CIC Video*   **H, P**
BEA 1077/VHA 1077

Videodrome   Fil-Ent '82
Science fiction
13609   90 mins   C
B, V
Deborah Harry, James Woods, Peter Dvorsky, Jack Creley, Sonja Smits, Les Carlson, directed by David Cronenberg
A chilling tale set in the near future about a television show that takes control and alters the lives of all its participants.
BBFC:18 — *A — EN*
Universal — *CIC Video*   **H, P**
1077

Videoslim to Lose Weight   Med-Sci '83
Physical fitness
13114   30 mins   C
B, V
Alf Fowles
This video combines soothing deep relaxation with visual messages aimed below the threshold of conscious perception resulting in weight-losses without dieting, drugs or other slimming aids.
A — I
Holiday Brothers Ltd. — *Holiday Brothers Ltd*
P

Videostars   Fil-Ent '81
Music-Performance
05316   80 mins   C
B, V
This tape includes twenty one hit tracks performed by twenty top artists and groups from 1977 to 1981, covering jazz-funk, disco, pop and new wave. Features Buggles, Kelly Marie, Hazel O'Connor, Korgis, Bad Manners, Japan, Linx, The Three Degrees, Genesis, Leo Sayer, Eddy Grant, 999, Imagination, Sky, Kiki Dee, Robert Palmer, Phil Collins, Depeche Mode, Barbara Jones and Dire Straits.
F — EN
Wienybuds Ltd — *THORN EMI*   **P**
TXE90 0550 4/TVE90 0550 2

Videotheque   Fil-Ent '82
Music-Performance
08574   84 mins   C
B, V
Directed by Stuart Orme

PALADIN VIDEO HOME ENTERTAINMENT GUIDE

This is a compilation of videos featuring 22 hits by original artists as Dexy's Midnight Runners, Roxy Music, Bow Wow Wow, John Cougar, Toni Basil, Elton John, Phil Collins and Dire Straits.
F — EN
Videotheque Ltd — THORN EMI   P
TXE 90 13044/TVE 90 1304 2

Vigilante   Fil-Ent '83
Drama/Suspense
12053   89 mins   C
V2, B, V
Robert Forster, Fred Williamson, Carol Lynley, Woody Strode, directed by William Lustig
This film depicts the aftermath of the collapse of law and order in an unprepared suburb of New York City. A man is driven to seek revenge for the murder of his young son and the disfiguration of his wife.
BBFC:18 — C,A — EN
Artists Releasing Corp — Intervision Video
H, P
A-A 0483

Vigilante Force   Fil-Ent '76
Drama
12675   86 mins   C
B, V
Kris Kristofferson, Jan-Michael Vincent, Victoria Principal, Bernadette Peters, directed by George Armitage
An embittered Vietnam war hero is hired to bring order to a violent oil boom town in California but he and his vigilante squad take over the community.
BBFC:18 — A — EN
Gene Corman — Warner Home Video   P
99425

Viking Invaders   Fil-Ent '??
War-Drama
07916   89 mins   C
V2, B, V
The only survivor of a bloody Viking battle, a small boy, vows that he will take revenge against those responsible for the brutal and savage massacre of his kinsmen.
S,A — EN
Unknown — Video Programme Distributors
P
Inter-Ocean—072

Villa Rides!   Fil-Ent '68
War-Drama
13280   117 mins   C
B, V
Robert Mitchum, Yul Brynner, Charles Bronson, Grazia Buccella, directed by Buzz Kulik

This story is set during the Mexican Revolution and tells how a gunrunner is won over to the Loyalist cause.
BBFC:15 — S,A — EN
Paramount — CIC Video   H, P
BEN 2091/VHN 2091

Village of the Giants   Fil-Ent '65
Adventure/Comedy
10072   77 mins   C
V2, B, V
Tommy Kirk, Johnny Crawford, Beau Bridges, Ronny Howard
Adapted from an H.G. Wells novel, this tells of a group of teenagers who discover a magic potion which makes anything grow. They take over a village, forcing the inhabitants to obey their commands.
F — EN
Bert I Gordon — Embassy Home Entertainment   P
2102

Villain   Fil-Ent '81
Crime-Drama
05881   91 mins   C
B, V
Richard Burton, Ian McShane, Nigel Davenport, Donald Sinden, Fiona Lewis, T P McKenna
The story of a contemptuous East End gangster and a robbery which goes wrong.
BBFC:X — A — EN
Alan Ladd Jr; Jay Kanker — THORN EMI
P
TXC 90 0261 4/TVC 90 0261 2

Violation of the Bitch, The   Fil-Ent '??
Drama
08628   85 mins   C
V2, B, V
Patricia Granada, Lydia Zuazu, Rafael Machado
Whilst travelling to England, a couple leave an orphan who is in their charge with an artist in a remote Spanish cottage. When a stranger tries to seduce the girl, the attempt leads to murder.
A — EN
Unknown — Hokushin Audio Visual Ltd
P
VM 59

Violent Breed, The   Fil-Ent '7?
Western
02121   85 mins   C
V2, B, V

(For Explanation of codes, see USE GUIDE and KEY)   699

PALADIN VIDEO HOME ENTERTAINMENT GUIDE

Violence explodes when Keoma's father is murdered and the Indian half-breed learns that his half-brothers, who detest him, are part of a notorious gang.
C,A — EN
Italian — Hokushin Audio Visual Ltd   P
VM-33

Violent Enemy, The Fil-Ent '68
Suspense/Drama
09021   94 mins   C
V2, B, V
Tom Bell, Susan Hampshire, Ed Begley
A group of IRA men plot to destroy a British factory in a desperate gesture of Irish independence. An imprisoned IRA leader is fighting for freedom, and shows the pathetic helplessness of the ordinary people of Ulster, who wish he'd never escaped.
C,A — EN
United Artists — Intervision Video   H, P
AA 0446

Violent Streets Fil-Ent '81
Drama
13016   122 mins   C
B, V
James Caan, Tuesday Weld, Willie Nelson, directed by Michael Mann
A highly honorable man who just happens to be a thief with a prison record foolishly agrees to join forces with a godfather type figure and finds himself caught between reality and his idealism.
BBFC:X — A — EN
United Artists — Warner Home Video   P
99294

Virgin and the Gypsy, The Fil-Ent '70
Romance/Drama
07651   95 mins   C
B, V
Franco Nero, Joanne Shimkus, Honor Blackman
Based on the controversial novel by D. H. Lawrence, this story follows the life of a young virgin who returns home to a claustrophobic Rectory in the North of England from a French finishing school. Finding the rebel in her awakened, she finds a man to satisfy her desires—the Gypsy, a stark, brooding character, a law unto himself and a man without conscience.
S,A — EN
Chevron Pictures — VCL Video Services   P
C198C

Virgin Campus Fil-Ent '8?
Drama/Romance
08828   76 mins   C
B, V
Nastassia Kinski, Gerry Sundquist
This film tells of a finishing school in Switzerland. The pupils are more interested in learning the facts of life than improving their education. It is based on the novel 'The Passion Flower Hotel' by Rosalind Erskine.
C,A — EN
Unknown — VCL Video Services   P
P282D

Virgin of Bali, The Fil-Ent '??
Adventure
06126   94 mins   C
V2, B, V
George Ardisson, Lea Lander, Pedro Sanchez, Haydee Politoff
A man, disillusioned by Western civilization, seeks peace in a South Sea Island. Among the gold-hunters evil exists, but the man's dream of a virgin island is too strong to resist.
S,A — EN
Unknown — Video Programme Distributors   P
Cinehollywood—V1740

Virgin Spring, The Fil-Ent '59
Drama
08668   88 mins   B/W
B, V
Max von Sydow, Birgitta Pettersson, Birgitta Valberg, directed by Ingmar Bergman
This story is based on a medieval ballad, and tells of a farmer's daughter who is raped and killed whilst riding to church. It continues with her father who wreaks a terrible vengeance on her murders. It is subtitled in English.
GA — EN
Svensk Filmindustri — Longman Video   P
LGBE 5009/LGVH 5009

Virgin Witch Fil-Ent '72
Horror
02494   93 mins   C
V2, B, V
Tension packed story of two lovely girls who become models in London and their first assignment is at a luxurious country house. Almost immediately after their arrival the girls are plunged into the depravity and orgiastic ritual of black witchcraft.
BBFC:X — A — EN
Joseph Brenner — Intervision Video   H
A-A 0077

Virginity Fil-Ent '76
Crime-Drama
07351   ? mins   C
B, V

PALADIN VIDEO HOME ENTERTAINMENT GUIDE

Vittorio Gassman, Ornella Muti
An intriguing plot of the Mafia's manoeuvring.
S,A — EN
Unknown — Precision Video Ltd P
BITC 2103/VITC 2103

Visa 3—From the Himalayas to Keilder-Action All the Way Spo-Lei '8?
Automobiles-Racing
09029 60 mins C (PAL, NTSC)
B, V
This tape features action from both the Himalayan and Lombard RAC Rallies. From the flat dusty plains north of Delhi to the snow of the high Himalayas, filmed from the ground and in the air, this film covers over 20 stages and includes candid interviews with the competitors.
F — EN
Motorsport Video Productions Ltd — Vintage Television Ltd H, P, E

Visa 4—The Best of Rallying on Video in 1982 Spo-Lei '82
Automobiles-Racing
09030 60 mins C
B, V
This tape features extracts from the 1982 World Championship events, including Monte Carlo, Sweden, Portugal, Acropolis, 1000 Lakes and RAC, as well as the UK home internationals and the Himalayan rally.
F — EN
Motorsport Video Productions Ltd — Vintage Television Ltd H, P, E

Visit With Maurice Chevalier, A Fil-Ent '7?
Variety
04364 60 mins C
B, V, PH17, 3/4U
Maurice Chevalier
A variety show starring Maurice Chevalier.
F — EN
Unknown — Vidpics International P

Visiting Hours Fil-Ent '82
Suspense
12008 105 mins C
B, V
Lee Grant, William Shatner, Linda Purl, directed by Jean Claude Lord
A psychopath is on the loose and will stop at nothing to kill the woman journalist he is terrorizing.
C,A — EN
20th Century Fox — CBS/Fox Video P
1171

Vital River, The Gen-Edu '8?
Ecology and environment/Wildlife
09101 26 mins C
B, V
This film looks at the worrying effects of some of the river management practices needed to meet the demands of modern life, which is very damaging to wildlife. However, it does suggest that with proper planning, the needs of man and wildlife can both be met.
BISFA '82: Silver Award S,A — ED
Royal Society for the Protection of Birds — Royal Society for the Protection of Birds H, P

Viva Knievel Fil-Ent '77
Drama
13166 100 mins C
B, V
Evel Knievel, Gene Kelly, Lauren Hutton, directed by Gordon Douglas
An irrepressible stunt genius signs up for a Mexican tour and finds himself unwittingly involved with sabotage, drug smuggling and syndicate hitmen.
BBFC:A — A — EN
Unknown — Warner Home Video P
61283

Viva Max Fil-Ent '69
Comedy
09204 93 mins C
B, V
Peter Ustinov, Pamela Tiffin, Jonathan Winters
A modern-day Mexican General and his men make their way across the Alamo.
F — EN
Montmorency Prods — Video Form Pictures H, P
DIP 1

Vivaldi's—The Four Seasons Fil-Ent '??
Music-Performance
07354 ? mins C
B, V
Filmed in the famous Pump Room in Cheltenham, Vivaldi's 'Four Seasons' is performed by The Montpellier Strings with soloist Raymond Cohen and readings by Michael Hordern.
F — EN
Unknown — Precision Video Ltd P
BMPV 2562/VMPV 2562

Voices Fil-Ent '73
Mystery/Suspense
07647 86 mins C
B, V

(For Explanation of codes, see USE GUIDE and KEY)

PALADIN VIDEO HOME ENTERTAINMENT GUIDE

David Hemmings, Gayle Hunnicutt, directed by Kevin Billington
A young couple find themselves fog-bound in a creaking Georgian country house. When the wife hears strange noises her disbelieving husband argues with her and they quarrel. Hysterical, the wife runs from the house into the fog. Suddenly her husband's doubts vanish as he too hears the noises and thinks he sees sinister shadowy figures.
S,A — EN
Hemdale — *VCL Video Services*   **P**
C212C

Voltron—Defender of the Universe, In the Castle of Lions
Chl-Juv '84
Science fiction
13679   77 mins   C
B, V
Animated
The evil King Zarcon shatters the peace of the united planets of the Galaxy Alliance and the evil forces of the planet Doom come into conflict with a team of young space explorers and the Legendary Voltron.
BBFC:U — F — EN
Unknown — *CBS/Fox Video*   **P**
6822

Voltron—Defender Of The Universe In The Invasion Of The Robeasts
Chl-Juv '84
Science fiction
13667   77 mins   C
B, V
Animated
In this episode the Drule's Empire Fleet, led by the evil Hazar, are forced to use their ultimate weapon, the Robeasts, to try to bring mighty Voltron to his knees.
BBFC:U — F — EN
Unknown — *CBS/Fox Video*   **P**
6823

Voltron—Defender of the Universe
Chl-Juv '84
Science fiction
13675   77 mins   C
B, V
Animated
The Galaxy Alliance is facing doom as their resources start to run out and a force is sent out to locate new planets suitable for settlement but when opposed by the deadly strength of the Drule Empire they combine to form the superobot Voltron.
BBFC:U — F — EN
Unknown — *CBS/Fox Video*   **P**
6810

Voltron—Defender Of The Universe In The Battle Of The Plant Arus
Chl-Juv '84
Cartoons
13654   77 mins   C
B, V
Animated
Intent on the destruction of the Voltron force, the evil King Zarkon and his wicked ally 'Hagar the Witch', try everything in their power to defeat the mighty Voltron once and for all.
BBFC:U — F — EN
Unknown — *CBS/Fox Video*   **P**
6824

Von Ryan's Express
Fil-Ent '65
War-Drama
01015   117 mins   C
B, V
Frank Sinatra, Trevor Howard, Brad Dexter, Edward Mulhare, directed by Mark Robson
American Air Force colonel leads a group of prisoners of war in taking control of a freight train.
F — EN
20th Century Fox; Saul David — *CBS/Fox Video*   **P**
3A-024

Voyage of the Damned
Fil-Ent '76
Drama
02038   178 mins   C
B, V
Max von Sydow, Faye Dunaway, Oskar Werner, Orson Welles, James Mason, Lee Grant, Katherine Ross
In 1939, 937 German Jewish refugees were permitted by the Nazis to leave their native land aboard the luxury linner, S.S. St. Louis. They believed they were receiving asylum in Cuba from the persecution at the hands of the Nazis.
S,A — EN
Robert Fryer — *Precision Video Ltd*   **P**
BITC 3033/VITC 3033

Voyage Round My Father, A
Fil-Ent '82
Biographical/Drama
12903   81 mins   C
B, V
Laurence Oliver, Alan Bates, Jane Asher, Elizabeth Sellars
Taken from John Mortimer's play, this is an affectionate anecdotal tribute to his own father, and through him to all fathers.
S,A — EN
Thames Video — *THORN EMI*   **P**
TXJ 90 17134/TVJ 90 17132

PALADIN VIDEO HOME ENTERTAINMENT GUIDE

Voyage to the Bottom of the Sea Fil-Ent '61
Science fiction
01026   105 mins   C
B, V
Walter Pidgeon, Joan Fontaine, Barbara Eden, Robert Sterling, Michael Ansara, Frankie Avalon
When an experimental atomic submarine discovers that Van Allen Belt radiation circling the earth has been burning for days, it speeds to the Marianas to explode the Belt into outer space.
F — EN
20th Century Fox — CBS/Fox Video   **P**
3A-026

VTV Magazine No. 1   Spo-Lei '79
Automobiles
04394   60 mins   C
B, V
This programme presents in separate segments the history of the Jaguar, how to rebuild a 1926 Citroen Tourer, the 1979 Jaguar Drivers Club race meeting at Silverstone, and the VSCC Pomeroy Trophy Competition of 1979.
F — EN
Vintage Television — *Vintage Television Ltd*
H, P, E

VTV Magazine No. 2   Spo-Lei '79
Automobiles
04395   60 mins   C
B, V
Five segments on this tape feature the Vintage Sports Car Club Race at Silverstone, interviews with Peter Morley and David Llewellyn, an update on the Citroen, a discussion about magnetos, and the BTRDA Celebrity Trial to aid the Gunnar Neilson Cancer Fund.
F — EN
Vintage Television — *Vintage Television Ltd*
H, P, E

VTV Magazine No. 3   Spo-Lei '79
Automobiles
04396   60 mins   C
B, V
A collection of automobile segments including the Lincolnshire Special State Rally, the 1979 Yorkshire Sports Car Club Hill Climb, the history of the Jaguar, and the Foden Historic Commercial Vehicle run from London to Brighton.
F — EN
Vintage Television — *Vintage Television Ltd*
H, P, E

VTV Magazine No. 4   Spo-Lei '79
Automobiles
04397   60 mins   C
B, V
Several short segments about auto racing in Britain, including the International Classic Car Weekend at Denington, the National Car Concourse, the 1979 Grand Transport Extravaganza at Crich, and the 1979 Yorkshire Evening Post Trans-Pennine Commercial Vehicle Run.
F — EN
Vintage Television — *Vintage Television Ltd*
H, P, E

W

Wackiest Wagon Train in the West, The   Fil-Ent '77
Comedy/Western
07926   86 mins   C
V2, B, V
Bob Denver, Forrest Tucker, Ivor Francis, Lynn Wood, Jeannine Riley, Lori Saunders
A wagon train master is stuck with a useless assistant as they guide a party of five characters across a trouble-laden West in a train consisting of one wagon and an elegant coach.
S,A — EN
Topar Films — *Video Programme Distributors*
P
Media—150

Wacky and Packy   Fil-Ent '83
Cartoons
12181   82 mins   C
B, V
Animated
Wacky the caveman and Packy the mammoth have a problem; they have been thrown forward in time to the twentieth century, they have enormous appetites and are constantly in search of food and cause havoc wherever they go.
F — EN
Filmation Associates — *Select Video Limited*
P
3623/43

Wacky Taxi   Fil-Ent '??
Comedy
01192   87 mins   C
V2, B, V
John Astin, Frank Sinatra Jr., Jackie Gayle, Allan Sherman

(For Explanation of codes, see USE GUIDE and KEY)   703

PALADIN VIDEO HOME ENTERTAINMENT GUIDE

The hilarious story of an unemployed man who buys an old jalopy and sets out to become a taxi driver.
F — EN
Unknown — *Intervision Video* **H, P**
A-AE 0198

Wacky World of Mother Goose, The Chi-Juv '66
Cartoons
12163   79 mins   C
V2, B, V
Animated
Mother Goose goes to visit her sister on the other side of the moon and finds lots of strange goings on in the land of Old King Cole.
PS,1 — EN
Avoc Embassy; Arthur Rankin Jr — *Embassy Home Entertainment* **P**
2084

Wagonmaster/Double Dynamite Fil-Ent '5?
Western/Comedy
05668   160 mins   B/W
B, V
Ben Johnson, Ward Bond, Harry Carey Jr, Joanne Dru, Jane Darwell, directed by John Ford, Frank Sinatra, Groucho Marx, Jane Russell, Don McGuire, directed by Irving Cummings
Two films are featured on one cassette. 'Wagonmaster' (Black/White, 82 mins, 1951) is the story of a wagon trains journey through the wilds, encountering a travelling medicine show, outlaws and Indians. 'Double Dynamite' (Black/White, 78 mins, 1952) is a yarn about a bank clerk who saves a gangster's life and his reward is a large sum of cash. He is unable to enjoy it because the bank where he works has just been robbed.
F — EN
RKO — *Kingston Video* **H, P**
KV44

Wait Till Your Mother Gets Home Fil-Ent '83
Comedy
12172   90 mins   C
B, V
Paul Michael Glaser, Dee Wallace, directed by Bill Persky
This is a true story of an American football coach who spends a summer as a house-husband, when his wife returns to work. All too soon he begins to wilt, while his wife blossoms and enjoys her new found freedom.
S,A — EN
NBC International — *Select Video Limited* **P**
3123/43

Waitress Fil-Ent '82
Comedy-Drama
09170   78 mins   C
V
Jim Harris, Carol Drake, Carol Bever
Set around a posh New York restaurant, where a group of macho characters find jobs. There is a menu of beautiful waitresses, who do much more than just serve their customers, with a mad Russian chef and a crazy salad man.
A — EN
Troma Inc — *Entertainment in Video* **H, P**

Waldo Kitty Fil-Ent '83
Cartoons
12183   69 mins   C
B, V
Animated
Waldo Kitty may look like an ordinary cat but in his dreams he becomes Catman, fighter of crime, or Catzan, King of the Jungle. His greatest enemy is the bulldog next door.
F — EN
Filmation Associates — *Select Video Limited* **P**
3610/43

Waldorf Travers Fil-Ent '80
Music-Performance
04405   30 mins   C
B, V
This pair of young singers perform songs from their recent album 'Night Blindness.'
F — EN
VCL — *VCL Video Services* **P**

Wales in Trust Gen-Edu '8?
Wales
13575   23 mins   C
V, 3/4U
HRH The Prince of Wales comperes this comprehensive film on the work of the National Trust in Wales where it now protects 90,000 acres of soil.
F — ED
Roderic Rees — *TFI Leisure Ltd* **H**

Walk a Crooked Path Fil-Ent '??
Mystery/Drama
05634   80 mins   C
V2, B, V
Tenniel Evans, Faith Brook, Robert Powell

PALADIN VIDEO HOME ENTERTAINMENT GUIDE

What appears to be an accident at an English public school unravels quickly to reveal a complex series of relationships culminating in a deadly calculated plot, involving a school master, his wife, a pupil and a housekeeper.
BBFC:A — S,A — EN
Unknown — *Video Unlimited* H, P
007

Walking The Edge   Fil-Ent '83
Drama
13657   90 mins   C
B, V
Nancy Kwan, Robert Forster, Joe Spinell, directed by Norbert Meisel
A heartbroken housewife seeks a bitter revenge on the mob who gunned down her husband and family and left her as the only survivor.
BBFC:18 — A — EN
Sergei Goncharoff — *CBS/Fox Video*   P
6813

Wall, The   Fil-Ent '82
Musical/Cartoons
08483   91 mins   C
B, V
Bob Geldof, directed by Alan Parker
This film contains both live action and animation and tells the story of a Rock 'n Roll superstar, played by Bob Geldof, whose life is one of increasing isolation, symbolised by the defensive wall he builds around himself. His story is told from early infancy, through his schooling, to stardom and eventual madness. Features music by Pink Floyd, written by Roger Waters and animated by Gerald Scarfe.
S,A — EN
Unknown — *THORN EMI*   P
TXA 90 1431 4/TVA 90 1431 2

Walls of Sin   Fil-Ent '??
Drama
06127   100 mins   C
V2, B, V
Peter Lawford, Francoise Prevost, Bernard Blier
A young man returns home after four years studying abroad. He is disgusted by the squalid changes in his former world and the decadence of his family and friends. He takes justice into his own hands and within forty-eight hours all is over.
S,A — EN
Unknown — *Video Programme Distributors*   P
Cinehollywood—V1710

Wanderers, The   Fil-Ent '79
Drama
01964   112 mins   C
B, V

Ken Wahl, Karen Allen
Set in 1963, this film follows the struggles of a group of New York City street gangs as they fight for supremacy.
C,A — EN
Warner Bros; Orion — *VCL Video Services*   P

Wanted Baby Sitter   Fil-Ent '75
Drama
08692   97 mins   C
V2, B, V
Maria Schneider, Sydne Rome, Robert Vaughn
This film tells the story of Ann, an aspiring actress who after a tragic accident is left disfigured, her career at an end. Through this accident she meets a young art student, surviving on the money she earns from babysitting. Ann irrationally blames her ex-lover for her misfortune and plans her revenge whilst also framing the student. A terrifying weekend follows.
BBFC:X — A — EN
Unknown — *Derann Film Services*   P
FCV 602

War in Concert   Fil-Ent '??
Music-Performance
06293   58 mins   C
V2, B, V
This film features the band War in concert; songs include 'The World is a Ghetto,' 'Cisco Kid,' 'All Bay Music,' 'Low Rider,' 'Why can't we be friends' and 'I'll take care of you.'
F — EN
Unknown — *World of Video 2000*   H, P
MV234

War of the Monsters   Fil-Ent '66
Science fiction
02392   89 mins   C
B, V
Minoru Takashima, Hiroshi Ishikawa
A number of incidents leads to the discovery of alien invaders from Space M, threatening the safety of the world.
S,A — EN
Daiei Motion Picture Company — *Derann Film Services*   H, P
DV 116B/DV 116

War of the Wizards   Fil-Ent '??
Adventure/Fantasy
10191   92 mins   C
B, V
Richard Kiel, Betty Noonan, Charles Lang
Set in the mystical Far East this follows the quest of Ty to regain possession of his magical artifacts stolen by the Flower Fox. Her sanctuary on a remote island is guarded by

(For Explanation of codes, see USE GUIDE and KEY)

705

PALADIN VIDEO HOME ENTERTAINMENT GUIDE

Grasshoper. Ty risks his life against a giant Phoenix, a massive tidal wave and an enormous stone warrior to stop her controlling the universe.
BBFC:15 — S,A — EN
Unknown — Video Form Pictures   H, P
MGS 25

War of the Worlds, The   Fil-Ent '54
Science fiction
05321   85 mins   C
B, V
Gene Barry, Ann Robinson, Les Tremayne, Jack Kruschen
An adaptation of H.G. Wells' novel of the invasion of Earth by Martians. The original story has been updated to include the atom bomb. The swan shaped Martian machines tick and hiss menacingly as they glide along, leaving a wake of destruction and panic.
Academy Awards '53: Best Special Effects.
S,A — EN
Paramount — CIC Video   H, P
BEA2018/VHA2018

Wargames   Fil-Ent '83
Adventure
12993   109 mins   C
B, V
Matthew Broderick, Ally Sheedy, Dabney Coleman, John Wood, directed by John Badham
A teenage computer genius connects his home computer up with the Defense Department's computer and triggers off a countdown to a third world war.
BBFC:PG — S,A — EN
Harold Schneider — Warner Home Video
P
99405

Warkill   Fil-Ent '68
War-Drama
05730   90 mins   C
V2, B, V
George Montgomery, Tom Drake
An American patrol in the Philippines is joined by an idealistic journalist who has just written a tribute to the Colonel of the patrol. As the patrol defends a hospital they are outnumbered by the Japanese; the Colonel has to decide whether to stick to his public image and fight, or run.
S,A — EN
Unknown — Video Unlimited   H, P

Warlock Moon   Fil-Ent '82
Horror
09308   90 mins   C
V2, B, V
Laurie Walters, Joe Spano
A young couple, after stumbling across an old abandoned health spa, are hunted by a bizarre axe-swinging man-animal said to come from a witches' coven.
A — EN
Unknown — ADB Video Distribution   P

Warlords of Atlantis   Fil-Ent '75
Science fiction/Adventure
05888   93 mins   C
B, V
Doug McClure, Peter Gilmore, Cyd Charisse, Daniel Massey, directed by Kevin Connor
The wicked leader of an ailing Martian colony under the Atlantic plans to conquer the world.
F — EN
John Dark — THORN EMI   P
TXB 90 0309 4/TVB 90 0309 2

Warm December, A   Fil-Ent '73
Drama/Romance
09472   103 mins   C
B, V
Sidney Poitier, Esther Anderson
This film tells the story of Catherine, a beautiful and clever girl, but incurably ill. She falls in love with a mysterious American stranger who comes into her life by chance and remains there with persistence.
BBFC:PG — F — EN
Veroon Prod. Ltd. — Guild Home Video
H, P, E

Warning, The   Fil-Ent '80
Adventure
02448   96 mins   C
V2, B, V, LV
Jack Palance, Martin Landau, Tarah Nutter, Cameron Mitchell, Christopher Nelson
Aliens from another galaxy land on earth and begin a murderous rampage against all humankind.
BBFC:X — A — EN
Unknown — Guild Home Video   H, P

Warrior of the Lost World   Fil-Ent '83
Fantasy/Drama
13703   90 mins   C
B, V
Robert Ginty, Persis Khambatta, Donald Pleasence, directed by David Worth
Set generations after the radiation wars and the collapse of nations, the rider of a supersonic speedcycle goes to the help of a beautiful girl battling against an evil force.
BBFC:18 — C,A — EN
Roberto Bessi; Frank E Hildebrand — THORN EMI   P
90 2574

PALADIN VIDEO HOME ENTERTAINMENT GUIDE

Warriors, The — Fil-Ent '79
Drama
01242 94 mins C
V2, B, V
Michael Beck, James Remer, Deborah Van Valkenburgh
A contemporary action story about a war between New York City street gangs that rages from Coney Island to the Bronx.
C,A — EN
Paramount — CIC Video H, P
CRA 2007/BEA 2007/VHA 2007

Washington Affair, The — Fil-Ent '82
Drama
09207 90 mins C
B, V
Tom Selleck, Barry Sullivan, Carol Lynley
A respectable airline executive is driven to blackmail by greed and desperation. A young and promising politician is the victim.
S,A — EN
Unknown — Video Form Pictures H, P
MGD 11

Watched — Fil-Ent '73
Drama
12872 93 mins C
B, V
Stacy Keach, directed by John Parsons
A man strikes back with insane violence when he discovers that all his actions are being mysteriously monitored.
BBFC:18 — A — EN
Unknown — Vestron Video International
P
14119

Watcher in the Woods, The — Fil-Ent '81
Suspense/Mystery
12564 83 mins C
B, V
Bette Davis, David McCallum
When an American composer moves to England to conduct his own opera, dark secrets from the past emerge as forces of the dark come to light.
F — EN
Walt Disney Productions — Rank Video Library
H
068

Water Babies, The — Fil-Ent '78
Adventure/Cartoons
08577 88 mins C
B, V
James Mason, Billie Whitelaw, Bernard Cribbins, Joan Greenwood, David Tomlinson, Paul Luty, Tommy Pender, Samantha Gates, directed by Lionel Jeffries
This tells the well-known, 19th-century story of the chimney sweep who discovers a mysterious underworld kingdom. It contains live action and animation. When a boy and his dog dive into a pool to escape from his cruel master, they become cartoon characters in a land where fish speak and evil spirits hide.
BBFC:U — F — EN
Ariadne Films — THORN EMI P
TXC 90 1007 4/TVC 90 1007 2

Water Babies — Spo-Lei '82
Sports/Infants
13878 20 mins C
B, V
This cassette demonstrates how very young children can be introduced more easily and happily to the water with an emphasis on safety precautions.
A — ED
Unknown — TFI Leisure Ltd H, P

Water Free — Gen-Edu '8?
Learning disabilities
13529 35 mins C
B, V
This film shows the methods and techniques by which disabled people can enjoy the support and freedom of movement that only water can give.
C,A — SE
Unknown — TFI Leisure Ltd H, P

Water Safety — Spo-Lei '8?
Boating/Safety education
13558 28 mins C
B, V
This film considers the care and maintenance of craft and equipment and the techniques of accident prevention in the water.
F — ED
Unknown — TFI Leisure Ltd H, P

Waterhole 3 — Fil-Ent '67
Comedy/Adventure
13294 92 mins C
B, V
Claude Atkins, Roy Jenson, James Coburn, Carroll O'Connor, Joan Blondell, directed by William Graham

(For Explanation of codes, see USE GUIDE and KEY)

PALADIN VIDEO HOME ENTERTAINMENT GUIDE

A gambler and adventurer sets out to steal a fortune in gold bullion that has been buried in a desert waterhole pursued by the local sheriff.
BBFC:15 — S,A — EN
Paramount — CIC Video   H, P
BEN 2087/VHN 2087

Watership Down   Fil-Ent '78
Cartoons/Fantasy
07472   88 mins   C
B, V
Animated, directed by Martin Rosen
This animated saga of survival is based on Richard Adams' best-selling modern classic. It tells the story of a warren of rabbits who leave home to find a new burrow on Watership Down. They encounter some menacing obstacles, from warring black rats to mined carrot fields, and have to fight a war with a rabbit dictator of a slave burrow. John Hurt, Sir Ralph Richardson, Richard Briers and Ray Kinnear provide some of the voices, with songs written by Mike Batt and sung by Art Garfunkel.
BBFC:U — F — EN
Nepenthe Productions — THORN EMI   P
TXA 90 0682 4/TVA 90 0682 2

Wavelength   Fil-Ent '82
Science fiction
12188   90 mins   C
V2, B, V
Robert Carradine, Cherie Currie, Keenan Wynn
Two weeks ago they landed on Earth. Now beneath a major American city the experiments begin and so do their cries for help.
BBFC:15 — S,A — EN
James M Rosenfield — Medusa Communications Ltd   H, P

Way of the Black Dragon   Fil-Ent '7?
Adventure/Martial arts
04607   88 mins   C
V2, B, V
A gang war breaks out between drug traffickers and white slavers in Indo China. Bill, an American kung-fu expert is sent by Interpol to investigate. He frees a pretty Thai girl, forced to act as a drug courier, when she is captured by a rival gang. Bill then entraps the big boss and brings the gang to justice.
C,A — EN
Unknown — Video Programme Distributors   P
Inter-Ocean—048

Way of the Dragon, The   Fil-Ent '74
Adventure/Martial arts
08063   88 mins   C
V2, B, V
Bruce Lee
In this Bruce Lee film he gets involved with the city gangsters in Rome.
BBFC:X — A — EN
Bryanston — Rank Video Library   H, P
0072 D

Way We Were, The   Fil-Ent '73
Romance/Drama
13076   113 mins   C
B, V
Robert Redford, Barbra Streisand, directed by Sydney Pollack
Set in the period between the thirties and the fifties, this is the story of the romance and marriage of a writer and a left-wing activist and their eventual divorce when her political ideals get in the way of their future.
C,A — EN
Ray Stark — RCA/Columbia Pictures Video UK   H, P
10152

We Dive at Dawn   Fil-Ent '43
War-Drama
12737   97 mins   B/W
B, V
John Mills, Eric Portman, directed by Anthony Asquith
The story of the British submarine 'Sea Tiger' and its mission to track down and sink the German warship Brandenburg which can only be achieved by having first faked its own sinking.
BBFC:U — C,A — EN
Edward Black — Rank Video Library   H, P
0196 E

We of The Never Never   Fil-Ent '82
Adventure/Drama
13770   127 mins   C
B, V
Angela Punch McGregor, directed by Igor Auzins
This is the story of a woman who sacrifices the comforts of civilization to be with her husband on a cattle ranch in the outback of Australia. It is based on a true story and set at the turn of the century.
BBFC:U — F — EN
Unknown — Odyssey Video   H, P
6990

Weapons of Death   Fil-Ent '7?
Suspense
04291   96 mins   C
V2, B, V
Henry Silva, Leonard Mann

PALADIN VIDEO HOME ENTERTAINMENT GUIDE

In his long and relentless fight against organised crime in Naples, Inspector Belli uncovers overwhelming evidence against Mafia boss Santoro. During an escape attempt Santoro is killed, temporarily leaving the underworld leaderless but other men are only too ready to step up and replace him, thus obliging Inspector Belli to fight on.
C,A — EN
Unknown — Video Programme Distributors
P
Inter-Ocean—006

Wedding Party, The   Fil-Ent '69
Comedy
08911   88 mins   C
V2, B, V
Jill Clayburgh, Robert DeNiro, directed by Brian DePalma
This is a comical look at a wedding in America.
S,A — EN
Ajay Films — Video Programme Distributors
P
Replay 1022

Wedge, The   How-Ins '80
Beauty
02052   50 mins   C
B, V
Kevin Murphy
The first in the planned 'Hair Tek Ladies' Hairdressing' series.
C,A — I
Hair Tek Video — VideoSpace Ltd   H, P

Weekend Murders   Fil-Ent '72
Mystery/Comedy
10164   94 mins   C
B, V
Lance Percival, Anna Moffo
An English family gather at the family home to hear the reading of the father's will. The main beneficiary is the favoured daughter and this starts of a chain of murders, first the butler and after that members of the family. A police inspector is called in to help solve the crimes.
BBFC:AA — C,A — EN
MGM; Jupiter Generale Cinematografica
Prod — MGM/UA Home Video   P
UMB 10266/UMV 10266

Weekend Warriors   Spo-Lei '8?
Sports
13541   30 mins   C
B, V

The staff of the Sports Injuries Rehabilitation Centre suggest how injuries might best be dealt with as they occur during play.
F — ED
Unknown — TFI Leisure Ltd   H, P

Welcome to Blood City   Fil-Ent '77
Science fiction/Western
05047   92 mins   C
B, V
Jack Palance, Keir Dullea, Samantha Eggar, directed by Peter Sasdy
A man is kidnapped and mentally transported, via computer electronics, to a strange kind of Western town, where a person's status depends on the number of people he or she can murder.
F — EN
Marilyn Stonehouse — THORN EMI   P
TXC 90 0316 4/TVC 90 0316 2

Welcome to Oshkosh '80   Gen-Edu '80
Aeronautics
06842   120 mins   C   (PAL, NTSC)
B, V
This film gives a personal view of the American Air Show filmed in 1980. It includes scenes of micro light, homebuilt and war planes showing the American Flying Fraternity at their best assisting each other when problems occur.
S,A — EN
Beattie/Forth Productions — Beattie-Edwards Aviation Ltd   P
BEA 002

Well Done, Noddy   Chl-Juv '7?
Fantasy
04685   58 mins   C
B, V
Narrated by Richard Briers
Poor old Big Ears has had an accident. His bicycle is smashed to pieces. Noddy takes him home to look after him. Big Ears is worried about his house, his cat, and his bicycle. Noddy solves the first two worries but he has no money for a new bicycle. So he sets out to earn some.
PS,I — EN
Spectrum — Polygram Video   P

Werewolf and the Yeti, The   Fil-Ent '??
Adventure/Horror
08861   84 mins   C
V2, B, V
Paul Naschy, Grace Mills

(For Explanation of codes, see USE GUIDE and KEY)

PALADIN VIDEO HOME ENTERTAINMENT GUIDE

A professor organises an expedition to Tibet, to find the Yeti monster. A member of the team is attacked by strange creatures.
BBFC:X — A — EN
Unknown — Video Programme Distributors
P
Canon 005

Werewolf Woman   Fil-Ent '??
Horror
06128   93 mins   C
V2, B, V
Frederick Stafford, Howard Ross
A woman raped in childhood has a violent repugnance for men. Fostered by a further tragedy, she disappears to a forest where she commits murder after murder in an uncontrollable frenzy of revenge.$aS?A
EN
Unknown — Video Programme Distributors
P
Cinehollywood—V1770

Werewolf's Shadow   Fil-Ent '??
Horror
12777   85 mins   C
V2, B, V
Paul Naschy, Gaby Fuchs, directed by Leon Klimovsky
Silver bullets are discovered during an autopsy of a long dead werewolf. Soon it becomes evident that the Black Queen of the Vampires has risen again.
A — EN
Unknown — Intervision Video   H, P
A-A0486

Werewolves on Wheels   Fil-Ent '??
Horror
05441   82 mins   C
V2, B, V
Stephen Oliver, Severn Darden, D. J. Anderson, directed by Michel Levesque
The Devils Advocates, a rebellious gang of bikers, enter into an evil conflict with a cloister of devil-worshipping monks. One of the Advocates' girls is selected to be the 'Bride of Satan;' her drugged companions are rendered powerless as the monks use their satanic powers.
BBFC:X — A — EN
Unknown — Iver Film Services   P

West and Soda   Chl-Juv '7?
Cartoons
12670   90 mins   C
V2, B, V
Animated

Clementine fights to save her ranch from her evil landlord and his henchmen with the help of Johnny the quick drawing cowboy.
PS,M — EN
Bruno Bozzetto — Videomedia   P
2113

West Side Story   Fil-Ent '61
Musical
01207   151 mins   C
V2, B, V
Natalie Wood, Richard Beymer, Russ Tamblyn, Rita Moreno, George Chakiris, directed by Robert Wise and Jerome Robbins
Gang rivalry on New York's West Side erupts in a ground-breaking musical that won ten Academy Awards. The Jets and the Sharks fight for their own turf and Tony and Maria fight for their own love. Amid the frenetic and brilliant choreography by Jerome Robbins, who directed the original Broadway show, and the high caliber score by Leonard Bernstein and Stephen Sondheim, there is the bittersweet message that tragedy breeds friendship.
Academy Awards '61: Best Picture; Best Supporting Actor (Chakiris); Best Direction (Wise/Robbins); Best Supporting Actress (Moreno); Best Cinematography: Color; Best Scoring Musical; Best Film Editing; Best Costume Design: Color; Best Art Direction: Color; Best Sound Recording.
BBFC:A — F — EN
United Artists; Robert Wise
Prods — Intervision Video   H
UA A B 5012

Westworld   Fil-Ent '73
Science fiction
07723   87 mins   C
B, V
Yul Brynner, Richard Benjamin, James Brolin, directed by Michael Crichton
A lawyer and a business man are among the visitors to Westworld, a futuristic 'theme-park' where robots are programmed to serve the guests' needs and fantasies. However, something goes wrong with their circuitry and a gunslinging humanoid turns the visit into a nightmare when it pursues the visitors who are powerless to stop the onslaught.
BBFC:AA — S,A — EN
MGM — MGM/UA Home Video   P
UMB 10097/UMV 10097

Whale for the Killing, A   Fil-Ent '81
Drama
09208   136 mins   C
B, V
Peter Strauss, Richard Widmark, Dee Wallace, Kathryn Walker, Bruce McGill, David Hollander, directed by Robert T. Heffron

PALADIN VIDEO HOME ENTERTAINMENT GUIDE

Set in a fishing village in Newfoundland, this film tells the story of one man's struggle and determination to save a stranded humpback whale from a group of hostile villages intent on selling it to the highest bidder. Based on the book by Farley Mowat.
F — EN
Playboy Prods; Robert Lovenheim and Peter Strauss — *Video Form Pictures* H, P
MGO 1

Whale of a Tale, A Fil-Ent '75
Adventure
02063 90 mins C
B, V
William Shatner
William Shatner plays a marine biologist in this touching story of a young boy's fascination with Marineland. The programme follows the boy's adventures during his summer vacations, and features all the underwater favourites.
F — EN
Unknown — *VCL Video Services* P

What a Picture!-Volume 1 Fin-Art '8?
Photography
09002 60 mins C
B, V
John Hedgecoe
The Professor of Photography at London's Royal College of Art gives an introduction to the art of photography in this four part series. Volume 1 contains two separate programmes; 'Making a Picture' which covers the basic elements of light, shape, form and pattern and 'The Vital Moment' featuring precision and timing in action photography.
S,A — I
Unknown — *THORN EMI* P
TXE 90 1623 4/TVE 90 1623 2

What a Picture!-Volume 2 How-Ins '83
Photography
09797 52 mins C
B, V
John Hedgecoe
The second programme of this four part series introduces us to Lighting and Composition and Faces and Figures. John Hedgecoe teaches us about selecting and arranging a studio still-life and the art of portrait photography.
S,A — I
Mitchell Beazley Television Ltd; Thorn EMI Video Programmes Ltd. — *THORN EMI*
P
TXF 90 0864 4/TVF 90 0864 2

What a Picture!-Volume 3 How-Ins '83
Photography
09793 52 mins C
B, V
John Hedgecoe
The third programme of this four part series introduces us to Landscape and Light and Perspectives of Space.
S,A — I
Mitchell Beazley Television Ltd; Thorn EMI Video Programmes Ltd. — *THORN EMI*
P
TXE 90 1723 4/TVE 90 1723 2

What a Picture!-Volume 4 How-Ins '83
Photography
09792 52 mins C
B, V
John Hedgecoe
The fourth programme in this series introduces us to Imagination and Technique and Travelling Light. The first part explores fantasy and imagination and the second part whisks us away to Egypt to cover holiday photography.
S,A — I
Mitchell Beazley Television Ltd; Thorn EMI Video Programmes Ltd. — *THORN EMI*
P
TXE 90 1993 4/TVE 90 1993 2

What Ever Happened to Aunt Alice? Fil-Ent '69
Horror
04271 98 mins C
B, V
Geraldine Page, Rosemary Forsyth, Ruth Gordon, Robert Fuller
Mrs. Marrable has a habit of hiring housekeepers who keep disappearing. A gruesome contemporary horror film with a bizarre and unexpected twist.
BBFC:A — S,A — EN
Cinerama Releasing — *Rank Video Library* H, P
0038

What Next? Fil-Ent '7?
Drama/Romance
08080 78 mins C
B, V
Monica Nordquist, Ollegard Wellton
This film is a Swedish love story from the country that started the sexual revolution.
BBFC:X — A — EN
Unknown — *Rank Video Library* H, P
0097 C

What Shall We Give Them to Eat? How-Ins '80
Cookery
04460 60 mins C
B
Prue Leith, Dilys Morgan

(For Explanation of codes, see USE GUIDE and KEY)

PALADIN VIDEO HOME ENTERTAINMENT GUIDE

International cookery expert Prue Leith talks about home entertaining with Dilys Morgan and demonstrates basic cooking methods for a wide variety of meals.
A — I
Michael Barratt Ltd; Sony — *Michael Barratt Ltd* **P**

Whatever Happened to Baby Jane?   Fil-Ent '62
Mystery/Suspense
06024   129 mins   B/W
B, V
Bette Davis, Joan Crawford, Victor Buono, directed by Robert Aldrich
This film covers the alarming and psychopathic relationship between two sisters. One is a former child vaudeville star, the other a crippled ex silent star of the screen. The cripple is terrorised by her sister who is consumed by hate and jealousy as she is forced to care for her after the suspicious 'accident.'
BBFC:X — A — EN
Warner Brother — *Warner Home Video* **P**
WEX1051/WEV1051

What's Good for the Goose   Fil-Ent '69
Comedy-Drama
08642   94 mins   C
V2, B, V
Norman Wisdom, Sally Geeson, Sally Bazeley, Derek Francis, Terence Alexander
An assistant bank manager, with a boring job and homelife, falls for a girl hitch-hiker and tries to recover his youth.
S,A — EN
Tigon — *Hokushin Audio Visual Ltd* **P**
VM44

What's New Pussycat?   Fil-Ent '65
Comedy
13011   108 mins   C
B, V
Peter O'Toole, Peter Sellers, Romy Schneider, Paula Prentiss, Woody Allen, Ursula Andress, Capucine
Being constantly surrounded by beautiful girls causes problems for a leading fashion magazine editor but when he confesses them to a mixed-up Viennese professor they only get worse!
BBFC:X — A — EN
Famous Artists Production — *Warner Home Video* **P**
99227

What's Up Doc?   Fil-Ent '72
Comedy
07875   87 mins   C
B, V
Barbra Streisand, Ryan O'Neal, Kenneth Mars, Austin Pendleton, directed by Peter Bogdanovich
An eccentric young girl and an equally absent-minded young professor get involved in a chase to recover four identical flight bags containing top secret documents, a wealthy woman's jewels, the professor's musical rocks and the girl's clothing.
BBFC:U — F — EN
Warner Bros — *Warner Home Video* **P**
WEX 61041/WEV 61041

What's Up Nurse   Fil-Ent '7?
Comedy
02104   82 mins   C
V2, B, V
John le Mesurier, Graham Stark, Kate Williams, Cardew Robinson
Star-studded cast in sexy comedy about a new young doctor arriving for his first ever hospital duty.
BBFC:X — A — EN
Unknown — *Hokushin Audio Visual Ltd* **P**
VM-10

What's Up Superdoc?   Fil-Ent '78
Comedy
02108   94 mins   C
V2, B, V
Hughie Green
Doctor Robert Todd is quietly going about his medical practice keeping his patients happy both in and out of bed, when his past catches up with him.
BBFC:X — A — EN
Blackwater Film Prods — *Hokushin Audio Visual Ltd* **P**
VM-21

When a Stranger Calls   Fil-Ent '80
Horror
06141   79 mins   C
V2, B, V
Charles Durning, Carol Kane, Colleen Dewhurst, Tony Beckley, Rachel Roberts, Ron O'Neal
A psychopathic murderer is apprehended by a detective and sent to an asylum. Years later he escapes to begin a new reign of terror, once again the same detective, now a lot older, sets out to find him. But not before he has caused terrifying chaos showing it could really happen anywhere, at anytime and to anyone.
BBFC:AA — S,A — EN
Columbia Pictures; Melvin Simon Productions — *Guild Home Video* **H, P, E**

PALADIN VIDEO HOME ENTERTAINMENT GUIDE

When Girls Undress   Fil-Ent '70
Comedy
05690   80 mins   C
B, V
Rinaldo Talamonti, Franz Muxeneder, Eva Mattern, Dorothea Rau, directed by Eberhard Schroeder
A young athlete is in training to win an important cycle race and has had strict instructions not to 'indulge' for six weeks. A rule he finds very difficult to keep when faced with temptation in the form of his girlfriend and her obsessed friends and harem of young ladies sent by a rival team.
BBFC:X — *A* — *EN*
Unknown — *Derann Film Services*   **H, P**
GS700B/GS700

When the North Wind Blows   Fil-Ent '74
Drama/Adventure
08051   109 mins   C
B, V
Henry Brandon, Herbet Nelson, Dan Haggarty, directed by Stewart Raffill
This film tells the story of an old man in Alaska. He lives alone, trapping his food and surviving the dangers and the elements. He befriends a snow tiger, with sad consequences.
BBFC:U — *F* — *EN*
Sunn Classic — *Rank Video Library*   **H, P**
0059 C

When Time Ran Out   Fil-Ent '80
Drama/Suspense
13161   121 mins   C
B, V
Paul Newman, Jacqueline Bisset, William Holden, directed by James Goldstone
A tropical island paradise attracting the rich, powerful and famous, and seething with emotional and commercial intrigues, becomes a burning hell when an inactive volcano suddenly erupts.
BBFC:A — *C,A* — *EN*
Warner Bros — *Warner Home Video*   **P**
61092

When You Comin' Back, Red Ryder?   Fil-Ent '79
Mystery/Suspense
08061   115 mins   C
B, V
Marjoe Gortner, Hal Linden, Peter Firth
This film is set in an isolated town in New Mexico. Violence finally flares on one hot sunny day, with horrifying consequences.
BBFC:X — *A* — *EN*
Columbia — *Rank Video Library*   **H, P**
0104 C

Where Danger Lives/Split Second   Fil-Ent '5?
Drama/Suspense
05666   160 mins   B/W
B, V
Robert Mitchum, Maureen O'Sullivan, Faith Domergue, Claude Rains, Charles Kemper, directed by John Farrow, Richard Egan, Jan Sterling, Stephen McNally, directed by Dick Powell
Two films are contained on one cassette. 'Where Danger Lives' (Black/white, 78 mins, 1951) is the story of a doctor who becomes involved with a patient, the wife of an older man on the verge of insanity; the result is murder. The doctor has to overcome the effects of serious injury before he can flee with the girl. 'Split Second' (Black/white, 82 mins, 1953) is the story of an escaped killer and his gang who, with hostages, hide in an old mining town which is due to be demolished any second by a nuclear explosion in the Nevada desert.
S,A — *EN*
RKO — *Kingston Video*   **H, P**
KV46

Where Does It Hurt?   Fil-Ent '72
Comedy
06196   85 mins   C
B, V
Peter Sellers, Jo-Ann Pflug, Rick Lens, directed by Ralph Amateau
A medical farce about a doctor 'on the fiddle.' Medical insurance swindles, unnecessary operations and costly treatment are all part of a phoney set-up. An unemployed construction worker becomes suspicious when he attends for an X-Ray and leaves minus his appendix.
S,A — *EN*
Cinerama — *VCL Video Services*   **P**
P183D

Where Eagles Dare   Fil-Ent '69
War-Drama
07721   150 mins   C
B, V
Richard Burton, Clint Eastwood, Mary Ure, Ingrid Pitt, Patrick Wymark, Michael Hordern, Donald Houston, directed by Brian Hutton
Two commandos are assigned to rescue an American General from the 'Eagle's Nest', an impregnable Nazi fortress which can only be reached by cable car. There are only three obstacles blocking their chances of success, getting up, getting down and getting away. Based on the novel by Alistair Maclean.
BBFC:A — *S,A* — *EN*
MGM — *MGM/UA Home Video*   **P**
UMB 10137/UMV 10137

(For Explanation of codes, see USE GUIDE and KEY)

PALADIN VIDEO HOME ENTERTAINMENT GUIDE

Where Have All the People Gone?   Fil-Ent '74
Drama/Science fiction
08014   72 mins   C
V2, B, V

Peter Graves, George O'Hanlon Jr, Kathleen Quinlan, Verna Bloom, Noble Willingham, Doug Chapin, directed by John Llewellyn Moxey

After a solar flare and an earthquake, a family on an archaeology expedition find themselves the only survivors, their guide having turned into a mysterious granular powder. After a journey back to the town they learn the reason for their survival.
BBFC:A — S,A — EN
Alpine-Jozak Prod; M P C — Iver Film Services   **P**
198

Where the Boys Are   Fil-Ent '84
Romance/Musical
13476   91 mins   C
V2, B, V

Lisa Hartman, Russel Todd, Lorna Luft, Wendy Schaal, Howard McGillan

A teenage movie that views the escapades and goings on from the girls' point of view. The soundtrack is in stereo Hi-Fi.
BBFC:15 — S,A — EN
Tri-star Pictures — Precision Video Ltd   **P**
3149

Where the Buffalo Roam   Fil-Ent '80
Comedy
13643   95 mins   C
B, V

Bill Murray, Peter Boyle, Bruno Kirby, directed by Art Linson

Comic action abounds when a drug-crazed journalist attempts to meet a writing deadline and enlists the help of an equally unpredictable lawyer with political aspirations.
BBFC:18 — A — EN
Universal — CIC Video   **H, P**
1145

Where the Red Fern Grows   Fil-Ent '74
Adventure/Drama
05490   93 mins   C
V2, B, V

James Whitmore, Beverly Garland, Jack Ging, Lonny Chapman, Stewart Peterson, directed by Nasman Tokar

Set in the 1930's, this is a story of a young boy who works hard to save enough money to buy a pair of hunting dogs. He trains them and is able to pitt them against the best top teams at the annual event. However, one night the dogs save his life when he is attacked by a mountain lion, a deed for which they pay a high price.
BBFC:U — F — EN
Lyman Dayton Prods — Iver Film Services   **P**

Whisky Galore   Fil-Ent '48
Comedy
01177   81 mins   B/W
B, V

Basil Radford, Joan Greenwood, directed by Alexander Mackendrick

A ship carrying a cargo of whiskey goes aground on a liquor-dry Scottish island. The men of the island hijack the cargo and spend many hilarious moments eluding the Customs officer.
BBFC:A — S,A — EN
Universal; J Arthur Rank — THORN EMI   **P**
TXE 90 0006 4/TVE 90 0006 2

Whispering Death   Fil-Ent '??
Horror/Drama
10192   90 mins   C
B, V

Christopher Lee, Trevor Howard, Sybil Danning, James Faulkener, Horst Frank, Sam Williams, Erik Schumann, Sascha Hehn, directed by Jurgen Goslar

Set in an Africa of tomorrow, Whispering Death, an albino Negro stalks the souls of white men, chanting and cursing them off African soil-an officer's daughter is ritualistically raped and tortured to death and a band of worshippers are mercilessly gunned down during a ceremonious plot.
BBFC:18 — A — EN
Unknown — Video Form Pictures   **H, P**
MGS 21

Whistle Down the Wind   Fil-Ent '61
Drama
05685   97 mins   B/W
B, V

Alan Bates, Hayley Mills, Bernard Lee, Diane Holgate, Alan Barnes, Norman Bird

The story of three children who discover an escaped murderer hiding in a barn and believe he is Jesus Christ. When adults call the police the man realises that a gun battle may injure the children and destroy their faith so he gives himself up.
BBFC:U — F — EN
Pathe — Rank Video Library   **H, P**
0053C

(For Explanation of codes, see USE GUIDE and KEY)

PALADIN VIDEO HOME ENTERTAINMENT GUIDE

White Buffalo, The   Fil-Ent '77
Western
08351   97 mins   C
V2, B, V
Charles Bronson, Jack Warden, Will Sampson, Clint Walker, Slim Pickens, Stuart Whitman, Kim Novak
This film is set during the Dakota Gold Rush. It tells of two men whose aim is to track down and destroy the legendary white buffalo.
S,A — EN
United Artists — *Guild Home Video*   H, P, E

White Comanche   Fil-Ent '67
Western
01691   98 mins   C
V2, B, V
Joseph Cotten, William Shatner
Twin sons of an Indian mother and a white settler are pitted against each other in a struggle for supremacy.
BBFC:A — S,A — EN
Spanish — *Intervision Video*   H, P
A-A 0089

White Dog   Fil-Ent '81
Drama
12037   89 mins   C
B, V
Kristy McNichol, Burl Ives, Paul Winfield, directed by Samuel Fuller
A stray white dog saves an actress from an intruder and she decides to keep it. However, she takes the dog on the set with her one day and it attacks a black actor. It is then discovered that the dog is trained to attack black people and it is decided to try and overcome this training by taking it to a special animal training centre.
BBFC:PG — S,A — EN
Paramount — *CIC Video*   H, P
BEA 2079/VHA 2079

White Heat   Fil-Ent '49
Drama/Adventure
13019   114 mins   B/W
B, V
James Cagney, Virginia Mayo, Edmund O'Brien
The authorities try to break a mother-fixated villain by planting one of their men in his gang.
BBFC:A — C,A — EN
United Artists — *Warner Home Video*   P
99245

White Lions, The   Fil-Ent '79
Wildlife/Adventure
08363   97 mins   C
V2, B, V
Michael York, Glynnis O'Conner, Donald Moffat, J.A. Preston, Roger E. Mosely, Lauri Lynn Meyers
This film set in October 1975 tells of the discovery of a totally new strain of lions in Africa, healthy but completely white. This film, based on the book 'The White Lions of Timbavati' by Chris McBride, tells of the efforts of the McBride family to protect the lions.
F — EN
Alan Landsburg Productions — *Guild Home Video*   H, P, E

White Rock   Spo-Lei '7?
Sports-Winter
01980   90 mins   C
B, V
Commentary by James Coburn
The raw elements of winter sports are brought to life with the explosive music of Rick Wakeman and the absorbing narration of James Coburn.
F — EN
Unknown — *Quadrant Video*   H, P

White Tower, The/Valley of the Sun   Fil-Ent '??
Drama/Comedy
05770   169 mins   C
B, V
Glenn Ford, Alida Valli, Lloyd Bridges, directed by Ted Tetzlaff, Lucille Ball, James Craig, Dean Jagger, directed by George Marshall
Two films are contained on one cassette. 'The White Tower' (colour, 94 minutes, 1951) features six people—a pretty girl, a U.S. pilot, two elderly men, an arrogant ex-Nazi, and a Swiss guide—who make an assault upon an unscaled Alpine Peak. 'Valley of the Sun' (black and white, 75 minutes, 1943) is set in the 1860's in Arizona. A Government agent has his work cut out in exposing a crooked Indian agent and preventing the Apaches from going on the warpath.
S,A — EN
RKO — *Kingston Video*   H, P
KV12

White Water Sam   Fil-Ent '7?
Adventure
07899   84 mins   C
V2, B, V
Keith Larsen
This is the story of a man, his dog and his adventures in the wilderness down an uncharted river. He comes close to death when

---

(For Explanation of codes, see USE GUIDE and KEY)

PALADIN VIDEO HOME ENTERTAINMENT GUIDE

attacked by a cougar, he risks his life while saving a drowning bear cub and is later saved himself when the cub's mother assists him in a brutal fight with wolves.
F — EN
Manson International — *Video Programme Distributors*   **P**
Inter-Ocean—062

Who, The   Fil-Ent '82
Music-Performance
12202   114 mins   C
B, V
Recorded at Toronto in stereo, this tape features many of The Who's hits including 'Pinball Wizard', 'My Generation', 'Won't Get Fooled Again', 'Long Live Rock', 'Squeezebox', 'Baba O'Reilly', 'I Can't Explain', 'See Me Feel Me' and 'Who Are You'.
F — EN
Bill Curbishley; Roy Baird — *CBS/Fox Video*
P
6234

Who Dares Wins   Fil-Ent '82
Crime-Drama/Suspense
08052   120 mins   C
B, V, LV
Lewis Collins, Richard Widmark, Judy Davis, Edward Woodward, Robert Webber, directed by Ian Sharp
This film portrays as accurately as possible the ways in which the legendary S.A.S. deals with violence, when an anti-nuclear group resorts to terror to secure their ends.
BBFC:AA — S,A — EN
Rank — *Rank Video Library*   **H, P**
0125 D

Who Finds a Friend Finds a Treasure   Fil-Ent '79
Comedy-Drama
12488   102 mins   C
B, V
Bud Spencer, Terence Hill
In this hilarious comedy Alan and Charlie go in search of a fortune hidden on a South Sea Island but encounter two major obstacles—a Japanese warrior who guards the treasure and the Boss of the American Underworld.
BBFC:PG — F — EN
Columbia; EMI — *RCA/Columbia Pictures Video UK*   **H, P**
10184

Who Mislaid My Wife?   Fil-Ent '82
Comedy
12846   101 mins   C
V2, B, V
A couple go away on holiday and fun develops when someone is discovered locked in a cupboard.
BBFC:18 — A — EN
Unknown — *Video Programme Distributors*
P

Who Slew Auntie Roo?   Fil-Ent '71
Horror
13460   91 mins   C
B, V
Shelley Winters, Mark Lester, Ralph Richardson, Judy Cornwell, Lionel Jeffries
A seemingly kindly old lady takes in orphans for Christmas dinner but some of the kids have their doubts and are not taken in so easily.
BBFC:18 — A — EN
Orion Pictures — *Rank Video Library*   **H, P**
2003

Who Will Love My Children?   Fil-Ent '82
Drama
12617   97 mins   C
V2, B, V
Ann-Margret, Frederic Forrest
A mother of ten children finds out she only has twelve months to live and sets out to find a happy home for each of her children.
Best Actress Golden Globe '82: Ann-Margret.
BBFC:PG — F — EN
ABC Pictures — *VideoSpace Ltd*   **P**

Who Will Save Our Children?   Fil-Ent '78
Drama
13493   92 mins   C
B, V
Shirley Jones, Len Cariou, Cassie Yates, Frances Sternhagen, David Hayward, Conchata Fenel, Jordan Charney
Two young children are abandoned by their parents and find a happy home with a couple to care for them but their world is shattered when their mother returns to the scene.
BBFC:PG — S,A — EN
George Schaefer — *Capricorn Entertainments*
P
103

Whodunit?   Fil-Ent '8?
Horror
09906   83 mins   C
B, V

PALADIN VIDEO HOME ENTERTAINMENT GUIDE

After answering an advertisement in a newspaper a girl rock singer participates in the making of a horror movie on the remote Creep Island, only to find that her now-found colleagues become victims of an unknown killer.
BBFC:18 — A — EN
Unknown — Entertainment in Video   **H, P**
EVB 1011/EVV 1011

Whoops Apocalypse   Fil-Ent '8?
Comedy/Satire
08985   137 mins   C
B, V

John Barron, John Cleese, Richard Griffiths, Peter Jones, Bruce Montague, Barry Morse, David Kelly, Geoffrey Palmer, Alexei Sayle, directed by John Reardon

This full length feature is the re-edited version of the acclaimed television series. It gives an hilarious account of the events leading up to World War III. With video-taped reports on events, this outrageous saga unfolds in the White House, at 10 Downing Street and in a gents loo on a cross-channel ferry.
S,A — EN
London Weekend Television — Palace Video Ltd   **P**
PVC 2025A

Who's Afraid of Virginia Woolf?   Fil-Ent '66
Drama
06041   124 mins   B/W
B, V

Elizabeth Taylor, Richard Burton, Sandy Dennis, George Segal, directed by Mike Nichols

After an evening out, a middle aged history professor and his wife invite a new young teacher and his wife over for a late night drinks party which lasts until dawn. The older couple constantly belittle and tear each other down, until, at last a glimmer of understanding is reached. Based on the Broadway play by Edward Albee.

Academy Awards '66: Best Acress (Taylor); Best Supporting Actress (Dennis); Best Cinematography—B/W; Best Costume Design—B/W.   BBFC:X — A — EN
Warner Bros; Ernest Lehman — Warner Home Video   **P**
WEX1056/WEV1056

Why Did You Pick On Me?   Fil-Ent '84
Drama/Comedy
13728   90 mins   C
V2, B, V

Bud Spencer, Cary Guffey, Raimund Harmstorf, directed by Michele Lupo

In this sequel to 'The Sheriff and the Satellite Kid' our truant from out of space is chased from town to town by the airforce soldiers.
BBFC:PG — F — EN
Elio Scardamaglia — Medusa Communications Ltd   **H, P**
MC 040

Why Not Stay for Breakfast?   Fil-Ent '78
Comedy/Romance
05739   95 mins   C
B, V

George Chakiris, Yvonne Wilder, Gemma Craven, directed by Terence Marcel

The life of a fussy, fortyish civil servant bachelor is shattered one evening by a knock at the door. His solitary existance with his pot plants and thirties music is put in turmoil by a pregnant girl who drops in to borrow money and promptly produces a baby. With nowhere else to go she stays; he immediately takes to fatherhood. His efforts to court her clash with her less than subtle attempts to get him into bed.
BBFC:A — M,A — EN
Artgrove Limited — Home Video Holdings   **H, P**
004

Why Would Anyone Want to Kill A Nice Girl Like You?   Fil-Ent '68
Adventure/Suspense
09012   99 mins   C
V2, B, V

Peter Vaughn, Eva Renzi, David Buck

A man is killed on the Dover to Boulogne ferry. The film follows the connections between that murder and the attempts on the life of the heroine as she speeds through the countryside to the Cote D'Azur.
F — EN
Group W — Intervision Video   **H, P**
AA 0447

Wicked Die Slow, The   Fil-Ent '7?
Western/Martial arts
08059   98 mins   C
B, V

Gary Allen, Steve Rivard

This film set in the old west involves harsh brutality, violence and unbridled passions with savage indians, ruthless outlaws and dangerous women.
BBFC:X — A — EN
Unknown — Rank Video Library   **H, P**
0108 C

(For Explanation of codes, see USE GUIDE and KEY)

PALADIN VIDEO HOME ENTERTAINMENT GUIDE

Wicked Lady, The   Fil-Ent '83
Drama
09463   94 mins   C
V2, B, V
Faye Dunaway, Alan Bates, John Gielgud, Deaholm Elliot, Prunella Scales, Oliver Tobias, Glynis Barber, directed by Michael Winner
This film tells the adventures of a 'lady highwayman', Lady Barbara Skelton who married a nobleman, lusted after a highwayman, and sought the love of the only man she would ever have.
BBFC:18 — A — EN
Golan-Globus Prod. — *Guild Home Video*
H, P, E

Wicker Man, The   Fil-Ent '73
Horror/Suspense
04662   83 mins   C
B, V
Edward Woodward, Britt Ekland, Diane Cilento, Ingrid Pitt, Christopher Lee
In response to an anonymous appeal, Police Sergeant Howie flies to the remote Scottish island of Summerisle to investigate the alleged disappearance of a child. Eventually suspecting her to be used as a 'sacrifice' he joins the celebrations intending to snatch her back, only to discover that she was the bait and he the sacrifice.
BBFC:X — A — EN
British Lion; Peter Snell — *THORN EMI*
H, P
TXC 90 0264 4/TVC 90 0264 2

Widows   Fil-Ent '83
Drama
09810   156 mins   C
B, V
When three members of a gang are killed before they can carry out their next hold-up, their widows determine to finish the job their husbands started.
S,A — EN
Euston Films Ltd. — *THORN EMI*   P
TXC 90 1716 4/TVC 90 1716 2

Wild and the Free, The   Fil-Ent '80
Adventure
05406   92 mins   C
B, V
Granville Van Dusen, Linda Gray
This film follows a group of chimpanzees through misadventures on a staid university campus to the African wilds. The chimps have been raised by an animal researcher as his own children. To save them he persuades another researcher to let him take them to her African facility. Problems arise over difference in opinion over the chimps welfare.
F — EN
BSR Production; Marble Arch Productions — *Precision Video Ltd*   P
BITC 2079/VITC 2079

Wild Angels, The   Fil-Ent '66
Drama
07403   83 mins   C
V2, B, V
Peter Fonda, Nancy Sinatra, Bruce Dern
A group of fanatical motorcyclists who live by their own violent rules terrorize a beach community in Southern California. When one of them is badly hurt they raid the hospital to take him out, an act which causes his death.
BBFC:X — A — EN
American International — *Guild Home Video*
H, P, E

Wild Babies   Gen-Edu '7?
Infants/Animals
02266   60 mins   C
V
Narrated by Marty Stouffer
A documentary about the very young, both animal and human, and their endless adventure of exploration and discovery.
F — ED
Unknown — *JVC*   P
PRT 45

Wild Birds and the Law—Can We Help You?   Gen-Edu '84
Birds/Law
13597   20 mins   C
V2, B, V
For use to police forces and training schools only, this video explains the operation of the law concerning the protection of wild birds in Britain and offers assistance and technical help in its interpretation.
A — I
Royal Society for the Protection of Birds — *Royal Society for the Protection of Birds*   H, P

Wild Bunch, The   Fil-Ent '69
Western
01257   127 mins   C
B, V
William Holden, Ernest Borgnine, Robert Ryan, directed by Sam Peckinpah

PALADIN VIDEO HOME ENTERTAINMENT GUIDE

A brutal, bloody western about a group of losers in the dying days of the lawless frontier, fighting and killing those in their path.
C,A — EN
Warner Bros — Warner Home Video   P

Wild Geese, The   Fil-Ent '78
War-Drama
04243   129 mins   C
B, V, LV
Richard Burton, Roger Moore, Richard Harris, Hardy Kruger, Stewart Granger
An all action war film with a powerful and dramatic theme. The Wild Geese are fifty crack mercenary paratroops commanded by fearless veteran Colonel Faulkner.
BBFC:AA — C,A — EN
Allied Artists — Rank Video Library   H, P
0013

Wild Heart, The   Fil-Ent '52
Drama
04220   82 mins   C
B, V
Jennifer Jones, David Farrar, Cyril Cusack, Sybil Thorndike, Esmond Knight
Strange tale of a Welsh country girl whose only guide to her wild emotions is an old book of legends.
BBFC:A — S,A — EN
RKO — Guild Home Video   H, P

Wild Horse Hank   Fil-Ent '8?
Western
07772   100 mins   C
V2, B, V
Linda Blair, Michael Wincott, Richard Crenna
This film follows the story of a ranch girl's love for the wild and her fight to keep it that way.
S,A — EN
Unknown — Fletcher Video   H, P
V152

Wild Little Bunch, The   Fil-Ent '74
Drama
04221   85 mins   C
B, V
Jack Wild, June Brown
A dying mother asks her eldest son to promise to keep the family of 14 children together. The Wild Little Bunch fight against plans to place them in care.
BBFC:U — F — EN
Unknown — Guild Home Video   H, P

Wild Party, The   Fil-Ent '74
Drama
13455   88 mins   C
B, V
James Coco, Raquel Welch
Set in Hollywood just before the advent of talking pictures in 1929, a fading film comedian and his voluptuous mistress throw a partyto attract producers which soon gives way to confusion and violence.
BBFC:18 — A — EN
Orion Pictures — Rank Video Library   H, P
0177 E

Wild Rovers   Fil-Ent '71
Western
12223   105 mins   C
B, V
Ryan O'Neal, William Holden, directed by Blake Edwards
This film is set against the scenery of Monument Valley and the Colorado River in the 1880s and tells the story of two poor cowboys who are determined to become rich at all costs.
F — EN
MGM; Blake Edwards — MGM/UA Home Video   P
10305

Wild Strawberries   Fil-Ent '57
Drama
08670   93 mins   B/W
B, V
Victor Sjostrom, Ingrid Thulin, Bibi Andersson, directed by Ingmar Bergman
This film tells the story of a distinguished doctor and his journey to his old university to receive an honorary doctorate. This ought to be a happy day for him, but on the way he is critised by his daughter-in-law, and this causes him to re-assess his life. As his memories and dreams reappear. The journey becomes a voyage into his soul and sins.
C,A — EN
Svensk Filmindustri — Longman Video   P
LGBE 5010/LGVH 5010

Wild Times   Fil-Ent '8?
Adventure/Western
12155   180 mins   C
V2, B, V
Sam Elliott, Ben Johnson, Bruce Boxleitner, Penny Peyser, Cameron Mitchell
A saga of American life that takes place in the 1880s which tells the story of the legendary hero, Hugh Cardiff, America's first wild west show impresario.
S,A — EN
Metromedia Producers — Guild Home Video
H, P, E

PALADIN VIDEO HOME ENTERTAINMENT GUIDE

Wild Women
Fil-Ent '70
Western
05184   72 mins   C
B, V
Hugh O'Brian, Anne Francis, Marilyn Maxwell, Sherry Jackson, Robert F Simon, John Nerris
A rollicking Western adventure in which five female convicts bargain for their liberty in exchange for acting as settlers on a wagon train which is to provide an un-military appearance for a team of US Army engineers setting out to map hostile territory along the Mexican frontier.
A — EN
Aaron Spelling — Rank Video Library   H, P
8002

Wildcat
Fil-Ent '80
Comedy/Western
12739   102 mins   C
B, V
Lee Marvin, Oliver Reed, Robert Culp, Elizabeth Ashley, Strother Martin, Sylvia Miles
A comedy western that kicks off with a cathouse raid and ends with a bare-knuckle brawl over a $60,000 fortune with lots of fun, fast-action and wild women in-between!
BBFC:PG — F — EN
Jules Buck — Rank Video Library   H, P
1062 Y

Wildcats of St. Trinians, The
Fil-Ent '80
Comedy/Adventure
05748   92 mins   C
B, V
Sheila Hancock, Michael Harden, Rodney Bewes, Maureen Lipman, Julia McKenzie, Joe Melia, Veronica Quilligan, Thorley Waters, directed by Frank Launder
The little horrors of St. Trinian's hatch yet another plot, this time to organise a union for schoolgirls. Their friend and mentor, Flash Harry, suggests a plan to kidnap girls from more respectable schools and to substitute their own 'agents.' They meet resistance from their headmistress, the Minister of Education, a private detective and an oil sheikh.
BBFC:A — M,A — EN
Wildcat Film Productions — Home Video Holdings   H, P
016

Wilde's Domain
Fil-Ent '8?
Drama/Romance
13485   73 mins   C
B, V
Kit Taylor, June Salter, Martin Vaughan, directed by Charles Tingwell
Set in Australia a large entertainment organisation decides to employ a Russian ballet company, a decision which triggers off a love story and a lot of opposition from the locals.
BBFC:U — F — EN
Unknown — Precision Video Ltd   P
2147

Wildlife USA
Gen-Edu '??
Documentary/Wildlife
06347   30 mins   C
V2, B, V
This film takes a journey through the thousands of miles of nature reserves in the U.S.A. whose task is to preserve and protect animals such as the Bison, the Alligator and the Bear.
F — EN
Unknown — Walton Film and Video Ltd   P
P1154

Will There Really Be a Morning?
Fil-Ent '83
Drama
13474   136 mins   C
B, V
Susan Blakely, Lee Grant, John Heard, directed by Fielder Cook
A filmed biography of the Hollywood star Frances Farmer, whose tormented spirit finally drove her into a mental institution and an eventual operation.
A — EN
Jaffe-Blakely Films; Sama Prods. — Rank Video Library   H, P
0218

Will to Die
Fil-Ent '8?
Drama/Mystery
09155   94 mins   C
V
John Carradine, Merry Anders, Norman Bartold, Rodolfo Acosta, Ivy Bethune, Richard Davalos, Faith Domergue, Buck Kartalian, Brooke Mills
A wealthy North American industrialist has recently died, and members of his family and his devoted staff gather together to hear the last recorded message from the old man. They are told that to inherit his fortune in various ways, the family and servants must stay in the house for seven days and nights. Motivated by greed they agree, but then the killing starts.
S,A — EN
Unknown — Cinema Indoors   H, P

Will to Win, The
Spo-Lei '7?
Sports
02269   30 mins   C
V

PALADIN VIDEO HOME ENTERTAINMENT GUIDE

An award winning programme of modern sport at its best. Full of action and excitement, it includes football, karate, surfing, and motorcycle racing.
F — EN
Unknown — *JVC* P
PRT 6

Willard Fil-Ent '71
Suspense/Drama
12690 95 mins C
B, V
Bruce Davison, Ernest Borgnine, Elsa Lanchester, Sondra Locke, directed by Daniel Mann
A young man possesses the power to communicate with rats and uses them in acts of vengeance against his enemies.
BBFC:18 — C,A — EN
Cinerama; BCP Productions — *Brent Walker Home Video Ltd* P
BW25

Willie and Phil Fil-Ent '81
Comedy
07717 116 mins C
V2, B, V
Michael Ontkean, Margot Kidder, Ray Sharkey, directed by Paul Mazursky
This compassionate satire explores love, friendship and the boundaries of commitment between Willie, a high school English teacher, and Phil, a photographer, who both discover and love Jeannette, a girl who came to New York determined to become somebody and is about to be evicted from her flat.
S,A — EN
Twentieth Century Fox — *CBS/Fox Video* P
1132

Willie Nelson and Family in Concert Fil-Ent '84
Music-Performance
13267 88 mins C
B, V
Twenty-eight great hits are featured in this video from the country and rock'n'roll star including 'On the Road Again,' 'Always on my Mind,' 'Stardust' and 'Georgia.'
F — EN
Opry House Productions — *CBS/Fox Video* P
6623

Willo the Wisp—Volume 1 Chi-Juv '??
Cartoons
08421 53 mins C
B, V
Animated, voices by Kenneth Williams, directed by Nicholas Spargo
Deep in Doyley Woods live Willo the Wisp and an assortment of creatures. The film tells the story of an overweight fairy and her caterpillar friend who frequently fall foul to a wicked witch in the form of a small, walking television. She casts horrid spells, turning the handsome Prince into the Beast.
BBFC:U — M,S — EN
Unknown — *THORN EMI* P
TXE 90 0965 4/TVE 90 0965 2

Willo the Wisp—Volume 2 Chi-Juv '??
Cartoons
08422 53 mins C
B, V
Animated, voices by Kenneth Williams, directed by Nicholas Spargo
This is the second volume of Willo the Wisp, featuring the strange collection of animals from Doyley Woods, including Mavis Cruet, the overweight fairy, the Beast, Twit, Carwash, The Moog, and the Astrognats. This tape contains 13 stories of approximately four minutes each.
M,S — EN
Unknown — *THORN EMI* P
TXE 90 0968 4/TVE 90 0968 2

Willy Wonka and the Chocolate Factory Chi-Juv '71
Adventure
12978 96 mins C
B, V
Gene Wilder, Jack Albertson
Five children are taken to see the wondrous sights in Willy Wonka's chocolate factory but strange fates await the spoilt and greedy children in the group.
BBFC:U — F — EN
David Wolper — *Warner Home Video* P
61206

Wimbledon, 1974 Spo-Lei '74
Tennis
04528 52 mins C
B, V
New young stars begin to emerge and unseat the old pros. Jimmy Connors, Chris Evert, Bjorn Borg, Ilie Nastase, Ken Rosewall, John Newcombe, Stan Smith, Virginia Wade, and others are seen both in action and behind the scenes.
F — EN
Trans World Intl — *Quadrant Video* H, P
W74

Wimbledon, 1975 Spo-Lei '75
Tennis
04529 52 mins C

PALADIN VIDEO HOME ENTERTAINMENT GUIDE

B, V
Narrated by Peter Ustinov
Jimmy Connors is upset by Arthur Ashe in the men's singles final. Peter Ustinov brings his own specialised, humourous and perceptive approach to the match highlights and their surroundings.
F — EN
Trans World Intl — *Quadrant Video* **H, P**
W75

Wimbledon, 1976   Spo-Lei '76
Tennis
04530   52 mins   C
B, V
Narrated by James Mason
Bjorn Borg and Chris Evert capture the singles crowns, prevailing over the likes of Jimmy Connors, Evonne Goolagong Cawley, Billie Jean King, and Manuel Orantes.
F — EN
Trans World Intl — *Quadrant Video* **H, P**
W76

Wimbledon, 1977   Spo-Lei '77
Tennis
04526   52 mins   C
B, V
Virginia Wade tells the story of her own major role in the historic Wimbledon classic. Champions of the past parade at Centre Court. Jimmy Connors, Bjorn Borg, Ilie Nastase, Chris Evert, Sue Barker, and 14-year-old Tracy Austin compete in some memorable matches.
F — EN
Trans World Intl — *Quadrant Video* **H, P**
W77

Wimbledon, 1978   Spo-Lei '77
Tennis
04527   52 mins   C
B, V
Narrated by John Newcombe
Bjorn Borg captures his third successive men's singles title, crushing Jimmy Connors in the finals.
F — EN
Trans World Intl — *Quadrant Video* **H, P**
W78

Wimbledon '81   Spo-Lei '81
Documentary/Tennis
07846   60 mins   C
B, V
Introduced by James Hunt and Dan Maskell
This film follows the events at the 1981 Wimbledon Lawn Tennis Championships, the year Borg lost the championship to McEnroe after five successive years. James Hunt takes a look behind the scenes and Dan Maskell comments on the matches.
F — EN
Unknown — *Polygram Video* **H, P**
790 375

Wimbledon, 1979   Spo-Lei '79
Tennis
01996   52 mins   C
B, V
Narrated by Charlton Heston
Bjorn Borg meets Roscoe Tanner in the historic Men's singles final. Billie Jean King teams with Martina Navratilova to win the Women's doubles title, setting a new record for career victories at Wimbledon.
F — EN
Trans World International — *Quadrant Video*
H, P
W79

Wimbledon, 1980   Spo-Lei '80
Tennis
01982   52 mins   C
B, V
Andrea Jaeger makes a name for herself, Yvonne Cawley wins the Women's singles, and Bjorn Borg and John McEnroe play a nail-biting finals match at the 1980 Wimbledon.
F — EN
Trans World International — *Quadrant Video*
H, P
W80

Wimbledon 1982   Spo-Lei '82
Tennis
09117   52 mins   C
B, V
Narrated by Dan Maskell
This maintains the almost traditional levels of excitement, showing Jimmy Connors and Martina Navratilova the eventual winners, of the mens and ladies singles titles.
F — EN
Trans World International — *Quadrant Video*
H, P
W82

Wimbledon '83   Spo-Lei '83
Tennis
12767   60 mins   C
V2, B, V

(For Explanation of codes, see USE GUIDE and KEY)

PALADIN VIDEO HOME ENTERTAINMENT GUIDE

This exciting review of the 1983 Championships features many of the stars, including Chris Evert Lloyd, Ivan Lendl, Jimmy Conners and John McEnroe, and also takes you behind the scenes at Wimbledon with Alan Mills and Virginia Wade.
F — EN
Trans World International — *VideoSpace Ltd*
P

Wind in the Willows, The   Fil-Ent '??
Cartoons
09838   92 mins   C
B, V
Animated
This is an old family favourite based on the original book. This tale of the riverbank tells of Mr. Toad's eccentricity, boastfullness and ultimate downfall.
F — EN
Unknown — *Polygram Video*   **H, P**
791 5622/791 5624

Wind in the Willows   Chi-Juv '83
Puppets
12889   75 mins   C
B, V
Animated
Kenneth Grahame's whimsical story is brought to life in an Edwardian setting with music and songs.
F — EN
Cosgrove Hall Production; Thames Video — *THORN EMI*   **P**
TXE 90 19374/TVE 90 19372

Wind in the   Fil-Ent '??
Willows—Cassette 1, The
Cartoons
08356   108 mins   C
V2, B, V
Animated
This film is about the well-known characters, Mr. Toad of Toad Hall, Ratty, Mole and the Wise Old Badger. In the first part Mr. Toad acquires a new motor car and Ratty teaches Mole about the river. From the book written by Kenneth Grahame.
F — EN
Unknown — *Guild Home Video*   **H, P, E**

Wind in the   Fil-Ent '??
Willows—Cassette 2, The
Cartoons
08357   108 mins   C
V2, B, V
Animated

This continues the story of Mr. Toad, Mole, Ratty and Badger and their battle with the evil stoats and weasels.
F — EN
Unknown — *Guild Home Video*   **H, P, E**

Windows: Animals at   Chi-Juv '7?
Work and Play
Animals
04682   54 mins   C
B, V
Animals are seen at work and play in Spain, the USSR, the United States, Thailand, The United Kingdom, Uruguay, Austria, Switzerland, Japan and France.
PS,I — EN
Spectrum — *Polygram Video*   **P**

Winds of Kitty Hawk, The   Fil-Ent '78
Biographical/Drama
00170   98 mins   C
B, V
Michael Moriarty, David Huffman, Kathryn Walker, Eugene Roche, John Randolph, Scott Hylands
On December 17, 1903, two uneducated bicycle mechanics, Wilbur and Orville Wright, successfully launched a power-driven craft, carrying a man. The film recounts the building of their aircrafts and the competition with Alexander Bell to produce the machines.
F — EN
Charles Fries Prods — *Video Form Pictures*
H, P
DD3

Wings of an Eagle   Fil-Ent '76
Adventure/Documentary
01191   90 mins   C
V2, B, V
Ed Durden
This documentary-adventure story follows the life of a rare California golden eagle from the time she was found as a nestling by wild bird trainer Ed Durden until her return to her natural wilderness environment as an adult.
F — EN
Martin Green — *Intervision Video*   **H**
A-AE 0185

Wings of the Wind/They   Spo-Lei '7?
Own the Sky
Sports-Minor/Aeronautics
02268   60 mins   C
V

(For Explanation of codes, see USE GUIDE and KEY)   723

PALADIN VIDEO HOME ENTERTAINMENT GUIDE

Two half-hour programmes on one tape dealing with man's age old desire to fly. Hand gliding and the RAF Falcons sky diving team are examined in stunning photography.
F — EN
Unknown — JVC   P
PRT 12

Winnie the Pooh and the Blustery Day   Chi-Juv '76
Cartoons
12587   72 mins   C
B, V
Animated
This cassette contains the title cartoon plus four other adventures; 'Baggage Bluster,' 'Bone Bandit,' 'Billposters,' 'Tea for Two Hundred' and 'Donald's Gold Mine.'
PS,I — EN
Walt Disney Productions — Rank Video Library
H
063

Winnie the Pooh and the Honey Tree   Fil-Ent '66
Cartoons/Fantasy
05580   38 mins   C
B, V
Animated
A cartoon presentation of one of A.A. Milne's 'Winnie the Pooh' stories, featuring Pooh, who in his search to satisfy his appetite for honey meets up with Eeyore, Owl, Kanga and Roo. This cassette also features 'Breezy Bear' in which Donald Duck deals with a honey stealing bear and 'Pluto and the Gopher.'
F — EN
Walt Disney Productions — Rank Video Library
H
06300

Winning   Fil-Ent '69
Drama
13611   121 mins   C
B, V
Paul Newman, Robert Wagner, Barry Ford, Joanne Woodward, directed by James Goldstone
An idol of the car racing circuits marries but then finds he is onto a losing streak as race after race goes to his best friend and his marriage also starts to get shaky.
BBFC:PG — S,A — EN
Universal — CIC Video   H, P
1138

Winning Streak   Fil-Ent '83
Crime-Drama
12666   94 mins   C
V2, B, V
Andra Millian, Kevin Costner, directed by Jim Wilson
Centreing round the gaming tables in the casinos, a young girl with an incredible knack for 'Blackjack' sets out to avenge her partner's death.
BBFC:PG — S,A — EN
Unknown — Videomedia   P
0805

Winslow Boy, The   Fil-Ent '48
Drama
05439   112 mins   B/W
B, V
Robert Donat, Cedric Hardwicke, Margaret Leighton, Frank Lawton, directed by Anthony Asquith
This film fictionalised the events of a famous Edwardian court-case, in which a cadet at the Royal Naval College was wrongly accused of theft and expelled. His father, with pig-headed idealism, fought through the courts to a satisfactory conclusion. From the play written by Terence Rattigan.
S,A — EN
British Lion — THORN EMI   P
TXC 90 0252 4/TVC 90 0252 2

Winston Churchill—Charles De Gaulle   Gen-Edu '??
History-Modern/World War II
06135   30 mins   B/W
V2, B, V
This authentic documentary footage depicts the biography of the two leaders from their boyhood to their successful political careers. An account of two men engaged in defending a common ideal: peace.
S,A — ED
Unknown — Video Programme Distributors
P
Cinehollywood—V800

Winter Comes Early   Fil-Ent '77
Romance
04333   85 mins   C
V2, B, V
Trudy Young, Art Hindle
Story of a love affair between a hockey player and a rock singer.
BBFC:A — A — EN
Agincourt Intl; J F Bassett — Intervision Video
H, P
A-A 0079

Winter Gardens   Gen-Edu '82
Flowers/Seasons
13574   16 mins   C
V, 3/4U

724   (For Explanation of codes, see USE GUIDE and KEY)

PALADIN VIDEO HOME ENTERTAINMENT GUIDE

This film shows the delicate but hardy winter flower garden of Polesden Lacey and different rhododendron woods in the winds, rain and snow.
F — EN
Unknown — *TFI Leisure Ltd* **H**

Winter Kills   Fil-Ent '79
Drama
07693   94 mins   C
V2, B, V
Jeff Bridges, John Huston, Anthony Perkins, Sterling Hayden, Eli Wallach, Dorothy Malone, Ralph Meeker, Toshiro Mifune, Richard Boone, directed by William Richert
The younger brother of an assassinated president of the United States sets out to find his brother's killers 19 years after the event. A dying man reveals to him that there was a conspiracy. Based on the novel by Richard Condon.
A — EN
Avco Embassy — *CBS/Fox Video* **P**
4061

Winter of Our Discontent,   Fil-Ent '83
The
Drama
13126   101 mins   C
B, V
Donald Sutherland, Teri Garr, Tuesday Weld, E.G. Marshall, directed by Waris Hussein
Based on John Steinbeck's book, a middle-aged American becomes involved in questionable double dealings in a vain bid to reclaim his lost social position.
BBFC:PG — S,A — EN
Lorimar Productions — *Polygram Video* **P**
041 0304/041 0302

Winter of Our Dreams   Fil-Ent '81
Drama
09831   85 mins   C
V2, B, V
Judy Davis, Bryan Brown
A prostitute and junkie meet a romantic man frantically searching for the love he'd lost.
A — EN
Vega Films — *Polygram Video* **H, P**
791 5365/791 5364/791 5362

Winter Sports Action   Spo-Lei '7?
(Volume One)
Sports-Winter
05200   60 mins   C
B, V

Winter Sports Action   Spo-Lei '7?
(Volume Two)
Sports-Winter
05201   60 mins   C
B, V
Two programmes on skiing are contained on this cassette: 'Garmisch 1978' and 'Just a Matter of Time,' which was filmed at the 1976 Winter Olympics in Innsbruck.
F — EN
Unknown — *Quadrant Video* **H, P**

Winter Sports Action   Spo-Lei '81
(Volume Three)
Sports-Winter
05202   25 mins   C
B, V
This cassette is devoted to the 1980 World Cup downhill races.
F — EN
Brunswick International — *Quadrant Video*
H, P

Witchfinder General   Fil-Ent '68
Suspense
02092   87 mins   C
V2, B, V
Vincent Price, Ian Ogilvy, Patrick Wymark
Conventional law collapses as civil war tears England apart in 1645. One man makes use of his natural talents in his chosen profession of witch hunter. American title is 'The Conqueror Worm.'
BBFC:X — A — EN
American International — *Hokushin Audio Visual Ltd* **P**
VM-16

Witching Time/The Silent   Fil-Ent '??
Scream
Horror
07362   202 mins   C
V2, B, V
Jon Finch, Patricia Quinn, Prunella Gee, Ian McCulloch, Peter Cushing, Brian Cox, Elaine Donnelly, Anthony Carrick
Two 'Hammer House of Horror' films are contained on one cassette. The first entitled 'Witching Time' (101 mins.) tells of a trail terror for a young man, which begins when he meets a girl in a long black cloak who tells him that seh was born in the farmhouse in which he lives, in

This cassette contains three programmes on skiing: 'Search for Speed,' 'Between Chaos and Beauty,' and 'Helix.'
F — EN
Unknown — *Quadrant Video* **H, P**

(For Explanation of codes, see USE GUIDE and KEY)

PALADIN VIDEO HOME ENTERTAINMENT GUIDE

1627. The second 'The Silent Scream' (101 mins.) tells of temptation and terror when a released convict finds himself caged again, only this time it is more horrifying than prison.
S,A — EN
Hammer Films — *Precision Video Ltd* P
CRITC 2116/BITC 2116/VITC 2116

Witchmaker, The Fil-Ent '69
Horror
02410 100 mins C
B, V
Anthony Eisley, Thoris Brandt, Alvy Moore, directed by William O. Brown

A remote, crocodile-infested bayou in Louisiana is the scene of bizarre murders. Since there is a suspicion of occult activities, a research team attempt to find a solution to the crimes.
S,A — EN
Excelsior — *Derann Film Services* H, P
DV 107B/DV 107

Without Reservations/Footlight Varieties Fil-Ent '??
Comedy-Drama/Variety
05773 162 mins B/W
B, V
John Wayne, Claudette Colbert, directed by Mervyn LeRoy, Liberace, Leon Errol, Frankie Carle, directed by Hal Yates

Two films are contained on one cassette. 'Without Reservations' (black and white, 102 minutes, 1947), is about an authoress who is off to Hollywood for the filming of her novel. She meets a man whom she thinks will make a perfect hero. In the comic confusions that follow, they are put off the train, nearly arrested, fall in love, break it off, and finally reach their destination. 'Footlight Varieties' (black and white, 60 minutes, 1952), features a number of variety acts, introduced by Jack Paar, and interwoven with movie clips.
S,A — EN
RKO — *Kingston Video* H, P
KV9

Wiz, The Fil-Ent '78
Musical/Fantasy
10101 127 mins C
B, V
Diana Ross, Michael Jackson, Richard Pryor, directed by Sidney Lumet

A modern day version of the 1939 film of ""The Wizard of Oz" the Scarecrow, Tinman and Cowardly Lion are found in a world of parking lots, garbage dumps and amusement parks, and the Yellow Brick Road leads down into the Subway.
BBFC:U — F — EN
Universal — *CIC Video* H, P
BEL 1065/VHL 1065

Wizard of Oz, The Fil-Ent '39
Musical/Fantasy
07958 98 mins C
B, V
Judy Garland, Jack Haley, Ray Bolger, Bert Lahr, Frank Morgan, Billie Burke, Margaret Hamilton

A Kansas farm girl dreams she and her dog are somewhere over the rainbow, in the wonderful land of Oz. On her adventure to find the 'Great Oz' she is joined by the Scarecrow, the Tin Woodsman and the Cowardly Lion. Based on the book by Frank L. Baum.
Academy Awards '39: Best Original Music Score; Best Song ('Over the Rainbow').
F — EN
MGM; Mervyn Le Roy — *MGM/UA Home Video* P
UMB 10001/UMV 10001

Wizards Fil-Ent '82
Cartoons/Fantasy
13269 94 mins C
B, V
Animated, directed by Ralph Bakshi

A visual spectacular set 3000 years after the world has been devastated by nuclear explosions leaving a few survivors, one a genial old wizard and his evil Hilter-inspired brother.
BBFC:PG — S,A — EN
Ralph Bakshi — *CBS/Fox Video* P
1342

Wolf Lake Fil-Ent '79
Drama/Horror
08055 83 mins C
B, V
Rod Steiger, David Hoffman

This film tells the story of a tough, sadistic World War II ex-Marine Sergeant. He arrives with a group of men at a resort, Wolf Lake, to find a young hippie couple living in the lodge. This sets the scene for the terror to begin.
BBFC:X — A — EN
Unknown — *Rank Video Library* H, P
0105 C

Woman's Paradise Or Hell Fil-Ent '??
Crime-Drama

PALADIN VIDEO HOME ENTERTAINMENT GUIDE

06851   90 mins   C
V2, B, V
Nadine Pascal, Monica Swinn
After Nazi Germany lost the war a group of SS Officers escaped to South America. There they built a fort where they keep women prisoners for their own pleasure. A group of people who have forgotten the war and its horrors decide to seek revenge and send a commando team to kill them all.
A — EN
Unknown — *European Video Company*
P

Wombles Very Own TV Show, The   Chi-Juv '7?
Fantasy
01974   60 mins   C
B, V
Animated
Twelve episodes of the Wombles of Wimbledon, featuring Orinoco, Uncle Bulgaria, Bungo, and other favourite characters.
PS,M — EN
Unknown — *Quadrant Video*   H, P

Wombling Free   Chi-Juv '78
Musical/Fantasy
01878   96 mins   C
B, V
David Tomlinson, Frances de la Tour, Bernard Spear, Bonnie Langford, the Wombles of Wimbledon, directed by Lionel Jeffries
A wonderful musical comedy starring the Wombles, enchanting for children of any age.
BBFC:U — *F — EN*
Rank — *Rank Video Library*   H, P
3000

Women Gladiators   Fil-Ent '??
Drama/Adventure
07918   90 mins   C
V2, B, V
This film is set in a land where men are slaves and the women fierce gladiators. They are ruled by a despotic Queen.
S,A — EN
Unknown — *Video Programme Distributors*
P
Inter-Ocean—069

Women in Love   Fil-Ent '69
Drama
12599   127 mins   C
B, V
Alan Bates, Glenda Jackson, Oliver Reed, Jennie Linden, directed by Ken Russell
Set against the sombre background of a small colliery town this film tells the story of two intense relationships that form and develop into a shinning climax that leads to the snow-covered mountains of Switzerland.
BBFC:18 — *C,A — EN*
Larry Kramer — *Warner Home Video*   P
99303

Women of the Prehistoric Planet   Fil-Ent '66
Science fiction
06877   85 mins   C
V2, B, V
Wendell Corey, Keith Larsen, John Agar, Paul Gilbert, Merry Anders, Irene Tsu
A space-ship heading for home makes a forced landing on an unexplored planet. After a series of events including an attack by savage planet women, the flagship returns in search of survivors. The commander leaves one of the survivors behind with a girl from his own rescue ship to create a new culture.
S,A — EN
Healart — *European Video Company*   P

Women Prisoners of Devil's Island, The   Fil-Ent '60
Drama
07781   115 mins   C
V2, B, V
Guy Madison, Michele Mercier
Set in the 18th century this film portrays the life of a group of women held prisoner on Devil's Island.
S,A — EN
American International — *Fletcher Video*   H, P
V115

Wonder Women   Fil-Ent '73
Suspense
04618   90 mins   C
B, V
Nancy Kwan, Ross Hagen
Top athletes disappear unaccountably. An insurance company sends an agent to Manilla to investigate, but he encounters an invisible wall of silence, constantly reaching a dead-end. Gradually, the agent makes progress until the climax of the film takes place on a remote volcanic island run by a beautiful Chinese woman.
C,A — EN
General Film Corp — *VCL Video Services*
P

Wonderful Life   Fil-Ent '64
Musical
12519   104 mins   C

(For Explanation of codes, see USE GUIDE and KEY)

PALADIN VIDEO HOME ENTERTAINMENT GUIDE

B, V
Cliff Richard, Susan Hampshire, Una Stubbs, The Shadows, directed by Sidney J. Furie
Set in the Canary Isles, this film tells the story of a young Rock 'n' Roll singer who inadvertently ends up as a stuntman in an ill fated motion picture. There is lots of fun, and many well known songs, including 'On the Beach,' 'Youth and Experience' and 'In a Matter of Moments.'
BBFC:U — F — EN
Ivy Productions Ltd — *THORN EMI*   **P**
TXJ 90 0970 4/TVJ 90 0970 2

Wooden Horse, The   Fil-Ent '50
War-Drama
01597   101 mins   B/W
B, V
Leo Genn, David Thomlinson, Anthony Steel
British prisoners of war dig a tunnel beneath a wooden gym horse to escape from a Nazi prison camp.
BBFC:U — S,A — EN
Ian Dalrymple — *THORN EMI*   **P**
TXC 90 0219 4/TVC 90 0219 2

Woody Woodpecker and His Friends II   Fil-Ent '83
Cartoons
10123   56 mins   C
B, V
Animated
This tape features eight Woody Woodpecker stories made between 1941 and 1955. Includes 'The Screwdriver', 'Wacky Bye Baby', 'Woody Dines Out', 'The Loose Nut', 'Convict Concerto', 'Poet and Peasant', 'Fish Fry' and 'Sh-h-h-h'.
BBFC:U — F — EN
Universal — *CIC Video*   **H, P**
BER 1075/VHR 1075

Woody Woodpecker and his Friends, Volume 3   Chi-Juv '84
Cartoons
13302   51 mins   C
B, V
Animated
Another collection of cartoons including Chilly Willy, Andy Panda, Wally Walrus and Maw and Paw created by Walter Lantz.
BBFC:U — F — EN
Universal — *CIC Video*   **H, P**
BER 1125/VHR 1125

Word, The   Fil-Ent '78
Mystery
09180   240 mins   C
B, V
David Janssen, Eddie Albert, Geraldine Chaplin, James Whitmore, Nicol Williamson, Ron Moody
The discovery of a centuries-old papyrus in the catacombs of Ostia, Italy triggers an international controversy. An archeologist uncovers what appears to be the writings of Jesus Christ's younger brother, James the Just. A publisher wishes to print an International New Testament, but is opposed by a powerful theologian dedicated to supressing it. A web of fear, secrecy, deceit, greed and violence is encountered by the man trying to authenticate the writings.
S,A — EN
Charles Fries Prods — *Video Form Pictures*
H, P
DD1

World According to Garp, The   Fil-Ent '82
Comedy
12489   131 mins   C
B, V
Robin Williams, John Lithgow, Mary Beth Hurt, directed by George Roy Hill
A young man grows up to be a novelist but his fame as an author is eclipsed when his mother writes a best-selling autobiography entitled 'A sexual suspect' which triggers off a feminist crusade.
BBFC:15 — C,A — EN
George Roy Hill — *Warner Home Video*
P
61261

World at War Parts 1 and 2, The   Gen-Edu '73
World War II/Documentary
04652   104 mins   C
B, V
Narrated by Laurence Olivier
'The World at War' tells the story of the Second World War. It uses dramatic film from national and private sources, much of it never screened before. It contains remarkable interviews with statesmen and military leaders of the time, along with the experiences of ordinary men and women. Two programmes are contained on one cassette: 'A New Germany 1933-39' and 'Distant War 1939-40.'
S,A — ED
Jeremy Isaacs; Thames Television — *THORN EMI*   **P**
TXB 90 6200 4/TVB 90 6200 2

World at War: Parts 1-4, The   Gen-Edu '73
World War II/Documentary
08915   208 mins   C
V2
Narrated by Laurence Olivier

---

728   (For Explanation of codes, see USE GUIDE and KEY)

PALADIN VIDEO HOME ENTERTAINMENT GUIDE

This cassette contains the first four segments of the 'World at War' series: 'A New Germany 1933-39,' 'Distant War 1939-40,' 'France Falls—May-June 1940' and 'Alone—Britain—May 1940-June 1941.'

S,A — ED

Jeremy Isaacs; Thames Television — *THORN EMI* P

TPA 90 0930 3

World at War Parts 3 and 4, The   Gen-Edu '73

World War II/Documentary

05291   104 mins   C

B, V

Narrated by Laurence Olivier

In the first programme, 'France Falls—May-June 1940,' the German invaders skirt the Maginot Line and France falls. The British Expeditionary Force retreats, leaving Hitler poised to invade Britain. The second shows the rescue of Allied troops from Dunkirk, and Hitler's decision to invade Russia and is titled 'Alone—Britain—May 1940-June 1941.'

S,A — ED

Jeremy Isaacs; Thames Television — *THORN EMI* P

TXB 90 6212 4/TVB 90 6212 2

World at War Parts 5 and 6, The   Gen-Edu '73

World War II/Documentary

05292   104 mins   C

B, V

Narrated by Laurence Olivier

The first programme, 'Barbarossa—June-December 1941,' shows the German offensive against Russia. The second, 'Banzai—Japan Strikes,' shows the Japanese attack on Pearl Harbour and their capture of the Far East.

S,A — ED

Jeremy Isaacs; Thames Television — *THORN EMI* P

TXB 90 6216 4/TVB 90 6216 2

World at War: Parts 5-8, The   Gen-Edu '73

World War II/Documentary

08916   208 mins   C

V2

Narrated by Laurence Olivier

This cassette contains the next four segments of the 'World at War' series: 'Barbarossa—June-December 1941,' 'Banzai—Japan Strikes,' 'On Our Way—America Enters the War' and 'Desert—The War in North Africa.'

S,A — ED

Jeremy Isaacs; Thames Television — *THORN EMI* P

TPA 90 0931 3

World at War Parts 7 and 8, The   Gen-Edu '73

World War II/Documentary

05290   104 mins   C

B, V

Narrated by Laurence Olivier

In the first programme on this cassette, 'On Our Way—America Enters the War,' the Americans get involved in the war in the Pacific, and Hitler declares war on the United States. The second programme, 'Desert—The War in North Africa,' traces the war in the desert to Montgomery's Desert Rats' defeat of Rommel's Afrika Korps at El Alamein in 1942.

S,A — ED

Jeremy Isaacs; Thames Television — *THORN EMI* P

TXB 90 6217 4/TVB 90 6217 2

World at War Parts 9 and 10, The   Gen-Edu '73

World War II/Documentary

05315   104 mins   C

B, V

Narrated by Laurence Olivier

In the first programme, the encirclement and defeat of the German army at Stalingrad is covered. In the second programme Germany attempts to starve Britain by attacking ships bringing supplies from North America. Many people who survived the U-boat attacks are featured on this cassette. Titles of the two programmes are 'Stalingrad' and 'Wolfpack.'

S,A — ED

Jeremy Isaacs; Thames Television — *THORN EMI* P

TXB 90 0549 4/TVB 90 0549 2

World at War Parts 11 and 12, The   Gen-Edu '73

World War II/Documentary

07412   104 mins   C

B, V

Narrated by Laurence Olivier

Part 11 entitled 'Red Star' follows the story of Russia's massive, lonely war with its 20,000,000 military and civilian casualties. Part 12 entitled

PALADIN VIDEO HOME ENTERTAINMENT GUIDE

'Whirlwind' looks at the Blitz on Britain, the public demand for revenge bombing and the change of attitude in Bomber Command by the arrival of Arthur 'Bomber' Harris.

S,A — ED

Jeremy Isaacs; Thames Television — *THORN EMI* **P**

TXB 90 0712 4/TVB 90 0712 2

World at War Parts 13 and 14, The   Gen-Edu '73

World War II/Documentary
07413   104 mins   C
B, V

Narrated by Laurence Olivier

Part 13 entitled 'Tough Old Gut' follows the defeat of Italy which proved tougher than predicted by Churchill in the Anglo-American advance from Sicily. Part 14 entitled 'It's a Lovely Day Tomorrow' covers the war in Burma where the Japanese are stopped at the Indian border.

S,A — ED

Jeremy Isaacs; Thames Television — *THORN EMI* **P**

TXB 90 0712 4/TVB 90 0712 2

World at War Parts 15 and 16, The   Gen-Edu '73

World War II/Documentary
07414   104 mins   C
B, V

Narrated by Laurence Olivier

Part 15 entitled 'Home Fires' looks at the change of direction by the Luftwaffe, after defeat in the Battle of Britain, when bombing raids took place in Portsmouth, Sheffield, Glasgow, Bristol, Coventry and Plymouth. Part 16 entitled 'Inside the Reich—Germany 1940-4' provides a picture of Germany where there is jubilation that the war is practically won and German cities remain intact.

S,A — ED

Jeremy Isaacs; Thames Television — *THORN EMI* **P**

TXB 90 0736 4/TVB 90 0736 2

World at War Parts 19 and 20, The   Gen-Edu '73

World War II/Documentary
08433   104 mins   C
B, V

Narrated by Laurence Olivier

With the liberation of Paris on August 25, 1944, in Part 19 entitled 'Pincers', the war seems to be over. The disparity of views between Montgomery and Eisenhower reaches a critical point. Part 20 entitled 'Genocide' looks at Heinrich Himmler and his aims in recreating an older 'Aryan' Germany.

S,A — ED

Jeremy Isaacs; Thames Television — *THORN EMI* **P**

TXB 90 0827 4/TVB 90 0827 2

World at War Parts 21 and 22, The   Gen-Edu '73

World War II/Documentary
08432   104 mins   C
B, V

Narrated by Laurence Olivier

Part 21 entitled 'Nemesis' looks at the desperate situation in Germany during the later stages of the war. Many thousands of Germans die as the RAF and the USAF attack by night and day. Part 22 entitled 'Japan 1941-45' looks at the Japanese. They were fearful when war was declared but after the victories of Hong Kong, Malaya and Singapore their fears were lost.

S,A — ED

Jeremy Isaacs; Thames Television — *THORN EMI* **P**

TXB 90 0828 4/TVB 90 0828 2

World at War Parts 23 And 24, The   Gen-Edu '73

World War II/Documentary
08431   104 mins   C
B, V

Narrated by Laurence Olivier

Part 23 entitled 'The Island to Island War' covers the war in the Pacific. The American commanders General MacArthur and Admiral Nimitz close in on the Japanese mainland. Part 24, entitled 'The Bomb' sees the dropping of the World's first Uranium bomb on Hiroshima. Four days later a second bomb is dropped. This brings about the Japanese surrender.

S,A — ED

Jeremy Isaccs; Thames Television — *THORN EMI* **P**

TXB 90 0832 4/TVB 90 0832 2

World at War Parts 25 And 26, The   Gen-Edu '73

World War II/Documentary
08430   104 mins   C
B, V

Narrated by Laurence Olivier

Part 25 entitled 'Reckoning' examines the end of the war in Central Europe, and the aftermath of the war. The intervention of outsiders from Russia and America meant that no European

PALADIN VIDEO HOME ENTERTAINMENT GUIDE

nation could win. The final, part 26, entitled 'Remember' counts the appalling losses of service-men and civilians whose lives were claimed by the war.
S,A — ED
Jeremy Isaacs; Thames Television — THORN EMI **P**
TXB 90 0833 4/TVB 90 08332

World Cup—Espana '82 Spo-Lei '82
Football
08544 60 mins C
B, V
Narrated by Brian Moore
This programme features edited highlights of the World's Premier Football tournament. It includes the final between Germany and Italy ending with the presentation of the World Cup Trophy to the Italians.
F — EN
Thames Television — THORN EMI **P**
TXE 90 1001 4/TVE 90 1001 2

World Cup—Mexico '70 Spo-Lei '70
Football
06217 30 mins C
B, V
Highlights from the three most outstanding games of the Mexico World Cup, Germany v Italy, Germany v England and Italy v Brazil.
F — EN
Unknown — VCL Video Services **P**
S145A

World Famous Fairy Tales FII-Ent '??
Cartoons/Fairy tales
05501 56 mins C
B, V
Animated
This programme presents animated fairy tales from around the world. From England—'Adventures of Robin Hood' and 'Jack and the Beanstalk', from Arabia—'Ali Baba and the Forty Thieves' and 'Aladdin's Lamp' and from Norway—'Gifts of the North Wind'.
BBFC:U — F — EN
Unknown — Derann Film Services **H, P**
BGS200B/BGS200

World in Flames, The: Gen-Edu '??
Part 1: From Hitler's Rise to Power to the Blitzkrieg
History-Modern/World War II
06136 99 mins B/W
V2, B, V
This film uses authentic footage from world archives. It deals with the re-arming of Germany, the dawn of World War II, the Germain invasion of Poland, the war between USSR and Finland, the German invasion of Norway and Denmark, the German campaign in France and Italy joining the Axis.
S,A — ED
Unknown — Video Programme Distributors **P**
Cinehollywood—V670

World in Flames, The: Gen-Edu '??
Part II: From the Battle of Britain to Stalingrad
History-Modern/World War II
06137 100 mins B/W
V2, B, V
This film uses authentic footage from world archives. It includes Britain's fight for life, the German campaign in the Balkans, the Battle of Moscow, war in the African desert, the Allied campaign in Africa, the Crimea and the battle of Stalingrad
S,A — ED
Unknown — Video Programme Distributors **P**
Cinehollywood—V680

World in Flames, The: Gen-Edu '??
Part III: The War on the Seas and the Fall of Japan
History-Modern/World War II
06138 95 mins B/W
V2, B, V
This film uses authentic footage from world archives. It includes the war on the seas, the Battle of Leningrad, the war in Italy, the invasion of Normandy, the Russians in Berlin, the fall of Germany and the fall of Japan.
S,A — ED
Unknown — Video Programme Distributors **P**
Cinehollywood—V690

World is Full of Married Men, The FII-Ent '80
Romance/Drama
06310 84 mins C
V2, B, V
Sherrie Lee Cronn, Anthony Franciosa
Based on the novel by Jackie Collins, this is the story of a twenty year old part-time model and her rise to the top. In the pursuit of her career she meets many men, including a forty year old married man. The film follows her exploits.
A — EN
Unknown — World of Video 2000 **H, P**
XF119

(For Explanation of codes, see USE GUIDE and KEY)

PALADIN VIDEO HOME ENTERTAINMENT GUIDE

World of Birds No. 1—Big Bill plus Speckle and Hide   Gen-Edu '7?
Birds
04501   56 mins   C
B, V
Narrated by Eric Thompson
This cassette includes two films. 'Big Bill—The Story of a Heron' (34 mins) tells the story of one of Europe's grey herons. Big Bill's life history is told in unique detail and in a light-hearted vein. 'Speckle and Hide' (22 mins) takes a look at the ptarmigan, woodcock, night jar, long-tailed tit and other masters of disguise. It examines how they use camouflage as a weapon in the battle for survival.
M,A — ED
Royal Society for the Protection of Birds — *Royal Society for the Protection of Birds*   H, P

World of Birds No. 2—Osprey   Gen-Edu '7?
Birds
04500   50 mins   C
B, V
Narrated by Robert Powell
This film tells the story of the osprey, from hatching in the Scottish Highlands, through migration to Africa and the eventual return to breed. The film takes the viewer through a year in the life of the species, including the sometimes comic moments of nest-building, family life, migration and hunting. Spectacular fishing scenes are featured. Music by Carl Davis.
S,A — EN
Royal Society for the Protection of Birds — *Royal Society for the Protection of Birds*   H, P

World of Morecambe and Wise Volume 1, The   Fil-Ent '80
Comedy
05038   104 mins   C
V2, B, V
Eric Morecambe, Ernie Wise, directed by John Ammonds
A record of the Morecambe and Wise Christmas Shows of 1978 and 1980, featuring several well-known personalities of stage and screen.
F — EN
John Ammonds — *THORN EMI*   P
TPB 90 0507 3/TXB 90 0507 4/TVB 90 0507 2

World of Survival—Hunters of the Plains, The   Gen-Edu '8?
Documentary/Wildlife
08420   45 mins   C
B, V
This programme studies the lives of two very different species of the big cat; the lion and the cheetah. It is filmed in the savannah of East Africa and contrasts the strength of the lion who hunts in group, with the greceful, slender cheethah who lives a solitary life catching his food on his own.
F — ED
Survival Anglia Ltd — *THORN EMI*   P
TXE 90 0854 4/TVE 90 0854 2

World of Survival—Man and the Great Apes, The   Gen-Edu '7?
Documentary/Animals
08418   59 mins   C
B, V
This film looks at man's closest relatives. It examines the lives of the mountain gorillas in the rain forests of Zaire. A Belgium Naturalist has spent years living close to one group, and has formed a bond between man and ape. A group of orang-utans are also looked at. To both these animals, their greatest enemy is man.
F — ED
Survival Anglia Ltd — *THORN EMI*   P
TXE 90 0749 4/TVE 90 0749 2

World of Survival—Migrants of the Arctic, The   Gen-Edu '7?
Documentary/Wildlife
08417   45 mins   C
B, V
This programme tells the remarkable story of two migrants of the Arctic, the caribou and the snow goose. Each year these animals travel hundreds of miles to reach their breeding grounds, the caribou's journey being perhaps the most dangerous to be undertaken by any animal. The snow goose flies 2500 miles from Southern America to the frozen wastelands.
F — ED
Survival Anglia Ltd — *THORN EMI*   P
TXE 90 0831 4/TVE 90 0831 2

World of Survival—Mysteries of the Great Whales, The   Fil-Ent '7?
Documentary/Animals
07431   58 mins   C
B, V
This programme follows the efforts of a group of dedicated scientists to learn something of the ways of this mysterious mammal. They spent several years investigating the haunting songs and behaviour of the Southern Right and

PALADIN VIDEO HOME ENTERTAINMENT GUIDE

Humpback whales. Accompanied by some of the best wildlife cameramen, the search took them to Patagonia, the Hawaiian Islands and Alaska.
F — EN
Survival Anglia Ltd — *THORN EMI* P
TXE 90 0589 4/TVE 90 0589 2

World of Survival—Penguins of the Falkland Islands, The
Gen-Edu '82
Documentary/Animals
08419   49 mins   C
B, V

This programme, made by Cindy Buxton and Annie Price who were trapped in South Georgia during the Argentine invasion, follows the life of penguins. It looks at the breeding season, when the eggs hatch, and the rearing of the young. The Penguins have little to fear from predators on the land, but in the sea the bull sealions hunt them, not for food, but for sport.
F — ED
Survival Anglia Ltd — *THORN EMI* P
TXE 90 0866 4/TVE 90 0866 2

World of Survival—The Last Kingdoms of the Elephants, The
Gen-Edu '7?
Documentary/Animals
07432   45 mins   C
B, V

This film examines whether the elephant can survive in the wild and whether it will be allowed to. While the elephant enjoys a protected life, its numbers are increasing and a herd eats an enormous quantity of the fast dwindling vegetation. The film includes footage shot in Sri Lanka, where an undrugged elephant charges straight for the cameraman, who leaves the camera running producing dramatic shots.
F — EN
Survival Anglia Ltd — *THORN EMI* P
TXE 90 0718 4/TVE 90 0718 2

World War III
Fil-Ent '80
Drama/Suspense
09181   180 mins   C
B, V

Rock Hudson, David Soul, Brian Keith, Cathy Lee Crosby
This film tells of a tense dramatic confrontation between the two world powers, America and Russia. At Wallace Radar Station, the American radar base in Alaska, Russians invade with a special force. Their aim is to capture an oil pipe line station, gaining a strength behind Russia's negotiations to lift the American embargo on grain.
S,A — EN
Finnegan Associates — *Video Form Pictures*
H, P
MGS 1

World's Greatest Athlete, The
Fil-Ent '73
Adventure
05596   89 mins   C
B, V

Tim Conway, Jan-Michael Vincent, John Amos, Roscoe Lee Browne, Dayle Haddon, Billy de Wolfe, directed by Rfobert Sheerer
A college coach on safari in Africa stumbles on a young boy who is obviously a brilliant athlete. Against the boy's witch doctor godfather's wishes he goes back to America with the coach. At the National Colleges Track and Field Meet it looks like he will win all events until the godfather arrives.
F — EN
Walt Disney Productions — *Rank Video Library*
H
05000

World's Greatest Paintings 1: Adoration, The
Fin-Art '8?
Arts/Documentary
08736   54 mins   C
LV

In this programme, five masterpieces of European painting are brought together. These include works by Van Eyck, Piero della Francesca, Botticelli, Rigaud and Tiepolo.
S,A — ED
Bill Morton; Kenneth Corden — *BBC Video*
H, P
BBCV 1013L

Woyzeck/How Much Wood Would a Woodchuck Chuck
Fil-Ent '79
Drama/Documentary
08982   125 mins   C
B, V

Klaus Kinski, Eva Mattes, Wolfgang Reichmann, directed by Werner Herzog
'Woyzeck' tells the story of a simple soldier whose life is completely determined by others. It tells of his relentless oppression and his final anguished protest against it. 'How Much Wood Would a Woodchuck Chuck' (black and white) tells of the 13th World Mastership of Livestock Auctioneers. The winner keeps in trim by

(For Explanation of codes, see USE GUIDE and KEY)

PALADIN VIDEO HOME ENTERTAINMENT GUIDE

working up fast speeds on tongue-twisters such as the title, whilst another practises by auctioning off telegraph poles along the highway.
BBFC:AA — C,A — EN
Unknown — Palace Video Ltd   P
PVC 2031A

World at War Parts 17 and 18, The   Gen-Edu '73
World War II/Documentary
07415   104 mins   C
B, V
Narrated by Laurence Olivier
part 17 entitled 'Morning' looks at the morning of 5 June 1944 when the largest amphibian invasion force ever reached the beaches of Normandy. Americans, British and Canadians attacked on five separate beaches. Part 18 entitled 'Occupation' examines the occupation of the Netherlands after Rotterdam is badly bombed.
S,A — ED
Jeremy Isaacs; Thames Television — THORN EMI   P
TXB 90 0757 4/TVB 90 0757 2

Wrong Man, The   Fil-Ent '56
Suspense
12997   126 mins   B/W
B, V
Henry Fonda, Vera Miles, Anthony Quayle, directed by Alfred Hitchcock
In this film a musician is accused of a robbery he did not commit. Based on a true story
C,A — EN
Warner Bros — Warner Home Video   P
61065

Wrong Way   Fil-Ent '??
Drama
06068   80 mins   C
V2, B, V
Laurel Kenyon, Candy Sweet
Two attractive girls seek help from a group of Nomadic Jeepers when their car breaks down. The girls are lured to the Jeepers camp and are raped, abused and humiliated. They are finally abandoned to even worse fate at the hands of a murderous band of hippies.
BBFC:X — A — EN
Unknown — Video Programme Distributors   P
Inter-Ocean—051

Wuthering Heights   Fil-Ent '70
Drama/Romance
08373   105 mins   C
V2, B, V
Anna Calder-Marshall, Timothy Dalton, Harry Andrews, Hugh Griffith, Ian Ogilvy, Judy Cornwell
This film is adapted from Emily Bronte's classic novel about a young girl's love for a stable lad. She forsakes her love for him and marries a country squire. The young man returns to take revenge.
BBFC:U — S,A — EN
AIP/Arkoff/Nicholson — Guild Home Video
H, P, E

X

X from Outer Space, The   Fil-Ent '66
Science fiction
05736   85 mins   C
V2, B, V
Toshiya Wazaki, Peggy Neal, Giji Okada, Hoko Harada, Franz Gruber, Mike Daneen, Shinichi Yanagisawa
A spacecraft on a mission in outerspace inadvertantly picks up an alien spore. Unknown to the crew the spore is bought back to earth; the spore uses high pressure electricity and atomic energy to magify itself into a monster of 15,000 tons, with devastating results.
F — EN
Japan — Video Unlimited   H, P
005

Xanadu   Fil-Ent '80
Musical/Fantasy
07960   96 mins   C
V2, B, V
Olivia Newton-John, Gene Kelly, Michael Beck
A beautiful muse comes down to earth and meets an artist and a nightclub owner. She helps them fulfill their dreams as they collaborate on a roller-disco venture.
S,A — EN
Universal — CIC Video   H, P
CRA1018/BEA1018/VHA1018

X-Ray   Fil-Ent '8?
Horror/Mystery
08067   78 mins   C
B, V
Barbie Benton, Chip Lucia

PALADIN VIDEO HOME ENTERTAINMENT GUIDE

This is the story of a young girl in hospital, believed to be terminally ill. However, her x-rays had been fixed to make it look as if she was dying. Everyone that comes to visit her is afterwards brutally murdered.
BBFC:X — A — EN
Unknown — *Rank Video Library*   **H, P**
2018 C

XTC-Look Look   **Fil-Ent '??**
Music-Performance
10130   45 mins   C
B, V
This tape is a collection of promotional videos featuring XTC performing hit singles that span their career. Also includes interview footage.
S,A — EN
Unknown — *Palace Video Ltd*   **P**
VIRV 013D

XTRO   **Fil-Ent '83**
Science fiction/Horror
09890   83 mins   C
B, V, LV
Bernice Stegers, Philip Sayer, Simon Nash, Maryam D'Abo, Danny Brainin
This film follows the bizarre events of a man who has been abducted by an alien civilisation and returns to earth, after three years absence from his wife and son, as a violent and brutal humanoid.
A — EN
New Line Cinema; Amalgamated Films — *Polygram Video*   **H, P**
790 6484/790 6482

Y

Yanks   **Fil-Ent '79**
Drama/Romance
12972   140 mins   C
B, V
Richard Gere, Vanessa Redgrave, William Devane, Lisa Eichorn, directed by John Schlesinger
Set in Britain during the war years, this film focuses on the lives of three American soldiers who are stationed in Lancashire and the women they meet and fall in love with.
BBFC:15 — S,A — EN
United Artists; CIP — *Warner Home Video*   **P**
99256

Year of Living Dangerously, The   **Fil-Ent '83**
Drama/Adventure
10149   115 mins   C
B, V
Mel Gibson, Linda Hunt, Jill Bryant, directed by Peter Weir
An ambitious Australian journalist is given his first overseas assignment in Indonesia. There he meets up with a cameraman and together they form a team, risking their lives to report stories from this tense land on the verge of civil war.
BBFC:18 — C,A — EN
MGM/UA — *MGM/UA Home Video*   **P**
UMB 10243/UMV 10243

Year of Sir Ivor, The   **Spo-Lei '7?**
Horse racing
01977   52 mins   C
B, V
The story of the great racehorse, Sir Ivor, and the man who rode him, Lester Piggott.
F — EN
Unknown — *Quadrant Video*   **H, P**

Year of the Quorn   **Spo-Lei '??**
Sports-Minor/Documentary
09122   44 mins   C
B, V
This is an entertaining and informative documentary about the Quorn Hunt. The film follows the hunt's year, including its social side, over 3 seasons.
F — EN
Unknown — *Quadrant Video*   **H, P**
EG

Yellow Emanuelle   **Fil-Ent '??**
Drama/Romance
08907   90 mins   C
V2, B, V
Ilono Staller, Claudio Giorgi, directed by Albert Thomas
Emanuelle falls in love with an airline pilot. He promises to marry her when he returns from Europe. However, a jealous woman intercepts his letters to her, and tells her he has married another woman.
BBFC:X — A — EN
Unknown — *Video Programme Distributors*   **P**
Inter-Ocean 010

Yellowbeard   **Fil-Ent '83**
Comedy
12740   95 mins   C
B, V

PALADIN VIDEO HOME ENTERTAINMENT GUIDE

Graham Chapman, Peter Boyle, Cheech and Chong, Peter Cook, Marty Feldman, Eric Idle, John Cleese
A star-studded pirate romp that sends up every swashbuckling pirate epic you have ever seen.
BBFC:PG — F — EN
Carter de Haven — Rank Video Library
H, P
1068 D

Yentl
Fil-Ent '84
Drama
12983   128 mins   C
B, V
Barbra Streisand, Mandy Patinkin, Amy Irving, Nehemiah Persoff, directed by Barbra Streisand
At the turn of the century, a young Jewish girl is determined to become educated and, flouting convention, enrols at school disguised as a boy.
BBFC:PG — S,A — EN
Barbra Streisand; Rusty Lemorande — Warner Home Video   **P**
99453

Yeoman of the Guard, The
Fil-Ent '??
Musical/Opera
05951   103 mins   C
B, V
Tommy Steele
A performance of one of Gilbert and Sullivan's operas adapted from the City of London Festival Production.
S,A — EN
City of London Festival Production; Stanley Dorfman — Precision Video Ltd   **P**
BITC 2022/VITC 2022

Yeomen of the Guard
Fil-Ent '8?
Opera
08925   100 mins   C
B, V
Joel Grey, Alfred Marks, Elizabeth Gale, David Hillman, Elizabeth Bainbridge, Peter Savidge, Geoffrey Chard, Michael Bulman, Claire Powell, Beryl Korman
This opera by Gilbert and Sullivan tells the story of an unfortunate jester who loses his sweetheart to a condemned man. However, he does not die, and she rejoices in her new-found love whilst the jester succumbs to a fatal despair. The music is performed by The London Symphony Orchestra conducted by Alexander Faris, with The Ambrosian Opera Chorus.
S,A — EN
Brent Walker Prods — Brent Walker Home Video Ltd   **P**

Yes, Giorgio
Fil-Ent '82
Comedy/Musical
10162   107 mins   C
B, V
Luciano Pavarotti, Kathryn Harrold
A famous Italian opera singer on tour in America is taken ill with throat trouble. A glamorous lady specialist is called in; she cures him and is consequently pursued and wooed by the opera singer. The songs include 'If We Were in Love', 'I Left My Heart in San Francisco', 'O Sole Mio' and 'Ave Maria'.
F — EN
MGM — MGM/UA Home Video   **P**
UMB 10208/UMV 10208

Yeti
Fil-Ent '7?
Science fiction
07762   110 mins   C
V2, B, V
Jim Sullivan, Tony Kendall, Phoenix Grant
This film follows the adventures of a Yeti, half man and half animal, who is brought back to life after a million years in hibernation.
S,A — EN
Unknown — Fletcher Video   **H, P**
V132

Ynys-Hir
Gen-Edu '81
Birds/Wildlife
04281   23 mins   C
B, V
Narrated by David Lloyd Meredith, music by Michael Omer, photography by Eamonde Buitlear
On the west coast of Wales, 630 acres bordering the south bank of the River Dyfi form the RSPB reserve of Ynys-hir. This programme looks at the varied habitats on the reserve and the abundance of animals and plants.
F — ED
Royal Society for the Protection of Birds — Royal Society for the Protection of Birds   **H, P**

YOC in Your School, The
Gen-Edu '84
Birds
13598   12 mins   C
V2, B, V
Designed primarily for leaders of the RSPB's Young Ornithologist Club, this cassette would also be helpful to anyone concerned with running a bird club.
A — ED
Royal Society for the Protection of Birds — Royal Society for the Protection of Birds   **H, P**

PALADIN VIDEO HOME ENTERTAINMENT GUIDE

Yoga for Health   Med-Sci '??
Yoga/Physical fitness
07366   110 mins   C
B, V
This tape provides a complete guide to yoga and how to keep in shape with expert tuition.
S,A — ED
Unknown — Precision Video Ltd   P
BOPV 2564/VOPV 2564

Yojimbo   Fil-Ent '62
Drama
10017   138 mins   B/W
B, V
Toshiro Mifune, Eijiro Tono, directed by Akira Kurosawa
Warring factions of a 19th century town are trying to gain control of the political situation. When a professional killer comes to town, both sides bid for his services. Japanese with English subtitles.
S,A — EN   JA
Japan — Palace Video Ltd   P
PVC 2044A

Yol (The Way)   Fil-Ent '82
Drama
09889   105 mins   C
B, V
Tarik Akan, Serif Sezer, Halil Ergun
This is a Turkish film with English subtitles. It is a dramatic tale focusing on five prisoners on a week's parole who each return home to face a domestic crisis fermented by the archaic social customs of the country.
C,A — EN
Yilmaz Guney; Cactus Films — Polygram Video   H, P
791 5474/791 5472

You and Me   Fil-Ent '76
Drama
12250   ? mins   C
B, V
David Carradine, Barbara Hershey, Chipper Chadbourne, directed by David Carradine
A brutal Hell's Angel biker teams up with a nine-year old boy. Both are on the run and together they stay one step ahead of the law.
S,A — EN
Billy Record; Filmmakers International — VCL Video Services   P

You and Your Child   Gen-Edu '??
Religion/Bible
06285   50 mins   C
B, V, PH15
4 pgms
This series of four films, each 50 mins, in colour, features Mr S. Thompson who brings a background of Bible and Jewish lessons to films on parent and child relationships.
1.Training Your Child 2.The Home Life of Jesus 4.Knowing Your Child 4.Marks a Maturity
S,A — R
Audio Visual Ministries — Audio Visual Ministries   H, L, P

You Light Up My Life   Fil-Ent '77
Drama
09284   90 mins   C
B, V
Didi Conn, Joe Silver, Michael Zaslow, Stephen Nathan, Melanie Mayron, directed by Joseph Brooks
A young singer/songwriter faces difficulties in achieving success in her career and in finding real meaning in her personal relationships. All this changes when she meets a young man with whom she has a one night stand.
Academy Awards '77: Best Song ('You Light Up My Life').   S,A — EN
Columbia — RCA/Columbia Pictures Video UK
H, P

You Only Live Twice   Fil-Ent '67
Adventure
13189   108 mins   C
B, V
Sean Connery, Donald Pleasence, Karin Dor, directed by Lewis Gilbert
Agent 007 battles Blofeld, the despicable head of Spectre, in this thriller set in Japan.
BBFC:A — C,A — EN
Danjaq SA; United Artists — Warner Home Video   P
99207

You Too Can Do the Cube   How-Ins '81
Hobbies/Games
07956   28 mins   C
B, V
Patrick Bossert
This programme features 13 year-old Patrick Bossert and his foolproof method of solving Rubik's cube. He demonstrates all stages step by step, then shows some other patterns and how to dismantle and improve the action of the cube.
F — I
Goldcrest Television; Penguin Books — THORN EMI   P
TXE 90 0548 4/TVE 90 0548 2

Young and Free   Fil-Ent '7?
Western
02128   83 mins   C
V2, B, V

(For Explanation of codes, see USE GUIDE and KEY)

PALADIN VIDEO HOME ENTERTAINMENT GUIDE

An Ohio farm boy finds himself on a wagon train heading west after his mother's death from cholera. His adventures in the wild and his love for an Indian girl make an exciting and warm story for all ages.
F — EN
Unknown — Hokushin Audio Visual Ltd
P
VM-40

Young and Innocent Fil-Ent '37
Suspense
04256   77 mins   B/W
B, V
Derrick de Marney, Percy Marmont, Mary Clare, George Curgon, Nova Pilbeam, Edward Rigby, John Longden, Basil Radford, directed by Alfred Hitchcock
A case of mistaken identity sends a young man off on a chase through the Cornish countryside to find the murderer who stole the raincoat that incriminates him.
BBFC:A — S,A — EN
Gaumont — Rank Video Library   H, P
0027

Young at Heart Fil-Ent '54
Musical-Drama
08722   113 mins   C
V2, B, V
Frank Sinatra, Doris Day, Gig Young, Ethel Barrymore, Dorothy Malone, Robert Keith, Elizabeth Fraser, Alan Hale Sr.
This is Fanny Hurst's lighthearted tale of a cynical hard-luck musician who finds happiness when he falls for a small-town girl. The songs include 'Young at Heart', the title song, 'You, My Love' and 'Just One of Those Things.'
F — EN
Warner Bros — BBC Video   H, P
BBCV 8002

Young Avenger, The Fil-Ent '83
Martial arts
12843   86 mins   C
V2, B, V
A young boy who works in an undertaker's is amazed when a 'ghost' tells him a story of betrayal and murder which he sets out to avenge.
BBFC:18 — C,A — EN
Unknown — Video Programme Distributors
P
VPD 240

Young Doctors in Love Fil-Ent '82
Comedy
12741   95 mins   C
B, V, LV
Michael McKean, Hector Elizondo, Patrick Macnee, Sean Young, Harry Dean-Stanton, Dabney Coleman
An uproarious, scandalous account of the goings-on in a sprawling general hospital, as seen through the eyes of the craziest bunch of interns who ever took the hippocratic oath.
BBFC:15 — C,A — EN
Jerry Bruckheimer — Rank Video Library
H, P
1064D

Young Graduates, The Fil-Ent '71
Adventure
06185   88 mins   C
B, V
Adam West, Ahna Capri
An adventure in which the teenagers discover the truth about the careless life they lead.
S,A — EN
Tempo — VCL Video Services   P

Young Joe-The Forgotten Kennedy Fil-Ent '77
Drama
10194   97 mins   C
B, V
Barbara Parkins, Peter Strauss, Stephen Elliott
This film tells the story of Joe Kennedy Jr. Groomed from boyhood to become the first Irish Catholic President of the United States he accepted glory as his destiny.
S,A — EN
ABC Circle Films — Video Form Pictures
H, P
6254-50

Young Lions, The Fil-Ent '58
Drama
01148   167 mins   B/W
B, V
Marlon Brando, Montgomery Clift, Dean Martin
An epic film, based on the Irwin Shaw novel, depicting the individual men and women caught up on both sides of World War II. Filmed on location with some documentary footage.
F — EN
20th Century Fox — CBS/Fox Video   P
4A-094

Young Love, First Love Fil-Ent '79
Romance
12094   95 mins   C
B, V
Timothy Hutton, Dee Wallace, Valerie Bertinelli, Arlen Dean Snyder, directed by Steve Stern

PALADIN VIDEO HOME ENTERTAINMENT GUIDE

A love story of two young people from conflicting backgrounds, and the confusing situation that arises when moral values threaten their love.
S,A — EN
Lorimar — *Polygram Video*   **H, P**
0401364/0401362

Young Master, The   Fil-Ent '84
Martial arts
13377   88 mins   C
V2, B, V
Jackie Chan
The action comes thick and fast in this film when Jackie Chan tries to save his best friend from a life of crime.
BBFC:18 — C,A — EN
Unknown — *Guild Home Video*   **H, P, E**
8289-3

Young Ones, The   Fil-Ent '61
Musical
05059   104 mins   C
B, V
Cliff Richard, Robert Morley, Carole Gray, The Shadows, directed by Sidney J Furie
This is the story of how a group of young Londoners produced a show to raise money and save their club from demolition.
F — EN
Kenneth Harper — *THORN EMI*   **P**
TXC 90 0242 4/TVC 90 0242 2

Young Ones, The   Fil-Ent '61
Musical
12518   104 mins   C
B, V
Cliff Richard, Robert Morley, Carole Gray, The Shadows, directed by Sidney J Furie
This is the story of a young man's battle to save his youth club's premises from demolition by his own father's company. The song track includes 'When the Girl in Your Arms is the Girl in Your Heart','Friday Night','Got a Funny Feeling','Nothing's Impossible' and 'Living Doll.'
BBFC:U — F — EN
Associated British Picture Corporation Ltd — *THORN EMI*   **P**
TXJ 90 0242 4/TVJ 90 0242 2

Young Warriors, The   Fil-Ent '84
Drama
13379   98 mins   C
V2, B, V
Ernest Borgnine, Richard Roundtree, Lynda Day George, James Van Patten
After a girl is brutally raped and killed, her brother and his friends set out to avenge her and become the ultimate weapon in the fight against crime.
BBFC:18 — A — EN
Cannon Films — *Guild Home Video*   **H, P, E**
8317-7

Your Money or Your Wife   Fil-Ent '72
Crime-Drama/Comedy
08015   72 mins   C
V2, B, V
Ted Bessell, Jack Cassidy, Richard Peabody, Elizabeth Ashley, Betsy Von Furstenberg, Graham Jarvis, directed by Allen Reisner
To take revenge on a beautiful actress who had walked out of a television series threatening many careers, a scriptwriter writes a kidnap plot with her as the victim. This imaginary plot turns into a nearly perfect crime. The story is based on the book 'If You Want to See Your Wife Again' by John Craig.
BBFC:A — S,A — EN
Brentwood TV Corp — *Iver Film Services*   **P**
197

Your Ticket Is No Longer Valid   Fil-Ent '80
Drama/Romance
09074   100 mins   C
B, V
Richard Harris, George Peppard, Jeanne Moreau, Jennifer Dale
Set in Paris, in a world of sophistication, luxury and romance, this film tells the story of an international business tycoon who at the age of sixty is facing a crisis with his financial empire crumbling. At the same time he falls in love with a twenty-year-old Brazilian girl.
A — EN
Unknown — *Video Tape Centre*   **P**
VTC 1029

You've Come a Long Way, Katie   Fil-Ent '8?
Drama
12141   153 mins   C
V2, B, V
Lolly Cadeau, directed by Vic Sarin
This is the story of Katie Forbes, a talented and successful TV chat show hostess and her struggle to overcome her dependence on alcoholism.
BBFC:PG — S,A — EN
Unknown — *Intervision Video*   **H, P**
A-A 0489

(For Explanation of codes, see USE GUIDE and KEY)

PALADIN VIDEO HOME ENTERTAINMENT GUIDE

Yum-Yum Girls   Fil-Ent '78
Comedy
06940   89 mins   C
B, V

Judy Landers, Tanya Roberts, Barbara Tully, Michelle Daw

A naive, innocent small-town girl travels to New York to fulfill her dreams of becoming a successful model. She soon learns that it is not that easy as she comes to terms with the nitty-gritty of the business.
BBFC:X — A — EN
Canon Releasing — *Rank Video Library*
H, P
1034C

Yuma   Fil-Ent '70
Western
04222   75 mins   C
B, V

Clint Walker, Barry Sullivan

A rough, tough lawman sets out to tame the wildest, most corrupt town of the old west—Yuma.
BBFC:U — F — EN
Spelling — *Guild Home Video*   **H, P**

Z

Zachariah   Fil-Ent '71
Western/Musical
05191   92 mins   C
B, V

John Rubinstein, Pat Quinn

Stunning photography and original heavy-metal rock music make 'Zachariah' a definitive surrealist cult film of the early seventies.
BBFC:A — C,A — EN
Cinerama Releasing — *Rank Video Library*
H, P
8003

Zapped   Fil-Ent '82
Comedy
13224   96 mins   C
V2, B, V

Scott Baio, Robert Mandan, directed by Robert J Rosenthal

After an accident in the chemistry laboratory, a shy young student finds he has super powers which lead him from one fun situation to the next.
BBFC:15 — S,A — EN
Embassy Pictures — *Embassy Home Entertainment*   **P**
1604

Zebra Force   Fil-Ent '76
Crime-Drama
02127   105 mins   C
V2, B, V

Mike Lane, Richard X Slattery, Rockne Tarkington

A group of Vietnam War veterans devise a scheme to use the talents that got them through the war, to get rich quick at the expense of organised criminals.
BBFC:X — A — EN
FAI Cinema II — *Video Programme Distributors*
P
Cinehollywood—V150

Zelig   Fil-Ent '83
Comedy
12968   76 mins   C
B, V

Woody Allen, Mia Farrow, directed by Woody Allen

In this mock documentary from the 1920-30 period, Woody Allen has combined authentic photographs and newsreels to appear as Zelig, the master of disguises. Filmed in black-and-white, with colour inserts.
BBFC:PG — S,A — EN
Orion Pictures — *Warner Home Video*   **P**
72027

Zero to Sixty   Fil-Ent '78
Comedy/Adventure
05759   87 mins   C
B, V

Darren McGavin, Dick Martin, Denise Nickerson, Joan Collins, directed by Don Weis

A man who worked hard for eighteen years and did all the 'right' things is framed by his wife and forced into an alimony bondage for the rest of his life. His only possession, his car, is repossessed and he gives chase. Now a victim of both sides of the law he joins the rowdy 'repo' gang and becomes involved in a series of unlikely escapades and romantic attachments.
BBFC:AA — C,A — EN
First Artists — *Home Video Holdings*   **H, P**
005

Ziegfeld Follies   Fil-Ent '46
Musical
13427   103 mins   C
B, V

Gene Kelly, Fred Astaire, Lucille Ball, Cyd Charisse, Judy Garland, Red Skelton, Lena Horne, Esther Williams, directed by Vincente Minnelli

PALADIN VIDEO HOME ENTERTAINMENT GUIDE

This extravaganza reveals a host of MGM's best-known stars taking turns to outshine each other and is the film in which Astaire and Kelly dance together.
BBFC:U — F — EN
MGM — *MGM/UA Home Video*   P
10173

Ziggy Stardust and the Spiders from Mars   Fil-Ent '82
Music-Performance
09804   95 mins   C
B, V
David Bowie, Mick Ronson, Trevor Bolder, Mick Woodmansy, directed by D.A. Pennebaker
This tape features David Bowie recorded live at the Hammersmith Odeon performing the story of The Rise and Fall of Ziggy Stardust and the Spiders from Mars. Songs include 'Ziggy Stardust', 'All the Young Dudes', 'Oh! You Pretty Things', 'Changes', 'Space Oddity' and many others.
BBFC:PG — F — EN
Bewlay Bros. — *THORN EMI*   P
TXJ 90 2113 4/TVJ 90 2113 2

Zoltan.....Hound of Dracula   Fil-Ent '77
Horror
07448   85 mins   C
B, V
Michael Pataki, Reggie Nalder, Jose Ferrer, directed by Albert Band
Count Dracula's dead servant is brought back to life when the tomb is inadvertently discovered by Russian soldiers. The servant becomes determined to track down the last exiled member of the Dracula clan. He sends his dog Zoltan to bite the man but is driven away by Alsatians. The servant is forced to follow the man when he goes on a caravaning holiday where he tries several times to 'vampirise' him.
BBFC:X — A — EN
VIC Cinema Productions — *THORN EMI*
P
TXC 90 02744/TVC 90 02742

Zombie, Creeping Flesh   Fil-Ent '??
Horror
08850   81 mins   C
B, V
Magrit Evelyn Newton, Frank Garfeeld, Selan Karay, Robert O'Neil, directed by Vincent Dawn
When a toxic gas explosion occurs in a factory, the workers become blood-crazed zombies.
BBFC:X — A — EN
Unknown — *VCL Video Services*   P
M264D

Zombies Dawn of the Dead   Fil-Ent '79
Horror
06806   121 mins   C
V2, B, V
David Emge, Ken Foree, Scott H. Reiniger, Gaylen Ross, directed by George A. Romero
A sequel to 'Night of the Living Dead,' in which the carnivorous corpses return to threaten extinction of the entire U.S. population.
S,A — EN
Richard P Rubinstein — *Intervision Video*
H, P
A-A 0358

Zorro   Fil-Ent '??
Cartoons/Adventure
09968   77 mins   C
B, V
Animated
When rich landowners and unscrupulous soldiers ruled California, only one man, Don Diego de Vega, Spain's greatest swordsman, stood against them. In his disguise of a black cloak and mask he rides out to help the people, known by them and all evil doers as Zorro.
F — EN
Unknown — *Select Video Limited*   P
3602/43

Zorro and the Three Musketeers   Fil-Ent '??
Adventure
06129   90 mins   C
V2, B, V
Gordon Scott, Maria Grazia Spina, James Stuart
Zorro sets out to free the cousin of the King of Spain. In spite of the help of the Three Musketeers, it is to prove a difficult enterprise.
F — EN
Unknown — *Video Programme Distributors*
P
Cinehollywood—V230

Zorro at the Spanish Court   Fil-Ent '77
Adventure
06130   90 mins   C
V2, B, V
George Ardisson, Alberto Lupo, Maria Grazia Spina
The Spanish Courts are the setting for this adventure with Zorro, who drives away the usurper of the Lusitania throne and liberates the dispossessed heiress.
F — EN
Unknown — *Video Programme Distributors*
P
Cinehollywood—V240

(For Explanation of codes, see USE GUIDE and KEY)

PALADIN VIDEO HOME ENTERTAINMENT GUIDE

Z.P.G. Fil-Ent '72
Science fiction/Drama
05604   95 mins   C
B, V
Oliver Reed, Geraldine Chaplin, Don Gordon, Diane Cilento, directed by Michael Campus
World leaders impose a thirty year ban on having children to attain Z.P.G.—Zero Population Growth. A couple are caught in the dilemma of desperately wanting their own baby and decide to defy the law.
S,A — EN
Paramount; Sagittarus Productions — *Home Video Merchandisers*   **H, P**
006

Zulu Dawn Fil-Ent '79
Adventure
06807   115 mins   C
V2, B, V
Burt Lancaster, Peter O'Toole, Simon Ward, Nigel Davenport, Denholm Elliot, John Mills
The tale of the Battle of Island Ihwana, wherein 1,500 redcoats were slaughtered by 16 times their number of Zulu warriors.
S,A — EN
American Cinema — *Intervision Video*   **H, P**
A-A 0340

SUBJECT CATEGORY INDEX

Adventure

Acapulco Gold
Across the Great Divide
Adventure in Ventana
Adventurers, The
Adventures of Buster the Bear, The
Adventures of Captain Future I, The
Adventures of Captain Future II, The
Adventures of Choppy and the Princess—1, The
Adventures of Choppy and the Princess—2, The
Adventures of Choppy and the Princess—3, The
Adventures of Curley and His Gang, The
Adventures of Frontier Fremont, The
Adventures of Gumdrop, The
Adventures of Huckleberry Finn, The
Adventures of Reddy the Fox, The
Adventures of Robin Hood, The
Adventures of Sinbad the Sailor, The
Adventures of the Wilderness Family
Adventures of the Wilderness Family—Part 2
Adventures of Tom Sawyer, The
Adventures of Ultraman, The
Africa Express
Africa—Texas Style
African Queen, The
Against a Crooked Sky
Aguirre, Wrath of God
Air Hawk
Airwolf
Alamo, The
All the Way Boys
Amateur, The
Amazing Dobermans, The
Amazing Spider-Man—Cassette 2, The
Amazing Spider-Man IV in Night of the Villains
Amazing Spider-Man-Cassette 3, The
America Screams
American Wilderness
Americano, The
Angel
Angry Dragon, The
Any Which Way You Can
Ark of the Sun God, The
Asterix and Cleopatra
Asterix the Gaul
Atlantic Adventure
Atom Ant—Cassette 1
Atom Ant—Cassette 2
Ator, the Fighting Eagle
Attack FORCE Z
Attila the Hun
Banana Splits Adventure Show-Cassette 2, The
Banana Splits Adventure Show, Cassette 3, The
Bad Man's River
Bang Bang Gang, The
Barbarosa
Bare Knuckles
Batfink-Cassette 1
Batfink II in Bat Patrol
Battle of the Stars
Battletruck
Beach Girls, The
Bear Island
Bears and I, The
Beat the Devil
Best of Walt Disney's True Life Adventures, The
Beyond the Poseidon Adventure
Big Cat, The
Big Fish Down Under—Away From It All
Big Fish Down Under—Black Marlin
Big Fish Down Under—Island Holiday
Big Fish Down Under—Professionals at Play
Big Fish Down Under—Sailfish
Big Fish Down Under—The Beginnings
Big Fish Down Under—The Ribbons
Big Red
Big Zapper
Black Arrow, The
Black Beard's Ghost
Black Beauty
Black Dragon, The
Black Island/Shooting Star
Black Pirate, The
Black Pirate, The
Black Stallion Returns, The
Black Tulip, The
Blackbeard the Pirate/Fish Feathers/Pal's Adventure/The Fireman
Blackstar
Blazing Stewardesses
Blue Fire Lady
Blue Jeans and Dynamite
Blue Thunder
Boatniks, The
Bobbie Jo and the Outlaw
Bonnie & Clyde
Bronco Billy
Bronx Warriors
Bronx Warriors 2-The Battle for Manhattan
Bruce Against Iron Hand
Bruce Lee Against Supermen
Bruce's Fingers
Buck Rogers in the 25th Century
Buckstone County Prison
Bulldog Drummond Escapes
Burglars, The
Bushido Blade, The
Cabo Blanco
Cahill
Calculus Affair, The
Call Him Mr Shatter
Call of the Wild
Canadian Pacific

743

Adventure — **SUBJECT CATEGORY INDEX**

Candleshoe
Capers
Captain America
Captain America—Cassette 2
Captain America-The Red Skull Lives
Captain Blood
Captain Micron's Electronic Comic
Caravan to Vaccares
Caravans
Carquake
Castaway Cowboy, The
Castle of Evil
Cat From Outer Space, The
Cavern Deep
Challenge, The
Challenge to Be Free
Charlie and the Talking Buzzard
Chisholms—Cassette 1, The
Chisholms—Cassette 2, The
Christmas Mountain
City Under the Sea
Cleopatra Jones
Clones of Bruce Lee, The
Cloud Dancer
Clutch of Power, The
Cody
Cold River
Comeback
Commando Attack
Companeros
Conan the Barbarian
Control Factor
Convoy
Cop in Blue Jeans
Copter Kids, The
Cormack
Corrupt Ones, The
Cotter/Island of Lost Women
Country Blue
Countryman
Crab with the Golden Claws, The
Creature from the Black Lagoon, The
Cry Wolf
Crystal Fist
Curley and His Gang in the Haunted Mansion
Cycles South
Daleks—Invasion Earth 2150 A.D.
Danger Mouse
Danger Mouse Volume 3
Dangerous Cargo
Dangerous Summer, A
Darby O'Fill and the Little People
Daring Game
Dark of the Sun
Fabulous Fantastic Four, The
Dastardly and Muttley-Cassette 1
Dastardly and Muttley—Cassette 2
Davy Crockett
Dead Man's Float
Deadly Impact
Deadly Trackers, The

Death Hunt
Death Race 2000
Death Raiders
Death Ship
Deathcheaters
Deep River Savages
Deerslayer, The
Deerslayer, The
Desert Chase
Desert Warrior
Desperate Ones, The
Desperate Women
Diamond Hunters
Diamonds Are Forever
Dick Deadeye
Dirty Dozen, The
Dirty Mary, Crazy Larry
Dr. No
Dr. Who and the Daleks
Doctor Who and the Revenge of the Cybermen
Dr. Who, the Brain of Moribus
Don't Play With Fire
Dot and Bunny
Dot and Santa Claus
Dot and the Kangaroo
Double Man, The
Double Nickles
Dove, The
Dr Syn—Alias the Scarecrow
Dragon Dies Hard, The
Dragon Lives, The
Dragon Lives Again, The
Dragon's Teeth
Dragonslayer
Dune
Dynamite Brothers, The
Dynamo
Eagles Attack at Dawn
Earthling, The
El Cid
Elephant Boy, The
Elephant Called Slowly, An
Elmer
Embassy
Enchanted Island/Westward Passage
Enter the Dragon
Enter the Streetfighter
Erotic Adventures of Zarro, The
Escapade in Japan/A Gift for Heidi
Escape from Angola
Escape from New York
Escape to Athena
Escape to Witch Mountain
Eureka Stockade
Every Which Way But Loose
Excalibur
Executioner on the High Seas, The
Exit the Dragon, Enter the Tiger
Explorers on the Moon
Exterminator, The
Exterminators of the Year 3000

SUBJECT CATEGORY INDEX — Adventure

Eye for an Eye, An
Famous Five—Five On A Secret Trail
Fantastic Plastic Machine, The
Fear Is the Key
Ferry to Hong Kong
Fiction Makers, The
Fiendish Plot of Dr Fu Manchu, The
Fifth Musketeer, The
Final Mission, The
Fire and Ice
Firebird 2015 A.D.
First Blood
Fist of Fear, Touch of Death
Fist of Fury II
Fistful of Dynamite, A
Fists of Vengeance, The
Fitzcarraldo
Five Days One Summer
Five Go to Smuggler's Top
Five Kung-Fu Dare Devil Heroes
5-Man Army, The
Five on Kirrin Island
Flash Gordon
Flash Gordon 2-The Big Battle
Flashpoint Africa
Flat Top
Flight of Dragons, The
Flight to Holocaust
Flower Angel, The
Flush
For Your Eyes Only
Forced Vengeance
40 Million Bucks on a Dead Man's Chest
Four Feathers, The
Four Feathers, The
Four Musketeers, The
Foxhole in Cairo
Freaky Friday
Free Wheelin'
From Russia with Love
From the Earth to the Moon
Fun and Fancy Free
Fury on Wheels
Game of Death
Gappa, The Triphibian Monster
Gauntlet, The
General Stone
Gentle Giant
Get Mean
Get Rita
Getaway, The
Ghosts from the Deep
Girls on the Road
Glen and Randa
Glove, The
Gnome Mobile, The
Gold of the Amazon Women
Golden Rendezvous
Golden Seal, The
Golden Triangle, The
Goldfinger
Goldrunner
Good Guys Wear Black
Good Time Outlaws
Goodbye, Bruce Lee
Goodbye Pork Pie
Greased Lightning
Great Alligator, The
Great Balloon Adventure, The
Great Escape, The
Great Expectations
Great Skycopter Rescue, The
Great Smokey Roadblock, The
Green Ice
Greystoke—The Legend of Tarzan, Lord of the Apes
Gulliver's Travels
Guns and the Fury, The
Guns of the Timberland/Bengazi
Gwendoline
Hawk the Slayer
He-Man and Masters of the Universe
He-Man and the Masters of the Universe
Heart Like a Wheel
Hercules in New York
Hi-Riders
High Ice
High Risk
High Road To China
Hijack!
Hitter, The
Honeybaby
Honky Tonk Freeway
Hoverbug
Huckleberry Finn
Hundra
Hunters of the Golden Cobra
Hurricane Express
I Walk the Line
Ice Station Zebra
Incredible Hulk, The
Incredible Hulk-Cassette 2, The
Incredible Hulk: Hulk vs The Metal Master, The
Incredible Journey, The
Incredible Rocky Mountain Race, The
Inside Out
International Velvet
Intrigue
Invaders of the Lost Gold
Invincible Barbarian, The
Invincible Super Chan
Iron Master, The
Island at the Top of the World, The
Island of Adventure, The
Island of the Lost
It Rained All Night The Day I Left
Italian Job, The
Ivanhoe
Ivanhoe
Jaws of the Dragon
Journey to the Centre of the Earth
Journey to the Centre of Time

745

Adventure — SUBJECT CATEGORY INDEX

Joy Ride
Jungle Book, The
Jungle Man
Kampuchea Express
Kashmiri Run
Kid Dynamite
Kidnapped
Kim
Kimba the White Lion-Part 2
King Kong
King of the Mountain
King Solomon's Treasure
Klondike Fever
Lama Avenger, The
Land of No Return, The
Land That Time Forgot, The
Lassie
Lassie
Lassie and the Rescue Rangers
Last American Hero, The
Last Chase, The
Last Flight of Noah's Ark, The
Last Giraffe, The
Last of the Mohicans
Last of the Vikings
Last Plane Out
Last Reunion, The
Last Roman, The
Last Valley, The
Legend of Loch Ness
Legend of the Northwest
Life and Times of Grizzly Adams, The
Light at the Edge of the World, The
Lion of Thebes
Lions for Breakfast
Lisbon
Little Ark, The
Little Big Man
Little Nezha Fights Great Dragon Kings
Little Super Man
Littlest Warrior, The
Live a Little, Steal a Lot
Live and Let Die
Lone Ranger, The
Lone Wolf Mc Quade
Long Riders, The
Longest Hunt, The
Losers, The
Love to Eternity
Lover of the Great Bear, The
Lt. Robin Crusoe U.S.N.
Lucky Luke
Macon County Line
Mad, Mad, Movie Makers
Mad Max
Mad Max 2
Mad Mission
Mad Mission Three
Magic of the Sea, The
Magnificent Seven, The
Malachi's Cove

Malibu Hot Summer
Man Friday
Man from Atlantis, The
Man from Button Willow, The
Man from Snowy River, A
Man Who Loved Bears, The
Man Who Would Not Die, The
Man with the Golden Gun, The
Manaos
Manions, The
Marco Polo
Mark of Zorro, The
Maroc 7
Match of Dragon and Tiger
Maui
Meet Captain Kidd/The Three Musketeers
Midas Run, The
Midnite Spares
Mighty Joe Young/Little Orvie
Mighty Thor, The
Mighty Thor-Cassette 2, The
Mighty Thor in the Power of Pluto, The
Mr Billion
Mr Horn
Mr. Robinson Crusoe
Moby Dick
Moby Dick
Modesty Blaise
Monsters Christmas, The
Moonraker
Moontrek
Mother Lode
Mountain Family Robinson
Mountain Man
Murderers Row
Muthers, The
My Favorite Martians
Mysterious Heroes
Needles of Death
Neopolitan Carousel
Neptune Disaster, The
New York Mystery
Night Crossing
No Deposit, No Return
No Mercy Man, The
North Country
North-East of Seoul
077 Fury in Istanbul
Off on a Comet
Old Yeller
Oliver Twist
On Her Majesty's Secret Service
One-Eyed Soldiers, The
One Little Indian
One of Our Dinosaurs Is Missing
Only Way to Spy, The
Orca...Killer Whale
Our Man Flint
Pacific Inferno
Panda and the Magic Serpent
Paradise

SUBJECT CATEGORY INDEX — Adventure

Piranha, Piranha
Pirate Movie, The
Plague Dogs, The
Poco
Popeye
Popeye and Friends at Sea
Popeye and Friends in Outer Space
Popeye Globetrotting
Popeye in the Wild West
Poppies Are Also Flowers
Poseidon Adventure, The
Postman Pat
Postman Pat 2
Prince Arthur Emerges
Probability Zero
Professionals, The
Professionals, The
Professionals III, The
Quo Vadis
Race for the Yankee Zephyr
Ragan
Ragewar
Raid on Entebbe
Raiders of the Lost Ark
Real Bruce Lee, The
Red Berets, The
Red Pony, The
Red Rackham's Treasure
Reilly—Ace of Spies
Remarkable Rocket
Return from Witch Mountain
Return of a Man Called Horse, The
Return of the Dragon
Return to Boggy Creek
Revenge of the Barbarians
Ride in a Pink Car
Ride the Hot Wind
Ride the Tiger
Riding High
Right Stuff, The
Ring of Bright Water
Rise and Rise of Casanova, The
Rivals of the Dragon
Roar
Robbers of the Sacred Mountain
Robin Hood
Robinson Crusoe
Rogue Lion
Romancing The Stone
Rome 2033
Roughnecks
Rover, The
Ruckus
Run, Angel, Run
Run For The Roses
Runners
Rush the Assassin
Safari Rally
Sahara
Sahara Cross
Saludos Amigos
Samson and Delilah
Sanjuro
Sartana
Savage Innocents, The
Savage Islands
Savage Sisters
Savages
Scandalous
Scarlet Pimpernel, The
Scavengers, The
Scott of the Antarctic
Scouts Honour
Scratch Harry
Sea Quest
Sellout, The
Seniors
Seven Alone
Seven Crystal Balls/Prisoners of the Sun
Seven Golden Men Strike Again
Seven Nights in Japan
Shalako
Shaolin Iron Finger
Shaolin Master and the Kid
Shark
Shark Hunter, The
Sharks' Treasure
Shazam
S*H*E
Sign of Four, The
Silence in the North
Silent Wilderness
Sinbad the Sailor/The Adventurer/An Apple in His Eye/Pal Fugitive Dog
Six Pack
Slavers
Sloane
Smokey and the Bandit—Part 3
Smokey and the Hotwire Gang
Smokey Bites the Dust
Snake in the Monkey's Shadow
Snow Treasure
Snowball Express
Some Girls Do
Somebody's Stolen Our Russian Spy
Son of Sinbad/Cyclone on Horseback/Pal's Return
Sons of the Musketeers/The Mysterians
S.O.S Pacific
Southern Comfort
Space Hijack
Space Riders
Spaceman and King Arthur, The
Spanish Main/Motor Maniacs/My Pal/Who's Zoo in Africa, The
Spasmo
Specialist, The
Speedtrap/Carquake
Spider-Man and The Dragon's Challenge
Spider-Woman
Spider-Woman-Cassette 2
Spider-Woman in Dracula's Revenge

Adventure — SUBJECT CATEGORY INDEX

Spirit of the Wind
Sporting Chance
Spy Who Loved Me, The
Stacey!
Star Trek—The Motion Picture
Star Trek:Whom Gods Destroy/Plato's Stepchildren
Starbird and Sweet William
Starflight One
Steelyard Blues
Stingray
Storm Over the Nile
Strange Brew
Stranger and the Gunfighter, The
Street Killers
Stunt Man, The
Stunts, the Deadly Game
Sub-Mariner, The
Sub-Mariner-Cassette 2, The
Sudden Death
Summer Night Fever
Summerdog
Sun Dragon
Sunday in the Country
Sunshine Run
Super Dragon
Super Seal
Superman
Superman III
Superman—The Movie
Supermen
Superpower
SuperTed-Cassette 1
Survival Run
Swallows and Amazons
Swingin' Summer
Swiss Family Robinson
Swiss Family Robinson
Switch, The
Sword and the Sorcerer, The
Sword of Monte Cristo
Sword of the Barbarians
Swordkill
Taboo Island
Taking of Pelham 123, The
Target Eagle
Target: Harry
Tarka the Otter
Tarzan the Ape Man
Te Deum
Team-Mates
Ten Fingers of Steel
Ten Violent Women
That Darn Cat
Theodora Queen of Byzantium
Thief of Bagdad, The
Thief of Bagdad, The
Thomas Crown Affair, The
Those Calloways
Three Musketeers, The
Thumbtripping
Thunder
Thunder and Lightning
Thunderball
Thunderbolt and Lightfoot
Tiger and the Flame, The
Tiger Strikes Again, The
Tigers Don't Cry
Time After Time
Time Bomb
Time Machine, The
To Be Twenty
To Build a Fire
Tor—Mighty Warrior
Town Called Bastard, A
Trap on Cougar Mountain
Treasure Island
Treasure Island
Treasure Island
Treasure Island
Treasure of Jamaica Reef
Treasure of Pancho Villa, The
Treasure of the Four Crowns
20,000 Leagues Under the Sea
240 Robert
Two in Black Belt
Tycoon/Six Gun Gold
UFO Journals
Ulysses
Undersea Adventures of Captain Nemo
Uranium Conspiracy, The
Vengeance of the Barbarians
Village of the Giants
Virgin of Bali, The
War of the Wizards
Wargames
Warlords of Atlantis
Warning, The
Water Babies, The
Waterhole 3
Way of the Black Dragon
Way of the Dragon, The
We of The Never Never
Werewolf and the Yeti, The
Whale of a Tale, A
When the North Wind Blows
Where the Red Fern Grows
White Heat
White Lions, The
White Water Sam
Why Would Anyone Want to Kill A Nice Girl Like You?
Wild and the Free, The
Wild Times
Wildcats of St. Trinians, The
Willy Wonka and the Chocolate Factory
Wings of an Eagle
Women Gladiators
World's Greatest Athlete, The
Year of Living Dangerously, The
You Only Live Twice
Young Graduates, The

SUBJECT CATEGORY INDEX — Adventure

Zero to Sixty
Zorro
Zorro and the Three Musketeers
Zorro at the Spanish Court
Zulu Dawn

Advertising

History of Advertising, The

Aeronautics

Above All
Biggin Hill '81
Challenge of the Sky
Colonel Culpeper's Flying Circus
Farnborough International '84
Farnborough International '82
History of Aviation, The
Iron Men and Steel Machines/Flames over the Sahara
Lancaster
Oshkosh Down Under '81
Red Arrows—Gnats and Hawks, The
Smoke On Go! The Red Arrows
Spitfire
Welcome to Oshkosh '80
Wings of the Wind/They Own the Sky

Africa

African Waterhole
From Africa with Love—Nature Film
Kwaheri
Under Kilimanjaro

Alcoholic beverages

Food, Wine and Friends: Volume 4
Food, Wine and Friends: Volume 5
Food, Wine and Friends: Volume 6
Food, Wine and Friends: Volume 1
Food, Wine and Friends: Volume 2
Food, Wine and Friends: Volume 3
Observer Guide to European Cookery, The

Anatomy and physiology

Body, The
Incredible, Indelible, Magical, Physical, Mystery Trip, The

Animals

Animal Kingdom
Animal Magic Presents Keeper (Johnny) Morris
Ape and Super Ape
Barbara Woodhouse Goes to Beverly Hills
Barbara Woodhouse's World of Horses and Ponies
Bruce Davidson's 'Champion's Way With Horses'
Care of the Horse
Disney's Greatest Dog Stars
Emma And Grandpa
Eye for a Horse, An
Farriery the Master Craft
First Aid for Horses, Part 1
First Aid for Horses, Part 2
Healthy Horse, The
Home of Rest for Horses
Horse Sense and Road Safety
It's Not Impossible
Last Of The Wild—Volume 1
Last Of The Wild—Volume 2
Last Of The Wild—Volume 3
Last of the Wild—Volume 6
Our Animals
Quick Dog Training with Barbara Woodhouse
Ringo's World
Royal Four in Hand
Taking Up the Reins, Parts 1-4
Tales from the Animal World
Tatters
Vaulting Horse, The
Wild Babies
Windows: Animals at Work and Play
World of Survival—Man and the Great Apes, The
World of Survival—Mysteries of the Great Whales, The
World of Survival—Penguins of the Falkland Islands, The
World of Survival—The Last Kingdoms of the Elephants, The

Anthropology

Brutes and Savages
Last Stone Age Tribes, The
Pigmies of the Rain Forest, The

Antiques

Story of English Furniture, The

Armed Forces-GB

Battle for the Falklands
Falklands—Task Force South
Salute to the Edinburgh Tattoo

Artists

Challenge, The
L S Lowry
Magritte

Arts

Andy Warhol and His Work
Challenge, The
Complete Potter, The
Flower Arranging
Flower Arranging: Part 1: The Basics

SUBJECT CATEGORY INDEX

Flower Arranging: Part 2: A Step Further
Living Form
Take Hart
Treasures of the British Crown
World's Greatest Paintings 1: Adoration, The

Asia

Dance and Music of India—Sanskritik Festival of Arts of India

Astronomy

Earth-Sun Relationship
Spacewatch

Australia

Giant Blacks and Great Whites, Part 4
Giant Blacks and Great Whites, Part 1
Giant Blacks and Great Whites, Part 2
Giant Blacks and Great Whites, Part 3

Automobiles

Crazy World of Cars
Jaguar Story, The
Me and My Car
Summer of Steam
VTV Magazine No. 1
VTV Magazine No. 2
VTV Magazine No. 3
VTV Magazine No. 4

Automobiles-Racing

Avon Tour 1974/3 Days in August 1975
Best of the Best 1972/Fast Company 1973
Dash of the Irish 1971, A/Road Time 1973
Decade of Grand Prix/The Frank Williams Story
Fast Company—Jackie Stewart
Fast Drive in the Country, A
Fastest Man on Earth, The
Flying Finns 1968, The/The Golden Age of Rallying
F.O.C.A Start to Finish
Forest Feast
Goodwind Nine Hours 1955/Final Victory 1959
Grand Prix 1978—The Shape of Things to Come/Grand Prix 1979—Car Wars
Grand Prix of the Decade 1970-1979
Grand Prix Trio 1955/Grand Prix d'Europe 1958
Greased Lightning
If You're Not Winning, You're Not Trying 1973
Inca Road 1970/Scene 72, Take 7
Iron Men and Steel Machines/Flames over the Sahara
James Hunt: World Champion/The Phoenix, 1977
Marlborough Safari Rally in Kenya 1981
Mintex International Rally 1981
Mountain Legend 1965

1980 1000 Lakes Rally
1980 Mintex International Rally
1981 Circuit of Ireland Rally
1981 Manx Rally
1981 1000 Lakes Rally
1979 Lombard RAC Rally, The
Nurburgring 100 KMS 1956/Monaco Grand Prix 1957
Once Upon a Wheel
Pole Position
Racecraft 1973/Collision Course 1976
Ringmasters 1967, The/Pause for Nostalgia
Ronde Infernale 1969, La
Rouen Round 1962/Brands Hatch Beat 1964
Scottish International Rally 1980
Scottish Rally 1973/12 Hours in Argyll 1974
Speed Fever
Speedway
Stages to Victory 1976
Swedish Rally 1981
Tale of Three Rallies
Time of Change 1976/Appointment at Penha 1977
Twice and Future King 1974, The/A Special Breed 1975
Uncrowned Champions 1970/House of Stewart 1971
Visa 3—From the Himalayas to Keilder-Action All the Way
Visa 4—The Best of Rallying on Video in 1982

Beauty

Asymmetric Cut (Two Styles), The
Body Massage
Paraffin and Parafango Waxing
Shave and Face Massage, The
Short Back and Sides, The
Wedge, The

Bible

David and Goliath
Genesis Flood, The
Greatest Heroes of the Bible
Phillip the Evangelist
Psalm 23
Resurrection, The
Training for Ministry
You and Your Child

Bicycling

Lightning Wheels

Biographical

Adventures of Frontier Fremont, The
Amazing Howard Hughes, The
Blood Queen
Bogie
Bruce Lee Story, The

SUBJECT CATEGORY INDEX — Biographical

Bruce Lee: The Man—The Myth
Bud and Lou
Buddy Holly Story, The
Chanel Solitaire
From a Far Country, Pope John Paul II
Gandhi
Gauguin—The Savage
Gentleman Tramp, The
Henry VIII and His Six Wives
I Am a Dancer
It's Good to be Alive
Jacqueline Bouvier Kennedy
James Dean Story, The
Jayne Mansfield Story, The
Joan Collins Video Special, The
Joan of Arc
John F Kennedy
Lennon-A Legend
Lenny
MacArthur
Mae West
Mahler
Monsieur Vincent
Piaf
Priest of Love
Princess
Scott of the Antarctic
Short Films 1
Song of Norway
Star 80
Stevie
Strauss Family—Part One, The
Strauss Family—Part Two, The
Voyage Round My Father, A
Winds of Kitty Hawk, The

Birds

Bird About Town
Early One Morning
Educational Release No 2
Flying Birds/Birds of the Lake/Osprey Watch
Gardening with Wildlife
Getting to Know Birds
Goshawk
Kingfisher—Secret Splendour of the Brooks
Language of Birds, The
Look Again at Garden Birds/Look Again at Gulls
Masterbuilders, The
Petersfinger Cuckoos, The
Round Robin
Sea Birds, The
Secret Reeds, The
Short-Eared Owl
Tony Soper's Birdquiz
Videobook of British Garden Birds
Wild Birds and the Law—Can We Help You?
World of Birds No. 1—Big Bill plus Speckle and Hide
World of Birds No. 2—Osprey
Ynys-Hir

YOC in Your School, The

Boating

Atlantic Adventure
Freedom Afloat
Sailing—The RYA Method, Part 1
Sailing—The RYA Method, Part 2
This Is Sailing I
This Is Sailing II
Water Safety

Boxing

Muhammed Ali vs Archie Moore

Building

Telford's Last Canal

Cartoons

Abbott and Costello
Adventures of Buster the Bear, The
Adventures of Captain Future I, The
Adventures of Captain Future II, The
Adventures of Chip 'n' Dale
Adventures of Choppy and the Princess, The
Adventures of Choppy and the Princess—1, The
Adventures of Choppy and the Princess—2, The
Adventures of Choppy and the Princess—3, The
Adventures of Gumdrop, The
Adventures of King Rollo, The
Adventures of Kum Kum, The
Adventures of Little Lulu — Volume 1, The
Adventures of Little Lulu—Volume 2, The
Adventures of Little Lulu—Volume 3, The
Adventures of Mole, The
Adventures of Popeye, The
Adventures of Reddy the Fox, The
Adventures of Sinbad the Sailor, The
Adventures of Superman, The
Adventures of Ultraman, The
Alex and His Dog
Alice in Wonderland
Amazing Adventures of Morph: Volume 1, The
Amazing Adventures of Morph: Volume 2, The
Amazing Adventures of Morph: Volume 3, The
Amazing Adventures of Morph: Volume 4, The
Amazing Adventures of Sherlock Holmes, Volume 2, The
Amazing Adventures of Sherlock Holmes, Volume 3, The
Amazing Adventures of Sherlock Holmes, The, Cassette 1
Amazing Spider-Man—Cassette 2, The
Amazing Spider-Man IV in Night of the Villains
Amazing Spider-Man-Cassette 3, The
Amazing Spiderman in The Terrible Triumph of Dr. Octopus, The
Amigo
Animal Kingdom

Cartoons **SUBJECT CATEGORY INDEX**

Animalympics
Animates, The
Archie and Sabrina
Archies, The
Asterix and Cleopatra
Asterix the Gaul
Asterix the Gaul
Atom Ant—Cassette 1
Atom Ant—Cassette 2
Atom Ant in How Now Bow Wow
Baldmoney, Sneezewort, Dodder and Cloudberry
Banana Splits Adventure Show, The
Banana Splits Adventure Show, Cassette 4
Banana Splits Adventure Show-Cassette 2, The
Banana Splits Adventure Show, Cassette 3, The
Bananaman
Barbapapa
Barbapapa Volume II
Batfink-Cassette 1
Batfink II in Bat Patrol
Battle of the Planets—Curse of the Cuttlefish
Battle of the Planets—G-Force Vs The Giant Insects
Battle of the Planets—The Jupiter Moon Menace
Battle of the Planets—Zoltar, Evil Master of Disguises
Battle Robot
BBC Children's Favourites
Beany and Cecil, Volume 1
Beebtots
Beetle Bailey
Beetle Bailey
Berenstain Bears Easter Surprise and Comic Valentine, The
Berenstein Bears, Volume 2, The
Best of Little Lulu, The
Black Arrow, The
Black Beauty
Black Island/Shooting Star
Blackstar
Bon Voyage, Charlie Brown
Boy Named Charlie Brown, A
Bruce Lee-Chinese Gods
Bugs Bunny/Road Runner Movie, The
Calculus Affair, The
Calimero
Calimero and the Wonderful Summer
Call of the Wild, The
Camberwick Green
Captain America
Captain America—Cassette 2
Captain America in The Super-Adaptoid
Captain America-The Red Skull Lives
Captain Harlock
Captain Micron's Electronic Comic
Cartoon Bonanza, Volumes 1-3
Cartoon Classics of the 1930's
Cartoon Festival I
Cartoon Festival II

Cartoon Festival III
Cartoon Hour
Cartoon Show No. 10
Cartoon Show No. 11
Cartoon Show No. 12
Cartoon Special
Cartoon Wonderland
Casper and the Angels
Casper and the Angels-Cassette 2
Chigley
Children's Cinema
Christmas Carol, A
Christmas Carol, A
Christmas Carol, A
Christmas Messenger, The
Crab with the Golden Claws, The
Daffy Duck's Movie: Fantastic Island
Daily Fable—Miss Ant
Danger Mouse
Danger Mouse Rides Again
Danger Mouse-Volume 2
Danger Mouse Volume 3
Dark Crystal, The
Fabulous Fantastic Four, The
Dastardly and Muttley-Cassette 1
Dastardly and Muttley—Cassette 2
Dastardly and Muttley in Home Sweet Homing Pigeon
David Copperfield
Day the Eiffel Tower Ran Away, The
Deputy Dawg
Destination Moon
Dick Deadeye
Disney Channel, Volume 5, The
Disney Channel, Volume 4, The
Disney Channel, Volume 1, The
Disney Channel, Volume 6, The
Disney Channel, Volume 3, The
Disney Channel, Volume 2, The
Disney's Greatest Dog Stars
Disney's Greatest Villains
Disney's Scary Tales
Dr Seuss Video Festival
Dr Snuggles
Donald Duck Goes West
Dot and Bunny
Dot and Santa Claus
Dumbo
Excalibur
Explorers on the Moon
Fabulous Fantastic Four, Cassette 2, The
Fabulous Fantastic Four in Meet Dr. Doom, The
Fabulous Funnies
Fairy Tales
Fearless Fly in Fly by Might
Felix the Cat—No. 1
Felix the Cat—No. 2
Felix the Cat—No. 3
Felix the Cat—No. 4
Felix the Cat—No. 5
Felix the Cat—No. 6

SUBJECT CATEGORY INDEX — Cartoons

Fire and Ice
Flash Gordon
Flash Gordon 2-The Big Battle
Flight of Dragons, The
Flower Angel, The
Flower Stories
Fox and the Hare, The
Fox and the Hare—Part 2, The
Fred Bassett
Freedom Force, The
From the Earth to the Moon
Fun and Fancy Free
Ghosts from the Deep
God's Story
Gold Wing
Golden Treasury of Classic Fairy Tales, The
Great Expectations
Great Stories 1
Great Stories 2
Great Stories 3
Great Stories 4
Great Stories 5
Great Stories 6
Great Stories 7
Great Stories 8
Great Stories 9: The Three Fools
Great Stories 10
Great Stories 11: The Mouse
Great Stories 12: The Dog Sharo
Great Toy Robbery, The
Groovie Ghouls
Gulliver's Travels
He-Man and Masters of the Universe
He-Man and the Masters of the Universe
Heckle and Jeckle
Henry's Cat and Friends, Cassette 1
Here Comes Noddy Again
Here Comes the Grump
Here Comes the Grump-Cassette 2
Hey, Good Looking!
Hollywood Cartoon Festival
Hoppity Goes to Town
Houndcats and the Barkleys, Volume 2, The
Houndcats and the Barkleys, Volume 3, The
Houndcats and the Barkleys, Volume 4, The
Houndcats and the Barkleys, Volume 6, The
Houndcats and the Barkleys, Volume 5, The
Houndcats and the Barkleys, Volume 1, The
Hugo the Hippo
Hurray for Betty Boop
Incredible Hulk-Cassette 2, The
Incredible Hulk: Hulk vs The Metal Master, The
Incredible Hulk in The Man Called Boomerang, The
Invaders from the Deep
Invincible Iron Man, The
Invincible Iron Man, Cassette 2, The
Invincible Iron Man in Enter Hawkeye, Cassette 3, The
Ivanhoe
Ivor the Engine and the Dragons
Johnny and the Wicked Giant
Journey to the Centre of the Earth
Just So Stories
Katy
Kidnapped
Kimba the White Lion-Part 2
Lassie
Lassie and the Rescue Rangers
Little Brown Burro, The
Little Drummer Boy, The
Little Miss Trouble and Friends
Little Nezha Fights Great Dragon Kings
Little Orbit the Astrodog
Little Women
Littlest Warrior, The
Lone Ranger, The
Looney, Looney, Looney, Bugs Bunny Movie, The
Looney Tunes Video Show, Volumes 14-19, The
Lord of the Rings
Lucky Luke
Lucky Luke and the Dalton Gang
Mad, Mad, Monsters
Mad Monster Party
Magic Adventure
Magic Ball, The
Magical Mystery Trip Through Little Red's Head
Many Adventures of Winnie the Pooh, The
Marco Polo
Mattie the Gooseboy
Michel's Mixed-Up Musical Bird
Mickey's Golden Jubilee
Mighty Mouse
Mighty Thor, The
Mighty Thor-Cassette 2, The
Mighty Thor in Molto the Lava Man, The
Mighty Thor in the Power of Pluto, The
Milton the Monster Show, The
Mr. Magoo in Sherwood Forest
Mister Men Volume 1
Mister Men Volume 2
Mister Men Volume 3
Mister Men Volume 4
Mr Rossi Looks for Happiness
Moby Dick
Moontrek
More Tales From Trumpton
Motion Epics Cartoon Show
Mouse and His Child, The
Mouse and his Child, The
Munch Bunch and Mumfie, The
My Bird to the Rescue
My Favorite Martians
Night Before Christmas, The
Nine Lives of Fritz the Cat, The
Noah's Animals
Nobody's Boy
Nursery Rhymes
Off on a Comet
Oliver Twist
Once Upon a Girl

753

Cartoons **SUBJECT CATEGORY INDEX**

1001 Rabbit Tales
Panda and the Magic Serpent
Peter-No-Tail
Pink Panther, Volume I, The
Pinocchio in Outer Space
Popeye and Friends at Sea
Popeye and Friends, Days Gone By
Popeye and Friends in Outer Space
Popeye and Friends-No Fun Like Snow Fun
Popeye And Superman
Popeye Globetrotting
Popeye in the Wild West
Prince Arthur Emerges
Princes and Princesses
Pugwash
Raccoons and the Lost Star, The
Raccoons on Ice/The Christmas Raccoons
Ragnarok
Red Baron, The
Red Rackham's Treasure
Remarkable Rocket
Return of the Dinosaurs
Return to Oz
Robin Hood
Robinson Crusoe
Roobarb and More Roobarb
Saludos Amigos
Santa and The Three Bears
Scooby and Scrappy-Doo—Cassette 1
Scooby and Scrappy-Doo—Cassette 2
Scooby and Scrappy-Doo-Cassette 3
Sealab 2020
Sealab 2020, Cassette 2
Secret Squirrel
Secret Squirrel-Cassette 2
Secret Squirrel-Cassette 3
Selfish Giant, The Happy Prince, The Little Mermaid, The
Seven Crystal Balls/Prisoners of the Sun
Shazam
Sherlock Holmes and the Baskerville Curse
Shinbone Alley
Silent Night
Sir Prancelot
Small One, The
Snowman, The
Song of the South
Sorcerer's Apprentice, The
Space Bandit
Space Firebird
Space Hijack
Space Sentinels
Spectreman
Spider-Woman
Spider-Woman-Cassette 2
Stingiest Man in Town, The
Sub-Mariner, The
Sub-Mariner-Cassette 2, The
Super Cartoon Show
Superman
Superstar Goofy

SuperTed-Cassette 1
SuperTed—Cassette 2
Swan Lake
Swiss Family Robinson
Tag the Intrepid Fox
Tales from the Animal World
Tales of Bobby Brewster and More Adventures of Gumdrop
Tales of Hoffnung
Tales of Magic
Tales of Washington Irving
Terrahawks
Terrahawks 2: The Menace from Mars
Terrahawks 3: Terror from Mars
Terry Toons
Terrytoons, Volume 1
Thief of Bagdad
3 Terrytoons
Tom and Jerry
Tom and Jerry II
Tom and Jerry III
Tom and Jerry, Volume IV
Top Cat
Top Cat—Cassette 2
Top Cat Falls in Love
Top Cat: The Great Alley Clean-Up Caper
Towser
Toytown Series No. 1
Toytown Series No. 2
Toytown Series No. 3
Toytown Series No. 4
Toytown Series No. 5
Treasure Island
Tubby the Tuba
Tukiki and His Search for a Merry Christmas
Twas the Night Before Christmas
Twelve Tasks of Asterix, The
Undersea Adventures of Captain Nemo
Unico
Victor and Maria
Video Cartoon Comic
Video Comic
Voltron—Defender Of The Universe In The Battle Of The Plant Arus
Wacky and Packy
Wacky World of Mother Goose, The
Waldo Kitty
Wall, The
Water Babies, The
Watership Down
West and Soda
Willo the Wisp—Volume 1
Willo the Wisp—Volume 2
Wind in the Willows, The
Wind in the Willows—Cassette 1, The
Wind in the Willows—Cassette 2, The
Winnie the Pooh and the Blustery Day
Winnie the Pooh and the Honey Tree
Wizards
Woody Woodpecker and His Friends II
Woody Woodpecker and his Friends, Volume 3

754

SUBJECT CATEGORY INDEX — Cartoons

World Famous Fairy Tales
Zorro

Childbirth

Having A Baby
New Good Birth Guide, The

Christianity

Story of Jesus, The

Christmas

Christmas Carol, A
Christmas Carol, A
Christmas Messenger, The
Handel's Messiah and Christmas Music
Nearly No Christmas
Night Before Christmas, The
Silent Night
Small One, The

Circus

Charlie Rivel—The Clown
Circus World Championships
Clowns—Magic—Sensations

Cities and towns

This Is London

Comedy

Abbott and Costello
Abigail's Party
Adult Fairytales
Adventures of a Plumber's Mate
Adventures of a Private Eye
Adventures of a Taxi Driver
Adventures of Curley and His Gang, The
Adventures of Sherlock Holmes' Smarter Brother, The
Africa Screams
Aib Ya Loulou (Shame on You Loulou)
Alice in Wonderland
All Coppers Are.....
All Night Long
All of Me
All the Loving Couples
All the Way Boys
American Candid Camera
American Candid Camera-Part 2
American Candid Camera-Part 3
American Raspberry
Amorous Milkman, The
And Now For Something Completely Different
Animal Crackers
Animal House
Annie Hall
Annie Hall
Any Which Way You Can
Any Which Way You Can
Apple Dumpling Gang, The
Apple Dumpling Gang Rides Again, The
Are You Being Served?
Arthur
At War with the Army
Attack of the Killer Tomatoes
Author! Author!
Avanti!
Baby Love
Baltimore Bullet, The
Bananas
Bang Bang Kid, The
Barefoot in the Park
Beach Girls, The
Bedazzled
Bedtime with Rosie
Beetle Bailey
Behave Yourself
Being There
Best Friends
Best Little Whorehouse in Texas, The
Best of Benny Hill Volume 1, The
Best of Benny Hill Volume 2, The
Best of Benny Hill—Volume 3, The
Best of Both Worlds
Best of George and Mildred, The
Best of Rising Damp, The
Best of the Two Ronnies, The
Big Bus, The
Big Meat Eater
Blackbeard the Pirate/Fish Feathers/Pal's Adventure/The Fireman
Blame It On Rio
Blazing Saddles
Blazing Stewardesses
Bless This House
Blood Relations
Bloodbath at the House of Death
Blue Fantasies
Blue Skies Again
Blues Brothers, The
Boatniks, The
Bogus Bandits
Bombay Talkie
Boys in Blue, The
Breakfast at Tiffany's
Breaking Away
Bringing Up Baby
Broadway Danny Rose
Brothers O'Toole, The
Bud and Lou
Buffalo Bill and the Indians
Bulldog Breed/The Square Peg, The
Bullshot
Bus Stop
Busting
By Design
By the Sea/The Picnic
Cactus Flower

Comedy   **SUBJECT CATEGORY INDEX**

Caddyshack
Cage Aux Folles, La
Can I Do It...Till I Need Glasses?
Can She Bake A Cherry Pie?
Candid Camera Classics—Volume 1
Candid Camera Classics—Volume 2
Candid Camera Classics—Volume 3
Candid Camera Classics—Volume 4
Candid Camera Classics—Volume 5
Candleshoe
Candy Stripe Nurses
Capers
Carry On Abroad
Carry On Again Doctor
Carry On Again Doctor
Carry On at Your Convenience
Carry On Behind
Carry On Camping
Carry On Cleo
Carry On Cowboy
Carry On Dick
Carry On Doctor
Carry On Emmannuelle
Carry On—Follow That Camel
Carry On Henry
Carry On Loving
Carry On Matron
Carry On Nurse
Carry On Up the Jungle
Carry On Up the Khyber
Caveman
CB Hustlers
Change of Seasons, A
Charley's Aunt/Mr Axelford's Angel
Charlie Chaplin I
Charlie Chaplin II
Charlie Chaplin III
Charlie Chaplin IV
Charlie Chaplin Comedy Theatre No. 2, The
Charlie Chaplin Comedy Theatre No. 1
Cheech and Chong's Next Movie
Cheerleaders Beach Party
Cheerleaders' Wild Weekend
Cherry Picker, The
Chicken Chronicles, The
Circus, The/A Day's Pleasure
City Lights
Class
Clinic, The
College
Come Play with Me
Comeback Kid, The
Comedy of Terrors, The
Comfort and Joy
Con Artist, The
Condorman
Confessions from the David Galaxy Affair
Confessions of a Pop Performer
Continental Divide
Kid with the 200 I.Q., The
Curley and His Gang in the Haunted Mansion
Curse of the Pink Panther
Dance of the Vampires
Dangerous Davies
Dead Men Don't Wear Plaid
Decameron, The
Deep Jaws
Dernier Milliardaire, Le
Desperate Living
Desperate Women
Devil and Max Devlin, The
Different Story, A
Diner
Doctor at Large
Doctor at Sea
Doctor Detroit
Dr. Heckyl and Mr. Hype
Doctor in Clover
Doctor in Distress
Doctor in the House
Don's Party
Don't Call Us
Double Agent 73
Down Memory Lane
Draws
Drum Beat/To Beat the Band
Duchess and the Dirtwater Fox, The
Duck Soup
DUTCH GIRLS
Eating Raoul
Elephant Parts
End, The
Every Home Should Have One
Every Which Way But Loose
Everything You Always Wanted to Know About Sex But Were Afraid to Ask
Everything You Always Wanted to Know About Sex (But Were Afraid to Ask)
Extra Girl, The
Fabulous Funnies
Family View Vol. 1
Farmer's Daughter, The
Fast Lady, The
Fatty Finn
Fawlty Towers, Tape 1, The Germans
Fawlty Towers, Tape 2, The Psychiatrist
Fawlty Towers, Tape 3, The Kipper and the Corpse
Fawlty Towers, Tape 4, Basil the Rat
Female Trouble
Femme Est une Femme, Une
Fiendish Plot of Dr Fu Manchu, The
Finally Sunday
Find the Lady
Firesign Theatre Presents Nick Danger
First Turn-On
Fish That Saved Pittsburgh, The
Flesh Gordon
Flush
Flying Deuces, The
Foolin' Around
Four Musketeers, The

756

SUBJECT CATEGORY INDEX — Comedy

Fox and the Hare, The
Fox and the Hare—Part 2, The
Freebie and the Bean
French Line, The/Texas Tough Guy/Murder in a Flat
Frisco Kid, The
Fritz the Cat
Funniest Man in the World, The
Futtock's End
Galaxina
Games That Lovers Play
Gas Pump Girls
Gay Deceivers
General, The
Genevieve
Gentlemen Prefer Blondes
George
George and Mildred
George Carlin—Live at Carnegie
Getting It On
Ghost Busters, The
Ghost in the Noonday Sun
Girl/Boy
Girl in Every Port, A/Return of the Badmen
Girl Who Couldn't Say No, The
Go Hog Wild
Goin' Coconuts
Goin' South
Going Berserk
Going Steady
Gold Rush, The/Pay Day
Gone are the Dayes
Good Time Outlaws
Good Times
Goodbye Girl, The
Goodies, The
Got It Made
Graduate, The
Grand Slam
Grand Theft Auto
Grass Is Greener, The
Great American Traffic Jam, The
Great Comedians of the Silents—Feed of Mud, The
Great Dictator, The
Great Golden Hits of the Monkees, The
Great Ice Rip-Off, The
Great McGonagall, The
Great Monkey Rip-Off, The
Great Muppet Caper, The
Great Race, The
Great Rock 'n' Roll Swindle, The
Great Skycopter Rescue, The
Great Smokey Roadblock, The
Great Train Robbery, The
Green Grow the Rushes
Guerillas in Pink Lace
Guess Who's Sleeping in My Bed?
Guide for the Married Man, A
Gumball Rally
Half a House
Happiest Millionaire, The
Happy Hooker, The
Happy Hooker Goes to Washington, The
Hard Day's Night, A
Harold and Maude
Harold Lloyd 'The Unsinkable'
Having It All
Heartbeeps
Hearts of the West
Heavens Above
Heavy Traffic
Herbie Goes Bananas
Herbie Rides Again
Hercules in New York
Hero at Large
Heroes of the Regiment
Higher and Higher/Strictly Dynamite
Hill's Angels
History of the World Part 1
Hobson's Choice
Holiday on the Buses
Home Movies
Homebodies
Honky Tonk Freeway
Hooper
Hot Bubblegum
Hot Rock, The
Hot T-Shirts
Hotel New Hampshire, The
H.O.T.S.
Hound of the Baskervilles, The
Householder, The
Hoverbug
How Do I Love Thee
How to Beat the High Cost of Living
How to Marry a Millionaire
Hullabaloo Over Georgie and Bonnie's Pictures
I Ought to Be in Pictures
I Wonder Who's Killing Her Now
If You Don't Stop It... You'll Go Blind
I'm All Right Jack
I'm For the Hippopotamus
In God We Trust
In-Laws, The
In Love With an Older Woman
Incoming Freshmen
Incredible Rocky Mountain Race, The
Inspector General, The
Intelligence Men, The
It Came From Hollywood
It Seemed Like a Good Idea at the Time
It Shouldn't Happen to a Vet
It's a Mad, Mad, Mad, Mad World
It's My Turn
Jasper Carrott Live
Jerk, The
Jesse and Lester: Two Brothers in a Place Called Trinity
Jim Davidson's Falklands Special
Jour de Fete
Joy Sticks

Comedy **SUBJECT CATEGORY INDEX**

Keep It Up Jack
Kenny Everett Video Show Volume 1, The
Kenny Everett Video Show Volume 2, The
Kenny Everett Video Show—Volume 3, The
Kentucky Fried Movie
Khatiat Mallak (An Angel's Sin)
Kid Blue
Kid Dynamite
Kid, The/The Idle Class
Kidco
Kimberly Jim
Kind Hearts and Coronets
King of Comedy
Kinky Coaches and the Pom-Pom Pussycats, The
Klassic Keystone Komedy Kapers
Knocking at Heaven's Door
Knowledge, The
Ladykillers, The
Last American Virgin, The
Last of the Summer Wine
Laughterhouse
Laurel and Hardy's Laughing Twenties
Lavender Hill Mob, The
Leave 'Em Laughing
Lemon Popsicle
Les Girls
Let George Do It
Let's Get Married
Let's Make a Dirty Movie
Likely Lads, The
Linda Lovelace for President
Lions for Breakfast
Little Rascals
Little Sex, A
Lonely Guy, The
Lonely Hearts
Loose Shoes
Loot
Losin' It
Lost and Found
Love and Death
Love at First Bite
Love Bug, The
Lovesick
Loving Couples
Lucky Jim
Lunch Wagon
Mad, Mad, Monsters
Mad, Mad, Movie Makers
Mad Monster Party
Maggie, The
Magic Christian, The
Magnificent 7 Deadly Sins
Magnificent Two, The
Main Event, The
Mame
Man, a Woman and a Bank, A
Man About the House
Man from Clover Grove, The
Man in the White Suit, The

Man of the East
Man Who Had Power Over Women, The
Man Who Loved Women, The
M*A*S*H
Mastermind
Matilda
Max Dugan Returns
Meatballs
Meet Captain Kidd/The Three Musketeers
Meet Me in St. Louis
Midas Run, The
Midnight Cowboy
Midnite Spares
Midsummer Night's Sex Comedy, A
Million Dollar Duck
Minder
Mr Blandings Builds His Dream House/Mexican Spitfire at Sea
Mr Hulot's Holiday
Mister Jerico
Mr Mum
Mister Roberts
Modern Times
Modesty Blaise
Mon Oncle
Mondo Erotico
Monster Club, The
Monty Python and the Holy Grail
Monty Python Live at the Hollywood Bowl
Monty Python's Life of Brian
Moon Is Blue, The
Morecambe & Wise Musical Extravaganzas
Morgan—A Suitable Case for Treatment
Move
Movie Movie
Muppet Movie, The
Mutiny on the Buses
My Favourite Year
My Learned Friend
My Mother, the General
My Pleasure is My Business
My Tutor
Myra Breckenridge
National Lampoon's Class Reunion
National Lampoon's Vacation
Never a Dull Moment
New York Mystery
Nickelodeon
Night at the Opera, A
Night Patrol
Night They Robbed Big Bertha's, The
9 to 5
1941
No Deposit, No Return
Not For Publication
Not Now, Darling
Not Tonight Darling
Nuts in May
Ocean's Eleven
Odds and Evens
Off the Wall

SUBJECT CATEGORY INDEX — Comedy

Oh! Calcutta!
Oh God!
Oh God! Book II
O'Hara'a Wife
On the Buses
One of Our Dinosaurs Is Missing
One Touch of Venus
Only Two Can Play
Only Way to Spy, The
Ooh.....You Are Awful
Open All Hours
Orders Are Orders
Partners
Peeper
Percy
Percy's Progress
Perfect Friday
Perils of Pauline, The
Picture Show Man, The
Pigs Versus the Freaks, The
Pink Flamingos
Pink Panther, The
Pink Panther Strikes Again, The
Pink Panther Strikes Again, The
Plank, The/Rhubarb, Rhubarb
Play It Again, Sam
Playboy of the Western World
Playtime
Plaza Suite
Please Sir
Polyester
Pom Pom Girls, The
Popeye
Porky's
Porridge
Press For Time
Private Benjamin
Private Eyes, The
Private Life of Sherlock Holmes, The
Private Nurse
Private Popsicle
Private School
Privates on Parade
Producers, The
P'tang Yang, Kipperbang
Quackser Fortune Has a Cousin in the Bronx
Rabbit Test
Rajab Faouka Safih Sakhen (Rajab on a Hot Tin Roof)
Rascals and Robbers
Rentadick
Return of the Pink Panther, The
Revenge of the Pink Panther
Revenge of the Pink Panther
Rhinestone
Ripping Yarns
Rise and Rise of Casanova, The
Rising Damp
Risky Business
Ritz, The
Road to Utopia

Rock 'n' Roll High School
Rocky Horror Picture Show, The
Romance with a Double Bass
Rutles, The: All You Need Is Cash
Sally of the Sawdust
Samurai
Satan's Brew
Saturday the 14th
Savannah Smiles
Scandalous
Scavenger Hunt
Schlock
Screamtime
Semi-Tough
Semi-Tough
Seniors
Sgt. Pepper's Lonely Hearts Club Band
Serial
Seven Per Cent Solution, The
Seven Year Itch, The
Sex Connection, The
Sex with a Smile
Sextette
Sexy Dozen, The
Sez Les
Shame, Shame on the Bixby Boys
She'll Follow You Anywhere
Sheriff and the Satellite Kid, The
Shillingbury Blowers, The
Silent Clowns: Big Moments from Little Pictures
Silent Clowns: Saturday Afternoon
Silent Movie, The
Silver Bears, The
Simon
Simon Simon
Sinbad the Sailor/The Adventurer/An Apple in His Eye/Pal Fugitive Dog
Six Pack
16 Candles
Slapstick Of Another Kind
Slightly Pregnant Man, The
Smokey and the Bandit
Smokey and the Bandit—Part 3
Smokey Bites the Dust
Snapshot
So Fine
S.O.B.
Soft Beds, Hard Battles
Soggy Bottom USA
Somebody Killed Her Husband
Son of Kong/You'll Find Out
Sooty Video Show, The
Spaceship
Spanish Main/Motor Maniacs/My Pal/Who's Zoo in Africa, The
S*P*Y*S
Squeeze a Flower
Starhops
Steelyard Blues
Steptoe and Son
Still Smokin'

Strange Brew
Stranger and the Gunfighter, The
Street Fleet
Stroker Ace
Stuck on You
Student Bodies
Suburban Wives
Suddenly Single
Sugarland Express
Sunburn
Super Seal
Superdad
Superknights
Supersnooper
Suppose They Gave a War and Nobody Came?
Surf II
Swim Team
Swinging Cheerleaders, The
Switch, The
Sykes
Take the Money and Run
Tall Story
"10"
Texas Across the River
That Darn Cat
That Lucky Touch
That Riviera Touch
That's Carry On
There Goes the Bride
There Was A Crooked Man
They All Laughed
They Call Me Hallelujah
They Call Me Trinity
They're a Weird Mob
This, That and the Other!
Those Magnificent Men in Their Flying Machines
Three in the Attic
Three of a Kind
Till Death Us Do Part
Time Bandits
Titfield Thunderbolt, The
To Be Or Not To Be
To See Such Fun
Tom and Jerry
Tom Jones
Tootsie
Top Cat
Top Cat—Cassette 2
Tough Enough
Toy, The
Trading Places
Traffic
Trail of the Pink Panther
Train Ride to Hollywood, A
Trenchcoat
Tricks of the Trade
Trouble With Harry, The
Tulips
Two-Way Stretch
Under the Cover Cops
Unfaithfully Yours

Up in Smoke
Up Pompeii
Up the Sandbox
Uptown Saturday Night
Utopia
Vals, The
Vampire Hookers
Very Important Person
Village of the Giants
Viva Max
Wackiest Wagon Train in the West, The
Wacky Taxi
Wagonmaster/Double Dynamite
Wait Till Your Mother Gets Home
Waterhole 3
Wedding Party, The
Weekend Murders
What's New Pussycat?
What's Up Doc?
What's Up Nurse
What's Up Superdoc?
When Girls Undress
Where Does It Hurt?
Where the Buffalo Roam
Whisky Galore
White Tower, The/Valley of the Sun
Who Mislaid My Wife?
Whoops Apocalypse
Why Did You Pick On Me?
Why Not Stay for Breakfast?
Wildcat
Wildcats of St. Trinians, The
Willie and Phil
World According to Garp, The
World of Morecambe and Wise Volume 1, The
Yellowbeard
Yes, Giorgio
Young Doctors in Love
Your Money or Your Wife
Yum-Yum Girls
Zapped
Zelig
Zero to Sixty

Comedy-Drama

Airplane II—The Sequel
Alfie Darling
Alice Doesn't Live Here Anymore
Alice in the Cities
Alice's Restaurant
Americathon
Apprenticeship of Duddy Kravitz, The
AWOL
Benji
Better Late Than Never
Better Late Than Never
Billy Liar
Butterflies
Captain's Table, The
Carbon Copy

SUBJECT CATEGORY INDEX — Comedy-Drama

Carry On England
Charley's Aunt/Mr. Axelford's Angel
C.H.O.M.P.S
Comedy of Errors, The
Commuter Husbands
Cul-de-Sac
Dixie Dynamite
Donkeys' Years
Double Nickles
Dribble
Early Bird, The
Entertaining Mr Sloane
Fall and Rise of Reginald Perrin, The
First Travelling Saleslady, The/A Lady Takes a Chance
For Love of Ivy
For the Love of Ada
Gator
Girl Next Door, The
Girls in the Office, The
Godmothers, The
Gods Must Be Crazy, The
Goin' All the Way
Good Life, The
Goodies and the Beanstalk, The
Heartbreak Kid, The
Hopscotch
How to Kill 400 Duponts
Hysterical
Indiscreet
Just a Gigolo
Kotch
Last Detail, The
Life with Father
Limelight
Local Hero
Lonely Hearts
Lookin' to Get Out
Marathon
Mean Machine ('The Longest Yard')
Midsummer Night's Dream, A
Missionary, The
My Therapist
My Wife Next Door
Naked Truth, The
Norman Conquests: Table Manners
Norman Conquests: Living Together, The
Norman Conquests: Round and Round the Garden, The
Nutcase
Optimists of Nine Elms, The
Outlaw Blues
Package Tour
Portnoy's Complaint
Prisoner of Second Avenue, The
Prize Fighter, The
Puberty Blues
Railway Children, The
Rattle of a Simple Man
Second Thoughts
Sensuous Nurse, The
Silence est D'Or, Le
Silver Streak
Stardust Memories
Stay Hungry
Sting, The
Sting II, The
Sunset Limousine
Sweatergirls
Sweet Sins of Sexy Susan, The
Take This Job and Shove It!
That Touch of Mink
They Call Me Bruce
Thief Who Came to Dinner, The
Three in the Cellar
Three Musketeers, The
Tiffany Jones
Trader Hornee
Trouble in store/On the Beat
Twelfth Night
28 Minutes for 3 Million Dollars
Ugly Dachshund, The
Up a Tree
Vampira
Waitress
What's Good for the Goose
Who Finds a Friend Finds a Treasure
Without Reservations/Footlight Varieties

Comedy-Performance

Best of the Two Ronnies, The
Big Banana Feet
Billy Connolly—'Bites Yer Bum'
Fundamental Frolics
Get Knighted!
Just a Carrott
Kelly Monteith-A Yank in London
Lenny Bruce Live in Concert
Mike Harding Goes Over the Top
Pam's Party
Peter Cook and Co
Rewind: Volume 3
Richard Pryor Live in Concert
Secret Policeman's Ball, The
Secret Policeman's Other Ball, The
Stanley Baxter Picture Show—Part 3, The
Stanley Baxter's Moving Picture Show

Cookery

Bar-b-q
Complete Dinner Party, A
Cooking Around the World
Cooking with Microwave
Delia Smith's Home Baking
Dinner at Seven
Food, Wine and Friends: Volume 4
Food, Wine and Friends: Volume 5
Food, Wine and Friends: Volume 6
Food, Wine and Friends: Volume 1
Food, Wine and Friends: Volume 2

Cookery — **SUBJECT CATEGORY INDEX**

Food, Wine and Friends: Volume 3
Kenneth Lo's Chinese Cooking Made Easy
Kenneth Lo's Taste of China
Madhur Jaffrey's Indian Cookery
Mary Berry's Country Cookery
Observer Guide to European Cookery, The
What Shall We Give Them to Eat?

Crime-Drama

Abduction
Abductors, The
Acapulco Gold
All Coppers Are.....
Ambush Murders, The
Amsterdam Kill
Anonymous Avenger
Arrival, The
Assassination Run, The
Assault on Precinct 13
Assignment, The
Atlantic City
Back to Bataan/Roadblock
Bad Boys
Badge
Bandits from Shantung
Barcelona Kill, The
Behave Yourself
Big Bad Mama
Big Combo, The
Big Sleep, The
Big Zapper
Black Gestapo
Black Gold
Black Hand, The
Black Marble, The
Black Panther, The
Blastfighter
Blood Relatives
Bloody Mary
Border U.S.A., The
Boss, The
Bullitt
Calibre 9
Call It Murder
Candy Man, The
Car-Napping
Checkmate
Cobra
Confessions of a Police Captain
Cool Breeze
Cop in Blue Jeans
Cormack
Cornered/The Woman on Pier Thirteen
Covert Action
Crackup/I Walked with a Zombie
Crimebusters
Cross Country
Crossfire
Cruising
Cynic, The Rat and The Fist, The

Dangerous Davies
Danny Travis
Dark Ride, The
Day of the Assassins
Day of the Cobra
Day of the Wolves/Gang Busters
Day of Violence
Deadly Chase
Deadly Force
Deadly Inheritance
Death Collector
Death Force
Death of a Snowman
Death Vengeance
Desperate Voyage
Detroit 9000
Devil with Seven Faces, The
Devil's Canyon/A Cry in the Night
Dirty Money
Dirty Money
Dirty Tricks
Dr Mabuse—The Gambler (Der Spieler)
Dolemite
Domino Killings, The
Doomed to Die
Double Agent 73
Double Crossers, The
Dragonfly for Each Corpse, A
Dressed to Kill
Early Frost
Eddie Macon's Run
Escape From Cell Block 3
Evidence of Power
Fake Out
Fast Kill, The
Father Brown, Detective
Firepower
First Deadly Sin, The
Flying Superboy, The
Force of One, A
Forced Impact
Fort Apache, The Bronx
48 Hrs.
Four for All
Foxy Brown
Framed
French Connection, The
French Connection II, The
From Corleone to Brooklyn/Convoy Busters
Fugitive, The
Funny Money
Fuzz
Gangster Wars
Gangster Wars II
Gangsters
Gardenia
General, The
Get Rita
Godchildren, The
Godfather of Hong Kong
Golden Lady, The

SUBJECT CATEGORY INDEX — Crime-Drama

Gone in 60 Seconds
Goodbye Paradise
Great Diamond Robbery, The
Great Guy
Great Kidnapping, The
Great Telephone Robbery, The
Great Texas Dynamite Chase, The
Ground Zero
Gypsy, The
H-Bomb
Heart of a Father
Heavenly Body
Hell Is Empty
Hell on Frisco Bay/The Mad Miss Manton
Hi-jackers, The/The Night Caller/Echo
High Crime
Hijack
Hit, The
Hit Man, The
Hitter, The
Hold-Up
Honor Thy Father
Hoodwink
Hostages, The
Hound of the Baskervilles, The
House of the Lost Girls
Hunter, The
Hustle
I'll Get You for This
Impulsion
In the Custody of Strangers
I, The Jury
It Takes All Kinds
Jane Doe
Janitor, The
Joy Ride
Kansas City Massacre
Kill
Killer Elite
Killerfish
Killer's Gold
Killing Machine
Killpoint
Kiss Me Killer
Klansman, The
Last Round, The
Left Hand of the Law, The
Little Laura and Big John
Live a Little, Steal a Lot
Long Arm of the Godfather
Long Good Friday, The
Loot
Los Angeles Connection, The
Love and Bullets
Lucky Luciano
Lucky the Inscrutable
Mafia Warfare
Magnum Force
Malibu High
Man from Chicago, The
Man from Hong Kong, The

Man Hunt
Man on the Run
Manipulator, The
Many Happy Returns
Mardi Gras Massacre
Marlowe-Private Eye
Massage Girls in Bangkok
Max
Medusa
Mirror Crack'd, The
Money Movers
Money to Burn
Moving Violation
Murder at Midnight
Murder Gang, The
Naked Fist
New Mafia Boss, The
Night Partners
Nightingale Sang in Berkeley Square, A
Nuclear Countdown
077 Fury in Istanbul
One Just Man
One-Man Jury
One Show Makes It Murder
Onion Field, The
Operation Black September
Ordeal of Patty Hearst, The
Out of the Past/Hell's Highway
Outlaw, The/Law of the Underworld
Perfect Crime, The
Perfect Friday
Perfect Killer, The
Photographer, The
Point Blank
Police Trap
Professionals, The
Professionals, The
Professionals III, The
Professionals IV, The
Projected Man, The/Guns Don't Argue
Puppet on a Chain
Pushing Up Daisies
Queen of the Blues
Queen's Ransom, A
Race for the Yankee Zephyr
Ransom
Rape Because of the Cats, The
Raw Deal
Recommendation for Mercy
Red Light Sting, The
Ride the Tiger
Rider on the Rain
Rivkin: Bounty Hunter
Robbery
Robbery
Rulers of the City
Run of the Arrow/Cry Danger
Scarface
Scarface
Scream for Vengeance
Seduced

Crime-Drama   **SUBJECT CATEGORY INDEX**

SEVEN
Sewers of Paradise, The
Shaft
Shalimar
Sharky's Machine
S*H*E
Sherlock Holmes and the Woman in Green
Shoestring
Sicilian Connection
Sicilian Cross
Sketches of a Strangler
Ski Bum, The
Slaughter
Slaughter in San Francisco
So Sweet, So Dead
South Hell Mountain
Special Cop in Action
Speedtrap/Carquake
Sporting Chance
Squeeze, The
S.T.A.B
Star Chamber, The
Stiletto
Stoner
Stranger Is Watching, A
Streethawk
Strike Back
Stunt Squad
Sudden Impact
Superfly
Suppose I Break Your Neck
Swedish Confessions
Sweeney 2
Switch, The
Target
Target/Shipment
Telefon
Terminate with Extreme Prejudice
They Made Me a Criminal
They Paid With Bullets
Thief
Thing from Another World, The/Stranger on the Third Floor
Three Guys Strike Again, The
Three Superguys, The
Three Superguys in the Snow, The
Thrillkill
Title Shot
Tomorrow Never Comes
Tomorrow Never Comes
Too Hot To Handle
Toolbox Murders, The
Toughest Man In The World
Trip to Kill
Two Female Spies with Flowered Panties
Underwater/The Big Steal
Valachi Papers, The
Vendetta for the Saint
Vice Squad
Victim
Villain
Virginity
Who Dares Wins
Winning Streak
Woman's Paradise Or Hell
Your Money or Your Wife
Zebra Force

Dance

Anchors Aweigh
Bal du Moulin Rouge
Barkleys of Broadway, The
Bizet's Carmen
Breakdance, The Movie
Breakdance—You Can Do It
Dance Fever
Dance Music
Dr. Coppelius
Fille Mal Gardee, La
Giselle
Giselle
Giselle
Giselle
Hip-Hop, a Street History
Hot Gossip
I Am a Dancer
Kids from Fame, The
Kiss Me Kate
Let's Break—The Definitive Guide to Break-Dancing
L'Incoronazione
Manon
Midsummer Night's Dream, A
New York City Ballet, The
Nutcracker, The
Nutcracker, The
Raks Shabi
Red Shoes, The
Romeo and Juliet
Shake Out with Mad Lizzie
Sleeping Beauty, The
Stories from a Flying Trunk
Swan Lake
Tales of Beatrix Potter

Dinosaurs

Dinosaurs—Fun, Fact and Fantasy

Disasters

Days Of Fury
Encounter with Disaster

Documentary

Adventure in Ventana
Alam Alhaiwan
Alaska Wilderness Adventure, The
Amag Elbehar
Andy Warhol and His Work
Angelo Branduardi—Concerto

SUBJECT CATEGORY INDEX — Documentary

Ape and Super Ape
Battle for the Falklands
Being Different
Bermuda Triangle, The
Best of Walt Disney's True Life Adventures, The
Beyond and Back
Big Banana Feet
Big Fish Down Under—Away From It All
Big Fish Down Under—Black Marlin
Big Fish Down Under—Island Holiday
Big Fish Down Under—Professionals at Play
Big Fish Down Under—Sailfish
Big Fish Down Under—The Beginnings
Big Fish Down Under—The Ribbons
Black Fox
Body, The
Britain's Royal Heritage
Brutes and Savages
Catastrophe
Challenge of the Sky
Charles and Diana
Colonel Culpeper's Flying Circus
Coming Soon
Crash of Flight 401, The
Crystal Voyager
D-Day—The Great Crusade
Dave Brubeck-A Musical Portrait
Edward and Mrs. Simpson Volume 1
Edward and Mrs. Simpson Volume 2
Edward and Mrs. Simpson Volume 3
Encounter with Disaster
Essential Mike Oldfield, The
Falklands—Task Force South
Farnborough International '84
Farnborough International '82
Fi Hob Allah
Finest Hours, The
Fleetwood Mac
Footsteps of Giants
Funniest Man in the World, The
Gandhi
Gentleman Tramp, The
Glittering Crowns, The
Great Event, The
In Search of Dracula
James Dean Story, The
James Dean—The First American Teenager
Joan Collins Video Special, The
Joan Sutherland—'A Life on the Move'
Jupiter Menace, The
Kelly Monteith-A Yank in London
KGB Connections, The
Kids Are Alright, The
King's Story, A
Kitty—Return to Auschwitz
Kwaheri
Land of Silence and Darkness/the Flying Doctors of East Africa
Last Of The Wild—Volume 1
Last Of The Wild—Volume 2
Last Of The Wild—Volume 3
Last of the Wild—Volume 4
Last of the Wild—Volume 5
Last of the Wild—Volume 6
Lawrence Durrell's Greece—'Spirit of the Place'
Legend of Boggy Creek, The
Let Me Die a Woman
Loners Plus Clipper Cup 'Hawaii 78,' The
Magic of Coronation Street—Distant Memories 1960-64, The
Manchester United Story, The
Metro-Land
Mighty Micro, The
Mysteries from Beyond Earth
Mysterious Monsters, The
Nasser
Never Cry Wolf
Night Bombers
147 Break
Pele: The Master and His Method
Pilgrimage to the Holy Land
Pole Position
Pope in the Park, The
Pope John Paul II in Ireland
Portrait of a Great Lady
Prince Charles: A Royal Portrait
Princess
Princess and the People
Private Life of Adolf Hitler, The/The Public Life of Adolf Hitler
Pumping Iron
Queen's Birthday Parade, The
Raks Shabi
Ringo's World
Rock, Rock, Rock!
Royal Wedding, The
Royal Wedding, The
Royal Wedding, The
Royal Wedding, The
Ruby and Oswald
Seapower
Short Films 1
Short Films 2
Silent Wilderness
Soccer: The Game of the Century: Part 2
Souvenir Video Guide to Royal London 1981
Spitfire
Story of Prince Charles and Lady Diana, The
Summer Festival
Tatters
That's Entertainment
That's Entertainment: Part 2
This Is London
This Year 1980
This Year 1981
UFO Journals
Unknown Chaplin
Unknown Powers
Videobook of British Garden Birds
Wildlife USA
Wimbledon '81
Wings of an Eagle

765

Documentary　　　　　　　**SUBJECT CATEGORY INDEX**

World at War Parts 1 and 2, The
World at War: Parts 1-4, The
World at War Parts 3 and 4, The
World at War Parts 5 and 6, The
World at War: Parts 5-8, The
World at War Parts 7 and 8, The
World at War Parts 9 and 10, The
World at War Parts 11 and 12, The
World at War Parts 13 and 14, The
World at War Parts 15 and 16, The
World at War Parts 19 and 20, The
World at War Parts 21 and 22, The
World at War Parts 23 And 24, The
World at War Parts 25 And 26, The
World of Survival—Hunters of the Plains, The
World of Survival—Man and the Great Apes, The
World of Survival—Migrants of the Arctic, The
World of Survival—Mysteries of the Great Whales, The
World of Survival—Penguins of the Falkland Islands, The
World of Survival—The Last Kingdoms of the Elephants, The
World's Greatest Paintings 1: Adoration, The
Woyzeck/How Much Wood Would a Woodchuck Chuck
World at War Parts 17 and 18, The
Year of the Quorn

Drama

Abducted
Abigail's Party
Abilene Town
Absolution
Accident
Ace Up My Sleeve
Act, The
Act Of Passion
Act of Vengeance
Adam
Adventurers, The
Adventures of Hambone and Hillie, The
Adventures of Huckleberry Finn, The
Affair, The
Agatha Christie Collection, Volume 1, The
Age of Innocence
Agency
Agony and the Ecstasy, The
Aguirre, Wrath of God
Airport '80—The Concorde
Airport '77
Airport SOS Hijack
Airwolf
Alcatraz
Alcatraz II—The Final Escape
All About Eve
All Creatures Great and Small
All Night Long
All That Jazz
All the Kind Strangers

All the President's Men
All the Right Moves
Allegheny Uprising/Back from Eternity
Alley Cat
Aloha, Bobby and Rose
Alpha Beta
Amateur, The
American Friend
Americana
Americano, The
Amorous Milkman, The
Anatomy of a Seduction
And Baby Comes Home
And Baby Makes Six
And Soon the Darkness
Andrea, the Nympho
Andy Warhol Presents Lonesome Cowboys
Angel
Angel
Angel City
Angel of Vengeance
Angel on My Shoulder
Angels Die Hard
Angels in Hell
Angry Breed, The
Anna Karenina
Anne of the Thousand Days
Another Time, Another Place
Antagonists, The
Antony and Cleopatra
Antony and Cleopatra
Arena, The
Ascendancy
Ash Wednesday
Ash Wednesday
Ashes and Diamonds
Asiad Wa Abeed (Masters and Slaves)
Assassination of Trotsky, The
Attack of the Normans
Attica
Attila the Hun
Audrey Rose
Autobiography of a Princess
Autumn Sonata
Baby, The
Baby Love
Baby Maker, The
Baby Sister
Babylon
Babysitter, The
Back Roads
Bad Timing
Badlands
Baffled
Bait, The
Balance, La
Balboa
Ballad of Joe Hill, The
Bang the Drum Slowly
Barbarian, The
Bare Knuckles

766

SUBJECT CATEGORY INDEX — Drama

Barrel Full of Dollars, A
Barry Lyndon
Battle for the Planet of the Apes
Beach House
Beastmaster, The
Beat Street
Because He's My Friend
Becket
Beguiled, The
Behind Convent Walls
Below the Belt
Belstone Fox, The
Ben Hur
Best of Friends, The
Best of the Sandbaggers, The
Best of Sandbaggers-Cassette 2, The
Best of Upstairs, Downstairs—Volume 1, The
Best of Upstairs, Downstairs—Volume 2, The
Best of Upstairs, Downstairs—Volume 4, The
Best of Upstairs, Downstairs—Volume 5, The
Best of Upstairs, Downstairs—Volume 6, The
Best of Upstairs, Downstairs—Volume 7, The
Best of Upstairs, Downstairs—Volume 3, The
Betsy, The
Beyond Atlantis
Beyond Death's Door
Beyond Reason
Beyond the Poseidon Adventure
Beyond the Valley of the Dolls
Bible, The
Bible—In the Beginning, The
Bicycle Thieves
Big Bird Cage, The
Big Chill, The
Big Fix, The
Big Red
Bilitis
Bill
Bill of Divorcement, A
Bill on his Own
Billy Jack
Bim
Birds of Prey
Birth of a Nation, The
Birthday Party, The
Bitch, The
Bitter Tears of Petra Von Kant, The
Bittersweet Love
Black Arrow, The
Black Beauty
Black Belt Jones
Black Carrion/A Distant Scream
Black Emmanuelle, White Emmanuelle
Black Pirate, The
Black Sunday
Black Veil for Lisa, A
Blade
Blazing Magnum
Blind Date
Blood and Black Lace
Blood and Guts

Blood and Sand
Blood Feud
Blood Queen
Bloodline
Bloody Kids
Blow-Up
Blue Belle
Blue Blood
Blue Jeans and Dynamite
Blue Max, The
Blue Thunder
Boardwalk
Bobby Deerfield
Body and Soul
Body and Soul
Body Heat
Bogie
Bombay Talkie
Border, The
Borderline
Born Again
Born Beautiful
Born Losers
Born to Be Sold
Born Wild
Born Winner
Bounty, The
Bounty Man, The
Boxcar Bertha
Boys from Brazil, The
Boys in the Band, The
Brainstorm
Brainwashed
Brainwaves
Breakdance, The Movie
Breaking Up-Love and Life
Breathless
Bride to Be
Brideshead Revisited—Vol. 1
Brideshead Revisited—Vol. 2
Brideshead Revisited—Vol. 3
Brideshead Revisited—Vol. 4
Brideshead Revisited—Vol. 5
Brideshead Revisited—Vol. 6
Brief Encounter
Brief Encounter
Brighton Rock
Brimstone and Treacle
Britannia Hospital
Broken Promise
Brotherhood of Death
Brothers
Brubaker
Brute, The
Buddy System, The
Bug
Bullet for the General
Burglars, The
Bury Me An Angel
Butterfly
Caddie

767

Drama
SUBJECT CATEGORY INDEX

Caesar and Cleopatra
Caged Heat
California Dolls, The
California Girls
Call to Glory
Camelot
Candidate, The
Cannibal
Card, The
Carefree/Easy Living
Carnal Knowledge
Carquake
Carrington, V.C.
Carthage in Flames
Casablanca
Casanova
Casey's Shadow
Cassandra Crossing, The
Cat and Mouse
Cat on a Hot Tin Roof
Catastrophe
Catch Me a Spy
Cathie's Child
Catwalk Killer, The
Caught
C.C. and Company
Celebrity
Chained Heat
Champ, The
Champion
Champions, The
Chanel Solitaire
Chant of Jimmie Blacksmith, The
Chant of Jimmie Blacksmith, The
Chariots of Fire
Charley's Aunt/Mr. Axelford's Angel
Charles Muffin
Charly
Charulata
Cheerleaders' Wild Weekend
Child Bride of Short Creek, The
Children of An-Lac, The
Children's Story, The
Child's Play/And the Wall Came Tumbling Down
China Rose
Choice, The
Choices
Chosen, The
Christiane F
Christmas to Remember, A
Cincinnati Kid, The
Circus World
Citizen Kane
City Lights
City on Fire
Clash By Night
Class of 1984
Class of '63
Cleopatra
Cloak and Dagger
Cloud Dancer

Club, the
Cocaine—One Man's Poison
Cold River
Coma
Come Back to the Five and Dime, Jimmy Dean, Jimmy Dean
Come Play With Me 2
Comeback
Comes a Horseman
Comfort and Joy
Coming Home
Coming Out Alive
Coming Out of the Ice
Concorde Affair
Concrete Jungle, The
Conduct Unbecoming
Confessions of the Sex Slaves
Connecting Rooms
Conquest of the Planet of the Apes
Constantine and the Cross
Contempt
Contract
Conversation Piece
Cool Hand Luke
Cornered/The Woman on Pier Thirteen
Corruption of Chris Miller
Count of Monte-Cristo, The
Countdown
Countryman
Cousins in Love
Cover Me Babe
Covergirl
Cradle Will Fall, The
Crash of Flight 401, The
Craze
Crazies
Cries and Whispers
Cross Creek
Cry of the Innocent
Cujo
Cutter's Way
Cyclone
Czech Mate/In Possession
Dain Curse, The
Dallas—Cassette 1
Dallas—Cassette 2
Dallas—Cassette 3
Dallas—Cassette 4
Dallas—Cassette 5
Dallas—Cassette 6
Dallas—Cassette 7
Dallas—Cassette 8
Dallas—Cassette 9
Dallas—Cassette 10
Dallas—Cassette 11
Dallas—Cassette 12
Dallas—Cassette 13
Dallas—Cassette 14
Dallas—Cassette 14
Dallas—Cassette 16
Dallas-Cassette 17

SUBJECT CATEGORY INDEX — Drama

Dallas-Cassette 18
Damned, The
Dance Fever
Dance Music
Dance of Love
Dangerous Summer, A
Dangerous Traffic
Danny
Daring Game
Dark Command
Dark Eyes
Dark Mirror, The
Darkroom, The
David and Goliath
Day After, The
Day of the Dolphin, The
Day of the Jackal, The
Day the Earth Moved, The
Days of Heaven
Dayton's Devil
Dead End Street
Dead Pigeon on Beethoven Street
Deadliest Season, The
Deadly Females, The
Deadly Hunt, The
Deadly Trap, The
Death Cruise
Death Drive
Death Flight
Death Hunt
Death in Venice
Death of a Centrefold
Death Raiders
Death Squad
Death Threat
Death Trap
Death Valley
Death Wish
Deathwatch
Deep Red
Deer Hunter, The
Deerslayer, The
Deerslayer, The
Delirium
Deliverance
Delta Factor
Demons of the Mind
Desert Chase
Deserter, The
Despair
Desperate Characters
Desperate Intruder
Devil and Leroy Bassett, The
Devil Doll/The Curse of Simba
Devil in Miss Jones Part II, The
Devils, The
Devil's Advocate, The
Devils Angels
Diamonds
Diary of Anne Frank, The
Die Screaming Marianne

Dimension 5
Dinah East
Dirty Deal
Dirty Harry
Disco Fever
Diva
Divorce His, Divorce Hers
Doctor Faustus
Doctor's Wives
Dog Day Afternoon
Dogpound Shuffle
Dollmaker, The
Doll's House, A
Dominique
Don is Dead, The
Donner Pass
Dorian Gray
Double Deal
Double Life, A
Dove, The
Downhill Racer
Dracula
Draughtman's Contract, The
Dream for Christmas, A
Dream of Passion
Dreamer, The
Driver
Drop Dead Dearest
Drum
Drum, The
Duel in the Sun
Duel of Champions
Duellists, The
Eagle in a Cage
East of Eden
East of Elephant Rock
East Side Hustle
Echoes
Educating Rita
Eiger Sanction, The
80,000 Suspects
Electric Horseman
Elephant Boy, The
Elephant Man, The
Elephant Man, The
Elmer
Elmer Gantry
Embassy
Emily
Emmanuelle
Emmanuelle 4
Emmanuelle—Queen of the Sados
Emmanuelle 3
Emmanuelle 2
End of August, The
Endangered Species
Endless Love
Enfants du Paradis, Les
Enforcer, The
England Made Me
Enigma

Drama   **SUBJECT CATEGORY INDEX**

Enigma of Kaspar Hauser, The
Equus
Eric
Eroticist, The
Escape from Alcatraz
Escape to the Sun
Eureka
Europeans, The
Evil that Men Do, The
Excalibur
Executioner's Song, The
Existance
Exorcist, The
Exorcist II—The Heretic
Exposed
Exterminators of the Year 3000
Eye of the Needle
Eyes of the Dragon
Eyewitness
Fall of the Roman Empire, The
Fallen Idol
Falling in Love Again
Falling Man, The
Fame
Family Enforcer
Family Life
Family Man, The
Family Plot
Fan, The
Fanny by Gaslight
Fanny Hill
Far from the Madding Crowd
Far Pavilions, The
Farewell My Lovely
Fast Times at Ridgemont High
Fast-Walking
Fatal Games
Fear Eats The Soul
Fear in the Night
Fedora
Fifth Musketeer, The
55 Days at Peking
Fighting Back
Fille Mal Gardee, La
Final Assignment
Final Countdown, The
Final Mission, The
Final Terror, The
Finally Sunday
Firefox
Fire Over England
Firechasers, The
Firehouse
Firestarter
First Love
First Monday in October
F.I.S.T.
Fitzcarraldo
Five Days from Home
Five Days One Summer
Five Desperate Women

Flame Trees of Thika, The
Flare-Up
Flashpoint Africa
Flight 90: Disaster on the Potomac
Flight of the Phoenix, The
Follow That Rainbow
Footsteps
For Ladies Only
For Whom the Bell Tolls
For Your Love Only
Forever Young
Forgotten Man, The
Formula, The
Fort Apache
49th Parallel
Four Feathers, The
Fourth Man, The
Fox and His Friends
Foxes
Frances
Fraud!
Freedom Road
French Lieutenant's Woman, The
French Way, The
Friendly Fire
Fright
From a Far Country, Pope John Paul II
From the Life of the Marionettes
Fruit Is Ripe, The
Fugitive, The/Follow Me Quietly
Funeral for an Assassin
Gambler, The
Gandhi
Garden of Allah, The
Gaugin—The Savage
Gauntlet, The
Generation, A
Gentle Savage
Gentle Sinners
Gentleman Bandit
Georgia
Getting of Wisdom, The
Girl Called Jules, A
Girl with Green Eyes
Girls on the Road
Glitter Dome
Godfather, The
God's Little Acre
Gold
Gold of the Amazon Women
Golden Needles
Golden Triangle, The
Goldengirl
Goliath and the Barbarians
Gone are the Dayes
Gone in 60 Seconds II
Gone with the Wind
Good Die Young, The
Goodbye, Norma Jean
Gorky Park
Got It Made

SUBJECT CATEGORY INDEX — Drama

Goya
Grace Kelly Story, The
Graduate, The
Grange Hill
Gray Lady Down
Great Expectations
Great Expectations
Great Gatsby, The
Great Houdinis, The
Great Waldo Pepper, The
Greatest Heroes of the Bible
Green Eyes
Green Horizon
Green Ice
Gregory's Girl
Griffin and Phoenix
Grissom Gang, The
Gun in the House, A
Guyana
Hamlet
Hammersmith is Out
Handgun
Happily Ever After—Love and Life
Hard Country
Harrad Experiment, The
Harry and Son
Harry's Game
Haunted Palace, The
Haunting Passion, The
Having It All
Head On
Heartaches
Heartbeat
Heartbreak Motel
Heartland
Hearts of the West
Heatwave
Heaven's Gate
Heidi
Heidi
Hell Drivers
Hellbenders, The
Hell's Angels on Wheels
Henry V
Henry VIII and His Six Wives
Hercules Challenge
Hide-Aways, The
Hide in Plain Sight
High Risk
High Rolling
Highpoint
Highway to Hell
Hills Have Eyes, The
Hit Lady
Hitch Hike
Hitler—The Last Ten Days
Hoax, The
Hoffman
Hollywood Boulevard
Hollywood Knight
Holocaust
Home Before Midnight
Home to Stay
Homework
Honey
Honeybaby
Honeymoon Killers, The
Honky
Honorary Consul, The
Hot Dog—The Movie
Hot Touch, The
Hound of the Baskervilles, The
House on Garibaldi Street, The
Howzer
Hullabaloo Over Georgie and Bonnie's Pictures
Human Factor, The
Hunchback of Notre Dame, The
Hunchback of Notre Dame, The
Hunger, The
Hunted, The
Hurricane
The Hustler
Hysteria
I Am a Camera
I Heard the Owl Call My Name
I Never Promised You a Rose Garden
I Walk the Line
I Will Fight No More Forever
Ibtisama Wahibda Takfi (One Smile Is Enough)
Ice Station Zebra
Iceman
Ideal Husband, An
I'll Be Seeing You
I'm Dancing As Fast As I Can
I'm Going To Be Famous
Images
Immoral Tales
In the Heat of the Night
Indiscretion of an American Wife
Inferno in Paradise
Initiation, The
Inn of the Damned
Inside Moves
Intermezzo
International Velvet
Intimate Relations
Intolerance
Irishman, The
Island, The
Island at the Top of the World, The
It Seemed Like a Good Idea at the Time
It's Good to be Alive
Italian Job, The
Italian Stallion
Jacqueline Bouvier Kennedy
Jailhouse Rock
Jane Austen in Manhattan
Jaws 3
Jayne Mansfield Story, The
Jennifer—A Woman's Story
Jenny
Jeremiah Johnson

Drama — SUBJECT CATEGORY INDEX

Jericho Mile, The
Jesse Owens Story, The
Jesus of Nazareth
Jesus Trip, The
Jet Lag
Joan of Arc
Joe
Joe Panther
Jour Se Leve, Le
Jour Se Leve, Le
Journalist, The
Journey Among Women
Jubilee
Julia
Julius Caesar
Jungle Warriors
Justine
Kansas City Bomber
Karamurat
Kashmiri Run
Kidnapped
Kidnapping of the President, The
Kill
Kill and Kill Again
Killer Inside Me, The
Killer Volcano
Killing of Sister George, The
Kind of Loving, A
King of Comedy
Kleinhoff Hotel
Klute
Knife in the Water
Knight Without Armour
Kramer Vs Kramer
Kublai Khan
Kuroneko
La Ya Oumi (No, Mother)
Lacemaker, The
Ladies' Doctor
Lady Caroline Lamb
Lady from Yesterday, The
Lady Grey
Lady Hamilton
Lady of the House
Lady, Stay Dead
Last Child, The
Last Days of Pompeii, The/The Mysterious Desperado
Last Embrace
Last Feelings
Last Fight, The
Last Moments
Last Roman, The
Last Snows of Spring
Last Song, The
Last Tango in Paris
Last Tango in Paris
Last Tycoon, The
Last Valley, The
Last Video and Testament/The Corvini Inheritance

Laura
Laura
Laura—Shadows of Summer
Lawrence of Arabia
Legend of Alfred Packer, The
Legend of Boggy Creek, The
Legend of the Northwest
Legend of Valentino, The
Lenny
Lenny
Leopard in the Snow
Les Miserables
Lianna
Liar's Moon
Lies
Life and Times of Grizzly Adams, The
Life Is Beautiful
Lifetaker, The
Lilacs in the Spring
Limbo Line, The
Lincoln Conspiracy, The
Line, The
Lion in Winter, The
Lisbon
Little Darlings
Little Lord Fauntleroy
Live Today, Die Tomorrow
Living Proof
Loaded Guns
Loneliest Runner, The
Lonely Lady, The
Loners, The
Long Day's Journey Into Night
Long Day's Journey Into Night
Long Hot Summer, The
Long Night of Veronique, The
Long Way Home, A
Longshot
Look Back in Anger
Looking for Mr. Goodbar
Looking Glass War, The
Loose Connections
Lords of Discipline, The
Lords of Flatbush, The
Losin' It
Lost Moment, The
Love Among the Ruins
Love by Appointment
Love Hate Love
Love Is a Splendid Illusion
Love Letters
Love, Lust and Ecstasy
Love Story
Loveless, The
Lover of the Great Bear, The
Lovers and Other Strangers
Lucky Star, The
Lust for Revenge
Macbeth
Mad Bomber, The
Mad Bull

SUBJECT CATEGORY INDEX — Drama

Mad Dog
Madame Sin
Madhouse
Mae West
Mafu Cage, The
Magic of Coronation Street—Distant Memories 1960-64, The
Magnificent Matador, The
Magnificent Tony Carrera, The
Mahler
Mako-Jaws of Death
Man at the Top
Man Called Intrepid, A
Man For All Seasons, A
Man Friday
Man in the Iron Mask, The
Man in the Steel Mask, The
Man of Flowers
Man Outside, The
Man, Pride, Vengeance
Man Who Knew Too Much, The
Mandingo
Manions, The
March or Die
Marciano
Margin For Murder
Mark, I Love You
Mark I Love You
Maroc 7
Marriage of Maria Braun
Mary and Joseph
Massacre at Fort Holman
Matter of Time, A
Maybe This Time
Mayerling
Mc Q
McVicar
Mean Streets
Mechanic, The
Medusa Touch, The
Megaforce 7-9
Melanie
Melody in Love
Memoirs of a Survivor
Memory of Us
Mephisto
Merchant of Venice, The
Meteor
Midnight Blue
Midnight Cowboy
Mighty Joe Young/Little Orvie
Million Pound Note, The
Minder
Miracle of Love
Miracle of the Bells, The
Miracle on Ice
Mirror, Mirror—Love and Life
Miss Julie
Missing
Missouri Breaks, The
Mrs R's Daughter

Mr Kingstreet's War/Ghost Ship
Mistral's Daughter
Mistress, The
Mistress of Paradise
Misunderstood
Mommie Dearest
Mongrel
Monsieur Verdoux
Monsieur Vincent
Monsignor
Monster, The
Montenegro
Month in the Country, A
Moon in the Gutter, The
Moonchild
Moses the Lawgiver
Moulin Rouge
Mountain Man
Mouse and the Woman, The
Mr Majestyk
Multiple Maniacs/Cocaine Fiends
Murder by Decree
Murder in Texas
Murder on Flight 502
Mutiny on the Bounty
My Boys Are Good Boys
My Brilliant Career
My Champion
My Nights With....Susan, Olga, Julie, Albert, Piet and Sandra
My Old Man
My Young Man
Nadia
Naked Civil Servant, The
Naked Kiss, The
Naked Truth, The
Name for Evil, A
Nana
Naou Minal Nisaa (A Type of Woman)
Natas
Natural, The
Natural Enemies
Neither the Sea Nor the Sand
Network
Never Say Never Again
Never to Love
New York After Midnight
New York Nights
Newsfront
Next Man, The
Next One, The
Nicholas Nickelby
Night Crossing
Night Strangler, The
Night The Lights Went Out In Georgia, The
Night the Prowler, The
Night to Remember, A
Night Train Murders
Nightcomers, The
Nightingale, the
Nights of Cabiria

Drama — SUBJECT CATEGORY INDEX

Nine Ages of Nakedness
92 in the Shade
Ninth Configuration, The
No Place to Hide
Norma Rae
North by Northwest
North Dallas Forty
North-East of Seoul
North Sea Hijack
Northville Cemetery Massacre, The
Notorious
Nowhere to Hide
Nuts in May
Obsessive Love
October Man, The
Octopussy
Odd Man Out
Of Mice and Men
Officer and a Gentleman, An
Oil
Old Boyfriends
Old Yeller
Oliver Twist
Oliver Twist
On Golden Pond
On the Nickel
Once Upon a Scoundrel
Once Upon a Time in America
One Away
One Blow Too Many
One Brief Summer
One-Eyed Soldiers, The
One Flew Over the Cuckoo's Nest
One Is a Lonely Number
One Million Years B.C.
One More Chance
One Night.....Only
One on Top of the Other
One Two Two
Oni Baba
Only Once in a Lifetime
Only One Winner
Operation Thunderbolt
Ordeal, The
Ordeal of Bill Carney, The
Ordeal of Dr. Mudd, The
Order of Death
Othello
Other Side of Madness, The
Other Side of Midnight, The
Out of Season
Out of the Past/Hell's Highway
Outback
Outrage
Outsiders, The
Over the Edge
Pacific Inferno
Paint Me a Murder/The Late Nancy Irving
Pancho Villa
Panic in Echo Park
Panic in Needle Park

Paper Chase, The
Paper Tiger
Paradine Case, The
Paradise Alley
Paranoia
Paris, Texas
Passione d'Amore
Pawnbroker, The
PayDay
Peeper
Penitentiary
Penitentiary II
Performance
Perversion Story
Phobia
Piaf
Picnic at Hanging Rock
Pilot, The
Pinball Summer
Pipe Dreams
Piranha, Piranha
Pixote
Play Dead
Playbirds, The
Playing with Fire
Plaza Suite
Pleasure Palace
Ploughman's Lunch, The
Poco
Policewoman Centrefold
Poor Albert, Little Annie
Pope Joan
Portes de la Nuit, Les
Portrait of a Showgirl
Portrait of a Stripper
Portrait of Jennie
Possession of Joel Delaney, The
Postman Always Rings Twice, The
Powderkeg
Power Play
Pranks
Preacherman
Premonition
Premonition
President's Mistress, The
Pretty Baby
Pretty Poison
Price of Power, The
Pride of Jesse Hallam, The
Priest of Love
Prime of Miss Jean Brodie-Cassette 1, The
Prince of the City
Princess Daisy
Private Parts
Prize of Peril, The
Psychopath
Punch and Jody
Purple Taxi, The
Pyx, The
Quackser Fortune Has a Cousin in the Bronx
Quartet

SUBJECT CATEGORY INDEX — Drama

Quartet
Queen for Caesar, A
Queen of Spades, The
Querelle
Quest for Love
Question of Love
Quinns, The
Quo Vadis
Rachel's Man
Racing Game, The
Racing with the Moon
Racquet
Rage
Raggedy Man
Raging Moon, The
Ragtime
Raid on Entebbe
Raise the Titanic
Ransom
Rape of the Third Reich
Rattlers
Ravagers, The
Ravine, The
Real Life
Rebecca
Rebecca of Sunnybrook Farm
Red Light in the White House
Redneck
Reds
Regle du Jeu, La
Reilly—Ace of Spies
Repo Man
Return Engagement
Return of the Soldier, The
Revenge
Rhinestone
Rich and Famous
Riddle of the Sands, The
Ride in a Pink Car
Rivals
Road Games
Road Hustlers
Robe, The
Rockers
Rocky
Rocky
Rocky II
Rocky III
Rocky II
Rodeo Girl
Rollermania
Rolling Man
Rolling Thunder
Rollover
Romantic Englishwoman, The
Ronde, La
Room at the Top
Roseland
Ruby and Oswald
Ruby Gentry
Rumble Fish

Run, Angel, Run
Run for Your Life
Runner Stumbles, The
Running
Running Brave/The Story of Zola Budd
Rush the Assassin
Russian Roulette
Ruthless
Ryan's Daughter
Safari Rally
Sahara Cross
Saigon—Year of the Cat
Sailor Who Fell from Grace with the Sea, The
Salahdin Al Ayoobi
Salamander, The
Salome—Where She Danced
Salvatore Giuliano
Samson and Delilah
Samson and Delilah
Sand Pebbles, The
Sandpiper, The
Sara Dane
Saturday Night at the Baths
Savage Bees, The
Savage Encounter
Savage Innocents, The
Savage Is Loose, The
Savage Islands
Savage Sisters
Savages
Say Hello to Yesterday
Sayonara
Scarecrow
Scared Straight-Another Story
Scarlet Pimpernel, The
Scarlet Woman, The
Scenes from a Marriage
School's Out at Sunset Cove
Scrubbers
Scum
Season for Assassins
Sebastiane
Second Chance/Great Day in the Morning
Second Hand Hearts
Second Wind
Secret Beyond the Door
Secret Places
Secrets
Seducer, The
Seduction of Joe Tynan, The
See How She Runs
Seed of Innocence
Seeds of Evil
Sense of Freedom, A
Sentinel, The
Separate Tables
Separate Ways
Serial
Serpent, The
Serpico
Servant, The

Drama — SUBJECT CATEGORY INDEX

Seventh Veil, The
Severed Arm, The
Sex Diary
Sex Madness/Mondo Trasho
Sex With the Stars
Sexy Dozen, The
Shadow of the Tiger
Shark Hunter, The
Shatter
She Came to the Valley
Sheriff and the Satellite Kid, The
Shock Corridor
Shock Waves
Shoot
Shout, The
Showbiz
Siege
Silence the Witness
Silent Partner, The
Silkwood
Silver Dream Racer
Simba
Simon Bolivar
Sin
Since You Went Away
Singer Not the Song, The
Single Room Furnished
Sins of Dorian Gray, The
Skag
Skeezer
Skokie
Sky Riders
Sky West and Crooked
Sky West and Crooked
Skyjacked
Slaughterhouse Five
Slayground
Sleeping Dogs
Smash Palace
Smithereens
Sneakers
Snowballing
So Long at the Fair
Some Kind of Hero
Someone Behind the Door
Someone Is Bleeding
Something Short of Paradise
Something Wicked This Way Comes
Sophie's Choice
Sorcerers, The
S.O.S. Titanic
Sounder
Space Riders
Spacehunter
Spellbound
Spetters
Sphinx
Spiral Staircase, The
Split Image
Spring Fever
Stage Struck/The Girl Most Likely

Star 80
Starbird and Sweet William
Starlet
Starstruck
Steps
Stevie
Still of the Night
Storm Boy
Story of Jesus, The
Story of O
Straight Time
Stranger in Sacramento
Stranger in the House
Strangers Kiss
Strauss Family—Part One, The
Strauss Family—Part Two, The
Straw Dogs
Street of the Damned
Streetcar Named Desire, A
Streets of Fire
Striptease
Stromboli/While the City Sleeps
Stroszek
Stud, The
Stunt Man, The
Stunts, the Deadly Game
Suburbia
Suddenly Single
Sugar Cookies
Sugarland Express
Suicide's Wife, The
Summer Lovers
Summer of Fear
Summer Of My German Soldier
Summer With Monika
Sunburst
Sunset Boulevard
Sunshine on the Skin
Supertrain
Surfacing
Survive!
Svengali
Swarm, The
Sweeney!
Sweet Revenge
Sweet Scent of Death/Mark of the Devil, The
Sweet William
Swiss Family Robinson
Switchblade Sisters, The
Take, The
Take an Easy Ride
Take Down
Tale of Two Cities, A
Tale of Two Cities, A
Tales of Ordinary Madness
Tamarind Seed, The
Tangier
Tank
Tarantulas
Taste of Evil, A
Tattoo

Taxi Zum Klo
Te Deum
Tempest, The
Tempest, The
Ten Commandments, The
Ten Violent Women
Tender Loving Care
Tender Mercies
Terminal Choice
Terms of Endearment
Terror
Terror from the Sky
Tess
Testament
That Championship Season
That Man Bolt
Theodora Queen of Byzantium
They Call Me Lucky
They Call That an Accident
They Shoot Horses, Don't They?
This Happy Breed
This Is Callan
This Sporting Life
Those Calloways
Three Cheers for Us
300 Miles for Stephanie
300 Year Weekend, The
Three Immoral Women
Three Sisters, The
Three Warriors
Threshold
Thursday's Child
Thursday's Game
Tiara Tahiti
Ticket to Heaven
Tiger Bay
Tiger Town
Tilt
Time After Time
Times Square
To Race the Wind
Together
Tomorrow Man, The
Too Late the Hero
Torn Between Two Lovers
Touch, The
Touch and Go
Touch-Me-Not
Touched
Touched by Love
Towering Inferno, The
Toy Soldiers
Train Killer, The
Trapped Beneath the Sea
Travelling Executioner, The
Treasure Island
Trenchcoat
Trespasser, The
Trial by Terror
Triangle Factory Fire Scandal, The
Triangle Factory Fire Scandal, The

Tribute
Trojan War, The
Trouble With Harry, The
Truck Stop Women
True Confessions
Turning Point, The
21 Hours at Munich
21 Hours at Munich
20,000 Leagues Under the Sea
Twice a Woman
Twinky
Twisted Nerve
2001: A Space Odyssey
Ulysses
Under Milk Wood
Under the Volcano
Underwater/The Big Steal
Union City
Unmarried Woman, An
Unsuitable Job for a Woman, An
Urban Cowboy
Valley of the Dolls
Vanishing Point
Vengeance
Vengeance Is Mine
Vengeance of the Barbarians
Venom
Vertigo
Very Like a Whale
Videodrome
Vigilante
Vigilante Force
Violation of the Bitch, The
Violent Enemy, The
Violent Streets
Virgin and the Gypsy, The
Virgin Campus
Virgin Spring, The
Viva Knievel
Voyage of the Damned
Voyage Round My Father, A
Walk a Crooked Path
Walking The Edge
Walls of Sin
Wanderers, The
Wanted Baby Sitter
Warm December, A
Warrior of the Lost World
Warriors, The
Washington Affair, The
Watched
Way We Were, The
We of The Never Never
Whale for the Killing, A
What Next?
When the North Wind Blows
When Time Ran Out
Where Danger Lives/Split Second
Where Have All the People Gone?
Where the Red Fern Grows
Whispering Death

Whistle Down the Wind
White Dog
White Heat
White Tower, The/Valley of the Sun
Who Will Love My Children?
Who Will Save Our Children?
Who's Afraid of Virginia Woolf?
Why Did You Pick On Me?
Wicked Lady, The
Widows
Wild Angels, The
Wild Heart, The
Wild Little Bunch, The
Wild Party, The
Wild Strawberries
Wilde's Domain
Will There Really Be a Morning?
Will to Die
Willard
Winds of Kitty Hawk, The
Winning
Winslow Boy, The
Winter Kills
Winter of Our Discontent, The
Winter of Our Dreams
Wolf Lake
Women Gladiators
Women in Love
Women Prisoners of Devil's Island, The
World Is Full of Married Men, The
World War III
Woyzeck/How Much Wood Would a Woodchuck Chuck
Wrong Way
Wuthering Heights
Yanks
Year of Living Dangerously, The
Yellow Emanuelle
Yentl
Yojimbo
Yol (The Way)
You and Me
You Light Up My Life
Young Joe-The Forgotten Kennedy
Young Lions, The
Young Warriors, The
Your Ticket Is No Longer Valid
You've Come a Long Way, Katie
Z.P.G.

Drawing

Drawing

Driver instruction

How to Pass Your Driving Test with the British School of Motoring

Drugs

Cocaine—One Man's Poison

Ear

Give Me A Signal

Earthquakes

Earthquake Below

Ecology and environment

Botanic Man Volume 1
Botanic Man Volume 2
Botanic Man Volume 3
Secret Reeds, The
Vital River, The

Education

BBC Micro Computer in Primary Education
BP Challenge to Youth
Children's Story, The
Play School

Electronic data processing

Acorn Electron, The
BBC Micro Computer in Primary Education
Commodore 64 Introduction to Programming—Level I
Commodore 64 Introduction to Programming—Level 2
Everything You Always Wanted to Know About Computers But Were Afraid to Ask
Further Basic With BBC Micro Computer No. 2
Getting Down to Basic
Graphics and Games for the BBC Micro Computer
Graphics and Games for the Electron Micro Computer
How to Use Your Computer, Starting to Program the Electron—No 1
How to Use Your Computer, Starting Basic with the BBC Micro Computer, No 1
How to Use Your Computer, Further Basic with the BBC Micro Computer, No 2
Master the Computer
Sinclair ZX Spectrum Introduction to Programming—Level I
Sinclair ZX Spectrum Introduction to Programming—Level 2
Starting Basic with BBC Micro Computer No. 1

Emergencies

Home First Aid

SUBJECT CATEGORY INDEX — Europe

Europe

Lawrence Durrell's Greece—'Spirit of the Place'
Our Animals

Exploitation

Assassin of Youth
Marihuana—The Devil's Weed
Multiple Maniacs/Cocaine Fiends
Sex Madness/Mondo Trasho

Fairy tales

Adult Fairytales
Adventures of Peter Cottontail, The
Aladdin
Aladdin's Lamp
Amazing Mr. Blunden, The
Belle et la Bete, La
Daily Fable
Fables of the Green Forest
Fairy Tales
Family View Vol. 1
Golden Treasury of Classic Fairy Tales, The
Goldilocks and the Three Bears
Goodies and the Beanstalk, The
Hansel and Gretel
Hansel and Gretel
Jack and the Beanstalk
Jack and the Beanstalk
Johnny and the Wicked Giant
Last Unicorn, The
Little Mermaid, The
Once Upon a Brothers Grimm
Peter Ustinov Tells Stories from Hans Christian Andersen
Pied Piper/Cinderella
Pinocchio
Pinocchio's Storybook Adventures
Poor Glassblower, The
Princes and Princesses
Princess and the Magic Frog, The
Princess and the Pea, The
Red Shoes, The
Sleeping Beauty
Slipper and the Rose, The
Snow White and the Seven Dwarfs
Sorcerer's Apprentice, The
Tales of Beatrix Potter
Tales of Magic
Tree Top Tales
World Famous Fairy Tales

Family

Marriage

Fantasy

Adventures of Choppy and the Princess, The
Aladdin
Altered States
Amazing Adventures of Baron Munchausen, The
Amazing Adventures of Morph: Volume 1, The
Amazing Adventures of Morph: Volume 2, The
Amazing Adventures of Morph: Volume 3, The
Amazing Adventures of Morph: Volume 4, The
Amazing Mr. Blunden, The
Angel on My Shoulder
Arabian Adventure
At the Earth's Core
Ator, the Fighting Eagle
Baldmoney, Sneezewort, Dodder and Cloudberry
Barbapapa
Barbapapa Volume II
Barbarella
Beastmaster, The
Beauty and the Beast
Bedknobs and Broomsticks
Beebtots
Bisexual
Brigadoon
Butterfly Ball, The
Calimero
Cartoon Wonderland
Chain Reaction, The
Challenge, The
Charlotte's Web
Chitty Chitty Bang Bang
Christmas Mountain
City Under the Sea
Clash Of The Titans
Dancing Princesses, The
Darby O'Fill and the Little People
Dark Crystal, The
Day the Eiffel Tower Ran Away, The
Desperate Living
Devil and Max Devlin, The
Dot and the Kangaroo
Dragonslayer
Dune
Electric Light Voyage
Empire Strikes Back, The
Eroticise
Escape to Witch Mountain
Excalibur
Fabulous Adventures of Baron Munchausen, The
Final Programme, The
Flash Gordon
Flower Stories
Fluteman, The
Freedom Force, The
Funny Forest
Gnome Mobile, The
Gulliver's Travels
Gulliver's Travels
Gwendoline
Hawk the Slayer
Heaven Can Wait
Here Comes the Grump

Fantasy · **SUBJECT CATEGORY INDEX**

Honey
Hundra
Jack and the Beanstalk
Joe and the Sleeping Beauty
Joe at the Kingdom of Ants
Joe at the Kingdom of the Bees
Jonathan Livingston Seagull
King Kong
Knocking at Heaven's Door
Land That Time Forgot, The
Lord of the Rings
Love Bug, The
Magic Ball, The
Magic Sword, The
Magical Mystery Trip Through Little Red's Head
Man Who Saw Tomorrow, The
March of the Wooden Soldiers
Mattie the Gooseboy
Merlin and the Sword
Mister Men Volume 1
Mister Men Volume 2
Mister Men Volume 3
Mister Men Volume 4
Mr Rossi Looks for Happiness
Mr. Sycamore
Monsters Christmas, The
Mouse and His Child, The
Nearly No Christmas
Next One, The
Nobody's Boy
Noddy Goes to Toyland
Now Voyager
Nutcracker Fantasy
Orphee
Paddington Goes to the Movies
Paddington's First 'Anywhen' T.V. Show
Paddington's Second 'Anywhen' T.V. Show
Paddington's Third 'Anywhen' T.V. Show
Paddington's Fourth 'Anywhen' T.V. Show
Paddington's Fifth 'Anywhen' T.V. Show
Paddington's Sixth 'Anywhen' T.V. Show
Paddington's Seventh 'Anywhen' T.V. Show
Paddington's Eighth 'Anywhen' T.V. Show
Paddington's Ninth 'Anywhen' T.V. Show
Peter-No-Tail
Pete's Dragon
Pied Piper, The
Pinocchio
Play-Box 1
Play-Box 2
Return from Witch Mountain
Rip Van Winkle
Roland Rat Roadshow, The
Santa and the Three Bears
Santa Claus Conquers the Martians
Secret Garden, The
Sharaz
Smurfs and the Magic Flute
Snowman, The
Something Wicked This Way Comes
Spider-Man and The Dragon's Challenge
Splash
Stories from a Flying Trunk
Superman—The Movie
Supermen
Swan Lake
Sword and the Sorcerer, The
Sword of the Barbarians
Swordkill
Tale of the Frog Prince, The
Tempest, The
Thief of Bagdad
Thief of Bagdad, The
Time Bandits
Time Machine, The
Tommy
Tor—Mighty Warrior
Twilight Zone, The
Two of a Kind
Up the Sandbox
War of the Wizards
Warrior of the Lost World
Watership Down
Well Done, Noddy
Winnie the Pooh and the Honey Tree
Wiz, The
Wizard of Oz, The
Wizards
Wombles Very Own TV Show, The
Wombling Free
Xanadu

Film making

Making of Star Wars, The
Making of Superman—The Movie, The

Film-Avant-garde

Blood of a Poet
Eraserhead
Testament d'Orphee

Film-History

Amazing Years of Early Cinema 1, The
Amazing Years of Early Cinema 2, The
Birth of a Nation, The
Charlie Chaplin III
Charlie Chaplin IV
To See Such Fun
Unknown Chaplin

First aid

Home First Aid

Fishing

Angler's Choice
Angler's Corner—Bream, Tench, Roach, Chubb
Angler's Corner—Salmon, Grayling, Trout
Carp Fishing with Duncan Kaye

SUBJECT CATEGORY INDEX — Fishing

Deep Sea Fishing
Distance Casting
Education on Pike Fishing, An
Education on Pole Fishing, An
Education on Stick Float Fishing, An
Giant Blacks and Great Whites, Part 4
Giant Blacks and Great Whites, Part 1
Giant Blacks and Great Whites, Part 2
Giant Blacks and Great Whites, Part 3
Go Fishing With Jack Charlton—Part 1: River Coarse Fishing
Go Fishing with Jack Charlton—Part 2: Still Water Coarse Fishing
Go Fishing With Jack Charlton—Part 4: Reservoir Trout Fishing
Go Fishing With Jack Charlton—Part 3: Sea Wreck Fishing
Go Fishing with Jack Charlton—Part 5: River Trout Fishing
Go Fishing with Jack Charlton-Part 6: Salmon Fishing
Lucky Jim Fishing Adventures
Porgy and Blue/High Island Pollack
Salmo the Leaper
Stillwater Trout Fishing from a Boat

Flowers

Emma And Grandpa
Flower Arranging
Flower Arranging: Part 1: The Basics
Flower Arranging: Part 2: A Step Further
Flower Arranging with Jean Taylor
House Plants with Percy Thrower
Houseplants and Patio Gardening
In Your Greenhouse with Percy Thrower
Mr. Smith's Flower Garden
Roses
Winter Gardens

Football

Best in Europe 1981, The
Best in Europe 1980, The
Best in Football—Cassette 1, The
Best in Football—Cassette 2, The
Best in Football—Cassette 3, The
Best in Football—Cassette 4, The
Cup Final
Europa '80
Football
Heading for Glory
Manchester United Story, The
Pele
Pele
Pele: The Master and His Method
Power of Football—World Cup 1978, The
Race for the Championship, The
Soccer is Fun
Soccer: Tactics and Skills
World Cup—Espana '82
World Cup—Mexico '70

Games

Bridge for Beginners
Chess Programme I
Chess Programme II
Chess Programme III
Chess Programme IV
Chess Programme V
Chess Programme VI
Chess Programme VII
Graphics and Games for the BBC Micro Computer
Graphics and Games for the Electron Micro Computer
How to Beat Home Video Games-Volume 1
How to Beat Home Video Games-Volume 2
How to Beat Home Video Games-Volume 3
How to Solve the Cube
Lesley Judd's Allsorts
Play School
Snooker Century Breakers
Snooker—Reardon Master Series, No 1
Snooker—Reardon Master Series, No 2
Snooker—Reardon Master Series, No 3
You Too Can Do the Cube

Gardening

Garden and Gardener
Gardening Calendar—April to June, The
Gardening Calendar—July to September, The
Gardening Calendar—January to March, The
Gardening Calendar—October to December, The
Gardening for Pleasure—Acid Soil and Alpines
Gardening for Pleasure—Herbacious Borders
Gardening for Pleasure—Propagation Part I and Hybrid Rhododendrons
Gardening with Wildlife
Grow Your Own Vegetables
Harkness on Roses
Houseplants and Patio Gardening
In Your Greenhouse with Percy Thrower
Mr. Smith's Flower Garden
Mr. Smith's Indoor Garden
Mr. Smith's Vegetable Garden
New Life in the Garden
Roses
Shrubs, Trees and Hedges with Percy Thrower

Geography

Amigo

Golf

British Open, 1971
British Open, 1972
British Open, 1973
British Open, 1974

British Open, 1975
British Open, 1976
British Open, 1977
British Open, 1978
British Open, 1979
British Open, 1980
British Open 1981
British Open 1982
British Open '83
Decade of British Open
Enjoy Better Golf: Basic Principles
Enjoy Better Golf 2: Tips from the Masters
Golf
Golf: Game of Power and Accuracy
Henry Cotton Celebrity Golf Lesson, The
History of Golf, I, The
History of Golf II, The
Jacklin and Palmer Play the Best 18 in Britain
Master Golf
Play Golf
Sweeten Your Swing
Tee to Green
US Golf on Video

Gun control

Safe Gun

Gymnastics

International Gymnastics

Handicapped

Give Me a Boat
Swimming for Disabled People

Handicraft

Blue Peter Makes...
Complete Potter, The
Flower Arranging with Jean Taylor

Health education

Incredible, Indelible, Magical, Physical, Mystery Trip, The

History

Alex and His Dog
Great Railways Volume I
History of Aviation, The

History-GB

Crooked Ditch, A

History-Modern

Adolph Hitler—Benito Mussolini
Glittering Crowns, The

Joseph Stalin—Leon Trotzkij
Men of Destiny I: World Political Figures
Men of Destiny II: Artists and Innovators
Milestones of the Century I: The Great Wars
Milestones of the Century II: 20th Century—Turning Points
This Year 1981
Winston Churchill—Charles De Gaulle
World in Flames, The: Part 1: From Hitler's Rise to Power to the Blitzkrieg
World in Flames, The: Part II: From the Battle of Britain to Stalingrad
World in Flames, The: Part III: The War on the Seas and the Fall of Japan

Hobbies

Blue Peter Makes...
Bridge for Beginners
Gardening for Pleasure—Acid Soil and Alpines
Gardening for Pleasure—Herbacious Borders
Gardening for Pleasure—Propagation Part I and Hybrid Rhododendrons
You Too Can Do the Cube

Home improvement

Making Your Own Home Cozy

Horror

Alchemist, The
Alien Terror
Alison's Birthday
Alone in the Dark
American Nightmare
American Werewolf in London, An
Amityville Horror, The
Amityville III
Amityville II-The Possession
And Now the Screaming Starts
Angry Joe Bass
Anthropohagous the Beast
Ants—Panic at Lakewood Manor
Astro Zombies
Asylum
Attack of the Killer Tomatoes
Attic, The
Awakening, The
Axe
Baron Blood
Basketcase
Bat, The
Bat People, The
Beast in the Cellar
Bees, The
Bells
Berlin Express/Isle of the Dead
Beyond, The
Big Meat Eater
Billy the Kid vs. Dracula

SUBJECT CATEGORY INDEX — Horror

Bird with the Crystal Plumage, The
Birds, The
Black Cat
Black Room, The
Black Sabbath
Black Sunday
Black Torment, The
Blackenstein
Blackout
Blob, The
Blood
Blood Bath
Blood Beach
Blood Beast Terror, The
Blood from the Mummy's Tomb
Blood on Satan's Claw
Blood Orgy of the She-Devils
Blood Relations
Blood Relatives
Blood Song
Blood Spattered Bride, The
Blood Tide
Bloodbath at the House of Death
Bloodbeat
Bloodlust
Bloodstained Shadow
Bloodsuckers
Bloody Birthday
Blow Out
Blue Eyes of the Broken Doll, The
Bluebeard
Brainwash
Brood, The
Bug
Burning, The
Cabinet of Dr. Caligari, The
Candle for the Devil, A
Cannibal
Cannibal Ferox
Cannibal Man, The
Cannibals
Captain Kronos Vampire Hunter
Carpathian Eagle/Guardian of the Abyss
Carrie
Castle of Evil
Cat in the Cage
Cataclysm
Cathy's Curse
Cauldron of Blood
Cemetery of the Living Dead
Centrefold Girls
Changeling, The
Charlie Boy/The Thirteenth Reunion
Child, The
Children of the Corn
Children of the Full Moon/Visitor from the Grave
Children Shouldn't Play with Dead Things
Christine
Christmas Evil
Circus of Horrors
City of the Dead

Claws
Clones, The
Comeback, The
Coming Soon
Communion
Corpse Grinders, The
Corridors of Blood
Count Dracula's Great Love
Countess Dracula
Crackup/I Walked with a Zombie
Crash
Craze
Crazed
Crazies
Creature from Black Lake
Creeping Flesh, The
Creepshow
Crocodile
Crucible of Terror
Cry of the Banshee
Crypt of Horror
Crypt of the Living Dead
Curse of the Crimson Altar
Curse of the Devil
Curtains
Cyclone
Damien Omen II
Dark, The
Dark Night of the Scarecrow
Dawn of the Mummy
Dead and Buried
Dead Kids
Dead of Night
Dead Zone, The
Deadly Blessing
Death Weekend
Deathdream
Deathhead Virgin, The
Demented
Demon
Demon, The
Demon Seed
Demonoid
Devil Doll/The Curse of Simba
Devil Hunter, The
Devil Times Five
Devil Within Her, The
Devil's Men
Devil's Nightmare
Devils of Darkness
Devil's Rain, The
Devil's Widow, The
Die Screaming Marianne
Die Sister, Die
Dinosaurus
Dr. Jekyll and Mr. Hyde
Dr. Jekyll and Mr. Hyde
Doctor Jekyll and Sister Hyde
Dogs, The
Don't Answer the Phone
Don't Be Afraid of the Dark

Horror — SUBJECT CATEGORY INDEX

Don't Go in the Woods.....Alone
Don't Look in the Basement
Don't Open the Door
Double Possession—The Doctor Cannot Die
Dracula
Dracula
Dracula
Dracula Saga, The
Dracula's Last Rites
Dracula's Virgin Lovers
Dunwich Horror, The
Dying Sea, The
Eaten Alive
Endangered Species
Enter the Devil
Entity, The
Equinox
Evil, The
Evil Dead, The
Exorcism
Fade to Black
Fall of the House of Usher, The
Fear No Evil
Fiend
Fiend, The
Final Exam
Final Hour, The
Final Terror, The
Five Bloody Graves
Flesh and Blood Show, The
Fog, The
Forbidden World
4D Man
Frankenstein
Frankenstein's Castle of Freaks
Frankenstein's Island
Friday the 13th Part 2
Fright
Frightmare
Frogs
Funhouse, The
Fury, The
Ghostkeeper
Ghoul, The
Giant Ant Invasion, The
Giant Salamander, The
Giant Spider Invasion, The
Godsend, The
Graduation Day
Grave of the Vampire
Grip of the Strangler/Fiend Without a Face/Goodness a Ghost
Halloween
Halloween II
Halloween III
Hands of the Ripper
Haunted
Haunted House of Horror, The
Haunted Palace, The
Hearse, The
Hell Night
Hills Have Eyes, The
Hills Have Eyes, Part 2, The
Home Sweet Home
Honeymoon Horror
Horror Hospital
Horror of Frankenstein
House by the Cemetery
House of Evil
House of Exorcism
House of the Long Shadows
House of Shadows
House of the Living Dead
House of the Seven Corpses, The
House of Wax
House of Whipcord
House That Bled to Death, The/Growing Pains
House That Dripped Blood, The
House That Wouldn't Die, The
Howling, The
Hunger, The
I Drink Your Blood
I, Monster
In Search of Dracula
Incubus
Island of Death
Island of Death
Island of Terror
Jesse James Meets Frankenstein's Daughter
Keep, The
Kill
Killer's Curse
Killer's Moon
King Kong
King of Kong Island
Kingdom of the Spiders
Kiss Daddy Goodbye
Kiss of the Tarantula
Knife for the Ladies
Last Horror Film, The
Last Victim, The
Legacy of Horror
Legacy of Satan
Legend of Blood Castle, The
Legend of the Werewolf
Lemora
Lift, The
Link, The
Loch Ness Horror, The
Long Weekend
Love Butcher, The
Love Me Deadly
Lunatic
Lust for a Vampire
Mad Foxes, The
Mafu Cage, The
Malpertius
Manitou, The
Mark of the Devil
Massacre at Central High
Mausoleum
Mephisto Waltz, The

SUBJECT CATEGORY INDEX — Horror

Messiah of Evil
Microwave Massacre
Midnight
Mirrors
Mongrel
Monster, The
Monster Club, The
Monstroid
Moonchild
Murders in the Rue Morgue
Mutant
My Bloody Valentine
My Nights With....Susan, Olga, Julie, Albert, Piet and Sandra
Naked Exorcism
Natas
New Barbarians, The
Night Creature
Night God Screamed, The
Night of the Bloody Apes
Night of the Demon
Night of the Living Dead
Nightmare City
No One Would Believe Her
Nosferatu: A Symphony of Horror
Nothing But the Night
Omen, The
Onibaba
Orphan, The
Parasite
Persecution
Phantasm
Phantom of the Opera, The
Phantom of the Opera
Pigs
Piranha
Pit and the Pendulum, The
Plan 9 from Outer Space
Poor White Trash
Possession
Pranks
Premature Burial, The
Prey
Prisoner of the Cannibal God
Projected Man, The/Guns Don't Argue
Prom Night
Prophecy
Psychomania
Psychopath
Rabid
Rats, The
Ravagers, The
Reflection of Fear, A
Repulsion
Return of the Evil Dead
Rituals
Road Games
Rosemary's Baby
Rosemary's Killer
Rottweiler—The Dogs of Hell
Ruby

Satan's Cheerleaders
Satan's Slave
Satan's Slave
Saturday the 14th
Savage Weekend
Scanners
Scared to Death
Scars of Dracula
Schizo
Schizoid
Schlock
Scream . . . . and Die
Scream Bloody Murder
Screamtime
Season of the Witch
Seizure
Sender, The
Sentinel, The
Seven x Dead
Shining, The
Shock
Shock Treatment
Shriek of the Mutilated
Siege
Silent Night Bloody Night
Simon, King of Witches
Sisters
Sisters of Death
Slithis
Sole Survivor
Son of Kong/You'll Find Out
Sorcerers, The
Spare Parts
Spectre of Edgar Allan Poe, The
Squirm
Squirm
Stepford Wives, The
Strangler of Vienna
Street Killers
Student Bodies
Study in Terror, A
Superstition
Survivor, The
Suspiria
Switchblade Sisters, The
Tales From The Crypt/Vault Of Horror
Tales of Terror
Tales that Witness Madness
Tempter, The
Tenebrae
Terror
Terror at Red Wolf Inn
Terror Express
Terror Eyes
Terror of Dr. Hitchcock, The
Terror on Tour
Terror Out of the Sky
Texas Chainsaw Massacre, The
Thing, The
Thirst
Thirsty Dead, The

Till Death
To All a Goodnight
To Kill a Stranger
To the Devil...a Daughter
Todd Killings, The
Tombs of the Blind Dead
Toolbox Murders, The
Torso
Torso
Touch of Satan, The
Tourist Trap
Tower of Evil
Track of the Moonbeast
Twilight Zone, The
Twins of Evil
Twisted Nerve
Two Faces of Evil, The/Rude Awakening
Uncanny, The
Unseen, The
Vampire Bat
Vampire Circus
Vampire Hookers
Vampyres
Velvet House, The
Vengeance of the Zombies
Venom
Victims
Virgin Witch
Warlock Moon
Werewolf and the Yeti, The
Werewolf Woman
Werewolf's Shadow
Werewolves on Wheels
What Ever Happened to Aunt Alice?
When a Stranger Calls
Whispering Death
Who Slew Auntie Roo?
Whodunit?
Wicker Man, The
Witching Time/The Silent Scream
Witchmaker, The
Wolf Lake
X-Ray
XTRO
Zoltan.....Hound of Dracula
Zombie, Creeping Flesh
Zombies Dawn of the Dead

Horse racing

Horse Called Nijinsky, A
Mill Reef
Riding to Win
Year of Sir Ivor, The

Industrial arts

Hand Made Bricks

Infants

Baby Care
Bringing Up Baby—The First Year
Water Babies
Wild Babies

Intelligence service

KGB Connections, The

Interior decoration

Dulux Videoguide to Colouring Your Home, The

Landscaping

Genius of the Place, The

Language arts

Animal Alphabet Parade
Rainbow

Languages-Instruction

Ensemble
Hello World—Chinese (Mandarin)
Hello World—English
Hello World—French
Hello World—German
Hello World—Hindi
Hello World—Italian
Hello World—Russian
Hello World—Spanish
Linguaphone-French

Law

Wild Birds and the Law—Can We Help You?

Learning disabilities

Able to Fish
Give Us The Chance
It's Not Impossible
Not Just a Spectator
Riding Towards Freedom
Right to Choose, The
Vaulting Horse, The
Water Free

Magic

Incredible Magic of Magic Volumes I and II, The
Paul Daniels—'Now You See It'
Tales of Magic
That's Magic

Martial arts

Angry Dragon, The

SUBJECT CATEGORY INDEX — Martial arts

Assassin
Assignment, The
Bamboo Brotherhood, The
Bandits from Shantung
Battle Creek Brawl
Beach of the War Gods
Big Boss, The
Big Risk, The
Black Belt Jones
Black Dragon, The
Brothers, The
Bruce Against Iron Hand
Bruce Lee Against Supermen
Bruce Lee-Chinese Gods
Bruce Lee Story, The
Bruce Lee: The Man—The Myth
Bruce's Fingers
Call Him Mr Shatter
Challenge of Young Bruce Lee
Chinese Hercules
Chinese Mechanic
Cleopatra Jones
Clones of Bruce Lee, The
Clutch of Power, The
Crystal Fist
Death Force
Death Promise
Dolemite
Dragon Dies Hard, The
Dragon Lives, The
Dragon Lives Again, The
Dragon Lord
Dragon's Executioner, The
Dragon's Teeth
Dynamite Brothers, The
Dynamo
Eagle's Killer, The
Enter the Dragon
Enter the Streetfighter
Exit the Dragon, Enter the Tiger
Eye for an Eye, An
Fighting Fist, The
Fighting Fists Of Shangai Joe, The
Fist of Fear, Touch of Death
Fist of Fury
Fist of Fury II
Fist of Fury 3
Fists of the Double K
Fists of Vengeance, The
Five Kung-Fu Dare Devil Heroes
Force of One, A
Forced Vengeance
Fury of the Dragon
Game of Death
General Stone
Goodbye, Bruce Lee
Goose Boxer
Hands Off!
Image of Bruce Lee
Invincible Super Chan
Jaguar Lives
Jaws of the Dragon
Judo Part 1-Basic
Karate Part 1
Karate Part 2
Kill and Kill Again
Kill the Golden Goose
Kung Fu Gang Busters
Kung Fu Girl
Kung-Fu Warriors, The
Lady Whirlwind
Lama Avenger, The
Little Godfather from Hong Kong
Lungwei Village
Man from Hong Kong, The
Mandarin Magician, The
Martial Arts
Master With Cracked Fingers
Match of Dragon and Tiger
Mysterious Heroes
Naked Fist
Needles of Death
Octagon, The
One Armed Boxer
One Down, Two To Go
Real Bruce Lee, The
Return of the Dragon
Return of the Tiger
Revenge of the Ninja
Rivals of the Dragon
Self Defence
Self Defence for Women
Shadow of the Tiger
Shaolin Iron Finger
Shaolin Master and the Kid
Six Directions Boxing, The
Slaughter in San Francisco
Snake in the Monkey's Shadow
Spirits of Bruce Lee
Stranger from Shaolin
Sun Dragon
Super Dragon
Superpower
Ten Brothers of Shao Lin
Ten Fingers of Steel
That Man Bolt
Tiger Strikes Again, The
Time Slip
Two in Black Belt
Velvet Smooth
Victim, The
Way of the Black Dragon
Way of the Dragon, The
Wicked Die Slow, The
Young Avenger, The
Young Master, The

Massage

Body Massage

Metalwork

Hand Rolling of Steel

Microbiology

Life?

Motorcycles

Agostini
American Challenge
Austrian Enduro
Catching Up
Island, The
Moto-Cross Professionals
Narrow Edge
Off Road Action
On Any Sunday
Race to the Top
Silver Dream Racer
Superbike 6
T. T. Tribute
Untamed Wheels—Agostini

Mountaineering

Conquest of Everest, The

Music

Beat, The
Beat Street
Billy Idol: Dancing with Myself
Buddy Holly Story, The
Cool Cats
David Grant
Elephant Parts
Hard to Hold
Learning the Guitar
Lennon-A Legend
Music-Image Odyssey
Sleeping Beauty, The
Songs of Praise
Tough Enough

Music video

American Heartbeat
Camel—Pressure Points
Far East & Far Out, Council Meeting in Japan
Heaven 17's—Industrial Revolution
Hits Video, The
Making Michael Jackson's Thriller
Making of 2 a.m. Paradise Cafe, The
Meatloaf—Hits Out of Hell
Motorhead, Deaf not Blind
Nik Kershaw—Single Pictures
Paul Young—The Video Singles
Rock Cocktail
Ronnie Lane Appeal for ARMS, The Royal Albert Hall Concert, Tape Two
Ronnie Lane Appeal for ARMS, The Royal Albert-Hall Concert, Tape One
Singalongamax; The Video
Streets of Fire, The Music Video
Test Dept.—Program for Progress
Ultravox 'The Collection'
Video Rewind—The Rolling Stones, Great Video Hits

Music-Performance

Abba Music Show 1
Abba Music Show 2
Abba—The Movie
ABC's Mantrap
Alan Price
'Alchemy'—Dire Straits Live
Alexis Korner-Eat a Little Rhythm and Blues
Alice Cooper
Amanda Lear—Live in Concert
America—Live in Central Park
American Heartbeat
Angelo Branduardi—Concerto
Ann-Margret from Hollywood with Love
April Wine—Live in London
Ashford and Simpson Video, The
Asia in Asia
Average White Band
Bananarama
Band Reunion Concert, The
Barclay James Harvest
Barry Manilow in Concert at the Greek Theater
Barry White
Beat in Concert
Belle Stars—Live Signs, Live Times, The
Benatar
Bert Kaempfert and His Orchestra
Best of Blondie, The
Best of Reggae Sunsplash-Part One
Best of Reggae Sunsplash-Part Two
Big Bands of the 30's and 40's—Volume 2, The
Big Bands of the '30s and '40s, The
Billy Squier—in the Dark
Black Sabbath
Black Sabbath/Blue Oyster Cult
Black Uhuru—Tear It Up
Blackjack
Blancmange—Hello, Good Evening
Blancmange-The Videosingles
Blondie—'Eat to the Beat'
Blondie Live!
Blood Sweat and Tears
Bob Marley and The Wailers
Bob Marley and the Wailers—Live
Bobby Darin
Body Music
Bolling: Concerto for Classic Guitar and Jazz Piano
Boomtown Rats Live!
Brahms Double Concerto for Violin and Cello
Brothers and Sisters

SUBJECT CATEGORY INDEX — Music-Performance

Castles and Concerts: The Polish Chamber Orchestra
CherylLadd-Fascinated
Chris Barber Band, The
Chris de Burgh—The Video
Christine McVie Concert, The
Christmas Carols from Cambridge
Christmas Music from York Minster/Handel's Messiah
Cliff Richard and The Shadows 'Thank You Very Much'
Cliff Richard-The Video Connection
Compleat Beatles, The
Concert for Bangla Desh, The
Count Basie
Culture Club, A Kiss Across the Ocean
Dance and Music of India—Sanskritik Festival of Arts of India
Dave Brubeck-A Musical Portrait
David Bowie Live
David Soul in Concert
Daylight Again: Crosby, Stills & Nash
Deep Purple—Concerto for Group and Orchestra
Deep Purple—California Jam April 6th 1974
Devo—'The Men Who Make the Music'
Dick Clark Show Music Programme 1
Dick Clark Show Music Programme 2
Dick Clark Show Music Programme 3
Dick Clark Show Music Programme 4
Dick Clark Show Music Programme 5
Dick Clark Show Music Programme 6
Dick Clark Show Music Programme 7
Dick Clark Show Music Programme 8
Dick Clark Show Music Programme 9
Dick Clark Show Music Programme 10
Dick Clark Show Music Programme 12
Dick Clark Show Music Programme 13
Dick Clark Show Music Programme 14
Dick Clark Show Music Programme 15
Dick Clark Show Music Programme 16
Dick Clark Show Music Programme 17
Dick Clark Show Music Programme 19
Dick Clark Show Music Programme 20
Dio Live in Concert
Dirt Band-Tonite, The
Divine Madness
Dolly in London
Duran Duran
Eddy Grant
Electric Light Orchestra
ELO—Live in Concert
Elton John
Elton John - The Fox
Elton John-The Videosingles
Elvis
Elvis in Hawaii
Elvis on Tour
Elvis—That's the Way It Is
Emerson Lake and Palmer
Eric Clapton, On Whistle Test

Essential Mike Oldfield, The
Evening with Charles Aznavour, An
Evening With Liza Minnelli, An
Everly Brothers—Album Flash, The
Everly Brothers Reunion Concert, The
Fifth Dimension with Dionne Warwick and The Carpenters, The
Fillmore Rock Festival
Fleetwood Mac
Fleetwood Mac in Concert
Four Seasons (Antonio Vivaldi), The
Fundamental Frolics
Garland
Gary Glitter—Live at the Rainbow
Gary Numan—The Touring Principle '79
Genesis-Three Sides Live
Girl Groups
Glen Campbell Live
Grace Jones: A One Man Show
'Graham Parker Live'
Great Golden Hits of the Monkees, The
Great Night with.....Chas and Dave, A
Handel's Messiah and Christmas Music
Herbie Hancock and the Rockit Band
History of Rock-Volume 4, The
Hoffnung
Hot Gossip
'Hot Summer Night'—Donna Summer, A
Human League-Video Single, The
Ian Hunter—'Ian Hunter Rocks'
Imagination in Concert
Iron Maiden
Iron Maiden, The Beast Over Hammersmith
Israel Philharmonic Orchestra 40th Anniversary Concert
Itzhak Perlman Beethoven Violin Concerto
Jack Mack and the Heart Attack in Concert
Jacksons in Concert, The
Jam, 'Trans-Global Unity Express,' The
Jam-Video Snap, The
James Brown Story—Soul Connection, The
James Galway and Kyung Wah Chung Play Bach
Japan—Instant Pictures
Jazz Festival
Jerry Lee Lewis
Jerry Lee Lewis Live
Jerry Lee Lewis—The Killer Performance
Jethro Tull—Slipstream
Joan Armatrading-'Track Record'
Joan Sutherland—'A Life on the Move'
Joan Sutherland in Concert
John Martyn — In Vision 1973-1981
John Miles
Johnny Winter Live
Judie Tzuke in Concert
Kaja GooGoo-White Feathers Tour
Kansas Live
Kate Bush Live at the Hammersmith Odeon
Kate Bush-The Single File
Kenny Ball and his Jazzmen

Music-Performance **SUBJECT CATEGORY INDEX**

Kevin Rowland and Dexy's Midnight Runners—The Bridge
Kid Creole and The Coconuts
Kid Creole and the Coconuts—The Lifeboat Party
Kids Are Alright, The
Kids from Fame, The
Kim Carnes Voyeur
Leroy Gomez
Linda Ronstadt with Nelson Riddle and his Orchestra in Concert—What's New
Little River Band — Live Exposure
Little Steven and the Disciples of Soul
London Bridge Special, The
London Rock 'n' Roll Show, The
Lords of the New Church Live from London, The
Lou Rawls
Love Machine from the U.S.A.
Love You Till Tuesday
Marillion-Recital of the Script
Marvin Gaye
Mary Wilson and the Supremes
Maze
Meatloaf
Meeting of the Spirits
Men at Work, Live at San Francisco or Was It Berkeley!
Micro Music—Gary Numan
Mina Live
Mink De Ville Live at the Savoy
Motorhead
Mozart
Mozart in Salzburg
Nancy Wilson
Nazareth—Live
Neil Diamond—Love at the Greek
Neville Marriner Conducts The Academy of St. Martin in the Fields at Longleat
New Edition-The Videosingles
Newman Numan
Night with Lou Reed, A
Nina von Pallandt
1981 Military Musical Pageant, The
Now Voyager
Olivia Newton-John: Live
Olivia Newton-John—Physical
Orchestral Manoeuvres in the Dark Live
Osibisa—Live at the Rainbow
Osmond Brothers Special/Tom Jones at Knott's
Osmonds, The
Other Side of Nashville, The
Outlaws Live in Concert, The
Paco de Lucia
Paul McCartney and Wings Rockshow
Paul Simon in Concert
Pavarotti
Pearls—The Video
Picture Music
Pink Floyd at Pompeii
Police Around the World
Queen: Greatest Flix
Queen—We Will Rock You
Rainbow—Live Between the Eyes
Randy Crawford
Randy Edelman
Raquel
Ready Steady Go!-Volume One
Reggae Sunsplash
Rewind: Volume 3
'Riding That Train'
Rock and Roll Revival
Rock Cocktail
Rock Gala
Rock Guitar—A Guide from the Greats
Rock 'n' Soul Live
Rock Revolution, The
Rod Stewart: Tonight He's Yours
Roger Daltrey—Ride A Rock Horse
Rolling Stones; Let's Spend the Night Together, The
Ronnie Lane Appeal for ARMS, The Royal Albert Hall Concert, Tape Two
Ronnie Lane Appeal for ARMS, The Royal Albert-Hall Concert, Tape One
Rostropovich
Roxy Music—The High Road
Royal Philharmonic Orchestra Plays Queen, The
Rush-Exit Stage Left
Rust Never Sleeps
Sad Cafe
Santana and Taj Mahal Live
Secret Policeman's Ball, The
Secret Policeman's Other Ball, The
Sheena Easton Live at the Palace
Side Kicks The Movie
Sinatra
Siouxsie and the Banshees-Nocturne (Live)
Siouxsie and the Banshees-Once Upon a Time
Sky at Westminster Abbey
Soft Cell
Sonny and Cher
Sounds of the Seventies
Spandau Ballet: Live Over Britain
Split Enz
Stamping Ground
Starfire
Stars on 45
Status Quo-Live in Concert at the N.E.C. Birmingham
Status Quo—Off the Road
Steve Miller Band Live
Stevie Nicks Live in Concert
Stones in the Park, The
Stranglers Video Collection 1977-82, The
Streisand
Style Council-The Videosingles, The
Styx—Caught in the Act—Live
Superstars
Susan George—Naturally
Swan's Way—History and Image
Sweet Dreams-The Video Album
Teardrop Explodes in Concert

SUBJECT CATEGORY INDEX — Music-Performance

Tears for Fears—In My Mind's Eye
Tears for Fears-The Videosingles
Teddy Pendergrass Live in London
10 cc Live at the International Music Show
10cc Live in Concert
Thin Lizzy
Thompson Twins—Into the Gap Live
Till Tomorrow
Times Square
Tina Turner
Tina Turner Nice 'N Rough
To Russia...with Elton
Tom Robinson 2-4-6-8
Toni Basil—Word of Mouth
Top of the Pops
Toyah at the Rainbow
Toyah—Good Morning Universe
Toyah! Toyah! Toyah!
Tubes Video, The
Twisted Sister, Stay Hungry
UB 40 Live
UB 40—Labour of Love
Ultravox: Monument
Urgh! A Music War
U2 'Under A Blood Red Sky"
Van Morrison in Ireland
Venom—The Seventh Gate of Hell
Video Rewind—The Rolling Stones, Great Video Hits
Video Rock Attack
Videostars
Videotheque
Vivaldi's—The Four Seasons
Waldorf Travers
War in Concert
Who, The
Willie Nelson and Family in Concert
XTC-Look Look
Ziggy Stardust and the Spiders from Mars
10cc Live at the International Show

Musical

American in Paris, An
Anchors Aweigh
Bal du Moulin Rouge
Bandwagon, The
Barkleys of Broadway, The
Best Little Whorehouse in Texas, The
Blue Hawaii
Boyfriend, The
Brigadoon
Butterfly Ball, The
Cabaret
Camelot
Can-Can
Can't Stop the Music
Carefree/Easy Living
Charlotte's Web
Chitty Chitty Bang Bang
Damsel in Distress, A/Old Man Rhythm
Dancing Years, The
Doctor Doolittle
Dr. Jekyll and Mr. Hyde
Easter Parade
Espresso Bongo
Fame
Fast Times at Ridgemont High
Fiddler on the Roof
Flower Out of Place, A
French Line, The/Texas Tough Guy/Murder in a Flat
From the Earth to the Moon/Jack and the Beanstalk
Fun in Acapulco
Getting Over
G.I. Blues
Gigi
Girls, Girls, Girls
Goin' Coconuts
Good Times
Grease
Grease 2
Great Caruso, The
Great Muppet Caper, The
Guys and Dolls
Hair
Hallelujah I'm a Tramp
Happiest Millionaire, The
Hard Day's Night, A
Hello, Dolly!
High Society
Higher and Higher/Strictly Dynamite
Hollywood on Parade
Jack and the Beanstalk
Jailhouse Rock
Jubilee
Kimberly Jim
King and I, The
Kismet
Kiss Me Kate
Les Girls
Lilacs in the Spring
Little Night Music, A
Loving You
Mame
Man from Button Willow, The
Mary Poppins
Meet Me In St Louis
Meet Me in St. Louis
Metal Messiah
My Fair Lady
New Adventures of Heidi, The
Night on the Town, A
Nutcracker, The
Oklahoma!
Orpheus in the Underworld
Paradise, Hawaiian Style
Perils of Pauline, The
Pete's Dragon
Pied Piper, The
Pinocchio

Musical — **SUBJECT CATEGORY INDEX**

Pippin
Pirate, The
Pirate Movie, The
Pirates of Penzance, The
Rockers
Rocky Horror Picture Show, The
Rose Marie
Rutles, The: All You Need Is Cash
Second Chorus
Sgt. Pepper's Lonely Hearts Club Band
Sextette
Shall We Dance
Shinbone Alley
Showboat
Silk Stockings
Singin' in the Rain
Sky's the Limit, The/Step Lively
Slipper and the Rose, The
Slumber Party '57
Smurfs and the Magic Flute
Song and Dance
Song of Norway
Song of the South
Stage Struck/The Girl Most Likely
Superman—The Musical
Swingin' Summer
That's Entertainment
That's Entertainment: Part 2
There's No Business Like Show Business
Till the Clouds Roll By
Top Hat
Train Ride to Hollywood, A
Treasure Island
Wall, The
West Side Story
Where the Boys Are
Wiz, The
Wizard of Oz, The
Wombling Free
Wonderful Life
Xanadu
Yeoman of the Guard, The
Yes, Giorgio
Young Ones, The
Young Ones, The
Zachariah
Ziegfeld Follies

Musical-Drama

Apple, The
Beggar's Opera, The
Body Rock
Breaking Glass
Bugsy Malone
Bundle of Joy/Montana Belle
Disco Dynamite
Elvis—The Movie
Footloose
Great Rock 'n' Roll Swindle, The
Harder They Come, The
Idolmaker, The
Jazz Singer, The
Jesus Christ Superstar
King Creole
Music Machine, The
On the Town
Quadrophenia
Rock 'n' Roll High School
Rock, Rock, Rock!
Roller Boogie
Rose, The
Roustabout
Saturday Night Fever
Seven Brides for Seven Brothers
Something to Sing About
Sound of Music, The
South Pacific
Star Is Born, A
Star Is Born, A
Stardust
Staying Alive
Summer Holiday
Swing High-Swing Low
That'll Be the Day
Tommy
Young at Heart

Mystery

Absurd
Agatha Christie Collection, Volume 1, The
Agency
All in a Night's Work
And Then There Were None
Assault
Audrey Rose
Barcelona Kill, The
Bermuda Triangle, The
Big Sleep, The
Bird with the Crystal Plumage, The
Blackmail
Blow-Up
Bounty Killers, The/Macao
Boxcar Bertha
Butcher, The
Cabo Blanco
Cat and the Canary, The
Catwalk Killer, The
Children of the Stones
Chinatown
Clifton House Mystery, The
Crazed
Dangerous Mission/Impact
Death Line
Death of a Hooker
Death on the Nile
Death Ship
Detective, The
Dominique
Double Exposure
Double Exposure

SUBJECT CATEGORY INDEX — Mystery

Evil Under the Sun
Family Plot
Fedora
Fiction Makers, The
Gorky Park
Great Ice Rip-Off, The
Halfbreed, The/Walk Softly, Stranger
Harlequin
Haunts
Hell on Frisco Bay/The Mad Miss Manton
Hound of the Baskervilles, The
House of Wax
Hue and Cry
Hurricane Express
Hysteria
Intrigue
Jane Doe
Journey into Fear
Killing of Angel Street, The
Lady Vanishes, The
London Conspiracy
Magician of Lublin, The
Magnificent Tony Carrera, The
Man Who Haunted Himself, The
Man Who Would Not Die, The
Mirror Crack'd, The
Mirrors
Mission: Monte Carlo
Murder at Midnight
Murder on the Orient Express
Murderers Row
New Years Evil
Night Moves
Night Stalker, The
Night They Robbed Big Bertha's, The
Night Train Murders
Old Man Who Cried Wolf, The
Picnic at Hanging Rock
Powers of Evil
Private Life of Sherlock Holmes, The
Purple Taxi, The
Puzzle
Red Light in the White House
Redeemer, The
Riddle of the Sands, The
Rings of Fear
Runner Stumbles, The
Salamander, The
Scarecrow, The
Schizoid
Seven Per Cent Solution, The
Seven x Dead
Shark's Cave
Sherlock Holmes Double Feature
Shock Waves
Sign of Four, The
Somebody Killed Her Husband
Stagecoach/Deadline at Dawn
Strangler of Vienna
Stromboli/While the City Sleeps
Study in Terror, A
Sunburn
Suspicion of Murder
Swap, The
Take, The
Tales of the Unexpected—Cassette 1
Tales of the Unexpected-Cassette 2
Third Man, The
Under Capricorn
Uranium Conspiracy, The
Venom
Voices
Walk a Crooked Path
Watcher in the Woods, The
Weekend Murders
Whatever Happened to Baby Jane?
When You Comin' Back, Red Ryder?
Will to Die
Word, The
X-Ray

National parks and reserves

Britain, Kingdom of the Seas
Genius of the Place, The

Nightclub

Mondo Erotico

Occult sciences

Amazing World of Psychic Phenomena, The
Beyond and Back
Liz Greene's Guide to Astrology

Occupations

Farriery the Master Craft

Oceanography

Amag Elbehar
Magic of the Sea, The
Ocean World

Opera

Aida
Aida
Boheme, La
Cenerentola, La
Contes d'Hoffmann, Les
Cox and Box
Don Pasquale
Ernani
Falstaff
Fanciulla del West, La
Gondoliers, The
HMS Pinafore
H.M.S. PINAFORE
Idomeno
Intermezzo

Iolanthe
Joan Sutherland in Concert
Lucia di Lammermoor
Madama Butterfly
Magic Flute, The
Manon Lescaut
Mary Stuart
Merry Wives of Windsor, The
Mikado, The
Mikado, The
Nabucco
Orpheus in the Underworld
Otello
Patience
Pavarotti
Peter Grimes
Pirates of Penzance, The
Princess Ida
Rigoletto
Ruddigore
Samson et Dalila
Sorcerer
Traviata, La
Traviata, La
Trial by Jury
Trittico, Il
Turandot
Yeoman of the Guard, The
Yeomen of the Guard

Outtakes and bloopers

Goofs from the Cutting Room Floor
It'll Be Alright on the Night 3

Painting

Landscape Painting
Paint!
Painting for Pleasure
Portrait Painting

Parades and festivals

Carnival '80
Feria de Abril
1981 Military Musical Pageant, The
Salute to the Edinburgh Tattoo
Summer Festival

Parapsychology

Mysteries from Beyond Earth
Unknown Powers

Pets

All You Need to Know About Dogs
Training Dogs the Woodhouse Way

Photography

Lichfield on Photography Part 1
Lichfield on Photography Part 2
Lichfield on Photography Part 3
So You Want to Be a Glamour Photographer
What a Picture!-Volume 1
What a Picture!-Volume 2
What a Picture!-Volume 3
What a Picture!-Volume 4

Physical fitness

Eroticise
Get Fit with the Green Goddess
Get Slim—Stay Slim
Home Body Care Part 1
If You Can Dance You Can Do It!
Jackie Genova-Work That Body
Keep in Shape System
Lotte Berk Exercise Class—Get Physical, The
Lyn Marshall's Everyday Yoga
Pumping Iron
Raquel—Total Beauty and Fitness
Shake Out with Mad Lizzie
Texersize
Videoslim to Lose Weight
Yoga for Health

Physical therapy

Going Well Over Sixty

Plants

House Plants with Percy Thrower

Pregnancy

Having A Baby

Presidency-US

John F Kennedy

Puppets

Amazing Adventures of Joe 90, The
Animates, The
Bubblies, Volumes I and II, The
Cosgrove Hall's Funtime
Countdown to Disaster
Incredible Voyage of Stingray, The
Kiri the Clown
Magic Roundabout, The
Mother's Hands
Nightingale, the
Nutcracker Fantasy
Nutcracker Fantasy
Pied Piper/Cinderella
Postman Pat
Postman Pat 2

SUBJECT CATEGORY INDEX — Puppets

Revenge of the Mysterons from Mars
Sooty Video Show, The
Sooty's Adventures
Terrahawks 6: Zero Strikes Back
Terrahawks 4: Hostages of Mars
Terrahawks 5: Flaming Thunderbolts
Thunderbirds in Outer Space
Thunderbirds to the Rescue
Toytown Series No. 1
Toytown Series No. 2
Toytown Series No. 3
Toytown Series No. 4
Toytown Series No. 5
Wind in the Willows

Religion

Divine Healing
Fi Hob Allah
Genesis Flood, The
God's Story
Jesus of Nazareth
Marriage
Mary and Joseph
Moses the Lawgiver
Mother's Hands
Phillip the Evangelist
Pilgrimage to the Holy Land
Pope in the Park, The
Pope John Paul II in Ireland
Psalm 23
Resurrection, The
Training for Ministry
You and Your Child

Romance

Affair, The
African Queen, The
Aloha, Bobby and Rose
Americana
Annie Hall
Another Time, Another Place
Arch of Triumph
Atlantic City
Baby Love
Baby Sister
Badlands
Beauty and the Beast
Best Friends
Best of Both Worlds
Best of Friends, The
Blame It On Rio
Blood and Sand
Blue Skies Again
Breakfast at Tiffany's
Breaking Up—Love and Life
Brief Encounter
Brief Encounter
Bus Stop
Change of Seasons, A

Charulata
Child of Love
Class
Class of '63
Comeback Kid, The
Continental Divide
Daughter of Emmanuelle
Days of Heaven
Different Story, A
DUTCH GIRLS
Educating Rita
Emily
Enchanted Island/Westward Passage
End of August, The
Endless Love
Escape to the Sun
Europeans, The
Falling in Love Again
Family Man, The
Far Pavilions, The
Farewell to Arms, A
Farewell to Arms, A
Fear Eats The Soul
First Love
For Love of Ivy
For Your Love Only
Ginger in the Morning
Girl Who Couldn't Say No, The
Go-Between, The
Great Gatsby, The
Greatest Attack, The
Griffin and Phoenix
Happily Ever After—Love and Life
Hard to Hold
Haunting Passion, The
Heaven Can Wait
Her First Affaire
Highway to Hell
Hollywood Knight
Householder, The
Ibtisama Wahibda Takfi (One Smile Is Enough)
In Love With an Older Woman
Incoming Freshmen
Indiscreet
Intermezzo
Intimate Relations
It's My Turn
Jenny
Lacemaker, The
Laura
Laura—Shadows of Summer
Let's Get Married
Letter from an Unknown Woman
Liar's Moon
Little Night Music, A
Little Sex, A
Lonely Guy, The
Lonely Hearts
Lonely Hearts
Loose Connections
Lost and Found

Romance **SUBJECT CATEGORY INDEX**

Love Among the Ruins
Love and Money
Love to Eternity
Lovesick
Man Who Had Power Over Women, The
Man Who Loved Cat Dancing, The
Man Who Loved Women, The
Maui
Maybe This Time
Melanie
Melody in Love
Mirror, Mirror—Love and Life
Montenegro
Month in the Country, A
Moon Is Blue, The
My Old Man
My Tutor
Neither the Sea Nor the Sand
New Black Emanuelle
Not Just Another Affair
Now and Forever
One Touch of Venus
Out of Season
Paradise
Private School
Quest for Love
Rachel's Man
Raging Moon, The
Reaching for the Moon
Return Engagement
Return of Martin Guerre, The
Rollover
Romance with a Double Bass
Romantic Englishwoman, The
Ronde, La
Sahara
Saigon—Year of the Cat
Sara Dane
Say Hello to Yesterday
Secrets
Seed of Innocence
Separate Tables
Seven Nights in Japan
Shakespeare Wallah
Sky West and Crooked
Sky West and Crooked
Something Short of Paradise
Son of the Sheik, The
Sophie's Choice
Splash
Star Is Born, A
Strangers Kiss
Summer Holiday
Summer Lovers
Summer Night Fever
Summer With Monika
Sunshine on the Skin
Swedish Confessions
Taboo Island
Tales of Ordinary Madness
"10"
That Touch of Mink
Top Hat
Torn Between Two Lovers
Touch, The
Touched
Trespasser, The
Triple Echo, The
Twice a Woman
Twinky
Two of a Kind
Unfaithfully Yours
Virgin and the Gypsy, The
Virgin Campus
Warm December, A
Way We Were, The
What Next?
Where the Boys Are
Why Not Stay for Breakfast?
Wilde's Domain
Winter Comes Early
World Is Full of Married Men, The
Wuthering Heights
Yanks
Yellow Emanuelle
Young Love, First Love
Your Ticket Is No Longer Valid

Royalty-GB

Britain's Royal Heritage
Charles and Diana
Edward and Mrs. Simpson Volume 1
Edward and Mrs. Simpson Volume 2
Edward and Mrs. Simpson Volume 3
King's Story, A
Portrait of a Great Lady
Prince Charles: A Royal Portrait
Queen in Arabia, The
Queen's Birthday Parade, The
Royal Jordan
Royal Wedding, The
Royal Wedding, The
Royal Wedding, The
Royal Wedding, The
Story of Prince Charles and Lady Diana, The
Treasures of the British Crown
25 Years Impressions

Running

Gillette London Marathon, The
Guinness Video Book, The Marathon Challenge, A

Safety education

Hit Back!
Safe Gun
Self Defence
Self Defence for Women
Think Ahead with Jackie Stewart

SUBJECT CATEGORY INDEX — Safety education

Water Safety

Satire

Animal Farm
Basketcase
Bonditis
Borsalino
Britannia Hospital
Comedy of Terrors, The
Duck Soup
Great Dictator, The
Hammersmith is Out
Hollywood Boulevard
I Wonder Who's Killing Her Now
It Came From Hollywood
Monty Python's Life of Brian
Monty Python's The Meaning of Life
Oh! What a Lovely War
Once Upon a Girl
Regle du Jeu, La
Silk Stockings
Whoops Apocalypse

Science

Mighty Micro, The

Science fiction

Alien
Alien Attack
Alien Encounters
Alien Factor, The
Alien Terror
Aliens from Spaceship Earth
Alpha Incident, The
Alphaville
Amazing Adventures of Joe 90, The
Android
Asphyx, The
At the Earth's Core
Atlantis Interceptors, The
Battle Beyond the Stars
Battle for the Planet of the Apes
Battle of the Planets—Curse of the Cuttlefish
Battle of the Planets—G-Force Vs The Giant Insects
Battle of the Planets—The Jupiter Moon Menace
Battle of the Planets—Zoltar, Evil Master of Disguises
Battle of the Stars
Battle of the Stars
Battlestar Galactica
Beneath the Planet of the Apes
Black Hole, The
Blade Runner
Body Stealers, The
Boy and His Dog, A
Buck Rogers in the 25th Century

Capricorn One
Captain Harlock
Cat From Outer Space, The
Chain Reaction, The
Chocky
Clones, The
Conquest
Conquest of the Planet of the Apes
Cosmic Princess
Countdown
Countdown to Disaster
Curious Female
Daleks—Invasion Earth 2150 A.D.
Dark Star
Day of the Triffids
Day the Earth Caught Fire, The
Day the Earth Stood Still, The
Day Time Ended, The
Deadly Harvest
Death Race 2000
Death Sport
Deathwatch
Demon
Demon Seed
Destination Inner Space/The Wizard of Mars
Destination Moonbase Alpha
Dr. Who and the Daleks
Doctor Who and the Revenge of the Cybermen
Dr. Who, the Brain of Moribus
Doomwatch
Dreamscape
Embryo
Empire Strikes Back, The
End of the World
Escape from Galaxy III
Escape from New York
Eyes Behind the Stars
Fantastic Voyage
Final Countdown, The
Final Programme, The
Flash Gordon
Flesh Gordon
Flight to Mars
Flight to Mars
Forbidden Planet
Forbidden World
From the Earth to the Moon/Jack and the Beanstalk
Futureworld
Galaxina
Gappa, The Triphibian Monster
Giant Spider Invasion, The
Glen and Randa
Godzilla vs. the Cosmic Monster
Gold Wing
Hangar 18
Heartbeeps
Henderson Monster, The
Hi-jackers, The/The Night Caller/Echo
Human Duplicators, The
Human Vapour, The

Science fiction — SUBJECT CATEGORY INDEX

Idaho Transfer
Incredible Hulk, The
Incredible Voyage of Stingray, The
Invaders from Mars
Invasion of the Body Snatchers
Invasion: UFO
Island of Dr Moreau, The
It Came from Outer Space
Journey to the Centre of Time
Jupiter Menace, The
Laserblast
Last War, The
Late Great Planet Earth, The
Little Orbit the Astrodog
Logan's Run
Love War, The
Lucifer Complex, The
Mad Max
Mad Max 2
Man Who Fell to Earth, The
Martian Chronicles—The Expeditions, The
Martian Chronicles—The Martians, The
Martian Chronicles—The Settlers, The
Master of the World
Megaforce
Memoirs of a Survivor
Metal Messiah
Metalstorm
Metropolis
Mission Galactica: The Cylon Attack
Mission Mars
Monsters from an Unknown Planet
Mysterious Two
New Barbarians, The
Night of the Big Heat
Octaman
Outland
Panic in the City
People, The
Philadelphia Experiment, The
Plan 9 from Outer Space
Planet of the Apes
Planet of the Dinosaurs
Puma Man, The
Quatermass
Ragewar
Ragnarok
Repo Man
Return, The
Revenge of the Mysterons from Mars
Rollerball
Rome 2033
Saturn 3
Scanners
Sealab 2020
Sealab 2020, Cassette 2
Shape of Things to Come, The
Shivers
Silent Running
Slithis
Sons of the Musketeers/The Mysterians
Soylent Green
Space Academy
Space Bandit
Space Cruiser
Space Firebird
Space Sentinels
Spacehunter
Spaceship
Spectreman
Star Fleet
Star Pilot
Star Trek II: The Wrath of Khan
Star Trek—Menagerie
Star Trek—Shore Leave
Star Trek: The Empath/Miri
Star Trek—The Motion Picture
Star Trek III: The Search for Spock
Star Trek: Whom Gods Destroy/Plato's Stepchildren
Star Wars
Starflight One
Starship Invasions
Strange Invaders
Stryker
Supersonic Man
Terrahawks 6: Zero Strikes Back
Terrahawks
Terrahawks 2: The Menace from Mars
Terrahawks 3: Terror from Mars
Terrahawks 4: Hostages of Mars
Terrahawks 5: Flaming Thunderbolts
Thing from Another World, The/Stranger on the Third Floor
Things to Come
Thunderbirds in Outer Space
Thunderbirds to the Rescue
THX 1138
Time Slip
Time Walker
Timerider
Tomorrow Man, The
Tron
2001: A Space Odyssey
Ultimate Warrior, The
Unknown World
Videodrome
Voltron—Defender of the Universe
Voltron—Defender Of The Universe In The Invasion Of The Robeasts
Voltron—Defender of the Universe, In the Castle of Lions
Voyage to the Bottom of the Sea
War of the Monsters
War of the Worlds, The
Warlords of Atlantis
Wavelength
Welcome to Blood City
Westworld
Where Have All the People Gone?
Women of the Prehistoric Planet
X from Outer Space, The

SUBJECT CATEGORY INDEX   Science fiction

XTRO
Yeti
Z.P.G.

Seasons

Garden and Gardener
Winter Gardens

Sewing

Sew Into Fashion

Sexuality

Learning to Love
Let Me Die a Woman

Smoking

So You Want to Stop Smoking
Stop Smoking

Soccer

Focus on Soccer 1-3
Giants of Brazil
Kick-Off Europe 1872-1968
Soccer: The Game of the Century: Part 2
Soccer: The Game of the Century

Space exploration

Apollo 4 Mission, The
Apollo 9: The Space Duet of Gumdrop and Spider
Apollo 10: Green Light for a Lunar Landing
Apollo 12: Pinpoint for Science
Apollo 13: 'Houston, We've Got a Problem'
Apollo 14: Mission to Fra Mauro
Apollo 15: In the Mountains of the Moon
Apollo 16: Nothing So Hidden
Apollo 17: On the Shoulders of Giants
Debrief: Apollo 8
Eagle Has Landed: The Flight of Apollo 11
Flight of Apollo 7, The
Footsteps of Giants
History of the Conquest of Space, The
Magnetic Effects in Space
New View of Space
Time of Apollo, The

Sports

Agostini
Basic Dressage
Better Rugby
Botham's Ashes: The 1981 Cornhill Test Series
Crowning Years, The
Daley's Decathlon
Danger Is My Business
England's Year 1979/80
Even Better Rugby
Feeling Fit
Female Mud Wrestling
First Chukkas
France's Year 1980/81
Gillette London Marathon, The
Great Event, The
Harry Carpenter's Videobook of Sport—Volume 2
Harry Carpenter's Videobook of Sport
Horseback
International Show Jumping
Ireland's Triple Crown
Lizzie Webb's Exercise Video
Match of the Century
Mini Rugby—It's the Real Thing
Montreal Olympics Equestrian Three-Day Event
Montreal Olympics 1976
147 Break
Red Arrows—Gnats and Hawks, The
Rollermania
Rugby—A Game for Everyone
Rugby—It's Childs Play
Rugby—Treatment of a Neck Injury
Scotland's Grand Slam
Secrets of the All Blacks
Secrets of the All Blacks II
Smirnoff Masters Squash 1981
Squash Coaching for School and Clubs
Status Quo—Off the Road
Steve Davis's World of Snooker Volume 1
Take Down
Water Babies
Weekend Warriors
Will to Win, The

Sports-Minor

American Challenge
Austrian Enduro
Darts - The John Lowe Way
Feria de Abril
International 'Supasquash' Championship
Moto-Cross Professionals
1978 British Open Squash Championship
1976 Irish Masters Squash Championship
People's Champion, The
Play Better Snooker
Reardon on Snooker
Ride
Squash Part 1
Squash Part 1-Elementary
Squash Part 2
Squash Part 2-Intermediate
Squash Part 3-Advanced
Squash Rackets 1
Squash Rackets 2
Table Tennis with Les Gresswell
Triangle of Suspense
Wings of the Wind/They Own the Sky
Year of the Quorn

Sports-Water

Crystal Voyager
Diving
Endless Summer, The
Flyer Flies Faster
Gold Medal Swimming, Part 1
Gold Medal Swimming, Part 2
How to Boardsail
Learning to Swim
Loners Plus Clipper Cup 'Hawaii 78,' The
Ocean World
Swimming Strokes

Sports-Winter

Games of the XXI Olympiad
In Search of Skiing
Leningrad Ice Show, The
Torvil and Dean—Path to Perfection
White Rock
Winter Sports Action (Volume One)
Winter Sports Action (Volume Two)
Winter Sports Action (Volume Three)

Suspense

Abductors, The
Absurd
Act, The
Africa Express
Airport '77
Airport SOS Hijack
All the Kind Strangers
Alligator
Amityville Horror, The
Angry Breed, The
Apocalypse—The Untold Story
Assault
Avalanche Express
Awakening, The
Baby, The
Baffled
Balance, La
Baltimore Bullet, The
Bang Bang Gang, The
Bear Island
Bells
Big Combo, The
Birds of Prey
Black Carrion/A Distant Scream
Black Veil for Lisa, A
Blazing Flowers
Blind Date
Blood and Black Lace
Bloodline
Blow Out
Bluebeard
Body Heat
Bomb at 10:10
Borsalino
Boston Strangler, The

Brainwash
Breathless
Bushido Blade, The
Butterfly
Candy Man, The
Caravan to Vaccares
Cat and Mouse
Child's Play/And the Wall Came Tumbling Down
Christmas Evil
City on Fire
Clairvoyant, The
Cloak and Dagger
Coma
Coming Out Alive
Concorde Affair
Cradle Will Fall, The
Crash
Crime Story
Crossfire
Crosstalk
Cry of the Innocent
Curtains
Czech Mate/In Possession
Dain Curse, The
Dangerous Cargo
Dangerous Summer, A
Dark Eyes
Dark Night of the Scarecrow
Day of the Assassins
Day of the Jackal, The
Day the Earth Moved, The
Dayton's Devil
Dead Zone, The
Deadly Games
Deadly Hero
Deadly Hunt, The
Deadly Impact
Deadly Revenge
Deadly Trap, The
Death Cruise
Death Dimension
Death Drive
Death Flight
Death Line
Death of a Snowman
Death Threat
Death Trap
Death Valley
Deep Red
Demons of the Mind
Despair
Desperate Voyage
Devouring Waves
Dial M for Murder
Diamonds
Dimension 5
Disappearance, The
Doctor Jekyll and Sister Hyde
Doll Squad, The
Don't Look Now
Double Exposure

SUBJECT CATEGORY INDEX — Suspense

- Eiger Sanction, The
- Enigma
- Erotic Inferno
- Evil Under the Sun
- Evilspeak
- Exorcist II—The Heretic
- Eye of the Needle
- Eyes of the Dragon
- Face of Fu Manchu, The
- Falling Man, The
- Fan, The
- Fatal Games
- Fear in the Night
- Fear Is the Key
- Final Exam
- Final Hour, The
- Firepower
- Firestarter
- 5-Man Army, The
- Flare-Up
- Flight of the Phoenix, The
- Florida Connection
- Flying Leathernecks, The/Beyond a Reasonable Doubt
- Fourth Man, The
- Freelance
- Fugitive, The/Follow Me Quietly
- Funeral for an Assassin
- Ghost Story
- Glove, The
- Gold
- Golden Needles
- Golden Rendezvous
- Great Alligator, The
- Grip of the Strangler/Fiend Without a Face/Goodness a Ghost
- Gun in the House, A
- Harlequin
- Harry's Game
- Haunting of Julia, The
- Haunts
- Hell Drivers
- High and Low
- High Ice
- Highpoint
- Hold-Up
- Homebodies
- House of Evil
- House of Whipcord
- House on Garibaldi Street, The
- Human Factor, The
- Humongous
- Hurricane
- In Broad Daylight
- Initiation, The
- Inn of the Damned
- Innocent Bystanders
- Ipcress File, The
- It Takes All Kinds
- Jaguar Lives
- Jaws
- Jaws II
- Jaws 3
- Journey
- Kidnapping of the President, The
- Killing Kind, The
- Klansman, The
- Kleinhoff Hotel
- Kwaidan
- Lady Vanishes, The
- Land of No Return, The
- Lassiter
- Last Horror Film, The
- Last Song, The
- Last Video and Testament/The Corvini Inheritance
- Laura
- League of Gentlemen, The
- Licensed to Kill
- Lies
- Lift, The
- Limbo Line, The
- Little Godfather from Hong Kong
- Loaded Guns
- Loners, The
- Long Live Your Death
- Long Night of Veronique, The
- Mad Bomber, The
- Mad Mission Three
- Madigan's Millions
- Magic Curse, The
- Magnum Force
- Man Called Intrepid, A
- Man in the Steel Mask, The
- Man Outside, The
- Man Who Haunted Himself, The
- Man Who Knew Too Much, The
- Manaos
- Margin For Murder
- Mastermind
- Mean Johnny Barrows
- Medusa Touch, The
- Mephisto Waltz, The
- Mission: Monte Carlo
- Mr Billion
- Money Movers
- Moon in the Gutter, The
- Murder by Decree
- Murder in Texas
- Murder on Flight 502
- Name for Evil, A
- New Years Evil
- Next Man, The
- Night of the Bloody Apes
- Night of the Juggler
- Night Partners
- Night Strangler, The
- Nightcomers, The
- Nightmares
- No One Would Believe Her
- No Place to Hide
- Nobody Runs Forever

Suspense — SUBJECT CATEGORY INDEX

North by Northwest
Notorious
Nowhere to Hide
No. 1—Licensed to Love and Kill
No. 1 of the Secret Service
Octagon, The
Octopussy
077 Mission Bloody Mary
One Away
One Down, Two To Go
Orca...Killer Whale
Order of Death
Osterman Weekend, The
Our Man Flint
Paint Me a Murder/The Late Nancy Irving
Panic City
Panic in the City
Partners
Patrick
Peking Blond
Photographer, The
Pimpernel Smith
Playing with Fire
Power Play
Premonition
President's Mistress, The
Pretty Poison
Private Parts
Private Right, The
Prize of Peril, The
Psycho
Psycho II
Pyx, The
Queen's Ransom, A
Quiller Memorandum, The
Ransom
Ransom
Rear Window
Red Berets, The
Reflection of Fear, A
Return of Martin Guerre, The
Return of the Tiger
Return to Boggy Creek
Revenge
Robbery
Rome Express
Run for Your Life
Runners
Running Scared
Sabotage
Savages
Scarecrow, The
Scream Bloody Murder
Search and Destroy
Second Chance/Great Day in the Morning
Secret of Seagull Island, The
Serpent, The
Serpico
Seven Golden Men
Shock Corridor
Silver Bears, The
Sisters
Sketches of a Strangler
Skyjacked
Slayground
Sleuth
Sloane
Snapshot—Australian Style
Some Girls Do
Somebody's Stolen Our Russian Spy
Someone Behind the Door
Someone Is Bleeding
Something to Hide
Sphinx
Spiral Staircase, The
Spy Killer, The
Spy Story
Still of the Night
Street of the Damned
Summer of Fear
Supertrain
Surabaya Conspiracy, The
Survivor, The
Swap, The
Sweet Scent of Death/Mark of the Devil, The
Sweet, Sweet Rachel
Taking of Pelham 123, The
Tales of the Unexpected—Cassette 1
Tales of the Unexpected-Cassette 2
Tamarind Seed, The
Tangier
Tarantulas
Target: Harry
Taste of Evil, A
Tension at Table Rock/Revenge Is My Destiny
Terminate with Extreme Prejudice
Terror Express
Terror Eyes
Terror from the Sky
Texas Chainsaw Massacre, The
Thief
Thirty Nine Steps, The
Thirty-Nine Steps, The
This Is Callan
Tigers Don't Cry
Tintorera
To Kill a Stranger
Towering Inferno, The
Train Killer, The
Trial by Terror
Ultimate Thrill, The
Under Capricorn
Union City
Unsuitable Job for a Woman, An
Venom
Vertigo
Victims
Vigilante
Violent Enemy, The
Visiting Hours
Voices
Watcher in the Woods, The

Weapons of Death
Whatever Happened to Baby Jane?
When Time Ran Out
When You Comin' Back, Red Ryder?
Where Danger Lives/Split Second
Who Dares Wins
Why Would Anyone Want to Kill A Nice Girl Like You?
Wicker Man, The
Willard
Witchfinder General
Wonder Women
World War III
Wrong Man, The
Young and Innocent

Television

Entertaining Electron, The
Showbiz

Tennis

Best of Wimbledon, The
Better Tennis
Decade of Wimbledon
Great English Garden Party, The
John McEnroe Story, The
Play Tennis
Playing Better Tennis
Tennis
Tennis with Mark Cox 1 and 2
Wimbledon, 1974
Wimbledon, 1975
Wimbledon, 1976
Wimbledon, 1977
Wimbledon, 1978
Wimbledon '81
Wimbledon, 1979
Wimbledon, 1980
Wimbledon 1982
Wimbledon '83

Trains

Great Little Trains of Wales, The
Great Railways Volume I
Metro-Land

Travel

Endless Summer, The

Variety

Abbe Lane Show, The
Allan Sherman Show, The
Barbara McNair Show, The
Bassey and Basie
Buddy Greco Show, The
Christy Minstrels, The
Cyd Charisse Show, The
Eartha Kitt Show, The
Evening With Liza Minnelli, An
Frankie Avalon Show, The
Jean-Pierre Aumont Show, The
Julie London Show, The
Kay Starr Show, The
Leslie Uggams Show, The
London Bridge Special, The
Mel Torme Show, The
Miss Nude Pageant, The
Osmond Brothers Special/Tom Jones at Knott's
Patti Page Show, The
Paul Anka Show, The
Pearl Bailey Show, The
Peggy Lee Show, The
Play-Box 1
Play-Box 2
Tony Martin Show, The
Vic Damone Show, The
Video Comic
Visit With Maurice Chevalier, A
Without Reservations/Footlight Varieties

Video

Beat, The
Billy Idol: Dancing with Myself
Blancmange-The Videosingles
David Grant
Elton John-The Videosingles
Entertaining Electron, The
How to Beat Home Video Games-Volume 1
How to Beat Home Video Games-Volume 2
How to Beat Home Video Games-Volume 3
Music-Image Odyssey
New Edition-The Videosingles
Style Council-The Videosingles, The
Tears for Fears-The Videosingles

Wales

Great Little Trains of Wales, The
Wales in Trust

War-Drama

Above Us the Waves
Aces High
All Quiet on the Western Front
All Quiet on the Western Front
Anzio
Apocalypse—The Untold Story
Arm of Fire
Attack FORCE Z
Back to Bataan/Roadblock
Battle of Britain, The
Battle of Okinawa
Battle of San Pasquale, The
Battle of the Bulge
Battle of the Commandos
Battle of the Japan Sea

War-Drama   SUBJECT CATEGORY INDEX

Battle of the River Plate, The
Battle on the River Neretva, The
Battle Squadron
Beach of the War Gods
Berlin Express/Isle of the Dead
Best of the Badmen/Sealed Cargo
Big Red One, The
Biggest Battle, The
Blood and Honour
Boat, The
Bomb at 10:10
Boys in Company C, The
Brave Bunch, The
Breaker Morant
Breakthrough
Bridge Too Far, A
Bridge Too Far, A
Bridges at Toko-Ri, The
Bunker, The
Churchill's Leopards
Colditz Story, The
Combat Killers
Commando Attack
Commandos
Corbari
Cross of Iron
Cruel Sea, The
Dam Busters, The
Deadly Commando
Death of Adolf Hitler, The
Desert Commando
Desert Fox, The
Desert Tigers
Dirty Dozen, The
Eagle Has Landed, The
Eagles Attack at Dawn
Eliminator, The
Enemy Below
Enola Gay
Escape to Victory
Fall of the Giants, The
Farewell to Arms, A
Farewell to Arms, A
Fifth Offensive, The
First of the Few, The
Flat Top
Flying Leathernecks, The/Beyond a Reasonable Doubt
Four Feathers, The
Frauleins in Uniforms
Game for Vultures
Greatest Attack, The
Green Berets, The
Guerillas in Pink Lace
Hard Way, The
Hell in the Pacific
Hero Bunker
Heroes of Telemark, The
High Velocity
How Sleep The Brave
Ice Cold in Alex

In Which We Serve
Inglorious Bastards, The
Kagemusha
Kanal
Last Day of the War, The
Last Train to Berlin
Lilli Marleen
Lionman
Long Ride, The
Longest Day, The
Losers, The
MacArthur
Massacre in Rome
Men in War
Merry Christmas Mr Lawrence
Missile-X
Missiles of October, The
Murphy's War
Mussolini
My Mother, the General
Naked and the Dead, The—Target
Night of the Assassin, The
Night of the Generals
1941
No Drums, No Bugles
No Place to Hide
Odd Angry Shot, The
Oh! What a Lovely War
One of Our Aircraft Is Missing
Only Way, The
Operation Amsterdam
Overlord
Passage, The
Pathfinders—Code Name 'Gomorrah'
Pathfinders—Fly There—Walk Back
Pathfinders—Fog
Pathfinders—For Better, For Worse
Pathfinders—In the Face of the Enemy
Pathfinders—Into the Fire
Pathfinders—Jonah Man
Pathfinders—Nightmare
Pathfinders—One Man's Lancaster
Pathfinders—Operation Pickpocket
Pathfinders—Our Daffodils Are Better Than Your Daffodils
Pathfinders—Sitting Ducks
Pathfinders—Sweets from a Stranger
Patton
Physical Assault
Pimpernel Smith
Place in Hell, A
Prisoner Without a Name, Cell Without a Number
Probability Zero
Purple Plain, The
Reach for the Sky
Red Flag
Red Nights of the Gestapo, The
Reluctant Heroes, The
Scarlet and the Black, The
Sea Wolves, The
Search and Destroy

Sergeant Klems
Shamwari
Shenandoah
Shout at the Devil
67 Days
Sky Rider Attack
Snow Treasure
Special Train for Hitler
SS Girls
Stalag 17
Suicide Commando
Suicide Mission
Surprise Attack
Survival Run
Taste of Hell, A
Tobruk
Tora! Tora! Tora!
Torn Allegiance
Tornado Strike Force
Town Like Alice, A
Toy Soldiers
Triple Cross
Triple Echo, The
Twelve O'Clock High
Uncommon Valour
Under Fire
Universal Soldier
Viking Invaders
Villa Rides!
Von Ryan's Express
Warkill
We Dive at Dawn
Where Eagles Dare
Wild Geese, The
Wooden Horse, The

Western

Abilene Town
Ace High
Acquasanta Joe
Adios Gringo
Against a Crooked Sky
Alamo, The
Allegheny Uprising/Back from Eternity
Alvarez Kelly
Angel and the Badman
Apache Massacre
Apple Dumpling Gang Rides Again, The
Ballad of Death Valley
Ballad of Gregorio Cortez, The
Bad Man's River
Bandidos
Bandits, The
Bandolero
Bang Bang Kid, The
Barbarosa
Barrel Full of Dollars, A
Belle Starr Story, The
Best of the Badmen/Sealed Cargo
Big Cat, The

Big Land, The/Pioneer Builders
Big Sky, The/Code of the West
Blood at Sundown
Boldest Job in the West
Born To Buck
Bounty Killers, The/Macao
Broken Sabre, The
Brothers O'Toole, The
Buffalo Bill and the Indians
Bullet for the General
Bundle of Joy/Montana Belle
Bury Them Deep
Butch and Sundance: The Early Days
Butch Cassidy and the Sundance Kid
Cahill
California Gold Rush
Captain Apache
Carry On Cowboy
Cattle Annie and Little Britches
Challenge of the McKennas, The
Charley-One-Eye
Chisum
Colorado Charlie
Colt Concert
Companeros
Cotter/Island of Lost Women
Cry Blood Apache
Dark Command
Davy Crockett
Deadly Trackers, The
Death at Owell Rock
Devil's Canyon/A Cry in the Night
Django
Django's Cut Price Corpses
Donner Pass
Drum Beat/To Beat the Band
Drummer of Vengeance
Duel in the Sun
Eagle's Wing
Face to Face
Father Murphy
Fighting Fists Of Shangai Joe, The
Find A Place To Die
First Travelling Saleslady, The/A Lady Takes a Chance
Fistful of Dollars, A
Five Bloody Graves
Five Guns West
Flaming Bullets
For a Few Dollars More
Fort Apache
Frisco Kid, The
Girl in Every Port, A/Return of the Badmen
Go Kill and Come Back!
God Forgives—I Don't
Goin' South
Gold Train
Gone with the West
Good, the Bad, and the Ugly, The
Good, The Bad and The Ugly, The
Grayeagle

Western — SUBJECT CATEGORY INDEX

Great Gundown, The
Gunfight, A
Gunfight at the O.K. Corral
Guns of the Timberland/Bengazi
Halfbreed, The/Walk Softly, Stranger
Hang 'Em High
Hannie Caulder
Harry Tracy—Desperado
Heaven's Gate
High Noon
High Plains Drifter
Hombre
Hunted, The
I'll Die For Vengeance
Jesse and Lester: Two Brothers in a Place Called Trinity
Jessi's Girls
Joe Kidd
Johnny Guitar
Jory
Junior Bonner
Keoma
Kid Blue
Kid from Not-So-Big, The
Killer Inside Me, The
Last Days of Pompeii, The/The Mysterious Desperado
Last Gun, The
Last of the Badmen
Last of the Mohicans, The
Last of the Mohicans
Last Rebel, The
Last Train from Gun Hill
Legend of Frank Woods, The
Legend of Frenchie King, The
Legend of the Lone Ranger, The
Little Big Man
Lone Wolf Mc Quade
Long Day of Massacre, The
Long Live Your Death
Long Riders, The
Longest Hunt, The
Lusty Men
Macho Callahan
Mackintosh & T.J.
Madron
Man Called Blade, A
Man Called Sledge, A
Man of the East
Man, Pride, Vengeance
Man Who Loved Cat Dancing, The
Massacre at Fort Holman
McMasters, The
Missouri Breaks, The
Mr Horn
Mohawk
Moment to Kill, The
Montana Trap
Mutiny at Fort Sharp
My Name Is Mallory
My Name Is Nobody

Naked and the Dead, The—Target
Northwest Frontier
Northwest Stampede
100 Rifles
One Little Indian
One Silver Dollar
Outlaw Josey Wales, The
Outlaw, The/Law of the Underworld
Paid In Blood
Pat Garrett and Billy the Kid
Pocket Money
Price of Death, The
Proud and Damned, The
Pushing Up Daisies
Raiders of the Treasures of Tayopa
Red Sun
Restless Breed, The
Return of a Man Called Horse, The
Ride to Glory
Rio Bravo
Rio Lobo
Rodeo Girl
Run, Man, Run
Run of the Arrow/Cry Danger
Samurai
Sartana
7 Winchesters for a Massacre
Shadow of Chikara, The
Shalako
Shame, Shame on the Bixby Boys
Shane
Shenandoah
Shoot the Sun Down
Soldier Blue
Son of Sinbad/Cyclone on Horseback/Pal's Return
Stagecoach/Deadline at Dawn
Stranger in Sacramento
Sweet Creek County War, The
Tell Them Willie Boy Is Here
Tension at Table Rock/Revenge Is My Destiny
Texas Across the River
Texas Adios
They Call Me Hallelujah
They Call Me Trinity
They called him Amen
Tom Horn
Too Much Gold For One Gringo
Town Called Bastard, A
Town That Dreaded Sundown, The
Trackers, The
Train Robbers, The
Treasure of Pancho Villa, The
True Grit
Tycoon/Six Gun Gold
Undefeated, The
Under California Skies
Valdez the Half-Breed
Vengeance with a Gun
Violent Breed, The
Wackiest Wagon Train in the West, The

SUBJECT CATEGORY INDEX — Western

Wagonmaster/Double Dynamite
Welcome to Blood City
White Buffalo, The
White Comanche
Wicked Die Slow, The
Wild Bunch, The
Wild Horse Hank
Wild Rovers
Wild Times
Wild Women
Wildcat
Young and Free
Yuma
Zachariah

Wildlife

African Waterhole
Alam Alhaiwan
Bird About Town
Early One Morning
Educational Release No 2
Elephant Called Slowly, An
Flying Birds/Birds of the Lake/Osprey Watch
From Africa with Love—Nature Film
Language of Birds, The
Last of the Wild—Volume 4
Last of the Wild—Volume 5
Life Among the Baboons/Run Cheetah Run
Man Who Loved Bears, The
Never Cry Wolf
Petersfinger Cuckoos, The
Predators, The
Round Robin
Under Kilimanjaro
Vital River, The
White Lions, The
Wildlife USA
World of Survival—Hunters of the Plains, The
World of Survival—Migrants of the Arctic, The
Ynys-Hir

Women

Female Mud Wrestling

Hands Off!
Hit Back!

World War II

Adolph Hitler—Benito Mussolini
Black Fox
Finest Hours, The
Great Escape, The
Joseph Stalin—Leon Trotzkij
Kitty—Return to Auschwitz
Lancaster
Night Bombers
Winston Churchill—Charles De Gaulle
World at War Parts 1 and 2, The
World at War: Parts 1-4, The
World at War Parts 3 and 4, The
World at War Parts 5 and 6, The
World at War: Parts 5-8, The
World at War Parts 7 and 8, The
World at War Parts 9 and 10, The
World at War Parts 11 and 12, The
World at War Parts 13 and 14, The
World at War Parts 15 and 16, The
World at War Parts 19 and 20, The
World at War Parts 21 and 22, The
World at War Parts 23 And 24, The
World at War Parts 25 And 26, The
World in Flames, The: Part 1: From Hitler's Rise to Power to the Blitzkrieg
World in Flames, The: Part II: From the Battle of Britain to Stalingrad
World in Flames, The: Part III: The War on the Seas and the Fall of Japan
World at War Parts 17 and 18, The

Yoga

Basic Introduction to Yoga, A
Learn About Yoga
Lyn Marshall's Everyday Yoga
Yoga for Health

Video Disc Index

For complete information on each programme, check the listing in the main body of this book.

LASER DISCS

A & M SOUND PICTURES
Pearls—The Video

BBC HOME VIDEO
BBC Children's Favourites
Blue Peter Makes
Chris Barber Band, The
Colonel Culpeper's Flying Circus
Deep Purple California Jam: April 6, 1974
Delia Smith's Home Baking
Falklands—Task Force South
Great Railways Vol. 1
Gulliver's Travels
Harry Carpenter's Videobook of Sport
Harry Carpenter's Videobook of Sport—Vol. 2
Horseback
Mike Harding Goes Over the Top
Mr. Smith's Flower Garden
Mr. Smith's Indoor Garden
Mr. Smith's Vegetable Garden
Paint!
Play Golf
Play Tennis
Queen's Birthday Parade, The
Royal Wedding, The Seapower
Sky at Westminster Abbey
Story of English Furniture, The
Toyah at the Rainbow
Training Dogs the Woodhouse Way
Treasures of the British Crow
Videobook of British Garden Birds
World's Greatest Paintings 1: Adoration, The

CBS/FOX VIDEO
Adventures of Sherlock Holmes' Smarter Brothers, The
Alien
All That Jazz
Author! Author!
Avalanche Express
Beneath the Planet of the Apes
Blue Hawaii
Blue Max, The
Boston Strangler, The
Breaking Away
Brubaker
Butch Cassidy and the Sundance Kid
Carnal Knowledge
Chariots of Fire
Damien Omen II
Day of the Dolphin
Death Hunt
Dirty Mary, Crazy Larry
Doctor Doolittle
Duchess and the Dirtwater Fox, The
Electric Light Orchestra—Live at Wembley
Enemy Below, The
Fantastic Voyage
French Connection, The
Fury, The
Hello, Dolly!
History of the World Part 1
Janitor, The
Julia
Kagemusha
King and I, The
Longest Day, The
M*A*S*H
My Fair Lady
9 to 5
Norma Rae
Omen, The
100 Rifles
Onion Field, The
Other Side of Midnight, The

Patton
Planet of the Apes, The
Poseidon Adventure, The
Producers, The
Rose, The

Sailor Who Fell from Grace with the Sea, The
Silver Streak
Sky Riders
Soldier Blue
Sound of Music, The
St. Valentine's Day Massacre, The
Those Magnificent Men in Their Flying Machines
Undefeated, The
Vanishing Point

CIC VIDEO
Best Little Whorehouse in Texas, The
Blues Brothers, The
Border, The
Buck Rogers in the 25th Century
Chinatown
Death Valley
Death Wish
Dracula
Electric Horseman, The
Escape from Alcatraz
Fan, The
48 Hours
Friday the 13th Part II
Grease
Grease II
Heaven Can Wait
Hunter, The
Island, The
Jaws
Jesus Christ Superstar
Lords of Discipline, The
Mission Galactica
Saturday Night Fever
Smokey and the Bandit
Star Trek—The Motion Picture
Star Trek II—The Wrath of Khan
Sting, The
Thing, The
Warriors, The
Xanadu

EMBASSY HOME ENTERTAINMENT
Black Marble, The
Dain Curse, The
Escape from New York
Eye for an Eye, An
Final Exam
Golden Girl
Howling, The
Man, a Woman & a Bank, A
Night the Lights Went Out in Georgia, The
Nightcomers, The
Olivia Newton-John: Live
Paradise
Prom Night
Raccoons on Ice/The Christmas Raccoons
Road Games
Rod Stewart: Tonight He's Yours
They Call Me Trinity
Vice Squad

GUILD HOME VIDEO
Carbon Copy
Dastardly & Muttley
Escape to Victory
High Risk
House of the Long Shadows
Last American Virgin, The
Love at First Bite
Mother Lode
Postman Always Rings Twice, The
Ring of Bright Water
Scanners
Scooby and Scrappy-Doo—Cassette 1
Scooby and Scrappy-Doo—Cassette 2
S.O.B.
Straw Dogs
Stunt Man, The
10cc Live at the International Music Show
Ugh! A Music War
Warning, The
When a Stranger Calls

HOME VIDEO HOLDINGS
Atlantic City
Why Not Stay for Breakfast
Wildcats of St. Trinians
Zero to Sixty

INTERVISION VIDEO LTD
El Cid
Exterminator, The
Fall of the Roman Empire, The
55 Days at Peking

MGM/UA HOME VIDEO
Bandwagon, The
Cat on a Hot Tin Roof
Champ, The
Clash of the Titans
Coma
Easter Parade
Fame
Gigi

My Favourite Year
On the Town
Pat Garrett and Billy the Kid
Showboat
Tarzan and Ape Man
20001: A Space Odyssey

POLYGRAM VIDEO
ABC's Mantrap
American Werewolf in London, An
Barclay James Harvest
Calimero
Coming Out of the Ice
Deadly Blessing
Endless Love
Flight of Dragons, The
Goin' All the Way
High Ice
Kids Are Alright, The
New York City Ballet
Nine Lives of Fritz the Cat, The
One Show Makes it Murder
Pavarotti
Peter Ustinov Tells Stories from Hans Christian Andersen
Pink Floyd Live at Pompeii
Rainbow—Live Between the Eyes
Red Sun
Roxy Road—The High Road
Sisters
Soccer—The Game of the Century
Status Quo—Live in Concert at the NEC Birmingham
Wind in the Willows, The
Xtro

PRECISION VIDEO
Animalympics
Barbarosa
Capricorn One
Dr Coppelius
Eagle Has Landed, The
Fruit Is Ripe, The
Great Muppet Caper, The
Green Ice
Hawk the Slayer
Hoodwink
Imagination in Concert
Invaders from the Deep
Moses the Lawgiver
Muppet Movie, The
On Golden Pond
Raise the Titanic
Return of the Pink Panther, The
Ruckus
Salamander, The
Saturn 3
Sophie's Choice
Thunderbirds in Outer Space
To Russia with Elton

RANK VIDEO LIBRARY
Alone in the Dark
Baltimore Bullet, The
Blow Out
Boys in Blue, The
Bugsy Malone
Cabaret
City on Fire
Feeling Fit
Focus on Soccer
Hands of the Ripper
Henry V
Hot Bubblegum
Ipcress File, The
Jaguar Lives
Just Before Dawn
Lady Vanishes, The *(1938)*
Lady Vanishes, The *(1978)*
Mikado, The
Riddle of the Sands, The
Sea Wolves, The
Silver Dream Racer
Squash Rackets
Starflight One
Sword and the Sorcerer, The
Tarka the Otter
Thirty-Nine Steps, The *(1935)*
Who Dares Wins
Wild Geese, The
Young Doctors in Love

SELECT VIDEO LTD
Asterix the Gaul
Lucky Luke
Popeye and Friends in Outer Space

THORN EMI
Best of the Benny Hill Show—Volume 1
Cliff Richard & The Shadows 'Thank You Very Much'
Kate Bush Live at the Hammersmith Odeon
Little River Band: Live Exposure
Olivia Newton-John—Physical
Pied Piper and Cinderella
Queen: Greatest Flix
Sheena Easton—Live at the Palace, Hollywood
Soft Cell—Non Stop Exotic Video Show
Tina Turner Live—Nice 'n Rough
Tubes Video, The

VESTRON VIDEO INTERNATIONAL
Linda Ronstadt—What's New?
Making Michael Jackson's Thriller
Video Rewind—The Rolling Stones

WARNER HOME VIDEO
Paul Simon in Concert

CED DISCS

RCA VIDEODISCS, a division of RCA/Columbia Pictures Video UK (see Video Programme Sources Index for address and telephone numbers).

Bugsy Malone
Elton John
Elvis—The Movie
Jasper Carrott Live
Moby Dick
Network
Silver Dream Racer
Stud, The
Swiss Family Robinson
Treasure Island
Videostars
Videotheque
West Side Story
Who Dares Wins

VESTRON VIDEO INTERNATIONAL
Christine McVie Concert, The
Linda Ronstadt—What's New?
Making Michael Jackson's Thriller

CAST INDEX

More than 275 performers and directors are listed in the cast index below. Cameo appearances, sound track narrations and other special situations have been included in performers' listings where known, to provide as complete a reference as possible.

Some selectivity has been applied, however, to keep this index from becoming too cumbersome. Cartoon characters, most "B" picture actors and actresses, character performers and low-budget Western stars have been omitted.

We have attempted to list those personalities that we feel most readers will be interested in looking for and have tried for a balanced mix of older names and newcomers.

ABBOTT AND COSTELLO
Abbott and Costello
Abbott and Costello Meet Captain Kidd
Africa Screams
From the Earth to the Moon/Jack and the Beanstalk
Meet Captain Kidd/The Three Musketeers

JENNY AGUTTER
American Werewolf in London, An
Dominique
Equus
Food, Wine and Friends: Vol. 3
Logan's Run
Man in the Iron Mask, The
Railway Children, The
Riddle of the Sands, The
Survivor, The

ALAN ALDA
Goofs from the Cutting Room Floor
Jenny
Mephisto Waltz, The
Seduction of Joe Tynan, The

WOODY ALLEN
Annie Hall
Bananas
Broadway Danny Rose
Everything You Always Wanted to Know...
Love and Death
Midsummer Night's Sex Comedy, A
Play It Again, Sam
Stardust Memories
Take the Money and Run
What's New Pussycat?
What's Up Tiger Lily
Zelig

ANTHONY ANDREWS
Mistress of Paradise
Percy's Progress
Under the Volcano

JULIE ANDREWS
Goofs from the Cutting Room Floor
Man Who Loved Women, The
Mary Poppins
S.O.B.
Sound of Music, The
Tamarind Seed, The
"10"

ANN-MARGRET
C.C. and Company
Cincinnati Kid, The
I Ought to Be in Pictures
Lookin' to Get Out
Murderers Row
Osmond Brothers Special, The
Return of the Soldier
Streetcar Named Desire, A
Tommy
Train Robbers, The
Who Will Love My Children?

FRED ASTAIRE
Amazing Dobermans, The
Bandwagon, The
Barkleys of Broadway, The
Carefree
Damsel in Distress, A
Easter Parade
Ghost Story
Hollywood on Parade
Midas Run, The
Purple Taxi, The
Second Chorus
Shall We Dance
Silk Stockings
Sky's the Limit, The/Step Lively
That's Entertainment

That's Entertainment: Part 2
Top Hat
Towering Inferno, The
Ziegfeld Follies

RICHARD ATTEN-BOROUGH
All Night Long
And Then There Were None
Bridge Too Far, A
Brighton Rock
Conduct Unbecoming
Doctor Doolittle
Flight of the Phoenix, The
Great Escape, The
Human Factor, The
League of Gentlemen, The
Loot
Magic Christian, The
Oh! What a Lovely War
Only Two Can Play
Sand Pebbles, The

LAUREN BACALL
Fan, The
How to Marry a Millionaire
Murder on the Orient Express
Northwest Frontier

ANNE BANCROFT
Graduate, The
Silent Movie, The
To Be or Not To Be

BRIGITTE BARDOT
Contempt
Doctor at Sea
Legend of Frenchie King, The
Shalako

ALAN BATES
Far from the Madding Crowd
Go-Between, The
Kind of Loving, A
Quartet
Return of the Soldier, The
Rose, The
Separate Tables
Shout, The
Three Sisters, The
Trespasser, The
Unmarried Woman, An
Very Like a Whale
Voyage Round My Father
Whistle Down the Wind
Wicked Lady, The
Women in Love

THE BEATLES
Caveman (Ringo)
Hard Day's Night, A

WARREN BEATTY
Bonnie & Clyde
Heaven Can Wait
Reds

CANDICE BERGEN
Carnal Knowledge
Domino Killings, The
Gandhi
Merlin and the Sword
Sand Pebbles, The
Soldier Blue

INGRID BERGMAN
Arch of Triumph
Autumn Sonata
Cactus Flower
Casablanca
For Whom the Bell Tolls
Hide-Aways, The
Indiscreet
Intermezzo
Joan of Arc
Matter of Time, A
Murder on the Orient Express
Notorious
Spellbound
Stromboli/While the City Sleeps
Under Capricorn

JACQUELINE BISSET
Bullitt
Class
Greek Tycoon, The
Mephisto Waltz, The
Murder on the Orient Express
Secrets
Thief Who Came to Dinner, The
Together
Under the Volcano
When Time Ran Out

COLIN BLAKELY
Donkey's Years
Equus
Evil Under the Sun
It Shouldn't Happen to a Vet
Little Lord Fauntleroy
Pink Panther Strikes Again, The
Private Life of Sherlock Holmes, The
Something to Hide

CLAIRE BLOOM
Clash of the Titans
Charly
80,000 Suspects
Limelight
Look Back in Anger
Separate Tables

DIRK BOGARDE
Accident
Bridge Too Far, A
Damned, The
Death in Venice
Despair
Doctor at Large
Doctor at Sea
Doctor in Distress
Doctor in the House
Modesty Blaise
Oh! What a Lovely War
Quartet
Serpent, The
Servant, The
Simba
Singer Not the Song, The
So Long at the Fair
Tale of Two Cities, A
Victim

HUMPHREY BOGART
African Queen, The
Beat the Devil
Call It Murder
Casablanca

DAVID BOWIE
Hunger, The
Just a Gigolo
Love You Till Tuesday
Man Who Fell to Earth, The
Merry Christmas, Mr. Lawrence
Ziggy Stardust and the Spiders from Mars

PETER BOYLE
Beyond the Poseidon Adventure
Candidate, The

F.I.S.T.
Hammett
In God We Trust
Joe
Kid Blue
Outland
Steelyard Blues
Where the Buffalo
    Roam
Yellowbeard

WILFRID BRAMBELL
Hard Day's Night, A
Holiday on the Buses
Island of Adventure,
    The
Steptoe and Son

MARLON BRANDO
Formula, The
Godfather, The
Guys and Dolls
Last Tango in Paris
Missouri Breaks, The
Mutiny on the Bounty
Nightcomers, The
Sayonara
Superman- The
    Movie
Young Lions, The

CHARLES BRONSON
Battle of the Bulge
Borderline
Cabo Blanco
Death Hunt
Death Wish
Dirty Dozen, The
Evil That Men Do, The
Great Escape, The
House of Wax
Love and Bullets
Magnificent Seven,
    The
Master of the World
Mechanic, The
Mr. Majestyk
Raid on Entebbe
Red Sun
Rider on the Rain
Run of the Arrow
Sandpiper, The
Someone Behind the
    Door
Telefon
10 to Midnight
Twinky
Valachi Papers, The
Villa Rides!
White Buffalo, The

MEL BROOKS
Blazing Saddles
History of the World
    Part 1
Muppet Movie, The
Producers, The
Silent Movie, The
To Be or Not To Be

RICHARD BURTON
Absolution
Anne of the Thousand
    Days
Assassination of
    Trotsky, The
Becket

Bluebeard
Breakthrough
Cleopatra
Divorce His, Divorce
    Hers
Doctor Faustus
Equus
Exorcist II—The
    Heretic
Fifth Offensive, The
Green Grow the
    Rushes
Hammersmith is Out
Klansman, The
Longest Day, The
Look Back in Anger
Massacre in Rome
Medusa Touch, The
Robe, The
Sandpiper, The
Under Milk Wood
Villain
Where Eagles Dare
Who's Afraid of
    Virginia Woolf?
Wild Geese, The

JAMES CAAN
Bridge Too Far, A
Comes a Horseman
Countdown
Freebie & the Bean
Gambler, The
Godfather, The
Gone with the West
Hide in Plain Sight
Killer Elite, The
Rollerball
Silent Movie, The
Violent Streets
White Heat

JAMES CAGNEY
Great Guy
Hollywood on Parade
Mister Roberts
One Blow Too Many
Ragtime
Something to Sing
    About
White Heat

MICHAEL CAINE
Battle of Britain, The
Beyond the Poseidon
    Adventure
Blame It on Rio
Bridge Too Far, A
Death Trap
Dressed to Kill
Eagle Has Landed,
    The
Educating Rita
Escape to Victory
Honorary Consul
Ipcress File, The
Island, The
Italian Job, The
Kidnapped
Last Valley, The
Peeper
Romantic
    Englishwoman, The
Silver Bears, The
Sleuth
Swarm, The
Too Late the Hero

RICHARD CHAMBERLAIN
Bells
Christmas Messenger,
    The
Count of Monte Cristo,
    The
Four Musketeers, The
Julius Caesar
Lady Caroline Lamb
Man in the Iron Mask,
    The
Only One Winner
Slipper and the Rose,
    The
Swarm, The
Three Musketeers,
    The

LON CHANEY
Hunchback of Notre
    Dame, The
Phantom of the
    Opera, The

CHARLIE CHAPLIN
Blackbeard the
    Pirate/Fish
    Feathers/Pal's
    Adventure/The
    Fireman
Charlie Chaplin
    Comedy Theatre
Charlie Chaplin
    Comedy Theatre
    No.2, The
Charlie Chaplin I-IV
Circus, The/A Day's
    Pleasure
City Lights
Funniest Man in the
    World, The

Gentleman Tramp, The
Gold Rush, The/Payday
Great Dictator, The
Kid, The/The Idle Class
Limelight
Modern Times
Monsieur Verdoux
Silent Clowns: Big Moments from Little Pictures
Sinbad the Sailor/The Adventurer
Unknown Chaplin

GERALDINE CHAPLIN
Buffalo Bill and the Indians
Innocent Bystanders
Mirror Crack'd, The
Roseland
Three Musketeers, The
Unknown Chaplin
Up a Tree
Word, The
Z.P.G.

JULIE CHRISTIE
Billy Liar
Demon Seed
Don't Look Now
Far from the Madding Crowd
Fast Lady, The
Go-Between, The
Heat and Dust
Heaven Can Wait
Memoirs of a Survivor
Return of the Soldier, The
Separate Tables

WINSTON CHURCHILL
Finest Hours, The
Winston Churchill— Charles De Gaulle

JILL CLAYBURGH
First Monday in October
Griffin and Phoenix
I'm Dancing as Fast as I Can
It's My Turn
Semi-Tough
Silver Streak
Thief Who Came to Dinner, The
Unmarried Woman, An
Wedding Party, The

MONTGOMERY CLIFT
Indiscretion of an American Wife
Young Lions, The

GLENN CLOSE
Big Chill, The
Natural, The
Hell Drivers
Meteor
Murder on the Orient Express
Never Say Never Again
Next Man, The
Outland
Ransom
Shalako
Thunderball
Time Bandits
You Only Live Twice

BILLY CONNOLLY
Absolution
Big Banana Feet
Billy Connolly—'Bites Yer Bum'
Bullshot
Rewind: Volume 3
Secret Policeman's Ball, The

TOM CONTI
Flame
Haunting of Julia, The
Merry Christmas, Mr. Lawrence
Norman Conquests, The
Princess and the Pea, The

PETER COOK
Bedazzled
Find the Lady
Hound of the Baskervilles, The
Peter Cook and Co.
Ready Steady Go!—Vol. 1
Secret Policeman's Ball, The
Yellowbeard

GARY COOPER
Farewell to Arms, A
For Whom the Bell Tolls
High Noon

NOEL COWARD
In Which We Serve
Italian Job, The
Kublai Khan

BERNARD CRIBBINS
Daleks—Invasion Earth 2150 A.D.
Plank, The/Rhubarb, Rhubarb
Porgy and Blue/High Island Pollack
Railway Children, The
To See Such Fun
Two-Way Stretch
Water Babies, The

BING CROSBY
High Society
Road to Utopia, The

TOM CRUISE
All the Right Moves
Outsiders, The
Risky Business

TONY CURTIS
Balboa
Boston Strangler, The
Brainwaves
Count of Monte Cristo, The
Great Race, The
It Rained All Night the Day I Left
Last Tycoon, The
London Conspiracy
Manitou, The
Mirror Crack'd, The
Mission: Monte Carlo
Portrait of a Showgirl
Rise and Rise of Casanova, The
Sextette
Sporting Chance
Suppose They Gave a War and Nobody Came
Switch, The
Title Shot

PETER CUSHING
And Now the Screaming Starts
Asylum
At the Earth's Core
Blood Beast Terror, The
Bloodsuckers
Call Him Mr. Shatter
Creeping Flesh, The
Daleks—Invasion Earth 2150 A.D.
Devil's Men
Dr. Who and the Daleks
Fear in the Night
Ghoul, The
Hamlet
House of the Long Shadows
House That Dripped Blood, The

I, Monster
Island of Terror
Legend of the Werewolf
Making of Star Wars, The
Night of the Big Heat
Nothing But the Night
Shock Waves
Star Wars
Tale of Two Cities, A
Tales from The Crypt/Vault of Horror
Twins of Evil
Uncanny, The
Witching Time/The Silent Scream

JIM DALE
Carry On Again, Doctor
Carry On Cleo
Carry On Cowboy
Dancing Princesses, The
Pete's Dragon
Scandalous
That's Carry On

BETTE DAVIS
All About Eve
Connecting Rooms
Death on the Nile
Madame Sin
Return from Witch Mountain
Watcher in the Woods, The
Whatever Happened to Baby Jane?

JAMES DEAN
James Dean Story, The

OLIVIA DE HAVILLAND
Airport '77
Dark Mirror, The
Gone with the Wind
Pope Joan
Swarm, The

CATHERINE DENEUVE
Dirty Money
Hunger, The
Love to Eternity
March or Die
Mayerling
Repulsion
Slightly Pregnant Man, The

ROBERT DeNIRO
Bang The Drum Slowly
Deer Hunter, The
King of Comedy
Last Tycoon, The
Once Upon a Time in America
Swap, The
True Confessions
Wedding Party, The

BO DEREK
Change of Seasons, A
Orca...Killer Whale
Tarzan the Ape Man
"10"

BRUCE DERN
Coming Home
Driver, The
Great Gatsby, The
Harry Tracy Desperado
Silent Running
Tattoo
That Championship Season
Thumbtripping
Wild Angels, The

MARLENE DIETRICH
Black Fox
Garden of Allah, The
Just a Gigolo
Knight Without Armour

MATT DILLON
Liar's Moon
Little Darlings
Outsiders, The
Over the Edge
Rumble Fish

ROBERT DONAT
Knight Without Armour
Thirty Nine Steps, The
Winslow Boy, The

KIRK DOUGLAS
Big Sky, The
Cat and Mouse
Catch Me a Spy
Champion
Dr. Jekyll and Mr. Hyde
Eddie Macon's Run
Fury, The
Gunfight, A
Gunfight at the OK Corral
Heroes of Telemark, The
Home Movies
Last Train from Gun Hill
Light at the Edge of the World, The
London Bridge Special, The
Man From Snowy River, The
Out of the Past
Saturn 3
There Was a Crooked Man
20,000 Leagues Under the Sea
Ulysses

RICHARD DREYFUSS
Apprenticeship of Duddy Kravitz, The
Big Fix, The
Buddy System, The
Goodbye Girl, The
Jaws

FAYE DUNAWAY
Bonnie & Clyde
Champ, The
Chinatown
Deadly Trap, The
First Deadly Sin, The
Four Musketeers, The
Little Big Man
Mommie Dearest
Network
Thomas Crown Affair, The
Three Musketeers, The
Towering Inferno, The
Voyage of the Damned
Wicked Lady, The

ROBERT DUVALL
Betsy, The
Bullitt
Countdown
Eagle Has Landed, The
Godfather, The
Joe Kidd
Killer Elite, The
M*A*S*H
Natural, The
Network
Seven Percent Solution, The
Tender Mercies
THX 1138
True Confessions
True Grit

CLINT EASTWOOD
Any Which Way You Can
Beguiled, The
Bronco Billy
Dirty Harry
Eiger Sanction, The
Enforcer, The
Escape from Alcatraz
Every Which Way But Loose
Firefox

First Travelling
  Saleslady, The/A
  Lady Takes a
  Chance
Fistful of Dollars, A
For a Few Dollars
  More
Gauntlet, The
Good, the Bad, and
  the Ugly, The
Hang 'Em High
High Plains Drifter
Joe Kidd
Magnum Force
Outlaw Josey Wales,
  The
Sudden Impact
Thunderbolt and
  Lightfoot
Where Eagles Dare

SAMANTHA EGGAR
All the Kind Strangers
Biggest Battle, The
Brood, The
Curtains
Demonoid
Doctor Doolittle
Doctor in Distress
Exterminator, The
Hot Touch, The
Light at the Edge of
  the World, The
Seven Percent
  Solution, The
Uncanny, The
Welcome to Blood
  City

DENHOLM ELLIOT
Apprenticeship of
  Duddy Kravitz, The
Bad Timing
Brimstone and Treacle
Cruel Sea, The
Donkey's Years
Hound of the
  Baskervilles, The
House That Dripped
  Blood, The
Madame Sin
Missionary, The
Percy
Percy's Progress
Quest for Love
Raiders of the Lost
  Ark, The
Rising Damp
Russian Roulette
Sweeney 2
To the Devil... A
  Daughter
Tales From the
  Crypt/Vault of
  Horror
Trading Places
Two Faces of Evil,
  The/Rude
  Awakening
Wicked Lady, The
Zulu Dawn

DAVID ESSEX
Christmas Messenger,
  The
Silver Dream Racer
Stardust
That'll Be the Day

EDITH EVANS
Look Back in Anger
Slipper and the Rose,
  The
Tom Jones

KENNY EVERETT
Kenny Everett Video
  Show, Vols. I–III,
  The
Rewind: Volume 3

DOUGLAS FAIRBANKS SR.
Black Pirate, The
Mark of Zorro, The
Mr. Robinson Crusoe
Reaching for the
  Moon
Thief of Bagdad, The

MIA FARROW
Broadway Danny
  Rose ·
Death on the Nile
Great Gatsby, The
Haunting of Julia, The
Hurricane
Last Unicorn, The
Midsummer Night's
  Sex Comedy, A
Rosemary's Baby

MARTY FELDMAN
Adventures of
  Sherlock Holmes'
  Smarter Brother,
  The
Every Home Should
  Have One
In God We Trust
Sex with a Smile
To See Such Fun
Yellowbeard

SALLY FIELD
Back Roads
Beyond the Poseidon
  Adventure
End, The
Norma Rae
Smokey and the
  Bandit
Stay Hungry

W.C. FIELDS
Down Memory Lane
Sally of the Sawdust
That's Entertainment:
  Part 2

PETER FINCH
Battle of the River
  Plate, The
England Made Me
Far from the Madding
  Crowd
Flight of the Phoenix,
  The
Girl with Green Eyes
Network
Operation Amsterdam
Raid on Entebbe
Rape of the Third
  Reich
Something to Hide
Town Like Alice, A

FRANK FINLAY
Assault
Death of Adolph Hitler,
  The
Doctor in Distress
Four Musketeers, The
Longest Day, The
Murder by Decree
Neither the Sea Nor
  the Sand
Othello
Ploughman's Lunch,
  The
Return of the Soldier,
  The
Robbery
Study in Terror, A
Three Musketeers,
  The
Twisted Nerve
Wild Geese, The

ALBERT FINNEY
Alpha Beta
Duellists, The
Murder on the Orient
  Express
Tom Jones
Under the Volcano

PETER FIRTH
Equus
Tales of the
  Unexpected—
  Cassette 1
Tess
When You Comin'
  Back, Red Ryder?

HENRY FONDA
Ash Wednesday
Battle of the Bulge
Biggest Battle, The
Boston Strangler, The
City on Fire

Fedora
Fort Apache
Fugitive, The
Great Smokey Roadblock, The
Hell on Frisco Bay/The Mad Miss Manton
Home to Stay
Man Who Loved Bears, The
Meteor
Mister Roberts
Mussolini
My Name is Nobody
On Golden Pond
Serpent, The
Stage Struck
Swarm, The
Too Late the Hero
Uptown Saturday Night
Wrong Man, The

JANE FONDA
Barbarella
Barefoot in the Park
Comes A Horseman
Coming Home
Dollmaker, The
Doll's House, A
Electric Horseman, The
Julia
Klute
9 to 5
On Golden Pond
Rollover
Steelyard Blues
Tall Story
They Shoot Horses, Don't They?
Powers of Evil

PETER FONDA
Dirty Mary, Crazy Larry
Futureworld
Idaho Transfer
92° in the Shade
Powers of Evil
Split Image
Wild Angels, The

JOAN FONTAINE
Damsel in Distress, A
Flying Leathernecks, The/Beyond a Reasonable Doubt
Ivanhoe
Letter from an Unknown Woman
Rebecca
Voyage to the Bottom of the Sea

GEORGE FORMBY
Let George Do It
To See Such Fun

CLARK GABLE
Gone with the Wind

AVA GARDNER
Bible—In the Beginning, The
City on Fire
Devil's Widow, The
55 Days at Peking
Kidnapping of the President, The
One Touch of Venus
Priest of Love
Sentinel, The
Showboat

JUDY GARLAND
Easter Parade
Garland
Meet Me in St. Louis
Pirate, The
That's Entertainment: Part 2
Till the Clouds Roll By
Wizard of Oz, The
Ziegfeld Follies

RICHARD GERE
Breathless
Honorary Consul, The
Yanks

SUSAN GEORGE
Die Screaming Marianne
Dirty Mary, Crazy Larry
Dr. Jekyll and Mr. Hyde
Eyewitness
Mandingo
Out of Season
Straw Dogs
Susan George —Naturally
Tintorera
Tomorrow Never Comes
Twinky
Venom

MEL GIBSON
Bounty, The
Mad Max
Mad Max II

SIR JOHN GIELGUD
Arthur
Becket
Chariots of Fire
Christmas Carols from Cambridge
Eagle in a Cage
Elephant Man, The
Gandhi
Gold
Human Factor, The
Julius Caesar
Les Miserables
Murder by Decree
Murder on the Orient Express
Oh! What a Lovely War
Scandalous
Scarlet and the Black, The
Sphinx
Wicked Lady, The

ELLIOT GOULD
Bridge Too Far, A
Busting
Capricorn One
Devil and Max Devlin, The
Dirty Tricks
Falling in Love Again
Jack and the Beanstalk
Lady Vanishes, The
Last Flight of Noah's Ark, The
London Bridge Special, The
Man in the Steel Mask, The
M*A*S*H
Mean Johnny Barrows
Move
Silent Partner, The
S*P*Y*S
Touch, The

CARY GRANT
Bringing Up Baby
Grass Is Greener, The
Hollywood on Parade
Indiscreet
Mr. Blandings Builds His Dream House
North by Northwest
Notorious
That Touch of Mink

D.W. GRIFFITH
Birth of a Nation
Intolerance
Sally of the Sawdust

ALEC GUINNESS
Card, The
Fall of the Roman Empire, The
Great Expectations
Hitler—The Last Ten Days
Kind Hearts and Coronets
Ladykillers, The
Lavender Hill Mob, The
Little Lord Fauntleroy
Lovesick
Making of Star Wars, The
Man in the White Suit, The

Oliver Twist
Quiller Memorandum, The
Raise the Titanic
Star Wars
Twelfth Night

SUSAN HAMPSHIRE
Baffled
Dr. Jekyll and Mr. Hyde
Feeling Fit
Malpertius
Neither the Sea Nor the Sand
Violent Enemy, The
Wonderful Life

SIR CEDRIC HARDWICKE
Desert Fox, The
Nicholas Nickelby
Rome Express
Things to Come
Tycoon
Winslow Boy, The

RICHARD HARRIS
Bible, The
Bible—In The Beginning, The
Cassandra Crossing, The
Camelot
Danny Travis
Deadly Trackers, The
Game for Vultures
Golden Rendezvous
Gulliver's Travels
Heroes of Telemark, The
Highpoint
Mutiny on the Bounty
Orca... Killer Whale
Ravagers, The
Return of a Man Called Horse, The
Tarzan the Ape Man
This Sporting Life
Wild Geese, The
Your Ticket Is No Longer Valid

REX HARRISON
Agony and the Ecstasy, The
Cleopatra
Doctor Doolittle
Fifth Musketeer, The
My Fair Lady
Shalimar

LAURENCE HARVEY
Alamo, The
Escape to the Sun
Expresso Bongo
I Am a Camera
Last Roman, The
Magic Christian, The
No One Would Believe Her
Room at the Top
Storm Over the Nile

JACK HAWKINS
Adventurers, The
Ben Hur
Cruel Sea, The
Escape to the Sun
Fallen Idol
Kidnapped
Lawrence of Arabia
League of Gentlemen, The
Poppies Are Also Flowers
Shalako
Sin
Sugarland Express
Twinky

GOLDIE HAWN
Best Friends
Cactus Flower
Duchess and the Dirtwater Fox, The
Private Benjamin

DAVID HEMMINGS
Airwolf
Barbarella
Blood Relations
Blow Up
Camelot
Christmas Messenger, The
Existance
Harlequin
Murder by Decree
Power Play
Race for the Yankee Zephyr
Squeeze, The
Survivor, The
Thirst
Voices

AUDREY HEPBURN
Bloodline
Breakfast at Tiffany's
My Fair Lady
They All Laughed

KATHARINE HEPBURN
African Queen, The
Bill of Divorcement, A
Bringing Up Baby
Great Balloon Adventure, The
Lion in Winter, The
Long Day's Journey Into Night
Love Among the Ruins
On Golden Pond

CHARLTON HESTON
Agony and the Ecstasy, The
Antony and Cleopatra
Awakening, The
Ben Hur
Beneath the Planet of the Apes
Call of the Wild
El Cid
55 Days at Peking
Gray Lady Down
Julius Caesar
Mother Lode
Planet of the Apes
Ruby Gentry
Skyjacked
Soylent Green
Ten Commandments, The
Three Musketeers, The
Wimbledon, 1979

BENNY HILL
Best of Benny Hill, Vols. I–III, The
Italian Job, The
To See Such Fun

TERENCE HILL
Ace High
All the Way Boys
Black Pirate, The
Carthage in Flames
Man of the East
March or Die
Mr. Billion
My Name Is Nobody
Odds and Evens
Who Finds a Friend Finds a Treasure

ALFRED HITCHCOCK
Birds, The
Blackmail
Dial M For Murder
Family Plot
Lady Vanishes, The
Notorious
Paradine Case, The
Psycho
Rear Window
Rebecca
Sabotage
Spellbound
Thirty Nine Steps, The
Trouble With Harry, The
Under Capricorn
Wrong Man, The
Young and Innocent

DUSTIN HOFFMAN
All the President's Men
Graduate, The

Kramer vs. Kramer
Lenny
Little Big Man
Madigan's Millions
Midnight Cowboy
Straight Time
Straw Dogs
Tootsie

WILLIAM HOLDEN
Alvarez Kelly
Bridges at Toko-Ri, The
Damien Omen II
Earthling, The
Fedora
Moon Is Blue, The
Network
S.O.B.
Stalag 17
Sunset Boulevard
Towering Inferno
21 Hours at Munich
When Time Ran Out
Wild Bunch, The
Wild Rovers

STANLEY HOLLOWAY
Beggar's Opera, The
Brief Encounter
Dr. Jekyll and Mr. Hyde
Hamlet
Lavender Hill Mob, The
My Fair Lady
Nicholas Nickelby
Target: Harry
This Happy Breed
Titfield Thunderbolt, The

IAN HOLM
Alien
All Quiet on the Western Front
Battle for the Falklands
Chariots of Fire
Holocaust
Les Miserables
Man in the Iron Mask, The
March or Die
Return of the Soldier, The
Shout at the Devil
S.O.S. Titanic
Time Bandits

BOB HOPE
Road to Utopia

ANTHONY HOPKINS
Audrey Rose
Bridge Too Far, A
Bunker, The
Change of Seasons, A
Elephant Man, The
International Velvet
Lion in Winter, The

LESLIE HOWARD
First of the Few, The
49th Parallel
Gone with the Wind
Intermezzo
Pimpernel Smith
Scarlet Pimpernel, The

TREVOR HOWARD
Brief Encounter
Catch Me a Spy
Conduct Unbecoming
Count of Monte Cristo, The
Doll's House, A
Flashpoint Africa
Gandhi
Hurricane
Kidnapped
Lunatic
Man in the Steel Mask, The
Missionary, The
Mutiny on the Bounty
Persecution
Pope Joan
Poppies Are Also Flowers
Ryan's Daughter
Sea Wolves, The
Shillingbury Blowers, The
Slavers
Stevie
Superman—The Movie
Third Man, The
Triple Cross
Twinky
Von Ryan's Express
Whispering Death

FRANKIE HOWERD
Carry On Doctor
Carry On Up the Jungle
Entertaining Electron, The
Ladykillers, The
Plank, The/Rhubarb, Rhubarb
To See Such Fun
Up Pompeii

ROCK HUDSON
Embryo
Farewell to Arms, A
Ice Station Zebra
Martian Chronicles, The
Mirror Crack'd, The
Tobruk
Undefeated, The
World War III

JOHN HURT
Alien
Champions, The
East of Elephant Rock
Elephant Man, The
Ghoul, The
Naked Civil Servant, The
Night Crossing
Osterman Weekend, The
Partners
Shout, The
Watership Down

WILLIAM HURT
Altered States
Big Chill, The
Body Heat
Gorky Park

JOHN HUSTON
African Queen, The
Beat the Devil
Bible—In the Beginning, The
Biggest Battle, The
Chinatown
Deserter, The
Head On
Jaguar Lives
Lovesick
Moby Dick
Myra Breckinridge
Phobia
Under the Volcano
Winter Kills

JEREMY IRONS
French Lieutenant's Woman, The
Moonlighting

GLENDA JACKSON
Boyfriend, The
Hopscotch
Lost and Found
Morecambe & Wise Musical Extravaganzas
Return of the Soldier, The
Romantic Englishwoman, The
Stevie
Triple Echo, The
Women in Love

DEREK JACOBI
Blue Blood
Day of the Jackal
Human Factor, The

SIDNEY JAMES
Bless This House
Carry On Aboard
Carry On Again Doctor

Carry On at Your Convenience
Carry On Behind
Carry On Camping
Carry On Cleo
Carry On Cowboy
Carry On Dick
Carry On—Follow that Camel
Carry On Henry
Carry On Loving
Carry On Matron
Carry On Up the Jungle
Carry On Up the Khyber
Lavender Hill Mob, The
Orders Are Orders
That's Carry On
To See Such Fun

AL JOLSON
Hallelujah, I'm a Tramp
Hollywood on Parade

BORIS KARLOFF
Berliner Express/Isle of the Dead
Black Sabbath
Cauldron of Blood
Comedy of Terrors, The
Corridors of Blood
Curse of the Crimson Altar
Doomed to Die
Frankenstein
Grip of the Strangler
Mad Monster Party
Scarface
Son of Kong/You'll Find Out
Sorcerers, The

DANNY KAYE
Skokie

BUSTER KEATON
American Candid Camera—Part 2
College
General, The
Hollywood on Parade
Limelight
Silent Clowns: Big Moments from Little Pictures

DIANE KEATON
Annie Hall
Godfather, The
Looking for Mr. Goodbar
Love and Death
Lovers and Other Strangers
Play It Again, Sam
Reds

PENELOPE KEITH
Donkey's Years
Every Home Should Have One
Good Life, The
Norman Conquests, The
Priest of Love

GENE KELLY
An American in Paris
Anchors Aweigh
Brigadoon
Guide for the Married Man, A
Hello, Dolly!
Jack and the Beanstalk
Les Girls
On the Town
Pirate, The
Singin' in the Rain
That's Entertainment
That's Entertainment: Part 2
Viva Knievel!
Xanadu
Ziegfeld Follies

GRACE KELLY
Bridge at Toko-Ri, The
Dial M for Murder
High Noon
High Society
Rear Window

KAY KENDALL
Genevieve
Les Girls

DEBORAH KERR
Grass Is Greener, The
King and I, The
Quo Vadis

NASTASSJA KINSKI
Paris, Texas
Unfaithfully Yours

KRIS KRISTOF-FERSON
Alice Doesn't Live Here Anymore
Convoy
Freedom Road
Osmond Brothers Special, The
Pat Garrett and Billy the Kid
Rollover
Sailor Who Fell from Grace with the Sea, The
Semi-Tough
Star Is Born, A
Vigilante Force

ALAN LADD
Big Land, The
Drum Beat/To Beat the Band
Duel of Champions
Guns of the Timberland
Hell on Frisco Bay
Shane

BURT LANCASTER
Atlantic City
Buffalo Bill and the Indians
Cassandra Crossing, The
Cattle Annie and Little Britches
Conversation Piece
Elmer Gantry
Gunfight at OK Corral
Island of Mr. Moreau, The
Local Hero
Moses the Lawgiver
Nuclear Countdown
Osterman Weekend, The
Zulu Dawn

HARRY LANGDON
Silent Clowns: Saturday Afternoon

JESSICA LANGE
All That Jazz
Frances
How to Beat the High Cost of Living
King Kong
Postman Always Rings Twice, The
Tootsie

FRANK LANGELLA
Deadly Trap, The
Dracula
Sphinx

ANGELA LANSBURY
Bedknobs and Broomsticks
Blue Hawaii
Death on the Nile
Lady Vanishes, The
Last Unicorn, The
Mirror Crack'd, The
Pirates of Penzance, The

CHARLES LAUGHTON
Abbott and Costello Meet Captain Kidd
Hobson's Choice
Hunchback of Notre Dame, The
Meet Captain Kidd/The Three Musketeers

Paradine Case, The
Samson and Delilah

LAUREL AND HARDY
Bogus Bandits
Flying Deuces, The
Heroes of the Regiment
Laurel and Hardy's Laughing Twenties
March of the Wooden Soldiers, The
Utopia

CHRISTOPHER LEE
Airport '77
Arabian Adventure
Bear Island
Caravans
Charles and Diana
Corridor of Blood
Creeping Flesh, The
Crypt of Horror
Curse of the Crimson Altar
Death Line
End of the World
Eye for an Eye, An
Far Pavilions
Face of Fu Manchu, The
Hannie Caulder
House of the Long Shadows
House That Dripped Blood, The
I, Monster
In Search of Dracula
Jaguar Lives
Last Unicorn, The
Man With The Golden Gun, The
Magic Christian, The
Night of the Big Heat
1941
Nothing But the Night
Nutcracker Fantasy
Oblong Box, The
Passage, The
Return from Witch Mountain
Salamander, The
Scars of Dracula
Serial
Starship Invasions
Tale of Two Cities, A
Three Musketeers, The
To the Devil...A Daughter
Whispering Death
Wicker Man, The

VIVIEN LEIGH
Anna Karenina
Caesar and Cleopatra
Fire Over England
Gone with the Wind

JACK LEMMON
Airport '77
Avanti!
Great Race, The
Missing
Mister Roberts
Prisoner of Second Avenue
Tribute

JERRY LEWIS
Slapstick of Another Kind

ROGER LIVESEY
Drum, The
Futtock's End
Green Grow the Rushes
League of Gentlemen, The

HAROLD LLOYD
Harold Lloyd 'The Unsinkable'
Silent Clowns: Big Moments from Little Pictures

SOPHIA LOREN
Aida
Attila the Hun
Blood Feud
Cassandra Crossing, The
El Cid
Fall of the Roman Empire, The
Firepower
Get Rita

PETER LORRE
Beat the Devil
Casablanca
Comedy of Terrors, The
Silk Stockings
Son of Kong/You'll Find Out
Tales of Terror
Things from Another World, The/Stranger on the Third Floor
20,000 Leagues Under the Sea

BELA LUGOSI
Dracula
Plan 9 from Outer Space
Scared to Death
Son of Kong/You'll Find Out

MALCOLM MacDOWELL
Aces High
Blue Thunder
Britannia Hospital
Merlin and the Sword
Passage, The
Raging Moon, The
Time After Time

ALI MacGRAW
China Rose
Convoy
Getaway, The
Love Story

SHIRLEY MacLAINE
All in a Night's Work
Being There
Can-Can
Change of Seasons, A
Desperate Characters
Loving Couples
Possession of Joel Delaney, The
Terms of Endearment
Trouble With Harry, The
Turning Point, The

LEE MARVIN
Avalanche Express
Death Hunt
Dirty Dozen, The
Gorky Park
Hell in the Pacific
Klansman, The
Pocket Money
Point Blank
Shout at the Devil
Wildcat

THE MARX BROTHERS/ GROUCHO MARX
Animal Crackers
Duck Soup
Girl in Every Port, A
Hollywood on Parade
Night at the Opera, A
That's Entertainment: Part 2
Wagonmaster/ Double Dynamite

JAMES MASON
Autobiography of a Princess
Bad Man's River
Bloodline
Blue Max, The
Boys from Brazil, The
Caught
Cross of Iron
Dangerous Summer, A
Desert Fox, The

Dirty Deal
Evil Under the Sun
Fall of the Roman
  Empire, The
Fanny by Gaslight
Fire Over England
Heaven Can Wait
Inside Out
Kill
Left Hand of the Law,
  The
Mandingo
Mayerling
Murder by Decree
North Sea Hijack
Odd Man Out
Passage, The
Seventh Viel, The
Tiara Tahiti
20,000 Leagues
  Under the Sea
Voyage of the
  Damned
Water Babies, The
Wimbledon, 1976

WALTER MATTHAU
Cactus Flower
Casey's Shadow
First Monday in
  October
Guide for the Married
  Man, A
Hello, Dolly!
Hopscotch
I Ought to Be in
  Pictures
King Creole
Kotch
Plaza Suite
Stingiest Man in
  Town, The
Taking of Pelham 123,
  The

RODDY McDOWALL
Battle for the Planet of
  the Apes
Bedknobs and
  Broomsticks
Cat from Outer Space,
  The
Class of 1984
Conquest of the
  Planet of the Apes
Dirty Mary, Crazy
  Larry
Embryo
Evil Under the Sun
Laserblast
Mae West
Martian Chronicles,
  The
Mean Johnny Barrows
Nutcracker Fantasy
Planet of the Apes
Scavenger Hunt
Taste of Evil, A
That Darn Cat

STEVE McQUEEN
Blob, The
Bullitt
Cincinnati Kid, The
Getaway, The
Great Escape, The
Hunter, The
Magnificent Seven,
  The
Sand Pebbles, The
Thomas Crown Affair,
  The
Tom Horn
Towering Inferno, The

SARAH MILES
Big Sleep, The
Blow Up
Bride to Be
Great Expectations
Lady Caroline Lamb
Man Who Loved Cat
  Dancing, The
Ryan's Daughter
Sailor Who Fell from
  Grace with the Sea,
  The
Servant, The
Those Magnificent
  Men in Their Flying
  Machines
Venom

SYLVIA MILES
Death of a Hooker
Evil Under the Sun
Farewell My Lovely
Funhouse, The
Sentinel, The
Shalimar
Wildcat

SPIKE MILLIGAN
Cherry Picker, The
Ghost in the Noonday
  Sun
Great McGonagall,
  The
Magic Christian, The
To See Such Fun

DONNA MILLS
Bait, The
Rolling Man

HAYLEY MILLS
Diamond Hunters
Flame Trees of Thika,
  The
Sky West and
  Crooked
That Darn Cat
Tiger Bay
Twisted Nerve
Whistle Down the
  Wind

JOHN MILLS
Above Us the Waves
Africa–Texas Style
Big Sleep, The
Black Veil for Lisa, A
Colditz Story, The
Devil's Advocate, The
Gandhi
Great Expectations
Hobson's Choice
Human Factor, The
Ice Cold in Alex
In Which We Serve
Lady Caroline Lamb
Lady Hamilton
October Man, The
Oh! What a Lovely
  War
Quatermass
Ryan's Daughter
Scott of the Antarctic
Singer Not the Song,
  The
Swiss Family
  Robinson
Thirty-Nine Steps, The
This Happy Breed
Tiara Tahiti
Tiger Bay
We Dive at Dawn
Zulu Dawn

LIZA MINNELLI
Arthur
Cabaret
Evening with
  Liza Minnelli, An
Garland
Matter of Time, A
Princess and the Pea,
  The
Silent Movie, The
That's Entertainment

MARILYN MONROE
All About Eve
Bus Stop
Clash by Night
Gentlemen Prefer
  Blondes
How to Marry a
  Millionaire
There's No Business
  Like Show
  Business

MONTY PYTHON
And Now for
  Something
  Completely
  Different
Fawlty Towers
  (*Cleese*)
Food, Wine and
  Friends: Vol. 1
  (*John Cleese*)
Great Muppet Caper,
  The (*John Cleese*)

Magic Christian, The
(*John Cleese*)
Missionary, The
(*Michael Palin*)
Monty Python and the
Holy Grail
Monty Python Live at
the Hollywood Bowl
Monty Python's Life of
Brian
Monty Python's
Meaning of Life
Peter Cook and Co.
(*John Cleese, Terry
Jones*)
Privates on Parade
(*John Cleese*)
Ripping Yarns
(*Michael Palin*)
Romance with a
Double Bass (*John
Cleese*)
Rutles, The: All You
Need Is Cash (*Eric
Idle*)
Secret Policeman's
Ball, The (*John
Cleese, Terry
Jones, Michael
Palin*)
Secret Policeman's
Other Ball, The
(*Graham Chapman,
John Cleese*)
Sez Les (*John
Cleese*)
Tale of the Frog
Prince, The (*Idle*)
Time Bandits (*John
Cleese, Terry
Gilliam, Michael
Palin*)
To See Such Fun
(*Eric Idle*)
Whoops Apocalypse
(*John Cleese*)
Yellowbeard (*Graham
Chapman, Eric
Idle, John Cleese*)

RON MOODY
Dogpound Shuffle
Dominique
Legend of the
Werewolf
Word, The

DUDLEY MOORE
Arthur
Bedazzled
Hound of the
Baskervilles, The
Lovesick
Ready Steady
Go!- Vol. One
"10"
Unfaithfully Yours

ROGER MOORE
Escape to Athena
For Your Eyes Only
Fiction Makers, The
Gold
Live and Let Die
London Conspiracy
Man Who Haunted
Himself, The
Man With the Golden
Gun
Mission: Monte Carlo
Moonraker
North Sea Hijack
Octopussy
Sea Wolves, The
Sicilian Cross
Shout at the Devil
Sporting Chance
Spy Who Loved Me,
The
Switch, The
That Lucky Touch
Vendetta for the Saint
Wild Geese, The

KENNETH MORE
Dark of the Sun
Doctor in the House
Genevieve
Leopard in the Snow
Longest Day, The
Night to Remember, A
Northwest Frontier
Reach for the Sky
Slipper and the Rose,
The
Spaceman and King
Arthur, The
Tale of Two Cities, A

**MORECAMBE AND
WISE**
Intelligence Men, The
Magnificent Two, The
Morecambe and Wise
Musical
Extravaganzas
Morecambe and Wise
Show, The
That Riviera Touch
World of Morecambe
and Wise Vol. 1,
The

ROBERT MORLEY
African Queen, The
Beat the Devil
Great Expectations
Great Muppet Caper,
The
High Road to China
Hugo the Hippo
Human Factor, The
Scavenger Hunt
Some Girls Do
Song of Norway
Study in Terror, A

Those Magnificent
Men in Their Flying
Machines
25 Years Impressions
Twinky
Young Ones, The

ZERO MOSTEL
Hot Rock, The
Mastermind
Producers, The

THE MUPPETS
Great Muppet Caper,
The
Muppet Movie, The

ANNA NEAGLE
Lilacs in the Spring
Victoria the Great

PAUL NEWMAN
Buffalo Bill and the
Indians
Butch Cassidy and the
Sundance Kid
Cat on a Hot Tin Roof
Cool Hand Luke
Fort Apache, The
Bronx
Harry and Son
Hombre
Hustler, The
Long Hot Summer,
The
Once Upon a Wheel
Pocket Money
Silent Movie, The
Sting, The
Towering Inferno, The
When Time Ran Out
Winning

ROBERT NEWTON
Odd Man Out
Oliver Twist
This Happy Breed
Treasure Island

JACK NICHOLSON
Border, The
Carnal Knowledge
Chinatown
Goin' South
Hell's Angels on
Wheels
Last Detail, The
Last Tycoon, The
Missouri Breaks, The
One Flew Over the
Cuckoo's Nest
Postman Always
Rings Twice, The
Reds
Shining, The
Terms of Endearment
Tommy

DAVID NIVEN
Better Late Than Never
Candleshoe
Carrington, V.C.
Curse of the Pink Panther
Death on the Nile
Escape to Athena
First of the Few, The
Man Called Intrepid, A
Moon Is Blue, The
Nightingale Sang in Berkeley Square, A
No Deposit, No Return
Paper Tiger
Pink Panther, The
Portrait of a Great Lady
Remarkable Rocket
Sea Wolves, The
Trail of the Pink Panther
Vampira

MAUREEN O'HARA
How Do I Love Thee
Hunchback of Notre Dame, The
Lisbon
Magnificent Matador, The
Never to Love
Sinbad the Sailor/The Adventurer
Sons of the Musketeers
Spanish Main

LORD LAURENCE OLIVIER
Battle of Britain, The
Beggar's Opera, The
Betsy, The
Boys from Brazil, The
Bridge Too Far, A
Bounty, The
Clash of the Titans
Dracula
Enchanted Island/Westward Passage
Fire Over England
49th Parallel
Hamlet
Henry V
Jazz Singer, The
Jesus of Nazareth
Lady Caroline Lamb
Long Day's Journey Into Night
Love Among the Ruins
Merchant of Venice, The
Oh! What a Lovely War
Othello
Rebecca
Seven Percent Solution
Sleuth
This Happy Breed
Three Sisters, The
Voyage Round My Father, A
World at War Parts 1–26, The

RYAN O'NEAL
Barry Lyndon
Bridge Too Far, A
Driver, The
Green Ice
Love Hate Love
Love Story
Main Event, The
Nickelodeon
Partners
So Fine
Thief Who Came to Dinner, The
What's Up Doc?
Wild Rovers

TATUM O'NEAL
Goldilocks and the Three Bears
International Velvet
Little Darlings
Nickelodeon

PETER O'TOOLE
Antagonists
Becket
Bible—In the Beginning, The
Kim
Lawrence of Arabia
Lion in Winter, The
Man Friday
Murphy's War
My Favourite Year
Night of the Generals
Power Play
Savage Innocents, The
Stunt Man, The
Svengali
Under Milk Wood
What's New Pussycat
Zulu Dawn

AL PACINO
Author! Author!
Bobby Deerfield
Cruising
Dog Day Afternoon
Godfather, The
Panic in Needle Park
Scarecrow
Scarface
Serpico

GREGORY PECK
Boys from Brazil, The
Duel in the Sun
I Walk the Line
MacArthur
Million Pound Note, The
Moby Dick
Omen, The
Paradine Case, The
Purple Plain, The
Scarlet and the Black, The
Sea Wolves, The
Spellbound
Twelve O'Clock High

ANTHONY PERKINS
Black Hole, The
Les Miserables
Murder on the Orient Express
North Sea Hijack
Pretty Poison
Psycho
Psycho II
Sins of Dorian Gray, The
Someone Behind the Door
Tall Story
Twice a Woman
Winter Kills

NOVA PILBEAM
Young and Innocent

DONALD PLEASANCE
All Quiet on the Western Front
Alone in the Dark
Better Late Than Never
Black Arrow, The
Blood Relatives
Cul-de-Sac
Death Line
Devil's Men
Dracula
Escape from New York
Escape to Witch Mountain
Fantastic Voyage
Gold of the Amazon Women
Halloween
Halloween II
Hearts of the West
Henry VIII and His Six Wives
Innocent Bystanders
Jaguar Lives
Journey Into Fear
Kidnapped
Last Tycoon, The
Malachi's Cove

Monster Club, The
Night Creature
Night of the Generals
Outback
Pied Piper, The
Power Play
Puma Man, The
Race for the Yankee Zephyr
Soldier Blue
Tale of Two Cities, A
Tales That Witness Madness
Telefon
THX 1138
To Kill A Stranger
Tomorrow Never Comes
Uncanny, The
Warrior of the Lost World
You Only Live Twice

CHRISTOPHER PLUMMER
Aces High
Assignment, The
Conduct Unbecoming
Desperate Voyage
Dreamscape
Fall of the Roman Empire, The
Highpoint
International Velvet
Janitor, The
Murder by Decree
Night of the Generals
Nobody Runs Forever
Pyx, The
Return of the Pink Panther, The
Scarlet and the Black, The
Silent Partner, The
Sound of Music, The
Stage Struck/The Girl Most Likely
Triple Cross

SIDNEY POITIER
For Love of Ivy
In the Heat of the Night
Warm December, A

DICK POWELL
Cornered
Run of the Arrow/Cry Danger
Where Danger Lives/Split Second

ELVIS PRESLEY
Blue Hawaii
Elvis
Elvis in Hawaii
Elvis on Tour
Elvis—That's the Way It Is
Fun in Acapulco
G.I. Blues
Girls, Girls, Girls
Jailhouse Rock
King Creole
Loving You
Paradise, Hawaiian Style
Roustabout

VINCENT PRICE
America Screams
Bat, The
Butterfly Ball, The
City Under the Sea
Comedy of Terrors
Cry of the Banshee
Dangerous Mission/Impact
Fall of the House of Usher
Haunted Palace, The
House of the Long Shadows
House of Wax
Journey Into Fear
Laura
Master of the World
Monster Club, The
Oblong Box, The
Percy's Progress
Pit and the Pendulum, The
Ruddigore
Snow White and the Seven Dwarfs
Son of Sinbad
Sorcerer's Apprentice, The
Stromboli/White the City Sleeps
Tales of Terror
Witchfinder General

ANTHONY QUAYLE
Antagonists, The
Battle of the River Plate, The
Everything You Always Wanted to Know...
Hamlet
Ice Cold in Alex
Mansions, The
Misunderstood
Murder by Decree
Poppies Are Also Flowers
Study in Terror, A
Tamarind Seed, The
21 Hours at Munich
Wrong Man, The

CHARLOTTE RAMPLING
Asylum
Caravan to Vaccares
Farewell My Lovely
Henry VIII and His Six Wives
Orca... Killer Whale
Purple Taxi, The
Ski Bum, The
Stardust Memories
Target: Harry

BASIL RATHBONE
Adventures of Robin Hood, The
Captain Blood
Comedy of Terrors, The
Garden of Allah, The
Last Days of Pompeii, The/The Mysterious Desperado
Magic Sword, The
Sherlock Holmes and the Women In Green
Sherlock Holmes Double Feature
Tales of Terror

ROBERT REDFORD
All the President's Men
Barefoot in the Park
Bridge Too Far, A
Brubaker
Butch Cassidy and the Sundance Kid
Candidate, The
Downhill Racer
Electric Horseman, The
Great Gatsby, The
Great Waldo Pepper, The
Hot Rock, The
Jeremiah Johnson
Natural, The
Sting, The
Way We Were, The

LYNN REDGRAVE
Big Bus, The
Everything You Always Wanted to Know...
Gaugin—The Savage
Girl with Green Eyes
Happy Hooker, The
Long Live Your Death

SIR MICHAEL REDGRAVE
Connecting Rooms
Dam Busters, The
Dr. Jekyll and Mr. Hyde
Go-Between, The
Heroes of Telemark, The
Lady Vanishes, The
Secret Beyond the Door

VANESSA REDGRAVE
Bear Island
Blow-Up
Camelot
Devils, The
Julia
Morecambe & Wise Musical Extravaganzas
Morgan—A Suitable Case for Treatment
Murder on the Orient Express
Oh! What a Lovely War
Out of Season
Seven Percent Solution
Snow White and The Seven Dwarfs
Yanks

OLIVER REED
And Then There Were None
Big Sleep, The
Black Arrow, The
Blue Blood
Brood, The
Condorman
Devils, The
Dr. Heckyl and Mr. Hype
Fanny Hill
Four Musketeers, The
Ransom
Sellout, The
Three Musketeers, The
Tommy
Tomorrow Never Comes
Triple Echo, The
Two of a Kind
Venom
Wildcat
Women in Love
Z.P.G.

CHRISTOPHER REEVE
Death Trap
Sleeping Beauty

BURT REYNOLDS
Best Friends
Best Little Whorehouse in Texas, The
End, The
Everything You Always Wanted to Know...
Fuzz
Gator
Hooper
Man Who Loved Cat Dancing, The
Man Who Loved Women, The
Mean Machine ('The Longest Yard')
Nickelodeon
100 Rifles
Ride to Glory
Semi-Tough
Shark
Sharkey's Machine
Silent Movie, The
Smokey and the Bandit
Stroker Ace

CLIFF RICHARD
Cliff Richard and the Shadows 'Thank You Very Much'
Cliff Richard—The Video Connection
Expresso Bongo
Morecambe and Wise Musical Extravaganzas
Riding High
Summer Holiday
Up the Sandbox
Wonderfull Life
Young Ones, the

SIR RALPH RICHARDSON
Anna Karenina
Charlie Muffin
Dragonslayer
Eagle in a Cage
Fallen Idol
Four Feathers, The
Greystoke
Lady Caroline Lamb
Long Day's Journey Into Night
Looking Glass War, The
Man in the Iron Mask, The
Midas Run, The
Tales From the Crypt/Vault of Horror
Things to Come
Time Bandits
Twelfth Night
Watership Down
Who Slew Auntie Roo

RACHEL ROBERTS
Alpha Beta
Belstone Fox, The
Murder on the Orient Express
Picnic at Hanging Rock
This Sporting Life
When a Stranger Calls

EDWARD G. ROBINSON
Cincinnati Kid, The
Never a Dull Moment
Old Man Who Cried Wolf
Peking Blond
Song of Norway
Soylent Green
Ten Commandments, The

GINGER ROGERS
Barkleys of Broadway, The
Carefree
First Travelling Saleslady, The/A Lady Takes a Chance
Hollywood on Parade
I'll Be Seeing You
Shall We Dance
Top Hat

ROY ROGERS
Dark Command
Hollywood on Parade
Mackintosh & T.J.
Under California Skies

MICKEY ROONEY
Bill
Bill on His Own
Breakfast at Tiffany's
Bridges at Toko-Ri, The
Domino Killings, The
Find the Lady
Godmothers, The
Hollywood on Parade
Leave 'Em Laughing
Pete's Dragon
Rachel's Man
That's Entertainment

THE ROYAL FAMILY
D-Day—The Great Crusade
Prince Charles: A Royal Portrait
Princess
Princess and the People
Queen's Birthday Parade, The
Royal Wedding, The
Story of Prince Charles and Lady Diana, The
This Year 1981
Treasures of the British Crown

JANE RUSSELL
Born Losers
Bounty Killers The

/Macao
Bundle of Joy/Montana Belle
French Line, The
Gentlemen Prefer Blondes
Outlaw, The/Law of the Underworld
Underwater/The Big Steal
Wagonmaster/ Double Dynamite

GEORGE SANDERS
All About Eve
Allegheny Uprising/Back from Eternity
Body Stealers, The
Candy Man, The
From the Earth to the Moon
Good Times
Ivanhoe
Night of the Assassin, The
Quiller Memorandum, The
Rebecca

PAUL SCOFIELD
Man for All Seasons, A

GEORGE C. SCOTT
Beauty and the Beast
Changeling, The
China Rose
Day of the Dolphin, The
Firestarter
Formula, The
Hustler, The
Movie Movie
Oliver Twist
Patton
Savage Is Loose, The

RANDOLPH SCOTT
Abilene Town
Girl in Every Port, A/Return of the Badman
Rebecca of Sunnybrook Farm

GEORGE SEGAL
Carbon Copy
Duchess and the Dirtwater Fox, The
Girl Who Couldn't Say No, The
Hot Rock, The
Lost and Found
Quiller Memorandum, The
Russian Roulette

Who's Afraid of Virginia Woolf?
What's New Pussycat
Where Does It Hurt?

TOM SELLECK
Concrete Cowboys
High Road to China
Lassiter

PETER SELLERS
Being There
Fiendish Plot of Dr. Fu Manchu, The
Ghost in the Noonday Sun
Great McGonagall, The
Heavens Above
Hoffman
I'm All Right Jack
Ladykillers, The
Magic Christian, The
Naked Truth, The
Only Two Can Play
Optimist of Nine Elms, The
Orders Are Orders
Pink Panther, The
Pink Panther Strikes Again, The
Return of the Pink Panther, The
Revenge of the Pink Panther
Soft Beds, Hard Battles
Sykes
To See Such Fun
Trail of the Pink Panther
Two-Way Stretch
What's New Pussycat
Where Does It Hurt?

OMAR SHARIF
Ace Up My Sleeve
Baltimore Bullet, The
Bloodline
Brainwashed
Burglars
Fall of the Roman Empire, The
Far Pavilions, The
Green Ice
Kublai Khan
Last Valley, The
Lawrence of Arabia
Mayerling
Night of the Generals
Pink Panther Strikes Again, The
Pleasure Palace
Poppies Are Also Flowers
S*H*E
Tamarind Seed, The

ROBERT SHAW
Avalanche Express
Battle of Britain, The
Battle of the Bulge
Birthday Party, The
Diamonds
From Russia With Love
Jaws
Man for All Seasons, A
Reflection of Fear, A
Taking of Pelham 123, The
Town Called Bastard, A

MOIRA SHEARER
Red Shoes, The

BROOKE SHIELDS
Communion
Endless Love
Sahara
Tilt

ALASTAIR SIM
Hue and Cry

FRANK SINATRA
Anchors Aweigh
Can-Can
Detective, The
First Deadly Sin, The
Guys and Dolls
High Society
Higher and Higher
Miracle of the Bells, The
Ocean's Eleven
On the Town
Sinatra
Sky's the Limit, The/Step Lively
That's Entertainment
That's Entertainment: Part 2
Till the Clouds Roll By
Von Ryan's Express
Wagonmaster/ Double Dynamite
Young at Heart

MAGGIE SMITH
Better Late Than Never
Clash of the Titans
Evil Under the Sun
Missionary, The
Othello
Quartet

ELKE SOMMER
And Then There Were None
Baron Blood
Carry On Behind

Corrupt Ones, The
40 Million Bucks on a
  Dead Man's Chest
House of Exorcism
Lisa and the Devil
Nightingale Sang in
  Berkeley Square, A
Percy
Percy's Progress

SISSY SPACEK
Bandlands
Carrie
Ginger in the Morning
Heartbeat
Missing
Raggedy Man

SYLVESTER STALLONE
Death Race 2000
Escape to Victory
First Blood
F.I.S.T.
Italian Stallion
Lords of Flatbush, The
No Place to Hide
Paradise Alley
Rhinestone
Rocky
Rocky II
Rocky III

TERENCE STAMP
Far from the Madding
  Crowd
Hit, The
Modesty Blaise
Powers of Evil
Striptease
Together

TOMMY STEELE
Twelfth Night
Yeoman of the Guard,
  The

JAMES STEWART
Airport '77
Bandolero
Big Sleep, The
Flight of the Phoenix,
  The
Green Horizon
Man Who Knew Too
  Much, The
Rear Window
Shenandoah
That's Entertainment

MERYL STREEP
Deadliest Season, The
Deer Hunter, The
French Lieutenant's
  Woman, The
Holocaust
Julia
Kramer vs. Kramer

Seduction of Joe
  Tynan, The
Silkwood
Sophie's Choice
Still of the Night

BARBRA STREISAND
All Night Long
Hello, Dolly!
Main Event, The
Star Is Born, A
Streisand
Up the Sandbox
Way We Were, The
What's Up Doc?
Yentl

DONALD SUTHERLAND
Animal House
Bear Island
Blood Relatives
Casanova
Disappearance, The
Don't Look Now
Eagle Has Landed,
  The
Eye of the Needle
Great Train Robbery,
  The
Klute
Man, A Woman and a
  Bank, A
M*A*S*H
Max Dugan Returns
Murder by Decree
S*P*Y*S
Steelyard Blues
Threshold
Winter of Our
  Discontent

JANET SUZMAN
Antony and Cleopatra
Draughtman's
  Contract, The
House on Garibaldi
  Street, The
Priest of Love

ELIZABETH TAYLOR
Ash Wednesday
Cat on a Hot Tin Roof
Cleopatra
Divorce His, Divorce
  Hers
Doctor Faustus
Hammersmith is Out
Ivanhoe
Life with Father
Little Night Music, A
Mirror Crack'd, The
Return Engagement
Sandpiper, The
That's Entertainment
Under Milk Wood
Who's Afraid of
  Virginia Woolf?

ROD TAYLOR
Birds, The
Charles and Diana
Cry of the Innocent
Dark of the Sun
Deadly Trackers, The
40 Million Bucks on a
  Dead Man's Chest
Jacqueline Bouvier
  Kennedy
Man Who Had Power
  Over Women, The
Nobody Runs Forever
Picture Show Man,
  The
Powderkeg
Time Machine, The
Train Robbers, The

SHIRLEY TEMPLE
Fort Apache
Heidi
Hollywood on Parade
I'll Be Seeing You
Rebecca of
  Sunnybrook Farm
Since You Went Away

TERRY-THOMAS
Cherry Picker, The
Hound of the
  Baskervilles, The
How to Kill 400
  Duponts
I'm All Right Jack
Lucky Jim
Naked Truth, The

DAVID TOMLINSON
Bedknobs and
  Broomsticks
City Under the Sea
Dominique
Fiendish Plot of Dr. Fu
  Manchu, The
Love Bug, The
Mary Poppins
Tom Jones
Water Babies, The
Wombling Free
Wooden Horse, The

SPENCER TRACY
It's a Mad, Mad, Mad,
  Mad World

JOHN TRAVOLTA
Blow Out
Carrie
Grease
Saturday Night Fever
Staying Alive
Two of a Kind
Urban Cowboy

ARTHUR TREACHER
Heidi
Little Princess, The

RITA TUSHINGHAM
Girl with Green Eyes
Green Eyes
Human Factor, The
Rachel's Man

TWIGGY
Boyfriend, The
Butterfly Ball, The
There Goes the Bride

LIV ULLMANN
Autumn Sonata
Bridge Too Far, A
Cries and Whispers
Food, Wine and
  Friends: Vol. 4
Lunatic
Prisoner Without a
  Name, Cell Without
  a Number
Scenes from a
  Marriage

PETER USTINOV
Black Beard's Ghost
Death on the Nile
Evil Under the Sun
Great English Garden
  Party, The
Great Muppet Caper,
  The
Hammersmith Is Out
Logan's Run
Mouse and His Child,
  The
One of Our Dinosaurs
  Is Missing
Peter Ustinov Tells
  Stories from Hans
  Christian Andersen
Purple Taxi, The
Quo Vadis
Tarka the Otter
Viva Max
Wimbledon, 1975

RUDOLPH VALENTINO
Son of the Sheik, The

JAN-MICHAEL VINCENT
Air Wolf
Bandits, The
Hard Country
Hooper
Last Plane Out
Mechanic, The
Return, The
Vigilante Force
World's Greatest
  Athlete, The

JON VOIGHT
Champ, The
Coming Home
Deliverance
Lookin' to Get Out
Midnight Cowboy

MAX VON SYDOW
Deathwatch
Dreamscape
Dune
Escape to Victory
Exorcist, The
Exorcist, II—The
  Heretic
Flash Gordon
Hurricane
Lunatic
March or Die
Quiller Memorandum,
  The
Target Eagle
Touch, The
Virgin Spring, The
Voyage of the
  Damned

DAVID WARNER
Age of Innocence
Cross of Iron
Doll's House, A
Island, The
Morgan—A Suitable
  Case for Treatment
Omen, The
Perfect Friday
Portrait of Jenny
Silver Bears, The
S.O.S. Titanic
Thirty Nine Steps, The
Time After Time
Tron

JOHN WAYNE
Alamo, The
Allegheny Uprising
Angel and the
  Badman
Back to Bataan
Cahill
Chisum
Circus World
Dark Command
First Travelling
  Saleslady, The/A
  Lady Takes a
  Chance
Flying Leathernecks,
  The
Fort Apache
Green Berets, The
Hurricane Express
Longest Day, The
McQ
Raquel
Rio Bravo
Rio Lobo
Stagecoach
Train Robbers, The
True Grit
Tycoon
Undefeated, The
Without Reservations

RAQUEL WELCH
Bandolero
Bedazzled
Bluebeard
Fantastic Voyage
Flare-Up
Four Musketeers, The
Fuzz
Hannie Caulder
Kansas City Bomber
Magic Christian, The
Myra Breckenridge
100 Rifles
One Million Years
  B.C.
Raquel
Sin
Swingin' Summer, A
Three Musketeers,
  The

ORSON WELLES
Battle on the River
  Neretva, The
Butterfly
Citizen Kane
David and Goliath
Ferry to Hong Kong
Finest Hours, The
Grande Breteche, La
Horse Called Nijinsky,
  A
King's Story, A
Kublai Khan
Last Roman, The
Late Great Planet
  Earth, The
Long Hot Summer,
  The
Macbeth
Malpertius
Man for All Seasons,
  A
Moby Dick
Third Man, The
To Build a Fire
Treasure Island
Voyage of the
  Damned

MAE WEST
Hollywood on Parade
Myra Breckenridge
Sextette

JACK WILD
Pied Piper, The
Wild Little Bunch, The

GENE WILDER
Adventures of Sherlock Holmes' Smarter Brother, The
Blazing Saddles
Cisco Kid
Everything You Always Wanted to Know...
Producers, The
Quackser Fortune Has A Cousin in the Bronx
Silver Streak
Thursday's Game

TREAT WILLIAMS
Prince of the City
Streetcar Named Desire, A

NICOL WILLIAMSON
Excalibur
Human Factor, The
I'm Dancing as Fast as I Can
Seven Percent Solution, The
Venom
Word, The

SHELLEY WINTERS
Behave Yourself
City on Fire
Cleopatra Jones
Diamonds
Double Life, A
Elvis—The Movie
Fanny Hill
Heartbreak Motel
How Do I Love Thee
I Am a Camera
Journey Into Fear
Pete's Dragon
Poseidon Adventure, The
Revenge
S.O.B.
Something to Hide
That Lucky Touch
Treasure of Pancho Villa, The
Who Slew Auntie Roo?

NATALIE WOOD
Affair, The
Brainstorm
Candidate, The
Devil's Canyon/A Cry in the Night
Great Race, The
Meteor
Peeper
West Side Story

MICHAEL YORK
Accident
Cabaret
Conduct Unbecoming
England Made Me
Fedora
Final Assignment
Four Musketeers, The
Great Expectations
Island of Dr. Moreau, The
Logan's Run
Man Called Intrepid, A
Murder on the Orient Express
Phantom of the Opera
Rape of the Third Reich
Riddle of the Sands, The
Seven Nights in Japan
Three Musketeers, The
White Lions, The

SUSANNAH YORK
Awakening, The
Battle of Britain, The
Conduct Unbecoming
Falling in Love Again
Food, Wine and Friends: Vol. 2
Gold
Images
Killing of Sister George, The
Man for All Seasons, A
Month in the Country, A
Oh! What a Lovely War
Shout, The
Silent Partner, The
Sky Rider
That Lucky Touch
They Shoot Horses, Don't They?
Tom Jones

Video Programme Sources Index

Below is an alphabetical index of companies or distributors whose video programmes are included in *The Paladin Video Home Entertainment Guide*. The corporate name, address and telephone number for each film are listed; contact the programme sources for further information on their titles, or your local video retailer.

A & M SOUND PICTURES
A & M Records Ltd.
Richard House
30-32 Mortimer Street
London
01-580 3176
(A & M titles are distributed by Place, Virgin and Gold.)

ABACUS VIDEO
D & M Video Services Ltd.
PO Box 85
Cullum House
North Orbital Road
Denham
Uxbridge
Middlesex UB9 5HL
(0895) 832494

ADB VIDEO DISTRIBUTION LTD
22 Arica Road
Brockley
London SE4 PX2
01-732 6842

ASTRA VIDEO LTD
8 Commerce Way
Waddon
Croydon
Surrey

AUDIO VISUAL MINISTRIES
"Cherith"
152 High Street
Holywood
Co. Down BT18 9HT
Northern Ireland
Holywood 4577

AVI VIDEO LTD
29 Great Pulteney Street
Suite 18-19
London W1R 3DD
01-734 8722

BBC VIDEO
Villiers House
The Broadway
London W5 2PA
01-579 0512 × 234

BEATTIE-EDWARDS AVIATION LTD
20 Normanhurst Close
Three Bridges
Crawley
Sussex RH10 1YL
Crawley 20565

BRENT WALKER VIDEO LTD
9 Chesterfield Street
London W1
01-491 4430

CAPRICORN ENTERTAINMENTS
Priest House
90 High Road
Broxbourne
Hartfordshire
(0992) 467216

CBS/FOX VIDEO
Perivale Industrial Estate
Greenford
Middlesex UB6 7RU
01-997 2552

CHANNEL VIDEO
Castleton House
High Street
Hamble
Hampshire SO3 5HA
(042122) 5744

CHRYSALIS VIDEO
The Chrysalis Group Ltd
12 Stratford Place
London W1
01-408 2355

CIC VIDEO
138/139 Piccadilly
London W1V 9FH
01-629 7211

CINEMA INDOORS
45 Kingswood Road
Chiswick
London W4

DERANN FILM SERVICES
Film House
99 High Street
Dudley
West Midlands DY1 1QP
(0384) 233191/2

DIRECT VIDEO SERVICES
BCM Direct Video
London WC1N 3XX

DUKE MARKETING LIMITED
32 Finch Road
Douglas
Isle of Man
0624 23634

EMBASSY HOME ENTERTAINMENT
Sloane Square House
Holbein Place
Sloane Square
London SW1W 8NT
01-409 1925

ENTERTAINMENT IN VIDEO LTD
National House
60/66 Wardour Street
London W1V 3HP

EUROPEAN VIDEO COMPANY LTD
17 Evans Street
Ashton-U-Lyne
Tameside OL6 9QD
061-339 9696

FLETCHER VIDEO
Unit 7
Space Waye
Pier Road
North Feltham Trading Estate
Feltham
Middlesex
01-751 2232
01-890 8610

FOURMATT VIDEO LTD
1st Floor
3B Hatherley Road
Sidcup
Kent DA14 4BH
01-302 7551

GO VIDEO LTD
PO Box 4BT
35/37 Wardour Street
London W1A 4BT
01-734 7195

GRANADA VIDEO
Granada Television International Ltd
36 Golden Square
London W1R 4AH

GREENPARK PRODUCTIONS LIMITED
St. Wilfrids
101 Honor Oak Park
London SE23 3LB
01-699 7234

GUILD HOME VIDEO
Woodston House
Oundle Road
Peterborough PE2 9PZ
(0733) 63122

HELLO VIDEO LIMITED
105 Heath Street
Hampstead
London NW3 6SS
01-431 0145

HOKUSHIN AUDIO VISUAL LTD
2 Ambleside Avenue
London SW16 6AD
01-769 0965

HOLIDAY BROTHERS (AUDIO & VIDEO) LTD
172 Finney Lane
Heald Green
Cheadle
Cheshire SK8 3PU
061-437 0538/9
061-436 4780

**HOME VIDEO
HOLDINGS**
61-65 Conduit
 Street
London W1R 9FD
01-439 1941

**HOME VIDEO
MERCHANDISERS
LTD**
61-65 Conduit
 Street
London W1R 9FD
01-439 6391

**I. A
RECORDINGS**
Unit 3
Maws Craft
 Centre
Ferry Road
Jackfield Telford
Shropshire TF8
 7LS
(090722) 4509

**INTERVISION
VIDEO LTD**
Unit 1
McKay Trading
 Estate
Kensal Road
London W10
01-969 8218
*Intervision titles
are distributed
by CBS/Fox
Video.)*

**ISLAND
PICTURES**
22 St. Peters
 Square
London W6
01-741 1511

**ISTEAD AUDIO
VISUAL**
38, The Tything
Worcester
(0905) 29713

**IVER FILM
SERVICES LTD**
Pinewood Studios
Iver
Buckinghamshire
 SL0 0NH
(0753) 651700

JVC
Eldonwall
 Trading Estate
Staples Corner
6-8 Priestley Way
London NW2 7AF
01-450 2621

**KINGSTON
VIDEO**
34 Windmill Street
Tottenham Court
 Road
London W1P 1HH
01-636 9242/4

**LINKED RING
TELEVISION
FILM
PRODUCTIONS
LTD**
82 Old Brompton
 Road
London SW7
01-581 8466

**LONGMAN
VIDEO**
21-27 Lambs
 Conduit Street
London WC1N
 3NJ
01-242 2548

**MEDUSA
COMMUNICATIONS
LTD**
109 Bancroft
Hitchin
Hertfordshire

**MGM/UA HOME
VIDEO**
Hammer House
113-117 Wardour
 Street
London W1V 3TD
01-437 8843
01-437 0514

**MICHAEL
BARRATT LTD**
108 Cromwell
 Road
London SW7 4ES
01-370 4391

**MOTION EPICS
VIDEO
COMPANY LTD**
122/24 Regent
 Street
London W1R 5FE
01-434 3751/2

**MOUNTAIN/
GRAPHIC**
45 New Oxford
 Street
London WC1
01-836 7038
01-836 5640

**MOUNTAIN
VIDEO**
45 New Oxford
 Street
London WC1
01-836 7038
01-836 5640

**NUCHRON
LIMITED**
107 Manningham
 Road
Bradford BD1 3BN
(0274 21871

**NUTLAND VIDEO
LTD**
200 London Road
Southend on Sea
Essex SS1 1PJ
(0702) 346355

ODYSSEY VIDEO LIMITED
11 Grape Street
London WC2H 8DR
01-735 8171

PALACE VIDEO
275/277
  Pentonville
  Road
London N1
01-278 0751

POLYGRAM VIDEO
1 Rockley Road
London W14 0DL
01-743 3474

PRECISION VIDEO LTD
ACC House
17 Great
  Cumberland
  Place
London W1A 1AG
01-262 8040

QUADRANT VIDEO
Surrey House
Throwley Way
Sutton
Surrey SM1 4QQ
01-643 8040

RADIAL CHOICE DISTRIBUTORS LTD
17 Nelson Road
Greenwich
London SE10 9JB
01-853 5899

RANK VIDEO LIBRARY
PO Box 70
Great West Road
Brentford
Middlesex TW8 9HR
01-568 9222

RCA/COLUMBIA PICTURES VIDEO UK
1 Bedford Avenue
London WC1 3DT
01-636 8373

REFERENCE TAPES LIMITED
Reference House
15 Lyon Road
London SW19 2SB
01-543 6144

REX
45 Kingswood
  Avenue
London W4

ROYAL SOCIETY FOR THE PROTECTION OF BIRDS
The Lodge
Sandy
Bedfordshire
  SG19 2DL
(0767) 80551

RPTA VIDEO LIMITED
Seymour Mews
  House
Seymour Mews
Wigmore Street
London W1H 9PE
01-486 1362
(RPTA titles are distributed by VideoSpace.)

SELECT VIDEO LTD
Regent House
Heaton Lane
Stockport
Cheshire SK4 1BS
061-477 8260

TEMPLE ENTERPRISES LTD
13A Apton Road
Bishops Stortford
Hertfordshire
(0279) 55225

TFI LEISURE LIMITED
21 Cheyne Row
Chelsea
London
01-352 7950

THORN EMI VIDEO PROGRAMMES LTD
Thorn House
Upper St. Martin's
  Lane
London WC2H 9ED
01-836 2444

VCL VIDEO SERVICES
VCL House
Dallington Street
London EC1
01-251 6131
(VCL titles are distributed by CBS/Fox Video.)

VESTRON VIDEO INTERNATIONAL
6-10 Bruton Street
London W1
01-499 3821

VIDEO BROKERS
105 Heath Street
Hampstead
London NW3 6SS

VIDEO FILM ORGANISATION
103-109 Wardour Street
London W1V 3TD
01-437 8473
01-437 8942

VIDEO FILM PROMOTIONS LTD
104 Wigmore Street
London W1H 9DR

VIDEO FORM PICTURES
Unit 4
Brunswick Industrial Park
Brunswick Park Road
London N11
01-368 9244

VIDEO NETWORK
7 First Avenue
Manor Park
London E12

VIDEO PROGRAMME DISTRIBUTORS
Building No. 1
GEC Estate
East Lane
Wembley
Middlesex HA9 7FF
01-904 0921

VIDEO SPORT FOR ALL
Marvic House
Bishops Road
London SW6 7AD
01-385 8443/4

VIDEO TAPE CENTRE (UK) LTD
No. 1 Newton Street
London WC2B 5EL
01-405 8484

VIDEO UNLIMITED
Patrick House
West Quay Road
Poole
Dorset BH15 1JF
(02013) 83335

VIDEOMEDIA
68/70 Wardour Street
London W1V 3HP
01-437 1333
(Videomedia titles are distributed by Guild Home Video.)

VIDEORAMA STUDIOS LTD
31 High Street
Hoddeson
Hertfordshire EN11 8TL
(09924) 60111

VIDEOSPACE LTD
272 London Road
Wallington
Surrey SM6 7DJ
01-773 0921

VIDPICS INTERNATIONAL
12 Golden Square
London W1R 3AS
01-434 3311

VINTAGE TELEVISION LTD
35 Petergate
Bradford
West Yorkshire
(0274) 29691

VIRGIN VIDEO
61-63 Portobello Road
London W11
01-221 7535

WALTON FILM & VIDEO LTD
Walton House
87 Richford Street
London W6 7HN
01-743 9421

WARNER HOME VIDEO
PO Box 59
Alperton Lane
Wembley
Middlesex HA0 1FS
01-998 8844

WARWICK VIDEO
79 Blythe Road
London W14
c/o Multiple Sound Distributors Ltd
3 Standard Road
London NW10 6EX
01-961 5646

WORLD OF VIDEO 2000
Cassette House
329 Hunslet Road
Leeds LS10 1NJ
(0532) 706066

Titles of General Interest now available in Panther Books

Malcolm MacPherson (Editor)
The Black Box: Cockpit Voice Recorder
Accounts of Nineteen Air Accidents £1.95 ☐

Isaac Asimov
Asimov on Science Fiction £2.50 ☐

Roy Harley Lewis
The Browser's Guide to Erotica £1.95 ☐

Charles Berlitz
Native Tongues £2.50 ☐

Carole Boyer
Names for Boys and Girls £1.25 ☐

José Silva and Michael Miele
The Silva Mind Control Method £2.50 ☐

Millard Arnold (editor)
The Testimony of Steve Biko £2.50 ☐

John Howard Griffin
Black Like Me £1.95 ☐

Desmond Morris
The Naked Ape £1.95 ☐
The Pocket Guide to Man Watching £2.95 ☐

Ivan Tyrell
The Survival Option £2.50 ☐

Peter Laurie
Beneath the City Streets £2.50 ☐

To order direct from the publisher just tick the titles you want and fill in the order form.

HB1082

Sports and activities handbooks now available in Panther Books

Pat Davis		
Badminton Complete (illustrated)	£1.25	☐
Bruce Tegner		
Karate (illustrated)	£1.50	☐
Bruce Tulloh		
The Complete Distance Runner (illustrated)	£1.95	☐
Meda Mander		
How to Trace Your Ancestors (illustrated)	£1.50	☐
Tom Hopkins		
How to Master the Art of Selling	£2.50	☐
William Prentice		
How to Start a Successful Business	£2.50	☐
Susan Glascock		
A Woman's Guide to Starting Her Own Business	£2.50	☐
Alfred Tack		
Sell Your Way to Success	£1.25	☐
Andrew Pennycook		
The Book of Card Games	£3.95	☐
C Lukács and E Tarjan		
Mathematical Games	£1.50	☐
Gyles Brandreth		
The Complete Puzzler	£1.50	☐
Patrick Duncan (ed.)		
The Panther Crossword Compendium (Vols 1 and 2)	£1.95 each	☐
Quizwords 1	£1.50	☐
Quizwords 2	£1.50	☐

To order direct from the publisher just tick the titles you want and fill in the order form.

HB1081

Paladin Reference Books

A Dictionary of Operations £2.50 ☐
Dr Andrew Stanway
A lucid commonsense guide to hospitals and how they affect the patient plus an A–Z of operations and an alphabetical list of procedures and investigations.

A Dictionary of Symbols £2.95 ☐
Tom Chetwynd
Tom Chetwynd has drawn from the collective wisdom of the great psychologists, particularly Jung, to create a comprehensive and thought-provoking guide to the language of symbols.

Trees and Bushes of Britain and Europe £2.95 ☐
Oleg Polunin
A superb and definitive guide. Fully illustrated in colour and carefully organized for use in the field

Halliwell's Film Guide (Fourth Edition) £7.95 ☐
Leslie Halliwell
A new edition of the indispensable film reference work.

Halliwell's Filmgoer's Companion (Seventh Edition) £5.95 ☐
A gargantuan compilation of film facts. 'Totally indispensable' – *Film Review Annual*.

A Dictionary of Mythologies £2.50 ☐
Max Shapiro and Rhoda Hendricks
The first concise yet comprehensive dictionary of world mythologies. It is fully cross-referenced, so that the universal themes in common to all myths are easily recognized, and the cultural differences easily compared.

The Encyclopaedia of Reality £2.25 ☐
Katinka Matson
An indispensable reference book of alternative thought and of the ideas of the key revolutionary thinkers of the past and modern times.

To order direct from the publisher just tick the titles you want and fill in the order form.

All these books are available at your local bookshop or newsagent, or can be ordered direct from the publisher.

To order direct from the publishers just tick the titles you want and fill in the form below.

Name _____

Address _____

_____

Send to:
**Paladin Cash Sales
PO Box 11, Falmouth, Cornwall TR10 9EN.**

Please enclose remittance to the value of the cover price plus:

UK 45p for the first book, 20p for the second book plus 14p per copy for each additional book ordered to a maximum charge of £1.63.

BFPO and Eire 45p for the first book, 20p for the second book plus 14p per copy for the next 7 books, thereafter 8p per book.

Overseas 75p for the first book and 21p for each additional book.

Paladin Books reserve the right to show new retail prices on covers, which may differ from those previously advertised in the text or elsewhere.